FILM COMPOSERS IN AMERICA

FILM COMPOSERS IN AMERICA

A Filmography, 1911–1970

Second Edition

Clifford McCarty

2000

OXFORD
UNIVERSITY PRESS

Oxford New York
Athens Auckland Bangkok Bogotá Buenos Aires Calcutta
Cape Town Chennai Dar es Salaam Delhi Florence Hong Kong Istanbul
Karachi Kuala Lumpur Madrid Melbourne Mexico City Mumbai
Nairobi Paris São Paulo Singapore Taipei Tokyo Toronto Warsaw

and associated companied in
Berlin Ibadan

Published by Oxford University Press, Inc.
198 Madison Avenue, New York, New York 10016

Library of Congress Cataloging-in-Publication Data
McCarty, Clifford, 1929–
Film composers in America : a filmography,
1911–1970 / Clifford McCarty. — 2nd ed.
p. cm.
Includes index.
ISBN 0-19-511473-6
1. Motion picture music—United States—Bibliography. I. Title
ML128.M7M3 2000
016.7815′42′09733—dc21 98-42710

1 3 5 7 9 8 6 4 2

Printed in the United States of Amrica
on acid-free paper

TO JOHN

Acknowledgments

Lawrence Morton was my friend and mentor from 1951 until his death in 1987. He was this country's finest film music critic, and he wrote an introduction to an early version of this filmography that is as valid today as it was in 1953. He was one of the best and wisest men I have ever known, and his knowledge, advice, and encouragement were invaluable. Although he was reluctant to receive any expression of gratitude, I expressed it to him then and I reaffirm it now.

Without the cooperation and assistance of many other people, my research would have been nearly impossible. First among them are the men and women in the studios' music libraries who made available scores and other primary materials: Harriet Crawford at Columbia; Harry Lojewski and Ruby Armstrong at Metro-Goldwyn-Mayer (MGM); Eldridge R. Walker and John Hammell at Paramount; John Hall and Vernon Harbin at RKO; Fred Combattente and Urban Thielmann at Twentieth Century–Fox; Julian Bratolyubov and Terry Wolff at Universal; Joel Franklin, Daniel Franklin, and Lois McGrew at Warner Bros.

Most of the research in secondary (and to a lesser extent in primary) materials was done at the Margaret Herrick Library of the Academy of Motion Picture Arts and Sciences. Without the publications and files at this extraordinary library, I can hardly imagine bringing my work to completion. My thanks go to the directors of the library, Elizabeth C. Franklin, Lillian N. Schwartz, Mildred Simpson, and Linda Harris Mehr for their unstinting aid. My special thanks go to Stacey Behlmer, Warren M. Sherk, and Samuel Gill, and no less to the many other librarians, archivists, and staff members who facilitated my research over a period of 48 years.

Two librarians who were unfailingly helpful were Stephen M. Fry of the Music Library at the University of California, Los Angeles (UCLA), and Ned Comstock of the Cinema-Television Library at the University of Southern California (USC). Also at USC are the Warner Bros. Archives, and I am indebted to Leith Adams and Stuart Ng for making many scores and other materials available.

For their several acts of kindness and assistance, I am especially grateful to Gillian B. Anderson and Jon Newsom in the Music Division of the Library of Congress. Other librarians, curators, and archivists who deserve mention are James V. D'Arc, Harold B. Lee Library, Brigham Young University; Brigitte Kueppers, Theater Arts Library, UCLA; Gene M. Gressley, Special Collections, University of Wyoming; Victoria Jones, Special Collections, University of Oregon Library; Pierre de Bellefeuille and Rowland Hill, National Film Board of Canada; Kathy Conner and Jan-Christopher Horak, George Eastman House.

Additional information and assistance came from Abe Meyer and Bobby Helfer of MCA Artists, Ltd.; Sara Kerber, Darryl Valdez, Lance Pope, and David A. Berry of the Index and Cue Sheet Department at ASCAP (American Society of Composers, Authors and Publishers); Ray W. Martin of the Colonial Williamsburg Foundation; Flo Renoudet and David R. Smith at Walt Disney Productions; Don Gillespie of the C. F. Peters Corporation; Richard P. May of the Turner Entertainment Company; Timothy M. Rogers of Unusual Films at Bob Jones University; Mona Grellson of World Wide Pictures; and Jeannie Pool, executive director of The Film Music Society.

Among the many individuals who aided my research, no one was more helpful than Jack Docherty, a Scottish film music historian whom

I have never met but whose correspondence for over three decades provided a veritable wealth of information. He called my attention to scores I had overlooked and to composers of whom I was ignorant, chiefly among those who worked outside Hollywood. He also saved me from some absurd blunders, in one memorable instance dissuading me from including Guillaume Dufay by pointing out that the man had died in 1474.

It gives me special pleasure to acknowledge the assistance of two old friends, Rudy Behlmer and Tony Thomas, who facilitated my work in countless ways, not the least of which was by example. Rudy's many books and articles on film history are marked by his conscientious regard for primary materials and by his punctilious scholarship. Tony was an indefatigable advocate of good film music, writing books and articles and producing films and record albums.

The most touching act of support came from my son John, then about seven or eight. Learning that I was collecting credits for cartoon composers, he began transcribing them on scraps of paper from viewings on television. He not only copied the names correctly, but often recorded the titles more accurately than some cartoon filmographers.

Others abetted my research in a variety of ways—by providing information or directing me to its sources, supplying cue sheets and other materials, furnishing taped or transcribed interviews, and introducing me to other helpful people. I take pleasure in thanking Clyde Allen, Verna Arvey (Mrs. William Grant Still), Irene Kahn Atkins, Leonard Atkins, Mainerd V. Baker, Ronald L. Bohn, Lance Bowling, Jon Burlingame, Richard H. Bush, Brendan G. Carroll, Alfred W. Cochran, Ken Darby, Tom DeMary, Carli D. Elinor, John Fitzpatrick, Eric A. Gordon, John Hora, Ron Hutchinson, George Korngold, Laura Kuhn, Randall D. Larson, Louis A. McMahon, Paul Mandell, Martin Miller Marks, Paul Mertz, Gerald Pratley, William H. Rosar, Anthony Slide, Steven C. Smith, Vernon Steele, Irvin Talbot, George E. Turner, John W. Waxman, and Leslie T. Zador.

I am especially grateful, of course, to the composers who responded to my inquiries: Van Alexander, Laurindo Almeida, Allan Alper, Daniele Amfitheatrof, George Antheil, Larry Austin, Donald Bagley, Tom Bähler, Buddy Baker, Robert Baksa, Leslie Bassett, George Bassman, John Bath, Irwin Bazelon, Charles Bernstein, Elmer Bernstein, Marc Blitzstein, Perry Botkin, Jr., Martin Bresnick, Lucien Cailliet, Gerard Carbonara, Benny Carter, Mario Castelnuovo-Tedesco, Jay Chernis, Buddy Collette, Alexander Courage, Sidney Cutner, Louis De Francesco, Milton Delugg, Adolph Deutsch, David Diamond, James Dietrich, Robert Drasnin, John Duffy, Vernon Duke, George Duning, Paul Dunlap, Robert Emenegger, David Epstein, Donald Erb, Richard Felciano, Ralph Ferraro, Amedeo de Filippi, Gerald Fried, René Garriguenc, Herschel Burke Gilbert, Jimmy Giuffre, Albert Glasser, Ernest Gold, Doug Goodwin, Morton Gould, Johnny Green, Richard Hageman, W. Franke Harling, Jimmie Haskell, Neal Hefti, Richard Hieronymus, Paul Horn, Werner Janssen, Dave Kahn, Bronislau Kaper, Elliot Kaplan, Sol Kaplan, Fred Karlin, Fred Katz, Bernhard Kaun, Samuel Kaylin, Roger Kellaway, Arthur Kleiner, Fred Kopp, Erich Wolfgang Korngold, Gail Kubik, Meyer Kupferman, Douglas Lackey, Ezra Laderman, Phillip Lambro, Benjamin Lees, John Leipold, Mort Lindsey, Colin McPhee, Eddy Manson, Richard Markowitz, Donald Martino, Charles Maxwell, Billy May, Mahlon Merrick, Michel Michelet, Phil Moody, Douglas Moore, Lucien Moraweck, Arthur Morton, Robert Muczynski, Gordon Mumma, Lyn Murray, Jack Nitzsche, Alex North, Pauline Oliveros, Louis S. Palange, Stephan Pasternacki, Stu Phillips, Daniel Pinkham, Edward B. Powell, Sid Ramin, Emil Richards, Milton Rosen, David Rosenboom, Miklós Rózsa, John Rubinstein, Michael Sahl, Hans J. Salter, Walter Scharf, Lalo Schifrin, Rudy Schrager, Gunther Schuller, William Schuman, Nathan Scott, Albert Sendrey, Walter Sheets, Bert Shefter, Marlin Skiles, Frank Skinner, Paul J. Smith, William O. Smith, Ronald Stein, Max Steiner, Alexander Steinert, Leith Stevens, David Stock, Robert W. Stringer, James Tenney, Dave Torbett, Gil Trythall, Emanuel Vardi, Clifford Vaughan, Don Vincent, Richard F. Wernick, Meredith Willson, Charles Wolcott, and—most of all—Hugo Friedhofer, David Raksin, and Fred Steiner.

My wife, Max, has been supportive of my continual (though not continuous) research for more years than she may care to recall. When the opportunity to publish the product of my labors presented itself, she voluntarily assumed the prodigious task of entering all of my typed data into the computer. For this, and for all her loving sustenance, I am ineffably grateful.

Contents

FILM COMPOSERS IN AMERICA

Introduction

This book represents the first attempt to identify all composers who have written musical scores for motion pictures in the United States through 1970 and to determine the authorship of as many American film scores as possible.

The film score, for the purpose of this book, is the original or adapted background score, composed expressly for a particular film. The score is usually the last component of a film, composed and recorded after the cinematography and film editing have been completed. In this, it differs from the source music, which normally is composed and recorded before filming begins. Another difference is that source music can be heard—and indeed is often performed—by the film's characters. The score, in contrast, is the only element of a film's soundtrack that cannot be heard by the film's characters but only by the audience.[1] Therefore, source music—the source of which is shown or implied—is ignored here, as are all songs, whether the film's characters can hear them or not. Also uncredited is preexistent music, whether it was published music from the popular, classical, or traditional repertoires or film music that was reused from previous pictures.

The chief purpose of this book is to establish the authorship of film scores. Composers' biographies and matters of film music history, theory, and aesthetics have been extensively (though far from completely) addressed elsewhere.[2]

FILMS

Films may be characterized as theatrical or nontheatrical. Those that most of us are familiar with are the former, meant to be exhibited in theaters. These films, which perhaps will be of greater interest to the user of this book, include narrative features, shorts, and cartoons and were usually the product of "Hollywood" (Los Angeles and its environs). The surviving and accessible music scores are largely for the Hollywood feature film, and most of the comments in this introduction address that category.

Nontheatrical films were made for purposes of education, instruction, and propaganda; their sponsors were business, industry, schools, and government. In this volume these nonfiction films—indeed, all factual films—are termed documentaries, although many of them, especially after the 1940s, are not documentaries in the traditional sense; the designation is only a convenient shorthand for indicating nonfiction films. Many of the shorts made by the Hollywood studios were factual films; here they are usually not termed documentaries, although their titles often suggest their nature.

Also to be found here are selected trailers, the short "previews of coming attractions" that heralded forthcoming features. Trailers were normally scored with music from their respective features, but some were composed expressly and occasionally not by the composer of the feature. Only those trailers that were scored by a composer other than that for the feature are included here. The reader will also find a number of experimental and avant-garde films, a few examples of the split-reel (two or more very short films on one reel), and several foreign-language pictures produced in this country.

Although generally composers who scored

films outside the United States are not credited with their foreign films, a few exceptions have been made. One example is Miklós Rózsa, whose early films were composed in England and some of whose later films were scored in Europe. Yet they were all English-language pictures and received widespread release in America, and I felt that to exclude them would be an undue distortion of Rózsa's career in films.

Whenever possible, the title and date given for a film are those on the film itself. When I have not seen the film—admittedly the case with most of the films listed here—I have taken the title and date from the following sources, in order of preference: *Catalog of Copyright Entries, Cumulative Series: Motion Pictures,* 1912–1969; *The American Film Institute Catalog of Motion Pictures Produced in the United States: Feature Films,* 1911–1940, 1961–1970; *The Library of Congress Author Catalog: Films, 1948–1952; The National Union Catalog: Motion Pictures and Filmstrips,* 1953–1972; *Index to 16mm Educational Films;* pressbooks, house organs, and film distributors' catalogs; reviews or notices in periodicals; information supplied by composers.

The title of each film is that of its original release. If the title was changed even shortly after release, that title is ignored, as are titles given to reissues, television showings, and releases in other countries. There are many instances of title changes and alternate titles, but with very few exceptions they are not included here.

In keeping with the lengths, or running times, established by the American Film Institute, a feature is a film of 40 minutes or more; a short is a film of less than 40 minutes. All of the films listed should be considered features or feature-length documentaries unless designated to the contrary (short, cartoon, trailer).

Films made for television are not included.

COMPOSERS

The dictionary tells us that a composer is one who creates or originates a musical work. A composer is expected to know the elements of composition—melody, harmony, form, rhythm, counterpoint, and so on—and, unless he or she is writing monophony, orchestration. A composer is also expected to notate the music so that it can be performed. Nearly all the composers in this book were musically educated and able to compose in this traditional manner.

A fact of film music, however, is that there is more than one way to produce a score, and some composers who lacked formal training but had some musical gifts are included here along with their more qualified colleagues. An obvious example is Charlie Chaplin, who is so widely acknowledged as the composer of the music for his films that he could not well be excluded. Although untrained in composition and notation, Chaplin could play the piano and the violin and could sing, whistle, and hum; in these ways, he was able to transmit his melodies and other musical ideas to trained musicians, who could notate, arrange, and orchestrate them.[3]

Another composer of questionable capabilities was George Stoll. André Previn once said that Stoll was "of no musical learning whatever" and concluded "that it was possible to be a rich, famous, highly considered, award-winning figure in Hollywood's musical world and still not know a goddam thing about music."[4]

Musically unschooled composers often came from the ranks of songwriters, but they also included Broadway pit conductors, performers, and even film directors. They were not highly regarded by trained musicians, who derisively called them "hummers," and although a number of them will be found here, I have been careful to also name their collaborators.

Others, whose composing credits I found to be entirely fallacious, appear only in the Supplementary List of Names, where their actual functions in film music are designated. Many of them were musical directors or music supervisors whose positions enabled them to add their names to, and even to sign, the music of others.

A further definition of composing is "to invest with a new function," which describes the arranging and/or adaptation that is included here when it actually constitutes composition. It is most observable in musical films, for which the composer extends and develops the tunes of a songwriter to form a background score. An example of this is *Till the Clouds Roll By* (1946), a film based on the life of Jerome Kern and naturally featuring many of his songs. The picture is here credited not to Kern (who in any case was dead a year earlier) but to those who adapted and composed the background score.

The question of plagiarism is not addressed here; it is a musical concern—and sometimes a legal concern as well—and is not within the scope of this book. It is often difficult to detect plagiarism without a careful analysis of the music, but it has been observed: one New York executive cautioned a colleague, "Such men as [David] Mendoza, [Erno] Rapée, and others are not above slipping something in, under their own name, composed by others."[5]

Bernard Herrmann suggested that one "might some day go see a lot of people, do an article on ghostwriting."[6] This is not so easy as it sounds, for most composers are reluctant to implicate their colleagues, whether ghost or client. Nor do musical materials offer any evidence, since true ghostwriting is so completely hidden that neither scores nor documents reveal any names other than that of the purported composer. One may hear anecdotes about ghostwriting, but they rarely concern a particular film; for the purpose of this book, they were unprovable and consequently are unreported.

Published accounts are not necessarily credible either. In his autobiography, Miklós Rózsa praises the score for *The Picture of Dorian Gray,* credited to Herbert Stothart, and says that it was "almost entirely [Mario Castelnuovo-Tedesco's] work."[7] The score, however, shows just the reverse: it was almost entirely Stothart's work; Castelnuovo-Tedesco's four cues total less than six minutes, and even they are based on Stothart's material. This is the most common form of so-called ghostwriting—that which is simply unacknowledged on the screen. Normally those composers who did not receive screen credit were denied it because of studio policy or because their contributions were relatively small; their names, however, usually appear on the scores and cue sheets.

Ghostwriting did sometimes occur on independent, low-budget pictures that were contracted for by an agent or business manager. This intermediary would strike a deal with the producer and hire a free-lance composer to provide the score, credit for which, on the screen and even on the cue sheet, would as likely as not be appropriated by the "music supervisor." That ghostwriting of one sort or another has occurred—probably from the very beginnings of film music—is undeniable, and it is not surprising to read that the practice continues to the present day.[8] But despite the space given here to the subject, it should be understood that most composers did not require either collaborators or ghosts and that when composers went uncredited, it had more to do with studio policies regarding accreditation than with attempts to conceal a score's authorship.

ORCHESTRATORS AND ARRANGERS

Studio composers usually were given one to six weeks to score a picture, the average time being perhaps three or four weeks. Under pressure to meet predetermined preview or release dates, most composers were obliged to use orchestrators to complete their scores on schedule. As will be seen in the filmographies, not only staff composers employed orchestrators but also such composers as Aaron Copland, Erich Korngold, and Virgil Thomson. Obviously they didn't need orchestrators for musical reasons; they simply didn't have time to write out the thousands of notes necessary to produce a performable score. Bernard Herrmann is often cited as a composer who never used orchestrators, but he was far from being the only one, for there were many others who routinely orchestrated their own music.

The composer's most common working method was to give the orchestrator a sketch that was complete in melody, harmony, counterpoint, and instrumentation, requiring only the distribution of parts to the various instruments of the orchestra. This might be followed by verbal discussions between the composer and orchestrator.

Other composers, who supplied only a melodic line or a piano score, required the services of an arranger, whose developments, embellishments, and counterpoint often constituted composition. Orchestrating and arranging frequently overlap, and their differences have been authoritatively described by Leo Arnaud.[9]

The credits for orchestrating and arranging in this book apply to the background score only, not to songs or any kind of source music.

MUSICAL DIRECTORS

No appellation in film music was more ambiguous than that of musical director, who could be responsible for any number of functions, from being head of the music department at a major studio to supplying tracked music to the smallest independent producer. The musical director could be an executive who managed only the business affairs of a studio's music department. He could be a composer, a conductor, a music supervisor, even an agent. One thing was almost certain: if anyone got a screen credit, it would be the musical director.

One of the most famous musical directors was Alfred Newman, who received more Academy Awards and nominations than any other musical director or composer. As a composer, in addition to writing his own scores, he often contributed to the scores of others, without screen credit. Other composers, by the same token, often contributed to his scores, also without screen credit. He was also a prolific conductor, both of his own scores and those of others.

At Columbia, Morris Stoloff was the musical director for 24 years, conducting a great many of the studio's pictures. Although not a composer, he occasionally added his name to a score even if it meant crossing out the name of the actual composer. Fifteen times he put his name on Academy Award–nominated films, and by doing so, picked up three undeserved Oscars.

Leo F. Forbstein at Warner Bros. put his name on several cue sheets and even a few pictures in the early 1930s, but he became a well-respected department head. Nat Finston, not so well respected at Paramount and later at MGM, at least once added his name to both the music and the cue sheet (of Dimitri Tiomkin's *Alice in Wonderland*).

And so it went. But musical directors are not the subject of this book, only the unavoidable consequence of conducting research for it. Their credits are not given here, with a few exceptions: when the only credit found for a picture was to the musical director, who also was known to be a composer (e.g., Alfred Newman), that picture is listed in the composer's filmography, followed by the abbreviation "(md)."

TERMS USED IN THIS BOOK

Before going any further, it might be well to define some terms used in this introduction and to some extent throughout the book. These are terms used in the motion picture industry and in published writings about film music, with the possible exception of "composite score," which may be my own invention.

Stock: preexistent music. In silent films it comprised music from the classical, popular, and traditional repertoires and/or from published collections of motion picture music. In sound films it was usually reused film music, that is, music composed for previous films that was used exclusively or in conjunction with original music to form a new score.

Original score: one newly composed or adapted for a specific film, for example, *The Best Years of Our Lives* (1946) by Hugo Friedhofer.

Collaborative score: an original score by two or more composers, for example, *The Egyptian* (1954) by Alfred Newman and Bernard Herrmann.

Composite score: one consisting of both original music and stock, for example, *Manhattan Melodrama* (1934) by William Axt (+ stock).

Compiled score: one assembled entirely from stock. This type was employed to score the vast majority of silent films, and a great many sound films as well.

Cue: a segment of music in a film score. In length it can be as short as one or two seconds or as long as necessary for the sequence it accompanies. The longest cue found in the research for this book was "Blind Flight" by Miklós Rózsa, running 19 minutes and 41 seconds, for *Men of the Fighting Lady* (1954).

A SHORT HISTORY OF FILM SCORES

From the very beginning, music was found to be an essential element in the presentation of silent films. This music ranged from Bach to the latest popular song, and its supply, of course, was limitless. Within a few years collections of original motion picture music began to appear, composed not for specific films but for specific moods and situations.[10] The scores for most silent films consisted entirely of these kinds of preexistent music, selected by such compilers as Max Winkler and James C. Bradford and published as "musical suggestions" for any theater that chose to use them. Composers for silent films appear in this book only if they wrote music for specific pictures; those who wrote solely for published collections of motion picture music are excluded.

Original scores for silent films were rare and as far as can be learned were not produced in this country until 1911, when Walter C. Simon composed the score for a three-reel film entitled *Arrah-Na-Pogue*. This fact was first published in a trade journal,[11] and no research has caused it to be superseded. Simon became a regular composer for the Kalem Company, his name publicized in the firm's house organ, *The Kalem Kalendar*, and on the scores the company published for distribution with its films. Although several Kalem scores survive, that for *Arrah-Na-Pogue* is not among them.

The Triangle Film Corporation, during the first two years (1915–1916) of its brief existence, ambitiously engaged no fewer than 10 composers and arrangers and, in doing so, established what was probably the first studio music department in Hollywood. The names of these composers appeared in advertisements for Triangle pictures and on the scores, published by G. Schirmer, that were circulated with the films.

With the phenomenal success of *The Birth of a Nation* in 1915, films of greater length became popular, and movie palaces in which to exhibit them sprang up in all the major cities. Most feature films had their premieres in New York, where scores were prepared that sometimes, though not necessarily, were subsequently sent to other cities. Hugo Riesenfeld, William Axt, and many other composer-conductors prepared the musical accompaniments at the larger New York theaters, often writing original themes in addition to compiling and arranging the stock music that made up the bulk of the scores. Although in this book the note "+ stock" does not appear after the titles of silent films, it is safe to say that even those scores that contained original music also consisted to some degree of preexistent music.

Original scores for silent films never became common; they took time and were costly and were usually commissioned only for prestigious films such as *The Fall of a Nation* (Victor Herbert), *When a Man Loves* (Henry Hadley), and Douglas Fairbanks's spectacles (Mortimer Wilson).[12]

The successful advent of sound in commercial films in 1927 had enormous repercussions in the film industry but not much effect in the way that scores were composed and compiled. The transition from silence to sound took about two years, with some residual films for another two.[13]

From 1927 to 1931, and unique to that period, films were distributed in a number of forms. (1) Silent films continued to be made and competed in theaters with the new "talkies," but their days, of course, were numbered. (2) Synchronized films took two forms: silent films that were released, or older silent films that were reissued, with recorded scores and sound effects; and so-called "foreign" versions of sound films, that is, nondialogue versions for the overseas market (with only sound effects and music on the soundtracks), whose scores were often lengthier than those for their domestic counterparts. (3) "Part-talkies" were usually conceived or produced as silents, with expeditiously added talking sequences. (4) Sound films ("all-talkies") became the dominant and, by 1930, virtually the sole form of motion pictures, although many sound films were released in silent versions for theaters not yet wired for sound.

Despite the variety of forms in which transitional films were released, pictures in general continued to be scored in much the same manner as silents had been—with a reliance on preexistent music (sometimes newly arranged), original music, or a combination of both. At the same time, musical films, made possible by the arrival of sound, provided an additional source of music: the underscoring of most early film musicals consisted of arrangements of the films' songs.

During 1928 and 1929 the major studios established music departments and hired musical directors. Composers were engaged and usually placed under contracts that ran from six months to seven years. Most of these composers came from the silent films and from New York, although a few had already worked in Hollywood.

Stock music continued to be a basic element in sound films, as it had been in silent pictures, and was widely used. It was entirely natural that music be reused. For one thing there was historical precedent: it always had been. For another, it was hardly the only film element to be used over and over if thought desirable; scenes from previous pictures—stock shots or stock footage—were edited into new films; stories, sets, props, and costumes were reused, so why not music? In the late 1920s and 1930s stock music consisted of phonograph recordings and old sound tracks that were edited into films wherever music was wanted, resulting in what were known as "tracked" scores. If a company's resources or a picture's budget permitted, stock music was rerecorded.

Just as the general repertoire provided a musical fund for silent films, preexisting film music came to provide a supply for sound films. After talkies had been in existence for a few years, music for early sound films constituted a new repertoire, and over the ensuing years studio music libraries continued to accumulate music that could be reused to score future pictures.

Sometimes composers wrote new pieces of stock music for a studio's library. William Grant Still, for example, in addition to composing music for several Columbia pictures, wrote a large number of sketches for the studio's catalog, for use in future pictures as needed.[14]

Scores compiled from stock were used, of course, to save money, most frequently in the low-budget films of independent producers and the B pictures of the major studios. But the use of compiled scores was not limited to cheaper pictures, and many A pictures, such as *Jesse James* (1939), *Detective Story* (1951), and *Home Before Dark* (1958) were scored entirely with music reused from previous films. By the end of the 1930s the Musicians' Union put an end to the use of tracked music, and thereafter all film music had to be newly recorded (though not newly composed).

During the first few years of sound, the majority of pictures had little or no underscoring beyond the almost obligatory main and end titles; actually a few films, for example, *Other Men's Women* (1931), had no underscoring whatever. Dialogue and sound effects were considered sufficient, and scoring under dialogue had not been perfected either artistically or technically. There was also a reluctance to use music unless it could be attributed to an on-screen source such as a radio or an orchestra, lest the audience wonder "where the music was coming from." A few pictures, such as *Fighting Caravans* (1931) and *Bird of Paradise* (1932) had substantial scores, the latter approaching 100 percent, but such scores were very infrequent.

Throughout the 1930s and 1940s the length of scores gradually increased, to the point where music averaged perhaps 30 or 40 percent of a film's running time. Large scores were so uncommon in the early 1930s that *King Kong* (1933) and *The Lost Patrol* (1934) were noticed in the press for the amount of music they contained. Twenty years later, underscoring had become so prevalent that the *absence* of scores in such films as *The Narrow Margin* (1952) and *Executive Suite* (1954) drew attention, even in film reviews.

SCREEN CREDITS

To the general public, the only evidence of a film score's authorship is the screen credit. Whereas these credits are generally accurate in what they state, what is unstated is often more complex. In compiling composers' filmographies, my purpose was to go behind these credits and determine from primary sources the true authorship of film scores.

Screen credits were never intended principally to inform the public, who generally didn't know or care who made movies except for the stars and a few producers and directors. They served largely to reflect the importance of individuals in the film industry. "What are your credits?" was likely to be the first question to a job-seeking composer.

It is hardly possible to know when a film composer first received screen credit. Actress Lillian Gish declared that D. W. Griffith "was the first director to include the name of the man who was responsible for the musical score in the list of film credits."[15] Whatever the case, Griffith would have been an exception: he traveled from city to city with his films *and* the orchestral parts, overseeing each new presentation. But with most silent films, the scores varied from theater to theater, and screen credits to composers would have been impractical.

With the coming of sound there was of course only one score, and composers gradually had a chance of seeing their names on the screen. Initially, most studios appeared reluctant to give music credits except to songwriters. When they did grant a credit, it usually went to the musical director. This was not unreasonable, as the musical director was responsible for the composing, arranging, and conducting of the music, even though he may not have accomplished all of those functions personally. Early screen credits were far more circumscribed than they became later, and the studios simply allotted them to department heads. The first four Academy Awards for music (1934–1937) went not to the composers but in each case to the studio music department and were received by the head of that department.

In general, credits to composers began to appear in 1932, although there were earlier exceptions. During the 1930s credits gradually became more and more common on A pictures and on some of those middle-range films called programmers, though not on most B pictures. Music credits rarely appeared on the many low-budget films, often westerns, produced and released by a host of small, independent companies. These cheap films normally received tracked music, provided by the Meyer Synchronizing Service and other suppliers of canned music, and often had no real scores, with music under the main and end titles only.

Even at the major studios, screen credits to composers did not become customary until the 1940s. Credit to more than one composer was very uncommon, although there were a few tandem credits. During the period covered in this book, only two pictures, both independent productions, acknowledged more than two composers: *Stagecoach* (1939) and *Abilene Town* (1946), each of which gave screen credit to five composers.

There is evidence that composers occasionally declined screen credit. R. H. Bassett, for example, is all but unknown, despite his prolific output, because he never received screen credit; he probably could have had credit, at least for his scores at MGM, since the studio at the time (1934–1935) was commonly granting credit for musical scores. Bernhard Kaun, an even more prolific composer, in an unpublished interview with Irene Kahn Atkins, avowed that he never wanted credit (although he once received it on a picture scored in Germany). Erich Korngold declined screen credit on *The Green Pastures* for his brief orchestral score, feeling that it would divert attention from the choral music arranged by Hall Johnson. On *Captain Blood,* his first original score for Warner Bros., Korngold scrupulously insisted that his credit read "Musical Arrangements" rather than "Music by," as he had used some 9 minutes of Liszt in the 65-minute score because the film's preview date had been advanced and he had only three weeks to compose the music.

A discussion of screen credits as allocated by the seven studios that I researched will be found under the name of each company.

METHODOLOGY

There are two primary sources for establishing the authorship of film scores: the music scores themselves and the music cue sheets. They must be used in combination, however, for each one, if used alone, presents perils.

Cue sheets exist in several forms for different purposes. The cue sheets used in my research are the legal documents that report the musical contents of a sound film. Although they vary in comprehensiveness, they include all or some of the following information: title of cue or name of musical composition, its composer and publisher, whether instrumental or vocal, whether background or visual, and its length in minutes and seconds. Cue sheets have two major shortcomings. One is that they do not always distinguish between original and preexistent music. Another is that adaptation is seldom credited, particularly on musical films, where only the composer of the songs is credited but not the adaptor who transformed the melodies into background music. Cue sheets alone, therefore, are unreliable evidence of a score's authorship; they are often inadequate and can even be misleading.

Music scores, though generally more helpful, present other problems. One is that they are not always signed, although this was found more often in the early years of sound than later. Another is that the music examined may not even be on the film's soundtrack. An example is *Just Imagine* (1930), for which I found a lengthy score by five composers. The cue sheet, however, revealed a much shorter score, retaining music by only one of those composers. This was further confirmed when I saw the film and indeed heard very little underscoring.

By using the music in conjunction with the cue sheet, however, I could determine who wrote the music; whether it was original; and in the case of a collaborative score, the relative importance (in length) of each composer's contribution. This was the method I employed at every studio and library where I conducted research.

The music examined was in most instances in the form of conductor's scores, that is, short scores, usually notated on from two to six staves. These were most often copyists' reproductions of the composer's sketches; occasionally they were reductions from the full scores. In most cases the composer's original sketches have disappeared. The full scores, in the hand of the composer or his orchestrator(s), have in many cases been lost or discarded by the studio or company concerned. (For more details on surviving materials, see the sections on individual companies.) Even when they do exist, both sketches and orchestral scores may be unsigned; sometimes only the folder containing them bears the composer's name. The full orchestral score for RKO's *Rio Rita* (1929), for example, bears no name or even initials, although studio documents identify the arranger as Roy Webb.

One is tempted to include composers as a primary source, but one example is enough to show why even they may be unreliable. George Antheil sent me a list of his films that included *The Scoundrel* (1935). (He apparently sent this list to others as well, for this film appears in at least two biographical dictionaries.) But though he did write a score for this picture, it was not used. Furthermore, Antheil did not mention instances of collaboration, and his list was incomplete. For nontheatrical films, I sometimes relied on information supplied by the composers, but in several instances their records or their memories were faulty, resulting in a number of question marks in the filmographies where dates, companies, or director's names should appear.

As for scores that were not found at studios or libraries, it was necessary to rely on secondary sources to determine their authorship. These scores include those for pictures produced or released by small companies and for most of the films designated here as documentaries. The scores for documentaries were almost invariably written by a single composer, all but eliminating the concern for cases of multiple authorship. Most of the scores for films produced by small companies (known as independents) seem to have vanished. These companies usually had no studios or music libraries, and the music probably went to the producers or composers, who subsequently lost or discarded it.

The authorship of these "lost" scores, where it could be determined, was established by a variety of secondary sources. I accepted screen credits when no contradictory evidence was found. Materials prepared by the producers, such as pressbooks and house organs, frequently proved useful. I made discretionary use of the *ASCAP Index of Performed Compositions,*[16] but because these volumes report information from cue sheets, they can be equally misleading and therefore were used with caution. I consulted a large number of periodicals, including newspapers, magazines, trade journals, and film and music publications. I also searched countless books in the fields of both film and music, among them biographies, histories, monographs, encyclopedias, and biographical dictionaries.

STUDIOS/COMPANIES

For most of the period covered in this book, especially after the coming of sound, Hollywood was dominated by motion picture companies that all but controlled the American film industry. The major companies not only produced and distributed films but also had their own theater chains. The actual production of films was the function of the studios, each of which, in its heyday, evolved a method of manufacturing approximately one feature film a week to keep the theaters supplied. Under this studio system, most creative talent was put under contract. Composers became members of the music staff and were assigned to pictures by the music director or the head of the music department.

Because most composers worked for studios, credit for each picture is here given to the studio; independent pictures are credited to the releasing company. Some accrediting exceptions have been made for such major independents as Walt Disney, Samuel Goldwyn, and David O. Selznick because their pictures were under their personal control, regardless of what company released them.

In Europe, and since the 1960s in this country, the director rather than a studio is often credited for a film, but with certain exceptions that was not the case under the studio system. There a director seldom participated in either preproduction (scripting, casting, etc.) or postproduction (editing, scoring, etc.), which normally were supervised by the film's producer or the studio head in charge of production.

In the 1950s and 1960s the studio system declined. Battered by television, which decimated movie audiences, and by antitrust suits that divested the companies of their theaters, the studios turned increasingly to the financing and distribution of independent pictures. The studios allowed the contracts of their creative personnel to lapse, and former staff composers found themselves competing in the free-lance market. By 1970 the studios had ceased making short subjects and cartoons and had all but stopped making features, leasing their facilities instead to independent producers whose products they also released. Nevertheless, pictures up through 1970 continue to be credited here to the studios and/or releasing companies.

The majority of surviving scores are at the studios where they were created, and most of my research in primary materials was accomplished there. The seven studios that I researched were Columbia, MGM, Paramount, RKO, Twentieth Century–Fox, Universal, and Warner Bros., and an account of each follows.

Columbia

The authorship of Columbia's scores before 1936 is almost impossible to determine. When the company moved in 1972 from its Hollywood lot to the Burbank Studios, the music for over half of its films was discarded. Whoever was responsible for saving some of the music chose that of the better known composers from 1936 on; but the only surviving music before 1936 is from a 1931 film, *The Flood,* which was preserved inadvertently and found in the folder for a later picture. Permission to examine cue sheets was refused by Columbia's legal department, so I determined the authorship of post-1936 scores from those conductor's scores and full scores that survive. When Columbia moved again, in 1990, this time to Sony Pictures Entertainment (on the former MGM lot in Culver City, California), these materials were transferred to a storage facility.

The only available evidence of authorship of pre-1936 scores is the *ASCAP Index of Performed Compositions,* which reports names from the cue sheets in some but far from all cases. This evidence suggests that much of the music for Columbia's pictures of the early sound period was supplied by the Meyer Synchronizing Service, and perhaps by other library services as well. *ASCAP Index* credits for Mischa Bakaleinikoff appear in 1930 and continue almost uninterrupted through 1960, although whether he at first worked for a library service or for Columbia is not clear.

The earliest screen credits for scores seem to have appeared in 1933, and beginning in 1934 Louis Silvers and Howard Jackson received credit for musical direction on several pictures. It was not until 1936, with the arrival of Morris Stoloff as head of the music department, that screen credits became common and even then usually went to musical directors. Most of the studio's scores, even into the 1950s, were either compiled or composite works, and composers worked largely in anonymity. These mostly uncredited composers included R. H. Bassett, Milan Roder, William Grant Still (the first African-American score composer in Hollywood), Ben Oakland, Gerard Carbonara, George Parrish, Joseph Nussbaum, Sidney Cutner, Gregory Stone, Leigh Harline, and Floyd Morgan.

Later composers associated with Columbia included Frederick Hollander, Werner Heymann, Carmen Dragon, John Leipold, Paul Sawtell, Mario Castelnuovo-Tedesco, George Duning,

Marlin Skiles, Heinz Roemheld, and Arthur Morton. Other composers were brought in on a per-picture basis.

Metro-Goldwyn-Mayer

Although MGM's full scores and orchestral parts were discarded in a 1969 housecleaning, conductor's scores and cue sheets were kept, along with recording logs. All these elements appear to have been made up or reassembled during 1951–1953, when Remington Rand was commissioned to supervise a reorganization of the music department to consolidate holdings, streamline access to files and records, and provide much-needed space. The materials from 1928 to 1930 are about 85 percent complete, and from 1931 onward virtually complete, including shorts and cartoons. (Since I researched this studio, these materials have been transferred to the Turner Entertainment Company.)

At MGM the transition from silence to sound was apparently smooth, perhaps because of the presence of William Axt. Axt, who had scored several of MGM's important silent films, ushered the studio into the sound era almost single-handedly, scoring more films through 1934 than all their other composers together. There is evidence that even compiled scores were assembled by him or under his direction. Except for his last score, all of his work during the sound period was for MGM.

Among subsequent composers associated with the studio were Arthur Lange, Herbert Stothart, Edward Ward, Franz Waxman, David Snell (who, like Stothart, spent his entire film career at MGM), Daniele Amfitheatrof, George Stoll, Bronislau Kaper, George Bassman, Mario Castelnuovo-Tedesco, Lennie Hayton, Sol Kaplan, Nathaniel Shilkret, Johnny Green, Conrad Salinger, Rudolph Kopp, Adolph Deutsch, Miklós Rózsa, André Previn, David Raksin, Carmen Dragon, David Rose, Jeff Alexander, Alexander Courage, and Robert Armbruster.

Stock music was used throughout the 1930s, both alone and in conjunction with original music; its use ceased in 1942, only to resurface in the early 1950s. Collaborative scores were equally common until the demise of the studio system in the late 1950s and 1960s, when freelance composers were engaged on a per-picture basis.

The studio began issuing screen credits in 1929, and they increased in frequency until 1934, when they became customary. The many pictures having composite or collaborative scores were usually credited only to the principal composer or to the musical director.

Paramount

Paramount has retained virtually all of its scores and cue sheets since the advent of sound. Missing are those for pictures made at its East Coast Studio and for independent productions that it only released. In 1996 the Society for the Preservation of Film Music (now renamed The Film Music Society) completed the task of cleaning, cataloging and preserving the 1500 scores and parts in Paramount's music library.

Compiled, composite, and collaborative scores, so prevalent in the 1930s, were gradually phased out in the 1940s, although a few cases were found in the 1950s. Screen credits for musical score were rare before 1936 and did not become customary until the 1940s.

Composers associated with Paramount included W. Franke Harling, Karl Hajos, Gerard Carbonara, John Leipold, Howard Jackson, Ralph Rainger, Rudolph Kopp, Herman Hand, Milan Roder, Heinz Roemheld, Frederick Hollander, Victor Young, Charles Bradshaw, Ernst Toch, George Antheil, Gregory Stone, Phil Boutelje, Leo Shuken, Robert Emmett Dolan, Joseph J. Lilley, Nathan Van Cleave, Walter Scharf, and Lyn Murray.

RKO Radio

RKO apparently never made up conductor's scores, although cue sheets and many full scores survive. I examined most of these at the RKO General warehouse in Los Angeles, and did additional research at UCLA, to whom RKO's music archives were donated.

Max Steiner and Roy Webb arrived in 1929, composing, conducting, or supervising most of the studio's music until 1935. Steiner left in 1936, but Webb remained, scoring RKO pictures as late as 1955.

Among subsequent composers at the studio were Alberto Colombo, Nathaniel Shilkret, Frank Tours, Robert Russell Bennett, Paul Sawtell, Anthony Collins, Leigh Harline, Hanns Eisler, and Frederick Hollander. In the 1950s and 1960s freelance composers were increasingly engaged to score both the company's own pictures and the many independent productions that RKO released.

Like most of the other studios, RKO made extensive use of stock music, although this gradually decreased over the years. Collaborative scores were few and never acknowledged in the credits. Screen credit to music directors started in 1929, and composers began receiving screen credit in 1931. RKO may have been the first studio to give screen credit to the orchestrator of a dramatic score, to Maurice de Packh in 1936 for *Mary of Scotland.*

Twentieth Century–Fox

Twentieth Century–Fox was formed in 1935 by the merger of Twentieth Century Pictures and Fox Film Corporation. Conductor's scores for both companies were mostly present from 1932 to 1963 but did not include those for independent productions released by them.

I determined authorship by consulting the surviving conductor's scores and cue sheets, in addition to card files arranged by composer and by cue title. Full scores were said to be in storage and inaccessible. Although I was welcomed warmly in 1963, when I applied in 1994 to conduct additional research, access to both scores and cue sheets was denied.

Screen credits began in 1929 but nearly always to musical directors. This policy, with a few exceptions, continued until 1943, when composers became routinely credited. During the first decade of sound, Fox composers included Arthur Kay, Peter Brunelli, George Lipschultz, Hugo Friedhofer, R. H. Bassett, Samuel Kaylin, Arthur Lange, Louis De Francesco, Cyril J. Mockridge, David Buttolph, Charles Maxwell, and Ernst Toch. Compiled, composite, and collaborative scores were common.

Among subsequent composers associated with Twentieth Century–Fox were David Raksin, Alfred Newman, Leigh Harline, Bernard Herrmann, Franz Waxman, Sol Kaplan, Alex North, Jerry Goldsmith, and Lionel Newman. In addition, the studio engaged several free-lance composers in the 1950s and 1960s.

Universal

Universal retains conductor's scores and cue sheets for nearly all of its pictures after 1935 and cue sheets and other documents for some pictures from 1929–1935. Whether conductor's scores existed before 1936 is not known; if they did, they may have been discarded in early 1936 when Carl Laemmle, who had founded the company in 1912, was deposed and the studio came under new management. In any event they could not be found in 1954, when a search for them was conducted. The whereabouts of Universal's full scores is unknown.

During the late 1920s and early 1930s the studio relied heavily on four composers, Sam A. Perry, Heinz Roemheld, Edward Ward, and Franz Waxman. Charles Previn arrived in 1936 as composer and head of the music department. In the late 1930s and 1940s the workhorses were Frank Skinner and Hans J. Salter. Later composers included Milton Rosen, Daniele Amfitheatrof, Miklós Rózsa, Walter Scharf, Herman Stein, Henry Mancini, William Lava, and Irving Gertz. In the 1960s, as at the other studios, free-lance composers predominated.

Although there were a few screen credits for musical direction in the early days of sound, score composers did not receive credits until 1933, and then only occasionally until 1946. The main reason for this was that most Universal pictures were scored with stock music or had collaborative scores. When Universal merged with International in 1946, scores were assigned to single composers, all of whom were credited. Within three years, however, the old method of composite and collaborative scores returned and was not completely abandoned until 1968, long after most studios had given up the practice.

Warner Bros.

Warner Bros. has preserved its music as well as any Hollywood studio. Full scores and orchestral parts for most of its films are in the Warner Bros.

Archives at the University of Southern California, along with cue sheets and other documents. The Warner studio music library has conductor's scores and cue sheets for nearly all of its pictures after 1931.

During the transition to sound (1928–1931) staff composers included Louis Silvers, David Mendoza, Cecil Copping, Alois Reiser, Leon Leonardi, and Rex Dunn. Ray Heindorf arrived in late 1931 and remained as a composer and arranger—and upon the death of Leo F. Forbstein in 1948 as Warners' musical director—until 1962.

Other composers associated with the studio included Bernhard Kaun, W. Franke Harling, Heinz Roemheld, Howard Jackson, Erich Wolfgang Korngold, Max Steiner, Adolph Deutsch, Hugo Friedhofer, William Lava, Frederick Hollander, Franz Waxman, David Buttolph, and Frank Perkins. In the 1950s and 1960s the staff was gradually supplanted by free-lance composers.

Unlike most of the other studios, Warners normally assigned a picture to a single composer. Collaborative scores were relatively uncommon and almost never acknowledged on the screen. Also unlike the other studios, Warners after 1931 rarely used stock music.

For a company that became famous for its furtherance of original music scores, Warners lagged notably behind the other studios in granting screen credit to composers (but they didn't credit producers either!). With the advent of sound, musical directors were routinely credited (before 1935 the credit usually read, "Vitaphone Orchestra conducted by . . . "). With the arrival of Korngold in 1935 and Steiner in 1936, screen credit to composers became more and more common, until by 1943 composers were not only consistently credited but were increasingly given a "solo card" as well (a card among the screen credits bearing only one name). At the same time, composers often received credit in paid advertising, a policy unique to Warner Bros. during the years of the studio system.

Other Companies

A word should be said about three companies, not previously mentioned, that released large numbers of films but whose scores are attributed here mostly from secondary sources.

Although United Artists (UA) had a studio until 1939, when Samuel Goldwyn took over the property, it was not a production company but a distributor for a large number of independent producers. The heads of UA's music department, Hugo Riesenfeld (1928–1930) and Alfred Newman (1931–1939), also composed the scores for many of the company's releases. After 1939 composers were engaged by the independent producer concerned. According to hearsay, the music for UA releases was destroyed in a fire at the Goldwyn Studios in 1974; in any event, it has not been found. The scores for many Samuel Goldwyn productions were donated to the Academy of Motion Picture Arts and Sciences, but as of this writing, access to them by researchers has been denied by the Samuel Goldwyn Foundation.

When Republic Pictures was in North Hollywood, my request to conduct research there was refused. Republic's music is now at Brigham Young University in Provo, Utah, but I have had neither the time nor the means to travel to Utah to examine it. The scores for Republic's pictures, therefore, are attributed on the basis of secondary sources and on the evaluation of a considerable number of annotated cue sheets that passed through my hands on the way to Utah from the Society for the Preservation of Film Music, which had rescued them from the former Republic premises. Credits from the *ASCAP Index* suggest that much of the music used during the first two years of the company's existence (1935–1936) was supplied by the Meyer Synchronizing Service. Composers at Republic after 1936 included Alberto Colombo, Raoul Kraushaar, William Lava, Cy Feuer, Mort Glickman, Walter Scharf, Joseph Dubin, R. Dale Butts, Charles Maxwell, Nathan Scott, and Stanley Wilson. Still, the majority of Republic's films bore compiled, composite, or collaborative scores. For their relatively few A pictures, the studio sometimes hired more prominent composers, Victor Young being a favorite. Republic issued screen credits almost from the beginning, but except for the A pictures, the credits, whether for musical direction or score, appear to be virtually meaningless.

The whereabouts of the music for Monogram Pictures (later Allied Artists) is unknown. Evidence from screen credits and the *ASCAP Index* indicates that most of Monogram's music from 1931–1938 was supplied by the Meyer Synchronizing Service. Credited composers after 1938 included Edward J. Kay, Frank Sanucci, the team of Johnny Lange and Lew Porter, Raoul Kraushaar, and Marlin Skiles, all of whom often received credit for musical direction and are believed to have frequently used stock music; their large number of credits alone suggests that not all of their films had original scores.

LENGTH OF SCORES

It is impossible to give the length of each score or of each composer's contribution. The amount of original music in films varies enormously, from a negligible main title to a full score of two hours or more.

When a composer is credited with a certain film, he or she was responsible for all of the original underscoring in that film. When two or more composers collaborated on a score, the picture's title appears in the filmographies of all the composers concerned; the Index of Film Titles, however, refers the user only to the composer of the greatest amount of music, with collaborators given in parentheses in descending order of their contribution.

Additional composition ("ac" in the filmographies) indicates an amount of music substantially less than the main score. Each contribution, however, has been evaluated in the context of a particular score; therefore the amount of additional composition in one film may be greater than the entire score for another film.

As a rule, the amount of music necessary for a composer to be credited is one minute in length. The length of each cue is usually stated on either the music or the cue sheet, but if it is not, I have allowed a minimum of two score pages to qualify (one page before 1936). There are actually hundreds of examples of film music that do not meet even these minimal requirements. An exception to the one minute or two pages rule is a film's main title, which is included regardless of length; in many pictures, especially early sound films, it often contains the film's only original music.

HOW TO USE THIS BOOK

If you want to know what films a composer scored, look under the name of that composer. If it is not there, look in the Supplementary List of Names, where that person's actual function in films is given.

If you want to know who scored a particular film, consult the Index of Film Titles, which will refer you to the name of the sole or principal composer and the date.

Notes

1. Another kind of music that can be heard only by the audience occurs when a film's character sings, alone, accompanied by an orchestra that is invisible to both the character *and* the viewer. This is a convention that has come to be understood by the audience and, because the music is composed and recorded before filming, is here considered to be source music.

2. The standard guides to film music literature are *A Comprehensive Bibliography of Music for Film and Television,* compiled by Steven D. Wescott (Detroit: Information Coordinators, 1985), and its supplement, *Additions and Corrections to Steven D. Wescott's A Comprehensive Bibliography of Music for Film and Television,* compiled by Gillian B. Anderson (Hollywood, Calif.: Society for the Preservation of Film Music, 1996).

3. For an account of Chaplin's working relationship with one of his collaborators, see David Raksin, "Life with Charlie," in *Wonderful Inventions,* ed. Iris Newsom (Washington, D.C.: Library of Congress, 1985), pp. 159–171.

4. Martin Bookspan and Ross Yockey, *André Previn: A Biography* (Garden City, N.Y.: Doubleday, 1981), pp. 70–71.

5. Letter from George Maxwell, of Ricordi music publishers, to E. H. Murphy, of Warner Bros., November 29, 1930 (Warner Bros. Archives, University of Southern California, Los Angeles).

6. "A Conversation with Bernard Herrmann," in *Film Music 1,* ed. Clifford McCarty (New York: Garland Publishing, 1989; reprint, Los Angeles: The Film Music Society, 1998), p. 249.

7. Miklós Rózsa, *Double Life* (New York: Hippocrene Books, 1982), p. 193n.

8. David Bell, *Getting the Best Score for Your Film* (Los Angeles: Silman-James Press, 1994), p. 50; Josef Woodard, "Scoring Some More Respect," *Los Angeles Times,* June 14, 1998, Calendar section, p. 53, in which Leonard Rosenman is quoted (p. 54): "there are a lot of [film composers] now who can't read or write music, who have ghostwriters."

9. Leo Arnaud, "Distinctly Different," in *Music and Dance in California and the West,* ed. Richard Drake Saunders (Hollywood, Calif.: Bureau of Musical Research, 1948), pp. 43, 140.

This short but informative article was overlooked by Wescott and Anderson (note 2).

10. A famous example of such a collection is *Motion Picture Moods,* compiled by Erno Rapée (New York: G. Schirmer, 1924; Arno Press, 1974).

11. *Moving Picture World,* Vol. 10, No. 7 (November 18, 1911), p. 536.

12. Three important books on music for the silent film are Charles Merrell Berg, *An Investigation of the Motives for and Realization of Music to Accompany the American Silent Film, 1896–1927* (New York: Arno Press, 1976); *Music for Silent Films, 1894–1929,* compiled by Gillian B. Anderson (Washington, D.C.: Library of Congress, 1988); and Martin Miller Marks, *Music and the Silent Film: Contexts and Case Studies, 1895–1924* (New York: Oxford University Press, 1997).

13. For an account of the evolution of the sound film, see Harry M. Geduld, *The Birth of the Talkies* (Bloomington: Indiana University Press, 1975).

14. *Films,* Vol. 1, No. 4 (Winter 1940), p. 7; reprinted in *Films,* ed. Lincoln Kirstein, Jay Leyda, Mary Losey, Robert Stebbins, Lee Strasberg (New York: Arno Press, 1968).

15. Lillian Gish, with Ann Pinchot, *Lillian Gish: The Movies, Mr. Griffith, and Me* (Englewood Cliffs, N.J.: Prentice-Hall, 1969), p. 153. The composer to whom Gish refers was Joseph Carl Breil, who scored *The Birth of a Nation* and several other films for D. W. Griffith. Breil himself wrote in 1922 that "the scorer of the great motion picture classics is finding his name flashed on the screen along with the name of other artists who have helped to make the picture." Joseph Carl Breil, "Making the Musical Adaptation," in *Opportunities in the Motion Picture Industry* (Los Angeles: Photoplay Research Society, 1922), Vol. II, p. 87. The editors state that Breil "has written scores for many hundreds of the finest motion picture productions," a claim that is hardly credible unless one observes that throughout his article Breil is referring to selecting music rather than composing it; even so, the claim seems greatly exaggerated and is probably unverifiable.

16. American Society of Composers, Authors and Publishers, *ASCAP Index of Performed Compositions* (New York: ASCAP, 1963, 3 vols.; 1978, 1 vol.; Supplement 1981, 1 vol.).

Abbreviations

a	arrangements; arranged by
ac	additional composition
an.	animated
doc.	documentary; a factual film
et	end title
m&e	main and end titles
md	musical director
mt	main title
o	orchestrations; orchestrated by

STUDIOS/ORGANIZATIONS

AA	Allied Artists
AAF	Army Air Forces
AIP	American International Pictures (including its predecessor, American Releasing Corp.)
CIAA	Coordinator of Inter-American Affairs
COL	Columbia Pictures
CR	Cinerama Releasing
CROWN	Crown International Pictures
CU	Commonwealth United
CW	Colonial Williamsburg
DCA	Distributors Corp. of America
EAMES	Charles and Ray Eames
EL	Eagle Lion; Eagle Lion Classics
EMB	Embassy Pictures (later Avco Embassy)
FC	Film Classics
FN	First National (also see WB)
FOX	Fox Film Corp.
GN	Grand National
IFF	International Film Foundation
JSP	John Sutherland Productions
LIP	Robert L. Lippert
MGM	Metro-Goldwyn-Mayer
MON	Monogram Pictures
NEA	National Education Association

NFBC	National Film Board of Canada
NG	National General
OWI	Office of War Information
PAR	Paramount Pictures
PDC	Producers Distributing Corp.
PFC	Protestant Film Commission
PRC	Producers Releasing Corp.
REP	Republic Pictures
RKO	RKO Radio Pictures
SG	Screen Guild
TCF	Twentieth Century-Fox
TS	Tiffany-Stahl Productions
U.	University
UA	United Artists
UCLA	University of California, Los Angeles
UNIV	Universal Pictures (including Universal-International, 1947–1963)
UPA	United Productions of America
USC	University of Southern California
USDA	U.S. Department of Agriculture
USIA	U.S. Information Agency
WB	Warner Bros. (including First National after 1928 and Warner Bros.–Seven Arts, 1967–1970)
WDP	Walt Disney Productions

A

ABRAMSON, ROBERT
1957
8 × 8 (see Townsend)
1959
The Ages of Time (doc. short) HAMILTON WATCH CO.
1965
Copper (doc. short) KENNECOTT COPPER

ACHRON, JOSEPH
1935
Spring Night (short; o: E. Powell) PAR

ACKERMAN, JACK
1968
Faces CONTINENTAL

ADDISON, JOHN
[English composer of many films since 1950. His only U.S. films before 1970 follow.]
1966
A Fine Madness WB
Torn Curtain (o: E. Powell) UNIV

ADDISS, STEVE
1968
In the Year of the Pig (doc.) EMILE DE ANTONIO

ADEN, ROBIN
1966
Take Me Naked AMERICAN FILM
1967
The Touch of Her Flesh AMERICAN FILM
1968
The Curse of Her Flesh AMERICAN FILM
The Kiss of Her Flesh AMERICAN FILM
A Thousand Pleasures AMERICAN FILM
1969
The Ultimate Degenerate AMERICAN FILM

ADLER, LARRY
1962
The Great Chase (compilation film; a: Bassman) CONTINENTAL
The Hook (o: R. Franklyn, Shuken, Hayes; ac: Sendrey, Armbruster) MGM
[Also composed music for several British films.]

ADOMIAN, LAN
Documentaries
1934
Ernst Thaelmann: Fighter Against Fascism GARRISON
1945
The Battle for the Beaches (short) U.S. NAVY
Behind Nazi Lines ?
1948
Tale of the Navajos MGM
1949
Dream No More PALESTINE FILMS
1951
Birthright COLUMBIA UNIVERSITY
Pictura (Grant Wood sequence) PICTURA FILMS
Features (composed in Mexico)
1956
Canasta de Cuentos Mexicanos (Basket of Mexican Tales) JOSÉ KOHN
Talpa CINEMATOGRAFICA LATINA
Yambaó (U.S. release 1962 as *Young and Evil*) DOMINÓ FILMS
1958
Ten Days to Tulara UA

AGOSTINI, LUCIO
[Canadian composer; his filmography includes both American and Canadian films.]
Documentary Shorts
1941
Nation Builders ALUMINUM CO. OF CANADA
1942
The Thousand Days ASSOCIATED SCREEN
1949
Beauty and the Blade TCF
Spring Comes to Niagara WB
1950
Sitzmarks the Spot WB
1951
Ski in the Sky WB
Rocky Eden WB
Hockey Stars' Summer ASSOCIATED SCREEN
The Roaring Game ASSOCIATED SCREEN
Making Mounties WB
Cowboy's Holiday WB
1952
All Joking Astride ASSOCIATED SCREEN
1954
Canine Crimebusters COL
Push Back the Edge COL
Circus on Ice WB
Documentary Shorts (NFBC)
1940
Letter from Aldershot
Wings of Youth
1941
Churchill's Island
Wings of a Continent
1942
Everywhere in the World
Forward Commandos
The Mask of Nippon (with Applebaum)
Quebec, Path of Conquest
This Is Blitz
Voice of Action
1943
Battle Is Their Birthright
Thought of Food
Train Busters
1944
Balkan Powder Keg
Our Northern Neighbour
When Asia Speaks
1945
Guilty Men
1953
The Newcomers

AGUILAR, JUAN
1933
Thunder Over Mexico (see Riesenfeld)
1935
Contra la Corriente (Spanish language) RAMÓN NOVARRO PRODS.

AIMÉE, MARCEL
1968
The Taming VICTORIA FILMS

AKRIDGE, LOYD
1944
The Singing Sheriff UNIV
See My Lawyer (ac: Sawtell; + stock) UNIV
1945
I'll Tell the World UNIV
[Also worked as an orchestrator.]

ALBAM, MANNY
1970
4 Clowns (compilation film) TCF

ALDERMAN, MYRL
1937
Something to Sing About GN

ALEXANDER, ARTHUR
1929
Paris Bound RKO PATHÉ
1931
Beyond Victory (mt; et: Gromon) RKO PATHÉ

ALEXANDER, ERNEST
1968
The Kill CANYON

ALEXANDER, JEFF
1951
Westward the Women (o: Sendrey) MGM
1953
Remains to Be Seen (o: Beittel) MGM
The Affairs of Dobie Gillis (o: Beittel) MGM
Escape from Fort Bravo (o: Beittel) MGM
1954
Prisoner of War MGM
1955
The Tender Trap (o: Beittel) MGM
Ransom! (o: Beittel) MGM
1956
These Wilder Years (o: Beittel) MGM

The Great American Pastime (o: A. Morton) MGM
Slander (o: A. Morton) MGM
1957
The Wings of Eagles (o: A. Morton) MGM
Gun Glory (o: A. Morton) MGM
Jailhouse Rock (o: A. Morton) MGM
The High Cost of Loving (o: A. Morton) MGM
1958
The Sheepman (o: A. Morton) MGM
Party Girl MGM
1959
The Mating Game (o: A. Morton, R. Raksin) MGM
Ask Any Girl (o: A. Morton, R. Raksin) MGM
It Started with a Kiss (o: A. Morton, R. Raksin) MGM
The Gazebo (o: A. Morton) MGM
1960
All the Fine Young Cannibals MGM
1961
The George Raft Story AA
1962
Kid Galahad UA
1964
The Rounders (o: R. Raksin) MGM
1966
Double Trouble MGM
1967
Clambake UA
1968
Day of the Evil Gun (o: Levene) MGM
Speedway MGM
1969
Support Your Local Sheriff! UA
1970
Dirty Dingus Magee (with Strange; o: Levene, A. Harris) MGM
Animated Shorts
1947
It's a Grand Old Nag REP
1964
From Here to There SAUL BASS
The Searching Eye SAUL BASS
1968
Why Man Creates SAUL BASS

ALEXANDER, SARAH
1951
As Others See Us (doc. short) U. OF NORTH CAROLINA

ALEXANDER, VAN
1954
The Atomic Kid REP
1955
The Twinkle in God's Eye REP
Jaguar REP
1956
When Gangland Strikes REP
1957
Baby Face Nelson UA
1958
Andy Hardy Comes Home MGM
Senior Prom COL
1959
The Last Mile UA
The Big Operator MGM
Girls Town MGM
The Private Lives of Adam and Eve UNIV
1960
Platinum High School MGM
1962
Safe at Home! COL
1963
13 Frightened Girls COL
Strait-Jacket COL
1965
I Saw What You Did UNIV
1966
Tarzan and the Valley of Gold AIP
1967
A Time for Killing COL
[Although Alexander's score was ostensibly replaced by Mundell Lowe's, both versions have apparently been shown.]

ALEXANDER, WILLIAM P.
1968
Face to Face—Walt Whitman: A Hundred Years Hence (doc. short) EDINBORO STATE COLLEGE

ALLEN, BILLY
[William Allen Castleman.]
1965
The Princess and the Magic Frog (with Dave Roberts) FANTASY FILMS
1966
The Devil's Mistress (with D. Warren) HOLIDAY PICTURES
1967
She Freak SONNEY-FRIEDMAN
Ski on the Wild Side (doc.) SIGMA III

1968

The Lustful Turk FPS VENTURES
The Acid Eaters FPS VENTURES
Brand of Shame FPS VENTURES

1969

Thar She Blows ENTERTAINMENT VENTURES
The Ecstasies of Women UNITED PICTURES
Starlet ENTERTAINMENT VENTURES

1970

Trader Hornee (with Loose) ENTERTAINMENT VENTURES

ALLEN, STEVE

1967

A Man Called Dagger (see R. Stein)

ALLEN, WAYNE

1938

Follow the Arrow (short) MGM

[Also a prolific orchestrator.]

ALMEIDA, LAURINDO

1954

Naked Sea (doc.; with G. Fields) RKO

1956

Goodbye, My Lady (with G. Fields) WB

1957

Escape from San Quentin COL

1958

Maracaibo PAR

1959

Cry Tough UA

1960

Flight SAN FRANCISCO FILMS

Shorts

1956

Goya (doc.) BEN BERG, IRVING BLOCK

1957

Day of the Dead EAMES

1966

Cowboy (doc.) USIA

1968

The Magic Pear Tree (cartoon) MURAKAMI-WOLF
19?? *A Day in the Life of Manolete* ?

ALPER, ALLAN

1970

The Bang Bang Gang E.S.I. PRODS.

ALPERSON, EDWARD L., JR.

1952

Rose of Cimarron (see Kraushaar)

1955

Mohawk TCF

1957

The Restless Breed TCF
Courage of Black Beauty TCF

1958

I, Mobster (see Fried)

1960

September Storm (see Kraushaar)

ALQUIST, SKEETS

1965

Laurel and Hardy's Laughing 20's (compilation film; ac: Kogen; + stock) MGM

ALTO, HENRY

1965

The Stones of Eden (doc. short) WILLIAM A. FURMAN

ALTSCHULER, MODEST

1912

The Life of John Bunyan F. W. HOCHSTETTER

1914

Spartacus (U.S. release of Italian film) GEORGE KLEINE

1929

She Goes to War UA

1938

It's All in Your Mind BERNARD B. RAY

1946

Buffalo Bill Rides Again SG

AMES, WILLIAM

1952

Philip Evergood (doc. short) HOWARD BIRD

AMFITHEATROF, DANIELE

1939

Bridal Suite (see Guttmann)
6,000 Enemies (see E. Ward)
Fast and Furious (with C. Bakaleinikoff) MGM
Nick Carter, Master Detective (o: Arnaud) MGM

1940

The Man from Dakota (see Snell)
Northwest Passage (see Stothart)
And One Was Beautiful (o: Raab, Marquardt, Skiles) MGM
Edison, the Man (see Stothart)
Phantom Raiders (see Snell)

New Moon (see Stothart)
We Who Are Young (see Kaper)
Boom Town (see Waxman)
Third Finger, Left Hand (see Snell)
Escape (see Waxman)
Gallant Sons (see Snell)
Comrade X (see Kaper)
Keeping Company (o: Raab, Maxwell, Marquardt) MGM

1941

Free and Easy (o: Nussbaum, Heglin, Altschuler) MGM
Billy the Kid (see Snell)
The Get-Away (o: Raab, Nussbaum) MGM
The Big Store (see Hayton)
They Met in Bombay (see Stothart)
Blossoms in the Dust (see Stothart)
The Stars Look Down (with Hans May; ac: Castelnuovo-Tedesco) MGM
Dr. Jekyll and Mr. Hyde (see Waxman)
Down in San Diego (with Snell, Cutter) MGM
Married Bachelor (with Hayton, S. Kaplan) MGM
When Ladies Meet (see Kaper)
Honky Tonk (see Waxman)
Unholy Partners (see Snell)
Kathleen (see Waxman)
H. M. Pulham, Esq. (see Kaper)
The Vanishing Virginian (o: Raab) MGM
Johnny Eager (see Kaper)
The Bugle Sounds (see Hayton)
Mr. and Mrs. North (o: Raab) MGM

1942

Joe Smith, American (o: Raab) MGM
Nazi Agent (with Hayton, Kaper, Snell; ac: Kaplan; o: Raab, Heglin, Nussbaum) MGM
We Were Dancing (see Kaper)
A Yank on the Burma Road (with Hayton; o: Raab, Heglin) MGM
Kid Glove Killer (see Hayton)
Fingers at the Window (see Kaper)
Sunday Punch (see Snell)
Mrs. Miniver (see Stothart)
Jackass Mail (m&e: Snell; o: Raab) MGM
Calling Dr. Gillespie (o: Raab, Heglin, Marquardt, Nussbaum) MGM
The Affairs of Martha (see Kaper)
Tish (see Snell)
The Talk of the Town (see Hollander)
Somewhere I'll Find You (see Kaper)
Cairo (see Stothart)
Whistling in Dixie (see Hayton)
Eyes in the Night (see Hayton)
The Omaha Trail (see Snell)
White Cargo (see Kaper)
Northwest Rangers (o: Raab, Nussbaum, Heglin) MGM
Random Harvest (see Stothart)
Dr. Gillespie's New Assistant (o: Nussbaum, Heglin, Raab) MGM
Andy Hardy's Double Life (o: Raab) MGM
Keeper of the Flame (see Kaper)
Tennessee Johnson (see Stothart)

1943

Slightly Dangerous (see Kaper)
A Stranger in Town (ac: N. Shilkret; o: Raab) MGM
Harrigan's Kid (ac: Castelnuovo-Tedesco; o: Heglin, Raab) MGM
Aerial Gunner PAR
High Explosive PAR
The Kansan (see Carbonara)
DuBarry Was a Lady (ac: Castelnuovo-Tedesco, Stoll, Bassman, D. Raksin) MGM
Dr. Gillespie's Criminal Case (o: Raab, Heglin) MGM
Above Suspicion (see Kaper)
Bataan (see Kaper)
I Dood It (see Bassman)
Lassie Come Home (o: Raab, Marquardt, Heglin) MGM
Lost Angel (o: Raab) MGM

1944

Cry Havoc (o: Raab) MGM
Days of Glory (o: Raab) RKO
Gaslight (see Kaper)
Bathing Beauty (see J. Green)
The Canterville Ghost (see Bassman)
Lost in a Harem (see N. Shilkret)
I'll Be Seeing You (o: Raab) SELZNICK

1945

Son of Lassie (see Stothart)
Week-End at the Waldorf (see J. Green)
Guest Wife UA
The Story of the DE-733 (doc.; o: Raab, Parrish) U.S. NAVY

1946

The Virginian (o: Shuken, Cutner, Raab, Parrish) PAR
Miss Susie Slagle's (o: Raab, Grau) PAR
Suspense (o: Raab, G. Rose) MON
O.S.S. (with Roemheld; o: Parrish, Shuken, Cutner, Raab) PAR

Song of the South (photoplay score; cartoon score: P. Smith; ac: Wolcott; o: Plumb) WDP
Temptation UNIV
1947
The Beginning or the End (o: Shuken, Cutner) MGM
Time Out of Mind (ac: Castelnuovo-Tedesco, based on Rozsa's score for *Lydia;* o: Shuken, Cutner, Zador) UNIV
Ivy (o: Tamkin, Shuken, Cutner) UNIV
Singapore (o: Tamkin) UNIV
The Lost Moment (o: Tamkin) UNIV
1948
The Senator Was Indiscreet (o: Tamkin; ac: L. Stevens, o: Torbett) UNIV
Another Part of the Forest (o: Tamkin) UNIV
Letter from an Unknown Woman (o: Tamkin) UNIV
Rogues' Regiment (o: Tamkin) UNIV
You Gotta Stay Happy (o: Tamkin) UNIV
An Act of Murder (o: Tamkin) UNIV
1949
The Fan (o: de Packh) TCF
Sand (o: de Packh) TCF
House of Strangers (o: de Packh, Hagen) TCF
1950
Backfire (o: Shuken, Cutner; ac: M. Steiner) WB
Under My Skin (o: de Packh) TCF
The Capture (o: Tamkin) RKO
The Damned Don't Cry (o: de Packh, Shuken, Cutner) WB
Devil's Doorway (o: Tamkin) MGM
Copper Canyon (o: Cutner, Parrish, Shuken, Tamkin) PAR
1951
Storm Warning (o: de Packh, Tamkin) WB
Bird of Paradise (o: E. Powell) TCF
The Painted Hills (o: Raab) MGM
A Place in the Sun (see Waxman)
Angels in the Outfield (o and ac: Plumb) MGM
Tomorrow Is Another Day (o: de Packh) WB
The Desert Fox (o: de Packh) TCF
1952
Carrie (see D. Raksin)
1953
Scandal at Scourie (o: Cutner, Shuken, Marquardt) MGM
Devil's Canyon (o: Grau) RKO
1954
The Naked Jungle (o: de Packh, Cutner) PAR
Human Desire (o: de Packh) COL
Day of Triumph CENTURY
1955
Trial MGM
The Desperate Hours (with Kubik) PAR
1956
The Last Hunt (o: Cutner, Sendrey) MGM
The Mountain (o: Van Cleave) PAR
1957
The Unholy Wife RKO
Spanish Affair (o: Van Cleave, Shuken, Hayes) PAR
1958
Fraulein (o: H. Spencer) TCF
From Hell to Texas (o: de Packh) TCF
That Kind of Woman (o: de Packh; ac: Van Cleave) PAR
1959
Edge of Eternity COL
1960
Heller in Pink Tights (o: Van Cleave, Shuken, Hayes) PAR
1965
Major Dundee (o: Tamkin, Raab) COL
Shorts (MGM)
1939
Prophet Without Honor (see Snell)
The Giant of Norway (see Snell)
The Story That Couldn't Be Printed (see Snell)
One Against the World (o: Marquardt)
The Ash Can Fleet (with C. Bakaleinikoff)
A Failure at Fifty (with C. Bakaleinikoff; o: Marquardt)
Ski Birds (with C. Bakaleinikoff; o: Marquardt)
Romance of the Potato (o: Marquardt)
Forgotten Victory (o: Marquardt)
1940
The Old South (o: Heglin, Marquardt)
Northward, Ho! (o: Raab)
Stuffie (see Snell)
The Flag Speaks (see Snell)
XXX Medico (o: Raab, Heglin)
The Hidden Master (see Snell)
Servant of Mankind (o: Marquardt, Heglin, Nussbaum)
A Way in the Wilderness (see Snell)
Trifles of Importance (o: Marquardt)
Soak the Old (mt)
Dreams (o: Heglin, Marquardt)

The Baron and the Rose (o: Heglin, Raab, Nussbaum)
Utopia of Death (o: Arnaud, Marquardt)
Eyes of the Navy (o: Marquardt)
The Miracle of Sound
The Great Meddler (o: Heglin)
You Can't Fool a Camera

1941
The Happiest Man on Earth (o: Maxwell)
Sea for Yourself (o: Raab)
Whispers (o: Raab, Marquardt, Heglin)
More Trifles of Importance (o: Marquardt, Raab)
Out of Darkness (o: Marquardt)
1-2-3-Go! (o: Marquardt, Raab)
This Is the Bowery (o: Nussbaum)
The Battle (o: Marquardt)
Coffins on Wheels (mt)
Memories of Europe (o: Nussbaum)
The Man Who Changed the World (o: Raab, Nussbaum)
Hobbies (o: Raab, Heglin, Marquardt)
Strange Testament (o: Raab; ac: Hayton, o: Heglin)
Scenic Grandeur
Viva Mexico

1942
Main Street on the March! (with Snell, S. Kaplan; o: Raab, Heglin)
Victory Quiz (o: Marquardt)
The Woman in the House (see Hayton)
Further Prophesies of Nostradamus (see Snell)
Vendetta (ac: Castelnuovo-Tedesco; o: Marquardt)
Mr. Blabbermouth! (with Castelnuovo-Tedesco; o: Nussbaum, Raab, Heglin, Marquardt)

1943
Brief Interval (o: Heglin)
Plan for Destruction (see N. Shilkret)
Sucker Bait (with N. Shilkret; ac: Terr; o: Raab, Nussbaum, Salinger, Heglin)

Shorts (PAR)

1942
A Letter from Bataan
We Refuse to Die
The Price of Victory

1943
The Aldrich Family Gets in the Scrap

Trailers

1941
A Woman's Face (o: Cutter) MGM
Smilin' Through (o: Marquardt) MGM

1943
Swing Shift Maisie (o: H. Taylor) MGM

1955
The Desperate Hours (o: Shuken) PAR

AMMON, MARTIN

1967
Professor Lust AMERICAN FILM

AMRAM, DAVID

1961
The Young Savages UA
Splendor in the Grass WB

1962
The Manchurian Candidate UA

1969
The Arrangement WB

Shorts

1957
Echo of an Era (doc.) HENRY FREEMAN

1959
Harmful Effects of Tobacco (doc.) PAUL NEWMAN
Pull My Daisy G-STRING ENTERPRISES

1967
To Be Alive EXPO 67

ANDERSEN, MICHAEL

1960
12 to the Moon COL

1961
Wings of Chance UNIV

1962
Tower of London UA
What Ever Happened to Baby Jane? (see De Vol)

1963
Terrified! CROWN

1967
Tell Me in the Sunlight MOVIE-RAMA

ANDERSON, HAROLD

Documentary Shorts (RKO PATHÉ)

1946
Great Lakes
Panama
Quarter Horses
Tenderfoot Trail
Winning Basketball

ANDES, MATT

1970
Joshua in a Box (an. short) STEPHEN BOSUSTOW

ANDREWS, DONALD JOHN
1952
Return of the Plainsman ASTOR

ANDREWS, JOEL
1965
Early Expressionists (doc. short) SUMMUS FILMS
1967
The Weaver (doc. short) PAUL HOEFLER
1969
Hildur and the Magician (with Ilger) LARRY JORDAN

ANDRIESSEN, JURRIAAN
1950
Yellowstone Park (doc. short) FORD MOTOR CO.
1965
Holland Off Guard (doc. short) PAR

ANTHEIL, GEORGE
1935
Once in a Blue Moon PAR
The Scoundrel (not used) PAR
1937
The Plainsman PAR
Make Way for Tomorrow (see V. Young)
1938
The Buccaneer (ac: Roder, Carbonara) PAR
1940
Angels Over Broadway COL
1946
Specter of the Rose (o: Maxwell) REP
Plainsman and the Lady (o: Gold, Butts, N. Scott) REP
That Brennan Girl (o: Gold) REP
1947
Repeat Performance EL
1949
Knock on Any Door (o: Gold) COL
We Were Strangers (o: Gold) COL
The Fighting Kentuckian (o: Butts) REP
Tokyo Joe (o: Gold) COL
1950
House by the River (o: Butts) REP
In a Lonely Place (o: Gold) COL
1951
Sirocco (o: Gold) COL
1952
The Sniper (o: A. Morton) COL
Actors and Sin (o: Gold) UA
1953
The Juggler (o: A. Morton) COL
Dementia (o: Gold) JOHN PARKER
1954
Hunters of the Deep (doc.; o: Cutner) DCA
1955
Not as a Stranger (o: Gold) UA
1957
The Young Don't Cry COL
The Pride and the Passion (o: Gold) UA
Shorts
1935
Harlem Sketches (doc.) VANGUARD FILMS
1939
N.Y. World's Fair doc. (title unknown) RALPH STEINER
1941
Orchids to Charlie ELIZABETH ARDEN

ANTONINI, ALFREDO
1939
The Miracle of Sister Beatrice PARK LANE
[Also composed music for importations of foreign silent films.]

APPLEBAUM, LOUIS
[Canadian composer; his filmography includes both American and Canadian films.]
1944
Tomorrow, the World! UA
1945
G. I. Joe (with Ronell) UA
1948
Dreams That Money Can Buy FILMS INT'L. OF AMERICA
(Continuity story and "Blue Man" [Hans Richter]; Paul Bowles: "Mobiles" [Alexander Calder] and "Desire" [Max Ernst]; John Cage: "Discs" [Marcel Duchamp]; David Diamond: "Circus" [Alexander Calder]; Darius Milhaud: "Ruth, Roses and Revolvers" [Man Ray])
1949
Lost Boundaries LOUIS DE ROCHEMONT
1951
Teresa MGM
The Whistle at Eaton Falls LOUIS DE ROCHEMONT
1952
Walk East on Beacon LOUIS DE ROCHEMONT
1961
The Mask (ac: Myron Schaeffer) WB
Documentary Features
1950
Farewell to Yesterday (with Robert McBride, Richard Mohaupt) TCF
1951
Royal Journey NFBC

1953
All My Babies GEORGIA DEPT. OF HEALTH
1954
And Now Miguel U.S. STATE DEPT.
The Stratford Adventure NFBC
1957
Canadian Profile NFBC
1967
Athabasca SUN OIL CO.

Documentary Shorts

1941
Plugger RAGAN ASSOCIATES
1945
Three Bears UNIV
Thrift Plan RAGAN ASSOCIATES
1946
Coal Gas (animated) CRAWLEY FILMS
1947
Rheumatic Fever WORLD TODAY
Starting Line WORLD TODAY
Searchlight on the Nations WORLD TODAY
Miracle of Living U.S. ARMY SIGNAL CORPS
Borrowing in Subtraction WORLD TODAY
National Rebuild WORLD TODAY
Lifeline WORLD TODAY
Round Trip WORLD TODAY
East by North U.S. STATE DEPT.
Puerto Rico PUERTO RICAN GOVT.
One World or None RAGAN ASSOCIATES
Wonder Eye WORLD TODAY
1948
First as a Child WORLD TODAY
Stuff for Stuff RAGAN ASSOCIATES
Tale in a Tea Cup (U.S. sequences) WORLD TODAY
Czechoslovakia MARCH OF TIME
Crystal of Energy SUGAR RESEARCH FOUNDATION
1949
Feeling All Right SOUTHERN EDUCATIONAL FILMS
Canadian Heritage ?
1950
Palmour Street SOUTHERN EDUCATIONAL FILMS
1952
Operation A-Bomb RKO PATHÉ
1953
Everybody's Handicapped GRAPHIC ASSOCIATES
1954
Hard Brought Up, A Child Welfare Story POTOMAC FILM PRODUCERS
1955
The Invader POTOMAC FILM PRODUCERS
1957
None Goes His Way Alone METHODIST CHURCH
1958
Assignment: Mankind CHRISTIAN SCIENCE PUBLISHING SOCIETY

Documentary Shorts (NFBC)

1940
Industrial Workers of Central Canada
1941
Dollar Dance (an.)
Call for Volunteers
1942
Victory Loan News Clips
The Mask of Nippon (see Agostini)
Art of Living
The Mouth
The Hand
The Eye
New Spirit
Wings for Victory
Inside Nazi Japan
1943
Wartime Housing
Northwest Passage
More Pigs (an.)
Military Law
A Man and His Job
Coal Face, Canada
Jimmy Jones
Handle with Care
Nutrition (an.)
13 Platoon
Industrial Workers
C.W.A.C. News Clip
Alexis Tremblay: Habitant (with Maurice Blackburn)
War for Men's Minds
Action Stations
Proudly She Marches
1944
Air Cadets
Flight 6
Proudest Girl in the World
Trans-Canada Express
Fortress Japan
Hoe to It
Grim Pastures
Target Berlin
Listen Soldier
Ships and Men
Money, Goods and Prices
Welcome Soldier

The Plots Thicken
Chansons Populaire (an.)
The Squirrel
1945
Ordeal by Ice
Food, Weapon of Conquest
VE-VJ
The Three Blind Mice
Third Victory Loan
Rackets (an.)
Suffer Little Children
Guests of Honour
Main Street, Canada (with Maurice Blackburn)
Wings Over Canada
1946
New Faces Come Back
Bronco Busters
Ten Little Indians (an.)
Barn Dance
Out of the Ruins
White Safari
A Little Phantasy on a 19th-Century Painting
1947
The Boy Who Stopped Niagara
Ten Little Farmers (an.)
The People Between
Montreal by Night
Tomorrow's Citizens
1948
Art for Everybody
Cartography
1949
Ballet Festival
1950
A Friend at the Door
Challenge—Science Against Cancer
1951
Around Is Around
Pen Point Percussion
The Fight: Science Against Cancer
1952
Arctic Saga
Opera School
1953
Varley
1954
Riches of the Earth
A Thousand Million Years
1955
The Jolifou Inn
Man Against a Fungus
1957
Bar Mitzvah
1959
Wheat Country
1965
The Forest
The Red Kite
1966
Paddle to the Sea

AREL, BÜLENT
1961
Wall Street Impressions (short) ?

ARMBRUSTER, ROBERT
1938
Steel—Man's Servant (doc. short) U.S. STEEL
1947
Northwest Outpost REP
1952
I Dream of Jeanie REP
1953
Sweethearts on Parade REP
1962
The Hook (see Adler)
1963
Dime with a Halo (see R. Stein)
1965
Clarence, the Cross-Eyed Lion (theme: S. Manne; + stock) MGM

ARNAUD, LEO
1937
Song of Revolt (short; see Cutter)
Broadway Melody of 1938 (see Cutter)
1940
Strike Up the Band (see Stoll)
1941
Blondie Goes Latin COL
I'll Wait for You (see Kaper)
Babes on Broadway (see Stoll)
1943
Presenting Lily Mars (see Stoll)
1944
Grandfather's Follies (short) WB
1946
The Thrill of Brazil COL
1947
Trail to San Antone (see M. Glickman)
Apache Rose (see Maxwell)
1949
Neptune's Daughter (see Stoll)
1953
Sombrero (o: Courage) MGM
1957
Day of Fear MARTIN GOSCH

1962
Jumbo (see Stoll)
1964
The Unsinkable Molly Brown (with Courage, C. Jackson) MGM
[Also a prolific arranger and orchestrator.]

ARNELL, RICHARD
1941
The Land (doc.) USDA
1942
Farm Front (doc. short) USDA
[Several subsequent films in Great Britain.]

ASHLEY, ROBERT
Shorts
1957
The Image in Time GEORGE MANUPELLI
1960
Bottleman GEORGE MANUPELLI
1961
The House GEORGE MANUPELLI
1963
Five Short Films (see Manupelli)
1964
Jenny and the Poet GEORGE MANUPELLI
1965
My May GEORGE MANUPELLI
1966
Goodbye to Captain Hook (doc.) U. OF MICHIGAN
1967
Overdrive GEORGE MANUPELLI
1969
Portraits, Self-Portraits, and Still Lifes (feature; with Sheff) GEORGE MANUPELLI
1970
Battery Davis P. MAKANNA
Dr. Chicago GEORGE MANUPELLI

AURANDT, RICHARD D.
1955
Gang Busters VISUAL DRAMA
1960
Walk Tall TCF
1961
The Silent Call TCF

AUSTIN, LARRY
Shorts (LARRY AUSTIN)
1966
Bass
1967
Brass
1968
The Magicians
1969
Black/White Study
Color Study

AXSOM, EILEEN
1952
Land of the Sleeping Fire (short) BERNARD E. CAWLEY

AXT, WILLIAM
1920
Passion (with Mendoza; U.S. release of 1919 German film, *Madame DuBarry*) FN
The Mark of Zorro UA
1921
The Four Horsemen of the Apocalypse (see Gottschalk)
The Birth of a Nation (see Breil, 1915)
1922
Nanook of the North PATHÉ
The Prisoner of Zenda (another score by Luz) METRO
1923
Richard the Lion-Hearted ALLIED
Scaramouche (another score by Kempinski) METRO
1924
The Sea Hawk (with Mendoza; another score by Copping, q.v.) FN
The Navigator METRO-GOLDWYN
He Who Gets Slapped METRO-GOLDWYN
1925
Greed (another score by Kempinski) METRO-GOLDWYN
The Merry Widow (a of Franz Lehar with Mendoza; o: Baron) MGM
The Big Parade (o: Baron) MGM
Ben-Hur (o: Baron) MGM
1926
The Torrent MGM
Don Juan (with Mendoza; o: Baron) WB
La Boheme (o: Baron) MGM
Mare Nostrum (with Mendoza; o: Baron) MGM
Bardelys the Magnificent (another score by Bassett, q.v.) MGM
Faust (U.S. release of German film) MGM
The Scarlet Letter (with Mendoza) MGM
1927
The Fire Brigade (with Mendoza) MGM
Flesh and the Devil MGM
Slide, Kelly, Slide (with Mendoza) MGM

Camille (with Mendoza) FN
Annie Laurie (with Mendoza) MGM

1928
Love (another score by Luz) MGM
The Student Prince in Old Heidelberg (with Mendoza) MGM
Our Dancing Daughters (+ stock) MGM
Excess Baggage (+ stock) MGM
While the City Sleeps (ac: Cupero; + stock) MGM
Show People (+ stock) MGM
The Wind (+ stock) MGM
The Masks of the Devil (ac: Stahlberg; + stock) MGM
White Shadows in the South Seas (+ stock) MGM
West of Zanzibar (with Stahlberg; + stock) MGM
A Woman of Affairs (+ stock) MGM
The Bellamy Trial (with Marquardt; m&e: Buffano; + stock) MGM

1929
The Flying Fleet (+ stock) MGM
Alias Jimmy Valentine (ac: Stahlberg; + stock) MGM
A Lady of Chance (+ stock) MGM
Wild Orchids (+ stock) MGM
Tide of Empire (ac: Stahlberg, Cupero; + stock) MGM
Desert Nights (+ stock) MGM
The Pagan (+ stock) MGM
Spite Marriage (see Stahlberg)
Where East Is East (+ stock) MGM
The Duke Steps Out (+ stock) MGM
The Trail of '98 (+ stock) MGM
Thunder (+ stock) MGM
The Last of Mrs. Cheyney (+ stock) MGM
Madame X (with Wineland; + stock) MGM
The Viking (+ stock) MGM
The Single Standard (+ stock) MGM
Our Modern Maidens (+ stock) MGM
Marianne (with Maxwell; + stock) MGM
Wonder of Women (see A. Lange)
Speedway (+ stock) MGM
Dynamite (with Lange; + stock) MGM
The Unholy Night (+ stock) MGM
The Mysterious Island (see Lamkoff)
The Thirteenth Chair (mt; + stock) MGM
The Kiss (+ stock) MGM
It's a Great Life (+ stock) MGM

1930
Navy Blues (+ stock) MGM
Their Own Desire (+ stock) MGM
Chasing Rainbows (+ stock) MGM
Devil May Care (+ stock) MGM
The Woman Racket MGM
The Ship from Shanghai (foreign version; + stock) MGM
Anna Christie (+ stock) MGM
Redemption (+ stock) MGM
The Rogue Song (+ stock) MGM
Free and Easy (foreign version; + stock) MGM
The Mysterious Lady (foreign version of 1928 film; + stock) MGM
Untamed (+ stock) MGM
The Cossacks (foreign version of 1928 film; with Lamkoff; + stock) MGM
Dynamite (foreign version of 1929 film) MGM
The Bishop Murder Case (+ stock) MGM
The Big House (mt) MGM
The Unholy Three (+ stock) MGM
Romance (o: Marquardt, Stahlberg, Lamkoff; + stock) MGM
Call of the Flesh (o: Lamkoff; + stock) MGM

1931
New Moon (ac) MGM
The Great Meadow (mt) MGM
Inspiration (o: Maxwell; + stock) MGM
Trader Horn (et; + stock) MGM
Madam Satan (foreign version of 1930 film; + stock) MGM
Jenny Lind (foreign version of 1930 film, *A Lady's Morals;* + stock) MGM
Doughboys (foreign version of 1930 film) MGM
Susan Lenox (o: Marquardt; + stock) MGM
Flying High (mt; o: Maxwell) MGM
Private Lives (+ stock) MGM

1932
Mata Hari (+ stock) MGM
Grand Hotel (mt; ac: Maxwell) MGM
Letty Lynton (mt; + stock) MGM
Are You Listening? MGM
As You Desire Me (+ stock) MGM
The Washington Masquerade (mt; + stock) MGM
Speak Easily (mt; + stock) MGM
Blondie of the Follies MGM
The Wet Parade MGM
Payment Deferred (o: Maxwell) MGM
Faithless (mt; + stock) MGM
The Mask of Fu Manchu MGM
Prosperity (+ stock) MGM

1933
Whistling in the Dark MGM

The Secret of Madame Blanche (o: Maxwell, Marquardt) MGM
Clear All Wires (o: Maxwell, Marquardt) MGM
Fast Workers (et; + stock) MGM
Gabriel Over the White House (o: Marquardt) MGM
Looking Forward (o: Marquardt) MGM
Today We Live (mt; + stock) MGM
Hell Below (o: Maxwell) MGM
Reunion in Vienna (o: Marquardt) MGM
Made on Broadway (mt; + stock) MGM
The Nuisance MGM
When Ladies Meet (o: Maxwell) MGM
Midnight Mary (o: Marquardt, Maxwell) MGM
Storm at Daybreak (o: Marquardt) MGM
Another Language (mt; o: Marquardt) MGM
Broadway to Hollywood (+ stock) MGM
Beauty for Sale (+ stock) MGM
Dinner at Eight MGM
Bombshell (+ stock) MGM
Should Ladies Behave? (o: de Packh) MGM

1934

Fugitive Lovers (o: Marquardt) MGM
Eskimo (o: Marquardt) MGM
You Can't Buy Everything (o: de Packh) MGM
This Side of Heaven (o: de Packh) MGM
The Mystery of Mr. X (o: Marquardt) MGM
Lazy River (o: Marquardt) MGM
Riptide (see Stothart)
Manhattan Melodrama (o: Marquardt, de Packh; + stock) MGM
Sadie McKee (o: de Packh, W. Allen) MGM
Hollywood Party MGM
The Thin Man (o: de Packh, W. Allen, Virgil) MGM
Operator 13 (o: Marquardt) MGM
Stamboul Quest (o: Marquardt; + stock) MGM
Paris Interlude (o: Marquardt) MGM
The Girl from Missouri MGM
Straight Is the Way (o: Marquardt) MGM
Hide-Out (o: Maxwell) MGM
Death on the Diamond (o: Marquardt) MGM
A Wicked Woman (o: Marquardt) MGM

1935

David Copperfield (see Stothart)
Pursuit (see Stothart)
O'Shaughnessy's Boy (o: Marquardt) MGM
It's In the Air (o: Marquardt) MGM
Rendezvous (o: Marquardt) MGM
Last of the Pagans (with Hajos, Roder; ac: Friedhofer, Harling; o: Reese, Virgil, Raab, Marquardt) MGM

1936

Three Live Ghosts (o: Virgil, W. Allen) MGM
Tough Guy (with Roemheld, Bassett; o: Maxwell, Marquardt, Virgil, W. Allen) MGM
The Garden Murder Case (o: Virgil, Marquardt) MGM
Three Godfathers (o: Marquardt, Virgil, Raab, Maxwell) MGM
The Unguarded Hour (o: Marquardt) MGM
The Great Ziegfeld (see A. Lange)
Three Wise Guys (o: Marquardt, W. Allen; + stock) MGM
We Went to College (o: Marquardt, W. Allen) MGM
Suzy (o: Marquardt, Bassman, W. Allen, Raab) MGM
Piccadilly Jim (o: Bassman, W. Allen, Marquardt) MGM
Old Hutch (o: Bassman, Marquardt, W. Allen) MGM
Libeled Lady (o: Bassman) MGM
All American Chump (o: Marquardt, Bassman) MGM
Mad Holiday (o: Marquardt) MGM

1937

Under Cover of Night (o: Marquardt, Virgil) MGM
The Last of Mrs. Cheyney (o: Bassman, Marquardt) MGM
Espionage (o: Marquardt) MGM
Song of the City (ac: Vaughan; o: Marquardt, Vaughan) MGM
Parnell (o: Marquardt, Bassman) MGM
Between Two Women (o: Bassman, Marquardt) MGM
London by Night (o: Marquardt, Vaughan) MGM
Big City (o: Bassman, Marquardt) MGM
Thoroughbreds Don't Cry (o: Cutter, Arnaud) MGM
Beg, Borrow, or Steal (o: Virgil, Marquardt, Bassman) MGM
The Bad Man of Brimstone (o: Marquardt, Vaughan) MGM

1938

Everybody Sing (o: Bassman, Marquardt) MGM
Of Human Hearts (see Stothart)

The First Hundred Years (o: Marquardt, Cutter, Arnaud, Virgil) MGM
Yellow Jack (o: Marquardt, Arnaud) MGM
Fast Company (o: Bassman) MGM
Rich Man, Poor Girl (o: Bassman) MGM
Listen, Darling (o: Bassman) MGM
Spring Madness (o: Bassman, Raab) MGM
The Girl Downstairs (o: Raab, Marquardt, Bassman) MGM
Pygmalion (additional music for U.S. version, supplementing Arthur Honegger's score for British version) MGM

1939
Stand Up and Fight (o: Marquardt, Raab) MGM
Sergeant Madden (o: Marquardt, Raab) MGM
The Kid from Texas (o: Marquardt, Virgil) MGM
Tell No Tales (o: Marquardt) MGM
Miracles for Sale (+ stock) MGM
Balalaika (see Stothart)

1940
Northwest Passage (see Stothart)
Untamed (o: Marquardt, de Packh) PAR

Shorts (MGM)

1930
Who Killed Rover? (+ stock)
China's Old Man River (+ stock)
Modern Madrid (mt)
The General (mt; o: R. Heindorf)
Dublin and Nearby (+ stock)

1931
The Big Dog House (+ stock)
Love-Tails of Morocco (+ stock)
Wild and Woolly (o: Marquardt; + stock)

1932
Microscopic Mysteries (+ stock)

1933
Whisperin' Bill (+ stock)
Menu
Plane Nuts (mt; o: Marquardt; + stock)

1934
Goofy Movies No. 2 (o: Marquardt)
Vital Victuals
Flying Hunters
Old Shep (o: Marquardt; + stock)
Dartmouth Days
Taking Care of Baby (o: Marquardt)

1935
Buried Loot
The Perfect Tribute (o: Marquardt)
Trained Hoofs (o: Marquardt)
Pitcairn Island Today

1936
Primitive Pitcairn (o: Marquardt)
The Jonker Diamond (o: Marquardt, Maxwell)
Wanted a Master (o: Bassman)

1937
Bar-Rac's Night Out (o: Marquardt)
Ski Skill (o: Marquardt)
Friend Indeed (o: Bassman)

1938
La Savate (o: Marquardt)
Modeling for Money (o: Marquardt)
The Story of Doctor Carver (o: Marquardt)

1939
Heroes at Leisure (with Snell; o: Marquardt, Raab)

Trailers (MGM)

1933
Rasputin and the Empress (o: Marquardt)

1934
Men in White (o: Marquardt)

1936
Petticoat Fever (o: Virgil)

B

BABBITT, MILTON

1949
Into the Good Ground (short) PATHESCOPE

BACHARACH, BURT

1965
What's New Pussycat? (o: C. Blackwell) UA

1966
After the Fox (o: C. Blackwell) UA

1967
Casino Royale (o: Shuken, Hayes) COL

1969
Butch Cassidy and the Sundance Kid (o: Shuken, Hayes) TCF

BADER, DON

1963
The Fat Black Pussycat STORMCO

BAER, MANNY (EMMANUEL)
1928
Marriage by Contract TS
1930
With Byrd at the South Pole (doc.) PAR

BAGLEY, DONALD
1961
Ole Rex (with Hinshaw) UNIV
1970
The Zodiac Couples S.A.E.

BÄHLER, TOM
1967
The Hippie Revolt (doc.; with John Bähler) HEADLINER

BAKALEINIKOFF, CONSTANTIN
1937
The Emperor's Candlesticks (see Waxman)
1939
Fast and Furious (see Amfitheatrof)
The Gentleman from Arizona MON
1940
Isle of Destiny RKO
Dr. Christian Meets the Women RKO
Escape (see Waxman)
Remedy for Riches RKO
1941
Scattergood Baines RKO
Melody for Three RKO
Power Dive PAR
Scattergood Pulls the Strings RKO
They Meet Again RKO
Shorts (MGM)
1936
Little Boy Blue (o: Arnaud, W. Allen; m&e: Kopp, o: Marquardt)
1938
The Forgotten Step (see Snell)
1939
Rural Hungary
Angel of Mercy (see Snell)
Colorful Caracao
A Day on Treasure Island
Captain Spanky's Show Boat (o: Marquardt, Heglin)
The Ash Can Fleet (see Amfitheatrof)
A Failure at Fifty (see Amfitheatrof)
Natural Wonders of Washington State
Let's Talk Turkey (o: Heglin)
Ski Birds (see Amfitheatrof)
Quaint St. Augustine
Valiant Venezuela
Night Descends on Treasure Island
1940
Beautiful Bali
Calling on Colombia
The Capital City, Washington, D.C.
Cavalcade of San Francisco
Glimpses of Kentucky
Glimpses of Washington State
Land of Alaska Nellie
Modern New Orleans
Old Natchez on the Mississippi
Old New Mexico
Old New Orleans
Red Men on Parade
Seattle, Gateway to the Northwest
Sitka and Juneau, A Tale of Two Cities
Suva, Pride of Fiji
1941
George Town, Pride of Penang
Glimpses of Florida
Haiti, Land of Dark Majesty
The Inside Passage
1943
Salt Lake Diversions

BAKALEINIKOFF, MISCHA
[Although he is credited on many cue sheets since 1930 for music for Columbia and independent films, whether this music was composed for specific films or for music libraries is not known. No music attributed to him before 1943 has been found. From 1944 to 1960, he received screen credit as musical director on many Columbia features and serials, mostly films with scores compiled wholly or in part from stock music. Only films for which his original music has been found are listed here, all of them for Columbia.]
1943
Crime Doctor (partial)
1944
Sergeant Mike (see Castelnuovo-Tedesco)
1946
Throw a Saddle on a Star (see Earl Lawrence)
The Secret of the Whistler (see Gilbert)
Lone Star Moonlight (see M. Glickman)
1947
Blondie's Big Moment (+ stock)
The Lone Wolf in Mexico (see Gertz)
Sport of Kings (+ stock)
The Son of Rusty (see Gertz)
Smoky River Serenade (ac: Gertz)
Blondie in the Dough (+ stock)
The Last Round-Up (see Dubin)
Blondie's Anniversary (see P. Smith)

1948
Glamour Girl (with P. Smith, Murphy)
Mary Lou (see Dubin)
The Arkansas Swing
The Strawberry Roan (m&e: Dubin)
The Big Sombrero (with Dubin; + stock)
1950
The Palomino (see Leipold)
Hoedown (see Leipold)
Beware of Blondie (see Leipold)
1953
Serpent of the Nile (+ stock)
Siren of Bagdad (see Leipold)
Mission Over Korea (+ stock)
The Stranger Wore a Gun (+ stock)
Valley of Headhunters (+ stock)
Slaves of Babylon (see Vars)
Gun Fury (with A. Morton; + stock)
1954
Battle of Rogue River (see Duning)
1955
New Orleans Uncensored (+ stock)
Cell 2455, Death Row (+ stock)
It Came from Beneath the Sea (+ stock)
The Crooked Web (+ stock)
1956
Over Exposed (+ stock)
Earth vs. the Flying Saucers (+ stock)
Miami Exposé (+ stock)
Reprisal! (+ stock)
The White Squaw (+ stock)
Rumble on the Docks (+ stock)
7th Cavalry (+ stock)
1957
Zombies of Mora Tau (+ stock)
The Guns of Fort Petticoat (ac: Greeley; + stock)
The Phantom Stagecoach (+ stock)
Hellcats of the Navy (mt: Greeley; + stock)
The Giant Claw (+ stock)
The 27th Day (mt: Duning; + stock)
No Time to Be Young (mt: Greeley; + stock)
Domino Kid (+ stock)
The Tijuana Story (+ stock)
The Hard Man (+ stock)
20 Million Miles to Earth (+ stock)
1958
Return to Warbow (+ stock)
Going Steady (+ stock)
The World Was His Jury (+ stock)
The True Story of Lynn Stuart (+ stock)
Screaming Mimi (+ stock)
The Case Against Brooklyn (+ stock)
The Lineup (+ stock)
Apache Territory (+ stock)
1959
Have Rocket, Will Travel (+ stock)
The Flying Fontaines (+ stock)
1960
Comanche Station (+ stock)
The Enemy General

BAKER, ABE
1962
The Brain That Wouldn't Die (with Restaino) AIP

BAKER, ALAN
1970
Changes (doc.) CINEX

BAKER, BILL
1956
The Man and the Bird (short) MEHRING

BAKER, BUDDY
1954
Wicked Woman (o: Mullendore) UA
1959
Toby Tyler (o: Sheets) WDP
1960
The Hound That Thought He Was a Raccoon (with Lava; o: Marks) WDP
1963
Summer Magic (o: Sheets, Hammack) WDP
The Misadventures of Merlin Jones (o: Brunner) WDP
1964
A Tiger Walks (o: Brunner) WDP
1965
The Monkey's Uncle (o: Sheets) WDP
1967
The Gnome-Mobile (o: W. Robinson) WDP
1969
Rascal (o: Sheets) WDP
King of the Grizzlies (o: Marks) WDP
Cartoons (WDP)
1956
3-D Jamboree
1959
Donald in Mathmagic Land
1961
Aquamania
Donald and the Wheel
The Litterbug

1965
Winnie the Pooh and the Honey Tree
1967
Winnie the Pooh and the Blustery Day
Animated Educational Shorts (WDP)
1960
I'm No Fool as a Pedestrian (with Dubin)
I'm No Fool in Water
1967
Family Planning

BAKER, EDNA RITCHIE
1968
The Road (doc.) FRONTIER NURSING SERVICE

BAKER, MICKEY
1968
The Story of a Three Day Pass (with Van Peebles) SIGMA III
1969
Float Like a Butterfly, Sting Like a Bee (doc.) GROVE PRESS

BAKSA, ROBERT
Documentary Shorts (HARRY ATWOOD)
1957
The Kress Collection
1958
New Horizons
1959
Projections in Indian Art
1960
Portrait of Europe
1962
Portrait of Mexico

BALAMOS, JOHN
1970
Hercules in New York RAF

BALES, RICHARD
1943
Your National Gallery (doc. short) ?
1960
The Society of the Cincinnati (doc. short) SOCIETY OF THE CINCINNATI

BALLANTINE, FRANCESCO
1967
Mundo Depravados MONIQUE PRODS.

BARBER, JOHN
1970
Norma EVE

BARKER, WARREN
1963
Strange Lovers GILLMAN
1965
Zebra in the Kitchen MGM

BARLOW, WAYNE
1938
Highlights and Shadows (see H. Hanson)

BARON, MAURICE
1926
The Better 'Ole WB
1928
Submarine COL
1929
The River FOX
1939
Back Door to Heaven PAR
[Also worked as an orchestrator.]

BARON, PAUL
1956
Toward the Unknown WB

BARRON, LOUIS AND BEBE
1956
Forbidden Planet MGM
Shorts
1950
Ai-Ye IAN HUGO
1953
Bells of Atlantis IAN HUGO
Miramagic W. LEWISOHN
1954
Jazz of Lights IAN HUGO
1959
Crystal Growing WESTERN ELECTRIC
1968
The Computer Age IBM

BARRYMORE, LIONEL
1929
His Glorious Night (+ stock) MGM

BARTLETT, MARY
1961
The Fountain of Faith (short) CLIFFORD B. WEST

BASSETT, LESLIE
1955
The Locks of Sault Ste. Marie (doc. short) U. OF MICHIGAN

BASSETT, R. H.
Silent Films (Los Angeles openings)
1926
The Volga Boatman (+ stock) PDC
Bardelys the Magnificent (+ stock) MGM
What Price Glory (+ stock) FOX
1927
Sunrise (+ stock) FOX
7th Heaven (+ stock) FOX
Loves of Carmen (based on music by Bizet et al.; + stock) FOX
Fazil (+ stock) FOX
The Devil Dancer (+ stock) UA
Sound Films
1929
Men Without Women (see Brunelli)
1930
High Society Blues (see Kaylin)
The Second Floor Mystery (see Kaylin)
The Arizona Kid (see Brunelli)
On the Level (see Lipschultz)
Rough Romance (see Brunelli)
Good Intentions (see Brunelli)
Man Trouble (ac: Fall, Gerstenberger, G. Knight) FOX
One Mad Kiss (see Brunelli)
The Sea Wolf (see Kaylin)
The Big Trail (see A. Kay)
Renegades (see A. Kay)
Part Time Wife (with G. Knight) FOX
Men on Call (see Kaylin)
1931
East Lynne (ac: G. Knight, Fall) FOX
Three Girls Lost (mt) FOX
Women of All Nations FOX
Goldie (mt; with Friedhofer) FOX
Transatlantic (with Friedhofer) FOX
The Spider (see Friedhofer)
Wicked FOX
Riders of the Purple Sage (with Knight) FOX
The Yellow Ticket (with Friedhofer) FOX
Surrender FOX
Good Sport FOX
The Rainbow Trail (see Brunelli)
Stepping Sisters FOX
1932
The Gay Caballero (+ stock) FOX
The Trial of Vivienne Ware (see Friedhofer)
While Paris Sleeps (see Arthur Kay)
Almost Married (see Friedhofer)
Bachelor's Affairs FOX
A Passport to Hell (see Friedhofer)
Chandu, the Magician (see Brunelli)
Wild Girl (see Zamecnik)
Six Hours to Live (see Brunelli)
Sherlock Holmes (with Friedhofer) FOX
Tess of the Storm Country (see De Francesco)
El Caballero de la Noche (Spanish language; with Brunelli, Friedhofer; ac: Lipschultz) FOX
Robbers' Roost (mt) FOX
Handle with Care (see Brunelli)
1933
The Face in the Sky (see Brunelli)
Dangerously Yours (see De Francesco)
Trick for Trick (ac: Kaylin; + stock) FOX
Zoo in Budapest (see Zamecnik)
Pilgrimage (ac: Kaylin, Friedhofer) FOX
The Warrior's Husband (see Zamecnik)
Hold Me Tight (o: Gerstenberger) FOX
It's Great to Be Alive (see Friedhofer)
Best of Enemies (see A. Lange)
Shanghai Madness (see Zamecnik)
Paddy the Next Best Thing (see De Francesco)
1934
La Ciudad de Cartón (see Kaylin)
No Greater Glory COL
The World Moves On (see De Francesco)
Have a Heart (o: Virgil) MGM
Un Capitán de Cosacos (see Kaylin)
Student Tour (o: Virgil) MGM
Evelyn Prentice MGM
The Gay Bride (o: Virgil) MGM
The Band Plays On MGM
1935
David Copperfield (see Stothart)
Society Doctor MGM
Shadow of Doubt MGM
Gypsy Night (short) MGM
Our Little Girl (see Brunelli)
Mad Love (see Tiomkin)
Curly Top (see Friedhofer)
The Black Room (see Silvers)
The Farmer Takes a Wife (see Buttolph)
Dante's Inferno (see Friedhofer)
1936
Tough Guy (see Axt)
Professional Soldier (o: E. Ross) TCF
The Prisoner of Shark Island (with Friedhofer) TCF
The Country Doctor (see Mockridge)
Song and Dance Man (see G. Rose)
The Country Beyond (+ stock) TCF
Under Two Flags (see Mockridge)

Sins of Man (see Friedhofer)
The Road to Glory (ac: Friedhofer, Buttolph) TCF
Craig's Wife (with Roder, Gerstenberger) COL
The Magnificent Brute (see Maxwell)
Dimples (see Mockridge)
Lloyd's of London (see Mockridge)

1937
Think Fast, Mr. Moto (with Kaylin; ac: G. Rose) TCF

1938
International Settlement (+ stock) TCF

1939
Susannah of the Mounties (see Maxwell)
Stanley and Livingstone (see Silvers)

BASSMAN, GEORGE

1936
Swing Banditry (short) MGM

1937
Double or Nothing (see V. Young)

1938
Poultry Pirates (cartoon; see E. Lewis)
Little Orphan Annie (see Forbes)

1939
The Wizard of Oz (see Stothart)
Lady of the Tropics (see Waxman)
Babes in Arms (see Stoll)
Blondie Brings Up Baby (see Harline)

1940
Broadway Melody of 1940 (see Stoll)
Two Girls on Broadway (see D. Raksin)
Forty Little Mothers (see Stringer)
Hullabaloo (ac: Snell) MGM
Too Many Girls RKO
Little Nellie Kelly (see Stoll)
Go West (see Stoll)

1941
Ziegfeld Girl (see Stothart)
The Big Store (see Hayton)
They Met in Bombay (see Stothart)
Lady Be Good (see Stoll)
Babes on Broadway (see Stoll)

1942
Ship Ahoy (see Stoll)
Cairo (see Stothart)
For Me and My Gal (see Edens)

1943
Cabin in the Sky (see Edens)
Presenting Lily Mars (see Stoll)
DuBarry Was a Lady (see Amfitheatrof)
Young Ideas (ac: Snell, Salinger; o: Heglin) MGM
I Dood It (with Amfitheatrof, Stoll, D. Raksin; o: Cutner, Nussbaum) MGM
Girl Crazy (see Stoll)
Whistling in Brooklyn (ac: S. Kaplan, Castelnuovo-Tedesco) MGM

1944
The Canterville Ghost (ac: Castelnuovo-Tedesco, Amfitheatrof, R. Franklyn, D. Raksin) MGM
Lost in a Harem (see N. Shilkret)
Main Street After Dark (ac: Castelnuovo-Tedesco) MGM

1945
The Clock (o: Duncan; ac: Castelnuovo-Tedesco, Cutner) MGM
Abbott and Costello in Hollywood (o: Duncan) MGM
A Letter for Evie (o: Sendrey; ac: Castelnuovo-Tedesco) MGM

1946
The Postman Always Rings Twice (o: Sendrey, Duncan) MGM
Two Smart People (o: Duncan, Sendrey) MGM
Little Mister Jim (o: Sendrey, Duncan; ac: R. Franklyn) MGM

1947
The Arnelo Affair (o: Arnaud, Cutner, Shuken; ac: R. Franklyn) MGM
The Romance of Rosy Ridge (o: Arnaud, Duncan, Sendrey) MGM

1950
Japan and the World Today (doc.) U.S. GOVT.

1953
The Joe Louis Story UA
Louisiana Territory (doc.) RKO PATHÉ

1955
Canyon Crossroads UA
Marty (see Webb)

1959
Middle of the Night COL

1962
Ride the High Country (o: Sendrey) MGM

1963
Mail Order Bride (o: Arnaud) MGM

BATH, JOHN

[Composed many features and documentary shorts in England, 1944–1958. His filmography includes both American and Canadian films.]

1958
Wolf Dog TCF
Flaming Frontier TCF

Now That April's Here KLENMAN-DAVIDSON
The Fast Ones KLENMAN-DAVIDSON

1961
1 + 1 (Exploring the Kinsey Reports) ARCH OBOLER

1963
Have Figure, Will Travel FANFARE
The Right Hand of the Devil ARAM KATCHER
The Skydivers CARDOZA-FRANCIS

1965
French Without Dressing TED LEVERSUCH

1966
Adulterous Affair TED LEVERSUCH
Flight of Birds (doc. short) PAUL BURNFORD
Night Train to Mundo Fine CARDOZA-FRANCIS

1967
Take Her by Surprise CANNON
Sex and the Lonely Woman VINCENT QUONDAMATEO

1968
Watch the Birdie . . . Die! CANYON

1969
Over 18, . . . and Ready! TED LEVERSUCH

1970
The Affairs of Aphrodite CANYON
The Politicians ELLMAN

BATTISTE, HAROLD R.

1967
Good Times (see Bono)

BAUER, MARION

1937
Pan (aka *Pan and Syrinx;* short) ?

BAXTER, LES

1954
Yellow Tomahawk UA

1955
A Life at Stake GIBRALTAR
Monika (U.S. release of 1953 Swedish film, *Summer with Monika*) HALLMARK

1956
Wetbacks BANNER
Hot Blood COL
Quincannon, Frontier Scout UA
The Black Sleep UA
Rebel in Town UA
Hot Cars UA
A Woman's Devotion REP
Tomahawk Trail UA

1957
The Vicious Breed CORONET
The Storm Rider TCF
Revolt at Fort Laramie UA
Voodoo Island UA
Pharaoh's Curse UA
War Drums UA
Untamed Youth WB
The Girl in Black Stockings UA
Bop Girl Goes Calypso UA
Outlaw's Son UA
Jungle Heat UA
The Invisible Boy (o: A. Harris) MGM
Hell Bound UA
Escape from Red Rock TCF
The Dalton Girls UA

1958
Fort Bowie UA
The Bride and the Beast AA
Macabre AA
The Lone Ranger and the Lost City of Gold UA

1959
Goliath and the Barbarians AIP

1960
The Fall of the House of Usher AIP
Goliath and the Dragon AIP

1961
Black Sunday AIP
Master of the World (o: A. Harris) AIP
Alakazam the Great (an.; o: A. Harris) AIP
Pit and the Pendulum AIP
Lisette MEDALLION

1962
Panic in Year Zero! AIP
Tales of Terror AIP
Marco Polo (U.S. release of Italian film) AIP
White Slave Ship (U.S. release of Italian film, *L'ammutinamento*) AIP
Daughter of the Sun God HERTS-LION
Reptilicus (ac for U.S. release of Danish film) AIP
Samson and the Seven Miracles of the World (U.S. release of 1961 Italian film) AIP
A House of Sand (see W. Jones)

1963
The Raven (ac: A. Harris) AIP
Operation Bikini AIP
The Young Racers AIP
Erik the Conqueror (U.S. release of 1961 Italian film, *Gli invasori*) AIP

Beach Party AIP
X—The Man with X-Ray Eyes AIP
A Boy Ten Feet Tall (U.S. release of British film, *Sammy Going South*) PAR
1964
The Comedy of Terrors AIP
Muscle Beach Party AIP
Black Sabbath (U.S. release of 1963 Italian film, *I tre volti della paura*) AIP
Evil Eye (U.S. release of 1963 Italian film, *La ragazza che sapeva troppo*) AIP
Bikini Beach AIP
The Mighty Jungle (U.S. release of 1959 Mexican film, *La Ciudad Sagrada*) PARADE
Pajama Party AIP
1965
Beach Blanket Bingo (a: Styner) AIP
How to Stuff a Wild Bikini (o: Easton) AIP
Sergeant Deadhead AIP
Dr. Goldfoot and the Bikini Machine (ac: A. Harris) AIP
1966
The Ghost in the Invisible Bikini (ac: A. Harris) AIP
Fireball 500 AIP
Dr. Goldfoot and the Girl Bombs AIP
1968
Cervantes (U.S. release of French-Italian-Spanish film) AIP
The Mini-Skirt Mob AIP
Wild in the Streets AIP
Terror in the Jungle CROWN INT'L
The Young Animals AIP
The Glass Sphinx (ac: Styner; U.S. release of 1967 Italian-Spanish film) AIP
1969
All the Loving Couples U-M FILM DIST.
Hell's Belles AIP
How to Make It INT'L FILM ORG.
Flareup MGM
1970
The Dunwich Horror AIP
Bora Bora (U.S. release of 1968 Italian film) AIP
Cry of the Banshee AIP
Documentaries
1953
Tanga-Tika DWIGHT LONG
1958
Mayan Secrets (short) WORLD WIDE ADVENTURES
1965
Taboos of the World AIP
1967
Sadismo TRANS AMERICAN
Animated Short
1954
Man-Made Miracles JSP

BAZELON, IRWIN
1968
Survival 1967 (doc.) JULES DASSIN
1970
The Glory of Their Times (doc.) BUD GREENSPAN
Documentary Shorts
1951
The Growing Years GIRL SCOUTS
1957
Eye in Space IBM
The Hope That Jack Built ROBERT LAWRENCE PRODS.
1962
Suffer Little Children LUTHERAN CHURCH
Inquiry IBM
1963
Girl Game AMERICAN WOOL PRODUCERS
The Human Element STANDARD OIL CO.
The Pond and the City KNICKERBOCKER PRODS.
Rice WILLARD VAN DYKE
1965
The Ivory Knife MARTHA JACKSON
Lasers and Atoms SCIENTIFIC AMERICAN
The Corbit-Sharp House WILLARD VAN DYKE
1966
Overture to Tomorrow HEWITT-ROBINS
1967
New York 100 MARTHA JACKSON
1968
Of Earth and Fire LENOX CHINA

BEATTIE, HERBERT
1958
Their Little World (short) U. OF BUFFALO

BECKER, JOHN
1950
Julius Caeser AVON PRODS.
1959
The Song of the Scaffold R.L. BRUCKBERGER

BECKMAN, IRVING
1951
Lifeguard (doc. short) LOS ANGELES COUNTY

BEHRENS, JACK
1959
The Old-Order Amish (doc. short) VINCENT R. TORTORA

BELASCO, JACQUES DALLIN
1940
The Ramparts We Watch (doc.; see De Francesco)
1941
They Dare Not Love (+ stock) COL
1942
Laugh Your Blues Away COL
1961
The Magic Fountain CLASSIC WORLD FILMS
1966
Rings Around the World (doc.) COL
Documentary Shorts (TCF)
1952
I Remember the Glory: The Art of Botticelli
Curtain Call: The Art of Degas
Light in the Window: The Art of Vermeer
Birth of Venus: Art of the Renaissance
The Young Immortal: The Art of Raphael
The Night Watch: The Art of Rembrandt
Joy of Living: The Art of Renoir

BENNETT, NORMAN
1967
The Cooper's Craft (doc. short) CW

BENNETT, ROBERT RUSSELL
1936
Show Boat UNIV
Swing Time RKO
1937
Shall We Dance (see N. Shilkret)
Artists and Models (see Jenkins)
High, Wide and Handsome PAR
Ali Baba Goes to Town (ac: W. Scharf) TCF
A Damsel in Distress (ac: Parrish) RKO
1938
Radio City Revels RKO
Joy of Living RKO
Carefree (o: Raab, Salinger) RKO
Fugitives for a Night (see Webb)
Suez (see Mockridge)
Annabel Takes a Tour RKO
1939
Pacific Liner RKO
Twelve Crowded Hours RKO
The Story of Vernon and Irene Castle RKO
Career (see Webb)
Stanley and Livingstone (see Silvers)
The Adventures of Sherlock Holmes (see Mockridge)
5th Avenue Girl RKO
Intermezzo (see M. Steiner)
Swanee River (see Schrager)
1940
Brigham Young (see A. Newman)
1942
Willow Run (doc. short) OEM
1955
Oklahoma! (see Deutsch)

BENNETT, TOM
1940
Oil Can—and Does (an. short) PETROLEUM INDUSTRY

BERGSMA, WILLIAM
1947
Titian (short) CHILDREN'S PRODS.
1956
A Desk for Billie (doc. feature) NEA
1957
Not by Chance (doc. short) NEA
1958
The Forgotten (short) RKS PRODS.

BERGUNKER, MAX
1928
The Whip (with Harling) FN
The Night Watch (see Bierman)
The Patriot (see Savino)
Show Girl (see Carbonara)
The Haunted House (with Hajos, Carbonara; + stock) FN
Adoration (see Hajos)
1929
The Shopworn Angel PAR
The Dummy (see Hajos)
Chinatown Nights (see Hajos)
Wolf Song (see Carbonara)
1930
Burning Up (see G. Lucas)
Young Eagles (see Leipold)
The Vagabond King (see Leipold)
Dangerous Nan McGrew PAR
1931
Fighting Caravans (see Leipold)
Rango (see Hajos)
1932
Forgotten Commandments (see Hand)

BERLINER, RUDOLPH
1931
The Spy (see Brunelli)
[Also compiled scores for many silent films.]

BERNSTEIN, CHARLES
1970
The Man from O.R.G.Y. CINEMATION
Documentary Shorts
1964
Beyond the Night ALAN CAPPS
1967
Marina del Rey L.A. COUNTY
1968
Chaim Soutine JACK LIEBERMAN
1969
A Time for Decision L.A. COUNTY
On Guard L.A. COUNTY
Czechoslovakia 1968 USIA
Helen Keller Story PROJECT 7 FILMS
1970
Abraham Lincoln and the Emancipation Proclamation PROJECT 7 FILMS
One Spring Day HOWARD & KURTZ

BERNSTEIN, ELMER
1951
Saturday's Hero (o: Grau) COL
Boots Malone (o: Grau) COL
1952
Battles of Chief Pontiac REALART
Sudden Fear RKO
1953
Never Wave at a WAC RKO
Cat Women of the Moon ASTOR
Robot Monster ASTOR
Miss Robin Crusoe TCF
1954
Make Haste to Live REP
Silent Raiders LIPPERT
1955
The Eternal Sea REP
It's a Dog's Life (o: F. Steiner, Woodbury) MGM
The View from Pompey's Head (o: F. Steiner) TCF
The Man with the Golden Arm (o: F. Steiner) UA
Storm Fear UA
1956
The Naked Eye (doc.; o: Gold) LOUIS CLYDE STOUMAN
The Ten Commandments (o: Cailliet, Shuken) PAR
1957
Drango UA
Men in War UA
Fear Strikes Out (o: Shuken, Hayes, Van Cleave) PAR
Sweet Smell of Success UA
The Tin Star (o: Van Cleave) PAR
Saddle the Wind (o: F. Steiner, Woodbury) MGM
1958
Desire Under the Elms (o: Van Cleave) PAR
God's Little Acre UA
Kings Go Forth (o: Shuken, Hayes) UA
Anna Lucasta UA
Some Came Running (o: Shuken, Hayes) MGM
The Buccaneer PAR
1959
The Story on Page One (o: E. Powell) TCF
The Miracle (o: Shuken) WB
1960
The Rat Race (o: Shuken, Hayes, Van Cleave) PAR
From the Terrace (o: E. Powell) TCF
The Magnificent Seven (o: Shuken, Hayes) UA
1961
By Love Possessed UA
The Young Doctors UA
The Comancheros (o: Shuken, Hayes, Sendrey) TCF
Summer and Smoke (o: Shuken, Hayes) PAR
1962
Walk on the Wild Side (o: Shuken, Hayes) COL
Birdman of Alcatraz (o: Shuken, Hayes) UA
A Girl Named Tamiko (o: E. Powell) PAR
Hud (a for guitar: Bain) PAR
1963
To Kill a Mockingbird (o: Shuken, Hayes) UNIV
The Caretakers UA
The Great Escape (o: Shuken, Hayes) UA
Rampage (o: Shuken, Hayes) WB
Kings of the Sun UA
Love with the Proper Stranger (o: Shuken, Hayes) PAR
The Carpetbaggers (o: Shuken, Hayes) PAR
1964
The World of Henry Orient UA

Baby the Rain Must Fall (o: Shuken, Hayes) COL
1965
The Hallelujah Trail (o: Shuken, Hayes, F. Steiner) UA
The Sons of Katie Elder (o: Shuken, Hayes) PAR
The Reward (o: Shuken, Hayes) TCF
Seven Women MGM
1966
The Silencers (o: Shuken, Hayes) COL
Cast a Giant Shadow (o: Shuken, Hayes) UA
Return of the Seven UA
Hawaii (o: Shuken, Hayes) UA
1967
Thoroughly Modern Millie (o: Shuken, Hayes, Sendrey) UNIV
1968
The Scalphunters UA
I Love You, Alice B. Toklas! (o: Shuken, Hayes) WB
1969
Where's Jack? PAR
Midas Run CR
True Grit (o: Shuken, Hayes) PAR
Guns of the Magnificent Seven (o: Shuken) UA
The Bridge at Remagen UA
1970
The Liberation of L. B. Jones (o: Shuken, Hayes) COL
A Walk in the Spring Rain (o: Shuken, Hayes) COL
Cannon for Cordoba UA
Shorts
1953
A Communications Primer EAMES
1954
S-73 (Sofa Compact) EAMES
Career: Medical Technologist CHURCHILL-WEXLER
1955
House—After Five Years of Living EAMES
1956
Eames Lounge Chair EAMES
1957
Toccata for Toy Trains EAMES
1958
The Information Machine (an.) EAMES
1959
Israel WB
Glimpses of the U.S.A. EAMES
Rainbow Valley FOCAL FILMS
1960
Introduction to Feedback EAMES
1961
Mathematica EAMES
1962
The House of Science EAMES
1964
Some Sort of Cage WILLIAM ALLYN, PETER BALDWIN
Think (multiscreen version)/*View from the People Wall* (single-screen version) EAMES
1965
Westinghouse in Alphabetical Order EAMES
The Smithsonian Institution EAMES
Computer Day at Midvale/Sherlock Holmes in the Singular Case of the Plural Green Mustache (two puppet films on same reel) EAMES
IBM at the Fair EAMES
1967
A Computer Glossary EAMES
1968
Powers of Ten EAMES
1969
Tops EAMES
1970
Harmony of Nature and Man ROGER TILTON
In Search of Lost Worlds MGM

BERNSTEIN, LEONARD
1954
On the Waterfront (o: Grau, Skiles) COL

BERRES, RICHARD
1961
Forbid Them Not (doc.) KAPLAN ASSOCIATES

BERTON, EUGENE
1930
Hell Harbor UA

BETTS, HARRY
1965
A Swingin' Summer UNITED SCREEN ARTS
Winter A-Go-Go COL
1967
The Big Mouth COL
1969
The Fantastic Plastic Machine (doc.) CROWN

BEYNON, GEORGE W.
1915
Peer Gynt (another score by Stickles) PAR
The Yankee Girl PAR
The Gentleman from Indiana PAR
Jane PAR
The Reform Candidate PAR
The Corner TRIANGLE
The Tongues of Men PAR
1916
Witchcraft PAR
1917
One Law for Both IVAN
Babbling Tongues IVAN
Rebecca of Sunnybrook Farm PAR
Sins of Ambition IVAN
1918
Lest We Forget METRO
Among the Cannibal Isles of the South Pacific (doc.) MARTIN JOHNSON
The Girl of My Dreams NATIONAL
1920
In Old Kentucky FN
1921
Mary Regan FN

BIBO, IRVING
[Cue sheets suggest that he was the sole or principal composer of the following films. However, he headed a music library, Bibo Music Inc., and his music sometimes appeared in films scored by the Meyer Synchronizing Service, so whether he wrote for music libraries or for specific films is problematical.]
1930
Headin' North TIFFANY
1931
Branded Men TIFFANY
Nice Women UNIV
A House Divided UNIV
1932
Racing Youth UNIV
Texas Gun Fighter TIFFANY

BICKFORD, JOHN
1955
The Beast with a Million Eyes AIP

BIERMAN, EMIL
1916
Ramona CLUNE
1928
The Good-bye Kiss (with M. Wilson; mt: Hajos; + stock) FN
The Night Watch (with M. Wilson; ac: Hajos, Bergunker, Hand, Cousminer; + stock) FN
1930
Burning Up (silent version; see G. Lucas)
1931
Fighting Caravans (see Leipold)

BIVIANO, JOSEPH
1951
The Knife Thrower (short) WB

BJOM, FRANK
1967
Catsup (short) BENJAMIN HAYEEM

BLACKTON, JAY
1952
The Merry Widow (o: Sendrey) MGM

BLAGMAN, NORMAN
1965
Goodbye in the Mirror (with Menkes) STORM DE HIRSCH

BLAND, ED
1960
The Searching Eye (short) MADELINE TOURTELOT

BLANFORD, ROBERT
1966
Nashville Rebel AIP

BLITZSTEIN, MARC
1928
Hands (short; filmed and composed in Germany) FAMA
1931
Surf and Seaweed (short) RALPH STEINER
1936
The Chesapeake Bay Retriever (doc. short) PEDIGREED PICTURES
1937
The Spanish Earth (doc.; a with Thomson) JORIS IVENS
1940
Valley Town (doc. short; o: Brant) WILLARD VAN DYKE
1942
Native Land (o: Brant) FRONTIER FILMS
Night Shift (doc. short) O.W.I.
1945
The True Glory (doc.; not used; scored by

British composer William Alwyn) O.W.I.

BLOOMFIELD, MIKE
1969
Medium Cool PAR

BLUESTONE, HARRY
1959
The Killer Shrews (with Cadkin) MCLENDON
1963
A Wish and Ticino (short) WB
1965
Mara of the Wilderness AA

BOCK, JERRY
1956
Wonders of Manhattan (doc. short) COL

BOND, JIMMY
1968
A Way Out of the Wilderness (doc. short) JSP

BONO, SONNY
1967
Good Times (adapted by Battiste; o: Van Cleave) COL
1969
Chastity (adapted by Peake) AIP

BORDEN, DAVID
1970
Branches CORNELL U. CINEMA

BORISOFF, ALEXANDER
[Pseudonym: Alex Alexander.]
1938
La Vida Bohemia (Spanish language) COL
1947
Sierra Journey (doc. short) C.M. MCCOY PRODS.
1950
Two Lost Worlds EL
1951
Gold Raiders (with Starr) UA
1952
Red Snow (with Starr) COL
1954
The World Dances (doc.) FESTIVAL PICTURES
1958
Alaska Passage TCF
1961
Operation Eichmann (with Starr; o: Doerfel) AA
1966
C'mon, Let's Live a Little (see Ralke)

BORNE, HAL
1942
Nightmare of a Goon (short) PAR
1946
Susie Steps Out (o: Cadkin) UA
1948
Heading for Heaven PRC
1961
The Explosive Generation UA
Not Tonight Henry FOREMOST
Flight of the Lost Balloon WOOLNER BROS.
1963
Promises! Promises! NOONAN-TAYLOR
1967
Hillbillys in a Haunted House WOOLNER BROS.

BOSSICK, BERNARD
1953
Guerilla Girl UA

BOTKIN, PERRY
1958
Murder by Contract COL
1960
Seventy Times Seven LLOYD YOUNG
1962
Saint of Devil's Island LLOYD YOUNG

BOTKIN, PERRY, JR.
1970
R. P. M. (with DeVorzon; o: Betts) COL

BOTTJE, WILL GAY
1963
Dissent Illusion (short) MORTON GOLDSHOLL

BOURGOIS, JIM
1968
Islands of the Sea (doc. short) DON MEIER

BOUTELJE, PHIL
1931
Paleface Pup (cartoon) VAN BEUREN
1936
Anything Goes (see Hollander)

Desire (see Hollander)
The Princess Comes Across (see Leipold)
Three Cheers for Love (with Leipold, Bradshaw) PAR

1937
Champagne Waltz (with Hollander, Stone, Bradshaw, Shuken) PAR
Swing High, Swing Low (see V. Young)

1938
The Arkansas Traveler (see Carbonara)

1939
Zaza (see Hollander)
The Magnificent Fraud PAR
The Great Victor Herbert (see A. Lange)

1941
You're the One (mt: Ralston) PAR
The Hard-Boiled Canary PAR
The Lady Eve (see Shuken)
Las Vegas Nights (see W. Scharf)

1943
Hi Diddle Diddle UA

BOWERS, ROBERT C.

1966
Come Spy with Me TCF

BOWERS, ROBERT HOOD

1914
Neptune's Daughter UNIVERSAL

1916
Patria (serial) INT'L. FILM SERVICE
A Daughter of the Gods FOX
War Brides HERBERT BRENON

BOWLES, PAUL

1933
Siva HARRY DUNHAM

1934
Innocent Island HARRY DUNHAM

1935
Venus and Adonis HARRY DUNHAM

1936
145 West 21 RUDOLF BURCKHARDT
Seeing the World: A Visit to New York RUDOLF BURCKHARDT

1937
America's Disinherited SHARECROPPER FILM COMMITTEE

1938
Too Much Johnson ORSON WELLES
How to Become a Citizen of the United States RUDOLF BURCKHARDT
Chelsea Through the Magnifying Glass RUDOLF BURCKHARDT
The Sex Life of the Common Film RUDOLF BURCKHARDT

1939
Film Made to Music Written by Paul Bowles RUDOLF BURCKHARDT

1940
Roots in the Earth USDA

1944
The Congo BELGIAN GOVT.

1948
Dreams That Money Can Buy (see Applebaum)

BOYELL, DICK

1964
First Impression (doc. short) MORTON GOLDSHOLL

1969
Up Is Down (an. short) MORTON GOLDSHOLL

BRACHER, WERNER

1956
Art and Motion (doc. short) PAUL BURNFORD

BRACKMAN, GEORGE

1963
San Fan See (short) TCF

1964
Only One New York (see Delugg)

1966
Gulliver's Travels Beyond the Moon (see Delugg)
Cinderella (see Delugg)

BRADFORD, JAMES C.

[Best known as a compiler of scores and cue sheets for hundreds of silent films, including *The Fall of the Romanoffs* (1917), *Richard the Lion-Hearted* (1923), and *The Son of the Sheik* (1926). There is some evidence that he composed music for the following features.]

1926
Moana (doc.) PAR

1932
Isle of Paradise (doc.) ADOLPH POLLAK

1933
Savage Gold (doc.) HAROLD AUTEN

1938
The Sheik (sound reissue of 1921 film) PAR

1939
Tumbleweeds (sound reissue of 1925 film; with Guttmann) ASTOR

BRADLEY, SCOTT

1946
Courage of Lassie (with Castelnuovo-Tedesco, Kaper; ac: Salinger, N. Shilkret, R. Franklyn) MGM
1948
The Kissing Bandit (see Stoll)
1950
The Yellow Cab Man (ac: Sendrey) MGM
1953
Dangerous When Wet (see Stoll)
1955
Blackboard Jungle (see Wolcott)

Shorts (MGM)
1941
Lions on the Loose (o: Marquardt)
1947
Football Thrills, No. 10 (o: Marquardt)
1949
Fishing for Fun
Football Thrills, No. 12
1952
Football Thrills, No. 15
1954
The Camera Caught It
Rough Riding

Cartoons (MGM)
1931
Movie Mad
The New Car
1932
Africa Squeaks
Fire! Fire!
Jail Birds
The Milkman
The Office Boy
The Phoney Express
Room Runners
School Days
Stormy Seas
The Village Specialist
1933
Techno-Cracked
1934
Bosko's Parlor Pranks
The Discontented Canary
The Old Pioneer
Tale of the Vienna Woods
Toyland Broadcast
1935
Alias St. Nick
Barnyard Babies
The Calico Dragon
The Chinese Nightingale
Good Little Monkeys
Hey-Hey Fever
Honeyland
The Lost Chick
The Old Plantation
Poor Little Me
When the Cat's Away
1936
Bottles
The Early Bird and the Worm
Little Cheeser
The Old House
The Old Mill Pond
The Pups' Christmas
The Pups' Picnic
Run Sheep Run
To Spring
Two Little Pups
1937
Bosko's Easter Egg
Circus Daze
The Hound and the Rabbit
Little Buck Cheeser
Little Ol' Bosko and the Cannibals
Little Ol' Bosko and the Pirates
Little Ol' Bosko in Bagdad
Swing Wedding
The Wayward Pups
1938
Baby Kittens LANTZ
The Little Bantamweight
Merbabies WDP
Pipe Dreams
1939
Art Gallery
The Bear That Couldn't Sleep
The Blue Danube
The Bookworm
Goldilocks and the Three Bears
The Little Goldfish
The Mad Maestro
One Mother's Family
Peace on Earth
1940
The Bookworm Turns
The Fishing Bear
Gallopin' Gals
Home on the Range
The Homeless Flea

The Lonesome Stranger
The Milky Way
Mrs. Lady Bug
Papa Gets the Bird
Puss Gets the Boot
A Rainy Day
Romeo in Rhythm
Swing Social
Tom Turkey and His Harmonica Humdingers

1941

Abdul the Bul-Bul Ameer
The Alley Cat
Dance of the Weed
The Field Mouse
The Flying Bear
The Goose Goes South
Little Cesario
The Little Mole
The Midnight Snack
The Night Before Christmas
Officer Pooch
The Prospecting Bear
The Rookie Bear

1942

Bats in the Belfry
The Bear and the Beavers
The Blitz Wolf
The Bowling Alley-Cat
Chips Off the Old Block
Dog Trouble
The Early Bird Dood It!
Fine Feathered Friend
The First Swallow
Fraidy Cat
The Hungry Wolf
Little Gravel Voice
Puss 'n Toots
Wild Honey

1943

Baby Puss
Bah Wilderness
Barney Bear's Victory Garden
The Boy and the Wolf
Dumb-Hounded
The Lonesome Mouse
One Ham's Family
Red Hot Riding Hood
The Stork's Holiday
Sufferin' Cats!
The Uninvited Pest
War Dogs
What's Buzzin' Buzzard
Who Killed Who?

1944

Batty Baseball
Bear Raid Warden
Big Heel-Watha
The Bodyguard
Happy-Go-Nutty
Innertube Antics
The Million Dollar Cat
Mouse Trouble
Polar Pest
Puttin' on the Dog
Screwball Squirrel
The Tree Surgeon
Yankee Doodle Mouse
The Zoot Cat

1945

Flirty Birdy
Jerky Turkey
The Mouse Comes to Dinner
Mouse in Manhattan
Quiet Please!
The Screwy Truant
The Shooting of Dan McGoo
Swing Shift Cinderella
Tee for Two
The Unwelcome Guest
Wild and Woolfy

1946

Henpecked Hoboes
The Hick Chick
Lonesome Lenny
The Milky Waif
Northwest Hounded Police
Solid Serenade
Springtime for Thomas
Trap Happy

1947

The Cat Concerto
Cat Fishin'
Dr. Jekyll and Mr. Mouse
Hound Hunters
The Invisible Mouse
King-Size Canary
A Mouse in the House
Part Time Pal
Red Hot Rangers
Salt Water Tabby
Slap Happy Lion
Uncle Tom's Cabaña

1948

The Bear and the Bean
The Bear and the Hare
The Cat That Hated People
Goggle Fishing Bear

Half-Pint Pygmy
Kitty Foiled
Little 'Tinker
Lucky Ducky
Mouse Cleaning
Old Rockin' Chair Tom
Professor Tom
The Truce Hurts
What Price Fleadom

1949

Bad Luck Blackie
The Cat and the Mermouse
The Counterfeit Cat
Doggone Tired
Hatch Up Your Troubles
Heavenly Puss
The House of Tomorrow
Jerry's Diary
The Little Orphan
Little Quacker
Little Rural Riding Hood
Love That Pup
Out-Foxed
Polka-Dot Puss
Saturday Evening Puss
Señor Droopy
Tennis Chumps
Wags to Riches

1950

Casanova Cat
The Chump Champ
Cock-a-Doodle Dog
The Cuckoo Clock
Cue Ball Cat
The Framed Cat
Garden Gopher
Jerry and the Lion
The Peachy Cobbler
Safety Second
Texas Tom
Tom and Jerry in the Hollywood Bowl
Ventriloquist Cat

1951

Car of Tomorrow
Cat Napping
Daredevil Droopy
Droopy's Double Trouble
Droopy's Good Deed
The Flying Cat
His Mouse Friday
Jerry and the Goldfish
Jerry's Cousin
Magical Maestro
Nit-Witty Kitty
Sleepy-Time Tom
Slicked-Up Pup
Symphony in Slang

1952

Barney's Hungry Cousin
Caballero Droopy
Cruise Cat
The Dog House
The Duck Doctor
Fit to Be Tied
Little Runaway
The Little Wise Quacker
One Cab's Family
Push Button Kitty
Rock-a-Bye Bear
Smitten Kitten
Triplet Trouble
The Two Mouseketeers

1953

Busybody Bear
Cobbs and Robbers
Half-Pint Palomino
Heir Bear
Jerry and Jumbo
Johann Mouse
Just Ducky
Life with Tom
Little Johnny Jet
Posse Cat
Puppy Tale
T.V. of Tomorrow
That's My Pup!
Two Little Indians
Wee-Willie Wildcat

1954

Baby Butch
Billy Boy
Bird-Brain Bird Dog
Dixieland Droopy
Downhearted Duckling
Drag-a-Long Droopy
The Farm of Tomorrow
Field and Scream
The Flea Circus
The Hic-cup Pup
Homesteader Droopy
The Impossible Possum
Little School Mouse
Mice Follies
Neapolitan Mouse
Pet Peeve
Sleepy-Time Squirrel
The Three Little Pups
Touché, Pussy Cat!

1955

Cellbound

Deputy Droopy
Designs on Jerry
The First Bad Man
Good Will to Men
Mouse for Sale
Pecos Pest
Pup on a Picnic
Smarty Cat
Southbound Duckling
That's My Mommy
Tom and Chérie

1956

Barbecue Brawl
Blackboard Jumble
Blue Cat Blues
Busy Buddies
Down Beat Bear
The Egg and Jerry
Feedin' the Kiddie
The Flying Sorceress
Grin and Share It
Happy Go Ducky
Millionaire Droopy
Mucho Mouse
Muscle Beach Tom
Scat Cats
Timid Tabby
Tom's Photo Finish

1957

Cat's Meow
Droopy Leprechaun
Give and Tyke
Mutts About Racing
One Droopy Knight
Robin Hoodwinked
Royal Cat Nap
Sheep Wrecked
Tops with Pops
Tot Watchers
The Vanishing Duck

Short Animated Training Films (MGM)

1944

A Few Quick Facts (#1) U.S. ARMY
A Few Quick Facts (#2) U.S. ARMY
A Few Quick Facts (#3) U.S. ARMY
A Few Quick Facts (#4) U.S. ARMY
A Few Quick Facts (#5): (Weapon of War) U.S. ARMY
A Few Quick Facts (#8): (The Case of the Disappearing Soldier) U.S. ARMY
History of Balloons U.S. NAVY

BRADSHAW, CHARLES

1935

Millions in the Air (mt) PAR

1936

Florida Special (with Leipold) PAR
Palm Springs (see Leipold)
Three Cheers for Love (see Boutelje)
My American Wife (see Hollander)

1937

Mind Your Own Business (see Shuken)
Champagne Waltz (see Boutelje)
Waikiki Wedding (see Shuken)
I Met Him in Paris (with Leipold) PAR

1938

Thanks for the Memory (ac: Leipold, Shuken) PAR
Say It in French (see Shuken)
Artists and Models Abroad (see Rainger)

1939

St. Louis Blues PAR
Boy Trouble (with Leipold) PAR
The Lady and the Mob (with Harline) COL
Never Say Die (see Roder)
Invitation to Happiness (see Hollander)
$1,000 a Touchdown (see Leipold)
Television Spy (see Leipold)
The Night of Nights (see V. Young)
Emergency Squad (see Shuken)

1940

Seventeen (with Leipold) PAR
The Farmer's Daughter (see V. Young)
Adventure in Diamonds (see Shuken)
Typhoon (see Hollander)

1941

The Lady Eve (see Shuken)
Road to Zanzibar (see V. Young)
Caught in the Draft (see V. Young)
Sullivan's Travels (see Shuken)
Remember the Day (see Mockridge)

1942

A Gentleman at Heart (o: D. Raksin, Moross) TCF
Silver Queen (see V. Young)

1943

Happy Go Lucky (see Dolan)
Henry Aldrich Swings It (see Sawtell)
Riding High (with V. Young, Shuken) PAR

1944

The Miracle of Morgan's Creek (see Shuken)
And the Angels Sing (with V. Young) PAR
Practically Yours (see V. Young)

1945

Out of This World (see Simeone)

1947

Ladies Man (see Webb)
Where There's Life (see V. Young)

Shorts
1944
Showboat Serenade (see Leipold)
Fun Time (see Schrager)
Bonnie Lassie (see Schrager)
1945
Naughty Nanette (see Schrager)
1946
A Tale of Two Cafés (see Schrager)
1948
Jingle, Jangle, Jingle (see Lilley)

BRADY, LAWRENCE W.
1962
Nature's Playmates DORE PRODS.

BRANDT, CARL
1954
The Cowboy (doc.) LIP
1955
Shotgun AA
Seven Angry Men AA
Bobby Ware Is Missing AA
Cartoons
1958
Gumshoe Magoo UPA
1966
Catty-Cornered MGM
Puss 'n' Boats MGM
1967
Rock 'n' Rodent MGM
Purr-Chance to Dream MGM

BRANT, HENRY
1947
My Father's House (doc.) HERBERT KLINE
1953
The Big Break JOSEPH STRICK
Documentary Shorts
1945
The Capitol Story IRVING JACOBY
1946
The Pale Horseman IRVING JACOBY
Journey Into Medicine WILLARD VAN DYKE
1948
Osmosis IRVING JACOBY
1949
Outbreak USDA
1954
Ode on a Grecian Urn LEWIS JACOBS
1956
The Secret Thief ?
Your Community ?
1957
Doctor "B" ?
Endowing Our Future HERMAN J. ENGEL
1959
United Nations Day ?
1961
Early Birds ?
Fire in Cities ?
1964
Voyage Four ?
Jack Levine VOYNOW-ROBINSON-ENGEL

BREESKIN, ELIAS
1948
Chase Me, Charlie (compilation film) CAPITAL
1950
Pancho Villa Returns HISPANO CONTINENTAL
1953
Captain Scarlett UA
1966
Chaplin's Art of Comedy (compilation film) HEMISPHERE

BREGMAN, BUDDY
1954
Five Guns West AIP
1956
Fighting Trouble AA
The Wild Party UA
1957
The Delicate Delinquent (o: Van Cleave, Shuken) PAR
1959
Guns, Girls and Gangsters UA
Born Reckless WB
1960
Valley of the Redwoods TCF
Secret of the Purple Reef TCF
1961
The Cat Burglar UA

BREIL, JOSEPH CARL
1912
Camille (U.S. release of French film, *La dame aux camélias*) FRENCH-AMERICAN
Mme. Sans-Gêne (U.S. release of 1911 French film) FRENCH-AMERICAN
Queen Elizabeth (U.S. release of French film, *La Reine Elisabeth*) FAMOUS PLAYERS
1913
The Prisoner of Zenda FAMOUS PLAYERS

Tess of the D'Urbervilles FAMOUS PLAYERS
In the Bishop's Carriage FAMOUS PLAYERS
[*Motion Picture News,* April 1, 1922, p. 1996, reported that Breil had scored *Queen Elizabeth* and "ten succeeding Famous Players productions, starting with *The Prisoner of Zenda,*" but this has not been confirmed nor that many films identified.]
1914
Cabiria (ac for U.S. release of 1913 Italian film) ITALA
1915
The Birth of a Nation D. W. GRIFFITH
[Los Angeles premiere as *The Clansman:* Overture by Nurnberger, score compiled by Carli Elinor and Lloyd Brown. New York revival, 1921: a by Rapee, Axt, Hand. Synchronized version (abridged) 1930: Breil's score adapted by Gottschalk.]
The Lamb (with Nurnberger) TRIANGLE
Old Heidelberg TRIANGLE
The Martyrs of the Alamo TRIANGLE
The Sable Lorcha (with Raynes) TRIANGLE
Double Trouble TRIANGLE
The Lily and the Rose (with Raynes) TRIANGLE
The Penitentes TRIANGLE
1916
The Missing Links TRIANGLE
The Wood Nymph TRIANGLE
Intolerance D. W. GRIFFITH
The Garden of Allah SELIG POLYSCOPE
1918
The Birth of a Race JOHN W. NOBLE
1919
The Betrayal LENOX
The Lost Battalion MACMANUS
1922
Tess of the Storm Country UA
1923
The White Rose (a: Pesce) D. W. GRIFFITH
The Green Goddess GOLDWYN-COSMOPOLITAN
The White Sister METRO
1924
America (with Fink) D. W. GRIFFITH
Abraham Lincoln ASSOCIATED FN
1925
The Phantom of the Opera UNIV
[World premiere, San Francisco. New York premiere: Hinrichs + stock. General release: stock. Reissue with sound sequences, 1929: Perry, Schiller, + stock.]

BRESKE, PAUL A.
1963
Circus Memories (doc. short) GEORGE W. SCOTT

BRESNICK, MARTIN
1968
Man Machine Meets Machine Man (short) ?
1969
Pour KATHY HANSEN

BRICKEN, CARL
1955
The Making of the River (doc. short) CONSERVATION FOUNDATION

BRITTON, D. GUYVER
1967
My Garden Japan (doc. short) EMPIRE PHOTOSOUND

BROEKMAN, DAVID
1932
Law and Order (mt; + stock) UNIV
Scandal for Sale UNIV
Stowaway (mt) UNIV
Tom Brown of Culver (mt; + stock) UNIV
Back Street (mt; + stock) UNIV
The Old Dark House (mt; + stock) UNIV
1956
Crowded Paradise TUDOR

BROWN, CHARLIE
1968
Wild 90 NORMAN MAILER

BROWN, HAROLD
1947
Your Child Is a Genius! (doc. short) DAVID ROBBINS PRODS.

BROWN, LAWRENCE
1968
The Angry Breed (see Curb)
Maryjane (see Curb)

BROWN, LOUIS Y.
1966
Three on a Couch (o: Betts, Byers, V. Feldman, A. Harris, Hazard, Holman) COL
Which Way to the Front? (see King)

BROWNING, MORTIMER
1951
Basic Dance (doc. short) A.F. FILMS

BRUBECK, DAVE
1965
Crocodile Tears (short) ROBERT DELPIRE
Jail Keys Made Here (doc. short) LEE BOLTIN
1967
Do Not Fold, Staple, Spindle, or Mutilate NFBC

BRUBECK, HOWARD
1948
Mother's Day (short) JAMES BROUGHTON
1951
Loony Tom (short) JAMES BROUGHTON
Daphni: Virgin of the Golden Laurels (short) GEORGE HOYNINGEN-HUENE

BRUCH, ALFRED E.
1954
Within Man's Power (short) NATIONAL TUBERCULOSIS ASSN.

BRUMMER, ANDRE S.
[Composed several film scores in Hungary before coming to the U.S.]
1954
Monster from the Ocean Floor LIP
1955
Air Strike LIP
1957
Love Slaves of the Amazon (see S. Wilson)
1958
The Rawhide Trail AA
1960
The Jailbreakers AIP
Three Blondes in His Life CINEMA ASSOCIATES
1965
Day of the Nightmare HERTS-LION
1969
Wild Gypsies MANSON

BRUNELLI, PETER
1929
The Bridge of San Luis Rey (+ stock) MGM
The Man and the Moment WB
Drag (see Copping)
South Sea Rose (with Knight; mt: Arthur Kay) FOX
Men Without Women (with Knight; ac: R. Bassett) FOX
1930
Such Men Are Dangerous (with Knight, Malotte) FOX
Song o' My Heart (with Lipschultz; ac: Malotte) FOX
3 Sisters (see Lipschultz)
The Arizona Kid (ac: R. Bassett) FOX
Born Reckless (with Lipschultz, Malotte, Talbot) FOX
Women Everywhere (with Lipschultz) FOX
Rough Romance (ac: R. Bassett, Lipschultz) FOX
Good Intentions (with R. Bassett, Knight) FOX
One Mad Kiss (with R. Bassett; ac: Knight) FOX
The Big Trail (see Arthur Kay)
A Devil with Women (ac: Lipschultz, Talbot, Friedhofer) FOX
Oh, for a Man FOX
The Princess and the Plumber (see Lipschultz)
Men on Call (see Kaylin)
The Man Who Came Back (with A. Kay; ac: Friedhofer, Knight, Lipschultz, Malotte) FOX
Fair Warning (see Arthur Kay)
1931
Seas Beneath (ac: Lipschultz) FOX
The Spy (with Talbot, Virgil, Berliner) FOX
Body and Soul (ac: Lipschultz) FOX
Not Exactly Gentlemen (with Arthur Kay; ac: Talbot, Virgil) FOX
Mr. Lemon of Orange (see Talbot)
The Flood (m&e) COL
Skyline (ac: Friedhofer) FOX
The Rainbow Trail (with R. Bassett; + stock) FOX
1932
El Caballero de la Noche (see R. Bassett)
Almost Married (see Friedhofer)
Chandu, the Magician (with R. Bassett, De Francesco; ac: Knight) FOX
Wild Girl (see Zamecnik)
Six Hours to Live (with R. Bassett) FOX
Tess of the Storm Country (see De Francesco)
Call Her Savage (see A. Lange)
Handle with Care (with R. Bassett; mt: Friedhofer) FOX
1933
Cavalcade (see De Francesco)

The Face in the Sky (with Zamecnik, R. Bassett, Friedhofer; ac: De Francesco) FOX
Dangerously Yours (see De Francesco)
Smoke Lightning (see A. Lange)
Pleasure Cruise FOX
Zoo in Budapest (see Zamecnik)
The Warrior's Husband (see Zamecnik)
Adorable (see A. Lange)
I Loved You Wednesday (see De Francesco)
The Power and the Glory (see Zamecnik)
Berkeley Square (see Zamecnik)
Paddy the Next Best Thing (see De Francesco)
Mr. Skitch (see De Francesco)
I Am Suzanne! (see Hollander)

1934
Carolina FOX
All Men Are Enemies (see De Francesco)
Springtime for Henry (ac: Friedhofer) FOX
Grand Canary (see De Francesco)
Caravan (with De Francesco, Reiser) FOX

1935
Angelina (see Sanders)
It's a Small World (see A. Lange)
Spring Tonic (with A. Lange, Buttolph) FOX
Our Little Girl (with R. Bassett; ac: Buttolph, Gerstenberger, Friedhofer) FOX
Daring Young Man (see A. Lange)
Under the Pampas Moon (see Mockridge)
Dressed to Thrill (with De Francesco; + stock) FOX
Dante's Inferno (see Friedhofer)

1940
The Ramparts We Watch (see De Francesco)

Trailer
1931
Merely Mary Ann FOX

BRUNNER, ROBERT F.

1965
That Darn Cat (o: Marks) WDP

1966
Lt. Robin Crusoe, U.S.N. (o: Crandall) WDP
Monkeys, Go Home! (o: Crandall) WDP

1967
Blackbeard's Ghost (o: Crandall) WDP

1968
Never a Dull Moment (o: Crandall) WDP

1969
Smith! (o: Sheets) WDP
The Computer Wore Tennis Shoes (o: Sheets) WDP

1970
The Boatniks (o: Marks) WDP

BRUNO, TONY

1969
Hell's Angels '69 (a: D'Andrea) AIP

BRUNS, GEORGE

1955
Davy Crockett, King of the Wild Frontier (o: Plumb) WDP

1956
Davy Crockett and the River Pirates (o: Plumb) WDP
Westward Ho the Wagons (o: Plumb) WDP

1957
Johnny Tremaine (o: Marks, Plumb) WDP

1958
Sleeping Beauty (based on Tchaikovsky) WDP

1960
One Hundred and One Dalmatians (o: Marks) WDP
The Absent-Minded Professor (o: Marks) WDP

1961
Babes in Toyland (o: Marks) WDP

1962
Son of Flubber (o: Marks) WDP

1963
The Sword and the Stone (o: Marks) WDP

1964
The Restless Sea (doc.) WDP

1965
The Ugly Dachshund (o: Marks) WDP

1966
The Fighting Prince of Donegal (o: Sheets) WDP
Follow Me, Boys! (o: Sheets) WDP
The Adventures of Bullwhip Griffin (o: Sheets) WDP

1967
The Jungle Book (o: Sheets) WDP
Island of the Lost PAR
The Daring Game PAR

1968
The Horse in the Gray Flannel Suit (o: Sheets) WDP
The Love Bug (o: Sheets) WDP

1970
The Aristocats (o: Sheets) WDP
Shorts (WDP)
1956
Man in Space
1959
Eyes in Outer Space
1960
I'm No Fool with Electricity
1964
A Country Coyote Goes Hollywood
Cartoons (UPA)
1952
Captains Outrageous
1953
The Little Boy with a Big Horn
Christopher Crumpet
Magoo's Masterpiece
1954
Ballet-Oop
Fudget's Budget
Kangaroo Courting
How Now Boing Boing
Cartoons (WDP)
1956
In the Bag
Jack and Old Mac
1957
The Truth About Mother Goose
1958
Paul Bunyan
1959
Goliath II
Noah's Ark
1961
The Saga of Windwagon Smith
1964
Freewayphobia, No. 1
1965
Goofy's Freeway Troubles
1969
It's Tough to Be a Bird

BUCCI, MARK
1967
A Time to Play (doc. short) POLAROID CORP.

BUCKNER, TEDDY
1964
The Legend of Jimmy Blue Eyes (short) ROBERT CLOUSE

BUDROW, MANUELA
1935
The Irish Gringo KEITH PRODS.

BUFFANO, JULES
1928
The Bellamy Trial (see Axt)

BURKE, SONNY
1944
Four Jills in a Jeep (see Friedhofer)
1961
Hand of Death TCF

BURNS, RALPH
1947
Rhapsody in Wood (cartoon) PAR

BURNS, SEYMOUR
1929
The Doctor's Secret PAR

BURROUGHS, JAMES A.
1970
Interplay TIMES
Ducks (doc. short) STELIOS ROCCOS
In, Out, Up, Down, Under, Upside Down (doc. short) STELIOS ROCCOS
Sun (doc. short) STELIOS ROCCOS
Wind (doc. short) STELIOS ROCCOS
Z Is for Zoo (doc. short) STELIOS ROCCOS

BURTON, VAL
[Because he often was credited as musical director and sometimes worked in association with the Meyer Synchronizing Service, it is likely that many of his films did not have original scores. He was best known as a songwriter.]
1926
College Days TIFFANY
1927
Resurrection UA
1930
Extravagance TIFFANY
Just Like Heaven TIFFANY
The Utah Kid TIFFANY
1931
The Drums of Jeopardy TIFFANY
The Two Gun Man TIFFANY
Waterloo Bridge UNIV
Murder at Midnight TIFFANY
1932
Hotel Continental (with Kilenyi) WORLD WIDE
Shop Angel TOWER
Lena Rivers TIFFANY
Strangers of the Evening TIFFANY
Igloo (with Kilenyi) UNIV

The Last Mile WORLD WIDE
Those We Love WORLD WIDE
The Crooked Circle WORLD WIDE
False Faces WORLD WIDE
Uptown New York WORLD WIDE
Tombstone Canyon WORLD WIDE

1933
The Death Kiss WORLD WIDE
A Study in Scarlet WORLD WIDE
Deluge (mt: Kilenyi, W. Spielter; + stock) ADMIRAL-RKO

BUSSATT, IVAN

1931
The Broken Doll (short) JUDEA FILMS

BUTENS, STAN

1963
Summit (short) STAN VANDERBEEK

BUTTOLPH, DAVID

1933
Mr. Skitch (see De Francesco)
Smoky FOX
I Am Suzanne! (see Hollander)

1934
Sleepers East (ac: Kaylin) FOX
La Cruz y la Espada (see Kaylin)
Hold That Girl (ac: Kaylin; + stock) FOX
Ever Since Eve (mt; + stock) FOX
I Believed in You (see Kaylin)
David Harum (o: Gerstenberger) FOX
George White's Scandals (see Friedhofer)
Murder in Trinidad (o: Gerstenberger; + stock) FOX
Call It Luck (see Kaylin)
Wild Gold (ac: Kaylin) FOX
She Learned About Sailors (ac: Kaylin; o: Gerstenberger) FOX
Baby Take a Bow (o: Gerstenberger; + stock) FOX
Charlie Chan's Courage (mt; + stock) FOX
Handy Andy (ac: Kaylin) FOX
Pursued (see Friedhofer)
The World Moves On (see De Francesco)
Servants' Entrance (see Friedhofer)
Love Time (see Kaylin)
Dos Más Uno, Dos (Spanish language; with Friedhofer, Zamecnik; ac: Kaylin) FOX
365 Nights in Hollywood (with Kaylin) FOX
Bright Eyes FOX

1935
Lottery Lover (see A. Lange)
One More Spring (with A. Lange) FOX
It's a Small World (see A. Lange)
Spring Tonic (see Brunelli)
Our Little Girl (see Brunelli)
Daring Young Man (see A. Lange)
Orchids to You (see A. Lange)
The Farmer Takes a Wife (with Mockridge, R. Bassett) FOX
Dante's Inferno (see Friedhofer)
This Is the Life FOX
Way Down East (see Friedhofer)
Navy Wife (with Friedhofer) FOX

1936
Everybody's Old Man (with Mockridge; + stock) TCF
Under Two Flags (see Mockridge)
Girls' Dormitory (see Maxwell)
The Road to Glory (see R. Bassett)
Ladies in Love (see Mockridge)
Dimples (see Mockridge)
Pigskin Parade (o: Virgil) TCF
Reunion (with Mockridge) TCF
Lloyd's of London (see Mockridge)

1937
One in a Million (with Maxwell) TCF
Nancy Steele Is Missing (with Mockridge; ac: W. Scharf) TCF
Seventh Heaven (with Mockridge; o: W. Scharf, H. Spencer, Cutter) TCF
Café Metropole (with Mockridge) TCF
You Can't Have Everything (see W. Scharf)
Thin Ice (with W. Scharf, Mockridge, Maxwell) TCF
Heidi (see Toch)

1938
Happy Landing (see Mockridge)

1939
The Three Musketeers (see Maxwell)
Made for Each Other (see Friedhofer)
The Hound of the Baskervilles (see Maxwell)
The Return of the Cisco Kid (see W. Scharf)
The Gorilla (o: D. Raksin) TCF
Susannah of the Mounties (see Maxwell)
Hotel for Women (see Mockridge)
Stanley and Livingstone (see Silvers)
The Adventures of Sherlock Holmes (see Mockridge)
Here I Am a Stranger TCF
Hollywood Cavalcade (see Schrager)
Barricade (o: D. Raksin, W. Scharf, H. Spencer) TCF
Swanee River (see Schrager)
Everything Happens at Night (with Mockridge; ac: A. Lange, Maxwell) TCF

1940
The Blue Bird (see A. Newman)
Star Dust (ac: A. Newman) TCF
I Was an Adventuress (o: H. Spencer) TCF
Lillian Russell (see Mockridge)
Girl in 313 (with Mockridge; theme: A. Newman) TCF
Four Sons (o: E. Powell, H. Spencer, Salinger) TCF
Maryland (ac: A. Lange, A. Newman) TCF
The Man I Married (o: E. Powell, Friedhofer) TCF
The Return of Frank James (o: E. Powell, H. Spencer) TCF
Foreign Correspondent (see A. Newman)
Public Deb No. 1 (with A. Newman; ac: Henderson; mt: G. Rose) TCF
Brigham Young (see A. Newman)
For Beauty's Sake (o: H. Spencer) TCF
The Mark of Zorro (see A. Newman)
Street of Memories (o: E. Powell, H. Spencer, Salinger) TCF
Chad Hanna (o: E. Powell, Salinger) TCF

1941
Hudson's Bay (see A. Newman)
Romance of the Rio Grande (see Mockridge)
Western Union (o: E. Powell, Salinger) TCF
Murder Among Friends (see Mockridge)
Tobacco Road (ac: A. Newman; o: E. Powell) TCF
Scotland Yard (see Mockridge)
That Night in Rio (see A. Newman)
Blood and Sand (see A. Newman)
The Bride Wore Crutches (o: E. Powell, H. Spencer) TCF
Man Hunt (o: E. Powell, H. Spencer) TCF
A Very Young Lady (with Mockridge; o: E. Powell, H. Spencer) TCF
Moon Over Miami (see Mockridge)
Dance Hall (see Mockridge)
Wild Geese Calling (with A. Newman, Mockridge; o: E. Powell, Salinger) TCF
Sun Valley Serenade (see Mockridge)
Belle Starr (with A. Newman, Mockridge; o: E. Powell, Salinger, Bradshaw) TCF
The Last of the Duanes (o: D. Raksin, Moross) TCF
Man at Large (o: E. Powell) TCF
Great Guns (o: Virgil) TCF
Week-End in Havana (see A. Newman)
Rise and Shine (with Mockridge, A. Newman; ac: D. Raksin) TCF
Cadet Girl (ac: D. Raksin, Friedhofer, Roemheld) TCF
Ball of Fire (see A. Newman)
Swamp Water (o: H. Spencer, D. Raksin, Friedhofer) TCF
Bahama Passage (o: Parrish, W. Scharf) PAR
Confirm or Deny (o: E. Powell, H. Spencer) TCF
Son of Fury (see A. Newman)
Remember the Day (see Mockridge)

1942
Lady for a Night REP
Castle in the Desert (with Mockridge; o: E. Powell, Salinger) TCF
Song of the Islands (with Mockridge; ac: D. Raksin) TCF
My Favorite Blonde (o: Shuken, Parrish) PAR
It Happened in Flatbush (with Mockridge; o: E. Powell, H. Spencer) TCF
The Mad Martindales (with Mockridge; m&e: Harline) TCF
Whispering Ghosts (see Harline)
Moontide (see Mockridge)
In Old California REP
This Gun for Hire (o: Parrish, Shuken, W. Scharf) PAR
Ten Gentlemen from West Point (see Mockridge)
This Above All (see A. Newman)
A-Haunting We Will Go (with Mockridge; + stock) TCF
The Loves of Edgar Allan Poe (with Mockridge, A. Newman) TCF
Berlin Correspondent (o: E. Powell, H. Spencer, Arnaud) TCF
Wake Island (o: Shuken, Parrish, Powell, Salinger, Hand) PAR
Street of Chance (o: Shuken, Parrish) PAR
Iceland (see Harline)
Girl Trouble (see A. Newman)
Manila Calling (see Mockridge)
Thunder Birds (o: Salinger, H. Spencer, Arnaud) TCF
China Girl (see Friedhofer)
The Black Swan (see A. Newman)
Immortal Sergeant (ac: A. Newman, L. Newman) TCF
He Hired the Boss (with D. Raksin, L. Newman) TCF
American Empire (see Carbonara)

1943
The Moon Is Down (see A. Newman)

Hello, Frisco, Hello (ac: Mockridge, Henderson, A. Newman) TCF
At the Front in North Africa (doc.; see A. Newman)
My Friend Flicka (see A. Newman)
Crash Dive (ac: A. Newman; o: de Packh, Salinger, D. Raksin, Parrish, Morton) TCF
Bomber's Moon (o: D. Raksin, Morton, Virgil) TCF
Wintertime (see A. Lange)
Corvette K-225 UNIV
Guadalcanal Diary (o: Morton, Virgil, D. Raksin) TCF
No Exceptions (doc. short; o: Salinger) TCF

1944

The Sullivans (see Mockridge)
Buffalo Bill (ac: A. Lange; o: D. Raksin, Morton) TCF
Tampico (see Raksin)
Roger Touhy, Gangster (see Friedhofer)
The Hitler Gang (o: Morton, Parrish) PAR
Greenwich Village (with G. Rose, D. Raksin; ac: A. Lange, Morton, Harline) TCF
Sweet and Low-Down (see Mockridge)
The Big Noise (o: Morton) TCF
Till We Meet Again (o: Parrish, Salinger, D. Raksin, Morton) PAR
This Is It (doc. short; o: Morton, Cutner) TCF
Sunday Dinner for a Soldier (see A. Newman)
The Fighting Lady (doc.; ac: A. Newman; o: Morton, de Packh, D. Raksin, Cutner) TCF

1945

Thunderhead (see Mockridge)
Circumstantial Evidence (o: D. Raksin, de Packh) TCF
Molly and Me (see Mockridge)
The Bullfighters (o: Morton, de Packh) TCF
Diamond Horseshoe (see H. Spencer)
Don Juan Quilligan (see D. Raksin)
Nob Hill (o: E. Powell, Morton) TCF
Caribbean Mystery (ac: A. Newman; o: Cutner, E. Powell) TCF
Junior Miss (o: de Packh) TCF
Within These Walls (o: Morton) TCF
The House on 92nd Street (ac: A. Newman; o: Marquardt, Morton) TCF
The Dolly Sisters (with A. Newman, Mockridge, Henderson) TCF
The Spider (o: Morton, Shuken, Cutner) TCF

1946

Doll Face (with Mockridge; o: Morton, Plumb) TCF
Shock (o: Morton) TCF
Johnny Comes Flying Home (o: Morton) TCF
Do You Love Me (o: E. Powell) TCF
Strange Triangle (o: Morton) TCF
Somewhere in the Night (o: Morton) TCF
It Shouldn't Happen to a Dog (o: Morton) TCF
Centennial Summer (see A. Newman)
Home Sweet Homicide (o: de Packh) TCF
Claudia and David (see Mockridge)
If I'm Lucky (see Mockridge)
Three Little Girls in Blue (with Mockridge; o: de Packh, Morton, E. Powell, Cutner, Shuken) TCF
Margie (see A. Newman)
My Darling Clementine (o: Parrish) TCF

1947

13 Rue Madeleine (o: E. Powell, Cutner, Marquardt, Morton) TCF
The Brasher Doubloon (o: de Packh) TCF
Blaze of Noon (see A. Deutsch)
Boomerang! (o: E. Powell, H. Spencer) TCF
Carnival in Costa Rica (with H. Spencer, Mockridge) TCF
Moss Rose (o: E. Powell, de Packh) TCF
I Wonder Who's Kissing Her Now (with A. Newman; o: E. Powell) TCF
Kiss of Death (o: Hagen) TCF
Mother Wore Tights (o: E. Powell, de Packh) TCF
The Foxes of Harrow (o: de Packh) TCF

1948

Bill and Coo (o: Shuken, Cutner) REP
To the Victor (o: Raab) WB
Give My Regards to Broadway (see Mockridge)
Rope (m&e and trailer) WB
Smart Girls Don't Talk (o: Raab) WB
June Bride (o: Raab, Shuken, Cutner) WB

1949

One Sunday Afternoon WB
John Loves Mary (o: Raab) WB
Colorado Territory (o: de Packh, Shuken, Cutner) WB
The Girl from Jones Beach (o: Raab, Cutner) WB
Look for the Silver Lining (o: Shuken, Cutner) WB

One Last Fling (o: Raab) WB
Roseanna McCoy (ac: Friedhofer; o: Moross, de Packh) GOLDWYN
Always Leave Them Laughing WB

1950
Montana (o: Shuken, Cutner) WB
Chain Lightning (o: de Packh) WB
The Daughter of Rosie O'Grady (o: de Packh) WB
The Story of Seabiscuit (o: de Packh) WB
Return of the Frontiersman (o: de Packh) WB
Pretty Baby (o: de Packh) WB
Three Secrets (o: de Packh) WB

1951
The Enforcer (o: de Packh) WB
The Redhead and the Cowboy (o: de Packh, Parrish, Shuken, Cutner) PAR
Fighting Coast Guard REP
Along the Great Divide (o: de Packh) WB
Fort Worth WB
Submarine Command (o: Parrish, Shuken, Cutner) PAR
Ten Tall Men (o: Morton) COL
The Sellout (o: Courage) MGM
Lone Star (o: Courage) MGM

1952
Talk About a Stranger (o: Courage) MGM
This Woman Is Dangerous (o: de Packh; ac: M. Steiner) WB
Carson City (o: Shuken, Cutner) WB
About Face (with R. Heindorf) WB
The Winning Team (o: de Packh) WB
My Man and I (o: de Packh) MGM
The Man Behind the Gun (o: de Packh) WB
Stop, You're Killing Me (with R. Heindorf, H. Jackson) WB

1953
She's Back on Broadway WB
The System (o: de Packh) WB
House of Wax (o: de Packh) WB
The Beast from 20,000 Fathoms (o: de Packh) WB
South Sea Woman (o: de Packh) WB
Calamity Jane (with R. Heindorf, H. Jackson) WB
Thunder Over the Plains (o: de Packh) WB

1954
The Eddie Cantor Story WB
Crime Wave (o: de Packh) WB
Riding Shotgun WB
Secret of the Incas (o: Van Cleave, de Packh) PAR
The Bounty Hunter (o: de Packh) WB
Long John Silver DCA
Phantom of the Rue Morgue WB

1955
Jump Into Hell (o: de Packh) WB
Pete Kelly's Blues (see R. Heindorf)
I Died a Thousand Times (o: de Packh, Levene) WB
Target Zero (o: de Packh) WB

1956
The Lone Ranger (o: Cutner) WB
The Steel Jungle (o: de Packh) WB
Santiago (o: Levene) WB
The Burning Hills (o: Levene) WB
A Cry in the Night (o: de Packh) WB

1957
The Big Land (o: Levene) WB
The D.I. (o: Levene; theme: R. Heindorf) WB

1958
The Deep Six (o: de Packh, Levene) WB
No Time for Sergeants (with R. Heindorf) WB
Onionhead (mt: R. Heindorf) WB

1959
Westbound (o: Levene) WB
Woman Obsessed (see Friedhofer)
The Horse Soldiers UA

1960
Guns of the Timberland (o: de Packh) WB

1963
PT 109 (see Lava)

1964
The Man from Galveston WB
The Raiders (see M. Stevens)

Trailers

1949
Under Capricorn (for U.S. release of British film) WB
The Hasty Heart (for U.S. release of British film) WB

BUTTOLPH, DAVID HEYMAN

1962
Looking Forward (short) GIRL SCOUTS OF THE U.S.A.

BUTTS, R. DALE

1944
The Yellow Rose of Texas (see Skiles)
My Buddy REP
Lights of Old Santa Fe (with Dubin, M. Glickman) REP

1945
Utah (with M. Glickman) REP

Flame of Barbary Coast (with M. Glickman) REP
Man from Oklahoma (with M. Glickman) REP
Sunset in El Dorado (with M. Glickman) REP
Don't Fence Me In (with M. Glickman) REP
An Angel Comes to Brooklyn REP
Dakota (see W. Scharf)

1946
Gay Blades REP
Song of Arizona (with M. Glickman) REP
Home on the Range (with M. Glickman) REP
One Exciting Week REP
Rainbow Over Texas (see Maxwell)
Night Train to Memphis (with M. Glickman) REP
The Catman of Paris (o: Maxwell) REP
My Pal Trigger (with Maxwell) REP
Roll On Texas Moon (with Dubin) REP
The Pilgrim Lady (with Dubin, M. Glickman, Law) REP
Heldorado REP

1947
The Crimson Key TCF
Second Chance TCF
The Invisible Wall TCF

1948
Eyes of Texas REP
Night Time in Nevada REP
Son of God's Country REP
The Denver Kid REP
The Plunderers REP

1949
The Far Frontier REP
The Last Bandit (o: S. Wilson) REP
Hellfire (o: S. Wilson) REP
Too Late for Tears UA
Down Dakota Way (o: S. Wilson) REP
Bells of Coronado (o: S. Wilson) REP

1950
Women from Headquarters (see S. Wilson)
Rock Island Trail (o: S. Wilson) REP
The Savage Horde (o: S. Wilson) REP
Trigger, Jr. (o: N. Scott, S. Wilson) REP
Sunset in the West REP
Hit Parade of 1951 (o: S. Wilson) REP

1951
Spoilers of the Plains REP
Oh! Susanna REP
The Sea Hornet REP
South of Caliente REP

1952
Colorado Sundown REP
The Last Musketeer REP
Bal Tabarin REP
Woman of the North Country REP
Toughest Man in Arizona REP
The WAC from Walla Walla REP

1953
San Antone REP
Old Overland Trail REP
City That Never Sleeps (with S. Wilson) REP
Champ for a Day REP
Sea of Lost Ships REP
Shadows of Tombstone REP
Geraldine REP
Red River Shore REP

1954
Trader Tom of the China Seas (serial) REP
Hell's Half Acre REP
Phantom Stallion REP
The Outcast REP
The Shanghai Story REP
Man with the Steel Whip (serial) REP
Hell's Outpost REP

1955
Panther Girl of the Kongo (serial) REP
Carolina Cannonball REP
Santa Fe Passage REP
I Cover the Underworld REP
Double Jeopardy REP
City of Shadows REP
King of the Carnival (serial) REP
Road to Denver REP
Lay That Rifle Down REP
Headline Hunters REP
The Vanishing American REP
The Fighting Chance REP
No Man's Woman REP

1956
Stranger at My Door REP
Terror at Midnight REP
Dakota Incident REP
Thunder Over Arizona REP
A Strange Adventure REP
The Man Is Armed REP
Accused of Murder REP

1957
Affair in Reno REP

BYERS, BILLY

1967
Young Americans (doc.) COL

[Also worked as an orchestrator.]

BYRD, CHARLIE
1961
Dead to the World UA
Shorts
1959
The Intruder E.L. BRUCE CO.
1962
The Refugee Story (doc.) EPISCOPAL CHURCH
1963
Swingin' West (doc.) PAR
1967
Another Way KETTLER BROS.
While I Run This Race (doc.) SUN DIAL FILMS
1968
A Voice in the City ?

BYRD, JOSEPH
1969
Lions Love AGNÈS VARDA

BYRNS, HAROLD
1951
Pickup COL
The Girl on the Bridge TCF
1965
Situation Hopeless—But Not Serious PAR
[Also worked as an orchestrator.]

C

CACIOPPO, GEORGE
1964
More Than Meets the Eye (doc. short) U.S. OFFICE OF EDUCATION
1970
What Next (short) MARSHALL FRANKE

CADKIN, EMIL
1947
The Devil on Wheels PRC
Three on a Ticket PRC
The Big Fix PRC
Heartaches PRC
Bury Me Dead EL
1959
The Killer Shrews (see Bluestone)
1964
The Devil's Bedroom (see Loose)
Navajo Run (see Loose)

CADMAN, CHARLES WAKEFIELD
1922
The Rubáiyat of Omar Khayyám (also released 1925 as *A Lover's Oath*) FERDINAND P. EARLE
1928
Drums of Love (with S. Cohen) D.W. GRIFFITH

CAGE, JOHN
1948
Dreams That Money Can Buy (see Applebaum)
1950
Works of Calder (short) HERBERT MATTER

CAILLIET, LUCIEN
1947
Fun on a Weekend UA
The Enchanted Valley EL
1948
The Winner's Circle TCF
Harpoon SG
Trouble Preferred TCF
Thunder in the Pines SG
1949
State Department—File 649 FC
Red Stallion in the Rockies EL
Special Agent PAR
1950
Captain China PAR
Tripoli PAR
1951
The Last Outpost PAR
Crosswinds PAR
Hong Kong PAR
1952
Confidence Girl UA
Caribbean PAR
The Blazing Forest PAR
1953
Tropic Zone PAR
Jamaica Run PAR
Sangaree PAR
The Vanquished PAR

1955

The Night Holds Terror COL

1965

The Secret of My Success (ac) MCM

[He orchestrated his own scores and those of several other composers.]

CAIRNCROSS, JAMES

1962

Ring of Terror PLAYSTAR

CALAHAN, MICHAEL

1963

Y (short) GERD STERN

CALE, JOHN

1965

Hedy ANDY WARHOL

CALELLO, CHARLES

1965

Who Killed Teddy Bear? MAGNA

CALKER, DARRELL

1941

Under Fiesta Stars (see M. Glickman)

1942

Miss Annie Rooney (with Michelet, C. Wheeler) UA

1945

Enemy Bacteria (an. doc.) U.S. NAVY

1946

Backlash TCF
Rolling Home SG
Renegade Girl SG
Dangerous Millions TCF

1947

Seven Were Saved PAR
Big Town PAR
Shoot to Kill SG
Jewels of Brandenburg TCF
Danger Street PAR
The Hat-Box Mystery SG
I Cover Big Town PAR
Jungle Flight PAR
Case of the Baby Sitter SG
Adventure Island PAR
Big Town After Dark PAR

1948

Half Past Midnight TCF
Albuquerque PAR
Silent Conflict UA
Arthur Takes Over TCF
Speed to Spare PAR
Sinister Journey UA
Borrowed Trouble UA
Fighting Back TCF
Big Town Scandal PAR

1949

Dynamite PAR
Ride, Ryder, Ride EL
Tucson TCF
El Paso PAR
Manhandled PAR
The Fighting Redhead EL
The Flying Saucer FC

1950

Forbidden Jungle EL
Federal Man EL
I Killed Geronimo EL
Border Outlaws EL
Cattle Queen EL

1951

Badman's Gold EL
Savage Drums LIP
The Hoodlum UA
Joe Palooka in Triple Cross MON
Slaughter Trail RKO
Superman and the Mole-Men LIP
F.B.I. Girl LIP

1953

Son of the Renegade UA
The Marshal's Daughter UA

1954

Outlaw Treasure AIP

1956

I Killed Wild Bill Hickok WHEELER
Voodoo Woman AIP

1957

From Hell It Came AA

1958

My World Dies Screaming HOWCO
Terror in the Haunted House HOWCO

1959

Beyond the Time Barrier AIP

1960

The Amazing Transparent Man AIP
Chartroose Caboose UNIV
Five Bold Women CITATION

Cartoons (UNIV)

1941

Andy Panda's Pop
Boogie Woogie Bugle Boy of Company B
Dizzy Kitty
Fair Today
Hysterical Highspots in American History
Man's Best Friend

Salt Water Daffy
The Screwdriver
Scrub Me Mama with a Boogie Beat
$21 a Day (Once a Month)
What's Cookin?
Woody Woodpecker

1942
Ace in the Hole
Andy Panda's Victory Garden
Boogie Woogie Sioux
Good-bye Mr. Moth
The Hams That Couldn't Be Cured
The Hollywood Matador
Juke Box Jamboree
The Loan Stranger
Mother Goose on the Loose
Nutty Pine Cabin
Pigeon Patrol
Under the Spreading Blacksmith Shop
Yankee Doodle Swing Shift

1943
Air Raid Warden
Boogie Woogie Man
Canine Commandos
Cow-Cow Boogie
The Dizzy Acrobat
Egg Cracker Suite
Meatless Tuesday
Pass the Biscuits Mirandy!
Ration Bored
The Screwball
Swing Your Partner

1944
Abou Ben Boogie
The Barber of Seville
The Beach Nut
Fish Fry
The Greatest Man in Siam
Jungle Jive
The Pied Piper of Basin Street
Ski for Two

1945
Andy Panda in Crow Crazy
Chew-Chew Baby
The Dippy Diplomat
The Loose Nut
The Painter and the Pointer
Sliphorn King of Polaroo
Woody Dines Out

1946
Apple Andy
Bathing Buddies
Fair Weather Fiends
Mousie Come Home
The Poet and Peasant
The Reckless Driver
Reddy Made Magic
The Wacky Weed
Who's Cookin' Who?

1947
The Coo Coo Bird
The Mad Hatter
Musical Moments from Chopin
The Overture to William Tell
Smoked Hams
Well Oiled

1948
Banquet Busters
Dog Tax Dodgers
Kiddie Koncert
Pixie Picnic
Playful Pelican
Solid Ivory
Wacky-Bye Baby
Wet Blanket Policy
Wild and Woody
Woody the Giant Killer

1949
Drooler's Delight
The Three Pigs
Scrappy Birthday
The Town Mouse and the Country Mouse

1961
Woody's Kook-Out

1962
Careless Caretaker
Punchy Pooch
Voo-Doo Boo-Boo

1963
Charlie's Mother-in-Law
Goose Is Wild

1964
The Case of the Maltese Chicken
Rah Rah Ruckus
Woody's Clip Joint

Cartoons (SCREEN GEMS)

1947
Boston Beanie
Kitty Caddy
Leave Us Chase It
Swiss Tease
Tooth or Consequences

1948
Flora
Short Snorts on Sports
Topsy Turkey

1949
Cat-Tastrophy

Coo-Coo Bird Dog
Grape Nutty
Animated Shorts (JSP)
1951
Inside Cackle Corners
Who Buys Your Livestock?

CAMBERN, DONN
1952
Broken Space (short) UCLA
1967
Venezuelan Adventure (doc. short) DOUGLAS AIRCRAFT

CAMPBELL, FRANCEAN
1946
The Potted Psalm (short) SIDNEY PETERSON

CARBONARA, GERARD
1928
Warming Up PAR
The Sawdust Paradise PAR
The Patriot (see Savino)
Waterfront (ac: Harling, Kaestner, Cousminer, Vaughan; + stock) FN
Show Girl (with Harling; ac: Bergunker, Vaughan; + stock) FN
The Haunted House (see Bergunker)
Adoration (see Hajos)
Naughty Baby (+ stock) FN
1929
Chinatown Nights (see Hajos)
Wolf Song (with Bergunker; ac: Hand, Arthur Kay) PAR
The Hole in the Wall PAR
Fast Company (mt) PAR
1930
Burning Up (see G. Lucas)
Young Eagles (see Leipold)
1931
Rango (see Hajos)
1935
The Land of Promise (doc.) URIM PALESTINE
1936
Desire (see Hollander)
The Trail of the Lonesome Pine (with Friedhofer) PAR
Too Many Parents (with Satterfield; + stock) PAR
Big Brown Eyes PAR
The Moon's Our Home PAR
The Sky Parade (see Leipold)
Fatal Lady (see V. Young)
The Case Against Mrs. Ames (+ stock) PAR
Forgotten Faces (see Leipold)
Palm Springs (see Leipold)
Girl of the Ozarks (with Leipold) PAR
Poppy (see Hollander)
Spendthrift (with Leipold) PAR
My American Wife (see Hollander)
The Texas Rangers (ac: Kaun, Hollander) PAR
The General Died at Dawn (see Janssen)
Wedding Present (see Skiles)
1937
Racketeers in Exile (see Nussbaum)
The Devil Is Driving! (see Nussbaum)
The Barrier PAR
1938
The Buccaneer (see Antheil)
The Texans PAR
Spawn of the North (see Tiomkin)
The Arkansas Traveler (ac: Leipold, Boutelje) PAR
Men with Wings (see Harling)
The Mysterious Rider PAR
Arrest Bulldog Drummond PAR
The Frontiersman (with Leipold; + stock) PAR
Tom Sawyer, Detective (ac: Leipold) PAR
Artists and Models Abroad (see Rainger)
1939
Disbarred (with Leipold) PAR
Ambush (with F. Morgan) PAR
Paris Honeymoon (see Rainger)
Stagecoach (see Leipold)
Sunset Trail (m&e; + stock) PAR
King of Chinatown (see Leipold)
Union Pacific (see Leipold)
Unmarried (see Leipold)
The Gracie Allen Murder Case (with Shuken; mt: V. Young) PAR
Grand Jury Secrets (see V. Young)
Our Leading Citizen (ac: Leipold, V. Young) PAR
The Renegade Trail (see Leipold)
1940
Geronimo! (with Leipold; o: Hand, Reese) PAR
Santa Fe Marshal (see Leipold)
Parole Fixer (with Shuken, Leipold; mt: V. Young) PAR
Women Without Names (with Leipold; o: Bradshaw, Hand) PAR
Dr. Cyclops (see Malotte)

Island of Doomed Men COL
I Married Adventure (doc.; o: Cutner) COL

1941
The Monster and the Girl PAR
The Shepherd of the Hills (o: Shuken, Bradshaw) PAR
Among the Living (o: Parrish, Bradshaw) PAR
The Night of January 16th (o and ac: Leipold; mt: V. Young) PAR
Pacific Blackout (mt: V. Young) PAR

1942
The Gold Rush (see C. Chaplin)
Tombstone (o: Marquardt) PAR
American Empire (with Buttolph; o: Marquardt, Nussbaum) UA

1943
Night Plane from Chungking (o: Parrish, Shuken) PAR
The Kansan (ac: Leipold, Amfitheatrof; o: Hand, Marquardt) UA
Appointment in Berlin (see Heymann)
Henry Aldrich Haunts a House (o: Marquardt) PAR

1944
The Town Went Wild PRC

1946
Abilene Town (see Terr)

1947
California (see V. Young)
Gunfighters (see Schrager)

1949
The Big Wheel (with Leipold; o: Nussbaum, Marquardt) UA

1950
High Lonesome (see Schrager)

1953
Road to Bali (see Lilley)

Shorts (MGM)

1944
By Your Command (o: Nussbaum)
Easy Life (o: Marquardt)
The Immortal Blacksmith (see Terr)

Doc. Shorts (EDUCATIONAL FILMS)

1932
Across America
Any Way to Get There
On the Farm
Traffic

Doc. Shorts (RAPHAEL G. WOLFF STUDIO)

1945
Clean Waters
Transit
Transportation
Welding

1946
More Power to America
More Power to the American Farmer
Of This We Are Proud
Running Water on the Farm

1948
"By Their Works"
Highway Highlights
The Textile Industry

CARLOS, WALTER

1964
Image (short) ROBERT SHAYE

CARLSON, JAMES C.

1956
Out of Darkness (short) HIGH CALL PRODS.

CARMICHAEL, RALPH

1951
Mr. Texas GREAT COMMISSION

1952
Oiltown, U.S.A. GREAT COMMISSION

1953
Queen of Sheba (short) GREAT COMMISSION
Sunday on the Range (short) GREAT COMMISSION

1954
Souls in Conflict GREAT COMMISSION

1955
Wiretapper GREAT COMMISSION

1957
The Persuader WORLD WIDE

1958
The Blob PAR

1959
4D Man UNIV

1962
Jerusalem (doc.) WORLD WIDE

1963
Lucia WORLD WIDE

1964
Man in the 5th Dimension (doc.) WORLD WIDE
So Little Time WORLD WIDE
World's Fair Encounter WORLD WIDE

1965
Copenhagen Crusade WORLD WIDE
The Restless Ones WORLD WIDE
Three Weeks of Love (see C. Jackson)
The Heart Is a Rebel WORLD WIDE

1966
For Pete's Sake WORLD WIDE
1969
His Land (doc.) WORLD WIDE
1970
The Cross and the Switchblade DICK ROSS

CARPENTER, JOHN
1970
The Resurrection of Broncho Billy (short) UNIV

CARPENTER, VINCENT
19??
Sculpture in Minnesota PAUL M. LAPORTE

CARRAS, NICHOLAS
1955
Jungle Hell NORMAN CERF
1956
Female Jungle AIP
1958
Hell's Five Hours AA
She Demons ASTOR
Frankenstein's Daughter ASTOR
Dragstrip Riot AIP
1959
Missile to the Moon ASTOR
1960
Date Bait FILMGROUP
High School Caesar FILMGROUP
1961
Honeymoon of Terror SONNEY
1963
Willy NG
1968
Girl in Gold Boots GENENI
The Astro-Zombies GENENI
1970
Do Not Throw Cushions Into the Ring TANHI PRODS.

CARROLL, JIMMY
1969
Harold and the Purple Crayon (an. short) WESTON WOODS

CARTER, BENNY
1966
A Man Called Adam EMBASSY
Animated Shorts (JOHN HUBLEY)
1957
Adventures of an Asterisk
1958
Harlem Wednesday
1966
The Cruise
1967
Urbanissimo

CASARINI, JACOB
1970
Melissa: The Total Female CANYON

CASTELNUOVO-TEDESCO, MARIO
1941
Rage in Heaven (see Kaper)
The Stars Look Down (see Amfitheatrof)
Dr. Jekyll and Mr. Hyde (see Waxman)
1942
Fingers at the Window (see Kaper)
Tortilla Flat (see Waxman)
The Affairs of Martha (see Kaper)
Somewhere I'll Find You (see Kaper)
A Yank at Eton (see Kaper)
White Cargo (see Kaper)
Journey for Margaret (see Waxman)
Reunion in France (see Waxman)
Keeper of the Flame (see Kaper)
1943
Harrigan's Kid (see Amfitheatrof)
DuBarry Was a Lady (see Amfitheatrof)
Above Suspicion (see Kaper)
Bataan (see Kaper)
Hitler's Madman (see N. Shilkret)
Whistling in Brooklyn (see Bassman)
The Cross of Lorraine (see Kaper)
The Return of the Vampire COL
1944
The Heavenly Body (see Kaper)
Rationing (with Snell, Salinger, S. Kaplan) MGM
In Our Time (see Waxman)
Two-Man Submarine COL
The Black Parachute COL
Gaslight (see Kaper)
The Canterville Ghost (see Bassman)
Address Unknown (see Toch)
She's a Soldier Too COL
Secret Command (see Sawtell)
Barbary Coast Gent (see Snell)
Mr. Winkle Goes to War (see Dragon)
Mrs. Parkington (see Kaper)
The Mark of the Whistler (with Moraweck) COL
Sergeant Mike (ac: M. Bakaleinikoff; + stock) COL

Main Street After Dark (see Bassman)
Dancing in Manhattan (+ stock) COL
Gentle Annie (see Snell)

1945

I Love a Mystery COL
The Crime Doctor's Courage COL
The Picture of Dorian Gray (see Stothart)
The Clock (see Bassman)
Without Love (see Kaper)
Son of Lassie (see Stothart)
The Valley of Decision (see Stothart)
Bewitched (see Kaper)
The Hidden Eye (see Snell)
The Strange Affair of Uncle Harry (see Salter)
Our Vines Have Tender Grapes (see Kaper)
And Then There Were None (with C. Previn) TCF
Voice of the Whistler (+ stock) COL
Prison Ship COL
A Letter for Evie (see Bassman)

1946

Bad Bascomb (see Snell)
Night Editor COL
Courage of Lassie (see Bradley)
Dangerous Business COL
Shadowed (+ stock) COL
Undercurrent (see Stothart)

1947

Time Out of Mind (see Amfitheatrof)
Desire Me (see Stothart)

1948

The Loves of Carmen COL

1950

Rogues of Sherwood Forest (with Morton, Roemheld) COL

1951

The Brave Bulls COL
Mask of the Avenger COL

1952

The Brigand COL

1954

The Long Wait UA

Shorts

1942

Vendetta (see Amfitheatrof)
Mr. Blabbermouth (see Amfitheatrof)

1943

Plan for Destruction (see N. Shilkret)
Inca Gold (see Terr)
Forgotten Treasure MGM
To My Unborn Son (see Terr)

1956

Day of the Fox (an.) UPA
Mr. Charmley Meets a Lady (an.) UPA

CASTILLO, DEL

Cartoons (UPA)

1948

Robin Hoodlum

1949

The Magic Fluke
The Ragtime Bear

1950

Punchy de Leon
Spellbound Hound

1951

Barefaced Flatfoot

1955

Madcap Magoo

1956

Meet Mother Magoo

CASWELL, OZZIE

1950

Blue Grass of Kentucky MON
Motor Patrol LIP
The Lost Volcano MON
County Fair MON
The Hidden City MON

1951

Blue Blood MON
Canyon Raiders MON
Blazing Bullets MON
Nevada Badmen MON

CEELY, ROBERT

1961

Spectrum (short) JOHN MCKEE FILMS

CHAITKIN, DAVID

1967

The Game (doc. short) ROBERTA HODES

CHAPIN, FREDERIC

1938

Unashamed CINE-GRAND FILMS

CHAPIN, STEVE

1967

The Legendary Champions (doc.) TURN OF THE CENTURY FIGHTS

CHAPLIN, CHARLES

1925

The Gold Rush UA

1931
City Lights (a: A. Johnston) UA
1936
Modern Times (a: D. Raksin; o: E. Powell, D. Raksin) UA
1940
The Great Dictator (with Willson; o: Dragon, Terr) UA
1942
The Gold Rush (sound reissue of 1925 film; with Terr, Carbonara) UA
1947
Monsieur Verdoux (a: Schrager) UA
1952
Limelight (a: Rasch, L. Russell) UA
[Chaplin left the United States in 1952 for Europe, where he composed music for his last two pictures and for reissues of 10 of his silent films.]

CHAPLIN, SAUL
1956
The Teahouse of the August Moon (a; o: R. Franklyn) MGM
1961
West Side Story (adapted with Ramin, Kostal; o: Ramin, Kostal) UA

CHARLES, JONATHAN
1970
Shut Up . . . I'm Crying (short) ROBERT SIEGLER

CHASE, NORMAN
1953
Heavenly Harmonies (short) BOB JONES U.

CHERNIS, JAY
1932
The Sign of the Cross (see Kopp)
1933
Song of the Eagle (see Harold Lewis)
1943
Harvest Melody PRC
1944
Trocadero REP
That's My Baby REP
1945
Identity Unknown REP

CHERRY, DON
1964
New York Eye and Ear Control (short) MICHAEL SNOW
1966
Zero in the Universe FILM-MAKERS
On Fighting Witches (short) ROBERT SHAYE

CHESSID, HERMAN
1949
An Adventure in Friendship (doc. short) BIG BROTHER MOVEMENT

CHILDS, BARNEY
1961
Campus International (doc. short) U. OF ARIZONA

CHOU WEN-CHUNG
1961
Tomorrow (short) ?
1964
A Day at the Fair (short) ?

CHUDACOFF, EDWARD
1951
Metamorphosis U. OF MISSISSIPPI
1957
The Expressionist Revolt (doc. short) DETROIT INSTITUTE OF ARTS

CHURCHILL, FRANK
1937
Snow White and the Seven Dwarfs (with Harline, P. Smith) WDP
1941
The Reluctant Dragon (ac: P. Smith, Wolcott) WDP
Dumbo (with Wallace; o: Plumb) WDP
1942
Bambi (with Plumb; o: P. Smith, Wolcott) WDP
Cartoons (WDP)
1930
The Chain Gang
1931
The Busy Beavers
The Castaway
The Cat's Nightmare
The China Plate
Egyptian Melodies
The Fox Hunt
In a Clock Store
1932
Barnyard Olympics
The Bears and Bees
The Bird Store

Bugs in Love
Building a Building
The Grocery Boy
The Klondike Kid
Mickey in Arabia
Musical Farmer
Santa's Workshop
Touchdown Mickey
The Whoopee Party

1933
Birds in the Spring (with E. Lewis)
Giantland
Lullaby Land (see Harline)
Mickey's Gala Premier
Mickey's Mellerdrammer
Mickey's Pal Pluto
Old King Cole (with E. Lewis)
Puppy Love
The Steeplechase
The Three Little Pigs
Ye Olden Days

1934
The Big Bad Wolf
Camping Out (with E. Lewis)
The Dognapper (see E. Lewis)
The Flying Mouse (with E. Lewis)
Funny Little Bunnies (with Harline)
Gulliver Mickey
Mickey Plays Papa (with E. Lewis)
Mickey's Steam Roller (see E. Lewis)
Orphans' Benefit
Playful Pluto
Shanghaied

1935
Cock o' the Walk (see Malotte)
The Golden Touch
Mickey's Man Friday (see E. Lewis)
On Ice (see E. Lewis)
Pluto's Judgment Day (with Harline)
The Robber Kitten
Three Orphan Kittens
The Tortoise and the Hare
Who Killed Cock Robin?

1936
Mickey's Polo Team (with P. Smith)
More Kittens
Three Little Wolves
Thru the Mirror (with P. Smith)
Toby Tortoise Returns (see Harline)

1941
Orphans' Benefit

1942
The Army Mascot
Sky Trooper

Cartoons (UNIV)

1937
The Lamplighter

1938
Barnyard Romeo
Cheese-Nappers
Feed the Kitty
Ghost Town Frolics
Happy Scouts
Hollywood Bowl
Movie Phoney News
Nellie, the Indian Chief's Daughter
Nellie, the Sewing Machine Girl
Problem Child
Silly Seals
Tail End
Voodoo in Harlem
Yokel Boy Makes Good

1939
The One-Armed Bandit
Snuffy's Party

1940
Kittens' Mittens

1941
Mouse Trappers

CLARK, PALMER

1913
The Last Days of Pompeii (U. S. release of Italian film) KLEINE

CLARK, ROBERT

1959
Circus (cartoon) WILLIS E. SIMMS

CLAYTON, JOHN

1950
In the Name of Freedom (doc. short) U. OF NORTH CAROLINA

CLAYTON, WILLIAM D.

1960
Tale of the Northern Lights (an.) CARTOON CLASSICS

1963
Mr. E. from Tau Ceti (an.) CARTOON CLASSICS

CLEMENTS, OTIS

1966
Change for the Better (doc. short) ALCOA

COBB, ED

1966
Breakaway (short) BRUCE CONNER

COBERT, ROBERT
1959
The Island (doc. short) CHARLES COLBY
1963
Ladybug, Ladybug UA
1970
House of Dark Shadows MGM

COHEN, NATHAN
1969
The Song and the Silence NATHAN COHEN

COHEN, SOL B.
1922
Skin Deep FN
The Hottentot FN
1923
Bell Boy 13 FN
Scars of Jealousy FN
1928
Drums of Love (see Cadman)

COHRSSEN, WALTER
1961
Little Blue and Little Yellow (an. short) DAVID HILBERMAN

COLBURN, GEORGE
1914
Antony and Cleopatra (U.S. release of 1913 Italian film) KLEINE

COLEMAN, CY
1964
The Troublemaker JANUS
Father Goose UNIV
1965
The Art of Love (ac: Skinner) UNIV
1968
Sweet Charity (o: R. Burns) UNIV

COLEMAN, ORNETTE
1963
O.K. End Here (short) ROBERT FRANK
1965
Who's Crazy? CINEMASTERS
1966
The Real Thing FILM-MAKERS' COOPERATIVE
1967
Population Explosion (an. short) PIERRE HÉBERT

COLICCHIO, MICHAEL
1966
Flame and the Fire (doc.) CONTINENTAL
1968
The Road Hustlers AIP

COLL, RICHARD H.
1963
What's a Nice Girl Like You Doing in a Place Like This? (short) MARTIN SCORSESE
1964
It's Not Just You, Murray! (short) MARTIN SCORSESE

COLLETTE, WILLIAM (BUDDY)
1962
Trauma PARADE
Shorts
1959
The George Washington Carver Story ARTISAN
1961
ECS (doc.) EAMES
1963
A Comedy Tale of Fanny Hill LESLIE GOODWINS
1967
National Fisheries Center and Aquarium (doc.) EAMES
Story Book Kiddles MATTEL TOYS
1968
Winter Geyser (doc.) PYRAMID
1970
The Fiberglass Chairs (doc.) EAMES
Soft Pad (doc.) EAMES
[Also others, titles and dates undetermined.]

COLLINS, ANTHONY
[English composer; his filmography includes both British and American films.]
1937
Victoria the Great HERBERT WILCOX
The Rat WILCOX
1938
A Royal Divorce WILCOX
Sixty Glorious Years (U.S.: *Queen of Destiny*) WILCOX
1939
Nurse Edith Cavell WILCOX
Allegheny Uprising RKO
1940
Swiss Family Robinson (adaptation of music by Schubert) RKO
Irene (with Webb) WILCOX
Tom Brown's School Days RKO
No, No, Nanette WILCOX

1941
Sunny WILCOX
Unexpected Uncle RKO
1942
The Nazis Strike (doc.; see Webb)
1943
Forever and a Day RKO
Destroyer COL
Around the World (see Duning)
1945
I Live in Grosvenor Square (U.S.: *A Yank in London*) WILCOX
1946
Piccadilly Incident WILCOX
1947
The Courtneys of Curzon Street WILCOX
The Fabulous Texan REP
1950
Odette WILCOX
1951
The Lady with the Lamp WILCOX
1952
Macao RKO
Derby Day (U.S.: *Four Against Fate*) WILCOX
Trent's Last Case WILCOX
1953
Laughing Anne WILCOX
1954
Adventures of Robinson Crusoe UA

COLOMBIER, MICHEL
1970
The Forbin Project UNIV

COLOMBO, ALBERTO
1934
Long Lost Father (m&e; + stock) RKO
Gridiron Flash (m&e; + stock) RKO
1935
Romance in Manhattan (+ stock) RKO
Murder on a Honeymoon RKO
Chasing Yesterday RKO
Village Tale RKO
Hooray for Love RKO
Jalna RKO
The Return of Peter Grimm RKO
His Family Tree (+ stock) RKO
Annie Oakley RKO
Seven Keys to Baldpate RKO
1936
Yellow Dust (+ stock) RKO
1937
Dick Tracy (serial; + stock) REP
The Hit Parade REP
Michael O'Halloran REP
Affairs of Cappy Ricks REP
Dangerous Holiday REP
Rhythm in the Clouds (o: C. Wheeler) REP
It Could Happen to You REP
The Sheik Steps Out (o: C. Wheeler) REP
Sea Racketeers REP
All Over Town REP
SOS Coast Guard (serial; + stock) REP
Escape by Night REP
Youth on Parole REP
The Wrong Road REP
Portia on Trial (o: C. Wheeler) REP
Manhattan Merry-Go-Round REP
Springtime in the Rockies (o: C. Wheeler) REP
The Duke Comes Back REP
Zorro Rides Again (serial; + stock) REP
Wild Horse Rodeo (+ stock) REP
Exiled to Shanghai REP
1938
Mama Runs Wild (+ stock) REP
The Purple Vigilantes REP
The Old Barn Dance (+ stock) REP
Outside of Paradise REP
Born to Be Wild REP
Hollywood Stadium Mystery REP
Prison Nurse REP
The Lone Ranger (serial; + stock) REP
Call the Mesquiteers (+ stock) REP
King of the Newsboys (+ stock) REP
Arson Gang Busters REP
Invisible Enemy REP
Call of the Yukon REP
Romance on the Run REP
Gangs of New York REP
The Fighting Devil Dogs (serial; mt: Feuer; + stock) REP
Ladies in Distress REP
Riders of the Black Hills (+ stock) REP
Gold Mine in the Sky REP
Dick Tracy Returns (serial) REP
Heroes of the Hills (see Feuer)
Swing That Cheer (+ stock) UNIV
Rhythm of the Saddle (with Lava; ac: Feuer) REP
1941
Federal Fugitives PRC
South of Panama PRC
Jungle Man PRC
1944
A Guy Named Joe (see Stothart)

1945
They Were Expendable (see Stothart)
1946
Adventure (see Stothart)
1948
Hills of Home (see Stothart)
1949
The Sickle or the Cross ROLAND REED
1950
The Pilgrimage Play ROLAND REED
Black Hand (o: Sendrey) MGM
Messenger of Peace ROLAND REED
1951
All That I Have FAMILY FILMS
Go for Broke (ac: Cutner, Shuken; o: Heglin, Sendrey, Marquardt) MGM
It's a Big Country (see Deutsch)
1952
Holiday for Sinners (+ stock) MGM
Rogue's March (o: Marquardt; + stock) MGM
1953
Code Two (o: Heglin; + stock) MGM
Fast Company (with Sendrey; + stock) MGM
A Slight Case of Larceny (with Sendrey; + stock) MGM
Shorts
1941
Oil for Aladdin's Lamp (doc.) SHELL OIL CO.
1945
Orders from Tokyo (doc.) WB
1947
It's Your Life, Brother (doc.) EDDIE ALBERT PRODS.
So They May Walk (doc.) HUDSON PRODS.
1949
A Boy and His Prayer FAMILY FILMS
Unto Thyself Be True FAMILY FILMS
Yesterday, Today, and Forever FAMILY FILMS
This Moving World (doc.) ROLAND REED
Trailin' West WB

COLVIG, RICHARD
1954
Let's Go to Art School (doc. short) COAST FILMS

COMPINSKY, MANUEL
1950
Sky House (doc. short) ERVEN JOURDAN
1953
Killers from Space RKO
1954
The Snow Creature UA
1955
The Big Bluff UA

COMSTOCK, FRANK
1955
Magoo Express (cartoon) UPA
1956
Magoo Goes West (cartoon) UPA
Trailblazer Magoo (cartoon) UPA
1961
The Last Time I Saw Archie UA
[Also worked as an orchestrator.]

CONRAD, TONY
1963
Flaming Creatures (+ stock) JACK SMITH
1964
Normal Love JACK SMITH
1966
The Flicker (short) TONY CONRAD
1970
Coming Attractions (short) BEVERLY CONRAD
Straight and Narrow (short) BEVERLY CONRAD

CONROY, FRANK
1968
Beyond the Law GROVE PRESS

CONVERSE, FREDERICK SHEPHERD
1923
Puritan Passions FILM GUILD

COOKERLY, JACK
1962
Shoot Out at Big Sag (see Loose)
Invasion of the Star Creatures (with E. Fisher) AIP

COOPER, BOB
1961
A Building Is Many Buildings (short) GRAPHIC FILMS
1963
Lonnie FUTURAMIC

COOPER, PAUL
1956
The Goldseeker (short) ARGUS FILMS

COOPERSMITH, J. M.
1930
Take the Heir BIG 4

COPLAND, AARON
1939
The City (doc.) CIVIC FILMS
1940
Of Mice and Men (o: Bassman) UA
Our Town UA
1943
The North Star (o: Grau, Moross, A. Morton) GOLDWYN
1945
The Cummington Story (doc. short) OWI
1949
The Red Pony (o: N. Scott, Butts) REP
The Heiress (o: Van Cleave) PAR
1961
Something Wild UA

COPPING, CECIL
Silent Films (New York Openings)
1924
The Hunchback of Notre Dame (see Riesenfeld, 1923)
The Sea Hawk FN
1925
The Lost World FN
Quo Vadis? (U.S. release of 1923 Italian film) FN
1927
The Patent Leather Kid FN
The Private Life of Helen of Troy FN
Chicago PATHÉ
1928
Lilac Time (synchronized version: see N. Shilkret) FN
Sound Films (WB)
1929
The Divine Lady
The Glad Rag Doll
On with the Show
Careers (with Reiser; + stock)
The Hottentot (see Reiser)
In the Headlines (mt)
Drag (with Brunelli)
Hearts in Exile
The Green Goddess (mt)
Her Private Life (see Reiser)
The Isle of Lost Ships (see Reiser)
1930
The Love Racket (see Reiser)
Loose Ankles (see Reiser)
No, No, Nanette (with Reiser)
A Notorious Affair (+ stock)
Spring Is Here (mt: Reiser)
Back Pay (see Reiser)
Dancing Sweeties (with Dunn)
1931
Father's Son (with Mendoza, Rosebrook)
Misbehaving Ladies
Gold Dust Gertie (see Mendoza)

COPPOLA, CARMINE
1961
Tonight for Sure! PREMIERE

CORWIN, ARLENE
1963
1,000 Shapes of a Female BARRY MAHON

COSTA, DON
1967
Rough Night in Jericho UNIV
1968
The Impossible Years (o: Feller) MGM
Madigan UNIV

COTTON, AL
1967
Hot Erotic Dreams COSMOS

COULTER, FRED
1965
Coronation (short) RICHARD MYERS
1969
Akran RICHARD MYERS

COURAGE, ALEXANDER
1950
Pagan Love Song (see A. Deutsch)
1951
Soldiers Three (see A. Deutsch)
Show Boat (see A. Deutsch)
1952
The Belle of New York (see A. Deutsch)
Million Dollar Mermaid (see A. Deutsch)
1953
The Band Wagon (see A. Deutsch)
Torch Song (see A. Deutsch)
1954
Deep in My Heart (see A. Deutsch)
1955
Interrupted Melody (see A. Deutsch)
It's Always Fair Weather (see A. Previn)
Kismet (see A. Previn)

1956
Meet Me in Las Vegas (see Stoll)
Hot Rod Girl AIP
Shake, Rattle, and Rock! AIP
1957
Funny Face (with Van Cleave; ac: Edens, A. Deutsch) PAR
Sierra Stranger COL
Hot Rod Rumble AA
My Gun Is Quick (see Skiles)
The Sun Also Rises (see Friedhofer)
Undersea Girl AA
Raintree County (see J. Green)
1958
Handle with Care MGM
Gigi (see Salinger)
The Left Handed Gun WB
Tokyo After Dark PAR
1959
Say One for Me (see Harline)
Day of the Outlaw UA
1960
Pepe (see J. Green)
1962
Jumbo (see Stoll)
1963
Follow the Boys (ac) MGM
1964
The Unsinkable Molly Brown (see Arnaud)
1965
The Pleasure Seekers (see L. Newman)
Do Not Disturb (see L. Newman)
1967
Doctor Dolittle (see L. Newman)
[Also a prolific arranger and orchestrator.]

COUSMINER, A.
1928
The Night Watch (see Bierman)
Waterfront (see Carbonara)
1930
Burning Up (silent version; see G. Lucas)
1931
Fighting Caravans (see Leipold)

COVE, RICHARD
1966
The Love Merchant JOE SARNO

COWELL, HENRY
1942
Mr. Flagmaker (short) MARY ELLEN BUTE
1956
Music for Ploesti (short) ?
1960
Here by the Water's Edge (short) LEO HURWITZ

COWEN, HENRY
1963
Gone are the Days! HAMMER BROTHERS

CRAIG, EDWARD
Documentary Features
1938
Dark Rapture (see Rochetti)
1941
Invasion (see Rapee)
1942
Kukan, the Battle Cry of China UA
1945
Behind Enemy Lines GLOBE
1946
The Story of the Pope CHAPEL FILMS
1948
Will It Happen Again? FC
Documentary Shorts
1940
Back to Missouri STACY & HORACE WOODARD
The Heritage We Guard USDA
Unveiling Algeria COL
Savoy in the Alps COL
Sojourn in Havana COL
From Singapore to Hong Kong COL
1941
Plows, Planes and Peace USDA
San Francisco, Metropolis of the West COL
1942
Great American Divide COL
A Journey to Denali COL
1943
The Tree in a Test Tube USDA
1947
Dividends for the Future AAF
1952
Clear Iron MARATHON
1953
Call Me Skinny PAR
Rowdy Raccoons PAR
Society Man PAR
1954
Drilling for Girls in Texas PAR
In Darkest Florida PAR
Killers at Bay PAR
The Nerve of Some People PAR
The Room That Flies PAR

Touchdown Highlights PAR
Wings to the North PAR
1955
All Chimps Ashore PAR
Five Hundred Horses PAR
Florida Aflame PAR
Just the Bear Facts Ma'am PAR
Let's Look at the Birds PAR
Pick a Pet PAR
Reunion in Paris PAR
Three Kisses PAR
Walk in the Deep PAR
You're a Trooper PAR
1956
There's Gold in Them Thrills PAR
Ups and Downs PAR

CRAIG, GEORGE
1965
Days of Sin and Nights of Nymphomania (U.S. release of 1963 Danish film) AUDUBON
1969
Shame, Shame, Everybody Knows Her Name DISTRIBPIX

CRESTON, PAUL
1945
Brought to Action! (doc. short) U.S. NAVY
1955
Tears of the Moon (short) TCF

CROOKS, MACK
1966
Film as an Art (doc. short) KARL HOLTSNIDER

CUGAT, XAVIER
1930
Captain Thunder (with Mendoza, Rosebrook) WB
The Lash (see Mendoza)

CUNNINGHAM, JAMES
1967
The Promise (doc. short) ILLINOIS BELL TELEPHONE

CUPERO, EDWARD
1928
While the City Sleeps (see Axt)
1929
Tide of Empire (see Axt)
Spite Marriage (see Stahlberg)
A Man's Man (+ stock) MGM

CURB, MIKE
1966
Skaterdater (short) BYWAY PRODS.
The Wild Angels AIP
1967
It's a Bikini World (with B. Summers) TRANS AMERICAN
Teenage Rebellion (doc.; with M. Summers) TRANS AMERICAN
Devil's Angels AIP
The Born Losers AIP
Mondo Hollywood (doc.) EMERSON
The Glory Stompers AIP
1968
Maryjane (with Lawrence Brown) AIP
The Wild Racers AIP
The Savage Seven (with Styner) AIP
The Angry Breed (with Lawrence Brown) CU
Killers Three (with Hatcher, Styner) AIP
The Golden Breed (doc.; with Styner, Hatcher) CONTINENTAL
1969
The Big Bounce (o: Styner) WB
The Devil's 8 AIP
Five the Hard Way (with Styner, Hemric) CROWN
Hot Rod Action (doc.) CR

CURTIN, HOYT
1951
For Men Only LIP
1953
Mesa of Lost Women HOWCO
1954
Jail Bait HOWCO
1969
Joniko and the Kush Ta Ka (with Loose) ALASKA
Shorts
1948
Music from the Mountains (with L. Dallin, D. Mackay, J. Oroop) USC
1950
The Magic Key (doc.) RAPHAEL G. WOLFF
1951
Within These Walls (doc.) GEORGE CARILLON
Cartoons
1950
Trouble Indemnity UPA
The Pop Corn Story UPA
Bungled Bungalow UPA

1951
Grizzly Golfer UPA
1952
Pete Hothead UPA
1953
Safety Spin UPA
1955
When Magoo Flew UPA
1956
Magoo's Canine Mutiny UPA
1960
Snoopy Loopy COL

CUTKOMP, THOMAS
1956
Calling Doctor Magoo (cartoon) UPA
1957
Magoo Breaks Par (cartoon) UPA
The Towers (short) WILLIAM HALE

CUTNER, SIDNEY
1935
Death from a Distance INVINCIBLE
The Girl Who Came Back CHESTERFIELD
1938
Holiday COL
City Streets (with Stringer; mt: Nussbaum; + stock) COL
The Lady Objects (ac: Parrish) COL
Flight to Fame COL
The Spider's Web (serial; + stock) COL
Homicide Bureau COL
1939
Flying G-Men (serial; + stock) COL
North of the Yukon COL
Romance of the Redwoods (see F. Morgan)
Mandrake the Magician (serial; with F. Morgan; + stock) COL
Overland with Kit Carson (serial; + stock) COL
Cafe Hostess (mt; + stock) COL
Music in My Heart COL
His Girl Friday (m&e theme: F. Mills) COL
1940
The Lone Wolf Strikes (+ stock) COL
Men Without Souls (mt: Parrish; + stock) COL
The Lone Wolf Meets a Lady (+ stock) COL
Out West with the Peppers (+ stock) COL
Five Little Peppers in Trouble (+ stock) COL
Escape to Glory (see Heymann)
The Lone Wolf Keeps a Date (+ stock) COL
1941
The Face Behind the Mask (+ stock) COL
Meet Boston Blackie (mt; + stock) COL
The Lone Wolf Takes a Chance (+ stock) COL
Here Comes Mr. Jordan (see Hollander)
Texas (with DiMaggio, Dragon; + stock) COL
1942
My Sister Eileen COL
1943
Appointment in Berlin (see Heymann)
1944
The Racket Man (+ stock) COL
Marriage Is a Private Affair (see Kaper)
Lost in a Harem (see N. Shilkret)
1945
The Clock (see Bassman)
Her Highness and the Bellboy (see Stoll)
Week-End at the Waldorf (see J. Green)
The Sailor Takes a Wife (see J. Green)
1949
Some of the Best (anniversary film; with Shuken; mt: Kopp) MGM
1950
Pagan Love Song (see A. Deutsch)
1951
Go for Broke (see Colombo)
Too Young to Kiss (see Kaper)
1953
This Is Cinerama (see M. Steiner)
Those Redheads from Seattle (see Shuken)
1955
Hold Back Tomorrow UNIV
1957
Raintree County (see J. Green)
1958
Gunsmoke in Tucson AA
1959
Green Mansions (see Kaper)
The Big Circus (see Sawtell and Shefter)
1960
The Lost World (see Sawtell and Shefter)
Pepe (see J. Green)
1962
What Ever Happened to Baby Jane? (see De Vol)
1963
Russia and the West (doc.) TITAN
1965
Indian Paint (see Skiles)
[Also a very prolific arranger and orchestrator.]

CUTTER, MURRAY
1937
The Girl from Scotland Yard (see Shuken)

Song of Revolt (short; with Arnaud) MGM
Broadway Melody of 1938 (with Arnaud) MGM
1938
Kentucky Moonshine (see Mockridge)
1940
The Man from Dakota (see Snell)
1941
Billy the Kid (see Snell)
Down in San Diego (see Amfitheatrof)
[Also a very prolific arranger and orchestrator.]

CUVA, CHARLEY
1969
Putney Swope ROBERT DOWNEY
1970
Pound ROBERT DOWNEY

D

DAHL, INGOLF
1963
Design for Correction (doc. short) SOUTHERN ILLINOIS U.

DALE, TED
1957
Zero Hour PAR
1962
Dangerous Charter CROWN

DALLIN, LEON
1948
Music from the Mountains (see Curtin)
1954
The Bishop (doc. short) BRIGHAM YOUNG U.

DAN, YOEL
1969
Artist in Manhattan—Jerome Myers (doc. short) BARRY DOWNES PRODS.

DANIEL, ELIOT
1946
Make Mine Music (see Wolcott)
1947
Fun and Fancy Free (see Wallace)
1948
Melody Time (with P. Smith) WDP
1950
And Then There Were Four (doc. short) GENERAL PETROLEUM
1953
Yesterday and Today (doc.) UA

DANIELS, HALL
1960
Squad Car TCF

DANT, CHARLES
1943
The Payoff PRC
Submarine Base PRC

DANZIGER, HOWARD
1970
The Delta Factor (see Kraushaar)

DARIAN, FRED
1966
Out of Sight (see de Lory)

DARIN, BOBBY
1964
The Lively Set UNIV
1965
That Funny Feeling UNIV
1967
Gunfight in Abilene (see M. Rogers)

DARREG, IVOR
1963
Prelude to an Afternoon with the Dentist (short) ?

DAUM, GLEN
1961
No, But I Saw the Movie (doc. short) SOUTHERN ILLINOIS U.
1968
Albatross (doc. short) SOUTHERN ILLINOIS U.

DAVENPORT, LANOUE
1952
The Drum (short) BRUMMER DEFOREST
1954
In Paris Parks (short) SHIRLEY CLARKE

DAVID, FREDERICK
1958
Lost, Lonely and Vicious HOWCO

DAVID, MARK
1970
The Love Doctors SIGMA III

DAVID, WILLIAM
1931
Alice in Wonderland POLLARD
1933
The Horror POLLARD

DAVIES, LEW
1957
Fright PLANET FILMPLAYS

DAVIS, DAVID H.
1968
Double-Stop WORLD ENTERTAINMENT

DAVIS, HERB C.
1967
Uncle Tomcat's House of Kittens SACK

DAVIS, MILES
1970
Jack Johnson (doc.) BIG FIGHTS

DEBEY, H.
1955
I Couldn't Marry FUTURITY

DE CENCO, ARTHUR
1960
The Black Cat (short) ROBERT BRAVERMAN

DEE, BILLY
1970
Dandy GENERAL FILM

DE FRANCESCO, LOUIS
1928
The Wedding March (see Zamecnik)
1929
Redskin (see Zamecnik)
Betrayal (see Zamecnik)
1932
Chandu, the Magician (see Brunelli)
Tess of the Storm Country (ac: Friedhofer, Brunelli, R. Bassett) FOX
1933
Cavalcade (with Brunelli, Zamecnik; ac: A. Lange) FOX
The Face in the Sky (see Brunelli)
Dangerously Yours (with R. Bassett, Brunelli, Zamecnik, Friedhofer) FOX
State Fair (o: Brunelli, A. Lange) FOX
Zoo in Budapest (see Zamecnik)
The Warrior's Husband (see Zamecnik)
Adorable (see Lange)
I Loved You Wednesday (with Brunelli; ac: A. Lange) FOX
The Devil's in Love (see Zamecnik)
Shanghai Madness (see Zamecnik)
The Power and the Glory (see Zamecnik)
Berkeley Square (see Zamecnik)
Paddy the Next Best Thing (with Brunelli; ac: R. Bassett, Friedhofer, Zamecnik) FOX
The Worst Woman in Paris? (with A. Lange; ac: Zamecnik) FOX
Hoop-la (o: Brunelli) FOX
Mr. Skitch (ac: Buttolph, Brunelli; + stock) FOX
I Am Suzanne! (see Hollander)
1934
All Men Are Enemies (o & ac: Brunelli) FOX
Change of Heart (o: Brunelli; + stock) FOX
Grand Canary (ac: Brunelli, A. Lange, Friedhofer) FOX
The World Moves On (with Friedhofer, R. Bassett, Buttolph, Mockridge) FOX
Caravan (see Brunelli)
Hell in the Heavens (mt; + stock) FOX
The White Parade (o: Brunelli, Buttolph) FOX
Helldorado (o: Brunelli; + stock) FOX
1935
George White's 1935 Scandals (see Friedhofer)
Dressed to Thrill (see Brunelli)
Here's to Romance (with Friedhofer) FOX
Documentary Features
1940
The Ramparts We Watch (with Belasco, Brunelli) THE MARCH OF TIME
1941
The Story of the Vatican THE MARCH OF TIME
1942
United We Stand TCF
Documentary Shorts (TCF)
1940
Bowling for Strikes
Spotlight on Indo-China
1941
Anzacs in Action
Arctic Springtime

Call of Canada
A Letter from Cairo
Playtime in Hawaii
Sagebrush and Silver
Symphony in Snow
Winter in Eskimo Land
Wonders of the Sea

1942

Along the Texas Range
Courageous Australia
Desert Wonderland
Dutch Guiana
Gay Rio
Heart of Mexico
Jewel of the Pacific
Men for the Fleet
Men of West Point
Neptune's Daughters
Secret of the Fjord
Snow Trails
Steelhead Fighters
Valley of Blossoms
Well-Rowed Harvard
When Winter Calls
Wings of Defense

1943

Accent on Courage
Champions Carry On
Climbing the Peaks
Flying Gunners
Fuss and Feathers
Jungle Land
Mormon Trails
Sails Aloft
A Volcano Is Born
Weapons for Victory

1944

Black Gold and Cactus
Blue Grass Gentlemen
City of Paradox
Fun for All
Girls Preferred
Jewels of Iran
Lew Lehr Makes the News
Mexican Majesty
Mystic India
Nymphs of the Lake
Sea-Food Mamas
Silver Wings
Ski Slopes
Steamboat on the River
Trolling for Strikes

1945

Alaskan Grandeur
Bountiful Alaska
Canyons of the Sun
China Carries On
Do You Remember
Down the Fairway
Empire State
Isle of Romance
Land of 10,000 Lakes
Louisiana Springtime
Magic of Youth
Memories of Columbus
Nova Scotia
Sikhs of Patiala
Ski Aces
Song of Sunshine
Steppin' Pretty
Time Out for Play
What It Takes to Make a Star

1946

Across the Great Divide
Along the Rainbow Trail
Behind the Footlights
Cradle of Liberty
Diving Dandies
Football Fanfare
Girls and Gags
Golden Horses
Here Comes the Circus
Historic Cape Town
Jamaica
Lost Lake
The Man from Missouri
Muscle Maulers
Pins and Cushions
Playtime's Journey
Sea Sirens
Sons of Courage
Summer Trails
Winter Holiday

1947

Alaska
Album of Animals
Aqua Capers
The Cape of Good Hope
Caravans of Trade
City Week End
Communications
Conservation Road
Copenhagen Pageantry
Draftsmen of Dreams
Fantasy of Siam
Fisherman's Nightmare
Gardens of the Sea
Gridiron Greatness

Harvest of the Sea
Holiday in South Africa
Home of the Danes
Horizons of Tomorrow
Jungle Close-Ups
Light and Power
Lobstertown
Monkey-Tone News
Romance of the Fjords
Royalty of the Range
Style of the Stars
Tanbark Champions
The Three R's Go Modern
Vacation—Two Weeks a Year
Vacation Magic
Wings of the Wind
Zululand

1948
Bermuda
Desert Lights
Dying to Live
Everglades Adventure
Fashioned for Action
Football Finesse
Majesty of Yellowstone
Neptune's Playground
Olympic Class
Olympic Water Wizards
Playtime in Scandinavia
Portrait of the West
Riddle of Rhodesia
Scenic Sweden
Sky Thrills
Something Old, Something New
Way of the Padres
Yankee Ski Doodle

1949
Aboard the Flattop Midway
Ahoy, Davy Jones
Fashions of Yesteryear
Foaled for Fame
Future Champs
Jewel of the Baltic
Landscape of the Norse
Maine Sail
Quaint Quebec
Realm of the Redwoods
Satisfied Saurians
Talented Beauties

DE HIRSCH, STORM
1963
Film Magazine of the Arts (short) JONAS MEKAS

DEKNIGHT, RENÉ
1969
Gun Runner GRADS CORP.

DE LANE, PETER
1959
Profile of an Alcoholic (doc.) WAYNE M. WELLMAN

DELINE, AL
1961
Confessions of a Wild Pair I.R.M.I.

DELLO JOIO, NORMAN
1952
Greentree Thoroughbred (short) BERNARD LIVINGSTON
19??
From Every Horizon: A Tone Poem to New York ?

DE LORY, AL
1966
Out of Sight (with Darian) UNIV
1970
Norwood (o: Levene) PAR

DELUGG, MILTON
1964
Only One New York (doc.; with Brackman) EMBASSY
Santa Claus Conquers the Martians EMBASSY
1966
Gulliver's Travels Beyond the Moon (with Anne Delugg, Brackman) CONTINENTAL
Cinderella (with Anne Delugg, Brackman) CHILDHOOD PRODS.

DEMARLOS, NORMAN
1955
Becoming (short) JAMES DAVIS

DE NAT, JOE
Cartoons (RKO)
1930
The Bug House
The Fiddler
The Miner
The Museum
The Showman
1931
Aces Up
The Brown Derby

The Bull Thrower
Circus Time
Down South
Halloween
The Milkman

Cartoons (COL)

1930

Alaskan Nights
The Apache Kid
The Bandmaster
Cinderella
Jazz Rhythm
Lambs Will Gamble
The Little Trail

1931

Bars and Stripes
Disarmament Conference
The Dog Snatcher
Hash House Blues
The Restless Sax
Rodeo Dough
Showing Off
Soda Poppa
The Stork Market
Svengarlic
Sunday Clothes
Taken for a Ride
Swiss Movements
Weenie Roast
Yelp Wanted

1932

The Bad Genius
The Birth of Jazz
The Black Sheep
Camping Out
The Chinatown Mystery
The Crystal Gazebo
Fare Play
Flop House
The Great Bird Mystery
Hollywood Goes Krazy
Light House Keeping
Love Krazy
Minding the Baby
The Minstrel Show
The Paper Hanger
The Pet Shop
Prosperity Blues
The Ritzy Hotel
Seeing Stars
Snow Time
Soldier Old Man
Stepping Stones
The Treasure Runt
What a Knight

1933

Antique Antics
The Beer Parade
The Bill Poster
The Broadway Malady
Bunnies and Bonnets
Curio Shop
The False Alarm
House Cleaning
Krazy Spooks
The Match Kid
The Medicine Show
Movie Struck
Out of the Ether
Russian Dressing
Sandman Tales
Sassy Cats
Scrappy's Auto Show
Scrappy's Party
Technoracket
Wedding Bells
Whacks Museum
Wolf at the Door
Wooden Shoes
The World's Affair

1934

The Autograph Hunter
Aw Nurse
Babes at Sea
Bowery Daze
Busy Bus
Cinder Alley
The Concert Kid
Goofy Gondolas
The Great Experiment
The Happy Butterfly
Holiday Land
The Katnips of 1940
Krazy's Waterloo
Scrappy's Art Gallery
Scrappy's Dog Show
Scrappy's Expedition
Scrappy's Relay Race
Scrappy's Television
Scrappy's Theme Song
Scrappy's Toy Shop
The Shoemaker and the Elves
Tom Thumb
The Trapeze Artist

1935

The Bon-Bon Parade
A Cat, a Mouse, and a Bell
Garden Gaities
The Gloom Chasers
The Gold Getters

The Graduation Exercises
A Happy Family
The Hotcha Melody
Kannibal Kapers
The King's Jester
Little Rover
Make Believe Revue
Monkey Love
Patch Mah Britches
Peace Conference
The Puppet Murder Case
Scrappy's Ghost Story
Scrappy's Trailer
Tetched in the Head

1936

The Bird Stuffer
Birds in Love
A Boy and His Dog
Dizzy Ducks
Dr. Blue Bird
Football Bugs
Gifts from the Air
Glee Worms
Highway Snobbery
In My Gondola
Krazy's News Reel
L'il an Jil
Loony Baloonists
Major Google
The Merry Cafe
The Merry Mutineers
The Novelty Shop
Playing Politics
Scrappy's Boy Scouts
Scrappy's Camera Troubles
Scrappy's Pony
Spark Plug
Two Lazy Crows
The Untrained Seal

1937

Air Hostess
Canine Capers
The Clock Goes Round and Round
The Fire Plug
Hollywood Picnic
I Want to Be an Actress
Indian Serenade
Krazy's Race of Time
Let's Go
The Little Match Girl
The Lyin' Hunter
The Masque Raid
Mother Hen's Holiday
The New Homestead
Puttin' Out the Kitten
Railroad Rhythm
Scary Crows
Scrappy's Band Concert
Scrappy's Music Lesson
Scrappy's News Flashes
Skeleton Frolic
The Spring Festival
The Stork Takes a Holiday
Swing, Monkey, Swing!

1938

The Animal Cracker Circus
The Auto Clinic
The Big Birdcast
Bluebirds' Baby
The City Slicker
The Early Bird
The Foolish Bunny
Gym Jams
Happy Birthday
Hollywood Graduation
Hot Dogs on Ice
The Kangaroo Kid
Krazy's Magic
The Little Buckaroo
Little Moth's Big Flame
The Lone Mountie
Poor Elmer
Poor Little Butterfly
The Sad Little Guinea Pigs
Scrappy's Playmates
Scrappy's Trip to Mars
Travel Squawks
Window Shopping

1939

A Boy, a Gun, and Birds
Charm Bracelet
Dreams on Ice
Golf Chumps
The Happy Tots
Hollywood Sweepstakes
The House That Jack Built
Krazy's Bear Tale
Krazy's Shoe Shop
The Little Lost Sheep
Lucky Pigs
The Millionaire Hobo
Mother Goose in Swingtime
Mountain Ears
The Mouse Exterminator
Park Your Baby
Peaceful Neighbors
Scrappy's Added Attraction
Scrappy's Rodeo
Scrappy's Side Show
A Worm's Eye View

1940
Barnyard Babies
Farmer Tom Thumb
Fish Follies
The Greyhound and the Rabbit
Happy Holidays
The Happytots' Expedition
The Mad Hatter
Man of Tin
Mouse Meets Lion
News Oddities
Paunch 'n Judy
A Peep in the Deep
The Pooch Parade
Practice Makes Perfect
Schoolboy Dreams
Tangled Television
The Timid Pup
1941
A Helping Paw
It Happened to Crusoe
Land of Fun
The Streamlined Donkey
There's Music in Your Hair
The Wallflower
The Way of All Pests

DENNI, LUCIEN
Cartoons (MGM)
1933
Bulloney
A Chinaman's Chance
Pale-Face

DENNISON, SAM
1953
Good Speech for Gary (doc. short) USC

DE PACKH, MAURICE
1933
Stage Mother (see Silvers)
Dancing Lady (see Silvers)
Goofy Movies No. 1 (short) MGM
1934
Riptide (see Stothart)
1942
My Gal Sal (see Mockridge)
1945
Diamond Horseshoe (see H. Spencer)
Where Do We Go from Here? (see D. Raksin)
Cartoons
1942
The Big Rock Candy Mountain SOUNDIES
1943
The Fly in the Ointment (see P. Worth)
The Truck That Flew PAR
Jasper Goes Fishing PAR
Good-Night Rusty PAR
1944
And to Think That I Saw It on Mulberry Street PAR
Jasper Goes Hunting PAR
Jasper's Paradise PAR
Two Gun Rusty PAR
[Also a very prolific arranger and orchestrator.]

DE SAXE, RUDY
1947
Bells of San Fernando SG
Beyond Our Own PFC
1949
Mystery Range SCREEN CRAFT
1950
The Texan Meets Calamity Jane COL
1954
The Lawless Rider UA

DESSAU, PAUL
[He scored many films in Germany and elsewhere from 1928 to 1939, when he came to the United States. In 1948 he returned to Germany, where he continued to score films.]
1944
Mr. Skeffington (see Waxman)
House of Frankenstein (see Salter)
1945
Hotel Berlin (see Waxman)
The Naughty Nineties (see Fairchild)
The Woman in Green (+ stock) UNIV
The Strange Affair of Uncle Harry (see Salter)
1946
Her Kind of Man (see Waxman)
The Wife of Monte Cristo PRC
1947
Nora Prentiss (see Waxman)
Winter Wonderland REP
The Pretender REP
The Paradine Case (see Waxman)
1948
Devil's Cargo FC
The Vicious Circle UA
Documentary Shorts
1941
Better Dresses—Fifth Floor VICTOR STOLOFF

1946
Combat Fatigue U.S. NAVY

DEUTSCH, ADOLPH
1930
The Dance of Life (see Duke)
Honeymoon (see Duke)
1937
Mr. Dodd Takes the Air WB
The Great Garrick (o: Friedhofer) WB
They Won't Forget WB
Swing Your Lady (o: Friedhofer) WB
1938
Fools for Scandal (ac: Roemheld) WB
A Slight Case of Murder (see Roemheld)
Cowboy from Brooklyn WB
Racket Busters (o: Friedhofer) WB
Valley of the Giants (see Friedhofer)
Heart of the North WB
1939
Off the Record WB
Dodge City (see M. Steiner)
The Man Who Dared WB
The Kid from Kokomo WB
The Oklahoma Kid (see M. Steiner)
Indianapolis Speedway WB
The Angels Wash Their Faces WB
Espionage Agent WB
1940
The Fighting 69th (o: Friedhofer) WB
Castle on the Hudson WB
Three Cheers for the Irish WB
Saturday's Children WB
Torrid Zone WB
They Drive by Night (o: Friedhofer, Moross, A. Lange) WB
Flowing Gold (ac: H. Jackson) WB
Tugboat Annie Sails Again WB
East of the River (with H. Jackson) WB
1941
High Sierra (o: Lange) WB
The Great Mr. Nobody (with H. Jackson; ac: Lava) WB
Singapore Woman WB
Underground (ac: Roemheld) WB
Kisses for Breakfast (ac: Roemheld) WB
Manpower (ac: Roemheld) WB
The Maltese Falcon (o: A. Lange) WB
1942
All Through the Night (ac: Roemheld) WB
Larceny, Inc. (ac: Lava, Roemheld) WB
This Was Paris (ac for U.S. release of British film) WB
Juke Girl (o: Moross, Friedhofer; ac: Roemheld) WB
The Big Shot (o: Moross; ac: Kaun) WB
Across the Pacific (o: Vaughan; ac: Roemheld) WB
You Can't Escape Forever WB
George Washington Slept Here WB
1943
Lucky Jordan (o: Parrish, Shuken) PAR
Action in the North Atlantic (o: Moross; ac: Lava) WB
Northern Pursuit (o: Moross) WB
1944
Uncertain Glory (o: Moross) WB
The Mask of Dimitrios (o: Moross) WB
The Doughgirls (o: Moross) WB
1945
Escape in the Desert (o: Moross) WB
Danger Signal (o: Cutter) WB
1946
Three Strangers (o: Moross, Cutter) WB
Her Kind of Man (see Waxman)
Shadow of a Woman (o: Cutter) WB
Nobody Lives Forever (o: Moross) WB
1947
Blaze of Noon (o: Parrish; ac: Buttolph, o: Shuken, Cutner) PAR
Ramrod UA
1948
Luxury Liner (o: Courage) MGM
Julia Misbehaves (o: Courage) MGM
1949
Little Women (o: Courage, R. Franklyn; ac: Kaper) MGM
Whispering Smith (o: Parrish, Cutner, Van Cleave, Shuken) PAR
The Stratton Story (o: Courage; + stock) MGM
Intruder in the Dust (o: Courage) MGM
1950
Stars in My Crown (o: Courage, R. Franklyn, Salinger) MGM
The Big Hangover (o: R. Franklyn, Conniff, Courage) MGM
Annie Get Your Gun (with Salinger, Edens; o: Courage, R. Franklyn, Marquardt) MGM
Father of the Bride (o: Shuken, Cutner, Courage) MGM
Mrs. O'Malley and Mr. Malone (o: R. Franklyn, Courage) MGM
Pagan Love Song (with Salinger, Edens, Courage; ac: Cutner, Shuken) MGM

1951

Soldiers Three (ac: Courage; o: Courage, Cutner, Shuken, Zador) MGM
Show Boat (with Salinger; ac: Courage; o: Franklyn, Courage) MGM
It's a Big Country (with Kaper, D. Rose, D. Raksin, Colombo, Wolcott, Kopp) MGM

1952

The Belle of New York (with Courage, Salinger; o: R. Franklyn) MGM
Million Dollar Mermaid (o and ac: Courage) MGM

1953

The Band Wagon (with Salinger, Courage; o: R. Franklyn) MGM
Torch Song (o and ac: Courage) MGM

1954

The Long, Long Trailer (o: Courage) MGM
Seven Brides for Seven Brothers (with Salinger; o: Courage, R. Franklyn) MGM
Deep in My Heart (with Courage; o: Courage, R. Franklyn) MGM

1955

Interrupted Melody (with Courage; o: Courage) MGM
Oklahoma! (with R. Bennett; o: Courage, Sendrey) magna

1956

The Rack (o: Courage) MGM
The Battle of Gettysburg (short; o: Courage; ac: Salinger, o: R. Franklyn) MGM
Tea and Sympathy (o: Courage) MGM

1957

Funny Face (see Courage)
Les Girls (o: Courage, Morton) MGM

1958

The Matchmaker (o: Van Cleave) PAR

1959

Some Like It Hot (o: Courage) UA

1960

The Apartment UA
Go Naked in the World (o: R. Franklyn, Courage) MGM

Trailer

1939

Confessions of a Nazi Spy WB

DEUTSCH, HERBERT

1964

Lines of Communication (doc. short) UNITED NATIONS

1965

Variable Studies (short) ED EMSHWILLER

DE VOL, FRANK

1951

Birthright (doc.) COLUMBIA U. PRESS

1954

World for Ransom AA

1955

Kiss Me Deadly (o: A. Harris) UA
The Big Knife UA
Paris Follies of 1956 (md) AA

1956

Pardners (o: Shuken, Hayes) PAR
Attack UA

1957

The Ride Back UA
Johnny Trouble WB

1959

Pillow Talk (o: de Packh) UNIV

1960

Murder, Inc. TCF

1961

Lover Come Back UNIV

1962

Boys' Night Out (o: Woodbury) MGM
What Ever Happened to Baby Jane? (o: Woodbury; ac: Cutner, R. Raksin, Andersen) WB

1963

The Wheeler Dealers (o: Woodbury) MGM
The Thrill of It All UNIV
For Love or Money UNIV
McLintock! UA
Under the Yum Yum Tree (o: Woodbury) COL

1964

Good Neighbor Sam (o: Woodbury) COL
Send Me No Flowers UNIV
Hush . . . Hush, Sweet Charlotte (o: Woodbury) TCF

1965

Cat Ballou (o: Woodbury) COL
The Flight of the Phoenix (o: Woodbury) TCF

1966

The Glass Bottom Boat (o: Woodbury) MGM
Texas Across the River UNIV

1967

The Ballad of Josie UNIV
The Happening (o: Woodbury, Pleis) COL
Caprice (o: Woodbury) TCF
The Dirty Dozen MGM
Guess Who's Coming to Dinner (o: Woodbury) COL

1968
The Legend of Lylah Clare (o: Woodbury) MGM
What's So Bad About Feeling Good? UNIV
Krakatoa, East of Java CR

DEXTER, VON
1958
House on Haunted Hill AA
1959
The Tingler COL
1960
13 Ghosts COL
1961
Mr. Sardonicus COL

DIAMOND, DAVID
1941
A Place to Live (doc. short) IRVING LERNER
1948
Dreams That Money Can Buy (see Applebaum)
Strange Victory (doc.) LEO HURWITZ
1949
Anna Lucasta (o: A. Morton) COL
1965
Lippold's The Sun (doc.) LEO HURWITZ
1966
Life in the Balance (doc.) GENE SEARCHINGER

DIAMOND, LEO
1944
Package for Jasper (cartoon) PAR

DIAZ CONDE, ANTONIO
[Mexican composer of many film scores; only his English-language films are listed here.]
1947
The Pearl RKO
1950
The Torch EL
1952
Stronghold LIP
1953
Plunder of the Sun (with Friedhofer; ac: A. Lange, R. Miller) WB
1954
The White Orchid UA
The Black Pirates LIP

DIETRICH, JAMES
1930
King of Jazz UNIV
1932
The Mummy (+ stock) UNIV
They Just Had to Get Married UNIV
1940
The Leopard Men of Africa (doc.; o: Lessner, R. Franklyn) ZEIDMAN
Shorts
1935
Father Knows Best UNIV
Old Age Pension UNIV
1940
Beautiful British Columbia (doc.) COL
Cartoons (UNIV)
1931
The Bandmaster
China
The Clown
College
Country School
The Farmer
The Fireman
The Fisherman
Hare Mail
Hot Feet
The Hunter
In Wonderland
Kentucky Belle
Mars
North Woods
Radio Rhythm
Shipwreck
The Stone Age
Sunny South
Trolley Troubles
1932
The Athlete
Beaus and Arrows
The Busy Barber
The Butcher Boy
Carnival Capers
Catnipped
Cats and Dogs
The Crowd Snores
Day Nurse
Foiled Again
Grandma's Pet
Great Guns
A Jungle Jumble
Let's Eat
Making Good
Mechanical Cow
Mechanical Man
Merry Dog
Oh, Teacher

Teacher's Pest
To the Rescue
The Underdog
A Wet Knight
Wild and Woolly
The Winged Horse
Wins Out

1933

Beau Best
Chicken Reel
Confidence
Five and Dime
Going to Blazes
Ham and Eggs
Hot and Cold
In the Zoo
King Klunk
The Lumber Champ
Merry Old Soul
Nature's Workshop
A New Deal
Parking Space
Pin Feathers
The Plumber
S.O.S. Icicle
She Done Him Right
The Shriek
The Terrible Troubadour

1934

Annie Moved Away
The Candy House
Chris Columbus, Jr.
The County Fair
The Dizzy Dwarf
The Ginger Bread Boy
Goldilocks and the Three Bears
Ye Happy Pilgrims
Jolly Little Elves
Kings Up
Robinson Crusoe Isle
Sky Larks
Spring in the Park
The Toy Shoppe
Toyland Premiere
Wax Works
William Tell
Wolf! Wolf!

1935

Amateur Broadcast
At Your Service
Bronco Buster
Candyland
The Case of the Lost Sheep
Do a Good Deed
Doctor Oswald
Elmer, the Great Dane
The Fox and the Rabbit
Gold Dust Oswald
The Hillbilly
Monkey Wretches
The Quail Hunt
Springtime Serenade
Three Lazy Mice
Towne Hall Follies
Two Little Lambs

1936

Alaska Sweepstakes
The Barnyard Five
Battle Royal
Beach Combers
Beauty Shoppe
Farming Fools
Fun House
The Golfers
Gopher Trouble
Kiddie Revue
Knights for a Day
Music Hath Charms
Night Life of the Bugs
Puppet Show
Slumberland Express
Soft Ball Game
Turkey Dinner
The Unpopular Mechanic

1937

The Air Express
The Big Race
The Birthday Party
The Country Store
Duck Hunt
Everybody Sing
Football Fever
House of Magic
Keeper of the Lions
The Lumber Camp
The Mechanical Handy Man
The Mysterious Jug
The Playful Pup
The Rest Resort
The Steel Workers
The Stevedores
Trailer Thrills
The Wily Weasel

DIMAGGIO, ROSS

1937

Murder in Swingtime (short) CONDOR
Prairie Swingaroo (short) CONDOR

1939

Water Rustlers GN
A Night in a Music Hall (short) COL
Ride 'Em Cowgirl GN
A Night at the Troc (short) COL
The Singing Cowgirl GN
Double Deal I.R.S.

1940

Mystery in Swing I.R.S.

1941

The Great Train Robbery (mt) REP
Adventures of Captain Marvel (see Glickman)
Kansas Cyclone (see Sawtell)
The Deadly Game MON
Reg'lar Fellers PRC
Texas (see Cutner)
Double Trouble MON

1946

Rancho in the Sky KEITH DANIELS PRODS.

[Also a music supervisor at Columbia, where he compiled and conducted stock scores, 1950–1962.]

DIMASE, SALVATORE

1962

The Theft of Fire (short) THORNE FILMS

DIPASQUALE, JAMES

1964

The Way Back (doc. short) ROBERT FORD PRODS.

DIVINA, VACLAV

1952

Strange Fascination (o: Raymond, Cadkin) HUGO HAAS/COL

1953

One Girl's Confession (o: Raymond, Cadkin) HUGO HAAS/COL
Thy Neighbor's Wife (based on music of Smetena) HUGO HAAS/TCF

1954

Bait (o: N. Scott) HUGO HAAS/COL

DLUGOSZEWSKI, LUCIA

1953

Visual Variations on Noguchi (short) MARIE MENKEN

1961

Guns of the Trees JONAS MEKAS

DODDS, MALCOLM

1970

The Lawyer PAR

DOLAN, ROBERT EMMETT

1941

Birth of the Blues (o: W. Scharf) PAR
Louisiana Purchase (o and ac: W. Scharf, Shuken) PAR

1942

True to the Army (with Harline; o: W. Scharf) PAR
Dr. Broadway (with Sawtell; o: Skiles) PAR
Are Husbands Necessary? (o: W. Scharf, Salinger, Shuken) PAR
Holiday Inn (ac: Scharf) PAR
The Major and the Minor (o: E. Powell, Salinger) PAR
Once Upon a Honeymoon (ac: Webb; o: E. Powell, H. Spencer, Raab, Salinger) RKO
Star Spangled Rhythm (o: Shuken, Bradshaw) PAR

1943

Happy Go Lucky (ac: Bradshaw) PAR
Henry Aldrich Gets Glamour (+ stock) PAR
Dixie (o: Parrish, Shuken, Bradshaw) PAR
Let's Face It (ac: Shuken, Grau) PAR

1944

Standing Room Only (ac: Lilley; o: Shuken, Parrish) PAR
Lady in the Dark (o: R. Bennett) PAR
Going My Way (o: Parrish, Shuken) PAR
I Love a Soldier (o: E. Powell, Shuken, Grau) PAR
Here Come the WAVES (o: Parrish, Cutner) PAR

1945

Bring On the Girls (ac: V. Young; o: Shuken, Grau, Parrish) PAR
Salty O'Rourke (o: Parrish; ac: Simeone) PAR
Murder, He Says (o: Parrish) PAR
Incendiary Blonde (ac: Leipold; o: Shuken, Parrish) PAR
Duffy's Tavern (o: Bradshaw, Parrish) PAR
The Bells of St. Mary's RKO
The Stork Club (o: Cutner, Shuken) PAR

1946

Monsieur Beaucaire (ac: Plumb; o: Parrish, Plumb) PAR
Blue Skies (o and ac: Parrish) PAR

1947

Cross My Heart (o: Bradshaw, de Packh) PAR
My Favorite Brunette (ac: Van Cleave; o: Parrish, Bradshaw) PAR

Welcome Stranger (o: Parrish, Bradshaw, Shuken, Cutner) PAR
The Trouble with Women (see V. Young)
The Perils of Pauline (o: Parrish, Bradshaw) PAR
Dear Ruth (o: Van Cleave, Bradshaw) PAR
Road to Rio (ac: Van Cleave; o: Parrish) PAR

1948
Saigon (o: Parrish) PAR
Good Sam RKO
Mr. Peabody and the Mermaid UNIV

1949
My Own True Love (o: Shuken, Cutner) PAR
Sorrowful Jones (o: Van Cleave, Parrish) PAR
The Great Gatsby (o: Van Cleave, Parrish, Cutner, Shuken) PAR
Top o' the Morning (o: Parrish, Van Cleave) PAR

1950
Let's Dance (o: Parrish, Cutner, Shuken, Levene) PAR

1952
My Son John (o: R. Bennett, Parrish) PAR

1957
The Three Faces of Eve (o: E. Powell) TCF

1959
The Man Who Understood Women (o: Hagen, E. Powell) TCF

DOWNING, TOM

1962
Stakeout! CROWN

DRAGON, CARMEN

1941
The Blonde from Singapore (mt; + stock) COL
Texas (see Cutner)
Sing for Your Supper COL

1944
Cover Girl (o: Cutner) COL
Mr. Winkle Goes to War (o: Cutner; ac: Castelnuovo-Tedesco, Sawtell, Skiles) COL

1946
Young Widow (o: Hallenbeck) UA
The Kid from Brooklyn GOLDWYN
The Strange Woman UA

1947
Dishonored Lady UA
Out of the Blue EL

1948
The Time of Your Life UA

1950
Kiss Tomorrow Goodbye WB

1951
Night Into Morning (o: Levene) MGM
The Law and the Lady (o: Sendrey, Zador, Levene) MGM
The People Against O'Hara (o: Sendrey) MGM

1952
When in Rome (o: Zador) MGM
Lovely to Look At (o: Arnaud) MGM

1955
At Gunpoint AA

1956
Invasion of the Body Snatchers AA

Documentary Short

19??
The Redwood Empire BUTLER PRODS.

DRAGON, DARYL

1969
Popsicle (short; with Dennis Dragon) GRANT ROHLOFF

DRASNIN, ROBERT

1956
One Way Ticket to Hell EXHIBITORS

1966
Ride in the Whirlwind FAVORITE
Picture Mommy Dead EMBASSY

1967
Harvest (doc.; see Rosmini)

1969
The Kremlin Letter TCF

DRUCKMAN, JACOB

1970
Look Park (short) ?
Traite du Rossignol ?

DUBIN, JOSEPH

1944
Cowboy and the Senorita (see Skiles)
Tucson Raiders (see M. Glickman)
The Tiger Woman (serial) REP
Marshal of Reno REP
Atlantic City (see W. Scharf)
Haunted Harbor (serial) REP
Code of the Prairie REP
Lights of Old Santa Fe (see Butts)
Faces in the Fog (o: M. Glickman) REP
Thoroughbreds REP
Lake Placid Serenade (see W. Scharf)

1945

Earl Carroll Vanities (see W. Scharf)
Bells of Rosarita (see Maxwell)
Tell It to a Star REP
Behind City Lights (o: M. Glickman) REP
Girls of the Big House REP
Mexicana (see W. Scharf)
Dakota (see W. Scharf)

1946

The Madonna's Secret (o: M. Glickman) REP
The Last Crooked Mile REP
Rendezvous with Annie (with N. Scott) REP
Roll On Texas Moon (see Butts)
Home in Oklahoma REP
The Pilgrim Lady (see Butts)
Sioux City Sue REP

1947

The Ghost Goes Wild (o: N. Scott) REP
Bulldog Drummond at Bay (see Leipold)
When a Girl's Beautiful (with Murphy; + stock) COL
The Last Round-Up (ac: Sawtell, M. Bakaleinikoff) COL

1948

Mary Lou (ac: M. Bakaleinikoff) COL
The Strawberry Room (see M. Bakaleinikoff)
The Big Sombrero (see M. Bakaleinikoff)

1949

Rim of the Canyon COL

Cartoons (WDP)

1949

Bee at the Beach

1950

Chicken in the Rough
Cold Storage
Cold War
Home Made Home
Out on a Limb
Plutopia
Tomorrow We Diet

1951

Donald Applecore
Father's Lion
Hello Aloha
Lambert, the Sheepish Lion
Man's Best Friend
Two Chips and a Miss

1952

How to Be a Detective
Pluto's Christmas Tree
Uncle Donald's Ants

1953

Don's Fountain of Youth
Father's Week-End
For Whom the Bulls Toil
How to Dance
Melody
Toot, Whistle, Plunk and Boom

1956

The Story of Anyburg U.S.A.

Documentary Shorts

1950

If You Don't Watch Out JSP

1959

Nature's Strangest Creatures WDP

Animated Educational Shorts (WDP)

1960

I'm No Fool as a Pedestrian (see Buddy Baker)
I'm No Fool Having Fun
I'm No Fool with a Bicycle
I'm No Fool with Fire

DUFFY, JOHN

Documentary Shorts

1962

Mexican Maize ROGER SANDALL

1965

The Days of Dylan Thomas ROLLIE MCKENNA
The Road to Carolina N. CAROLINA FILM BOARD

196?

The Beginning ROBERT LOWE
A Chance to Be Somebody ROBERT KAYLOR PRODS.
The Changing Image TIME FOUR PRODS.
Children of the World AMRAM NOWAK PRODS.
The Driving Scene THOMAS CRAVEN FILMS

DUGAN, WILLIAM FRANCIS

1929

Mawas (doc.) BOWES

DUKE, VERNON

1930

The Dance of Life (foreign version of 1929 film; with A. Deutsch) PAR
Honeymoon (foreign version of 1928 film, *The Wedding March*, Part Two; with Deutsch) PAR
The Sap from Syracuse (see J. Green)
Follow Thru PAR
Laughter PAR

1931
Honor Among Lovers (see J. Green)
Tarnished Lady PAR
The Night Angel (see Goulding)
Secrets of a Secretary (see J. Green)
1943
Battle Stations (doc. short; o: Grundman) U.S. COAST GUARD
1948
The Angry God UA

DUNCAN, TED
1943
My Tomato (short; see Terr)
1944
Broadway Rhythm (see J. Green)
1945
Her Highness and the Bellboy (see Stoll)
1946
Easy to Wed (see J. Green)
[Also an arranger and orchestrator.]

DUNHAM, KAYE
1953
Obmaru (short) PATRICIA MARX

DUNING, GEORGE
1943
Around the World (with Collins, Harline) RKO
1944
Kansas City Kitty (o: Maxwell) COL
Strange Affair (see Skiles)
Meet Miss Bobby Socks (o: Grau) COL
Carolina Blues (o: A. Morton; + stock) COL
She's a Sweetheart (o: A. Morton; + stock) COL
Tahiti Nights (see M. Glickman)
1945
Let's Go Steady COL
Youth on Trial (see Skiles)
Eadie Was a Lady (with Skiles; + stock) COL
Sing Me a Song of Texas COL
Tonight and Every Night (see Skiles)
Eve Knew Her Apples COL
1946
Meet Me on Broadway COL
Mysterious Intruder (+ stock) COL
The Devil's Mask (with Gertz; + stock) COL
The Man Who Dared (+ stock) COL
The Return of Rusty COL
Sing While You Dance COL
It's Great to Be Young COL
The Jolson Story (see Skiles)
1947
Johnny O'Clock (o: A. Morton) COL
The Guilt of Janet Ames (o: A. Morton) COL
The Corpse Came C.O.D. (o: A. Morton) COL
Down to Earth (see Roemheld)
Her Husband's Affairs COL
Two Blondes and a Redhead (with Shuken; + stock) COL
I Love Trouble (o: A. Morton) COL
1948
To the Ends of the Earth (o: A. Morton) COL
Adventures in Silverado (+ stock) COL
The Man from Colorado (o: A. Morton) COL
The Untamed Breed (o: A. Morton) COL
The Gallant Blade (o: A. Morton) COL
The Return of October (o: A. Morton) COL
1949
The Dark Past (o: Gilbert) COL
Shockproof (o: A. Morton) COL
Ladies of the Chorus COL
Slightly French (o: A. Morton) COL
Undercover Man (o: A. Morton) COL
Lust for Gold (ac: Morton; o: A. Morton) COL
Johnny Allegro (ac: Morton; o: A. Morton) COL
The Doolins of Oklahoma (o: A. Morton) (with Sawtell, Skiles) COL
Jolson Sings Again (o: A. Morton) COL
And Baby Makes Three (o: A. Morton) COL
All the King's Men (see Gruenberg)
1950
Cargo to Capetown (o: Grau) COL
No Sad Songs for Me (o: A. Morton) COL
Convicted (o: A. Morton) COL
When You're Smiling COL
The Petty Girl (o: A. Morton) (with Heymann, o: Byrns) COL
Between Midnight and Dawn (o: A. Morton) COL
Harriet Craig (o: A. Morton) COL
The Flying Missile (o: A. Morton) COL
1951
Lorna Doone (o: A. Morton) COL
Her First Romance (+ stock) COL
Two of a Kind (o: A. Morton) COL

The Lady and the Bandit (o: A. Morton) COL
The Family Secret (o: A. Morton) COL
Sunny Side of the Street (o: A. Morton) COL
The Mob (o: A. Morton) COL
The Barefoot Mailman (o: A. Morton) COL
Man in the Saddle (o: A. Morton) COL
Purple Heart Diary (o: A. Morton; + stock) COL

1952
Scandal Sheet (o: A. Morton) COL
Paula (o: A. Morton) COL
Sound Off (o: A. Morton) COL
Affair in Trinidad (o: A. Morton) COL
Captain Pirate (o: A. Morton) COL
Rainbow 'Round My Shoulder (o: A. Morton) COL
Assignment—Paris (o: A. Morton) COL
Last of the Comanches (o: A. Morton) COL

1953
Salome (o: A. Morton) COL
All Ashore (o: A. Morton) COL
Let's Do It Again (o: A. Morton) COL
Cruisin' Down the River (o: A. Morton) COL
From Here to Eternity (o: A. Morton) COL
Miss Sadie Thompson (o: A. Morton) COL

1954
Battle of Rogue River (with M. Bakaleinikoff; + stock) COL
Drive a Crooked Road (o: A. Morton) COL
The Long Gray Line (o: A. Morton) COL

1955
Three for the Show (o: A. Morton) COL
Tight Spot (o: A. Morton) COL
5 Against the House (o: A. Morton) COL
Man from Laramie (o: A. Morton) COL
Bring Your Smile Along (o: A. Morton) COL
Count Three and Pray (o: A. Morton) COL
My Sister Eileen COL
Three Stripes in the Sun (o: A. Morton) COL
Queen Bee (o: A. Morton) COL

1956
Picnic (o: A. Morton) COL
The Eddy Duchin Story (o: A. Morton) COL
Autumn Leaves (see Salter)
Storm Center (o: A. Morton) COL
The Solid Gold Cadillac (o: A. Morton; ac: Mockridge) COL
You Can't Run Away from It (o: A. Morton) COL
Nightfall (o: A. Morton) COL

1957
Full of Life (o: A. Morton) COL
The Shadow on the Window (o: A. Morton) COL
The 27th Day (see M. Bakaleinikoff)
The Brothers Rico (o: A. Morton) COL
Jeanne Eagels (o: A. Morton) COL
3:10 to Yuma (o: A. Morton) COL
Operation Mad Ball (o: A. Morton) COL
Pal Joey (o: A. Morton) COL

1958
Cowboy (o: A. Morton) COL
Gunman's Walk (o: A. Morton) COL
Me and the Colonel COL
Houseboat (o: A. Morton, Van Cleave) PAR
Bell, Book and Candle COL

1959
It Happened to Jane (o: A. Morton) COL
The Last Angry Man (o: A. Morton) COL
The Wreck of the Mary Deare (o: A. Morton) MGM
1001 Arabian Nights (an.) (o: A. Morton) COL

1960
Man on a String (o: A. Morton) COL
Strangers When We Meet (o: A. Morton) COL
Stop! Look! and Laugh! (o: A. Morton; + stock) COL
All the Young Men (o: A. Morton) COL
Let No Man Write My Epitaph (o: A. Morton) COL
The World of Susie Wong PAR

1961
The Wackiest Ship in the Army (o: A. Morton) COL
Cry for Happy (o: A. Morton) COL
Gidget Goes Hawaiian COL
Two Rode Together (o: A. Morton) COL
The Devil at 4 O'Clock (o: A. Morton) COL

1962
Sail a Crooked Ship (o: A. Morton) COL
13 West Street (o: A. Morton) COL
That Touch of Mink UNIV
The Notorious Landlady (o: A. Morton) COL
Who's Got the Action? (o: A. Morton) PAR

1963
Critic's Choice (o: A. Morton) WB
Island of Love (o: A. Morton) WB
Toys in the Attic UA
Who's Been Sleeping in My Bed? (o: A. Morton) PAR

1964
Ensign Pulver (o: A. Morton) WB
1965
Dear Brigitte (o: A. Morton) TCF
My Blood Runs Cold (o: A. Morton) WB
Brainstorm (o: A. Morton) WB
1966
Any Wednesday WB

DUNLAP, PAUL
1950
The Baron of Arizona LIP
Hi-Jacked LIP
Cry Danger (themes: Friedhofer, A. Lange) RKO
1951
The Steel Helmet LIP
Little Big Horn LIP
Lost Continent LIP
Journey Into Light (with Friedhofer) TCF
1952
The San Francisco Story (with Friedhofer) WB
Breakdown REALART
Park Row UA
Big Jim McLain (with A. Lange, R. Miller; themes: Friedhofer) WB
Hellgate LIP
1953
Fort Vengeance AA
Hannah Lee REALART
The Royal African Rifles AA
Combat Squad COL
Dragonfly Squadron AA
1954
Loophole AA
Duffy of San Quentin WB
Fangs of the Wild LIP
Return from the Sea AA
Ring of Fear (with A. Lange) WB
Shield for Murder UA
Target Earth AA
Cry Vengeance AA
Black Tuesday UA
1955
Big House, U.S.A. UA
Stranger on Horseback UA
Robber's Roost UA
Fingerman AA
Desert Sands UA
Fort Yuma UA
The Return of Jack Slade AA
Shack Out on 101 AA
1956
Three Bad Sisters UA
Last of the Desperadoes ASSOCIATED
Ghost Town UA
The Come On AA
The Wild Dakotas ASSOCIATED
Crime Against Joe UA
The Broken Star UA
Walk the Dark Streets DOMINANT
Emergency Hospital UA
Frontier Gambler ASSOCIATED
The Three Outlaws ASSOCIATED
Magnificent Roughnecks AA
Strange Intruder AA
The Cruel Tower AA
Stagecoach to Fury TCF
The Women of Pitcairn Island TCF
Dance with Me, Henry UA
The Brass Legend UA
1957
The Quiet Gun TCF
Crime of Passion UA
Dragoon Wells Massacre AA
Lure of the Swamp TCF
I Was a Teenage Werewolf AIP
Apache Warrior TCF
God Is My Partner TCF
Portland Expose AA
Under Fire TCF
Young and Dangerous TCF
Rockabilly Baby TCF
Blood of Dracula AIP
I Was a Teenage Frankenstein AIP
Guns Don't Argue! VISUAL DRAMA
Hooked MANHATTAN
1958
Oregon Passage AA
Gun Fever UA
Gang War TCF
Toughest Gun in Tombstone UA
Frankenstein—1970 AA
How to Make a Monster AIP
Wolf Larsen AA
Frontier Gun TCF
Lone Texan TCF
1959
The Four Skulls of Jonathan Drake UA
Invisible Invaders UA
Here Come the Jets TCF
The Rebel Set AA
The Oregon Trail TCF
Five Gates to Hell TCF
The Rookie TCF
Gunfighters of Abilene UA

1960
The Purple Gang AA
The Angry Red Planet AIP
Twelve Hours to Kill TCF
Walk Like a Dragon PAR
Desire in the Dust TCF
Stump Run EMERALD
The Crowning Experience MORAL REARMAMENT
1961
Seven Women from Hell TCF
1962
The Three Stooges Meet Hercules COL
The Three Stooges in Orbit COL
1963
Black Zoo AA
The Three Stooges Go Around the World in a Daze COL
Shock Corridor AA
Law of the Lawless PAR
Stage to Thunder Rock PAR
1964
The Naked Kiss AA
Young Fury PAR
1965
The Outlaws Is Coming COL
Operation CIA AA
1966
Destination Inner Space MAGNA
Castle of Evil UNITED
Cyborg 2087 FEATURE FILM
Dimension 5 FEATURE FILM
1967
The Sweet and the Bitter COMMONWEALTH
The Money Jungle UNITED
1968
The Destructors FEATURE FILM
Panic in the City UNITED

DUNN, REX
1929
No Defense (with Reiser) WB
Skin Deep (+ stock) WB
Evidence WB
The Aviator (mt) WB
Little Johnny Jones (mt) WB
General Crack (mt) WB
1930
Golden Dawn WB
Dancing Sweeties (see Copping)
Sweet Kitty Bellairs (with Leonardi; ac: Mendoza) WB
Big Boy (see Reiser)
The Dawn Patrol WB
1931
Sit Tight (foreign version; + stock) WB
The Right of Way (see Reiser)
1939
The Spellbinder (o: R. Bennett) RKO
Private Detective WB
1940
Calling All Husbands (see H. Jackson)
Father Is a Prince WB
Always a Bride WB
1948
Panhandle AA
Documentary Shorts (WB)
1940
Fly Fishing
1941
Fight, Fish, Fight
Hunting the Hard Way
King Salmon
Kings of the Turf
Lions for Sale
Miracle Makers
Monsters of the Deep
Sail Ho
The Seeing Eye
1942
Argentine Horses
Hatteras Honkers
A Hunter's Paradise
Rocky Mountain Big Game
1943
King of the Archers
The Man Killers
Our African Frontier
1944
Blue Nose Schooner
Hunting the Devil Cat
The Struggle for Life
1945
Alice in Jungleland
Arabians in the Rockies
The Birds and the Beasts Were There
Cavalcade of Archery
Facing Your Danger
Flivver Flying
The Forest Commandos
Let's Go Gunning
Mexican Sea Sports
Michigan Ski-Daddle
1946
Down Singapore Way
King of the Everglades
Let's Go Camping
South of Monterrey

1947
Carnival of Sports
Fishing the Florida Keys
Kingdom of the Wild
Land of Romance

DUNSTEDTER, EDDIE
1953
Donovan's Brain UA

DuPAGE, RICHARD
1945
Cap'n Cub (cartoon) FC
1950
Cassino to Korea (doc.; see G. Steiner)
1958
Terror from the Year 5000 AIP

E

EAMES, HENRY PURMORT
1920
The Gamesters (with Goodell) AMERICAN FILM CO.
The Blue Moon (with Goodell) AMERICAN FILM CO.

EARLS, PAUL
1968
No Handouts for Mrs. Hedgepeth (doc. short) NORTH CAROLINA FUND

EASTON, JACK
1955
Baby Boogie (cartoon) UPA

EATON, JOHN RANDOLPH
1968
Robby BLUEWOOD

EDENS, ROGER
1940
Little Nellie Kelly (see Stoll)
1942
For Me and My Gal (mt and o: Bassman) MGM
1943
Cabin in the Sky (with Bassman) MGM
1944
Meet Me in St. Louis (see Salinger)
1946
Ziegfeld Follies (with Hayton, Salinger) MGM
Till the Clouds Roll By (see Salinger)
1947
Good News (see Salinger)
1948
Easter Parade (see Salinger)
1949
Take Me Out to the Ball Game (with Salinger; o: R. Franklyn, Marquardt) MGM
1950
Annie Get Your Gun (see A. Deutsch)
Pagan Love Song (see A. Deutsch)
1956
Invitation to the Dance (see A. Previn)
1957
Funny Face (see Courage)
1962
Jumbo (see Stoll)

EDOUARDE, CARL
1920
Kismet ROBERTSON-COLE
1924
The Hunchback of Notre Dame (see Riesenfeld)
1931
Blonde Captive (doc.) IMPERIAL
[Musical director of *Aesop's Sound Fables,* 1929; whether he composed any scores for this cartoon series is unknown.]

EDWARDS, LEO
1922
Heroes of the Street WB

EISLER, HANNS
[He scored several German, Dutch, French, and British films before coming to the United States in 1938. In 1948 he returned to Germany, where he scored many films.]
1939
The 400 Million (doc.) JORIS IVENS
Pete Roleum and His Cousins (an. short) JOSEPH LOSEY
Soil (doc.) USDA

1940
White Flood (doc. short) FRONTIER FILMS
1941
A Child Went Forth (doc. short) U.S. STATE DEPT.
The Forgotten Village (doc.) HERBERT KLINE
1943
Hangmen Also Die! UA
1944
None But the Lonely Heart RKO
1945
Jealousy REP
The Spanish Main (o: Grau) RKO
1946
Deadline at Dawn (o: Grau) RKO
A Scandal in Paris (o: Byrns) UA
1947
The Woman on the Beach (o: Grau) RKO
So Well Remembered RKO

ELLENHORN, MAURY
1958
Merry Minstrel Magoo (cartoon) UPA

ELLINGTON, DUKE
1959
Anatomy of a Murder COL
1961
Paris Blues UA
1965
Astro-Freight (doc. short) AMERICAN AIRLINES
1966
Assault on a Queen (a and o: Comstock, Van Cleave) PAR
1968
Racing World (doc. short) SAM SHAW
1969
Change of Mind CR

ELLIOTT, CLINTON
1954
Moses (short) VICTOR KAYFETZ
1956
Secrets of the Reef (doc.) CONTINENTAL

ELLIOTT, DEAN
1960
Sex Kittens Go to College AA
College Confidential UNIV
1969
The Phantom Tollbooth MGM
Cartoons
1956
Magoo's Puddle Jumper UPA
1957
Magoo's Glorious Fourth UPA
Rockhound Magoo UPA
1958
Magoo's Young Manhood UPA
1966
The A-tom-inable Snowman MGM
Duel Personality MGM
Filet Meow MGM
Jerry, Jerry, Quite Contrary MGM
Matinee Mouse MGM
Time for Decision AMERICAN CANCER SOCIETY
1967
Advance and Be Mechanized MGM
The Bear That Wasn't MGM
Cannery Rodent MGM
The Mouse from H.U.N.G.E.R. MGM
Shutter Bugged Cat MGM
Surf-Bored Cat MGM

ELLIOTT, DON
Documentary Shorts
1960
A Number of Things ELECTRA STUDIOS
1963
Que Puerto Rico TIBOR HIRSCH
Reflections of New York FIMA NOVECK
1964
Reflections of Paris FIMA NOVECK
I Wonder Why ROBERT ROSENTHAL
1965
Architecture USA TIBOR HIRSCH
1966
Atoms on the Move U.S. ATOMIC ENERGY COMMISSION
1967
Atomic Power Today U.S. ATOMIC ENERGY COMMISSION
Tapline in Arabia ?
Transportation USA ?

ELLIOTT, JACK
1967
The Happiest Millionaire WDP
Valley of Mystery (ac: S. Wilson, S. Fine; + stock) UNIV
1968
The One and Only, Genuine, Original Family Band WDP
1969
The Comic COL
1970
Where's Poppa? UA

ELLIOTT, VERN
1918
Tarzan of the Apes NATIONAL
Indian Life (doc.) NORTHWESTERN
1951
Hidden Treasures (doc.; with Boersma) MOODY BIBLE INSTITUTE

ELLIS, DOLAN
1967
Peace for a Gunfighter CROWN

ELLIS, RAY
1962
Wonders of Arkansas (doc. short) COL

EMENEGGER, ROBERT
1960
California Gray Whale (doc. short) PYRAMID
1964
Passion Street, U.S.A. GILLMAN

ENGEL, LEHMAN
1954
Roogie's Bump REP
Documentary Shorts
1944
N. P. Patients U.S. NAVY
1945
Irritability U.S. NAVY
Fury in the Pacific U.S. NAVY
Report to Judy U.S. NAVY
The Fleet That Came to Stay U.S. NAVY
Well Done (o: Palange) U.S. NAVY
Unconditional Surrender U.S. NAVY
War Days U.S. NAVY
1949
Berlin Powderkeg RKO PATHÉ
On Watch RKO PATHÉ
1955
Tuesday's Child INFORMATION PRODS.
1959
Beyond Gauguin WILLARD

ENGLEMAN, MAURICE
1963
Surf (doc. short) JANTZEN, INC.

ENOS, JOSEPH T.
1952
Yellowstone Legend (doc. short) MUSICALE PUBLICATIONS

EPSTEIN, DAVID M.
1952
Union in the Mill (doc. short) PAPER MAKERS UNION
1956
The Summoning of Everyman (short) RICHARD HILLIARD
1960
Frontiers (doc. short) STATE OF UTAH
1963
By the Sea (short) ?
1964
The Count Down Under (doc. short) UNITED NATIONS
No Other Choice (doc. short) UNITED NATIONS

ERB, DONALD
1963
Texture in Painting (doc. short) PHOEBE FLORY

ERDODY, LEO
1928
Lilac Time (see N. Shilkret)
1941
Under Fiesta Stars (see M. Glickman)
1942
Murder in the Big House (see H. Jackson)
Prisoner of Japan PRC
Baby Face Morgan PRC
Tomorrow We Live PRC
City of Silent Men PRC
The Boss of Big Town PRC
1943
The Kid Rides Again PRC
Dead Men Walk PRC
Queen of Broadway PRC
Wild Horse Rustlers PRC
Overland Stagecoach PRC
Fugitive of the Plains PRC
Behind Prison Walls PRC
Corregidor PRC
My Son, the Hero PRC
Girls in Chains PRC
Western Cyclone PRC
Isle of Forgotten Sins PRC
A Hunting We Won't Go (cartoon; see Kilfeather)
Jive Junction (md) PRC
1944
Bluebeard PRC
1945
Out of the Night PRC
White Pongo (o: Bernie) PRC
Apology for Murder PRC
Detour PRC
1946
I Ring Doorbells PRC

The Flying Serpent PRC
Murder Is My Business PRC
Larceny in Her Heart PRC
Blonde for a Day PRC
Gas House Kids PRC

1947
The Return of Rin Tin Tin EL
Blonde Savage EL

1948
Money Madness FC
Lady at Midnight EL
Miraculous Journey FC

ERICKSON, JAMIE
1933
Her Secret IDEAL

ERICSON, BILL
1958
What Is a Man? (short) SARA-KATHRYN ARLEDGE

ESPOSITO, GENE
1957
Texoprint (doc. short) MORTON GOLDSHOLL

ETO, KIMIO
1957
Pictures in Pure Light Painting (short) BETTY SCHEYER

EVANS, GIL
1967
Fragments D. NOGATA

1968
Days in My Father's House MPO VIDEOTRONICS

1969
Parachute to Paradise A. GITTLER

1970
The Sea in Your Future O. LEE

F

FAGAS, JIMMIE
1969
Once You Kiss a Stranger WB

FAIRCHILD, EDGAR
1944
Penthouse Rhythm UNIV

1945
Her Lucky Night UNIV
The Naughty Nineties (with Dessau) UNIV
The Crimson Canary UNIV
Senorita from the West UNIV

1946
Little Giant UNIV
She Wrote the Book UNIV

1948
If You Knew Susie RKO

FAITH, PERCY
1961
Tammy Tell Me True UNIV

1964
I'd Rather Be Rich UNIV

1965
The Love Goddesses (compilation film) CONTINENTAL
The Third Day (o: Garcia) WB

1966
The Oscar (o: Shuken, Hayes) EMBASSY

FALCK, EDWARD
1918
The Blue Bird (see Riesenfeld)

1923
The Ten Commandments (see Riesenfeld)

FALIKS, KEN
1963
Dumpson's Place (short) ED EMSHWILLER

FALL, RICHARD
1930
Man Trouble (see R. Bassett)
Liliom (with Kaylin; o: Friedhofer, Gerstenberger, Dalby, W. Spielter) FOX
The Princess and the Plumber (see Lipschultz)

1931
East Lynne (see R. Bassett)
Their Mad Moment (o: Gerstenberger, Dalby, Virgil) FOX
Merely Mary Ann (o: Friedhofer, Virgil, R. Bassett) FOX

FARNON, DENNIS
1966
Arrivederci, Baby! PAR
Cartoons (UPA)
1955
Spare the Child
Magoo's Check Up
Four Wheels, No Brakes
Christopher Crumpet's Playmate
Stage Door Magoo
The Rise of Duton Lang
Magoo Makes News
1956
Magoo Beats the Heat
Magoo's Problem Child
1957
Magoo Saves the Bank
Magoo's Moose Hunt
Magoo's Private War
1958
Scoutmaster Magoo
Magoo's Three-Point Landing
Magoo's Cruise

FEIERABEND, JACK
1966
Saint Louis: Gateway to the West (doc. short) SOUTHWESTERN BELL

FELCIANO, RICHARD
1967
Si See Sunni (short) CHARLES I. LEVINE

FELDMAN, MORTON
1951
Jackson Pollock (doc. short) PAUL FALKENBERG, HANS NAMUTH
1954
Sculpture by Lipton (doc. short) NATHAN BOXER
1961
The Sin of Jesus (short) ROBERT FRANK
1966
Willem de Kooning (doc. short) PETER FALKENBERG, HANS NAMUTH
1968
Time of the Locust (doc. short) PETER GESSNER

FENYO, THOMAS
1957
Once Upon a Sunday (doc. short) ALBA PRODS.

FERGUSON, ALLYN
1961
The Devil's Hand CROWN
The Magic Tide (short; with Hinshaw) SOMBRERO PICTURES
1962
Airborne (with Hinshaw) GILLMAN
1967
Sofi GOLDEN BEAR

FERRARO, RALPH
1966
The She Beast PAUL MASLANSKY
1967
The King's Pirate UNIV

FEUER, CY
1938
The Fighting Devil Dogs (see Colombo)
Heroes of the Hills (with Lava; ac: Colombo) REP
Pals of the Saddle REP
The Higgins Family (see Lava)
The Night Hawk REP
I Stand Accused REP
Rhythm of the Saddle (see Colombo)
Storm Over Bengal (with Lava) REP
Come On, Rangers (see Lava)
Western Jamboree (see Lava)
Orphans of the Street REP
Hawk of the Wilderness (serial; see Lava)
Federal Man Hunt REP
1939
Fighting Thoroughbreds (with Lava) REP
The Mysterious Miss X (see Lava)
Pride of the Navy REP
Woman Doctor (see Lava)
Forged Passport REP
I Was a Convict REP
Mexicali Rose (with Lava; ac: Sawtell; + stock) REP
Street of Missing Men REP
Blue Montana Skies (see Lava)
My Wife's Relatives (with Lava) REP
S.O.S.—Tidal Wave REP
Mountain Rhythm (with Lava; + stock) REP
Daredevils of the Red Circle (serial; see Lava)
Mickey the Kid (with Lava) REP
She Married a Cop (with Lava) REP
Should Husbands Work? (see Lava)
Smuggled Cargo REP
Flight at Midnight REP

Calling All Marines REP
Sabotage REP
Jeepers Creepers REP
Main Street Lawyer (see Lava)
The Covered Trailer (see Lava)
Zorro's Fighting Legion (serial; see Lava)
Thou Shalt Not Kill REP
Money to Burn (with Sawtell; + stock) REP

1940
Heroes of the Saddle (with Lava, Sawtell; + stock) REP
Village Barn Dance REP
Pioneers of the West REP
Forgotten Girls REP
Drums of Fu Manchu (serial; with Sawtell; + stock) REP
In Old Missouri REP
Covered Wagon Days (see Sawtell)
Rocky Mountain Rangers REP
Women in War REP
Wagons Westward REP
One Man's Law REP
Sing, Dance, Plenty Hot REP
Oklahoma Renegades (see Sawtell)
Girl from Havana REP
King of the Royal Mounted (serial; with Lava, Sawtell) REP
Frontier Vengeance REP
Melody and Moonlight REP
Hit Parade of 1941 REP
Who Killed Aunt Maggie? REP
Texas Terrors REP
Meet the Missus REP
Barnyard Follies REP
Lone Star Raiders REP

1941
Wyoming Wildcat REP
Arkansas Judge REP
Petticoat Politics REP
The Phantom Cowboy REP
Prairie Pioneers REP
The Great Train Robbery REP
Mr. District Attorney REP
Pals of the Pecos REP
The Gay Vagabond REP
Desert Bandit REP
Saddlemates REP
Nevada City REP
Gangs of Sonora REP
Citadel of Crime REP
Ice-Capades REP
Mercy Island (with Scharf) REP
Public Enemies REP
A Missouri Outlaw REP
West of Cimarron REP
Mr. District Attorney in the Carter Case REP
Dick Tracy vs. Crime, Inc. (serial) REP

1942
Arizona Terrors REP
Code of the Outlaw REP
A Tragedy at Midnight REP
Stagecoach Express REP
Raiders of the Range REP
Affairs of Jimmy Valentine REP
Jesse James, Jr. REP
Sunset on the Desert REP
The Girl from Alaska REP
Westward Ho REP
The Yukon Patrol REP
The Cyclone Kid REP
Moonlight Masquerade REP
Sons of the Pioneers REP

1945
Swim and Live (doc. short) A.A.F.

FIELDING, JERRY

1962
Advise and Consent COL
The Nun and the Sergeant UA

1964
For Those Who Think Young UA
McHale's Navy UNIV

1965
The Crazy World of Laurel and Hardy (compilation film) BRENNER
McHale's Navy Joins the Air Force UNIV

1969
The Wild Bunch WB

1970
Suppose They Gave a War and Nobody Came CR

FIELDS, FRANK G.

1954
Abstract in Concrete (short) JOHN ARVONIO

FIELDS, GEORGE

1954
Naked Sea (see Almeida)

1956
Goodbye, My Lady (see Almeida)

FILIPPI, AMEDEO DE

1928
Blockade FBO

1929
The Jazz Age FBO

The Leatherneck PATHÉ
Trial Marriage COL
1939
Everything's on Ice (with Terr) RKO
The Housekeeper's Daughter (with Moraweck) UA

FINCKEL, JOHN ALDEN
1941
Harvests for Tomorrow (doc. short) USDA

FINE, SIDNEY
1967
Valley of Mystery (see J. Elliott)
[Also worked as an orchestrator.]

FINE, VIVIAN
1954
New Ways of Seeing (doc. short) ROGER TILTON

FINK, ADOLPH
1924
America (see Breil)

FIRESTONE, ELIZABETH
1949
Once More, My Darling UNIV
1953
That Man from Tangier UA

FISHER, LAWRENCE V.
1963
Stark Fear ELLIS FILMS

FLANAGAN, WILLIAM
1948
The Climate of New York (doc. short) RUDOLPH BURKHARDT
1951
See Naples and the Island of Ischia RUDOLPH BURKHARDT

FLETCHER, GRANT
1953
Magic (short) ?
1956
The Fourth Opinion (doc. short) ARIZONA SOCIETY FOR HANDICAPPED CHILDREN
1970
Arcosantos (short) ?

FONTAINE, BILL
1949
Holiday in Havana (mt; + stock) COL
[Also worked as an orchestrator.]

FORBES, LOUIS
1938
Little Orphan Annie (with Nussbaum; ac: Bassman) PAR
1941
Pot o' Gold UA
1947
The Spirit of West Point FC
Intrigue UA
1948
Pitfall UA
1949
The Crooked Way UA
1950
Johnny One-Eye (with H. Jackson; o: Strech) UA
Second Chance PFC
The Man Who Cheated Himself TCF
1951
Home Town Story MGM
A Wonderful Life PFC
1953
Count the Hours (with H. Jackson) RKO
Appointment in Honduras (with H. Jackson) RKO
For Every Child PFC
The Hidden Heart PFC
1954
Silver Lode (with H. Jackson) RKO
City Story PAUL F. HEARD
Passion (with H. Jackson) RKO
Cattle Queen of Montana (with Lava, H. Jackson) RKO
1955
Escape to Burma (with H. Jackson) RKO
Pearl of the South Pacific (with H. Jackson, Lava) RKO
Tennessee's Partner (with H. Jackson, Lava) RKO
Slightly Scarlet (with H. Jackson) RKO
1957
The River's Edge TCF
1958
Hong Kong Affair AA
From the Earth to the Moon WB
1959
The Bat AA
Jet Over the Atlantic INTERCONTINENT

1961
Most Dangerous Man Alive COL

FORRELL, GENE
1958
The Big Country (doc.) EDGAR M. QUEENY
1960
Music of Williamsburg (doc.) CW
1965
Willy McBean and His Magic Machine (puppet film) MAGNA
Shorts
1943
Henry Browne, Farmer USDA
Farm Battle Lines USDA
Farmers at War OWI
1945
The Private Life of a Cat ALEXANDER HAMMID
1946
Children of Russia (with Lloyd) IFF
Mary Visits Poland IFF
Bolivia CIAA
How Russians Play IFF
1947
Boundary Lines (an.) IFF
Italy Rebuilds IFF
1949
World Friendship IFF
Picture in Your Mind (an.) IFF
Sampan Family IFF
1950
The Story of a Girl Scout Troop GIRL SCOUTS OF THE U.S.A.
Japanese Family IFF
The Story of a Brownie Troop GIRL SCOUTS OF THE U.S.A.
1952
British Factory Foreman IFF
British Mill Owner IFF
English Farm Family IFF
Oxford Student IFF
Sadler's Wells Ballerina IFF
Scottish Miner IFF
1953
House of the Child CRAFTSMAN
Lincoln Speaks at Gettysburg LEWIS JACOBS
The Warning Shadow AMER. CANCER SOCIETY
A People Without Fear IFF
1954
With One Voice IFF
1956
Adventuring in the Arts GIRL SCOUTS OF THE U.S.A.
The Petrified River—The Story of Uranium UNION CARBIDE
1957
This Is Kilmer LEO BEEBE
Your Share in Tomorrow N.Y. STOCK EXCHANGE
1958
For All Time ROGER WADE PRODS.
The Miracle of the Bulb JOHN OTT
N.Y., N.Y. FRANCIS THOMPSON
1959
The Middle East IFF
1960
South America (with Lloyd, Horst) IFF
1962
Amazon Family (with Lloyd, Horst) IFF
1964
To Be Alive! FRANCIS THOMPSON
To the Fair FRANCIS THOMPSON
1967
Symmetry NATL. SCIENCE FOUNDATION
19??
Corn's Hidden Enemies ?
Hereford Heritage ?

FOSS, LUKAS
1962
Search Into Darkness (doc. short) WILLARD VAN DYKE

FOX, CHARLES
1967
The Incident (see T. Knight)
1968
The Green Slime (ac for U.S. release of Japanese film) MGM
1969
Goodbye, Columbus PAR
1970
Pufnstuf UNIV

FOX, DAN
1970
Women Women Women Moira MORTON LEWIS

FOX, J.C.
1969
Swingtail COSMOS FILMS

FRAN, PAUL
1964
Papillote (short) BENJAMIN HAYEEM

FRANK, MARCEL
1958
Ellen in Windowland (short) FILM IMAGES

FRANKLIN, DAVE
1946
Romance of the West PRC

FRANKLYN, MILTON J.
Cartoons (WB)
1942
The Impatient Patient
1943
Coal Black and de Sebben Dwarfs
1953
Bugs and Thugs
Devil May Hare
Sheep Ahoy
1954
Baby Buggy Bunny
By Word of Mouse
Dime to Retire
Double or Mutton
Feather Dusted
Hare Brush
The Hole Idea
My Little Duckaroo
Past Perfumance
Pests for Guests
Rabbit Rampage
Sahara Hare
Stork Naked
Tweety's Circus
Yankee Doodle Bugs
1955
Broom-Stick Bunny
Bugs' Bonnets
Heaven Scent
Heir-Conditioned
A Hitch in Time (for U.S. Air Force)
A Kiddie's Kitty
Knight-Mare Hare
Lighthouse Mouse
Lumber Jerks
Mixed Master
One Froggy Evening
Pizzicato Pussycat
Rabbitson Crusoe
Red Riding Hoodwinked
Rocket Squad
Roman Legion-Hare
This Is a Life?
Too Hop to Handle
Tree-Cornered Tweety
Tweet and Sour
Two Scents Worth
Weasel Stop
1956
Deduce, You Say!
Go Fly a Kit
The Honey-Mousers
90 Day Wondering (for U.S. Army)
Rocket-Bye Baby
A Star Is Bored
To Hare Is Human
Tugboat Granny
Tweet Zoo
Tweety and the Beanstalk
Yankee Dood It
1957
Bedevilled Rabbit
Birds Anonymous
Boston Quackie
Boyhood Daze
Don't Axe Me
Drafty, Isn't It? (for U.S. Army)
Ducking the Devil
Feather Bluster
Greedy for Tweety
Hare-less Wolf
Hare-way to the Stars
Knighty Knight Bugs
Now, Hare This
A Pizza Tweety-Pie
Rabbit Romeo
Robin Hood Daffy
Show Biz Bugs
Steal Wool
Tortilla Flaps
Touché and Go
Waggily Tale
What's Opera Doc?
Whoa, Be Gone!
1958
Baton Bunny
Cat Feud
Cat's Paw
China Jones
Dog Tales
Hare-abian Nights
Hot Rod and Reel

Mexicali Shmoes
Mouse-Placed Kitten
The Mouse That Jack Built
A Mutt in a Rut
Really Scent
Trick or Tweet

1959

Apes of Wrath
Backwoods Bunny
Bonanza Bunny
A Broken Leghorn
Crockett-Doodle-Do
Fastest with the Mostest
Goldimouse and the Three Cats
Here Today, Gone Tamale
High Note
Horse Hare
Hyde and Go Tweet
Mice Follies
The Mouse on 57th Street
People Are Bunny
Person to Bunny
Ready, Woolen and Able
Tweet and Lovely
Tweet Dreams
Unnatural History
West of the Pesos
Who Scent You?
Wild About Hurry
Wild and Woolly Hare
Wild, Wild World
A Witch's Tangled Hare

1960

Cannery Woe
The Dixie Fryer
Doggone People
From Heir to Heir
Hopalong Casualty
Hoppy Days
Lighter Than Hare
Mouse and Garden
Rabbit's Feat
Strangled Eggs
Trip for Tat
Zip 'n Snort

1961

The Abominable Snow Rabbit
Beep Prepared
Birds of a Father
Compressed Hare
Crow's Feat
D' Fightin' Ones
Daffy's Inn Trouble
Fish and Slips
The Last Hungry Cat
Lickety-Splat
Mexican Boarders
Nelly's Folly
The Pied Piper of Guadalupe
Prince Violent
Quackodile Tears
The Rebel Without Claws
A Scent of the Matterhorn
A Sheep in the Deep
What' s My Lion?

1962

Adventures of the Road-Runner
Bill of Hare
Honey's Money
Louvre Come Back to Me
Mother Was a Rooster
Slick Chick
Wet Hare
Zoom at the Top

FRANKLYN, ROBERT

1944

The Canterville Ghost (see Bassman)
Maisie Goes to Reno (see Snell)
Marriage Is a Private Affair (see Kaper)
Barbary Coast Gent (see Snell)
Lost in a Harem (see N. Shilkret)

1945

Anchors Aweigh (see Stoll)
Week-End at the Waldorf (see J. Green)
Dangerous Partners (see Snell)
The Sailor Takes a Wife (see J. Green)
Up Goes Maisie (see Snell)

1946

Bad Bascomb (see Snell)
Easy to Wed (see J. Green)
Courage of Lassie (see Bradley)
Little Mister Jim (see Bassman)
The Cockeyed Miracle (see Snell)
The Secret Heart (see Kaper)

1947

The Arnelo Affair (see Bassman)
Undercover Maisie (see Snell)
Cynthia (see Kaper)
Dark Delusion (see Snell)
Merton of the Movies (see Snell)
Song of the Thin Man (see Snell)

1948

Alias a Gentleman (see Snell)
B. F.'s Daughter (see Kaper)
A Date with Judy (see Stoll)

A Southern Yankee (see Snell)
Hills of Home (see Stothart)
The Secret Land (see Kaper)
1949
Big Jack (see Stothart)
That Midnight Kiss (see C. Previn)
1957
Raintree County (see J. Green)
1960
Pepe (see J. Green)
1962
Jumbo (see Stoll)
Shorts (MGM)
1944
Twenty Years After (see Snell)
1947
It Can't Be Done (with Snell; o: Heglin)
1948
Good-bye, Miss Turlock
My Old Town (with Snell; o: Heglin)
Souvenirs of Death
The Fabulous Fraud
[Also a prolific orchestrator.]

FREE, STAN
1966
Moonlighting Wives JOE SARNO
1967
My Body Hungers JOE SARNO

FREEBAIRN-SMITH, IAN
1964
Voice of the Hurricane MORAL RE-ARMAMENT
1970
The Strawberry Statement MGM
Dreams of Glass UNIV

FREEDMAN, ROBERT
1970
Ezra Jack Keats (doc. short) WESTON WOODS

FREEMAN, ERNIE
1967
The Cool Ones (a: Strange) WB
What Am I Bid? EMERSON
The Double Man WB
1968
The Pink Jungle UNIV
Duffy (o: A. Freeman) COL
1970
Dinah East (see Nash)

FREEMAN, NED
1952
Ride the Man Down REP

FRIED, GERALD
1953
Fear and Desire BURSTYN
1955
Killer's Kiss UA
1956
The Killing UA
1957
Trooper Hook UA
The Vampire UA
Bayou UA
Dino AA
Paths of Glory UA
1958
Machine Gun Kelly AIP
The Flame Barrier UA
The Return of Dracula UA
The Cry Baby Killer AA
I Bury the Living UA
Curse of the Faceless Man UA
Terror in a Texas Town UA
Timbuktu UA
The Lost Missile UA
I, Mobster (with Alperson) TCF
1959
Cast a Long Shadow UA
1961
A Cold Wind in August AIDART
Twenty Plus Two AA
The Second Time Around TCF
1962
The Cabinet of Caligari TCF
1964
One Potato, Two Potato CINEMA V
1966
Deathwatch BEVERLY
1968
The Killing of Sister George CR
1969
What Ever Happened to Aunt Alice? CR
1970
Too Late the Hero CR
Shorts
1950
The Legend of the Thirsting Stones FILMS FOR CHILDREN
1951
Day of the Fight (doc.) RKO PATHÉ
Icebreaker (doc.) RKO PATHÉ

1952
The Big Lie (doc.) MGM
1956
The Princess in the Tower AMERICAN JEWISH COMMITTEE
1963
The Great Rights (an.) BRANDON
1965
Bio-Satellite (doc.) ?
1969
Image of the City (doc.) EAMES

FRIEDHOFER, HUGO
1929
Seven Faces (see Lipschultz)
1930
The Golden Calf (with Arthur Kay, Talbot) FOX
Scotland Yard (see Arthur Kay)
A Devil with Women (see Brunelli)
The Dancers (see Talbot)
Just Imagine FOX
The Princess and the Plumber (see Lipschultz)
Under Suspicion (see Kaylin)
Men on Call (see Kaylin)
The Man Who Came Back (see Brunelli)
1931
Always Goodbye (mt; + stock) FOX
Daddy Long Legs FOX
Goldie (see R. Bassett)
Transatlantic (see R. Bassett)
The Spider (with R. Bassett, G. Knight) FOX
Skyline (see Brunelli)
Heartbreak (ac: Virgil; + stock) FOX
The Yellow Ticket (see R. Bassett)
La Ley del Harem (Spanish language; + stock) FOX
1932
After Tomorrow (theme: Hanley) FOX
Devil's Lottery (mt; + stock) FOX
Careless Lady FOX
Amateur Daddy FOX
The Trial of Vivienne Ware (with R. Bassett) FOX
The Woman in Room 13 (+ stock) FOX
Almost Married (with R. Bassett, Brunelli) FOX
Mystery Ranch (+ stock) FOX
Rebecca of Sunnybrook Farm (see A. Lange)
A Passport to Hell (with R. Bassett, A. Lange) FOX
The First Year FOX
The Painted Woman (with A. Lange; ac: Lipschultz) FOX
Sherlock Holmes (see R. Bassett)
Tess of the Storm Country (see De Francesco)
El Caballero de la Noche (see R. Bassett)
Handle with Care (see Brunelli)
Second Hand Wife (see Lipschultz)
1933
The Face in the Sky (see Brunelli)
Dangerously Yours (see De Francesco)
El Último Varón Sobre la Tierra (Spanish language) FOX
Broadway Bad (see A. Lange)
Zoo in Budapest (see Zamecnik)
Pilgrimage (see R. Bassett)
It's Great to Be Alive (ac: R. Bassett, Kaylin; o: Gerstenberger) FOX
My Lips Betray (o: Gerstenberger, R. Bassett) FOX
The Man Who Dared (see Kaylin)
The Good Companions (U.S. release of British film; based on themes of George Posford) FOX
La Melodía Prohibida (see Kaylin)
Paddy the Next Best Thing (see De Francesco)
As Husbands Go (o: Gerstenberger, Brunelli) FOX
Jimmy and Sally (see A. Lange)
I Am Suzanne! (see Hollander)
1934
Orient Express (with A. Lange; ac: Kaylin) FOX
Coming Out Party FOX
George White's Scandals (with Buttolph) FOX
Now I'll Tell (with A. Lange) FOX
Springtime for Henry (see Brunelli)
Grand Canary (see De Francesco)
Pursued (with Buttolph, Kaylin; o: Gerstenberger) FOX
The World Moves On (see De Francesco)
Servants' Entrance (with Buttolph, A. Lange; o: E. Ross) FOX
Dos Más Uno, Dos (see Buttolph)
1935
Lottery Lover (see A. Lange)
The Little Colonel (see Mockridge)
George White's 1935 Scandals (ac: De Francesco) FOX
Our Little Girl (see Brunelli)
The Call of the Wild (see A. Newman)

Orchids to You (see A. Lange)
Curly Top (with R. Bassett, A. Lange) FOX
Dante's Inferno (with Kaylin, R. Bassett, Brunelli; ac: Buttolph, Lange, G. Rose) FOX
Here's to Romance (see De Francesco)
Way Down East (with Mockridge, Buttolph; + stock) FOX
Peter Ibbetson (see Toch)
So Red the Rose (see Harling)
Navy Wife (see Buttolph)
Last of the Pagans (see Axt)

1936

Rose of the Rancho (with Roemheld, Leipold, Hollander; mt: Satterfield) PAR
The Prisoner of Shark Island (see R. Bassett)
The Trail of the Lonesome Pine (see Carbonara)
The Great Ziegfeld (see Lange)
Sins of Man (with R. Bassett; + music sent from Europe by Alexis Archangelsky; o: E. Ross, Maxwell) TCF
White Fang (with Maxwell) TCF
The Road to Glory (see R. Bassett)

1937

Beloved Enemy (see A. Newman)
You Only Live Once (see A. Newman)
The Prisoner of Zenda (see A. Newman)

1938

The Adventures of Marco Polo (o: E. Powell) GOLDWYN
Valley of the Giants (with A. Deutsch) WB

1939

Topper Takes a Trip (with E. Powell) UA
Made for Each Other (with E. Powell, Buttolph; theme: Levant) SELZNICK
The Oklahoma Kid (see M. Steiner)
Gone with the Wind (see M. Steiner)

1940

The Mark of Zorro (see A. Newman)
Santa Fe Trail (see M. Steiner)

1941

Cadet Girl (see Buttolph)
Son of Fury (see A. Newman)
Remember the Day (see Mockridge)

1942

Secret Agent of Japan (see Harline)
The Pied Piper (see A. Newman)
The Battle of Midway (see A. Newman)
Desperate Journey (see M. Steiner)
Prelude to War (see Harline)
China Girl (ac: Lange, Harline, Mockridge, Buttolph; o: H. Spencer, Morton, E. Powell, de Packh) TCF
The Black Swan (see A. Newman)

1943

Chetniks! (ac: Mockridge; o: Salinger, H. Spencer, de Packh, Morton, D. Raksin, E. Powell) TCF
My Friend Flicka (see A. Newman)
They Came to Blow Up America (ac: Harline, Lange; o: D. Raksin, Morton, de Packh) TCF
Wintertime (see Lange)
Paris After Dark (o: Morton, H. Spencer, E. Powell, D. Raksin) TCF
The Gang's All Here (see A. Newman)
Heaven Can Wait (see A. Newman)

1944

The Lodger (ac: Mockridge; o: Morton, D. Raksin, H. Spencer) TCF
Lifeboat TCF
The Sullivans (see Mockridge)
Four Jills in a Jeep (with Burke, Mockridge, A. Lange) TCF
Roger Touhy, Gangster (ac: A. Lange, Buttolph; o: Morton, D. Raksin) TCF
Home in Indiana (o: Morton, de Packh, D. Raksin) TCF
Take It or Leave It (see Mockridge)
Wing and a Prayer (o: Morton, de Packh) TCF
The Woman in the Window (with A. Lange, Maxwell; ac: B. Mason) INTERNATIONAL
The Conspirators (see M. Steiner)
Belle of the Yukon (see A. Lange)

1945

Brewster's Millions (o: Morton, Byrns) UA
Along Came Jones (see A. Lange)
Getting Gertie's Garter (o: Morton, R. Franklyn, Byrns) UA

1946

The Bandit of Sherwood Forest (o: Morton) COL
Gilda (o: Morton) COL
One More Tomorrow (see M. Steiner)
The Jolson Story (see Skiles)
So Dark the Night (o: Morton) COL
The Best Years of Our Lives (o: Moross, Cutner, Shuken, E. Powell) GOLDWYN

1947

Dead Reckoning (see Skiles)
Body and Soul (o: Moross, Grau) UA
Wild Harvest (o: Shuken, Cutner) PAR

The Bishop's Wife (o: Moross, Skiles) GOLDWYN
The Swordsman (o and ac: Morton, Skiles) COL
A Song Is Born (ac: Moross) GOLDWYN

1948
Adventures of Casanova (o: Cadkin, Byrns) EL
Black Bart (see L. Stevens)
Sealed Verdict (o: Parrish) PAR
Joan of Arc (o: Moross, Byrns, Dessau) RKO
Enchantment (o: Moross, Skiles, de Packh) GOLDWYN

1949
Bride of Vengeance (o: Cutner, Shuken, Van Cleave, Raab) PAR
Roseanna McCoy (see Buttolph)

1950
Guilty of Treason (ac: A. Lange; o: Skiles) EL
Three Came Home (o: E. Powell) TCF
Captain Carey, U.S.A. (o: Parrish, Cutner, Shuken, Van Cleave) PAR
No Man of Her Own (o: Shuken, Cutner, Parrish) PAR
Broken Arrow (o: E. Powell) TCF
Edge of Doom (o: Skiles) GOLDWYN
Two Flags West (o: de Packh) TCF
The Sound of Fury (o: Moross) UA
Cry Danger (see Dunlap)

1951
Queen for a Day (with A. Lange; o: Skiles, Maxwell) UA
Ace in the Hole (o: Shuken, Cutner, Parrish, Van Cleave) PAR
Journey Into Light (see Dunlap)

1952
Rancho Notorious (ac: A. Lange) RKO
The Marrying Kind (o: A. Morton) COL
The San Francisco Story (see Dunlap)
The Outcasts of Poker Flat (o: E. Powell) TCF
Lydia Bailey (o: E. Powell) TCF
Just for You (o and ac: Van Cleave) PAR
Big Jim McLain (see Dunlap)
Above and Beyond (o: R. Franklyn, Byrns) MGM
Face to Face (*The Secret Sharer* and *The Bride Comes to Yellow Sky;* o: Byrns) RKO

1953
Thunder in the East (o: Parrish, Byrns) PAR
Plunder of the Sun (see Diaz Conde)
Island in the Sky (ac: A. Lange) WB
Hondo WB

1954
Vera Cruz (o: Raul Lavista) UA

1955
White Feather (o: F. Steiner) TCF
Violent Saturday (o: E. Powell) TCF
Soldier of Fortune (o: E. Powell) TCF
Love Is a Many-Splendored Thing (see A. Newman)
Seven Cities of Gold (o: E. Powell) TCF
The Rains of Ranchipur (o: de Packh, Arnaud) TCF

1956
The Harder They Fall (o: A. Morton) COL
The Revolt of Mamie Stover (o: Hagen) TCF
Between Heaven and Hell (o: E. Powell) TCF
Love Me Tender (see L. Newman)
The Girl Can't Help It (see Harline)

1957
Oh, Men! Oh, Women! (see Mockridge)
Boy on a Dolphin (o: E. Powell) TCF
An Affair to Remember (o: E. Powell, King, Mayers, Morton) TCF
The Sun Also Rises (Spanish music: Courage; o: de Packh, Mayers, Morton, Shuken) TCF

1958
The Gift of Love (see A. Newman)
The Young Lions (o: E. Powell, Hagen, Morton) TCF
The Bravados (see A. Newman)
The Barbarian and the Geisha TCF
In Love and War (ac: A. Newman; o: E. Powell, Mayers) TCF

1959
Woman Obsessed (ac: A. Newman, Buttolph, Harline; o: Courage, E. Powell, Levene, Morton) TCF
This Earth Is Mine (o: Tamkin) UNIV
The Blue Angel (o: Mayers, Courage, Hagen) TCF
Never So Few (o: R. Franklyn, H. Spencer, Grau) MGM

1960
One-Eyed Jacks (o: Van Cleave, Shuken, Hayes) PAR

1961
Homicidal COL

1962
Geronimo (ac: Gilbert) UA
Beauty and the Beast UA

1964
The Secret Invasion UA
1965
The Greatest Story Ever Told (see A. Newman)
1970
Airport (see A. Newman)
[Also a very prolific orchestrator and arranger.]

FRIEDMAN, MARK
1969
Take a Giant Step (doc. short) SUNBURST FILMS

FRONTIERA, MARY JO
1970
Sticks and Stones FILMTEAM

FRONTIERE, DOMINIC
1957
Ten Thousand Bedrooms (see Stoll)
1959
Seven Thieves (o: E. Powell) TCF
1960
One Foot in Hell (ac: E. Powell) TCF
The Marriage-Go-Round TCF
1961
The Right Approach TCF
1962
Hero's Island (adapted by Van Eps) UA
1963
A Global Affair (o: E. Powell) MGM
1965
Billie UA
1966
Incubus PREMIERE
1968
Hang 'Em High (o: E. Powell) UA
1969
Popi UA
Number One UA
1970
Barquero UA
Chisum WB
Lost Flight UNIV

FRYE, MARY JANE
1948
Chucky Lou—The Story of a Woodchuck (doc. short) INDIANA U.

FULLER, DONALD
1954
The Peppermint Tree (an. short; o: Moross) ARIES PRODS.

FULLER, JEFF
1969
The Hurdler (doc. short) REDISCOVERY PRODS.

FULLER, LORENZO
1968
Devil in Velvet LARRY CRANE
Beware the Black Widow (a of music by L. Crane) LARRY CRANE

FURST, WILLIAM
1915
My Valet TRIANGLE
The Lamb (see Breil)
The Iron Strain (see Nurnberger)
1916
Let Katie Do It TRIANGLE
The Green Swamp (with Kerr) TRIANGLE
Joan the Woman CARDINAL

G

GABLE, JOHN
1938
The Thunder of the Sea (doc. short) UNITED LUTHERAN CHURCH

GAGE, EDWARD
1930
Ingagi (semi-doc.) CONGO PICTURES

GALBRAITH, BARRY
1965
Whistle for Willie (an. short) WESTON WOODS

GALE, ERIC
1970
Events GROVE PRESS

GALLEZ, DOUGLAS W.
1956
The Black Cat (short) USC

GAMA, RAPHAEL
1931
La Cautivadora (Spanish language) IBERIA
1944
Mexican Sportland (short) WB
1947
Romance and Dance (short; see H. Jackson)

GAMSON, ARNOLD
1966
Alberto Giacometti (doc. short) COLUMBIA U.

GARCIA, RUSSELL
1950
Radar Secret Service (with Hazard) LIP
Operation Haylift (with Hazard) LIP
1960
The Time Machine MGM
Atlantis, the Lost Continent MGM
1966
The Pad (and How to Use It) UNIV
1968
Three Guns for Texas UNIV

GARDNER, MAURICE
1953
Conquest of Ungava (short) RKO PATHÉ

GARF, GENE
1954
Hollywood Thrillmakers LIP
1955
King Dinosaur LIP
1957
The Delinquents (see Palange)
1958
Man or Gun (with Idriss) REP

GARLOCK, FRANK
1967
Gateway to a Miracle (doc. short) BOB JONES U.

GARRIGUENC, RENÉ
1944
The Whistler (see Moraweck)
1946
Avalanche (see Moraweck)
1947
High Conquest (see Moraweck)
1948
16 Fathoms Deep (see Moraweck)
1951
New Mexico (see Moraweck)

GARSON, MORT
1970
Kinestasis 60 (doc. short) PYRAMID FILMS

GART, JOHN
1952
Log Jam (short) RKO PATHÉ
1953
Where the Heart Is (short) WILDING

GARY, ELEANOR
1970
Love Is a Carousel ROMA PRODS.

GATES, CRAWFORD
1956
It's the Ward Teachers (short) BRIGHAM YOUNG U.
How Near to the Angels BRIGHAM YOUNG U.
1957
Feed My Sheep (short) BRIGHAM YOUNG U.

GATES, DAVID
1967
Journey to Shiloh UNIV

GAY, B.
1915
A Fool There Was FOX

GEESIN, RON
Shorts (STEVE DWOSKIN)
1961
Asleep
1963
Alone
Chinese Checkers
1968
Take Me (with Dwoskin)

GELLER, HARRY
1949
Creation (doc. short) HERMAN BOXER
[Also worked as an arranger.]

GEORGE, EARL
1956
Eye of an Artist (doc. short) INT'L. FILM BUREAU

GERENS, ALEXANDER
1950
Korea Patrol UA
1954
The Fast and the Furious AIP

GERSCHEFSKI, EDWIN
1940
Tarantella MARY ELLEN BUTE

GERSHWIN, GEORGE
1931
Delicious ("Rhapsody in Rivets") FOX
1937
Shall We Dance ("Walking the Dog") (see N. Shilkret)

GERSTENBERGER, EMIL
1930
Man Trouble (see R. Bassett)
Scotland Yard (see Arthur Kay)
Renegades (see Arthur Kay)
1932
Down to Earth (mt) FOX
1934
Judge Priest (see Kaylin)
1935
Our Little Girl (see Brunelli)
1936
Craig's Wife (see R. Bassett)
Can This Be Dixie? (see Kaylin)
[Also a prolific orchestrator.]

GERTZ, IRVING
1946
The Devil's Mask (see Duning)
1947
The Lone Wolf in Mexico (with M. Bakaleinikoff; + stock) COL
Cigarette Girl (with Kilfeather; mt: L. Murphy; + stock) COL
Over the Santa Fe Trail (+ stock) COL
The Millerson Case (+ stock) COL
The Son of Rusty (with C. Wheeler, M. Bakaleinikoff; + stock) COL
Dragnet SG
The Last of the Redmen (+ stock) COL
Smoky River Serenade (see M. Bakaleinikoff)
Bulldog Drummond Strikes Back (+ stock) COL
The Lone Wolf in London (+ stock) COL
Sweet Genevieve (mt: L. Murphy; + stock) COL
1948
Blonde Ice FC
The Counterfeiters TCF
Jungle Goddess SG
Adventures of Gallant Bess EL
1949
Prejudice PFC
Daughter of the West FC
1950
Again—Pioneers! PFC
Destination Murder RKO
Experiment Alcatraz RKO
1951
Skipalong Rosenbloom UA
Two Dollar Bettor REALART
1953
I Beheld His Glory CATHEDRAL
Bandits of Corsica UA
White Goddess LIP
East of Sumatra (see H. Stein)
Gun Belt UA
Eyes of the Jungle LIP
It Came from Outer Space (see Mancini)
The Golden Blade (see H. Stein)
Shark River UA
1954
Overland Pacific UA
The Lone Gun UA
Francis Joins the WACs (with F. Skinner, Mancini) UNIV
Khyber Patrol UA
1955
Smoke Signal (see Lava)
Abbott and Costello Meet the Mummy (see Maury)
Cult of the Cobra (see Lava)
The Man from Bitter Ridge (with Lava, Mancini) UNIV
Kentucky Rifle HOWCO
Francis in the Navy (see Lava)
To Hell and Back (see Lava)
Top Gun UA
1956
A Day of Fury (with Mancini; mt: H. Stein; + stock) UNIV
Creature Walks Among Us (see Mancini)
Congo Crossing (see Mancini)
Raw Edge (with Lava; ac: Salter) UNIV
The First Traveling Saleslady RKO

Gun Brothers UA
Everything but the Truth (see H. Stein)
Gun for a Coward (see F. Skinner)
Four Girls in Town (see North)
Istanbul (with Roemheld; ac: F. Skinner) UNIV

1957
The Incredible Shrinking Man (with Salter, E. Lawrence, H. Stein) UNIV
The Deadly Mantis (with Lava) UNIV
Joe Butterfly (see Mancini)
Badlands of Montana TCF
Joe Dakota (see Salter)
The Kettles on Old MacDonald's Farm (see Mancini)
Hell on Devil's Island TCF
Hell Canyon Outlaws REP
Jonah and the Highway (short) JSP
The Monolith Monsters (ac: Mancini, H. Stein) UNIV
Plunder Road TCF
Love Slaves of the Amazon (see S. Wilson)

1958
Thundering Jets TCF
Girls on the Loose (see Vars)
Live Fast, Die Young (see S. Wilson)
Wild Heritage (see Vars)
Badman's Country WB
The Fearmakers UA
Money, Women and Guns (see H. Stein)

1959
No Name on the Bullet (see H. Stein)
Curse of the Undead UNIV
The Alligator People TCF
Hound Dog Man (see Mockridge)
The Leech Woman (with Vars, Salter) UNIV

1960
Hell Bent for Leather (with Lava) UNIV
13 Fighting Men TCF
Young Jesse James TCF
Seven Ways from Sundown (with Lava) UNIV
North to Alaska (see Mockridge)
The Wizard of Baghdad TCF
Flaming Star (see Mockridge)

1961
All Hands on Deck (see Mockridge)
The Fiercest Heart TCF
Marines, Let's Go! (with Lava; ac: Morton) TCF

1962
Brushfire! PAR

1963
He Rides Tall UNIV

1964
Fluffy UNIV

1966
Daffy Rents (cartoon) WB

1968
Nobody's Perfect (o: Barker) UNIV

GIANNINI, VITTORIO

1942
High Over the Borders (doc. short) IRVING JACOBY

GIGAGUSKY, IGOR

1966
Suburbia Confidential SCA

1967
Bachelor's Dream SCA
Motel Confidential SCA

1968
Office Love-In, White Collar Style SCA

GILBERT, HENRY F.

1922
Down to the Sea in Ships HODKINSON

GILBERT, HERSCHEL BURKE

1946
The Secret of the Whistler (ac: M. Bakaleinikoff; + stock) COL

1947
Mr. District Attorney (o: Sheets) COL

1948
Open Secret (o: Mullendore, Sheets) EL

1949
An Old Fashioned Girl (o: Mullendore, Sheets) EL
Shamrock Hill EL
There's a Girl in My Heart (o: Cadkin, Mullendore, Sheets) AA

1950
The Jackie Robinson Story (o: Mullendore, Sheets) EL
Three Husbands (o: Mullendore, Sheets) UA

1951
The Scarf (o: Mullendore, Sheets) UA
The Highwayman (o: Mullendore, Sheets) AA
The Magic Face (o: Mullendore, Sheets) COL

1952
Without Warning (o: Mullendore, L. Morton) UA
Kid Monk Baroni (o: Mullendore, Sheets) REALART

Models, Inc. (ac: Mullendore, Sheets) MUTUAL
The Ring (o: Mullendore, Sheets) UA
The Thief (o: Sheets, L. Morton; ac and o: Mullendore) UA
No Time for Flowers RKO
1953
The Moon Is Blue (o: Mullendore) UA
Vice Squad (o: Mullendore) UA
Sabre Jet UA
Project Moon Base (o: Mullendore) LIP
1954
Riot in Cell Block 11 (o: Mullendore) AA
Witness to Murder (o: Mullendore) UA
Carmen Jones (based on music of Bizet) TCF
1955
Naked Dawn UNIV
1956
Comanche UA
The Bold and the Brave (o: Mullendore, Sheets) RKO
While the City Sleeps (o: Mullendore, Sheets) RKO
Nightmare UA
The Naked Hills AA
Beyond a Reasonable Doubt RKO
No Place to Hide (ac: Mullendore; o: Sheets) AA
1957
Slaughter on Tenth Avenue UNIV
1959
Crime and Punishment, U.S.A. (o: E. Hughes) AA
1962
Geronimo (see Friedhofer)
1969
Sam Whiskey UA
1970
The Secret of the Sacred Forest (o: E. Hughes) SHERMART

GILBERT, RALPH
1953
Dance in the Sun (short) SHIRLEY CLARKE

GILLETTE, PAUL J.
1963
Goldilocks and the Three Bares DORE
1965
Sylvia's Girls CENTRAL

GILLIS, DON
1957
No Teacher Alone (doc. short) NEA

GILSON, PAUL
1955
Belgium—Where the Past Meets the Present (doc. short; with Legley) ERNEST KLEINBERG

GIRVIN, RICHARD
1951
Macbeth BOB JONES U.
1952
Pound of Flesh (short) BOB JONES U.

GIUFFRE, JIMMY
1964
Smiles (short) JOHN G. AVILDSEN
1967
Sighet, Sighet (short) HAROLD BECKER
1969
Discovery in a Landscape (doc. short) LEO HURWITZ
1970
This Island (short) LEO HURWITZ

GLANVILLE-HICKS, PEGGY
1949
Tulsa (doc. short) U.S. STATE DEPT.
1950
Tel (an. short) FILM GRAPHICS
1956
All Our Children (doc.) UNITED NATIONS
1960
A Scary Time (an. doc. short) UNITED NATIONS

GLASS, PAUL
1957
The Abductors TCF
1960
George Grosz' Interregnum (short) EDUCATIONAL COMMUNICATIONS
1961
Fear No More SUTTON
1963
Lady in a Cage PAR
1964
Nightmare in the Sun ZODIAC
1965
Bunny Lake Is Missing COL
1969
A Test of Violence (short) SAWBUCK PRODS.

GLASS, PHILIP
1968
Railroaded (short) MORNINGSIDE

GLASSER, ALBERT

1941
Under Fiesta Stars (see M. Glickman)

1943
Klondike Kate COL

1944
The Negro Soldier (doc.; see Tiomkin)
The Monster Maker PRC
The Contender PRC
Call of the Jungle MON

1945
The Kid Sister PRC
The Cisco Kid Returns MON
The Cisco Kid in Old New Mexico MON
Her Highness and the Bellboy (see Stoll)

1946
Abilene Town (see Terr)

1947
Law of the Lash PRC
Border Feud PRC
Killer at Large PRC
Philo Vance Returns PRC
The Gas House Kids in Hollywood PRC
Where the North Begins SG
Trail of the Mounties SG

1948
The Cobra Strikes EL
Assigned to Danger EL
In This Corner EL
Urubu (doc.) UA
The Return of Wildfire SG
Behind Locked Doors EL
Last of the Wild Horses SG

1949
Valiant Hombre UA
I Shot Jesse James SG
The Gay Amigo UA
Omoo-Omoo, the Shark God SG
The Daring Caballero UA
Grand Canyon SG
Satan's Cradle UA
Treasure of Monte Cristo SG
Apache Chief LIP
Tough Assignment LIP
Showdown at Sunup (short) LIP
The White Phantom (short) LIP

1950
Hollywood Varieties LIP
The Girl from San Lorenzo UA
Western Pacific Agent LIP
Everybody's Dancin' LIP
Gunfire LIP
I Shot Billy the Kid LIP
Train to Tombstone LIP
Border Rangers LIP
Bandit Queen LIP

1951
Three Desperate Men LIP
Tokyo File 212 RKO
The Bushwhackers REALART

1952
Geisha Girl REALART
Oriental Evil CLASSIC
Paradise for Buster (short) WILDING
Invasion, U.S.A. COL
Port Sinister RKO

1953
Problem Girls COL
The Neanderthal Man UA
Man of Conflict ATLAS
Dragon's Gold UA
Paris Model COL
Captain John Smith and Pocahontas UA

1955
Murder Is My Beat AA
Top of the World UA

1956
Please Murder Me! DCA
Indestructible Man AA
Huk! UA
The Boss UA
Flight to Hong Kong UA

1957
Four Boys and a Gun UA
Monster from Green Hell DCA
The Big Caper UA
The Buckskin Lady UA
Bail Out at 43,000 UA
Street of Sinners UA
Valerie UA
Destination 60,000 AA
Beginning of the End REP
The Cyclops AA
Cop Hater UA
The Amazing Colossal Man AIP
The Hired Gun MGM
Motorcycle Gang AIP
Girl in the Woods REP

1958
Viking Women and the Sea Serpent AIP
Giant from the Unknown ASTOR
Snowfire AA
High School Confidential MGM
War of the Colossal Beast AIP
Attack of the Puppet People AIP
Teenage Caveman AIP
Earth vs. the Spider AIP
When Hell Broke Loose PAR

The Mugger UA
Oklahoma Territory UA

1959
Night of the Quarter Moon MGM
The Beat Generation MGM
Inside the Mafia UA
What It Takes (doc. short) WILDING

1960
The Boy and the Pirates UA
The High-Powered Rifle TCF
Kipling's Women (with Bruce Locke) KROGER BABB
Tormented (additional modern jazz sequences: C. Jackson) AA
Talent for Disaster (doc. short) GEO. FOX CORP.

1961
20,000 Eyes TCF

1962
Confessions of an Opium Eater AA
Air Patrol TCF

1963
Girlsapoppin FAVORITE

1964
Lecoque (doc. short) HENRY TRAVELL

1966
Magnificence in Trust (doc.) U.S. DEPT. OF THE INTERIOR

GLAZER, TOM

1957
A Face in the Crowd WB

GLICKMAN, LOREN

1963
The Doughnuts (short) WESTON WOODS

1964
This Is Venice (short) WESTON WOODS

GLICKMAN, MORT

1940
Mysterious Doctor Satan (serial) REP
Behind the News REP
Bowery Boy REP

1941
Adventures of Captain Marvel (serial; with DiMaggio) REP
Angels with Broken Wings REP
Bad Man of Deadwood REP
Country Fair REP
The Devil Pays Off REP
Doctors Don't Tell REP
Down Mexico Way REP
Jungle Girl (serial) REP
Lady from Louisiana REP
A Man Betrayed REP
Mountain Moonlight REP
Mountain Rhythm REP
Puddin' Head (see W. Scharf)
Rags to Riches REP
Ridin' on a Rainbow REP
Robin Hood of the Pecos (+ stock) REP
Rookies on Parade REP
Sis Hopkins (see W. Scharf)
Tuxedo Junction REP
Under Fiesta Stars (with Calker, Erdody, Glasser, Skiles; + stock) REP

1942
Bells of Capistrano REP
Heart of the Golden West REP
Hi, Neighbor! REP
Joan of Ozark REP
King of the Mounties (serial) REP
The Old Homestead REP
Outlaws of Pine Ridge REP
Pardon My Stripes REP
Perils of Nyoka (serial) REP
Remember Pearl Harbor! REP
Secrets of the Underground (see W. Scharf)
Shadows on the Sage REP
Shepherd of the Ozarks REP
Sleepytime Gal REP
The Sombrero Kid REP
South of Santa Fe REP
Spy Smasher REP
The Sundown Kid REP
The Traitor Within REP
Valley of Hunted Men REP
Yokel Boy REP

1943
Beyond the Last Frontier REP
The Black Hills Express REP
The Blocked Trail REP
Bordertown Gun Fighters REP
California Joe REP
Calling Wild Bill Elliott REP
Canyon City REP
Captain America (serial) REP
Carson City Cyclone REP
Daredevils of the West (serial) REP
Days of Old Cheyenne REP
Dead Man's Gulch REP
Death Valley Manhunt REP
Fugitive from Sonora REP
G-Men vs. the Black Dragon (serial) REP
Hands Across the Border (with Skiles) REP
Headin' for God's Country REP

Hoosier Holiday REP
In Old Oklahoma (see W. Scharf)
King of the Cowboys REP
The Man from the Rio Grande REP
The Man from Thunder River REP
The Mantrap REP
The Masked Marvel (serial) REP
Minesweeper PAR
Mystery Broadcast REP
Overland Mail Robbery REP
Pride of the Plains REP
The Purple V REP
Raiders of Sunset Pass REP
Riders of the Rio Grande REP
Santa Fe Scouts REP
A Scream in the Dark REP
Secret Service in Darkest Africa (serial) REP
Song of Texas (with Skiles) REP
Swing Your Partner REP
Thundering Trails REP
Wagon Tracks West REP
The West Side Kid REP
Whispering Footsteps REP

1944

Beneath Western Skies REP
Cowboy and the Senorita (see Skiles)
The Fighting Seabees (see W. Scharf)
Forty Thieves (see Leipold)
Gambler's Choice PAR
Hidden Valley Outlaws REP
The Laramie Trail REP
Lights of Old Santa Fe (see Butts)
Machine Gun Mama PRC
Mojave Firebrand REP
Outlaws of Santa Fe REP
San Fernando Valley REP
Sensations of 1945 (see Merrick)
Song of Nevada REP
Tahiti Nights (with Duning) COL
Tucson Raiders (ac: Van Loan, Dubin; + stock) REP

1945

Bells of Rosarita (see Maxwell)
The Big Bonanza REP
Dakota (see Scharf)
Don't Fence Me In (see Butts)
Flame of Barbary Coast (see Butts)
Gangs of the Waterfront REP
Lone Texas Ranger (+ stock) REP
Man from Oklahoma (see Butts)
Manhunt of Mystery Island (serial) REP
The Phantom Rider (serial) REP
Sunset in El Dorado (see Butts)
Utah (see Butts)

1946

Along the Navajo Trail REP
The Crimson Ghost (serial) REP
Daughter of Don Q REP
Home on the Range (see Butts)
The Inner Circle REP
The Invisible Informer REP
King of the Forest Rangers (serial; + stock) REP
Lone Star Moonlight (ac: M. Bakaleinikoff; + stock) COL
The Magnificent Rogue (see N. Scott)
Man from Rainbow Valley REP
Murder in the Music Hall (see W. Scharf)
The Mysterious Mr. Valentine REP
Night Train to Memphis (see Butts)
Passkey to Danger REP
The Pilgrim Lady (see Butts)
Red River Renegades (+ stock) REP
Rio Grande Raiders REP
Santa Fe Uprising REP
Song of Arizona (see Butts)
Stagecoach to Denver REP
Traffic in Crime REP
Under Nevada Skies (with Butts) REP

1947

Along the Oregon Trail REP
The Black Widow (serial) REP
Blackmail REP
G-Men Never Forget (serial) REP
Homesteaders of Paradise Valley REP
Jesse James Rides Again (serial; + stock) REP
Last Frontier Uprising REP
Marshal of Cripple Creek REP
On the Old Spanish Trail REP
Oregon Trail Scouts REP
Robin Hood of Texas (see N. Scott)
Rustlers of Devil's Canyon REP
Saddle Pals REP
Son of Zorro (serial) REP
Spoilers of the North REP
Springtime in the Sierras REP
Trail to San Antone (with Arnaud, Perkins) REP
The Trespasser REP
Under Colorado Skies REP
Vigilantes of Boomtown REP
Web of Danger REP
The Wild Frontier REP

1948

Bandits of Dark Canyon REP

The Bold Frontiersman REP
California Firebrand REP
Carson City Raiders REP
Dangers of the Canadian Mounted (serial) REP
The Gallant Legion REP
King of the Gamblers REP
Lightnin' in the Forest REP
Madonna of the Desert REP
Oklahoma Badlands REP
Slippy McGee REP
The Timber Trail REP
Under California Stars REP

[For the following films, see Kraushaar and the note at the beginning of his filmography.]

1950
Prehistoric Women
You Can Beat the A-Bomb (doc. short)

1951
Bride of the Gorilla
Galahad Jones
Elephant Stampede
The Longhorn
The Sword of Monte Cristo

1952
Bomba and the Jungle Girl
Fargo
The Maverick
Rose of Cimarron
Untamed Women
Waco

1953
Invaders from Mars

GLOVER, HENRY

1949
Souls of Sin (with S. Churchill, William Greaves) WILLIAM ALEXANDER

1961
Hey, Let's Twist! PAR

1962
Two Tickets to Paris COL

GLOVER, JOE

1936
Can This Be Dixie? (see Kaylin)

1938
Walking Down Broadway TCF

[Also worked as an orchestrator.]

GOBERMAN, MAX

19??
Builders of a Nation (doc. short) HISTADRUT

GOETZL, ANSELM

1919
Deliverance KLEINE

GOHMAN, DON

1962
Wonders of Philadelphia (doc. short) COL
Wonders of Dallas (doc. short) COL

GOLD, ERNEST

1945
The Girl of the Limberlost COL

1946
The Falcon's Alibi (m&e: Sawtell; + stock) RKO
Smooth as Silk UNIV
G. I. War Brides REP

1947
Lighthouse PRC
Wyoming (see N. Scott)
Exposed REP

1948
Old Los Angeles REP

1951
Unknown World LIP

1953
Jennifer AA
Man Crazy TCF

1954
Karamoja (doc.) HALLMARK
The Other Woman TCF

1955
The Naked Street UA
Tender Hearts HUGO HAAS

1956
Unidentified Flying Objects (doc.) UA
Edge of Hell UNIV
Running Target UA

1957
Affair in Havana AA
Man on the Prowl UA

1958
Too Much, Too Soon WB
Wink of an Eye UA
Tarzan's Fight for Life MGM
The Defiant Ones (o: J. Marshall) UA
The Screaming Skull AIP

1959
The Young Philadelphians WB
Battle of the Coral Sea COL
On the Beach UA

1960
Inherit the Wind UA
Exodus (o: Schürmann) UA

1961
A Fever in the Blood WB
The Last Sunset UNIV
Judgment at Nuremberg UA
1962
Pressure Point UA
A Child Is Waiting UA
1963
It's a Mad, Mad, Mad, Mad World (o: E. Powell) UA
1965
Ship of Fools COL
1969
The Secret of Santa Vittoria UA
Shorts
1948
Picnic CURTIS HARRINGTON
Architecture of Frank Lloyd Wright ERVEN JOURDAN
1953
Thc Assignation CURTIS HARRINGTON
1957
The True Story of the Civil War CAMERA EYE FILMS
Cartoons (UPA)
1951
Family Circus
Georgie and the Dragon
1952
Willie the Kid
1953
Gerald McBoing Boing's Symphony
Magoo Slept Here
1956
Gerald McBoing Boing on Planet Moo

GOLDENBERG, WILLIAM (BILLY)
1969
Change of Habit UNIV
1970
The Grasshopper NG

GOLDFADEN, ABRAHAM
1931
Shulamith (Yiddish language) JUDEA FILMS
The Voice of Israel (doc.; Yiddish language) JUDEA FILMS

GOLDMAN, MAURICE
1946
Lady in the Lake (see Snell)
1958
Wild Heritage (see Vars)

GOLDMAN, PETER EMANUEL
1965
Pestilent City (short) P.E. GOLDMAN

GOLDSMITH, JERRY
1957
Black Patch WB
1959
City of Fear COL
Face of a Fugitive COL
1960
Studs Lonigan UA
Flaming Star (see Mockridge)
1962
Lonely Are the Brave UNIV
The General with the Cockeyed Id (doc. short) JSP
The Spiral Road UNIV
Freud UNIV
1963
The Stripper TCF
The List of Adrian Messenger UNIV
A Gathering of Eagles UNIV
Lilies of the Field UA
The Prize (o: A. Morton, Tamkin, Shuken, Hayes) MGM
Take Her, She's Mine (o: A. Morton) TCF
1964
Seven Days in May PAR
Shock Treatment TCF
Fate Is the Hunter (o: Barker) TCF
Rio Conchos (o: A. Morton) TCF
1965
The Satan Bug (o: A. Morton) UA
In Harm's Way PAR
Von Ryan's Express (o: A. Morton) TCF
Morituri (o: A. Morton) TCF
The Artist Who Did Not Want to Paint (doc. short) TCF
A Patch of Blue MGM
Our Man Flint (o: A. Morton) TCF
1966
The Trouble with Angels (o: A. Morton) COL
Stagecoach (o: Morton) TCF
The Blue Max TCF
Seconds (o: A. Morton) PAR
The Sand Pebbles (o: Tamkin, A. Morton) TCF
Warning Shot PAR
1967
In Like Flint (o: A. Morton) TCF
The Flim-Flam Man (o: A. Morton) TCF

Hour of the Gun UA
Sebastian PAR
Planet of the Apes (o: A. Morton) TCF

1968

The Detective (o: Barker) TCF
Bandolero! (o: H. Spencer) TCF
100 Rifles (o: Tamkin) TCF

1969

The Illustrated Man WB
The Chairman TCF
Justine (o: A. Morton) TCF
Patton (o: A. Morton) TCF

1970

The Ballad of Cable Hogue (o: A. Morton) WB
Tora! Tora! Tora! (o: A. Morton, Courage) TCF
The Traveling Executioner (o: A. Morton) MGM
Rio Lobo NG

GOLSON, BENNY

1959

Stop Driving Us Crazy (an. short) METHODIST CHURCH

1966

Ski Fascination (doc.) ?

1969

Where It's At UA

GOMEZ, VICENTE

1941

Blood and Sand (see A. Newman)

1952

The Fighter UA

1956

Goya (short) ARTEMIS PRODS.

GONZALES, AARON

1939

Behind the Cup (doc. short) HILLS BROS. COFFEE

GOODELL, WALTER J.

1920

The Gamesters (see Eames)
The Blue Moon (see Eames)

GOODWIN, DOUG

Cartoons (UA)

1969

The Ant and the Aardvark
The Ant from U.N.C.L.E.
The Deadwood Thunderball
Dune Bug
Extinct Pink
Hasty But Tasty
Isle of Caprice
I've Got Ants in My Plans
Mumbo Jumbo
Never Bug an Ant
A Pair of Sneakers
Sweet and Sourdough
Technology, Phooey
Tijuana Toads

1970

Ants in the Pantry
Don't Hustle an Ant with Muscle
The Froggy Froggo Duo
Odd Ant Out
Robin Goodhood
Science Friction
Scratch a Tiger

GOOSSENS, EUGENE

1944

The Cowboy (doc. short) OWI

GORGONI, AL

1964

Before It's Too Late (doc. short) AT&T

1970

I Never Sang for My Father (with B. Mann) COL

GOTTLIEB, JACK S.

1967

Golden Gate ?

GOTTSCHALK, LOUIS F.

1914

The Patchwork Girl of Oz OZ FILM CO.
The Magic Cloak of Oz OZ FILM CO.
His Majesty, the Scarecrow of Oz OZ FILM CO.
The Last Egyptian OZ FILM CO.

1916

The Despoilers TRIANGLE
Honor's Altar TRIANGLE

1917

The Curse of Eve CORONA

1918

Old Wives for New FPL
The Great Love GRIFFITH

1919

Broken Blossoms GRIFFITH
The Fall of Babylon GRIFFITH
The Mother and the Law GRIFFITH

1920
A Splendid Hazard FN
1921
The Four Horsemen of the Apocalypse (other scores by Axt, Luz, and Riesenfeld) METRO
The Three Musketeers UA
Little Lord Fauntleroy UA
Orphans of the Storm (with Peters) GRIFFITH
1922
Shadows LICHTMAN
1923
Rosita UA
A Woman of Paris UA
1924
Romola METRO-GOLDWYN
1929
The Rainbow Man PAR
1930
The Birth of a Nation (see Breil, 1915)

GOULD, GLEN
1966
Poetry of Polymers (doc. short) WAYNE STATE U.

GOULD, MORTON
1942
Ring of Steel (doc. short) OWI
1945
Delightfully Dangerous UA
1946
San Francisco Conference (doc. short) OWI
1955
Cinerama Holiday (doc.; ac: Van Cleave) LOUIS DE ROCHEMENT
1958
Windjammer (doc.; o: Cutner) LOUIS DE ROCHEMENT

GOULD, STEPHEN M.
Documentary Shorts (IFF)
1967
Children of Israel
1968
The Russian Consumer
Women of Russia

GOULDING, EDMUND
1930
The Devil's Holiday (a: H. Jackson, Leipold) PAR
1931
The Night Angel (with Duke, Tours) PAR

GRANELLI, JERRY
1967
Jim the Man MAX KATZ

GRANT, RON E.
1969
The Activist (+ stock) REGIONAL

GRAU, GILBERT
1941
The Lady Eve (see Shuken)
1943
Redhead from Manhattan (with Leipold) COL
Mardi Gras (short; see Leipold)
Let's Face It (see Dolan)
Rookies in Burma RKO
1944
You Can't Ration Love (see Heymann)
Halfway to Heaven (short; see Schrager)
The National Barn Dance (see Schrager)
[Also a prolific orchestrator.]

GRAY, JAN
1944
Lady in the Death House PRC

GREELEY, GEORGE
1950
Beyond the Purple Hills (+ stock) COL
1951
A Watch for Joe HAL R. MAKELIM PRODS.
1956
The Peacemaker UA
1957
The Guns of Fort Petticoat (see M. Bakaleinikoff)
Hellcats of the Navy (see M. Bakaleinikoff)
No Time to Be Young (see M. Bakaleinikoff)

GREEN, BERNARD
1961
Everything's Ducky COL
1962
Zotz! COL
30 Years of Fun (compilation film; with Shaindlin; o: B. Green, Weinstein) TCF
1963
The Brass Bottle UNIV
All the Way Home PAR

The Big Parade of Comedy (compilation film) MGM
1965
Sunflower (cartoon; see Pintoff)
Harvey Middleman, Fireman (see Pintoff)

GREEN, JOHN (JOHNNY)
1930
The Sap from Syracuse (with Duke) PAR
1931
Honor Among Lovers (with Duke) PAR
The Girl Habit PAR
Secrets of a Secretary (with Duke) PAR
My Sin (with Tours) PAR
1932
Wayward PAR
The Wiser Sex PAR
The Misleading Lady PAR
1943
You, John Jones (short; with N. Shilkret) MGM
Pilot #5 (see Hayton)
1944
Broadway Rhythm (ac and o: Duncan) MGM
Bathing Beauty (with Amfitheatrof; ac: Skiles, D. Raksin) MGM
1945
Week-End at the Waldorf (o: Duncan; ac: R. Franklyn, Cutner, Amfitheatrof) MGM
The Sailor Takes a Wife (ac: R. Franklyn, Cutner) MGM
1946
Easy to Wed (ac: R. Franklyn, Duncan) MGM
1947
It Happened in Brooklyn (o: Duncan, R. Franklyn) MGM
Fiesta (o: Duncan; ac and o: Sendrey) MGM
Something in the Wind (o: Duncan) UNIV
1948
Up in Central Park (o: Duncan) UNIV
1949
The Inspector General WB
1951
Royal Wedding (see Sendrey)
The Great Caruso (o: Sendrey, Salinger, Cutner) MGM
An American in Paris (see Salinger)
1952
Because You're Mine (o: Sendrey, Cutner, Shuken) MGM
1953
All the Brothers Were Valiant (see Rozsa)
1954
Brigadoon (see Salinger)
1956
High Society (with Salinger; o: R. Franklyn) MGM
1957
Raintree County (ac: Sendrey, Salinger, Courage, Cutner, R. Franklyn) MGM
1960
Pepe (ac: Courage, Cutner, R. Franklyn, Woodbury) COL
1963
Bye Bye Birdie (o: J. Green, Woodbury) COL
Twilight of Honor MGM
1966
Johnny Tiger UNIV
Alvarez Kelly (o: R. Franklyn) COL
1968
Oliver! COL
1969
They Shoot Horses, Don't They? (o: J. Green, Woodbury) CR

GREEN, PHIL
1953
A Night in Hollywood BROADWAY ROADSHOWS

GREENE, BURTON
1967
Anything for Money DISTRIBPIX
Skin Deep in Love DISTRIBPIX

GREENE, JOE
1962
A Public Affair PARADE
1966
On Her Bed of Roses FAMOUS PLAYERS
Movie Star, American Style FAMOUS PLAYERS
1969
A Boy . . . a Girl JACK HANSON
Childish Things FILMWORLD
The Girl Who Knew Too Much CU
1970
Tiger by the Tail CU

GREENE, RICHARD
1970
Riverrun (with Peter Berg) COL

GREENE, WALTER

1945

Crime, Inc. PRC
Why Girls Leave Home PRC

1946

Danny Boy PRC
Queen of Burlesque PRC
Lady Chaser PRC

1947

Pioneer Justice PRC
Ghost Town Renegades PRC
Hollywood Barn Dance SG
Return of the Lash EL
Black Hills EL
Cheyenne Takes Over EL
The Westward Trail EL
Stage to Mesa City EL
The Fighting Vigilantes EL
Shadow Valley EL
The Hawk of Powder River EL

1948

Check Your Guns EL
Tornado Range EL
Prairie Outlaws (ac for new scenes in reissue of 1946 film *Wild West*) EL
Dead Man's Gold SG
Mark of the Lash SG
Shep Comes Home SG
Frontier Revenge SG
Outlaw Country SG

1949

Son of a Bad Man SG
Son of Billy the Kid SG
Rimfire SG
Ringside SG
The Dalton Gang SG
Square Dance Jubilee SG
Red Desert SG

1950

West of the Brazos LIP
Crooked River LIP
Marshal of Heldorado LIP
Hostile Country LIP
Colorado Ranger LIP
Fast on the Draw LIP
The Daltons' Women REALART
King of the Bullwhip REALART

1951

Kentucky Jubilee LIP
The Thundering Trail REALART
G. I. Jane LIP
Yes Sir, Mr. Bones LIP
Varieties on Parade LIP
The Vanishing Outpost REALART
The Black Lash REALART
The Frontier Phantom REALART
Outlaw Women LIP

1954

Jesse James' Women UA

1956

Frontier Woman EXCLUSIVE
Naked Gun ASSOCIATED

1957

Teenage Thunder HOWCO
Carnival Rock HOWCO
Teenage Doll AA
The Brain from Planet Arous HOWCO
Teenage Monster HOWCO

1958

War of the Satellites AA

1960

Thunder in Carolina HOWCO
Louisiana Hussy HOWCO

1961

Natchez Trace PANORAMA
I Bombed Pearl Harbor PARADE

1962

Twist All Night AIP

Cartoons (UNIVERSAL)

1962

Coming Out Party
Fish and Chips

1963

Greedy Gabby Gator
Science Friction
The Tenant's Racket

1964

The Case of the Elephant's Trunk
Dumb Like a Fox
Fractured Friendship
Lighthouse Keeping Blues
Roof Top Razzle-Dazzle
Saddle-Sore Woody
Ski-Napper
Skinfolks
Three Little Woodpeckers

1965

Astronut Woody
Birds of a Feather
Davey Cricket
Foot Brawl
Guess Who?
Half Baked Alaska
Janie Get Your Gun
Lonesome Ranger
Pesty Guest

Practical Yolk
Snow Place Like Home
Woody and the Beanstalk
1966
Operation Shanghai
Polar Fright
South Pole Pals
Teeny Weeny Meany
Vicious Viking
Window Pains
1967
Chilly and the Woodchopper
Chilly Chums
Hot Time on Ice
Mouse in the House
Secret Agent Woody Woodpecker
1968
Chiller Dillers
Cartoons (WB)
1966
Daffy's Diner
Feather Finger
A Squeak in the Deep
Sugar and Spies
Swing Ding Amigo
A Taste of Catnip
Cartoons (UA)
1966
Genie with the Light Pink Fur
Le Escape Goat
Pink-a-Boo
Pink, Plunk, Plink
Rock a Bye Pinky
That's No Lady—That's Notre Dame
Unsafe and Seine
1967
Bomb Voyage
Canadian Can-Can
In the Pink
Jet Pink
Le Pig-Al Patrol
London Derriere
Pink of the Litter
Pinknic
The Shooting of Caribou Lou
1968
G.I. Pink
Little Beaux Pink
Lucky Pink
Pink in the Clink
Pink Valiant
Pinkadilly Circus
Psychedelic Pink
Put-Put Pink
1969
In the Pink of the Night
Pink-a-Rella
Pink Pest Control
Slink Pink
Think Before You Pink
1970
Pink-In

GRENNELL, DEAN
1966
The Agony of Love BOXOFFICE INT'L

GREVER, MARIA
Shorts (MGM)
1936
Cherry Blossom Time in Japan
1937
Oriental Paradise
Floral Japan

GRIMSON, S. B.
1936
The Alchemist's Hourglass (short) NORTON CO.

GROFÉ, FERDE
1944
Minstrel Man (o: Erdody) PRC
1950
Rocketship X-M (o: Glasser) LIP
The Return of Jesse James LIP

GROMON, FRANCIS
1928
Sal of Singapore (see Zuro)
1929
Geraldine RKO PATHÉ
1930
Sin Takes a Holiday (see Zuro)
1931
The Painted Desert RKO PATHÉ
Lonely Wives RKO PATHÉ
Beyond Victory (see Arthur Alexander)
Born to Love RKO PATHÉ
Marius (French language) PAR
Mistigri (French language) PAR
1938
Barefoot Boy (md) MON

GRON, LEE
1940
And So They Live (doc. short) NEW YORK U.

GROSS, CHARLES
1965
Across the River FRANCHI
1966
The Group UA
Shorts
1964
Commuting for Adventure PAR
1966
The Agent's Secret EL AL ISRAEL AIRLINES
1967
Post No Bills EVERETT AISON

GRUEN, JOHN
1955
The Mechanics of Love (short) WILLARD MAAS
1957
8 × 8 (see Townsend)

GRUENBERG, LOUIS
1940
The Fight for Life (semi-doc.) PARE LORENTZ
1941
So Ends Our Night UA
1942
The Nazis Strike (see Webb)
1943
Commandos Strike at Dawn (o: Nussbaum, Cutner; ac: Leipold) COL
1944
An American Romance (with N. Shilkret; o: Nussbaum, Cutner, Marquardt, Salinger, Glasser) MGM
1945
Counter-Attack COL
1947
The Gangster AA
1948
Arch of Triumph (o: Raab, Nussbaum) UA
Smart Woman AA
1949
All the King's Men (o: Nussbaum; ac: Duning, Skiles) COL
1950
Quicksand UA

GRUNDMAN, CLARE
Documentary Shorts (RKO PATHÉ)
1946
Two Million Rooms
Palmetto Quail
1951
Railroad Special Agent
1952
Men of Science
1954
Dog Scents

GRUSIN, DAVE
1967
Divorce American Style (o: Hazard, Byers) COL
Waterhole #3 PAR
The Graduate EMB
1968
Where Were You When the Lights Went Out? (o: Shuken, Hayes) MGM
A Man Called Gannon UNIV
The Heart Is a Lonely Hunter WB
Candy CR
1969
The Mad Room (o: Hazard) COL
Winning UNIV
Tell Them Willie Boy Is Here UNIV
Generation EMB
1970
Halls of Anger UA
Adam at 6 A.M. NG

GRYCE, GIGI
1963
On the Sound (short) FRED BAKER

GUARALDI, VINCE
1965
San Francisco, San Francisco, San Francisco (doc. short; see Tjader)
1969
A Boy Named Charlie Brown (an.) NG

GUBERNICK, HY
1963
Greenwich Village Story JACK O'CONNELL

GUSTAFSON, DWIGHT L.
1956
Shadow Over Italy (doc. short) BOB JONES U.
1959
Fortress of Faith (doc. short) BOB JONES U.
1963
Red Runs the River BOB JONES U.

GUTERSON, MISCHA
1921
Hail the Woman THOMAS H. INCE
1924
The Siren of Seville PDC
The Lover of Camille WB

GUTMAN, CARL
1923
The Ten Commandments (see Riesenfeld)

GUTTMANN, ARTHUR
[He composed music for many films in Germany, 1929–1934.]
1939
Tumbleweeds (see Bradford)
Bridal Suite (with Amfitheatrof) MGM
1940
I Take This Woman (see Kaper)
1944
Enemy of Women MON

H

HADJIDAKIS, MANOS
1968
Blue (o: Arnaud, Shuken, Hayes) PAR
[Also scores for many Greek films and films produced in Greece.]

HADLEY, HENRY
1926
When a Man Loves WB

HAGEMAN, RICHARD
1938
Men with Wings (see Harling)
If I Were King (ac: Roder; o: Cailliet) PAR
1939
Stagecoach (see Leipold)
Hotel Imperial (o: Cailliet) PAR
Rulers of the Sea (o: Hand, Maxwell) PAR
1940
The Howards of Virginia (o: Cailliet, Hand) COL
The Long Voyage Home UA
1941
This Woman Is Mine UNIV
Paris Calling UNIV
The Shanghai Gesture UA
1946
Angel and the Badman REP
1947
The Fugitive (o: Cailliet) RKO
Mourning Becomes Electra (o: Cailliet) RKO
1948
Fort Apache (o: Cailliet) RKO
3 Godfathers (o: Cailliet) MGM
1949
She Wore a Yellow Ribbon (o: Cailliet) RKO
1950
Wagon Master RKO

HAGEN, EARLE
1948
Sitting Pretty (see A. Newman)
Apartment for Peggy (see D. Raksin)
1949
Oh, You Beautiful Doll (see Mockridge)
1951
On the Riviera (with A. Newman, Mockridge) TCF
1952
Monkey Business (see Harline)
1954
There's No Business Like Show Business (see A. Newman)
1955
The Girl Rush (see Mockridge)
1956
Love Me Tender (see L. Newman)
1957
Spring Reunion (with H. Spencer) UA
1958
Mardi Gras (see L. Newman)
1959
Say One for Me (see Harline)
1960
Let's Make Love (with Mockridge; ac: H. Spencer) TCF
1964
The New Interns (o: A. Morton, Carpenter, Barker) COL
[Also a prolific arranger and orchestrator.]

HAGGH, RAYMOND
1956
Shiloh—Portrait of a Battle (short; with Eaheart) NAT'L PARK SERVICE

HAGUE, ALBERT
1967
The Funniest Man in the World (compilation film) FUNNYMAN, INC.
1968
The Great Stone Face (compilation film) FUNNYMAN, INC.

HAHN, CARL
1917
Hate FAIRMOUNT

HAJOS, KARL
1928
The Good-bye Kiss (see Bierman)
Loves of an Actress PAR
The Night Watch (see Bierman)
Beggars of Life PAR
The Haunted House (see Bergunker)
The Woman from Moscow PAR
Outcast (see Schertzinger)
Adoration (ac: Bergunker, Carbonara; + stock) FN
Scarlet Seas (+ stock) FN
1929
The Wolf of Wall Street PAR
The Canary Murder Case PAR
Homecoming PAR
The Dummy (with Potoker, Bergunker) PAR
Chinatown Nights (with Bergunker; ac: Carbonara; + stock) PAR
A Dangerous Woman (m&e; + stock) PAR
The Studio Murder Mystery (mt) PAR
Thunderbolt (mt) PAR
River of Romance (mt) PAR
Charming Sinners PAR
The Greene Murder Case PAR
Illusion PAR
Woman Trap PAR
The Love Doctor PAR
The Virginian PAR
Darkened Rooms PAR
1930
Slightly Scarlet (ac: Potoker) PAR
The Vagabond King (foreign version; see Leipold)
A Man from Wyoming PAR
The Silent Enemy (see Midgely)
Manslaughter PAR
Grumpy PAR
Anybody's Woman (mt) PAR
The Sea God (foreign version; with Pasternacki, Rainger) PAR
The Spoilers (with Leipold) PAR
Monte Carlo (see Harling)
The Virtuous Sin (mt) PAR
Derelict (mt) PAR
Morocco PAR
The Right to Love (see Harling)
1931
Scandal Sheet PAR
Fighting Caravans (see Leipold)
Rango (with Leipold, Harling, Hand; ac: Carbonara, Bergunker, Krumgold, G. Steiner) PAR
Unfaithful PAR
Dishonored PAR
City Streets (with Rainger) PAR
Ladies' Man (see Hand)
The Magnificent Lie (see Leipold)
Gente Alegre (Spanish language; see Leipold)
Once a Lady (see Kopp)
1933
Tonight Is Ours (with Leipold; ac: Marquardt; + stock) PAR
A Bedtime Story (see Rainger)
Supernatural (with H. Jackson, Roder) PAR
The Story of Temple Drake (see Kaun)
I Love That Man (see Kaun)
Jennie Gerhardt (see Leipold)
The Song of Songs (with Kaun, Roder, Hand) PAR
White Woman (ac: Leipold) PAR
The Thundering Herd (m&e; + stock) PAR
Girl Without a Room (with H. Jackson) PAR
1934
Eight Girls in a Boat (see H. Lewis)
All of Me PAR
Four Frightened People (with Roemheld, Leipold, Roder) PAR
1935
Werewolf of London (+ stock) UNIV
Manhattan Moon UNIV
She Gets Her Man UNIV
Last of the Pagans (see Axt)
1936
Happy Go Lucky (+ stock) REP
1937
The Bold Caballero REP
Two Wise Maids REP

Circus Girl (with Riesenfeld; + stock) REP
The Painted Stallion (serial; + stock) REP

1943
Hitler's Madman (see N. Shilkret)

1944
Charlie Chan in the Secret Service MON
The Sultan's Daughter MON
Summer Storm UA

1945
Fog Island PRC
The Man Who Walked Alone PRC
The Phantom of 42nd Street PRC
The Missing Corpse PRC
Shadow of Terror PRC
Dangerous Intruder (o: Bernie) PRC

1946
The Mask of Diijon PRC
Colorado Serenade PRC
The Caravan Trail PRC
Down Missouri Way (o: W. Greene) PRC
Secrets of a Sorority Girl PRC
Driftin' River (o: W. Greene) PRC
Tumbleweed Trail PRC
Stars Over Texas PRC
Wild West (o: W. Greene) PRC

1947
Wild Country (o: W. Greene) PRC
Range Beyond the Blue PRC
West to Glory (o: W. Greene) PRC

1948
Appointment with Murder FC
The Daring Miss Jones PINNACLE

1949
Search for Danger FC
The Lovable Cheat FC
Call of the Forest LIP

1950
Kill or Be Killed (themes: Jurmann) EL
It's a Small World EL

HALL, BETTY
1970
Her and She and Him AUDUBON FILMS

HALLIGAN, RICHARD
1970
The Owl and the Pussycat COL

HALLSTROM, HENRY
1955
The Oresteia of Aeschylus RANDOLPH-MACON WOMAN'S COLLEGE

HALPER, JONATHAN
1949
Puce Moment (short) KENNETH ANGER

HAMBRO, LENNY
1970
Dirtymouth (see Vardi)

HAMES, BILL
1966
Bad Girls for the Boys (with Tarwater) SACK

HAMILTON, FOREST (CHICO)
1961
Litho (doc. short) ELEKTRA

1967
Peacemeal (doc. short) ALBERT ALLOTTA

1970
How to Succeed with Sex (with Bonniwell) MEDFORD

HAMILTON, FRANK
1954
A Time Out of War (short) CARNIVAL

1967
Surfers (short) FLEETWOOD

HAMILTON, WADE
1947
The Greatest Treasure (short) NORRIS EWING

1957
Guarded Treasure (short) NORRIS EWING

HAMLISCH, MARVIN
1968
The Swimmer (o: Shuken, Hayes) COL

1969
The April Fools NG
Take the Money and Run (o: Levinsky) CR

1970
Flap WB
Move (o: Shuken, Hayes, R. Burns) TCF

HAMMOND, JOHN PAUL
1970
Little Big Man NG

HANAGAN, LOU
1970
Happy Birthday, Davy ZENITH

HAND, HERMAN
1921
The Birth of a Nation (see Breil, 1915)
1928
The Night Watch (see Bierman)
1929
Wolf Song (see Carbonara)
1930
Young Eagles (see Leipold)
The Vagabond King (see Leipold)
Monte Carlo (see Harling)
Her Wedding Night (with Pasternacki) PAR
1931
Fighting Caravans (see Leipold)
Rango (see Hajos)
Man of the World PAR
Ladies' Man (ac: Leipold, Hajos) PAR
Gente Alegre (see Leipold)
Once a Lady (see R. Kopp)
Rich Man's Folly (see Leipold)
The False Madonna (see Leipold)
1932
Dr. Jekyll and Mr. Hyde (m&e, based on music of Bach) PAR
Tomorrow and Tomorrow (with R. Kopp, Leipold) PAR
The Miracle Man (see Harling)
The World and the Flesh (with Leipold, Pasternacki) PAR
Forgotten Commandments (with R. Kopp; ac: Kaun, Leipold [m&e], Bergunker, Krumgold) PAR
The Man from Yesterday (see Leipold)
Devil and the Deep (with R. Kopp, Leipold) PAR
Under-Cover Man (mt; et: Leipold; + stock) PAR
1933
A Farewell to Arms (see Harling)
King of the Jungle (with Leipold, R. Kopp) PAR
Terror Aboard (et with Leipold; + stock) PAR
The Song of Songs (see Hajos)
I'm No Angel (see H. Jackson)
Hell and High Water (mt; et: H. Jackson) PAR
Lone Cowboy PAR
1934
The Last Round-Up (+ stock) PAR
Here Comes the Groom (mt: Leipold) PAR
1935
The Lives of a Bengal Lancer (see Roemheld)
The Devil Is a Woman (see Leipold)
The Crusades (see Kopp)
[Also active as an orchestrator.]

HANDY, JOHN, III
1967
Poem Posters (short) CHARLES HENRI FORD

HANKS, FREDERICK O.
1917
The Barrier (see S. Levy)
The Bar Sinister (see S. Levy)

HANSON, HOWARD
1938
Highlights and Shadows (doc; with B. Rogers, B. Phillips, Barlow) EASTMAN KODAK

HANSON, JO
1965
One Way Wahine UNITED SCREEN ARTS

HANSON, ROBERT
1961
Autumn (short) U. OF IOWA

HARLAN, PHILIP
1955
The Wormwood Star (short; with Leona Wood) CURTIS HARRINGTON

HARLINE, LEIGH
1937
Snow White and the Seven Dwarfs (an.; with Churchill, P. Smith) WDP
1938
Blondie (+ stock) COL
There's That Woman Again COL
1939
Blondie Meets the Boss COL
The Lady and the Mob (see Bradshaw)
Good Girls Go to Paris (mt) COL
Beware Spooks! (m&e; + stock) COL
Blondie Brings Up Baby (with Stone, Bassman) COL
1940
Pinocchio (an.; with P. Smith; ac: Plumb; o: Stark, Wolcott) WDP
Blondie on a Budget (+ stock) COL
Blondie Has Servant Trouble COL
So You Won't Talk? COL
Blondie Plays Cupid COL

1941
Blondie in Society (mt) COL
Mr. Bug Goes to Town (an.; o: Shuken, Parrish, Bradshaw, W. Scharf) PAR
The Lady Has Plans (with Shuken; o: Grau, W. Scharf, Skiles) PAR
On the Sunny Side (see Mockridge)

1942
Right to the Heart (o: Parrish, Moross) TCF
The Night Before the Divorce (ac: Mockridge; o: D. Raksin) TCF
Henry and Dizzy (o: Shuken, Bradshaw) PAR
True to the Army (see Dolan)
Rings on Her Fingers (with Mockridge; o: E. Powell, H. Spencer, G. Rose, Salinger, de Packh) TCF
Secret Agent of Japan (with Mockridge, Friedhofer; add. themes: A. Newman; o: E. Powell, H. Spencer, Salinger) TCF
My Gal Sal (see Mockridge)
The Mad Martindales (see Buttolph)
Whispering Ghosts (with Buttolph, Mockridge; mt: D. Raksin; o: E. Powell, H. Spencer, Salinger) TCF
The Magnificent Dope (see Mockridge)
The Postman Didn't Ring (see D. Raksin)
The Pride of the Yankees GOLDWYN
Wings for the Eagle (see Hollander)
Orchestra Wives (with A. Newman; o: E. Powell, de Packh) TCF
Careful, Soft Shoulder (o: Plumb, Powell, Morton) TCF
Iceland (with Buttolph, Mockridge; ac: A. Newman, C. Henderson, D. Raksin; o: Morton, Virgil, Plumb, de Packh, Arnaud, E. Powell, H. Spencer, Wolcott, G. Rose) TCF
Girl Trouble (see A. Newman)
Manila Calling (see Mockridge)
You Were Never Lovelier (o: Cutner, Grau, Plumb, Salinger) COL
Prelude to War (doc.; with A. Newman, Friedhofer, Lange; ac: D. Raksin, Mockridge; o: E. Powell, Salinger, H. Spencer, Bradshaw, de Packh, Virgil, Morton; + stock) TCF
The Nazis Strike (doc.; see Webb)
China Girl (see Friedhofer)
Life Begins at Eight-Thirty (see A. Newman)
They Got Me Covered GOLDWYN
Silver Queen (see V. Young)

1943
Margin for Error (o: de Packh) TCF
The More the Merrier (o: Cutner) COL
They Came to Blow Up America (see Friedhofer)
Jitterbugs (o: Raksin) TCF
Coney Island (see Mockridge)
The Sky's the Limit (o: de Packh, Cutner) RKO
Johnny Come Lately UA
Wintertime (see Lange)
Sweet Rosie O'Grady (see Mockridge)
Government Girl (o: de Packh) RKO
Around the World (see Duning)
Tender Comrade (o: de Packh) RKO

1944
Follow the Boys (with F. Skinner, Wallace) UNIV
Show Business RKO
A Night of Adventure RKO
Step Lively RKO
The Falcon in Mexico (+ stock) RKO
Greenwich Village (see Buttolph)
Music in Manhattan RKO
Heavenly Days (o: de Packh) RKO
Girl Rush RKO
Something for the Boys (see Mockridge)
Having Wonderful Crime RKO

1945
What a Blonde RKO
Pan-Americana RKO
The Brighton Strangler (o: Grau, L. Morton) RKO
China Sky (o: Grau, Bradshaw) RKO
Mama Loves Papa RKO
Johnny Angel (o: Grau) RKO
Isle of the Dead (o: Grau) RKO
First Yank Into Tokyo (o: Grau) RKO
Man Alive (o: Grau, L. Morton) RKO
Ding Dong Williams RKO

1946
From This Day Forward (o: Grau) RKO
Road to Utopia (o: Shuken, Parrish, Grau, Bradshaw) PAR
The Truth About Murder RKO
Crack-Up RKO
Till the End of Time (o: Grau) RKO
Lady Luck RKO
Child of Divorce RKO

1947
Nocturne RKO
Beat the Band RKO
The Farmer's Daughter (o: Grau) RKO
A Likely Story RKO

Honeymoon RKO
The Bachelor and the Bobby-Soxer RKO
Tycoon (o: Grau) RKO

1948
The Miracle of the Bells RKO
Mr. Blandings Builds His Dream House RKO
The Velvet Touch RKO
The Boy with Green Hair (o: Grau) RKO
Every Girl Should Be Married RKO
They Live by Night RKO

1949
It Happens Every Spring (o: E. Powell) TCF
The Judge Steps Out RKO
The Big Steal RKO
I Married a Communist RKO

1950
Perfect Strangers (o: de Packh) WB
My Friend Irma Goes West (o: Shuken, Cutner, Parrish) PAR
The Happy Years (o: Plumb) MGM
Fancy Pants (see Van Cleave)
The Company She Keeps RKO

1951
Call Me Mister (ac: A. Newman; o: Mayers, E. Powell) TCF
The Guy Who Came Back (o: de Packh, Mayers) TCF
That's My Boy (o: Shuken, Cutner, Plumb, Parrish, Van Cleave) PAR
His Kind of Woman RKO
On the Loose RKO
Behave Yourself RKO
Sailor Beware (see Lilley)
Double Dynamite RKO
I Want You GOLDWYN

1952
The Las Vegas Story RKO
Down Among the Sheltering Palms (see Lange)
Monkey Business (o: Grau; ac and o: Hagen) TCF
My Wife's Best Friend (o: Mayers) TCF
Bloodhounds of Broadway (o: Mayers) TCF
My Pal Gus (o: Powell, de Packh) TCF

1953
Taxi (o: E. Powell) TCF
The Desert Rats (o: E. Powell) TCF
Pickup on South Street (o: Mayers) TCF
Gentlemen Prefer Blondes (see H. Schaefer)
A Blueprint for Murder (o: E. Powell; + stock) TCF
Vicki (o: E. Powell) TCF

1954
Money from Home (o: Van Cleave, Shuken, Cutner, Levene) PAR
The New Venezuela (short; o: E. Powell, Arnaud) TCF
River of No Return (with Mockridge; o: E. Powell) TCF
Susan Slept Here RKO
Broken Lance (o: E. Powell) TCF
Black Widow (o: E. Powell, Mayers) TCF

1955
House of Bamboo (o: E. Powell) TCF
Love is a Many-Splendored Thing (see A. Newman)
The Girl in the Red Velvet Swing (ac: L. Newman; o: Mayers, de Packh) TCF
Good Morning, Miss Dove (o: F. Steiner) TCF

1956
The Last Frontier (o: Morton) COL
The Bottom of the Bottle (o: Mayers, H. Spencer; ac: L. Martin) TCF
23 Paces to Baker Street (o: de Packh) TCF
The Best Things in Life Are Free (o: de Packh) TCF
Teenage Rebel (o: E. Powell) TCF
Love Me Tender (see L. Newman)
The Girl Can't Help It (with L. Newman; ac: Friedhofer; o: E. Powell) TCF

1957
The True Story of Jesse James (o: E. Powell) TCF
The Wayward Bus (o: E. Powell) TCF
No Down Payment (o: E. Powell, Morton) TCF
The Enemy Below (o: E. Powell, de Packh) TCF

1958
Sing Boy Sing (see L. Newman)
The Gift of Love (see A. Newman)
Ten North Frederick (o: E. Powell) TCF
Man of the West UA
These Thousand Hills (o: Hagen, E. Powell, King) TCF
The Remarkable Mr. Pennypacker (o: E. Powell, A. Morton) TCF

1959
Warlock (ac: A. Morton, Mockridge; o: E. Powell, Arnaud) TCF
Woman Obsessed (see Friedhofer)
Say One for Me (with Hagen, A. Morton, L. Newman, Courage) TCF
Holiday for Lovers (o: Hagen, H. Spencer, Mayers) TCF
Hound Dog Man (see Mockridge)

Visit to a Small Planet (o: Shuken, Hayes) PAR
1960
Wake Me When It's Over (see Mockridge)
The Facts of Life UA
Flaming Star (see Mockridge)
1961
All Hands on Deck (see Mockridge)
The Honeymoon Machine (o: Levene) MGM
1962
The Wonderful World of the Brothers Grimm (o: Levene) MGM
1963
7 Faces of Dr. Lao (o: Levene) MGM
1965
Strange Bedfellows UNIV
Cartoons (WDP)
1933
The China Shop
Father Noah's Ark
Lullaby Land (ac: Churchill)
Mickey's Mechanical Man
The Night Before Christmas
The Pet Store
The Pied Piper
1934
Funny Little Bunnies (see Churchill)
The Goddess of Spring
The Grasshopper and the Ants
Peculiar Penguins
Two-Gun Mickey
The Wise Little Hen
1935
The Band Concert
The Cookie Carnival
Mickey's Garden
Mickey's Service Station
Music Land
On Ice (see E. Lewis)
Pluto's Judgment Day (see Churchill)
Water Babies
1936
The Country Cousin
Elmer Elephant
Mickey's Grand Opera
Mickey's Rival
Mother Pluto
Toby Tortoise Returns (ac: Churchill)
1937
The Old Mill
Woodland Cafe
1938
Farmyard Symphony
Wynken, Blynken and Nod
1940
Mr. Mouse Takes a Trip (with Wallace)
Pluto's Dream House
1941
The Art of Self Defense
The Baggage Buster
Donald's Camera
Golden Eggs
A Good Time for a Dime
Lend a Paw
Old MacDonald Duck
Pantry Pirate
The Recruit (an. short)
Truant Officer Donald
1942
Pluto, Junior
The Sleep Walker

HARLING, W. FRANKE
1928
The Whip (see Bergunker)
Waterfront (see Carbonara)
Show Girl (see Carbonara)
1929
Interference PAR
Dangerous Curves (+ stock) PAR
Sweetie (mt) PAR
Pointed Heels (mt) PAR
The Marriage Playground PAR
1930
Behind the Make-Up (with Leipold) PAR
The Kibitzer PAR
The Love Parade (see Leipold)
Only the Brave (with Leipold) PAR
Men Are Like That PAR
The Vagabond King (see Potoker)
The Vagabond King (foreign version; see Leipold)
The Silent Enemy (see Midgely)
Monte Carlo (with Leipold, Hand, Krumgold, Hajos) PAR
The Right to Love (ac: Hajos) PAR
1931
Rango (see Hajos)
Tabu (see Riesenfeld)
Rich Man's Folly (see Leipold)
The False Madonna (see Leipold)
1932
Shanghai Express (o: Hand; m&e: Kopp) PAR
Broken Lullaby PAR
Fireman, Save My Child (mt & trailer) WB
The Expert (trailer) WB
Beauty and the Boss (o: Potoker; theme:

Perry, o: Gerstenberger; mt: Lange) WB
One Hour with You (see Leipold)
The Miracle Man (with Hand, Potoker) PAR
This Is the Night (with Leipold, Rainger; ac: Lange, Kopp) PAR
Two Seconds WB
Street of Women (mt) WB
Week-End Marriage (o: R. Heindorf) WB
The Rich Are Always With Us WB
Play Girl (mt) WB
Winner Take All WB
Stranger in Town (mt) WB
One Way Passage (theme, o: Kaun, R. Heindorf; mt and trailer: Kaun) WB
Blonde Venus (with Marquardt, Leipold, Potoker) PAR
A Bill of Divorcement (see M. Steiner)
Trouble in Paradise PAR
Men Are Such Fools RKO
You Said a Mouthful (mt) WB
The Crash WB
The Match King (see Kaun)
The Bitter Tea of General Yen COL

1933
A Farewell to Arms (with Hand, Kaun, Leipold, Roder, Rainger, Marquardt) PAR
Madame Butterfly (based on Puccini) PAR
Destination Unknown UNIV
The Keyhole (o: Heindorf) WB
The Kiss Before the Mirror UNIV
Cradle Song (o: Hand, Reese) PAR
Man's Castle COL
The House on 56th Street (see Kaun)
By Candlelight UNIV

1934
He Was Her Man (see Kaun)
One More River UNIV
The Scarlet Empress (see Leipold)

1935
Peter Ibbetson (see Toch)
So Red the Rose (ac: Friedhofer, Hollander; o: Hand, Leipold, Reese) PAR
Last of the Pagans (see Axt)

1936
I Married a Doctor (see Roemheld)
The Golden Arrow (see Roemheld)
Parole (see Maxwell)
Give Me Your Heart (see Roemheld)
China Clipper (see Kaun)
Mountain Justice (see Kaun)

1937
Souls at Sea (with Leipold, Roder; ac: Stone, V. Young) PAR

1938
You and Me (see Weill)
Spawn of the North (see Tiomkin)
Men with Wings (with Carbonara; ac: Hageman, Shuken) PAR

1939
Stagecoach (see Leipold)

1941
Adam Had Four Sons COL
Penny Serenade (o: Raab, Cutner, C. Dragon) COL
Adventure in Washington COL

1942
The Lady Is Willing (o: Cutner) COL

1943
I Escaped from the Gestapo MON
Soldiers of the Soil (doc. short) DU PONT

1944
Three Russian Girls UA
Johnny Doesn't Live Here Any More MON
When the Lights Go On Again PRC

1945
Red Wagon (doc.) AMERICAN FILM CENTER

HARPER, FRED

1968
The Young Man's Bride GEORGE GUNTER

HARRIS, ALBERT

1958
Showdown at Boot Hill TCF
Queen of Outer Space (see Skiles)

1963
The Raven (see Baxter)

1964
The Great Space Adventure (see Skiles)

1965
Dr. Goldfoot and the Bikini Machine (see Baxter)

1966
The Ghost in the Invisible Bikini (see Baxter)

1967
The Violent Ones (see Skiles)

HARRIS, ROY

1940
One-Tenth of a Nation (doc. short) FILM ASSOCIATES

HARRISON, LOU

1969
Nuptiae (short) JAMES BROUGHTON

HART, DANIEL
1962
Nude on the Moon MOON PRODS.
The Small Hours BELL
1965
The Dirty Girls AUDUBON
1967
Carmen, Baby AUDUBON

HARTMAN, PETER
1962
Serenity GREGORY J. MARKOPOULOS

HASKELL, JIMMIE
1961
Love in a Goldfish Bowl PAR
1963
The Gun Hawk AA
Surf Party TCF
1964
Black Spurs PAR
1965
I'll Take Sweden UA
Town Tamer PAR
Wild on the Beach TCF
Love and Kisses (see Loose)
Apache Uprising PAR
Johnny Reno PAR
1966
Waco PAR
Red Tomahawk PAR
1967
Fort Utah PAR
Hostile Guns PAR
Arizona Bushwhackers PAR
1968
The Wicked Dreams of Paula Schultz UA
Buckskin PAR
Rogue's Gallery PAR
1969
The 1,000 Plane Raid UA

HASTINGS, HAL
1966
Safety Is Golden (doc. short) GOTHAM FILM PRODS.

HATCHER, HARLEY
1968
Killers Three (see Curb)
The Golden Breed (see Curb)
Jennie, Wife/Child EMERSON
1969
Satan's Sadists INDEPENDENT-INTERNATIONAL
Wild Wheels FANFARE
1970
Cain's Way FANFARE
A Bullet for Pretty Boy AIP

HATLEY, MARVIN
1933
Sons of the Desert (+ stock) HAL ROACH
1935
Bonnie Scotland (with Shield) HAL ROACH
1936
Kelly the Second HAL ROACH
Mister Cinderella HAL ROACH
General Spanky HAL ROACH
1937
Way Out West HAL ROACH
Nobody's Baby HAL ROACH
Pick a Star (see A. Morton)
Topper (o: A. Morton) HAL ROACH
1938
Merrily We Live (o: A. Morton) HAL ROACH
Swiss Miss (o: A. Morton) HAL ROACH
Block-Heads HAL ROACH
There Goes My Heart (with E. Powell) HAL ROACH
1939
Zenobia HAL ROACH
Captain Fury HAL ROACH
1940
A Chump at Oxford HAL ROACH
Saps at Sea HAL ROACH
1941
City of Missing Girls SELECT
Broadway Limited (+ stock) HAL ROACH
I'll Sell My Life SELECT
1945
Life of Thomas Edison (o: Lindoff) GENERAL SERVICE
Hollywood and Vine (o: Lindoff, Miessner) PRC
Shorts
1931
Beau Hunks HAL ROACH
1933
Midsummer Mush HAL ROACH
1934
Movie Daze HAL ROACH
1937
Our Gang Follies of 1938 HAL ROACH

1941
Melody Comes to Town WILDING

HAYES, JACK
1955
David and the Giant (short) WESTERN SCREEN
1957
Hear Me Good (see Shuken)
1968
Fade In (see Lauber)
[Also a prolific orchestrator.]

HAYTON, LENNIE
1941
I'll Wait for You (see Kaper)
Love Crazy (see Snell)
Billy the Kid (see Snell)
The Big Store (with Amfitheatrof, Stoll, Bassman) MGM
Barnacle Bill (see Kaper)
Married Bachelor (see Amfitheatrof)
Shadow of the Thin Man (see Snell)
The Bugle Sounds (o: Marquardt, Raab, Heglin; ac: Amfitheatrof, o: Nussbaum) MGM
1942
Born to Sing (see Snell)
Nazi Agent (see Amfitheatrof)
A Yank on the Burma Road (see Amfitheatrof)
This Time for Keeps (o: Heglin, Raab; + stock) MGM
Kid Glove Killer (with Snell, Amfitheatrof) MGM
Mokey (o: Heglin, Raab) MGM
Grand Central Murder (with Snell) MGM
Maisie Gets Her Man (o: Heglin, Raab) MGM
Pierre of the Plains (o: Raab) MGM
Somewhere I'll Find You (see Kaper)
A Yank at Eton (see Kaper)
Whistling in Dixie (ac: Snell, Amfitheatrof; o: Raab, Heglin) MGM
Eyes in the Night (ac: Amfitheatrof; o: Raab, Heglin) MGM
Stand By for Action (o: Heglin, Raab) MGM
1943
Assignment in Brittany (o: Raab, Heglin) MGM
Pilot #5 (with J. Green; ac: Snell; o: Raab, Heglin, Duncan; + stock) MGM
Swing Shift Maisie (o: Heglin) MGM
Best Foot Forward (o: Heglin) MGM
Salute to the Marines (o: Heglin, Marquardt, Cutner) MGM
1944
See Here, Private Hargrove (see Snell)
Meet the People (o: Heglin; ac: Salinger) MGM
Maisie Goes to Reno (see Snell)
Lost in a Harem (see N. Shilkret)
Meet Me in St. Louis (see Salinger)
The Thin Man Goes Home (see Snell)
1945
Yolanda and the Thief (o: Heglin; ac: Salinger) MGM
The Harvey Girls (see Salinger)
1946
Adventure (see Stothart)
Ziegfeld Follies (see Edens)
The Secret Heart (see Kaper)
Till the Clouds Roll By (see Salinger)
1947
Living in a Big Way (o: Heglin) MGM
The Hucksters (o: Heglin) MGM
Summer Holiday (see Salinger)
1948
Alias a Gentleman (see Snell)
The Pirate (with Salinger; o: Heglin) MGM
Words and Music (with Salinger; o: Heglin, R. Franklyn) MGM
1949
The Barkleys of Broadway (o: Heglin; ac: Salinger) MGM
Any Number Can Play (o: Heglin) MGM
Battleground (o: Heglin) MGM
Side Street (o: Salinger, Heglin) MGM
1951
Inside Straight (o: Heglin) MGM
Strictly Dishonorable (o: Heglin) MGM
Love Is Better Than Ever (o: Heglin) MGM
1952
Singin' in the Rain (o: Heglin) MGM
1953
Battle Circus (o: R. Franklyn) MGM
1968
Star! TCF
1969
Hello, Dolly! (with L. Newman) TCF
Shorts (MGM)
1941
Your Last Act
Ghost Treasure
Triumph Without Drums (with Raab)
Changed Identity

Strange Testament (see Amfitheatrof)
We Must Have Music (with Snell)
1942
The Woman in the House (with Amfitheatrof)
Doin' Their Bit
Personalities
Chinese Training Pilot
Trailer
1942
Ship Ahoy (o: Bassman) MGM

HAYWARD, DAVID
1969
The Stud Farm MCABEE PICTURES

HAZARD, RICHARD
1950
Radar Secret Service (see Garcia)
Operation Haylift (see Garcia)
1951
Disc Jockey AA
1952
Bela Lugosi Meets a Brooklyn Gorilla REALART
1957
Calypso Joe AA
1970
Company of Killers UNIV
[Also an orchestrator for many films.]

HAZZARD, PETER
1968
Laughing Till It Hurt: The Comedy of Charles Chaplin (compilation film) WHOLESOME FILM CENTER

HAZZARD, TONY
1970
Daddy, Darling JOE SARNO

HEAPS, PORTER
1949
Wilderness Canoe Country (doc. short) QUETICO-SUPERIOR COMMITTEE

HECKMAN, DON
1962
Dylan Thomas' A Child's Christmas in Wales (short) MARGIN PRODS.

HEFTI, NEAL
1957
Jamboree (with O. Blackwell) WB
1964
Sex and the Single Girl (o: A. Morton) WB
1965
How to Murder Your Wife UA
Synanon (o: Grau) COL
Harlow (o: Van Cleave) PAR
Boeing Boeing (o: Van Cleave) PAR
1966
Lord Love a Duck UA
Duel at Diablo UA
1967
Oh Dad, Poor Dad, Mamma's Hung You in the Closet and I'm Feelin' So Sad (o: Comstock) PAR
P. J. UNIV
Barefoot in the Park (o: Van Cleave, Levene) PAR
1968
The Odd Couple (o: L. Martin, Mooney) PAR
1970
The Moonshine War (see Karger)

HEGLIN, WALLY
1946
Adventure (see Stothart)
[Also a prolific orchestrator.]

HEIDEN, BERNHARD
1953
Conspiracy in Kyoto (short) INDIANA U.

HEIFETZ, VLADIMIR
1937
The Dybbuk CHIAM LUDWIG PRYWES
Green Fields (Yiddish language) COLLECTIVE FILM
1939
Mirele Efros (Yiddish language) CREDO PICTURES
1966
The Last Chapter (doc.) BEN-LAR PRODS.

HEIN, SILVIO
1916
Charity? MUTUAL

HEINDORF, RAY
1932
Crooner WB
Big City Blues (with Kaun) WB
Central Park WB
1933
Picture Snatcher (mt) WB
Lilly Turner (mt) WB

1934
Desirable (see Roemheld)
A Lost Lady (see Roemheld)
Murder in the Clouds (m&e and trailer: Kaun) WB
1935
Broadway Hostess (with Roemheld) WB
1936
Dangerous (see Roemheld)
The Singing Kid (see Roemheld)
1937
Varsity Show (see Roemheld)
Hollywood Hotel (see Roemheld)
1938
Gold Diggers in Paris (see Roemheld)
Boy Meets Girl (with H. Jackson) WB
1939
Naughty But Nice (see Roemheld)
On Your Toes (see Roemheld)
The Roaring Twenties (see Roemheld)
1941
Blues in the Night (see Roemheld)
1942
Yankee Doodle Dandy (with Roemheld) WB
1943
This Is the Army (with M. Steiner) WB
1945
Wonder Man (see Roemheld)
1948
April Showers (with M. Steiner) WB
1950
Young Man with a Horn (see M. Steiner)
1951
Goodbye, My Fancy WB
Come Fill the Cup (ac: M. Steiner; + stock) WB
I'll See You in My Dreams (ac: H. Jackson) WB
1952
About Face (see Buttolph)
Where's Charley? (with H. Jackson) WB
April in Paris (see H. Jackson)
Stop, You're Killing Me (see Buttolph)
1953
Calamity Jane (see Buttolph)
Three Sailors and a Girl (with H. Jackson) WB
1954
Lucky Me (with H. Jackson) WB
A Star Is Born (ac: H. Jackson) WB
1955
Young at Heart WB
Pete Kelly's Blues (with Buttolph) WB
Sincerely Yours (ac: H. Jackson) WB
1956
Miracle in the Rain (see Waxman)
Serenade WB
1957
The D. I. (see Buttolph)
The Pajama Game (with H. Jackson) WB
The Helen Morgan Story WB
1958
No Time for Sergeants (see Buttolph)
Damn Yankees WB
Onionhead (see Buttolph)
1959
-30- WB
1961
The Music Man WB
1968
Finian's Rainbow WB
[Also a very prolific arranger and orchestrator.]

HELLER, KEN
1970
Is It Always Right to Be Right? (short) STEPHEN BOSUSTOW

HEMMER, EUGENE
1956
The World of Mosaic (doc. short) UCLA

HEMRIC, GUY
1969
Five the Hard Way (see Curb)

HENDERSON, CHARLES
1937
We Have Our Moments (+ stock) UNIV
Behind the Mike (mt; + stock) UNIV
Merry-Go-Round of 1938 (mt with F. Skinner; + stock) UNIV
You're a Sweetheart UNIV
1938
Wives Under Suspicion (with F. Skinner, C. Previn) UNIV
The Rage of Paris (see F. Skinner)
Little Tough Guy (see F. Skinner)
The Road to Reno (mt: F. Skinner; + stock) UNIV
Youth Takes a Fling (see C. Previn)
Service De Luxe UNIV
The Storm (with F. Skinner; + stock) UNIV
1940
Public Deb No. 1 (see Buttolph)
1941
Moon Over Miami (see Mockridge)
Week-End in Havana (see A. Newman)

1942
My Gal Sal (see Mockridge)
Footlight Serenade (ac: Mockridge, A. Newman) TCF
Iceland (see Harline)
Springtime in the Rockies (with A. Newman) TCF
1943
Hello, Frisco, Hello (see Buttolph)
Coney Island (see Mockridge)
Sweet Rosie O'Grady (see Mockridge)
1944
Irish Eyes Are Smiling (see Mockridge)
1945
Diamond Horseshoe (see H. Spencer)
The Dolly Sisters (see Buttolph)

HENDERSON, LUTHER
1969
Recess EDWIN PRODS.

HENDERSON, SKITCH
1960
Zero to Sixth (doc. short) AMERICAN OIL CO.
1961
Royal Purple (doc. short) MONARCH WINE CO.
1964
Act One WB
1970
The Gifts (doc. short) FEDERAL WATER QUALITY ADMIN.

HENKEL, TED
1926
The Winning of Barbara Worth UA

HENNEMAN, ALEXANDER
1923
Fabiola (U.S. release of 1918 Italian film) FABIOLA PHOTOPLAY CORP.

HENNINGER, GEORGE
1934
Playthings of Desire PINNACLE
Chloe PINNACLE
Hired Wife PINNACLE

HERBERT, VICTOR
1916
The Fall of a Nation NATIONAL FILMS

HERMAN, DAVE
1966
Invitation to Lust RON WERTHEIM
1969
The Spy Who Came RON WERTHEIM
1970
Baby, Light My Fire LOU CAMPA
It's Not My Body RON WERTHEIM

HERRMANN, BERNARD
1941
Citizen Kane RKO
All That Money Can Buy RKO
1942
The Magnificent Ambersons (ac: Webb) RKO
1944
Jane Eyre TCF
1945
Hangover Square TCF
1946
Anna and the King of Siam TCF
1947
The Ghost and Mrs. Muir TCF
1951
The Day the Earth Stood Still TCF
On Dangerous Ground RKO
1952
5 Fingers TCF
The Snows of Kilimanjaro TCF
1953
White Witch Doctor TCF
Beneath the 12-Mile Reef TCF
King of the Khyber Rifles TCF
1954
Garden of Evil TCF
The Egyptian (see A. Newman)
1955
Prince of Players TCF
The Kentuckian UA
The Trouble with Harry PAR
1956
The Man in the Gray Flannel Suit TCF
The Man Who Knew Too Much PAR
1957
The Wrong Man WB
Williamsburg, the Story of a Patriot (short) CW
A Hatful of Rain TCF
1958
Vertigo PAR
The Naked and the Dead WB
The 7th Voyage of Sinbad COL
1959
North by Northwest MGM
Blue Denim TCF
Journey to the Center of the Earth TCF

1960
Psycho PAR
The 3 Worlds of Gulliver COL
1961
Mysterious Island COL
Cape Fear UNIV
Tender Is the Night TCF
1963
Jason and the Argonauts COL
1964
Marnie UNIV
Joy in the Morning MGM
1966
Torn Curtain (not used) UNIV
1967
Fahrenheit 451 UNIV
1968
The Bride Wore Black LOPERT
1969
Twisted Nerve NG

HERSCHENSOHN, BRUCE
Documentaries (USIA)
1966
John F. Kennedy: Years of Lightning, Day of Drums (o: Loose, Cookerly)
USA: The Seventh Generation

HERTH, ROBIN
1968
Blow the Man Down CANYON
Tropic of Scorpio CANYON
1969
Hedonistic Pleasures CANYON

HESS, DEAN
1969
Incident in a Glass Blower's Shop (short) BYRON BAUER

HEYMANN, WERNER R.
[He scored several films in Germany, 1926–1932, and at least one after returning to Germany in 1950.]
1937
The King and the Chorus Girl WB
Angel (see Hollander)
1938
Bluebeard's Eighth Wife (see Hollander)
1939
Ninotchka (o: Cutter, Raab, de Packh) MGM
1940
The Earl of Chicago (o: Cutter, Maxwell, Arnaud, Bassman) MGM
The Shop Around the Corner (o: Heglin) MGM
Primrose Path RKO
One Million B.C. UA
He Stayed for Breakfast COL
Escape to Glory (with Cutner; + stock) COL
1941
This Thing Called Love COL
That Uncertain Feeling (o: Cutner) UA
Topper Returns UA
She Knew All the Answers (o: Cutner) COL
My Life with Caroline RKO
Bedtime Story COL
1942
To Be or Not to Be (ac: Rozsa) UA
The Wife Takes a Flyer (o: Cutner, Leipold) COL
They All Kissed the Bride COL
Flight Lieutenant (+ stock) COL
A Night to Remember (o: Cutner) COL
1943
Appointment in Berlin (ac: Carbonara, Cutner; o: Cutner, Sawtell) COL
Caribbean Romance (short; o: Parrish) PAR
1944
Henry Aldrich, Boy Scout (o: Parrish, Shuken) PAR
You Can't Ration Love (o: Cutner; ac: Marquardt, Lilley; m&e: Grau) PAR
Knickerbocker Holiday UA
Hail the Conquering Hero (o: Parrish, Shuken, Marquardt) PAR
Henry Aldrich Plays Cupid (o: Cutner; + stock) PAR
Mademoiselle Fifi RKO
Our Hearts Were Young and Gay (o: Parrish, Shuken) PAR
My Pal Wolf RKO
3 Is a Family UA
Together Again (o: Cutner) COL
1945
It's In the Bag UA
Kiss and Tell (o: Sawtell) COL
Hold That Blonde! (o: Shuken, Cutner) PAR
1946
Mad Wednesday (o: Shuken, Cutner) UA
1947
Lost Honeymoon EL
1948
Always Together (o: Raab) WB
The Mating of Millie (o: H. Gilbert) COL
Let's Live a Little EL

1949
Tell It to the Judge (o: Byrns) COL
A Kiss for Corliss UA
1950
A Woman of Distinction (o: Byrns) COL
The Petty Girl (see Duning)
Emergency Wedding (o: Byrns) COL

HEYWOOD, DONALD
1931
The Exile OSCAR MICHEAUX
1932
Ten Minutes to Live (a) OSCAR MICHEAUX
1939
Moon Over Harlem (a: Calduel, Macomber) EDGAR G. ULMER
1941
Murder on Lenox Avenue ARTHUR DREIFUSS
Sunday Sinners (a: Macomber) ARTHUR DREIFUSS

HIBBARD, WILLIAM
1963
Portraits for Eternity (short) ?
1966
Girl on a Landscape (short) DAVID ABRAMSON

HIERONYMOUS, RICHARD
1970
Westward (doc. short) PHIL GIRIODI
Angels Die Hard! NEW WORLD

HIGGINS, DICK
1965
For the Dead (short) DICK HIGGINS

HILB, EMIL
1929
Coquette (see Riesenfeld)
1931
Fighting Caravans (see Leipold)

HILLER, LEJAREN A., JR.
1961
Time of the Heathen ED EMSHWILLER

HILTON, LESESNE
1965
Dropouts Anonymous (doc. short) ROBERT M. QUITTNER

HINRICHS, GUSTAV
1925
The Phantom of the Opera (see Breil)

HINSHAW, WILLIAM
1961
Ole Rex (see Bagley)
The Magic Tide (see Ferguson)
1962
Airborne (see Ferguson)

HOCHMAN, I. J.
1932
Joseph in the Land of Egypt (Yiddish language) GEORGE ROLAND
1933
A Daughter of Her People (Yiddish language) GEORGE ROLAND
The Wandering Jew (Yiddish language) GEORGE ROLAND

HOFFMAN, DAVID
1963
The Outriders (short) ?

HOFFMAN, MICHAEL
1925
Baree, Son of Kazan VITAGRAPH
Big Pal RUSSELL-ROYAL
Wandering Footsteps BANNER
1926
A Desperate Moment ROYAL-BANNER
The Checkered Flag BANNER
1927
Outcast Souls STERLING
1928
Burning Up Broadway STERLING
Marry the Girl STERLING
1932
Dangers of the Arctic (doc.) PRINCIPAL
1934
My People's Dream (doc.) PALESTINE-AMERICAN FILM CO.
1949
The Eagle (sound reissue of 1925 film) HOFFBERG
1952
Uncommon Clay (doc. short) THOMAS CRAVEN

HOLCOMBE, WILFORD
[Pseudonym: Bill Holmes.]
1961
What Is a Painting? (short) METROPOLITAN MUSEUM OF ART
1963
Wild Is My Love RICHARD HILLIARD
Violent Midnight RICHARD HILLIARD
The Horror of Party Beach TCF
The Curse of the Living Corpse TCF

HOLLANDER, FREDERICK
[Wrote music for several films in Germany, 1930–1933.]

1933
I Am Suzanne! (with De Francesco; ac: Buttolph, Friedhofer, Brunelli) FOX

1935
College Scandal (with Leipold) PAR
Paris in Spring (with Leipold, Satterfield, Roemheld) PAR
Shanghai PAR
Every Night at Eight (with Vaughan) PAR
Accent on Youth (with Satterfield) PAR
Here Comes Cookie (+ stock) PAR
The Crusades (see Kopp)
Hands Across the Table (see Roemheld)
So Red the Rose (see Harling)

1936
Collegiate (with Leipold, Satterfield) PAR
Rose of the Rancho (see Friedhofer)
Anything Goes (ac: Boutelje, V. Young, Leipold) PAR
Desire (ac: Boutelje, Carbonara) PAR
Till We Meet Again (ac: Leipold; + stock) PAR
Forgotten Faces (see Leipold)
Poppy (ac: Leipold, Carbonara, V. Young) PAR
A Son Comes Home (see Leipold)
My American Wife (with V. Young, Bradshaw, Carbonara) PAR
The Texas Rangers (see Carbonara)
Valiant Is the Word for Carrie PAR
Hideaway Girl (ac: Leipold) PAR

1937
Champagne Waltz (see Boutelje)
John Meade's Woman (ac: Stone) PAR
Internes Can't Take Money (see Stone)
Mountain Music (see Leipold)
Easy Living (see Jenkins)
Angel (with Heymann) PAR
Blossoms on Broadway (see Leipold)
True Confession PAR

1938
Bluebeard's Eighth Wife (with Heymann; ac: Leipold, Parrish) PAR

1939
Zaza (with Boutelje) PAR
Midnight (o: Shuken) PAR
Invitation to Happiness (o and ac: Shuken, Bradshaw) PAR
Man About Town (ac: V. Young, Leipold) PAR
Honeymoon in Bali (with V. Young) PAR
Disputed Passage (ac: Leipold) PAR

1940
Remember the Night (o: Bradshaw, Shuken) PAR
Too Many Husbands (o: Parrish) COL
Typhoon (ac: V. Young, Leipold, Shuken, Bradshaw) PAR
The Biscuit Eater (o: Shuken, Leipold) PAR
Safari PAR
Queen of the Mob (ac: Leipold; + stock) PAR
Golden Gloves (with Marquardt; + stock) PAR
The Great McGinty (with Leipold) PAR
Rangers of Fortune (ac: Leipold) PAR
Cherokee Strip (see Leipold)
Arise My Love (see V. Young)
South of Suez (ac: Roemheld, Lava) WB

1941
Victory (o: Shuken, Bradshaw) PAR
Life with Henry (o: Leipold) PAR
Footsteps in the Dark WB
Million Dollar Baby WB
Here Comes Mr. Jordan (ac: Schoop, Cutner) COL
You Belong to Me (o: Cutner) COL

1942
The Man Who Came to Dinner WB
Wings for the Eagle (ac: Harline) WB
The Talk of the Town (ac: Amfitheatrof) COL

1943
Background to Danger (ac: Kaun, Roemheld) WB
Princess O'Rourke WB

1944
Once Upon a Time (o: Moross; ac: Skiles) COL

1945
The Affairs of Susan (o: Moross, Bradshaw, Grau) PAR
Pillow to Post (o: Moross) WB
Conflict (o: Moross) WB
Christmas in Connecticut (o: Moross) WB

1946
Cinderella Jones (o: Moross) WB
The Bride Wore Boots (o: Parrish, Cutner, Shuken) PAR
Janie Gets Married (o: Raab) WB
The Perfect Marriage (with Webb; o: Bradshaw, Shuken, Cutner, Parrish) PAR
Two Guys from Milwaukee (o: Raab; ac: Lava) WB
Never Say Goodbye (o: Raab) WB
The Verdict (o: Raab) WB

The Time, the Place, and the Girl (o: Raab) WB
1947
That Way with Women (o: Raab) WB
Stallion Road (o: Raab) WB
The Red Stallion EL
1948
Berlin Express RKO
Wallflower (o: Raab) WB
Romance on the High Seas WB
A Foreign Affair (o: Van Cleave, Shuken, Cutner) PAR
Two Guys from Texas (cartoon sequence: Stalling) WB
1949
Caught MGM
A Woman's Secret RKO
Adventure in Baltimore RKO
Strange Bargain RKO
Bride for Sale RKO
A Dangerous Profession RKO
Walk Softly, Stranger RKO
1950
Born to Be Bad RKO
Never a Dull Moment RKO
My Forbidden Past RKO
1951
Born Yesterday (o: A. Morton) COL
Darling, How Could You! (o: Van Cleave, Grau) PAR
1952
The First Time (o: A. Morton, Grau) COL
Androcles and the Lion (ac: Webb) RKO
The 5,000 Fingers of Dr. T. (with Salter, Roemheld; o: A. Morton, Grau) COL
1954
It Should Happen to You (o: A. Morton) COL
Sabrina (o: Van Cleave) PAR
Phffft (ac: Roemheld; o: A. Morton) COL
1955
We're No Angels (o: Van Cleave) PAR

HOLLISTER, DAVID
1958
Highway (doc. short) HILARY HARRIS
1962
The Walk (short) ?
1963
The Squeeze (doc. short) HILARY HARRIS

HOLMAN, WILLIS (BILL)
1956
Swamp Women WOOLNER BROS.
1960
Get Outta Town MILLER CONSOLIDATED
[Also worked as an orchestrator.]

HOLOP, ARNOLD
1962
Night of Evil ASTOR

HOOD, MANTLE
1952
Dr. Gloom and Dr. Cheer (short) UCLA

HOOVEN, JOSEPH D.
1962
Rider on a Dead Horse AA

HOPKINS, ARTHUR
1961
Capture That Capsule! RIVIERA

HOPKINS, KENYON
1956
Baby Doll WB
1957
12 Angry Men UA
The Strange One COL
1960
The Fugitive Kind UA
Wild River TCF
1961
Wild in the Country TCF
The Hustler TCF
1963
The Yellow Canary TCF
1964
Lilith COL
1965
Mister Buddwing MGM
1966
This Property Is Condemned PAR
Doctor, You've Got to Be Kidding! MGM
1968
A Lovely Way to Die UNIV
1969
The First Time UA
The Tree GUENETTE
Downhill Racer PAR
Documentary Shorts
1960
Pennsylvania: Keystone of the Nation BELL TELEPHONE CO.
1963
One Week in October U.S. DEPT. OF DEFENSE

HORMEL, GEORDIE
1962
Money in My Pocket ERVEN JOURDAN
1966
Intimacy VICTOR STOLOFF

HORN, PAUL
1963
Lullaby (short) ROBERT S. LEVY
1965
The Bird (cartoon) FRED WOLF

HOROWITZ, DAVID
1970
Adagio (short) PYRAMID FILMS

HORST, LOUIS
1943
Lamentation (short) SIMON MOSELSIO
1949
Pacific Island (doc. short) IFF
1953
Flower Arrangements of Williamsburg (doc. short) CW
1960
South America (see Forrell)
1962
Amazon Family (see Forrell)

HOSMER, JAMES
1952
The Handwritten Word (short) PAPER STATIONERY ASSN.

HOSSEINI, ANYAR
1960
Nineteen Trees (doc. short) HARRY COOPER

HOVEY, SERGE
1952
The Magic Hat ?
1964
Hangman (an. short) MELROSE PRODS.
1970
A Storm of Strangers (doc. short) NAT'L. COMMUNICATIONS FOUNDATION
Denmark 43 (doc. short) NAT'L. COMMUNICATIONS FOUNDATION

HOVHANESS, ALAN
1956
Narcissus WILLARD MAAS

HOWARD, OLIVER
1970
Casting Call SACK
Matinee Wives SACK

HOWE, EDWARD J.
1916
Less Than the Dust ARTCRAFT

HOWELL, JACK
1964
The Love of Living—At the Kahala Hilton (doc. short) DON HORTER PRODS.

HUGHES, ROBERT
1970
The Golden Positions (short) JAMES BROUGHTON

HULETTE, DON
1963
They Saved Hitler's Brain (+ stock) CROWN
1969
Dracula's Castle (+ stock) PARAGON

HUMPHREYS, A. W.
1959
Piegan Medicine Lodge (short) DEPT. OF INDIAN AFFAIRS

HUMPHREYS, NANCY
1963
Galvani and Volta, an Early Debate in Science (short) GILBERT ALTSCHUL PRODS.

HUTTON, J. WARDE
1918
The Unbeliever KLEINE

HYAMS, ALAN
1969
Big Daddy CARL K. HITTLEMAN

I

IDRISS, RAMEZ
1956
Hidden Guns REP
1957
The Badge of Marshal Brennan AA
1958
Man or Gun (see Garf)
1961
Buffalo Gun GLOBE

ITO, TEIJI
1961
Maeva MAYA DEREN
1968
The Virgin President NEW LINE CINEMA
Shorts
1958
The Very Eye of Night MAYA DEREN
1959
Henry James' Memories of Old New York CHARLES BOULTENHOUSE
Meshes of the Afternoon (music added to 1943 silent film) MAYA DEREN
Dwightiana MARIE MENKEN
Handwritten CHARLES BOULTENHOUSE
1960
Lifelines ED EMSHWILLER
1961
Arabesque for Kenneth Anger MARIE MENKEN
The Language of Faces JOHN KORTY
Bagatelle for Willard Maas MARIE MENKEN
1962
Moonplay MARIE MENKEN
1963
Dionysus CHARLES BOULTENHOUSE
1965
Flora BENJAMIN HAYEEM
A Valentine for Marie WILLARD MAAS
1967
Orgia WILLARD MAAS

IVERS, PETER
1967
Desire Is Fire (short) ?
1970
The Devil's Bargain (short) ?
Saturday (short) ?

IVEY, JEAN EICHELBERGER
1962
Montage IV (short) ?
1964
The Exception and the Rule (short) ?
1965
Montage V: How to Play Pinball (short) ?

J

JACKSON, CALVIN
1944
The Negro Soldier (doc.; see Tiomkin)
Two Girls and a Sailor (see Stoll)
Meet Me in St. Louis (see Salinger)
Music for Millions (see Michelet)
1945
Thrill of a Romance (see Stoll)
Her Highness and the Bellboy (see Stoll)
Anchors Aweigh (see Stoll)
1946
Two Sisters from Boston (see Salinger)
Holiday in Mexico (see Stoll)
No Leave, No Love (see Stoll)
1947
This Time for Keeps (see Stoll)
1959
Blood and Steel TCF
1960
Tormented (see Glasser)
Where the Boys Are (see Stoll)
1964
The Unsinkable Molly Brown (see Arnaud)

1965

Three Weeks of Love (with Carmichael) WESTMINSTER

JACKSON, HOWARD

1930

Young Eagles (see Leipold)
The Devil's Holiday (see Goulding)
Paramount on Parade PAR
True to the Navy PAR
The Social Lion PAR
Love Among the Millionaires PAR
The Silent Enemy (see Midgely)
Playboy of Paris (with Leipold) PAR

1933

Goldie Gets Along RKO
Man Hunt RKO
A Bedtime Story (see Rainger)
Supernatural (see Hajos)
International House (see Rainger)
Jennie Gerhardt (see Leipold)
College Humor (see Leipold)
Her Bodyguard (mt; + stock) PAR
Midnight Club (see Rainger)
Big Executive PAR
This Day and Age (mt) PAR
Ladies Must Love (mt) UNIV
Lady for a Day COL
I'm No Angel (with Roemheld, Hand, Kopp, Leipold) PAR
The Way to Love (see Rainger)
Hell and High Water (see Hand)
Good-bye Love (see Roder)
Girl Without a Room (see Hajos)

1934

Eight Girls in a Boat (see H. Lewis)
Beloved (see Schertzinger)
It Happened One Night COL
Bottoms Up FOX
Glamour UNIV
We're Not Dressing PAR
Thirty Day Princess (see Leipold)
Murder at the Vanities (see Roder)
One Night of Love (see Schertzinger)
Blind Date (partial) COL
Wake Up and Dream UNIV
Belle of the Nineties (see Leipold)
Broadway Bill COL

1935

The Best Man Wins (partial) COL
Eight Bells (partial) COL
Air Hawks (partial) COL
Dizzy Dames LIBERTY
The Old Homestead LIBERTY
Personal Maid's Secret WB
Moonlight on the Prairie WB

1936

The Lone Wolf Returns COL
The Widow from Monte Carlo (see Roemheld)
Song of the Saddle (m&e: Kaun) WB
The Music Goes 'Round COL
Mr. Deeds Goes to Town COL
Treachery Rides the Range WB
Devil's Squadron COL
And So They Were Married COL
Counterfeit COL
Meet Nero Wolfe COL
Earthworm Tractors (ac: Roemheld) WB
Love Begins at Twenty WB
Bengal Tiger (ac: Roemheld) WB
Trailin' West WB
Isle of Fury WB
Here Comes Carter WB
California Mail WB
Three Men on a Horse WB
Polo Joe WB
Fugitive in the Sky WB
Conflict (+ stock) UNIV
King of Hockey WB
The Captain's Kid WB
Down the Stretch WB
Guns of the Pecos WB

1937

Her Husband's Secretary WB
Penrod and Sam WB
Men in Exile WB
Land Beyond the Law WB
That Man's Here Again WB
The Cherokee Strip WB
Blazing Sixes WB
Fly-Away Baby WB
Public Wedding WB
Empty Holsters WB
Talent Scout WB
The Footloose Heiress WB
Wine, Women and Horses WB
Prairie Thunder WB
Dance Charlie Dance WB
The Devil's Saddle Legion WB
Love Is On the Air WB
The Adventurous Blonde WB
Sergeant Murphy WB
Over the Wall WB
Accidents Will Happen WB
Mystery House WB
She Loved a Fireman WB

Blondes at Work WB
He Couldn't Say No WB

1938
The Daredevil Drivers WB
Penrod and His Twin Brother WB
Love, Honor and Behave (see Roemheld)
The Beloved Brat WB
A Slight Case of Murder (see Roemheld)
Torchy Blane in Panama WB
Penrod's Double Trouble WB
Little Miss Thoroughbred WB
Boy Meets Girl (see R. Heindorf)
My Bill WB
Mr. Chump WB
Girls on Probation WB
Torchy Gets Her Man WB

1939
Devil's Island WB
Torchy Blane in Chinatown WB
The Adventures of Jane Arden WB
Torchy Runs for Mayor WB
Sweepstakes Winner WB
The Cowboy Quarterback WB
Torchy Blane—Playing with Dynamite WB
Everybody's Hobby WB
Pride of the Blue Grass WB
Kid Nightingale WB
The Dead End Kids on Dress Parade WB

1940
Brother Rat and a Baby (see Roemheld)
Gambling on the High Seas WB
Granny Get Your Gun WB
It All Came True (see Roemheld)
An Angel from Texas WB
Tear Gas Squad WB
A Fugitive from Justice (with Lava) WB
Ladies Must Live WB
River's End (see Vaughan)
Flowing Gold (see A. Deutsch)
Calling All Husbands (ac: Dunn, Vaughan) WB
East of the River (see A. Deutsch)
She Couldn't Say No WB

1941
Father's Son WB
The Great Mr. Nobody (see A. Deutsch)
A Shot in the Dark (see Lava)
Here Comes Happiness WB
Knockout (ac: Lava) WB
Strange Alibi (with Lava) WB
Bad Men of Missouri WB
Three Sons o' Guns WB
Law of the Tropics (ac: Lava) WB
The Body Disappears (ac: Kaun) WB
You're In the Army Now WB

1942
Wild Bill Hickok Rides (ac: Roemheld) WB
Bullet Scars (see Lava)
I Was Framed (with Lava) WB
Murder in the Big House (with Lava, Erdody) WB
Lady Gangster (see Lava)
Escape from Crime (see Lava)
Spy Ship (see Lava)
Busses Roar (see Lava)
Secret Enemies (with Lava) WB

1943
Truck Busters WB
The Mysterious Doctor (see Lava)
Murder on the Waterfront WB

1944
Up in Arms (see M. Steiner)

1945
Club Havana PRC

1946
How Doooo You Do PRC

1949
My Dream Is Yours WB
It's a Great Feeling WB

1950
Johnny One-Eye (see Forbes)
Tea for Two WB
The Breaking Point (see M. Steiner)
The West Point Story WB

1951
Lullaby of Broadway WB
Painting the Clouds with Sunshine WB
Starlift WB

1952
I'll See You in My Dreams (see R. Heindorf)
She's Working Her Way Through College WB
Where's Charley? (see R. Heindorf)
April in Paris (with R. Heindorf) WB
Stop, You're Killing Me (see Buttolph)

1953
Count the Hours (see Forbes)
Appointment in Honduras (see Forbes)
Three Sailors and a Girl (see R. Heindorf)
Calamity Jane (see Buttolph)

1954
Lucky Me (see R. Heindorf)
Silver Lode (see Forbes)
Tobor the Great (with Lava) REP

A Star Is Born (see R. Heindorf)
Passion (see Forbes)
Cattle Queen of Montana (see Forbes)
1955
Run for Cover (o: Cailliet) PAR
Escape to Burma (see Forbes)
Pearl of the South Pacific (see Forbes)
Tennessee's Partner (see Forbes)
Sincerely Yours (see R. Heindorf)
Slightly Scarlet (see Forbes)
1956
The Amazon Trader WB
The Search for Bridey Murphy (see Webb)
1957
Deep Adventure WB
China Gate (see M. Steiner)
The Pajama Game (see R. Heindorf)
1958
Cry Terror! MGM
Manhunt in the Jungle WB
1959
The Miracle of the Hills (see Sawtell and Shefter)
Yellowstone Kelly WB
1960
Noose for a Gunman (see Shefter)
Sergeant Rutledge WB
Cage of Evil (see Sawtell and Shefter)
The Lost World (see Sawtell and Shefter)
Five Guns to Tombstone (see Sawtell and Shefter)
1961
Gold of the Seven Saints WB
Claudelle Inglish WB
House of Women (+ stock) WB
1962
Merrill's Marauders WB
1963
Black Gold WB
1964
F.B.I. Code 98 (based on M. Steiner's themes for *The FBI Story*) WB
Documentary Features
1943
The Navy Gets Rough WB
The Battle of Britain (see M. Steiner)
Know Your Ally: Britain (o: Vaughan) U.S. WAR DEPT.
1944
The Negro Soldier (see Tiomkin)
1950
50 Years Before Your Eyes (see Lava)
1953
This Is Cinerama (see M. Steiner)
1955
Wakamba RKO
1957
Forbidden Desert WB
Shorts (UNIV)
1934
Good Time Henry
Henry's Social Splash
Just We Two
1935
Hollywood Trouble
Shorts (WB)
1935
Husband's Holiday
Keystone Hotel
Reg'lar Kids
Romance of the West
Springtime in Holland
1936
Echo Mountain
Lonesome Trailer
The Lucky Swede
Okay, José
Romance in the Air
1937
A Day at Santa Anita
Little Pioneer
Romance of Louisiana
Romance Road
1938
The Declaration of Independence
The Littlest Diplomat
The Man Without a Country
Sons of the Plains
1939
American Saddle Horses
The Bill of Rights
Lincoln in the White House
The Monroe Doctrine
Quiet, Please
The Right Way
Slapsie Maxie's
Sons of Liberty
1940
Alex in Wonderland
California Thoroughbreds
Cinderella's Feller
Diary of a Racing Pigeon
Dogs You Seldom See
Famous Movie Dogs
The Flag of Humanity
Gun Dog Life
Just a Cute Kid
The Lady and the Lug

March On, Marines
Mechanix Illustrated No. 3
Mechanix Illustrated No. 4
Meet the Fleet
Men Wanted
Mexican Jumping Beans
New Horizons
Old Hickory
Pony Express Days
Riding Into Society
The Singing Dude
Sockeroo
Spills for Thrills
Take the Air
Teddy, the Rough Rider
The Valley
Wild Boar Hunt

1941

At the Stroke of Twelve
Carioca Serenaders (mt)
The Dog in the Orchard
Here Comes the Cavalry
Points on Arrows
Polo with the Stars
Rodeo Round-Up
Soldiers in White
The Tanks Are Coming
Then and Now
White Sails
Wings of Steel

1942

Battle for Beauty
Beyond the Line of Duty (with Lava)
Calling All Girls
The Daughter of Rosie O'Grady
Horses! Horses! Horses!
March On, America
Maybe Darwin Was Right
Men of the Sky (with Lava)
The Pacific Frontier (see Lava)
South American Sports
Sporting Dogs
Winning Your Wings

1943

Behind the Big Top
Cuba, Land of Adventure and Sport
Dude Ranch Buckaroos
Eagles of the Navy (with Lava)
The Fighting Engineers
Mountain Fighters
On Your Own (+ stock)
The Rear Gunner
Secret Weapon
This Is Your Enemy
The Voice That Thrilled the World
Wagon Wheels West (+ stock)
With Rod and Reel on Anticosti Island
With the Marines at Tarawa (with Lava)

1944

Baa, Baa, Black Sheep
Backyard Golf
Bees a' Buzzin'
Bikes and Skis
California, Here We Are
Cattlemen's Days
Champions of the Future
Chinatown Champs
Colorado Trout
Combat Patrol (see Lava)
Coney Island Honeymoon
Cuba Calling
Desert Playground
Gun to Gun
It's Your War Too (see Lava)
Jungle Thrills
Let's Go Fishing
Marine Anniversary (see Lava)
Nautical But Nice
Our Alaskan Frontier
Outdoor Living
Over the Wall
Roaring Guns (+ stock)
Ski Whizz
Their Dizzy Day
Wells Fargo Days
The Winner's Circle (+ stock)

1945

Adventures in South America
Are Animals Actors?
Bahama Sea Sports
Barbershop Ballads
Congo
Days of '76
Fashions for Tomorrow
Fin 'n Feathers
Flying Sportsman in the West Indies
Frontier Days
Glamor in Sports
Hawaiian Memories
Holiday on Horseback
In Old Santa Fe
Law of the Badlands
Musical Mexico
Overseas Roundup (with Lava)
Overseas Roundup No. 2
Overseas Roundup No. 3
Peeks at Hollywood
Snow Eagles

Sports Go to War
Swimcapades
Under Water Spear Fishing (o: Maxwell)
Water Babies
With Rod and Gun in Canada

1946

All Aboard! (o: Vaughan)
Battle of Champs
Beach Days
Beautiful Bali
Dixieland Jamboree
The Dominion of Sports
Girls and Flowers (o: Vaughan)
Las Vegas, Frontier Town
The Lazy Hunter
Ranch in White (o: Vaughan)
The Riding Hannefords

1947

Action in Sports
Arrow Magic
Celebration Days
The Circus Horse
Flying Sportsman in Jamaica
Glamour Town
Holiday for Sports
Hollywood Wonderland
Let's Go Swimming
The Race Rider
Romance and Dance (with Gama)
Rubber River (o: Vaughan)
Saddle Up
Sportsman's Playground
Tennis Town

1948

Built for Speed
Camera Angles
A Day at the Fair
King of the Carnival
Living with Lions
A Nation on Skis
Pie in the Eye (with Lava)
Playtime in Rio
Ride, Ranchero, Ride
So You Want to Be in Politics
So You Want to Be on the Radio
Sun Valley Fun
Sports Down Under
Trip to Sportland
What's Hatchin'?

1949

Cinderella Horse
Daredevils on Wheels
Dude Rancheroos
English Outings
Highland Games
Horse and Buggy Days
The Little Archer
Snow Carnival
Sport of Millions
Treachery Rides the Trail
Water Wizards
Water Wonderland
Women of Tomorrow

1950

Charlie McCarthy and Mortimer Snerd in Sweden
Grandad of Races
Paddle Your Own Canoe
Those Who Dance
Wild Water Champions

1951

Animal Antics
Anything for Laughs (ac: Lava)
Enchanted Islands
Hawaiian Sports
Kings of the Outdoors
The Naughty Twenties
Stranger in the Lighthouse
The Wanderers' Return
Winter Wonders

1952

Cruise of the Zaca
Dutch Treat in Sports
Glamour in Tennis
Killers of the Swamp
Land of Everyday Miracles
No Pets Allowed
Orange Blossoms for Violet
Switzerland Sportland
They Fly Through the Air

1953

Black Fury (with Lava)
Cheyenne Days (see Lava)
Gone Fishin'
Heart of a Champion
Here We Go Again
Hit 'Im Again
Ride a White Horse
Three Lives (see Lava)
Under the Little Big Top

1954

Aloha Nui!
Below the Rio Grande
Born to Ski
Coney Island Holiday
Hold Your Horses
Mariners Ahoy
North of the Sahara

Valley of the Sun
When Fish Fight
Where Winter Is King
1955
The Adventures of Alexander Selkirk
Aqua Queens
Carnival in Rio
Festival Days
Football Royal
G. I. Holiday
The Golden Tomorrow
Italian Holiday
Mississippi Traveler
Riviera Revelries
Sportsman's Holiday
Uranium Fever
Wave of the Flag
Who's Who in the Zoo
1956
Beauty and the Bull (see Lava)
Chasing the Sun
Copters and Cows
East Is East (ac: Lava)
Fish Are Where You Find Them
Green Gold
Heart of an Empire
Hero on Horseback
Howdy, Partner
Italian Memories
Journey to the Sea
The Legend of El Dorado
Magic in the Sun
Miracle in the Caribbean
Out of the Desert
Playtime Pals
Ski Valley
South of the Himalayas
The Sporting Irish
Springtime in Holland
Time Stood Still
Viva Cuba
The Wonders of Araby (see Lava)
1957
Alpine Glory
The Blue Danube
I'll Be Doggoned
Pearls of the Pacific
Under Carib Skies
1963
Philbert
Shorts (DUDLEY)
1948
New York City
1951
Italy
Southern California Holiday
Texas, the Big State
1953
Sports of the Southwest
1954
Speed Sub-Zero
1955
Fortress of Freedom
Pacific Sports
The Queen's Guard
Venezuela
VistaVision Visits Hawaii
1956
Days of Our Years
Everybody Dances
Frozen Frontier
Hula Happy
Screwball Sports
VistaVision Visits Austria
VistaVision Visits Gibraltar
Where All Roads Lead
1958
VistaVision Visits Spain
Trailers (WB)
1936
The Green Pastures
1937
Marry the Girl
Back in Circulation
1938
Racket Busters
1939
Off the Record
Private Detective
1940
A Dispatch from Reuter's
Tugboat Annie Sails Again
1941
Kisses for Breakfast
1952
About Face

JACOBS, AL
1964
Racing Fever AA
1966
The Devil's Sisters THUNDERBIRD
Sting of Death THUNDERBIRD
1967
The Wild Rebels CROWN

JACOBS, HENRY
Shorts (JANE CONGER)
1957
Logos

1959

Odds and Ends

JAFFE, RICHARD

1953

Two Nymphs of the Well (short) ?

JANSSEN, WERNER

1936

The General Died at Dawn (ac: Carbonara, Toch) PAR

1938

Blockade UA

1939

Winter Carnival UA
Eternally Yours UA

1940

Slightly Honorable UA
The House Across the Bay UA
Lights Out in Europe (doc.) HERBERT KLINE

1944

Guest in the House UA

1945

The Southerner UA
Captain Kidd UA

1946

A Night in Casablanca UA

1948

Ruthless EL

195?

Safety First (doc. short) UNION PACIFIC
Soil (doc. short) UNION PACIFIC

1958

Uncle Vanya CONTINENTAL

JARRE, MAURICE

[He scored many French films, but only his English-language films, whether or not scored in the United States, are listed here.]

1960

Crack in the Mirror TCF
The Big Gamble TCF

1962

The Longest Day TCF
Lawrence of Arabia (o: Schürmann) COL

1964

Behold a Pale Horse COL
The Train UA

1965

The Collector COL
Doctor Zhivago (o: Arnaud) MGM

1966

The Professionals (o: Arnaud) COL
Is Paris Burning? PAR
Grand Prix MGM

1967

Gambit UNIV
The Night of the Generals COL

1968

Villa Rides PAR
5 Card Stud (o: Arnaud) PAR
The Fixer (o: Arnaud) MGM
Isadora UNIV
Barbarella PAR
The Extraordinary Seaman (o: Arnaud) MGM
The Damned WB
Topaz UNIV
The Only Game in Town TCF

1970

El Condor NG
Ryan's Daughter MGM

JENCKS, GARDNER

1955

Karl Knaths' Cape Cod (doc. short) DOCUFILM

JENKINS, GORDON

1937

Easy Living (with Stone, Hollander, V. Young) PAR
Exclusive (see Leipold)
Artists and Models (with R. Bennett, Leipold, Shuken) PAR
This Way Please (see Leipold)
Blossoms on Broadway (see Leipold)

1938

Thrill of a Lifetime (with Leipold) PAR
The Big Broadcast of 1938 (see Leipold)
College Swing PAR
Doctor Rhythm (with Leipold) PAR
Tropic Holiday PAR

1943

The Last Will and Testament of Tom Smith (short) PAR

1945

Strange Holiday ARCH OBOLER

1952

Time for Beanie (puppet short; o: Neff) ARCH OBOLER

1953

Bwana Devil ARCH OBOLER

JENKS, HARRY

1966

Santa's Christmas Circus GOLD STAR PICTURES

JENNINGS, WILLIAM DALE
1962
Barbara (short) WILLIAM DALE JENNINGS

JEPSON, WARNER
1968
The Bed (short) JAMES BROUGHTON

JEROME, M. K.
1934
Housewife (see Roemheld)
Friends of Mr. Sweeney (theme) WB
Big Hearted Herbert (theme) WB
I Sell Anything (theme) WB
Babbitt (themes; o: Skiles) WB
6 Day Bike Rider (theme) WB
1935
Red Hot Tires (mt; o: Skiles; ac: Kaun) WB
What, No Men? (short; theme) WB
Alibi Ike (theme; o: R. Heindorf) WB
1936
Hot Money (theme) WB

JOHNS, VAL
1969
The Big Cube WB
1970
Waves of Change (doc.) GREG MACGILLIVRAY

JOHNSON, HALL
1953
The House on Cedar Hill (short) CARLTON MOSS

JOHNSON, HAROLD
1964
Hop on the Melrose Distillers Bandwagon (doc. short) MELROSE DISTILLERS

JOHNSON, JOE
1963
Free, White and 21 AIP

JOHNSON, MICHAEL
1955
My Name Is Mary Brown (short) ILGWU

JOHNSON, TOM
1970
T'ai Chi Ch'uan (doc. short) TOM DAVENPORT FILMS

JOHNSTON, BEN
1969
Museum Piece ?

JOHNSTON, GENE
1936
I'll Name the Murderer PURITAN
The Reckless Way PURITAN
Ellis Island (see Zahler)

JONES, BOOKER T.
1968
Uptight PAR

JONES, QUINCY
1961
The Boy in the Tree ARNE SUCKSDORFF
1965
The Pawnbroker (o: Hazard, Byers) LANDAU
Mirage UNIV
The Slender Thread (o: Shuken, Hayes) PAR
1966
Walk Don't Run (o: Shuken, Hayes, Hazard) COL
1967
The Deadly Affair (o: Shuken, Hayes) COL
Enter Laughing (o: Shuken, Hayes) COL
In the Heat of the Night UA
Banning UNIV
In Cold Blood (o: Shuken, Hayes) COL
1968
A Dandy in Aspic COL
For Love of Ivy CR
The Counterfeit Killer UNIV
The Split (o: Shuken, Hayes) MGM
Jigsaw UNIV
The Hell with Heroes UNIV
1969
Mackenna's Gold (o: Shuken, Hayes, Arnaud, Levene) COL
The Lost Man UNIV
The Italian Job PAR
Bob & Carol & Ted & Alice (o: Shuken, Hayes) COL
Cactus Flower (o: Shuken, Hayes, Mooney, Haskell) COL
John and Mary (o: Shuken, Hayes) TCF
The Out-of-Towners (o: Shuken, Hayes) PAR
1970
The Last of the Mobile Hotshots WB
Up Your Teddy Bear GENENI
They Call Me MISTER Tibbs UA

Animated Shorts (JOHN HUBLEY)
1970
Of Men and Demons
Eggs

JONES, VITO
1966
Adam Lost His Apple DORE

JONES, WILLARD
1962
A House of Sand (based on themes by Les Baxter) DARWIN

JORDAN, LOUIS
1949
Look Out Sister ASTOR

JURIST, IRMA
1951
Ballet by Degas (doc. short) JEAN LENAUER

JURMANN, WALTER
1935
Escapade (see Kaper)
1950
Kill or Be Killed (see Hajos)

K

KAESTNER, JOSEPH
1928
Waterfront (see Carbonara)

KAHN, DAVE
[For the following films, see Kraushaar and the note at the beginning of his filmography.]
1953
The Blue Gardenia
Marry Me Again
Vigilante Terror
1957
Back from the Dead
The Unknown Terror
Copper Sky
Ride a Violent Mile
Blood Arrow
1958
Desert Hell
The Cool and the Crazy
1959
Island of Lost Women

KAISER, KURT
1966
Way Out PREMIERE

KALAJIAN, BERGE
1968
Mission Mars (with Pardalis) AA
1969
The Candy Man (with Pardalis) AA

KANDER, JOHN
1970
Something for Everyone NG

KAPER, BRONISLAU
1935
Escapade (with Jurmann; a: Marquardt, Raab, Virgil, Maxwell, W. Allen) MGM
1940
I Take This Woman (with Guttmann; o: Marquardt, Arnaud, Bassman) MGM
Florian (see Waxman)
The Mortal Storm (with Zador; o: Bassman, Marquardt, Raab, Nussbaum, Cutter, Maxwell) MGM
The Captain Is a Lady (o: Raab, Bassman, Marquardt) MGM
We Who Are Young (with Amfitheatrof) MGM
Dulcy (o: Marquardt, Heglin) MGM
Comrade X (with Amfitheatrof; o: Cutter, Raab) MGM
1941
Blonde Inspiration (o: Harrington, Marquardt) MGM
Rage in Heaven (ac: Zador, Castelnuovo-Tedesco; o: Raab, Bassman) MGM
A Woman's Face (o: Raab, Bassman, Marquardt) MGM
I'll Wait for You (with Hayton, D. Raksin; m&e: Arnaud) MGM
Barnacle Bill (with Hayton; ac: Snell; o: Heglin, Raab) MGM

Whistling in the Dark (m&e; o: Marquardt; + stock) MGM
When Ladies Meet (ac: Amfitheatrof; o: Arnaud, Raab, Heglin) MGM
The Chocolate Soldier (see Stothart)
H. M. Pulham, Esquire (with Amfitheatrof) MGM
Johnny Eager (ac: Amfitheatrof; o: Raab, Heglin) MGM

1942

Two-Faced Woman (o: Heglin, W. Greene) MGM
Nazi Agent (see Amfitheatrof)
We Were Dancing (ac: Amfitheatrof; o: Marquardt, Raab, Heglin) MGM
Fingers at the Window (ac: Amfitheatrof, Castelnuovo-Tedesco; o: Raab) MGM
Crossroads (o: Raab) MGM
The Affairs of Martha (ac: Amfitheatrof, Castelnuovo-Tedesco) MGM
Somewhere I'll Find You (ac: Amfitheatrof, Hayton, Castelnuovo-Tedesco; o: Raab, Heglin, Arnaud) MGM
A Yank at Eton (ac: Castelnuovo-Tedesco, Hayton; o: Raab, Heglin, Arnaud) MGM
White Cargo (with Amfitheatrof; ac: Castelnuovo-Tedesco; o: Raab, Nussbaum) MGM
Keeper of the Flame (with Amfitheatrof, Castelnuovo-Tedesco; o: Raab, Heglin) MGM

1943

Slightly Dangerous (ac: Amfitheatrof, Zeisl; o: Raab, Heglin) MGM
Above Suspicion (with Zeisl, Castelnuovo-Tedesco; ac: Amfitheatrof, N. Shilkret; o: Raab, Nussbaum) MGM
Bataan (with Amfitheatrof; ac: Castelnuovo-Tedesco, Zeisl; o: Raab) MGM
The Man from Down Under (see Snell)
The Cross of Lorraine (with Castelnuovo-Tedesco, Zeisl; o: Raab, Cutner) MGM

1944

The Heavenly Body (ac: Castelnuovo-Tedesco; o: Raab, Heglin) MGM
Gaslight (ac: Amfitheatrof, Castelnuovo-Tedesco; o: Cutner, Salinger, R. Franklyn) MGM
Maisie Goes to Reno (see Snell)
Marriage Is a Private Affair (o and ac: Cutner, R. Franklyn) MGM
Mrs. Parkington (ac: Castelnuovo-Tedesco, N. Shilkret; o: Cutner, R. Franklyn, Duncan, Nussbaum, Glasser) MGM
The Thin Man Goes Home (see Snell)

1945

Keep Your Powder Dry (see Snell)
Without Love (ac: Castelnuovo-Tedesco; o: R. Franklyn, Heglin) MGM
Bewitched (ac: Castelnuovo-Tedesco) MGM
Our Vines Have Tender Grapes (ac: Castelnuovo-Tedesco, N. Shilkret; o: R. Franklyn, Duncan, Glasser) MGM

1946

Courage of Lassie (see Bradley)
Three Wise Fools (o: R. Franklyn) MGM
The Stranger (o: Byrns, Cutner, Shuken) INTERNATIONAL
The Secret Heart (ac: R. Franklyn, Hayton; o: R. Franklyn, Heglin) MGM

1947

Cynthia (ac: R. Franklyn; o: Byrns, Heglin) MGM
Green Dolphin Street (o: R. Franklyn, Byrns) MGM

1948

High Wall (o: R. Franklyn) MGM
B. F.'s Daughter (with Vaughan; ac: R. Franklyn, Salinger) MGM
Homecoming (o: R. Franklyn, Byrns) MGM
The Secret Land (doc.; ac: R. Franklyn; o: R. Franklyn, Byrns) MGM
Act of Violence (o: R. Franklyn) MGM

1949

Little Women (see A. Deutsch)
The Secret Garden (o: R. Franklyn) MGM
The Great Sinner (o: R. Franklyn, Salinger) MGM
That Forsyte Woman (o: R. Franklyn) MGM
Malaya (o: R. Franklyn) MGM

1950

Key to the City (o: R. Franklyn) MGM
The Skipper Surprised His Wife (o: R. Franklyn) MGM
A Life of Her Own (o: R. Franklyn, Heglin) MGM
To Please a Lady (o: R. Franklyn, Marquardt) MGM
Grounds for Marriage (o: R. Franklyn) MGM
Kim (see A. Previn)

1951

Three Guys Named Mike (o: R. Franklyn, Heglin) MGM

Mr. Imperium (o: Shuken, Cutner) MGM
The Red Badge of Courage (o: R. Franklyn) MGM
Too Young to Kiss (based on music of Grieg; ac: Cutner, Shuken) MGM
It's a Big Country (see A. Deutsch)
Shadow in the Sky (o: R. Franklyn) MGM

1952
The Wild North (o: Byrns, R. Franklyn) MGM
Invitation (o: R. Franklyn, Rugolo, Heglin) MGM

1953
The Naked Spur (o: R. Franklyn) MGM
Lili (o: R. Franklyn) MGM
Ride, Vaquero! (o: R. Franklyn) MGM
The Actress (o: R. Franklyn) MGM
Saadia (o: R. Franklyn) MGM

1954
Her Twelve Men (o: R. Franklyn) MGM
Them! (o: R. Franklyn) WB

1955
The Glass Slipper (o: R. Franklyn) MGM
The Prodigal (o: R. Franklyn) MGM
Quentin Durward (ac: Salinger; o: R. Franklyn) MGM
Forever, Darling (o: R. Franklyn, Woodbury) MGM

1956
The Swan (o: R. Franklyn) MGM
Somebody Up There Likes Me (o: R. Franklyn) MGM
The Power and the Prize (o: R. Franklyn) MGM

1957
The Barretts of Wimpole Street (o: R. Franklyn) MGM
Jet Pilot RKO
Don't Go Near the Water (o: R. Franklyn) MGM
The Brothers Karamazov (o: R. Franklyn) MGM

1958
Auntie Mame WB
The Scapegoat (o: R. Franklyn) MGM

1959
Green Mansions (+ adaptation of music from Heitor Villa-Lobos; o: R. Franklyn; ac and o: Cutner) MGM
Home from the Hill (o: R. Franklyn) MGM

1960
The Angel Wore Red MGM
BUtterfield 8 (o: R. Franklyn) MGM

1961
Two Loves (o: R. Franklyn) MGM
Ada (o: Raab) MGM

1962
Mutiny on the Bounty (o: R. Franklyn) MGM

1964
Kisses for My President (o: R. Franklyn) WB

1965
Lord Jim (o: R. Franklyn) COL

1967
Tobruk UNIV
The Way West UA

1968
Counterpoint UNIV
A Flea in Her Ear (o: H. Spencer) TCF

KAPLAN, ELLIOT

1962
Coing Up (short) D. W. CANNON

1964
The Square Root of Zero WILLIAM CANNON

1965
The Playground RICHARD HILLIARD

1966
Passages from "Finnegans Wake" MARY ELLEN BUTE

1967
I, Marquis de Sade RICHARD HILLIARD

1968
The Challenge of Six Billion (doc. short) REID H. RAY

1970
Cry Blood, Apache GOLDEN EAGLE

KAPLAN, SOL

1941
Married Bachelor (see Amfitheatrof)

1942
Nazi Agent (see Amfitheatrof)
Apache Trail (o: Raab, Marquardt) MGM
Journey for Margaret (see Waxman)
Tales of Manhattan (o: C. Wheeler, Bradshaw, Friedhofer) TCF

1943
Whistling in Brooklyn (see Bassman)

1944
Rationing (see Castelnuovo-Tedesco)

1948
Hollow Triumph EL

1949
Reign of Terror (o: Parrish) EL
Down Memory Lane (compilation film) EL

Trapped EL
Port of New York EL
1950
711 Ocean Drive COL
Mister 880 (o: E. Powell) TCF
1951
Halls of Montezuma (o: E. Powell, de Packh) TCF
I'd Climb the Highest Mountain (o: de Packh, E. Powell) TCF
I Can Get It for You Wholesale (ac: A. Newman; o: de Packh, Mayers) TCF
Rawhide (o: de Packh) TCF
House on Telegraph Hill (o: de Packh, Mayers) TCF
The Secret of Convict Lake (o: Mayers, Parrish, H. Spencer, Hagen) TCF
Alice in Wonderland LOU BUNIN
1952
Red Skies of Montana (o: Mayers, Hagen) TCF
Return of the Texan (o: de Packh, H. Spencer) TCF
Deadline—U.S.A. (see Mockridge)
Kangaroo (o: E. Powell) TCF
Diplomatic Courier (o: E. Powell) TCF
Way of a Gaucho (o: E. Powell) TCF
1953
Something for the Birds (o: Mayers) TCF
Niagara (o: E. Powell) TCF
Treasure of the Golden Condor (o: E. Powell) TCF
Destination Gobi (o: E. Powell) TCF
Titanic (o: E. Powell) TCF
1954
Salt of the Earth HERBERT BIBERMAN
1957
The Burglar COL
Happy Anniversary (with Robert Allen) UA
1960
Girl of the Night (o: H. Kay) WB
1963
The Victors (o: Wally Stott) COL
1964
The Young Lovers MGM
1965
The Spy Who Came In from the Cold (o: David Lindup) PAR
Judith (o: Wally Stott) PAR
1970
Explosion (o: McCauley) AIP
Documentaries
1945
Appointment in Tokyo U.S. ARMY
1956
Seven Wonders of the World (see D. Raksin)
1960
The Patterns of Progress (short) MPO PRODS.
1961
Got It Made MPO PRODS.
1963
The World of Henry Ford (short) MPO PRODS.
1964
The Guns of August UNIV
1965
Beyond All Barriers (short) AT&T
The Colonial Naturalist CW
1967
Pancho (short) U.S. OFFICE OF ECONOMIC OPPORTUNITY
1968
New York City—The Most N.Y. TIMES
1969
Doorway to the Past (short) CW
Once There Was a City (short) SCHOENFELD
Shorts (MGM)
1941
The Tell-Tale Heart (o: Raab, Heglin)
1942
Main Street on the March! (see Amfitheatrof)
The Greenie (with Snell; o: Raab)
The Lady or the Tiger? (o: Raab)
Self-Defense (mt; et: Snell, o: Heglin)
It's a Dog's Life (o: Raab)
A.T.C.A. (o: Heglin, Raab)
Calling All Pa's (o: Heglin)
Madero of Mexico (o: Raab, Heglin)
Unexpected Riches (o: Raab)
1943
For God and Country (o: Raab, Duncan, Salinger; ac: N. Shilkret, o: Nussbaum, Cutner)
1944
Shoe Shine Boy (o: Duncan)
The Kid in Upper 4 (o: Raab, Salinger)

KARGER, FRED
1962
Twist Around the Clock (+ stock) COL
Don't Knock the Twist COL
1963
Hootenanny Hoot (o: Stafford, Bowers, Strange) MGM

1964

Kissin' Cousins (o: Stafford, Stern) MGM

Your Cheatin' Heart MGM

Get Yourself a College Girl MGM

1965

Harum Scarum MGM

When the Boys Meet the Girls MGM

Hold On! (o: Stafford, Stern) MGM

1966

Frankie and Johnny UA

The Fastest Guitar Alive (o: Stafford, Stern) MGM

Hot Rods to Hell MGM

1967

Riot on Sunset Strip AIP

The Love-Ins (o: Stafford) COL

1968

For Singles Only (o: Stafford, Stern) COL

A Time to Sing (o: Stafford, Stern) MGM

The Young Runaways MGM

1969

Angel, Angel, Down We Go AIP

1970

The Moonshine War (ac: Hefti) MGM

KARLIN, FRED

1965

The Last Man (short) BRAUER PRODS.

1967

Up the Down Staircase WB

1968

Yours, Mine and Ours UA

The Stalking Moon NG

1969

The Sterile Cuckoo PAR

Cover Me Babe TCF

1970

Lovers and Other Strangers CR

The Baby Maker NG

KARMEN, STEVE

1963

Hollywood Nudes Report CINEMA SYNDICATE

1964

The Candidate (with Sid Robin) ATLANTIC

The Beautiful, the Bloody, and the Bare ESQUIRE

1965

The Sexploiters OLYMPIC INT'L.

Nudes on Tiger Reef BARRY MAHON

1966

Misconduct CIP LTD.

Teenage Gang Debs CIP LTD.

1967

Teenage Mother CINEMATION

1970

What Do You Say to a Naked Lady? UA

KATZ, BERNARD

1948

Street Corner WILSHIRE

KATZ, ERICH

1952

Tropical Noah's Ark (short) IAN HUGO

KATZ, FRED

1958

Never Alone (doc.) CAMERA EYE

1959

A Bucket of Blood AIP

The Wasp Woman FILMGROUP

1960

Ski Troop Attack FILMGROUP

Shorts

1958

T Is for Tumbleweed CAMERA EYE

1961

The Puppet's Dream (an.) PYRAMID

1962

Leaf PYRAMID

1963

College PYRAMID

196?

The Sorcerer (an.) PYRAMID

1966

Quest for Freedom DAVE HILBERMAN

19??

The Life of Gauguin ?

Rebel in Paradise ?

The Birth of Aphrodite LELAND AUSLENDER

KAUER, GUENTHER (GENE)

1956

The Outlaw Queen GLOBE

1958

The Astounding She Monster AIP

Girl with an Itch SONNEY

1959

Mission in Morocco JAYARK

1960

The Cape Canaveral Monsters CCM

Ma Barker's Killer Brood FILMSERVICE

1961

Five Minutes to Live SUTTON

[In collaboration with Lackey:]

1962
The Silent Witness EMERSON
1963
A Swingin' Affair EMERSON
The Starbuilders (doc.) JAMES FITZPATRICK
Monstrosity EMERSON
1964
Guerillas in Pink Lace GEORGE MONTGOMERY
From Hell to Borneo GEORGE MONTGOMERY
1965
Fortress of the Dead FERDE GROFÉ JR.
1966
Agent for H.A.R.M. UNIV
Mother Goose a Go-Go JACK H. HARRIS
1967
Cottonpickin' Chickenpickers SOUTHEASTERN
Warkill UNIV
1969
The Ice House HOLLYWOOD CINEMART

KAUN, BERNHARD
1931
The Midnight Sun (mt: Roemheld; + stock; nondialogue sound version of 1926 film) UNIV
Frankenstein (mt) UNIV
Rich Man's Folly (see Leipold)
Heaven on Earth UNIV
The False Madonna (see Leipold)
Under Eighteen (mt; o: R. Heindorf) WB
1932
The Woman from Monte Carlo (and trailer) WB
High Pressure (mt and trailer) WB
The Hatchet Man (and trailer) WB
Alias the Doctor (and trailer; waltz theme: Perry) WB
The Heart of New York (mt) WB
The Crowd Roars (mt) WB
The Mouthpiece (mt) WB
The Famous Ferguson Case WB
Man Wanted WB
The Strange Love of Molly Louvain WB
Forgotten Commandments (see Hand)
Westward Passage (m&e; + stock) RKO
Miss Pinkerton (and trailer) WB
Jewel Robbery WB
Doctor X (and trailer) WB
Big City Blues (see R. Heindorf)
Tiger Shark (and trailer) WB
One Way Passage (see Harling)
A Successful Calamity (and trailer) WB
I Am a Fugitive from a Chain Gang (and trailer) WB
The Match King (love theme: Harling) WB
20,000 Years in Sing Sing (and trailer; o: R. Heindorf) WB
Lawyer Man WB
1933
A Farewell to Arms (see Harling)
Employees' Entrance (mt and trailer) WB
Luxury Liner (mt; o: Hand; + stock) PAR
Mystery of the Wax Museum (et and trailer) WB
Our Betters (ac: Webb) RKO
The King's Vacation WB
Grand Slam WB
Girl Missing (mt and trailer) WB
The Mind Reader (and trailer; themes: F. Mills) WB
Central Airport WB
The Story of Temple Drake (with Hajos; ac: Rainger, Leipold) PAR
The Silk Express (and trailer) WB
I Love That Man (with Kopp, H. Lewis, Hajos, Leipold) PAR
The Life of Jimmy Dolan (mt and trailer) WB
Mary Stevens, M.D. WB
Heroes for Sale (and trailer) WB
The Mayor of Hell (and trailer) WB
The Narrow Corner (and trailer) WB
Private Detective 62 WB
Voltaire (with Roder) WB
Captured! (and trailer) WB
The Song of Songs (see Hajos)
Bureau of Missing Persons (mt and trailer) WB
Wild Boys of the Road WB
I Loved a Woman WB
College Coach WB
Ever in My Heart WB
From Headquarters WB
The World Changes WB
The Kennel Murder Case (and trailer; o: R. Heindorf) WB
The House on 56th Street (and trailer; theme: Harling) WB
Lady Killer WB
The Big Shakedown (and trailer) WB
1934
Man of Two Worlds (m&e; + stock) RKO
Massacre WB
Hi, Nellie! (and trailer) WB
Dark Hazard (and trailer; mt: Marquardt) WB

Bolero (see Rainger)
Gambling Lady WB
Spitfire (m&e; + stock) RKO
Upperworld (and trailer) WB
Death Takes a Holiday (see Roder)
Success at Any Price (m&e; + stock) RKO
Bedside (and trailer) WB
I've Got Your Number WB
Heat Lightning (mt and trailer) WB
Jimmy the Gent WB
A Very Honorable Guy WB
As the Earth Turns (see Roemheld)
The Merry Frinks WB
He Was Her Man (love theme: Harling) WB
Fog Over Frisco (and trailer) WB
The Personality Kid WB
Murder on the Blackboard (see M. Steiner)
Return of the Terror (and trailer) WB
The Man with Two Faces (and trailer) WB
Side Street (see Roemheld)
Housewife (see Roemheld)
Midnight Alibi (see Roemheld)
The Scarlet Empress (see Leipold)
The Dragon Murder Case (and trailer) WB
Desirable (see Roemheld)
The Case of the Howling Dog (and trailer) WB
A Lost Lady (see Roemheld)
British Agent (see Roemheld)
The St. Louis Kid WB
The Firebird (et and trailer; music of Stravinsky) WB
Gentlemen Are Born (see Roemheld)
Murder in the Clouds (see R. Heindorf)
The Secret Bride WB
Bordertown (and trailer) WB

1935

Red Hot Tires (see Jerome)
The Right to Live WB
The White Cockatoo WB
Devil Dogs of the Air WB
The Woman in Red WB
Sweet Music WB
Gold Diggers of 1935 (see Roemheld)
Living on Velvet (see Roemheld)
I Am a Thief (and trailer) WB
The Florentine Dagger WB
While the Patient Slept WB
The Case of the Curious Bride (and trailer) WB
Black Fury (and trailer) WB
Traveling Saleslady WB
"G" Men (and trailer) WB
The Girl from 10th Avenue (see Roemheld)
Mary Jane's Pa (see Roemheld)
Dinky (see Roemheld)
Oil for the Lamps of China (see Roemheld)
Go Into Your Dance WB
Stranded (see Roemheld)
Going Highbrow (with Roemheld) WB
Don't Bet on Blondes (theme: H. Lewis) WB
We're In the Money (see Roemheld)
The Irish in Us (see Roemheld)
In Caliente WB
The Goose and the Gander (see Roemheld)
Special Agent WB
Dr. Socrates (and trailer; with Roemheld) WB
The Last Outpost (with Roemheld, Lynch, Roder) PAR
Shipmates Forever WB
The Payoff (see Roemheld)
The Frisco Kid WB
Man of Iron (and trailer) WB
The Murder of Dr. Harrigan WB

1936

Dangerous (see Roemheld)
Ceiling Zero (and trailer) WB
The Widow from Monte Carlo (see Roemheld)
Man Hunt WB
The Story of Louis Pasteur (see Roemheld)
The Petrified Forest (and trailer) WB
Song of the Saddle (see H. Jackson)
The Walking Dead WB
Colleen (see Roemheld)
Bullets or Ballots WB
Parole (see C. Previn)
Hearts Divided (see Roemheld)
Satan Met a Lady (with Roemheld) WB
The Case of the Velvet Claws (with Roemheld; and trailer) WB
Public Enemy's Wife WB
Two Against the World (and trailer) WB
Jailbreak WB
The Texas Rangers (see Carbonara)
Draegerman Courage (see Roemheld)
China Clipper (with Roemheld; theme: Harling) WB
Mountain Justice (with Roemheld; theme: Harling) WB
Black Legion WB

1937

Marked Woman (with Roemheld) WB
The Go Getter WB
Internes Can't Take Money (see Stone)
Back in Circulation (with Roemheld; mt: Still) WB

Missing Witnesses WB
The Patient in Room 18 WB
The Invisible Menace WB
1938
When Were You Born WB
1939
Secret Service of the Air WB
Blackwell's Island WB
On Trial WB
Code of the Secret Service WB
Smashing the Money Ring WB
The Return of Doctor X WB
1940
British Intelligence WB
Money and the Woman WB
1941
The Case of the Black Parrot WB
Shadows on the Stairs WB
Bullets for O'Hara WB
The Smiling Ghost (ac: Lava) WB
The Body Disappears (see H. Jackson)
1942
The Big Shot (see A. Deutsch)
1943
Background to Danger (see Hollander)
Shorts
1934
Business Is a Pleasure WB
Morocco Nights WB
The Singer of Naples WB
1963
Forest Murmers (doc.) INTERLUDE
Trailers (WB)
1932
The Man Who Played God
So Big
Life Begins
The Crash
Scarlet Dawn
Central Park
1933
Frisco Jenny
Parachute Jumper
Ladies They Talk About
The Working Man
Lilly Turner
Convention City
1934
Journal of a Crime
A Modern Hero
Desirable
Madame Du Barry
1936
Road Gang
The Law in Her Hands
Murder by an Aristocrat
The Case of the Black Cat
1937
The Case of the Stuttering Bishop

KAY, AL
1933
The Eternal Jew JEWISH TALKING PICTURES

KAY, ARTHUR
1920
The Last of the Mohicans MAURICE TOURNEUR
1928
The Gaucho UA
1929
Wolf Song (see Carbonara)
William Fox Movietone Follies of 1929 (mt) FOX
The Exalted Flapper FOX
The One Woman Idea FOX
Chasing Through Europe FOX
Frozen Justice FOX
Married in Hollywood FOX
Seven Faces (see Lipschultz)
South Sea Rose (see Brunelli)
Let's Go Places FOX
1930
City Girl FOX
The Golden Calf (see Friedhofer)
Common Clay FOX
Scotland Yard (ac: Friedhofer, Gerstenberger, G. Knight) FOX
The Big Trail (with Virgil, R. Bassett; ac: Brunelli) FOX
Renegades (ac: R. Bassett, Talbot, Gerstenberger, Lipschultz, Malotte) FOX
Lightnin' FOX
The Princess and the Plumber (see Lipschultz)
Men on Call (see Kaylin)
Once a Sinner (with Kaylin) FOX
The Man Who Came Back (with Brunelli; ac: Friedhofer, G. Knight, Lipschultz, Malotte) FOX
Fair Warning (ac: Virgil, Brunelli) FOX
1931
Not Exactly Gentlemen (see Brunelli)
A Connecticut Yankee FOX
Ambassador Bill (mt; + stock) FOX
1932
While Paris Sleeps (with R. Bassett) FOX

1934

Little Man, What Now? UNIV
The Human Side (mt) UNIV
Young and Beautiful (md) MASCOT
There's Always Tomorrow UNIV

1935

Harmony Lane (md) MASCOT
Streamline Empress (mt) MASCOT
The Fighting Marines (serial; md) MASCOT

1936

I Conquer the Sea! ACADEMY
Hitch Hike Lady REP
Darkest Africa (serial; + stock) REP
The House of a Thousand Candles (+ stock) REP
The Girl from Mandalay (+ stock) REP
Tundra (with Riesenfeld; + stock) BURROUGHS-TARZAN
Down to the Sea (+ stock) REP
The Vigilantes Are Coming (serial; + stock) REP
Daniel Boone (see Riesenfeld)

1937

The Girl Said No (md) GN
Renfrew of the Royal Mounted (md) GN
Wallaby Jim of the Islands (md) GN

KAY, EDWARD J.

[Several cue sheets from 1935–1936 indicate partial contributions by Kay, but they appear to be stock library cues and are not included here. This filmography is compiled entirely from secondary sources, and it is unlikely that every film had an original score. The number of films is inordinately large, and on the majority of them Kay received credit for musical direction. There is some evidence that stock music was often used and that many of the scores were ghostwritten. Unless otherwise stated, the films were released by Monogram (later renamed Allied Artists).]

1936

With Love and Kisses AMBASSADOR

1937

Sing While You're Able AMBASSADOR

1938

Mr. Wong, Detective
Gangster's Boy

1939

Tough Kid
Navy Secrets
The Mystery of Mr. Wong
Undercover Agent
Streets of New York
Boys' Reformatory
Wolf Call
Mr. Wong in Chinatown
Girl from Rio
Irish Luck
Mutiny in the Big House

1940

On the Spot
Hidden Enemy
Chasing Trouble
The Fatal Hour
Son of the Navy
Tomboy
Doomed to Die
Haunted House
Laughing at Danger
Up in the Air
Queen of the Yukon
The Ape
Drums of the Desert
The Old Swimmin' Hole
Phantom of Chinatown

1941

Secret Evidence PRC
Sign of the Wolf
No Greater Sin UNIVERSITY
Roar of the Press
King of the Zombies
The Gang's All Here
Arizona Bound
Father Steps Out
Let's Go Collegiate
The Gunman from Bodie

1942

Forbidden Trails
Road to Happiness
Man from Headquarters
Below the Border
Klondike Fury
Ghost Town Law
So's Your Aunt Emma!
Down Texas Way
Smart Alecks
Lure of the Islands
Isle of Missing Men
Foreign Agent
Bowery at Midnight
'Neath Brooklyn Bridge
Rhythm Parade

1943

Cosmo Jones in Crime Smasher
Dawn on the Great Divide
Kid Dynamite
Silent Witness

You Can't Beat the Law
Silver Skates
The Ape Man
Clancy Street Boys
Sarong Girl
The Stranger from Pecos
Wings Over the Pacific
Spy Train
Ghosts on the Loose
Melody Parade
Six-Gun Gospel
Here Comes Kelly
Revenge of the Zombies
Spotlight Scandals
Outlaws of Stampede Pass
Nearly Eighteen
Campus Rhythm
The Texas Kid
Mr. Muggs Steps Out
Smart Guy
Women in Bondage
Million Dollar Kid

1944

What a Man!
Raiders of the Border
Voodoo Man
Where Are Your Children?
Lady, Let's Dance
Partners of the Trail
Hot Rhythm
Law Men
Detective Kitty O'Day
Follow the Leader
Return of the Ape Man
Range Law
Are These Our Parents?
Three of a Kind
West of the Rio Grande
Block Busters
Oh, What a Night
Land of the Outlaws
Law of the Valley
Alaska
Ghost Guns
Adventures of Kitty O'Day
Bowery Champs
Army Wives
The Jade Mask (see Torbett)
Mom and Dad (see Torbett) HYGIENIC PRODS.
Crazy Knights
The Navajo Trail

1945

G.I. Honeymoon
There Goes Kelly
Brenda Starr, Reporter (serial) COL
Docks of New York
Fashion Model
The Scarlet Clue
Trouble Chasers
Come Out Fighting
Mr. Muggs Rides Again
Divorce
The Shanghai Cobra
South of the Rio Grande
Sunbonnet Sue
The Strange Mr. Gregory
Captain Tugboat Annie REP
Black Market Babies
The Red Dragon

1946

Fear
Live Wires
The Face of Marble
Drifting Along
The Shadow Returns
Swing Parade of 1946
The Gay Cavalier
Dark Alibi
Behind the Mask
In Fast Company
Under Arizona Skies
Don't Gamble with Strangers
The Gentleman from Texas
South of Monterey
Bowery Bombshell
Shadows Over Chinatown
The Missing Lady
Below the Deadline
Shadows on the Range
Spook Busters
Trigger Fingers
Decoy
High School Hero
Dangerous Money
Gentleman Joe Palooka
Wife Wanted
Silver Range
Bringing Up Father
Beauty and the Bandit
The Trap
Ginger
Sweetheart of Sigma Chi
Mr. Hex

1947

Raiders of the South
Vacation Days
Riding the California Trail

Valley of Fear
Fall Guy
Land of the Lawless
Hard Boiled Mahoney
Trailing Danger
Violence
The Law Comes to Gunsight
Sarge Goes to College
Song of the Wasteland
Kilroy Was Here
News Hounds
Code of the Saddle
Robin Hood of Monterey
Flashing Guns
Ridin' Down the Trail
Black Gold
Joe Palooka in The Knockout
Prairie Express
Louisiana
King of the Bandits
The Hunted
Bowery Buckaroos
The Chinese Ring
Gun Talk
Jiggs and Maggie in Society

1948

Smart Politics
Song of the Drifter
Joe Palooka in Fighting Mad
Overland Trails
Rocky (see Torbett)
Angels Alley
Docks of New Orleans
Oklahoma Blues
Campus Sleuth
Crossed Trails
French Leave
Partners of the Sunset
Frontier Agent
I Wouldn't Be in Your Shoes
Range Renegades
Stage Struck
The Checkered Coat TCF
Triggerman
Jinx Money
Cowboy Cavalier
The Shanghai Chest
Back Trail
The Fighting Ranger
Silver Trails
The Golden Eye
The Music Man
Winner Take All
The Sheriff of Medicine Bow
The Rangers Ride
Kidnapped (see Torbett)
Smuggler's Cove
Outlaw Brand
Bungalow 13 TCF
Gunning for Justice
Courtin' Trouble
Hidden Danger
Jiggs and Maggie in Court
Incident
Trouble Makers

1949

Crashing Thru
The Feathered Serpent
Gun Runner
Henry, the Rainmaker
Joe Palooka in The Big Fight
Law of the West
I Cheated the Law TCF
Gun Law Justice
Fighting Fools
Bomba, the Jungle Boy
The Lawton Story of the Prince of Peace (see Torbett) HALLMARK
Trail's End
Tuna Clipper
Sky Dragon
Stampede
Across the Rio Grande
Mississippi Rhythm
West of Eldorado
Leave It to Henry
Hold That Baby
Brand of Fear
Forgotten Women
Shadows of the West
Trail of the Yukon
Range Justice
Joe Palooka in The Counterpunch
Haunted Trails
Jiggs and Maggie in Jackpot Jitters
Roaring Westward
Angels in Disguise
Black Midnight
Western Renegades
Riders of the Dusk
The Wolf Hunters
Lawless Code
Master Minds
Bomba on Panther Island
Range Land

1950

Joe Palooka Meets Humphrey
Blonde Dynamite

Fence Riders
West of Wyoming
Young Daniel Boone
Over the Border
The Great Plane Robbery UA
Killer Shark
Square Dance Katy
Gunslingers
Jiggs and Maggie Out West
Six Gun Mesa
Father Makes Good
Lucky Losers
Joe Palooka in Humphrey Takes a Chance
Sideshow
Arizona Territory
Snow Dog
The Admiral Was a Lady UA
Triple Trouble
Silver Raiders
Big Timber
Law of the Panhandle
A Modern Marriage
Cherokee Uprising
Hot Rod
Blues Busters
Joe Palooka in The Squared Circle
Outlaw Gold
Father's Wild Game
Outlaws of Texas
Call of the Klondike
Short Grass
Sierra Passage

1951
Colorado Ambush
Bowery Battalion
Abilene Trail
Rhythm Inn
Navy Bound
Man from Sonora
I Was an American Spy
Ghost Chasers
According to Mrs. Hoyle
Casa Mañana
Father Takes the Air
Montana Desperado
Yukon Manhunt
Let's Go Navy
Yellow Fin
Crazy Over Horses
Northwest Territory

1952
The Steel Fist
Hold That Line
Jet Job
Here Come the Marines
Desert Pursuit
Feudin' Fools
Sea Tiger
Yukon Gold
Arctic Flight
No Holds Barred
Torpedo Alley

1953
Fangs of the Arctic
Tangier Incident
Cow Country
Trail Blazers
Murder Without Tears
Northern Patrol
Mexican Manhunt

1954
Yukon Vengeance
Highway Dragnet
Racing Blood TCF
Security Risk
Thunder Pass LIP
Port of Hell

1955
Treasure of Ruby Hills
The Big Tip-Off
Las Vegas Shakedown
Betrayed Women
Night Freight
The Toughest Man Alive

1956
Yaqui Drums

1958
Johnny Rocco
Arson for Hire
Revolt in the Big House

1962
The Creation of the Humanoids EMERSON

KAY, ULYSSES

1948
The Quiet One (doc.) SIDNEY MEYERS

1952
The Lion, the Griffin, and the Kangaroo (doc. short) PETER HOLLANDER

1958
New York, City of Magic (doc. short) WNYC

1962
Going Home (short) PETER HOLLANDER
Nosotros (short) PETER HOLLANDER

1966
A Thing of Beauty (doc. short) FISK U.

KAY, WILLIAM
1953
Black Bear Twins (doc. short) ENCYCLOPAEDIA BRITANNICA

KAYDEN, MILDRED
1960
The Procession (doc. short) UNITED CHURCH OF CHRIST
The Pumpkin Coach (an. short) UNITED CHURCH OF CHRIST
19??
Leaven for the Cities ?

KAYLIN, SAMUEL
1929
Harmony at Home FOX
1930
The Second Floor Mystery (mt: R. Bassett) WB
High Society Blues (ac: R. Bassett) FOX
Wild Company (ac: Malotte) FOX
The Last of the Duanes (ac: Virgil) FOX
The Sea Wolf (ac: R. Bassett) FOX
Liliom (see Fall)
Under Suspicion (ac: Friedhofer, Virgil) FOX
Men on Call (ac: R. Bassett, Brunelli, A. Kay, Friedhofer) FOX
Once a Sinner (see Arthur Kay)
1931
Charlie Chan Carries On (mt; + stock) FOX
Doctors' Wives FOX
The Black Camel (mt) FOX
1933
Infernal Machine (ac: A. Lange; o: Gerstenberger) FOX
Bondage (mt; + stock) FOX
Trick for Trick (see R. Bassett)
Pilgrimage (see R. Bassett)
It's Great to Be Alive (see Friedhofer)
El Rey de los Gitanos (Spanish language) FOX
The Man Who Dared (with Friedhofer, Reiser) FOX
Doctor Bull (o: Gerstenberger) FOX
Una Viuda Romántica (Spanish language; + stock) FOX
La Melodía Prohibida (Spanish language; with Friedhofer; ac: A. Lange) FOX
Walls of Gold (o: Gerstenberger) FOX
No Dejes la Puerta Abierta (Spanish language) FOX
1934
Orient Express (see Friedhofer)
Sleepers East (see Buttolph)
La Cruz y la Espada (Spanish language; ac: Buttolph) FOX
I Believed in You (ac: Buttolph) FOX
Hold That Girl (see Buttolph)
La Ciudad de Cartón (Spanish language; ac: R. Bassett) FOX
Three on a Honeymoon (o: W. Spielter; + stock) FOX
Call It Luck (ac: Buttolph, Mockridge; o: Gerstenberger) FOX
Wild Gold (see Buttolph)
She Learned About Sailors (see Buttolph)
Handy Andy (see Buttolph)
Pursued (see Friedhofer)
Granaderos del Amor (Spanish language) FOX
Un Capitán de Cosacos (Spanish language; ac: R. Bassett) FOX
Love Time (based on music of Schubert; ac: Buttolph) FOX
Judge Priest (o and ac: Gerstenberger) FOX
Dos Mas Uno, Dos (see Buttolph)
365 Nights in Hollywood (see Buttolph)
Las Fronteras del Amor (Spanish language; with Sanders) FOX
Bachelor of Arts (o: Gerstenberger) FOX
1935
Charlie Chan in Paris (+ stock) FOX
Life Begins at Forty (mt; + stock) FOX
Ginger (o: Gerstenberger) FOX
Dante's Inferno (see Friedhofer)
Steamboat Round the Bend (o: Gerstenberger) FOX
Piernas de Seda (Spanish language; + stock) FOX
Thunder in the Night (o: Gerstenberger) FOX
1936
Paddy O'Day (o: Gerstenberger; + stock) TCF
Song and Dance Man (see G. Rose)
Gentle Julia (o: Gerstenberger) TCF
The First Baby (o: G. Rose, Gerstenberger) TCF
Little Miss Nobody (o: G. Rose) TCF
Star for a Night (see Maxwell)
Can This Be Dixie? (with G. Rose, J. Glover, Gerstenberger) TCF
Crack-Up (o: G. Rose) TCF
1937
Angel's Holiday (+ stock) TCF

One Mile from Heaven (mt; + stock) TCF
Think Fast, Mr. Moto (see R. Bassett)
45 Fathers (+ stock) TCF

1938
Five of a Kind (see G. Rose)
Sharpshooters (see G. Rose)
Up the River (o: G. Rose) TCF

1939
Charlie Chan in Honolulu (o: G. Rose) TCF
Mr. Moto in Danger Island (o: G. Rose, Maxwell) TCF
Winner Take All (o: G. Rose) TCF
Mr. Moto Takes a Vacation (o: G. Rose) TCF
Frontier Marshal (with Maxwell, W. Scharf, D. Raksin) TCF
Chicken-Wagon Family (o: G. Rose) TCF
Charlie Chan at Treasure Island (o: G. Rose) TCF
Pack Up Your Troubles (o: G. Rose) TCF
20,000 Men a Year (o: G. Rose; + stock) TCF
Heaven with a Barbed Wire Fence (o: G. Rose) TCF
The Honeymoon's Over (o: W. Scharf) TCF
The Cisco Kid and the Lady (o: Maxwell) TCF

1940
City of Chance (o: G. Rose) TCF
The Man Who Wouldn't Talk (o: Maxwell) TCF
The Jones Family in Young as You Feel (o: G. Rose) TCF
Charlie Chan in Panama (o: Maxwell, G. Rose) TCF
Free, Blonde and 21 (o: W. Scharf, H. Spencer) TCF
Shooting High (o: G. Rose; + stock) TCF
The Jones Family in On Their Own (o: E. Powell, H. Spencer) TCF
Sailor's Lady (o: E. Powell, W. Scharf) TCF

1942
Leather Burners (o: Marquardt; + stock) UA

KAZ, ERIC
1968
Greetings SIGMA III
1970
Hi, Mom! SIGMA III

KAZ, FRED
1969
The Monitors CU

KEANE, DAVID
1965
City of Tanguy (short) ?
1966
A Matter of Consequence (short) ?

KEATING, JOHNNY
1967
Hotel WB

KEEFER, KARL
1951
Light of the World (short) BOB JONES U.
1952
You Can't Win (short) BOB JONES U.
1953
Miracle (short; with Donna Perry) BOB JONES U.

KEES, WELDON
1950
Adventures of Jimmy (short) JAMES BROUGHTON

KELLAWAY, ROGER
1968
Paper Lion UA

KELLER, HOMER
1954
The First Hundred U. OF MICHIGAN

KEMPINSKI, LEO
1923
Scaramouche (see Axt)
1925
Greed (see Axt)

KENDRICK, MERRIL
1949
Kenji Comes Home (doc. short) PFC

KENNEDY, DAVE
1966
We Like it Here (doc.) STATE OF WISCONSIN

KENT, CHARLES
1955
Color Lithography, an Art Medium (doc. short) U. OF MISSISSIPPI

KENTON, STAN
1965
Fraternity for Life (doc. short; o: Rugolo) TAU KAPPA EPSILON

KENZIE, DAVID
1970
Come One, Come All! ENTERTAINMENT VENTURES

KERN, JEROME
1916
Gloria's Romance (serial) KLEINE
1935
The Flame Within (o: Maxwell, Virgil, W. Allen) MGM

KERR, C. HERBERT
1916
The Green Swamp (see Furst)

KILENYI, EDWARD
[Compiled scores for many silent films.]
1929
Abie's Irish Rose (see Zamecnik)
1931
Three Loves (ac for U.S. release of 1929 German film, *Die Frau, nach der man sich sehnt*) ASSOCIATED CINEMAS
1932
Hotel Continental (see Burton) WORLD WIDE
Igloo (see Burton)
1933
Deluge (see Burton)
1935
Angelina (see Sanders)
1937
African Holiday (doc.) HARRY C. PEARSON
Nation Aflame TREASURE PICTURES
Zamboanga GN
Adventures of Chico (with W. Spielter) MON
Headin' East COL
1938
Topa Topa PENNANT
The Overland Express COL
The International Crime GN
Two Gun Justice MON
Clipped Wings ACE
The Terror of Tiny Town COL
1941
Tillie's Punctured Romance (abridged reissue of 1914 film) MON
1942
Ravaged Earth CRYSTAL
1947
The Tender Years TCF
A Fortune in Two Old Trunks (short) SUNSWEET
1948
The Story of Life CRUSADE
Belle Starr's Daughter TCF

KILFEATHER, EDDIE
Cartoons (COL)
1937
The Foxy Pup
Merry Mannequins
1938
The Frog Pond
The Horse on the Merry-Go-Round
Midnight Frolics
Snowtime
1939
Crop Chasers
The Gorilla Hunt
Nell's Yells
1940
Blackboard Revue
The Egg Hunt
Wise Owl
Ye Olde Swap Shoppe
1941
The Crystal Gazer
The Cute Recruit
Dumb Like a Fox
The Fox and the Grapes
Kitty Gets the Bird
The Little Theatre
Playing the Pied Piper
Tom Thumb's Brother
Who's Zoo in Hollywood
1942
A Battle for a Bottle
Concerto in B Flat Minor
Dog Meets Dog
The Gullible Canary
Malice in Slumberland
Red Riding Hood Rides Again
Song of Victory
Toll Bridge Troubles
Under the Shedding Chestnut Tree
Woodman Spare That Tree
1943
A Hunting We Won't Go (with Erdody)
The Cocky Bantam
He Can't Make It Stick
The Playful Pest
Plenty Below Zero
Polly Wants a Doctor
Prof. Small and Mr. Tall

Room and Board
Slay It with Flowers
The Vitamin G-Man
Way Down Yonder in the Corn
1944
As the Fly Flies
Be Patient, Patient
The Dream Kids
Giddy-Yapping
The Herring Murder Mystery
Mr. Fore by Fore
Mr. Moocher
Mutt 'n Bones
A Pee-kool-yar Sit-chee-ay-shun
Porkuliar Piggy
Sadie Hawkins Day
Tangled Travels
1945
Booby Socks
Carnival Courage
Dog, Cat and Canary
The Egg-Yegg
Fiesta Time
Goofy News Views
Hot Foot Lights
Kickapoo Juice
Ku-Ku-Nuts
Phoney Baloney
Simple Siren
Treasure Jest
1946
Cagey Bird
Catnipped
Foxey Flatfoots
Kongo-Roo
Mysto Fox
Picnic Panic
Polar Playmates
River Ribber
The Schooner the Better
Silent Tweetment
Snap Happy Traps
Unsure-Runts
1947
Big House Blues
Cockatoos for Two
Fowl Brawl
Loco Lobo
Mother Hubba-Hubba Hubbard
The Uncultured Vulture
Up 'n' Atom
Feature
1947
Cigarette Girl (see Gertz)

KILPATRICK, JACK FREDERICK
Shorts
1950
Hello, Baby ?
1961
Beauty and the Cave ?
1964
Bob Hope Talks Texas ?

KIMMEL, WALTER
1969
Steps Towards Art (short) ?

KING, PETE
1958
Mardi Gras (see L. Newman)
1965
The Family Jewels (o: Comstock) PAR
1966
The Last of the Secret Agents? (o: Comstock) PAR
1970
Which Way to the Front? (with Louis Brown) WB
[Also worked as an orchestrator.]

KINGSLEY, GERSHON
1970
The Dreamer CANNON

KIRK, LESLEY
Shorts
1949
Mighty Manhattan, New York's Wonder City MGM
1951
Voices of Venice (with Salvador Pastori) MGM
A Word for the Greeks MGM
Romantic Riviera MGM
Glimpses of Morocco and Algiers MGM
Visiting Italy MGM
1968
Come Back to Erin PAR

KIRK, WILBUR
1964
Nothing But a Man (+ stock) CINEMA V

KLATZKIN, LEON
1948
Inner Sanctum FC
1951
As You Were LIP
Tales of Robin Hood LIP

1952
Mr. Walkie Talkie LIP
1953
Captain Scarface ASTOR
1954
The Fifty-First Dragon (cartoon) UPA
1955
The Silver Star LIP
The Lonesome Trail LIP
1956
Two-Gun Lady ASSOCIATED
1959
Go, Johnny, Go! HAL ROACH

KLAUSS, KENNETH
1953
Ballad of the Little Square (short) PORTIA MANSFIELD
1955
Louisiana's Koasati (short) ?

KLEIN, JOHN
1953
Canadian Mounties (doc. short) RKO PATHÉ
[Published sources state that in 1944 he scored two documentary shorts for the U.S. Navy and three for RKO Pathé, but the titles given cannot be verified.]

KLEIN, MANUEL
1914
Soldiers of Fortune ALL STAR
Paid in Full ALL STAR
In Mizzoura ALL STAR
Pierre of the Plains ALL STAR
America ALL STAR
The Jungle ALL STAR
Dan ALL STAR
The Nightingale ALL STAR

KLEIN, MARTIN
1964
St. Francis of Assisi (short) KARL HOLTSNIDER
1965
That They May See (short) KARL HOLTSNIDER
Elements of the Film (doc. short) KARL HOLTSNIDER
Language of the Film (doc. short) KARL HOLTSNIDER

KLEINER, ARTHUR
Shorts
1943
Alexander Calder: Sculpture and Constructions MUSEUM OF MODERN ART
1948
The Singing Earth NELL DORR
1953
In the Street FILM DOCUMENT
1955
The Mantel of Protection FILM DOCUMENT
1958
Inside Connecticut STATE OF CONNECTICUT
Shorts (WESTON WOODS)
1955
Andy and the Lion
Hercules
Make Way for Ducklings
Millions of Cats
The Red Carpet
Stone Soup
The Story About Ping
1956
The Circus Baby
Georgie
Jenny's Birthday Book
The Little Red Lighthouse and the Great Gray Bridge
Mike Mulligan and His Steam Shovel
1958
The Camel Who Took a Walk
Curious George Rides a Bike
The Five Chinese Brothers
Lentil
1960
Caps for Sale
In the Forest
Magic Michael
Pancho
1961
Frog Went A-Courtin'
Time of Wonder
1962
This Is New York

KLEINSINGER, GEORGE
1964
The Inheritance (doc.) MAYER
1970
Shinbone Alley (an.) AA
Shorts
1951
The Telephone and the Farmer (doc.) USDA

1952
Woodland Manners (doc.) USDA
1953
The Big Gamble (doc.) USDA
Grass: The Big Story (doc.) USDA
Gypsy Moth (doc.) USDA
Little Smokey (doc.) USDA
Skippy and the 3 R's (doc.) NEA
1954
Freedom to Learn NEA
Men, Women and Children (doc.) USDA
Rainbow Valley: The Story of a Forest Ranger (doc.) USDA
The Small Sawmill (doc.) USDA
The United Way (an.) COMMUNITY CHEST
1955
Better Seeds for Better Grasslands (doc.) USDA
From the Ground Up (doc.) USDA
From the Ridge to the River (doc.) USDA
Modernizing Marketing Facilities (doc.) USDA
Out of the Woods (doc.) USDA
This Is Your Forest (doc.) USDA
1956
Days of a Tree (doc.) USDA
The Town Musicians (an.) PIPER PRODS.
Tree Bank (doc.) USDA
1957
The Japanese Beetle (doc.) USDA
Our Magic Land (doc.) USDA
A Piece of Wood (doc.) USDA
Wonders of New Orleans (doc.) COL
1958
Back the Attack on Brucellosis (doc.) USDA
The Eternal Harvest ALBERT PRODS.
1960
Eastern White Pine (doc.) USDA
The REA Story (doc.) USDA
1961
The Dust Is Dying (doc.) USDA
Jet Terminal PAN AMERICAN
The Little Star of Bethlehem MKR FILMS
Voice of the Forest USDA
1962
Challenging Careers in Chemistry (doc.) USDA
Emma Belle Sweet (doc.) NEA
Forest in a Museum (doc.) USDA
Heritage Restored (doc.) USDA
It's the Farmers' Business (doc.) USDA
1963
This Is Israel WESTON WOODS
Watch Out for Witchweed (doc.) USDA
1964
Silent Snow, Secret Snow GENE KEARNEY
Our Schools Have Kept Us Free (doc.) NEA
1966
Design for Dreaming (ballet film) SPECTRA PRODS.
1969
Children's Letters to God LEE MENDELSON
Hurricane (doc.) AETNA LIFE & CASUALTY

KNIGHT, GLENN
1929
South Sea Rose (see Brunelli)
Men Without Women (see Brunelli)
1930
Such Men Are Dangerous (see Brunelli)
Good Intentions (see Brunelli)
Man Trouble (see R. Bassett)
One Mad Kiss (see Brunelli)
Scotland Yard (see Arthur Kay)
Part Time Wife (see R. Bassett)
The Man Who Came Back (see Brunelli)
1931
East Lynne (see R. Bassett)
Hush Money FOX
The Spider (see Friedhofer)
Riders of the Purple Sage (see R. Bassett)
1932
Chandu, the Magician (see Brunelli)
1933
Arizona to Broadway (see A. Lange)

KNIGHT, TERRY
1967
The Incident (adapted by Charles Fox) TCF

KNUDSON, THURSTON
1941
Hoola Boola (cartoon) PAR

KOFF, CHARLES
1946
Abilene Town (see Terr)
1951
The Man from Planet X UA
1952
Captive Women RKO
Sword of Venus RKO
1953
Mahatma Gandhi—20th Century Prophet (doc.) UA
1956
Down Liberty Road (doc.; with C. Wheeler) WB

Documentary Shorts
1950
The New Pioneers PAR
1953
America for Me (with C. Wheeler) WB
1956
They Seek Adventure (with C. Wheeler) WB

KOGEN, LAWRENCE
1965
Laurel and Hardy's Laughing 20's (see Alquist)
1967
The Further Perils of Laurel and Hardy (see Parker)

KOMEDA, KRZYSZTOF (CHRISTOPHER)
1968
Rosemary's Baby (o: Hazard) PAR
Riot (o: Hazard) PAR
[Also composed scores for several Polish films.]

KOMROFF, M.
1912
Fighting Dan McCool (short) KALEM

KOOPER, AL
1969
My Girlfriend's Wedding PARADIGM
1970
The Landlord UA

KOPP, FRED
1963
The Smile of Recife (short) FAMILY THEATRE
1964
The Creeping Terror TELEDYN
1968
Air Freight Specialist (short) FLYING TIGER AIRLINES

KOPP, RUDOLPH G.
1931
Gente Alegre (see Leipold))
The Vice Squad (see Rainger)
Forbidden Adventure (mt) PAR
I Take This Woman (see Rainger)
El Príncipe Gondolero (Spanish language; with Leipold; ac: Krumgold) PAR
The Secret Call PAR
The Magnificent Lie (see Leipold)
Daughter of the Dragon (with Leipold) PAR
The Mad Parade (see Leipold)
24 Hours (see Leipold)
The Road to Reno (see Leipold)
The Beloved Bachelor (see Leipold)
Once a Lady (with Hand, Hajos, Potoker) PAR
Rich Man's Folly (see Leipold)
The False Madonna (see Leipold)
1932
Two Kinds of Women (see Leipold)
Tomorrow and Tomorrow (see Hand)
Shanghai Express (see Harling)
Strangers in Love (with Pasternacki, Leipold) PAR
The Broken Wing (see Leipold)
One Hour with You (see Leipold)
This Is the Night (see Harling)
Sinners in the Sun (see Leipold)
Forgotten Commandments (see Hand)
Merrily We Go to Hell (with Leipold; + stock) PAR
The Man from Yesterday (see Leipold)
Million Dollar Legs (see Leipold)
Devil and the Deep (see Hand)
The Sign of the Cross (with Marquardt, Roder; ac: Chernis) PAR
1933
The Woman Accused (m&e; + stock) PAR
From Hell to Heaven (mt; + stock) PAR
King of the Jungle (see Hand)
Pick Up (see Rainger)
Murders in the Zoo (with Leipold) PAR
I Love That Man (see Kaun)
I'm No Angel (see H. Jackson)
1934
Cleopatra (o: Roder, Reese) PAR
1935
The Crusades (ac: Roemheld, Roder, Hollander, Leipold, Hand) PAR
1936
The Voice of Bugle Ann (see Roemheld)
1946
Gallant Bess (o: Sendrey, Byrns) MGM
My Brother Talks to Horses (o: Byrns) MGM
1947
Tenth Avenue Angel (with A. Previn; o: Byrns) MGM
1948
The Bride Goes Wild (o: Byrns; mt: A. Previn) MGM
1949
Some of the Best (see Cutner)
The Doctor and the Girl (o: Cutner, Shuken) MGM

Ambush (o: R. Franklyn; ac and o: Sendrey) MGM
1950
Mystery Street (o: Shuken, Cutner) MGM
1951
Vengeance Valley (o: Marquardt) MGM
Bannerline (o: Heglin) MGM
Calling Bulldog Drummond (o: Heglin) MGM
It's a Big Country (see A. Deutsch)
1952
Fearless Fagan (o: Heglin; + stock) MGM
1953
Arena (o: Marquardt) MGM
1954
Gypsy Colt (ac: Sendrey; o: Sendrey, Marquardt) MGM
Shorts (MGM)
1936
Little Boy Blue (see C. Bakaleinikoff)
No Place Like Rome
1937
A Girl's Best Years
1946
The Horse with the Human Mind
1947
Able Baker
The Amazing Mr. Nordill (o: R. Franklyn)
Miracle in a Cornfield (o: R. Franklyn)
1949
Annie Was a Wonder
Mr. Whitney Had a Notion
Clues to Adventure
The City of Children (o: Marquardt)
1950
Wrong Son (o: Sendrey)
1953
Nostradamus Says So
Let's Ask Nostradamus
Nostradamus and the Queen
Trailers (MGM)
1946
Lady in the Lake
1947
Cynthia
The Unfinished Dance
1951
The Tall Target

KORB, ARTHUR
1965
Demo Derby (doc. short) JAMES A. PIKE
1966
Feelin' Good JAMES A. PIKE

KORN, RICHARD
1964
Return No More (short) AMERICAN COUNCIL FOR JUDAISM

KORNGOLD, ERICH WOLFGANG
1935
A Midsummer Night's Dream (a of Mendelssohn and ac) WB
Captain Blood (o: Friedhofer, Roder, Heindorf) WB
1936
Give Us This Night (o: Friedhofer) PAR
Hearts Divided (see Roemheld)
The Green Pastures (o: Friedhofer) WB
Anthony Adverse (o: Friedhofer, Roder) WB
1937
The Prince and the Pauper (o: Friedhofer, Roder) WB
Another Dawn (o: Friedhofer, Roder) WB
1938
The Adventures of Robin Hood (o: Friedhofer, Roder, R. Bassett) WB
1939
Juarez (o: Friedhofer, Roder) WB
The Private Lives of Elizabeth and Essex (o: Friedhofer, Roder) WB
1940
The Sea Hawk (o: Friedhofer, Roder, Heindorf, Bucharoff) WB
1941
The Sea Wolf (o: Friedhofer, Heindorf) WB
1942
Kings Row (o: Friedhofer, Roder, Heindorf, Kaun) WB
1943
The Constant Nymph (o: Friedhofer) WB
1944
Between Two Worlds (o: Friedhofer, Bucharoff, Raab) WB
1946
Devotion (o: Friedhofer, Bucharoff, Toch, Raab, Kaun, Roder) WB
Of Human Bondage (o: Bucharoff, Friedhofer) WB
Deception (o: Cutter) WB
1947
Escape Me Never (o: Friedhofer, Heindorf) WB
1955
Magic Fire (a of Wagner) REP

KOSTAL, IRWIN
1961
West Side Story (see S. Chaplin)
1964
Mary Poppins WDP
1965
The Sound of Music TCF
1967
Half a Sixpence PAR
1968
Chitty Chitty Bang Bang UA

KRAFT, WILLIAM
1958
Desire in a Public Dump (short) ROBERT PIKE
1962
Hud (trailer only) PAR

KRAININ, LEW
1966
Hide and Seek (short) COLUMBIA U. PRESS

KRAUSHAAR, RAOUL
[He received screen credit for musical direction or music supervision on many Republic pictures from 1937 to 1942. Those films are not included here because the Republic archives have not been sufficiently researched. Among his later pseudonyms are Ralph Stanley and Stanley C. Rogers.]

A single asterisk (*) indicates that the score was ghostwritten or has some music by Mort Glickman, according to the Glickman estate.

A double asterisk (**) indicates music ghostwritten by Dave Kahn, according to Kahn, and "many more I don't remember."
1947
The Adventures of Don Coyote UA
Stork Bites Man UA
The Burning Cross SG
The Marauders UA
Dangerous Years TCF
Road to the Big House SG
1948
Let's Live Again TCF
The Argyle Secrets FC
The Dead Don't Dream UA
Shaggy PAR
False Paradise UA
Shed No Tears EL
Strange Gamble UA
Night Wind TCF
The Gay Intruders TCF
Unknown Island FC
1949
Highway 13 SG
Roll, Thunder, Roll! EL
Riders of the Pony Express SCREENCRAFT
Arson, Inc. SG
Zamba EL
Sky Liner SG
Wild Weed FRANKLIN
Cowboy and the Prize Fighter EL
1950
*Prehistoric Women** EL
Timber Fury EL
The Second Face EL
1951
*The Sword of Monte Cristo** TCF
Stagecoach Driver MON
Oklahoma Justice MON
The Basketball Fix REALART
Wanted: Dead or Alive MON
*Bride of the Gorilla** REALART
Whistling Hills MON
*Galahad Jones** WILDING
*Elephant Stampede** MON
Lawless Cowboys MON
*The Longhorn** MON
Texas Lawmen MON
Stage to Blue River MON
1952
Texas City MON
Night Raiders MON
*Waco** MON
Rose of Cimarron (with Alperson)* TCF
Man from the Black Hills MON
The Gunman MON
Kansas Territory MON
African Treasure MON
Dead Man's Trail MON
Montana Incident MON
*Fargo** MON
*Untamed Women** UA
Operation Mexico (doc.) WILDING
Canyon Ambush MON
Wyoming Roundup MON
*Bomba and the Jungle Girl** MON
*The Maverick** AA
Abbott and Costello Meet Captain Kidd WB
1953
Star of Texas AA
The Homesteaders AA
*The Blue Gardenia*** WB

The Marksman AA
*Invaders from Mars** TCF
Run for the Hills REALART
Rebel City AA
Topeka AA
The Fighting Lawman AA
*Marry Me Again*** RKO
*Vigilante Terror*** AA
Texas Bad Man AA

1954
Bitter Creek AA
The Forty-Niners AA
The Desperado AA
Two Guns and a Badge AA
The Golden Mistress UA
Sitting Bull UA
The Outlaw's Daughter TCF

1955
The Magnificent Matador TCF

1956
Curucu, Beast of the Amazon UNIV
The Black Whip TCF

1957
The Wayward Girl REP
*Back from the Dead*** TCF
*The Unknown Terror*** TCF
*Copper Sky*** TCF
*Ride a Violent Mile*** TCF
*Blood Arrow*** TCF

1958
The Unchained Goddess ayer
*Desert Hell*** TCF
*The Cool and the Crazy*** AIP

1959
Mustang UA
*Island of Lost Women*** WB
The 30-Foot Bride of Candy Rock COL

1960
September Storm (with Alperson) TCF

1964
Vengeance CROWN

1966
Billy the Kid Versus Dracula EMBASSY
Jesse James Meets Frankenstein's Daughter EMBASSY
An Eye for an Eye (with R. Raksin) EMBASSY

1967
They Ran for Their Lives MASTERPIECE

1968
The Bamboo Saucer WORLD

1970
The Delta Factor (with Danziger) CONTINENTAL

Documentary Shorts

1945
Army training films (VARIETY, 9 MARCH)

1950
*You Can Beat the A-Bomb** RKO

1952
Insurance Against Fire Losses (an.) ENCYCLOPAEDIA BRITANNICA
New Tools for Learning U. OF CHICAGO

KREIDER, NOBLE

1914
Samson UNIV

KREMENLIEV, BORIS

1953
The Tell Tale Heart (an. short) UPA

1955
Crucifixion (doc. short) UCLA

KREUTZ, ARTHUR

1942
Salvage (doc. short) OWI

1969
Theatre and Your Community (doc. short) U. OF MISSISSIPPI

KROCULICK, JOSEPH A.

1964
Every Sparrow Must Fall DCA

KROLL, NATHAN

1958
Israel, an Adventure (doc. short) TRIBUNE FILMS

KRUMGOLD, SIGMUND

1930
Monte Carlo (see Harling)

1931
Fighting Caravans (see Leipold)
Rango (see Hajos)
El Príncipe Gondolero (see R. Kopp)

1932
Forgotten Commandments (see Hand)
Thunder Below (with Pasternacki) PAR

1933
A Lady's Profession (see Leipold)

1935
The Gilded Lily (see Satterfield)

1940
Adventure in Diamonds (see Shuken)
Opened by Mistake (see Leipold)

1941

The Lady Eve (see Shuken)

KRUMMEL, CONSTANTINE

1935

Soviet Russia Through the Eyes of an American (doc.) IMPERIAL

KUBIK, GAIL

1949

C-Man FC

1951

Two Gals and a Guy UA

1955

The Desperate Hours (see Amfitheatrof)

Documentaries

1940

Men and Ships U.S. MARITIME COMMISSION

1942

The World at War OWI
Manpower (short) OWI
Dover (short) OWI
Colleges at War (short) OWI

1943

Paratroops (short) OWI
Earthquakers (short) AAF

1944

The Memphis Belle AAF

1945

Air Pattern Pacific (short) AAF
Thunderbolt AAF

Cartoons

1950

The Miner's Daughter UPA

1951

Gerald McBoing Boing UPA

1952

Trans Atlantic LES FILMS MADELEINE

KUDO, KAZUE

1970

Hand and Clay: A Celebration (doc. short) DAVE BELL ASSOCIATES

KUPFERMAN, MEYER

1961

Blast of Silence UNIV

1963

Hallelujah the Hills ADOLFAS MEKAS

1964

Black Like Me CONTINENTAL

1965

Goldstein ALTURA
The Double-Barrelled Detective Story ADOLFAS MEKAS

1969

Trilogy AA
Fearless Frank AIP

Documentary Shorts

1959

Chinese Dressmaking CHINA FILM ENTERPRISES
Chinese Firecrackers CHINA FILM ENTERPRISES
Nanking CHINA FILM ENTERPRISES
Peking CHINA FILM ENTERPRISES
Tsientsien CHINA FILM ENTERPRISES

1964

Cool Wind ?

1965

Faces of America U.S. STATE DEPT.
High Arctic EXPLORER'S CLUB, USA

KURTZ, SAUNDERS

1927

Twin Flappers AYWON

1928

The City Without Jews AYWON

KYNARD, CHARLES E.

1969

Midtown Madness ?

KYTE, BENNY

1952

Inside Harvester WILDING

L

LACKEY, DOUGLAS
[In the 1950s, he scored several student films at UCLA.]
Features (see Kauer)
Documentary Shorts
1962
The Far Sound JSP
1964
Your Union DONALD A. DAVIS PRODS.
Your Voice and Vote DONALD A. DAVIS PRODS.
1966
Arizona and Its Natural Resources U.S. BUREAU OF MINES
1967
Ready on Arrival GRUMMAN AIRCRAFT
Sea of Contention GRUMMAN AIRCRAFT
1968
The Long Shadow USC

LADERMAN, EZRA
Documentary Features
1962
Black Fox LOUIS CLYDE STOUMEN
1964
The Image of Love LOUIS CLYDE STOUMEN
1965
The Eleanor Roosevelt Story RICHARD KAPLAN
1970
The Burden of the Mystery JOHN BARNES
Documentary Shorts
1958
The Invisible Atom ?
1960
The Charter UNITED NATIONS
1961
The Question Tree HENRY STRAUSS PRODS.
1964
Odyssey ?
1967
The Meaning of Modern Art JOHN BARNES
1968
Confrontation RICHARD KAPLAN
1969
Magic Prison JOHN BARNES

LAKE, M. L.
1917
The Submarine Eye (+ stock) WILLIAMSON

LAKE, OLIVER
1968
Jazzoo (short) JOHN CAMIE

LAMBRO, PHILLIP
1964
Energy on the Move (doc. short) COLUMBIA GAS SYSTEM
1965
Git! EMBASSY
1966
And Now Miguel UNIV

LAMKOFF, PAUL
1929
The Mysterious Island (with Axt; love theme: Broones; + stock) MGM
1930
The Cossacks (see Axt)
Three Faces East (love theme) WB
[Also worked as an orchestrator.]

LANCE, VIC
1968
Mantis in Lace BOXOFFICE INT'L
1969
Weekend Lover BOXOFFICE INT'L
1970
The Notorious Cleopatra BOXOFFICE INT'L
The Joys of Jezebel P. O. FILMS

LANDAU, IRVING
1952
FDR—Hyde Park (doc. short) PICTORIAL FILMS

LANDAU, SIEGFRIED
1948
Displaced Persons (doc. short) ?

LANGE, ARTHUR
1929
Wonder of Women (with Wineland, Axt) MGM
Dynamite (see Axt)
The Hollywood Revue MGM
1931
Millie RKO
The Common Law RKO
A Woman of Experience RKO

The Big Gamble RKO
Rebound RKO
Bad Company RKO
The Tip-Off (mt) RKO
Freighters of Destiny RKO
Suicide Fleet RKO
The Big Shot RKO

1932
Prestige (with Harold Lewis) RKO
Carnival Boat (with H. Lewis) RKO
Lady with a Past (see H. Lewis)
Beauty and the Boss (see Harling)
This Is the Night (see Harling)
Week Ends Only FOX
Rebecca of Sunnybrook Farm (with Friedhofer) FOX
A Passport to Hell (see Friedhofer)
The Painted Woman (see Friedhofer)
Hat Check Girl FOX
The Golden West (+ stock) FOX
Rackety Rax (o: Marquardt) FOX
Call Her Savage (with Brunelli; + stock) FOX

1933
Cavalcade (see De Francesco)
Infernal Machine (see Kaylin)
Smoke Lightning (with Brunelli) FOX
Broadway Bad (with Friedhofer) FOX
Hello, Sister! (+ stock) FOX
The Warrior's Husband (see Zamecnik)
Adorable (ac: Zamecnik, Brunelli, De Francesco) FOX
I Loved You Wednesday (see De Francesco)
Best of Enemies (with R. Bassett; ac: W. Spielter) FOX
Arizona to Broadway (with G. Knight, Van Loan; + stock) FOX
La Melodía Prohibida (see Kaylin)
My Weakness (ac: Mockridge; o: W. Spielter) FOX
The Worst Woman in Paris? (see De Francesco)
Jimmy and Sally (ac: Friedhofer) FOX

1934
Orient Express (see Friedhofer)
Stand Up and Cheer! FOX
Now I'll Tell (see Friedhofer)
Grand Canary (see De Francesco)
Servants' Entrance (see Friedhofer)
Marie Galante (o: Van Loan) FOX

1935
Lottery Lover (ac: Friedhofer, Buttolph) FOX
One More Spring (see Buttolph)
It's a Small World (with Zamecnik; ac: Brunelli, Buttolph) FOX
Spring Tonic (see Brunelli)
Daring Young Man (with Buttolph, Brunelli) FOX
Orchids to You (with Buttolph, Friedhofer) FOX
Curly Top (see Friedhofer)
Dante's Inferno (see Friedhofer)
In Old Kentucky (o: Haring, Gerstenberger; + stock) FOX

1936
The Great Ziegfeld (ac: Maxwell, Friedhofer, Axt) MGM
Girls' Dormitory (see Maxwell)
The Magnificent Brute (see Maxwell)
Under Your Spell (see Maxwell)
White Hunter (see Maxwell)
Banjo on My Knee (see Maxwell)

1937
This Is My Affair (see Maxwell)
Love Under Fire (with Maxwell) TCF
The Lancer Spy (see Maxwell)

1938
Sally, Irene and Mary (see W. Scharf)
Kidnapped (see Maxwell)
Submarine Patrol (see Maxwell)

1939
Let Freedom Ring (ac: Snell; o: Raab) MGM
Everything Happens at Night (see Buttolph)
The Great Victor Herbert (with Boutelje) PAR

1940
Married and in Love RKO
Maryland (see Buttolph)

1942
It's Everybody's War (doc. short; o: Virgil) TCF
Prelude to War (see Harline)
The Other Woman (o: Maxwell) TCF
Dixie Dugan (with Maxwell; o: A. Morton) TCF
The Undying Monster (see D. Raksin)
China Girl (see Friedhofer)
Quiet, Please, Murder (with Maxwell; o: A. Morton) TCF

1943
Substitution and Conversion (doc.; see Tiomkin)
Lady of Burlesque (with Maxwell; o: de Packh) UA
They Came to Blow Up America (see Friedhofer)

Coney Island (see Mockridge)
Wintertime (with Friedhofer, Harline, Buttolph, Maxwell) TCF
The Dancing Masters (o: A. Morton) TCF
The Gang's All Here (with Friedhofer, A. Newman, Mockridge, G. Rose) TCF

1944
Four Jills in a Jeep (see Friedhofer)
Buffalo Bill (see Buttolph)
Bermuda Mystery (o: A. Morton) TCF
Pin Up Girl (see Mockridge)
Roger Touhy, Gangster (see Friedhofer)
Greenwich Village (see Buttolph)
Casanova Brown (with Maxwell, Vaughan, H. Jackson; o: De Saxe, Schoepp, Leftwich) INTERNATIONAL
The Woman in the Window (see Friedhofer)
Belle of the Yukon (with Friedhofer; ac: D. Raksin; o: Schoepp, De Saxe, Virgil) INTERNATIONAL

1945
It's a Pleasure (ac: Roemheld, B. Mason, Sheets; o: Maxwell, Schoepp) INTERNATIONAL
Along Came Jones (with Friedhofer, Maxwell; o: Vaughan, R. Franklyn, Schoepp, Leftwich) INTERNATIONAL

1946
Rendezvous 24 (o: A. Morton) TCF
The Time of Their Lives (see M. Rosen)
The Fabulous Suzanne (o: De Saxe) REP

1948
Texas, Brooklyn, and Heaven UA
Jungle Patrol TCF

1950
The Groom Wore Spurs UNIV
The Vicious Years FC
Guilty of Treason (see Friedhofer)
The Golden Gloves Story (with Skiles) EL
Woman on the Run UNIV
Cry Danger (see Dunlap)

1951
Queen for a Day (see Friedhofer)

1952
Japanese War Bride TCF
The Lady Says No UA
Rancho Notorious (see Friedhofer)
The Pride of St. Louis (o: Arnaud) TCF
Down Among the Sheltering Palms (with Harline; o: Arnaud) TCF
Big Jim McLain (see Dunlap)

1953
War Paint UA
Plunder of the Sun (see Diaz Conde)
99 River Street UA
Island in the Sky (see Friedhofer)
The Steel Lady UA

1954
Beachhead UA
The Mad Magician COL
Southwest Passage UA
Ring of Fear (see Dunlap)

LANGE, JOHNNY
[In collaboration with Lew Porter:]

1938
Where the West Begins MON

1939
Code of the Fearless SPECTRUM
Port of Hate METROPOLITAN
Code of the Cactus VICTORY
The Pal from Texas METROPOLITAN
El Diablo Rides METROPOLITAN
Midnight Shadow SACK

1940
Texas Renegades PDC
Pride of the Bowery MON
The Cheyenne Kid MON
Wild Horse Valley METROPOLITAN
Danger Ahead MON
Murder on the Yukon MON
Covered Wagon Trails MON
Pinto Canyon METROPOLITAN
Riders from Nowhere MON
The Golden Trail MON
Wild Horse Range MON
Land of the Six Guns MON

1941
Ridin' the Cherokee Trail MON
The Lone Rider Crosses the Rio PRC
Flying Wild MON
Invisible Ghost MON
The Lone Rider in Ghost Town PRC
The Texas Marshal PRC
Paper Bullets PRC
Billy the Kid in Santa Fe PRC
Zis Boom Bah MON
The Lone Rider in Frontier Fury PRC
The Lone Rider Ambushed PRC
Billy the Kid Wanted PRC
The Lone Rider Fights Back PRC
Spooks Run Wild MON
Swamp Woman PRC
Billy the Kid's Round-Up PRC
I Killed That Man MON

1942
Today I Hang PRC

Billy the Kid Trapped PRC
The Lone Rider in Cheyenne PRC
Mr. Wise Guy MON
Black Dragons MON
Rolling Down the Great Divide PRC
The Corpse Vanishes MON
Billy the Kid's Smoking Guns PRC
Let's Get Tough MON
The Lone Rider in Texas Justice PRC
Tumbleweed Trail PRC
Texas Manhunt PRC

1943
Along the Sundown Trail PRC
Sheriff of Sage Valley PRC
Outlaws of Boulder Pass PRC
Border Roundup PRC
Prairie Pals PRC

LANHAM, GENE

1949
The Judge FC

LANNIN, PAUL

1933
The Poor Fish (short) COL

1937
The Little Maestro (short; o: Bassman) MGM

LANTZ, GARY

1967
Marvin Digs (cartoon) PAR

LAPHAM, CLAUDE

1930
Feet First PAR
Charley's Aunt COL

LaSALLE, RICHARD

1958
Tank Battalion AIP

1959
Speed Crazy AA

1960
The Big Night PAR
Why Must I Die? AIP

1961
Sniper's Ridge TCF
When the Clock Strikes UA
You Have to Run Fast UA
Flight That Disappeared UA
Wild Youth CINEMA ASSOC.
Secret of Deep Harbor UA
The Purple Hills TCF
The Boy Who Caught a Crook UA
Gun Street UA
Saintly Sinners UA
The Broken Land TCF

1962
Incident in an Alley UA
Deadly Duo UA
The Clown and the Kid UA
Hands of a Stranger AA
The Mermaids of Tiburon FILMGROUP
The Firebrand TCF
The Day Mars Invaded Earth TCF

1963
California AIP
Diary of a Madman UA
Police Nurse TCF
Twice Told Tales UA

1964
The Quick Gun COL
Apache Rifles TCF
Blood on the Arrow AA
The Time Travelers AIP
A Yank in Viet-Nam AA

1965
War Party TCF
Fort Courageous TCF
Arizona Raiders COL
Convict Stage TCF
The Desert Raven AA

1966
Runaway Girl UNITED SCREEN ARTS
Don't Worry, We'll Think of a Title UA
Ambush Bay UA
Boy, Did I Get a Wrong Number! UA

1967
40 Guns to Apache Pass COL

1969
This Is My Alaska (doc.) LEROY SHEBAL

LASKO, EDWARD

1959
The Immoral Mr. Teas EVE

LASKO, EMIL

1961
Symphony in Motion (doc. short) PAR

LASZLO, ALEXANDER

1944
The Chinese Cat MON
Black Magic MON
One Body Too Many PAR
Double Exposure PAR
Dangerous Passage PAR

1945
High Powered PAR
The Great Flamarion REP
Scared Stiff PAR
Midnight Manhunt PAR
Follow That Woman PAR
1946
They Made Me a Killer PAR
Strange Impersonation REP
The Glass Alibi REP
Hot Cargo PAR
Joe Palooka, Champ MON
The French Key REP
Accomplice PRC
1947
Yankee Fakir REP
Untamed Fury PRC
Banjo RKO
1948
The Spiritualist EL
Parole, Inc EL
Tarzan's Magic Fountain RKO
1949
Song of India (based on music of Rimsky-Korsakov) COL
Amazon Quest FC
Alimony EL
1957
Fincho SAM ZEBBA
1958
The Narcotics Story (semi-doc.) HARRY STERN
Ghost of the China Sea COL
Night of the Blood Beast AIP
Forbidden Island COL
Submarine Seahawk AIP
1959
Attack of the Giant Leeches AIP
The Atomic Submarine AA
1961
The Legend of Aku-Aku, the Mysterious Land of Easter Island (doc.) DE ROSNER PRODS.
Shorts
1947
My Pal RKO
1948
Pal's Adventure RKO
Pal's Return RKO
1949
I Found a Dog RKO
Dog of the Wild RKO
Pal, Canine Detective RKO
1950
Pal, Fugitive Dog RKO
Pal's Gallant Journey RKO
1954
People Without Place (doc.) ERNEST KLEINBERG
The Story of Colonel Drake ROLAND REED
1955
Every Moment Thine (doc.) TRINITY FILMS
The Honorable Mountain RAY FIELDING PRODS.
The Invisible Moustache of Raoul Dufy (cartoon) UPA
Lost in the Night RELIGIOUS FILM FOUNDATION

LAUBER, KEN
1967
Press On Regardless (doc. short) PAR
The Drifter FILM-MAKERS
1968
Fade In (ac: Shuken, Hayes) PAR
1969
To Ingrid My Love, Lisa CANNON
1970
Scratch Harry CANNON
Brand X C.M.B.

LAVA, WILLIAM
1938
Heroes of the Hills (see Feuer)
The Higgins Family (with Feuer, Nussbaum) REP
Billy the Kid Returns (+ stock) REP
Rhythm of the Saddle (see Colombo)
Storm Over Bengal (see Feuer)
Santa Fe Stampede REP
Come On, Rangers (with Feuer, Nussbaum; + stock) REP
Western Jamboree (with Feuer, Nussbaum; + stock) REP
Hawk of the Wilderness (serial; with Nussbaum, Feuer; + stock) REP
Red River Range REP
1939
Fighting Thoroughbreds (see Feuer)
The Mysterious Miss X (with Feuer) REP
Woman Doctor (with Sawtell, Feuer) REP
Rough Riders' Round-Up (mt; + stock) REP
Mexicali Rose (see Feuer)
The Night Riders REP
Blue Montana Skies (with Feuer; ac: Nussbaum; + stock) REP

Three Texas Steers REP
My Wife's Relatives (see Feuer)
Mountain Rhythm (see Feuer)
Daredevils of the Red Circle (serial; with Feuer; ac: Tamkin; + stock) REP
Wyoming Outlaw REP
Mickey the Kid (see Feuer)
She Married a Cop (see Feuer)
Should Husbands Work? (with Feuer) REP
New Frontier REP
Dick Tracy's G-Men (serial) REP
Wall Street Cowboy (mt; + stock) REP
The Kansas Terrors REP
Main Street Lawyer (with Feuer) REP
The Covered Trailer (with Feuer) REP
Zorro's Fighting Legion (serial; with Feuer; ac: Nussbaum, Tamkin) REP
Days of Jesse James (with Morgan; + stock) REP

1940

Heroes of the Saddle (see Feuer)
Wolf of New York (+ stock) REP
The Courageous Dr. Christian RKO
King of the Lumberjacks WB
Murder in the Air WB
Grandpa Goes to Town (see Sawtell)
A Fugitive from Justice (see H. Jackson)
Adventures of Red Ryder (serial; with Sawtell) REP
Girl from God's Country REP
Oklahoma Renegades (see Sawtell)
Earl of Puddlestone (+ stock) REP
King of the Royal Mounted (see Feuer)
The Crooked Road (+ stock) REP
Gangs of Chicago (+ stock) REP
Under Texas Skies (with Sawtell; + stock) REP
South of Suez (see Hollander)
The Border Legion (see Rosen)

1941

The Great Mr. Nobody (see A. Deutsch)
A Shot in the Dark (ac: H. Jackson) WB
Knockout (see H. Jackson)
Strange Alibi (see H. Jackson)
The Nurse's Secret (o: Maxwell) WB
Passage from Hong Kong (o: Maxwell) WB
Nine Lives Are Not Enough (o: Maxwell) WB
The Smiling Ghost (see Kaun)
Highway West (o: Maxwell) WB
Law of the Tropics (see H. Jackson)
International Squadron (o: Maxwell) WB
Steel Against the Sky (o: Maxwell) WB

1942

Dangerously They Live (o: Maxwell) WB
Bullet Scars (with Roemheld, H. Jackson) (o: Maxwell) WB
I Was Framed (see H. Jackson)
Murder in the Big House (see H. Jackson)
Larceny, Inc. (see A. Deutsch)
Lady Gangster (with H. Jackson) (o: Maxwell) WB
Escape from Crime (ac: H. Jackson; o: Maxwell) WB
Spy Ship (ac: H. Jackson; o: Maxwell) WB
Busses Roar (with H. Jackson; o: Maxwell) WB
Secret Enemies (see H. Jackson)
The Hidden Hand (o: Maxwell) WB

1943

The Gorilla Man (o: Maxwell) WB
The Mysterious Doctor (with H. Jackson, Sommer; o: Maxwell) WB
Action in the North Atlantic (see A. Deutsch)
The Strange Death of Adolph Hitler (ac: Sawtell, Salter) UNIV

1944

Destination Tokyo (see Waxman)
Make Your Own Bed (see Roemheld)
The Invisible Man's Revenge (see Salter)
Crime by Night (o: Maxwell) WB
The Last Ride (o: Maxwell) WB
Murder in the Blue Room (ac: Salter) UNIV

1945

That's the Spirit (see Salter)
The Horn Blows at Midnight (see Waxman)
Shady Lady UNIV
House of Dracula (+ stock) UNIV

1946

Saratoga Trunk (see M. Steiner)
She-Wolf of London UNIV
Her Kind of Man (see Waxman)
Two Guys from Milwaukee (see Hollander)

1948

The Big Punch (o: Maxwell) WB
Embraceable You (o: Maxwell) WB
Moonrise REP

1949

Whiplash (see Waxman)
Flaxy Martin (o: Maxwell) WB
Homicide (o: Maxwell) WB
The Younger Brothers (o: Maxwell) WB
The House Across the Street (o: Maxwell) WB

1950

Barricade (o: Maxwell) WB
Colt .45 (o: Maxwell) WB
This Side of the Law (o: Maxwell) WB
The Great Jewel Robber (o: Maxwell) WB
Breakthrough (o: Maxwell) WB
Highway 301 (o: Maxwell) WB

1951

Inside the Walls of Folsom Prison (o: Maxwell) WB
Five (see H. Russell)
The Tanks Are Coming (o: Maxwell) WB

1952

Retreat, Hell! (o: Maxwell) WB
Cattle Town (o: Maxwell) WB

1953

Border River (see Mancini)
Phantom from Space UA
Stormy, the Thoroughbred with an Inferiority Complex WDP
All American (+ stock) UNIV

1954

Yankee Pasha (see Salter)
War Arrow (see H. Stein)
Ma and Pa Kettle at Home (see H. Stein)
Saskatchewan (see Mancini)
Tanganyika (see Salter)
Black Horse Canyon (see F. Skinner)
Fireman, Save My Child (with Mancini; ac: H. Stein) UNIV
Tobor the Great (see H. Jackson)
The Littlest Outlaw WDP
Ricochet Romance (with Mancini; ac: Rosen) UNIV
Cattle Queen of Montana (see Forbes)
Abbott and Costello Meet the Keystone Kops (see Mancini)

1955

Smoke Signal (with Mancini, Gertz) UNIV
Revenge of the Creature (ac: H. Stein; + stock) UNIV
Cult of the Cobra (with Maury, S. Wilson, Gertz) UNIV
The Man from Bitter Ridge (see Gertz)
Francis in the Navy (with Gertz; ac: S. Wilson) UNIV
The Private War of Major Benson (with S. Wilson, Mancini; mt: H. Stein) UNIV
Pearl of the South Pacific (see Forbes)
To Hell and Back (with Gertz, Maury; ac: Mancini) UNIV
Tennessee's Partner (see Forbes)

1956

Walk the Proud Land (see Salter)
Raw Edge (see Gertz)
Pillars of the Sky (with Roemheld) UNIV
Kelly and Me (see Mancini)

1957

The Deadly Mantis (see Gertz)
Flood Tide (see Mancini)

1958

The Sign of Zorro WDP

1960

Hell Bent for Leather (see Gertz)
The Hound That Thought He Was a Raccoon (see Buddy Baker)
Seven Ways from Sundown (see Gertz)
The Horse with the Flying Tail WDP

1961

Marines, Let's Go! (see Gertz)

1963

PT 109 (with Buttolph) (o: Strech, Brandt, Levene) WB
Wall of Noise (o: Strech) WB

1964

The Tattooed Police Horse WDP

1966

Chamber of Horrors (o: Strech) WB

1968

Chubasco WB
In Enemy Country UNIV

1969

Assignment to Kill WB
The Good Guys and the Bad Guys WB

1970

Rabbit, Run WB

Documentary Features

1943

The Battle of Britain (see M. Steiner)
Divide and Conquer U.S. WAR DEPT.
Substitution and Conversion (see Tiomkin)

1950

50 Years Before Your Eyes (with H. Jackson) WB

1953

Man with a Thousand Hands INT'L. HARVESTER
Mystery Lake LANSBURGH
Boy Scout Jamboree of 1953 (with Rosoff) U.S. STATE DEPT.

1955

On-Stream (ac and o: Maury) SOCONY MOBIL OIL

1962

Freedom and You WB

Shorts
1941
The Miracle of Hydro (doc.) GUNTHER V. FRITSCH
1944
The Battle of Saipan (doc.) WB
1945
To the Shores of Iwo Jima (doc.) OWI
1946
Traffic with the Devil (doc.) MGM
1947
Give Us the Earth (doc.) MGM
1948
Going to Blazes (doc.) MGM
1949
Heart to Heart (doc.) MGM
1951
Tree Farm (with Maxwell) HERBERT MORGAN
1955
Arizona Sheepdog (o: Maxwell) WDP
1956
Cow Dog WDP
Alaska Lifeboat (doc.) HERBERT MORGAN
The Wetback Hound WDP
Shorts (WB)
1940
Sky Sailing
Love's Intrigue
1941
Big Bill Tilden
Happy Faces
It Happens on Rollers
Perils of the Jungle
Soldiers in White
Water Sports
West of the Rockies
1942
Beyond the Line of Duty (see H. Jackson)
Hunting Dogs at Work
Men of the Sky (see H. Jackson)
The Pacific Frontier (with H. Jackson)
The Right Timing
Shoot Yourself Some Golf
Sniffer Soldiers
There Ain't No Such Animal
Wedding Yells
1943
Baptism of Fire
Champions Training Champions
Concealment of Vehicles
Daytime Reconnaisance Patrol
Eagles of the Navy (see H. Jackson)
Food and Magic
Grey, White and Blue
Happy Times and Jolly Moments
Heroes
Interior Guard Duty
Little Isles of Freedom
Mechanized Patrol
Rover's Rangers
A Ship Is Born
Snow Sports
Stars on Horseback
Sweeney Steps Out
This Is Your Enemy (see H. Jackson)
Tropical Sportland
Women at War
With the Marines at Tarawa (see H. Jackson)
Women in Sports
Young and Beautiful
1944
America's Hidden Weapon
The Battle for the Marianas
Combat Patrol (with H. Jackson)
Devil Boats
Dogie Round Up
Filipino Sports Parade
I Am an American
I Won't Play
Into the Clouds
It's Your War Too (with H. Jackson)
Junior Jive Bombers
Marine Anniversary (with H. Jackson)
Once Over Lightly
Our Frontier in Italy
Proudly We Serve
Swinging Into Step
1945
All Star Musical Revue
America the Beautiful
Beachhead to Berlin
Camouflage Principles
Good Old Corn
Hitler Lives? (o: Maxwell)
It Happened in Springfield
Learn and Live
Men of Tomorrow
Navy Nurse
Overseas Roundup (see H. Jackson)
Pledge to Bataan
So You Think You're Allergic
Star in the Night
Story of a Dog
1946
Gem of the Ocean

Okay for Pictures
Okay for Sound
Smart as a Fox
So You Think You're a Nervous Wreck
So You Want to Play the Horses
Star Spangled City
Sunset in the Pacific

1947

American Sports Album
Big Time Revue
A Boy and His Dog
Dad Minds the Baby
A Day at Hollywood Park
Harness Racing
Power Behind the Nation
So You Want an Apartment
So You Want to Be a Salesman
So You Want to Be in Pictures
So You Want to Hold Your Wife
So You Want to Keep Your Hair
So You're Going on a Vacation
So You're Going to Be a Father

1948

Bannister's Bantering Babies
Circus Town
Cradle of the Republic
Drums of India
Fighting Athletes
Gauchos of the Pampas
Jungle Man Killers
The Man from New Orleans
My Own United States
Pie in the Eye (see H. Jackson)
Rhythm of a Big City
Royal Duck Shoot
So You Want to Be a Baby Sitter
So You Want to Be a Detective
So You Want to Be a Gambler
So You Want to Be Popular
So You Want to Build a House
Soap Box Derby

1949

Calgary Stampede
Cavalcade of Egyptian Sports
Down the Nile
The Grass Is Always Greener
Happy Holidays
Heart of Paris
Hunting the Fox
Jungle Terror
Kings of the Rockies
Let's Go Boating
Mysterious Ceylon
Princely India
So You Want to Be a Muscle Man
So You Want to Be an Actor
So You Want to Get Rich Quick
So You're Having In-Law Trouble
Sports New and Old
Sportsmen of the Far East
That's Bully
This Sporting World

1950

Alpine Champions
Champions of Tomorrow
Danger Is My Business
Hands Tell the Story
Just for Fun
Racing Thrills
Riviera Days
Slap Happy
So You Think You're Not Guilty
So You Want a Raise
So You Want to Hold Your Husband
So You Want to Move
So You Want to Throw a Party
So You're Going to Have an Operation
Wish You Were Here

1951

Ace of Clubs
Anything for Laughs (see H. Jackson)
A Laugh a Day
My Country 'Tis of Thee
The Neighbor Next Door
So You Want to Be a Bachelor
So You Want to Be a Cowboy
So You Want to Be a Handyman
So You Want to Be a Paperhanger
So You Want to Buy a Used Car
To Bee or Not to Bee
Will to Win

1952

Ain't Rio Grand?
The Art of Archery
Centennial Sports
Emperor's Horses
Every Dog Has His Day
Just for Sport
Land of the Trembling Earth
Open Up That Golden Gate
The Seeing Eye
So You Never Tell a Lie
So You Want to Be a Musician
So You Want to Be a Plumber
So You Want to Enjoy Life
So You Want to Get It Wholesale
So You Want to Go to a Convention
So You Want to Wear the Pants

So You're Going to the Dentist
Stop! Look and Laugh
Snow Frolics
Unfamiliar Sports

1953
Birthplace of Hockey
Black Fury (see H. Jackson)
Cheyenne Days (with H. Jackson)
Danish Sport Delights
Desert Killer
Fiesta for Sports
So You Love Your Dog
So You Want a Television Set
So You Want to Learn to Dance
Sporting Courage
Thar She Blows
Three Lives (with H. Jackson)
Where the Trade Winds Play

1954
Don't Forget to Write
In Fourteen Hundred Ninety-Two
Off to the Races
Rodeo Roundup
The Royal Mounties
Sea Sports of Tahiti
So You Think You Can't Sleep
So You Want to Be an Heir
So You Want to Be Your Own Boss
So You Want to Know Your Relatives
So You're Having Neighbor Trouble
So You're Taking In a Roomer
Winter Paradise

1955
Caribbean Playgrounds
Continental Holiday
Silver Blades
So You Don't Trust Your Wife
So You Want a Model Railroad
So You Want to Be a Banker
So You Want to Be a Gladiator
So You Want to Be a Policeman
So You Want to Be a V.P.
So You Want to Be on a Jury
So You Want to Go to a Night Club

1956
Beauty and the Bull (with H. Jackson)
Crossroads of the World
East Is East (see H. Jackson)
So You Think the Grass Is Greener
So You Want to Be Pretty
So You Want to Play the Piano
So Your Wife Wants to Work
24-Hour Alert
The Wonders of Araby (ac: H. Jackson)

1957
Tales of the Black Forest

Cartoons (UPA)

1951
Fuddy Duddy Buddy
Man on the Land

1952
The Dog Snatcher

Cartoons (WB)

1962
Banty Raids
Devil's Feud Cake
Fast Buck Duck
Good Noose
I Was a Teenage Thumb
The Jet Cage
Martian Thru Georgia
The Million-Hare
Now Hear This
Shishkabugs
Woolen Under Where

1963
Aqua Duck
Bartholomew Versus the Wheel
Chili Weather
Claws in the Lease
Dr. Devil and Mr. Hare
Dumb Patrol
False Hare
Freudy Cat
Hare-Breadth Hurry
Hawaiian Aye Aye
The Iceman Ducketh
Mad as a Mars Hare
A Message to Gracias
Mexican Cat Dance
Nuts and Volts
Senorella and the Glass Huarache
To Beep or Not to Beep
Transylvania 6–5000
The Unmentionables
War and Pieces

1964
It's Nice to Have a Mouse Around the House
Pancho's Hideaway
Road to Andalay

1965
Assault and Peppered
The Astroduck
Boulder Wham!
Cats and Bruises
Chaser on the Rocks
Chili Corn Corny

Corn on the Cop
Go Go Amigo
Harried and Hurried
Highway Runnery
Just Plane Beep
Moby Duck
Run, Run, Sweet Road Runner
Rushing Roulette
Shot and Bothered
Suppressed Duck
Tease for Two
Tired and Feathered
Well Worn Daffy
The Wild Chase

1966
A Haunting We Will Go
Clippety Clobbered
Mexican Mousepiece
Out and Out Rout
Snow Excuse
The Solid Tin Coyote

1967
Cool Cat
Fiesta Fiasco
Go Away Stowaway
Merlin the Magic Mouse
The Music Mice-tro
Norman Normal
Rodent to Stardom
Speedy Ghost to Town
The Spy Swatter

1968
Big Game Haunt
Bunny and Claude—We Rob Carrot Patches
Chimp & Zee
Feud with a Dude
Flying Circus
The Great Carrot Train Robbery
Hippydrome Tiger
Hocus Focus Powwow
See Ya Later Gladiator
Skyscraper Caper
3-Ring Wing-Ding

1969
Bugged by a Bee
Fistic Mystic
Injun Trouble
Rabbit Stew and Rabbits Too
Shamrock and Roll

Cartoons (UA)

1964
Pink Phink

1965
An Ounce of Pink
Pickled Pink
Pink Ice
The Pink Tail Fly
Pinkfinger
Shocking Pink
Sink Pink
We Give Pink Stamps

1966
Napoleon Blown-Aparte
The Pink Blueprint
Pink Pistons
Plastered in Paris
Smile Pretty, Say Pink
Vitamin Pink

Trailers (WB)

1942
Flying Fortress

1947
Dark Passage

1949
"G" Men (reissue of 1935 film)

1950
Stage Fright
Kiss Tomorrow Goodbye
The Breaking Point

1951
Tomorrow Is Another Day
Come Fill the Cup

1952
Big Jim McLain

1955
The Dam Busters

LAVRY, MARK

1954
Deadline for Danny BARUCH DIENAR

LAVSKY, RICHARD

1966
Brighty of the Grand Canyon FEATURE FILM

1969
People Soup (short) COL

LAW, ALEX

1944
That's My Baby (see Chernis)

1946
The Pilgrim Lady (see Butts)

1947
Winter Wonderland (see Dessau)

LAWRENCE, EARL
1941
Tillie the Toiler (mt) COL
Two Latins from Manhattan (+ stock) COL
1943
Dangerous Blondes COL
1946
Throw a Saddle on a Star (with M. Bakaleinikoff) COL
1957
The Incredible Shrinking Man (see Gertz)
Joe Butterfly (see Mancini)

LAWRENCE, ELLIOT
1957
The Violators RKO
1963
You Are France to Me (doc.) FRENCH GOVT.
1965
Light! (doc. short) GENERAL ELECTRIC
Thunder in Dixie MPI
1966
Hot Rod Hullabaloo AA

LAWRENCE, MARK
1962
David and Lisa (a: Paris) CONTINENTAL

LAWS, MAURY
1966
The Daydreamer EMBASSY
1967
Mad Monster Party (an.) EMBASSY
The Wacky World of Mother Goose EMBASSY

LEE, BILL
1967
One Fine Day (doc. short; with S. Scharf) AMERICAN HEART ASSN.

LEE, DAI-KEONG
1944
Letter from Australia (doc. short) AUSTRALIAN DEPT. OF INFORMATION

LEES, BENJAMIN
1952
Man Alive (an. short) UPA
Pink and Blue Blues (cartoon) UPA
1953
The Emperor's New Clothes (cartoon) UPA
1954
Bringing Up Mother (cartoon) UPA
1957
Theatre (doc.short) T. J. SARKKA

LEGRAND, MICHEL
[He scored many films in France; only his American films are listed here.]
1967
How to Save a Marriage and Ruin Your Life COL
1968
Sweet November WB
The Thomas Crown Affair UA
Ice Station Zebra MGM
1969
Castle Keep COL
The Happy Ending UA
1970
The Plastic Dome of Norma Jean COMPTON
Pieces of Dreams UA

LEICHTLING, ALAN
1970
Item 72-D (short) EDWARD TOBY SUMMER

LEIPOLD, JOHN
1929
The Wild Party (mt; + stock) PAR
Close Harmony (+ stock) PAR
Innocents of Paris (m&e; + stock) PAR
The Dance of Life (+ stock) PAR
The Saturday Night Kid PAR
1930
Behind the Make-Up (see Harling)
The Love Parade (with Terr, Potoker, Harling) PAR
Seven Days Leave (mt) PAR
Street of Chance PAR
Dangerous Paradise (mt) PAR
Only the Brave (see Harling)
Young Eagles PAR
Young Eagles (silent; with Carbonara, Bergunker; ac: Hand, H. Jackson) PAR
The Vagabond King (see Potoker)
The Vagabond King (silent; with Hajos, Potoker; ac: Bergunker, Hand, Terr, Harling) PAR
The Devil's Holiday (see Goulding)
The Silent Enemy (see Midgely)
The Cock-Eyed News (short) PAR
The Spoilers (see Hajos)
Monte Carlo (see Harling)

Playboy of Paris (see H. Jackson)
Tom Sawyer (mt with Rainger) PAR

1931

The Gang Buster (mt) PAR
Fighting Caravans (with Hand, Potoker, Hajos; ac: Bergunker, Bierman, Krumgold, Cousminer, Hilb) PAR
The Conquering Horde (with Rainger) PAR
Rango (see Hajos)
Skippy PAR
Gente Alegre (Spanish language; with Hajos, Rainger; ac: R. Kopp, Hand) PAR
Ladies' Man (see Hand)
Up Pops the Devil PAR
Confessions of a Co-ed PAR
El Príncipe Gondolero (Spanish language; see R. Kopp)
The Magnificent Lie (with Hajos, R. Kopp) PAR
Huckleberry Finn (mt) PAR
An American Tragedy (see Rainger)
Silence (mt; + stock) PAR
Daughter of the Dragon (see R. Kopp)
Monkey Business (with Rainger) PAR
The Mad Parade (with R. Kopp) PAR
24 Hours (with Kopp) PAR
The Road to Reno (ac: R. Kopp) PAR
The Beloved Bachelor (ac: R. Kopp, Potoker) PAR
Touchdown PAR
Rich Man's Folly (with Hand, Kaun, Harling, Potoker, R. Kopp) PAR
The False Madonna (with Harling; ac: Kaun, R. Kopp, Hand) PAR
Husband's Holiday PAR
Ladies of the Big House (ac: Rainger) PAR

1932

This Reckless Age PAR
Two Kinds of Women (ac: R. Kopp) PAR
Tomorrow and Tomorrow (see Hand)
Dancers in the Dark (see Pasternacki)
The Broken Wing (with R. Kopp) PAR
One Hour with You (with Harling, R. Kopp) PAR
This Is the Night (see Harling)
The World and the Flesh (see Hand)
Sky Bride (m&e; + stock) PAR
Strangers in Love (see R. Kopp)
The Strange Case of Clara Deane PAR
Sinners in the Sun (ac: R. Kopp) PAR
Forgotten Commandments (see Hand)
Merrily We Go to Hell (see R. Kopp)
The Man from Yesterday (with R. Kopp; ac: Hand) PAR
Make Me a Star PAR
Million Dollar Legs (with R. Kopp) PAR
Lady and Gent PAR
Madame Racketeer PAR
Devil and the Deep (see Hand)
Horse Feathers (+ stock) PAR
The Night of June 13th (mt) PAR
Blonde Venus (see Harling)
Love Me Tonight PAR
The Phantom President PAR
The Big Broadcast (see Rainger)
Hot Saturday (+ stock) PAR
He Learned About Women PAR
If I Had a Million (m&e; + stock) PAR
Wild Horse Mesa PAR

1933

A Farewell to Arms (see Harling)
Tonight Is Ours (see Hajos)
She Done Him Wrong PAR
The Crime of the Century (mt; + stock) PAR
A Lady's Profession (with Krumgold) PAR
King of the Jungle (see Hand)
Pick Up (see Rainger)
Murders in the Zoo (see R. Kopp)
Terror Aboard (see Hand)
A Bedtime Story (see Rainger)
Song of the Eagle (see Harold Lewis)
The Story of Temple Drake (see Kaun)
The Eagle and the Hawk (m&e; + stock) PAR
The Girl in 419 (mt; + stock) PAR
Sunset Pass (mt; + stock) PAR
International House (see Rainger)
I Love That Man (see Kaun)
Jennie Gerhardt (with Hajos; ac: H. Jackson) PAR
College Humor (with H. Jackson) PAR
Disgraced PAR
Three Cornered Moon PAR
One Sunday Afternoon PAR
I'm No Angel (see H. Jackson)
The Way to Love (see Rainger)
White Woman (see Hajos)
Duck Soup PAR
Design for Living PAR

1934

Eight Girls in a Boat (see Harold Lewis)
Four Frightened People (see Hajos)
Search for Beauty (+ stock) PAR
Six of a Kind PAR
Bolero (see Rainger)
Death Takes a Holiday (see Roder)
You're Telling Me (with Satterfield) PAR

The Witching Hour PAR
Thirty Day Princess (with H. Jackson) PAR
Here Comes the Groom (see Hand)
Kiss and Make-Up (see Rainger)
The Old-Fashioned Way PAR
The Notorious Sophie Lang (+ stock) PAR
Elmer and Elsie (mt) PAR
The Scarlet Empress (with Harling, Roder, Potoker, Kaun; based on music of Tchaikovsky, Mendelssohn, and Wagner) PAR
Wagon Wheels (m&e; + stock) PAR
Belle of the Nineties (with Satterfield, H. Jackson) PAR
The Lemon Drop Kid (see Satterfield)
Ready for Love (see Satterfield)
Mrs. Wiggs of the Cabbage Patch (+ stock) PAR
Limehouse Blues PAR
It's a Gift PAR
Behold My Wife! PAR
Here Is My Heart (with Roemheld) PAR

1935

The Lives of a Bengal Lancer (see Roemheld)
All the King's Horses (see Roemheld)
McFadden's Flats (+ stock) PAR
Stolen Harmony PAR
The Devil Is a Woman (with Roemheld; ac: Hand) PAR
Goin' to Town (see Satterfield)
College Scandal (see Hollander)
Men Without Names (+ stock) PAR
Paris in Spring (see Hollander)
Annapolis Farewell PAR
The Big Broadcast of 1936 PAR
The Virginia Judge (m&e; + stock) PAR
The Crusades (see R. Kopp)
Hands Across the Table (see Roemheld)
Coronado (see Satterfield)
It's a Great Life! (m&e; + stock) PAR

1936

The Bride Comes Home (see Roemheld)
Collegiate (see Hollander)
Rose of the Rancho (see Friedhofer)
Anything Goes (see Hollander)
Klondike Annie (see V. Young)
Till We Meet Again (see Hollander)
Florida Special (see Bradshaw)
Forgotten Faces (with Hollander; ac: Carbonara) PAR
Border Flight PAR
Palm Springs (with Bradshaw; ac: Carbonara) PAR
Three Cheers for Love (see Boutelje)
Spendthrift (see Carbonara)
The Sky Parade (with Carbonara) PAR
Fatal Lady (see V. Young)
The Princess Comes Across (ac: Boutelje, V. Young) PAR
Girl of the Ozarks (see Carbonara)
Poppy (see Hollander)
Rhythm on the Range PAR
A Son Comes Home (ac: Hollander) PAR
I'd Give My Life PAR
Lady Be Careful PAR
Three Married Men (+ stock) PAR
Wedding Present (see Skiles)
Rose Bowl PAR
Hideaway Girl (see Hollander)
College Holiday (see Skiles)

1937

When's Your Birthday? (with Skiles) RKO
I Met Him in Paris (see Bradshaw)
Turn Off the Moon PAR
Mountain Music (with V. Young, Hollander) PAR
Exclusive (with Roder; mt: Jenkins) PAR
Artists and Models (see Jenkins)
Souls at Sea (see Harling)
Double or Nothing (see V. Young)
This Way Please (ac: Jenkins, Shuken, Stone) PAR
Blossoms on Broadway (with Jenkins, Hollander) PAR
Wells Fargo (see V. Young)

1938

Thrill of a Lifetime (see Jenkins)
Scandal Street (+ stock) PAR
The Big Broadcast of 1938 (with V. Young, Parrish, Rainger, Jenkins) PAR
Romance in the Dark (see V. Young)
Bluebeard's Eighth Wife (see Hollander)
Doctor Rhythm (see Jenkins)
Stolen Heaven (ac) PAR
Cocoanut Grove (with Shuken) PAR
You and Me (see Weill)
Give Me a Sailor (ac: D. Rose) PAR
Spawn of the North (see Tiomkin)
Campus Confessions PAR
Touchdown Army PAR
The Arkansas Traveler (see Carbonara)
Illegal Traffic (ac: Shuken) PAR
Thanks for the Memory (see Bradshaw)
Say It in French (see Shuken)
The Frontiersman (see Carbonara)
Tom Sawyer, Detective (see Carbonara)
Artists and Models Abroad (see Rainger)

1939
Disbarred (see Carbonara)
Paris Honeymoon (see Rainger)
Persons in Hiding (with Shuken, Morgan) PAR
Boy Trouble (see Bradshaw)
Stagecoach (with Shuken, Carbonara, Harling, Hageman) UA
King of Chinatown (with Carbonara) PAR
Silver on the Sage (with Pasternacki) PAR
Sudden Money (with Shuken) PAR
I'm from Missouri (ac: Morgan, Shuken) PAR
Never Say Die (see Roder)
The Lady's from Kentucky (see Shuken)
Union Pacific (with Carbonara, V. Young, Shuken) PAR
Unmarried (ac: Carbonara) PAR
Undercover Doctor (see V. Young)
Bulldog Drummond's Bride PAR
Man About Town (see Hollander)
Million Dollar Legs (+ stock) PAR
Island of Lost Men (ac: V. Young) PAR
Our Leading Citizen (see Carbonara)
Death of a Champion (ac: Shuken, V. Young) PAR
The Renegade Trail (with Carbonara) PAR
$1,000 a Touchdown (with Shuken, Bradshaw) PAR
What a Life PAR
Television Spy (m&e: V. Young and Bradshaw) PAR
Disputed Passage (see Hollander)
The Flying Deuces (with Shuken) RKO
Law of the Pampas (see V. Young)
The Llano Kid (see V. Young)
All Women Have Secrets (ac: V. Young) PAR
Emergency Squad (see Shuken)

1940
Geronimo! (see Carbonara)
Santa Fe Marshal (with V. Young, Carbonara) PAR
Parole Fixer (see Carbonara)
Knights of the Range (with V. Young) PAR
Seventeen (see Bradshaw)
The Showdown PAR
Women Without Names (see Carbonara)
The Farmer's Daughter (see V. Young)
Adventure in Diamonds (see Shuken)
Opened by Mistake (ac: Krumgold) PAR
Typhoon (see Hollander)
Buck Benny Rides Again (see V. Young)
Queen of the Mob (see Hollander)
Stagecoach War PAR
The Great McGinty (see Hollander)
Rangers of Fortune (see Hollander)
The Quarterback (mt: Parrish) PAR
Cherokee Strip (with Malotte; ac: Hollander) PAR
Christmas in July (see Shuken)
The Fargo Kid RKO
Texas Rangers Ride Again PAR

1941
Doomed Caravan (+ stock) PAR
In Old Colorado (+ stock) PAR
The Lady Eve (see Shuken)
The Round Up (see V. Young)
Border Vigilantes (+ stock) PAR
Pirates on Horseback (see Malotte)
West Point Widow (with Shuken; + stock) PAR
The Parson of Panamint PAR
Wide Open Town (+ stock) PAR
The Night of January 16th (see Carbonara)
Stick to Your Guns (o: Hand) PAR
Hold Back the Dawn (see V. Young)
Secret of the Wastelands PAR
Go West, Young Lady (o: Cutner) COL
Outlaws of the Desert PAR
Riders of the Timberline (+ stock) PAR
Twilight on the Trail (o: Hand) PAR

1942
Cadets on Parade (+ stock) COL
Shut My Big Mouth COL
Adventures of Martin Eden (+ stock) COL
Two Yanks in Trinidad COL
Blondie's Blessed Event COL
Hello, Annapolis COL
Not a Ladies' Man (+ stock) COL
Sweetheart of the Fleet COL
Submarine Raider (+ stock) COL
Parachute Nurse (+ stock) COL
The Nazis Strike (doc.; see Webb)
Blondie for Victory COL
Sabotage Squad (mt; + stock) COL
The Spirit of Stanford (+ stock) COL
A Man's World (+ stock) COL
The Daring Young Man COL
The Boogie Man Will Get You (mt; + stock) COL
Stand By All Networks (mt; + stock) COL

1943
Commandos Strike at Dawn (see Gruenberg)
Reveille with Beverly COL
Something to Shout About (with D. Raksin) COL

The Desperadoes (o: Cutner) COL
After Midnight with Boston Blackie (mt; + stock) COL
Redhead from Manhattan (see Grau)
The Kansan (see Carbonara)
Good Luck, Mr. Yates COL
What's Buzzin' Cousin? COL
First Comes Courage (see Toch)
Footlight Glamour (+ stock) COL
Mardi Gras (short; ac: Grau, Shuken) PAR
Doughboys in Ireland COL
My Kingdom for a Cook COL
Is Everybody Happy? COL
The Heat's On COL
There's Something About a Soldier COL
What a Woman (o: Cutner) COL
Hey, Rookie COL

1944
Swing Out the Blues (+ stock) COL
Cowboy Canteen (with Sawtell) COL
Nine Girls (+ stock) COL
Beautiful But Broke COL
Sailor's Holiday (mt; + stock) COL
Showboat Serenade (short; ac: L. Russell, Bradshaw) PAR
Girl in the Case (+ stock) COL
Henry Aldrich's Little Secret (ac: Sawtell) PAR
Forty Thieves (with Glickman) UA
Abroad with Two Yanks (see Moraweck)
The National Barn Dance (see Schrager)

1945
Incendiary Blonde (see Dolan)

1946
Breakfast in Hollywood (with Mayfield) UA
Partners in Time (see Moraweck)

1947
King of the Wild Horses (see Steinert)
Bulldog Drummond at Bay (with Dubin; + stock) COL

1949
Massacre River (with Moraweck) AA
The Big Wheel (see Carbonara)
Riders in the Sky (+ stock) COL

1950
The Traveling Saleswoman (mt; + stock) COL
Hoedown (with M. Bakaleinikoff; + stock) COL
The Palomino (ac: M. Bakaleinikoff; + stock) COL
Beware of Blondie (with M. Bakaleinikoff; + stock) COL
Gene Autry and the Mounties (+ stock) COL

1951
Whirlwind (+ stock) COL
Roar of the Iron Horse (serial; m&e; + stock) COL

1952
Thief of Damascus (mt: A. Morton; + stock) COL

1953
Siren of Bagdad (ac: M. Bakaleinikoff; + stock) COL

LEONARD, CLAIRE

1952
Wilderness River Trail (doc. short) SIERRA CLUB

1961
She Goes to Vassar (score added to 1931 doc. short) MARVIN BRECKINRIDGE

LEONARDI, LEONID S.

1929
Dark Streets (+ stock) WB
The Careless Age (with Mendoza) WB

1930
Sally WB
Bride of the Regiment (overture) WB
Sweethearts and Wives WB
Oh Sailor Behave (ac: Mendoza) WB
Sweet Kitty Bellairs (see Dunn)
The Bad Man WB
Top Speed (+ stock) WB
The Girl of the Golden West (love theme: Mendoza) WB

1931
Captain Applejack (o: E. Ross; + stock) WB

LERMAN, RICHARD

1967
The Reef and Beyond, Or Darrow's Scope (short) RICHARD LERMAN

1969
The Ring Masters (short) RICHARD LERMAN

LERNER, STEPHEN

1970
Cowards SIMON NUCHTERN

LESKO, JOE

1965
Murder in Mississippi HERBERT S. ALTMAN

LESSNER, GEORGE
1936
The Border Patrolman TCF
Cartoons (UNIV)
1937
A Firemen's Picnic
Ostrich Feathers
Lovesick
The Dumb Cluck

LEVANT, OSCAR
1930
Leathernecking (ac) RKO
1934
Crime Without Passion (see Tours)
1937
Nothing Sacred (o: A. Deutsch, D. Raksin) SELZNICK
1939
Made for Each Other (see Friedhofer)
1942
Fellow Americans (doc. short) OWI

LEVENE, GUS
1952
Somebody Loves Me (see Van Cleave)
1953
Road to Bali (see Lilley)
1954
White Christmas (see Lilley)
[Also a prolific orchestrator.]

LEVEY, HAROLD
1930
The Nightingale (short) WB
The Royal Box (+ stock) WB
1931
Rhythms of a Big City (short) WB

LEVI, MAURICE
1915
Silver Threads Among the Gold K. & R. FILM CO.

LEVIN, ALVIN
1947
Born to Speed PRC
It's a Joke, Son! EL
Philo Vance's Gamble EL
Too Many Winners PRC
Railroaded EL

LEVIN, MARC LEONARD
1970
Buttons (doc. short) INDIANA U.

LEVIN, SUSA
1967
Brandeis University in Israel—Hiatt Institute (short) BRANDEIS U.

LEVINE, EDDIE
1970
Barbie's Hospital Affair CARL R. CARTER PRODS.
My Sister's Business CARL R. CARTER PRODS.
Trucker's Girl CARL R. CARTER PRODS.

LEVINE, HANK
1963
The Young Swingers TCF
1964
Raiders from Beneath the Sea TCF

LEVY, MARVIN
1960
The Neighboring Shore (doc. short) SEXTANT, INC.

LEVY, SOL P.
1914
Sealed Orders DE LUXE ATTRACTIONS
1917
The Barrier (with Hanks) EDGAR LEWIS
The Bar Sinister (with Hanks) EDGAR LEWIS

LEWIN, FRANK
1969
The Plot Against Harry NEW YORKER FILMS
Shorts
1951
The Flop ?
1953
Pertaining to Marin (doc.) JAMES DAVIS
1955
The Golden Leaf (doc.) AMERICAN TOBACCO CO.
1957
Color and Texture in Aluminum Finishes (doc.) ALUMINUM CO. OF AMERICA
1959
The Sign of Plexiglas (doc.) ROHM & HAAS CO.
The Mayflower Story (doc.) AERO MAYFLOWER TRANSIT
1966
A Year Toward Tomorrow (doc.) SUN DIAL FILMS

1967

The Brookhaven Spectrum (doc.) OWEN MURPHY PRODS.

1968

Spirit in the Tree OWEN MURPHY PRODS.

1969

Fathomless JAMES DAVIS

London Bridge Is Falling Down CONNECTICUT FILMS

To Market, to Market CONNECTICUT FILMS

1970

Pixillation (an.) LILLIAN SCHWARTZ

LEWINE, RICHARD

1965

The Days of Wilfred Owen (doc. short) RICHARD LEWINE, BOB BACH

LEWIN-RICHTER, ANDRÉS

1963

The Gondola Eye (short) IAN HUGO

1964

Sublimated Birth (short) EFFECTS-U-ALL CORP.

LEWIS, ELBERT C. (BERT)

Cartoons (WDP)

1930

Pioneer Days

1931

The Barnyard Broadcast

Fishin' Around

The Moose Hunt

Playful Pan

1932

Babes in the Woods

Just Dogs

King Neptune

The Mad Dog

Mickey's Good Deed

Trader Mickey

The Wayward Canary

1933

Birds in the Spring (see Churchill)

The Mad Doctor

The Mail Pilot

Old King Cole (see Churchill)

1934

Camping Out (see Churchill)

The Dognapper (ac: Churchill)

The Flying Mouse (see Churchill)

Mickey Plays Papa (see Churchill)

Mickey's Steam-Roller (ac: Churchill)

1935

Mickey's Fire Brigade

Mickey's Kangaroo

Mickey's Man Friday (ac: Churchill)

On Ice (ac: Churchill, Harline)

Cartoons (MGM)

1938

Blue Monday

Buried Treasure

The Captain's Christmas

The Captain's Pup (o: Cutter)

Cleaning House

A Day at the Beach (o: Bassman)

The Honduras Hurricane

Petunia Natural Park

Poultry Pirates (with Bassman)

The Pygmy Hunt

What a Lion!

The Winning Ticket

1939

Jitterbug Follies

Mama's New Hat

Seal Skinners

Wanted: No Master

LEWIS, HAROLD

1932

Panama Flo RKO PATHÉ

Prestige (see Arthur Lange) RKO PATHÉ

Carnival Boat (see Arthur Lange) RKO PATHÉ

Lady with a Past (mt; et: Arthur Lange) RKO PATHÉ

70,000 Witnesses PAR

Madison Square Garden (o: Marquardt, Gerstenberger) PAR

1933

Song of the Eagle (with Leipold; ac: Chernis) PAR

I Love That Man (see Kaun)

Golden Harvest (a: Roemheld, Hand) PAR

1934

Eight Girls in a Boat (with Leipold, Hajos, H. Jackson, Roder) PAR

1935

Don't Bet on Blondes (see Kaun)

LEWIS, HERSCHELL G.

1963

Blood Feast HERSCHELL G. LEWIS

1964

Two Thousand Maniacs! (a: Wellington) HERSCHELL G. LEWIS

LEWIS, JACK

1966

What's Up, Tiger Lily? AIP

LEWIS, JOHN

1959

Odds Against Tomorrow UA

Exposure (doc. short) UNITED NATIONS

LEWIS, MORGAN

1955

Helen Keller in Her Story (doc.; o: R. Bennett) LOUIS DE ROCHEMONT

LIEBLING, JOSEPH

1953

Dimitri Works in Black Wax (doc. short) PETER HOLLANDER

LIEBMAN, JOSEPH

1961

Roof Tops of New York (short) COL

Force of Impulse sutton

1964

Light Fantastic EMBASSY

LILLEY, JOSEPH J.

1944

Standing Room Only (see Dolan)

You Can't Ration Love (see Heymann)

1945

Out of This World (see Simeone)

1947

Ladies Man (see Webb)

Variety Girl (Puppetoon sequence: Plumb; o: Bradshaw, Van Cleave) PAR

1948

Isn't It Romantic? (o: Van Cleave) PAR

1949

A Connecticut Yankee in King Arthur's Court (see V. Young)

Red, Hot and Blue (ac: F. Skinner; o: Van Cleave, Cutner, Shuken) PAR

The Great Lover (ac: Webb, Plumb; o: Shuken, Cutner, Bradshaw) PAR

1950

Dear Wife (ac: Van Cleave) PAR

1951

At War with the Army (o: Levene, Shuken, Cutner, Parrish) PAR

Mr. Music (o: Van Cleave) PAR

The Mating Season (o: Parrish, Cutner, Levene) PAR

Here Comes the Groom (m&e; o: B. Jones) PAR

Sailor Beware (with Harline; o: Van Cleave, Parrish, Virgil, Levene, Shuken, Cutner) PAR

1952

Jumping Jacks (o: Levene, Shuken, Cutner) PAR

Somebody Loves Me (see Van Cleave)

1953

Road to Bali (ac: Van Cleave, Shuken, Carbonara, Levene) PAR

The Stooge (o: Shuken, Cutner, Levene, Parrish) PAR

The Caddy (o: Shuken, Levene, Van Cleave) PAR

1954

Red Garters (o: Van Cleave, Levene, Shuken) PAR

White Christmas (with Van Cleave, Levene; ac: Mayers) PAR

1955

The Seven Little Foys (o: Parrish, Levene, Shuken, Cutner) PAR

1956

That Certain Feeling (o: Van Cleave, Shuken, Hayes) PAR

1957

Beau James (o: Van Cleave, Hayes) PAR

1958

Paris Holiday UA

1959

Alias Jesse James (o: Levene) UA

Li'l Abner (o: Parrish, Van Cleave) PAR

1960

G. I. Blues (o: Levene) PAR

Blue Hawaii (o: Levene) PAR

1962

Girls! Girls! Girls! (o: Levene) PAR

1963

Papa's Delicate Condition (o: Levene) PAR

Fun in Acapulco (o: Levene) PAR

Who's Minding the Store? (o: Levene) PAR

1964

Roustabout (o: Levene) PAR

The Disorderly Orderly (o: Levene) PAR

1965

Paradise—Hawaiian Style (o: Levene) PAR

1967

Easy Come, Easy Go (o: Levene, Van Cleave) PAR

1969

How to Commit Marriage CR

Shorts

1944

Fun Time (see Schrager)

1945

Boogie Woogie (see Schrager)

1946
Double Rhythm PAR
A Tale of Two Cafés (see Schrager)
1947
Midnight Serenade PAR
1948
Jingle, Jangle, Jingle (with Bradshaw) PAR
Gypsy Holiday PAR
Big Sister Blues PAR
Trailers (PAR)
1948
Dream Girl
1949
A Connecticut Yankee in King Arthur's Court

LINDAHL, ROBERT
1961
The Right to Live (doc. short) UNITED GOOD NEIGHBORS

LINDSAY, ARTHUR
1969
The Abnormal Female DISTRIBPIX

LINDSEY, MORT
1962
40 Pounds of Trouble UNIV
The Seducers BRENNER
Gay Purr-ee (an.) WB
1963
I Could Go On Singing UA
Stolen Hours UA
1964
The Best Man UA

LINN, ROBERT
1954
The Story Tellers of the Canterbury Tales (doc. short) USC

LIPSCHULTZ, GEORGE
1929
They Had to See Paris FOX
Seven Faces (with Arthur Kay; ac: Friedhofer) FOX
Cameo Kirby FOX
1930
Song o' My Heart (see Brunelli)
3 Sisters (with Brunelli, Malotte) FOX
Temple Tower (ac: Malotte, W. Wheeler) FOX
Double Cross Roads (ac: Malotte, Talbot, Virgil) FOX
Movietone Follies of 1930 (ac: Talbot, Malotte) FOX
Born Reckless (see Brunelli)
On the Level (ac: Malotte, Talbot, R. Bassett) FOX
Not Damaged (with Malotte, Talbot) FOX
Women Everywhere (see Brunelli)
Rough Romance (see Brunelli)
On Your Back (with Talbot) FOX
Renegades (see Arthur Kay)
A Devil with Women (see Brunelli)
The Princess and the Plumber (with Friedhofer, Brunelli, Arthur Kay; ac: Fall) FOX
The Man Who Came Back (see Brunelli)
1931
Seas Beneath (see Brunelli)
Body and Soul (see Brunelli)
Annabelle's Affairs FOX
1932
El Caballero de la Noche (see Bassett)
The Painted Woman (see Friedhofer)
Second Hand Wife (with Friedhofer) FOX

LISKA, ZDENEK
1970
The Angel Levine UA

LITTAU, JOSEPH
1929
The Rainbow TS
Moulin Rouge (U.S. release of 1928 British film) WORLD WIDE

LLOYD, MICHAEL
1968
Amblin' (short) STEVEN SPIELBERG

LLOYD, NORMAN
1951
Williamsburg Restored (doc.) IFF
Documentary Shorts
1944
Valley of the Tennessee OWI
Peru JULIEN BRYAN
1945
Northwest U.S.A. OWI
Argentine Primer JULIEN BRYAN
1946
Children of Russia (see Forrell)
1948
My Name Is Han IFF
1950
The Greatest Good USDA

1951
Lament WALTER STRATE
1955
Mike Makes His Mark NEA
Japanese House MUSEUM OF MODERN ART
Bullfight SHIRLEY CLARKE
1957
A Moment in Love SHIRLEY CLARKE
1960
South America (see Forrell)
1961
Tropical Africa IFF
1962
Amazon Family (see Forrell)
Yugoslavia IFF
1963
The Ancient Egyptian IFF

LOBODA, SAMUEL R.
19??
O'er the Ramparts We Watched N.Y. WORLD'S FAIR
Headquarters, USA U.S. ARMY
Retreat U.S. ARMY
We're a Team U.S. ARMY

LOCKE, BRUCE
1960
Kipling's Women (see Glasser)

LOCKWOOD, WILLIAM
1966
Weekend of Fear JOE DANFORD

LONG, JERRY
1966
Wild, Wild Winter UNIV
1967
Catalina Caper CROWN

LONG, NEWELL
Shorts (INDIANA U.)
1954
Square Dance 1: Take a Little Peek
Square Dance 2: Split the Ring

LOOSE, WILLIAM
1962
Shoot Out at Big Sag (with Cookerly) PARALLEL
1963
The Man in the Water (with Aldeen) KEY WEST
1964
The Devil's Bedroom (with Cadkin) MANSON
Navajo Run (with Cadkin) AIP
1965
Love and Kisses (with Haskell) UNIV
1967
Tarzan and the Great River PAR
Tarzan and the Jungle Boy PAR
1968
Ballet in the Blue (short) PAR
1969
Joniko and the Kush Ta Ka (see Curtin)
Cherry, Harry & Raquel EVE
1970
Cougar Country (doc.) AMERICAN NATIONAL
Trader Hornee (see B. Allen)
The Rebel Rousers FOUR STAR

LOPEZ, ROBERT
1946
Operation Underground (short) TELENEWS PRODS.

LOWE, MUNDELL
1962
Satan in High Heels COSMIC FILMS
1965
Miracle at Your House (doc. short) AMERICAN GAS ASSN.
1967
A Time for Killing (see V. Alexander)

LUBIN, HARRY
1931
Style & Class (short) JUDEA FILMS
1948
Caged Fury PAR
Mr. Reckless PAR
Waterfront at Midnight PAR
Disaster PAR
1950
Wyoming Mail (+ stock) UNIV

LUCAS, CLYDE
1936
Music, Music Everwhere (short) PAR

LUCAS, GENE
1929
Half Way to Heaven PAR
1930
Burning Up PAR

Burning Up (silent version; with Carbonara; ac: Bergunker, Bierman, Cousminer) PAR
Silent Enemy (see Midgely)

LUCKHARDT, HILMAR F.
1951
Face of Youth (short) U. OF WISCONSIN

LUDWIG, EDWIN E.
1938
Hurricane's Challenge (doc. short) BELL TELEPHONE
1939
The Middleton Family at the New York World's Fair (doc.) WESTINGHOUSE
1943
Western Crossing (doc. short) AT&T

LUND, EDDIE
1950
The Control of Filariasis in Tahiti (doc. short) USC
1956
The Tahitian (a: Kilenyi) CRANE-KNOTT-LONG

LUZ, ERNST
[From 1915 to 1929 he compiled scores and music cue sheets for a large number of films. Evidence has been found that he composed at least some original music only for those films listed here.]
1921
The Four Horsemen of the Apocalypse (see Gottschalk)
1922
The Prisoner of Zenda (see Axt)
1926
The Temptress MGM
1928
Love (see Axt)
1936
Robinson Crusoe (short) GUARANTEED

LYNCH, WILLIAM E.
1934
Murder at the Vanities (see Roder)
1935
The Last Outpost (see Kaun)
1936
The Voice of Bugle Ann (see Roemheld)

M

MAASZ, GERHARD
1958
Crowded Out (doc. short) NEA

MacDERMOT, GALT
1970
Cotton Comes to Harlem UA

MACHAN, BEN
1945
Power Unlimited (doc. short) RKO
1946
Seeds of Destiny (doc. short) U.S. WAR DEPT.

MacISAAC, DON
1955
Susan's Wonderful Adventure (doc. short) CLARKE SCHOOL

MACKAY, DANIEL
1948
Music from the Mountains (see Curtin)
1949
A Place in the Sun (doc. short) USC

MacKAY, HARPER
1970
Guess What We Learned in School Today? CANNON

MacLAINE, CHRISTOPHER
1954
Moods in Motion (abstract short) ETTILIE WALLACE

MacLISE, ANGUS
1964
Chumlum (short) RON RICE

MacNEIL, ALAN
1950
Green Mountain Land (doc. short) VERMONT DEVELOPMENT COMMISSION

MACPHERSON, CAMERON
1933
Dawn to Dawn DUWORLD

MACERO, TEO
1970
End of the Road AA
A.K.A. Cassius Clay (doc.) UA
Shorts
1958
Bridges-Go-Round (doc.) SHIRLEY CLARKE
1959
Skyscraper (doc.) SHIRLEY CLARKE
1960
Faces and Fortunes (doc.) MORTON GODSHOLL
1967
Opus Op (ballet film) KING SCREEN PRODS.
1969
The Transplanters (doc.) MEDICAL COMMUNICATIONS
[Apparently many other documentaries, titles and dates unknown or unconfirmed.]

MALIK, AHMED ABDUL
1967
Kali (short; with Caro Scott) UNITED GERANIUMS

MALNECK, MATTY
1938
Sing You Sinners (mt) PAR
1957
Witness for the Prosecution (o: Raab) UA

MALOOF, ALEXANDER
1931
Father Nile (short) COL
Jerusalem, City of Peace (short) COL
1934
Mediterranean Blues (short) EDUCATIONAL

MALOTTE, ALBERT HAY
1929
Black Magic FOX
1930
Such Men Are Dangerous (see Brunelli)
Song o' My Heart (see Brunelli)
The 3 Sisters (see Lipschultz)
Temple Tower (see Lipschultz)
Double Cross Roads (see Lipschultz)
Movietone Follies of 1930 (see Lipschultz)
Born Reckless (see Brunelli)
On the Level (see Lipschultz)
Not Damaged (see Lipschultz)
Wild Company (see Kaylin)
Renegades (see Arthur Kay)
The Man Who Came Back (see Brunelli)
1932
The Girl from Calgary MON
1935
Hi, Gaucho! RKO
1940
Dr. Cyclops (with Toch, Carbonara) PAR
Forty Little Mothers (see Stringer)
Mystery Sea Raider (with V. Young) PAR
Cherokee Strip (see Leipold)
1941
Pirates on Horseback (with Leipold) PAR
1945
The Enchanted Forest (o: Bernie) PRC
1959
The Big Fisherman (o: Tamkin) WDP
Shorts
1932
A Firehouse Honeymoon RKO
1942
The Incredible Stranger MGM
The Greatest Gift MGM
Cartoons (WDP)
1935
Cock o' the Walk
1936
Broken Toys
Orphans' Picnic
Moving Day
Alpine Climbers
Mickey's Elephant
Three Blind Mouseketeers
1937
Magician Mickey
Little Hiawatha
Lonesome Ghosts
1938
The Moth and the Flame
The Whalers
Brave Little Tailor
Ferdinand the Bull
1939
The Ugly Duckling

MALTBY, RICHARD
1964
Something for Mrs. Gibbs (short) PITTSBURGH PLATE GLASS

MAMORSKY, MORRIS
1950
With These Hands (doc.) ILGWU

Documentary Shorts
1947
The New Tobaccoland, U.S.A. LIGGETT & MYERS
1949
A Circus Wakes Up ARGO FILMS
Best of Breed PAR
Fairway Champions PAR
Top Figure Champs PAR
Running the Keyes PAR
Water Speed PAR
1950
Wild Goose Chase PAR
Down Stream Highway PAR
The Sporting Suwannee PAR
Operation Jack Frost PAR
Desert High-Jinks PAR
Glacier Fishing PAR
Dobbin Steps Out PAR
1951
The Isle of Sports PAR
The Jumping Off Place PAR
Follow the Game Trails PAR
Allen's Animal Kingdom PAR
Ridin' the Rails PAR
Fresh Water Champs PAR
Ski-Lark in the Rockies PAR
Water Jockey Hi-Jinks PAR
Wings to the Word PFC
1952
The Dog-Gonedest Dog PAR
Unsuspected NAT'L. TUBERCULOSIS ASSN.
Playmates of the Sea PAR
They All Like Boats PAR
Sails of Acapulco PAR
Battle of the Beetles USDA
The Impressionable Years U.S. STATE DEPT
River Run LEE PRATHER & DICK MOSHER
1953
Britannia's Athletic Cadets PAR
The Wizard of Clubs PAR
Flying Horseshoes PAR
Rocky Mountain River Thrills PAR
Choosing Canines PAR
1954
A Gift from Dirk UNIV
Shorts (NATIONAL COUNCIL OF CHURCHES OF CHRIST)
1952
Joseph and His Brethren
Joseph in Egypt
Moses and His People
Moses and the Ten Commandments
Moses in Egypt

MANCINI, HENRY
1952
Lost in Alaska (ac: M. Rosen; + stock) UNIV
Horizons West (see H. Stein)
Willie and Joe in Back at the Front (with H. Stein) UNIV
The Raiders (with H. Stein) UNIV
1953
City Beneath the Sea (see H. Stein)
Girls in the Night (with H. Stein; + stock) UNIV
Border River (with H. Stein, Lava) UNIV
Abbott and Costello Go to Mars (see H. Stein)
Column South (see H. Stein)
Law and Order (see M. Rosen)
Lone Hand (see H. Stein)
All I Desire (see H. Stein)
East of Sumatra (see H. Stein)
The Great Sioux Uprising (see H. Stein)
Take Me to Town (see H. Stein)
It Came from Outer Space (with H. Stein, Gertz) UNIV
The Golden Blade (see H. Stein)
Veils of Bagdad (with H. Stein; + stock) UNIV
Tumbleweed (with H. Stein; ac: M. Rosen; + stock) UNIV
Walking My Baby Back Home UNIV
The Glenn Miller Story UNIV
1954
Ma and Pa Kettle at Home (see H. Stein)
Creature from the Black Lagoon (see Salter)
Saskatchewan (with H. Stein, F. Skinner, Lava, Salter) UNIV
Rails Into Laramie (see H. Stein)
Johnny Dark (see Salter)
Drums Across the River (see H. Stein)
Tanganyika (see Salter)
The Far Country (see F. Skinner)
Fireman, Save My Child (see Lava)
Black Horse Canyon (see F. Skinner)
Destry (see F. Skinner)
Francis Joins the WACs (see Gertz)
Ricochet Romance (see Lava)
Four Guns to the Border (see H. Stein)
The Yellow Mountain (with H. Stein, S. Wilson) UNIV
So This Is Paris (with H. Stein) UNIV
Abbott and Costello Meet the Keystone Kops (with Lava, H. Stein) UNIV
1955
Smoke Signal (see Lava)

Abbott and Costello Meet the Mummy (see Maury)
This Island Earth (see H. Stein)
The Man from Bitter Ridge (see Gertz)
Ma and Pa Kettle at Waikiki (+ stock) UNIV
Ain't Misbehavin' (ac: F. Skinner) UNIV
The Private War of Major Benson (see Lava)
The Second Greatest Sex UNIV
To Hell and Back (see Lava)
The Benny Goodman Story UNIV
The Spoilers (with Salter, H. Stein) UNIV
The Kettles in the Ozarks (with H. Stein; + stock) UNIV

1956
A Day of Fury (see Gertz)
Creature Walks Among Us (with Gertz, Roemheld; ac: Salter) UNIV
World in My Corner (with Roemheld) UNIV
Toy Tiger (with S. Wilson, H. Stein; ac: F. Skinner, Roemheld) UNIV
Congo Crossing (with Gertz) UNIV
Francis in the Haunted House (with F. Skinner, Stein) UNIV
The Unguarded Moment (see H. Stein)
Everything but the Truth (see H. Stein)
The Great Man (see H. Stein)
Kelly and Me (ac: Lava, S. Wilson, F. Skinner) UNIV

1957
Rock, Pretty Baby UNIV
Mister Cory (see H. Stein)
Man Afraid UNIV
Joe Butterfly (with S. Wilson, Earl Lawrence, Gertz) UNIV
The Kettles on Old MacDonald's Farm (with H. Stein, Gertz) UNIV
Joe Dakota (see Salter)
The Land Unknown (see Salter)
The Monolith Monsters (see Gertz)
Flood Tide (with Lava) UNIV
Damn Citizen UNIV
Summer Love UNIV
The Big Beat UNIV

1958
Touch of Evil UNIV
This Happy Feeling (see F. Skinner)
The Thing That Couldn't Die (+ stock) UNIV
Voice in the Mirror UNIV
Never Steal Anything Small UNIV

1960
High Time (o: E. Powell) TCF
The Great Imposter UNIV

1961
Breakfast at Tiffany's (o: Shuken, Hayes) PAR
Bachelor in Paradise (o: Shuken, Hayes) MGM
Hatari (o: Shuken, Hayes) PAR

1962
Experiment in Terror (o: Shuken, Hayes) COL
Mr. Hobbs Takes a Vacation (o: Shuken, Hayes) TCF
Days of Wine and Roses WB

1963
Man's Favorite Sport? UNIV
Soldier in the Rain AA
Charade UNIV

1964
The Pink Panther UA
A Shot in the Dark (o: Douglas Gamley) UA

1965
Dear Heart (o: Shuken, Hayes) WB
The Great Race WB

1966
Moment to Moment UNIV
What Did You Do in the War, Daddy? UA
Arabesque (o: Gamley) UNIV
Two for the Road (o: Gamley) TCF

1967
Gunn PAR
Wait Until Dark (o: Shuken, Hayes) WB

1968
The Party UA

1969
Me, Natalie NG
Gaily, Gaily UA
Darling Lili (o: Shuken, Hayes) PAR

1970
The Molly Maguires (o: Shuken, Hayes) PAR
The Hawaiians UA
Sunflower EMB

Shorts (UNIV)

1952
The World's Most Beautiful Girls

1953
Andy Russell and Della in House Party

1955
A World of Beauty
Queens of Beauty (+ stock)

1956
Cool and Groovy

MANDEL, JOHN (JOHNNY)

1958
I Want to Live UA

1960
The Third Voice TCF
1963
Drums of Africa MGM
1964
The Americanization of Emily (o: Courage) MGM
1965
The Sandpiper (o: Byers) MGM
1966
Harper (o: Holman) WB
The Russians Are Coming The Russians Are Coming UA
An American Dream (o: Holman) WB
1967
Point Blank (o: Byers) MGM
1968
Pretty Poison TCF
1969
Heaven with a Gun (o: A. Harris) MGM
That Cold Day in the Park CU
Some Kind of a Nut UA
MASH (o: H. Spencer) TCF
1970
The Man Who Had Power Over Women EMB

MANERI, JOSEPH
1955
Labyrinth (short) J. WEDEEN, K. SINGH, L. FEINSTEIN

MANN, BARRY
1970
I Never Sang for My Father (see Gorgoni)

MANN, BOBBY
1970
Divorce Las Vegas Style (with C. Stevens) WILLIAM WHITE

MANNE, SHELLY
1958
T-Bird Gang FILMGROUP
1959
The Proper Time UA
1965
Clarence, the Cross-Eyed Lion (see Armbruster)
The Young Sinner UNITED SCREEN ARTS
1967
The Box (an. short) MURAKAMI-WOLF
1969
Young Billy Young UA

MANSON, EDDY
1953
Little Fugitive MORRIS ENGEL
1956
Lovers and Lollipops MORRIS ENGEL
1960
Weddings and Babies MORRIS ENGEL
1966
Three Bites of the Apple MGM
Shorts
1956
The Friendly Towns HERALD TRIBUNE
1957
Mirror in the Mountains (doc.) BERNIE HABER
Future Tense (doc.) YMCA
1960
The Day of the Painter EZRA BAKER
1962
The Cliff Dwellers GROUP 11
1964
The Supermarket EZRA BAKER
King of the Ice GROUP 11
1965
The Boudoir EZRA BAKER
Gideon's Trumpet (doc.) USIA
1967
What Time Is It Now? (doc.) GARGANO ASSOCIATES
1970
Crash EZRA BAKER

MANUPELLI, GEORGE
1963
Five Short Films [on one reel:] GEORGE MANUPELLI
A Film for Hooded Projector (music: Manupelli)
I Love You, Do Not Be Afraid (music: Robert Ashley)
Say Nothing About This to Anyone (music: Mumma)
I Must See You Regarding a Matter of the Utmost Urgency (music: Robert Ashley)
If You Leave Me I Will Kill Myself (music: Mumma)

MARAIS, JOSEPH
1965
Rainshower (doc. short) CHURCHILL FILMS
1967
Land of the Book (Ancient Israel) (doc. short) RAY GARNER

MARCELLI, ULDERICO
1922
Salome ALLIED

MARCELLINO, MUZZY
1959
Terror Faces Magoo (cartoon) UPA

MARGULIES, STEVE
1970
Don't Just Lay There MATTIS-PINE PRODS.

MARINI, PIR
1967
Bed of Violence JOE SARNO
Come Ride the Wild Pink Horse JOE SARNO
The Love Rebellion JOE SARNO
1968
Deep Inside JOE SARNO
Wall of Flesh JOE SARNO
1969
Passion in Hot Hollows JOE SARNO

MARKOWITZ, RICHARD
1958
Roadracers AIP
Stake Out on Dope Street WB
The Hot Angel PAR
The Young Captives PAR
1959
Operation Dames AIP
1961
The Hoodlum Priest UA
1962
The Magic Sword UA
1963
A Face in the Rain EMB
Cry of Battle AA
1964
One Man's Way (o: W. Jones) UA
1965
Bus Riley's Back in Town (ac: M. Stevens) UNIV
Wild Seed UNIV
The Shooting JACK H. HARRIS
1966
Ride Beyond Vengeance (o: W. Jones) COL
1969
A Black Veil for Lisa (o: W. Jones) CU
Documentaries
1965
The Bus HARRISON
1967
The Summer Children (short) SPECIAL PURPOSE FILMS
Lab School (short) SPECIAL PURPOSE FILMS
19??
Central Market (short) USIS
The Bridge (short) USIS
[And numerous industrial films.]

MARKS, FRANKLYN
1956
How to Have an Accident in the Home (cartoon) WDP
1961
The First Noel (short) CATHEDRAL FILMS
1967
Scrooge McDuck and Money (cartoon) WDP
The Legend of the Boy and the Eagle (o: Sheets) WDP
Charlie, the Lonesome Cougar (o: W. Robinson) WDP

MARQUARDT, PAUL
1928
Bellamy Trial (see Axt)
1932
Blonde Venus (see Harling)
The Sign of the Cross (see R. Kopp)
1933
A Farewell to Arms (see Harling)
Tonight Is Ours (see Hajos)
Tugboat Annie (+ stock) MGM
1934
Dark Hazard (see Kaun)
1935
Baby Face Harrington (see E. Ward)
Murder in the Fleet (m&e; + stock) MGM
1937
Bad Boy GATEWAY
1940
Golden Gloves (see Hollander)
1944
You Can't Ration Love (see Heymann)
[Also a very prolific arranger and orchestrator.]

MARSALES, FRANK
Cartoons (WB)
1930
Sinkin' in the Bathtub
Congo Jazz
Hold Anything
The Booze Hangs High
Box Car Blues
Big Man from the North
Ain't Nature Grand

1931

Battling Bosko
Big-Hearted Bosko
Bosko at the Zoo
Bosko Shipwrecked
Bosko the Doughboy
Bosko's Fox Hunt
Bosko's Holiday
Bosko's Party
Bosko's Soda Fountain
The Dumb Patrol
Hittin' the Trail to Hallelujah Land
Lady Play Your Mandolin
One More Time
Pagan Moon
Red-Headed Baby
Smile, Darn Ya, Smile
The Tree's Knees
Ups'n Downs
Yodeling Yokels
You Don't Know What You're Doing

1932

Bosko and Bruno
Bosko and Honey
Bosko at the Beach
Bosko the Lumberjack
Bosko's Dog Race
Bosko's Store
Crosby, Columbo and Vallee
Freddie the Freshman
Goopy Gear
It's Got Me Again
Moonlight for Two
The Queen Was in the Parlor

1933

Beau Bosko
Bosko in Dutch
Bosko in Person
Bosko the Drawback
Bosko the Musketeer
Bosko the Sheepherder
Bosko the Speed King
Bosko's Dizzy Date
Bosko's Knight-Mare
Bosko's Mechanical Man
Bosko's Picture Show
Bosko's Woodland Daze
The Dish Ran Away with the Spoon
A Great Big Bunch of You
I Like Mountain Music
I Love a Parade
I Wish I Had Wings
One Step Ahead of My Shadow
The Organ Grinder
Ride Him, Bosko
The Shanty Where Santy Claus Lives
Shuffle Off to Buffalo
Three's a Crowd
Wake Up the Gypsy in Me
We're in the Money
Young and Healthy
You're Too Careless with Your Kisses

Cartoons (UNIV)

1938

The Big Cat and the Little Mousie
The Cat and the Bell
The Disobedient Mouse
Little Blue Blackbird
Man Hunt
Pixie Land
Queen's Kittens
The Rabbit Hunt
Sailor Mouse

1939

A-Haunting We Will Go
Arabs with Dirty Fezzes
The Bird on Nellie's Hat
The Birth of a Toothpick
Bolo-Mola Land
Charlie Cuckoo
Crackpot Cruise
I'm Just a Jitterbug
Life Begins for Andy Panda
Little Tough Mice
The Magic Beans
Scrambled Eggs
Slaphappy Valley
The Sleeping Princess
Soup to Mutts
The Stubborn Mule

1940

Adventures of Tom Thumb, Jr.
Knock Knock

MARSH, GEORGE

Shorts (AAA FOUNDATION)

1953

Mickey's Big Chance
The Talking Car

1956

Lakewood Learns to Live

MARSHALL, CLIFFORD

Documentary Shorts (VIRGINIA DEPT. OF EDUCATION)

1948

Operations Wildlife
The Oyster and Virginia

1949
New Fields in the Old Dominions

MARSHALL, DENNIS
1966
Fragile (doc. short) U. OF PENNSYLVANIA

MARSHALL, JACK
1957
The Missouri Traveler C. V. WHITNEY
1958
Thunder Road UA
1959
The Giant Gila Monster MCLENDON
The Rabbit Trap UA
Take a Giant Step UA
1960
My Dog Buddy COL
1966
Munster, Go Home! UNIV
1967
Tammy and the Millionaire UNIV
1968
Stay Away, Joe (o: A. Harris) MGM
Kona Coast WB
1969
Backtrack (+ stock) UNIV

MARTEL, PIERRE
1962
The House on Bare Mountain OLYMPIC INT'L.

MARTELL, CHRIS
1968
The Hooked Generation AA

MARTIN, DAVID
1963
Moses Soyer—Paintings in a Low Voice (doc. short) SIDNEY MEYERS

MARTIN, DENNY
1968
Hot Spur OLYMPIC INT'L.

MARTIN, GENE
1961
True Gang Murders (doc.) SAGITTARIUS FILMS

MARTIN, HUGH
1950
Grandma Moses (doc. short; a: Alec Wilder) JEROME HILL

MARTIN, JAMES
1956
Calvary (doc. short) BOB JONES U.

MARTIN, LLOYD (SKIP)
1956
The Bottom of the Bottle (see Harline)
The Opposite Sex (see Stoll)
1957
Ten Thousand Bedrooms (see Stoll)
Bernardine (see L. Newman)
[Also an arranger and orchestrator.]

MARTIN, RAY
1964
Focus on a Century of Communications (doc. short) VICTOR KAYFETZ
1966
New York: The Anytime City (doc. short) JOHN BRANSBY PRODS.
The Spy Who Came In for the Olds (doc.) MPO PRODS.
1967
One Hundred Million Dollars a Day (doc. short) MPO PRODS.
[Also scored several films in Britain in the 1950s.]

MARTINEZ, GILBERT M.
1970
Threshold (short) HOLLYWOOD FILM ASSOC.

MARTINO, DONALD
1953
The White Rooster (short) ?
1958
The Lonely Crime RICHARD HILLIARD

MARTYN, ARLING
1943
Jasper's Music Lesson (cartoon) PAR

MARX, DICK
1958
Mag (doc. short) LIFE MAGAZINE
1960
Kaleidoscope Jazz Chair (short) EAMES

MARX, WILLIAM
1961
Weekend Pass PAUL VON SCHREIBER
Walk the Angry Beach JOHN PATRICK HAYES
1970
Count Yorga, Vampire AIP

MASAGNI, LOUIS
1964
Peaches and Cream (short) PAUL MORRISSEY

MASON, BRUNO
1944
The Woman in the Window (see Friedhofer)
1945
It's a Pleasure (see A. Lange)

MASON, JACK
1948
Linda, Be Good EL

MASON, WILTON
Documentary Shorts
1950
North Carolina, Variety Vacationland NORTH CAROLINA DEPT. OF CONSERVATION
1952
Dare, Birthplace of America U. OF NORTH CAROLINA
Spring of Our Faith U. OF NORTH CAROLINA

MATLOVSKY, SAMUEL
1962
Third of a Man UA
1966
Namu the Killer Whale UA
Birds Do It COL
1967
Games UNIV
Gentle Giant PAR

MATZ, PETER
1968
Bye Bye Braverman WB
1969
Marlowe MGM

MAURY, LOU
1955
Abbott and Costello Meet the Mummy (with Gertz, Salter; ac: Mancini) UNIV
Cult of the Cobra (see Lava)
To Hell and Back (see Lava)
On-Stream (doc.; see Lava)
Cartoons (UPA)
1951
The Wonder Gloves
1954
The Man on the Flying Trapeze
Magoo Goes Skiing
Destination Magoo

MAXWELL, CHARLES
1929
Marianne (see Axt)
1931
Possessed (+ stock) MGM
1932
Grand Hotel (see Axt)
1935
The Winning Ticket MGM
West Point of the Air MGM
Calm Yourself MGM
1936
West Point of the South (short) MGM
The Great Ziegfeld (see A. Lange)
Parole (see C. Previn)
White Fang (see Friedhofer)
Girls' Dormitory (with Buttolph; ac: A. Lange) TCF
Star for a Night (with Kaylin) TCF
The Magnificent Brute (with A. Lange; ac: Van Loan, Roemheld, R. Bassett) UNIV
Under Your Spell (with A. Lange) TCF
White Hunter (with A. Lange) TCF
Banjo on My Knee (mt; et: A. Lange) TCF
Charlie Chan at the Opera (+ stock) TCF
1937
One in a Million (see Buttolph)
On the Avenue (see Mockridge)
This Is My Affair (with A. Lange) TCF
You Can't Have Everything (see W. Scharf)
Love Under Fire (see A. Lange)
Thin Ice (see Buttolph)
San Quentin (see Roemheld)
Lancer Spy (with A. Lange) TCF
Heidi (see Toch)
1938
Kidnapped (with A. Lange) TCF
Three Blind Mice (ac: Mockridge) TCF
We're Going to Be Rich (ac for U.S. release of British film) TCF
Gateway (with Mockridge) TCF
Mysterious Mr. Moto (+ stock) TCF
Suez (see Mockridge)
Submarine Patrol (with A. Lange) TCF
1939
The Three Musketeers (with Toch, Mockridge; ac: Buttolph, W. Scharf) TCF
Wife, Husband and Friend (ac: Mockridge) TCF
The Little Princess (see Mockridge)

The Hound of the Baskervilles (with Buttolph, Mockridge, D. Raksin) TCF
The Return of the Cisco Kid (see W. Scharf)
Susannah of the Mounties (with R. Bassett, Buttolph) TCF
Frontier Marshal (see Kaylin)
Everything Happens at Night (see Buttolph)

1940
The Gay Caballero (o: Virgil) TCF

1941
Romance of the Rio Grande (see Mockridge)
Ride Kelly Ride TCF

1942
Prelude to War (see Harline)
Dixie Dugan (see A. Lange)
Quiet, Please, Murder (see A. Lange)

1943
Lady of Burlesque (see A. Lange)
Wintertime (see A. Lange)

1944
Cowboy and the Senorita (see Skiles)
Secrets of Scotland Yard (o: Vaughan) REP
Storm Over Lisbon REP
The Merry Monahans (see Salter)
Casanova Brown (see A. Lange)
The Woman in the Window (see Friedhofer)
Lake Placid Serenade (see W. Scharf)

1945
Bells of Rosarita (with Dubin, M. Glickman) REP
Along Came Jones (see A. Lange)
Scotland Yard Investigator (o: M. Glickman) REP

1946
In Old Sacramento (o: Vaughan) REP
Rainbow Over Texas (with Butts) REP
My Pal Trigger (see Butts)

1947
Apache Rose (with Arnaud, Perkins, S. Wilson) REP
Twilight on the Rio Grande (partial) REP
Bells of San Angelo (partial) REP

1948
Black Bart (see L. Stevens)

1951
Five (see H. Russell)
Tree Farm (short; see Lava)

[Also a very prolific orchestrator.]

MAY, BILLY

1955
Tara the Stone-Cutter (cartoon) FINE ARTS

1956
The Jay Walker (cartoon) UPA

1957
Bernardine (see L. Newman)
The Fuzzy Pink Nightgown UA

1962
Sergeants 3 UA

1963
Johnny Cool UA

1967
Tony Rome TCF

1968
The Secret Life of an American Wife TCF

MAYERS, BERNARD

1953
The I Don't Care Girl (see H. Spencer)

1954
White Christmas (see Lilley)
There's No Business Like Show Business (see A. Newman)

1958
Mardi Gras (see L. Newman)

[Also a prolific orchestrator.]

MAYFIELD, JAMES K.

1946
Abilene Town (see Terr)
Breakfast in Hollywood (see Leipold)
God's Country SG
Scared to Death SG
Death Valley SG
North of the Border SG
'Neath Canadian Skies SG
Flight to Nowhere SG

Shorts (MGM)

1946
Looking Down at London
Over the Seas to Belfast

1947
Visiting Virginia

1948
Wandering Through Wales
Scholastic England

1949
Roaming Through Northern Ireland
From Liverpool to Stratford
A Wee Bit of Scotland

1950
The Land of Auld Lang Syne

McBRIDE, DOMINIC
1937
Angkor (doc.) ROAD SHOW ATTRACTIONS

McBRIDE, ROBERT
1946
Magazine Magic (doc. short) CURTIS PUBLISHING
1950
Farewell to Yesterday (doc.; see Applebaum)
1951
Rodney (cartoon) FILM GRAPHICS
The Man with My Face UA
1953
Sea-Going Smoke Eaters (doc. short) RKO PATHÉ
1954
Garden of Eden EXCELSIOR

McCOSH, CAMERON
1957
A Dancer's World (doc. short) NATHAN KROLL

McCURDY, RICHARD
1965
Toward a Better Life (doc. short) L.A. ATHLETIC CLUB

McDOWELL, JOHN HERBERT
196?
Whispers (short) MARK SADAN
1962
Woton's Wake (short) BRIAN DE PALMA
1965
Deadly Sins (short) ?
Three Dances (short) ?
1968
Tappy Toes (short) RED GROOMS
Murder a la Mod BRIAN DE PALMA
1969
The Wedding Party BRIAN DE PALMA

McELHENY, HUGH
1957
Six, Seven and Eight-Year Olds (doc. short) VASSAR COLLEGE

McGINNIS, DON
1965
Psycho a Go-Go! (with Billy Storm) AL ADAMSON
1970
Hell's Bloody Devils (themes: Riddle) AL ADAMSON

McGLOHON, LOONIS
1969
The Travel Door (doc. short) DELTA AIR LINES

McHUGH, JIMMY
1958
Jack the Ripper (see Rugolo)
[He composed the trademark fanfare for Universal Pictures used from 1936–1946.]

McINTOSH, TOM
1969
The Learning Tree (see Parks)

McINTYRE, CHET
1963
One Naked Night SACK

McKENNA, WILLIAM J.
1918
The Crucible of Life AUTHORS' FILM CO.

McPARTLAND, MARIAN
1963
Mark (short) GEORGE F. JOHNSTON

McPHEE, COLIN
1931
Mechanical Principles (doc. short) RALPH STEINER
H_2O (doc. short) RALPH STEINER
1957
Airskills (doc. short) UNITED NATIONS
Blue Vanguard (doc.) UNITED NATIONS
1959
In Our Hands (doc. short) UNITED NATIONS

McRITCHIE, GREIG
1962
This Is Not a Test FREDERIC GADETTE

McVANE, SANDY
1969
Vibrations JOE SARNO

MEAKIN, JACK
1953
The Twonky UA

1956

A Hotel Is Born (doc. short) PARTHENON
Tools of Telephony (doc. short) PARTHENON

1957

The Next Ten (doc. short) PARTHENON

1959

Magoo's Lodge Brother (cartoon) UPA

1961

Locked On (doc.) PARTHENON

[Also many other non-theatrical films, titles unknown.]

MEEKER, JESS

1959

Youth Dances (doc. short) DANCE IN EDUCATION FUND

MEKAS, ADOLFAS

1968

Windflowers (with Chapelle; a: Blume) ADOLFAS MEKAS

MELTZER, RAYMOND

1951

An Adventure in Casein Painting (short) DYNAMIC FILMS

MENDEL, YUSHO

1965

The Doctor and the Playgirl EMERSON

MENDELSOHN, DANIEL

1953

Quebec Camera Hunt (doc. short) RKO PATHÉ

1956

Invitation to New York (short) UNIV

MENDOZA, DAVID

1920

Passion (see Axt)

1924

The Sea Hawk (see Axt)

1925

The Merry Widow (see Axt)

1926

Don Juan (see Axt)
Mare Nostrum (see Axt)
The Scarlet Letter (see Axt)
The Fire Brigade (see Axt)
Slide, Kelly, Slide (see Axt)
Camille (see Axt)
Annie Laurie (see Axt)

1928

The Student Prince in Old Heidelberg (see Axt)
Glorious Betsy WB

1929

Gold Diggers of Broadway (with Reiser) WB
The Careless Age (see Leonardi)
Disraeli WB

1930

Young Man of Manhattan (mt) PAR
Song of the Flame WB
Oh Sailor Behave (see Leonardi)
Sweet Kitty Bellairs (see Dunn)
The Girl of the Golden West (see Leonardi)
Captain Thunder (see Cugat)
Mother's Cry WB
The Lash (with Cugat, Rosebrook) WB
Little Caesar (mt; + stock) WB

1931

My Past (+ stock) WB
Kiss Me Again (+ stock) WB
Father's Son (see Copping)
The Public Enemy (mt) WB
God's Gift to Women (o: E. Ross) WB
Svengali (o: Potoker) WB
Gold Dust Gertie (with Copping) WB
Smart Money (mt; o: Potoker) WB
Chances (mt; o: Potoker; + stock) WB
Men of the Sky WB
Children of Dreams WB
The Reckless Hour (o: Potoker; + stock) WB
The Bargain WB
Penrod and Sam (mt; + stock) WB
I Like Your Nerve (o: Potoker; + stock) WB
Alexander Hamilton (o: Potoker; + stock) WB
The Ruling Voice (m&e; o: Potoker; + stock) WB
Honor of the Family (m&e; + stock) WB
Compromised (o: Potoker; + stock) WB
The Mad Genius (+ stock) WB
Local Boy Makes Good (mt; o: Potoker; + stock) WB

MENDOZA-NAVA, JAIME

1961

The Grass Eater GLOBE

1962

Fallguy FAIRWAY-INT'L.

1963

The Quick and the Dead BECKMAN
Ballad of a Gunfighter PARADE

1964

Shell Shock PARADE
No Man's Land CINEMA-VIDEO
Handle with Care CINEMA-VIDEO

1965

Orgy of the Dead F.O.G.
A Hot Summer Game EUROPEAN

1966

Marine Battleground MANSON
The Black Klansman U.S. FILMS
The Hostage CROWN INT'L.
The Talisman GILLMAN

1968

High, Wild and Free (doc.) AIP
Fever Heat PAR

1969

The Witchmaker EXCELSIOR
The Stewardesses SHERPIX

1970

The Savage Wild (doc.) AIP
Equinox VIP
Brother Cry for Me FINE
The Wild Scene FOUR STAR
The Hard Road FOUR STAR
Royal Flesh ALL-STATE
The Midnight Graduate GRADS

Shorts

1965

On This Mountain DORIAN FILMS

1966

1966 Indianapolis 500 (doc.) PAR

1967

The Silent Screamer (doc.) PAR
Quiet Revolution (doc.) STUDEBAKER

1969

Up and Over—Exploring on the Stegel (doc.) BRADLEY WRIGHT

MENOTTI, GIAN-CARLO

1940

Mr. Trull Finds Out (short) FILM ASSOCIATES

MENTION, MICHEL

1969

A Day with the Boys (doc. short) CLU GULAGER

MERKUR, J. L.

1933

Devil's Playground (doc.) GEORGE VANDERBILT PRODS.

1944

John, the Drunkard P.A.L. PICTURES

MERRICK, MAHLON

1943

Silver Skates MON
The Girl from Monterey PRC

1944

Sensations of 1945 (with Roemheld, M. Glickman) UA

1948

Alaska Patrol FC
This Is Nylon (doc. short) APEX

1949

Miss Mink of 1949 TCF
Deputy Marshal LIP

1950

The Lawless PAR
The U.C.L.A. Story (doc.) APEX
The Du Pont Story (doc.) APEX

1951

Passage West PAR
One Man's Lifetime (doc.) APEX

1952

Red Planet Mars UA

MERRIMAN, THOMAS C.

1962

Copper, the Oldest Modern Metal (doc. short) PHELPS DODGE CORP.

MERSEY, ROBERT

1965

Terror in the City AA

1968

With Six You Get Eggroll NG

MEYERS, SHEPARD

1970

All Together Now (with L. Rosen) CANNON

MICHAELIDES, GEORGE

1966

The Last Moment HEADLINER PRODS.

MICHALSKY, DONAL

1950

Hast Any Philosophy in Thee? (short) USC

MICHELET, MICHEL

[He scored nearly a hundred features and shorts in France, 1929–1940.]

1942

Miss Annie Rooney (see Calker)

1943

The Crime Doctor's Strangest Case (partial) COL
Voice in the Wind UA

1944
Up in Mabel's Room UA
The Hairy Ape UA
Music for Millions (o: Nussbaum; ac: Stoll, C. Jackson) MGM
1946
The Diary of a Chambermaid (o: Cailliet) UA
The Chase (o: Cailliet) UA
1947
Lured (o: Herschel Gilbert) UA
1948
Siren of Atlantis (o: Herschel Gilbert) UA
1949
Outpost in Morocco (o: Herschel Gilbert) UA
Impact (o: Herschel Gilbert) UA
The Man on the Eiffel Tower RKO
1950
Once a Thief UA
Double Deal RKO
1951
M COL
Tarzan's Peril RKO
1953
Fort Algiers UA
1954
Miss Body Beautiful PHOENIX
1960
Journey to the Lost City AIP
The Goddess of Love TCF
1961
Desert Warrior MEDALLION
1963
Captain Sinbad MGM

MIDDLEBROOKS, HARRY
1966
The Gold Guitar CRADDOCK

MIDGELY, CHARLES
1930
The Benson Murder Case (mt) PAR
The Light of Western Skies PAR
The Silent Enemy (with Potoker, G. Lucas, Hajos, Terr, H. Jackson, Harling, Leipold; based on themes by Massard Kur-Zhene) PAR

MILHAUD, DARIUS
1947
The Private Affairs of Bel Ami UA
1948
Dreams That Money Can Buy (see Applebaum)
[He composed many films in France, 1924–1959.]

MILLER, ALAN
1966
Sunflight (an. short) IFF

MILLER, ROBERT WILEY
1952
Big Jim McLain (see Dunlap)
1953
Plunder of the Sun (see Diaz Conde)
1957
Death in Small Doses AA
Gun Battle at Monterey AA

MILLS, CHARLES
1957
On the Bowery (doc.) LIONEL ROGOSIN

MILLS, FELIX
1933
The Mind Reader (see Kaun)
1939
The Amazing Mr. Williams (+ stock) COL
His Girl Friday (see Cutner)

MINGUS, CHARLES
1959
Shadows (ac) JOHN CASSAVETES

MITCHEL, EDMUND
1966
Aroused CAMBIST

MIZZY, VIC
1964
The Night Walker UNIV
1965
A Very Special Favor UNIV
1966
The Ghost and Mr. Chicken UNIV
The Spirit Is Willing (o: Levene) PAR
1967
The Busy Body (o: Levene) PAR
The Reluctant Astronaut UNIV
Did You Hear the One About the Traveling Saleslady? UNIV
The Shakiest Gun in the West UNIV
Don't Make Waves (o: Levene) MGM
The Caper of the Golden Bulls (o: Levene) EMBASSY
The Perils of Pauline UNIV
1969
The Love God? UNIV

MOCKRIDGE, CYRIL J.
1933
My Weakness (see A. Lange)

1934

Call It Luck (see Kaylin)
The World Moves On (see De Francesco)

1935

The Little Colonel (with Friedhofer) FOX
Under the Pampas Moon (ac: Brunelli; o: Friedhofer) FOX
The Farmer Takes a Wife (see Buttolph)
Way Down East (see Friedhofer)
The Man Who Broke the Bank at Monte Carlo (+ stock) TCF
The Littlest Rebel (o: Buttolph) TCF

1936

King of Burlesque (o: H. Spencer)
The Country Doctor (with R. Bassett; o: H. Spencer) TCF
Everybody's Old Man (see Buttolph)
Captain January (o: H. Spencer) TCF
Under Two Flags (with R. Bassett, Buttolph) TCF
Private Number (o: H. Spencer) TCF
Poor Little Rich Girl (o: H. Spencer) TCF
To Mary—With Love (o: H. Spencer) TCF
Sing, Baby, Sing (o: H. Spencer) TCF
Ladies in Love (with Buttolph; ac: Silvers) TCF
Dimples (with R. Bassett; ac: Buttolph) TCF
Reunion (see Buttolph)
Lloyd's of London (with Buttolph, R. Bassett) TCF

1937

On the Avenue (with Maxwell; o: H. Spencer) TCF
Nancy Steele Is Missing (see Buttolph)
Seventh Heaven (see Buttolph)
Wake Up and Live (o: W. Scharf) TCF
Café Metropole (see Buttolph)
Wee Willie Winkie (see A. Newman)
You Can't Have Everything (see W. Scharf)
Thin Ice (see Buttolph)
Danger—Love at Work TCF
Second Honeymoon (o: H. Spencer) TCF

1938

Happy Landing (with Toch, Buttolph) TCF
In Old Chicago (o: H. Spencer) TCF
Kentucky Moonshine (with G. Rose, Cutter) TCF
Three Blind Mice (see Maxwell)
Always Goodbye (o: H. Spencer) TCF
I'll Give a Million (+ stock) TCF
Gateway (see Maxwell)
Suez (with Bennett, Maxwell, Toch, D. Raksin) TCF

1939

The Three Musketeers (see Maxwell)
Wife, Husband and Friend (see Maxwell)
Inside Story (o: G. Rose) TCF
The Little Princess (with Maxwell; o: H. Spencer) TCF
The Hound of the Baskervilles (see Maxwell)
Second Fiddle (with D. Raksin) TCF
Hotel for Women (with Buttolph) TCF
Stanley and Livingstone (see Silvers)
The Adventures of Sherlock Holmes (with Bennett, Buttolph; ac: Raksin) TCF
Hollywood Cavalcade (see Schrager)
Swanee River (see Schrager)
Everything Happens at Night (see Buttolph)

1940

Johnny Apollo (o: W. Scharf) TCF
Lillian Russell (with A. Newman, Buttolph; o: E. Powell, H. Spencer) TCF
Girl in 313 (see Buttolph)
Lucky Cisco Kid (o: W. Scharf) TCF
Manhattan Heartbeat (o: Scharf, H. Spencer) TCF
Girl from Avenue A (o: E. Powell, H. Spencer) TCF
Pier 13 (o: W. Scharf, H. Spencer) TCF
Young People (o: H. Spencer) TCF
Charlie Chan at the Wax Museum (o: E. Powell, H. Spencer) TCF
Yesterday's Heroes (o: E. Powell, Salinger, Arnaud) TCF
Brigham Young (see A. Newman)
Down Argentine Way (o: Salinger, E. Powell, H. Spencer)
Laddie (see Webb)
The Great Profile (o: D. Raksin, H. Spencer) TCF
The Mark of Zorro (see A. Newman)
Tin Pan Alley (see A. Newman)
Youth Will Be Served (o: Salinger, E. Powell) TCF
Murder Over New York (o: Arnaud) TCF
Jennie (o: H. Spencer) TCF

1941

Hudson's Bay (see A. Newman)
Michael Shayne, Private Detective (o: W. Scharf) TCF
Golden Hoofs (o: E. Powell, Salinger) TCF
Romance of the Rio Grande (ac: Maxwell, Buttolph, A. Morton) TCF
Tall, Dark and Handsome (o: W. Scharf) TCF

Murder Among Friends (with Buttolph; o: W. Scharf; + stock) TCF
Sleepers West (o: Salinger) TCF
Scotland Yard (with Buttolph; o: H. Spencer, Moross, E. Powell) TCF
The Great American Broadcast (theme: A. Newman; o: Salinger) TCF
The Cowboy and the Blonde (o: E. Powell, H. Spencer) TCF
A Very Young Lady (see Buttolph)
Moon Over Miami (with C. Henderson, Buttolph, A. Newman) TCF
Accent on Love (o: E. Powell, H. Spencer) TCF
Dance Hall (with G. Rose; ac: Buttolph) TCF
Charley's Aunt (o: Salinger) TCF
Dressed to Kill (o: G. Rose) TCF
Wild Geese Calling (see Buttolph)
Sun Valley Serenade (with Buttolph; o: Salinger, D. Raksin) TCF
Charlie Chan in Rio (o: G. Rose) TCF
Belle Starr (see Buttolph)
We Go Fast (o: G. Rose) TCF
A Yank in the R.A.F. (see A. Newman)
Riders of the Purple Sage (o: G. Rose) TCF
Week-End in Havana (see A. Newman)
Moon Over Her Shoulder (o: H. Spencer, E. Powell) TCF
I Wake Up Screaming (o: H. Spencer) TCF
Rise and Shine (see Buttolph)
Marry the Boss's Daughter (o: G. Rose) TCF
On the Sunny Side (with Harline, D. Raksin; o: Parrish, Moross) TCF
Lone Star Ranger (o: E. Powell) TCF
The Perfect Snob (o: D. Raksin, H. Spencer) TCF
Son of Fury (see A. Newman)
Blue, White and Perfect (o: W. Scharf, G. Rose) TCF
Remember the Day (with D. Raksin, Buttolph, Friedhofer, Bradshaw; theme: A. Newman; o: Salinger, E. Powell, H. Spencer, Arnaud) TCF

1942

Roxie Hart (see A. Newman)
Castle in the Desert (see Buttolph)
The Night Before the Divorce (see Harline)
Song of the Islands (see Buttolph)
Rings on Her Fingers (see Harline)
Sundown Jim (mt; o: E. Powell) TCF
Secret Agent of Japan (see Harline)
It Happened in Flatbush (see Buttolph)
My Gal Sal (with Harline; ac: de Packh, C. Henderson) TCF
The Mad Martindales (see Buttolph)
Whispering Ghosts (see Harline)
Moontide (with Buttolph; o: E. Powell, Bradshaw, H. Spencer) TCF
The Magnificent Dope (with D. Raksin, Harline; o: H. Spencer, E. Powell) TCF
Thru Different Eyes (mt, o: H. Spencer; et: D. Raksin) TCF
Ten Gentlemen from West Point (with Buttolph; o: E. Powell, de Packh, Salinger) TCF
Footlight Serenade (see C. Henderson)
A-Haunting We Will Go (see Buttolph)
The Pied Piper (see A. Newman)
The Loves of Edgar Allan Poe (see Buttolph)
The Meanest Man in the World (o: G. Rose, E. Powell) TCF
Prelude to War (see Harline)
Iceland (see Harline)
Girl Trouble (see A. Newman)
Manila Calling (with Buttolph, D. Raksin; ac: Harline) TCF
The Man in the Trunk (o: H. Spencer, de Packh) TCF
The Ox-Bow Incident (o: Salinger, H. Spencer) TCF
The Undying Monster (see D. Raksin)
China Girl (see Friedhofer)
Time to Kill (see D. Raksin)
Over My Dead Body (o: de Packh) TCF
Life Begins at Eight-Thirty (see A. Newman)

1943

Chetniks! (see Friedhofer)
Hello, Frisco, Hello (see Buttolph)
At the Front in North Africa (see A. Newman)
My Friend Flicka (see A. Newman)
Tonight We Raid Calais (o: Salinger) TCF
Coney Island (ac: C. Henderson, Harline, A. Newman, A. Lange) TCF
Stormy Weather (o: G. Rose, A. Morton) TCF
Heaven Can Wait (see A. Newman)
Holy Matrimony (o: A. Morton, H. Spencer) TCF
Sweet Rosie O'Grady (with H. Spencer, C. Henderson, Harline) TCF
Happy Land (ac: A. Newman; o: D. Raksin, H. Spencer, A. Morton) TCF
The Gang's All Here (see A.Lange)

1944
The Lodger (see Friedhofer)
The Sullivans (with Buttolph, Friedhofer; ac: A. Newman; o: E. Powell, D. Raksin, A. Morton, de Packh) TCF
Four Jills in a Jeep (see Friedhofer)
Pin Up Girl (with A. Lange; o: G. Rose, A. Morton, de Packh) TCF
Ladies of Washington (o: A. Morton, Virgil) TCF
The Eve of St. Mark (ac: G. Rose; o: A. Morton, E. Powell, de Packh) TCF
Take It or Leave It (ac: Friedhofer; o: G. Rose) TCF
Sweet and Low-Down (ac: Buttolph, G. Rose; o: de Packh, D. Raksin) TCF
In the Meantime, Darling (o: A. Morton) TCF
Irish Eyes Are Smiling (with A. Newman; ac: C. Henderson, D. Raksin) TCF
Something for the Boys (with Harline; o: A. Morton, Plumb) TCF
Sunday Dinner for a Soldier (see A. Newman)

1945
Thunderhead (ac: A. Newman, Buttolph; o: de Packh, A. Morton, Parrish) TCF
Molly and Me (ac: Buttolph; o: A. Morton, de Packh) TCF
A Royal Scandal (see A. Newman)
The All-Star Bond Rally (short; o: A. Morton, de Packh) TCF
Where Do We Go from Here? (see D. Raksin)
Captain Eddie (o: de Packh, A. Morton) TCF
State Fair (see E. Powell)
Colonel Effingham's Raid (o: A. Morton, de Packh, Maxwell) TCF
The Dolly Sisters (see Buttolph)

1946
Doll Face (see Buttolph)
Sentimental Journey (ac: A. Newman; o: de Packh, H. Spencer, A. Morton) TCF
Cluny Brown (o: de Packh, A. Morton, Salinger) TCF
Centennial Summer (see A. Newman)
Claudia and David (with Buttolph; based on Newman's themes from *Claudia;* o: E. Powell) TCF
If I'm Lucky (with Buttolph; o: de Packh, E. Powell) TCF
Three Little Girls in Blue (see Buttolph)
Margie (see A. Newman)
Wake Up and Dream (o: Plumb, G. Rose, A. Morton) TCF

1947
The Late George Apley (o: de Packh) TCF
Carnival in Costa Rica (see Buttolph)
Miracle on 34th Street (o: E. Powell, de Packh) TCF
Thunder in the Valley (o: de Packh, E. Powell) TCF
Nightmare Alley (o: de Packh) TCF

1948
You Were Meant for Me (o: Powell, H. Spencer) TCF
Scudda-Hoo! Scudda-Hay! (o: H. Spencer, de Packh, Hagen) TCF
Green Grass of Wyoming (o: de Packh) TCF
Give My Regards to Broadway (with A. Newman; Buttolph; o: E. Powell, de Packh) TCF
Deep Waters (with A. Newman; o: E. Powell, de Packh) TCF
That Lady in Ermine (see A. Newman)
The Luck of the Irish (o: de Packh, E. Powell) TCF
Apartment for Peggy (see D. Raksin)
Unfaithfully Yours (o: E. Powell) TCF
That Wonderful Urge (o: de Packh, E. Powell, H. Spencer) TCF

1949
Mother Is a Freshman (see A. Newman)
The Beautiful Blonde from Bashful Bend (o: E. Powell) TCF
Come to the Stable (o: E. Powell) TCF
Slattery's Hurricane (o: de Packh) TCF
I Was a Male War Bride (o: H. Spencer) TCF
Father Was a Fullback (o: Virgil) TCF
Thieves' Highway (o: de Packh) TCF
Oh, You Beautiful Doll (see Hagen)
Dancing in the Dark (with H. Spencer; o: Hagen) TCF

1950
Mother Didn't Tell Me (o: de Packh, Hagen) TCF
Cheaper by the Dozen (with A. Newman; o: E. Powell, de Packh) TCF
Wabash Avenue (o: E. Powell) TCF
A Ticket to Tomahawk (o: Hagen, H. Spencer, Virgil) TCF
Love That Brute (o: E. Powell, H. Spencer) TCF
Where the Sidewalk Ends (o: de Packh) TCF

Stella (theme: A. Newman; o: E. Powell) TCF
I'll Get By (o: E. Powell) TCF
American Guerrilla in the Philippines (o: de Packh) TCF
For Heaven's Sake (see A. Newman)

1951
You're in the Navy Now (o: E. Powell, Mayers) TCF
Follow the Sun (o: E. Powell, Mayers) TCF
Half Angel (ac: A. Newman; o: de Packh, E. Powell) TCF
On the Riviera (see Hagen)
As Young as You Feel (o: de Packh) TCF
The Frogmen (o: Mayers, H. Spencer) TCF
Mr. Belvedere Rings the Bell (o: Parrish) TCF
Love Nest (o: Mayers) TCF
Let's Make It Legal (o: Mayers) TCF
Elopement (with A. Newman; o: E. Powell) TCF

1952
Golden Girl (see A. Newman)
The Model and the Marriage Broker (ac: A. Newman; o: E. Powell) TCF
Deadline—U.S.A. (with S. Kaplan; o: E. Powell, Mayers) TCF
Belles on Their Toes (o: Mayers) TCF
We're Not Married! (o: Mayers, E. Powell) TCF
Dreamboat (o: Mayers) TCF
Night Without Sleep (o: Mayers) TCF

1953
The I Don't Care Girl (see H. Spencer)
The Girl Next Door (o: Hagen) TCF
The Farmer Takes a Wife (o: Courage, Mayers) TCF
City of Bad Men (ac: D. Raksin; o: E. Powell, Hagen, de Packh, Mayers) TCF
The Kid from Left Field (see L. Newman)
Mister Scoutmaster (o: E. Powell, Courage) TCF
How to Marry a Millionaire (ac: A. Newman; o: E. Powell, Mayers) TCF
Dancers of the Deep (short; o: de Packh, Mayers) TCF

1954
Tournament of Roses (short; + stock) TCF
Siege at Red River (ac: L. Newman; o: Mayers) TCF
Night People (o: Mayers) TCF
River of No Return (see Harline)
Woman's World (ac: A. Newman; o: Mayers, Arnaud, Raab, de Packh) TCF

1955
Many Rivers to Cross (o: Courage, Woodbury) MGM
Daddy Long Legs (with A. Newman; o: E. Powell, Mayers) TCF
The Seven Year Itch (see A. Newman)
How to Be Very, Very Popular (ac: A. Newman; o: Mayers) TCF
The Girl Rush (see Hagen)
Guys and Dolls (o: Courage) GOLDWYN
The Lieutenant Wore Skirts (o: Mayers, H. Spencer) TCF

1956
Bus Stop (see A. Newman)
The Last Wagon (see L. Newman)
The Solid Gold Cadillac (see Duning)
I Married a Woman RKO

1957
Oh, Men! Oh, Women! (with Friedhofer; o: E. Powell) TCF
Desk Set (o: E. Powell) TCF
Will Success Spoil Rock Hunter? (o: E. Powell, Mayers) TCF
Kiss Them for Me (o: E. Powell) TCF
April Love (see A. Newman)

1958
The Gift of Love (see A. Newman)
Rally 'Round the Flag, Boys! (o: Hagen, Mayers, E. Powell) TCF

1959
Thunder in the Sun PAR
Warlock (see Harline)
A Private's Affair (o: Hagen, King) TCF
Hound Dog Man (with Gertz, Harline; o: Mayers, E. Powell, King) TCF

1960
Tall Story WB
Wake Me When It's Over (ac: Harline; o: E. Powell, H. Spencer) TCF
Let's Make Love (see Hagen)
North to Alaska (theme: L. Newman; ac: Gertz; o: Mayers, E. Powell, A. Morton) TCF
Flaming Star (with Gertz; ac: A. Morton, Harline, Murray, Goldsmith; o: E. Powell, H. Spencer) TCF

1961
All Hands on Deck (with Harline, Gertz, Murray; o: Mayers, E. Powell, H. Spencer) TCF

1962
The Man Who Shot Liberty Valance (o: Shuken, Hayes) PAR
1963
Donovan's Reef (o: Shuken, Hayes) PAR

MOHAUPT, RICHARD
1950
Farewell to Yesterday (doc.; see Applebaum)
1955
Herman Melville's Moby Dick (doc. short) JERRY WINTERS

MONACHELLI, JOE
1956
Festival of Judo (short) LEO-COSTA FILM PRODS.

MONTENEGRO, HUGO
1963
Advance to the Rear (see Sparks)
1966
Hurry Sundown PAR
1967
The Ambushers (o: Woodbury, Hazard, J. Hill, Grove) COL
1968
Lady in Cement (o: May) TCF
1969
The Wrecking Crew (o: Capps, J. Hill, Holman, Bahler, Hazard) COL
Churro! NG
The Undefeated (o: H. Spencer, Shuken, Hayes) TCF
Viva Max! CU

MOODY, PHIL
1964
Three Nuts in Search of a Bolt HARLEQUIN INT'L

MOORE, DOUGLAS
1940
Power and the Land (doc. short; o: Brant) USDA
Youth Gets a Break (doc. short; o: Brant) NAT'L YOUTH ADMINISTRATION
1941
Bip Goes to Town (doc. short; o: Brant) USDA

MOORE, FRANK LEDLIE
1964
Yugoslav Farm Family (doc. short) IFF

1966
The American Vision (doc. short) NATIONAL GALLERY OF ART

MOORE, GENE
1962
Carnival of Souls HERTS-LION

MOORE, PHIL
1944
The Negro Soldier (doc.; see Tiomkin)
1952
Rooty Toot Toot (cartoon) UPA
[Also worked as an arranger.]

MORAWECK, LUCIEN
1939
The Man in the Iron Mask UA
The Housekeeper's Daughter (see Filippi)
Cuando Canta la Ley (Spanish language) PAR
1940
The Lady in Question COL
Dreaming Out Loud RKO
Li'l Abner RKO
1941
They Met in Argentina RKO
International Lady UA
1942
Friendly Enemies UA
1943
Two Weeks to Live RKO
So This Is Washington! RKO
1944
The Whistler (with Garriguenc) COL
Abroad with Two Yanks (with Leipold) UA
Goin' to Town RKO
The Mark of the Whistler (see Castelnuovo-Tedesco)
1946
Strange Voyage MON
Partners in Time (ac: Leipold) RKO
Avalanche (with Garriguenc) PRC
The Return of Monte Cristo COL
1947
High Conquest (with Garriguenc, Murray) MON
1948
16 Fathoms Deep (with Garriguenc) MON
Michael O'Halloran (with Skiles) MON
1949
Massacre River (see Leipold)
1950
Boy from Indiana (with Skiles) EL

1951

New Mexico (with Garriguenc) UA

MORE, CHET

1966

The Notorious Daughter of Fanny Hill (with Sam Brown) SONNEY

1970

Caged Desires (with Jim More) HOLLYWOOD CINEMA

MOREY, LARRY

1953

Southern Cross (doc. short) TRINITY FILMS

1955

Going His Way? (short) TRINITY FILMS

MORGAN, FLOYD V.

1939

Ambush (see Carbonara)
Persons in Hiding (see Leipold)
Romance of the Redwoods (ac: Parrish, Cutner; + stock) COL
I'm from Missouri (see Leipold)
Outside These Walls COL
Missing Daughters (+ stock) COL
Mandrake the Magician (see Cutner)
The Arizona Kid (+ stock) REP
Days of Jesse James (see Lava)

MORGAN, TOMMY

1961

Dondi AA
Erotica RUSS MEYER

MORGENSTERN, SAM

1940

Americaner Schadchen (Yiddish language) EDGAR G. ULMER

MORLEY, GLEN

1954

Quality in Photographic Lenses (doc. short) EASTMAN KODAK

MOROSS, JEROME

1947

A Song Is Born (see Friedhofer)

1948

Close-Up EL

1951

When I Grow Up UA

1952

The Captive City UA

1956

Seven Wonders of the World (see D. Raksin)
The Sharkfighters UA

1958

The Proud Rebel (o: Mayers) FORMOSA
The Big Country (o: Mayers, Grau, Salinger, Courage) UA

1959

The Jayhawkers! (o: Van Cleave) PAR
The Mountain Road (o: A. Morton) COL

1960

The Adventures of Huckleberry Finn (o: R. Franklyn) MGM

1962

Five Finger Exercise (o: R. Franklyn) COL

1963

The Cardinal COL

1965

Forget Me Not (short) GR CO.
The War Lord (with Salter) UNIV

1968

Rachel, Rachel WB

1969

The Valley of Gwangi WB
Hail, Hero! NG

[Also worked as an orchestrator.]

MORRIS, JOHN

1967

The Producers SIDNEY GLAZIER

1970

The Gamblers SIDNEY GLAZIER
The Twelve Chairs SIDNEY GLAZIER

MORTON, ARTHUR

1935

Night Life of the Gods UNIV
Princess O'Hara (o: Vaughan) UNIV

1937

Pick a Star (with Hatley) HAL ROACH
Riding on Air (with Skiles) RKO
Fit for a King RKO

1939

The Day the Bookies Wept RKO

1940

Turnabout HAL ROACH

1941

Romance of the Rio Grande (see Mockridge)

1944

Greenwich Village (see Buttolph)
Strange Affair (see Skiles)

1945
She Gets Her Man (see F. Skinner)
1946
The Walls Came Tumbling Down (see Skiles)
The Jolson Story (see Skiles)
1947
Framed (see Skiles)
The Thirteenth Hour (+ stock) COL
Millie's Daughter COL
Down to Earth (see Roemheld)
It Had to Be You (see Roemheld)
The Swordsman (see Friedhofer)
1948
Loaded Pistols COL
1949
The Walking Hills COL
Lust for Gold (see Duning)
Johnny Allegro (see Duning)
1950
Father Is a Bachelor (o: Plumb) COL
The Nevadan (o: Fontaine) COL
Rogues of Sherwood Forest (see Castelnuovo-Tedesco)
On the Isle of Samoa (+ stock) COL
1951
Never Trust a Gambler (o: L. Morton) COL
The Harlem Globetrotters COL
The Magic Carpet (+ stock) COL
1952
Thief of Damascus (see Leipold)
Hiawatha (see Skiles)
1953
The Maze (see Skiles)
The Big Heat (see Vars)
Hot News (see Skiles)
Gun Fury (see M. Bakaleinikoff)
Charge of the Lancers (+ stock) COL
1954
Paris Playboys (see Skiles)
Arrow in the Dust (see Skiles)
Pushover (o: N. Scott) COL
1955
High Society (see Skiles)
Kismet (see A. Previn)
1956
He Laughed Last COL
Hot Shots (see Skiles)
1957
Calypso Heat Wave (+ stock) COL
1958
Fort Massacre (see Skiles)
1959
Juke Box Rhythm COL
Gidget COL
Warlock (see Harline)
Say One for Me (see Harline)
1960
Flaming Star (see Mockridge)
1961
Marines, Let's Go! (see Gertz)
Swingin' Along TCF
1964
The Great Space Adventure (see Skiles)
[Also a very prolific orchestrator.]

MOTTOLA, TONY
1953
Violated PANTHER
1965
Fashion Horizons (doc. short) ESQUIRE MAGAZINE

MOWSCHINE, MICHEL
1916
The Crisis SELIG POLYSCOPE

MUCZYNSKI, ROBERT
Documentary Shorts (HARRY ATWOOD)
1963
The Great Unfenced
1964
Yankee Painter: The Work of Winslow Homer
1965
American Realists
Cajititlán
1966
Charles Burchfield: Fifty Years of His Art
1967
The Clowns Never Laugh: The Work of Walt Kuhn
1969
Terra Sancta: A Film of Israel
Bellota

MULHOBERAC, LARRY
1968
My Name Is Paul (short) HUMBLE OIL

MULLENDORE, JOSEPH
1952
Models, Inc. (see Herschel Gilbert)
The Thief (see Herschel Gilbert)
1955
New York Confidential (o: Sheets) WB
1956
No Place to Hide (see Herschel Gilbert)
[Also worked as an orchestrator.]

MULLER, EDWARD
Shorts
1948
Light Reflections JAMES DAVIS
1950
Color and Light No. 1 JAMES DAVIS
1954
The Pardoner's Tale DYNAMIC FILMS

MULLIGAN, GERRY
1964
Help! My Snowman's Burning Down (short) CARSON DAVIDSON
1967
Luv (o: Holman) COL
1968
Fat People, Skinny People (short) LEE SAVAGE

MUMMA, GORDON
Shorts
1963
The Analog Computer and Its Application to Partial Differential Equations U. OF MICHIGAN
Greys DONALD SCAVARDA
Love in Truro MILTON COHEN
Five Short Films (see Manupelli)

MURI, JOHN
1967
The Lost World Revisited (doc. short) SPECTRA PICTURES
1968
The Gold Rush '68 (60-min. abridgement of Chaplin's 1925 film, with music and narration added) SPECTRA PICTURES

MURPHY, LYLE (SPUD)
1947
Cigarette Girl (see Gertz)
When a Girl's Beautiful (see Dubin)
Sweet Genevieve (see Gertz)
1948
Glamour Girl (see M. Bakaleinikoff)
[Also worked as an arranger.]

MURPHY, MELVIN E. (TURK)
1960
Nothing to Sneeze At (an. short) FILM GRAPHICS

MURRAY, LYN
1947
High Conquest (see Moraweck) MON
1951
The Prowler (o: F. Steiner) UA
The Big Night UA
1952
The Return of Gilbert and Sullivan (short) UA
Son of Paleface (o: Shuken, Cutner, Van Cleave, F. Steiner) PAR
1953
The Girls of Pleasure Island (o: Shuken, Cutner, F. Steiner) PAR
Here Come the Girls (o: Levene, Shuken, Cutner) PAR
1954
Casanova's Big Night (o: F. Steiner, Cutner, Shuken) PAR
1955
The Bridges at Toko-Ri PAR
To Catch a Thief PAR
1956
On the Threshold of Space (o: E. Powell, Mayers) TCF
D-Day, the Sixth of June (o: de Packh) TCF
1957
Magoo's Masquerade (cartoon) UPA
Energetically Yours (an. doc. short) STANDARD OIL
1960
Flaming Star (see Mockridge)
1961
All Hands on Deck (see Mockridge)
Snow White and the Three Stooges (o: A. Morton, E. Powell, F. Steiner) TCF
Escape from Zahrain (o: E. Powell) PAR
1962
Period of Adjustment (o: E. Powell) MGM
1963
Come Fly With Me (o: Wally Stott) MGM
Wives and Lovers PAR
1964
Signpost to Murder MGM
1965
Promise Her Anything (o: Keating) PAR
1967
Rosie UNIV
1969
Strategy of Terror UNIV
Angel in My Pocket UNIV
1970
The Cockeyed Cowboys of Calico County UNIV

MURTAUGH, JOHN
1965
Howard (an. short) LEONARD GLASSER

MYROW, FRED
1970
Leo the Last UA

N

NAFSHUN, IRWIN
1961
The Beast of Yucca Flats (with Romington) CROWN

NASE, RALPH J.
1930
The Call of the Circus C. C. BURR

NASH, GENE
1970
Dinah East (a: E. Freeman) EMERSON

NEFF, JERRY
1970
Miner's Ridge (doc. short) SIERRA CLUB

NELSON, OLIVER
1965
Encounter and Response (educational film) LUTHERAN CHURCH
1969
Death of a Gunfighter UNIV
1970
Skullduggery UNIV
Zig Zag MGM

NELSON, RON
Documentary Shorts
1954
Neighborhood Story SYRACUSE U.
1960
Before the Day SOCIAL SECURITY ADMIN.
1962
The Social Security Story SOCIAL SECURITY ADMIN.
1963
The Long Haul SOCIAL SECURITY ADMIN.

NERO, PETER
1963
Sunday in New York (o: Van Eps, Woodbury, Arnaud) MGM

NEWCOMER, W. W.
1914
The Volunteer Organist WILLIAM B. GRAY

NEWMAN, ALFRED
1930
Whoopee! (md; o: R. Heindorf) UA
1931
The Devil to Pay UA
Reaching for the Moon (md) UA
Kiki UA
Indiscreet (md) UA
Street Scene (o: R. Heindorf) UA
The Unholy Garden UA
Palmy Days (o: R. Heindorf) UA
The Age for Love UA
Corsair (o: R. Heindorf) UA
Tonight or Never UA
1932
Arrowsmith (o: R. Heindorf) UA
Cock of the Air UA
The Greeks Had a Word for Them (o: Heindorf) UA
Sky Devils UA
Night World UNIV
Movie Crazy HAROLD LLOYD
Mr. Robinson Crusoe UA
Rain UA
Flesh MGM
Cynara UA
1933
The Kid from Spain (o: R. Heindorf) UA
Hallelujah, I'm a Bum (o: R. Heindorf) UA
Secrets (o: Heindorf) UA
I Cover the Waterfront UA
The Masquerader UA
The Bowery UA
[First use of Newman's trademark fanfare for 20th Century Pictures and, after the merger with Fox in 1935, for 20th Century–Fox.]
Broadway Thru a Keyhole UA
Blood Money UA
Advice to the Lovelorn UA
Roman Scandals (o: R. Heindorf) UA

1934
Gallant Lady UA
Moulin Rouge (md) UA
Looking for Trouble UA
Nana UA
The House of Rothschild UA
Born to Be Bad UA
The Affairs of Cellini UA
The Last Gentleman UA
Bulldog Drummond Strikes Back (o: R. Heindorf) UA
The Cat's-Paw HAROLD LLOYD
Our Daily Bread (o: E. Powell) UA
Kid Millions (o: E. Powell) UA
Transatlantic Merry-Go-Round UA
We Live Again (o: E. Powell) UA
The Count of Monte Cristo UA

1935
The Mighty Barnum UA
Clive of India (o: E. Powell) UA
Folies Bergere UA
The Wedding Night (o: E. Powell) UA
Les Misérables UA
Cardinal Richelieu UA
The Call of the Wild (ac: Friedhofer; o: E. Powell) UA
The Dark Angel (o: E. Powell) UA
Red Salute UA
Barbary Coast (o: E. Powell) UA
The Melody Lingers On UA
Splendor (o: E. Powell) UA

1936
Strike Me Pink (o: E. Powell) UA
These Three (o: E. Powell, D. Raksin) UA
One Rainy Afternoon (o: E. Powell, Friedhofer) UA
Dancing Pirate RKO
Ramona (o: E. Powell, Friedhofer) TCF
Dodsworth (o: E. Powell) UA
The Gay Desperado UA
Come and Get It (o: E. Powell) UA

1937
Beloved Enemy (ac: Friedhofer; o: E. Powell, Friedhofer, Mockridge) UA
You Only Live Once (ac: Friedhofer) UA
When You're in Love (o: E. Powell) COL
History Is Made at Night UA
Woman Chases Man (o: E. Powell) UA
Slave Ship (o: E. Powell) TCF
Wee Willie Winkie (ac: Mockridge; o: E. Powell) TCF
Stella Dallas (ac: D. Raksin; o: E. Powell) UA
Dead End (o: E. Powell) UA
The Prisoner of Zenda (ac: Friedhofer; o: E. Powell, Friedhofer) UA
52nd Street (ac: D. Raksin) UA

1938
The Hurricane (o: E. Powell, Friedhofer) UA
The Goldwyn Follies (o: E. Powell, D. Raksin, Friedhofer) UA
The Cowboy and the Lady (o: E. Powell, Friedhofer, Salinger) UA
Trade Winds UA

1939
Gunga Din (o: R. Bennett, E. Powell, Salinger) RKO
Wuthering Heights (o: E. Powell) GOLDWYN
Young Mr. Lincoln (o: E. Powell) TCF
They Shall Have Music GOLDWYN
The Star Maker PAR
Beau Geste (o: E. Powell) PAR
The Rains Came (o: E. Powell) TCF
The Real Glory (o: E. Powell) GOLDWYN
Drums Along the Mohawk (o: E. Powell, Salinger) TCF
The Hunchback of Notre Dame (o: E. Powell, Salinger, R. Bennett, Raab) RKO

1940
The Blue Bird (ac: D. Raksin, Buttolph; o: Salinger, E. Powell) TCF*
The Grapes of Wrath (o: E. Powell) TCF
Vigil in the Night (o: E. Powell) RKO
Little Old New York (o: E. Powell, H. Spencer, Salinger) TCF
Star Dust (see Buttolph)
Lillian Russell (see Mockridge)
Girl in 313 (see Buttolph)
Earthbound (o: E. Powell, Salinger) TCF
Maryland (see Buttolph)
Foreign Correspondent (ac: Buttolph, G. Rose; o: E. Powell, Salinger) UA
Public Deb No. 1 (see Buttolph)
Brigham Young (with Bennett, Buttolph, Mockridge; o: Salinger, E. Powell, H. Spencer) TCF
The Westerner (see Tiomkin)
They Knew What They Wanted RKO
The Mark of Zorro (with Friedhofer, Buttolph, Mockridge; o: E. Powell, Salinger, W. Scharf) TCF
Tin Pan Alley (with Mockridge)

*From here through 1959 Newman was also the studio's General Music Director.

1941
Hudson's Bay (with Buttolph, Mockridge; o: Salinger, E. Powell, W. Scharf, H. Spencer) TCF
Tobacco Road (see Buttolph)
That Night in Rio (ac: Buttolph; o: H. Spencer, W. Scharf) TCF
The Great American Broadcast (see Mockridge)
Blood and Sand (with Buttolph; o: E. Powell; guitar music: Gomez) TCF
Moon Over Miami (see Mockridge)
Wild Geese Calling (see Buttolph)
Belle Starr (see Buttolph)
A Yank in the R.A.F. (ac: Mockridge; o: E. Powell, H. Spencer) TCF
Week-End in Havana (with Mockridge, C. Henderson, Buttolph) TCF
Rise and Shine (see Buttolph)
Ball of Fire (ac: Buttolph) GOLDWYN
Son of Fury (with Buttolph; ac: D. Raksin, Mockridge, Friedhofer; o: Salinger, E. Powell, Parrish, H. Spencer, Arnaud) TCF
How Green Was My Valley (o: E. Powell, Friedhofer) TCF

1942
Roxie Hart (ac: Mockridge; o: G. Rose) TCF
Secret Agent of Japan (see Harline)
To the Shores of Tripoli (o: Arnaud, H. Spencer, G. Rose) TCF
This Above All (ac: Buttolph; o: E. Powell, Salinger) TCF
Footlight Serenade (see C. Henderson)
The Pied Piper (ac: Mockridge, Friedhofer; o: E. Powell) TCF
The Loves of Edgar Allan Poe (see Buttolph)
Orchestra Wives (see Harline)
Iceland (see Harline)
Girl Trouble (with Harline, Buttolph; ac: Mockridge; o: E. Powell, Plumb, de Packh, Friedhofer) TCF
Springtime in the Rockies (see C. Henderson)
The Black Swan (with Buttolph; ac: Friedhofer; o: E. Powell, H. Spencer, Salinger, Parrish, de Packh) TCF
Immortal Sergeant (see Buttolph)
Life Begins at Eight-Thirty (ac: Harline, Mockridge; o: E. Powell, Salinger, de Packh) TCF

1943
The Moon Is Down (ac: Buttolph; o: E. Powell) TCF
Hello, Frisco, Hello (see Buttolph)
My Friend Flicka (with Buttolph; ac: Mockridge, Friedhofer; o: E. Powell, D. Raksin, H. Spencer, A. Morton, Parrish) TCF
Crash Dive (see Buttolph)
Coney Island (see Mockridge)
Heaven Can Wait (with Mockridge; ac: Friedhofer; o: E. Powell) TCF
Claudia (o: E. Powell) TCF
Happy Land (see Mockridge)
The Gang's All Here (see A. Lange)
The Song of Bernadette (o: E. Powell) TCF

1944
The Sullivans (see Mockridge)
The Purple Heart (o: E. Powell) TCF
Wilson (o: E. Powell) TCF
Irish Eyes Are Smiling (see Mockridge)
Sunday Dinner for a Soldier (with Buttolph; ac: Mockridge; o: E. Powell, de Packh, A. Morton, Salinger, D. Raksin) TCF
The Keys of the Kingdom (o: E. Powell) TCF

1945
Thunderhead (see Mockridge)
A Royal Scandal (ac: Mockridge; o: E. Powell) TCF
A Caribbean Mystery (see Buttolph)
A Bell for Adano (o: E. Powell) TCF
State Fair (see E. Powell)
The House on 92nd Street (see Buttolph)
The Dolly Sisters (see Buttolph)

1946
Leave Her to Heaven (o: E. Powell) TCF
Sentimental Journey (see Mockridge)
Dragonwyck (o: E. Powell) TCF
Centennial Summer (ac: Mockridge, Buttolph, H. Spencer, Plumb; o: E. Powell, de Packh, H. Spencer, A. Morton) TCF
Margie (ac: Buttolph, Mockridge; o: H. Spencer) TCF
The Razor's Edge (o: E. Powell) TCF

1947
I Wonder Who's Kissing Her Now (see Buttolph)
Gentleman's Agreement (o: E. Powell) TCF
Captain from Castile (o: E. Powell) TCF

1948
Call Northside 777 (o: E. Powell) TCF
Sitting Pretty (o: E. Powell; ac and o: Hagen) TCF

Give My Regards to Broadway (see Mockridge)
Deep Waters (see Mockridge)
The Walls of Jericho (o: E. Powell) TCF
That Lady in Ermine (with Mockridge; o: E. Powell, de Packh) TCF
Cry of the City (o: E. Powell, Hagen) TCF
Apartment for Peggy (see D. Raksin)
Road House (o: E. Powell) TCF
The Snake Pit (o: E. Powell) TCF
Yellow Sky (o: E. Powell) TCF

1949
Chicken Every Sunday (o: E. Powell) TCF
A Letter to Three Wives (o: E. Powell) TCF
Down to the Sea in Ships (o: E. Powell) TCF
Mother Is a Freshman (ac: Mockridge; o: E. Powell) TCF
Mr. Belvedere Goes to College (o: E. Powell, H. Spencer) TCF
You're My Everything (o: E. Powell) TCF
Pinky (o: E. Powell) TCF
Prince of Foxes (o: E. Powell) TCF
Twelve O'Clock High (o: E. Powell) TCF

1950
When Willie Comes Marching Home (o: E. Powell) TCF
Cheaper by the Dozen (see Mockridge)
The Big Lift (o: E. Powell) TCF
The Gunfighter (o: E. Powell) TCF
Panic in the Streets (o: H. Spencer) TCF
Stella (see Mockridge)
No Way Out (o: E. Powell) TCF
All About Eve (o: E. Powell) TCF
For Heaven's Sake (ac: Mockridge; o: E. Powell) TCF

1951
Call Me Mister (see Harline)
I Can Get It for You Wholesale (see S. Kaplan)
Fourteen Hours (o: E. Powell) TCF
Half Angel (see Mockridge)
On the Riviera (see Hagen)
Take Care of My Little Girl (o: E. Powell, Mayers) TCF
David and Bathsheba (o: E. Powell) TCF
The Guest (short; development: S. Kaplan; o: E. Powell) TCF
Elopement (see Mockridge)

1952
Golden Girl (with Mockridge; o: E. Powell, Mayers) TCF
The Model and the Marriage Broker (see Mockridge)
With a Song in My Heart (o: E. Powell) TCF
Wait Till the Sun Shines, Nellie (o: E. Powell) TCF
What Price Glory (o: E. Powell) TCF
O. Henry's Full House (o: E. Powell) TCF
Stars and Stripes Forever (o: E. Powell, Mayers) TCF

1953
Tonight We Sing (o: E. Powell) TCF
Call Me Madam (o: E. Powell) TCF
The President's Lady (o: E. Powell, Mayers, H. Spencer) TCF
The Robe (o: E. Powell) TCF
How to Marry a Millionaire (see Mockridge)

1954
Land of Legend (short; o: E. Powell; + stock) TCF
Hell and High Water (o: E. Powell) TCF
The Egyptian (with Herrmann) TCF
Woman's World (see Mockridge)
The CinemaScope Parade (short) TCF
There's No Business Like Show Business (with H. Spencer, H. Schaefer, Hagen, Mayers, L. Newman) TCF

1955
A Man Called Peter (o: E. Powell) TCF
Daddy Long Legs (see Mockridge)
The Seven Year Itch (ac: Mockridge; o: E. Powell) TCF
How to Be Very, Very Popular (see Mockridge)
Love Is a Many-Splendored Thing (ac: Friedhofer, Harline; o: E. Powell) TCF

1956
Carousel (o: E. Powell) TCF
The King and I (o: E. Powell) TCF
Bus Stop (with Mockridge; o: Mayers, de Packh, E. Powell) TCF
The Last Wagon (see L. Newman)
Anastasia (o: E. Powell) TCF

1957
April Love (with Mockridge; o: E. Powell) TCF

1958
The Gift of Love (with Mockridge; ac: Friedhofer, Harline; o: E. Powell, Hagen) TCF
South Pacific (o: E. Powell, King, Mayers) TCF
The Bravados (with Friedhofer) TCF
A Certain Smile TCF
In Love and War (see Friedhofer)

1959

The Diary of Anne Frank (o: E. Powell, Hagen) TCF

Woman Obsessed (see Friedhofer)

The Best of Everything (o: H. Spencer, Hagen) TCF

1961

The Pleasure of His Company (o: H. Spencer, E. Powell, Mayers) PAR

Flower Drum Song UNIV

The Counterfeit Traitor (o: Shuken, Hayes) PAR

1962

State Fair (o: Levene, Mayers) TCF

How the West Was Won (o: Shuken, Hayes) MGM

1965

The Greatest Story Ever Told (ac: Friedhofer, F. Steiner; o: Shuken, Hayes) UA

Nevada Smith (o: Shuken, Hayes) PAR

1967

Camelot (o: Shuken, Hayes, King, Sendrey) WB

Firecreek WB

1970

Airport (ac: Friedhofer, F. Steiner; o: Shuken, Hayes, Levene) UNIV

Documentaries

1931

Around the World in Eighty Minutes with Douglas Fairbanks UA

1942

The Battle of Midway (short; ac: Friedhofer) U.S. NAVY

Prelude to War (see Harline)

1943

At the Front in North Africa (with Mockridge, Buttolph) U.S. ARMY

December 7th U.S. NAVY

1944

The Fighting Lady (see Buttolph)

Trailer

1950

Whirlpool TCF

NEWMAN, LIONEL

[All for 20th Century–Fox unless otherwise stated.]

1942

Immortal Sergeant (see Buttolph)

He Hired the Boss (see Buttolph)

1953

Gentlemen Prefer Blondes (see H. Schaefer)

The Kid from Left Field (ac: Mockridge; o: E. Powell)

1954

Siege at Red River (see Mockridge)

Princess of the Nile (+ stock)

Calypso Cruise (short; o: Mayers; + stock)

The Gambler from Natchez (o: Arnaud, Dunlap; + stock)

There's No Business Like Show Business (see A. Newman)

1955

The Girl in the Red Velvet Swing (see Harline)

1956

The Killer Is Loose UA

The Proud Ones (o: Arnaud, de Packh, L. Martin)

A Kiss Before Dying (o: May, Riddle) UA

The Last Wagon (ac: A. Newman, Mockridge; o: E. Powell, Mayers)

Love Me Tender (ac: Hagen, Friedhofer, Harline; o: E. Powell, A. Morton)

The Girl Can't Help It (see Harline)

1957

The Way to the Gold (o: E. Powell, de Packh)

Bernardine (with L. Martin, May; o: Mayers)

1958

Sing Boy Sing (ac: Harline; o: E. Powell)

Mardi Gras (ac: Hagen, King, Mayers)

1959

Compulsion (o: Hagen, Mayers)

Say One for Me (see Harline)

1960

North to Alaska (see Mockridge)

1963

Move Over, Darling (o: A. Morton, Barker)

1965

The Pleasure Seekers (with Courage; o: H. Spencer, Barker, May)

Do Not Disturb (with Courage; o: Garson, Barker)

1967

Doctor Dolittle (with Courage)

1968

The Boston Strangler (partial)

1969

Hello, Dolly! (see Hayton)

NEWMAN, THEODORE

1962

The Orozco Murals: Quetzalcoatl (doc. short) ROBERT CANTON

NICHOLS, TED
1966
The Man Called Flintstone (see Paich)

NIKOLAIS, ALWIN
1963
Totem—The World of Nikolais (short) ED EMSHWILLER
1966
Space Rendezvous (doc. short) U.S. AIR FORCE
1967
Fusion (short) ED EMSHWILLER

NILSSON, HARRY
1968
Skidoo (a: Tipton) PAR

NITZSCHE, JACK
1965
Village of the Giants EMB
1970
Performance WB

NORLIN, LLOYD
1953
Once Upon the Wabash (doc. short) WABASH RAILROAD
1954
The Germ (doc. short) U.S. STEEL
1956
Knowing's Not Enough (doc. short) U.S. STEEL
Heaven to Betsy DEERE & CO.
1958
A Product of the Imagination (doc. short) ALCOA
1960
The New World of Stainless Steel (doc. short) REPUBLIC STEEL
The Blacksmith's Gift (doc. short) DEERE & CO.
[Many others, titles undetermined.]

NORMAN, LEE
1939
Keep Punching M. C. PICTURES

NORMAN, LON E.
1964
Zombies DEL TENNEY PRODS.
1966
Sting of Death (see Al Jacobs)

NORMAN, RALPH
1946
Aquaqueens (doc. short) RKO PATHÉ

NORTH, ALEX
1951
The 13th Letter (o: de Packh) TCF
A Streetcar Named Desire (o: de Packh) WB
Death of a Salesman (o: de Packh) COL
1952
Viva Zapata! (o: de Packh) TCF
Les Misérables (o: E. Powell) TCF
Pony Soldier (o: E. Powell) TCF
1953
The Member of the Wedding (o: de Packh) COL
1954
Go, Man, Go! UA
Désirée (o: E. Powell) TCF
1955
The Racers (o: E. Powell, Mayers) TCF
Unchained (o: de Packh) WB
Man with the Gun (o: H. Kay) UA
The Rose Tattoo (o: de Packh) PAR
1956
I'll Cry Tomorrow (o: de Packh) MGM
The Bad Seed (o: de Packh) WB
The Rainmaker (o: de Packh) PAR
Four Girls in Town (with Gertz, H. Stein) UNIV
The King and Four Queens (o: H. Kay) UA
1957
The Bachelor Party UA
1958
The Long, Hot Summer (o: de Packh) TCF
Stage Struck RKO
Hot Spell (o: Van Cleave) PAR
1959
The Sound and the Fury (o: E. Powell) TCF
The Wonderful Country (o: de Packh) UA
1960
Spartacus (o: de Packh, Matlovsky, E. Powell, Tamkin) UNIV
1961
The Misfits UA
Sanctuary (o: E. Powell) TCF
The Children's Hour UA
1962
All Fall Down (o: E. Powell, Tamkin, Van Cleave) MGM
1963
Cleopatra (o: Brant, H. Spencer, Tamkin) TCF

1964
The Outrage MGM
1965
Cheyenne Autumn (o: Grau, Brant) WB
The Agony and the Ecstasy (o: Courage) TCF
1966
Who's Afraid of Virginia Woolf? (o: Brant) WB
1968
2001: A Space Odyssey (not used) MGM
The Devil's Brigade (o: Brant) UA
The Shoes of the Fisherman (o: Tamkin) MGM
1969
Hard Contract TCF
A Dream of Kings NG
Documentary Features
1953
The American Road FORD FOUNDATION
Decision for Chemistry MONSANTO CHEMICAL
1958
South Seas Adventure (o: H. Kay) CINERAMA
Documentary Shorts
1937
Heart of Spain FRONTIER FILMS
China Strikes Back FRONTIER FILMS
People of the Cumberland FRONTIER FILMS
1944
A Better Tomorrow OWI
1945
Library of Congress OWI
Venezuela USDA
1946
City Pastorale U.S. STATE DEPT.
Recreation USDA
Rural Nurse WILLARD PICTURES
1949
Mount Vernon WILLARD VAN DYKE
1950
Coney Island, U.S.A. VALENTINE SHERRY

NOWELL, WEDGEWOOD
1915
Matrimony (see Nurnberger)
Aloha Oe TRIANGLE
The Winged Idol (see Nurnberger)
The Golden Claw (see Nurnberger)
Between Men (see Nurnberger)
1916
The Conqueror (see Schertzinger)
D'Artagnan (see Nurnberger)

NURNBERGER, JOSEPH E.
1915
The Birth of a Nation (see Breil)
The Iron Strain TRIANGLE
The Coward TRIANGLE
The Lamb (see Breil)
Matrimony (with Nowell) TRIANGLE
The Disciple TRIANGLE
The Winged Idol (with Schertzinger, Nowell) TRIANGLE
The Golden Claw (with Schertzinger, Nowell) TRIANGLE
The Edge of the Abyss (see Schertzinger)
Between Men (with Schertzinger, Nowell) TRIANGLE
1916
D'Artagnan (with Schertzinger, Nowell) TRIANGLE
1918
Hearts of the World (Los Angeles opening) GRIFFITH

NUSSBAUM, JOSEPH
1937
The Devil Is Driving! (with Carbonara, Parrish; + stock) COL
Racketeers in Exile (with Carbonara) COL
1938
City Streets (see Cutner)
The Higgins Family (see Lava)
Frontier Scout GN
Come On, Rangers (see Lava)
Western Jamboree (see Lava)
Little Orphan Annie (see Forbes)
Hawk of the Wilderness (see Lava)
1939
The Lone Wolf Spy Hunt (+ stock) COL
Blue Montana Skies (see Lava)
Meet Doctor Christian RKO
Zorro's Fighting Legion (see Lava)
1947
Song of My Heart (based on music of Tchaikovsky) AA
1951
The Second Woman (based on music of Tchaikovsky) UA
Shorts (MGM, unless otherwise noted)
1946
The Mission Trail
1947
Cradle of a Nation
1948
Cape Breton Island

Chicago, the Beautiful
Night Life in Chicago
1949
Calling on Michigan
Glimpses of Old England
In Old Amsterdam
Playlands of Michigan
Quebec in Summertime
1950
Colorful Holland
Land of Tradition
Life on the Thames
Pastoral Panoramas
Roaming Through Michigan
To the Coast of Devon
Touring Northern England
1951
Land of the Zuider Zee
Springtime in the Netherlands
1952
Ancient India
Beautiful Brazil
Calling on Cape Town
Glimpses of Argentina (+ stock)
Jasper National Park
Land of the Taj Mahal
Life in the Andes
Pretoria to Durban
Seeing Ceylon
1953
In the Land of Diamonds
In the Valley of the Rhine
1958
Old Testament Series: Moses, Leader of God's People CONCORDIA FILMS

Shorts, with Zeisl (MGM, unless otherwise noted)
1941
Colorful North Carolina
1942
Exotic Mexico
Glacier Park and Waterton Lakes
Glimpses of Ontario
Historic Maryland
Land of Orizaba
Land of the Quintuplets
Minnesota, Land of Plenty
Modern Mexico City
Motoring in Mexico
Picturesque Massachusetts
Picturesque Patzcuaro
West Point on the Hudson
1943
Mighty Niagara
People of Russia
Romantic Nevada
Scenic Oregon
Through the Colorado Rockies
Wood Goes to War
1944
Along the Cactus Trail
Colorful Colorado
A Day in Death Valley
Grand Canyon, Pride of Creation
Mackinac Island
On the Road to Monterrey
Over the Andes
Roaming Through Arizona
Throwing the Bull WB
Visiting St. Louis
Wandering Here and There
1945
Modern Guatemala City
Merida and Campeche
Seeing El Salvador
Shrines of Yucatan
Where Time Stands Still
1946
Glimpses of California
Glimpses of Guatemala
Land of the Mayas
Visiting Vera Cruz
1947
Around the World in California
Calling on Costa Rica
Glimpses of New Scotland
On the Shores of Nova Scotia
1949
Ontario—Land of Lakes

[Also a prolific orchestrator.]

O

OAKLAND, BEN
1937
Criminals of the Air COL
The Awful Truth (o: Parrish) COL
1940
Glamour for Sale COL
1962
When the Girls Take Over PARADE

O'DAY, ALAN
1962
Wild Guitar FAIRWAY INT'L.

OHMAN, PHIL
1940
Captain Caution UA
1946
Dick Tracy vs. Cueball (see Sawtell)
1948
Million Dollar Weekend (o: H. Jackson) EL

O'HORGAN, TOM
1964
Babo 73 ROBERT DOWNEY
1965
The Sweet Smell of Sex ROBERT DOWNEY
1967
Chafed Elbows ROBERT DOWNEY
1969
Futz CU
1970
Alex in Wonderland MGM

OLIVEROS, PAULINE
1958
4H Club (doc. short) ?
1963
Art in Woodcut (doc. short) PROCTER JONES
1965
Covenant (short) RONALD CHASE
1969
Events (short) LYNN LONIDIER

OLSHANETSKY, ALEXANDER
1937
The Cantor's Son (Yiddish language) ERON PICTURES
1939
My Son (Yiddish language) JEWISH TALKING PICTURES
1940
Overture to Glory (Yiddish language) G. & L.
1941
Mazel Tov, Jews (see Secunda)
1949
Three Daughters CINEMA SERVICE
1950
Catskill Honeymoon MARTIN COHEN

ORLANDO, NICHOLAS
1919
The Spirit of Lafayette JAMES VINCENT

OROOP, JOSEPH
1948
Music from the Mountains (short; see Curtin)

ORTIZ, MANUEL
1963
Scum of the Earth! HERSCHELL G. LEWIS

OSBORN, BRUCE
1966
From Scratch (abstract short) BRUCE OSBORN

OTIS, CLYDE
1964
Olga's Girls AMERICAN FILM

OVERTON, HALL
1959
The New Look Is the Anxious Look (short) E. F. MEDARD

P

PADDOCK, JOHN
1952
Quetzalcoatl (doc. short) USC

PAGE, GENE
1970
Brewster McCloud MGM

PAICH, MARTY
1964
Hey There, It's Yogi Bear (an.) COL
1966
The Man Called Flintstone (an.; with Ted Nichols) COL
The Swinger (o: Comstock) PAR

PALANGE, LOUIS S.
1955
Dark Venture JOHN CALVERT PRODS.
1957
The Delinquents (with Garf) UA
Documentary Shorts (U.S. NAVY)
1945
Guam
Midnight
The 957th Day
Radar
Rockets Bursting in Air
Target Dead Ahead
Voice of Truth
1946
D-Day
Iwo Jima
My Japan

PALMER, CARLETON
1968
Speed Lovers JEMCO

PALMER, SOLITA
Documentary Shorts
1940
New Hampshire COL
1948
This Way to Nursing EMERSON YORKE
1954
This Is Baseball (m&e) EMERSON YORKE
1965
Our Heritage EMERSON YORKE

PALMIERI, CHARLIE
1965
Heroina (Spanish language) ROYAL FILMS

PARIS, NORMAN
1962
History's Brew (doc. short) GENERAL FOODS
The Old Man and the Flower (see Pintoff)
David and Lisa (see M. Lawrence)

PARISI, FRANK D.
1951
Before the Sacrifice: Sacristy and Sanctuary (doc. short) WILLIAM A. WINCHESTER
1952
Call the Priest (doc. short) WILLIAM A. WINCHESTER

PARKER, JOHN
1967
The Further Perils of Laurel and Hardy (compilation film; ac: Kogen) TCF
1970
Darker Than Amber NG

PARKS, GORDON
1969
The Learning Tree (with McIntosh) WB

PARRISH, GEORGE
1936
Four Days' Wonder (see C. Previn)
1937
The League of Frightened Men (mt) COL
The Devil Is Driving! (see Nussbaum)
It's All Yours (+ stock) COL
A Damsel in Distress (see R. Bennett)
Start Cheering (+ stock) COL
1938
The Big Broadcast of 1938 (see Leipold)
Bluebeard's Eighth Wife (see Hollander)
There's Always a Woman (m&e; + stock) COL
I Am the Law COL
The Lady Objects (see Cutner)
1939
My Son Is a Criminal (o: Hand) COL
First Offenders COL

Romance of the Redwoods (see F. Morgan)
Blind Alley (+ stock) COL
Exile Express GN
Coast Guard COL
Konga, the Wild Stallion (+ stock) COL

1940
Men Without Souls (see Cutner)
The Quarterback (see Leipold)
Nobody's Children (o: Nussbaum) COL

1941
I Was a Prisoner on Devil's Island (+ stock) COL

1944
Lucky Cowboy (short; see Shuken)
Brazil (see W. Scharf)

1946
Blue Skies (see Dolan)

[Also a prolific orchestrator.]

PARTCH, HARRY

1958
Windsong (short) MADELINE TOURTELOT

1961
Rotate the Body in All Its Planes MADELINE TOURTELOT

PASTERNACKI, STEPHAN

1930
The Sea God (see Hajos)
Her Wedding Night (see Hand)

1932
Strangers in Love (see R. Kopp)
Dancers in the Dark (with Leipold) PAR
The World and the Flesh (see Hand)
Thunder Below (see Krumgold)

1935
Goin' to Town (see Satterfield)

1939
Silver on the Sage (see Leipold)

PAUL, MYRON

1967
I Crave Your Body DOVE

PAUL, STEPHEN

1964
The Starfighters PARADE

PEAKE, DON

1969
Chastity (see Bono)

PEASLEE, RICHARD

1965
Where Time Is a River (doc. short) RADRICK PRODS.

PELLEGRINI, AL

1960
Heroes Die Young AA

1961
The Choppers FAIRWAY-INT'L.

PERITO, NICK

1968
Don't Just Stand There! UNIV

PERKINS, FRANK

1944
Make Your Own Bed (see Roemheld)
Janie (see Roemheld)

1947
Trail to San Antone (see M. Glickman)
Apache Rose (see Maxwell)

1955
Glory RKO

1961
The Couch (o: Brandt) WB

1963
Gypsy (o: Brandt) WB
Mary Mary (o: Brandt) WB
Palm Springs Weekend (o: Brandt) WB

1964
The Incredible Mr. Limpet (o: Brandt) WB
Ready for the People WB

1967
Quacker Tracker (cartoon) WB

PERKINSON, COLERIDGE-TAYLOR

1970
King: A Filmed Record . . . Montgomery to Memphis (doc.) CU
The McMasters CHEVRON

PERL, LOTHAR

1943
This Land Is Mine (o: Raab, Cutner) RKO

1947
The Unfinished Dance (see Stothart)

1948
Three Daring Daughters (see Stothart)
Big City (ac: Stoll, Sendrey) MGM

PERRY, SAM A.

1929
The Last Performance UNIV

Tarzan the Tiger (serial) UNIV
The Long, Long Trail (mt) UNIV
Shanghai Lady UNIV
The Phantom of the Opera (see Breil, 1925)
Hell's Heroes UNIV
Hell's Heroes (foreign version; with Roemheld; + stock) UNIV

1930
Night Ride UNIV
Undertow UNIV
The Jade Box (serial) UNIV
Lightning Express (serial) UNIV
All Quiet on the Western Front (see Roemheld)
Young Desire UNIV
Song of the Caballero UNIV
Terry of the Times (serial) UNIV
Outside the Law (see Roemheld)
The Indians Are Coming (serial) UNIV
East Is West (see Roemheld)
Spell of the Circus (serial) UNIV
See America Thirst (see Roemheld)

1932
Alias the Doctor (see Kaun)
Beauty and the Boss (see Harling)

Trailers (WB)

1932
Taxi!
Winner Take All

1933
Silver Dollar

PERSICHETTI, VINCENT

1969
Beyond Niagara (short) RALPH STEINER

PESCE, ALBERT

1919
The Greatest Question GRIFFITH

1920
The Love Flower GRIFFITH

1922
One Exciting Night GRIFFITH

PETERS, WILLIAM FREDERICK

1920
Way Down East (see Silvers)

1921
Orphans of the Storm (see Gottschalk)

1922
When Knighthood Was in Flower COSMOPOLITAN

1923
The Enemies of Women COSMOPOLITAN
Little Old New York COSMOPOLITAN

1924
Under the Red Robe COSMOPOLITAN
Yolanda COSMOPOLITAN

1929
Hungarian Rhapsody (U.S. release of 1928 German film, *Ungarische Rhapsodie*) PAR
The Four Feathers PAR

PETERSON, JAMES

1961
Fiend of Dope Island ESSANJAY

PHILLIPS, BURRILL

1938
Highlights and Shadows (see H. Hanson)

1964
Nine from Little Rock ?

PHILLIPS, ROBERT

1969
Down and Dirty JEMCO

PHILLIPS, STU

1961
Mad Dog Coll COL
Katie's Lot (short) THALIA

1963
The Man from the Diners' Club (o: A. Morton) COL

1964
Ride the Wild Surf COL

1966
Dead Heat on a Merry-Go-Round COL

1967
Hell's Angels on Wheels FANFARE

1968
The Name of the Game Is Kill! FANFARE
Angels from Hell FANFARE

1969
2000 Years Later WB
Run, Angel, Run! FANFARE
Follow Me (doc.) CR
The Gay Deceivers FANFARE
The Curious Female FANFARE

1970
The Appointment MGM
The Losers FANFARE
Beyond the Valley of the Dolls TCF
The Red, White and Black HIRSCHMAN-NORTHERN

PIERCE, ALEX
1960
Code of Silence STERLING

PIERCE, ARTHUR C.
1962
Invasion of the Animal People (ac for U.S. release of 1958 Swedish film) A.D.P. PRODS.

PIERCE, VICTOR
1965
The Farmer's Other Daughter UNITED PRODUCERS

PILHOFER, HERB
1960
Mahnomen, Harvest of the North (doc. short) FILM RESEARCH CO.

PINKHAM, DANIEL
1960
Land of White Alice (doc. short) WILLARD VAN DYKE
1968
Structures (doc. short) ?

PINSKY, DANIEL
1967
The Possibilities of Agam (doc. short) WARREN FORMA

PINSKY, MILTON
1954
The Lion and the Mouse (cartoon) REYNERTSON & DUVALL

PINTOFF, ERNEST
1957
Flebus (cartoon) TCF
1959
The Violinist (cartoon; a: G. Steiner) COL
1961
The Shoes (short) UNION
1962
The Old Man and the Flower (cartoon; a: Paris) UNION
1965
Sunflower (cartoon; with B. Green) JOSHUA WHITE
Harvey Middleman, Fireman (a: B. Green) COL

PISERCHIO, GINO
1969
Once Upon a Time (doc. short) UNITED AIR LINES

PITTON, ROBERT
1949
Forms in Space: The Art of Sculpture (doc. short) USC

PITTS, CLAY
1968
Inga (U.S. release of Swedish film) CINEMATION
1969
Fanny Hill (U.S. release of 1968 Swedish film) CINEMATION
1970
Female Animal (U.S. release of Spanish film) CINEMATION
I Drink Your Blood CINEMATION

PLAGENS, RAY
1961
The Naked Witch ALEXANDER ENTERPRISES

PLEIS, JACK
1964
Diary of a Bachelor AIP

PLUMB, EDWARD
1940
Pinocchio (see Harline)
1942
Bambi (see Churchill)
Saludos Amigos (see Wolcott)
1943
Victory Through Air Power (with P. Smith, Wallace; o: S. Fine, A. Morton, Stark, Vaughan) WDP
1944
Ever Since Venus (+ stock) COL
The Three Caballeros (see Wolcott)
1945
The Phantom Speaks REP
Woman Who Came Back REP
1946
Murder in the Music Hall (see W. Scharf)
Valley of the Zombies REP
Centennial Summer (see A. Newman)
Monsieur Beaucaire (see Dolan)
1947
Variety Girl (see Lilley)

1949
The Great Lover (see Lilley)
1951
Quebec (see Van Cleave)
Angels in the Outfield (see Amfitheatrof)
Cartoons
1938
Mother Goose Goes Hollywood WDP
1945
Donald's Crime WDP
1952
The Missing Mouse MGM
1953
The New Neighbor WDP
Football (Now and Then) WDP
How to Sleep WDP
Donald's Diary WDP
Animated Shorts (WDP)
1942
The Grain that Built a Hemisphere CIAA
South of the Border with Disney CIAA
1943
Water—Friend or Enemy CIAA
1944
Quick Facts on Fear U.S. ARMY
1945
Something You Didn't Eat USDA
[Also worked as an orchestrator.]

POCKRISS, LEE
1965
Holiday with Light (doc. short) WILDING
1968
The Subject Was Roses MGM

PODDANY, EUGENE F.
Cartoons (WB)
1950
The Fair-Haired Hare (see Stalling)
French Rarebit
Leghorn Swoggled
Lovelorn Leghorn
1951
Room and Bird
The Wearing of the Grin
Cartoons (UNIV)
1956
The Ostrich Egg and I
Plumber of Seville
1957
The Goofy Gardener
1959
Billion Dollar Boner
Kiddie League
Mouse Trapped
1960
Fish Hooked
Freeloading Feline
Heap Big Hepcat
Southern Fried Hospitality
1961
Doc's Last Stand
Eggnapper
Gabby's Diner
Poop Deck Pirate
Rough and Tumbleweed
1962
Mackerel Moocher
Phoney Express
Rock-a-Bye Gator
Cartoons (MGM)
1963
Pent-House Mouse
1964
The Cat Above and the Mouse Below
The Cat's Me-Ouch
Is There a Doctor in the Mouse?
Much Ado About Mousing
Snowbody Loves Me
Tom-ic Energy
The Unshrinkable Jerry Mouse
1965
Ah, Sweet Mouse-Story of Life
Bad Day at Cat Rock
The Dot and the Line
The Haunted Mouse
I'm Just Wild About Jerry
Jerry-Go-Round
Of Feline Bondage
The Year of the Mouse
1966
The Brothers Carry-Mouse-Off
Guided Mouse-ille
Love Me, Love My Mouse
O-Solar-Meow
1967
Cat and Dupli-cat
Shorts (JSP)
1952
What Makes Us Tick N.Y. STOCK EXCHANGE
1953
A Is for Atom GENERAL ELECTRIC
Dear Uncle HARDING COLLEGE
1954
Horizons of Hope SLOAN FOUNDATION
1956
The Voice Beneath the Sea AT&T
1957
Your Safety First (an.) AUTOMOBILE MANUF. ASSN.

1968
Money and Banking SLOAN FOUNDATION

PODOLOR, RICHARD
1964
Kings of the Wild Waves (doc. short) PAR
1970
Bigfoot ELLMAN

POLONSKY, SAMUEL
1932
Uncle Moses (Yiddish language) YIDDISH TALKING PICTURES

POPE, ROBERT
1964
The Narcotics Trade (doc. short) OCEANIA PRODS.

POPKIN, LEONARD
1963
Pianissimo (short) CARMEN D'AVINO

PORÉE, GREG
1968
Like It Is LIMA PRODS.
1969
Over-Exposed LIMA PRODS.

PORTER, LEW
1938
Harlem on the Prairie ASSOCIATED FEATURES
The Rangers' Round-Up SPECTRUM
Phantom Ranger MON
Renfrew on the Great White Trail GN
1939
The Bronze Buckaroo SACK
Trigger Pals GN
Harlem Rides the Range SACK
Six-Gun Rhythm GN
1940
Death Rides the Range COLONY
Yukon Flight MON
East Side Kids MON
Phantom Rancher COLONY
Gang War SACK
The Kid from Santa Fe MON
Frontier Crusader PRC
Lightning Strikes West COLONY
Billy the Kid Outlawed PRC
Boys of the City MON
Gun Code PRC
Arizona Gang Busters PRC
That Gang of Mine MON
Billy the Kid in Texas PRC
Riders of Black Mountain PRC
1941
Billy the Kid's Range War PRC
Emergency Landing PRC
Bowery Blitzkrieg MON
1942
Jungle Siren PRC
[Also many films in collaboration with J. Lange, q.v.]

PORTER, QUINCY
1956
Music for a Film on the Yale Library ?

POTOKER, OSCAR
1929
The Dummy (see Hajos)
The Wheel of Life (mt; + stock) PAR
Fashions in Love PAR
The Mysterious Dr. Fu Manchu PAR
The Mighty PAR
1930
The Love Parade (see Leipold)
Slightly Scarlet (see Hajos)
Sarah and Son PAR
The Vagabond King (with Leipold; ac: Terr, Harling) PAR
The Vagabond King (silent version; see Leipold)
Ladies Love Brutes PAR
Shadow of the Law (mt) PAR
The Border Legion PAR
The Silent Enemy (see Midgely)
1931
Fighting Caravans (see Leipold)
The Beloved Bachelor (see Leipold)
Once a Lady (see R. Kopp)
Rich Man's Folly (see Leipold)
1932
The Miracle Man (see Harling)
Blonde Venus (see Harling)
Trailing the Killer WORLD WIDE
1934
The Scarlet Empress (see Leipold)
1935
Hei Tiki (doc.) PRINCIPAL
[Also worked as an orchestrator.]

POTTS, GREGORY
1969
Dr. Masher CINEX INT'L.

POWELL, EDWARD B.
1935
The President Vanishes (see Riesenfeld)

1938
There Goes My Heart (see Hatley)
1939
Topper Takes a Trip (see Friedhofer)
Made for Each Other (see Friedhofer)
Stanley and Livingstone (see Silvers)
1945
State Fair (with A. Newman, G. Rose, Mockridge) TCF
1955
Gods of the Road (short; mt; + stock) TCF
1960
One Foot in Hell (see Frontiere)
1965
The Great Sioux Massacre COL
[Also a very prolific arranger and orchestrator.]

POWELL, MEL
Documentaries (WILLARD VAN DYKE)
1952
American Frontier (short)
The Lonely Night
New York University (short)
1953
There Is a Season (short)

PREISNER, JACK
1970
Machismo—40 Graves for 40 Guns BOXOFFICE INTERNATIONAL

PREVIN, ANDRÉ
1947
Tenth Avenue Angel (see R. Kopp)
1948
The Bride Goes Wild (see R. Kopp)
The Kissing Bandit (see Stoll)
The Sun Comes Up (o: R. Franklyn) MGM
1949
Big Jack (see Stothart)
Scene of the Crime (o: Courage, Heglin) MGM
Border Incident (o: R. Franklyn) MGM
Challenge to Lassie (o: R. Franklyn) MGM
Tension (o: Heglin) MGM
Shadow on the Wall (o: Courage) MGM
1950
The Outriders (o and ac: Sendrey) MGM
Three Little Words (o: Heglin, R. Franklyn) MGM
Dial 1119 (o: R. Franklyn) MGM
Kim (with Kaper; o: R. Franklyn, Arnaud) MGM
1951
Cause for Alarm (o: Arnaud, Heglin) MGM
1953
Small Town Girl (with Sendrey; o: Heglin) MGM
The Girl Who Had Everything (o: Heglin, Rugolo) MGM
Kiss Me Kate (with Salinger; o: R. Franklyn, Heglin) MGM
Give a Girl a Break (o: Heglin) MGM
1954
Bad Day at Black Rock (o: Courage) MGM
1955
It's Always Fair Weather (ac: Salinger, Courage; o: Heglin, Woodbury, R. Franklyn) MGM
Kismet (with Salinger; ac: A. Morton, Courage; o: Heglin, R. Franklyn) MGM
1956
The Catered Affair (o: Heglin) MGM
Invitation to the Dance ("Ring Around the Rosy" sequence; o: Heglin. "Sinbad the Sailor" sequence: Edens, Salinger, adapted from music of Rimsky-Korsakov; o: R. Franklyn. "Circus" sequence: Jacques Ibert) MGM
The Fastest Gun Alive (o: R. Franklyn, Heglin) MGM
1957
Hot Summer Night (o: Heglin) MGM
Designing Woman (o: Woodbury, R. Franklyn) MGM
Silk Stockings (see Salinger)
House of Numbers (o: Woodbury) MGM
1958
Gigi (see Salinger)
1959
Porgy and Bess (o: Courage) GOLDWYN
1960
Who Was That Lady? (o: Courage) COL
The Subterraneans (o: Woodbury) MGM
Bells Are Ringing MGM
Elmer Gantry (o: Woodbury) UA
All in a Night's Work (o: Woodbury) PAR
1961
One, Two, Three UA
The Four Horsemen of the Apocalypse (o: Woodbury) MGM
1962
Long Day's Journey Into Night EMB
Two for the Seesaw UA
1963
Irma La Douce (o: Courage) UA

1964
Dead Ringer WB
My Fair Lady (o: Courage, R. Franklyn, Woodbury) WB
Goodbye Charlie (o: Woodbury) TCF
Kiss Me, Stupid LOPERT
1965
Inside Daisy Clover (o: Woodbury) WB
1966
The Fortune Cookie UA

PREVIN, CHARLES
1936
Parole (with Maxwell; mt: Kaun) UNIV
My Man Godfrey UNIV
The Man I Marry (ac: Roemheld) UNIV
Three Smart Girls (see Roemheld)
Four Days' Wonder (with Vaughan, Parrish) UNIV
1937
The Mighty Treve (see D. Raksin)
One Hundred Men and a Girl (see F. Skinner)
Prescription for Romance (+ stock) UNIV
1938
Mad About Music (with F. Skinner) UNIV
Wives Under Suspicion (see C. Henderson)
The Rage of Paris (see F. Skinner)
Youth Takes a Fling (with F. Skinner, C. Henderson) UNIV
1939
For Love or Money (mt; + stock) UNIV
Hero for a Day (+ stock) UNIV
First Love (see F. Skinner)
1941
The Flame of New Orleans (see F. Skinner)
It Started with Eve (see Salter)
Never Give a Sucker an Even Break (+ stock) UNIV
The Wolf Man (see Skinner)
1942
Get Hep to Love (mt: F. Skinner) UNIV
Between Us Girls (see F. Skinner)
1944
Song of the Open Road UA
1945
And Then There Were None (see Castelnuovo-Tedesco)
1949
That Midnight Kiss (with Salinger; mt: R. Franklyn; o: Marquardt) MGM

PRICE, HENRY
1962
Eegah! FAIRWAY-INTERNATIONAL
1964
The Incredibly Strange Creatures Who Stopped Living and Became Crazy Mixed-Up Zombies FAIRWAY-INTERNATIONAL
1965
Rope of Flesh EVE
The Thrill Killers HOLLYWOOD-INTERNATIONAL
1966
Moonwolf (ac with Sendrey for U.S. release of 1959 German film) AA
Rat Pfink and Boo Boo CRADDOCK
1968
Sappho Darling CAMBIST
1970
Sinthia, the Devil's Doll SUN ART

PRICE, HERMAN
1952
The Colonial Printer (doc. short) CW
1957
Williamsburg in the American Heritage (doc. short) CW

PRICE, WILL
1955
The Flesh Merchant SONNEY

PRINCE, HUGH
1940
Recruiting Daze (cartoon) UNIV
1950
Strip Tease Murder Case FUTURITY
1955
Harlem Follies FUTURITY

PRINCE, ROBERT
1962
Strangers in the City EMBASSY
1965
Andy UNIV
1966
You're a Big Boy Now (o: Schroeck) SEVEN ARTS
1968
A Great Big Thing ARGO FILM

PROVENZANO, ALDO
1962
Jacktown PICTORIAL INT'L.

PRYDATEKYCH, ROMAN
1938
Marusia (Ukrainian language) UKRAFILM

PRYOR, ARTHUR
1919
Soldiers of Fortune MAYFLOWER

Q

QUICK, AL
1969
Wanda (The Sadistic Hypnotist) FALU PRODS.

QUINCY, GEORGE
1967
Splendor in the Sand (doc. short) ARTHUR WHITNEY

R

RAAB, LEONID
1935
David Copperfield (see Stothart)
1941
Triumph Without Drums (short; see Hayton)
1948
He Walked by Night EL
1949
Follow Me Quietly (ac: Sawtell) RKO
The Sundowners (see Schrager)
[Also a very prolific orchestrator.]

RAGLAND, ROBERT O.
1969
The Babysitter CROWN
1970
Cindy and Donna CROWN
Weekend with the Babysitter CROWN

RAIM, WALTER
1965
Open Your Eyes (doc. short) GIRL SCOUTS OF THE U.S.A.
1966
Yoo Hoo! I'm a Bird (doc. short) UNITED AIR LINES
1967
The King of Madison Avenue (doc. short) PAR

RAINGER, RALPH
1930
The Sea God (see Hajos)
Tom Sawyer (see Leipold)
Sea Legs PAR
Only Saps Work (mt) PAR
1931
Gente Alegre (see Leipold)
Finn and Hattie (mt) PAR
The Conquering Horde (see Leipold)
City Streets (see Hajos)
The Vice Squad (with R. Kopp) PAR
I Take This Woman (with R. Kopp) PAR
Women Love Once (o: Leipold) PAR
An American Tragedy (with Leipold) PAR
Monkey Business (see Leipold)
Girls About Town (o: Leipold, R. Heindorf) PAR
Working Girls (o: Leipold) PAR
Ladies of the Big House (see Leipold)
1932
No One Man (with Reese; + stock) PAR
This Is the Night (see Harling)
The Big Broadcast (with Leipold; o: Leipold, Marquardt) PAR
1933
A Farewell to Arms (see Harling)
Pick Up (with Leipold, R. Kopp) PAR
A Bedtime Story (with Leipold, Hajos; ac: H. Jackson) PAR
The Story of Temple Drake (see Kaun)
International House (with Leipold, H. Jackson) PAR
Midnight Club (with H. Jackson; + stock) PAR
Torch Singer (o: H. Jackson, Leipold) PAR

The Way to Love (with H. Jackson, Leipold) PAR
1934
Bolero (with Kaun, Leipold) PAR
Come On Marines! (+ stock) PAR
The Trumpet Blows PAR
Little Miss Marker (o: Satterfield; + stock) PAR
Kiss and Make-Up (with Leipold, Satterfield) PAR
1935
Rumba (o: Leipold, Satterfield, Hand) PAR
1936
Allegretto (short) PAR
1937
Swing High, Swing Low (see Young)
Artists and Models Abroad (with Leipold, Carbonara; ac: Bradshaw, D. Rose) PAR
Hula Heaven (short; mt) PAR
1938
The Big Broadcast of 1938 (see Leipold)
1939
Paris Honeymoon (with Leipold, Shuken, Carbonara) PAR

RAKSIN, DAVID
1936
Modern Times (see C. Chaplin)
Three Smart Girls (see Roemheld)
1937
The Mighty Treve (with C. Previn) UNIV
She's Dangerous (+ stock) UNIV
Midnight Court (o: Nussbaum) WB
As Good as Married (with F. Skinner) UNIV
Wings Over Honolulu (+ stock) UNIV
San Quentin (see Roemheld)
Marry the Girl (see Roemheld)
Stella Dallas (see A. Newman)
52nd Street (see A. Newman)
Sh! The Octopus (see Roemheld)
The Kid Comes Back WB
1938
Suez (see Mockridge)
1939
Mr. Moto's Last Warning (+ stock) TCF
The Hound of the Baskervilles (see Maxwell)
Second Fiddle (see Mockridge)
Frontier Marshal (see Kaylin)
Stanley and Livingstone (see Silvers)
The Adventures of Sherlock Holmes (see Mockridge)
1940
The Blue Bird (see A. Newman)
Two Girls on Broadway (with Stringer; mt: Bassman; + stock) MGM
Forty Little Mothers (see Stringer)
Storm Warning (doc.) PAUL BURNFORD
1941
Ride On, Vaquero TCF
I'll Wait for You (see Kaper)
Dead Men Tell TCF
Rise and Shine (see Buttolph)
Cadet Girl (see Buttolph)
The Men in Her Life (o: Cutner) COL
On the Sunny Side (see Mockridge)
Son of Fury (see A. Newman)
Remember the Day (see Mockridge)
1942
Song of the Islands (see Buttolph)
Who Is Hope Schuyler? TCF
The Man Who Wouldn't Die (o: Bradshaw) TCF
Whispering Ghosts (see Harline)
The Magnificent Dope (see Mockridge)
Thru Different Eyes (see Mockridge)
The Postman Didn't Ring (with Harline; o: A. Morton, E. Powell, de Packh) TCF
Just Off Broadway TCF
Prelude to War (doc.; see Harline)
Iceland (see Harline)
Manila Calling (see Mockridge)
The Undying Monster (with A. Lange, Mockridge; o: E. Powell, A. Morton) TCF
Time to Kill (with Mockridge; + stock) TCF
Dr. Renault's Secret (o: A. Morton) TCF
He Hired the Boss (see Buttolph)
1943
City Without Men (o: A. Morton, Cutner) COL
Something to Shout About (see Leipold)
DuBarry Was a Lady (see Amfitheatrof)
I Dood It (see Bassman)
1944
Tampico (ac: Buttolph; o: A. Morton, Virgil, de Packh) TCF
Bathing Beauty (see J. Green)
The Canterville Ghost (see Bassman)
Greenwich Village (see Buttolph)
Laura (o: A. Morton) TCF
Irish Eyes Are Smiling (see Mockridge)
Belle of the Yukon (see A. Lange)
1945
Attack in the Pacific (doc.; partial) U.S. NAVY
It's a Pleasure (see A. Lange)
Diamond Horseshoe (see H. Spencer)
Where Do We Go from Here? (with Buttolph; ac: Mockridge, de Packh) TCF

Don Juan Quilligan (ac: Buttolph; o: de Packh, A. Morton) TCF
Fallen Angel (o: A. Morton) TCF

1946
Smoky (o: A. Morton) TCF
The Shocking Miss Pilgrim (o: A. Morton, de Packh) TCF

1947
The Homestretch (o: Hagen, E. Powell) TCF
The Secret Life of Walter Mitty GOLDWYN
Forever Amber (o: de Packh, Spencer, E. Powell) TCF
Daisy Kenyon (o: E. Powell) TCF

1948
Fury at Furnace Creek (o: de Packh) TCF
Apartment for Peggy (mt; ac: Mockridge, A. Newman, Hagen) TCF

1949
Force of Evil (o: R. Raksin, L. Morton) MGM

1950
Whirlpool (o: E. Powell) TCF
The Reformer and the Redhead (o: R. Raksin, Arnaud, R. Franklyn) MGM
A Lady Without Passport (o: R. Franklyn) MGM
Right Cross (o: R. Franklyn) MGM
The Next Voice You Hear MGM
The Magnificent Yankee (o: Arnaud, R. Franklyn) MGM

1951
Kind Lady (o: R. Franklyn, Zador, Arnaud) MGM
Across the Wide Missouri (ac: Sendrey; o: Arnaud, R. Raksin, L. Morton) MGM
The Man with a Cloak (o: R. Raksin, Salinger) MGM
It's a Big Country (see A. Deutsch)

1952
The Girl in White (o: de Packh, R. Franklyn) MGM
Pat and Mike (o: R. Raksin) MGM
Carrie (ac: Amfitheatrof; o: R. Raksin, Van Cleave) PAR
The Bad and the Beautiful (o: L. Morton, R. Raksin) MGM

1953
City of Bad Men (see Mockridge)

1954
Apache (o: de Packh) UA
Suddenly UA

1955
The Big Combo AA

1956
Jubal (o: A. Morton) COL
Seven Wonders of the World (doc.; with Moross, S. Kaplan) CINERAMA
Hilda Crane (o: E. Powell) TCF
Bigger Than Life (o: E. Powell) TCF

1957
The Vintage (o: Courage, R. Franklyn, R. Raksin) MGM
Man on Fire (o: R. Raksin, R. Franklyn) MGM
Gunsight Ridge UA
Until They Sail (o: R. Raksin, R. Franklyn) MGM

1958
Twilight for the Gods UNIV
Separate Tables UA

1959
Al Capone AA

1960
Pay or Die AA

1961
Night Tide AIP
Too Late Blues PAR

1962
Two Weeks in Another Town (o: R. Raksin, R. Franklyn) MGM

1964
The Patsy (o: Van Cleave, R. Raksin) PAR
Invitation to a Gunfighter (o: Friedhofer) UA
Sylvia (o: E. Powell, R. Raksin, Van Cleave) PAR
Love Has Many Faces (o: Van Cleave, R. Raksin) COL

1965
The Redeemer (U.S. release of 1959 Spanish film; o: Friedhofer) EMPIRE

1966
A Big Hand for the Little Lady (o: E. Powell) WB

1967
Will Penny (o: R. Raksin, Van Cleave) PAR

Shorts

1944
Main Street Today (o: Salinger) MGM
Inflation (o: A. Morton) MGM

1961
To Be as One (doc.) JEWISH CENTERS

1967
The Leading Edge (doc.) EAMES

196?
Moment to Act (doc.) ROGER TILTON
The Shelter (doc.) ROGER TILTON

Cartoons
1941
Western Daze PAR
Dipsy Gypsy PAR
1950
Giddyap UPA
1952
Sloppy Jalopy UPA
Madeline (o: R. Raksin) UPA
1953
The Unicorn in the Garden (o: R. Raksin) UPA

RAKSIN, RUBY
1961
Valley of the Dragons COL
1962
What Ever Happened to Baby Jane? (see De Vol)
1965
The Lollipop Cover CONTINENTAL
1966
An Eye for an Eye (see Kraushaar)
[Also worked as an orchestrator.]

RALF, RICHARD
1957
Five Miles West (short) VOLKSWAGEN OF AMERICA

RALKE, DON
1966
C'mon, Let's Live a Little (ac: Borisoff) PAR

RAM, BUCK
1957
Rock All Night AIP

RAMIN, SID
1961
West Side Story (see S. Chaplin)
1969
Stiletto EMBASSY

RAMSIER, PAUL
1962
Turkey—A Nation in Transition (doc. short) IFF

RANDI, DON
1970
Bloody Mama AIP
Up in the Cellar AIP

RAPÉE, ERNO
1920
Over the Hill FOX
Passion (U.S. release of 1919 German film, *Madame DuBarry;* another score by Axt and Mendoza) FN
A Connecticut Yankee at King Arthur's Court FOX
1921
The Queen of Sheba FOX
The Birth of a Nation (see Breil, 1915)
1922
Nero (U.S. release of Italian film) FOX
1923
If Winter Comes FOX
1924
The Last Man on Earth FOX
The Iron Horse FOX
1925
The Man Without a Country FOX
1926
Monte Carlo MGM
Film Record of the Eucharistic Congress (doc.; with Otto Singenberger) FOX
What Price Glory (New York opening; o: M. Baron. Los Angeles opening: R. Bassett + stock) FOX
1927
The Missing Link WB
Sunrise (New York opening; o: M. Baron. Los Angeles opening: R. Bassett + stock. 1928 synchronized score: Riesenfeld) FOX
7th Heaven (New York opening; o: M. Baron. Los Angeles opening: R. Bassett + stock) FOX
Fazil (New York opening. Los Angeles opening: R. Bassett; + stock) FOX
1928
Mother Machree FOX
Four Sons (o: M. Baron) FOX
Street Angel (o: M. Baron) FOX
The Red Dance FOX
Dry Martini FOX
Mother Knows Best FOX
Four Devils (o: M. Baron) FOX
1929
Making the Grade FOX
The Bachelors' Club PARTHENON
1937
The Dead March (doc.) IMPERIAL
1941
Invasion (ac: Craig) ADVENTURE FILMS

RAPOSO, JOE
1969
An Impression of John Steinbeck: Writer (doc. short) USIA

RASCH, RAYMOND
1952
Limelight (see C. Chaplin)

RATHAUS, KAROL
[He scored several films in Germany, France, and England, 1931–1937.]
1939
Let Us Live COL
1942
Jaguas (doc.) DOCUMENTARY FILM
1945
Histadruth (doc.) DOCUMENTARY FILM
1948
Clearing the Way (doc. short) UNITED NATIONS
Before Your Telephone Rings (doc. short) BELL TELEPHONE CO.
1950
Out of Evil (doc.) JOSEPH KRUMGOLD
Preface to a Life (doc.) SUN DIAL FILMS

RAY, MATTHEW
1934
Are We Civilized? (see Wachtel)

RAYNES, J. A.
1915
The Sable Lorcha (see Breil)
The Lily and the Rose (see Breil)
Jordan Is a Hard Road TRIANGLE
Cross Currents TRIANGLE
1916
The Price of Power TRIANGLE
The Flying Torpedo TRIANGLE

READ, JOHN T.
1918
Restitution (with Alford) MENA FILM CO.

RECHLIN, EDWARD
1924
Martin Luther, His Life and Time (see H. Spielter)

REDD, FREDDIE
1962
The Connection SHIRLEY CLARKE

REESE, MAX
1930
Animal Crackers PAR
1932
No One Man (see Rainger)
1961
The Big Show (see Sawtell and Shefter)
[Also a prolific orchestrator.]

REGAN, WARREN
1969
Linda and Abilene UNITED PICTURES

REICH, STEVE
Shorts (ROBERT NELSON)
1963
The Plastic Haircut
1965
Oh Dem Watermelons
Thick Pucker

REICHERT, JAMES A.
1965
The Way of a Ship (doc. short) MARATHON
1966
Of Sea and Ships (doc. short) MARATHON

REISER, ALOIS
1929
The House of Horror WB
No Defense (see Dunn)
Saturday's Children (o: E. Ross) WB
From Headquarters (+ stock) WB
Two Weeks Off WB
Noah's Ark (+ stock) WB
The Time, the Place, and the Girl WB
The Gamblers WB
Careers (see Copping)
The Girl in the Glass Cage (mt; + stock) WB
Honky Tonk WB
The Hottentot (with Copping; + stock) WB
Gold Diggers of Broadway (see Mendoza)
Hard to Get WB
Her Private Life (with Copping) WB
The Isle of Lost Ships (with Copping) WB
Footlights and Fools WB
The Painted Angel WB
1930
The Love Racket (with Copping) WB
Loose Ankles (with Copping) WB
No, No, Nanette (see Copping)
Spring Is Here (see Copping)
Murder Will Out WB

In the Next Room WB
The Flirting Widow (m&e; + stock) WB
Back Pay (with Copping; + stock) WB
Big Boy (with Dunn; + stock) WB
Office Wife (+ stock) WB

1931
The Right of Way (with Dunn; + stock) WB
My Past (foreign version; + stock) WB
The Millionaire (foreign version; + stock) WB
The Lady Who Dared (+ stock) WB
Star Witness (mt; + stock) WB

1933
The Man Who Dared (see Kaylin)

1934
Caravan (see Brunelli)

1938
Man's Paradise (doc.) HUNTINGTON

RENO, DON

1968
Basketmaking in Colonial Virginia (doc. short) CW

REPINE, BURT

1963
Folk Artist of the Blue Ridge (doc. short) CW

1968
New England Folk Painter, Erastus Salisbury Field (doc. short) CW

RESNICK, FELIX

1957
Line (short) PORTAFILMS

REYNOLDS, DICK

1969
Finney (with Les Hooper, Eli Wolf) BILL HARE

RICH, FREDERIC EFREM (FREDDIE)

1942
Torpedo Boat PAR
Wildcat PAR
I Live on Danger PAR
Wrecking Crew PAR

1943
Stage Door Canteen UA
Submarine Alert PAR
Tornado PAR
Alaska Highway PAR
Jack London UA

1944
A WAVE, a WAC and a Marine MON

1945
A Walk in the Sun TCF

RICHARDS, EMIL

1967
Stoked—The Surfer Generation (doc.) ?

RICHARDS, JOHNNY

1952
Gold Fever MON

1959
Kiss Her Goodbye ALBERT LIPTON

RICHARDSON, BOB

1963
From Eight to Five (doc. short) AUBURN U.

RICHARDSON, JAMES

1958
Hell Squad AIP

RIDDLE, NELSON

1955
Flame of the Islands REP

1956
Johnny Concho (o: A. Morton) UA
Lisbon REP

1957
The Girl Most Likely RKO

1958
Merry Andrew (o: A. Morton) MGM
St. Louis Blues (o: Shuken, Hayes) PAR

1959
A Hole in the Head UA

1960
Can-Can TCF
Ocean's Eleven (o: A. Morton) WB

1961
Lolita (o: Grau) MGM

1963
Come Blow Your Horn (o: Grau) PAR
Paris—When It Sizzles (o: A. Morton) PAR

1964
4 for Texas (o: Grau) WB
What a Way to Go! (o: A. Morton) TCF
Robin and the 7 Hoods (o: Grau) WB

1965
Harlow MAGNA
A Rage to Live (o: Grau) UA
Marriage on the Rocks WB
Red Line 7000 PAR

1966

Batman (o: Grau) TCF

El Dorado (o: Grau) PAR

1967

How to Succeed in Business Without Really Trying UA

1969

The Maltese Bippy (o: Grau) MGM

The Great Bank Robbery (o: Grau) WB

Paint Your Wagon (o: W. Jones) PAR

1970

Hell's Bloody Devils (see McGinnis)

On a Clear Day You Can See Forever PAR

RIDDLE, RON

1963

Art in Exhibition (doc. short) YALE U.

1966

Art of the Conservator (doc.) CW

RIESENFELD, HUGO

1915

Carmen (a of music by Bizet) PAR

1916

Hoodoo Ann TRIANGLE

The Habit of Happiness TRIANGLE

The Aryan TRIANGLE

1918

The Blue Bird (with Falck) PAR

Woman MAURICE TOURNEUR

1919

Sahara (see Schertzinger)

The Miracle Man MAYFLOWER

The Mystery of the Yellow Room MAYFLOWER

1920

Dr. Jekyll and Mr. Hyde PAR

Humoresque PAR

Always Audacious PAR

Conrad in Quest of His Youth PAR

Idols of Clay PAR

1921

The Four Horsemen of the Apocalypse (see Gottschalk)

Reputation UNIV

Deception (U.S. release of 1920 German film, *Anna Boleyn;* ac: Stahlberg) PAR

La Tosca (reissue of 1918 film) PAR

1922

The Loves of Pharaoh (U.S. release of 1921 German film, *Das Weib des Pharao*) PAR

1923

The Ten Commandments (with Roder, Saminsky, Gutman, Falck; 1924 score: Snyder) PAR

The Covered Wagon (with Zamecnik) PAR

Bella Donna PAR

The Hunchback of Notre Dame (New York premiere, Astor Theatre. Popular-price run, Strand Theatre, 1924: Copping and Edouarde. Reissue with sound, 1929: Perry. Foreign version, 1931: Roemheld, + stock) UNIV

1924

Monsieur Beaucaire PAR

1925

The Swan PAR

Madame Sans-Gêne PAR

Siegfried (a of music by Wagner; U.S. release of 1923 German film) UFA

Beggar on Horseback PAR

The Pony Express PAR

Les Misérables UNIV

Three Faces East PDC

1926

The Wanderer PAR

The Flaming Frontier UNIV

The Vanishing American PAR

The Volga Boatman (New York opening. Los Angeles opening: R. Bassett, + stock) PDC

Grass (doc.) PAR

Beau Geste (o: Savino; ac: Bradford, Spialek) PAR

1927

The Sorrows of Satan PAR

The Cat and the Canary UNIV

Old San Francisco WB

Old Ironsides (with Zamecnik) PAR

Chang (doc.) PAR

The King of Kings PATHÉ

The Rough Riders (with Zamecnik) PAR

Tempest UA

1928

Ramona UA

Two Lovers UA

The Cavalier TS

The Toilers TS

The Godless Girl PATHÉ

Uncle Tom's Cabin (sound reissue of 1927 silent film) UNIV

The Woman Disputed UA

Revenge UA

The Battle of the Sexes (another score by Schildkret) UA

Sunrise (see Rapée, 1927)

The Awakening UA
Sins of the Fathers PAR

1929
The Rescue UA
Lucky Boy TS
Lady of the Pavements UA
Molly and Me TS
The Iron Mask UA
Looping the Loop PAR
The Three Passions UA
*Coquette** UA
Alibi UA
Eternal Love UA
My Lady's Past TS
Two Men and a Maid TS
This Is Heaven UA
Evangeline UA
Bulldog Drummond UA
Three Live Ghosts UA
Midstream TS
New Orleans TS
Whispering Winds TS
The Taming of the Shrew UA
Condemned UA

1930
Lummox UA
Be Yourself! UA
One Romantic Night UA
The Bad One UA
Hell's Angels UA
Kathleen Mavourneen TS
Abraham Lincoln UA
The Lottery Bride UA

1931
Tabu (with Harling; ac: Roder; + stock) PAR

1933
This Is America (doc.) BEEKMAN
Thunder Over Mexico (AC: Aguilar) PRINCIPAL
The Wandering Jew TWICKENHAM

*The score actually shows nothing by Riesenfeld; it was arranged and orchestrated by Emil Hilb and Erwin Nyiregyhazi from music of Chopin, Liszt, and Schumann, + stock from the Hugo Riesenfeld Reference Library. No other Riesenfeld scores from 1928–30 have been seen, but this example suggests how he may have been able to score over forty films in three years: i.e., by using a combination of newly composed or arranged music, some of it ghost-written, and/or stock music from his library, which in the 1920s was reported in the press to consist of several thousand orchestral scores and other compositions.

1934
The Doctor (short; a: W. Scharf) EDUCATIONAL
Two Heads on a Pillow LIBERTY
Peck's Bad Boy PRINCIPAL
Flirtation SALIENT
Little Men MASCOT

1935
The President Vanishes (with Vaughan, E. Powell) PAR
Hard Rock Harrigan ATHERTON

1936
Tundra (see Arthur Kay)
Let's Sing Again PRINCIPAL
Hearts in Bondage REP
Follow Your Heart (ac: Skiles) REP
The Devil on Horseback GN
The President's Mystery REP
Daniel Boone (with Arthur Kay) RKO
White Legion GN
Rainbow on the River PRINCIPAL

1937
Circus Girl (see Hajos)
Make a Wish PRINCIPAL
Stan (short) STANDARD OIL
The Californian PRINCIPAL

1938
Tarzan's Revenge PRINCIPAL
Wide Open Faces (md) COL
Hawaii Calls PRINCIPAL
Rose of the Rio Grande (md) MON
El Trovador de la Radio (md; Spanish language) PAR
King of the Sierras GN
The Sunset Strip Case (md) GN

RIESMAN, MICHAEL

1969
Sand, Or Peter and the Wolf (an. short) HARVARD U.

RILEY, TERRY

1970
Corridor (short) STANDISH D. LAWDER

ROBERTS, ARTHUR

1967
LINK (doc. short) ATOMIC ENERGY COMMISSION

ROBERTS, DES

1970
Guess What Happened To Count Dracula (a: D. Roberts, Andy Wilder) MERRICK INT'L.

ROBERTS, KAI
1963
All of Me BRENNER

ROBERTS, TRUDI
1961
Pineapple Country, Hawaii (doc. short) PINEAPPLE GROWERS ASSN.

ROBERTSON, HUGH
1970
Wheel of Ashes (U. S. release of 1968 French film) PETER EMANUEL GOLDMAN

ROBINSON, EARL
1941
It's Up to You (doc.) USDA
1944
The Negro Soldier (doc.; see Tiomkin)
1947
The Roosevelt Story (doc.) UA
1948
Man from Texas (o: Cadkin) EL
Documentary Shorts
1939
United Action UNITED AUTO WORKERS
1944
Hell Bent for Election (an.) UNITED AUTO WORKERS
1948
Muscle Beach JOSEPH STRICK, IRVING LERNER
1951
When We Grow Up NEIGHBORHOOD FILMS
1956
Giants in the Land GENERAL MOTORS
1959
Something New Under the Sun PAN AMERICAN
More Than Words HENRY STRAUSS PRODS.
1969
The Concept of Intensive Coronary Care JSP

ROBINSON, McNEIL
1966
Nine Variations on a Dance Theme (short) HILARY HARRIS

ROCHETTI, JOHN
1933
The Fighting President (doc.) UNIV
His Double Life PAR
1934
The First World War (doc.) FOX
1935
Gigolette RKO
1937
Borneo (doc.) TCF
1938
Dark Rapture (doc.; with Sharples) UNIV
Documentary Shorts (TCF)
1938
Fall (Fashion Forecast)
Winter (Fashion Forecast)
1939
Spring Styles (Fashion Forecast)
The Evergreen Empire
1940
Flying Stewardess
Tales of the East
Eskimo Trails
Florida, Land of Flowers

RODEMICH, GENE
1929
Gridiron Glory (short) PATHÉ
Body Building (short) PATHÉ
1932
Bring 'Em Back Alive (doc.; mt; + stock) RKO
1933
Hook & Ladder Hokum (cartoon) RKO

RODER, MILAN
1923
The Ten Conmandments (see Riesenfeld)
1931
Tabu (see Riesenfeld)
1932
The Sign of the Cross (see R. Kopp)
Scarlet Dawn WB
1933
A Farewell to Arms (see Harling)
Silver Dollar WB
Supernatural (see Hajos)
Voltaire (see Kaun)
The Song of Songs (see Hajos)
Good-Bye Love (with Wallace, Wineland, H. Jackson) RKO
1934
Eight Girls in a Boat (see Harold Lewis)
Four Frightened People (see Hajos)
Death Takes a Holiday (with Leipold; ac: Kaun) PAR
Murder at the Vanities (with Lynch, H. Jackson) PAR
You Belong to Me (with Roemheld) PAR
The Scarlet Empress (see Leipold)

1935
The Lives of a Bengal Lancer (see Roemheld)
All the King's Horses (see Roemheld)
The Black Room (see Silvers)
The Last Outpost (see Kaun)
The Crusades (see R. Kopp)
Last of the Pagans (see Axt)
1936
The Voice of Bugle Ann (see Roemheld)
Craig's Wife (see R. Bassett)
1937
Exclusive (see Leipold)
Souls at Sea (see Harling)
1938
The Buccaneer (see Antheil)
Bulldog Drummond in Africa (+ stock) PAR
Spawn of the North (see Tiomkin)
If I Were King (see Hageman)
1939
Never Say Die (with Leipold, Bradshaw; ac: Shuken) PAR
[Also worked as an orchestrator.]

ROEMHELD, HEINZ
1929
Hell's Heroes (foreign version; see Perry)
1930
The Cohens and the Kellys in Scotland UNIV
The Hide-Out UNIV
Captain of the Guard (o: Fink, Pinter, Schiller; + stock) UNIV
Czar of Broadway (foreign version) UNIV
All Quiet on the Western Front (foreign version; with Perry; + stock) UNIV
White Hell of Pitz Palu (U.S. release of 1929 German film, *Die weisse Hölle vom Piz Palü*) UNIV
What Men Want (foreign version) UNIV
The Leather Pushers (serial; foreign version) UNIV
Outside the Law (foreign version; with Perry; ac: C. Arnold; + stock) UNIV
A Lady Surrenders UNIV
East Is West (with Perry; + stock) UNIV
The Cat Creeps (mt) UNIV
See America Thirst (foreign version; with Perry) UNIV
The Boudoir Diplomat UNIV
Free Love UNIV
The Cohens and Kellys in Africa UNIV
1931
Many a Slip UNIV
The Midnight Sun (foreign version of 1926 film; see Kaun)
Seed (+ stock) UNIV
Up for Murder (+ stock) UNIV
The Hunchback of Notre Dame (see Riesenfeld, 1923)
1933
Golden Harvest (see Harold Lewis)
Too Much Harmony (+ stock) PAR
I'm No Angel (see H. Jackson)
The Invisible Man UNIV
The Sin of Nora Moran MAJESTIC
Easy to Love WB
1934
Bombay Mail UNIV
Madame Spy UNIV
Cross Country Cruise UNIV
Pirate Treasure (serial; mt; + stock) UNIV
Four Frightened People (see Hajos)
Mandalay WB
The Poor Rich (mt) UNIV
Love Birds UNIV
The Wharf Angel (mt) PAR
Registered Nurse WB
Fashions of 1934 WB
Journal of a Crime WB
A Modern Hero WB
Merry Wives of Reno WB
The Black Cat UNIV
As the Earth Turns (mt and trailer: Kaun) WB
The Circus Clown (+ stock) WB
Dr. Monica WB
Side Streets (mt: Kaun) WB
Housewife (mt and trailer: Kaun; theme: Jerome) WB
Midnight Alibi (mt: Kaun) WB
You Belong to Me (see Roder)
Desirable (with Kaun, R. Heindorf) WB
A Lost Lady (with R. Heindorf; ac: Kaun) WB
British Agent (with Kaun) WB
The Lemon Drop Kid (see Satterfield)
Dames WB
One Exciting Adventure UNIV
Madame DuBarry WB
Happiness Ahead WB
Ready for Love (see Satterfield)
The Pursuit of Happiness (see Satterfield)
Flirtation Walk WB
Imitation of Life UNIV
Gentlemen Are Born (ac: E. Ward; et and trailer: Kaun) WB
The Man Who Reclaimed His Head UNIV

Father Brown, Detective (mt) PAR
Maybe It's Love WB
Here Is My Heart (see Leipold)

1935

Enter Madame! (+ stock) PAR
Sweet Adeline WB
A Notorious Gentleman UNIV
The Lives of a Bengal Lancer (with Roder, Leipold, Hand) PAR
The Gilded Lily (see Satterfield)
Wings in the Dark (+ stock) PAR
The Good Fairy UNIV
Ruggles of Red Gap (mt) PAR
Gold Diggers of 1935 (with Kaun) WB
All the King's Horses (with Leipold, Roder) PAR
Living on Velvet (ac: Kaun) WB
Love in Bloom PAR
Four Hours to Kill! (ac: Satterfield) PAR
Private Worlds PAR
The Devil Is a Woman (see Leipold)
The Girl from 10th Avenue (m&e: Kaun) WB
The Glass Key (mt) PAR
The Dinky (m&e: Kaun) WB
Mary Jane's Pa (ac and trailer: Kaun) WB
Oil for the Lamps of China (ac: Kaun) WB
Stranded (with Kaun) WB
Going Highbrow (see Kaun)
Kliou (The Tiger) BENNETT
Paris in Spring (see Hollander)
Front Page Woman WB
Broadway Gondolier WB
Page Miss Glory WB
We're In the Money (ac: Kaun) WB
The Irish in Us (mt: Kaun) WB
Bright Lights WB
Little Big Shot WB
The Goose and the Gander (m&e: Kaun) WB
I Live for Love WB
Dr. Socrates (see Kaun)
The Last Outpost (see Kaun)
The Crusades (see R. Kopp)
The Payoff (ac and trailer: Kaun) WB
Hands Across the Table (with Hollander, Leipold) PAR
Stormy UNIV
Three Kids and a Queen (see Waxman)
Storm Over the Andes (with Vaughan) UNIV
Peter Ibbetson (see Toch)
Mary Burns, Fugitive PAR
Broadway Hostess (see R. Heindorf)
East of Java (see Waxman)
The Great Impersonation (with Vaughan) UNIV
Stars Over Broadway WB
I Found Stella Parish WB

1936

Dangerous (with R. Heindorf, Kaun) WB
The Bride Comes Home (with Leipold, Satterfield) PAR
Rose of the Rancho (see Friedhofer)
The Widow from Monte Carlo (with H. Jackson, Kaun) WB
Her Master's Voice PAR
Tough Guy (see Axt)
The Story of Louis Pasteur (m&e and trailer: Kaun) WB
The Voice of Bugle Ann (with Roder; ac: R. Kopp, Lynch) MGM
Klondike Annie (see V. Young)
Boulder Dam WB
Road Gang WB
Snowed Under WB
Colleen (ac: Kaun) WB
Brides Are Like That WB
Sutter's Gold (see Waxman)
The Singing Kid (with R. Heindorf) WB
The Law in Her Hands WB
I Married a Doctor (theme: Harling) WB
The Golden Arrow (theme: Harling) WB
Dracula's Daughter UNIV
Sons o' Guns WB
The Big Noise WB
The White Angel (o: Friedhofer) WB
Hearts Divided (ac: Korngold, Kaun) WB
Satan Met a Lady (see Kaun)
The Case of the Velvet Claws (see Kaun)
Earthworm Tractors (see H. Jackson)
Draegerman Courage (m&e, trailer: Kaun) WB
Bengal Tiger (see H. Jackson)
Stage Struck WB
Two in a Crowd (ac: Vaughan) UNIV
Give Me Your Heart (theme: Harling) WB
China Clipper (see Kaun)
The Girl on the Front Page (+ stock) UNIV
The Magnificent Brute (see Maxwell)
The Man I Marry (see C. Previn)
Cain and Mabel WB
The Case of the Black Cat WB
The Luckiest Girl in the World UNIV
Mountain Justice (see Kaun)
Three Smart Girls (ac: C. Previn, F. Skinner; mt: D. Raksin) UNIV

Smart Blonde WB
Once a Doctor WB
The Great O'Malley WB
Sing Me a Love Song WB
Gold Diggers of 1937 WB

1937
Stolen Holiday WB
Ready, Willing, and Able WB
Marked Woman (see Kaun)
Call It a Day WB
Slim (see M. Steiner)
Kid Galahad (with M. Steiner) WB
Melody for Two WB
The Case of the Stuttering Bishop WB
The Singing Marine WB
Ever Since Eve WB
Varsity Show (with Heindorf) WB
San Quentin (with Maxwell; mt: D. Raksin) WB
Marry the Girl (m&e: D. Raksin) WB
Confession (adaptation of Peter Kreuder's score for 1935 German film, *Mazurka*, of which this was a remake) WB
Expensive Husbands WB
Back in Circulation (see Kaun)
Alcatraz Island WB
West of Shanghai WB
The Perfect Specimen WB
Over the Goal WB
It's Love I'm After WB
Stand-In UA
Sh! The Octopus (mt: D. Raksin) WB
Hollywood Hotel (with R. Heindorf) WB
Women Are Like That WB

1938
Fools for Scandal (see A. Deutsch)
I Met My Love Again UA
Love, Honor, and Behave (ac: H. Jackson) WB
A Slight Case of Murder (ac: A. Deutsch; mt: H. Jackson) WB
Men Are Such Fools (o: R. Heindorf) WB
Gold Diggers in Paris (with R. Heindorf) WB
Four's a Crowd WB
Garden of the Moon WB
Secrets of an Actress WB
Brother Rat WB
Broadway Musketeers WB
Hard to Get WB
Nancy Drew—Detective WB
Comet Over Broadway WB
The Young in Heart (see Waxman)
Going Places WB

1939
King of the Underworld WB
Wings of the Navy WB
Nancy Drew—Reporter WB
Yes, My Darling Daughter WB
You Can't Get Away with Murder (o: Friedhofer, A. Kay, R. Kopp) WB
Nancy Drew—Trouble Shooter WB
Naughty But Nice (with R. Heindorf) WB
Hell's Kitchen WB
Waterfront WB
No Place to Go WB
Nancy Drew and the Hidden Staircase WB
On Your Toes (with R. Heindorf) WB
The Roaring Twenties (with R. Heindorf) WB
The Mad Empress (+ stock) WB
Invisible Stripes (o: R. Heindorf) WB
A Child Is Born WB

1940
Brother Rat and a Baby (ac: H. Jackson) WB
Calling Philo Vance WB
It All Came True (ac: H. Jackson) WB
Zanzibar (see F. Skinner)
'Til We Meet Again (o: R. Heindorf) WB
Flight Angels WB
Brother Orchid (o: R. Heindorf) WB
The Man Who Talked Too Much (o: R. Heindorf) WB
My Love Came Back (o: R. Heindorf) WB
No Time for Comedy (o: R. Heindorf) WB
Knute Rockne—All American (o: R. Heindorf) WB
South of Suez (see Hollander)
Lady with Red Hair (o: Friedhofer) WB

1941
Four Mothers (o: R. Heindorf) WB
Honeymoon for Three (o: R. Heindorf) WB
Flight from Destiny (o: R. Heindorf) WB
The Strawberry Blonde (o: R. Heindorf) WB
The Wagons Roll at Night (o: R. Heindorf) WB
Thieves Fall Out WB
Affectionately Yours (o: R. Heindorf) WB
Out of the Fog WB
Underground (see A. Deutsch)
Kisses for Breakfast (see A. Deutsch)
Manpower (see A. Deutsch)
Navy Blues WB
Blues in the Night (with R. Heindorf) WB
The Prime Minister (ac; score: Jack Beaver) WB
Cadet Girl (see Buttolph)

1942

All Through the Night (see A. Deutsch)
Wild Bill Hickok Rides (see H. Jackson)
Always in My Heart WB
Bullet Scars (see Lava)
Sons of the Sea (ac; score: Jack Beaver) WB
The Male Animal (o: R. Heindorf) WB
Larceny, Inc. (see A. Deutsch)
Juke Girl (see A. Deutsch)
Across the Pacific (see A. Deutsch)
Gentleman Jim (o: R. Heindorf) WB
Yankee Doodle Dandy (see R. Heindorf)

1943

Background to Danger (see Hollander)
The Hard Way (o: Friedhofer) WB
Thank Your Lucky Stars WB
Adventure in Iraq WB
Find the Blackmailer WB
The Desert Song WB

1944

Shine On, Harvest Moon WB
Make Your Own Bed (ac: Lava; mt: Perkins) WB
Sensations of 1945 (see Merrick)
Janie (ac: Waxman, Perkins) WB

1945

Hollywood Canteen WB
It's a Pleasure (see A. Lange)
Wonder Man (with Heindorf) GOLDWYN
Too Young to Know WB

1946

O.S.S. (see Amfitheatrof)
Mr. Ace UA

1947

Down to Earth (with Duning; ac: A. Morton) COL
Curley UA
The Fabulous Joe UA
Heaven Only Knows UA
Christmas Eve (o: Herschel Gilbert) UA
The Flame REP
It Had to Be You (with A. Morton) COL

1948

I, Jane Doe REP
Here Comes Trouble UA
The Lady from Shanghai (o: A. Morton, Herschel Gilbert) COL
The Fuller Brush Man (o: Herschel Gilbert, Vaughan) COL
On Our Merry Way (o: H. Russell, Herschel Gilbert) UA
The Girl from Manhattan (o: Heglin) UA
Station West RKO
My Dear Secretary (o: Herschel Gilbert) UA

1949

The Lucky Stiff UA
Mr. Soft Touch (o: Herschel Gilbert) COL
Miss Grant Takes Richmond COL

1950

The Good Humor Man (o: Herschel Gilbert) COL
Kill the Umpire (o: Herschel Gilbert) COL
Rogues of Sherwood Forest (see Castelnuovo-Tedesco)
Union Station (o: Van Cleave, Parrish; + stock) PAR
The Fuller Brush Girl (o: A. Morton, Herschel Gilbert) COL

1951

Valentino COL

1952

Chicago Calling UA
The Big Trees (o: de Packh, Shuken, Cutner) WB
Jack and the Beanstalk WB
Loan Shark LIP
3 for Bedroom C WB
The 5,000 Fingers of Dr. T (see Hollander)
Ruby Gentry TCF

1953

The Moonlighter WB

1954

Phffft (see Hollander)

1955

Captain Lightfoot (see H. Stein)
The Looters (with Zeisl) UNIV
The Purple Mask (with Zeisl, H. Stein; ac: Salter) UNIV
Female on the Beach (see H. Stein)
Kiss of Fire (see Salter)
There's Always Tomorrow (see H. Stein)
Red Sundown (see Salter)
The Square Jungle UNIV
Hell's Horizon COL

1956

Creature Walks Among Us (see Mancini)
The Price of Fear UNIV
World in My Corner (see Mancini)
Toy Tiger (see Mancini)
Away All Boats (see F. Skinner)
Pillars of the Sky (see Lava)
The Mole People (ac: Salter, H. Stein) UNIV
Istanbul (see Gertz)

1957

The Night Runner (see H. Stein)
The Tall T COL
The Land Unknown (see Salter)

The Monster That Challenged the World UA
Decision at Sundown COL
This Is Russia (see H. Stein)
The Lady Takes a Flyer (see H. Stein)
1959
Ride Lonesome COL
1961
Lad: A Dog WB
Shorts (WB)
1934
The Fortune Teller
1936
Changing of the Guard
1964
World of Pleasure
Trailers (WB)
1936
Man Hunt
1942
This Was Paris
You Can't Escape Forever

ROGERS, BERNARD
1938
Highlights and Shadows (see H. Hanson)

ROGERS, MILTON (SHORTY)
1959
Tarzan, the Ape Man MGM
1965
Young Dillinger AA
Taffy and the Jungle Hunter AA
1967
Gunfight in Abilene (with Darin) UNIV
The Tiger Makes Out (o: Florence) COL
1970
Like It Is SEYMOUR BORDE
Fools CR
Cartoons
1952
Hotsy Footsy UPA
1956
Blues Pattern ERNEST PINTOFF
Sappy Homiens UPA
1957
The Three Little Bops WB
1968
The Wacky World of Numburrs STEPHEN BOSUSTOW

ROMAN, MARTIN
1963
50,000 B. C. (Before Clothing) WALDORF

ROMANIS, GEORGE
1967
8 on the Lam UA

ROMBERG, SIGMUND
1922
Foolish Wives (o: J. Frank Cork) UNIV
1937
They Gave Him a Gun (o: Marquardt, Hand) MGM

ROMEO, BOB
1956
Fantasy of the Sky (short) GERARD H. WAYNE

RONELL, ANN
1945
G. I. Joe (see Applebaum)
1948
One Touch of Venus (md: Arnaud) UNIV
1950
Love Happy (o: Geller) UA
1953
Main Street to Broadway (o: Arnaud) MGM
1966
Meeting at a Far Meridian (unreleased)

ROOD, HALE
1963
Melody for Machines (doc. short) MARATHON
1967
Images (doc. short) MARATHON

ROSE, DAVID
1938
Give Me a Sailor (see Leipold)
Artists and Models Abroad (see Rainger)
1944
Resisting Enemy Interrogation (quasi doc.) A.A.F.
The Princess and the Pirate GOLDWYN
Winged Victory (o: de Packh) TCF
1947
Do You Know What the Army Air Force Is? (doc. short) A.A.F.
1950
The Underworld Story (o: Cadkin) UA
1951
Rich, Young and Pretty (o: Arnaud, Heglin) MGM
Texas Carnival (o: Sendrey) MGM
It's a Big Country (see A. Deutsch)

1952

Just This Once (o: Sendrey) MGM
Young Man with Ideas (o: Heglin) MGM
Everything I Have Is Yours (o: Sendrey) MGM
The Clown (o: Sendrey) MGM

1953

Confidentially Connie (o: Sendrey) MGM
Bright Road (o: Sendrey) MGM

1955

Jupiter's Darling (o: R. Franklyn, Courage) MGM

1956

Public Pigeon No. 1 RKO

1959

Operation Petticoat UNIV

1960

Please Don't Eat the Daisies (o: de Packh) MGM
This Rebel Breed (o: Shuken, Hayes) WB

1964

Quick, Before It Melts (o: Shuken, Hayes) MGM

1965

Never Too Late (o: Shuken, Hayes) WB

1966

Hombre (o: Shuken, Hayes) TCF

ROSE, GENE

1935

Dante's Inferno (see Friedhofer)
Music Is Magic TCF

1936

Song and Dance Man (with R. Bassett; ac: Kaylin) TCF
Can This Be Dixie? (see Kaylin)

1937

The Holy Terror TCF
She Had to Eat TCF
Sing and Be Happy TCF
Think Fast, Mr. Moto (see R. Bassett)

1938

Kentucky Moonshine (see Mockridge)
Five of a Kind (ac: Kaylin) TCF
Sharpshooters (with Kaylin) TCF
Road Demon TCF

1939

Pardon Our Nerve TCF
Rose of Washington Square TCF
The Jones Family in Hollywood TCF
The Jones Family in Quick Millions TCF
Stop, Look and Love TCF
Too Busy to Work TCF

1940

High School TCF
Public Deb No. 1 (see Buttolph)
Foreign Correspondent (see A. Newman)

1941

Dance Hall (see Mockridge)

1942

Priorities on Parade (see V. Young)

1943

The Gang's All Here (see A. Lange)

1944

The Eve of St. Mark (see Mockridge)
Greenwich Village (see Buttolph)
Sweet and Low-Down (see Mockridge)

1945

State Fair (see E. Powell)

[Also a prolific arranger and orchestrator.]

ROSE, WILFRED N.

1952

Love Moods (short) ROADSHOW ATTRACTIONS

ROSEBROOK, LEONARD

1930

Captain Thunder (see Cugat)
The Lash (see Mendoza)
Kismet WB

1931

Sit Tight (mt) WB
Father's Son (see Copping)
The Hot Heiress WB

ROSEN, HERMAN

1926

Stella Dallas (+ stock) UA

ROSEN, MILTON

[All for Universal unless otherwise stated.]

1940

The Border Legion (mt: Lava; + stock) REP

1941

Riders of Death Valley (serial; + stock)
Sea Raiders (serial; mt; + stock)
Swing It Soldier (mt; + stock)
Arizona Cyclone (with Salter; + stock)
Stagecoach Buckaroo (+ stock)

1942

Drums of the Congo (+ stock)
Junior G-Men of the Air (serial; + stock)
The Adventures of Smilin' Jack (serial; + stock)
Don Winslow of the Coast Guard (serial; mt; + stock)

1943
Good Morning, Judge
Hi Ya, Sailor (+ stock)
1944
Enter Arsene Lupin
1945
Sudan
Men in Her Diary (+ stock)
1946
The Scarlct Horseman (serial; m&e; + stock)
Tangier
The Spider Woman Strikes Back
Her Adventurous Night
Cuban Pete
The Time of Their Lives (ac: A. Lange)
White Tie and Tails
1947
Slave Girl
Pirates of Monterey
1948
The Challenge TCF
13 Lead Soldiers TCF
The Story of Bob and Sally SOCIAL GUIDANCE
The Creeper TCF
1950
The Milkman
Kansas Raiders (+ stock)
Mystery Submarine (mt; + stock)
Under the Gun (+ stock)
1951
Target Unknown (+ stock)
Cattle Drive (mt: F. Skinner; + stock)
Iron Man (+ stock)
Mark of the Renegade (see F. Skinner)
1952
Just Across the Street (see H. Stein)
Francis Goes to West Point (see H. Stein)
Lost in Alaska (see Mancini)
Yankee Buccaneer (+ stock)
Meet Me at the Fair (with H. Stein; + stock)
1953
City Beneath the Sea (see H. Stein)
Abbott and Costello Go to Mars (see H. Stein)
Law and Order (with Mancini, H. Stein; + stock)
All I Desire (see H. Stein)
Take Me to Town (see H. Stein)
The Glass Web (see H. Stein)
Tumbleweed (see Mancini)
Ride Clear of Diablo (see H. Stein)
1954
Yankee Pasha (see Salter)
Rails Into Laramie (see H. Stein)
Ricochet Romance (see Lava)
1967
The Young Warriors
Shorts
1940
Rhythm Jamboree (mt)
Bullets and Ballads
1948
Abraham's Faith CHURCH-CRAFT
And Forbid Them Not CHURCH-CRAFT
Daniel in the Lions' Den CHURCH-CRAFT
The Raising of Lazarus CHURCH-CRAFT
1950
Rustlers' Ransom
Western Courage (+ stock)

ROSENBERG, BERNARD
1958
The Wilderness of Zin (doc. short) ISRAEL OFFICE OF INFORMATION

ROSENBOOM, DAVID
1967
I'll Be Damned (short) GALE WILEY
1968
Pére Facts (an. short) ROBERT LIEBERMAN
1969
Involuntary?Control (doc. short) PHILIP MENDLO, JERRY MURPHY

ROSENMAN, LEONARD
1949
Form Evolution (an. experimental short) FRANK STAUFFACHER, MARTIN METAL
1955
East of Eden WB
The Cobweb MGM
Rebel Without a Cause WB
1956
Edge of the City (o: de Packh) MGM
1957
The Young Stranger (o: de Packh) RKO
Bombers B-52 WB
1958
Lafayette Escadrille (o: de Packh) WB
The Hidden World (doc.) SMALL WORLD
1959
Pork Chop Hill UA
The Savage Eye TRANS-LUX
1960
The Bramble Bush WB

The Rise and Fall of Legs Diamond WB
The Crowded Sky WB
The Plunderers AA

1961
The Outsider UNIV
Hell Is for Heroes PAR

1962
Convicts 4 AA
The Chapman Report WB

1966
Fantastic Voyage TCF

1967
A Covenant with Death WB

1968
Countdown WB
Hellfighters UNIV

1969
Beneath the Planet of the Apes (o: Ferraro) TCF

1970
A Man Called Horse (o: Ferraro) NG

ROSENTHAL, LAURENCE

1955
Yellowneck REP

1957
Naked in the Sun AA

1961
A Raisin in the Sun COL
Dark Odyssey ERA

1962
The Miracle Worker UA
Requiem for a Heavyweight COL

1964
Becket PAR

1966
Hotel Paradiso MGM

1967
The Comedians MGM

1969
Three UA

ROSMINI, DICK

1967
Harvest (doc.; with Sahl, Drasnin; + stock) CARROLL BALLARD

1969
Rodeo (doc. short) CARROLL BALLARD

ROSOFF, CHARLES

1934
Southern Exposure (cartoon) COL

1935
The Bird Man (cartoon) COL

1953
Boy Scout Jamboree of 1953 (doc.; see Lava)

ROSS, GILBERT

1970
Metamorphosis (an. short) EDWARD ROSS

ROTH, CARL

1965
Eve and the Merman THUNDERBIRD

ROYAL, TED

1959
When Comedy Was King (compilation film; o: Royal, Cooke) TCF

1961
Days of Thrills and Laughter (compilation film; o: Royal) TCF

ROZNYAI, ZOLTAN

Documentary Shorts (JULES POTOCSNY)

1962
Steel by Stopwatch

1964
Search

1965
The Ohio Story

ROZSA, MIKLOS

1937
Thunder in the City ATLANTIC
Knight Without Armour ALEXANDER KORDA
The Squeaker (U.S.: *Murder on Diamond Row*) KORDA
Four Dark Hours (U.S.: *The Green Cockatoo*) NEW WORLD

1938
The Divorce of Lady X KORDA
The Drum (U.S.: *Drums;* ac; score: John Greenwood) KORDA

1939
The Spy in Black (U.S.: *U-Boat 29*) KORDA
The Four Feathers KORDA
Ten Days in Paris (U.S.: *Missing Ten Days*) ASHER
On the Night of the Fire (U.S.: *The Fugitive*) G&S FILMS

1940
The Thief of Bagdad (o: Sendrey) KORDA

1941
That Hamilton Woman (o: Sendrey, Zador) KORDA

New Wine (based on music of Schubert; o: Sendrey) UA
Lydia (o: Sendrey, Zador) KORDA
Sundown (o: Sendrey, Zador) UA

1942
To Be or Not to Be (see Heymann)
Jungle Book (o: Sendrey, Zador) KORDA
Jacaré (doc.; o: Zador) UA

1943
Five Graves to Cairo (o: Zador) PAR
So Proudly We Hail! (o: Zador, Parrish, Shuken) PAR
Sahara (o: Zador, Cutner) COL
The Woman of the Town (o: Zador) UA

1944
The Hour Before the Dawn (o: Zador) PAR
Double Indemnity (o: Zador) PAR
Dark Waters UA
The Man in Half Moon Street (o: Zador) PAR
Ministry of Fear (see Young)
A Song to Remember (based on music of Chopin) COL

1945
Blood on the Sun UA
The Lost Weekend (o: Zador, Parrish, Cutner, Shuken) PAR
Lady on a Train UNIV
Spellbound (o: Zador) SELZNICK

1946
Because of Him UNIV
The Strange Love of Martha Ivers (o: Zador) PAR
The Killers (o: Zador) UNIV

1947
The Red House UA
Song of Scheherazade (based on music of Rimsky-Korsakov) UNIV
The Macomber Affair UA
Desert Fury (o: Zador) PAR
Brute Force (o: Zador) UNIV
The Other Love UA

1948
Secret Beyond the Door (o: Zador) UNIV
A Woman's Vengeance (o: Zador) UNIV
A Double Life (o: Zador) UNIV
The Naked City (o: Zador) (with F. Skinner) UNIV
Kiss the Blood Off My Hands UNIV
Criss Cross UNIV

1949
Command Decision (o: Zador) MGM
The Bribe (o: Zador) MGM
Edward, My Son (ac; o: Zador; score: John Wooldridge) MGM
Madame Bovary (o: Zador) MGM
The Red Danube (o: Zador) MGM
Adam's Rib (o: Zador) MGM
East Side, West Side (o: Zador) MGM

1950
The Asphalt Jungle (o: Zador) MGM
Crisis (o: Zador) MGM
King Solomon's Mines (trailer only; o: Zador) MGM
The Miniver Story (based on Stothart's score for *Mrs. Miniver*) (o: Zador) MGM

1951
The Light Touch (o: Zador) MGM
Quo Vadis (o: Zador) MGM

1952
Ivanhoe (o: Zador) MGM
Plymouth Adventure (o: Zador, R. Franklyn) MGM

1953
Julius Caesar (o: Zador) MGM
The Story of Three Loves (o: Zador) MGM
Young Bess (o: Zador) MGM
All the Brothers Were Valiant (o: Zador) (ac: Salinger, J. Green; o: R. Franklyn) MGM
Knights of the Round Table (o: Zador) MGM

1954
Men of the Fighting Lady (o: Zador) MGM
Valley of the Kings (o: Zador) MGM
Beau Brummell (ac; o: Zador; score: Richard Addinsell) MGM
Crest of the Wave (o: Zador) MGM
Green Fire (o: Zador) MGM

1955
Moonfleet (o: Zador) MGM
The King's Thief (o: Zador) MGM
Diane (o: Zador) MGM

1956
Tribute to a Bad Man (o: Zador) MGM
Bhowani Junction (o: Zador) MGM
Lust for Life (o: Zador) MGM

1957
Something of Value (o: Zador) MGM
The Seventh Sin (o: Zador) MGM
Tip on a Dead Jockey (o: Zador) MGM

1958
A Time to Love and a Time to Die UNIV
The World, the Flesh and the Devil (o: Zador) MGM

1959
Ben-Hur (o: Zador) MGM

1961
King of Kings (o: Zador) MGM
El Cid AA
1962
Sodom and Gomorrah TCF
1963
The V.I.P.s (o: Zador) MGM
1967
The Power MGM
1968
The Green Berets (o: Tamkin) WB
1970
The Private Life of Sherlock Holmes (o: Tamkin) UA

RUBAG, MIKLOS
1967
Free Love Confidential BOXOFFICE INT'L.

RUBENSTEIN, MARTIN
1960
The Prime Time (with B. Frye) ESSANJAY
1962
Envelope Jive (an. short) KAROTTON ENVELOPE CO.
1969
I've Got This Problem (short) RON CLASKY

RUBINI, JAN
1927
The Love of Sunya UA

RUBINSTEIN, GEORGE M.
1918
Salome FOX

RUBINSTEIN, JOHN
1970
Paddy AA

RUDDY, CHARLES
1955
Dance Hall Racket SCREEN CLASSICS

RUDIN, ANDREW
1966
For Ages 10 to Adult (doc. short) AMERICAN FRIENDS SERVICE

RUFF, WILLIE
1968
Prelude (short) PRELUDE CO.

RUGOLO, PETE
1951
The Strip (see Stoll)
1952
Skirts Ahoy! (see Stoll)
Glory Alley (see Stoll)
1958
Jack the Ripper (U.S. release of British film; with McHugh) PAR
1964
The Killers (see F. Steiner)
1967
The Sweet Ride TCF

RUMSHINSKY, JOSEPH
1935
Shir Hashirim (Yiddish language) GLOBE
1938
Two Sisters (Yiddish language) GRAPHIC

RUSSELL, HENRY
1948
Lulu Belle COL
1951
Five (with Lava, Maxwell; o: Maxwell) COL
1956
Gun for a Coward (see F. Skinner)
1958
Wild Heritage (see Vars)

RUSSELL, LARRY
1943
She's for Me (+ stock) UNIV
1944
Showboat Serenade (short; see Leipold)
Chip Off the Old Block UNIV
Hat Check Honey (see F. Skinner)
1952
Limelight (see C. Chaplin)

RYBNER, C.
1929
Abbie's Irish Rose (see Zmacnik)

S

SACK, ALBERT E.
1944
Once Upon a Wintertime (an. short) WDP
[Also worked as an orchestrator.]

SAHL, MICHAEL
1967
Pigs! (short) CARROLL BALLARD
Harvest (see Rosmini)

SAINT-SANEZ, GREGOR
1969
The Fabulous Bastard from Chicago GRADS CORP.

SALINGER, CONRAD
[All for MGM unless otherwise noted.]
1943
Girl Crazy (see Stoll)
The Man from Down Under (see Snell)
Young Ideas (see Bassman)
1944
Rationing (see Castelnuovo-Tedesco)
Meet the People (see Hayton)
Meet Me in St. Louis (with Edens; ac: C. Jackson, Hayton, Stoll; o: R. Franklyn, Nussbaum, Cutner, Heglin)
1945
Yolanda and the Thief (see Hayton)
The Harvey Girls (with Hayton; o: R. Franklyn, Heglin, Duncan, Marquardt)
1946
Ziegfeld Follies (see Edens)
Two Sisters from Boston (with Stoll, C. Jackson; o: R. Franklyn, Duncan)
Courage of Lassie (see Bradley)
Till the Clouds Roll By (ac: Hayton, Edens; o: Shuken, Cutner, R. Franklyn, Heglin)
1947
Dark Delusion (see Snell)
Summer Holiday (ac: Hayton; o: Salinger, Heglin, Glasser)
Good News (ac: Edens; o: Cutner, Shuken, R. Franklyn, Heglin)
1948
B. F.'s Daughter (see Kaper)
The Pirate (see Hayton)
Easter Parade (ac: Edens; o: R. Franklyn, Marquardt, Cutner, Shuken)
Words and Music (see Hayton)
1949
Take Me Out to the Ball Game (see Edens)
The Barkleys of Broadway (see Hayton)
That Midnight Kiss (see C. Previn)
On the Town
1950
Nancy Goes to Rio (with Stoll; o: Sendrey, R. Franklyn, Van Eps)
Annie Get Your Gun (see A. Deutsch)
Summer Stock (o: R. Franklyn)
Pagan Love Song (see A. Deutsch)
1951
Royal Wedding (see Sendrey)
Show Boat (see A. Deutsch)
An American in Paris (ac: J. Green; o: Sendrey)
The Unknown Man (o: R. Franklyn)
1952
The Belle of New York (see A. Deutsch)
Carbine Williams (o: R. Franklyn)
Washington Story (o: R. Franklyn)
The Prisoner of Zenda (adaptation of Newman's 1937 score; o: Sendrey)
1953
Dream Wife (o: R. Franklyn)
The Band Wagon (see A. Deutsch)
All the Brothers Were Valiant (see Rozsa)
Kiss Me Kate (see A. Previn)
1954
Tennessee Champ (o: R. Franklyn)
Seven Brides for Seven Brothers (see A. Deutsch)
Brigadoon (ac: J. Green; o: R. Franklyn, Sendrey)
The Last Time I Saw Paris (o: R. Franklyn)
1955
Hit the Deck (see Stoll)
The Scarlet Coat (o: R. Franklyn)
It's Always Fair Weather (see A. Previn)
Quentin Durward (see Kaper)
Kismet (see A. Previn)
1956
Gaby (o: R. Franklyn)
Invitation to the Dance (see A. Previn)

The Battle of Gettysburg (short; see A. Deutsch)
High Society (see J. Green)

1957
Silk Stockings (ac: A. Previn, Woodbury; o: R. Franklyn)
Raintree County (see J. Green)

1958
Gigi (with A. Previn; ac: Courage; o: R. Franklyn, Woodbury)
Lonelyhearts UA

1962
Jumbo (see Stoll)

[Also a prolific arranger and orchestrator.]

SALTER, HANS J.

[All for Universal unless otherwise noted.]

1938
The Rage of Paris (see F. Skinner)
Danger on the Air (m&e; + stock)
Little Tough Guy (see F. Skinner)

1939
Ex-Champ (see F. Skinner)
The Great Commandment CATHEDRAL
Missing Evidence (mt; + stock)
Call a Messenger (+ stock)
Miracle on Main Street COL
West of Carson City (+ stock)
First Love (see F. Skinner)
The Big Guy (with F. Skinner)

1940
The Invisible Man Returns (with F. Skinner; + stock)
Honeymoon Deferred (+ stock)
Zanzibar (see F. Skinner)
Black Friday (with F. Skinner; + stock)
The Mummy's Hand (see F. Skinner)
Spring Parade
Dark Streets of Cairo (+ stock)
San Francisco Docks (ac: F. Skinner)
Trail of the Vigilantes (+ stock)

1941
Meet the Chump (with F. Skinner; + stock)
Man Made Monster (ac: F. Skinner)
The Man Who Lost Himself (ac: F. Skinner)
Model Wife (+ stock)
The Black Cat (with F. Skinner; + stock)
Bachelor Daddy (m&e with F. Skinner; + stock)
Cracked Nuts (see F. Skinner)
Raiders of the Desert (+ stock)
Hold That Ghost (mt: F. Skinner; + stock)
Badlands of Dakota (see F. Skinner)
The Kid from Kansas (+ stock)
It Started with Eve (ac: C. Previn)
Arizona Cyclone (see M. Rosen)
The Wolf Man (see F. Skinner)

1942
The Strange Case of Doctor Rx (see F. Skinner)
The Ghost of Frankenstein
The Spoilers
Top Sergeant (+ stock)
The Silver Bullet (+ stock)
Invisible Agent
Sin Town (+ stock)
Pittsburgh (see F. Skinner)
Frankenstein Meets the Wolf Man (+ stock)

1943
Keep 'Em Slugging (see F. Skinner)
The Amazing Mrs. Holliday (see F. Skinner)
Get Going (+ stock)
Frontier Badmen (mt; + stock)
The Strange Death of Adolph Hitler (see Lava)
Son of Dracula (mt; + stock)
Never a Dull Moment (+ stock)
His Butler's Sister
The Spider Woman (+ stock)

1944
The Invisible Man's Revenge (with Lava, Zeisl)
Christmas Holiday
The Merry Monahans (ac: Maxwell)
San Diego, I Love You
Murder in the Blue Room (see Lava)
House of Frankenstein (with Dessau)
Patrick the Great
Can't Help Singing

1945
Assignment Home (doc.) U.S. NAVY
That's the Spirit (with Lava)
The Strange Affair of Uncle Harry (with Dessau, Castelnuouvo-Tedesco)
That Night with You
River Gang (+ stock)
This Love of Ours
Scarlet Street

1946
So Goes My Love
Lover Come Back
The Dark Horse (+ stock)
Little Miss Big (+ stock)
Magnificent Doll (o: Tamkin)

1947
Michigan Kid (ac: F. Skinner)
That's My Man REP
The Web (o: Tamkin)
The Vigilantes Return (see F. Skinner)
Love from a Stranger (o: Cadkin) EL
The Wistful Widow of Wagon Gap (see Schumann)
1948
The Sign of the Ram (o: A. Morton, H. Gilbert) COL
Black Bart (see L. Stevens)
An Innocent Affair UA
Man-Eater of Kumaon
1949
Cover-Up (o: Byrns) UA
They Went That-a-Way (short; + stock)
The Reckless Moment (o: A. Morton) COL
1950
Please Believe Me (o: Byrns, Heglin) MGM
Borderline
The Killer That Stalked New York (o: Byrns, A. Morton) COL
Frenchie
1951
Tomahawk
The Fat Man (see F. Skinner)
Apache Drums
The Prince Who Was a Thief
Thunder on the Hill
You Never Can Tell
The Golden Horde
Finders Keepers
1952
Bend of the River (ac: F. Skinner)
Flesh and Fury
The Battle at Apache Pass
Untamed Frontier
Against All Flags
The 5,000 Fingers of Dr. T. (see Hollander)
1954
Yankee Pasha (with Lava, M. Rosen; mt: F. Skinner)
Creature from the Black Lagoon (with Mancini, H. Stein)
Saskatchewan (see Mancini)
Johnny Dark (ac: Mancini; mt: H. Stein)
Tanganyika (with H. Stein, Lava, Mancini)
The Far Country (see F. Skinner)
Black Horse Canyon (see F. Skinner)
The Black Shield of Falworth (with H. Stein, F. Skinner)
Naked Alibi (with Skinner; ac: H. Stein)
Four Guns to the Border (see F. Skinner)
The Human Jungle AA
Bengal Brigade (see S. Wilson)
Sign of the Pagan (see F. Skinner)
1955
Captain Lightfoot (see H. Stein)
Abbott and Costello Meet the Mummy (see Maury)
This Island Earth (see H. Stein)
Man Without a Star (see H. Stein)
The Purple Mask (see Roemheld)
The Far Horizons (o: Van Cleave, Parrish, Cailliet, Shuken) PAR
Wichita AA
Lady Godiva of Coventry (see F. Skinner)
Kiss of Fire (with H. Stein, Roemheld)
The Spoilers (see Mancini)
Red Sundown (ac: Roemheld)
The Rawhide Years (see F. Skinner)
1956
Creature Walks Among Us (see Mancini)
Navy Wife AA
Autumn Leaves (o: Grau; m&e: Duning; o: N. Riddle) COL
Walk the Proud Land (with H. Stein, Lava)
Raw Edge (see Gertz)
Hold Back the Night AA
The Mole People (see Roemheld)
1957
Three Brave Men (o: E. Powell; + stock) TCF
The Incredible Shrinking Man (see Gertz)
The Oklahoman AA
Joe Dakota (with Gertz, Mancini, H. Stein)
The Land Unknown (with Roemheld, H. Stein; ac: Mancini)
The Midnight Story (ac: F. Skinner; + stock)
The Tall Stranger AA
Man in the Shadow (see H. Stein)
Love Slaves of the Amazon (see S. Wilson)
The Female Animal
Day of the Bad Man
1958
The Last of the Fast Guns (with H. Stein)
Wild Heritage (see Vars)
Raw Wind in Eden
Appointment with a Shadow (with Vars; + stock)
1959
The Wild and the Innocent
The Man in the Net UA
The Gunfight at Dodge City UA
The Leech Woman (see Gertz)

1961

Follow That Dream UA
Come September
Hitler AA

1962

If a Man Answers

1963

Bedtime Story

1965

The War Lord (see Moross)

1966

Beau Geste

SALTONSTALL, SAMMY

1964

Clay (short) ELIOT NOYES

SAMINSKY, L.

1923

The Ten Commandments (see Riesenfeld)

SANDERS, TROY

1934

Las Fronteras del Amor (see Kaylin)

1935

Angelina o el Honor de un Brigadier (Spanish language; with Kilenyi, Brunelli; + stock) FOX

SANDFORD, ALEX

1962

Bachelor Tom Peeping PAUL MART PRODS.

SANFORD, BLAINE

1953

The Magnetic Monster UA

SANFORD, WILLIAM

1960

Pretty Boy Floyd (with Serino) CONTINENTAL

SANUCCI, FRANK

[Of 12 Universal films credited to him, only two (1938) had original music, suggesting that many of his other scores may have consisted of or included stock music.]

1936

Song of the Gringo GN
Headin' for the Rio Grande GN

1937

Arizona Days GN
Trouble in Texas GN
Hittin' the Trail GN
Sing, Cowboy, Sing GN
Riders of the Rockies GN
Riders of the Dawn MON
The Mystery of the Hooded Horsemen GN
God's Country and the Man MON
Stars Over Arizona MON
Tex Rides with the Boy Scouts GN
Frontier Town GN

1938

Rollin' Plains GN
Prison Break UNIV
The Utah Trail GN
Starlight Over Texas MON
The Black Bandit UNIV
Where the Buffalo Roam MON
Song of the Buckaroo MON

1939

Feud of the Range METROPOLITAN
Sundown on the Prairie MON
Rollin' Westward MON
Mystery Plane MON
Lure of the Wasteland AL LANE
Smoky Trails METROPOLITAN
Mesquite Buckaroo METROPOLITAN
Down the Wyoming Trail MON
Stunt Pilot MON
The Man from Texas MON
Riders of the Frontier MON
Riders of the Sage METROPOLITAN

1940

Roll Wagons Roll MON
Westbound Stage MON
Rhythm of the Rio Grande MON
Cowboy from Sundown MON
The Golden Trail MON
Rainbow Over the Range MON
Arizona Frontier MON
The Range Busters MON
Trailing Double Trouble MON
West of Pinto Basin MON
Take Me Back to Oklahoma MON
Rollin' Home to Texas MON

1941

The Trail of the Silver Spurs MON
The Kid's Last Ride MON
Tumbledown Ranch in Arizona MON
The Pioneers MON
Silver Stallion MON
Wrangler's Roost MON
Wanderers of the West MON
Fugitive Valley MON
Dynamite Canyon MON
Saddle Mountain Roundup MON

Gentleman from Dixie MON
The Driftin' Kid MON
Riding the Sunset Trail MON
Tonto Basin Outlaws MON
Underground Rustlers MON
Riot Squad MON

1942
Thunder River Feud MON
Western Mail MON
Rock River Renegades MON
Arizona Round-Up MON
Man with Two Lives MON
Boot Hill Bandits MON
Where Trails End MON
Texas Trouble Shooters MON
One Thrilling Night MON
Arizona Stage Coach MON
King of the Stallions MON
Phantom Killer MON
Texas to Bataan MON
War Dogs MON
The Living Ghost MON
Trail Riders MON
Two-Fisted Justice MON

1943
Haunted Ranch MON
Land of Hunted Men MON
Wild Horse Stampede MON
Cowboy Commandos MON
The Law Rides Again MON
Black Market Rustlers MON
Blazing Guns MON
Bullets and Saddles MON
Death Valley Rangers MON
Westward Bound MON

1944
Arizona Whirlwind MON
Outlaw Trail MON
Marked Trails MON
Sonora Stagecoach MON
Trigger Law MON

1945
Youth Aflame CONTINENTAL
Stranger from Santa Fe MON
His Brother's Ghost PRC
Flame of the West MON
Springtime in Texas MON
Border Badmen PRC
Riders of the Dawn MON
Frontier Feud MON
Fighting Bill Carson PRC
Border Bandits MON
The Lonesome Trail MON
Northwest Trail SG

1946
Moon Over Montana MON
West of the Alamo MON
Trail to Mexico MON
Song of the Sierras MON
Rainbow Over the Rockies MON

1947
Six-Gun Serenade MON

1948
Fighting Mustang ASTOR
Deadline ASTOR
Sunset Carson Rides Again ASTOR

1952
Buffalo Bill in Tomahawk Territory UA

SARGENT, CHARLES

1936
Three on the Trail PAR

SASSOVER, NATE

1970
The Way We Live Now (with Tamkus) UA

SATTERFIELD, TOM

[All for Paramount.]

1934
You're Telling Me (see Leipold)
Kiss and Make-Up (see Rainger)
Ladies Should Listen
She Loves Me Not
Belle of the Nineties (see Leipold)
The Lemon Drop Kid (with Roemheld; ac: Leipold)
Ready for Love (with Leipold, Roemheld)
The Pursuit of Happiness (with Roemheld)
College Rhythm
One Hour Late (+ stock)

1935
The Gilded Lily (with Roemheld, Krumgold)
Four Hours to Kill (see Roemheld)
Goin' to Town (with Leipold, Pasternacki)
Paris in Spring (see Hollander)
Accent on Youth (see Hollander)
Ship Cafe (+ stock)
Coronado (with Leipold)

1936
The Bride Comes Home (see Roemheld)
Collegiate (see Hollander)
Rose of the Rancho (see Friedhofer)
The Milky Way (see V. Young)

Klondike Annie (see V. Young)
Too Many Parents (see Carbonara)

[Also worked as an arranger and orchestrator.]

SAUTER, EDDIE

1965

Mickey One COL

SAVINE, ALEXANDER

1925

The Man Nobody Knows PICTORIAL CLUBS

1926

As We Forgive PICTORIAL CLUBS

SAVINO, DOMENICO

1922

Burning Sands (theme) PAR

1928

The Patriot (with Carbonara, Bergunker) PAR

SAWTELL, PAUL

1939

Woman Doctor (see Lava)
Mexicali Rose (see Feuer)
In Old Monterey (+ stock) REP
The Marshal of Mesa City RKO
Money to Burn (see Feuer)

1940

Legion of the Lawless RKO
Heroes of the Saddle (see Feuer)
Mexican Spitfire RKO
Little Orvie RKO
Drums of Fu Manchu (see Feuer)
Millionaire Playboy RKO
Ghost Valley Raiders (+ stock) REP
Bullet Code RKO
Grandpa Goes to Town (with Lava) REP
Covered Wagon Days (with Feuer; + stock) REP
Prairie Law RKO
Pop Always Pays RKO
Adventures of Red Ryder (see Lava)
Stage to Chino RKO
Oklahoma Renegades (with Lava; + stock) REP
Triple Justice RKO
King of the Royal Mounted (see Feuer)
Under Texas Skies (see Lava)
Wagon Train RKO

1941

Along the Rio Grande RKO
Play Girl RKO
Redhead MON
Kansas Cyclone (with DiMaggio; + stock) REP
Dude Cowboy RKO
The Bandit Trail (with Webb) RKO
The Gay Falcon RKO
A Date with the Falcon RKO
No Hands on the Clock (+ stock) PAR

1942

Valley of the Sun RKO
Dr. Broadway (see Dolan)
Night in New Orleans (+ stock) PAR
Scattergood Rides High RKO
Hillbilly Blitzkrieg MON
Bandit Ranger (mt; + stock) RKO
Scattergood Survives a Murder RKO
Hoppy Serves a Writ (+ stock) UA
Fighting Frontier (mt; + stock) RKO
Undercover Man (+ stock) UA
Lost Canyon (+ stock) UA
Border Patrol (+ stock) UA
Sagebrush Law (m&e; + stock) RKO

1943

Lady Bodyguard PAR
Tarzan Triumphs RKO
The Great Gildersleeve RKO
Cinderella Swings It RKO
Colt Comrades (+ stock) UA
Substitution and Conversion (doc.; see Tiomkin)
Bar 20 (m&e; + stock) UA
Hit the Ice UNIV
Henry Aldrich Swings It (ac: Shuken; m&e: Bradshaw) PAR
Power of the Press (+ stock) COL
The Strange Death of Adolph Hitler (see Lava)
False Colors (+ stock) UA
Riders of the Deadline (+ stock) UA
Tarzan's Desert Mystery RKO
Texas Masquerade (+ stock) UA
Calling Dr. Death (+ stock) UNIV

1944

So Many Hands (doc.) U.S. NAVY
One Mysterious Night (+ stock) COL
Cowboy Canteen (see Leipold)
Weird Woman (+ stock) UNIV
Lumberjack (+ stock) UA
The Scarlet Claw (+ stock) UNIV
Stars on Parade COL
Gildersleeve's Ghost RKO
Mystery Man (+ stock) UA
Henry Aldrich's Little Secret (see Leipold)
Jungle Woman (+ stock) UNIV

Secret Command (ac: Castelnuovo-Tedesco) COL
Youth Runs Wild RKO
Mr. Winkle Goes to War (see C. Dragon)
Pearl of Death (+ stock) UNIV
Dead Man's Eyes (+ stock) UNIV
See My Lawyer (see Akridge)
The Mummy's Curse (+ stock) UNIV
Beyond the Pecos (+ stock) UNIV
The House of Fear (+ stock) UNIV
Jungle Captive (+ stock) UNIV

1945

Under Western Skies (+ stock) UNIV
She Gets Her Man (see F. Skinner)
Tarzan and the Amazons RKO
Rockin' in the Rockies (+ stock) COL
The Power of the Whistler (+ stock) COL
The Fighting Guardsman (o: Reese) COL
Rhythm Round-Up (+ stock) COL
West of the Pecos (+ stock) RKO
Blonde from Brooklyn (+ stock) COL
The Falcon in San Francisco RKO
The Crime Doctor's Warning (+ stock) COL
Wanderer of the Wasteland RKO
Snafu (o: Reese) COL
A Game of Death (+ stock) RKO
Girl on the Spot UNIV
Tarzan and the Leopard Woman RKO

1946

The Falcon's Alibi (see Gold)
Perilous Holiday (+ stock) COL
The Cat Creeps (+ stock) UNIV
The Bamboo Blonde RKO
Renegades COL
Step by Step RKO
Sunset Pass (+ stock) RKO
Genius at Work (with Webb) RKO
Criminal Court RKO
Vacation in Reno RKO
Crime Doctor's Man Hunt (+ stock) COL
Dick Tracy vs. Cueball (with Ohman) RKO
San Quentin RKO
Alias Mr. Twilight (o: Reese) COL

1947

The Falcon's Adventure RKO
Blind Spot (+ stock) COL
Code of the West RKO
Trail Street RKO
Tarzan and the Huntress RKO
Born to Kill RKO
Dick Tracy's Dilemma RKO
Desperate RKO
Under the Tonto Rim RKO
Keeper of the Bees COL
Seven Keys to Baldpate RKO
The Sea Hound (serial; + stock) COL
Dick Tracy Meets Gruesome RKO
The Last Round-Up (see Dubin)
Wild Horse Mesa RKO
For You I Die FC

1948

T-Men (o: Cadkin) EL
Black Bart (see L. Stevens)
The Arizona Ranger RKO
Design for Death (doc.) RKO
Raw Deal EL
The Black Arrow COL
Four Faces West UA
Guns of Hate RKO
River Lady (o: Tamkin) UNIV
Return of the Bad Men RKO
Mystery in Mexico RKO
Northwest Stampede (o: Cadkin) EL
Variety Time RKO
Bodyguard RKO
Walk a Crooked Mile COL
Indian Agent RKO

1949

Gun Smugglers RKO
Brothers in the Saddle RKO
Bad Boy AA
The Clay Pigeon RKO
Rustlers RKO
The Big Cat EL
Roughshod (see Webb)
Follow Me Quietly (see Raab)
Stagecoach Kid RKO
The Doolins of Oklahoma (see Duning)
Savage Splendor (doc.) RKO
Black Magic UA
The Mysterious Desperado RKO
Masked Raiders RKO
Fighting Man of the Plains TCF
Riders of the Range RKO
The Threat RKO
Spotlight on Mexico (doc. short) RKO
Storm Over Wyoming RKO

1950

Davy Crockett, Indian Scout UA
Tarzan and the Slave Girl RKO
Fortunes of Captain Blood (o: Reese, H. Gilbert, Cadkin, Raab) COL
Armored Car Robbery RKO
Rider from Tucson RKO
The Cariboo Trail TCF
Bunco Squad RKO
Border Treasure RKO
Outrage RKO

Rio Grande Patrol RKO
Southside 1–1000 AA
Rogue River EL
Law of the Badlands RKO
Stage to Tucson (o: Reese, H. Gilbert) COL
Saddle Legion RKO
Jungle Headhunters (doc.) RKO

1951
Hunt the Man Down RKO
Santa Fe (o: Reese, H. Gilbert) COL
The Great Missouri Raid (o: Reese) PAR
Gun Play RKO
Best of the Badmen RKO
Pistol Harvest RKO
Roadblock RKO
Warpath (o: Reese) PAR
Hot Lead RKO
The Son of Dr. Jekyll COL
Last of the Wild West (short) RKO
The Whip Hand RKO
The Racket RKO
Fort Defiance UA
Silver City (o: Reese) PAR
Overland Telegraph RKO
Flaming Feather (o: Reese) PAR
Trail Guide RKO

1952
Another Man's Poison (U.S. release of 1951 British film) UA
The Pace That Thrills RKO
Tarzan's Savage Fury RKO
Target RKO
Denver & Rio Grande (o: Reese) PAR
The Half-Breed RKO
Desert Passage RKO
And Now Tomorrow WESTMINSTER
Hurricane Smith (o: Cailliet) PAR
Sky Full of Moon (o: R. Franklyn) MGM
The Savage (o: Cailliet) PAR
Kansas City Confidential UA

1953
Pony Express (o: Raab, Reese, Leipold) PAR
Raiders of the Seven Seas UA
Below the Sahara (doc.) RKO
Tarzan and the She-Devil RKO
The Sea Around Us (doc.) RKO
Inferno (o: E. Powell) TCF
Half a Hero (o: R. Franklyn) MGM
Arrowhead (o: Cailliet) PAR
The Diamond Queen (o: Cailliet) WB
Flight to Tangier (o: Cailliet) PAR

1954
Captain Kidd and the Slave Girl UA
Return to Treasure Island UA
Three Hours to Kill COL
Down Three Dark Streets UA
They Rode West COL
Africa Adventure (doc.) RKO
Quest of the Lost City (doc.) RKO

1955
Ten Wanted Men COL
Tarzan's Hidden Jungle RKO
Rage at Dawn RKO
The Marauders (o: R. Franklyn, Reese) MGM
Tall Man Riding (o: Reese) WB
The Living Swamp (doc. short) TCF
Texas Lady RKO
Lawless Street COL

1956
The Animal World (doc.) WB

1957
Last of the Badmen AA
Pawnee REP
The Black Scorpion (o: Shefter) WB
Stopover Tokyo (o: E. Powell, Levene) TCF
The Story of Mankind WB

1958
The Hunters TCF

1962
Five Weeks in a Balloon (o: Reese, Cutner) TCF

1964
Island of the Blue Dolphins UNIV

(In collaboration with Shefter:)

1956
Scandal, Inc. REP
The Desperados Are in Town TCF

1957
5 Steps to Danger UA
Gun Duel in Durango UA
Kronos TCF
She Devil TCF
Monkey on My Back UA
The Deerslayer TCF
Ghost Diver TCF
Hell Ship Mutiny REP

1958
Ambush at Cimarron Pass TCF
Cattle Empire TCF
The Fly TCF
Sierra Baron TCF
It! The Terror from Beyond Space UA
The Fiend Who Walked the West TCF
Villa TCF
Wind Across the Everglades WB

Hong Kong Confidential UA
Machete UA

1959
The Cosmic Man AA
The Sad Horse (o: Cutner) TCF
Gigantis the Fire Monster WB
The Big Circus (ac: Cutner) AA
The Miracle of the Hills (ac: H. Jackson) TCF
Return of the Fly (ac: Webb; o: Cutner) TCF
Counterplot UA
A Dog's Best Friend UA
Virgin Sacrifice R.C.I.P.
A Dog of Flanders TCF

1960
Three Came to Kill UA
The Music Box Kid UA
Cage of Evil (ac: H. Jackson) UA
The Lost World (ac: H. Jackson, Cutner; o: Cutner, Reese) TCF
The Police Dog Story UA
Tess of the Storm Country TCF
Five Guns to Tombstone (ac: H. Jackson) UA

1961
The Long Rope TCF
Frontier Uprising UA
Operation Bottleneck UA
Misty (o: Reese) TCF
Gun Fight UA
The Big Show (ac: Reese) TCF
Voyage to the Bottom of the Sea (o: Reese) TCF
Pirates of Tortuga (o: Reese) TCF
Wild Harvest SUTTON

1962
Jack the Giant Killer UA
Young Guns of Texas TCF

1963
Cattle King MGM
Harbor Lights TCF
Thunder Island TCF

1964
The Last Man on Earth AIP

1965
Motorpsycho EVE

1966
Faster, Pussycat! Kill! Kill! EVE
The Bubble ARCH OBOLER

1967
Texas Today (short) PAR
Texas Longhorns (short) PAR

1970
The Christine Jorgensen Story UA

SAXON, DAVID

1969
That Tender Touch RUSSEL VINCENT

SCHAEFER, HAL

1953
Gentlemen Prefer Blondes (with Harline, L. Newman, H. Spencer) TCF

1954
There's No Business Like Show Business (see A. Newman)

1965
The Money Trap MGM

SCHAEFER, WILLIAM

1966
To the Shores of Hell CROWN

SCHAEFER, WILLIS

1951
The American Cowboy (doc. short) FORD MOTOR CO.

SCHAEFFER, PIERRE

1948
The Petrified Dog (short) SIDNEY PETERSON

SCHARF, STUART

1965
What Is a Tree? (short) GEORGE & SHERRY ZABRISKIE

1967
One Fine Day (see B. Lee)

SCHARF, WALTER

1933
Day Dreams (short) EDUCATIONAL
Poppin' the Cork (short) EDUCATIONAL

1937
Nancy Steele Is Missing (see Buttolph)
You Can't Have Everything (with Mockridge; ac: Maxwell, Buttolph) TCF
Thin Ice (see Buttolph)
Ali Baba Goes to Town (see R. Bennett)

1938
Sally, Irene and Mary (see A. Lange)
Josette TCF

1939
The Three Musketeers (see Maxwell)
The Return of the Cisco Kid (with Toch, Buttolph, Maxwell) TCF
Frontier Marshal (see Kaylin)

1940
Hit Parade of 1941 REP

1941
Las Vegas Nights (with Boutelje) PAR
Sis Hopkins (with M. Glickman) REP
Puddin' Head (with M. Glickman) REP
Henry Aldrich for President (+ stock) PAR
Mercy Island (see Feuer)
Louisiana Purchase (see Dolan)
1942
Holiday Inn (see Dolan)
Henry Aldrich, Editor (see Shuken)
Youth on Parade REP
The Glass Key (see V. Young)
Secrets of the Underground (with M. Glickman) REP
Ice-Capades Revue (with Skiles) REP
London Blackout Murders REP
Johnny Doughboy REP
1943
Hit Parade of 1943 REP
Chatterbox REP
Shantytown REP
Someone to Remember REP
Thumbs Up REP
Sleepy Lagoon REP
Nobody's Darling (with Skiles) REP
In Old Oklahoma (ac: Skiles, M. Glickman) REP
Casanova in Burlesque (with Skiles) REP
1944
The Fighting Seabees (ac: M. Glickman, Skiles, Webb) REP
The Lady and the Monster (with Skiles) REP
Atlantic City (with Dubin) REP
Brazil (with Parrish) REP
Lake Placid Serenade (with Maxwell, Dubin) REP
1945
Earl Carroll Vanities (with Dubin; o: Parrish) REP
The Cheaters REP
Mexicana (with Dubin) REP
Dakota (ac: Butts, Dubin, M. Glickman) REP
1946
Murder in the Music Hall (with M. Glickman, Plumb) REP
I've Always Loved You REP
1948
Casbah UNIV
Are You With It? (+ stock) UNIV
The Saxon Charm (o: Tamkin) UNIV
The Countess of Monte Cristo (o: Tamkin) UNIV
Mexican Hayride (+ stock) UNIV
1949
Red Canyon UNIV
City Across the River (+ stock) UNIV
Take One False Step UNIV
Yes Sir, That's My Baby UNIV
1950
South Sea Sinner UNIV
Buccaneer's Girl UNIV
Curtain Call at Cactus Creek UNIV
Sierra (+ stock) UNIV
Spy Hunt (+ stock) UNIV
Peggy (with F. Skinner; o: Tamkin; + stock) UNIV
Winchester '73 (mt; + stock) UNIV
Deported (o: Tamkin) UNIV
1951
Two Tickets to Broadway (o: Shuken, Cutner) RKO
1952
Hans Christian Andersen (o: Moross, Shuken, Cutner) GOLDWYN
1953
The French Line RKO
1954
Living It Up (o: Levene, Van Cleave, Shuken) PAR
Three Ring Circus (o: Van Cleave, Shuken, Cutner) PAR
1955
You're Never Too Young (o: Shuken, Cutner, Hayes) PAR
Artists and Models (o: Shuken, Hayes) PAR
1956
The Court Jester (see Schoen)
Timetable UA
The Birds and the Bees (o: Shuken, Hayes, Van Cleave) PAR
Three for Jamie Dawn AA
Hollywood or Bust (o: Shuken, Hayes) PAR
Bundle of Joy RKO
1957
Three Violent People (o: Shuken, Hayes) PAR
Loving You (o: Shuken, Hayes, Van Cleave) PAR
The Joker Is Wild (o: Shuken, Hayes) PAR
The Sad Sack (o: Shuken, Hayes, Van Cleave) PAR
1958
King Creole (o: Shuken, Hayes) PAR
Rock-a-Bye Baby PAR
The Geisha Boy PAR
1959
Don't Give Up the Ship (o: Shuken, Hayes, Van Cleave) PAR

1960
The Bellboy (o: Shuken, Hayes, Van Cleave) PAR
Cinderfella (o: Shuken, Hayes) PAR
1961
The Ladies' Man (o: Shuken, Hayes) PAR
The Errand Boy (o: Shuken, Hayes) PAR
Pocketful of Miracles (o: Grau) UA
1962
Harold Lloyd's World of Comedy (compilation film; o: Shuken, Hayes) CONTINENTAL
It's Only Money (o: Shuken, Hayes) PAR
My Six Loves PAR
1963
The Nutty Professor PAR
Harold Lloyd's Funny Side of Life (compilation film) JANUS
1964
Honeymoon Hotel MGM
Where Love Has Gone PAR
1965
Tickle Me AA
1968
Funny Girl (o: Shuken, Hayes, H. Spencer) COL
1969
Pendulum COL
If It's Tuesday, This Must Be Belgium UA
1970
The Cheyenne Social Club NG

SCHEIB, PHILIP A.
1931
The Struggle (md) GRIFFITH
Cartoons (WB)
1931
'Neath the Bababa Tree
Put on the Spout
Cartoons (TERRYTOONS)
[Terrytoons often incorporated character names into its official titles, e.g., *Mighty Mouse in The Jail Break* and *Heckle and Jeckle, the Talking Magpies, in Cat Trouble*. These prefixes have usually been omitted in this filmography, and the titles appear as *The Jail Break* (1946) and *Cat Trouble* (1947).]
1930
Bully Beef
Chop Suey
Codfish Balls
Dutch Treat
French Fried
Fried Chicken
Golf Nuts
Hungarian Goulash
Irish Stew
Jumping Beans
Kangaroo Steak
Monkey Meat
Pigskin Capers
Salt Water Taffy
Scotch Highball
Swiss Cheese
1931
Aladdin's Lamp
Around the World
The Black Spider
Blues
By the Sea
Canadian Capers
The Champ
China
Clowning
Club Sandwich
A Day to Live
The Explorer
The Fireman's Bride
Go West, Big Boy
Her First Egg
Jazz Mad
Jesse and James
Jingle Bells
The Lorelei
Popcorn
Quack, Quack
Razzberries
Sing Sing Song
The Sultan's Cat
Summer Time
2000 B.C.
1932
Bluebeard's Brother
Bull-Ero
Burlesque
Cocky Cockroach
College Spirit
Farmer Al Falfa's Ape Girl
Farmer Al Falfa's Bedtime Story
Farmer Al Falfa's Birthday Party
The Forty Thieves
Hollywood Diet
Hook and Ladder No. 1
Ireland or Bust
The Mad King
Noah's Outing
Peg Leg Pete
Play Ball
Radio Girl
Romance

Sherman Was Right
Southern Rhythm
The Spider Talks
Spring Is Here
Toyland
The Villain's Curse
Woodland
Ye Olde Songs

1933

The Banker's Daughter
Beanstalk Jack
Cinderella
Down on the Levee
Fanny in the Lion's Den
Fanny's Wedding Day
Grand Uproar
A Gypsy Fiddler
Hansel and Gretel
Hypnotic Eyes
In Venice
The Jealous Lover
King Zilch
Little Boy Blue
Oh! Susanna
The Oil Can Mystery
Pick-Necking
The Pirate Ship
Robin Hood
Romeo and Juliet
Shipwrecked Brothers
The Sunny South
The Tale of a Shirt
Tropical Fish
The Village Blacksmith
Who Killed Cock-Robin?

1934

The Black Sheep
Busted Blossoms
The Dog Show
Holland Days
Hot Sands
Irish Sweepstakes
Jack's Shack
Jail Birds
Joe's Lunch Wagon
Just a Clown
The King's Daughter
The Last Straw
The Lion's Friend
A Mad House
The Magic Fish
Mice in Council
My Lady's Garden
The Owl and the Pussycat
Pandora
Rip Van Winkle
See the World
Slow But Sure
South Pole or Bust
The Three Bears
Tom, Tom, the Piper's Son
Why Mules Leave Home

1935

Aladdin's Lamp
Amateur Night
Birdland
The Bull Fight
Chain Letters
Circus Days
Fireman, Save My Child
The First Snow
Five Puplets
Flying Oil
Foiled Again
Football
The Foxy Fox
Hey Diddle Diddle
A June Bride
King Looney XIV
The Mayflower
Moans and Groans
A Modern Red Riding Hood
The Moth and the Spider
Old Dog Tray
Opera Night
Peg Leg Pete the Pirate
Southern Horse-pitality
What a Night
Ye Olde Toy Shop

1936

The Alpine Yodeler
Barnyard Amateurs
A Battle Royal
A Bully Frog
The Busy Bee
Cats in a Bag
Farmer Al Falfa and the Runt
Farmer Al Falfa's Prize Package
Farmer Al Falfa's 20th Anniversary
The Feud
The Health Farm
Home Town Olympics
The Hot Spell
Kiko and the Honey Bears
Kiko Foils the Fox
The 19th Hole Club
Off to China
Puddy the Pup and the Gypsies

Robin Hood in an Arrow Escape
Rolling Stones
The Sailor's Home
Skunked Again
Sunken Treasures
A Tough Egg
The Western Trail
A Wolf in Cheap Clothing

1937

Barnyard Boss
The Big Game Hunt
The Billy Goat's Whiskers
Bug Carnival
A Close Shave
The Dancing Bear
The Dog and the Bone
Flying South
The Hay Ride
The Homeless Pup
Kiko's Cleaning Day
The Mechanical Cow
Ozzie Ostrich Comes to Town
The Paper Hangers
Pink Elephants
Play Ball
Puddy the Pup in the Book Shop
Puddy's Coronation
Red Hot Music
Salty McGuire
The Saw Mill Mystery
School Birds
The Timid Rabbit
The Tin Can Tourist
Trailer Life
The Villain Still Pursued Her

1938

The Big Top
Bugs Beetle and His Orchestra
Chris Columbo
Devil of the Deep
Doomsday
Eliza Runs Again
The Frame-Up
Gandy the Goose
The Glass Slipper
The Goose Flies High
Happy and Lucky
Here's to Good Old Jail
His Day Off
Housewife Herman
Just Ask Jupiter
The Last Indian
The Lion Hunt
Maid in China
Milk for Baby
Mrs. O'Leary's Cow
A Mountain Romance
The Newcomer
Robinson Crusoe's Broadcast
The Stranger Rides Again
String Bean Jack
The Village Blacksmith
The Wolf's Side of the Story

1939

Africa Squawks
Barnyard Baseball
Barnyard Egg-citement
A Bully Romance
The Cuckoo Bird
The First Robin
Frozen Feet
G Man Jitters
The Golden West
The Hitch-Hiker
Hook, Line and Sinker
The Ice Pond
Nick's Coffee Pot
The Nutty Network
The Old Fire Horse
One Gun Gary in the Nick of Time
One Mouse in a Million
The Orphan Duck
The Owl and the Pussy Cat
The Prize Guest
Sheep in the Meadow
Their Last Bean
The Three Bears
Two Headed Giant
The Watchdog
A Wicky, Wacky Romance

1940

All's Well That Ends Well
Billy Mouse's Akwakade
Catnip Capers
Club Life in the Stone Age
A Dog in a Mansion
Edgar Runs Again
Happy Haunting Grounds
Hare and Hounds
Harvest Time
How Wet Was My Ocean
It Must Be Love
Just a Little Bull
Landing of the Pilgrims
Love in a Cottage
The Lucky Duck
The Magic Pencil
Much Ado About Nothing

Plane Goofy
Prof. Offkeysky
Rover's Rescue
Rupert the Runt
The Snow Man
Swiss Ski Yodelers
The Temperamental Lion
Touchdown Demons
Wot's All th' Shootin' Fer

1941
The Baby Seal
Back to the Soil
The Bird Tower
Bringing Home the Bacon
A Dog's Dream
Fishing Made Easy
Flying Fever
The Frozen North
Good Old Irish Tunes
Hairless Hector
The Home Guard
Horsefly Opera
The Ice Carnival
The Magic Shell
Mississippi Swing
The Old Oaken Bucket
The One Man Navy
Slap Happy Hunters
Twelve O'Clock and All Ain't Well
Uncle Joey
Uncle Joey Comes to Town
Welcome Little Stranger
What a Little Sneeze Will Do
What Happens at Night
When Knights Were Bold
A Yarn About Yarn

1942
All About Dogs
All Out for "V"
Barnyard WAAC
The Big Build-Up
Cat Meets Mouse
Doing Their Bit
Eat Me Kitty Eight to the Bar
Frankenstein's Cat
Funny Bunny Business
Happy Circus Days
Ickle Meets Pickle
Life with Fido
Lights Out
The Mouse of Tomorrow
Neck and Neck
Night Life in the Army
Oh Gentle Spring
The Outpost
School Daze
Sham Battle Shenanigans
The Stork's Mistake
Tire Trouble
A Torrid Toreador
Tricky Business
Wilful Willie

1943
Aladdin's Lamp
Barnyard Blackout
Camouflage
Down with Cats
He Dood It Again
The Hopeful Donkey
Keep 'Em Growing
The Last Round-Up
The Lion and the Mouse
Mopping Up
Pandora's Box
Patriotic Pooches
Scrap for Victory
Shipyard Symphony
Somewhere in Egypt
Somewhere in the Pacific
Super Mouse Rides Again
Yokel Duck Makes Good

1944
The Butcher of Seville
Carmen's Veranda
The Cat Came Back
The Champion of Justice
A Day in June
Dear Old Switzerland
Eliza on the Ice
The Frog and the Princess
Gandy's Dream Girl
The Ghost Town
The Green Line
The Helicopter
Mighty Mouse and the Two Barbers
Mighty Mouse at the Circus
Mighty Mouse Meets Jekyll and Hyde Cat
My Boy Johnny
The Sultan's Birthday
Wolf! Wolf!
A Wolf's Tale
The Wreck of the Hesperus

1945
Ants in Your Pantry
The Exterminator
Fishermen's Luck
The Fox and the Duck
Gypsy Life

Krakatoa
Mighty Mouse and the Kilkenny Cats
Mighty Mouse and the Pirates
Mighty Mouse and the Wolf
Mighty Mouse Meets Bad Bad Bill Bunion
The Mosquito
Mother Goose Nightmare
Port of Missing Mice
Post War Inventions
Raiding the Raiders
The Silver Streak
Smoky Joe
Swooning the Swooners
The Watchdog
Who's Who in the Jungle

1946

Beanstalk Jack
The Crackpot King
Dinky Finds a Home
The Electronic Mouse Trap
Fortune Hunters
The Golden Hen
The Housing Problem
It's All in the Stars
The Jail Break
The Johnstown Flood
Mighty Mouse and the Hep Cat
My Old Kentucky Home
Peace-Time Football
The Snow Man
Svengali's Cat
The Talking Magpies
Throwing the Bull
The Tortoise Wins Again
The Trojan Horse
The Uninvited Pests
The Wicked Wolf
Winning the West

1947

Cat Trouble
Crying Wolf
A Date for Dinner
The Dead End Cats
A Fight to the Finish
The First Snow
Fishing by the Sea
Flying South
Happy Go Lucky
The Hitch Hikers
The Intruders
Lazy Little Beaver
McDougal's Rest Farm
Mexican Baseball
Mighty Mouse Meets Deadeye Dick
One Note Tony
The Sky Is Falling
The Super Salesman
Swiss Cheese Family Robinson
The Wolf's Pardon

1948

Felix the Fox
The Feudin' Hillbillies
Free Enterprise
Gandy Goose and the Chipper Chipmunk
Goony Golfers
The Hard Boiled Egg
Hounding the Hares
Love's Labor Won
The Magic Slipper
Magpie Madness
Mighty Mouse and the Magician
The Mysterious Stranger
Mystery in the Moonlight
Out Again, In Again
The Power of Thought
The Racket Buster
Seeing Ghosts
A Sleepless Night
Taming the Cat
Triple Trouble
The Witch's Cat
The Wooden Indian

1949

Aladdin's Lamp
The Catnip Gang
A Cold Romance
Comic Book Land
The Covered Pushcart
Dancing Shoes
Flying Cups and Saucers
Happy Landing
Hula Hula Land
The Kitten Sitter
The Lion Hunt
The Lyin' Lion
Mrs. Jones' Rest Farm
Paint Pot Symphony
The Perils of Pearl Pureheart
Sourpuss in Dingbat Land
Stop, Look and Listen
The Stowaways
A Truckload of Trouble

1950

Aesop's Fable—Foiling the Fox
All This and Rabbit Stew
Anti-Cats
Beauty on the Beach
The Beauty Shop

Better Late Than Never
Cat Happy
The Dog Show
Dream Walking
The Fox Hunt
If Cats Could Sing
King Tut's Tomb
Law and Order
A Merry Chase
Mother Goose's Birthday Party
Mouse and Garden
The Red Headed Monkey
Rival Romeos
Sour Grapes
Squirrel Crazy
Stage Struck
Sunny Italy
Three Is a Crowd
Wide Open Spaces
Woodman Spare That Tree

1951

Aesop's Fable—Golden Egg Goosie
Beaver Trouble
Bulldozing the Bull
A Cat's Tale
City Slicker
The Elephant Mouse
Goons from the Moon
The Haunted Cat
The Helpful Genie
Injun Trouble
Little Problems
The Mechanical Bird
Movie Madness
Musical Madness
Papa's Day of Rest
Papa's Little Helpers
Pastry Panic
Prehistoric Perils
The Rainmakers
Seasick Sailors
Seaside Adventure
'Sno Fun
Songs of Erin
Spring Fever
Steeple Jacks
A Swiss Miss
Tall Timber Tale

1952

Aesop's Fable—Happy Valley
Flat Foot Fledgling
Flipper Frolics
Flop Secret
The Foolish Duckling
Good Mousekeeping
Hair Cut-Ups
Hansel and Gretel
The Happy Cobblers
Happy Holland
Hero for a Day
House Busters
Hypnotized
Little Anglers
Moose on the Loose
Mouse Meets Bird
The Mysterious Cowboy
Nice Doggy
Off to the Opera
Picnic with Papa
Pill Peddlers
Sink or Swim
Snappy Snapshots
A Soapy Opera
Thrifty Cubs
Time Gallops On
Wise Quacks

1953

Aesop's Fable—Sparky, the Firefly
Bargain Daze
Blind Date
Featherweight Champ
Friday the 13th
Growing Pains
The Helpless Hippo
Hot Rods
How to Keep Cool
How to Relax
Log Rollers
Mouse Menace
Nonsense Newsreel
Open House
The Orphan Egg
Playful Puss
Plumber's Helpers
The Reluctant Pup
Runaway Mouse
Spare the Rod
Ten Pin Terrors
The Timid Scarecrow
When Mousehood Was in Flower

1954

Arctic Rivals
Blue Plate Symphony
The Cat's Revenge
A Howling Success
Pet Problems
Prescription for Percy
Pride of the Yard
The Reformed Wolf
Satisfied Customers

The Tall Tale Teller
A Yokohama Yankee

1955

Aesop's Fable—The First Flying Fish
African Jungle Hunt
Baffling Bunnies
Barnyard Actor
Bird Symphony
The Clockmaker's Dog
Daddy's Little Darling
Duck Fever
Foxed by a Fox
Good Deed Daly
Hep Mother Hubbard
An Igloo for Two
The Last Mouse of Hamelin
The Little Red Hen
Miami Maniacs
No Sleep for Percy
Park Avenue Pussycat
Phony News Flashes
Scouts to the Rescue
Uranium Blues

1956

The Brave Little Brave
Cloak and Stagger
A Hare-Breadth Finish
Lucky Dog
Oceans of Love
Pirate's Gold
Police Dogged

1957

The Bone Ranger
Bum Steer
Clint Clobber's Cat
Gag Buster
Gaston Is Here
Gaston's Baby
It's a Living
The Juggler of Our Lady
Love Is Blind
Shove Thy Neighbor
Springtime for Clobber
Topsy TV

1958

Camp Clobber
Dustcap Doormat
Gaston Go Home
Gaston's Easel Life
Old Mother Clobber
Sick, Sick Sidney
Sidney's Family Tree
Signed, Sealed and Clobbered

1959

Another Day, Another Doormat
Clobber's Ballet Ache
The Fabulous Fireworks Family
The Flamboyant Arms
Foofle's Picnic
Foofle's Train Ride
Gaston's Mama Lisa
Hashimoto-San
Hide and Go Sidney
The Leaky Faucet
The Minute and 1/2 Man
The Misunderstood Giant
Outer Space Visitor
The Tale of a Dog
Wild Life

1960

Aesop's Fable—The Tiger King
Cat Alarm
Daniel Boone, Jr.
Deep Sea Doodle
The Famous Ride
Hearts and Glowers
House of Hashimoto
The Littlest Bully
Mint Men
The Mysterious Package
Night Life in Tokyo
So Sorry, Pussycat
Stunt Men
Thousand Smile Check-Up
Tin Pan Alley Cat
Trapeze Pleeze
Tusk, Tusk
Two Ton Baby Sitter
The Wayward Hat

1962

Home Life

1963

A Bell for Philadelphia

1964

Brother from Outer Space

1966

Messed Up Movie Makers

SCHENK, ELLIOT

1915

The Battle Cry of Peace (premiere)
VITAGRAPH

SCHERTZINGER, VICTOR L.

1915

The Winged Idol (see Nurnberger)
The Golden Claw (see Nurnberger)
Between Men (see Nurnberger)
The Edge of the Abyss (with Nurnberger)
TRIANGLE

1916
The Beckoning Flame TRIANGLE
Peggy TRIANGLE
The Conqueror (with Nowell) TRIANGLE
D'Artagnan (see Nurnberger)
Hell's Hinges TRIANGLE
Civilization THOMAS H. INCE
1917
The Princess of the Dark THOMAS H. INCE
1919
Forbidden Fire (premiere; later released as *Sahara;* see Riesenfeld) J. PARKER READ, JR.
Other Men's Wives THOMAS H. INCE
1922
Robin Hood UA
1924
Dorothy Vernon of Haddon Hall UA
1925
Zander the Great METRO-GOLDWYN
The Pinch Hitter ASSOCIATED EXHIBITORS
1928
Outcast (theme; mt: Hajos; + stock) FN
1931
The Woman Between RKO
Caught Plastered RKO
Friends and Lovers RKO
1932
Strange Justice RKO
1933
Cocktail Hour COL
1934
Beloved (with H. Jackson) UNIV
One Night of Love (with Silvers, H. Jackson) COL
1935
Love Me Forever (with Silvers, R. Bassett) COL

SCHICKELE, PETER
1965
Israel (doc. short) IFF
Poland (doc. short) IFF
1966
Crazy Quilt JOHN KORTY
1967
Big People—Little People (short) JOHN KORTY
1968
Funnyman JOHN KORTY
Texas Hemisphere (short) ?

SCHIFRIN, LALO
1963
Rhino! MGM
1964
Joy House MGM
Once a Thief MGM
1965
Gone with the Wave (doc.) PHIL WILSON
The Cincinnati Kid MGM
Dark Intruder UNIV
The Liquidator MGM
1966
Blindfold UNIV
Way . . . Way Out! TCF
The Venetian Affair MGM
Murderers' Row (o: Hazard) COL
1967
Cool Hand Luke WB
Sullivan's Empire UNIV
Who's Minding the Mint? (o: Hazard) COL
The President's Analyst PAR
Sol Madrid (o: Del Barrio) MGM
The Fox WB
Where Angels Go . . . Trouble Follows! (o: Hazard) COL
1968
The Brotherhood PAR
Coogan's Bluff UNIV
Bullitt WB
Hell in the Pacific CR
1969
Che! TCF
Eye of the Cat UNIV
1970
Pussycat, Pussycat, I Love You UA
Kelly's Heroes (o: Hazard) MGM
WUSA (o: Hazard) PAR
Imago EMERSON
I Love My Wife UNIV
A Long Way from Nowhere (doc. short) ROBERT ALLER

SCHILDKRET, R.
1928
The Battle of the Sexes (see Riesenfeld)

SCHILLER, WILLIAM
1929
The Phantom of the Opera (see Breil, 1925)
1934
City Limits (see Wallace)
[Also worked as an orchestrator.]

SCHMIDT, ADOLPH
1916
The Dumb Girl of Portici UNIV

SCHMIDT, HARVEY
1964
A Texas Romance, 1909 (short) ROBERT BENTON, ELINOR JONES

SCHMIDT, KENNETH
1962
Come with Me My Brother (short) WOMEN'S AMERICAN ORT

SCHMOLL, JOSEPH
1955
Wine of Morning BOB JONES U.

SCHOEN, VIC
1943
Mister Big (mt) UNIV
1956
The Court Jester (with W. Scharf; mt: Van Cleave) PAR

SCHOOP, PAUL
1941
Here Comes Mr. Jordan (see Hollander)

SCHRAGER, RUDY
1939
Stanley and Livingstone (see Silvers)
Hollywood Cavalcade (with Mockridge; ac: Buttolph) TCF
Swanee River (with R. Bennett, Buttolph, Mockridge) TCF
1942
Private Snuffy Smith MON
1944
Career Girl PRC
Take It Big PAR
Dixie Jamboree PRC
The National Barn Dance (with Grau, Leipold) PAR
1945
Tokyo Rose PAR
1946
People Are Funny PAR
Deadline for Murder TCF
Swamp Fire PAR
Strange Journey TCF
1947
Fear in the Night PAR
The Guilty MON
Gunfighters (ac: Carbonara; o: H. Gilbert) COL
High Tide MON
Monsieur Verdoux (see C. Chaplin)
Roses Are Red TCF
1948
Sleep, My Love UA
Perilous Waters MON
Coroner Creek COL
Strike It Rich AA
1949
The Green Promise RKO
The Great Dan Patch UA
The Sundowners (with Raab; o: Nussbaum, Raab, Parrish) EL
1950
The Eagle and the Hawk PAR
The Iroquois Trail UA
High Lonesome (ac: Carbonara) EL
1960
The Last Voyage (a of music by Andrew and Virginia Stone) MGM
Shorts (PAR)
1944
Fun Time (with Bradshaw, Wallace, Lilley)
Halfway to Heaven (with Grau)
Bonnie Lassie (m&e: Bradshaw)
Star Bright
1945
The Isle of Tabu
Boogie Woogie (m&e: Lilley)
You Hit the Spot (with Simeone)
Naughty Nanette (with Bradshaw)
1946
A Tale of Two Cafés (with Lilley, Bradshaw)
Trailers
1931
Safe in Hell WB
1945
Murder, He Says PAR
1948
The Paleface PAR

SCHRAMM, RUDOLF
1947
Nanook of the North (sound reissue of 1922 doc.) ROBERT FLAHERTY

SCHULLER, GUNTHER
1962
The Gift (doc.) HERB DANSKA
Journey to the Stars (doc. short) SPACEARIUM
1963
Yesterday in Fact (short) ?

SCHULMAN, JIM
1969
Promises to Keep (doc. short) NEA

SCHUMAN, WILLIAM
1944
Steeltown (doc. short) WILLARD VAN DYKE
1957
The Earth Is Born (doc. short) LIFE MAGAZINE

SCHUMANN, WALTER
1947
Buck Private Come Home (o: Tamkin) UNIV
The Wistful Widow of Wagon Gap (o: Tamkin; ac: L. Stevens, F. Skinner, Salter) UNIV
1948
The Noose Hangs High (o: A. Morton) EL
1949
Africa Screams UA
1954
Dragnet (o: N. Scott) WB
1955
The Night of the Hunter (o: A. Morton) UA

SCHUTT, ARTHUR
1941
Road Show (see Stoll)
[Also worked as an orchestrator.]

SCHWARTZ, ABE
1936
Love and Sacrifice (Yiddish language) JEWISH TALKING PICTURES

SCHWARTZ, ROBERT
1968
The Wicked Die Slow CANNON

SCHWARZWALD, MILTON
1934
World in Revolt (doc.) MENTONE
1939
Snow Follies (short) UNIV

SCIANNI, JOSEPH
1964
Another Time, Another Voice (short) LEWIS JACOBS

SCOLOFF, NEKI
1949
I Married a Savage FUTURITY

SCOTT, BOBBY
1969
Slaves CONTINENTAL
1970
Joe CANNON
Who Says I Can't Ride a Rainbow! TRANSVUE

SCOTT, JOSEPH
1969
Pinocchio (U.S. release of 1967 German film) CHILDHOOD PRODS.

SCOTT, NATHAN
[All for Republic unless otherwise noted.]
1946
Rendezvous with Annie (see Dubin)
Affairs of Geraldine
Earl Carroll Sketchbook
Out California Way
The Magnificent Rogue (with M. Glickman)
1947
Calendar Girl
Robin Hood of Texas (with M. Glickman)
Wyoming (with Gold)
Driftwood
1948
Campus Honeymoon
The Inside Story
Angel in Exile
Grand Canyon Trail
Angel on the Amazon
1949
Wake of the Red Witch (o: S. Wilson)
The Red Menace (o: S. Wilson)
Brimstone (o: S. Wilson)
The Kid from Cleveland (o: S. Wilson)
The Golden Stallion (o: S. Wilson)
1950
Singing Guns (o: S. Wilson, Arnaud)
The Avengers (o: S. Wilson)
Surrender (o: S. Wilson)
California Passage (o: S. Wilson)
Trail of Robinhood (o: S. Wilson)
1951
Heart of the Rockies
Lady Possessed (o: S. Wilson)
Montana Belle (o: Butts, S. Wilson) RKO
1952
Oklahoma Annie (o: S. Wilson)
Hoodlum Empire (o: S. Wilson)
1961
X-15 (o: Sendrey) UA

SCOTT, RANDY
1970
101 Acts of Love FILMS INT'L.

SCOTT, RAYMOND
1958
Never Love a Stranger (o: Van Cleave) AA
1959
The Pusher UA

SCOTT, TOM
1954
Summer Sequence JOE SLEVIN

SCOTT, TONY
1959
The New Girl (short) ON FILM

SEBESKY, DON
1965
Time Piece (short) MUPPETS, INC.
1970
The People Next Door EMBASSY

SECUNDA, SHOLOM
1929
East Side Sadie WORLDART
1931
Eli Eli (short) JUDEA FILMS
An Evening in a Jewish Camp (short) JUDEA FILMS
The Jewish Melody (short) JUDEA FILMS
Sailor's Sweetheart (short) JUDEA FILMS
Unsana Takoff (short) JUDEA FILMS
1933
Laughter Through Tears (U.S. release of 1928 Yiddish language Russian film) WORLDKINO
1939
Kol Nidre (Yiddish language) CINEMA SERVICE
Tevya (Yiddish language) MAYMON FILMS
Motl, the Operator (Yiddish language) CINEMA SERVICE
1940
The Jewish Melody (Yiddish language) CINEMA SERVICE
Eli Eli (Yiddish language) CINEMA SERVICE
Her Second Mother (Yiddish language) CINEMA SERVICE
1941
Mazel Tov, Jews (Yiddish language; with Olshanetsky) CINEMA SERVICE
1950
God, Man, and Devil AARON FILMS

SEGÁLL, BERNARDO
1950
Congolaise (doc.) FC
1959
The Great St. Louis Bank Robbery (o: H. Kay) UA
1964
The Luck of Ginger Coffey CONTINENTAL
1966
Hallucination Generation AIP
1967
Custer of the West CR
1970
Loving (o: Byers, Levene) COL
Shorts
1950
The Desperate Heart WALTER STRATE
Honolulu (doc.) UNITED AIR LINES
1963
The Air Force on Canvas (doc.) PELICAN FILMS
1964
The Tale of Truthful George OWEN MURPHY PRODS.
Hope Is Eternal ?
Sunday Lark CRESCENDO FILMS
1969
Bartleby ENCYCLOPAEDIA BRITANNICA

SEIDEL, EMIL
1943
Silver Skates MON

SELDEN, EDGAR
1912
Odyssey (U.S. release of Italian short film) MONOPOL

SELETSKY, HAROLD
1966
A Nose (an. short) PELICAN FILMS

SELINSKY, WLADIMIR
1952
More Than Meets the Eye (cartoon) UPA

SEMMLER, ALEXANDER
1949
Game Birds (doc. short) RKO PATHÉ
1961
The Legend of Rudolph Valentino JANUS
1964
The Minnesota Story (doc. short) MARTIN BOVEY, JR.

SENDREY, ALBERT
1946
The Hoodlum Saint (see N. Shilkret)

1947
Fiesta (see J. Green)
1948
Big City (see Perl)
On an Island with You (see Stoll)
A Date with Judy (see Stoll)
Hills of Home (see Stothart)
The Three Musketeers (see Stothart)
The Kissing Bandit (see Stoll)
1949
Ambush (see Kopp)
1950
The Yellow Cab Man (see Bradley)
The Outriders (see A. Previn)
Duchess of Idaho (see Stoll)
The Toast of New Orleans (see Stoll)
Two Weeks with Love (see Stoll)
Watch the Birdie (see Stoll)
1951
Royal Wedding (ac: J. Green, Salinger) MGM
Father's Little Dividend MGM
Across the Wide Missouri (see D. Raksin)
1952
Skirts Ahoy! (see Stoll)
Glory Alley (see Stoll)
The Rose Bowl Story (see Skiles)
1953
Kansas Pacific (ac: Skiles) AA
Small Town Girl (see A. Previn)
Fast Company (see Colombo)
A Slight Case of Larceny (see Colombo)
Dangerous When Wet (see Stoll)
Latin Lovers (see Stoll)
Easy to Love (see Stoll)
1954
Gypsy Colt (see R. Kopp)
Rose Marie (see Stoll)
Flame and the Flesh (see Stoll)
The Student Prince (see Stoll)
Athena (see Stoll)
1956
Meet Me in Las Vegas (see Stoll)
1957
Let's Be Happy (with Nicholas Brodszky) AA
Raintree County (see J. Green)
1962
The Hook (see Adler)
1966
Moonwolf (see H. Price)
1968
Hello Down There (adaptation of music by Jeff Barry) PAR
[Also a prolific arranger and orchestrator.]

SENTESI, JOHN
1951
Stop That Cab LIPPERT

SEVERI, GINO
1923
Hunting Big Game in Africa with Gun and Camera (doc.) AFRICAN EXPEDITION CORP.

SHAINDLIN, JACK
[He was a composer who also operated a music library service from the 1930s to the 1960s, providing music for hundreds of shorts and documentaries produced in the East for Universal, RKO, Columbia, 20th Century–Fox, and many other companies. From 1942–1951 he supplied music for *The March of Time,* employing ghostwriters such as Robert McBride and even Bernard Herrmann, who stated that "for years I wrote piles of music every week for *The March of Time.*" It is both pointless and impossible to list all his films, but following are the documentary features on which he is credited as musical director or co-composer.]
1942
We Are the Marines (with Frederick Block) MARCH OF TIME
1944
Norway Replies HOFFBERG PRODS.
1950
The Golden Twenties MARCH OF TIME
Modern Arms and Free Men (commercially released 1952 as *If Moscow Strikes*) MARCH OF TIME
1951
And a Voice Shall Be Heard MARCH OF TIME
1954
This Is Your Army FOX MOVIETONE NEWS
1962
30 Years of Fun (see B. Green)

SHANK, BUD
1959
Slippery When Wet BRUCE BROWN
1961
Barefoot Adventure BRUCE BROWN
1962
War Hunt UA

SHANKAR, RAVI
1959
The Sword and the Flute (doc. short) JAMES IVORY

1966

Lapis (short) JAMES WHITNEY
Chappaqua CONRAD ROOKS

1968

Charly CR
Not Enough (doc. short) BERT HAENSTRA
Primordium (short) AMRAM NOWAK

[He also scored many films in India.]

SHANKLIN, WAYNE

1961

Angel Baby (o: Beau) AA

SHAPIRO, MICHAEL

Documentary Shorts

1966

The Odds Against VISION ASSOCIATES

1968

The Price of a Life VISION ASSOCIATES
The Revolving Door VISION ASSOCIATES

1969

Anatomy of a Parade VISION ASSOCIATES
Beloved Island S.A. FILMS

1970

Geronimo Jones BERT SALZMAN PRODS.

SHARPLES, WILLIAM

1968

The America's Cup Races, 1967 (doc.) THOMAS J. LIPTON, INC.

SHARPLES, WIN, JR.

1967

A Voyage from Tahiti (doc. short) PAR

SHARPLES, WINSTON

Documentary Features (VAN BEUREN–RKO)

1934

Wild Cargo
Joan Lowell, Adventure Girl

1935

Fang and Claw

1938

Dark Rapture (see Rochetti)

1950

Cassino to Korea (see G. Steiner)

Documentary Shorts (PAR unless otherwise specified)

1935

A World Within VAN BEUREN

1942

Cactus Capers RKO

1946

Brooklyn, I Love You

1947

Radio, Take It Away!
Try and Catch Me!
It Could Happen to You
Babies, They're Wonderful

1948

Bundle from Brazil
A Model Is Born

1949

Make Mine Monica
The Macademy Awards
My Silent Love
Roller Derby Girl
Neighbors in the Night
The Football Fan
Strawhat Cinderella

1950

Sing Me Goodbye
Flatbush, Florida
Cowboy Crazy
The City of Beautiful Girls

1951

Music Circus

Cartoons (VAN BEUREN–RKO)

1933

Croon Crazy
The Last Mail
Pals

1934

Along Came a Duck
Art for Art's Sake
The Cactus King
Cubby's Stratosphere Flight
Fiddlin' Fun
Goode Knight
Grandfather's Clock
How's Crops?
Jest of Honor
Jolly Good Felons
The Lion Tamer
A Little Bird Told Me
Mild Cargo
The Parrotville Fire Department
The Pastry Town Wedding
The Rasslin' Match
A Royal Good Time
Sinister Stuff
Sultan Pepper

1935

Bird Scouts
The Foxy Terrier
The Hunting Season
Japanese Lanterns
The Merry Kittens

Molly Moo-Cow and Rip Van Winkle
Molly Moo-Cow and the Butterflies
Molly Moo-Cow and the Indians
Parrotville Old Folks
Parrotville Post Office
The Picnic Panic
The Rag Doll
Scottie Finds a Home
Spinning Mice
The Sunshine Makers

1936
Bold King Cole
Cupid Gets His Man
Felix the Cat and the Goose That Laid the Golden Egg
It's a Greek Life
Molly Moo-Cow and Robinson Crusoe
Neptune Nonsense
Toonerville Picnic
Toonerville Trolley
Trolley Ahoy
A Waif's Welcome

Cartoons (PAR)

1940
Bring Himself Back Alive (see Timberg)
The Constable (see Timberg)
Doing Impossikible Stunts (see Timberg)
Fightin' Pals (see Timberg)
The Foul Ball Player
The Fulla Bluff Man (see Timberg)
King for a Day (see Timberg)
Little Lambkin (see Timberg)
Mommy Loves Puppy (see Timberg)
My Pop, My Pop
Nurse Mates (see Timberg)
Shakespearian Spinach
Sneak, Snoop and Snitch (see Timberg)
Springtime in the Rockage (see Timberg)
The Ugly Dino (see Timberg)
Way Back When a Razzberry Was a Fruit
Wedding Belts (see Timberg)
Wimmin Is a Myskery (see Timberg)

1941
All's Well (see Timberg)
Copy Cat (see Timberg)
Gabby Goes Fishing (see Timberg)
I'll Never Crow Again (see Timberg)
It's a Hap-Hap-Happy Day (see Timberg)
Nix on Hypnotricks (see Timberg)
Olive's Boithday Presink (see Timberg)
Olive's Sweepstake Ticket (see Timberg)
Pest Pilot (see Timberg)
Popeye Meets Rip Van Winkle (see Timberg)
Raggedy Ann and Raggedy Andy (see Timberg)
Sneak, Snoop and Snitch in Triple Trouble (see Timberg)
Superman (see Timberg)
Superman in The Mechanical Monsters (see Timberg)
Swing Cleaning (see Timberg)
Twinkletoes Gets the Bird (see Timberg)
Two for the Zoo (see Timberg)
Vitamin Hay (see Timberg)
The Wizard of Arts (see Timberg)
Zero, the Hound (see Timberg)

1942
Many Tanks (see Timberg)
Me Musical Nephews (see Timberg)
Olive Oyl and Water Don't Mix (see Timberg)
Pip-Eye, Pup-Eye, Poop-Eye and Peep-Eye (see Timberg)
The Raven (see Timberg)
Scrap the Japs (see Timberg)
Superman in Billion Dollar Limited (see Timberg)
Superman in Destruction, Inc. (see Timberg)
Superman in Electric Earthquake (see Timberg)
Superman in Showdown (see Timberg)
Superman in Terror on the Midway (see Timberg)
Superman in The Arctic Giant (see Timberg)
Superman in The Bulleteers
Superman in The Eleventh Hour (see Timberg)
Superman in The Japoteurs (see Timberg)
Superman in The Magnetic Telescope (see Timberg)
Superman in Volcano (see Timberg)
You're a Sap, Mr. Jap (see Timberg)

1943
The Marry-Go-Round
Spinach fer Britain (see Timberg)
Superman in Jungle Drums (see Timberg)
Superman in The Mummy Strikes (see Timberg)
Too Weak to Work (see Timberg)

1944
Cilly Goose
Gabriel Churchkitten
Henpecked Rooster (see Timberg)
Lucky Lulu

Lulu Gets the Birdie
Lulu's Indoor Outing
Moving Aweigh
Spinach Packin' Popeye
Suddenly It's Spring!
We're on Our Way to Rio

1945
Daffydilly Daddy
For Better or Nurse
The Friendly Ghost
A Lamb in a Jam
Magicalulu
Man's Pest Friend
Mess Production
Old MacDonald Had a Farm
Pop-Pie a la Mode
Scrappily Married
A Self-Made Mongrel
Shape Ahoy
Snap Happy
Tops in the Big Top
When G.I. Johnny Comes Home

1946
Bargain Counter Attack
Bored of Education
Cheese Burglar
Chick and Double Chick
The Fistic Mystic
The Goal Rush
Klondike Casanova
Musicalulu
Peep in the Deep
Rocket to Mars
Rodeo Romeo
Sheep Shape
Spree for All
Sudden Fried Chicken

1947
Abusement Park
All's Fair at the Fair
The Baby Sitter
A Bout with a Trout
Cad and Caddy
The Circus Comes to Clown
The Enchanted Square
I'll Be Skiing Ya
The Island Fling
Loose in the Caboose
Madhattan Island
The Mild West
Much Ado About Mutton
Naughty But Mice
Popeye and the Pirates
The Royal Four-Flusher
Safari So Good
Santa's Surprise
A Scout with the Gout
Stupidstitious Cat
Super Lulu
The Wee Men
Wotta Knight

1948
Base Brawl
The Bored Cuckoo
Butterscotch and Soda
Camptown Races
Cat o' Nine Ails
The Dog Show-Off
Flip Flap
The Golden State
Hector's Hectic Life
Hep Cat Symphony
The Land of the Lost
Little Brown Jug
The Lone Star State
The Mite Makes Right
The Old Shell Game
Olive Oyl for President
Popeye Meets Hercules
Pre-Hysterical Man
Readin', Ritin', and Rhythmetic
Robin Hood Winked
Sing or Swim
Snow Place Like Home
Spinach vs Hamburgers
There's Good Boos Tonight
We're in the Honey
Wigwam Whoopee
Winter Draws On
Wolf in Sheik's Clothing

1949
A-Haunting We Will Go
The Balmy Swami
Barking Dogs Don't Fite
The Big Drip
The Big Flame-Up
Campus Capers
Comin' Round the Mountain
Farm Foolery
Fly's Last Flight
The Funshine State
Leprechaun's Gold
Little Cut Up
Little Red School Mouse
The Lost Dream
Lumber Jack and Jill

Marriage Wows
A Mutt in a Rut
Our Funny Finny Friends
Popeye's Premiere
Silly Hillbilly
The Ski's the Limit
Snow Foolin'
Song of the Birds
Spring Song
Stork Market
Strolling Thru the Park
Tar with a Star
Toys Will Be Toys

1950

Baby Wants Spinach
Beach Peach
Blue Hawaii
Boos in the Night
Casper's Spree Under the Sea
Detouring Thru Maine
Fiesta Time
Fresh Yeggs
Gobs of Fun
Goofy Goofy Gander
Gym Jam
Heap Hep Injuns
Helter Swelter
How Green Is My Spinach
Jingle, Jangle, Jungle
Jitterbug Jive
Land of the Lost Jewels
Mice Meeting You
Once Upon a Rhyme
Pleased to Eat You
Popeye Makes a Movie
Quack a Doodle Doo
Quick on the Vigor
Riot in Rhythm
Saved by the Bell
Shortenin' Bread
Sock-a-Bye Kitty
Tarts and Flowers
Teacher's Pest
Ups an' Downs Derby
Voice of the Turkey
Win, Place and Showboat

1951

Alpine for You
As the Crow Lies
Boo Hoo Baby
Boo Scout
By Leaps and Hounds
Casper Comes to Clown
Casper Takes a Bow-Wow
Cat-Choo
Cat Tamale
Double-Cross-Country Race
Drippy Mississippi
The Farmer and the Belle
Land of Lost Watches
Let's Stalk Spinach
Mice Paradise
Miners Forty Niners
One Quack Mind
Party Smarty
Pilgrim Popeye
Punch and Judo
Scout Fellow
Sing Again of Michigan
Slip Us Some Redskin
Snooze Reel
Thrill of Fair
To Boo or Not to Boo
Tweet Music
Vacation with Play
Vegetable Vaudeville

1952

The Awful Tooth
Big Bad Sindbad
Cage Fright
The Case of the Cockeyed Canary
Cat Carson Rides Again
City Kitty
Clown on the Farm
The Deep Boo Sea
Dizzy Dinosaurs
Feast and Furious
Forest Fantasy
Friend or Phoney
Fun at the Fair
Gag and Baggage
Ghost of the Town
Law and Audrey
Lunch with a Punch
Mice-Capades
Off We Glow
Pig-a-Boo
Popalong Popeye
Popeye's Pappy
Shuteye Popeye
Spunky Skunky
Swimmer Take All
Tots of Fun
True Boo

1953

Aero-Nutics
Ancient Fistory
Baby Wants a Battle

Better Bait Than Never
Boos and Saddles
By the Old Mill Scream
Child Sockology
Do or Diet
Drinks on the Mouse
Firemen's Brawl
Frightday the 13th
Herman the Catoonist
Huey's Ducky Daddy
Hysterical History
Invention Convention
Little Boo-Peep
No Place Like Rome
North Pal
Northwest Mousie
Of Mice and Magic
Philharmaniacs
Popeye, the Ace of Space
Popeye's Mirthday
Shaving Muggs
Spook No Evil
Starting from Hatch
Surf Bored
Toreadorable
Winner by a Hare

1954

Boo Moon
Boo Ribbon Winner
Boos and Arrows
Bride and Gloom
Candy Cabaret
Casper Genie
Crazytown
Fido Beta Kappa
Floor Flusher
Fright to the Finish
Gopher Spinach
Greek Mirthology
Hair Today, Gone Tomorrow
No Ifs, Ands or Butts
Of Mice and Menace
The Oily Bird
Popeye's 20th Anniversary
Private Eye Popeye
Puss 'n Boos
Rail Rodents
The Seapreme Court
Ship A-Hooey
Surf and Sound
Taxi-Turvy
Zero the Hero

1955

Beaus Will Be Beaus
A Bicep Built for Two
Boo Kind to Animals
Bull Fright
Car-azy Drivers
Cookin' with Gags
Cops Is Tops
Dizzy Dishes
Gift of Gag
Git Along Li'l Duckie
Hide and Shriek
Hillbilling and Cooing
A Job for a Gob
Keep Your Grin Up
Kitty Coronered
Little Audrey Riding Hood
Mister and Mistletoe
Mouse Trapeze
Mousieur Herman
News Hound
Nurse to Meet Ya
Penny Antics
Poop Goes the Weasel
Rabbit Punch
Red, White and Boo
Robin Rodenthood
Spooking with a Brogue

1956

Assault and Flattery
Dutch Treat
Fright from Wrong
Ground Hog Play
A Haul in One
Hide and Peak
I Don't Scare
Insect to Injury
Line of Screammage
Lion in the Roar
Mousetro Herman
Mouseum
Out to Punch
Parlez Vous Woo
Pedro and Lorenzo
Penguin for Your Thoughts
Popeye for President
Sir Irving and Jeames
Sleuth But Sure
Swab the Duck
Will Do Mousework

1957

Boo Bop
Cat in the Act
Cock-a-Doodle Dino
The Crystal Brawl
Dante Dreamer

Fishing Tackler
From Mad to Worse
Ghost of Honor
Hooky Spooky
Ice Scream
Jolly, the Clown
Jumping with Toy
L'Amour the Merrier
Mr. Money Gags
Nearlyweds
One Funny Knight
Patriotic Popeye
Peekaboo
Pest Pupil
Possum Pearl
Sky Scrappers
Spooking About Africa
Spooky Swabs
Spree Lunch

1958

The Animal Fair
Chew Chew Baby
Dawg Gawn
Felineous Assault
Finnegan's Flea
Fit to Be Toyed
Frighty Cat
Ghost Writers
Good Scream Fun
Grateful Gus
Heir Restorer
Okey Dokey Donkey
Right Off the Bat
Spook and Span
Sportickles
Stork Raving Mad
Travelaffs
Which Is Witch
You Said a Mouseful

1959

The Boss Is Always Right
Casper's Birthday Party
Doing What's Fright
Down to Mirth
Fiddle Faddle
Fun on Furlough
Houndabout
Katnip's Big Day
La Petite Parade
Mike the Masquerader
Not Ghoulty
Out of This Whirl
Owly to Bed
Spooking of Ghosts
Talking Horse Sense
TV Fuddlehead

1960

Be Mice to Cats
Bouncing Benny
Busy Buddies
Cool Cat Blues
Counter Attack
Disguise the Limit
Electronica
Fine Feathered Fiend
From Dime to Dime
Galaxia
The Kid from Mars
Miceniks
Monkey Doodles
Northern Mites
Peck Your Own Home
The Planet Mouseola
Samson Scrap
Scouting for Trouble
The Shoe Must Go On
Shootin' Stars
Silly Science
Terry the Terror
Top Cat
Trigger Treat
Trouble Date
Turning the Fables

1961

Abner the Baseball
Alvin's Solo Flight
Bopin' Hood
Cane and Able
Cape Kidnaveral
Crumley Cogwheel
Giddy Gadgets
Good and Guilty
Goodie, the Gremlin
Hound About That
In the Nicotine
The Inquisit Visit
Kozmo Goes to School
The Lion's Busy
The Mighty Termite
Perry Popgun
The Phantom Moustacher
The Plot Sickens
Popcorn and Politics
Trick or Tree
Turtle Scoop
Without Time or Reason

1962

Drum Up a Tenant

Et Tu Otto
Fiddlin' Around
Frog Legs
Funderful Suburbia
Good Snooze Tonight
Hi-Fi Jinx
Hound for Pound
It's for the Birdies
Keeping Up with Krazy
The Method and Maw
Mouse Blanche
Ollie the Owl
One of the Family
One Weak Vacation
Penny Pals
Psychological Testing
The Ringading Kid
The Robot Ringer
A Sight for Squaw Eyes
Snuffy's Song
Take Me to Your Gen'rul
Trash Program
A Tree Is a Tree Is a Tree?
TV or No TV
Yule Laff

1963

Goodie's Good Deed
Gramps to the Rescue
Harry Happy
Hiccup Hound
Hobo's Holiday
Laddy and His Lamp
Muggy-Doo Boycat
The Pigs' Feat
The Sheepish Wolf
Sour Gripes
Tell Me a Badtime Story
Whiz Quiz Kid

1964

Accidents Will Happen
And So Tibet
The Bus Way to Travel
Call Me a Taxi
Fix That Clock
Fizzicle Fizzle
A Friend in Tweed
Highway Slobbery
Hip Hip Olé
Homer on the Range
Horning In
Near Sighted and Far Out
The Once Over
Panhandling on Madison Avenue
Reading, Writhing and 'Rithmetic
Robot Rival
Sailing Zero
Service with a Smile
A Tiger's Tail

1965

Cagey Business
Getting Ahead
A Hair-Raising Tale
Inferior Decorator
The Itch
A Leak in the Dike
Les Boys
Ocean Bruise
Op, Pop, Wham and Bop
The Outside Dope
Poor Little Witch Girl
Shoeflies
Sick Transit
Solitary Refinement
The Story of George Washington
Tally-Hokum
Two by Two

1966

Baggin' the Dragon
A Balmy Knight
The Blacksheep Blacksmith
The Defiant Giant
From Nags to Witches
Geronimo and Son
I Want My Mummy
Potions and Notions
Space Kid
Throne for a Loss
Trick or Cheat
A Wedding Knight

1967

Alter Egotist
A Bridge Grows in Brooklyn
Clean Sweep
The Fuz
Halt, Who Grows There?
Keep the Cool, Baby
Mini Squirts
Mouse Trek
My Daddy the Astronaut
The Opera Caper
The Plumber
Robin Hoodwinked
The Squaw-Path
Think or Sink
The Trip

Cartoon (B.C.O. ASSOC.)

1962

The Adventures of Dolly and Daniel Whale

SHAW, ARTIE
1941
Second Chorus (a: E. Paul, Stone, Guarnieri) PAR

SHEARING, GEORGE
1966
The Shooting of Dan McGrew (short) ED GRAHAM
1969
80 Steps to Jonah (a: D. Vincent) WB

SHEETS, WALTER
1945
It's a Pleasure (see A. Lange)
1952
Models, Inc. (see Herschel Gilbert)
[Also worked as an orchestrator.]

SHEFF, ROBERT
1964
Peace in the Valley (short) ?
1969
Portraits, Self-Portraits, and Still Lives (see Ashley)

SHEFTER, BERT
1950
Holiday Rhythm LIP
1951
One Too Many HALLMARK
Fingerprints Don't Lie LIP
Mask of the Dragon LIP
Danger Zone LIP
Roaring City LIP
Pier 23 LIP
Sky High LIP
Leave It to the Marines LIP
1953
The Tall Texan LIP
A Day in the Country (short) LIP
College Capers (short) LIP
No Escape UA
Bandit Island (short) LIP
The Great Jesse James Raid LIP
Sins of Jezebel LIP
1954
The Big Chase LIP
1955
Mixed-Up Women HALLMARK
1959
Pier 5 Havana UA
Vice Raid UA
1960
Noose for a Gunman (with H. Jackson) UA
Walking Target UA
Pacific Paradise (short) UNIV
1961
The Gambler Wore a Gun UA
1965
Curse of the Fly (o: Pearson) TCF
1968
The Last Shot You Hear (o: Len Stevens) TCF
[Also many collaborations with Sawtell, q.v.]

SHELDON, JAMES
1968
Single Room Furnished CROWN

SHEPARD, ROBERT
1956
Abraham, Man of Faith (an. short) CHRISTIAN MISSION FILMS
1958
Life to Life (semi-doc.) CHURCH OF THE FOURSQUARE GOSPEL

SHERMAN, RAY
1951
The Oompahs (cartoon) UPA

SHETLER, DONALD
1959
Telling Stories to Children (doc. short) U. OF MICHIGAN

SHIELD, LEROY
[He worked exclusively for Hal Roach Studios, where he wrote over 110 short compositions for the music library; apparently not written for specific films, they were used in many shorts and features from 1930 to 1938. Although no scores have been found, following are pictures in which his music appears, based solely on information from cue sheets.]
1931
Pardon Us
1932
Pack Up Your Troubles
1933
The Devil's Brother (md; music from Auber's *Fra Diavolo*)
1935
Bonnie Scotland (see Hatley)
1936
Our Relations

Shorts
1930
Doctor's Orders
Helping Grandma
1931
Air Tight
Laughing Gravy
The Panic Is On
Catch as Catch Can
Call a Cop!
Come Clean
Mama Loves Papa
The Pajama Party
War Mamas
1932
Sealskins
Any Old Port
County Hospital
Scram
1933
Bring 'Em Back a Wife
Towed in a Hole
The Kid from Borneo
1935
The Misses Stooge
Twin Tripletts
Hot Money
1936
The Pinch Singer
Two Too Young

SHILKRET, JACK
1939
Lying Lips SACK
1940
The Notorious Elinor Lee SACK
Documentary Shorts (MGM unless otherwise noted)
1936
Colorful Islands—Madagascar and Seychelles
Yellowstone Park
1937
Chile, Land of Charm
Copenhagen
Glimpses of Peru
India on Parade
Land of the Incas
Rocky Mountain Grandeur (see N. Shilkret)
Stockholm, Pride of Sweden
1938
Ancient Egypt
Beautiful Budapest
Cairo, City of Contrast
Czechoslovakia on Parade
Glimpses of Austria
Glimpses of New Brunswick
Imperial Delhi
Jaipur, the Pink City
Java Journey
Madeira, Isle of Romance
Natural Wonders of the West
Paris on Parade
Rural Sweden
1939
Picturesque Udaipur
1941
Alluring Alaska
Mediterranean Ports of Call
Yosemite the Magnificent
1942
Home on the Range USDA
1943
The Champ of Champions COL
Ten Pin Aces COL
1944
Follow Thru with Sam Byrd COL
G. I. Sports COL
Golden Gloves COL
Hedge Hoppers COL
Table Tennis Topnotchers COL
1945
Hi-Ho Rodeo COL
Salmon Fishing COL

SHILKRET, NATHANIEL
1928
Lilac Time (synchronized version; ac: Stahlberg, Erdody; + stock. New York premiere of silent version: Copping, q.v.) FN
Synthetic Sin FN
1929
Children of the Ritz FN
1930
The Break Up (doc.) TALKING PICTURE EPICS
The Lady of the Lake (U.S. release of 1928 British film) FITZPATRICK
1931
Puss in Boots PICTURE CLASSICS
1932
It Happened in Paris PICTURE CLASSICS
1934
Social Register (md) COL
1935
George Washington's Railroad (doc.) CHESAPEAKE & OHIO

1936

The Bohemian Girl HAL ROACH

Mary of Scotland (o: de Packh) RKO

Walking on Air (o: R. Bennett, de Packh) RKO

Smartest Girl in Town (o: Nussbaum; + stock) RKO

Winterset (o: de Packh) RKO

That Girl from Paris (o: de Packh, Nussbaum) RKO

1937

The Soldier and the Lady (o: de Packh) RKO

Shall We Dance (with R. Bennett, Gershwin) RKO

Border Café (+ stock) RKO

The Toast of New York RKO

Music for Madame (o: R. Bennett) RKO

Hitting a New High RKO

1938

Di que me quieres (Spanish language; md) RKO

1939

. . . One Third of a Nation . . . PAR

1941

Frank Buck's Jungle Cavalcade (doc.) RKO

Stolen Paradise MON

1943

A Stranger in Town (see Amfitheatrof)

Air Raid Wardens (o: Leipold) MGM

Presenting Lily Mars (see Stoll)

Above Suspicion (see Kaper)

Hitler's Madman (with Hajos, Castelnuovo-Tedesco; ac: Zeisl; mt: A. Morton; o: Nussbaum, Marquardt, Raab, de Packh, Altschuler) MGM

1944

Three Men in White (o: R. Franklyn, Cutner) MGM

An American Romance (see Gruenberg)

Lost in a Harem (ac: Amfitheatrof, Hayton, Snell, R. Franklyn, Cutner, Bassman; o: R. Franklyn, Glasser, Duncan, W. Greene, Heglin) MGM

Mrs. Parkington (see Kaper)

Nothing But Trouble (o: Nussbaum, Glasser) MGM

Blonde Fever (o: Nussbaum, R. Franklyn) MGM

1945

This Man's Navy (o: R. Franklyn, Glasser, Nussbaum) MGM

Our Vines Have Tender Grapes (see Kaper)

She Went to the Races (o: Byrns, Glasser, P. Smith, Heglin) MGM

1946

The Hoodlum Saint (o and ac: Sendrey) MGM

Boys' Ranch (o: Sendrey, Glasser) MGM

Courage of Lassie (see Bradley)

Faithful in My Fashion (o: Sendrey, Duncan, R. Franklyn) MGM

Shorts (1929–1939)

[ASCAP credits him with "several hundred short subjects," but only those whose titles have been confirmed are listed here.]

1929

People Born in September FITZPATRICK

1930

Blotto MGM

The Laurel-Hardy Murder Case MGM

1932

Leningrad—The Gateway to Soviet Russia MGM

Rio the Magnificent MGM

1933

Iceland—Land of the Vikings MGM

Cuba, the Land of Rhumba MGM

Beer Is Here STANDARD

1934

Ireland—The Emerald Isle MGM

1935

Los Angeles—Wonder City of the West MGM

1937

Glimpses of Java and Ceylon MGM

Hong Kong, the Hub of the Orient MGM

Serene Siam MGM

Rocky Mountain Grandeur (with J. Shilkret) MGM

1938

Quintupland RKO PATHÉ

Windward Way RKO PATHÉ

Sydney, Pride of Australia MGM

Singapore and Jahore MGM

1939

Glimpses of Australia MGM

Yankee Doodle Home COL

Montmartre Madness COL

Shorts (MGM)

1942

The Last Lesson (o: Raab, Marquardt)

1943

You, John Jones (see J. Green)

Portrait of a Genius (see Terr)

Plan for Destruction (with Amfitheatrof,

Castelnuovo-Tedesco, Zeisl; o: Nussbaum, Raab, Marquardt)
Heavenly Music (o: Nussbaum, Heglin, Altschuler)
Here at Home (o: Nussbaum, Altschuler)
That's Why I Left You (see Terr)
Memories of Australia
Nursery Rhyme Mysteries (see Terr)
Ode to Victory
Sucker Bait (see Amfitheatrof)
Storm (o: Cutner)
This Is Tomorrow (o: Duncan, Schutt)
For God and Country (sec S. Kaplan)

1944
A Great Day's Coming (o: Glasser)
Patrolling the Ether (o: Glasser)
Grandpa Called It Art (o: Glasser)
Nostradamus IV (with Terr; o: Glasser, R. Franklyn, Nussbaum)
Tomorrow John Jones (with Terr)
A Lady Fights Back (o: Nussbaum)
Dark Shadows (ac: Terr; o: Glasser)
Return from Nowhere (o: Glasser)

1945
It Looks Like Rain (o: Glasser, Cutner)

Shorts (RKO PATHÉ)

1946
Beauty for Sale
Courtship to Courthouse
Hail Notre Dame
Highway Mania
Kentucky Basketeers
Northern Rampart
Skating Lady
Steeplechasers
White House

1947
The Big Party
Campus Boom
Chasing Rainbows
College Climbers
Forgotten Island
The 49th State
Golf Doctor
I Am an Alcoholic
Ice Skippers
A Nation Is Born
Passport to Nowhere
Pin Games
Racing Sleuths
Reading and Riding
San Francisco—Pacific Gateway
Ski Belles
Smoke Eaters
Switzerland Today
Whistle in the Night
Wild Turkey

1948
Athletic Stars
Athletic Varieties
Block Party
Children's Village
Doggone Clever
Fighting Tarpon
Frozen Fun
Glamour Street
Ladies in Waiting
Letter to a Rebel
Muscles and the Lady
Sports Coverage
Strikes to Spare
Teen Age Tars
Texas Redheads

1949
Airline Glamour Girls
The Boy and the Eagle
Canada Unlimited
Fraud Fighters
I Like Soap Because . . .
The Kentucky Derby Story
Men of the Shooting Stars
Mighty Marlin
Rolling Thrills

1950
The Bauer Girls

1951
Ambulance Doctor
Cleopatra's Playground
Feathered Bullets
Florida Cowhands
Flying Padre
Lady Marines
Lake Texoma
Rainbow Chasers
Riders of the Andes
Slammin' Sammy Snead

1952
Caution, Danger Ahead
Male Vanity
Second Sight
That Man Rickey

1954
Riding the Wind

SHINBERG, ROBERT

1960
Genesis of an Idea (doc. short) ALLEN LEEPA

SHOLOGON, DORIS
1954
Lonely by the Sea (doc. short) STEWART WILENSKY

SHORES, RICHARD
1953
Cheechako—Tale of Alaska (doc.) MERCURY MOTORS
The Street (doc. short) PACIFIC GARDEN MISSION
1954
Farm Petroleum Safety (doc. short) AMERICAN PETROLEUM INSTITUTE
1961
Tomboy and the Champ UNIV
Look in Any Window AA
1965
Run, Appaloosa, Run WDP
1967
The Last Challenge MGM

SHRYER, ART
1932
The Unfortunate Bride JUDEA FILMS

SHUKEN, LEO
1936
Go West, Young Man (see Stoll)
1937
Mind Your Own Business (with Bradshaw) PAR
Champagne Waltz (see Boutelje)
Waikiki Wedding (ac: Bradshaw, V. Young) PAR
The Girl from Scotland Yard (mt: Cutter) PAR
Artists and Models (see Jenkins)
This Way Please (see Leipold)
1938
Every Day's a Holiday PAR
Cocoanut Grove (see Leipold)
Men with Wings (see Harling)
Illegal Traffic (see Leipold)
Thanks for the Memory (see Bradshaw)
Say It in French (with Leipold; ac: Bradshaw) PAR
1939
Paris Honeymoon (see Rainger)
Persons in Hiding (see Leipold)
Stagecoach (see Leipold)
Cafe Society PAR
Sudden Money (see Leipold)
I'm from Missouri (see Leipold)
Never Say Die (see Roder)
The Lady's from Kentucky (with Leipold) PAR
Union Pacific (see Leipold)
The Gracie Allen Murder Case (see Carbonara)
Invitation to Happiness (see Hollander)
Death of a Champion (see Leipold)
$1,000 a Touchdown (see Leipold)
The Flying Deuces (see Leipold)
Emergency Squad (with Leipold; m&e: Bradshaw) PAR
1940
Parole Fixer (see Carbonara)
The Farmer's Daughter (see V. Young)
Adventure in Diamonds (with Krumgold; ac: Bradshaw, Leipold) PAR
Typhoon (see Hollander)
Christmas in July (with Leipold) PAR
Arise My Love (see V. Young)
1941
Virginia (mt) PAR
The Lady Eve (ac: Boutelje, Krumgold, Grau, Bradshaw, Leipold) PAR
Her First Beau (+ stock) COL
The Richest Man in Town (o: Bradshaw; + stock) COL
One Night in Lisbon (see V. Young)
West Point Widow (see Leipold)
Our Wife (o: Parrish, Bradshaw, Grau) COL
New York Town PAR
Skylark (see Young)
Louisiana Purchase (see Dolan)
Sullivan's Travels (with Bradshaw) PAR
The Lady Has Plans (see Harline)
1942
The Fleet's In (with V. Young) PAR
Meet the Stewarts COL
Henry Aldrich, Editor (mt: W. Scharf; + stock) PAR
1943
My Heart Belongs to Daddy (with V. Young) PAR
Henry Aldrich Swings It (see Sawtell)
Mardi Gras (short; see Leipold)
Let's Face It (see Dolan)
Good Fellows PAR
Riding High (see Bradshaw)
1944
The Miracle of Morgan's Creek (with Bradshaw; o: Parrish) PAR
Lucky Cowboy (short; with Wallace, Parrish) PAR

1947
The Fabulous Dorseys UA
Two Blondes and a Redhead (see Duning)
1949
Some of the Best (see Cutner)
1950
Pagan Love Song (see A. Deutsch)
1951
Go for Broke (see Colombo)
Too Young to Kiss (see Kaper)
1953
Road to Bali (see Lilley)
Those Redheads from Seattle (with Cutner; ac: Van Cleave) PAR
1954
Alaska Seas (with Webb; + stock) PAR
1957
Hear Me Good (with Hayes; + stock) PAR
[Also a very prolific arranger and orchestrator.]

SHULMAN, ALAN
1945
T.V.A. (doc. short) RKO PATHÉ
1946
Port of New York (doc. short) RKO PATHÉ
1950
The Tattooed Stranger RKO
1954
The Big Port (doc. short) RKO PATHÉ

SHVEDOFF, C. N.
1936
Natalka Poltavka (Ukranian language) AVRAMENKO

SIEGEL, LOUIS
1933
Lot in Sodom (short) J.S.WATSON, M. WEBBER

SIEGEL, SID
1960
Mural: Midwest Metropolis (doc. short; a: Boyell) FRED A. NILES PRODS.
1962
Two Before Zero (doc.) MOTION PICTURE CORP.
1963
Bounty Without Boundaries (doc. short) FRED A. NILES PRODS.
1965
The First 100 Years (doc. short) FRED A. NILES PRODS.
1966
Discover Greyhound America (doc. short) FRED A. NILES PRODS.

SIEGMEISTER, ELIE
1959
They Came to Cordura (o: A. Morton) COL

SILVA, GUILIO
1952
True Peace (an. short) DAMASCENE PICTURES

SILVA, MARIO
1947
Stepchild PRC

SILVERS, LOUIS
1920
Way Down East (with Peters) GRIFFITH
1921
Dream Street GRIFFITH
1925
Isn't Life Wonderful (with Sodero) GRIFFITH
Sally of the Sawdust GRIFFITH
1927
The Jazz Singer (o: E. Ross) WB
1928
The Barker FN
The Singing Fool (o: E. Ross) WB
1929
Weary River WB
Frozen River WB
Sonny Boy (o: E. Ross) WB
Madonna of Avenue A WB
1930
Mammy WB
1933
Stage Mother (with de Packh) MGM
Dancing Lady (with de Packh) MGM
1934
One Night of Love (see Schertzinger)
1935
Love Me Forever (see Schertzinger)
The Black Room (with R. Bassett; ac: Roder) COL
1939
Stanley and Livingstone (with R. Bennett, Buttolph, Mockridge, R. Bassett, D. Raksin, Schrager; mt: E. Powell) TCF
1943
The Powers Girl UA

SIMEONE, HARRY
1945
Bombalera (short) PAR
Salty O'Rourke (see Dolan)
Out of This World (ac: Lilley, Bradshaw) PAR
You Hit the Spot (short; see Schrager)
Little Witch (short) PAR
[Also worked as an arranger.]

SIMMONS, RUTH AND RUBY
1957
Otto Nobetter and the Railroad Gang (an. short) TED ESHBAUGH STUDIOS

SIMMS, ALICE
1963
The Checkered Flag MERCURY

SIMON, JOHN
1968
You Are What You Eat (doc.) CU
1969
Last Summer AA

SIMON, TED
1965
Love Hunger CAMBIST FILMS

SIMON, WALTER C.
Short Films (KALEM)
1911
Arrah-na-Pogue
1912
A Spartan Mother
The Spanish Revolt of 1836
Under a Flag of Truce
The Fighting Dervishes of the Desert
The Drummer Girl of Vicksburg
An Arabian Tragedy
Captured by Bedouins
Tragedy of the Desert
The Bugler of Battery B. [and] *Hungry Hank's Hallucination* (split-reel)
A Prisoner of the Harem [and] *Egyptian Sports* (split-reel)
The Siege of Petersburg
The Soldier Brothers of Susanna
The Confederate Ironclad
1913
The Tragedy of Big Eagle Mine
Features
1915
Midnight at Maxim's KALEM
1916
The Black Crook KALEM
1919
The Echo of Youth GRAPHIC

SINATRA, FRANK, JR.
1965
The Beach Girls and the Monster (a: Slagle) U.S. FILMS

SINGMAN, ELSA
1969
The Hanging of Jake Ellis (a and ac: A. Mancini) HOLLYWOOD CINEMART
1970
Love Me Like I Do HOLLYWOOD CINEMART

SKILES, MARLIN
1936
Follow Your Heart (see Riesenfeld)
The Big Broadcast of 1937 (with V. Young) PAR
Wedding Present (with Leipold, Carbonara) PAR
College Holiday (with Leipold) PAR
1937
Great Guy GN
When's Your Birthday? (see Leipold)
23 1/2 Hours Leave GN
Sweetheart of the Navy GN
Riding on Air (see A. Morton)
1941
Hurricane Smith (+ stock) REP
Under Fiesta Stars (see M. Glickman)
Bad Man of Deadwood (see M. Glickman)
Outlaws of Cherokee Trail (+ stock) REP
1942
Ice-Capades Revue (see W. Scharf)
1943
Song of Texas (see M. Glickman)
Nobody's Darling (see W. Scharf)
In Old Oklahoma (see W. Scharf)
O, My Darling Clementine (+ stock) REP
Casanova in Burlesque (see W. Scharf)
Captain America (see M. Glickman)
1944
The Fighting Seabees (see W. Scharf)
My Best Gal (+ stock) REP
The Lady and the Monster (see W. Scharf)
Cowboy and the Senorita (with Maxwell, M. Glickman, Dubin) REP
Man from Frisco (o: A. Morton, Dubin, Vaughan, Maxwell) REP
Once Upon a Time (see Hollander)

The Yellow Rose of Texas (with Butts; + stock) REP
Call of the South Seas (+ stock) REP
Bathing Beauty (see J. Green)
Mr. Winkle Goes to War (see Dragon)
The Impatient Years (o: Duning, A. Morton, Maxwell) COL
Strange Affair (with A. Morton, Duning) COL

1945
Youth on Trial (with Duning; + stock) COL
Eadie Was a Lady (see Duning)
Tonight and Every Night (with Duning) COL
A Guy, a Gal, and a Pal (o: A. Morton) COL
Rough, Tough and Ready (+ stock) COL
A Thousand and One Nights (o: A. Morton, Sawtell) COL
Over 21 (o: A. Morton) COL
The Adventures of Rusty (+ stock) COL
Outlaws of the Rockies COL
She Wouldn't Say Yes (o: A. Morton) COL
Hit the Hay COL
One Way to Love (+ stock) COL

1946
Tars and Spars (o: A. Morton) COL
Talk About a Lady COL
That Texas Jamboree (+ stock) COL
The Walls Came Tumbling Down (ac: A. Morton) COL
The Jolson Story (with Friedhofer, Duning, A. Morton) COL
Gallant Journey (o: A. Morton) COL

1947
Dead Reckoning (o: A. Morton, Dubin; ac: Friedhofer) COL
Framed (o and ac: A. Morton) COL
For the Love of Rusty (+ stock) COL
The Swordsman (see Friedhofer)

1948
Relentless (o: A. Morton) COL
Mickey EL
Michael O'Halloran (see Moraweck)

1949
The Doolins of Oklahoma (see Duning)
All the King's Men (see Gruenberg)

1950
The Golden Gloves Story (see A. Lange) EL
Boy from Indiana (see Moraweck)
The Great Wilderness (doc.) ?

1951
The Lion Hunters MON
Cavalry Scout MON
Excuse My Dust (see Stoll)
Callaway Went Thataway (o: Sendrey) MGM
Flight to Mars MON
Fort Osage MON

1952
Aladdin and His Lamp MON
Rodeo MON
Wild Stallion MON
Wagons West MON
The Rose Bowl Story (m&e: Sendrey) MON
Army Bound MON
Battle Zone AA
Flat Top MON
Hiawatha (ac: A. Morton) MON

1953
Kansas Pacific (see Sendrey)
Jalopy AA
White Lightning AA
Son of Belle Starr AA
Loose in London AA
The Roar of the Crowd AA
Safari Drums AA
The Maze (ac: A. Morton) AA
Clipped Wings AA
Hot News (ac: A. Morton) AA
Private Eyes AA
Fighter Attack AA

1954
The Golden Idol AA
Pride of the Blue Grass AA
Paris Playboys (ac: A. Morton) AA
Arrow in the Dust (ac: A. Morton) AA
The Bowery Boys Meet the Monsters AA
Challenge the Wild (doc.) UA
Jungle Gents AA
Killer Leopard AA
Bowery to Bagdad AA

1955
Annapolis Story AA
Dial Red O AA
High Society (mt: A. Morton) AA
Skabenga (doc.) AA
Lord of the Jungle AA
Spy Chasers AA
Jail Busters AA
Dig That Uranium AA
Sudden Danger AA

1956
Crashing Las Vegas AA
Canyon River AA
The Young Guns AA
Calling Homicide AA

Chain of Evidence AA
Hot Shots (ac: A. Morton) AA
1957
Hold That Hypnotist AA
Footsteps in the Night AA
Spook Chasers AA
My Gun Is Quick (ac: Courage, J. Williams) UA
The Disembodied AA
Looking for Danger AA
Up in Smoke AA
Sabu and the Magic Ring AA
The Beast of Budapest AA
1958
Man from God's Country AA
In the Money AA
Cole Younger, Gunfighter AA
Quantrill's Raiders AA
Fort Massacre (ac: A. Morton) UA
Queen of Outer Space (ac: A. Harris) AA
Joy Ride AA
1959
King of the Wild Stallions AA
Battle Flame AA
1960
The Hypnotic Eye AA
1961
The Deadly Companions PATHÉ-AMERICA
1962
The Immoral West—And How It Was Lost PACIFICA
1963
Europe in the Raw (doc.) EVE
The Shepherd of the Hills HOWCO
Gunfight at Comanche Creek AA
The Crawling Hand HANSEN ENTERPRISES
1964
The Great Space Adventure (ac: A. Morton, A. Harris) FAMOUS PLAYERS
The Strangler AA
Space Monster AIP
The Lure of Bali (doc.) RICHARD FOOTE
1965
Indian Paint (ac: Cutner) CROWN
The First Woman Into Space AIP
1967
Dr. Terror's Gallery of Horrors AMERICAN GENERAL
Journey to the Center of Time AMERICAN GENERAL
The Violent Ones (ac: A. Harris) MADISON
1968
Dayton's Devils MADISON

SKINNER, DONALD
1970
Meat/Rack SHERPIX

SKINNER, FRANK
[All for Universal unless otherwise stated.]
1936
Three Smart Girls (see Roemheld)
1937
When Love Is Young
Top of the Town
As Good as Married (see D. Raksin)
One Hundred Men and a Girl (with C. Previn)
Merry-Go-Round of 1938 (see C. Henderson)
1938
Mad About Music (see C. Previn)
Reckless Living (mt; + stock)
Wives Under Suspicion (see C. Henderson)
The Rage of Paris (with C. Henderson, C. Previn; ac: Salter)
Letter of Introduction
Freshman Year
The Road to Reno (see C. Henderson)
Little Tough Guy (with Salter, C. Henderson; + stock)
Youth Takes a Fling (see C. Previn)
That Certain Age
The Storm (see C. Henderson)
Strange Faces
Exposed
Secrets of a Nurse (+ stock)
Little Tough Guys in Society (+ stock)
Swing, Sister, Swing
Newsboys Home (+ stock)
1939
Son of Frankenstein (o: Salter)
Pirates of the Skies (m&e; + stock)
Code of the Streets
You Can't Cheat an Honest Man (+ stock)
Spirit of Culver
Big Town Czar
Three Smart Girls Grow Up
The Family Next Door (mt; + stock)
East Side of Heaven
Ex-Champ (ac: Salter; + stock)
They Asked for It
The Sun Never Sets
The Forgotten Woman
Unexpected Father (+ stock)
I Stole a Million
When Tomorrow Comes
The Under-Pup

Two Bright Boys (+ stock)
Tropic Fury (mt; + stock)
Rio
Little Accident
First Love (ac: Salter, C. Previn)
Tower of London (o: Salter)
The Big Guy (see Salter)
Destry Rides Again
Green Hell
Charlie McCarthy, Detective
Framed (+ stock)

1940
The Invisible Man Returns (see Salter)
My Little Chickadee
Double Alibi (+ stock)
Zanzibar (with Salter; ac: Roemheld; + stock)
Black Friday (see Salter)
The House of the Seven Gables
It's a Date
Ski Patrol (+ stock)
La Conga Nights (+ stock)
Black Diamonds (+ stock)
The Boys from Syracuse
When the Daltons Rode
The Mummy's Hand (ac: Salter)
Hired Wife
Argentine Nights
A Little Bit of Heaven
Seven Sinners
One Night in the Tropics
The Bank Dick
San Francisco Docks (see Salter)
The Invisible Woman

1941
Meet the Chump (see Salter)
Buck Privates (mt)
Back Street
Nice Girl?
Man Made Monster (see Salter)
The Man Who Lost Himself (see Salter)
The Lady from Cheyenne
The Flame of New Orleans (with C. Previn)
The Black Cat (see Salter)
Too Many Blondes (+ stock)
In the Navy
Hello, Sucker (+ stock)
Bachelor Daddy (see Salter)
Cracked Nuts (see Salter)
Sing Another Chorus (mt)
Hold That Ghost (see Salter)
Moonlight in Hawaii (+ stock)
Badlands of Dakota (with Salter)
South of Tahiti
Appointment for Love
Jail House Blues
Ride 'Em Cowboy (+ stock)
Melody Lane (+ stock)
The Wolf Man (with Salter, C. Previn)
Hellzapoppin' (+ stock)

1942
Don't Get Personal
North to the Klondike (+ stock)
Mississippi Gambler (+ stock)
The Strange Case of Doctor Rx (with Salter; + stock)
There's One Born Every Minute (+ stock)
Butch Minds the Baby
Saboteur
Broadway
Lady in a Jam
Eagle Squadron
Pardon My Sarong (+ stock)
Sherlock Holmes and the Voice of Terror (+ stock)
Get Hep to Love (see C. Previn)
Between Us Girls (ac: C. Previn)
It Comes Up Love (+ stock)
Who Done It? (+ stock)
Nightmare
Pittsburgh (with Salter)
Arabian Nights

1943
Keep 'Em Slugging (with Salter; + stock)
The Amazing Mrs. Holliday (ac: Salter)
It Ain't Hay (+ stock)
Follow the Band (mt)
White Savage
Two Tickets to London
Hers to Hold
Honeymoon Lodge (+ stock)
We've Never Been Licked
Top Man
Fired Wife
This Is the Life
Sing a Jingle (+ stock)
Gung Ho!
The Mumny's Ghost (+ stock)

1944
Week-End Pass
Hat Check Honey (with L. Russell; + stock)
Follow the Boys (see Harline)
South of Dixie
Twilight on the Prairie
Allergic to Love
In Society

Reckless Age
Hi, Beautiful!
I'll Remember April
Night Club Girl
Destiny (see Tansman)

1945
The Suspect
She Gets Her Man (with Sawtell; ac: A. Morton)
Honeymoon Ahead (+ stock)
Blonde Ransom
Easy to Look At
Strange Confession (+ stock)
Pillow of Death
The Daltons Ride Again (+ stock)
Frontier Gal

1946
Idea Girl (+ stock)
Night in Paradise
The Runaround
Inside Job (+ stock)
Canyon Passage
The Black Angel
Wild Beauty
The Dark Mirror (see Tiomkin)
Swell Guy (o: Tamkin)

1947
Michigan Kid (see Salter)
I'll Be Yours (o: Tamkin)
Smash-Up (o: Tamkin)
The Egg and I (o: Tamkin)
The Vigilantes Return (ac: Salter)
Ride the Pink Horse (o: Tamkin)
The Wistful Widow of Wagon Gap (see Schumann)

1948
The Exile (o: Tamkin)
The Naked City (see Rozsa)
Black Bart (see L. Stevens)
Hazard (o: Parrish, Shuken, Cutner) PAR
Tap Roots (o: Tamkin)
For the Love of Mary (o: Tamkin)
Family Honeymoon (o: Tamkin)
The Fighting O'Flynn (o: Tamkin)

1949
West of Laramie (short; + stock)
The Life of Riley
Tulsa (o: Tamkin) EL
The Lady Gambles
Abbott and Costello Meet Frankenstein (o: Tamkin)
The Gal Who Took the West
Sword in the Desert
Red, Hot and Blue (see Lilley)
Bagdad (+ stock)
Free for All

1950
Kid from Texas (mt; + stock)
Francis
One Way Street
Comanche Territory
Louisa
Peggy (see W. Scharf)
The Desert Hawk
The Sleeping City
Harvey
Double Crossbones (o: Tamkin)

1951
Bedtime for Bonzo
Hollywood Story (+ stock)
The Fat Man (with Salter; + stock)
Katie Did It
Francis Goes to the Races
Mark of the Renegade (theme: M. Rosen)
Cattle Drive (see M. Rosen)
Bright Victory
The Lady Pays Off
The Raging Tide
Weekend with Father
The Treasure of Lost Canyon (+ stock)

1952
Bend of the River (see Salter)
No Room for the Groom
Francis Covers the Big Town (with H. Stein; + stock)
Sally and Saint Anne
The World in His Arms
Francis Goes to West Point (see H. Stein)
Bonzo Goes to College
It Grows on Trees
Because of You

1953
Forbidden
The Mississippi Gambler
Taza, Son of Cochise
Desert Legion
The Man from the Alamo
Thunder Bay
The Stand at Apache River (+ stock)
Wings of the Hawk
The Glass Web (see H. Stein)
Back to God's Country

1954
Yankee Pasha (see Salter)
Saskatchewan (see Mancini)
Magnificent Obsession
The Far Country (ac: Mancini, H. Stein, Salter)

Black Horse Canyon (with Salter, Lava, Mancini; ac: H. Stein)
Playgirl (ac: H. Stein; + stock)
The Black Shield of Falworth (see Salter)
Dawn at Socorro (with H. Stein; + stock)
Naked Alibi (see Salter)
Francis Joins the WACs (see Gertz)
Destry (with Mancini, H. Stein)
Four Guns to the Border (see H. Stein)
Dear Myrtle (short; + stock)
Sign of the Pagan (with Salter; ac: H. Stein)

1955
Chief Crazy Horse
Six Bridges to Cross (see H. Stein)
Captain Lightfoot (see H. Stein)
Ain't Misbehavin' (see Mancini)
Foxfire
The Shrike
One Desire
Lady Godiva of Coventry (with Salter)
Never Say Goodbye
All That Heaven Allows
The Rawhide Years (with Salter)

1956
Star in the Dust
Toy Tiger (see Mancini)
Away All Boats (ac: Roemheld)
Francis in the Haunted House (see Mancini)
Gun for a Coward (with Gertz, H. Russell)
Written on the Wind
Kelly and Me (see Mancini)
Istanbul (see Gertz)

1957
The Night Runner (see H. Stein)
Battle Hymn
The Tattered Dress
Tammy and the Bachelor
Kathy O'
Interlude
Man of a Thousand Faces
My Man Godfrey
The Tarnished Angels

1958
This Happy Feeling (ac: Mancini)
Once Upon a Horse
The Restless Years (+ stock)
The Perfect Furlough

1959
Imitation of Life
The Snow Queen

1960
Portrait in Black
Midnight Lace

1961
Back Street

1963
The Ugly American

1964
Captain Newman, M.D.

1965
The Art of Love (see Coleman)
Shenandoah

1966
Madame X
The Appaloosa

SMALL, MICHAEL

1965
Rendezvous (short) ROBERT GRAND PRODS.

1966
Worthington (doc. short) PELICAN FILMS

1967
Draw Me a Telephone (short) PELICAN FILMS

1969
Out of It UA

1970
Jenny CR
The Revolutionary UA
Puzzle of a Downfall Child UNIV

SMITH, A. L.

1958
The Chinese Village (an. short) CW

SMITH, E. JESSUP

1923
Youthful Cheaters HODKINSON

SMITH, HALE

1966
Bold New Approach (doc.) IRVING JACOBY

SMITH, JOLAINE E.

1966
The Birth of a Legend (doc. short) MARY PICKFORD CORP.

SMITH, PAUL J.

1937
Snow White and the Seven Dwarfs (see Churchill)

1940
Pinocchio (see Harline)

1941
The Reluctant Dragon (see Churchill)

1942
Saludos Amigos (see Wolcott)

1943
Victory Through Air Power (see Plumb)
1944
The Three Caballeros (see Wolcott)
1946
Song of the South (see Amfitheatrof)
1947
Fun and Fancy Free (see Wallace)
Blondie's Anniversary (with M. Bakaleinikoff, C. Wheeler; + stock) COL
1948
Glamour Girl (see M. Bakaleinikoff)
Melody Time (see Daniel)
So Dear to My Heart (o: Plumb) WDP
The Strange Mrs. Crane EL
1949
Cinderella (see Wallace)
1954
20,000 Leagues Under the Sea (o: Dubin) WDP
1956
The Great Locomotive Chase (o: Marks) WDP
1957
Perri (o: Brandt, Marks) WDP
1958
The Light in the Forest (o: Marks) WDP
1959
The Shaggy Dog (o: Mullendore) WDP
1960
Pollyanna (o: Marks) WDP
1961
The Parent Trap (o: Marks) WDP
Moon Pilot (o: Oroop) WDP
1962
Bon Voyage! (o: Marks) WDP
1963
Miracle of the White Stallions (o: Marks) WDP
The Three Lives of Thomasina (o: Sheets) WDP

Documentary Features (WDP)
1953
The Living Desert (o: Plumb, Dubin)
1954
The Vanishing Prairie (o: Plumb, Dubin)
1955
The African Lion (o: Dubin)
1956
Secrets of Life (o: Marks, Plumb)
1963
Yellowstone Cubs (o: von Hallberg)

Documentary Shorts (WDP)
1950
Beaver Valley (o: Plumb)
1951
Nature's Half Acre (o: Plumb, Dubin)
The Olympic Elk (o: Plumb)
1952
Water Birds (o: Plumb)
Prowlers of the Everglades (o: Vaughan)
Bear Country (o: Plumb)
1955
Switzerland
1958
The Seven Cities of Antarctica

Animated shorts and cartoons (JSP)
1944
The Crosseyed Bull UA
1945
The Lady Said No UA
Choo-Choo Amigo UA
1946
Pipito's Serenade UA
1947
The Flying Jeep UA
The Fatal Kiss UA
1948
Make Mine Freedom MGM
1949
Meet King Joe HARDING COLLEGE
Why Play Leap Frog? HARDING COLLEGE
1950
Albert in Blunderland HARDING COLLEGE
Fresh Laid Plans HARDING COLLEGE

Animated Shorts
1946
Expanding World Relationships UPA
1947
Public Opinion Polls UPA
Brotherhood of Man UPA
1949
Romantic Rumbolia REP

Animated Shorts (WDP)
1942
The Admiral's Strut U.S. GOVT.
Men of the Navy U.S. GOVT.
The Mosquito and Malaria U.S. GOVT.
Our Battle-Wagons Are Rolling U.S. GOVT.
Food Will Win the War USDA
Out of the Frying Pan Into the Firing Line WAR PRODUCTION BOARD
1943
The Spirit of '43 U.S. GOVT.
1945
Personal Cleanliness U.S. GOVT.
Transmission of Disease U.S. GOVT.
Hold Your Horsepower THE TEXAS CO.

José Come Bem (The Unseen Enemy) CIAA
Hookworm CIAA
The Human Body CIAA
Tuberculosis CIAA
The Dawn of Better Living WESTINGHOUSE
Light Is What You Make It BETTER LIGHT BUREAU
Jet Propulsion GENERAL ELECTRIC

1946
The ABC of Hand Tools GENERAL MOTORS
The Building of a Tire FIRESTONE
Bathing Time for Baby JOHNSON & JOHNSON
Environmental Sanitation CIAA

1951
How to Catch a Cold KLEENEX

Cartoons (WDP)

1936
Don Donald
Donald and Pluto
Mickey's Circus
Mickey's Polo Team (see Churchill)
Thru the Mirror (see Churchill)
The Worm Turns

1937
Clock Cleaners
Hawaiian Holiday
Moose Hunters
Pluto's Quin-Puplets

1938
Polar Trappers

1939
Beach Picnic
Goofy and Wilbur
The Pointer
The Practical Pig

1940
Fire Chief
Window Cleaners (with Wallace)

1941
Canine Caddy
A Gentleman's Gentleman
The Olympic Champ
Pluto's Playmate

1942
Donald Gets Drafted
How to Fish
How to Play Baseball
How to Swim
Pluto and the Armadillo

1943
Fall Out—Fall In
Figaro and Cleo
Home Defense
How to Be a Sailor
The Old Army Game
Reason and Emotion

1944
Contrary Condor
Donald's Day Off
How to Play Football
Tiger Trouble

1945
Californy er Bust!
The Eyes Have It
Hockey Homicide

1949
Camp Dog
Food for Feudin'
Hook, Lion and Sinker
Pests of the West
Puss-Cafe
Toy Tinkers
Trailer Horn

1950
Dude Duck
Hold That Pose
Lion Down
Lucky Number
Morris, the Midget Moose
Motor Mania
R'coon Dawg
Test Pilot Donald

1951
Cold Turkey
Fathers Are People
Get Rich Quick
No Smoking
Out of Scale

1952
Father's Day Off
The Little House
The Simple Things
Susie, the Little Blue Coupe
Trick or Treat
Two Gun Goofy

1956
A Cowboy Needs a Horse

SMITH, ROLAND

1964
The Widening Circle (doc. short) CONTINENTAL CAN CO.

SMITH, WILLIAM O.

1951
Four in the Afternoon (short) JAMES BROUGHTON

SMYTH, HARPER GARCIA
1914
The Seats of the Mighty (with Marum)
COLONIAL

SNELL, DAVID
[All at MGM.]
1937
Married Before Breakfast (o: W. Allen)
My Dear Miss Aldrich (o: Bassman, W. Allen)
Madame X (o: W. Allen, Marquardt)
You're Only Young Once (o: W. Allen, Bassman)
1938
Judge Hardy's Children (o: Raab)
Love Finds Andy Hardy (o: Bassman)
Young Dr. Kildare (o: Raab)
Out West with the Hardys (o: Arnaud)
A Christmas Carol (see Waxman)
1939
Let Freedom Ring (see A. Lange)
The Hardys Ride High (o: Marquardt)
They All Come Out (with E. Ward)
Andy Hardy Gets Spring Fever (see E. Ward)
These Glamour Girls (see E. Ward)
The Women (see E. Ward)
Blackmail (see E. Ward)
Joe and Ethel Turp Call on the President (see E. Ward)
1940
The Man from Dakota (with Cutter, Amfitheatrof)
The Ghost Comes Home (o: Bassman, Maxwell)
20 Mule Team (o: Heglin)
Phantom Raiders (with Amfitheatrof; o: Heglin)
Andy Hardy Meets Debutante (o: Heglin)
Gold Rush Maisie (o: Heglin)
The Golden Fleecing (o: Raab)
Wyoming (o: Raab)
Third Finger, Left Hand (ac: Amfitheatrof, E. Ward; o: Raab)
Hullabaloo (see Bassman)
Gallant Sons (with Amfitheatrof, Zador; o: Raab, Heglin, Marquardt)
1941
Maisie Was a Lady
The Wild Man of Borneo (o: Maxwell, Heglin)
The Penalty (o: Heglin)
Washington Melodrama (o: Raab)
Love Crazy (with Hayton)
Billy the Kid (with Hayton, Cutter; ac: Amfitheatrof; o: Raab, Heglin)
Barnacle Bill (see Kaper)
Down in San Diego (see Amfitheatrof)
Ringside Maisie (+ stock)
Unholy Partners (with Amfitheatrof; o: Heglin, Maxwell, Nussbaum, Raab)
Shadow of the Thin Man (ac: Hayton)
1942
Born to Sing (with Hayton; o: Raab, Heglin)
Nazi Agent (see Amfitheatrof)
The Courtship of Andy Hardy (o: Heglin, Nussbaum)
Kid Glove Killer (see Hayton)
Sunday Punch (with Amfitheatrof; o: Raab, Heglin)
Grand Central Murder (see Hayton)
Pacific Rendezvous (o: Marquardt, Heglin, Raab)
Jackass Mail (see Amfitheatrof)
Tish (with Amfitheatrof; o: Heglin, Raab)
The War Against Mrs. Hadley (o: Raab, Heglin)
Whistling in Dixie (see Hayton)
The Omaha Trail (ac: Amfitheatrof; o: Heglin, Raab)
1943
The Youngest Profession (o: Heglin)
Pilot #5 (see Hayton)
Young Ideas (see Bassman)
The Man from Down Under (ac: Salinger, Kaper; o: Heglin, Raab)
1944
Rationing (see Castelnuovo-Tedesco)
See Here, Private Hargrove (with Hayton; o: Heglin)
Andy Hardy's Blonde Trouble (o: Heglin)
Maisie Goes to Reno (with Kaper, Hayton, R. Franklyn; o: Heglin)
Barbary Coast Gent (with R. Franklyn, Castelnuovo-Tedesco; o: Heglin, Duncan)
Lost in a Harem (see N. Shilkret)
The Thin Man Goes Home (with Kaper, Hayton; o: Heglin)
Between Two Women (o: Heglin)
Gentle Annie (ac: Castelnuovo-Tedesco; o: Heglin)
1945
Keep Your Powder Dry (ac: Kaper; o: Heglin)
Twice Blessed (o: Heglin)

The Hidden Eye (ac: Castelnuovo-Tedesco; o: Heglin)
Dangerous Partners (ac: R. Franklyn; o: Heglin)
What Next, Corporal Hargrove? (o: Heglin)
Up Goes Maisie (ac: R. Franklyn; o: Heglin, Duncan)

1946
Bad Bascomb (ac: R. Franklyn, Castelnuovo-Tedesco; o: Heglin, Duncan)
The Cockeyed Miracle (ac: R. Franklyn; o: Heglin)
The Show-Off (o: Heglin)
The Mighty McGurk (o: Heglin; + stock)
Lady in the Lake (with M. Goldman; o: Heglin)
Love Laughs at Andy Hardy (o: Heglin)

1947
Undercover Maisie (m&e; ac: R. Franklyn; o: Heglin; + stock)
Dark Delusion (with R. Franklyn, Salinger; o: Heglin)
Merton of the Movies (with R. Franklyn; o: Heglin)
Song of the Thin Man (ac: R. Franklyn; o: Heglin; + stock)
Killer McCoy (o: Heglin)

1948
Alias a Gentleman (ac: R. Franklyn, Hayton; o: Heglin; + stock)
A Southern Yankee (with R. Franklyn; o: Heglin, Marquardt)

Shorts

1931
The Geography Lesson (+ stock)

1935
Prince, King of Dogs
Windy

1936
Behind the Headlines (mt)

1937
Bars and Stripes
Candid Cameramaniacs (o: Vaughan)
Carnival in Paris (o: W. Allen)
Equestrian Acrobatics (o: Marquardt)
The Man in the Barn (o: Virgil)
Some Time Soon

1938
Aladdin's Lantern (o: Raab, Bassman)
Anaesthesia (o: Allen)
Billy Rose's Casa Mañana Revue (o: Arnaud, Cutter)
Bravest of the Brave (o: Raab)
The Canary Comes Across (o: Raab, W. Allen, Marquardt)
Captain Kidd's Treasure (o: Raab)
Football Thrills (o: Marquardt)
The Forgotten Step (with C. Bakaleinikoff; o: Bassman, Marquardt)
The Great Heart (o: Raab)
Grid Rules (o: Bassman)
It's In the Stars (o: Arnaud, Marquardt, Salinger)
Joaquin Murrieta (o: Marquardt, Bassman)
John Nesbitt's Passing Parade (o: Raab)
The Little Ranger (o: Arnaud)
The Magician's Daughter (o: W. Allen)
The Man on the Rock (o: Raab)
Men of Steel (o: Raab, Bassman)
The Miracle of Salt Lake (o: Raab)
Music Made Simple (o: Arnaud)
Nostradamus (o: Raab)
Once Over Lightly (o: Raab, Bassman)
An Optical Poem (o: Marquardt)
Party Fever (o: Allen, Marquardt)
Snow Gets in Your Eyes (o: W. Allen, Arnaud, Bassman)
Strange Glory (o: Marquardt, Raab)
That Mothers Might Live (o: Raab, Bassman)
They Live Again (o: Bassman, Raab)
Tracking the Sleeping Death (o: Marquardt, Raab)
Tupapaoo (o: W. Allen, Bassman, Marquardt)
What Do You Think? No. 3 (o: Raab, Arnaud, Cutter, W. Allen)

1939
Angel of Mercy (ac: C. Bakaleinikoff; o: Raab, Virgil, Heglin)
A Door Will Open (mt; o: Heglin)
Electrical Power
Football Thrills of 1938 (o: Marquardt)
From the Ends of the Earth (see E. Ward)
The Giant of Norway (with Amfitheatrof; o: Heglin)
The Greener Hills (o: Virgil)
Happily Buried (o: Raab, Bassman)
Heroes at Leisure (see Axt)
Ice Antics
Marine Circus (o: Raab)
Miracle at Lourdes (o: Raab)
Prophet Without Honor (ac: Amfitheatrof; o: Heglin, Virgil)
Radio Hams (o: Virgil)
Somewhat Secret (o: Raab, Heglin)
The Story of Alfred Nobel (o: Raab)

The Story of Dr. Jenner (o: Raab)
The Story That Couldn't Be Printed (with Amfitheatrof; o: Heglin)
The World Is Ours
Yankee Doodle Goes to Town (o: Virgil, Heglin)

1940
The Big Premiere (o: Bleyer)
The Flag Speaks (with Amfitheatrof; o: Raab, Heglin, Arnaud, Marquardt)
Football Thrills of 1939 (o: Marquardt)
The Hidden Master (with Amfitheatrof; o: Heglin)
Hollywood: Style Center of the World
Know Your Money (mt; o: Heglin)
Maintain the Right (o: Heglin)
Sky Murder
Stuffie (with Amfitheatrof; o: Heglin, Marquardt)
Third Dimensional Murder (with Zador; o: Raab)
A Way in the Wilderness (with Amfitheatrof; o: Heglin)

1941
Army Champions (o: Maxwell)
Football Thrills of 1940 (o: Marquardt)
How to Hold Your Husband—Back (mt; o: Heglin)
Melodies Old and New (o: Heglin)
We Must Have Music (see Hayton)
Ye Olde Minstrels (o: Heglin)

1942
Acro-Batty (o: Raab)
Barbee-Cues (mt; o: Heglin)
First Aid (o: Heglin)
Football Thrills of 1941 (o: Marquardt)
Further Prophecies of Nostradamus (with Amfitheatrof; o: Raab, Nussbaum)
The Greenie (see S. Kaplan)
Main Street on the March! (see Amfitheatrof)
Victory Vittles (o: Heglin)
What About Daddy? (o: Raab)

1944
Twenty Years After (with R. Franklyn)

1947
It Can't Be Done (see R. Franklyn)

1948
My Old Town (see R. Franklyn)

SNYDER, JACK

1924
The Ten Commandments (see Riesenfeld, 1923)

SODERO, CESARE

1925
Isn't Life Wonderful (see Silvers)

SODJA, JOE

1957
The Parson and the Outlaw COL

SOMMER, HANS

1943
The Mysterious Doctor (see Lava)

1946
Her Sister's Secret PRC
Boston Blackie and the Law (+ stock) COL
Singin' in the Corn (+ stock) COL

1947
Gas House Kids Go West (o: Glasser) PRC

1951
The First Legion UA

SORACI, JESS

1970
Before the Mountain Was Moved (doc.) ROBERT K. SHARPE PRODS.

SPARKS, RANDY

1964
Advance to the Rear (adapted by Montenegro) MGM

1970
Angel Unchained AIP

SPECHT, DON

1965
The Top (an. short) MURAKAMI-WOLF

SPENCER, HERBERT

1940
He Married His Wife TCF

1943
Sweet Rosie O'Grady (see Mockridge)

1945
Diamond Horseshoe (ac: C. Henderson, de Packh, D. Raksin, Buttolph) TCF

1946
Centennial Summer (see A. Newman)

1947
Carnival in Costa Rica (see Buttolph)

1949
Dancing in the Dark (see Mockridge)

1953
The I Don't Care Girl (ac: Mayers, Mockridge) TCF

Gentlemen Prefer Blondes (see H. Schaefer)
1954
There's No Business Like Show Business (see A. Newman)
1957
Spring Reunion (with Hagen) UA
1960
Let's Make Love (see Hagen)
[Also a very prolific arranger and orchestrator.]

SPENCER, NORMAN
Cartoons (WB)
1933
Buddy's Day Out
I've Got to Sing a Torch Song
1934
Beauty and the Beast
Buddy and Towser
Buddy of the Apes
Buddy the Detective
Buddy the Gob
Buddy the Woodsman
Buddy's Bearcats
Buddy's Beer Garden
Buddy's Circus
Buddy's Garage
Buddy's Show Boat
Buddy's Trolley Troubles
The Girl at the Ironing Board
Goin' to Heaven on a Mule
Honeymoon Hotel
How Do I Know It's Sunday?
The Miller's Daughter
Pettin' in the Park
Shake Your Powder Puff
Sittin' on a Backyard Fence
Those Were Wonderful Days
Viva Buddy
Why Do I Dream Those Dreams?
1935
Along Flirtation Walk
Buddy in Africa
Buddy of the Legion
Buddy Steps Out
Buddy the Dentist
Buddy the Gee Man
Buddy's Adventures
Buddy's Bug Hunt
Buddy's Pony Express
Buddy's Theatre
The Country Boy
The Country Mouse
I Haven't Got a Hat
Into Your Dance
The Merry Old Soul
Mr. & Mrs. Is the Name
My Green Fedora
Pop Goes Your Heart
Rhythm in the Bow
Those Beautiful Dames
1936
Alpine Antics
At Your Service Madame
Billboard Frolics
Bingo Crosbyana
The Blow-Out
Boom Boom
Buddy's Lost World
A Cartoonist's Nightmare
The Cat Came Back
The Fire Alarm
Fish Tales
Flowers for Madame
Gold Diggers of '49
Hollywood Capers
I Love to Singa
I Wanna Play House
I'd Love to Take Orders from You
I'm a Big Shot Now
A Lady in Red
Let It Be Me
The Little Dutch Plate
Miss Glory
The Phantom Ship
Plane Dippy
Porky the Rainmaker
Porky's Pet
Shanghaied Shipmates
Sunday Go to Meetin' Time
Westward Whoa
When I Yoo Hoo

SPICE, IRVING
1969
Gathering of Evil ABRAMS & PARISI

SPIELTER, HERMANN
1924
Martin Luther, His Life and Time (with Rechlin) LUTHERAN FILM DIVISION

SPIELTER, WILLIAM
1933
Hot Pepper (partial) FOX
The Warrior's Husband (see Zamecnik)
Best of Enemies (see A. Lange)
Deluge (see Burton)

1937
Adventures of Chico (see Kilenyi)
[Also worked as an orchestrator.]

SPITALNY, PHIL
1918
Virtuous Wives FN

SPRINGER, PHILIP
1967
Kill a Dragon UA
1968
I Sailed to Tahiti with an All Girl Crew WORLD
1969
More Dead Than Alive UA
Impasse UA
Tell Me That You Love Me, Junie Moon PAR

SPRINGER, ROBERT
1966
Her Name Was Ellie, His Name Was Luke (short) PUBLIC HEALTH SERVICE

STABILE, DICK
1968
Born to Buck (doc.) PANDORA
1969
Hook, Line and Sinker COL

STACK, LENNY
1970
C. C. and Company EMB

STAHL, WILLY
1934
Dealers in Death (doc.) TOPICAL FILMS
1936
La última cita (Spanish language) COL
1944
Timber Queen PAR
Nabonga (Gorilla) PRC
The Navy Way PAR
Dark Mountain PAR
1946
A Boy, a Girl and a Dog FC

STAHLBERG, FREDERICK
1921
Deception (see Riesenfeld)
1923
A Woman of Paris UA
1928
Lilac Time (see N. Shilkret)
The Wind (see Axt)
The Masks of the Devil (see Axt)
West of Zanzibar (see Axt)
1929
Alias Jimmy Valentine (see Axt)
Tide of Empire (see Axt)
Spite Marriage (ac: Axt, Cupero; + stock) MGM
1930
Billy the Kid (+ stock) MGM

STALLING, CARL W.
Cartoons (WDP)
1928
The Barn Dance
The Gallopin' Gaucho
Plane Crazy
1929
Barnyard Battle
The Haunted House
Hell's Bells
The Jazz Fool
Jungle Rhythm
The Karnival Kid
The Merry Dwarfs
Mickey's Choo Choo
Mickey's Follies
The Opry House
Plow Boy
The Skeleton Dance
Springtime
El Terrible Toreador
When the Cat's Away
Wild Waves
1930
Autumn
Summer
Cartoons (CELEBRITY)
1931
The Cuckoo Murder Case
Fiddlesticks
Flying Fists
Laughing Gas
Ragtime Romeo
The Soup Song
The Village Barber
The Village Smitty
1932
Nurse Maid
1933
Coo-Coo, the Magician
Jack and the Beanstalk
Play Ball
Spite Flight
Stratos-Fear

1934

Aladdin and the Wonderful Lamp
The Brave Tin Soldier
The Cave Man
Davy Jones' Locker
Don Quixote
A Good Scout
The Headless Horseman
Hell's Fire
Insultin' the Sultan
Jack Frost
Jungle Jitters
The Little Red Hen
Puss in Boots
The Queen of Hearts
Rasslin' Round
Reducing Creme
Robin Hood, Jr.
The Valiant Tailor
Viva Willie

1935

Balloonland
Bremen Town Musicians
Humpty Dumpty
Little Black Sambo
Mary's Little Lamb
Old Mother Hubbard
Simple Simon
Sinbad the Sailor
Summertime
The Three Bears

1936

Ali Baba
Dick Whittington's Cat
Happy Days
Little Boy Blue
Tom Thumb

Cartoons (WB)

1936

Boulevardier from the Bronx
Coocoonut Grove
Don't Look Now
Little Beau Porky
Milk and Money
Porky in the Northwoods
Porky the Wrestler
Porky's Moving Day
Porky's Poultry Plant
Toy Town Hall
The Village Smithy

1937

Ain't We Got Fun
The Case of the Stuttering Pig
Clean Pastures
Daffy Duck and Egghead
Dog Daze
Egghead Rides Again
The Fella with the Fiddle
Get-Rich-Quick Porky
He Was Her Man
I Only Have Eyes for You
I Wanna Be a Sailor
Little Red Walking Hood
The Lyin' Mouse
My Little Buckaroo
Picador Porky
Pigs Is Pigs
Plenty of Money and You
Porky and Gabby
Porky at the Crocadero
Porky's Badtime Story
Porky's Building
Porky's Double Trouble
Porky's Duck Hunt
Porky's Garden
Porky's Hero Agency
Porky's Phoney Express
Porky's Poppa
Porky's Railroad
Porky's Road Race
Porky's Romance
Porky's Super Service
Rover's Rival
September in the Rain
She Was an Acrobat's Daughter
The Sneezing Weasel
Speaking of the Weather
A Star Is Hatched
Streamlined Greta Green
A Sunbonnet Blue
Sweet Siox
Uncle Tom's Bungalow
The Woods Are Full of Cuckoos

1938

Cinderella Meets Fella
Count Me Out
Cracked Ice
The Daffy Doc
Daffy Duck in Hollywood
Dog Gone Modern
A Feud There Was
Hamateur Night
Have You Got Any Castles
Injun Trouble
The Isle of Pingo Pongo
Johnny Smith and Poker-Huntas
Jungle Jitters
Katnip Kollege
A Lad in Bagdad
Little Pancho Vanilla

The Lone Stranger and Porky
Love and Curses
The Major Lied Till Dawn
The Mice Will Play
The Night Watchman
Now That Summer Is Gone
The Penguin Parade
Porky & Daffy
Porky in Egypt
Porky in Wackyland
Porky the Fireman
Porky's Five and Ten
Porky's Hare Hunt
Porky's Naughty Nephew
Porky's Party
Porky's Spring Planting
What Price Porky
Wholly Smoke
You're an Education

1939

Bars and Stripes Forever
Believe It or Else
Chicken Jitters
The Curious Puppy
Dangerous Dan McFoo
A Day at the Zoo
Detouring America
The Early Worm Gets the Bird
Fagin's Freshmen
The Film Fan
Fresh Fish
Gold Rush Daze
The Good Egg
Hare-um Scare-um
Hobo Gadget Band
It's an Ill Wind
Jeepers Creepers
Kristopher Kolumbus, Jr.
Land of the Midnight Fun
Little Brother Rat
Little Lion Hunter
Naughty But Mice
Naughty Neighbors
Old Glory
Pied Piper Porky
Polar Pals
Porky and Teabiscuit
Porky the Giant Killer
Porky the Gob
Porky's Hotel
Porky's Last Stand
Porky's Movie Mystery
Porky's Picnic
Porky's Tire Trouble
Prest-o Change-o
Robin Hood Makes Good
Scalp Trouble
Screwball Football
Sioux Me
Sniffles and the Bookworm
Snow Man's Land
Thugs with Dirty Mugs
Wise Quacks

1940

Africa Squeaks
Ali Baba Bound
The Bear's Tale
Bedtime for Sniffles
Busy Bakers
Calling Dr. Porky
Ceiling Hero
The Chewin' Bruin
Circus Today
Confederate Honey
Cross Country Detours
The Egg Collector
Elmer's Candid Camera
Elmer's Pet Rabbit
The Fighting 69½th
A Gander at Mother Goose
Ghost Wanted
Good Night Elmer
The Hardship of Miles Standish
Holiday Highlights
Little Blabbermouse
Malibu Beach Party
Mighty Hunters
Of Fox and Hounds
Patient Porky
Pilgrim Porky
Porky's Baseball Broadcast
Porky's Hired Hand
Porky's Poor Fish
Porky's Snooze Reel
Prehistoric Porky
Shop, Look, and Listen
Slap Happy Pappy
Sniffles Bells the Cat
Sniffles Takes a Trip
The Sour Puss
Stage Fright
The Timid Toreador
Tom Thumb in Trouble
Wacky Wild Life
A Wild Hare
You Ought to Be in Pictures

1941

All This and Rabbit Stew

Aviation Vacation
The Brave Little Bat
The Bug Parade
The Cagey Canary
The Cat's Tale
A Coy Decoy
The Crackpot Quail
Farm Frolics
Goofy Groceries
The Haunted Mouse
The Heckling Hare
The Henpecked Duck
Hiawatha's Rabbit Hunt
Hollywood Steps Out
Inki and the Lion
Joe Glow, the Firefly
Meet John Doughboy
Notes to You
Porky's Aunt
Porky's Bear Facts
Porky's Midnight Matinee
Porky's Pooch
Porky's Preview
Porky's Prize Pony
Rhapsody in Rivets
Robinson Crusoe, Jr.
Rookie Revue
Saddle Silly
Snow Time for Comedy
Sport Chumpions
Tortoise Beats Hare
Toy Trouble
The Trial of Mr. Wolf
Wabbit Trouble
The Wacky Worm
We the Animals Squeak

1942

Aloha Hooey
The Bird Came C.O.D.
Bugs Bunny Gets the Boid
The Case of the Missing Hare
Conrad, the Sailor
Crazy Cruise
Daffy Duckaroo
Daffy's Southern Exposure
Ding Dog Daddy
Dog Tired
Double Chaser
The Dover Boys
The Draft Horse
The Ducktators
Eatin' on the Cuff
Foney Fables
Fox Pop
Fresh Hare
Gopher Goofy
The Hare-Brained Hypnotist
The Hep Cat
Hobby Horse-Laffs
Hold the Lion, Please
Hop Skip and a Chump
Horton Hatches the Egg
Lights Fantastic
Nutty News
Porky's Cafe
Porky's Pastry Pirates
Saps in Chaps
The Sheepish Wolf
The Squawkin' Hawk
A Tale of Two Kitties
The Wabbit Who Came to Supper
Wacky Blackout
The Wacky Wabbit
Who's Who in the Zoo

1943

The Aristo-Cat
Confusions of a Nutzy Spy
A Corny Concerto (a of music by Tchaikovsky)
Daffy the Commando
Falling Hare
Fifth Column Mouse
Fin 'n Catty
Flop Goes the Weasel
Greetings Bait!
Hiss and Make Up
Hop and Go
Inki and the Minah Bird
An Itch in Time
Jack-Wabbit and the Beanstalk
Meatless Flyday
My Favorite Duck
Pigs in a Polka (a of music by Brahms)
Porky Pig's Feat
Puss 'n Booty
Scrap Happy Daffy
Super-Rabbit
Tin Pan Alley Cats
To Duck or Not to Duck
Tokio Jokio
Tortoise Wins by a Hare
The Unbearable Bear
Wackiki Wabbit
The Wise Quacking Duck
Yankee Doodle Daffy

1944

Angel Puss
Birdy and the Beast

Booby Hatched
Brother Brat
Buckaroo Bugs
Bugs Bunny and the Three Bears
Bugs Bunny Nips the Nips
Draftee Daffy
Duck Soup to Nuts
Goldilocks and the Jivin' Bears
Hare Force
Hare Ribbin'
Herr Meets Hare
I Got Plenty of Mutton
Little Red Riding Rabbit
Lost and Foundling
The Odor-able Kitty
The Old Grey Hare
Plane Daffy
Russian Rhapsody
Slightly Daffy
The Stupid Cupid
The Swooner Crooner
Tick, Tock, Tuckered
Tom Turk and Daffy
The Unruly Hare
The Weakly Reporter
What's Cookin' Doc?

1945

Ain't That Ducky
Baby Bottleneck
The Bashful Buzzard
Behind the Meat Ball
Book Revue
Daffy Doodles
The Eager Beaver
Fresh Airedale
From Hand to Mouse
A Gruesome Twosome
Hair Raising Hare
Hare Conditioned
Hare Remover
Hare Tonic
Hare Trigger
Holiday for Shoestrings
Hollywood Canine Canteen
Hush My Mouse
Life with Feathers
Nasty Quacks
Peck Up Your Troubles
Quentin Quail
Stage Door Cartoon
Tale of Two Mice
Trap Happy Porky
Wagon Heels

1946

Acrobatty Bunny
Along Came Daffy
Bacall to Arms
Baseball Bugs
The Big Snooze
Easter Yeggs
Fair and Worm-er
A Feather in His Hare
The Gay Anties
Goofy Gophers
The Great Piggy Bank Robbery
Hollywood Daffy
Kitty Kornered
Mouse Menace
The Mouse-merized Cat
Of Thee I Sting
Rabbit Transit
Racketeer Rabbit
Rhapsody Rabbit
Roughly Squeaking
Slick Hare
Walky Talky Hawky

1947

Birth of a Notion
Bone Sweet Bone
Bugs Bunny Rides Again
Catch as Cats Can
Crowing Pains
Daffy Duck Slept Here
Doggone Cats
The Foxy Duckling
Gorilla My Dreams
Hare Do
A Hare Grows in Manhattan
Haredevil Hare
A Hick, a Slick and a Chick
High Diving Hare
Hobo Bobo
Hop, Look, and Listen
A Horse Fly Fleas
House Hunting Mice
I Taw a Putty Tat
Inki at the Circus
Kit for Kat
Little Orphan Airedale
Mexican Joy Ride
Mouse Wreckers
Nothing But the Tooth
One Meat Brawl
Paying the Piper
A Pest in the House
The Pest That Came to Dinner
Porky Chops
Rabbit Punch
Rebel Rabbit
Scent-imental Over You

Tweetie Pie
Two Gophers from Texas
What's Brewin' Bruin?

1948

A-Lad-in His Lamp
Awful Orphan
Back Alley Oproar
Bad Ol' Putty Tat
Bear Feat
The Bee-Deviled Bruin
Big House Bunny
Boobs in the Woods
Bowery Bugs
Buccaneer Bunny
Curtain Razor
Daffy Dilly
Dough for the Do-Do
Dough Ray Me-ow
Each Dawn I Crow
Fast and Furry-ous
The Foghorn Leghorn
For Scent-imental Reasons
Frigid-Hare
The Gray Hounded Hare
A Ham in a Role
Hare Splitter
Henhouse Henery
Hippety Hopper
Holiday for Drumsticks
Hot Cross Bunny
Hurdy-Gurdy Hare
The Leghorn Blows at Midnight
Mouse Mazurka
Mutiny on the Bunny
My Bunny Lies Over the Sea
Odor of the Day
Often an Orphan
The Rattled Rooster
Riff Raffy Daffy
Scaredy Cat
The Scarlet Pumpernickel
The Shell-Shocked Egg
Strife with Father
The Stupor Salesman
Swallow the Leader
The Upstanding Sitter
What Makes Daffy Duck?
Which Is Witch
The Windblown Hare
Wise Quackers
You Were Never Duckier

1949

All Abir-r-r-d
A Bone for a Bone
Bunker Hill Bunny
Bushy Hare
Bye, Bye, Bluebeard
Canary Road
Canned Feud
Caveman Inki
Daffy Duck Hunt
Dog Collared
The Ducksters
An Egg Scramble
8 Ball Bunny
A Fox in a Fix
A Fractured Leghorn
Golden Yeggs
Hare We Go
His Bitter Half
Home Tweet Home
Homeless Hare
The Hypo-Chondri-Cat
It's Hummer Time
Knights Must Fall
The Lion's Busy
Long-Haired Hare
Mississippi Hare
Pop 'Im Pop
Rabbit Hood
The Rabbit of Seville
Scent-imental Romeo
Two's a Crowd
What's Up, Doc?

1950

Ballot Box Bunny
A Bear for Punishment
Big Top Bunny
Bunny Hugged
Cheese Chasers
Chow Hound
Corn Plastered
Dog Gone South
Drip-Along Daffy
Early to Bet
The Fair-Haired Hare (with Poddany)
Foxy by Proxy
Hillbilly Hare
His Hare Raising Tale
A Hound for Trouble
Operation Rabbit
The Prize Pest
Putty Tat Trouble
Rabbit Every Monday
Rabbit Fire
Sleepy Time Possum
Stooge for a Mouse
Thumb Fun
Tweet Tweet Tweety
Tweety's S.O.S.

Water, Water Every Hare
Who's Kitten Who?

1951

Ain't She Tweet?
Beep, Beep
A Bird in a Guilty Cage
Cracked Quack
Duck Amuck
The EGGcited Rooster
Feed the Kitty
Fool Coverage
14 Carrot Rabbit
Gift Wrapped
Going, Going, Gosh!
Hare Lift
The Hasty Hare
Hoppy Go Lucky
Kiddin' the Kitten
Kiss Me Cat
Little Beau Pepe
Little Red Rodent Hood
A Mouse Divided
Oily Hare
A Peck o' Trouble
Rabbit Seasoning
Rabbit's Kin
Snow Business
Sock-a-Doodle-Do
The Super Snooper
Tree for Two
The Turn-Tale Wolf

1952

Ant Pasted
Bully for Bugs
Cats A-Weigh
Catty Cornered
Duck Dodgers in the 24th$^{1}/_{2}$ Century
Duck! Rabbit, Duck!
Easy Peckin's
Forward March Hare
Fowl Weather
Hare Trimmed
Mousewarming
Much Ado About Nutting
Muscle Tussle
Of Rice and Hen
Punch Trunk
Robot Rabbit
Southern Fried Rabbit
A Street Cat Named Sylvester
Terrier Stricken
There Auto Be a Law
Tom-Tom Tomcat
Upswept Hare
Wild Over You
Zipping Along

1953

Bell Hoppy
Bewitched Bunny
Cat-Tails for Two
The Cat's Bah
Claws for Alarm
Design for Leaving
Doctor Jerkyl's Hide
Dog Pounded
Don't Give Up the Sheep
Feline Frame-Up
Gone Batty
Goo, Goo, Goliath
I Gopher You
Little Boy Boo
Lumber Jack-Rabbit
Muzzle Tough
No Barking
No Parking Hare
The Oily American
Quack Shot
Satan's Waitin'
Stop, Look, & Hasten!
Wild Wife

1954

All Fowled Up
Beanstalk Bunny
Captain Hareblower
Jumpin' Jupiter
Plop Goes the Weasel
Ready, Set, Zoom!
Sandy Claws

1955

From A to Z-Z-Z
Gee Whiz-z-z-z-z-z-z!
Guided Muscle
The High and the Flighty
Hyde and Hare
Pappy's Puppy
Speedy Gonzales
Stupor Duck
The Unexpected Pest

1956

Ali Baba Bunny
Barbary Coast Bunny
Half-Fare Hare
Napoleon Bunny-Part
Raw! Raw! Rooster
Scrambled Aches
The Slap-Hoppy Mouse

There They Go-Go-Go!
Two Crows from Tacos
Wideo Wabbit
1957
Bugsy and Mugsy
Cheese It, the Cat!
Fox Terror
Gonzales' Tamales
Mouse-Taken Identity
Piker's Peak
Tabasco Road
To Itch His Own
Zoom and Bored
Private Snafu Cartoons (WB for U.S. ARMY)
1943
Coming Snafu
Fighting Tools
The Goldbrick
Gripes
The Home Front
The Infantry Blues
Rumors
Spies
1944
Booby Traps
Censored
The Chow Hound
Gas
A Lecture on Camouflage
Outpost
Pay Day
Private Snafu vs. Malaria Mike
Snafuperman
Target Snafu
The Three Brothers
1945
Hot Spot
In the Aleutians
It's Murder She Says
No Buddy Atoll
Operation Snafu
Animated Documentary Short
1949
So Much for So Little U.S. HEALTH SERVICE
Features
1945
The Horn Blows at Midnight (see Waxman)
1948
Two Guys from Texas (see Hollander)
1964
Kitten with a Whip (+ stock) UNIV

STALLINGS, KENDALL
1969
Exchanges I (short) JOHN J. CAMIE

STALLWORTH, DOTTIE
1966
The Love Statue VANSAN

STAMPER, DAVE
1928
The Ghost Talks (mt; o: Cokayne) FOX

STANLEIGH, BERTRAM
1956
Suez (doc. short) IFF

STARR, JUNE
1951
Gold Raiders (see Borisoff)
1952
Red Snow (see Borisoff)
1960
Israel Today (doc. short) MARTIN MURRAY
1961
Operation Eichmann (see Borisoff)

STARR, PAULA
1968
Of the Same Gender DISTRIBPIX

STEIN, HERMAN
[All for Universal unless otherwise stated.]
1950
Career for Two (doc. short) ?
1951
Here Come the Nelsons (+ stock)
1952
Has Anybody Seen My Gal (+ stock)
Just Across the Street (ac: M. Rosen; + stock)
Francis Covers the Big Town (see F. Skinner)
The Duel at Silver Creek (+ stock)
Francis Goes to West Point (ac: F. Skinner, M. Rosen; + stock)
Son of Ali Baba (+ stock)
Horizons West (with Mancini; + stock)
Willie and Joe in Back at the Front (see Mancini)
The Raiders (see Mancini)
The Lawless Breed (+ stock)
Meet Me at the Fair (see M. Rosen)
1953
The Redhead from Wyoming (+ stock)

City Beneath the Sea (with M. Rosen, Mancini; + stock)
Gunsmoke (+ stock)
Girls in the Night (see Mancini)
Border River (see Mancini)
Ma and Pa Kettle on Vacation (+ stock)
Abbott and Costello Go to Mars (with Mancini; ac: M. Rosen; + stock)
Column South (with Mancini; + stock)
Law and Order (see M. Rosen)
Lone Hand (with Mancini; + stock)
All I Desire (with Mancini; ac: M. Rosen)
East of Sumatra (with Mancini, Gertz)
The Great Sioux Uprising (with Mancini; + stock)
It Happens Every Thursday (+ stock)
Take Me to Town (with M. Rosen, Mancini)
It Came from Outer Space (see Mancini)
The Golden Blade (with Mancini, Gertz; + stock)
The Glass Web (with F. Skinner, M. Rosen)
Veils of Bagdad (see Mancini)
Tumbleweed (see Mancini)
Ride Clear of Diablo (with M. Rosen; + stock)

1954

War Arrow (ac: Lava; + stock)
Ma and Pa Kettle at Home (with Mancini, Lava; + stock)
Creature from the Black Lagoon (see Salter)
Saskatchewan (see Mancini)
Rails Into Laramie (with Mancini, M. Rosen; + stock)
Johnny Dark (see Salter)
Drums Across the River (with Mancini; + stock)
Tanganyika (see Salter)
The Far Country (see F. Skinner)
Black Horse Canyon (see F. Skinner)
Fireman, Save My Child (see Lava)
Playgirl (see F. Skinner)
The Black Shield of Falworth (see Salter)
Dawn at Socorro (see F. Skinner)
Naked Alibi (see Salter)
Destry (see F. Skinner)
Four Guns to the Border (with F. Skinner, Salter; ac: Mancini)
The Yellow Mountain (see Mancini)
So This Is Paris (see Mancini)
Bengal Brigade (see S. Wilson)
Sign of the Pagan (see F. Skinner)
Abbott and Costello Meet the Keystone Kops (see Mancini)

1955

Six Bridges to Cross (with F. Skinner)
Captain Lightfoot (with Roemheld; ac: Salter; mt: F. Skinner)
This Island Earth (ac: Mancini, Salter)
Revenge of the Creature (see Lava)
Man Without a Star (with Salter)
The Purple Mask (see Roemheld)
The Private War of Major Benson (see Lava)
Female on the Beach (with Roemheld)
Kiss of Fire (see Salter)
There's Always Tomorrow (with Roemheld)
The Spoilers (see Mancini)
Tarantula (+ stock)
The Kettles in the Ozarks (see Mancini)

1956

A Day of Fury (see Gertz)
Backlash
Toy Tiger (see Mancini)
I've Lived Before
Walk the Proud Land (see Salter)
Francis in the Haunted House (see Mancini)
The Mole People (see Roemheld)
The Unguarded Moment (ac: Mancini)
Everything But the Truth (with Mancini, Gertz)
The Great Man (with Mancini; + stock)
Four Girls in Town (see North)

1957

The Night Runner (with F. Skinner, Roemheld; + stock)
Mister Cory (with Mancini)
The Incredible Shrinking Man (see Gertz)
Joe Dakota (see Salter)
The Kettles on Old MacDonald's Farm (see Mancini)
The Land Unknown (see Salter)
Quantez
Slim Carter
The Monolith Monsters (see Gertz)
Man in the Shadow (with Salter)
Love Slaves of the Amazon (see S. Wilson)
This Is Russia (doc.; with Roemheld)
The Lady Takes a Flyer (ac: Roemheld)

1958

The Last of the Fast Guns (see Salter)
The Saga of Hemp Brown (+ stock)
Money, Women and Guns (with Gertz; + stock)

1959

No Name on the Bullet (with Gertz)

1962

The Intruder PATHÉ-AMERICA

1965

Muchos Locos (cartoon) WB

STEIN, JULIAN

1964

The Flesh Eaters CINEMA DISTRIBUTORS

STEIN, RONALD

1955

Apache Woman AIP
Day the World Ended AIP
The Phantom from 10,000 Leagues AIP

1956

The Oklahoma Woman AIP
The Gunslinger AIP
Girls in Prison AIP
It Conquered the World AIP
The She Creature AIP
Flesh and the Spur AIP
Runaway Daughters AIP
The Undead AIP

1957

Naked Paradise AIP
Not of This Earth AA
Dragstrip Girl AIP
Attack of the Crab Monsters AA
Invasion of the Saucer Men AIP
Reform School Girl AIP
Sorority Girl AIP

1958

Jet Attack AIP
Suicide Battalion AIP
Attack of the 50 Foot Woman AA
The Bonnie Parker Story AIP
Hot Rod Gang AIP
High School Hellcats AIP
The Littlest Hobo AA
She Gods of Shark Reef AIP
Paratroop Command AIP

1959

Tank Commando AIP
The Legend of Tom Dooley COL
The Diary of a High School Bride AIP
Ghost of Dragstrip Hollow AIP
Too Soon to Love UNIV

1960

Raymie AA
The Threat WB
Dinosaurus! UNIV
The Girl in Lover's Lane FILMGROUP
The Last Woman on Earth FILMGROUP

1961

War Is Hell AA
Atlas FILMGROUP
Just Between Us PAX
The Devil's Partner FILMGROUP
Guns of the Black Witch AIP
Lost Battalion AIP
Journey to the Seventh Planet AIP

1962

The Bashful Elephant AA
The Underwater City COL
The Premature Burial AIP
Warriors 5 AIP

1963

Dime with a Halo (ac: Armbruster) MGM
Battle Beyond the Sun AIP
The Young and the Brave MGM
The Terror AIP
Of Love and Desire TCF
The Haunted Palace AIP
Dementia 13 AIP

1964

Mars Needs Women AIP

1965

The Eye Creatures AIP
Voyage to a Prehistoric Planet AIP
Portrait in Terror AIP
The Bounty Killer EMBASSY
Requiem for a Gunfighter EMBASSY
Rat Fink CINEMA DISTRIBUTORS

1966

Queen of Blood AIP
Blood Bath AIP
Women of the Prehistoric Planet REALART
Curse of the Swamp Creature AIP
Zontar: The Thing from Venus AIP

1967

A Man Called Dagger (adaptation of music by Steve Allen and ac) MGM

1968

Spider Baby AMERICAN GENERAL
Psych-Out AIP
National Parks—A Road for the Future (doc. short) U.S. EDUCATIONAL FILMS
Little Dreamer (short) UPA FOR BANK OF AMERICA

1969

The Rain People WB

1970

Getting Straight COL

STEINER, FRED

1956

Run for the Sun UA
Man from Del Rio UA

1957

Time Limit UA

1964

The Killers (theme: J. Williams; ac: Rugolo; + stock) UNIV

1965

The Greatest Story Ever Told (see A. Newman)

1967

First to Fight WB

The St. Valentine's Day Massacre TCF

1970

Airport (see A. Newman)

STEINER, GEORGE

1931

Rango (see Hajos)

1950

Cassino to Korea (doc.; with DuPage; ac: Sharples) PAR

1957

The Golden Age of Comedy (compilation film) DCA

Shorts

1935

Manhattan Rhythm PAR

1936

Lulu's Love PAR

1939

Busy Little Bears PAR

In Tune with Tomorrow (doc.) CHRYSLER CORP.

1943

Three Bears in a Boat PAR

1947

Party Lines BIL BAIRD'S MARIONETTES

The Wee Cooper o' Fife BIL BAIRD'S MARIONETTES

1949

Adventure in Telezonia BIL BAIRD'S MARIONETTES

1959

The Violinist (see Pintoff)

Cartoons (PAR)

1930

Accordion Joe

Fire Bugs

Hot Dog

Row, Row, Row

Up to Mars

1931

The Cow's Husband

Dizzy Red Riding Hood

Jack and the Beanstalk

Minding the Baby

1933

Mother Goose Land

Parade of the Wooden Soldiers

Reaching for the Moon

Song Shopping

1934

Lazybones

Little Dutch Mill

There's Something About a Soldier

This Little Piggie Went to Market

1935

Baby Be Good

Choose Your Weppins

The Kids in the Shoe

No! No! A Thousand Times No!!

1936

Little Nobody

STEINER, MAX

[Steiner stated in an interview (Bernard Rosenberg and Harry Silverstein, *The Real Tinsel,* New York, 1970) that he wrote an original score for *The Bondman* (Fox, 1916) for its presentation at the 14th Street Playhouse in New York City.]

[All pictures through 1935 were for RKO.]

1930

Side Street (foreign version of 1929 film; with Webb)

The Delightful Rogue (foreign version of 1929 film; with Webb)

The Case of Sergeant Grischa (mt; + stock)

Dixiana

Cimarron

Beau Ideal (m&e; + stock)

1931

Kept Husbands (m&e; + stock)

Bachelor Apartment (+ stock)

Cracked Nuts (o: Marquardt)

Young Donovan's Kid (mt; + stock)

Transgression

The Public Defender (o: E. Ross)

The Runaround

High Stakes (+ stock)

The Gay Diplomat

Fanny Foley Herself

Consolation Marriage (o: Gerstenberger)

Way Back Home (o: Gerstenberger)

Secret Service (o: Gerstenberger)

Are These Our Children?

Peach-o-Reno (o: R. Heindorf)

1932

Men of Chance (o: Gerstenberger)

Girl of the Rio (o: Gerstenberger)
Ladies of the Jury (mt; o: R. Heindorf; + stock)
The Lost Squadron
Girl Crazy (ac)
Symphony of Six Million (o: Kaun)
State's Attorney (o: R. Heindorf)
Is My Face Red? (o: R. Heindorf, Kaun)
What Price Hollywood? (o: Kaun)
Roar of the Dragon (o: Kaun, Gerstenberger)
Bird of Paradise (o: Kaun, R. Bassett)
The Most Dangerous Game (o: Kaun, Gerstenberger)
A Bill of Divorcement (mt: Harling; o: Kaun)
Thirteen Women (o: Kaun, Gerstenberger)
The Conquerors (o: Kaun)
The Half Naked Truth
Penguin Pool Murder (mt)
The Animal Kingdom
The Monkey's Paw (o: Kaun)

1933
The Cheyenne Kid (+ stock)
Lucky Devils
King Kong (o: Kaun)
Christopher Strong (o: Kaun; ac: Webb, o: Sharpe)
Sweepings (o: Kaun)
Diplomaniacs (with Webb; o: Kaun, Sharpe)
The Silver Cord (+ stock)
Melody Cruise
Morning Glory (o: Kaun)
Little Women (o: Kaun)
The Right to Romance (see Webb)
The Son of Kong (o: Kaun)

1934
The Lost Patrol (o: Kaun)
Stingaree (o: Kaun)
Murder on the Blackboard (with Kaun)
The Life of Vergie Winters (o: Kaun)
Of Human Bondage (o: Kaun)
The Fountain
The Age of Innocence (o: Kaun)
The Gay Divorcee
The Little Minister (o: Kaun)

1935
Roberta
Star of Midnight (+ stock)
The Informer (o: Kaun, de Packh)
Break of Hearts (o: Kaun)
She (o: Kaun, de Packh, E. Powell)
Alice Adams (see Webb)
The Three Musketeers (o: Kaun)
I Dream Too Much

1936
Follow the Fleet RKO
Little Lord Fauntleroy (o: Kaun) SELZNICK
The Charge of the Light Brigade (o: Friedhofer, Parrish, de Packh, R. Bassett) WB
The Garden of Allah (o: Kaun, E. Powell, R. Bassett, Parrish, Friedhofer) SELZNICK
God's Country and the Woman (o: Friedhofer) WB

1937
Green Light (o: Friedhofer) WB
Slim (with Roemheld; o: Friedhofer) WB
Kid Galahad (see Roemheld)
A Star Is Born (o: Kaun, Parrish, Friedhofer) SELZNICK
The Life of Emile Zola (o: Friedhofer) WB
That Certain Woman (o: Friedhofer) WB
First Lady (o: Friedhofer) WB
Submarine D-l (o: Friedhofer) WB
Tovarich (o: Friedhofer) WB
[First use of Steiner's trademark fanfare, "Warner Bros. Presents", subsequently used on hundreds of pictures.]

1938
Gold Is Where You Find It (o: Friedhofer, Kaun) WB
Jezebel (o: Friedhofer) WB
The Adventures of Tom Sawyer (o: Parrish, Kaun; + stock) SELZNICK
Crime School (o: Friedhofer, Parrish) WB
White Banners WB
The Amazing Dr. Clitterhouse (o: Parrish) WB
Four Daughters (o: Friedhofer) WB
The Sisters (o: Friedhofer) WB
Angels with Dirty Faces (o: Friedhofer) WB
The Dawn Patrol (o: Friedhofer) WB

1939
They Made Me a Criminal (o: Friedhofer) WB
The Oklahoma Kid (ac: A. Deutsch, Friedhofer; o: Friedhofer, A. Deutsch, Parrish, Cutter) WB
Dodge City (ac: A. Deutsch; o: Friedhofer) WB
Dark Victory (o: Friedhofer) WB
Confessions of a Nazi Spy WB
Daughters Courageous (o: R. Heindorf) WB
Each Dawn I Die (o: Friedhofer) WB
The Old Maid (o: Friedhofer) WB
Dust Be My Destiny (o: Friedhofer) WB
Intermezzo, a Love Story (ac: R. Bennett; o: R. Bennet t, Friedhofer, Raab, de Packh, R. Bassett, Salinger) SELZNICK

We Are Not Alone (o: Friedhofer) WB
Gone with the Wind (ac: Friedhofer, A. Deutsch, Roemheld; o: Friedhofer, Kaun, R. Bassett, Deutsch, et al.) SELZNICK

1940
Four Wives (o: Friedhofer, R. Heindorf) WB
Dr. Ehrlich's Magic Bullet (o: Friedhofer) WB
Virginia City (o: Friedhofer) WB
All This, and Heaven Too (o: Friedhofer) WB
City for Conquest (o: Friedhofer, R. Heindorf) WB
A Dispatch from Reuter's (o: Friedhofer) WB
The Letter (o: Friedhofer) WB
Santa Fe Trail (o and ac: Friedhofer) WB

1941
The Great Lie (o: Friedhofer, R. Heindorf) WB
Shining Victory (o: Friedhofer) WB
The Bride Came C.O.D. (o: Friedhofer, R. Heindorf) WB
Dive Bomber (o: Friedhofer) WB
Sergeant York (o: Friedhofer) WB
One Foot in Heaven (o: Friedhofer) WB

1942
They Died with Their Boots On (o: Friedhofer, Kaun) WB
Captains of the Clouds (o: Friedhofer) WB
In This Our Life (o: Friedhofer) WB
The Gay Sisters (o: Friedhofer) WB
Desperate Journey (o and ac: Friedhofer) WB
Now, Voyager (o: Friedhofer) WB

1943
Casablanca (o: Friedhofer) WB
Mission to Moscow (o: Kaun, Friedhofer) WB
Watch on the Rhine (o: Friedhofer) WB
This Is the Army (see R. Heindorf)
The Battle of Britain (doc.; with Lava, H. Jackson) WB

1944
Up in Arms (ac: H. Jackson) GOLDWYN
Passage to Marseille (o: Raab) WB
The Adventures of Mark Twain (o: Kaun) WB
Since You Went Away (o: Grau, Raab, Moross, Zador) SELZNICK
Arsenic and Old Lace (o: Friedhofer) WB
The Conspirators (o: Raab; ac: Friedhofer) WB

1945
Roughly Speaking (o: Friedhofer) WB
The Corn Is Green (o: Friedhofer) WB
Rhapsody in Blue (o: Friedhofer) WB
Mildred Pierce (o: Friedhofer) WB
Tomorrow Is Forever (o: Kaun) INTERNATIONAL

1946
San Antonio (o: Friedhofer) WB
My Reputation (o: Friedhofer) WB
Saratoga Trunk (o: Kaun; ac: Lava) WB
Her Kind of Man (see Waxman)
One More Tomorrow (mt: Friedhofer) WB
A Stolen Life (o: Friedhofer) WB
Night and Day (o: Friedhofer) WB
The Big Sleep (o: Bucharoff) WB
Cloak and Dagger (o: Friedhofer) WB

1947
The Man I Love (o: Friedhofer) WB
The Beast with Five Fingers (o: Cutter) WB
Pursued (o: Cutter) WB
Love and Learn (o: Cutter) WB
Cheyenne (o: Friedhofer) WB
The Unfaithful (o: Cutter) WB
Deep Valley (o: Cutter) WB
Life with Father (o: Cutter) WB
Dark Passage (see Waxman)
The Voice of the Turtle (o: Cutter) WB
My Wild Irish Rose (o: Cutter) WB

1948
The Treasure of the Sierra Madre (o: Cutter) WB
My Girl Tisa (o: Cutter) WB
April Showers (see R. Heindorf)
Winter Meeting (o: Cutter) WB
The Woman in White (o: Cutter) WB
Silver River (o: Cutter) WB
Key Largo (o: Cutter) WB
Johnny Belinda (o: Cutter) WB
Fighter Squadron (o: Cutter) WB
The Decision of Christopher Blake (o: Cutter) WB
A Kiss in the Dark (o: Cutter) WB

1949
Adventures of Don Juan (o: Cutter) WB
South of St. Louis (o: Cutter) WB
Flamingo Road (o: Cutter) WB
The Fountainhead (o: Cutter) WB
Without Honor (o: Cutter) UA
Beyond the Forest (o: Cutter) WB
White Heat (o: Cutter) WB
Mrs. Mike (ac: Lava) UA
The Lady Takes a Sailor (o: Cutter) WB

1950
Backfire (see Amfitheatrof)
Young Man with a Horn (theme: R. Heindorf) WB
Caged (o: Cutter) WB
The Flame and the Arrow (o: Cutter) WB
The Breaking Point (ac: H. Jackson) WB
The Glass Menagerie (o: Cutter) WB
Rocky Mountain (o: Cutter) WB
Sugarfoot (o: Cutter) WB
Dallas (o: Cutter) WB
1951
Operation Pacific (o: Cutter) WB
Lightning Strikes Twice (o: Cutter) WB
Raton Pass (o: Cutter) WB
I Was a Communist for the F.B.I. (o: Cutter) WB
On Moonlight Bay (o: Cutter) WB
Jim Thorpe—All-American (o: Cutter) WB
Force of Arms (o: Cutter) WB
Come Fill the Cup (see R. Heindorf)
Close to My Heart (o: Cutter) WB
Distant Drums (o: Cutter) WB
1952
I'll See You in My Dreams (see R. Heindorf)
This Woman Is Dangerous (see Buttolph)
Room for One More (o: Cutter) WB
The Lion and the Horse (o: Cutter) WB
Mara Maru (o: Cutter) WB
The Miracle of Our Lady of Fatima (o: Cutter) WB
Springfield Rifle (o: Cutter) WB
The Iron Mistress (o: Cutter) WB
1953
The Jazz Singer (o: Cutter) WB
This Is Cinerama (doc.; ac: Webb, Sawtell, Shuken, Cutner) CINERAMA
Trouble Along the Way (o: Cutter) WB
By the Light of the Silvery Moon (o: Cutter) WB
The Desert Song (o: Cutter) WB
House of Wax (trailer only) (o: Cutter) WB
The Charge at Feather River (o: Cutter) WB
So This Is Love (o: Cutter) WB
So Big (o: Cutter) WB
1954
The Boy from Oklahoma (o: Cutter) WB
The Caine Mutiny (o: Cutter) COL
King Richard and the Crusaders (o: Cutter) WB
The Violent Men (o: Cutter) COL
1955
Battle Cry (o: Cutter) WB
The Last Command (o: Cutter) REP
The McConnell Story (o: Cutter) WB
Illegal (o: Cutter) WB
Come Next Spring (o: Cutter) REP
1956
Hell on Frisco Bay (o: Cutter) WB
Helen of Troy (o: Cutter) WB
The Searchers (o: Cutter) WB
Bandido (o: Cutter) UA
Death of a Scoundrel (o: Cutter) RKO
1957
China Gate (with H. Jackson; theme: V. Young) TCF
Band of Angels (o: Cutter) WB
Escapade in Japan (o: Cutter) RKO
All Mine to Give (o: Cutter) RKO
1958
Fort Dobbs (o: Cutter) WB
Darby's Rangers (o: Cutter) WB
Marjorie Morningstar (o: Cutter) WB
1959
The Hanging Tree (o: Cutter) WB
John Paul Jones (o: Cutter) WB
The FBI Story (o: Cutter) WB
A Summer Place (o: Cutter) WB
1960
Cash McCall (o: Cutter) WB
Ice Palace (o: Cutter) WB
The Dark at the Top of the Stairs (o: Cutter) WB
1961
The Sins of Rachel Cade (o: Cutter) WB
Parrish (o: Cutter) WB
Susan Slade (o: Cutter) WB
A Majority of One (o: Cutter) WB
1962
Rome Adventure (o: Cutter) WB
1963
Spencer's Mountain (o: Cutter) WB
1964
A Distant Trumpet (o: Cutter) WB
Those Calloways (o: Cutter) WDP
Youngblood Hawke (o: Cutter) WB
Two on a Guillotine (o: Cutter) WB

STEINERT, ALEXANDER

1942
Camouflage (doc. short) A.A.F.
Learn and Live (doc. short) A.A.F.
Radio Operator (doc. short) A.A.F.
Target for Today (doc. short) A.A.F.
1946
Strangler of the Swamp PRC
Devil Bat's Daughter PRC

The Unknown (+ stock) COL
Personality Kid (+ stock) COL
Little Iodine UA
Blondie Knows Best (+ stock) COL
Don Ricardo Returns PRC
1947
King of the Wild Horses (with Leipold; + stock) COL
1948
The Prairie SG
1962
Xmas (short) HERBERT NAGLE

STEININGER, FRANZ
1957
Hit and Run HUGO HAAS
1958
Born to Be Loved HUGO HAAS
1962
Paradise Alley HUGO HAAS
Stagecoach to Dancer's Rock UNIV

STEVENS, LEITH
1942
Syncopation (o: Torbett) RKO
1947
The Wistful Widow of Wagon Gap (see Schumann)
Night Song RKO
1948
The Senator Was Indiscreet (see Amfitheatrof)
Black Bart (with Friedhofer, F. Skinner, Salter, Sawtell, Maxwell) UNIV
All My Sons (o: Tamkin, Torbett) UNIV
Feudin', Fussin' and A-Fightin' UNIV
Larceny (o: Torbett) UNIV
1949
Not Wanted FC
Never Fear (o: Torbett) FILMAKERS
1950
The Great Rupert (o: C. Wheeler) EL
The Sun Sets at Dawn EL
Destination Moon (o: Torbett; an. sequence: C. Wheeler) EL
1951
No Questions Asked (o: R. Franklyn) MGM
When Worlds Collide (o: Shuken, Cutner) PAR
Navajo LIP
Storm Over Tibet (ac; + music by Arthur Honegger from 1935 German film, *Der Dämon des Himalaya,* of which this was a remake) COL
1952
The Atomic City (o: Cailliet) PAR
Eight Iron Men (o: Cailliet) COL
Beware, My Lovely FILMAKERS
1953
The Hitch-Hiker FILMAKERS
The Glass Wall (o: Levene) COL
Scared Stiff (mt: Van Cleave; o: Cailliet) PAR
The War of the Worlds (o: Parrish) PAR
Crazylegs REP
The Bigamist FILMAKERS
The Wild One (o: A. Morton) COL
1954
Private Hell 36 FILMAKERS
The Bob Mathias Story AA
1955
Crashout FILMAKERS
Mad at the World FILMAKERS
The Treasure of Pancho Villa RKO
1956
World Without End AA
The Scarlet Hour (o: Shuken, Hayes, Van Cleave) PAR
Great Day in the Morning RKO
Julie MGM
1957
Lizzie MGM
The Garment Jungle (o: A. Morton, Grau) COL
The James Dean Story (doc.; o: Mandel, Holman) WB
The Careless Years UA
Eighteen and Anxious REP
The Green-Eyed Blonde WB
1958
Ride Out for Revenge UA
Seven Guns to Mesa (o: Courage) AA
Bullwhip AA
Violent Road WB
The Gun Runners (o: Courage) UA
1959
The Five Pennies (o: Van Cleave) PAR
But Not for Me (o: Van Cleave, Shuken, Hayes) PAR
The Gene Krupa Story (o: N. Scott) COL
1960
Hell to Eternity (o: N. Scott) AA
1961
On the Double (o: Van Cleave, Parrish) PAR
Man-Trap (o: Van Cleave, Beau, H. von Hallberg, Crawford) PAR
1962
The Interns (o: Van Cleave) COL

It Happened at the World's Fair (o: Van Cleave) MGM
1963
A New Kind of Love (o: Van Cleave) PAR
1966
The Night of the Grizzly (o: H. Spencer) PAR
Smoky (o: H. Spencer) TCF
1967
Chuka (o: Van Cleave, Grau) PAR

STEVENS, MORTON
1964
The Raiders (with Buttolph) UNIV
Wild and Wonderful UNIV
1965
Bus Riley's Back in Town (see Markowitz)
1966
The Spy with My Face MGM

STEWART, CECIL
1935
On Probation PEERLESS PICTURES

STEWART, FRED
1940
Men and Dust (doc. short) DIAL FILMS
The Children Must Learn (doc. short) WILLARD VAN DYKE
Day After Day (short) DIAL FILMS

STICKLES, WILLIAM
1915
Peer Gynt (+ music of Grieg; another score by Beynon) PAR
1916
The Parson of Panamint PAR
[Also compiled scores for many silent films.]

STILL, WILLIAM GRANT
1936
Lady of Secrets (partial) COL
Adventure in Manhattan (+ stock) COL
Theodora Goes Wild (+ stock) COL
Pennies from Heaven (+ stock) COL
Dodge City Trail (partial) COL
1937
Back in Circulation (see Kaun)
[Also composed many pieces for Columbia's stock catalog.]

STILLMAN, JACK
1934
The Youth of Russia (Yiddish language) HENRY LYNN
1935
Bar-Mitzvah (Yiddish language) HENRY LYNN
1937
Where Is My Child? (Yiddish language) HENRY LYNN
The Holy Oath (Yiddish language) HENRY LYNN
1938
The Power of Life (Yiddish language) HENRY LYNN

ST. JEAN, GENE
1965
Mme. Olga's Massage Parlor AMERICAN FILM

STOCK, DAVID
1964
Evolution of a Shadow (short) KEN JOHNSON

STOLL, GEORGE
1936
Go West, Young Man (with H. Taylor; mt: Shuken) PAR
1937
Midnight Madonna (mt) PAR
On Such a Night (see Toch)
1939
The Wizard of Oz (see Stothart)
Babes in Arms (with Bassman; o: Bassman, Heglin, Cutter) MGM
1940
Broadway Melody of 1940 (with Bassman; o: Bassman, Heglin, Cutter) MGM
Forty Little Mothers (see Stringer)
Strike Up the Band (with Arnaud; o: Van Eps, Bassman) MGM
Little Nellie Kelly (with Bassman, Edens; o: Salinger, Schutt) MGM
Go West (with Bassman; o: Bassman) MGM
1941
Road Show (with Schutt) HAL ROACH
Ziegfeld Girl (see Stothart)
The Big Store (see Hayton)
Lady Be Good (with Bassman; o: Bassman, Salinger) MGM
Babes on Broadway (with Arnaud, Bassman; o: Arnaud, Bassman, Salinger) MGM
1942
Ship Ahoy (with Bassman; o: Bassman, Arnaud) MGM

Panama Hattie (o: Adlam, H. Taylor, Bassman, Van Eps) MGM

1943

Du Barry Was a Lady (see Amfitheatrof)
Presenting Lily Mars (ac: Van Eps, Bassman, N. Shilkret, Arnaud; o: Bassman, Van Eps, Heglin, Arnaud, Raab, Nussbaum, Marquardt) MGM
I Dood It (see Bassman)
Girl Crazy (with Salinger; mt: Bassman; o: Salinger, Nussbaum, D. Raksin, A. Morton) MGM
Swing Fever (o: Nussbaum, Salinger, H. Taylor) MGM

1944

Two Girls and a Sailor (with C. Jackson; o: C. Jackson, Salinger, Duncan, H. Taylor) MGM
Meet Me in St. Louis (see Salinger)
Music for Millions (see Michelet)

1945

Thrill of a Romance (with C. Jackson; o: Duncan, Nussbaum, C. Jackson, Salinger) MGM
Her Highness and the Bellboy (with C. Jackson; ac: Cutner, Duncan, Glasser; o: R. Franklyn, Nussbaum, Duncan, Cutner, C. Jackson, Glasser) MGM
Anchors Aweigh (with C. Jackson; ac: R. Franklyn; o: Nussbaum, Franklyn, C. Jackson) MGM

1946

Two Sisters from Boston (see Salinger)
Holiday in Mexico (with C. Jackson; o: Nussbaum, R. Franklyn, Duncan, Heglin) MGM
No Leave, No Love (with C. Jackson; o: Sendrey, Byrns, Duncan, R. Franklyn) MGM

1947

This Time for Keeps (with C. Jackson; o: Byrns, Duncan, Heglin) MGM

1948

Big City (see Perl)
On an Island with You (with Sendrey; o: Sendrey) MGM
A Date with Judy (with Sendrey; ac: R. Franklyn; o: Sendrey) MGM
The Kissing Bandit (with Sendrey; ac: Bradley, A. Previn; o: Sendrey, Arnaud, Van Eps, Marquardt) MGM

1949

Neptune's Daughter (with Arnaud; o: Arnaud) MGM
In the Good Old Summertime (with Van Eps; o: Van Eps) MGM

1950

Nancy Goes to Rio (see Salinger)
Duchess of Idaho (with Sendrey; o: Sendrey) MGM
The Toast of New Orleans (with Sendrey; o: Sendrey) MGM
Two Weeks with Love (with Sendrey; o: Sendrey) MGM
Watch the Birdie (with Sendrey; o: Sendrey) MGM

1951

Excuse My Dust (with Skiles; o: Arnaud, Skiles) MGM
The Strip (with Rugolo; o: Rugulo) MGM

1952

Skirts Ahoy! (with Sendrey, Rugolo; o: Sendrey) MGM
Glory Alley (with Sendrey; ac: Rugolo; o: Sendrey) MGM

1953

I Love Melvin (o: Van Eps) MGM
Dangerous When Wet (with Sendrey; cartoon sequence: Bradley; o: Sendrey) MGM
Latin Lovers (with Sendrey; o: Sendrey) MGM
Easy to Love (with Van Eps; ac: Sendrey; o: Van Eps, Sendrey) MGM

1954

Rose Marie (with Van Eps, Sendrey; o: Van Eps, Sendrey) MGM
Flame and the Flesh (with Van Eps, Sendrey; o: Van Eps, Sendrey) MGM
The Student Prince (with Van Eps, Sendrey; o: Van Eps, Sendrey) MGM
Athena (with Van Eps, Sendrey; o: Van Eps, Sendrey) MGM

1955

Hit the Deck (with Van Eps, Salinger; o: Van Eps, R. Franklyn) MGM
Love Me or Leave Me (with Van Eps; o: Van Eps) MGM

1956

Meet Me in Las Vegas (with Sendrey, Van Eps; ac: Courage) MGM
The Opposite Sex (with Van Eps; ac: L. Martin; o: Van Eps) MGM

1957

Ten Thousand Bedrooms (with Van Eps; ac: Frontiere, L. Martin) MGM
This Could Be the Night (with Van Eps; o: Van Eps) MGM

Seven Hills of Rome MGM
1959
For the First Time MGM
1960
Where the Boys Are (ac: C. Jackson) MGM
1961
The Horizontal Lieutenant (o: Sendrey) MGM
1962
Jumbo (with Edens, Salinger, Arnaud, Van Eps, R. Franklyn, Courage) MGM
The Courtship of Eddie's Father (with Van Eps) MGM
1963
A Ticklish Affair (with Van Eps; o: Sendrey, Van Eps) MGM
Viva Las Vegas (with Van Eps; o: Van Eps) MGM
1964
Looking for Love (with Van Eps; o: Van Eps) MGM
Girl Happy (with Van Eps; o: Van Eps) MGM
1965
The Man from Button Willow (an.; with Van Eps) UNITED SCREEN ARTS
Made in Paris (with Van Eps; o: Van Eps) MGM
1966
Spinout (with Van Eps; o: Van Eps) MGM

STOLLER, MIKE
1970
The Phynx (o: Cutner, Haskell) WB

STOLZ, ROBERT
1944
It Happened Tomorrow (a: Maxwell) UA

STONE, ANDREW AND VIRGINIA
1960
The Last Voyage (a: Schrager) MGM

STONE, GREGORY
1936
Hollywood Boulevard PAR
Along Came Love (+ stock) PAR
Easy to Take PAR
The Jungle Princess PAR
1937
Champagne Waltz (see Boutelje)
John Meade's Woman (see Hollander)
Her Husband Lies PAR
Internes Can't Take Money (with Hollander; ac: Kaun) PAR
Easy Living (see Jenkins)
Souls at Sea (see Harling)
This Way Please (see Leipold)
1938
Her Jungle Love PAR
In Old Mexico PAR
Girls' School COL
Smashing the Spy Ring COL
Ride a Crooked Mile PAR
1939
Blondie Brings Up Baby (see Harline)
1940
Her First Romance MON
1943
The Boy from Stalingrad COL
1954
Jivaro PAR

STOTHART, HERBERT
1928
The End of St. Petersburg (New York showing of 1927 Russian silent film) ARTHUR HAMMERSTEIN
[All of the following films were for MGM.]
1931
The Squaw Man (o: Maxwell)
The Cuban Love Song (o: Maxwell, Marquardt)
1932
The Son-Daughter (o: Maxwell, Marquardt)
1933
Rasputin and the Empress (o: Marquardt, Maxwell)
The White Sister (o: Maxwell, Marquardt)
The Barbarian (o: Maxwell)
Peg o' My Heart (o: Maxwell, Marquardt)
Turn Back the Clock
Night Flight (o: Maxwell)
Christopher Bean (o: Marquardt)
Going Hollywood
1934
Queen Christina (o: de Packh)
The Cat and the Fiddle (o: Maxwell)
Riptide (ac: Axt, de Packh; o: Maxwell, W. Allen, Marquardt)
Laughing Boy (o: Maxwell, Marquardt, W. Allen, de Packh)
Tarzan and His Mate (trailer only; o: Marquardt)
Viva Villa! (o: Maxwell, Marquardt, de Packh, W. Allen)
Treasure Island (o: Maxwell, Marquardt, de Packh, Lamkoff, W. Allen)

The Barretts of Wimpole Street
Chained (o: Raab, Maxwell, W. Allen, R. Bassett, Virgil)
The Spectacle Maker (short; o: W. Allen)
What Every Woman Knows (o: Maxwell, Raab)
The Merry Widow (o: Maxwell, Marquardt, Raab)
The Painted Veil (o: Raab, Maxwell, Marquardt, W. Allen)
Biography of a Bachelor Girl (trailer only; o: Marquardt)

1935
Sequoia (o: Maxwell, Marquardt, W. Allen, Virgil, Lamkoff, R. Bassett)
The Night Is Young (o: Virgil, Maxwell, Marquardt, Raab, W. Allen, R. Bassett)
David Copperfield (with Axt; ac: R. Bassett, Raab; o: Raab, R. Bassett, Stringer, Virgil, W. Allen, Marquardt, Maxwell)
Vanessa: Her Love Story (o: Raab, Maxwell, Marquardt)
Naughty Marietta (o: Maxwell, Raab, Marquardt, Virgil)
Reckless (see Virgil)
Pursuit (m&e: Axt; o: Maxwell)
China Seas (o: Raab, Maxwell, Marquardt, Virgil)
Anna Karenina (o: Raab, Maxwell, Marquardt, W. Allen)
Here Comes the Band (see E. Ward)
A Night at the Opera (o: W. Allen, Virgil, Raab, Maxwell, Marquardt, Zweifel)
Mutiny on the Bounty (o: Raab, Maxwell)
Ah, Wilderness! (see E. Ward)
A Tale of Two Cities (o: Raab, Maxwell, Marquardt)

1936
Rose Marie (o: Raab, Maxwell)
Wife vs. Secretary (with E. Ward; o: Raab, W. Allen, Virgil, Maxwell)
The Robin Hood of El Dorado (ac: E. Ward; o: Raab, W. Allen, Maxwell, Marquardt)
Small Town Girl (with E. Ward; o: Raab, Marquardt, Maxwell, Virgil, W. Allen)
San Francisco (with E. Ward; o: Raab, Marquardt, W. Allen, Virgil, Maxwell)
Master Will Shakespeare (short; o: Raab)
The Gorgeous Hussy (ac: E. Ward; o: Raab, Marquardt, W. Allen)
Romeo and Juliet (ac: E. Ward; o: Raab, W. Allen, R. Bennett, Marquardt, Vaughan, Maxwell)
Camille (ac: E. Ward; o: Raab, Marquardt, Maxwell, W. Allen)

1937
The Good Earth (ac: E. Ward; o: Raab, Vaughan, W. Allen)
Maytime (ac: E. Ward; o: Raab, Marquardt, W. Allen)
The Firefly (ac: E. Ward; o: Raab, Marquardt, W. Allen, Maxwell)
Conquest (o: Raab, Marquardt, Cutter, Arnaud, Bassman)
Rosalie (o: Raab, Cutter, Arnaud, Marquardt)

1938
Of Human Hearts (ac: Axt, E. Ward; o: Raab, Marquardt, Arnaud, Cutter)
The Girl of the Golden West (o: Raab, Cutter, Arnaud, Marquardt)
Marie Antoinette (o: Raab, Cutter, Arnaud, Marquardt, Bassman, Stringer)
Sweethearts (o: Cutter, Bassman, Marquardt)

1939
Idiot's Delight (o: Cutter, Raab, Marquardt)
Broadway Serenade (with E. Ward; o: Raab, Arnaud, Bassman, Marquardt)
The Wizard of Oz (ac: Bassman, Stoll, Stringer; o: Cutter, Bassman, Marquardt)
Balalaika (ac: Axt; o: Cutter, Marquardt, Raab)

1940
Northwest Passage (ac: Amfitheatrof, Axt; o: Raab, Cutter, Marquardt, Maxwell)
Edison, the Man (ac: Amfitheatrof, Zador)
Waterloo Bridge (o: Raab, Cutter, Marquardt)
Susan and God (o: Cutter, Raab)
New Moon (ac: Amfitheatrof; o: Cutter, Marquardt, Raab, Maxwell, Bassman)
Pride and Prejudice (o: Cutter, Raab, Marquardt)
Bitter Sweet (o: Cutter)

1941
Come Live with Me (o: Cutter)
Men of Boys Town (o: Cutter, Heglin)
Ziegfeld Girl (ac: Bassman, Stoll; o: Cutter, Bassman)
They Met in Bombay (ac: Amfitheatrof, Bassman; o: Cutter, Marquardt, Nussbaum, Heglin)
Blossoms in the Dust (ac: Amfitheatrof; o: Cutter, Raab, Arnaud)
Smilin' Through (o: Cutter, Raab, Nussbaum)

The Chocolate Soldier (with Kaper; o: Cutter)

1942

Rio Rita (o: Cutter; + stock)
Mrs. Miniver (o: Cutter; ac: Amfitheatrof, o: Raab, Marquardt)
I Married an Angel (o: Cutter, Marquardt)
Cairo (o: Cutter; ac: Amfitheatrof, Bassman, o: Bassman, Nussbaum)
Random Harvest (ac: Amfitheatrof; o: Cutter, Marquardt, Raab)
Tennessee Johnson (ac: Amfitheatrof; o: Cutter, Marquardt)

1943

Three Hearts for Julia (o: Cutter; + stock)
The Human Comedy (o: Cutter, Heglin)
Thousands Cheer (o: Cutter, Marquardt)
Madame Curie (o: Cutter)

1944

Song of Russia (based on music of Tchaikovsky and Rimsky-Korsakov; o: Cutter)
A Guy Named Joe (ac: Colombo; o: Cutter)
The White Cliffs of Dover (o: Cutter)
Dragon Seed (o: Cutter, Marquardt)
Kismet (o: Cutter)
Combat America (doc.)
Thirty Seconds Over Tokyo (o: Cutter, Heglin)
National Velvet (o: Cutter)

1945

The Picture of Dorian Gray (ac: Castelnuovo-Tedesco; o: Cutter, Duncan)
Son of Lassie (with Castelnuovo-Tedesco, Amfitheatrof; o: Cutter, R. Franklyn, Cutner)
The Valley of Decision (ac: Castelnuovo-Tedesco; o: Cutter)
They Were Expendable (ac: Colombo; o: Cutter, Byrns, Heglin)

1946

Adventure (ac: Heglin, Colombo, Hayton; o: Cutter, Heglin)
The Green Years (o: Cutter)
Undercurrent (ac: Castelnuovo-Tedesco; o: Sendrey)
The Sea of Grass (o: Sendrey)
The Yearling (based on music of Delius; o: Sendrey, R. Bassett, Heglin)

1947

High Barbaree (o: Sendrey)
The Unfinished Dance (ac: Perl; o: Sendrey)
Desire Me (o: Sendrey; ac: Castelnuovo-Tedesco, o: R. Franklyn)
If Winter Comes (o: Sendrey)

1948

Three Daring Daughters (with Perl; o: Sendrey)
Hills of Home (ac: R. Franklyn, Colombo, Sendrey; o: Sendrey)
The Three Musketeers (based on music of Tchaikovsky; o and ac: Sendrey)

1949

Big Jack (ac: R. Franklyn, A. Previn; o: Heglin, R. Franklyn)

ST. PIERRE, WILLIAM G.

1970

Big Sin City FRANK-EFRAIN PRODS.

STRANGE, BILLY

1968

Live a Little, Love a Little MGM

1969

The Trouble with Girls (o: L. Taylor) MGM
De Sade AIP

1970

Dirty Dingus Magee (see J. Alexander)

STRASSBURG, ROBERT

1954

Village of the Poor (short) ALAN SHILIN

STRINGER, ROBERT W.

1938

City Streets (see Cutner)

1939

The Wizard of Oz (see Stothart)

1940

Two Girls on Broadway (see D. Raksin)
Forty Little Mothers (with D. Raksin, Malotte, Stoll, Bassman) MGM

1949

Jigsaw UA

1950

So Young, So Bad UA

1951

St. Benny the Dip UA

Documentary Shorts (RKO PATHÉ unless otherwise stated)

1946

Report on Japan
Street of Shadows
Black Ducks and Broadbills
No Place Like Home
Ben Hogan

1947
Pueblo Boy FORD MOTOR CO.
1952
Pampas Sky Targets

STROKIN, AGNES
1967
Strange Rampage MONIQUE PRODS.

STRONACH, ROBERT
1914
The Spoilers SELIG POLYSCOPE

STROUSE, CHARLES
1957
The Other City (doc. short) AMERICAN CANCER SOCIETY
1967
Bonnie and Clyde (a: Bassman) WB
1968
The Night They Raided Minsky's (o: Lang) UA
1970
Replay (short) ROBERT DEUBEL
There Was a Crooked Man . . . WB

STUART, CHAD
1968
3 in the Attic AIP

STYNER, JERRY
1968
The Savage Seven (see Curb)
Killers Three (see Curb)
The Golden Breed (see Curb)
1969
Ski Fever (with Hemric) AA
The Cycle Savages AIP
Five the Hard Way (see Curb)
Tick . . . Tick . . . Tick MGM
1970
The Magic Garden of Stanley Sweetheart MGM

SUKMAN, HARRY
1954
Riders to the Stars (o: Vars) UA
Gog (o: Vars) UA
1955
Battle Taxi UA
A Bullet for Joey (o: Vars) UA
The Phenix City Story (o: Vars) AA
1956
Screaming Eagles (o: Vars) AA
1957
Fury at Showdown UA
Forty Guns TCF
Underwater Warrior MGM
1958
Outcasts of the City REP
1959
Verboten COL
The Hangman (o: Shuken, Hayes) PAR
The Crimson Kimono (o: Shuken, Hayes) COL
1960
Fanny WB
Song Without End (based on music of Liszt; o: Shuken, Hayes) COL
1961
Underworld, U.S.A. (o: Shuken, Hayes) COL
A Thunder of Drums (o: Shuken, Hayes) MGM
Madison Avenue (o: Shuken, Hayes) TCF
1962
Belle Sommers COL
1965
Around the World Under the Sea MGM
1966
The Singing Nun (o: Shuken, Hayes, Levene) MGM
Welcome to Hard Times MGM
The Naked Runner (o: H. Spencer) WB
1968
The Private Navy of Sgt. O'Farrell UA
If He Hollers, Let Him Go! (o: Sendrey) CR
1970
Mister Kingstreet's War H.R.S. FILMS

SULLIVAN, IRA
1964
The Lullaby of Bareland GRIFFITH PRODS.

SULLIVAN, JOE
1962
Who's Enchanted? (short) ?

SUMMERLIN, EDGAR
1963
We Shall Return CARI
1967
Ciao DAVAL

SUMMERS, BOB
1967
It's a Bikini World (see Curb)

SUMMERS, MIKE
1967
Teenage Rebellion (see Curb)

SURINACH, CARLOS
1954
Pump Trouble (an. short) UPA
1962
Genesis (short) ELEKTRA

SUTTON, HENRY
1960
Boats A-Poppin' (doc. short) PAR

SUTTON, JON
1960
The Mask of Comedy (doc. short) PIZZO FILMS

SWANSEN, CHRIS
1968
Tue. Afternoon (short) RIVERBANK

SWEETEN, CLAUDE
1952
Tembo (doc.) RKO

SWINNEN, FIRMIN
1921
The Old Nest GOLDWYN

SZABO, GABOR
1967
The Senses (doc. short) SIGMA

SZARVAS, LES
1965
SINderella and the Golden Bra (a: Sorenson) MANSON

T

TALBOT, JEAN
1930
The Golden Calf (see Friedhofer)
Double Cross Roads (see Lipschultz)
Movietone Follies of 1930 (see Lipschultz)
Born Reckless (see Brunelli)
On the Level (see Lipschultz)
Not Damaged (see Lipschultz)
On Your Back (see Lipschultz)
Renegades (see Arthur Kay)
A Devil with Women (see Brunelli)
The Dancers (with Friedhofer) FOX
1931
The Spy (see Brunelli)
Not Exactly Gentlemen (see Brunelli)
Mr. Lemon of Orange (with Brunelli) FOX

TAMKIN, DAVID
1939
Daredevils of the Red Circle (serial; see Lava)
Zorro's Fighting Legion (serial; see Lava)
[Also a very prolific orchestrator.]

TANDLER, ADOLPH
1930
Mamba TIFFANY
1931
Queen Kelly GLORIA SWANSON
1932
Scarface UA
1935
Struggle for Life (doc.) C.COURT TREATT

TANSMAN, ALEXANDER
[Scored several films in France in the 1930s and 1950s.]
1943
Flesh and Fantasy UNIV
1944
Destiny (with F. Skinner) UNIV
1945
Paris-Underground UA
1946
Sister Kenny RKO

TAUBMAN, PAUL
1962
The Painting (short) JAMEL PRODS.

TAYLOR, BILLY
1960
A Morning for Jimmy (doc. short) NATIONAL URBAN LEAGUE

TAYLOR, DEEMS
1925
Janice Meredith METRO-GOLDWYN

TAYLOR, HERB
1931
Broad Minded WB
1936
Go West, Young Man (see Stoll)
[Also a prolific arranger and orchestrator.]

TAYLOR, ROWAN
1954
Running for Sheriff (short) ED-VENTURE FILMS

TCHEREPNIN, IVAN
1968
Post Office (short) DEREK LAMB

TENNEY, JAMES
1953
Interim (short) STAN BRAKHAGE
1954
Desistfilm (short) STAN BRAKHAGE
1966
Viet Flakes (short) CAROLEE SCHNEEMANN

TEPPER, AL
1966
Relativity (short) ED EMSHWILLER

TERR, MAX
1930
The Love Parade (see Leipold)
The Vagabond King (sound; see Potoker)
The Vagabond King (silent; see Leipold)
The Silent Enemy (see Midgely)
1937
Double or Nothing (see V. Young)
1939
Everything's on Ice (see Filippi)
1942
The Gold Rush (see C. Chaplin)
1946
Abilene Town (with Carbonara, Mayfield, Glasser, Koff) UA
Shorts (MGM)
1943
Calling All Kids (o: Nussbaum, Heglin)
Dog-House
Don't You Believe It (o: Altschuler, Nussbaum)
Fala (o: Nussbaum)
Football Thrills of 1942 (o: Marquardt)
Inca Gold (with Castelnuovo-Tedesco; o: Nussbaum, Terr)
Marines in the Making (o: Heglin)
My Tomato (with Duncan; o: Duncan)
No News Is Good News (o: Salinger)
Nursery Rhyme Mysteries (with N. Shilkret; o: Salinger, Nussbaum)
Portrait of a Genius (with N. Shilkret; o: Raab)
Seeing Hands (o: Nussbaum)
Sky Science
Sucker Bait (see Amfitheatrof)
That's Why I Left You (with N. Shilkret; o: Nussbaum, P. Moore)
Tips on Trips (mt; o: Heglin)
To My Unborn Son (with Castelnuovo-Tedesco; o: Cutner)
Trifles That Win Wars
Who's Superstitious? (o: Nussbaum)
Wild Horses
1944
Dancing Romeo (o: Duncan)
Dark Shadows (see N. Shilkret)
Football Thrills of 1943 (o: Marquardt)
Groovie Movie (o: Duncan)
The Immortal Blacksmith (with Carbonara; o: Nussbaum)
Important Business (o: Duncan)
Journey to Yesterday (o: Nussbaum)
Moments That Made History
Nostradamus IV (see N. Shilkret)
Somewhere, U.S.A. (o: Duncan)
Sportsman's Memories (mt; o: Duncan)
Tomorrow John Jones (see N. Shilkret)
Why Daddy? (o: R. Franklyn)
1945
Christmas in Australia
Fall Guy (o: Duncan, Glasser)
Football Thrills of 1944 (o: Marquardt)
The Golden Hunch (o: Glasser)
The Great American Mug (o: Glasser)
The Great Morgan (o: Heglin)
A Gun in His Hand (o: Glasser)
The Last Installment (o: Duncan)
Little White Lie (o: Marquardt, Glasser, Cutner)
Magic on a Stick (o: Glasser)
People on Paper (o: Glasser, Heglin)
Phantoms, Inc. (o: Glasser)
Purity Squad (o: Heglin)
The Seesaw and the Shoes (o: Glasser)
Stairway to Light (o: Glasser)
Strange Destiny (o: Glasser)
Track and Field Quiz (o: Glasser)
1946
Bikini—The Atom Island (o: Glasser)
Football Thrills of 1945 (o: Marquardt)

I Love My Husband, But (o: Heglin)
Musical Masterpieces (mt; o: Glasser)
Our Old Car (o: Glasser, Heglin)
Sure Cures (o: Glasser)
1947
The Luckiest Guy in the World (o: Glasser)
A Really Important Person (o: Glasser)
Trailers (MGM)
1944
The Thin Man Goes Home
1945
Our Vines Have Tender Grapes
1946
The Green Years
Three Wise Fools

TERRY, CLARK
1967
The Door (an. short) KEN MUNDIE

TERRY, ROBERT
1942
A Report to the People (doc. short) NAT'L. FOUND. FOR INFANTILE PARALYSIS

THAYER, EDWIN
1969
Gunsmith of Williamsburg (doc.) CW

THOMAS, WHITEY
1970
Mark of the Witch PRESIDIO

THOMPSON, DONALD
1950
Spelling and Learning (doc. short) USC

THOMPSON, JOHN
1947
Killer Dill SG
1948
Campus Honeymoon (see N. Scott)

THOMSON, VIRGIL
1936
The Plow That Broke the Plains (doc. short; o: Brant) PARE LORENTZ
1937
The Spanish Earth (see Blitzstein)
The River (doc. short; o: Brant) PARE LORENTZ
1945
Tuesday in November (doc. short; o: Marquardt) JOHN HOUSEMAN
1948
Louisiana Story (o: Brant) ROBERT FLAHERTY
1958
The Goddess COL
1959
Power Among Men (doc.) UNITED NATIONS
1964
Voyage to America (doc. short) JOHN HOUSEMAN

THORNE, FRED G.
1968
Alternative (doc.) FRED G. THORNE

THORNE, OAKLEIGH
1959
Autumn Color (doc. short) THORNE FILMS

TIMBERG, SAMMY
Cartoons (PAR)
1935
An Elephant Never Forgets
A Little Soap and Water
Time for Love
1936
Bridge Ahoy!
Christmas Comes But Once a Year
The Cobweb Hotel
Greedy Humpty Dumpty
Hawaiian Birds
I Wanna Be a Life Guard
I-Ski Love-Ski You-Ski
The Little Stranger
Making Friends
More Pep
Play Safe
Popeye the Sailor Meets Sindbad the Sailor
A Song a Day
Training Pigeons
We Did It
What, No Spinach?
You're Not Built That Way
1937
Bunny-Mooning
The Candid Candidate
A Car-Tune Portrait
Chicken a la King
Ding Dong Doggie
Educated Fish
The Football Toucher Downer
Fowl Play
The Foxy Hunter

House Cleaning Blues
The Impractical Joker
I Never Changes My Altitude
Little Lamby
Lost and Foundry
The Paneless Window Washer
Peeping Penguins
Popeye the Sailor Meets Ali Baba's Forty Thieves
Protek the Weakerist
Pudgy Picks a Fight
Pudgy Takes a Bow-Wow
Whoops! I'm a Cowboy
Zula Hula

1938

All's Fair at the Fair
Be Up to Date
Big Chief Ugh-Amugh-Ugh
Buzzy Boop
A Date to Skate
Goonland
Hunky and Spunky
The Jeep
The Playful Polar Bears
Plumbing Is a Pipe
Pudgy and the Lost Kitten
Pudgy the Watchman
Riding the Rails
The Tears of an Onion

1939

Aladdin and His Wonderful Lamp
Always Kickin!
Barnyard Brat
Customers Wanted
The Fresh Vegetable Mystery
Ghosks Is the Bunk
Leave Well Enough Alone
Musical Mountaineers
My Friend the Monkey
Never Sock a Baby
The Scared Crows
So Does the Automobile

1940

Ants in the Plants
Bring Himself Back Alive (with Winston Sharples)
The Constable (with Winston Sharples)
The Dandy Lion
Doing Impossikible Stunts (with Winston Sharples)
Females Is Fickle
Fightin' Pals (with Winston Sharples)
The Fulla Bluff Man (with Winston Sharples)
Granite Hotel
A Kick in Time
King for a Day (with Winston Sharples)
Little Lambkin (with Winston Sharples)
Mommy Loves Puppy (with Winston Sharples)
Nurse Mates (with Winston Sharples)
Poopdeck Pappy
Sneak, Snoop and Snitch (with Winston Sharples)
Springtime in the Rockage (with Winston Sharples)
The Ugly Dino (with Winston Sharples)
Way Back When a Nag Was Only a Horse
Way Back When a Night Club Was a Stick
Way Back When a Triangle Had Its Points
Way Back When Women Had Their Weigh
Wedding Belts (with Winston Sharples)
Wimmin Is a Myskery (with Winston Sharples)

1941

All's Well (with Winston Sharples)
Child Psykolojiky
Copy Cat (with Winston Sharples)
Gabby Goes Fishing (with Winston Sharples)
I'll Never Crow Again (with Winston Sharples)
It's a Hap-Hap-Happy Day (with Winston Sharples)
Nix on Hypnotricks (with Winston Sharples)
Olive's Boithday Presink (with Winston Sharples)
Olive's Sweepstake Ticket (with Winston Sharples)
Pest Pilot (with Winston Sharples)
Popeye Meets Rip Van Winkle (with Winston Sharples)
Raggedy Ann and Raggedy Andy (with Winston Sharples)
Sneak, Snoop and Snitch in Triple Trouble (with Winston Sharples)
Superman (with Winston Sharples)
Superman in The Mechanical Monsters (with Winston Sharples)
Swing Cleaning (with Winston Sharples)
Twinkletoes Gets the Bird (with Winston Sharples)
Two for the Zoo (with Winston Sharples)
Vitamin Hay (with Winston Sharples)
The Wizard of Arts (with Winston Sharples)
Zero, the Hound (with Winston Sharples)

1942

Baby Wants a Bottleship

Fleets of Stren'th
Kickin' the Conga 'Round
Many Tanks (with Winston Sharples)
Me Musical Nephews (with Winston Sharples)
Olive Oyl and Water Don't Mix (with Winston Sharples)
Pip-Eye, Pup-Eye, Poop-Eye and Peep-Eye (with Winston Sharples)
The Raven (with Winston Sharples)
Scrap the Japs (with Winston Sharples)
Superman in Billion Dollar Limited (with Winston Sharples)
Superman in Destruction, Inc. (with Winston Sharples)
Superman in Electric Earthquake (with Winston Sharples)
Superman in Showdown (with Winston Sharples)
Superman in Terror on the Midway (with Winston Sharples)
Superman in The Arctic Giant (with Winston Sharples)
Superman in The Eleventh Hour (with Winston Sharples)
Superman in The Japoteurs (with Winston Sharples)
Superman in The Magnetic Telescope (with Winston Sharples)
Superman in Volcano (with Winston Sharples)
You're a Sap, Mr. Jap (with Winston Sharples)

1943
Cartoons Ain't Human
Eggs Don't Bounce
A Jolly Good Furlough
No Mutton fer Nuttin'
Ration fer the Duration
Seein' Red, White 'n' Blue
Spinach fer Britain (with Winston Sharples)
Superman in Jungle Drums (with Winston Sharples)
Superman in Secret Agent
Superman in The Mummy Strikes (with Winston Sharples)
Superman in The Underground World
Too Weak to Work (with Winston Sharples)
Wood-Peckin'

1944
Henpecked Rooster (with Winston Sharples)
I'm Just Curious
It's Nifty to Be Thrifty
Lulu at the Zoo
Lulu in Hollywood
Lulu's Birthday Party
Puppet Love
Pitchin' Woo at the Zoo
Yankee Doodle Donkey

Shorts
1931
Ambitious People MGM
Puff Your Blues Away PAR
Musical Justice PAR

1932
The Musical Doctor PAR

TIMMENS, JAMES F. (JIM)
Cartoons (TCF)
1964
The Astronut in Molecular Mixup
The Astronut in Outer Galaxy Gazette

1965
Don't Spill the Beans
Dress Reversal
Freight Fright
The Sky's the Limit
Twinkle, Twinkle, Little Telestar
Weather Magic

1966
Big Bad Bobcat
The Cowardly Watchdog
Dr. Ha Ha
Dreamnapping
Gems from Gemini
Rain Drain
Scuba Duba Do

1967
Baron von Go-Go
Bugged by a Bug
Dr. Rhinestone's Theory
Fancy Plants
Frozen Sparklers
The Heat's Off
It's for the Birds
Mr. Winlucky

1968
Dribble Drabble
Judo Kudos

TIMMERMAN, JOHN PAUL
1951
Hansel and Gretel AUSTIN PRODS.

TIOMKIN, DIMITRI
1931
Resurrection UNIV

1933
Alice in Wonderland (o: H. Jackson, Leipold, Potoker, Hand, Virgil, Reese) PAR
1935
The Casino Murder Case (o: Raab, Marquardt, R. Bassett, Maxwell) MGM
Mad Love (mt: R. Bassett; o: Marquardt, Virgil, Raab, Maxwell) MGM
I Live My Life (mt: E. Ward; o: Virgil, Maxwell) MGM
1936
More Than a Secretary (mt; o: Parrish; + stock) COL
1937
Lost Horizon (o: Parrish, R. Bennett, Still, Friedhofer, Maxwell, Reese, Kaun) COL
The Road Back (o: Maxwell, D. Raksin, Hand, R. Bennett, Schiller) UNIV
1938
Spawn of the North (ac: Leipold, Harling, Roder, Carbonara; o: Shuken, Parrish, Reese) PAR
You Can't Take It With You (o: Reese, Parrish) COL
The Great Waltz (adaptation of music by Johann Strauss) MGM
1939
Only Angels Have Wings (o: Parrish; + stock) COL
Mr. Smith Goes to Washington COL
1940
Lucky Partners (o: Parrish, R. Bennett, Maxwell) RKO
The Westerner (with A. Newman; o: Friedhofer, Parrish, E. Powell, Salinger) GOLDWYN
1941
Meet John Doe (o: Parrish, Maxwell, Harline, Reese, Cailliet, Friedhofer, Raab, Bassman, Bucharoff, Tamkin) WB
Forced Landing PAR
Scattergood Meets Broadway RKO
Flying Blind PAR
The Corsican Brothers (o: Nussbaum) UA
1942
A Gentleman After Dark UA
Twin Beds UA
The Moon and Sixpence (o: Nussbaum, Reese) UA
Shadow of a Doubt UNIV
1943
Unknown Guest MON
1944
The Imposter UNIV
The Bridge of San Luis Rey (o: Nussbaum) UA
Ladies Courageous (o: Cailliet, Tamkin, Marquardt, Nussbaum, L. Russell, Still) UNIV
When Strangers Marry MON
Forever Yours MON
1945
Dillinger (o: Marquardt, Nussbaum) MON
China's Little Devils (o: Marquardt) MON
Pardon My Past (o: Nussbaum) COL
1946
Whistle Stop (o: Nussbaum, Marquardt, Herschel Gilbert) UA
Black Beauty (o: Nussbaum, Marquardt) TCF
Angel on My Shoulder (o: Cailliet, Marquardt) UA
The Dark Mirror (with F. Skinner; o: Cailliet, Nussbaum) UNIV
Duel in the Sun (o: Nussbaum, Tamkin, Marquardt, Herschel Gilbert, Parrish, Cailliet) SELZNICK
1947
It's a Wonderful Life (o: Marquardt, Tamkin, Herschel Gilbert, N. Scott; + stock) RKO
The Long Night (o: Marquardt, H. Taylor, Dubin, Maxwell, Kahn) RKO
1948
Tarzan and the Mermaids RKO
The Dude Goes West (o: Tamkin) AA
So This Is New York (o: Tamkin) UA
Red River (o: Cailliet, Marquardt) UA
1949
Canadian Pacific (o: H. Taylor, Marquardt) TCF
Champion (o: Marquardt, H. Taylor, Emanuel, Dubin) UA
Portrait of Jennie (based on music of Debussy; o: Parrish, Marquardt, Emanuel, Dubin, Byrns, de Packh) SELZNICK
Home of the Brave (o: Marquardt, H. Taylor, Emanuel) UA
Red Light (o: Marquardt, H. Taylor) UA
1950
Dakota Lil (o: Marquardt, H. Taylor) TCF
Guilty Bystander (o: Jack Andrews) FC
Champagne for Caesar (o: H. Taylor, Marquardt, Parrish) UA
D.O.A. (o: H. Taylor, Marquardt) UA

The Men (o: Parrish, Marquardt, H. Taylor) UA
Cyrano de Bergerac (o: Parrish, Emanuel, Marquardt, H. Taylor) UA
Mr. Universe (o: Marquardt, H. Taylor) UA

1951
The Thing RKO
Strangers on a Train WB
Peking Express (o: Parrish, Shuken, Cutner, Marquardt) PAR
The Well (o: Marquardt, H. Taylor) UA
Drums in the Deep South (o: Marquardt, Emanuel, H. Taylor) RKO
Bugles in the Afternoon WB

1952
Mutiny (o: H. Taylor, Marquardt, Emanuel) UA
My Six Convicts (o: Marquardt, Emanuel, Parrish, H. Taylor) COL
Lady in the Iron Mask (o: Marquardt) TCF
The Happy Time (o: Parrish, Marquardt, Emanuel) COL
The Big Sky RKO
High Noon (o: Marquardt, H. Taylor, Emanuel) UA
The Four Poster (o: Marquardt, H. Taylor, Parrish, Maxwell, Emanuel) COL
The Steel Trap (o: Marquardt, Cailliet) TCF
Angel Face RKO

1953
Jeopardy (o: Marquardt, Parrish, Emanuel) MGM
I Confess (o: Parrish, Marquardt, H. Taylor) WB
Return to Paradise (o: Marquardt, Cailliet, Emanuel) UA
Blowing Wild (o: Cailliet) WB
Take the High Ground! (o: Parrish, Emanuel, Marquardt, Cailliet) MGM

1954
Cease Fire! (o: Parrish, Emanuel, Marquardt, Cailliet) PAR
His Majesty O'Keefe (U.S. release of British film) WB
The Command WB
Dial M for Murder WB
The High and the Mighty (o: Parrish, Marquardt, Maxwell, H. Taylor, Emanuel, Tamkin) WB
A Bullet Is Waiting (o: Parrish, Marquardt, Emanuel, H. Taylor) COL
The Adventures of Hajji Baba (o: Marquardt, Parrish, Emanuel, Cailliet, Levene, H. Taylor) TCF

1955
Strange Lady in Town WB
Land of the Pharaohs (o: Parrish, Marquardt, Emanuel, H. Taylor, Cailliet, Raab) WB
The Court-Martial of Billy Mitchell WB

1956
Friendly Persuasion (o: Marquardt, Parrish, H. Taylor) AA
Tension at Table Rock RKO
Giant (o: Cailliet, Marquardt, Parrish, H. Taylor, Raab, Emanuel, M. Heindorf, Levene) WB

1957
Gunfight at the O. K. Corral (o: Parrish, H. Taylor, Marquardt, M. Heindorf, Hayes, Raab, Cailliet) PAR
Night Passage UNIV
The Young Land (o: Parrish, Emanuel, H. Taylor, M. Heindorf) COL

1958
Wild Is the Wind (o: Parrish, Van Cleave, de Packh, Emanuel, Raab, H. Taylor) PAR
The Old Man and the Sea WB

1959
Rio Bravo (o: M. Heindorf, Emanuel, Parrish, Levene, de Packh, H. Taylor, Raab, Cutner) WB
Last Train from Gun Hill (o: Parrish, Emanuel, M. Heindorf, H. Taylor, de Packh) PAR

1960
The Unforgiven UA
The Alamo (o: H. Taylor, Parrish, Emanuel, Haskell) UA
The Sundowners WB

1961
The Guns of Navarone (o: H. Taylor, M. Heindorf, Parrish, Raab, Maxwell) COL
Town Without Pity UA

1962
Without Each Other ALLEN KLEIN

1963
55 Days at Peking (o: H. Taylor, Emanuel) AA

1964
The Fall of the Roman Empire (o: Parrish, H. Taylor, Comstock, Bolton, Docker, Tamkin) PAR
Circus World (o: H. Taylor, Tamkin) PAR
36 Hours (o: Tamkin) MGM

1967
The War Wagon (o: Grau, Raab et al.) UNIV

1968

Great Catherine (o: Tamkin) WB

Documentaries

1942

Moscow Strikes Back (a; U.S. release of Soviet film, *Defeat of the German Armies Near Moscow*) REP

The Nazis Strike (see Webb)

1943

Substitution and Conversion (based on music of Gershwin; with Lava, Sawtell, A. Lange; o: Moross, Maxwell, Nussbaum, Schoepp) U.S. ARMY

The Battle of Russia (based on music of Russian composers; o: Nussbaum, Marquardt, Maxwell, Arnaud, Glasser) U.S. ARMY

1944

Tunisian Victory (with William Alwyn; o: Nussbaum, Still, Marquardt) BRITISH ARMY AND U.S. ARMY

The Negro Soldier (with C. Jackson, H. Jackson, E. Robinson, Glasser; o: Marquardt, Still, Cailliet, Arnaud, P. Moore) U.S. ARMY

The Battle of China (o: Marquardt, Nussbaum, Tamkin, Cailliet, Maxwell) U.S. ARMY

Attack! The Battle for New Britain (o: Marquardt, Nussbaum, + stock) U.S. ARMY

1945

San Pietro (short; o: Cailliet, Marquardt) U.S. ARMY

Two Down and One to Go! (short) U.S. ARMY

War Comes to America (o: Marquardt, Nussbaum) U.S. ARMY

Know Your Enemy—Japan (o: Nussbaum, Tamkin, Marquardt) U.S. ARMY

Here Is Germany (+ stock) U.S. ARMY

1957

Search for Paradise (o: Marquardt, Parrish, Raab, King, de Packh, J. Mason, H. Taylor, Cailliet, Emanuel) CINERAMA

1959

Rhapsody of Steel (an. short for U.S. Steel) JSP

1965

A President's Country (adapted from several of his earlier scores) USIA

TJADER, CAL

1958

Hot Car Girl AA

1965

San Francisco, San Francisco, San Francisco (doc. short; with Guaraldi, Sete) PAR

TOCH, ERNST

1934

Catherine the Great LONDON FILMS

Little Friend GAUMONT-BRITISH

The Private Life of Don Juan LONDON FILMS

1935

Peter Ibbetson (ac: Roemheld, Harling, Friedhofer) PAR

1936

The General Died at Dawn (see Janssen)

1937

Outcast PAR

On Such a Night (ac: Stoll) PAR

Heidi (with Maxwell, Buttolph) TCF

1938

Happy Landing (see Mockridge)

Four Men and a Prayer (mt; + stock) TCF

Suez (see Mockridge)

1939

The Three Musketeers (see Maxwell)

The Story of Alexander Graham Bell (mt) TCF

The Return of the Cisco Kid (see W. Scharf)

The Cat and the Canary PAR

1940

Dr. Cyclops (see Malotte)

The Ghost Breakers (ac: V. Young) PAR

1941

Ladies in Retirement COL

1943

First Comes Courage (ac: Leipold) COL

1944

None Shall Escape COL

Address Unknown (ac: Castelnuovo-Tedesco) COL

1945

The Unseen PAR

TORBETT, DAVE

*Torbett claimed to have ghostwritten these pictures (credited to Edward J. Kay), along with many Johnny Mack Brown and Jimmy Wakely westerns and several "Charlie Chan" films, totalling over fifty. He stated that his papers were destroyed in a flood and that he could not recall other specific titles. He also worked as an orchestrator.

1938
Down in "Arkansaw" (partial) REP
1939
Cowboys from Texas (partial) REP
1940
Friendly Neighbors (partial) REP
1944
*The Jade Mask**
*Mom and Dad**
1948
*Rocky**
*Kidnapped**
1949
*The Lawton Story of the Prince of Peace**

TOSCANA, MARIO
1970
All the Lovin' Kinfolk CLOVER
Fandango CLOVER

TOSCO, SOL
1968
My Third Wife George MONIQUE
1969
Campus Heat CINEX

TOURS, FRANK
1929
The Cocoanuts PAR
Glorifying the American Girl (md) PAR
1930
One Heavenly Night (md) GOLDWYN
1931
The Night Angel (see Goulding)
My Sin (see J. Green)
His Woman PAR
1933
The Emperor Jones UA
1934
Crime Without Passion (with Levant) PAR
Gambling (md) FOX
1938
Mother Carey's Chickens (o: R. Bennett) RKO
Smashing the Rackets RKO
Tarnished Angel RKO
1939
The Duke of West Point UA
Boy Slaves (o: Parrish) RKO
Beauty for the Asking (with Webb) RKO
King of the Turf UA
Trouble in Sundown (see Webb)
Almost a Gentleman RKO
Conspiracy (o: Parrish) RKO
1940
Beyond Tomorrow RKO
Men Against the Sky (o: de Packh) RKO
The Villain Still Pursued Her RKO

TOWNSEND, DOUGLAS
1951
Rules and Laws (short) RITTER YOUNG LERNER ASSOC.
1955
Man Against Hunger (short) AMERICANA PRODS.
1956
Pastoral (short) IRVING KRIESBERG
Old Bangum (short) HARLEQUIN FILMS
Heart of a Neighborhood (short) DYNAMIC FILMS
1957
8 × 8 (with Gruen, Abramson) HANS RICHTER

TRACEY, HUGH
1968
No Room for Wilderness? (doc. short) SIERRA CLUB

TRAVIS, MERLE
1963
Born Hunters (doc. short) PAR

TRENTHAM, BRIAN
1970
The Sky Pirate ANDREW MEYER

TROTTER, JOHN SCOTT
1946
Abie's Irish Rose UA

TRUE, GISDON
1928
Top Sergeant Mulligan ANCHOR
Hearts of Men ANCHOR

TRYTHALL, GIL
Shorts (DON EVANS; dates unknown)
Laundromat Symphony
This Is a Test
Global Morality

TUCHMAN, WILLIAM
1933
Missing Daughters QUALITY PICTURES

TUCKER, GREGORY
1947
Clinic of Stumble (short) SIDNEY PETERSON

TULANE, HUGH
1936
Señor Jim BEAUMONT PICTURES

TULLIS, WALTER
1939
Baby Rabbit in I Wanted Red Wings (short) CONTEMPORARY FILMS
1947
Chata (short) CONTEMPORARY FILMS
1949
The Maya Through the Ages (doc.) UNITED FRUIT CO.

TURECK, JEROME
1967
In Lewis and Clark's Footsteps Across Montana (doc. short) UNION OIL CO.

U

USHER, GARY
1965
The Girls on the Beach PAR
Ski Party AIP

USSACHEVSKY, VLADIMIR
1940
Circle of Fire (doc. short) ?
1958
The Boy Who Saw Through (short) MARY ELLEN BUTE
1962
No Exit ZENITH INTERNATIONAL
1967
Line of Apogee LLOYD WILLIAMS
1969
2 Images for the Computer Piece (short) LLOYD WILLIAMS
1970
Duck, Duck (short) ?

V

VALENTINE, DeWAIN
1963
The Doors (short) ARNOLD GASSAN

VAN CAMP, R. C.
1951
Frontiers Unlimited (doc. short) CENTRAL AND SOUTH WEST CORP.
1952
Forecast—Continued Prosperity (doc. short) SOUTHWESTERN GAS & ELECTRIC CO.
1953
Opportunity America (doc. short) THE JEFFERSON MILLS

VAN CLEAVE, NATHAN
[All for Paramount unless otherwise stated.]
1947
Ladies Man (see Webb)
My Favorite Brunette (see Dolan)
The Trouble with Women (see V. Young)
Road to Rio (see Dolan)
Where There's Life (see V. Young)
1948
The Sainted Sisters (o: Plumb)
1949
Song of Surrender (see V. Young)
1950
Dear Wife (see Lilley)
Fancy Pants (ac: Harline, Webb; o: Cutner, Parrish, Plumb, Shuken)
1951
Molly
Quebec (with Plumb)

Dear Brat
Rhubarb
1952
Aaron Slick from Punkin Crick
Just for You (see Friedhofer)
Somebody Loves Me (ac: Levene, Lilley)
1953
Road to Bali (see Lilley)
Off Limits (o: Parrish)
Scared Stiff (see L. Stevens)
Those Redheads from Seattle (see Shuken)
1954
White Christmas (see Lilley)
1955
Cinerama Holiday (see Gould)
Conquest of Space (o: de Packh, Shuken, Cutner, Grau)
Lucy Gallant (o: F. Steiner)
1956
The Court Jester (see Schoen)
Anything Goes
1957
Funny Face (see Courage)
The Lonely Man (o: Shuken, Hayes)
The Devil's Hairpin (+ stock)
1958
The Colossus of New York (o: F. Steiner)
The Space Children
That Kind of Woman (see Amfitheatrof)
1959
Hey Boy! Hey Girl! COL
1960
Blueprint for Robbery
1964
Robinson Crusoe on Mars (o: F. Steiner)
1967
Project X (o: Loose, F. Steiner, Levene, P. Carpenter)
Shorts
1946
College Queen
1947
Sweet and Low
Champagne for Two
Smooth Sailing
Paris in the Spring
1948
Samba-Mania
Footlight Rhythm (o: Plumb)
Tropical Masquerade
Curtain Time
Catalina Interlude
1950
On Stage Everybody (doc.)
Trailers
1948
Isn't It Romantic? (see Lilley)
1949
My Own True Love
1950
Riding High
1953
Sangaree
1954
White Christmas
1963
Come Blow Your Horn
1964
Sylvia
1967
Chuka
[Also a prolific arranger and orchestrator.]

VAN EPS, ROBERT
1943
Presenting Lily Mars (see Stoll)
1949
In the Good Old Summertime (see Stoll)
1953
Easy to Love (see Stoll)
1954
Rose Marie (see Stoll)
Flame and the Flesh (see Stoll)
The Student Prince (see Stoll)
Athena (see Stoll)
1955
Hit the Deck (see Stoll)
Love Me or Leave Me (see Stoll)
1956
Meet Me in Las Vegas (see Stoll)
The Opposite Sex (see Stoll)
1957
Ten Thousand Bedrooms (see Stoll)
This Could Be the Night (see Stoll)
1962
Jumbo (see Stoll)
Hero's Island (see Frontiere)
The Courtship of Eddie's Father (see Stoll)
1963
A Ticklish Affair (see Stoll)
Viva Las Vegas (see Stoll)
1964
Looking for Love (see Stoll)
Girl Happy (see Stoll)
1965
The Man from Button Willow (see Stoll)
Made in Paris (see Stoll)

1966
Spinout (see Stoll)
[Also worked as an arranger.]

VAN GROVE, ISAAC
1951
The Song of Mid-America (doc.) ILLINOIS CENTRAL RAILROAD
1952
Adam to Atom (short) JOHN OTT PICTURES

VAN LATTMAN, LAWRENCE
1966
Mondo Bizarro (doc.) OLYMPIC INT'L

VAN LOAN, PAUL
1933
Arizona to Broadway (see A. Lange)
1936
The Magnificent Brute (see Maxwell)
1944
Tucson Raiders (see M. Glickman)
[Also worked as an arranger and orchestrator.]

VANN, TEDDY
1963
The Moving Finger MOYER

VAN PEEBLES, MELVIN
1968
The Story of a Three Day Pass (see M. Baker)
1970
Watermelon Man (o: R. Matthews) COL

VAN SLYCK, NICHOLAS
1949
A Touch of the Times MICHAEL ROEMER

VARDI, EMANUEL
1966
Once Before I Die JOHN DEREK
1967
Hawaii—USA (doc. short) AMERICAN EXPRESS
1969
From Sea to Shining Sea (doc. short) READER'S DIGEST
1970
Dirtymouth (with Hambro) HERBERT S. ALTMAN

VARÈSE, EDGARD
1943
Fernand Leger in America (doc. short) THOMAS BOUCHARD
1955
Around and About Joan Miró (doc.; one sequence) THOMAS BOUCHARD

VARGES, THEODORE A.
1955
Why Vandalism? (doc. short) ENCYCLOPAEDIA BRITANNICA

VARNER, RED
1952
Waiting (short) FLORA MOCK

VARS, HENRY
[Scored over 50 films in Poland, 1930–1939.]
1951
Chained for Life RENATA SPERA FILMS
1953
Slaves of Babylon (ac: M. Bakaleinikoff; + stock) COL
The Big Heat (mt: A. Morton; + stock) COL
1955
Ski Crazy (doc.; o: Kaun, Vars) GORDON MACLEAN
Man in the Vault RKO
1956
Seven Men from Now WB
Gun the Man Down UA
1957
The Unearthly REP
Love Slaves of the Amazon (see S. Wilson)
1958
Girls on the Loose (with Gertz, S. Wilson) UNIV
Wild Heritage (with H. Russell, M. Goldman, Salter, Gertz) UNIV
China Doll UA
Appointment with a Shadow (see Salter)
1959
Escort West UA
The Leech Woman (see Gertz)
1960
Freckles TCF
The Little Shepherd of Kingdom Come TCF
1961
Battle at Bloody Beach TCF
The Two Little Bears TCF
Woman Hunt TCF
1963
Flipper MGM
House of the Damned TCF
1964
Flipper's New Adventure MGM
[Also worked as an orchestrator.]

VAUGHAN, CLIFFORD
1928
Waterfront (see Carbonara)
Show Girl (see Carbonara)
1934
Life Returns (see Wallace)
Successful Failure MON
1935
The President Vanishes (see Riesenfeld)
The Raven (+ stock) UNIV
Every Night at Eight (see Hollander)
Storm Over the Andes (see Roemheld)
East of Java (see Waxman)
The Great Impersonation (see Roemheld)
1936
Tango INVINCIBLE
Flash Gordon (serial; + stock) UNIV
Sutter's Gold (see Waxman)
Trouble for Two (see Waxman)
Postal Inspector (+ stock) UNIV
Yellowstone UNIV
Two in a Crowd (see Roemheld)
Ace Drummond (serial; mt; + stock) UNIV
Four Days' Wonder (see C. Previn)
1937
Song of the City (see Axt)
Captains Courageous (see Waxman)
White Bondage WB
The Emperor's Candlesticks (see Waxman)
1938
The Shining Hour (see Waxman)
1940
River's End (with H. Jackson) WB
Calling All Husbands (see H. Jackson)
1948
B. F.'s Daughter (see Kaper)
1952
Harem Girl (+ stock) COL
1953
Flame of Calcutta (+ stock) COL
Shorts
1936
King of the Islands WB
Slide, Nellie, Slide WB
Violets in Spring MGM
1937
Dancing on the Ceiling MGM
Servant of the People MGM
The Romance of Robert Burns WB
[Also a prolific orchestrator.]

VAUGHN, BILLY
1965
Wonders of Kentucky (doc. short) COL

VERRALL, JOHN
1938
Minnesota Document (doc.) U. OF MINNESOTA

VINCENT, DON
1969
80 Steps to Jonah (see Shearing)
1970
Blood Mania CROWN

VINCENT, JOHN
1948
Red Cross ?

VINCENT, PAUL
Shorts (EDUCATIONAL PICTURES)
1932
Hypnotizing for Love
Burned at the Steak
In the Clutches of Death
Gaslit Nineties
1933
The Evil Eye Conquers
When Dad Was a Boy
Puffs and Bustles
Highlights of the Past
An Old Fashioned News Reel

VIRGIL, JACK
1930
Double Cross Roads (see Lipschultz)
The Last of the Duanes (see Kaylin)
The Big Trail (see Arthur Kay)
Under Suspicion (see Kaylin)
Fair Warning (see Arthur Kay)
1931
The Spy (see Brunelli)
Not Exactly Gentlemen (see Brunelli)
Heartbreak (see Friedhofer)
Business and Pleasure (mt; + stock) FOX
1935
Baby Face Harrington (see E. Ward)
Reckless (ac: Stothart, E. Ward) MGM
[Also a prolific arranger and orchestrator.]

VITO, EDWARD
1955
Still Going Places (doc.) GEORGE C. STONEY
195?
Active Management of Disability in the Aged (doc. short) GEORGE C. STONEY
1956
The Proud Years (doc. short) GEORGE C. STONEY

VOEGELI, DON
1956
The London of William Hogarth (doc. short) BARNARD-CORNWELL FILMS

VON HADEN, LLOYD
1955
Come In, Jupiter (short) USC

VON OTTENFELD, EDDISON
[Pseudonym: William Eddison.]
1947
The Way of Peace (an. puppet short) EAST-WEST STUDIO
1948
Sword of the Avenger EL
1954
Soaring Over the Everglades (doc.) EVINRUDE OUTBOARD MOTORS

George Pal Puppetoons (PAR)
1941
The Gay Knighties
Rhythm in the Ranks
1942
Jasper and the Haunted House
Jasper and the Watermelons
Mr. Strauss Takes a Walk
The Sky Princess
Tulips Shall Grow
1943
The 500 Hats of Bartholomew Cubbins
Bravo, Mr. Strauss
Jasper and the Choo-Choo
1944
Say Ah, Jasper

W

WACHTEL, MUSSINA
1931
Explorers of the World (doc.) RASPIN PRODS.
1934
Are We Civilized? (with Matthew Ray) RASPIN PRODS.

WAGNER, ROGER
1960
The Gallant Hours UA

WAGNER, THOMAS
1967
The Ancient Peruvian (doc. short) IFF
1969
The Ancient Africans (doc. short) IFF
Anansi the Spider (an. short) GERALD MCDERMOTT
1970
The Magic Tree (an. short) GERALD MCDERMOTT

WAKEFIELD, FOSTER
1965
Saturday Night Bath in Apple Valley EMERSON

WALDMAN, ROBERT
1963
The Sound of Laughter (compilation film) UNION

WALDRON, MAL
1964
The Cool World SHIRLEY CLARKE
1967
Sweet Love, Bitter HERBERT DANSKA

WALKER, DON
1965
A Thousand Clowns UA

WALLACE, OLIVER
1933
Good-bye Love (see Roder)
1934
Sixteen Fathoms Deep MON
City Limits (with Schiller) MON
The Girl in the Case DUWORLD
Life Returns (with Vaughan) SCIENART PICTURES
1935
It Happened in New York (o: Vaughan) UNIV

Alias Mary Dow (o: Vaughan; + stock) UNIV
Murder by Television IMPERIAL
1936
Bulldog Courage PURITAN
Black Gold CONN
Roarin' Guns PURITAN
High Hat IMPERIAL
1938
Sinners in Paradise (+ stock) UNIV
1940
Straight Shooter VICTORY
1941
Dumbo (see Churchill)
1943
Victory Through Air Power (see Plumb)
1944
Follow the Boys (see Harline)
1946
Make Mine Music (see Wolcott)
1947
Fun and Fancy Free (with P. Smith, Daniel; o: Plumb, S. Fine) WDP
1949
The Adventures of Ichabod and Mr. Toad (with Wolcott; o: Dubin) WDP
Cinderella (with P. Smith; o: Dubin, Plumb) WDP
1951
Alice in Wonderland (o: Dubin) WDP
1952
Peter Pan (o: Plumb) WDP
1955
Lady and the Tramp (o: Plumb, S. Fine) WDP
1956
Disneyland, U.S.A. (doc.) WDP
1957
Old Yeller (o: Vaughan) WDP
1958
White Wilderness (doc.; o: Vaughan) WDP
Tonka (o: Vaughan) WDP
1959
Darby O'Gill and the Little People (o: Vaughan) WDP
Jungle Cat (doc.; o: Vaughan) WDP
1960
Ten Who Dared (o: Dubin) WDP
1961
Nikki, Wild Dog of the North (o: Vaughan) WDP
1962
Big Red (o: Sheets) WDP
The Legend of Lobo (o: Sheets) WDP
1963
Savage Sam (o: Sheets) WDP
The Incredible Journey (o: Sheets) WDP

Shorts (WDP)
1944
Lucky Cowboy (see Shuken)
Fun Time (see Schrager)
1948
Seal Island (o: Dubin, Stark)
1952
The Alaskan Eskimo (o: Plumb)
1954
Siam
1955
Blue Men of Morocco
Men Against the Arctic
1956
Sardinia
Alaskan Sled Dog
Samoa
1957
Lapland
Portugal
1958
Ama Girls
The Danube
Japan
Cruise of the Eagle
1959
Mysteries of the Deep
Islands of the Sea

Cartoons (WDP)
1937
Donald's Ostrich
Mickey's Amateurs
Modern Inventions
1938
Boat Builders
Donald's Better Self
Donald's Golf Game
Donald's Lucky Day
Donald's Nephews
Donald's Penguin
Good Scouts
Mickey's Parrot
Mickey's Trailer
Self Control
1939
Autograph Hound
Donald's Cousin Gus
The Hockey Champ
Mickey's Surprise Party
Officer Duck

Sea Scouts
Society Dog Show

1940

Billposters
Bone Trouble
Donald's Dog Laundry
Donald's Vacation
Mr. Mouse Takes a Trip (see Harline)
Put-Put Troubles
The Riveter
Tugboat Mickey
Window Cleaners (see P. Smith)

1941

Early to Bed
The Little Whirlwind
Timber

1942

Bellboy Donald
Der Fuehrer's Face
Donald's Garden
Donald's Gold Mine
Donald's Snow Fight
Donald's Tire Trouble
Education for Death
Pluto at the Zoo
T-Bone for Two
The Vanishing Private

1943

Chicken Little
The Flying Jalopy
The Pelican and the Snipe
Private Pluto
Victory Vehicles

1944

The Clock Watcher
Commando Duck
Donald Duck and the Gorilla
First Aiders
How to Play Golf
The Plastics Inventor
Springtime for Pluto
Trombone Trouble

1945

African Diary
Canine Casanova
Canine Patrol
Cured Duck
Dog Watch
Duck Pimples
In Dutch
A Knight for a Day
The Legend of Coyote Rock
No Sail
Old Sequoia
Pluto's Kid Brother

1946

Bath Day
Clown of the Jungle
Donald's Double Trouble
Double Dribble
Dumb-Bell of the Yukon
Figaro and Frankie
Frank Duck Brings 'Em Back Alive
Lighthouse Keeping
Pluto's Housewarming
The Purloined Pup
Rescue Dog
Sleepy Time Donald
Squatter's Rights
Straight Shooters
Wet Paint

1947

The Big Wash
Bone Bandit
Bootle Beetle
Cat Nap Pluto
Chip 'n' Dale
Crazy with the Heat
Daddy Duck
Donald's Dilemma
Donald's Dream Voice
Drip Dippy Donald
Foul Hunting
Inferior Decorator
Mail Dog
Mickey Down Under
Mickey's Delayed Date
Pluto's Blue Note
Pluto's Fledgling
Pluto's Purchase
Soup's On
They're Off
Three for Breakfast
The Trial of Donald Duck
Wide Open Spaces

1948

All in a Nutshell
Bubble Bee
Donald's Happy Birthday
Goofy Gymnastics
The Greener Yard
Honey Harvester
Mickey and the Seal
Pluto's Surprise Package
Pluto's Sweater
Pueblo Pluto

Sea Salts
Sheep Dog
Slide, Donald, Slide
Tea for Two Hundred
Tennis Racquet
Winter Storage
The Wonder Dog
1949
Crazy Over Daisy
Lion Around
Pluto and the Gopher
Pluto's Heart Throb
Primitive Pluto
1950
Corn Chips
1951
Bee on Guard
1952
Let's Stick Together
Pluto's Party
Teachers Are People
Two Weeks Vacation
1953
Ben and Me
Canvas Back Duck
Casey Bats Again
Pigs Is Pigs
Rugged Bear
Spare the Rod
Working for Peanuts
1954
Dragon Around
The Flying Squirrel
Grand Canyonscope
Grin and Bear It
The Lone Chipmunks
No Hunting
Social Lion
1955
Bearly Asleep
Breezy Bear
Chips Ahoy
Up a Tree
1956
Hooked Bear
1959
How to Have an Accident at Work
Animated Educational Shorts (WDP)
1941
The Seven Wise Dwarfs
The Thrifty Pig
1942
All Together
Donald's Decision
The New Spirit
1945
Insects as Carriers of Disease

WALTERS, INGRAM P.
1962
The Case of Patty Smith LEO HANDEL

WARD, EDWARD
1932
A Fool's Advice FRANK FAY
Hypnotized WORLD WIDE
1933
The Sweetheart of Sigma Chi MON
1934
I Like It That Way UNIV
The Countess of Monte Cristo UNIV
Let's Be Ritzy UNIV
Uncertain Lady UNIV
Affairs of a Gentleman UNIV
Embarrassing Moments UNIV
Romance in the Rain UNIV
Million Dollar Ransom UNIV
Gift of Gab UNIV
Great Expectations UNIV
Cheating Cheaters UNIV
Gentlemen Are Born (see Roemheld)
Strange Wives UNIV
Girl o' My Dreams MON
1935
Mystery of Edwin Drood (o: Vaughan) UNIV
Times Square Lady (o: W. Allen, Marquardt, Vaughan, Raab) MGM
Baby Face Harrington (ac: Marquardt, Virgil; o: W. Allen, R. Bassett) MGM
Reckless (see Virgil)
Public Hero No. 1 MGM
No More Ladies MGM
Here Comes the Band (ac: Stothart; o: Virgil, Raab, Marquardt, W. Allen, Maxwell) MGM
The Bishop Misbehaves MGM
I Live My Life (see Tiomkin)
Ah, Wilderness! (o: Virgil, Vaughan, W. Allen, Marquardt; m&e: Stothart, o: Raab) MGM
Kind Lady (o: Virgil, Maxwell, Marquardt, W. Allen, Vaughan) MGM
Whipsaw MGM
1936
Riff Raff (o: W. Allen, Virgil, Maxwell) MGM

Exclusive Story (o: Marquardt, Virgil) MGM
Wife vs. Secretary (see Stothart)
The Robin Hood of El Dorado (see Stothart)
Moonlight Murder (o: Marquardt, Maxwell, Virgil, W. Allen) MGM
Small Town Girl (see Stothart)
Absolute Quiet (see Waxman)
Speed (o: Raab, Maxwell, Marquardt, W. Allen) MGM
San Francisco (see Stothart)
Women Are Trouble (o: W. Allen, Marquardt, Arnaud) MGM
Sworn Enemy (o: Raab, W. Allen, Arnaud) MGM
The Gorgeous Hussy (see Stothart)
Romeo and Juliet (see Stothart)
The Longest Night (o: Raab, Marquardt) MGM
After the Thin Man (o: Raab, Marquardt, W. Allen) MGM
Sinner Take All (o: W. Allen) MGM
Camille (see Stothart)

1937

Man of the People (o: Marquardt) MGM
Mama Steps Out (o: Marquardt, W. Allen) MGM
The Good Earth (see Stothart)
Maytime (see Stothart)
The Good Old Soak (o: W. Allen) MGM
Night Must Fall (o: W. Allen, Marquardt) MGM
Saratoga (o: Marquardt, W. Allen, Zweifel) MGM
The Women Men Marry (o: Marquardt, W. Allen, Cutter, Arnaud) MGM
The Firefly (see Stothart)
Double Wedding (o: Bassman, Arnaud, Cutter, W. Allen, Marquardt) MGM
Live, Love and Learn (o: W. Allen, Bassman, Marquardt) MGM
The Last Gangster (o: W. Allen, Bassman, Marquardt) MGM
Navy Blue and Gold (o: Marquardt, W. Allen, Arnaud, Cutter) MGM

1938

Love Is a Headache (+ stock) MGM
Mannequin (o: W. Allen, Cutter, Arnaud, Marquardt, Virgil) MGM
Paradise for Three (o: Marquardt, Raab, W. Allen) MGM
Of Human Hearts (see Stothart)
A Yank at Oxford (with Hubert Bath) MGM
Hold That Kiss MGM
The Toy Wife (o: Raab) MGM
Lord Jeff (o: Marquardt, Raab) MGM
The Shopworn Angel (o: W. Allen, Virgil, Raab, Marquardt, Arnaud) MGM
The Chaser (+ stock) MGM
The Crowd Roars (o: W. Allen, Raab, Arnaud, Maxwell, Marquardt) MGM
Boys Town (o: Arnaud, Raab, Marquardt) MGM
Vacation from Love (o: Arnaud, Salinger, Marquardt) MGM
Stablemates (o: Raab, Marquardt) MGM

1939

Broadway Serenade (see Stothart)
Society Lawyer (o: Raab, Bassman, Arnaud) MGM
It's a Wonderful World (o: Heglin, Bassman) MGM
6,000 Enemies (ac: Amfitheatrof) MGM
Maisie (o: Heglin) MGM
Stronger Than Desire (o: Heglin, Bassman) MGM
They All Come Out (see Snell)
Andy Hardy Gets Spring Fever (with Snell) MGM
These Glamour Girls (with Snell; o: Heglin) MGM
The Women (ac: Snell; o: Raab, Heglin, Marquardt, Bassman, Maxwell, Schutt) MGM
Blackmail (with Snell; o: Heglin, Raab) MGM
Thunder Afloat (o: Raab) MGM
Dancing Co-Ed (o: Heglin, Bassman, Maxwell, Marquardt) MGM
Bad Little Angel (o: Heglin) MGM
Remember? (o: Heglin, Raab, Marquardt) MGM
Another Thin Man (o: Heglin, Marquardt, Raab) MGM
Joe and Ethel Turp Call on the President (o: Heglin; ac: Snell, o: Raab) MGM

1940

Congo Maisie (o: Heglin) MGM
Young Tom Edison (o: Raab, Heglin, Marquardt) MGM
My Son, My Son! (o: Raab, Heglin, Schutt) UA
South of Pago Pago (o: Heglin) UA
Dance, Girl, Dance (o: Heglin, G. Rose) RKO
Kit Carson UA
The Son of Monte Cristo UA

1941

Cheers for Miss Bishop UA
Mr. & Mrs. Smith RKO
Tanks a Million UA
Niagara Falls UA
All-American Co-Ed UA
Miss Polly UA
Hay Foot UA
Fiesta UA

1942

Brooklyn Orchid UA
Dudes Are Pretty People UA
About Face UA
Men of Texas UNIV
Flying with Music UA
The Devil with Hitler UA
The McGuerins from Brooklyn UA
Nazty Nuisance UA

1943

Calaboose UA
Fall In UA
Taxi, Mister UA
Prairie Chickens UA
Yanks Ahoy UA
Phantom of the Opera (o: Schutt, Zweifel) UNIV
Ali Baba and the Forty Thieves (o: Zweifel) UNIV
Cobra Woman (o: Zweifel) UNIV

1944

Her Primitive Man UNIV
Ghost Catchers (o: Zweifel) UNIV
Gypsy Wildcat (o: Zweifel) UNIV
The Climax (o: Zweifel) UNIV
Bowery to Broadway UNIV
My Gal Loves Music UNIV

1945

Frisco Sal (o: Zweifel) UNIV
Salome, Where She Danced (o: Zweifel) UNIV
Song of the Sarong UNIV

1947

It Happened on Fifth Avenue AA
Copacabana UA

1948

The Babe Ruth Story AA

Shorts

1934

Show Kids WB

1935

Vacation Daze WB
Radio Scout WB
Memories and Melodies (o: Marquardt) MGM
A Trip Thru a Hollywood Studio WB
Get Rich Quick WB
Two Hearts in Wax Time (o: Virgil, W. Allen) MGM

1936

The Perfect Set-Up (+ stock) MGM
New Shoes (o: W. Allen, Marquardt) MGM
Greater Movie Season MGM
Hollywood Extra (o: Bassman, Arnaud) MGM
Annie Laurie (o: W. Allen, Arnaud, Raab) MGM

1938

Another Romance of Celluloid MGM
The City of Little Men (o: Arnaud) MGM
Hot on Ice (o: Raab) MGM
Man's Greatest Friend (o: Raab) MGM

1939

From the Ends of the Earth (with Snell) MGM

1943

Sweetheart Serenade WB

Trailers (MGM)

1935

After Office Hours
Broadway Melody of 1936
The Casino Murder Case
China Seas
Mark of the Vampire
One New York Night
Shadow of Doubt
Vanessa: Her Love Story
West Point of the Air

WARD, ROBERT

1964

Adventures in Sharps and Flats (doc. short) REID H. RAY

WARING, FRED

1953

You'll Never Walk Alone (doc. short) CHICAGO FILM LABORATORY

WARREN, DOUGLAS

1966

The Devil's Mistress (see B. Allen)

WARREN, HARRY

1932

Cabin in the Cotton (theme; o: R. Heindorf) WB

1933

Parachute Jumper (theme; o: R. Heindorf) WB

WATT, JAY
1957
What, Who, How (short) STAN VANDERBEEK
1964
Breathdeath (short) STAN VANDERBEEK

WATTS, JOHN
1968
War (doc. short) SYLVAN MARKMAN

WAXMAN, FRANZ
[Scored several films in Germany and France, 1930–1934.]
1934
Music in the Air (partial adaptation; o: Friedhofer) FOX
1935
Bride of Frankenstein (o: Vaughan) UNIV
Diamond Jim (o: Vaughan) UNIV
The Affair of Susan (o: Vaughan) UNIV
Three Kids and a Queen (with Roemheld) UNIV
Remember Last Night? (o: Vaughan) UNIV
East of Java (with Roemheld; ac and o: Vaughan) UNIV
Magnificent Obsession (o: Vaughan) UNIV
1936
The Invisible Ray (o: Vaughan) UNIV
Dangerous Waters (+ stock) UNIV
Next Time We Love (o: Vaughan) UNIV
Don't Get Personal (o: Vaughan) UNIV
Love Before Breakfast (o: Vaughan) UNIV
Sutter's Gold (ac: Roemheld, Vaughan) UNIV
Absolute Quiet (mt; ac: E. Ward; + stock) MGM
Trouble for Two (ac: Vaughan) MGM
Fury (o: Marquardt, Vaughan) MGM
The Devil-Doll (o: Marquardt, Vaughan, W. Allen) MGM
His Brother's Wife (o: Bassman, W. Allen, Maxwell) MGM
Love on the Run (o: Marquardt, Bassman, Vaughan, Arnaud) MGM
1937
Personal Property (o: Bassman, W. Allen, Vaughan) MGM
Captains Courageous (o: Marquardt, Maxwell; ac and o: Vaughan) MGM
A Day at the Races (o: Bassman, W. Allen, Marquardt) MGM
The Emperor's Candlesticks (ac: Vaughan, C. Bakaleinikoff; o: Marquardt, Vaughan, Bassman) MGM
The Bride Wore Red (o: Marquardt) MGM
Man-Proof (o: W. Allen) MGM
1938
Test Pilot (o: Marquardt; + stock) MGM
Port of Seven Seas (o: Marquardt) MGM
Three Comrades (o: Raab, Marquardt, Bassman, W. Allen) MGM
Too Hot to Handle (o: Bassman, Cutter) MGM
The Shining Hour (ac: Vaughan; o: Raab, Marquardt) MGM
The Young in Heart (ac: Roemheld; o: Raab, Friedhofer, Bassman, Cutter) SELZNICK
Dramatic School (o: Raab, Marquardt, Cutter, Bassman) MGM
A Christmas Carol (ac: Snell; o: Raab, Marquardt) MGM
1939
Honolulu (o: Raab, Satterfield, Bassman, Glover) MGM
The Adventures of Huckleberry Finn (o: Raab, Marquardt) MGM
The Ice Follies of 1939 (o: Raab, Bassman) MGM
Lucky Night (o: Marquardt, Bassman) MGM
On Borrowed Time (o: Raab, Marquardt) MGM
Lady of the Tropics (ac: Bassman; o: Raab, Marquardt, Arnaud) MGM
At the Circus (o: Marquardt, Cutter, Heglin) MGM
1940
Strange Cargo (o: Marquardt) MGM
Florian (ac: Zador, Kaper; o: Marquardt, Raab, Maxwell, Cutter) MGM
Rebecca (o: R. Bennett, Raab, Friedhofer, Marquardt, Nussbaum) SELZNICK
Sporting Blood (o: Marquardt, Raab, Arnaud) MGM
Boom Town (o: Raab, Marquardt; ac: Amfitheatrof, o: Maxwell) MGM
I Love You Again (o: Bassman) MGM
Escape (ac: Amfitheatrof, Zador, C. Bakaleinikoff; o: Raab, Marquardt, Cutter) MGM
The Philadelphia Story (o: Raab, Arnaud) MGM
Flight Command (o: Raab, Cutter, Hand, Nussbaum, Marquardt) MGM
1941
The Bad Man (o: Marquardt) MGM
Dr. Jekyll and Mr. Hyde (ac: Amfitheatrof, Castelnuovo-Tedesco; o: Raab,

Marquardt, Nussbaum) MGM
Unfinished Business (o: Raab) UNIV
The Feminine Touch (o: Bassman; + stock) MGM
Honky Tonk (ac: Amfitheatrof; o: Raab, Nussbaum) MGM
Kathleen (ac: Amfitheatrof; o: Raab, Heglin, Adlam) MGM
Suspicion (o: Raab) RKO
Design for Scandal (o: Raab, Arnaud, Bassman) MGM

1942
Woman of the Year (o: Raab, Marquardt, Maxwell, Heglin) MGM
Tortilla Flat (with Castelnuovo-Tedesco; o: Bassman, Raab, Marquardt, Arnaud) MGM
Her Cardboard Lover (o: Raab, Bassman; + stock) MGM
Seven Sweethearts (o: Raab, Heglin, Marquardt) MGM
Journey for Margaret (with Castelnuovo-Tedesco, S. Kaplan, Zeisl; o: Raab, Marquardt, Nussbaum) MGM
Reunion in France (o: Raab; ac: Castelnuovo-Tedesco, o: Marquardt; Zeisl, o: Nussbaum) MGM

1943
Air Force (o: Raab) WB
Edge of Darkness (o: Raab) WB
Old Acquaintance (o: Raab) WB

1944
Destination Tokyo (ac: Lava; o: Raab) WB
In Our Time (ac: Castelnuovo-Tedesco; o: Raab) WB
Mr. Skeffington (ac: Dessau; o: Raab) WB
Janie (see Roemheld)
The Very Thought of You (o: Raab) WB

1945
To Have and Have Not (o: Raab) WB
Objective, Burma! (o: Raab) WB
Hotel Berlin (ac: Dessau; o: Raab) WB
God Is My Co-Pilot (o: Moross) WB
The Horn Blows at Midnight (ac: Lava, Stalling; o: Raab) WB
Pride of the Marines (o: Raab) WB
Confidential Agent (o: Raab) WB

1946
Her Kind of Man (with M. Steiner, A. Deutsch, Dessau, Lava) WB

1947
Humoresque (o: Raab) WB
Nora Prentiss (ac: Dessau; o: Raab) WB
The Two Mrs. Carrolls (o: Raab) WB
Possessed (o: Raab) WB
Cry Wolf (o: Raab) WB
Dark Passage (ac: M. Steiner; o: Raab) WB
The Unsuspected (o: Raab) WB
That Hagen Girl (o: Raab) WB
The Paradine Case (ac: Dessau; o: Raab, Byrns) SELZNICK

1948
Sorry, Wrong Number (o: Raab, Parrish, Cutner, Shuken) PAR
No Minor Vices (o: Raab) MGM

1949
Whiplash (ac: Lava; o: Raab) WB
Alias Nick Beal (o: Raab, Parrish, Cutner, Shuken) PAR
Night Unto Night (o: Raab) WB
Rope of Sand (o: Raab, Parrish, Van Cleave) PAR
Task Force (o: Raab) WB

1950
Johnny Holiday (o: Raab) UA
Night and the City (o: E. Powell) TCF
The Furies (o: Raab, Cutner, Shuken, Parrish) PAR
Sunset Blvd. (o: Raab, Parrish, Shuken, Cutner) PAR
Dark City (o: Raab, Shuken, Cutner, Van Cleave) PAR

1951
Only the Valiant (o: Raab) WB
He Ran All the Way (o: Raab) UA
A Place in the Sun (ac: Amfitheatrof, V. Young; o: Raab, Cutner, Shuken, Parrish, Van Cleave) PAR
Anne of the Indies (o: Raab, E. Powell) TCF
The Blue Veil (ac: Webb; o: Raab) RKO
Red Mountain (o: Raab, Shuken, Cutner, Parrish, Van Cleave) PAR
Decision Before Dawn (o: Raab) TCF

1952
Phone Call from a Stranger (o: Raab) TCF
Lure of the Wilderness (o: Raab) TCF
My Cousin Rachel (o: E. Powell, Raab) TCF

1953
Come Back, Little Sheba (o: Raab, Van Cleave) PAR
Man on a Tightrope (o: Hagen) TCF
Stalag 17 (o: Raab) PAR
I, the Jury (o: Raab) UA
A Lion Is in the Streets (o: Raab) WB
Botany Bay (o: Raab, Shuken, Cutner) PAR

1954

Prince Valiant TCF
Elephant Walk (o: Raab, Van Cleave) PAR
Demetrius and the Gladiators (o: E. Powell; including themes by A. Newman from *The Robe*) TCF
Rear Window (o: Raab, Shuken, Cutner, Van Cleave, Levene) PAR
This Is My Love (o: Raab) RKO

1955
The Silver Chalice (o: Raab) WB
Untamed (o: E. Powell) TCF
Mister Roberts (o: Raab) WB
The Virgin Queen (o: Raab, E. Powell) TCF
The Indian Fighter (o: Raab) UA

1956
Miracle in the Rain (ac: R. Heindorf; o: Raab) WB
Crime in the Streets (o: Courage) AA
Back from Eternity (o: Raab) RKO

1957
The Spirit of St. Louis (ac: Webb; o: Raab) WB
Love in the Afternoon (o: Sendrey) AA
Peyton Place (o: E. Powell) TCF
Sayonara (o: Raab) WB

1958
Run Silent, Run Deep (o: Raab) UA

1959
Count Your Blessings (o: Raab, Arnaud) MGM
The Nun's Story WB
Career (o: Raab) PAR
Beloved Infidel (o: E. Powell, Raab) TCF

1960
The Story of Ruth (o: E. Powell, Raab) TCF
Sunrise at Campobello WB
Cimarron (o: Raab, E. Powell) MGM

1961
King of the Roaring '20's (o: Raab) AA
Return to Peyton Place (o: Raab, E. Powell) TCF
My Geisha (o: Raab) PAR

1962
Ernest Hemingway's Adventures of a Young Man (o: Raab) TCF
Taras Bulba (o: Raab) UA

1966
Lost Command (o: Raab) COL

WEAVER, EDDIE

1963
Around the World in Eighty Feet (doc. short) CW

WEBB, ROY

[All for RKO unless otherwise noted.]

1930
Side Street (see M. Steiner)
The Delightful Rogue (see M. Steiner)
Night Parade (foreign version of 1929 film; + stock)
Seven Keys to Baldpate (foreign version; + stock)
Girl of the Port
Alias French Gertie
Shooting Straight
Inside the Lines
Conspiracy

1933
Our Betters (see Kaun)
Topaze
Christopher Strong (see M. Steiner)
Diplomaniacs (see M. Steiner)
Emergency Call (+ stock)
Ann Vickers (m&e; + stock)
A Preferred List (short; m&e)
The Right to Romance (o: Hand, Malotte; m&e: M. Steiner)
Aggie Appleby, Maker of Men (m&e; o: Kaun)
If I Were Free (+ stock)

1934
Hips, Hips, Hooray!
This Man Is Mine (m&e; + stock)
Strictly Dynamite
Cockeyed Cavaliers
We're Rich Again (mt; + stock)
Down to Their Last Yacht
Kentucky Kernels (+ stock)

1935
The Nitwits (o: de Packh)
Becky Sharp (o: de Packh, Kaun)
Alice Adams (waltz theme: M. Steiner; o: de Packh)
The Rainmakers (o: G. Rose, de Packh)
The Last Days of Pompeii (o: de Packh, Friedhofer)
In Person (o: de Packh)

1936
Sylvia Scarlett (o: de Packh)
Silly Billies (o: G. Rose, C. Wheeler)
The Last of the Mohicans (o: Friedhofer) UA
Mummy's Boys
A Woman Rebels (o: de Packh)
Night Waitress (+ stock)

1937
The Plough and the Stars (o: de Packh)

Racing Lady (mt; + stock)
We're on the Jury (mt; + stock)
Quality Street (o: de Packh)
The Woman I Love (ac; + music by Arthur Honegger & Maurice Thiriet from 1935 French film, *L'Équipage,* of which this was a remake)
Meet the Missus (+ stock)
New Faces of 1937
On Again—Off Again
The Life of the Party (o: de Packh)
Stage Door (o: R. Bennett)
High Flyers

1938
Bringing Up Baby (o: R. Bennett)
Vivacious Lady (o: R. Bennett)
Having Wonderful Time (o: R. Bennett)
Sky Giant (o: R. Bennett)
I'm from the City (m&e; + stock)
The Affairs of Annabel
The Renegade Ranger
Room Service (o: R. Bennett)
Fugitives for a Night (m&e: R. Bennett)
Mr. Doodle Kicks Off
A Man to Remember (o: R. Bennett)
The Mad Miss Manton (o: R. Bennett)
Lawless Valley (o: R. Bennett)
The Law West of Tombstone (o: R. Bennett)
Next Time I Marry

1939
The Great Man Votes (o: Parrish, R. Bennett)
Arizona Legion (o: R. Bennett, Bucharoff, Reese)
Beauty for the Asking (see Tours)
The Saint Strikes Back (o: R. Bennett)
Love Affair (o: Parrish, R. Bennett, Buttolph, D. Raksin)
Trouble in Sundown (with Tours; o: Nussbaum, Parrish, Bucharoff)
The Flying Irishman
They Made Her a Spy
Fixer Dugan
The Rookie Cop
Sorority House
Panama Lady (o: Parrish)
The Girl from Mexico (o: Parrish)
The Girl and the Gambler (o: Parrish)
Five Came Back (o: Parrish)
Timber Stampede (o: Van Loan)
Bachelor Mother (o: Parrish)
Career (with R. Bennett; o: Parrish)
Bad Lands
In Name Only
Full Confession
Three Sons
Sued for Libel
Reno
Two Thoroughbreds
That's Right—You're Wrong

1940
Abe Lincoln in Illinois
The Saint's Double Trouble
The Marines Fly High
Curtain Call
Irene (see Collins)
A Bill of Divorcement
My Favorite Wife
The Saint Takes Over
You Can't Fool Your Wife
Anne of Windy Poplars
Cross Country Romance
Millionaires in Prison
One Crowded Night (o: de Packh)
Stranger on the Third Floor (o: Parrish, de Packh)
I'm Still Alive (o: de Packh)
Laddie (ac: Mockridge; o: G. Rose, de Packh, Maxwell, Parrish)
Mexican Spitfire Out West (o: G. Rose)
You'll Find Out
Kitty Foyle

1941
Little Men
Let's Make Music
The Saint in Palm Springs
A Girl, a Guy and a Gob
The Devil and Miss Jones
Hurry, Charlie, Hurry
Tom, Dick and Harry
Parachute Battalion
Father Takes a Wife
Look Who's Laughing
Obliging Young Lady
The Bandit Trail (see Sawtell)
Weekend for Three
Playmates

1942
Joan of Paris
Mayor of 44th Street
The Tuttles of Tahiti
My Favorite Spy
The Big Street
The Magnificent Ambersons (see Herrmann)
Mexican Spitfire's Elephant
The Navy Comes Through
Here We Go Again

Once Upon a Honeymoon (see Dolan)
Army Surgeon
Seven Days' Leave
I Married a Witch (o: Parrish, Shuken) UA
Conquer by the Clock (doc. short)
The Nazis Strike (doc.; with Leipold, Harline, Collins, Tiomkin, Gruenberg) U.S. WAR DEPT.

1943
Cat People
Ladies' Day
Hitler's Children (o: de Packh)
I Walked with a Zombie (o: de Packh, Raab)
Flight for Freedom (o: de Packh, Raab)
Bombardier (o: de Packh)
The Leopard Man
Mr. Lucky (o: de Packh, Raab)
Behind the Rising Sun (o: de Packh)
The Fallen Sparrow (o: de Packh)
The Adventures of a Rookie
The Seventh Victim (o: de Packh)
A Lady Takes a Chance (o: de Packh)
The Iron Major (o: de Packh)
Gangway for Tomorrow
The Ghost Ship
Higher and Higher (o: de Packh)

1944
The Fighting Seabees (see W. Scharf)
Action in Arabia
The Curse of the Cat People
Passport to Destiny
The Falcon Out West
Seven Days Ashore
Marine Raiders (o: de Packh)
The Seventh Cross (o: de Packh, A. Morton) MGM
Bride by Mistake
Rainbow Island (o: Parrish, Grau, Shuken) PAR
Tall in the Saddle
The Master Race (o: Grau)
Experiment Perilous

1945
The Body Snatcher (o: Grau)
The Enchanted Cottage (o: Grau)
Murder, My Sweet (o: Grau)
Zombies on Broadway
Those Endearing Young Charms (o: Grau)
Back to Bataan (o: Grau)
George White's Scandals
Radio Stars on Parade
Love, Honor and Goodbye (o: Butts, Dubin) REP
Cornered (o: Grau)
Sing Your Way Home
The Spiral Staircase

1946
Dick Tracy
Riverboat Rhythm
The Well Groomed Bride (o: Parrish, Simeone, Bradshaw, Marquardt, Cutner, Shuken) PAR
Bedlam (o: Grau)
Badman's Territory (o: Grau)
Without Reservations (o: Grau)
The Perfect Marriage (see Hollander)
Genius at Work (see Sawtell)
Notorious (o: Grau)
The Locket
Sinbad the Sailor (o: Grau)

1947
Ladies Man (with Lilley, Van Cleave, Bradshaw) PAR
Easy Come, Easy Go (o: Cutner, Parrish, Shuken) PAR
The Devil Thumbs a Ride (+ stock)
They Won't Believe Me
Riffraff
Crossfire
Magic Town
Cass Timberlane (o: Grau) MGM
Out of the Past

1948
I Remember Mama
Fighting Father Dunne
Race Street
Rachel and the Stranger
Blood on the Moon (o: Grau)
Bad Men of Tombstone AA

1949
The Window
Roughshod (with Sawtell; o: Grau)
Mighty Joe Young (o: Grau)
My Friend Irma (o: Shuken, Cutner, Parrish, Bradshaw) PAR
Make Mine Laughs
Easy Living
Holiday Affair
The Great Lover (see Lilley)

1950
The Secret Fury
The White Tower (o: Grau, Raab)
Fancy Pants (see Van Cleave)
Where Danger Lives (o: Grau, Raab)
Vendetta (o: Raab)

1951
Branded (o: Van Cleave, Parrish) PAR

Gambling House
Sealed Cargo
Hard, Fast and Beautiful
Flying Leathernecks
The Blue Veil (see Waxman)
Fixed Bayonets! (o: de Packh) TCF

1952
A Girl in Every Port
At Sword's Point
Clash by Night
The Lusty Men
Operation Secret (o: Shuken, Cutner) WB
Androcles and the Lion (see Hollander)

1953
Split Second (o: Grau, Raab)
Affair with a Stranger
Houdini (o: Parrish, Grau, Shuken, Cutner, Van Cleave) PAR
Second Chance

1954
Alaska Seas (see Shuken)
She Couldn't Say No
Dangerous Mission
The Raid (o: Arnaud, E. Powell, Raab) TCF
Track of the Cat (o: de Packh) WB
The Americano
Underwater!

1955
Marty (ac: Bassman) UA
The Sea Chase (o: de Packh, Raab) WB
Bengazi
Blood Alley (o: de Packh, Levene) WB

1956
Our Miss Brooks (o: Levene) WB
The River Changes (o: Levene) WB
The First Texan AA
The Search for Bridey Murphy (o: Grau; ac and o: H. Jackson) PAR
The Girl He Left Behind (o: Levene) WB

1957
Top Secret Affair (o: Levene, de Packh) WB
The Spirit of St. Louis (see Waxman)
Shoot-Out at Medicine Bend (o: de Packh) WB

1958
Teacher's Pet (o: Van Cleave) PAR

1959
Return of the Fly (see Sawtell and Shefter)

WEBER, BEN

1948
Image in the Snow (short) WILLARD MAAS

WEDBERG, CONRAD, JR.

1949
The Thinnest Slice (doc. short) USC

WEILL, KURT

1938
You and Me (ac: Harling, Leipold; dance hall sequences and et: Shuken; a and o: Roder, Leipold, Hand, A. Siegel, Jenkins, Bradshaw) PAR

1944
Salute to France (doc. short) OWI

WEINBERG, JACOB

1938
The Singing Blacksmith (Yiddish language) EDGAR G. ULMER

1952
To Save One Life HADASSAH

WEINER, PETER

1969
Lady Godiva Rides SCA DISTRIBUTORS

WEINMAN, EDWARD

1962
The Legend of Soupspoon (doc.) DAN-GLENN PRODS.

WEINSTOCK, JACOB

1917
The Chosen Prince CREST

WEISS, JOSEPH

1964
A House Is Not a Home EMB

WELLINGTON, LARRY

1963
Bell, Bare and Beautiful GRIFFITH PRODS.

1964
Two Thousand Maniacs! (see Herschell Lewis)

1967
The Gruesome Twosome HERSCHELL G. LEWIS
A Taste of Blood HERSCHELL G. LEWIS
The Girl, the Body, and the Pill HERSCHELL G. LEWIS

1968
She-Devils on Wheels HERSCHELL G. LEWIS
How to Make a Doll HERSCHELL G. LEWIS
Just for the Hell of It HERSCHELL G. LEWIS

1970
The Wizard of Gore HERSCHELL G. LEWIS

WELLS, HOWARD
1962
Out of the Tiger's Mouth PATHÉ-AMERICA

WERLE, FLOYD
1960
The Devil to Pay! (short) RODEL PRODS.

WERNICK, RICHARD F.
Shorts
1960
Bowl of Cherries WILLIAM KRONICK
1961
The Fur-Lined Foxhole GEORGE C. STONEY ASSOC.
The Purple Turtle STELIOS ROCOS
1962
Something for the Girls GEORGE C. STONEY ASSOC.
Worship, a Family's Heritage METHODIST CHURCH

WHEELER, CLARENCE
1941
Combat (an. doc.) GENERAL CHEMICAL
Dangerous Lady PRC
The Miracle Kid PRC
Law of the Timber PRC
1942
Too Many Women PRC
Miss Annie Rooney (see Calker)
1944
I'm from Arkansas PRC
1947
Blondie's Holiday (+ stock) COL
The Son of Rusty (see Gertz)
Blondie's Anniversary (see P. Smith)
1950
The Fighting Stallion EL
Destination Moon (see L. Stevens)
1956
Down Liberty Road (see Koff)
Shorts
[From 1941–1949 he composed the scores for *Speaking of Animals* (at least 38 of the 48 in the series) for Paramount.]
1953
America for Me (see Koff)
1956
They Seek Adventure (see Koff)
Animated Shorts
1946
Haste Makes Waste PLANET
1948
Prospecting for Petroleum SHELL OIL CO.
1949
Birth of an Oil Field SHELL OIL CO.
1952
Wheat Smut Control UNION PACIFIC
1955
Fresh from the West UNION PACIFIC
Cartoons
1938
Old Smokey MGM
1941
Broken Treaties COL
The Carpenters COL
How War Came COL
1945
A Hatful of Dreams PAR
Hotlip Jasper PAR
Jasper and the Beanstalk PAR
Jasper Tell PAR
Jasper's Boobytraps PAR
Jasper's Close Shave PAR
Jasper's Minstrels PAR
My Man Jasper PAR
1946
Jasper in a Jam PAR
Jasper's Derby PAR
John Henry and the Inky-Poo PAR
Olio for Jasper PAR
Together in the Weather PAR
1947
Shoe Shine Jasper PAR
Tubby the Tuba (md) PAR
Wilbur the Lion PAR
1949
Beyond Civilization to Texas REP
The Three Minnies REP
Cartoons (WALTER LANTZ/UNIV)
1951
Puny Express
The Redwood Sap
Sleep Happy
Sling Shot $6\frac{7}{8}$
Wicket Wacky
1952
Born to Peck
Destination Meat Ball
The Great Who-Dood-It
Scalp Treatment

Stage Hoax
Woodpecker in the Rough
The Woody Woodpecker Polka

1953
Belle Boys
Buccaneer Woodpecker
The Dog That Cried Wolf
The Flying Turtle
Hot Noon
Hypnotic Hick
Maw and Paw
The Mouse and the Lion
Operation Sawdust
Plywood Panic
Termites from Mars
What's Sweepin'
Wrestling Wrecks

1954
Alley to Bali
Broadway Bow-Wows
Convict Concerto
Dig That Dog
A Fine Feathered Frenzy
Hay Rube
A Horse's Tale
Hot Rod Huckster
Pig in a Pickle
Real Gone Woody
Socko in Morocco
Under the Counter Spy

1955
Bedtime Bedlam
Bunco Busters
Chilly Willy in The Legend of Rockabye Point
Crazy Mixed-up Pup
Flea for Two
Helter Shelter
Hot and Cold Penguin
I'm Cold
Paw's Night Out
Private Eye Pooch
Sh-h-h-h-h
Square Shootin' Square
The Tree Medic
Witch Crafty

1956
After the Ball
Arts and Flowers
Box Car Bandit
Calling All Cuckoos
Chief Charlie Horse
Get Lost
Hold That Rock
Niagara Fools
Pigeon Holed
Room and Wrath
The Talking Dog
Woodpecker from Mars
Woody Meets Davy Crewcut

1957
The Bongo Punch
Dopey Dick, the Pink Whale
Fodder and Son
Fowled Up Party
International Woodpecker
Misguided Missile
Operation Cold Feet
Red Riding Hoodlum
Round Trip to Mars
To Catch a Woodpecker
The Unbearable Salesman

1958
Everglade Raid
His Better Elf
Jittery Jester
Polar Pests
Salmon Yeggs
Three Ring Fling
Tree's a Crowd
Truant Student
Watch the Birdie

1959
Bee Bopped
Log Jammed
Space Mouse
The Tee Bird
Woodpecker in the Moon

1960
Ballyhooey
Bats in the Belfry
Fowled Up Falcon
How to Stuff a Woodpecker
Hunger Strife

1961
The Bird Who Came to Dinner
Busman's Holiday
Papoose on the Loose
Phantom of the Horse Opera

1962
Born to Peck
Crowin' Pains
Home Sweet Homewrecker
Little Woody Riding Hood
Robin Hoody Woody
Rocket Racket
Room and Bore
Tragic Magic

1963
Calling Dr. Woodpecker
Coy Decoy
Short in the Saddle
Shutter Bug
Stowaway Woody
Tepee for Two
1964
Deep Freeze Squeeze
Freeway Fracus
Get Lost! Little Doggy
Roamin' Roman
Woodpecker Wanted
1965
The Big Bite
Canned Dog Feud
Hassle in a Castle
Rough Riding Hood
Sioux Me
What's Peckin'
1966
Monster of Ceremonies
Sissy Sheriff

WHEELER, WALLACE
1930
Temple Tower (see Lipschultz)
[Also worked as an orchestrator.]

WHITE, DALE
Documentary Shorts (CHET HENSON)
1964
Isle of Women
Mayaland Safari
Toltec Mystery

WHITE, JOHNNY
1966
The Undertaker and His Pals HOWCO

WHITE, LEW
1932
Devil of the Matterhorn HARRY J. REVIER
1934
The Shepherd of the Seven Hills (doc.) VATICAN PICTURES
Documentary Shorts (ANDRÉ DE LAVARRE)
1936
Colourful Cairo
Damascus and Jerusalem
Glimpses of Picturesque Java
Through Normandy to Mont St. Michel

WHITE, RUTH
1954
Railroad Rhythms (doc. short) PAUL BURNFORD

WILDER, ALEC
1950
Grandma Moses (see H. Martin)
1955
The Grocer and the Dragon (short) TRANSFILM
1957
Albert Schweitzer (doc.) JEROME HILL
1959
The Fall of the House of Usher (music added to 1928 short) J.S.WATSON, M. WEBBER
1961
The Sand Castle JEROME HILL
Since Life Began (doc. short) LIFE MAGAZINE
1964
Open the Door and See All the People JEROME HILL

WILDING-WHITE, RAYMOND
1965
Ecce Homo—Behold the Man (doc. short) PAULIST PRODS.

WILLIAMS, AUDREY
1965
Second Fiddle to a Steel Guitar MARATHON

WILLIAMS, GLENN
1961
From Inner Space (short) JOSEPH MARZANO

WILLIAMS, JOHN
1957
My Gun Is Quick (see Skiles)
1959
Daddy-'O' AIP
1960
I Passed for White AA
Because They're Young COL
1961
The Secret Ways UNIV
Bachelor Flat (o: R. Franklyn) TCF
1963
Diamond Head (o: A. Morton) COL
Gidget Goes to Rome (o: A. Morton) COL

1964

The Killers (see F. Steiner)

John Goldfarb, Please Come Home! (o: A. Morton) TCF

1965

None But the Brave (o: Woodbury) WB

1966

The Rare Breed UNIV

How to Steal a Million (o: Harbert) TCF

The Plainsman UNIV

Penelope (o: Woodbury, Bryant) MGM

Not With MY Wife, You Don't! WB

The Kathryn Reed Story (short) ROBERT ALTMAN

1967

A Guide for the Married Man (o: H. Spencer) TCF

Valley of the Dolls (o: H. Spencer) TCF

Fitzwilly UA

1968

Sergeant Ryker UNIV

1969

Daddy's Gone A-Hunting NG

Goodbye, Mr. Chips MGM

The Reivers NG

1970

Story of a Woman UNIV

WILLIAMS, PATRICK

1968

How Sweet It Is! (o: Van Cleave) NG

1969

Don't Drink the Water EMB

A Nice Girl Like Me EMB

1970

Macho Callahan EMB

The Sidelong Glances of a Pigeon Kicker (with Lee Holdridge, Edd Kalehoff, Chris Dedrick, Warren Marley) MGM

WILLIS, T. RALPH

1934

Tubal-Cain (short) NATIONAL

WILLSON, MEREDITH

1929

Peacock Alley (partial) TS

The Lost Zeppelin (partial) TS

1940

The Great Dictator (see C. Chaplin)

1941

The Little Foxes (o: C. Dragon, Terr, Zador) GOLDWYN

WILSON, FRANK

1965

Beach Ball PAR

WILSON, JOHN

Dance Shorts (PORTIA MANSFIELD)

1953

Smith College

1954

Dance Demonstration

Basic Movement

1956

The Barrel

WILSON, MORTIMER

1923

The Covered Wagon (Overture "1849"; score: see Riesenfeld)

1924

The Thief of Bagdad UA

1925

Don Q, Son of Zorro UA

1926

The Black Pirate UA

1928

The Good-bye Kiss (see Bierman)

The Night Watch (see Bierman)

WILSON, STANLEY

[All pictures through 1953 for Republic.]

1947

Apache Rose (see Maxwell)

1948

Federal Agents vs. Underworld, Inc. (serial)

1949

Rose of the Yukon

Sheriff of Wichita

Death Valley Gunfighters

Duke of Chicago

Susanna Pass

Frontier Investigator

Law of the Golden West

King of the Rocket Men (serial)

South of Rio

Bandit King of Texas

The James Brothers of Missouri (serial)

Flame of Youth

San Antone Ambush

Navajo Trail Raiders

Alias the Champ

Ranger of Cherokee Strip

Powder River Rustlers

The Blonde Bandit
Pioneer Marshal
Radar Patrol vs. Spy King (serial)

1950
Belle of Old Mexico
Unmasked
Gunmen of Abilene
Tarnished
Federal Agent at Large
Code of the Silver Sage
Harbor of Missing Men
The Vanishing Westerner
Arizona Cowboy
Twilight in the Sierras
Women from Headquarters (with Butts)
Hills of Oklahoma
Destination Big House
Covered Wagon Raid
Trial Without Jury
The Old Frontier
Vigilante Hideout
The Showdown
Lonely Hearts Bandits
Frisco Tornado
Redwood Forest Trail
Prisoners in Petticoats
Rustlers on Horseback
Flying Disc Man from Mars (serial)
The Missourians
Under Mexicali Stars

1951
Rough Riders of Durango
Missing Women
Night Riders of Montana
Silver City Bonanza
Cuban Fireball
Buckaroo Sheriff of Texas
Thunder in God's Country
Don Daredevil Rides Again (serial)
Wells Fargo Gunmaster
Million Dollar Pursuit
The Dakota Kid
Government Agents vs. Phantom Legion (serial)
Rodeo King and the Señorita
Utah Wagon Train
Fort Dodge Stampede
Havana Rose
Arizona Manhunt
Desert of Lost Men
Captive of Billy the Kid
Woman in the Dark

1952
Radar Men from the Moon (serial)
The Fabulous Señorita
Gobs and Gals
Wild Horse Ambush
Border Saddlemates
Black Hills Ambush
Thundering Caravans
Old Oklahoma Plains
Zombies of the Stratosphere (serial)
Tropical Heat Wave
Desperadoes' Outpost
The Lady Wants Mink

1953
Marshal of Cedar Rock
Commando Cody (serial)
The Woman They Almost Lynched
Iron Mountain Trail
City That Never Sleeps (see Butts)
Savage Frontier
Down Laredo Way
Bandits of the West
El Paso Stampede

1954
Untamed Heiress REP
The Yellow Mountain (see Mancini)
Bengal Brigade (with H. Stein; ac: Salter; + stock) UNIV

1955
Cult of the Cobra (see Lava)
Francis in the Navy (see Lava)
The Private War of Major Benson (see Lava)

1956
Toy Tiger (see Mancini)
Kelly and Me (see Mancini)

1957
The Halliday Brand UA
Joe Butterfly (see Mancini)
Love Slaves of the Amazon (with Vars, H. Stein, Gertz; ac: Brummer, Salter) UNIV

1958
Girls on the Loose (see Vars)
Live Fast, Die Young (with Gertz) UNIV
The Explosive Mr. Magoo (cartoon) UPA
The Mating Urge HOWARD C. BROWN
Ride a Crooked Trail (+ stock) UNIV

1967
Valley of Mystery (see J. Elliott)

WILSON, TALBERT

1970
The Dispossessed (doc. short) GEORGE BALLIS

WINELAND, SAMUEL K.
1929
Madame X (see Axt)
Wonder of Women (see A. Lange)
1930
Gems of M.G.M. (short; + stock) MGM
1933
Good-bye Love (see Roder)
[Also worked as a musical director.]

WING, EDWIN O.
1963
The Fifth Freedom (short) WING PRODS.

WINSLOW, RICHARD
1953
A Poem of Life (doc. short) FOCAL POINT FILMS

WOLCOTT, CHARLES
1941
The Reluctant Dragon (see Churchill)
1942
Saludos Amigos (with P. Smith, Plumb) WDP
1944
The Three Caballeros (with Plumb, P. Smith) WDP
1946
Make Mine Music (with Wallace, Daniel; o: Hand, Plumb, Schoen) WDP
Song of the South (see Amfitheatrof)
1949
The Adventures of Ichabod and Mr. Toad (see Wallace)
1951
It's a Big Country (see A. Deutsch)
1955
Blackboard Jungle (cartoon sequence: Bradley) MGM
1960
Key Witness MGM
Shorts
1943
Defense Against Invasion (an.) WDP
1951
Football Thrills, No. 14 MGM
1952
Gymnastic Rhythm MGM
Cartoons (WDP)
1940
Goofy's Glider
Mr. Duck Steps Out
1941
The Art of Skiing
Chef Donald
Mickey's Birthday Party
The Nifty Nineties
The Village Smithy

WOLDIN, JUDD
1966
Poppycock! (short) CARSON DAVIDSON

WOLF, ROBERT ERICH
1951
Bird Hunt (short) UCLA

WOLFF, F. ROGER
1951
You, Chicago! (doc. short) ?
1964
The Silent Crisis (doc. short) NED BOSNICK

WOLFF, TOM
1967
Wavelength MICHAEL SNOW

WOLPE, STEFAN
1942
Palestine at War (doc.) PALESTINE LABOR COMMISSION

WOODBURY, ALBERT
1957
Silk Stockings (see Salinger)
1960
Pepe (see J. Green)
1961
Sweet Bird of Youth (mt; + stock) MGM
[Also a prolific orchestrator.]

WOODE, HENRI
1964
Bunny Yeager's Nude Las Vegas CINEMA SYNDICATE
1965
Naughty Nudes CINEMA SYNDICATE

WORTH, DON
1957
Ansel Adams, Photographer (doc. short) LARRY DAWSON PRODS.

WORTH, FRANK
1956
Bride of the Monster BANNER

1958
Street of Darkness REP

WORTH, PAUL
Cartoons (SCREEN GEMS/COL)
1941
The Cuckoo I. Q.
The Great Cheese Mystery
The Merry Mouse Cafe
1942
The Bulldog and the Baby
Cholly Polly
Cinderella Goes to a Party
The Dumbconscious Mind
A Hollywood Detour
King Midas, Junior
Old Blackout Joe
The Tangled Angler
Tito's Guitar
Wacky Wigwams
The Wild and Woozy West
Wolf Chases Pigs
1943
Dizzy Newsreel
Duty and the Beast
The Fly in the Ointment (with de Packh)
Imagination
Kindly Scram
Mass Mouse Meeting
Nursery Crimes
There's Something About a Soldier
Tree for Two
Willoughby's Magic Hat
1944
Amoozin' But Confoozin'
The Disillusioned Blue Bird
1945
Rippling Romance

WORTH, STAN
1966
The Cat EMB
1967
You've Got to Be Smart ELLIS KADISON

WYKES, ROBERT
Documentary Shorts
1964
Children Without GUGGENHEIM PRODS.
1966
Time of the West GUGGENHEIM PRODS.
1967
Quality and Promise WASHINGTON U.
1968
Monument to the Dream GUGGENHEIM PRODS.
Robert Kennedy Remembered GUGGENHEIM PRODS.

Y

YEAWORTH, JEAN
1955
Mission of the Bells (short) SCHULMERICH CARILLONS

YOUNG, LA MONTE
1964
Warhol (film loop of four silent Andy Warhol films: *Sleep, Kiss, Haircut, Eat*) DAVID BOURDON

YOUNG, VICTOR
(1889–1968)
1929
In Old California AUDIBLE PICTURES

YOUNG, VICTOR
(1900–1956)
1936
Anything Goes (see Hollander)
The Milky Way (m&e; ac: Satterfield; + stock) PAR
Klondike Annie (with Leipold, Satterfield; ac: Roemheld) PAR
Frankie and Johnnie REP
Fatal Lady (ac: Carbonara, Leipold; o: Shuken, Bradshaw) PAR
The Princess Comes Across (see Leipold)
Poppy (see Hollander)
My American Wife (see Hollander)
The Big Broadcast of 1937 (see Skiles)
1937
Maid of Salem PAR
Swing High, Swing Low (with Boutelje, Rainger) PAR
Waikiki Wedding (see Shuken)
Make Way for Tomorrow (with Antheil) PAR
Mountain Music (see Leipold)
Easy Living (see Jenkins)

Souls at Sea (see Harling)
Vogues of 1938 UA
Double or Nothing (with Leipold; ac: Bassman, Terr) PAR
Ebb Tide PAR
Wells Fargo (ac: Leipold) PAR

1938

The Big Broadcast of 1938 (see Leipold)
Romance in the Dark (with Leipold) PAR
Army Girl (o: Hand) REP
The Gladiator COL
Breaking the Ice RKO
Peck's Bad Boy with the Circus RKO
Flirting with Fate MGM

1939

Fisherman's Wharf RKO
Union Pacific (see Leipold)
Man of Conquest REP
Undercover Doctor (with Leipold) PAR
The Gracie Allen Murder Case (see Carbonara)
Heritage of the Desert PAR
Grand Jury Secrets (ac: Carbonara; + stock) PAR
Man About Town (see Hollander)
Way Down South RKO
Island of Lost Men (see Leipold)
Our Leading Citizen (see Carbonara)
Golden Boy (o: Shuken) COL
Death of a Champion (see Leipold)
Range War PAR
Honeymoon in Bali (see Hollander)
Television Spy (see Leipold)
Law of the Pampas (with Leipold) PAR
Our Neighbors—The Carters (o: Leipold, Shuken, Bradshaw) PAR
The Night of Nights (ac: Bradshaw; o: Shuken, Leipold) PAR
The Llano Kid (with Leipold; o: Shuken, Leipold) PAR
All Women Have Secrets (see Leipold)
Escape to Paradise RKO
Gulliver's Travels (an.; o: Parrish, Shuken, Bassman, Bradshaw) PAR

1940

Raffles GOLDWYN
Santa Fe Marshal (see Leipold)
Parole Fixer (see Carbonara)
The Light That Failed (o: Parrish, Shuken, Bradshaw) PAR
Knights of the Range (see Leipold)
Road to Singapore PAR
The Farmer's Daughter (with Leipold, Bradshaw; m&e: Shuken) PAR
Dark Command REP
The Light of Western Stars PAR
Typhoon (see Hollander)
Buck Benny Rides Again (ac: Leipold; o: Shuken) PAR
Those Were the Days PAR
The Ghost Breakers (see Toch)
The Way of All Flesh (o: Leipold, Shuken, Bradshaw) PAR
Three Faces West (o: Hand) REP
Mystery Sea Raider (see Malotte)
Rhythm on the River (o: Shuken, Bradshaw) PAR
I Want a Divorce (o: Shuken, Bradshaw) PAR
Moon Over Burma PAR
Dancing on a Dime PAR
Arise, My Love (ac: Shuken; mt: Hollander) PAR
Three Men from Texas (o: Leipold; + stock) PAR
North West Mounted Police (o: Shuken, Parrish, Bradshaw, Hand, Leipold) PAR
Arizona (o: Cutner, Hand) COL
A Night at Earl Carroll's (o: Shuken) PAR
Love Thy Neighbor PAR
The Mad Doctor PAR

1941

The Outlaw UA
The Round Up (with Leipold; o: Hand, Leipold) PAR
Road to Zanzibar (ac: Bradshaw; o: W. Scharf, Parrish, Bassman) PAR
Reaching for the Sun (o: Parrish) PAR
Caught in the Draft (ac: Bradshaw; o: Shuken, Leipold) PAR
I Wanted Wings (o: Bradshaw, Parrish, Shuken, W. Scharf, Hand, Leipold) PAR
One Night in Lisbon (o and ac: Shuken) PAR
Kiss the Boys Goodbye (o: Shuken, Bradshaw) PAR
World Premiere (o: Parrish) PAR
Aloma of the South Seas (o: Shuken, Parrish) PAR
The Night of January 16th (see Carbonara)
Hold Back the Dawn (ac: Leipold; o: Parrish, Leipold) PAR
Buy Me That Town (o: Parrish, Leipold) PAR
Skylark (ac: Shuken; o: Shuken, Parrish, Bradshaw) PAR
Glamour Boy (o: Parrish, Shuken) PAR
Pacific Blackout (see Carbonara)

1942

The Remarkable Andrew (o: Parrish, Shuken) PAR

Reap the Wild Wind (o: Parrish, Shuken, W. Scharf) PAR
The Great Man's Lady (o: Parrish, Shuken) PAR
The Fleet's In (see Shuken)
Beyond the Blue Horizon (o: Parrish, Shuken) PAR
Sweater Girl (o: Shuken) PAR
Take a Letter, Darling (o: Parrish, Shuken, Bradshaw, W. Scharf, Grau) PAR
Priorities on Parade (mt: G. Rose; o: Shuken, W. Scharf) PAR
The Forest Rangers (o: Shuken) PAR
The Road to Morocco (o: Shuken, Parrish, Bradshaw) PAR
Mrs. Wiggs of the Cabbage Patch (o: Parrish, Shuken, Grau, W. Scharf) PAR
Flying Tigers REP
Young and Willing (o: Shuken) UA
The Glass Key (with W. Scharf; o: Shuken, Parrish) PAR
The Palm Beach Story (o: Parrish, W. Scharf, Shuken) PAR
The Crystal Ball (o: Shuken, Bradshaw) UA
Silver Queen (ac: Harline, Bradshaw; o: Hand, Parrish) UA

1943
My Heart Belongs to Daddy (see Shuken)
Buckskin Frontier (o: Shuken, Parrish; + stock) UA
China (o: Parrish) PAR
For Whom the Bell Tolls (o: Parrish, Shuken) PAR
Salute for Three (o: Parrish) PAR
Hostages (o: Parrish, Shuken) PAR
True to Life (o: Shuken) PAR
Riding High (see Bradshaw)
No Time for Love (o: Shuken, Parrish, Hand, Bradshaw) PAR

1944
The Uninvited (o: Shuken, Parrish) PAR
The Story of Dr. Wassell (o: Shuken, Parrish) PAR
And the Angels Sing (see Bradshaw)
The Great Moment (o: Parrish, Shuken) PAR
The Sign of the Cross (new prologue to reissue of 1932 film; o: Parrish) PAR
Frenchman's Creek (o: Parrish, Shuken) PAR
Ministry of Fear (o: Parrish, Shuken; ac: Rozsa, o: Zador) PAR
And Now Tomorrow (o: Parrish, Shuken) PAR
Practically Yours (o: Shuken; ac and o: Bradshaw) PAR

1945
Bring On the Girls (see Dolan)
A Medal for Benny (o: Parrish, Shuken) PAR
The Great John L. UA
You Came Along (o: Parrish, Shuken, Cutner) PAR
Kitty (o: Parrish, Cutner, Shuken) PAR
Love Letters (o: Parrish, Shuken, Cutner) PAR
Masquerade in Mexico (o: Parrish, Shuken, Cutner) PAR

1946
The Blue Dahlia (o: Parrish; trailer: Bradshaw) PAR
The Searching Wind (o: Parrish, Cutner, Shuken) PAR
Our Hearts Were Growing Up (o: Parrish) PAR
To Each His Own (o: Parrish, Shuken, Cutner) PAR
Two Years Before the Mast (o: Parrish, Shuken, Zador, Cutner) PAR

1947
Suddenly It's Spring (o: Parrish, Shuken, Cutner) PAR
California (ac: Carbonara; o: Parrish, Shuken, Cutner) PAR
The Imperfect Lady (o: Cutner, Shuken) PAR
Calcutta (o: Shuken, Cutner, Parrish, Plumb) PAR
The Trouble with Women (with Dolan, Van Cleave; o: Bradshaw, Cutner, Shuken, Parrish) PAR
I Walk Alone (o: Parrish, Shuken, Cutner) PAR
Unconquered (o: Parrish, Cutner, Shuken, Hand) PAR
Golden Earrings (o: Parrish, Cutner, Shuken) PAR
Where There's Life (with Bradshaw, Van Cleave; o: Shuken, Cutner; + stock) PAR

1948
State of the Union (o: Shuken, Cutner, Parrish) MGM
The Big Clock (o: Shuken, Cutner, Parrish) PAR
The Emperor Waltz (o: Parrish, Cutner, Shuken, Bradshaw) PAR

Dream Girl (o: Shuken, Cutner) PAR
So Evil My Love (with William Alwyn; o: Shuken, Cutner) PAR
Beyond Glory (o: Cutner, Shuken, Parrish) PAR
The Night Has a Thousand Eyes (o: Parrish, Cutner, Van Cleave, Shuken) PAR
Miss Tatlock's Millions (o: Shuken, Cutner, Parrish, Van Cleave) PAR
The Paleface (o: Parrish, Shuken, Cutner) PAR

1949
The Accused (o: Van Cleave, Shuken, Plumb, Parrish, Cutner) PAR
A Connecticut Yankee in King Arthur's Court (ac: Lilley; o: Parrish, Shuken, Cutner, Van Cleave) PAR
Streets of Laredo (o: Van Cleave, Cutner, Shuken, Parrish) PAR
The File on Thelma Jordan (o: Van Cleave, Shuken, Cutner, Parrish, Raab) PAR
Samson and Delilah (o: Shuken, Cutner, Parrish, Van Cleave) PAR
Song of Surrender (m&e: Van Cleave; o: Parrish, Cutner, Shuken) PAR
Chicago Deadline (o: Cutner, Shuken, Van Cleave, Parrish) PAR
Sands of Iwo Jima (o: Shuken, Cutner, Gold) REP
Deadly Is the Female (o: Shuken, Cutner) UA
My Foolish Heart (o: Shuken, Cutner) GOLDWYN
Our Very Own (o: Shuken, Cutner) GOLDWYN

1950
Paid in Full (o: Shuken, Cutner, Van Cleave, Parrish) PAR
Riding High PAR
Bright Leaf (o: Shuken, Cutner) WB
The Fireball (o: Shuken, Cutner) TCF
Rio Grande REP

1951
September Affair (o: Parrish, Shuken, Cutner, Van Cleave) PAR
Belle Le Grand REP
Payment on Demand RKO
Bullfighter and the Lady REP
The Lemon Drop Kid (o: Parrish, Cutner, Shuken, Van Cleave) PAR
Appointment with Danger (o: Van Cleave, Cutner, Shuken, Parrish) PAR
This Is Korea (doc.) REP
Honeychile REP
A Place in the Sun (see Waxman)
A Millionaire for Christy (o: Shuken, Cutner) TCF
The Wild Blue Yonder REP
My Favorite Spy (o: Parrish, Shuken, Cutner) PAR

1952
The Quiet Man (o: Shuken, Cutner) REP
Anything Can Happen (o: Shuken, Cutner, Parrish) PAR
Something to Live For (o: Parrish, Shuken, Cutner) PAR
The Greatest Show on Earth (o: Parrish, Shuken, Cutner) PAR
Scaramouche (o: Shuken, Cutner) MGM
The Story of Will Rogers (o: Shuken, Cutner) WB
One Minute to Zero RKO
Thunderbirds (o: Cutner) REP
Blackbeard the Pirate RKO
The Star (o: Cutner) TCF

1953
Fair Wind to Java (o: Shuken, Cutner) REP
The Stars Are Singing (o: Shuken, Cutner) PAR
A Perilous Journey (o: Shuken, Cutner) REP
The Sun Shines Bright REP
Shane (o: Shuken, Cutner, Parrish) PAR
Roman Holiday (mt, o: Shuken; score: Georges Auric) PAR
Flight Nurse (o: Shuken) REP
Little Boy Lost (o: Shuken, Van Cleave, Cutner) PAR
Forever Female (o: Shuken, Van Cleave, Cutner) PAR

1954
Jubilee Trail (o: S. Wilson) REP
Johnny Guitar (o: S. Wilson) REP
Three Coins in the Fountain (o: E. Powell, Shuken, Cutner) TCF
Trouble in the Glen (o: Cutner) REP
Knock on Wood (o: Shuken, Cutner) PAR
About Mrs. Leslie (o: Shuken, Cutner) PAR
Drum Beat (o: Shuken, Cutner) WB
The Country Girl (o: Shuken, Cutner) PAR
Timberjack REP

1955
Strategic Air Command (o: Shuken, Cutner, Parrish) PAR
Son of Sinbad (o: Grau) RKO
A Man Alone REP

The Left Hand of God (o: Shuken, Cutner) TCF
The Tall Men (o: Cutner, Shuken) TCF
The Conqueror (o: Shuken, Cutner) RKO
1956
The Maverick Queen (o: Cutner) REP
The Vagabond King (o: Shuken, Cutner) PAR
The Proud and Profane (o: Shuken, Cutner, Van Cleave) PAR
Around the World in 80 Days (o: Shuken, Cutner) UA
The Brave One (o: Cutner) RKO
1957
The Buster Keaton Story (o: Shuken, Cutner) PAR
Run of the Arrow (o: Cutner) RKO
China Gate (see M. Steiner)
Omar Khayyam (o: Shuken, Cutner) PAR
Trailer
1950
Going My Way (reissue of 1944 film; m&e) PAR

YOUNGMEYER, DELL
1931
Call of the Rockies (a) ROAD SHOW PICTURES

Z

ZADOR, EUGENE
1940
Florian (see Waxman)
Edison, the Man (see Stothart)
The Mortal Storm (see Kaper)
Escape (see Waxman)
Gallant Sons (see Snell)
More About Nostradamus (short; o: Raab, Heglin) MGM
Third Dimensional Murder (short; see Snell)
1941
Rage in Heaven (see Kaper)
[Also worked as an orchestrator.]

ZAHLER, LEE
[He was a composer who also operated a music service, and it is impossible to distinguish original scores from library compilations. No scores have been seen, and this filmography is based solely on screen credits and other secondary sources.]
1929
College Love UNIV
Mister Antonio TS
Woman to Woman TS
Dark Skies BILTMORE
1931
The Silver Lining UA
Chinatown After Dark ACTION
A Private Scandal HEADLINE
Sporting Chance PEERLESS
Air Eagles CONTINENTAL
1932
The Monster Walks ACTION
Murder at Dawn BIG FOUR
The Vanishing Frontier PAR
Tangled Destinies MAYFAIR
The Savage Girl FREULER
Midnight Warning MAYFAIR
1933
Cheating Blondes EQUITABLE
The Flaming Signal IMPERIAL
Laughing at Life MASCOT
The Big Bluff TOWER
Dance Girl Dance INVINCIBLE
Secret Sinners MAYFAIR
The Woman Who Dared IMPERIAL
1934
The Film Parade (compilation doc.) J. STUART BLACKTON
In Love With Life INVINCIBLE
When Lightning Strikes REGAL
Port of Lost Dreams INVINCIBLE
1935
Symphony of Living INVINCIBLE
Public Opinion INVINCIBLE
Mutiny Ahead MAJESTIC
Night Cargo PEERLESS
Social Error WILLIAM BERKE
Kentucky Blue Streak PURITAN
Adventurous Knights ASTOR
The Outlaw Deputy PURITAN
Reckless Roads MAJESTIC
Motive for Revenge MAJESTIC
Western Frontier COL

Gunners and Guns BEAUMONT
The Man from Guntown PURITAN
The Drunkard STAGE AND SCREEN
Heir to Trouble COL
Melody Trail REP
Just My Luck NEW CENTURY
Toll of the Desert COMMODORE
Lawless Riders COL

1936
The Fire Trap EMPIRE
Ghost Town COMMODORE
Heroes of the Range COL
Song of the Trail AMBASSADOR
Hair-Trigger Casey BERKE-PERRIN
The Little Red Schoolhouse CHESTERFIELD
Desert Justice BERKE-PERRIN
The Fugitive Sheriff COL
Gun Grit BERKE-PERRIN
The Unknown Ranger COL
Ranger Courage COL
North of Nome COL
What Becomes of the Children? SENTINEL
Rio Grande Ranger COL
Ellis Island (with G. Johnston) INVINCIBLE
The Lash of the Penitentes STEWART

1937
Borderland PAR
Guns in the Dark REP
Hills of Old Wyoming PAR
Law and Lead COLONY
Reckless Ranger COL
The Rangers Step In COL
Shadows of the Orient MON

1938
Rolling Caravans COL
Spirit of Youth GN
Stagecoach Days COL
Knight of the Plains SPECTRUM
Pioneer Trail COL
Phantom Gold COL
Songs and Saddles COLONY
Rebellious Daughters PROGRESSIVE
Slander House PROGRESSIVE
In Early Arizona COL
Frontiers of '49 COL

1939
Lone Star Pioneers COL
In Old Montana SPECTRUM
Verbena trágica (Spanish language) COL
The Law Comes to Texas COL
Hidden Power COL
Daughter of the Tong METROPOLITAN

1940
Outside the 3-Mile Limit COL
Midnight Limited MON
Passport to Alcatraz COL
Fugitive from a Prison Camp COL
The Last Alarm MON
The Great Plane Robbery COL
Ellery Queen, Master Detective COL

1941
Ellery Queen's Penthouse Mystery COL
The Great Swindle COL
Ellery Queen and the Perfect Crime COL
Ellery Queen and the Murder Ring COL

1942
Duke of the Navy PRC
A Close Call for Ellery Queen COL
Girls' Town PRC
A Night for Crime PRC
House of Errors PRC
The Dawn Express PRC
The Panther's Claw PRC
A Desperate Chance for Ellery Queen COL
Gallant Lady PRC
Bombs Over Burma PRC
A Yank in Libya PRC
Enemy Agents Meet Ellery Queen COL
Miss V from Moscow PRC

1943
Secrets of a Co-Ed PRC
The Rangers Take Over PRC
The Yanks Are Coming PRC
Man of Courage PRC
Lady from Chungking PRC
No Place for a Lady COL
Bad Men of Thunder Gap PRC
The Ghost and the Guest PRC
A Gentle Gangster REP
West of Texas PRC
Border Buckaroos PRC
Fighting Valley PRC
Trail of Terror PRC
Tiger Fangs PRC
The Underdog PRC
Return of the Rangers PRC
Boss of Rawhide PRC

1944
Gunsmoke Mesa PRC
Outlaw Roundup PRC
Guns of the Law PRC
Shake Hands with Murder PRC
The Pinto Bandit PRC
Waterfront PRC
Spook Town PRC
Brand of the Devil PRC
Seven Doors to Death PRC
Delinquent Daughters PRC
Shadow of Suspicion MON

Gangsters of the Frontier PRC
Dead or Alive PRC
The Great Mike PRC
Men on Her Mind PRC
I Accuse My Parents PRC
The Whispering Skull PRC

1945
Rogues' Gallery PRC
Marked for Murder PRC
Enemy of the Law PRC
The Lady Confesses PRC
The White Gorilla LOUIS WEISS
Three in the Saddle PRC
Jeep-Herders PLANET
Frontier Fugitives PRC
Arson Squad (o: Bernie) PRC
Flaming Bullets PRC
Prairie Rustlers PRC
Navajo Kid PRC
Lightning Raiders PRC

1946
Six Gun Man PRC
Junior Prom MON
Detour to Danger PLANET
The People's Choice PLANET
Freddie Steps Out MON
Ghost of Hidden Valley PRC
Ambush Trail PRC
Thunder Town PRC
Gentlemen with Guns PRC
Prairie Badmen PRC
Terrors on Horseback PRC
Overland Riders PRC
Outlaws of the Plains PRC
Queen of the Amazons SG

Serials

1929
King of the Kongo MASCOT

1931
The Galloping Ghost MASCOT
The Vanishing Legion MASCOT
King of the Wild MASCOT
The Phantom of the West MASCOT
The Lightning Warrior MASCOT

1932
The Last of the Mohicans MASCOT
The Shadow of the Eagle MASCOT
The Hurricane Express MASCOT

1933
The Whispering Shadow MASCOT
The Three Musketeers MASCOT
Fighting with Kit Carson MASCOT

1934
Mystery Mountain MASCOT

1935
The Phantom Empire MASCOT
The Miracle Rider MASCOT
The Lost City REGAL

1936
The Black Coin STAGE AND SCREEN
The Clutching Hand STAGE AND SCREEN
Custer's Last Stand STAGE AND SCREEN

1940
The Shadow COL
Terry and the Pirates COL
Deadwood Dick COL
The Green Archer COL

1941
White Eagle COL
The Spider Returns COL
The Iron Claw COL
Holt of the Secret Service COL

1942
Captain Midnight COL
Perils of the Royal Mounted COL
The Secret Code COL
The Valley of Vanishing Men COL

1943
Batman COL
The Phantom COL

1944
The Desert Hawk COL
Black Arrow COL

1945
The Monster and the Ape COL
Jungle Raiders COL
Who's Guilty? COL

1946
Hop Harrigan COL
Chick Carter, Detective COL
Son of the Guardsman COL

1947
Jack Armstrong COL

Shorts

1930
Old Vamps for New DARMOUR
Men Without Skirts DARMOUR
Pure and Simple DARMOUR

1931
Mickey's Crusaders DARMOUR
Big Business DARMOUR
Mickey's Golden Rule DARMOUR

1933
Campus Codes COL
Marriage Humor PAR
Kid'n' Africa EDUCATIONAL

1934
Old Kentucky Hounds DARMOUR

1937

The Herald of the Skies COL
The Fifty Year Barter COL
Little Jack Horner COL
Silver Threads COL
The Boy Who Saved a Nation COL

1940

What's Your I.Q.? MGM

1947

Branding Irons WB

ZAMECNIK, J. S.

1923

The Covered Wagon (see Riesenfeld)

1927

The Rough Riders (see Riesenfeld)
Old Ironsides (see Riesenfeld)
Wings PAR

1928

The Wedding March (with De Francesco) PAR
Abie's Irish Rose (with Kilenyi, Rybner) PAR

1929

Redskin (with De Francesco) PAR
Betrayal (with De Francesco) PAR

1932

Wild Girl (ac: R. Bassett, Brunelli) FOX

1933

Cavalcade (see De Francesco)
The Face in the Sky (see Brunelli)
Dangerously Yours (see R. Bassett)
Zoo in Budapest (with Brunelli, Friedhofer, De Francesco; ac: R. Bassett) FOX
The Warrior's Husband (with De Francesco, Brunelli, R. Bassett, A. Lange, W. Spielter) FOX
Adorable (see A. Lange)
The Devil's in Love (ac: De Francesco) FOX
Shanghai Madness (with R. Bassett, De Francesco; + stock) FOX
The Power and the Glory (with Brunelli, De Francesco) FOX
Berkeley Square (with De Francesco, Brunelli) FOX
Paddy the Next Best Thing (see De Francesco)
The Worst Woman in Paris? (see De Francesco)

1934

Dos Más Uno, Dos (see Buttolph)

1935

It's a Small World (see A. Lange)

[The 1934–1935 *Motion Picture Almanac* reported that he also composed scores for "more than 200 newsreels and Magic Carpet travelogues."]

ZAPPA, FRANK

1962

The World's Greatest Sinner TIMOTHY CAREY

1965

Run Home Slow EMERSON

1969

Naked Angels CROWN

ZEISL, ERIC

1942

Journey for Margaret (see Waxman)
Reunion in France (see Waxman)

1943

Slightly Dangerous (see Kaper)
Plan for Destruction (short; see N. Shilkret)
Above Suspicion (see Kaper)
Bataan (see Kaper)
Hitler's Madman (see N. Shilkret)
The Cross of Lorraine (see Kaper)

1944

The Invisible Man's Revenge (see Salter)

1955

The Looters (see Roemheld)
The Purple Mask (see Roemheld)

[For additional shorts, see Nussbaum.]

ZEKLEY, MICKIE

1968

Shorts (PETER SPOECKER)
Meditation
Pot-Pourri
Yin-Yang

ZIMMERMAN, HARRY

1961

The Steel Claw WB
Samar WB

ZORNIG, CHARLES, JR.

1958

The National Gallery of Art, Washington, D.C. (doc. short) ENCYCLOPAEDIA BRITANNICA

ZURO, JOSIAH

[He usually was credited as musical director and may not always have composed the scores.]

1928

The Perfect Crime FBO
Taxi 13 FBO
Hit of the Show FBO
Gang War FBO
Captain Swagger PATHÉ
The Circus Kid FBO
Annapolis PATHÉ
Show Folks PATHÉ
Marked Money PATHÉ
Sal of Singapore (with Gromon) PATHÉ
The Spieler PATHÉ

1929

The Leatherneck PATHÉ
Square Shoulders PATHÉ
High Voltage PATHÉ
The Trespasser UA
Red Hot Rhythm PATHÉ

1930

Swing High PATHÉ
Night Work PATHÉ
Holiday PATHÉ
Pardon My Gun PATHÉ
What a Widow! UA
Her Man PATHÉ
Big Money PATHÉ
Sin Takes a Holiday (with Gromon) PATHÉ

Supplementary List of Names

Included here are individuals whose names have appeared in screen credits, on scores, on cue sheets, and/or in print but who are not listed among the composers. The list includes composers with a single collaborative credit; arrangers and orchestrators mentioned in the main list whose first names were omitted there to save space and others who worked on source music rather than scores; and those who have been credited with scores that in fact they did not compose. All are assigned to one or more categories (musical director, arranger, etc.); these designations should not be construed as limiting their contributions in other fields of music or during other periods of time but only as describing their functions in American film music insofar as my research has indicated.

Aberbach, Jean J. European composer whose name, as well as his pseudonym, Jean de la Roche, were put on many American cue sheets of the 1930s in order to collect European royalties.
Adlam, Basil. Arranger and orchestrator.
Adrian, Louis. Music director.
Ahlert, Fred. Orchestrator.
Aldeen, Nat. See Loose, 1963.
Alexander, Alex. Pseudonym of Alexander Borisoff, q.v.
Alford, Harry. See Read.
Allen, Robert. See S. Kaplan, 1959.
Altshuler, Bernard. Conductor.
Anderson, Richard H. Orchestrator.
Andrews, Jack. Orchestrator.
Anthens, William. Arranger.
Arnheim, Gus. Music director.
Arnold, Cecil. 1930 *Outside the Law* (see Roemheld).
Bähler, John. Orchestrator.
Bain, Bob. Arranger.
Ballard, Robert H. Arranger.
Baravalle, Victor. Music director and conductor.
Barnett, John. Pseudonym of John Bath.
Barrett, Curt. Orchestrator.
Barroso, José. Arranger.
Barry, Jeff. See Sendrey, 1968.
Baskerville, David. Arranger.
Bay, Victor. Conductor.
Beau, Henry (Heine). Arranger.
Beittel, Will. Orchestrator.
Benavie, Samuel. Music director from at least 1938 to 1959 for the Jam Handy Organization, producer of business and industrial films.
Berg, Peter. See R. Greene.
Berg, S. M. Compiler of scores and cue sheets for silent films.
Berman, Lenny. Arranger.
Bernie, Saul. Orchestrator.
Blackburn, Maurice. Canadian composer.
Blackwell, Charles. Orchestrator.
Blackwell, Otis. See Hefti, 1957.
Blau, Victor. Music supervisor.
Block, Frederick. See Shaindlin, 1942.
Blume, Dave. Arranger.
Boersma, James. See V. Elliott, 1951.
Bolton, Cecil. Orchestrator.
Bonniwell, Sean. See Forest Hamilton, 1970.
Bourdon, Rosario. Music director.
Bowers, Gil. Orchestrator.
Bradley, David. Music supervisor.
Bradley, Oscar. Conductor and music director.
Brand, Oscar. Music director.
Breen, Michael. Music supervisor.
Brent, Earl. Song writer.
Brito, Alfredo. Arranger.
Broady, J. K. Unidentified; a fictitious name?
Bromberg, Erich. Music director.

Brooks, Harvey. Music director.
Broones, Martin. See Lamkoff, 1929.
Brown, Bernard B. Sound recorder.
Brown, Lloyd. Compiler of music for silent films.
Brown, Sam. See Chet More.
Bryant, Jimmy. Orchestrator.
Bucharoff, Simon. Orchestrator.
Bunchuk, Yasha. Arranger and music director.
Butler, Lauretta. Music director.

Calduel, Lorenzo. Arranger.
Camarata, Salvador. Arranger.
Cameron, Ken. Vocal arranger.
Caper, John, Jr. Music supervisor.
Capps, Al. Orchestrator.
Carpenter, Elliot J. Arranger.
Carpenter, Pete. Orchestrator.
Carruth, Richard. Music supervisor.
Casanova. Pseudonym of Les Baxter, q.v.
Cascales, John. Arranger.
Castellanos, Alberto. Music director.
Cathcart, Jack. Vocal arranger.
Cesana, Otto. Arranger.
Chambers, Dudley. Arranger, choral director, and music supervisor.
Chapelle, Pola. See Mekas.
Chasnoff, Hal. Music director and supervisor.
Cheever, Russ. Orchestrator.
Cherniavsky, Joseph. Conductor and music director.
Cherwin, Richard. Music director and supervisor.
Chiaffarelli, Alfred. Arranger.
Chudnow, Byron. Music supervisor.
Chudnow, David. Music supervisor.
Cleave, Van. See Van Cleave.
Cokayne, A. H. (Harry). Arranger and orchestrator.
Compinsky, Alec. Music director and supervisor.
Conniff, Ray. Arranger and orchestrator.
Conte, Eugene. Compiler of scores for silent films; conductor.
Cooke, Charles L. Orchestrator.
Corelli, Alfonso. Music director and partner in Corelli-Jacobs music library.
Cork, J. Frank. Orchestrator.
Cramer, Lawrence F. Arranger.
Crandall, Cecil A. Orchestrator.
Crane, Larry. See L. Fuller.
Crawford, Harriet. Orchestrator.
Crozier, George. Orchestrator.

Dalby, Alfred. Arranger.
Dallin, Jacques. See Belasco.
D'Andrea, John. Arranger.
de Angelis, Pete. Arranger.
de la Roche, Jean. See Aberbach.
Del Barrio, George. Orchestrator.
Del Castillo, Lloyd. See Castillo.
DeMule, Firth. Music editor.
DeVorzon, Barry. See Botkin, Jr.
Dickinson, Sanford H. Music consultant; a fictitious name?
Docker, Robert. Orchestrator.
Doerfel, Herbert. Orchestrator.
Donatelli, Nicola. Music director.
Dryer, Dave. Music director.
Ducloux, W. Conductor.
Dukelsky, Vladimir. Real name of Vernon Duke, q.v.
Dupré, Serge. Unidentified; a fictitious name?
Dutreil, Edward. Music director and supervisor.
Dweir, Irv. Arranger and conductor.
Dwoskin, Steve. See Geesin.

Eaheart, Paul. See Haggh.
Easton, Lynn. Orchestrator.
Eddison, William. Pseudonym of Eddison von Ottenfeld, q.v.
Elinor, Carli D. Music director and conductor; compiler of scores for silent films.
Ellfeldt, William. Arranger.
Ellington, L. W. Pseudonym of Larry Wellington, q.v.
Emanuel, Manuel. Orchestrator.

Farber, Nathaniel C. Orchestrator.
Feldman, Victor. Orchestrator.
Felice, Ernie. Arranger.
Felix, Hugo. Orchestrator.
Feller, Sid. Orchestrator.
Findlay, Hal. Music supervisor.
Finston, Nathaniel W. Music director and conductor.
Fisher, Elliott. See Cookerly.
Fiske, Bert. Music director.
Fleischer, Mark. Orchestrator.
Flesher, Chuck. Arranger.
Florence, Bob. Orchestrator.
Forbstein, Leo F. Music director and conductor. Head of Warner Bros.' music department, 1932–1948. Brother of Louis Forbes, q.v.
Foster, Bill. Arranger.
Francisco, Manuel. Pseudonym of Mischa Terr, q.v.

Franklin, Arthur. Arranger.
Freeman, Arthur. Orchestrator.
Frey, Hugo. Arranger and orchestrator.
Friedman, Irving. Music supervisor.
Frohman, Lou. Music supervisor.
Frye, Buddy. See Rubenstein.
Fuchs, Herman (Hi). Music supervisor.

Gaffney, Ross. Proprietor of the Ross-Gaffney music library.
Gelman, Harold. Music supervisor.
George, Don. Music director.
Germaine, Ortala Le Clerc. Unidentified; probably a European composer whose name was put on many American cue sheets in order to collect European royalties.
Gerson, Murray. Arranger.
Gibeling, Howard. Arranger.
Gluskin, John. Music supervisor.
Gluskin, Lud. Music director.
Goering, Al. Arranger.
Gogliano, Oswaldo. Arranger.
Golden, Ray. Music supervisor.
Goodman, Al. Conductor.
Gool, Danny. Arranger.
Gordon, Bob. Orchestrator.
Gorney, Jay. Music supervisor.
Graeff, Tom. Music supervisor.
Grant, Tommy and Frances. Arrangers.
Grass, Clancy B., III. Music supervisor.
Grayson, Hal. Music supervisor.
Greaves, William. See H. Glover, 1949.
Grey, Harry. Music supervisor.
Grier, Jimmie. Arranger.
Griselle, Tom. Arranger.
Grove, Dick. Orchestrator.
Guarnieri, Johnny. Arranger.
Guentzel, George (Gus). Arranger.
Gutman, Carl. 1923 *The Ten Commandments* (see Riesenfeld).

Hairston, Jester. Choral arranger.
Hall, George. Music director.
Hallenbeck, Ralph. Orchestrator.
Haller, Hans. See Saxon.
Halley, Glenn. Arranger.
Halmy, Lou. Arranger.
Hamilton, Harley. Compiler of music for *A Romance of Happy Valley* (D. W. Griffith, 1918).
Hammack, Bobby. Arranger and orchestrator.
Handman, Lou. Arranger.
Haney, Ray. From 1956 to 1967 he is credited with the music for over 100 documentary shorts, most of them produced by Norwood Studios for the AFL-CIO.
Hanley, James F. Songwriter.
Harbert, James. Orchestrator.
Haring, Robert C. Orchestrator.
Harrington, Ray. Arranger and orchestrator.
Hart, Lloyd. Arranger.
Heathcock, Bill. Arranger.
Heindorf, Michael. Orchestrator.
Helfer, Bobby. Conductor.
Heller, Adolph. Conductor.
Heller, Herman. Music director and conductor.
Henshel, James G. Music director.
Herbert, Bert. Compiler of music for silent films.
Hess, Cliff. Arranger and music supervisor.
Higgins, James. Arranger.
Hill, Jay. Orchestrator.
Hill, Tommy. Music director.
Hoefle, Carl. Music director.
Holmes, Bill. Pseudonym of Wilford Holcombe, q.v.
Holst, Ernest. Music director.
Hooper, Les. See Reynolds.
Hopper, Hal. Music supervisor.
Howell, Ken. Arranger and orchestrator.
Hubbell, Frank. Arranger.
Hughes, Ernest. Orchestrator.
Humphrey, Stetson. Music director.
Huxley, Carroll. Arranger.

Ilger, Julie. See J. Andrews.

Jackson, Harry. Music director.
Jacobs, Fred. Partner in Corelli-Jacobs music library.
Jacobson, Hy. Arranger and conductor.
Jacoby, Elliot. Orchestrator.
James, Harry. Arranger.
Johnson, Ray. Arranger.
Johnston, Arthur. Arranger and orchestrator.
Jones, Bill. Arranger and orchestrator.
Jonson, Tom. Unidentified; a fictitious name?

Kane, Edward. A fictitious name.
Kantor, Igo. Music supervisor and music editor.
Karaski, Nico. See Carras.
Karnes, Joe. Arranger.
Kay, Hershy. Orchestrator.
Kelsey, Carlton. Music director.
Kendall, Ben. Arranger.
King, Dudley. Arranger.
King, Howard. Arranger.
Klatzkin, David. Music director.

Knowlton, Arthur. Orchestrator.
Kostelanetz, André. Music director and conductor.
Krandel, Sol. Pseudonym of Sol Kaplan, q.v.
Kuder, Morton. Music director.
Kugler, Harvey. Music director.
Kurland, Gilbert. Music supervisor and sound recorder.
Kur-Zhene, Massard. 1930 *The Silent Enemy* (see Midgely).

Lane, Ken. Arranger.
Lang, Philip J. Orchestrator.
La Rondelle, Louis. Arranger.
Lawrence, Maurice. Music supervisor.
Leahy, Joe. Music director.
Leftwich, Vernon. Orchestrator.
Legley, Victor. See Gilson.
Lenard, Melvyn. Music supervisor.
Levant, Mark. Music director.
Levin, Erma E. Music editor.
Levinsky, Kermit. Orchestrator.
Lindoff, Harold. Orchestrator.
Lipman, Joseph. Orchestrator.
Livingston, Joseph A. Arranger.
Lofthouse, Pete. Arranger.
Lowry, Mark. Pseudonym of Ronald Stein, q.v.
Luboff, Norman. Vocal arranger.
Lyman, Abe. Music director.

Macomber, Kenneth. Arranger.
Madison, Marion. Orchestrator.
Mahr, Curley. Vocal arranger.
Mancini, Arthur. Arranger.
Mann, Dave. Orchestrator.
Mann, Edward. Music director.
Manne, Max. Music supervisor.
Marino, Joe. Arranger.
Martin, Lowell. Arranger.
Martinez, Ray. Arranger.
Marum, Ludwig. See Smyth.
Matlock, Matty. Arranger.
Matthews, Dave. Arranger.
Matthews, Robert. Orchestrator.
Matthias, Jack. Arranger.
May, Hans. Composer for German and British films.
Mazzu, Joe. Arranger.
McCauley, William. Orchestrator.
Menkes, Jeffrey. See Blagman.
Mertz, Paul. Arranger; music director; music supervisor.
Meyer, Abe. Proprietor of the Meyer Synchronizing Service, Ltd., Hollywood's largest supplier in the 1930s of canned music (and, occasionally, original scores). He later worked for the talent agency, MCA Artists, Ltd., where he represented film composers.
Miessner, George E. Orchestrator.
Miller, Jack. Music director.
Molina, Carlos. Music director.
Mooney, Hal. Arranger and orchestrator.
Moore, Morrill. Music director.
Morand, Leonard. Pseudonym of Ronald Stein, q.v.
More, Jim. See Chet More.
Morgan, Stephen M. Arranger.
Morros, Boris. Music director.
Morton, Lawrence. Orchestrator.
Moss, Rod. Music director.
Mundy, James. Arranger.
Mundy, Thomas. Arranger.
Murray, Don. Music director.

Neff, Fred. Orchestrator.
Newman, Emil. Music director and conductor.
Nichols, Red. Arranger.
Nichols, Ted. See Paich, 1966.
Noble, Ray. Arranger.
Norton, Ed. Music editor and head of Ed Norton Music Service.
Norvo, Red. Arranger.
Nyiregyhazy, Erwin. 1929 *Coquette* (see Riesenfeld).

Ogerman, Claus. Arranger.
Oliver, Eddie. Arranger.
Oliver, Sy. Arranger.
Oulton, Dick. Arranger.

Pacheco, José. Arranger.
Pagel, Hayes. Music editor.
Pallos, Charles. Arranger.
Pardalis, Gus. See Kalajian.
Parker, Andy. Arranger.
Paul, Edward. Music director and arranger.
Payne, Benny. Arranger.
Pearson, Johnny. Orchestrator.
Pendleton, Edmund. Orchestrator.
Penso, Raffaelo. European composer whose name was put on many American cue sheets of the 1930s in order to collect European royalties.
Peralta, Lou. Music director.
Perry, Donna. See Keefer, 1953.
Phillips, Jerry. Vocal arranger.
Pickering, John F. Arranger.
Pinter, Andor. Arranger and orchestrator.

Polk, Rudolph. Music director and conductor.
Potter, James G. Arranger.
Powell, Loren. Music director.
Prince, Charles A. Music director.

Quadling, Lew. His entry in the *ASCAP Biographical Dictionary* (1948) claims scores for 17 Army Signal Corps films but gives no titles or dates.

Rabinowitsh, Max. Arranger.
Radin, Oscar. Arranger, music director, and conductor.
Raeburn, Boyd. Music supervisor.
Raff, Robert. Music supervisor.
Ralston, Everett. 1941 *You're the One* (see Boutelje).
Ray, Matthew. See Wachtel.
Raymond, Lew. Orchestrator.
Reed, Gus. Music director.
Rehsen, F. Compiler of music for silent films.
Remington, Al. See Nafshun.
Restaino, Tony. See Abe Baker.
Rittman, Trude. Vocal arranger.
Roberts, Dave. See B. Allen, 1965.
Roberts, Gerald. Music director.
Roberts, Jerry. Music supervisor.
Robillard, Paul. Orchestrator.
Robin, Sid. See Karmen, 1964.
Robinson, Gordon. Arranger.
Robinson, Wayne. Orchestrator.
Rogers, Stanley C. Pseudonym of Raoul Kraushaar, q.v.
Rolontz, Robert. Music director.
Rommell, Rox. Pseudonym of Heinz Roemheld, q.v.
Rose, Gordon. Arranger.
Rosen, Larry. See S. Meyers.
Ross, Angelo. Music editor.
Ross, Byron. See B. Chudnow.
Ross, Edmund. Orchestrator.
Rothapfel (later Rothafel), S. L. Compiler of music for silent films.
Rowles, Jimmy. Arranger.
Rubens, Maurie. Music director.
Rudisill, Ivan. Compiler of music for silent films.
Ruick, Walter. Arranger.

Sanns, Joe. Arranger.
Schaeffer, Myron. See Applebaum, 1961.
Schoepp, Arthur. Orchestrator.
Schroeck, Arthur. Orchestrator.
Schürmann, Gerard. Orchestrator.
Score, Phil. Music supervisor.
Scott, Caro. See Malik.
Scott, Francis. Arranger.
Scott, Morton. Music director.
Seely, John. Music supervisor.
Sells, Paul L. Arranger.
Serino, Del. See W. Sanford.
Setaro, Andrea. Music supervisor and conductor.
Sete, Bola. See Tjader.
Sharpe, Eddie. Orchestrator.
Sharvell, Sidney W. Music director.
Shephard, Alan. Music director.
Shepherd, Robert A. Arranger.
Sherman, Garry. Arranger.
Sherman, Joseph. Arranger.
Short, Al. Music director.
Siegel, Al. Arranger.
Silvern, Henry. Music supervisor.
Simpson, Don. Arranger.
Simson, George. Music director.
Sinatra, Ray. Music director.
Siravo, George. Arranger.
Slagle, Chuck. Arranger.
Sorenson, Paul. Arranger.
Spector, Phil. Music director.
Spialek, Hans. Arranger and composer.
Stafford, Bill. Orchestrator.
Stanley, Ralph. Pseudonym of Raoul Kraushaar, q.v.
Stark, Frederick. Orchestrator.
Stern, Jack. Orchestrator.
Stevens, Carl. See Bobby Mann.
Stevens, Len. Orchestrator.
Stewart, Leon A. Arranger.
Stoloff, Morris W. Musical director and conductor. Head of Columbia Pictures' music department, 1936–1960.
Stordahl, Axel. Arranger.
Storm, Billy. See McGinnis, 1965.
Strange, William E. Orchestrator.
Strech, Dave. Orchestrator.
Subotsky, Milton. Music director.

Talbot, Irvin. Music director and conductor.
Tamkus, Daniel. See Sassover.
Tarwater, Robert. See Hames.
Taylor, Bob. Orchestrator.
Taylor, Les. Orchestrator.
Terr, Mischa. Music supervisor. Pseudonyms: Manuel Francisco, Richard Teri, Michael Terr, Michael Terresco.
Terresco, Michael. Pseudonym of Mischa Terr.
Terry, David. Arranger.
Tipton, George. Arranger.
Tresselt, Frank. Arranger.

Tucci, Terig. Music director.
Tucker, Robert. Vocal arranger.
Turchen, Louis. Music supervisor.

Valentino, Thomas J. Music supervisor and proprietor of a music library.
Velazco, Emil Robert. Proprietor of a music library.
Virgil, Frank J. Vocal arranger.
Vodery, Will. Orchestrator.
von Hallberg, Gene. Orchestrator.
von Hallberg, Henry. Orchestrator.

Walden, Charles. Music supervisor.
Warner, Eddie. Music director.
Warren, Douglas, See B. Allen, 1966
Watson, Ernest C. Arranger.
Weinstein, Milton. Orchestrator.
West, Alvy. Music director.
Wetstein, Paul. Arranger.
Wetstein, Paul, Jr. Orchestrator.
Whittle, Raynard. Music director.
Wilder, Andy. Arranger.
Winkler, Max. Compiler of scores and cue sheets for silent films.
Winslow, Alfred. Arranger.
Winterhalter, Hugo. Arranger.
Wolf, Eli. See Reynolds.
Wonder, Leo. Music director.
Wood, Howard T. Compiler of scores for silent films.
Wood, J. H. British composer whose name appears on many American cue sheets of the 1930s in order to collect European royalties.
Wood, Leona. See Harlan.
Wright, Marvin. Arranger.

Zahler, Gordon. Music supervisor and proprietor of General Music Corp., a music library.
Zimanich, Joseph. Music supervisor.
Zinner, Peter. Music supervisor.
Zivelli, Joseph Ernest. Compiler of scores for silent films.
Zweifel, Harold. Orchestrator.

Index of Film Titles

This index is arranged alphabetically by title, but omits articles (a, an, the) that may precede a title. Titles in foreign languages, however, *begin* with articles, if any; therefore *El Cid* appears under E and *Les Girls* under L.

Each title is followed by its date and the surname of the sole or principal composer. This index should not be used alone to learn the name of the composer, but only as a referral to that name, under which will appear other information such as the names of collaborators or orchestrators, the type and length of the film, and the name of the producer or distributor.

If a film's title in fact does not appear, there are several possible explanations for its absence: (1) The film had no score. (2) The score consisted of musical arrangements rather than original music. (3) The score was compiled entirely from stock (pre-existent) music. (4) The score was composed outside the United States by a foreign composer. (5) The score's composer is unknown to me.

1+1 (Exploring the Kinsey Reports) (1961) Bath
1-2-3-Go! (1941) Amfitheatrof
2 Images for the Computer Piece (1969) Ussachevsky
3:10 to Yuma (1957) Duning
3-D Jamboree (1956) Baker, Buddy
3 for Bedroom C (1952) Roemheld
3 Godfathers (1948) Hageman
3 in the Attic (1968) Stuart
3 Is a Family (1944) Heymann
3-Ring Wing-Ding (1968) Lava
3 Sisters (1930) Lipschultz
3 Worlds of Gulliver (1960) Herrmann
4 Clowns (1970) Albam
4D Man (1959) Carmichael
4 for Texas (1964) Riddle
4H Club (1958) Oliveros
5 Against the House (1955) Duning
5 Card Stud (1968) Jarre
5 Fingers (1952) Herrmann
5 Steps to Danger (1957) Sawtell
5th Avenue Girl (1939) Bennett, R. R.
6 Day Bike Rider (1934) Jerome
7 Faces of Dr. Lao (1963) Harline
7th Cavalry (1956) Bakaleinikoff, M.
7th Heaven (1927) Bassett, R. H.
7th Heaven (1928) Rapée
7th Voyage of Sinbad (1958) Herrmann
8 × 8 (1957) Townsend
8 Ball Bunny (1949) Stalling
8 on the Lam (1967) Romanis
12 Angry Men (1957) Hopkins, K.
12 to the Moon (1960) Andersen
13 Fighting Men (1960) Gertz
13 Frightened Girls (1963) Alexander, V.
13 Ghosts (1960) Dexter
13 Lead Soldiers (1948) Rosen, M.
13 Platoon (1943) Applebaum
13 Rue Madeleine (1947) Buttolph, David
13th Letter (1951) North
13 West Street (1962) Duning
14 Carrot Rabbit (1951) Stalling
16 Fathoms Deep (1948) Moraweck
19th Hole Club (1936) Scheib
20 Mule Team (1940) Snell
$21 a Day (Once a Month) (1941) Calker
23 Paces to Baker Street (1956) Harline
23½ Hours Leave (1937) Skiles
24-Hour Alert (1956) Lava
24 Hours (1931) Leipold
27th Day (1957) Bakaleinikoff, M.
-30- (1959) Heindorf
30-Foot Bride of Candy Rock (1959) Kraushaar
30 Years of Fun (1962) Green, B.
36 Hours (1964) Tiomkin
40 Guns to Apache Pass (1967) LaSalle
40 Pounds of Trouble (1962) Lindsey
45 Fathers (1937) Kaylin
49th State (1947) Shilkret, N.
50 Years Before Your Eyes (1950) Lava
52nd Street (1937) Newman
55 Days at Peking (1963) Tiomkin
80 Steps to Jonah (1969) Shearing
90 Day Wondering (1956) Franklyn
99 River Street (1953) Lange
100 Rifles (1968) Goldsmith
101 Acts of Love (1970) Scott, Randy
145 West 21 (1936) Bowles
365 Nights in Hollywood (1934) Buttolph, David
500 Hats of Bartholomew Cubbins (1943) von Ottenfeld
711 Ocean Drive (1950) Kaplan, S.
957th Day (1945) Palange
$1,000 a Touchdown (1939) Leipold
1,000 Plane Raid (1969) Haskell
1,000 Shapes of a Female (1963) Corwin
1001 Arabian Nights (1959) Duning
1966 Indianapolis 500 (1966) Mendoza-Nava
2000 B.C. (1931) Scheib
2000 Years Later (1969) Phillips, S.
2001: A Space Odyssey (1968) North
5,000 Fingers of Dr. T. (1952) Hollander
6,000 Enemies (1939) Ward, E.
20,000 Eyes (1961) Glasser
20,000 Leagues Under the Sea (1954) Smith, P.
20,000 Men a Year (1939) Kaylin
20,000 Years in Sing Sing (1932) Kaun
50,000 B. C. (1963) Roman
70,000 Witnesses (1932) Lewis, Harold
20 Million Miles to Earth (1957) Bakaleinikoff, M.
400 Million (1939) Eisler

A Haunting We Will Go (1966) Lava
A-Haunting We Will Go (1939) Marsales
A-Haunting We Will Go (1942) Buttolph, David
A-Haunting We Will Go (1949) Sharples, Winston
A Hunting We Won't Go (1943) Kilfeather
A Is for Atom (1953) Poddany
A-Lad-in His Lamp (1948) Stalling
A-tom-inable Snowman (1966) Elliott, Dean
A.K.A. Cassius Clay (1970) Macero
A.T.C.A. (1942) Kaplan, S.
Aaron Slick from Punkin Crick (1952) Van Cleave
Abbott and Costello Go to Mars (1953) Stein, H.
Abbott and Costello in Hollywood (1945) Bassman
Abbott and Costello Meet Captain Kidd (1952) Kraushaar
Abbott and Costello Meet Frankenstein (1949) Skinner, F.
Abbott and Costello Meet the Keystone Kops (1954) Mancini
Abbott and Costello Meet the Mummy (1955) Maury
ABC of Hand Tools (1946) Smith, P.
Abductors (1957) Glass, Paul
Abdul the Bul-Bul Ameer (1941) Bradley
Abe Lincoln in Illinois (1940) Webb
Abie's Irish Rose (1928) Zamecnik

Abie's Irish Rose (1946) Trotter
Abilene Town (1946) Terr
Abilene Trail (1951) Kay, Edward
Able Baker (1947) Kopp, R.
Abner the Baseball (1961) Sharples, Winston
Abnormal Female (1969) Lindsay
Aboard the Flattop Midway (1949) De Francesco
Abominable Snow Rabbit (1961) Franklyn
Abou Ben Boogie (1944) Calker
About Face (1942) Ward, E.
About Face (1952) Buttolph, David
About Face (Trailer, 1952) Jackson, H.
About Mrs. Leslie (1954) Young, V.
Above and Beyond (1952) Friedhofer
Above Suspicion (1943) Kaper
Abraham Lincoln (1924) Breil
Abraham Lincoln (1930) Riesenfeld
Abraham Lincoln and the Emancipation Proclamation (1970) Bernstein, C.
Abraham, Man of Faith (1956) Shepard
Abraham's Faith (1948) Rosen, M.
Abroad with Two Yanks (1944) Moraweck
Absent-Minded Professor (1960) Bruns
Absolute Quiet (1936) Waxman
Abstract in Concrete (1954) Fields, F.
Abusement Park (1947) Sharples, Winston
Accent on Courage (1943) De Francesco
Accent on Love (1941) Mockridge
Accent on Youth (1935) Hollander
Accidents Will Happen (1937) Jackson, H.
Accidents Will Happen (1964) Sharples, Winston
Accomplice (1946) Laszlo
According to Mrs. Hoyle (1951) Kay, Edward
Accordion Joe (1930) Steiner, G.
Accused (1949) Young, V.
Accused of Murder (1956) Butts
Ace Drummond (1936) Vaughan
Ace in the Hole (1942) Calker
Ace in the Hole (1951) Friedhofer
Ace of Clubs (1951) Lava
Aces Up (1931) De Nat
Acid Eaters (1968) Allen, B.
Acro-Batty (1942) Snell
Acrobatty Bunny (1946) Stalling
Across America (1932) Carbonara
Across the Great Divide (1946) De Francesco
Across the Pacific (1942) Deutsch
Across the Rio Grande (1949) Kay, Edward
Across the River (1965) Gross
Across the Wide Missouri (1951) Raksin
Act of Murder (1948) Amfitheatrof
Act of Violence (1948) Kaper
Act One (1964) Henderson, S.
Action in Arabia (1944) Webb
Action in Sports (1947) Jackson, H.
Action in the North Atlantic (1943) Deutsch
Action Stations (1943) Applebaum
Active Management of Disability in the Aged (19??) Vito
Activist (1969) Grant
Actors and Sin (1952) Antheil
Actress (1953) Kaper
Ada (1961) Kaper
Adagio (1970) Horowitz
Adam at 6 A.M (1970) Grusin
Adam Had Four Sons (1941) Harling
Adam Lost His Apple (1966) Jones, V.
Adam to Atom (1952) van Grove
Adam's Rib (1949) Rozsa
Address Unknown (1944) Toch
Admiral Was a Lady (1950) Kay, Edward
Admiral's Strut (1942) Smith, P.
Adorable (1933) Lange
Adoration (1928) Hajos
Adulterous Affair (1966) Bath
Advance and Be Mechanized (1967) Elliott, Dean
Advance to the Rear (1964) Sparks
Adventure (1946) Stothart
Adventure in Baltimore (1949) Hollander
Adventure in Casein Painting (1951) Meltzer
Adventure in Diamonds (1940) Shuken
Adventure in Friendship (1949) Chessid
Adventure in Iraq (1943) Roemheld
Adventure in Manhattan (1936) Still
Adventure in Telezonia (1949) Steiner, G.
Adventure in Washington (1941) Harling
Adventure Island (1947) Calker
Adventures in Sharps and Flats (1964) Ward, R.
Adventures in Silverado (1948) Duning
Adventures in South America (1945) Jackson, H.
Adventures of a Rookie (1943) Webb
Adventures of Alexander Selkirk (1955) Jackson, H.
Adventures of an Asterisk (1957) Carter
Adventures of Bullwhip Griffin (1966) Bruns
Adventures of Captain Marvel (1941) Glickman, M.
Adventures of Casanova (1948) Friedhofer
Adventures of Chico (1937) Kilenyi
Adventures of Dolly and Daniel Whale (1962) Sharples, Winston
Adventures of Don Coyote (1947) Kraushaar
Adventures of Don Juan (1949) Steiner, M.
Adventures of Gallant Bess (1948) Gertz
Adventures of Hajji Baba (1954) Tiomkin
Adventures of Huckleberry Finn (1939) Waxman
Adventures of Huckleberry Finn (1960) Moross
Adventures of Ichabod and Mr. Toad (1949) Wallace
Adventures of Jane Arden (1939) Jackson, H.
Adventures of Jimmy (1950) Kees
Adventures of Kitty O'Day (1944) Kay, Edward
Adventures of Marco Polo (1938) Friedhofer
Adventures of Mark Twain (1944) Steiner, M.
Adventures of Martin Eden (1942) Leipold
Adventures of Red Ryder (1940) Lava
Adventures of Robin Hood (1938) Korngold
Adventures of Robinson Crusoe (1954) Collins

Adventures of Rusty (1945) Skiles
Adventures of Sherlock Holmes (1939) Mockridge
Adventures of Smilin' Jack (1942) Rosen, M.
Adventures of the Road-Runner (1962) Franklyn
Adventures of Tom Sawyer (1938) Steiner, M.
Adventures of Tom Thumb, Jr. (1940) Marsales
Adventuring in the Arts (1956) Forrell
Adventurous Blonde (1937) Jackson, H.
Adventurous Knights (1935) Zahler
Advice to the Lovelorn (1933) Newman
Advise and Consent (1962) Fielding
Aerial Gunner (1943) Amfitheatrof
Aero-Nutics (1953) Sharples, Winston
Aesop's Fable—Foiling the Fox (1950) Scheib
Aesop's Fable—Golden Egg Goosie (1951) Scheib
Aesop's Fable—Happy Valley (1952) Scheib
Aesop's Fable—Sparky, the Firefly (1953) Scheib
Aesop's Fable—The First Flying Fish (1955) Scheib
Aesop's Fable—The Tiger King (1960) Scheib
Affair in Havana (1957) Gold
Affair in Reno (1957) Butts
Affair in Trinidad (1952) Duning
Affair of Susan (1935) Waxman
Affair to Remember (1957) Friedhofer
Affair with a Stranger (1953) Webb
Affairs of a Gentleman (1934) Ward, E.
Affairs of Annabel (1938) Webb
Affairs of Aphrodite (1970) Bath
Affairs of Cappy Ricks (1937) Colombo
Affairs of Cellini (1934) Newman
Affairs of Geraldine (1946) Scott, N.
Affairs of Jimmy Valentine (1942) Feuer
Affairs of Martha (1942) Kaper
Affairs of Susan (1945) Hollander
Affectionately Yours (1941) Roemheld
Africa Adventure (1954) Sawtell
Africa Screams (1949) Schumann
Africa Squawks (1939) Scheib
Africa Squeaks (1932) Bradley
Africa Squeaks (1940) Stalling
African Diary (1945) Wallace
African Holiday (1937) Kilenyi
African Jungle Hunt (1955) Scheib
African Lion (1955) Smith, P.
African Treasure (1952) Kraushaar
After Midnight with Boston Blackie (1943) Leipold
After Office Hours (Trailer, 1935) Ward, E.
After the Ball (1956) Wheeler
After the Fox (1966) Bacharach
After the Thin Man (1936) Ward, E.
After Tomorrow (1932) Friedhofer
Again—Pioneers! (1950) Gertz
Against All Flags (1952) Salter
Age for Love (1931) Newman
Age of Innocence (1934) Steiner, M.
Agent for H.A.R.M. (1966) Kauer
Agent's Secret (1966) Gross
Ages of Time (1959) Abramson
Aggie Appleby, Maker of Men (1933) Webb
Agony and the Ecstasy (1965) North
Agony of Love (1966) Grennell
Ah, Sweet Mouse-Story of Life (1965) Poddany
Ah, Wilderness! (1935) Ward, E.
Ahoy, Davy Jones (1949) De Francesco
Ai-Ye (1950) Barron
Ain't Misbehavin (1955) Mancini
Ain't Nature Grand (1930) Marsales
Ain't Rio Grand? (1952) Lava
Ain't She Tweet? (1951) Stalling
Ain't That Ducky (1945) Stalling
Ain't We Got Fun (1937) Stalling
Air Cadets (1944) Applebaum
Air Eagles (1931) Zahler
Air Express (1937) Dietrich
Air Force (1943) Waxman
Air Force on Canvas (1963) Segßll
Air Freight Specialist (1968) Kopp, F.
Air Hawks (1935) Jackson, H.
Air Hostess (1937) De Nat
Air Patrol (1962) Glasser
Air Pattern Pacific (1945) Kubik
Air Raid Warden (1943) Calker
Air Raid Wardens (1943) Shilkret, N.
Air Strike (1955) Brummer
Air Tight (1931) Shield
Airborne (1962) Ferguson
Airline Glamour Girls (1949) Shilkret, N.
Airport (1970) Newman
Airskills (1957) McPhee
Akran (1969) Coulter
Al Capone (1959) Raksin
Aladdin and His Lamp (1952) Skiles
Aladdin and His Wonderful Lamp (1939) Timberg
Aladdin and the Wonderful Lamp (1934) Stalling
Aladdin's Lamp (1931) Scheib
Aladdin's Lamp (1935) Scheib
Aladdin's Lamp (1943) Scheib
Aladdin's Lamp (1949) Scheib
Aladdin's Lantern (1938) Snell
Alakazam the Great (1961) Baxter
Alamo (1960) Tiomkin
Alaska (1944) Kay, Edward
Alaska (1947) De Francesco
Alaska Highway (1943) Rich
Alaska Lifeboat (1956) Lava
Alaska Passage (1958) Borisoff
Alaska Patrol (1948) Merrick
Alaska Seas (1954) Shuken
Alaska Sweepstakes (1936) Dietrich
Alaskan Eskimo (1952) Wallace
Alaskan Grandeur (1945) De Francesco
Alaskan Nights (1930) De Nat
Alaskan Sled Dog (1956) Wallace
Albatross (1968) Daum
Albert in Blunderland (1950) Smith, P.
Albert Schweitzer (1957) Wilder
Alberto Giacometti (1966) Gamson

Album of Animals (1947) De Francesco
Albuquerque (1948) Calker
Alcatraz Island (1937) Roemheld
Alchemist's Hourglass (1936) Grimson
Aldrich Family Gets in the Scrap (1943) Amfitheatrof
Alex in Wonderland (1940) Jackson, H.
Alex in Wonderland (1970) O'Horgan
Alexander Calder: Sculpture and Constructions (1943) Kleiner
Alexander Hamilton (1931) Mendoza
Alexis Tremblay: Habitant (1943) Applebaum
Ali Baba (1936) Stalling
Ali Baba and the Forty Thieves (1943) Ward, E.
Ali Baba Bound (1940) Stalling
Ali Baba Bunny (1956) Stalling
Ali Baba Goes to Town (1937) Bennett, R. R.
Alias a Gentleman (1948) Snell
Alias French Gertie (1930) Webb
Alias Jesse James (1959) Lilley
Alias Jimmy Valentine (1929) Axt
Alias Mary Dow (1935) Wallace
Alias Mr. Twilight (1946) Sawtell
Alias Nick Beal (1949) Waxman
Alias St. Nick (1935) Bradley
Alias the Champ (1949) Wilson, S.
Alias the Doctor (1932) Kaun
Alibi (1929) Riesenfeld
Alibi Ike (1935) Jerome
Alice Adams (1935) Webb
Alice in Jungleland (1945) Dunn
Alice in Wonderland (1931) David, W.
Alice in Wonderland (1933) Tiomkin
Alice in Wonderland (1951) Kaplan, S.
Alice in Wonderland (1951) Wallace
Alimony (1949) Laszlo
All Abir-r-r-d (1949) Stalling
All Aboard! (1946) Jackson, H.
All About Dogs (1942) Scheib
All About Eve (1950) Newman
All American (1953) Lava
All American Chump (1936) Axt
All-American Co-Ed (1941) Ward, E.
All Ashore (1953) Duning
All Chimps Ashore (1955) Craig, E.
All Fall Down (1962) North
All Fowled Up (1954) Stalling
All Hands on Deck (1961) Mockridge
All I Desire (1953) Stein, H.
All in a Night's Work (1960) Previn, A.
All in a Nutshell (1948) Wallace
All Joking Astride (1952) Agostini
All Men Are Enemies (1934) De Francesco
All Mine to Give (1957) Steiner, M.
All My Babies (1953) Applebaum
All My Sons (1948) Stevens, L.
All of Me (1934) Hajos
All of Me (1963) Roberts, K.
All Our Children (1956) Glanville-Hicks
All Out for "V" (1942) Scheib
All Over Town (1937) Colombo
All Quiet on the Western Front (1930) Roemheld
All-Star Bond Rally (1945) Mockridge
All Star Musical Revue (1945) Lava
All That Heaven Allows (1955) Skinner, F.
All That I Have (1951) Colombo
All That Money Can Buy (1941) Herrmann
All the Brothers Were Valiant (1953) Rozsa
All the Fine Young Cannibals (1960) Alexander, J.
All the King's Horses (1935) Roemheld
All the King's Men (1949) Gruenberg
All the Lovin' Kinfolk (1970) Toscana
All the Loving Couples (1969) Baxter
All the Way Home (1963) Green, B.
All the Young Men (1960) Duning
All This, and Heaven Too (1940) Steiner, M.
All This and Rabbit Stew (1941) Stalling
All This and Rabbit Stew (1950) Scheib
All Through the Night (1942) Deutsch
All Together (1942) Wallace
All Together Now (1970) Meyers
All Women Have Secrets (1939) Leipold
All's Fair at the Fair (1938) Timberg
All's Fair at the Fair (1947) Sharples, Winston
All's Well (1941) Timberg
All's Well That Ends Well (1940) Scheib
Allegheny Uprising (1939) Collins
Allegretto (1936) Rainger
Allen's Animal Kingdom (1951) Mamorsky
Allergic to Love (1944) Skinner, F.
Alley Cat (1941) Bradley
Alley to Bali (1954) Wheeler
Alligator People (1959) Gertz
Alluring Alaska (1941) Shilkret, J.
Almost a Gentleman (1939) Tours
Almost Married (1932) Friedhofer
Aloha Hooey (1942) Stalling
Aloha Nui! (1954) Jackson, H.
Aloha Oe (1915) Nowell
Aloma of the South Seas (1941) Young, V.
Alone (1963) Geesin
Along Came a Duck (1934) Sharples, Winston
Along Came Daffy (1946) Stalling
Along Came Jones (1945) Lange
Along Came Love (1936) Stone
Along Flirtation Walk (1935) Spencer, N.
Along the Cactus Trail (1944) Nussbaum
Along the Great Divide (1951) Buttolph, David
Along the Navajo Trail (1946) Glickman, M.
Along the Oregon Trail (1947) Glickman, M.
Along the Rainbow Trail (1946) De Francesco
Along the Rio Grande (1941) Sawtell
Along the Sundown Trail (1943) Lange, J.
Along the Texas Range (1942) De Francesco
Alpine Antics (1936) Spencer, N.
Alpine Champions (1950) Lava
Alpine Climbers (1936) Malotte
Alpine for You (1951) Sharples, Winston

Alpine Glory (1957) Jackson, H.
Alpine Yodeler (1936) Scheib
Alter Egotist (1967) Sharples, Winston
Alternative (1968) Thorne, F.
Alvarez Kelly (1966) Green, J.
Alvin's Solo Flight (1961) Sharples, Winston
Always a Bride (1940) Dunn
Always Audacious (1920) Riesenfeld
Always Goodbye (1931) Friedhofer
Always Goodbye (1938) Mockridge
Always in My Heart (1942) Roemheld
Always Kickin! (1939) Timberg
Always Leave Them Laughing (1949) Buttolph, David
Always Together (1948) Heymann
Ama Girls (1958) Wallace
Amateur Broadcast (1935) Dietrich
Amateur Daddy (1932) Friedhofer
Amateur Night (1935) Scheib
Amazing Colossal Man (1957) Glasser
Amazing Dr. Clitterhouse (1938) Steiner, M.
Amazing Mr. Nordill (1947) Kopp, R.
Amazing Mr. Williams (1939) Mills, F.
Amazing Mrs. Holliday (1943) Skinner, F.
Amazing Transparent Man (1960) Calker
Amazon Family (1962) Forrell
Amazon Quest (1949) Laszlo
Amazon Trader (1956) Jackson, H.
Ambassador Bill (1931) Kay, Arthur
Ambitious People (1931) Timberg
Amblin' (1968) Lloyd, M.
Ambulance Doctor (1951) Shilkret, N.
Ambush (1939) Carbonara
Ambush (1949) Kopp, R.
Ambush at Cimarron Pass (1958) Sawtell
Ambush Bay (1966) LaSalle
Ambush Trail (1946) Zahler
Ambushers (1967) Montenegro
America (1914) Klein, Manuel
America (1924) Breil
America for Me (1953) Koff
America the Beautiful (1945) Lava
America's Cup Races (1968) Sharples, William
America's Disinherited (1937) Bowles
America's Hidden Weapon (1944) Lava
American Cowboy (1951) Schaefer, Willis
American Dream (1966) Mandel
American Empire (1942) Carbonara
American Frontier (1952) Powell, M.
American Guerrilla in the Philippines (1950) Mockridge
American in Paris (1951) Salinger
American Realists (1965) Muczynski
American Road (1953) North
American Romance (1944) Gruenberg
American Saddle Horses (1939) Jackson, H.
American Sports Album (1947) Lava
American Tragedy (1931) Rainger
American Vision (1966) Moore, F.
Americaner Schadchen (1940) Morgenstern
Americanization of Emily (1964) Mandel
Americano (1954) Webb
Among the Cannibal Isles of the South Pacific (1918) Beynon
Among the Living (1941) Carbonara
Amoozin' But Confoozin (1944) Worth, P.
Anaesthesia (1938) Snell
Analog Computer and Its Application to Partial Differential Equations (1963) Mumma
Anansi the Spider (1969) Wagner, T.
Anastasia (1956) Newman
Anatomy of a Murder (1959) Ellington
Anatomy of a Parade (1969) Shapiro
Anchors Aweigh (1945) Stoll
Ancient Africans (1969) Wagner, T.
Ancient Egypt (1938) Shilkret, J.
Ancient Egyptian (1963) Lloyd, N.
Ancient Fistory (1953) Sharples, Winston
Ancient India (1952) Nussbaum
Ancient Peruvian (1967) Wagner, T.
And a Voice Shall Be Heard (1951) Shaindlin
And Baby Makes Three (1949) Duning
And Forbid Them Not (1948) Rosen, M.
And Now Miguel (1954) Applebaum
And Now Miguel (1966) Lambro
And Now Tomorrow (1944) Young, V.
And Now Tomorrow (1952) Sawtell
And One Was Beautiful (1940) Amfitheatrof
And So They Live (1940) Gron
And So They Were Married (1936) Jackson, H.
And So Tibet (1964) Sharples, Winston
And the Angels Sing (1944) Bradshaw
And Then There Were Four (1950) Daniel
And Then There Were None (1945) Castelnuovo-Tedesco
And to Think That I Saw It on Mulberry Street (1944) de Packh
Androcles and the Lion (1952) Hollander
Andy (1965) Prince, R.
Andy and the Lion (1955) Kleiner
Andy Hardy Comes Home (1958) Alexander, V.
Andy Hardy Gets Spring Fever (1939) Ward, E.
Andy Hardy Meets Debutante (1940) Snell
Andy Hardy's Blonde Trouble (1944) Snell
Andy Hardy's Double Life (1942) Amfitheatrof
Andy Panda in Crow Crazy (1945) Calker
Andy Panda's Pop (1941) Calker
Andy Panda's Victory Garden (1942) Calker
Andy Russell and Della in House Party (1953) Mancini
Angel (1937) Hollander
Angel and the Badman (1946) Hageman
Angel, Angel, Down We Go (1969) Karger
Angel Baby (1961) Shanklin
Angel Comes to Brooklyn (1945) Butts
Angel Face (1952) Tiomkin
Angel from Texas (1940) Jackson, H.
Angel in Exile (1948) Scott, N.

Angel in My Pocket (1969) Murray
Angel Levine (1970) Liska
Angel of Mercy (1939) Snell
Angel on My Shoulder (1946) Tiomkin
Angel on the Amazon (1948) Scott, N.
Angel Puss (1944) Stalling
Angel Unchained (1970) Sparks
Angel Wore Red (1960) Kaper
Angel's Holiday (1937) Kaylin
Angelina o el Honor de un Brigadier (1935) Sanders
Angels Alley (1948) Kay, Edward
Angels Die Hard! (1970) Hieronymous
Angels from Hell (1968) Phillips, S.
Angels in Disguise (1949) Kay, Edward
Angels in the Outfield (1951) Amfitheatrof
Angels Over Broadway (1940) Antheil
Angels Wash Their Faces (1939) Deutsch
Angels with Broken Wings (1941) Glickman, M.
Angels with Dirty Faces (1938) Steiner, M.
Angkor (1937) McBride, D.
Angry Breed (1968) Curb
Angry God (1948) Duke
Angry Red Planet (1960) Dunlap
Animal Antics (1951) Jackson, H.
Animal Cracker Circus (1938) De Nat
Animal Crackers (1930) Reese
Animal Fair (1958) Sharples, Winston
Animal Kingdom (1932) Steiner, M.
Animal World (1956) Sawtell
Ann Vickers (1933) Webb
Anna and the King of Siam (1946) Herrmann
Anna Christie (1930) Axt
Anna Karenina (1935) Stothart
Anna Lucasta (1949) Diamond
Anna Lucasta (1958) Bernstein, E.
Annabel Takes a Tour (1938) Bennett, R. R.
Annabelle's Affairs (1931) Lipschultz
Annapolis (1928) Zuro
Annapolis Farewell (1935) Leipold
Annapolis Story (1955) Skiles
Anne of the Indies (1951) Waxman
Anne of Windy Poplars (1940) Webb
Annie Get Your Gun (1950) Deutsch
Annie Laurie (1927) Axt
Annie Laurie (1936) Ward, E.
Annie Moved Away (1934) Dietrich
Annie Oakley (1935) Colombo
Annie Was a Wonder (1949) Kopp, R.
Another Dawn (1937) Korngold
Another Day, Another Doormat (1959) Scheib
Another Language (1933) Axt
Another Man's Poison (1952) Sawtell
Another Part of the Forest (1948) Amfitheatrof
Another Romance of Celluloid (1938) Ward, E.
Another Thin Man (1939) Ward, E.
Another Time, Another Voice (1964) Scianni
Another Way (1967) Byrd, C.
Ansel Adams, Photographer (1957) Worth, D.
Ant and the Aardvark (1969) Goodwin
Ant from U.N.C.L.E. (1969) Goodwin
Ant Pasted (1952) Stalling
Anthony Adverse (1936) Korngold
Anti-Cats (1950) Scheib
Antique Antics (1933) De Nat
Antony and Cleopatra (1914) Colburn
Ants in the Pantry (1970) Goodwin
Ants in the Plants (1940) Timberg
Ants in Your Pantry (1945) Scheib
Any Number Can Play (1949) Hayton
Any Old Port (1932) Shield
Any Way to Get There (1932) Carbonara
Any Wednesday (1966) Duning
Anybody's Woman (1930) Hajos
Anything Can Happen (1952) Young, V.
Anything for Laughs (1951) Jackson, H.
Anything for Money (1967) Greene, B.
Anything Goes (1936) Hollander
Anything Goes (1956) Van Cleave
Anzacs in Action (1941) De Francesco
Apache (1954) Raksin
Apache Chief (1949) Glasser
Apache Drums (1951) Salter
Apache Kid (1930) De Nat
Apache Rifles (1964) LaSalle
Apache Rose (1947) Maxwell
Apache Territory (1958) Bakaleinikoff, M.
Apache Trail (1942) Kaplan, S.
Apache Uprising (1965) Haskell
Apache Warrior (1957) Dunlap
Apache Woman (1955) Stein, R.
Apartment (1960) Deutsch
Apartment for Peggy (1948) Raksin
Ape (1940) Kay, Edward
Ape Man (1943) Kay, Edward
Apes of Wrath (1959) Franklyn
Apology for Murder (1945) Erdody
Appaloosa (1966) Skinner, F.
Apple Andy (1946) Calker
Appointment (1970) Phillips, S.
Appointment for Love (1941) Skinner, F.
Appointment in Berlin (1943) Heymann
Appointment in Honduras (1953) Forbes
Appointment in Tokyo (1945) Kaplan, S.
Appointment with a Shadow (1958) Salter
Appointment with Danger (1951) Young, V.
Appointment with Murder (1948) Hajos
April Fools (1969) Hamlisch
April in Paris (1952) Jackson, H.
April Love (1957) Newman
April Showers (1948) Heindorf
Aqua Capers (1947) De Francesco
Aqua Duck (1963) Lava
Aqua Queens (1955) Jackson, H.
Aquamania (1961) Baker, Buddy
Aquaqueens (1946) Norman, R.
Arabesque (1966) Mancini
Arabesque for Kenneth Anger (1961) Ito
Arabian Nights (1942) Skinner, F.

Arabian Tragedy (1912) Simon, W.
Arabians in the Rockies (1945) Dunn
Arabs with Dirty Fezzes (1939) Marsales
Arch of Triumph (1948) Gruenberg
Architecture of Frank Lloyd Wright (1948) Gold
Architecture USA (1965) Elliott, Don
Arcosantos (1970) Fletcher
Arctic Flight (1952) Kay, Edward
Arctic Rivals (1954) Scheib
Arctic Saga (1952) Applebaum
Arctic Springtime (1941) De Francesco
Are Animals Actors? (1945) Jackson, H.
Are Husbands Necessary? (1942) Dolan
Are These Our Children? (1931) Steiner, M.
Are These Our Parents? (1944) Kay, Edward
Are We Civilized? (1934) Wachtel
Are You Listening? (1932) Axt
Are You With It? (1948) Scharf, W.
Arena (1953) Kopp, R.
Argentine Horses (1942) Dunn
Argentine Nights (1940) Skinner, F.
Argentine Primer (1945) Lloyd, N.
Argyle Secrets (1948) Kraushaar
Arise, My Love (1940) Young, V.
Aristo-Cat (1943) Stalling
Aristocats (1970) Bruns
Arizona (1940) Young, V.
Arizona and Its Natural Resources (1966) Lackey
Arizona Bound (1941) Kay, Edward
Arizona Bushwhackers (1967) Haskell
Arizona Cowboy (1950) Wilson, S.
Arizona Cyclone (1941) Rosen, M.
Arizona Days (1937) Sanucci
Arizona Frontier (1940) Sanucci
Arizona Gang Busters (1940) Porter
Arizona Kid (1930) Brunelli
Arizona Kid (1939) Morgan, F.
Arizona Legion (1939) Webb
Arizona Manhunt (1951) Wilson, S.
Arizona Raiders (1965) LaSalle
Arizona Ranger (1948) Sawtell
Arizona Round-Up (1942) Sanucci
Arizona Sheepdog (1955) Lava
Arizona Stage Coach (1942) Sanucci
Arizona Territory (1950) Kay, Edward
Arizona Terrors (1942) Feuer
Arizona to Broadway (1933) Lange
Arizona Whirlwind (1944) Sanucci
Arkansas Judge (1941) Feuer
Arkansas Swing (1948) Bakaleinikoff, M.
Arkansas Traveler (1938) Carbonara
Armored Car Robbery (1950) Sawtell
Army Bound (1952) Skiles
Army Champions (1941) Snell
Army Girl (1938) Young, V.
Army Mascot (1942) Churchill
Army Surgeon (1942) Webb
Army Wives (1944) Kay, Edward
Arnelo Affair (1947) Bassman
Around and About Joan Miró (1955) Varèse
Around Is Around (1951) Applebaum
Around the World (1931) Scheib
Around the World (1943) Duning
Around the World in 80 Days (1956) Young, V.
Around the World in California (1947) Nussbaum
Around the World in Eighty Feet (1963) Weaver
Around the World in Eighty Minutes (1931) Newman
Around the World Under the Sea (1965) Sukman
Aroused (1966) Mitchel
Arrah-na-Pogue (1911) Simon, W.
Arrangement (1969) Amram
Arrest Bulldog Drummond (1938) Carbonara
Arrivederci, Baby! (1966) Farnon
Arrow in the Dust (1954) Skiles
Arrow Magic (1947) Jackson, H.
Arrowhead (1953) Sawtell
Arrowsmith (1932) Newman
Arsenic and Old Lace (1944) Steiner, M.
Arson for Hire (1958) Kay, Edward
Arson Gang Busters (1938) Colombo
Arson, Inc. (1949) Kraushaar
Arson Squad (1945) Zahler
Art and Motion (1956) Bracher
Art for Art's Sake (1934) Sharples, Winston
Art for Everybody (1948) Applebaum
Art Gallery (1939) Bradley
Art in Exhibition (1963) Riddle, R.
Art in Woodcut (1963) Oliveros
Art of Archery (1952) Lava
Art of Living (1942) Applebaum
Art of Love (1965) Coleman, C.
Art of Self Defense (1941) Harline
Art of Skiing (1941) Wolcott
Art of the Conservator (1966) Riddle, R.
Arthur Takes Over (1948) Calker
Artist in Manhattan—Jerome Myers (1969) Dan
Artist Who Did Not Want to Paint (1965) Goldsmith
Artists and Models (1937) Jenkins
Artists and Models (1955) Scharf, W.
Artists and Models Abroad (1937) Rainger
Arts and Flowers (1956) Wheeler
Aryan (1916) Riesenfeld
As Good as Married (1937) Raksin
As Husbands Go (1933) Friedhofer
As Others See Us (1951) Alexander, S.
As the Crow Lies (1951) Sharples, Winston
As the Earth Turns (1934) Roemheld
As the Fly Flies (1944) Kilfeather
As We Forgive (1926) Savine
As You Desire Me (1932) Axt
As You Were (1951) Klatzkin
As Young as You Feel (1951) Mockridge
Ash Can Fleet (1939) Amfitheatrof
Ask Any Girl (1959) Alexander, J.
Asleep (1961) Geesin
Asphalt Jungle (1950) Rozsa

Assault and Flattery (1956) Sharples, Winston
Assault and Peppered (1965) Lava
Assault on a Queen (1966) Ellington
Assignation (1953) Gold
Assigned to Danger (1948) Glasser
Assignment Home (1945) Salter
Assignment in Brittany (1943) Hayton
Assignment to Kill (1969) Lava
Assignment: Mankind (1958) Applebaum
Assignment—Paris (1952) Duning
Astounding She Monster (1958) Kauer
Astro-Freight (1965) Ellington
Astro-Zombies (1968) Carras
Astroduck (1965) Lava
Astronut in Molecular Mixup (1964) Timmens
Astronut in Outer Galaxy Gazette (1964) Timmens
Astronut Woody (1965) Greene, W.
At Gunpoint (1955) Dragon
At Sword's Point (1952) Webb
At the Circus (1939) Waxman
At the Front in North Africa (1943) Newman
At the Stroke of Twelve (1941) Jackson, H.
At War with the Army (1951) Lilley
At Your Service (1935) Dietrich
At Your Service Madame (1936) Spencer, N.
Athabasca (1967) Applebaum
Athena (1954) Stoll
Athlete (1932) Dietrich
Athletic Stars (1948) Shilkret, N.
Athletic Varieties (1948) Shilkret, N.
Atlantic City (1944) Scharf, W.
Atlantis, the Lost Continent (1960) Garcia
Atlas (1961) Stein, R.
Atomic City (1952) Stevens, L.
Atomic Kid (1954) Alexander, V.
Atomic Power Today (1967) Elliott, Don
Atomic Submarine (1959) Laszlo
Atoms on the Move (1966) Elliott, Don
Attack (1956) De Vol
Attack in the Pacific (1945) Raksin
Attack of the 50 Foot Woman (1958) Stein, R.
Attack of the Crab Monsters (1957) Stein, R.
Attack of the Giant Leeches (1959) Laszlo
Attack of the Puppet People (1958) Glasser
Attack! The Battle for New Britain (1944) Tiomkin
Auntie Mame (1958) Kaper
Auto Clinic (1938) De Nat
Autograph Hound (1939) Wallace
Autograph Hunter (1934) De Nat
Autumn (1930) Stalling
Autumn (1961) Hanson, R.
Autumn Color (1959) Thorne, O.
Autumn Leaves (1956) Salter
Avalanche (1946) Moraweck
Avengers (1950) Scott, N.
Aviation Vacation (1941) Stalling
Aviator (1929) Dunn
Aw Nurse (1934) De Nat
Awakening (1928) Riesenfeld
Away All Boats (1956) Skinner, F.
Awful Orphan (1948) Stalling
Awful Tooth (1952) Sharples, Winston
Awful Truth (1937) Oakland

B. F.'s Daughter (1948) Kaper
Baa, Baa, Black Sheep (1944) Jackson, H.
Babbitt (1934) Jerome
Babbling Tongues (1917) Beynon
Babe Ruth Story (1948) Ward, E.
Babes at Sea (1934) De Nat
Babes in Arms (1939) Stoll
Babes in the Woods (1932) Lewis
Babes in Toyland (1961) Bruns
Babes on Broadway (1941) Stoll
Babies, They're Wonderful (1947) Sharples, Winston
Babo 73 (1964) O'Horgan
Baby Be Good (1935) Steiner, G.
Baby Boogie (1955) Easton
Baby Bottleneck (1945) Stalling
Baby Buggy Bunny (1954) Franklyn
Baby Butch (1954) Bradley
Baby Doll (1956) Hopkins, K.
Baby Face Harrington (1935) Ward, E.
Baby Face Morgan (1942) Erdody
Baby Face Nelson (1957) Alexander, V.
Baby Kittens (1938) Bradley
Baby, Light My Fire (1970) Herman
Baby Maker (1970) Karlin
Baby Puss (1943) Bradley
Baby Rabbit in I Wanted Red Wings (1939) Tullis
Baby Seal (1941) Scheib
Baby Sitter (1947) Sharples, Winston
Baby Take a Bow (1934) Buttolph, David
Baby the Rain Must Fall (1964) Bernstein, E.
Baby Wants a Battle (1953) Sharples, Winston
Baby Wants a Bottleship (1942) Timberg
Baby Wants Spinach (1950) Sharples, Winston
Babysitter (1969) Ragland
Bacall to Arms (1946) Stalling
Bachelor and the Bobby-Soxer (1947) Harline
Bachelor Apartment (1931) Steiner, M.
Bachelor Daddy (1941) Salter
Bachelor Flat (1961) Williams, J.
Bachelor in Paradise (1961) Mancini
Bachelor Mother (1939) Webb
Bachelor of Arts (1934) Kaylin
Bachelor Party (1957) North
Bachelor Tom Peeping (1962) Sandford
Bachelor's Affairs (1932) Bassett, R. H.
Bachelor's Dream (1967) Gigagusky
Bachelors' Club (1929) Rapée
Back Alley Oproar (1948) Stalling
Back Door to Heaven (1939) Baron, M.
Back from Eternity (1956) Waxman
Back from the Dead (1957) Kraushaar
Back in Circulation (1937) Kaun
Back in Circulation (Trailer, 1937) Jackson, H.

Back Pay (1930) Copping
Back Pay (1930) Reiser
Back Street (1932) Broekman
Back Street (1941) Skinner, F.
Back Street (1961) Skinner, F.
Back the Attack on Brucellosis (1958) Kleinsinger
Back to Bataan (1945) Webb
Back to God's Country (1953) Skinner, F.
Back to Missouri (1940) Craig, E.
Back to the Soil (1941) Scheib
Back Trail (1948) Kay, Edward
Backfire (1950) Amfitheatrof
Background to Danger (1943) Hollander
Backlash (1946) Calker
Backlash (1956) Stein, H.
Backtrack (1969) Marshall, J.
Backwoods Bunny (1959) Franklyn
Backyard Golf (1944) Jackson, H.
Bad and the Beautiful (1952) Raksin
Bad Bascomb (1946) Snell
Bad Boy (1937) Marquardt
Bad Boy (1949) Sawtell
Bad Company (1931) Lange
Bad Day at Black Rock (1954) Previn, A.
Bad Day at Cat Rock (1965) Poddany
Bad Genius (1932) De Nat
Bad Girls for the Boys (1966) Hames
Bad Lands (1939) Webb
Bad Little Angel (1939) Ward, E.
Bad Luck Blackie (1949) Bradley
Bad Man (1930) Leonardi
Bad Man (1941) Waxman
Bad Man of Brimstone (1937) Axt
Bad Man of Deadwood (1941) Glickman, M.
Bad Men of Missouri (1941) Jackson, H.
Bad Men of Thunder Gap (1943) Zahler
Bad Men of Tombstone (1948) Webb
Bad Ol' Putty Tat (1948) Stalling
Bad One (1930) Riesenfeld
Bad Seed (1956) North
Badge of Marshal Brennan (1957) Idriss
Badlands of Dakota (1941) Skinner, F.
Badlands of Montana (1957) Gertz
Badman's Country (1958) Gertz
Badman's Gold (1951) Calker
Badman's Territory (1946) Webb
Baffling Bunnies (1955) Scheib
Bagatelle for Willard Maas (1961) Ito
Bagdad (1949) Skinner, F.
Baggage Buster (1941) Harline
Baggin' the Dragon (1966) Sharples, Winston
Bah Wilderness (1943) Bradley
Bahama Passage (1941) Buttolph, David
Bahama Sea Sports (1945) Jackson, H.
Bail Out at 43,000 (1957) Glasser
Bait (1954) Divina
Bal Tabarin (1952) Butts
Balalaika (1939) Stothart
Balkan Powder Keg (1944) Agostini
Ball of Fire (1941) Newman
Ballad of a Gunfighter (1963) Mendoza-Nava
Ballad of Cable Hogue (1970) Goldsmith
Ballad of Josie (1967) De Vol
Ballad of the Little Square (1953) Klauss
Ballet by Degas (1951) Jurist
Ballet Festival (1949) Applebaum
Ballet in the Blue (1968) Loose
Ballet-Oop (1954) Bruns
Balloonland (1935) Stalling
Ballot Box Bunny (1950) Stalling
Ballyhooey (1960) Wheeler
Balmy Knight (1966) Sharples, Winston
Balmy Swami (1949) Sharples, Winston
Bambi (1942) Churchill
Bamboo Blonde (1946) Sawtell
Bamboo Saucer (1968) Kraushaar
Band Concert (1935) Harline
Band of Angels (1957) Steiner, M.
Band Plays On (1934) Bassett, R. H.
Band Wagon (1953) Deutsch
Bandido (1956) Steiner, M.
Bandit Island (1953) Shefter
Bandit King of Texas (1949) Wilson, S.
Bandit of Sherwood Forest (1946) Friedhofer
Bandit Queen (1950) Glasser
Bandit Ranger (1942) Sawtell
Bandit Trail (1941) Sawtell
Bandits of Corsica (1953) Gertz
Bandits of Dark Canyon (1948) Glickman, M.
Bandits of the West (1953) Wilson, S.
Bandmaster (1930) De Nat
Bandmaster (1931) Dietrich
Bandolero! (1968) Goldsmith
Bang Bang Gang (1970) Alper
Banjo (1947) Laszlo
Banjo on My Knee (1936) Maxwell
Bank Dick (1940) Skinner, F.
Banker's Daughter (1933) Scheib
Bannerline (1951) Kopp, R.
Banning (1967) Jones
Bannister's Bantering Babies (1948) Lava
Banquet Busters (1948) Calker
Banty Raids (1962) Lava
Baptism of Fire (1943) Lava
Bar 20 (1943) Sawtell
Bar Mitzvah (1957) Applebaum
Bar-Mitzvah (1935) Stillman
Bar-Rac's Night Out (1937) Axt
Bar Sinister (1917) Levy, S.
Barbara (1962) Jennings
Barbarella (1968) Jarre
Barbarian (1933) Stothart
Barbarian and the Geisha (1958) Friedhofer
Barbary Coast (1935) Newman
Barbary Coast Bunny (1956) Stalling
Barbary Coast Gent (1944) Snell
Barbecue Brawl (1956) Bradley
Barbee-Cues (1942) Snell

Barber of Seville (1944) Calker
Barbershop Ballads (1945) Jackson, H.
Barbie's Hospital Affair (1970) Levine, E.
Bardelys the Magnificent (1926) Axt
Bardelys the Magnificent (1926) Bassett, R. H.
Baree, Son of Kazan (1925) Hoffman, M.
Barefaced Flatfoot (1951) Castillo
Barefoot Adventure (1961) Shank
Barefoot Boy (1938) Gromon
Barefoot in the Park (1967) Hefti
Barefoot Mailman (1951) Duning
Bargain (1931) Mendoza
Bargain Counter Attack (1946) Sharples, Winston
Bargain Daze (1953) Scheib
Barker (1928) Silvers
Barking Dogs Don't Fite (1949) Sharples, Winston
Barkleys of Broadway (1949) Hayton
Barn Dance (1928) Stalling
Barn Dance (1946) Applebaum
Barnacle Bill (1941) Kaper
Barney Bear's Victory Garden (1943) Bradley
Barney's Hungry Cousin (1952) Bradley
Barnyard Actor (1955) Scheib
Barnyard Amateurs (1936) Scheib
Barnyard Babies (1935) Bradley
Barnyard Babies (1940) De Nat
Barnyard Baseball (1939) Scheib
Barnyard Battle (1929) Stalling
Barnyard Blackout (1943) Scheib
Barnyard Boss (1937) Scheib
Barnyard Brat (1939) Timberg
Barnyard Broadcast (1931) Lewis
Barnyard Egg-citement (1939) Scheib
Barnyard Five (1936) Dietrich
Barnyard Follies (1940) Feuer
Barnyard Olympics (1932) Churchill
Barnyard Romeo (1938) Churchill
Barnyard WAAC (1942) Scheib
Baron and the Rose (1940) Amfitheatrof
Baron of Arizona (1950) Dunlap
Baron von Go-Go (1967) Timmens
Barquero (1970) Frontiere
Barrel (1956) Wilson, J.
Barretts of Wimpole Street (1934) Stothart
Barretts of Wimpole Street (1957) Kaper
Barricade (1939) Buttolph, David
Barricade (1950) Lava
Barrier (1917) Levy, S.
Barrier (1937) Carbonara
Bars and Stripes (1931) De Nat
Bars and Stripes (1937) Snell
Bars and Stripes Forever (1939) Stalling
Bartholomew versus the Wheel (1963) Lava
Bartleby (1969) Segáll
Base Brawl (1948) Sharples, Winston
Baseball Bugs (1946) Stalling
Bashful Buckaroo (1937) Paterson
Bashful Buzzard (1945) Stalling
Bashful Elephant (1962) Stein, R.
Basic Dance (1951) Browning
Basic Movement (1954) Wilson, J.
Basket of Mexican Tales (1956) Adomian
Basketball Fix (1951) Kraushaar
Basketmaking in Colonial Virginia (1968) Reno
Bass (1966) Austin
Bat (1959) Forbes
Bataan (1943) Kaper
Bath Day (1946) Wallace
Bathing Beauty (1944) Green, J.
Bathing Buddies (1946) Calker
Bathing Time for Baby (1946) Smith, P.
Batman (1943) Zahler
Batman (1966) Riddle
Baton Bunny (1958) Franklyn
Bats in the Belfry (1942) Bradley
Bats in the Belfry (1960) Wheeler
Battery Davis (1970) Ashley
Battle (1941) Amfitheatrof
Battle at Apache Pass (1952) Salter
Battle at Bloody Beach (1961) Vars
Battle Beyond the Sun (1963) Stein, R.
Battle Circus (1953) Hayton
Battle Cry (1955) Steiner, M.
Battle Cry of Peace (1915) Schenk
Battle Flame (1959) Skiles
Battle for a Bottle (1942) Kilfeather
Battle for Beauty (1942) Jackson, H.
Battle for the Beaches (1945) Adomian
Battle for the Marianas (1944) Lava
Battle Hymn (1957) Skinner, F.
Battle Is Their Birthright (1943) Agostini
Battle of Britain (1943) Steiner, M.
Battle of Champs (1946) Jackson, H.
Battle of China (1944) Tiomkin
Battle of Gettysburg (1956) Deutsch
Battle of Midway (1942) Newman
Battle of Rogue River (1954) Duning
Battle of Russia (1943) Tiomkin
Battle of Saipan (1944) Lava
Battle of the Beetles (1952) Mamorsky
Battle of the Coral Sea (1959) Gold
Battle of the Sexes (1928) Riesenfeld
Battle Royal (1936) Dietrich
Battle Royal (1936) Scheib
Battle Stations (1943) Duke
Battle Taxi (1955) Sukman
Battle Zone (1952) Skiles
Battleground (1949) Hayton
Battles of Chief Pontiac (1952) Bernstein, E.
Battling Bosko (1931) Marsales
Batty Baseball (1944) Bradley
Bauer Girls (1950) Shilkret, N.
Bayou (1957) Fried
Be Mice to Cats (1960) Sharples, Winston
Be Patient, Patient (1944) Kilfeather
Be Up to Date (1938) Timberg
Be Yourself! (1930) Riesenfeld
Beach Ball (1965) Wilson, F.

Beach Blanket Bingo (1965) Baxter
Beach Combers (1936) Dietrich
Beach Days (1946) Jackson, H.
Beach Girls and the Monster (1965) Sinatra
Beach Nut (1944) Calker
Beach Party (1963) Baxter
Beach Peach (1950) Sharples, Winston
Beach Picnic (1939) Smith, P.
Beachhead (1954) Lange
Beachhead to Berlin (1945) Lava
Beanstalk Bunny (1954) Stalling
Beanstalk Jack (1933) Scheib
Beanstalk Jack (1946) Scheib
Bear and the Bean (1948) Bradley
Bear and the Beavers (1942) Bradley
Bear and the Hare (1948) Bradley
Bear Country (1952) Smith, P.
Bear Feat (1948) Stalling
Bear for Punishment (1950) Stalling
Bear Raid Warden (1944) Bradley
Bear That Couldn't Sleep (1939) Bradley
Bear That Wasn't (1967) Elliott, Dean
Bear's Tale (1940) Stalling
Bearly Asleep (1955) Wallace
Bears and Bees (1932) Churchill
Beast from 20,000 Fathoms (1953) Buttolph, David
Beast of Budapest (1957) Skiles
Beast of Yucca Flats (1961) Nafshun
Beast with a Million Eyes (1955) Bickford
Beast with Five Fingers (1947) Steiner, M.
Beat Generation (1959) Glasser
Beat the Band (1947) Harline
Beau Best (1933) Dietrich
Beau Bosko (1933) Marsales
Beau Brummell (1954) Rozsa
Beau Geste (1926) Riesenfeld
Beau Geste (1939) Newman
Beau Geste (1966) Salter
Beau Hunks (1931) Hatley
Beau Ideal (1930) Steiner, M.
Beau James (1957) Lilley
Beaus and Arrows (1932) Dietrich
Beaus Will Be Beaus (1955) Sharples, Winston
Beautiful Bali (1940) Bakaleinikoff, C.
Beautiful Bali (1946) Jackson, H.
Beautiful Blonde from Bashful Bend (1949) Mockridge
Beautiful Brazil (1952) Nussbaum
Beautiful British Columbia (1940) Dietrich
Beautiful Budapest (1938) Shilkret, J.
Beautiful But Broke (1944) Leipold
Beautiful, the Bloody, and the Bare (1964) Karmen
Beauty and the Bandit (1946) Kay, Edward
Beauty and the Beast (1934) Spencer, N.
Beauty and the Beast (1962) Friedhofer
Beauty and the Blade (1949) Agostini
Beauty and the Boss (1932) Harling
Beauty and the Bull (1956) Lava
Beauty and the Cave (1961) Kilpatrick
Beauty for Sale (1933) Axt
Beauty for Sale (1946) Shilkret, N.
Beauty for the Asking (1939) Tours
Beauty on the Beach (1950) Scheib
Beauty Shop (1950) Scheib
Beauty Shoppe (1936) Dietrich
Beaver Trouble (1951) Scheib
Beaver Valley (1950) Smith, P.
Because of Him (1946) Rozsa
Because of You (1952) Skinner, F.
Because They're Young (1960) Williams, J.
Because You're Mine (1952) Green, J.
Becket (1964) Rosenthal
Beckoning Flame (1916) Schertzinger
Becky Sharp (1935) Webb
Becoming (1955) DeMarlos
Bed (1968) Jepson
Bed of Violence (1967) Marini
Bedevilled Rabbit (1957) Franklyn
Bedlam (1946) Webb
Bedside (1934) Kaun
Bedtime Bedlam (1955) Wheeler
Bedtime for Bonzo (1951) Skinner, F.
Bedtime for Sniffles (1940) Stalling
Bedtime Story (1933) Rainger
Bedtime Story (1941) Heymann
Bedtime Story (1963) Salter
Bee at the Beach (1949) Dubin
Bee Bopped (1959) Wheeler
Bee-Deviled Bruin (1948) Stalling
Bee on Guard (1951) Wallace
Beep, Beep (1951) Stalling
Beep Prepared (1961) Franklyn
Beer Is Here (1933) Shilkret, N.
Beer Parade (1933) De Nat
Bees a' Buzzin' (1944) Jackson, H.
Before It's Too Late (1964) Gorgoni
Before the Day (1960) Nelson, R.
Before the Mountain Was Moved (1970) Soraci
Before the Sacrifice: Sacristy and Sanctuary (1951) Parisi
Before Your Telephone Rings (1948) Rathaus
Beg, Borrow, or Steal (1937) Axt
Beggar on Horseback (1925) Riesenfeld
Beggars of Life (1928) Hajos
Beginning (196?) Duffy
Beginning of the End (1957) Glasser
Beginning or the End (1947) Amfitheatrof
Behave Yourself (1951) Harline
Behind City Lights (1945) Dubin
Behind Enemy Lines (1945) Craig, E.
Behind Locked Doors (1948) Glasser
Behind Nazi Lines (1945) Adomian
Behind Prison Walls (1943) Erdody
Behind the Big Top (1943) Jackson, H.
Behind the Cup (1939) Gonzales
Behind the Footlights (1946) De Francesco
Behind the Headlines (1936) Snell

Behind the Make-Up (1930) Harling
Behind the Mask (1946) Kay, Edward
Behind the Meat Ball (1945) Stalling
Behind the Mike (1937) Henderson, C.
Behind the News (1940) Glickman, M.
Behind the Rising Sun (1943) Webb
Behold a Pale Horse (1964) Jarre
Behold My Wife! (1934) Leipold
Bela Lugosi Meets a Brooklyn Gorilla (1952) Hazard
Belgium—Where the Past Meets the Present (1955) Gilson
Believe It or Else (1939) Stalling
Bell, Bare and Beautiful (1963) Wellington
Bell, Book and Candle (1958) Duning
Bell Boy 13 (1923) Cohen, S.
Bell for Adano (1945) Newman
Bell for Philadelphia (1963) Scheib
Bell Hoppy (1953) Stalling
Bella Donna (1923) Riesenfeld
Bellamy Trial (1928) Axt
Bellboy (1960) Scharf, W.
Bellboy Donald (1942) Wallace
Belle Boys (1953) Wheeler
Belle Le Grand (1951) Young, V.
Belle of New York (1952) Deutsch
Belle of Old Mexico (1950) Wilson, S.
Belle of the Nineties (1934) Leipold
Belle of the Yukon (1944) Lange
Belle Sommers (1962) Sukman
Belle Starr (1941) Buttolph, David
Belle Starr's Daughter (1948) Kilenyi
Belles on Their Toes (1952) Mockridge
Bellota (1969) Muczynski
Bells Are Ringing (1960) Previn, A.
Bells of Atlantis (1953) Barron
Bells of Capistrano (1942) Glickman, M.
Bells of Coronado (1949) Butts
Bells of Rosarita (1945) Maxwell
Bells of San Angelo (1947) Maxwell
Bells of San Fernando (1947) De Saxe
Bells of St. Mary's (1945) Dolan
Beloved (1934) Schertzinger
Beloved Bachelor (1931) Leipold
Beloved Brat (1938) Jackson, H.
Beloved Enemy (1937) Newman
Beloved Infidel (1959) Waxman
Beloved Island (1969) Shapiro
Below the Border (1942) Kay, Edward
Below the Deadline (1946) Kay, Edward
Below the Rio Grande (1954) Jackson, H.
Below the Sahara (1953) Sawtell
Ben and Me (1953) Wallace
Ben Hogan (1946) Stringer
Ben-Hur (1925) Axt
Ben-Hur (1959) Rozsa
Bend of the River (1952) Salter
Beneath the 12-Mile Reef (1953) Herrmann
Beneath the Planet of the Apes (1969) Rosenman
Beneath Western Skies (1944) Glickman, M.
Bengal Brigade (1954) Wilson, S.
Bengal Tiger (1936) Jackson, H.
Bengazi (1955) Webb
Benny Goodman Story (1955) Mancini
Benson Murder Case (1930) Midgely
Berkeley Square (1933) Zamecnik
Berlin Correspondent (1942) Buttolph, David
Berlin Express (1948) Hollander
Berlin Powderkeg (1949) Engel
Bermuda (1948) De Francesco
Bermuda Mystery (1944) Lange
Bernardine (1957) Newman, L.
Best Foot Forward (1943) Hayton
Best Man (1964) Lindsey
Best Man Wins (1935) Jackson, H.
Best of Breed (1949) Mamorsky
Best of Enemies (1933) Lange
Best of Everything (1959) Newman
Best of the Badmen (1951) Sawtell
Best Things in Life Are Free (1956) Harline
Best Years of Our Lives (1946) Friedhofer
Betrayal (1919) Breil
Betrayal (1929) Zamecnik
Betrayed Women (1955) Kay, Edward
Better Bait Than Never (1953) Sharples, Winston
Better Dresses—Fifth Floor (1941) Dessau
Better Late Than Never (1950) Scheib
Better 'Ole (1926) Baron, M.
Better Seeds for Better Grasslands (1955) Kleinsinger
Better Tomorrow (1944) North
Between Heaven and Hell (1956) Friedhofer
Between Men (1915) Nurnberger
Between Midnight and Dawn (1950) Duning
Between Two Women (1937) Axt
Between Two Women (1944) Snell
Between Two Worlds (1944) Korngold
Between Us Girls (1942) Skinner, F.
Beware, My Lovely (1952) Stevens, L.
Beware of Blondie (1950) Leipold
Beware Spooks! (1939) Harline
Beware the Black Widow (1968) Fuller, L.
Bewitched (1945) Kaper
Bewitched Bunny (1953) Stalling
Beyond a Reasonable Doubt (1956) Gilbert, H.
Beyond All Barriers (1965) Kaplan, S.
Beyond Civilization to Texas (1949) Wheeler
Beyond Gauguin (1959) Engel
Beyond Glory (1948) Young, V.
Beyond Niagara (1969) Persichetti
Beyond Our Own (1947) De Saxe
Beyond the Blue Horizon (1942) Young, V.
Beyond the Forest (1949) Steiner, M.
Beyond the Last Frontier (1943) Glickman, M.
Beyond the Law (1968) Conroy
Beyond the Line of Duty (1942) Jackson, H.
Beyond the Night (1964) Bernstein, C.
Beyond the Pecos (1944) Sawtell

Beyond the Purple Hills (1950) Greeley
Beyond the Time Barrier (1959) Calker
Beyond the Valley of the Dolls (1970) Phillips, S.
Beyond Tomorrow (1940) Tours
Beyond Victory (1931) Alexander, A.
Bhowani Junction (1956) Rozsa
Bicep Built for Two (1955) Sharples, Winston
Big Bad Bobcat (1966) Timmens
Big Bad Sindbad (1952) Sharples, Winston
Big Bad Wolf (1934) Churchill
Big Beat (1957) Mancini
Big Bill Tilden (1941) Lava
Big Birdcast (1938) De Nat
Big Bite (1965) Wheeler
Big Bluff (1933) Zahler
Big Bluff (1955) Compinsky
Big Bonanza (1945) Glickman, M.
Big Bounce (1969) Curb
Big Boy (1930) Reiser
Big Break (1953) Brant
Big Broadcast (1932) Rainger
Big Broadcast of 1936 (1935) Leipold
Big Broadcast of 1937 (1936) Skiles
Big Broadcast of 1938 (1938) Leipold
Big Brown Eyes (1936) Carbonara
Big Build-Up (1942) Scheib
Big Business (1931) Zahler
Big Caper (1957) Glasser
Big Cat (1949) Sawtell
Big Cat and the Little Mousie (1938) Marsales
Big Chase (1954) Shefter
Big Chief Ugh-Amugh-Ugh (1938) Timberg
Big Circus (1959) Sawtell
Big City (1937) Axt
Big City (1948) Perl
Big City Blues (1932) Heindorf
Big Clock (1948) Young, V.
Big Combo (1955) Raksin
Big Country (1958) Forrell
Big Country (1958) Moross
Big Cube (1969) Johns
Big Daddy (1969) Hyams
Big Dog House (1931) Axt
Big Drip (1949) Sharples, Winston
Big Executive (1933) Jackson, H.
Big Fisherman (1959) Malotte
Big Fix (1947) Cadkin
Big Flame-Up (1949) Sharples, Winston
Big Gamble (1960) Jarre
Big Gamble (1931) Lange
Big Gamble (1953) Kleinsinger
Big Game Haunt (1968) Lava
Big Game Hunt (1937) Scheib
Big Guy (1939) Salter
Big Hand for the Little Lady (1966) Raksin
Big Hangover (1950) Deutsch
Big-Hearted Bosko (1931) Marsales
Big Hearted Herbert (1934) Jerome
Big Heat (1953) Vars
Big Heel-Watha (1944) Bradley
Big House (1930) Axt
Big House Blues (1947) Kilfeather
Big House Bunny (1948) Stalling
Big House, U.S.A. (1955) Dunlap
Big Jack (1949) Stothart
Big Jim McLain (1952) Dunlap
Big Jim McLain (Trailer, 1952) Lava
Big Knife (1955) De Vol
Big Land (1957) Buttolph, David
Big Lie (1952) Fried
Big Lift (1950) Newman
Big Man from the North (1930) Marsales
Big Money (1930) Zuro
Big Mouth (1967) Betts
Big Night (1951) Murray
Big Night (1960) LaSalle
Big Noise (1936) Roemheld
Big Noise (1944) Buttolph, David
Big Operator (1959) Alexander, V.
Big Pal (1925) Hoffman, M.
Big Parade (1925) Axt
Big Parade of Comedy (1963) Green, B.
Big Party (1947) Shilkret, N.
Big People—Little People (1967) Schickele
Big Port (1954) Shulman
Big Premiere (1940) Snell
Big Punch (1948) Lava
Big Race (1937) Dietrich
Big Red (1962) Wallace
Big Rock Candy Mountain (1942) de Packh
Big Shakedown (1933) Kaun
Big Shot (1931) Lange
Big Shot (1942) Deutsch
Big Show (1961) Sawtell
Big Sin City (1970) St. Pierre
Big Sister Blues (1948) Lilley
Big Sky (1952) Tiomkin
Big Sleep (1946) Steiner, M.
Big Snooze (1946) Stalling
Big Sombrero (1948) Bakaleinikoff, M.
Big Steal (1949) Harline
Big Store (1941) Hayton
Big Street (1942) Webb
Big Timber (1950) Kay, Edward
Big Time Revue (1947) Lava
Big Tip-Off (1955) Kay, Edward
Big Top (1938) Scheib
Big Top Bunny (1950) Stalling
Big Town (1947) Calker
Big Town After Dark (1947) Calker
Big Town Czar (1939) Skinner, F.
Big Town Scandal (1948) Calker
Big Trail (1930) Kay, Arthur
Big Trees (1952) Roemheld
Big Wash (1947) Wallace
Big Wheel (1949) Carbonara
Bigamist (1953) Stevens, L.
Bigfoot (1970) Podolor

Bigger Than Life (1956) Raksin
Bikes and Skis (1944) Jackson, H.
Bikini Beach (1964) Baxter
Bikini—the Atom Island (1946) Terr
Bill and Coo (1948) Buttolph, David
Bill of Divorcement (1932) Steiner, M.
Bill of Divorcement (1940) Webb
Bill of Hare (1962) Franklyn
Bill of Rights (1939) Jackson, H.
Bill Poster (1933) De Nat
Billboard Frolics (1936) Spencer, N.
Billie (1965) Frontiere
Billion Dollar Boner (1959) Poddany
Billposters (1940) Wallace
Billy Boy (1954) Bradley
Billy Goat's Whiskers (1937) Scheib
Billy Mouse's Akwakade (1940) Scheib
Billy Rose's Casa Mañana Revue (1938) Snell
Billy the Kid (1930) Stahlberg
Billy the Kid (1941) Snell
Billy the Kid in Santa Fe (1941) Lange, J.
Billy the Kid in Texas (1940) Porter
Billy the Kid Outlawed (1940) Porter
Billy the Kid Returns (1938) Lava
Billy the Kid Trapped (1942) Lange, J.
Billy the Kid versus Dracula (1966) Kraushaar
Billy the Kid Wanted (1941) Lange, J.
Billy the Kid's Range War (1941) Porter
Billy the Kid's Round-Up (1941) Lange, J.
Billy the Kid's Smoking Guns (1942) Lange, J.
Bingo Crosbyana (1936) Spencer, N.
Bio-Satellite (1965) Fried
Biography of a Bachelor Girl (1934) Stothart
Bip Goes to Town (1941) Moore, D.
Bird (1965) Horn
Bird-Brain Bird Dog (1954) Bradley
Bird Came C.O.D. (1942) Stalling
Bird Hunt (1951) Wolf
Bird in a Guilty Cage (1951) Stalling
Bird Man (1935) Rosoff
Bird of Paradise (1932) Steiner, M.
Bird of Paradise (1951) Amfitheatrof
Bird on Nellie's Hat (1939) Marsales
Bird Scouts (1935) Sharples, Winston
Bird Store (1932) Churchill
Bird Stuffer (1936) De Nat
Bird Symphony (1955) Scheib
Bird Tower (1941) Scheib
Bird Who Came to Dinner (1961) Wheeler
Birdland (1935) Scheib
Birdman of Alcatraz (1962) Bernstein, E.
Birds and the Beasts Were There (1945) Dunn
Birds and the Bees (1956) Scharf, W.
Birds Anonymous (1957) Franklyn
Birds Do It (1966) Matlovsky
Birds in Love (1936) De Nat
Birds in the Spring (1933) Churchill
Birds of a Father (1961) Franklyn
Birds of a Feather (1965) Greene, W.
Birdy and the Beast (1944) Stalling
Birth of a Legend (1966) Smith, J.
Birth of a Nation (1915) Breil
Birth of a Notion (1947) Stalling
Birth of a Race (1918) Breil
Birth of a Toothpick (1939) Marsales
Birth of an Oil Field (1949) Wheeler
Birth of Aphrodite (196?) Katz, F.
Birth of Jazz (1932) De Nat
Birth of the Blues (1941) Dolan
Birth of Venus: Art of the Renaissance (1952) Belasco
Birthday Party (1937) Dietrich
Birthplace of Hockey (1953) Lava
Birthright (1951) Adomian
Birthright (1951) De Vol
Biscuit Eater (1940) Hollander
Bishop (1954) Dallin
Bishop Misbehaves (1935) Ward, E.
Bishop Murder Case (1930) Axt
Bishop's Wife (1947) Friedhofer
Bitter Creek (1954) Kraushaar
Bitter Sweet (1940) Stothart
Bitter Tea of General Yen (1932) Harling
Black Angel (1946) Skinner, F.
Black Arrow (1944) Zahler
Black Arrow (1948) Sawtell
Black Bandit (1938) Sanucci
Black Bart (1948) Stevens, L.
Black Bear Twins (1953) Kay, W.
Black Beauty (1946) Tiomkin
Black Camel (1931) Kaylin
Black Cat (1934) Roemheld
Black Cat (1941) Salter
Black Cat (1956) Gallez
Black Cat (1960) De Cenco
Black Coin (1936) Zahler
Black Crook (1916) Simon, W.
Black Diamonds (1940) Skinner, F.
Black Dragons (1942) Lange, J.
Black Ducks and Broadbills (1946) Stringer
Black Fox (1962) Laderman
Black Friday (1940) Salter
Black Fury (1935) Kaun
Black Fury (1953) Jackson, H.
Black Gold (1936) Wallace
Black Gold (1947) Kay, Edward
Black Gold (1963) Jackson, H.
Black Gold and Cactus (1944) De Francesco
Black Hand (1950) Colombo
Black Hills (1947) Greene, W.
Black Hills Ambush (1952) Wilson, S.
Black Hills Express (1943) Glickman, M.
Black Horse Canyon (1954) Skinner, F.
Black Klansman (1966) Mendoza-Nava
Black Lash (1951) Greene, W.
Black Legion (1936) Kaun
Black Like Me (1964) Kupferman
Black Magic (1929) Malotte

Black Magic (1944) Laszlo
Black Magic (1949) Sawtell
Black Market Babies (1945) Kay, Edward
Black Market Rustlers (1943) Sanucci
Black Midnight (1949) Kay, Edward
Black Parachute (1944) Castelnuovo-Tedesco
Black Patch (1957) Goldsmith
Black Pirate (1926) Wilson, M.
Black Pirates (1954) Diaz Conde
Black Room (1935) Silvers
Black Sabbath (1964) Baxter
Black Scorpion (1957) Sawtell
Black Sheep (1932) De Nat
Black Sheep (1934) Scheib
Black Shield of Falworth (1954) Salter
Black Sleep (1956) Baxter
Black Spider (1931) Scheib
Black Spurs (1964) Haskell
Black Sunday (1961) Baxter
Black Swan (1942) Newman
Black Tuesday (1954) Dunlap
Black Veil for Lisa (1969) Markowitz
Black Whip (1956) Kraushaar
Black/White Study (1969) Austin
Black Widow (1947) Glickman, M.
Black Widow (1954) Harline
Black Zoo (1963) Dunlap
Blackbeard the Pirate (1952) Young, V.
Blackbeard's Ghost (1967) Brunner
Blackboard Jumble (1956) Bradley
Blackboard Jungle (1955) Wolcott
Blackboard Revue (1940) Kilfeather
Blackmail (1939) Ward, E.
Blackmail (1947) Glickman, M.
Blacksheep Blacksmith (1966) Sharples, Winston
Blacksmith's Gift (1960) Norlin
Blackwell's Island (1939) Kaun
Blast of Silence (1961) Kupferman
Blaze of Noon (1947) Deutsch
Blazing Bullets (1951) Caswell
Blazing Forest (1952) Cailliet
Blazing Guns (1943) Sanucci
Blazing Sixes (1937) Jackson, H.
Blind Alley (1939) Parrish
Blind Date (1934) Jackson, H.
Blind Date (1953) Scheib
Blind Spot (1947) Sawtell
Blindfold (1966) Schifrin
Blitz Wolf (1942) Bradley
Blob (1958) Carmichael
Block Busters (1944) Kay, Edward
Block Party (1948) Shilkret, N.
Block-Heads (1938) Hatley
Blockade (1928) Filippi
Blockade (1938) Janssen
Blocked Trail (1943) Glickman, M.
Blonde Bandit (1949) Wilson, S.
Blonde Captive (1931) Edouarde
Blonde Dynamite (1950) Kay, Edward
Blonde Fever (1944) Shilkret, N.
Blonde for a Day (1946) Erdody
Blonde from Brooklyn (1945) Sawtell
Blonde from Singapore (1941) Dragon
Blonde Ice (1948) Gertz
Blonde Inspiration (1941) Kaper
Blonde Ransom (1945) Skinner, F.
Blonde Savage (1947) Erdody
Blonde Venus (1932) Harling
Blondes at Work (1937) Jackson, H.
Blondie (1938) Harline
Blondie Brings Up Baby (1939) Harline
Blondie for Victory (1942) Leipold
Blondie Goes Latin (1941) Arnaud
Blondie Has Servant Trouble (1940) Harline
Blondie in Society (1941) Harline
Blondie in the Dough (1947) Bakaleinikoff, M.
Blondie Knows Best (1946) Steinert
Blondie Meets the Boss (1939) Harline
Blondie of the Follies (1932) Axt
Blondie on a Budget (1940) Harline
Blondie Plays Cupid (1940) Harline
Blondie's Anniversary (1947) Smith, P.
Blondie's Big Moment (1947) Bakaleinikoff, M.
Blondie's Blessed Event (1942) Leipold
Blondie's Holiday (1947) Wheeler
Blood Alley (1955) Webb
Blood and Sand (1941) Newman
Blood and Steel (1959) Jackson, C.
Blood Arrow (1957) Kraushaar
Blood Bath (1966) Stein, R.
Blood Feast (1963) Lewis, Herschell
Blood Mania (1970) Vincent, D.
Blood Money (1933) Newman
Blood of Dracula (1957) Dunlap
Blood on the Arrow (1964) LaSalle
Blood on the Moon (1948) Webb
Blood on the Sun (1945) Rozsa
Bloodhounds of Broadway (1952) Harline
Bloody Mama (1970) Randi
Blossoms in the Dust (1941) Stothart
Blossoms on Broadway (1937) Leipold
Blotto (1930) Shilkret, N.
Blow-Out (1936) Spencer, N.
Blow the Man Down (1968) Herth
Blowing Wild (1953) Tiomkin
Blue (1968) Hadjidakis
Blue Angel (1959) Friedhofer
Blue Bird (1918) Riesenfeld
Blue Bird (1940) Newman
Blue Blood (1951) Caswell
Blue Cat Blues (1956) Bradley
Blue Dahlia (1946) Young, V.
Blue Danube (1939) Bradley
Blue Danube (1957) Jackson, H.
Blue Denim (1959) Herrmann
Blue Gardenia (1953) Kraushaar
Blue Grass Gentlemen (1944) De Francesco
Blue Grass of Kentucky (1950) Caswell

Blue Hawaii (1950) Sharples, Winston
Blue Hawaii (1960) Lilley
Blue Max (1966) Goldsmith
Blue Men of Morocco (1955) Wallace
Blue Monday (1938) Lewis
Blue Montana Skies (1939) Lava
Blue Moon (1920) Eames
Blue Nose Schooner (1944) Dunn
Blue Plate Symphony (1954) Scheib
Blue Skies (1946) Dolan
Blue Vanguard (1957) McPhee
Blue Veil (1951) Waxman
Blue, White and Perfect (1941) Mockridge
Bluebeard (1944) Erdody
Bluebeard's Brother (1932) Scheib
Bluebeard's Eighth Wife (1938) Hollander
Bluebirds' Baby (1938) De Nat
Blueprint for Murder (1953) Harline
Blueprint for Robbery (1960) Van Cleave
Blues (1931) Scheib
Blues Busters (1950) Kay, Edward
Blues in the Night (1941) Roemheld
Blues Pattern (1956) Rogers
Boat Builders (1938) Wallace
Boatniks (1970) Brunner
Boats A-Poppin' (1960) Sutton, H.
Bob & Carol & Ted & Alice (1969) Jones
Bob Hope Talks Texas (1964) Kilpatrick
Bob Mathias Story (1954) Stevens, L.
Bobby Ware Is Missing (1955) Brandt
Body and Soul (1931) Brunelli
Body and Soul (1947) Friedhofer
Body Building (1929) Rodemich
Body Disappears (1941) Jackson, H.
Body Snatcher (1945) Webb
Bodyguard (1944) Bradley
Bodyguard (1948) Sawtell
Boeing Boeing (1965) Hefti
Bohemian Girl (1936) Shilkret, N.
Bold and the Brave (1956) Gilbert, H.
Bold Caballero (1937) Hajos
Bold Frontiersman (1948) Glickman, M.
Bold King Cole (1936) Sharples, Winston
Bold New Approach (1966) Smith, H.
Bolero (1934) Rainger
Bolivia (1946) Forrell
Bolo-Mola Land (1939) Marsales
Bomb Voyage (1967) Greene, W.
Bomba and the Jungle Girl (1952) Kraushaar
Bomba on Panther Island (1949) Kay, Edward
Bomba, the Jungle Boy (1949) Kay, Edward
Bombalera (1945) Simeone
Bombardier (1943) Webb
Bombay Mail (1934) Roemheld
Bomber's Moon (1943) Buttolph, David
Bombers B-52 (1957) Rosenman
Bombs Over Burma (1942) Zahler
Bombshell (1933) Axt
Bon Voyage! (1962) Smith, P.
Bonanza Bunny (1959) Franklyn
Bon-Bon Parade (1935) De Nat
Bondage (1933) Kaylin
Bondman (1916) Steiner, M.
Bone Bandit (1947) Wallace
Bone for a Bone (1949) Stalling
Bone Ranger (1957) Scheib
Bone Sweet Bone (1947) Stalling
Bone Trouble (1940) Wallace
Bongo Punch (1957) Wheeler
Bonnie and Clyde (1967) Strouse
Bonnie Lassie (1944) Schrager
Bonnie Parker Story (1958) Stein, R.
Bonnie Scotland (1935) Hatley
Bonzo Goes to College (1952) Skinner, F.
Boo Bop (1957) Sharples, Winston
Boo Hoo Baby (1951) Sharples, Winston
Boo Kind to Animals (1955) Sharples, Winston
Boo Moon (1954) Sharples, Winston
Boo Ribbon Winner (1954) Sharples, Winston
Boo Scout (1951) Sharples, Winston
Boobs in the Woods (1948) Stalling
Booby Hatched (1944) Stalling
Booby Socks (1945) Kilfeather
Booby Traps (1944) Stalling
Boogie Man Will Get You (1942) Leipold
Boogie Woogie (1945) Schrager
Boogie Woogie Bugle Boy of Company B (1941) Calker
Boogie Woogie Man (1943) Calker
Boogie Woogie Sioux (1942) Calker
Book Revue (1945) Stalling
Bookworm (1939) Bradley
Bookworm Turns (1940) Bradley
Boom Boom (1936) Spencer, N.
Boom Town (1940) Waxman
Boomerang! (1947) Buttolph, David
Boos and Arrows (1954) Sharples, Winston
Boos and Saddles (1953) Sharples, Winston
Boos in the Night (1950) Sharples, Winston
Boot Hill Bandits (1942) Sanucci
Bootle Beetle (1947) Wallace
Boots Malone (1951) Bernstein, E.
Booze Hangs High (1930) Marsales
Bop Girl Goes Calypso (1957) Baxter
Bopin' Hood (1961) Sharples, Winston
Bora Bora (1970) Baxter
Border Badmen (1945) Sanucci
Border Bandits (1945) Sanucci
Border Buckaroos (1943) Zahler
Border Cafe (1937) Shilkret, N.
Border Feud (1947) Glasser
Border Flight (1936) Leipold
Border Incident (1949) Previn, A.
Border Legion (1930) Potoker
Border Legion (1940) Rosen, M.
Border Outlaws (1950) Calker
Border Patrol (1942) Sawtell
Border Patrolman (1936) Lessner

Border Rangers (1950) Glasser
Border River (1953) Mancini
Border Roundup (1943) Lange, J.
Border Saddlemates (1952) Wilson, S.
Border Treasure (1950) Sawtell
Border Vigilantes (1941) Leipold
Borderland (1937) Zahler
Borderline (1950) Salter
Bordertown (1934) Kaun
Bordertown Gun Fighters (1943) Glickman, M.
Bored Cuckoo (1948) Sharples, Winston
Bored of Education (1946) Sharples, Winston
Born Hunters (1963) Travis
Born Losers (1967) Curb
Born Reckless (1930) Brunelli
Born Reckless (1959) Bregman
Born to Be Bad (1934) Newman
Born to Be Bad (1950) Hollander
Born to Be Loved (1958) Steininger
Born to Be Wild (1938) Colombo
Born to Buck (1968) Stabile
Born to Kill (1947) Sawtell
Born to Love (1931) Gromon
Born to Peck (1952) Wheeler
Born to Peck (1962) Wheeler
Born to Sing (1942) Snell
Born to Ski (1954) Jackson, H.
Born to Speed (1947) Levin
Born Yesterday (1951) Hollander
Borneo (1937) Rochetti
Borrowed Trouble (1948) Calker
Borrowing in Subtraction (1947) Applebaum
Bosko and Bruno (1932) Marsales
Bosko and Honey (1932) Marsales
Bosko at the Beach (1932) Marsales
Bosko at the Zoo (1931) Marsales
Bosko in Dutch (1933) Marsales
Bosko in Person (1933) Marsales
Bosko Shipwrecked (1931) Marsales
Bosko the Doughboy (1931) Marsales
Bosko the Drawback (1933) Marsales
Bosko the Lumberjack (1932) Marsales
Bosko the Musketeer (1933) Marsales
Bosko the Sheepherder (1933) Marsales
Bosko the Speed King (1933) Marsales
Bosko's Dizzy Date (1933) Marsales
Bosko's Dog Race (1932) Marsales
Bosko's Easter Egg (1937) Bradley
Bosko's Fox Hunt (1931) Marsales
Bosko's Holiday (1931) Marsales
Bosko's Knight-Mare (1933) Marsales
Bosko's Mechanical Man (1933) Marsales
Bosko's Parlor Pranks (1934) Bradley
Bosko's Party (1931) Marsales
Bosko's Picture Show (1933) Marsales
Bosko's Soda Fountain (1931) Marsales
Bosko's Store (1932) Marsales
Bosko's Woodland Daze (1933) Marsales
Boss (1956) Glasser
Boss Is Always Right (1959) Sharples, Winston
Boss of Big Town (1942) Erdody
Boss of Rawhide (1943) Zahler
Boston Beanie (1947) Calker
Boston Blackie and the Law (1946) Sommer
Boston Quackie (1957) Franklyn
Boston Strangler (1968) Newman, L.
Botany Bay (1953) Waxman
Bottleman (1960) Ashley
Bottles (1936) Bradley
Bottom of the Bottle (1956) Harline
Bottoms Up (1934) Jackson, H.
Boudoir (1965) Manson
Boudoir Diplomat (1930) Roemheld
Boulder Dam (1936) Roemheld
Boulder Wham! (1965) Lava
Boulevardier from the Bronx (1936) Stalling
Bouncing Benny (1960) Sharples, Winston
Boundary Lines (1947) Forrell
Bountiful Alaska (1945) De Francesco
Bounty Hunter (1954) Buttolph, David
Bounty Killer (1965) Stein, R.
Bounty Without Boundaries (1963) Siegel, S.
Bout with a Trout (1947) Sharples, Winston
Bowery (1933) Newman
Bowery at Midnight (1942) Kay, Edward
Bowery Battalion (1951) Kay, Edward
Bowery Blitzkrieg (1941) Porter
Bowery Bombshell (1946) Kay, Edward
Bowery Boy (1940) Glickman, M.
Bowery Boys Meet the Monsters (1954) Skiles
Bowery Buckaroos (1947) Kay, Edward
Bowery Bugs (1948) Stalling
Bowery Champs (1944) Kay, Edward
Bowery Daze (1934) De Nat
Bowery to Bagdad (1954) Skiles
Bowery to Broadway (1944) Ward, E.
Bowl of Cherries (1960) Wernick
Bowling Alley-Cat (1942) Bradley
Bowling for Strikes (1940) De Francesco
Box (1967) Manne
Box Car Bandit (1956) Wheeler
Box Car Blues (1930) Marsales
Boy . . . a Girl (1969) Greene, J.
Boy, a Girl and a Dog (1946) Stahl
Boy, a Gun, and Birds (1939) De Nat
Boy and His Dog (1936) De Nat
Boy and His Dog (1947) Lava
Boy and His Prayer (1949) Colombo
Boy and the Eagle (1949) Shilkret, N.
Boy and the Pirates (1960) Glasser
Boy and the Wolf (1943) Bradley
Boy, Did I Get a Wrong Number! (1966) LaSalle
Boy from Indiana (1950) Moraweck
Boy from Oklahoma (1954) Steiner, M.
Boy from Stalingrad (1943) Stone
Boy in the Tree (1961) Jones
Boy Meets Girl (1938) Heindorf
Boy Named Charlie Brown (1969) Guaraldi

Boy on a Dolphin (1957) Friedhofer
Boy Scout Jamboree of 1953 (1953) Lava
Boy Slaves (1939) Tours
Boy Ten Feet Tall (1963) Baxter
Boy Trouble (1939) Bradshaw
Boy Who Caught a Crook (1961) LaSalle
Boy Who Saved a Nation (1937) Zahler
Boy Who Saw Through (1958) Ussachevsky
Boy Who Stopped Niagara (1947) Applebaum
Boy with Green Hair (1948) Harline
Boyhood Daze (1957) Franklyn
Boys from Syracuse (1940) Skinner, F.
Boys of the City (1940) Porter
Boys Town (1938) Ward, E.
Boys' Night Out (1962) De Vol
Boys' Ranch (1946) Shilkret, N.
Boys' Reformatory (1939) Kay, Edward
Brain from Planet Arous (1957) Greene, W.
Brain That Wouldn't Die (1962) Baker, Abe
Brainstorm (1965) Duning
Bramble Bush (1960) Rosenman
Branches (1970) Bordon
Brand of Fear (1949) Kay, Edward
Brand of Shame (1968) Allen, B.
Brand of the Devil (1944) Zahler
Brand X (1970) Lauber
Branded (1951) Webb
Branded Men (1931) Bibo
Brandeis (1967) Levin, S.
Branding Irons (1947) Zahler
Brasher Doubloon (1947) Buttolph, David
Brass (1967) Austin
Brass Bottle (1963) Green, B.
Brass Legend (1956) Dunlap
Bravados (1958) Newman
Brave Bulls (1951) Castelnuovo-Tedesco
Brave Little Bat (1941) Stalling
Brave Little Brave (1956) Scheib
Brave Little Tailor (1938) Malotte
Brave One (1956) Young, V.
Brave Tin Soldier (1934) Stalling
Bravest of the Brave (1938) Snell
Bravo, Mr. Strauss (1943) von Ottenfeld
Brazil (1944) Scharf, W.
Break of Hearts (1935) Steiner, M.
Break Up (1930) Shilkret, N.
Breakaway (1966) Cobb
Breakdown (1952) Dunlap
Breakfast at Tiffany's (1961) Mancini
Breakfast in Hollywood (1946) Leipold
Breaking Point (1950) Steiner, M.
Breaking Point (Trailer, 1950) Lava
Breaking the Ice (1938) Young, V.
Breakthrough (1950) Lava
Breathdeath (1964) Watt
Breezy Bear (1955) Wallace
Bremen Town Musicians (1935) Stalling
Brenda Starr, Reporter (1945) Kay, Edward
Brewster McCloud (1970) Page
Brewster's Millions (1945) Friedhofer
Bribe (1949) Rozsa
Bridal Suite (1939) Guttmann
Bride and Gloom (1954) Sharples, Winston
Bride and the Beast (1958) Baxter
Bride by Mistake (1944) Webb
Bride Came C.O.D. (1941) Steiner, M.
Bride Comes Home (1936) Roemheld
Bride for Sale (1949) Hollander
Bride Goes Wild (1948) Kopp, R.
Bride of Frankenstein (1935) Waxman
Bride of the Gorilla (1951) Kraushaar
Bride of the Monster (1956) Worth, F.
Bride of the Regiment (1930) Leonardi
Bride of Vengeance (1949) Friedhofer
Bride Wore Black (1968) Herrmann
Bride Wore Boots (1946) Hollander
Bride Wore Crutches (1941) Buttolph, David
Bride Wore Red (1937) Waxman
Brides Are Like That (1936) Roemheld
Bridge (196?) Markowitz
Bridge Ahoy! (1936) Timberg
Bridge at Remagen (1969) Bernstein, E.
Bridge Grows in Brooklyn (1967) Sharples, Winston
Bridge of San Luis Rey (1929) Brunelli
Bridge of San Luis Rey (1944) Tiomkin
Bridges at Toko-Ri (1955) Murray
Bridges-Go-Round (1958) Macero
Brief Interval (1943) Amfitheatrof
Brigadoon (1954) Salinger
Brigand (1952) Castelnuovo-Tedesco
Brigham Young (1940) Newman
Bright Eyes (1934) Buttolph, David
Bright Leaf (1950) Young, V.
Bright Lights (1935) Roemheld
Bright Road (1953) Rose
Bright Victory (1951) Skinner, F.
Brighton Strangler (1945) Harline
Brighty of the Grand Canyon (1966) Lavsky
Brimstone (1949) Scott, N.
Bring 'Em Back a Wife (1933) Shield
Bring 'Em Back Alive (1932) Rodemich
Bring Himself Back Alive (1940) Timberg
Bring On the Girls (1945) Dolan
Bring Your Smile Along (1955) Duning
Bringing Home the Bacon (1941) Scheib
Bringing Up Baby (1938) Webb
Bringing Up Father (1946) Kay, Edward
Bringing Up Mother (1954) Lees
Britannia's Athletic Cadets (1953) Mamorsky
British Agent (1934) Roemheld
British Factory Foreman (1952) Forrell
British Intelligence (1940) Kaun
British Mill Owner (1952) Forrell
Broad Minded (1931) Taylor, H.
Broadway (1942) Skinner, F.
Broadway Bad (1933) Lange
Broadway Bill (1934) Jackson, H.

Broadway Bow-Wows (1954) Wheeler
Broadway Gondolier (1935) Roemheld
Broadway Hostess (1935) Heindorf
Broadway Limited (1941) Hatley
Broadway Malady (1933) De Nat
Broadway Melody of 1936 (Trailer, 1935) Ward, E.
Broadway Melody of 1938 (1937) Cutter
Broadway Melody of 1940 (1940) Stoll
Broadway Musketeers (1938) Roemheld
Broadway Rhythm (1944) Green, J.
Broadway Serenade (1939) Stothart
Broadway Thru a Keyhole (1933) Newman
Broadway to Hollywood (1933) Axt
Broken Arrow (1950) Friedhofer
Broken Blossoms (1919) Gottschalk
Broken Doll (1931) Bussatt
Broken Lance (1954) Harline
Broken Land (1961) LaSalle
Broken Leghorn (1959) Franklyn
Broken Lullaby (1932) Harling
Broken Space (1952) Cambern
Broken Star (1956) Dunlap
Broken Toys (1936) Malotte
Broken Treaties (1941) Wheeler
Broken Wing (1932) Leipold
Bronco Buster (1935) Dietrich
Bronco Busters (1946) Applebaum
Bronze Buckaroo (1939) Porter
Brookhaven Spectrum (1967) Lewin
Brooklyn, I Love You (1946) Sharples, Winston
Brooklyn Orchid (1942) Ward, E.
Broom-Stick Bunny (1955) Franklyn
Brother Brat (1944) Stalling
Brother Cry for Me (1970) Mendoza-Nava
Brother from Outer Space (1964) Scheib
Brother Orchid (1940) Roemheld
Brother Rat (1938) Roemheld
Brother Rat and a Baby (1940) Roemheld
Brotherhood (1968) Schifrin
Brotherhood of Man (1947) Smith, P.
Brothers Carry-Mouse-Off (1966) Poddany
Brothers in the Saddle (1949) Sawtell
Brothers Karamazov (1957) Kaper
Brothers Rico (1957) Duning
Brought to Action! (1945) Creston
Brown Derby (1931) De Nat
Brushfire! (1962) Gertz
Brute Force (1947) Rozsa
Bubble (1966) Sawtell
Bubble Bee (1948) Wallace
Buccaneer (1938) Antheil
Buccaneer (1958) Bernstein, E.
Buccaneer Bunny (1948) Stalling
Buccaneer Woodpecker (1953) Wheeler
Buccaneer's Girl (1950) Scharf, W.
Buck Benny Rides Again (1940) Young, V.
Buck Privates (1941) Skinner, F.
Buck Privates Come Home (1947) Schumann
Buckaroo Bugs (1944) Stalling
Buckaroo Sheriff of Texas (1951) Wilson, S.
Bucket of Blood (1959) Katz, F.
Buckskin (1968) Haskell
Buckskin Frontier (1943) Young, V.
Buckskin Lady (1957) Glasser
Buddy and Towser (1934) Spencer, N.
Buddy in Africa (1935) Spencer, N.
Buddy of the Apes (1934) Spencer, N.
Buddy of the Legion (1935) Spencer, N.
Buddy Steps Out (1935) Spencer, N.
Buddy the Dentist (1935) Spencer, N.
Buddy the Detective (1934) Spencer, N.
Buddy the Gee Man (1935) Spencer, N.
Buddy the Gob (1934) Spencer, N.
Buddy the Woodsman (1934) Spencer, N.
Buddy's Adventures (1935) Spencer, N.
Buddy's Bearcats (1934) Spencer, N.
Buddy's Beer Garden (1934) Spencer, N.
Buddy's Bug Hunt (1935) Spencer, N.
Buddy's Circus (1934) Spencer, N.
Buddy's Day Out (1933) Spencer, N.
Buddy's Garage (1934) Spencer, N.
Buddy's Lost World (1936) Spencer, N.
Buddy's Pony Express (1935) Spencer, N.
Buddy's Show Boat (1934) Spencer, N.
Buddy's Theatre (1935) Spencer, N.
Buddy's Trolley Troubles (1934) Spencer, N.
Buffalo Bill (1944) Buttolph, David
Buffalo Bill in Tomahawk Territory (1952) Sanucci
Buffalo Bill Rides Again (1946) Altschuler
Buffalo Gun (1961) Idriss
Bug Carnival (1937) Scheib
Bug House (1930) De Nat
Bug Parade (1941) Stalling
Bugged by a Bee (1969) Lava
Bugged by a Bug (1967) Timmens
Bugle Sounds (1941) Hayton
Bugler of Battery B. (1912) Simon, W.
Bugles in the Afternoon (1951) Tiomkin
Bugs and Thugs (1953) Franklyn
Bugs Beetle and His Orchestra (1938) Scheib
Bugs' Bonnets (1955) Franklyn
Bugs Bunny and the Three Bears (1944) Stalling
Bugs Bunny Gets the Boid (1942) Stalling
Bugs Bunny Nips the Nips (1944) Stalling
Bugs Bunny Rides Again (1947) Stalling
Bugs in Love (1932) Churchill
Bugsy and Mugsy (1957) Stalling
Builders of a Nation (19??) Goberman
Building a Building (1932) Churchill
Building Is Many Buildings (1961) Cooper, B.
Building of a Tire (1946) Smith, P.
Built for Speed (1948) Jackson, H.
Bull-Ero (1932) Scheib
Bull Fight (1935) Scheib
Bull Fright (1955) Sharples, Winston
Bull Thrower (1931) De Nat
Bulldog and the Baby (1942) Worth, P.
Bulldog Courage (1936) Wallace

Bulldog Drummond (1929) Riesenfeld
Bulldog Drummond at Bay (1947) Leipold
Bulldog Drummond in Africa (1938) Roder
Bulldog Drummond Strikes Back (1934) Newman
Bulldog Drummond Strikes Back (1947) Gertz
Bulldog Drummond's Bride (1939) Leipold
Bulldozing the Bull (1951) Scheib
Bullet Code (1940) Sawtell
Bullet for Joey (1955) Sukman
Bullet for Pretty Boy (1970) Hatcher
Bullet Is Waiting (1954) Tiomkin
Bullet Scars (1942) Lava
Bullets and Ballads (1940) Rosen, M.
Bullets and Saddles (1943) Sanucci
Bullets for O'Hara (1941) Kaun
Bullets or Ballots (1936) Kaun
Bullfight (1955) Lloyd, N.
Bullfighter and the Lady (1951) Young, V.
Bullfighters (1945) Buttolph, David
Bullitt (1968) Schifrin
Bulloney (1933) Denni
Bullwhip (1958) Stevens, L.
Bully Beef (1930) Scheib
Bully for Bugs (1952) Stalling
Bully Frog (1936) Scheib
Bully Romance (1939) Scheib
Bum Steer (1957) Scheib
Bunco Busters (1955) Wheeler
Bunco Squad (1950) Sawtell
Bundle from Brazil (1948) Sharples, Winston
Bundle of Joy (1956) Scharf, W.
Bungalow 13 (1948) Kay, Edward
Bungled Bungalow (1950) Curtin
Bunker Hill Bunny (1949) Stalling
Bunnies and Bonnets (1933) De Nat
Bunny and Claude—We Rob Carrot Patches (1968) Lava
Bunny Hugged (1950) Stalling
Bunny Lake Is Missing (1965) Glass, Paul
Bunny-Mooning (1937) Timberg
Bunny Yeager's Nude Las Vegas (1964) Woode
Burden of the Mystery (1970) Laderman
Bureau of Missing Persons (1933) Kaun
Burglar (1957) Kaplan, S.
Buried Loot (1935) Axt
Buried Treasure (1938) Lewis
Burlesque (1932) Scheib
Burned at the Steak (1932) Vincent, P.
Burning Cross (1947) Kraushaar
Burning Hills (1956) Buttolph, David
Burning Sands (1922) Savino
Burning Up (1930) Lucas, G.
Burning Up Broadway (1928) Hoffman, M.
Bury Me Dead (1947) Cadkin
Bus (1965) Markowitz
Bus Riley's Back in Town (1965) Markowitz
Bus Stop (1956) Newman
Bus Way to Travel (1964) Sharples, Winston
Bushwhackers (1951) Glasser
Bushy Hare (1949) Stalling
Business and Pleasure (1931) Virgil
Business Is a Pleasure (1934) Kaun
Busman's Holiday (1961) Wheeler
Busses Roar (1942) Lava
Busted Blossoms (1934) Scheib
Buster Keaton Story (1957) Young, V.
Busy Bakers (1940) Stalling
Busy Barber (1932) Dietrich
Busy Beavers (1931) Churchill
Busy Bee (1936) Scheib
Busy Body (1967) Mizzy
Busy Buddies (1956) Bradley
Busy Buddies (1960) Sharples, Winston
Busy Bus (1934) De Nat
Busy Little Bears (1939) Steiner, G.
Busybody Bear (1953) Bradley
But Not for Me (1959) Stevens, L.
Butch Cassidy and the Sundance Kid (1969) Bacharach
Butch Minds the Baby (1942) Skinner, F.
Butcher Boy (1932) Dietrich
Butcher of Seville (1944) Scheib
BUtterfield 8 (1960) Kaper
Butterscotch and Soda (1948) Sharples, Winston
Buttons (1970) Levin, M.
Buy Me That Town (1941) Young, V.
Buzzy Boop (1938) Timberg
Bwana Devil (1953) Jenkins
By Candlelight (1933) Harling
By Leaps and Hounds (1951) Sharples, Winston
By Love Possessed (1961) Bernstein, E.
By the Light of the Silvery Moon (1953) Steiner, M.
By the Old Mill Scream (1953) Sharples, Winston
By the Sea (1931) Scheib
By the Sea (1963) Epstein
"By Their Works" (1948) Carbonara
By Word of Mouse (1954) Franklyn
By Your Command (1944) Carbonara
Bye Bye Birdie (1963) Green, J.
Bye, Bye, Bluebeard (1949) Stalling
Bye Bye Braverman (1968) Matz

C'mon, Let's Live a Little (1966) Ralke
C-Man (1949) Kubik
C. C. and Company (1970) Stack
C.W.A.C. News Clip (1943) Applebaum
Caballero Droopy (1952) Bradley
Cabin in the Cotton (1932) Warren
Cabin in the Sky (1943) Edens
Cabinet of Caligari (1962) Fried
Cabiria (1914) Breil
Cactus Capers (1942) Sharples, Winston
Cactus Flower (1969) Jones
Cactus King (1934) Sharples, Winston
Cad and Caddy (1947) Sharples, Winston
Caddy (1953) Lilley
Cadet Girl (1941) Buttolph, David
Cadets on Parade (1942) Leipold

Cafe Hostess (1939) Cutner
Café Metropole (1937) Buttolph, David
Cafe Society (1939) Shuken
Cage Fright (1952) Sharples, Winston
Cage of Evil (1960) Sawtell
Caged (1950) Steiner, M.
Caged Desires (1970) More
Caged Fury (1948) Lubin
Cagey Bird (1946) Kilfeather
Cagey Business (1965) Sharples, Winston
Cagey Canary (1941) Stalling
Cain and Mabel (1936) Roemheld
Cain's Way (1970) Hatcher
Caine Mutiny (1954) Steiner, M.
Cairo (1942) Stothart
Cairo, City of Contrast (1938) Shilkret, J.
Cajititlán (1965) Muczynski
Calaboose (1943) Ward, E.
Calamity Jane (1953) Buttolph, David
Calcutta (1947) Young, V.
Calendar Girl (1947) Scott, N.
Calgary Stampede (1949) Lava
Calico Dragon (1935) Bradley
California (1947) Young, V.
California (1963) LaSalle
California Firebrand (1948) Glickman, M.
California Gray Whale (1960) Emenegger
California Joe (1943) Glickman, M.
California Mail (1936) Jackson, H.
California Passage (1950) Scott, N.
California Thoroughbreds (1940) Jackson, H.
California, Here We Are (1944) Jackson, H.
Californian (1937) Riesenfeld
Californy er Bust! (1945) Smith, P.
Call a Cop! (1931) Shield
Call a Messenger (1939) Salter
Call for Volunteers (1941) Applebaum
Call Her Savage (1932) Lange
Call It a Day (1937) Roemheld
Call It Luck (1934) Kaylin
Call Me a Taxi (1964) Sharples, Winston
Call Me Madam (1953) Newman
Call Me Mister (1951) Harline
Call Me Skinny (1953) Craig, E.
Call Northside 777 (1948) Newman
Call of Canada (1941) De Francesco
Call of the Circus (1930) Nase
Call of the Flesh (1930) Axt
Call of the Forest (1949) Hajos
Call of the Jungle (1944) Glasser
Call of the Klondike (1950) Kay, Edward
Call of the Rockies (1931) Youngmeyer
Call of the South Seas (1944) Skiles
Call of the Wild (1935) Newman
Call of the Yukon (1938) Colombo
Call the Mesquiteers (1938) Colombo
Call the Priest (1952) Parisi
Callaway Went Thataway (1951) Skiles
Calling All Cuckoos (1956) Wheeler
Calling All Girls (1942) Jackson, H.
Calling All Husbands (1940) Jackson, H.
Calling All Kids (1943) Terr
Calling All Marines (1939) Feuer
Calling All Pa's (1942) Kaplan, S.
Calling Bulldog Drummond (1951) Kopp, R.
Calling Doctor Magoo (1956) Cutkomp
Calling Dr. Death (1943) Sawtell
Calling Dr. Gillespie (1942) Amfitheatrof
Calling Dr. Porky (1940) Stalling
Calling Dr. Woodpecker (1963) Wheeler
Calling Homicide (1956) Skiles
Calling on Cape Town (1952) Nussbaum
Calling on Colombia (1940) Bakaleinikoff, C.
Calling on Costa Rica (1947) Nussbaum
Calling on Michigan (1949) Nussbaum
Calling Philo Vance (1940) Roemheld
Calling Wild Bill Elliott (1943) Glickman, M.
Calm Yourself (1935) Maxwell
Calvary (1956) Martin, J.
Calypso Cruise (1954) Newman, L.
Calypso Heat Wave (1957) Morton
Calypso Joe (1957) Hazard
Camel Who Took a Walk (1958) Kleiner
Camelot (1967) Newman
Cameo Kirby (1929) Lipschultz
Camera Angles (1948) Jackson, H.
Camera Caught It (1954) Bradley
Camille (1912) Breil
Camille (1927) Axt
Camille (1936) Stothart
Camouflage (1942) Steinert
Camouflage (1943) Scheib
Camouflage Principles (1945) Lava
Camp Clobber (1958) Scheib
Camp Dog (1949) Smith, P.
Camping Out (1932) De Nat
Camping Out (1934) Churchill
Camptown Races (1948) Sharples, Winston
Campus Boom (1947) Shilkret, N.
Campus Capers (1949) Sharples, Winston
Campus Codes (1933) Zahler
Campus Confessions (1938) Leipold
Campus Heat (1969) Tosco
Campus Honeymoon (1948) Scott, N.
Campus International (1961) Childs
Campus Rhythm (1943) Kay, Edward
Campus Sleuth (1948) Kay, Edward
Can-Can (1960) Riddle
Can This Be Dixie? (1936) Kaylin
Can't Help Singing (1944) Salter
Canada Unlimited (1949) Shilkret, N.
Canadian Can-Can (1967) Greene, W.
Canadian Capers (1931) Scheib
Canadian Heritage (1949) Applebaum
Canadian Mounties (1953) Klein, J.
Canadian Pacific (1949) Tiomkin
Canadian Profile (1957) Applebaum
Canary Comes Across (1938) Snell

Canary Murder Case (1929) Hajos
Canary Road (1949) Stalling
Canasta de Cuentos Mexicanos (1956) Adomian
Candid Cameramaniacs (1937) Snell
Candid Candidate (1937) Timberg
Candidate (1964) Karmen
Candy (1968) Grusin
Candy Cabaret (1954) Sharples, Winston
Candy House (1934) Dietrich
Candy Man (1969) Kalajian
Candyland (1935) Dietrich
Cane and Able (1961) Sharples, Winston
Canine Caddy (1941) Smith, P.
Canine Capers (1937) De Nat
Canine Casanova (1945) Wallace
Canine Commandos (1943) Calker
Canine Crimebusters (1954) Agostini
Canine Patrol (1945) Wallace
Canned Dog Feud (1965) Wheeler
Canned Feud (1949) Stalling
Cannery Rodent (1967) Elliott, Dean
Cannery Woe (1960) Franklyn
Cannon for Cordoba (1970) Bernstein, E.
Canterville Ghost (1944) Bassman
Cantor's Son (1937) Olshanetsky
Canvas Back Duck (1953) Wallace
Canyon Ambush (1952) Kraushaar
Canyon City (1943) Glickman, M.
Canyon Crossroads (1955) Bassman
Canyon Passage (1946) Skinner, F.
Canyon Raiders (1951) Caswell
Canyon River (1956) Skiles
Canyons of the Sun (1945) De Francesco
Cap'n Cub (1945) DuPage
Cape Breton Island (1948) Nussbaum
Cape Canaveral Monsters (1960) Kauer
Cape Fear (1961) Herrmann
Cape Kidnaveral (1961) Sharples, Winston
Cape of Good Hope (1947) De Francesco
Caper of the Golden Bulls (1967) Mizzy
Capital City, Washington, D.C. (1940) Bakaleinikoff, C.
Capitol Story (1945) Brant
Caprice (1967) De Vol
Caps for Sale (1960) Kleiner
Captain America (1943) Glickman, M.
Captain Applejack (1931) Leonardi
Captain Blood (1935) Korngold
Captain Carey, U.S.A. (1950) Friedhofer
Captain Caution (1940) Ohman
Captain China (1950) Cailliet
Captain Eddie (1945) Mockridge
Captain from Castile (1947) Newman
Captain Fury (1939) Hatley
Captain Hareblower (1954) Stalling
Captain Is a Lady (1940) Kaper
Captain January (1936) Mockridge
Captain John Smith and Pocahontas (1953) Glasser
Captain Kidd (1945) Janssen
Captain Kidd and the Slave Girl (1954) Sawtell
Captain Kidd's Treasure (1938) Snell
Captain Lightfoot (1955) Stein, H.
Captain Midnight (1942) Zahler
Captain Newman, M.D. (1964) Skinner, F.
Captain of the Guard (1930) Roemheld
Captain Pirate (1952) Duning
Captain Scarface (1953) Klatzkin
Captain Scarlett (1953) Breeskin
Captain Sinbad (1963) Michelet
Captain Spanky's Show Boat (1939) Bakaleinikoff, C.
Captain Swagger (1928) Zuro
Captain Thunder (1930) Cugat
Captain Tugboat Annie (1945) Kay, Edward
Captain's Christmas (1938) Lewis
Captain's Kid (1936) Jackson, H.
Captain's Pup (1938) Lewis
Captains Courageous (1937) Waxman
Captains of the Clouds (1942) Steiner, M.
Captains Outrageous (1952) Bruns
Captive City (1952) Moross
Captive of Billy the Kid (1951) Wilson, S.
Captive Women (1952) Koff
Capture (1950) Amfitheatrof
Capture That Capsule! (1961) Hopkins, A.
Captured by Bedouins (1912) Simon, W.
Captured! (1933) Kaun
Car-azy Drivers (1955) Sharples, Winston
Car of Tomorrow (1951) Bradley
Car-Tune Portrait (1937) Timberg
Caravan (1934) Brunelli
Caravan Trail (1946) Hajos
Caravans of Trade (1947) De Francesco
Carbine Williams (1952) Salinger
Cardinal (1963) Moross
Cardinal Richelieu (1935) Newman
Career (1939) Webb
Career (1959) Waxman
Career for Two (1950) Stein, H.
Career Girl (1944) Schrager
Career: Medical Technologist (1954) Bernstein, E.
Careers (1929) Copping
Carefree (1938) Bennett, R. R.
Careful, Soft Shoulder (1942) Harline
Careless Age (1929) Leonardi
Careless Caretaker (1962) Calker
Careless Lady (1932) Friedhofer
Careless Years (1957) Stevens, L.
Caretakers (1963) Bernstein, E.
Cargo to Capetown (1950) Duning
Caribbean (1952) Cailliet
Caribbean Mystery (1945) Buttolph, David
Caribbean Playgrounds (1955) Lava
Caribbean Romance (1943) Heymann
Cariboo Trail (1950) Sawtell
Carioca Serenaders (1941) Jackson, H.
Carmen (1915) Riesenfeld

Carmen, Baby (1967) Hart
Carmen Jones (1954) Gilbert, H.
Carmen's Veranda (1944) Scheib
Carnival Boat (1932) Lange
Carnival Capers (1932) Dietrich
Carnival Courage (1945) Kilfeather
Carnival in Costa Rica (1947) Buttolph, David
Carnival in Paris (1937) Snell
Carnival in Rio (1955) Jackson, H.
Carnival of Souls (1962) Moore, G.
Carnival of Sports (1947) Dunn
Carnival Rock (1957) Greene, W.
Carolina (1934) Brunelli
Carolina Blues (1944) Duning
Carolina Cannonball (1955) Butts
Carousel (1956) Newman
Carpenters (1941) Wheeler
Carpetbaggers (1963) Bernstein, E.
Carrie (1952) Raksin
Carson City (1952) Buttolph, David
Carson City Cyclone (1943) Glickman, M.
Carson City Raiders (1948) Glickman, M.
Cartography (1948) Applebaum
Cartoonist's Nightmare (1936) Spencer, N.
Cartoons Ain't Human (1943) Timberg
Casa Mañana (1951) Kay, Edward
Casablanca (1943) Steiner, M.
Casanova Brown (1944) Lange
Casanova Cat (1950) Bradley
Casanova in Burlesque (1943) Scharf, W.
Casanova's Big Night (1954) Murray
Casbah (1948) Scharf, W.
Case Against Brooklyn (1958) Bakaleinikoff, M.
Case Against Mrs. Ames (1936) Carbonara
Case of Patty Smith (1962) Walters
Case of Sergeant Grischa (1930) Steiner, M.
Case of the Baby Sitter (1947) Calker
Case of the Black Cat (1936) Roemheld
Case of the Black Cat (Trailer, 1936) *Kaun*
Case of the Black Parrot (1941) Kaun
Case of the Cockeyed Canary (1952) Sharples, Winston
Case of the Curious Bride (1935) Kaun
Case of the Elephant's Trunk (1964) Greene, W.
Case of the Howling Dog (1934) Kaun
Case of the Lost Sheep (1935) Dietrich
Case of the Maltese Chicken (1964) Calker
Case of the Missing Hare (1942) Stalling
Case of the Stuttering Bishop (1937) Roemheld
Case of the Stuttering Bishop (Trailer, 1937) Kaun
Case of the Stuttering Pig (1937) Stalling
Case of the Velvet Claws (1936) Kaun
Casey Bats Again (1953) Wallace
Cash McCall (1960) Steiner, M.
Casino Murder Case (1935) Tiomkin
Casino Murder Case (Trailer, 1935) Ward, E.
Casino Royale (1967) Bacharach
Casper Comes to Clown (1951) Sharples, Winston
Casper Genie (1954) Sharples, Winston
Casper Takes a Bow-Wow (1951) Sharples, Winston
Casper's Birthday Party (1959) Sharples, Winston
Casper's Spree Under the Sea (1950) Sharples, Winston
Cass Timberlane (1947) Webb
Cassino to Korea (1950) Steiner, G.
Cast a Giant Shadow (1966) Bernstein, E.
Cast a Long Shadow (1959) Fried
Castaway (1931) Churchill
Casting Call (1970) Howard
Castle in the Desert (1942) Buttolph, David
Castle Keep (1969) Legrand
Castle of Evil (1966) Dunlap
Castle on the Hudson (1940) Deutsch
Cat (1966) Worth, S.
Cat Above and the Mouse Below (1964) Poddany
Cat Alarm (1960) Scheib
Cat, a Mouse, and a Bell (1935) De Nat
Cat and Dupli-cat (1967) Poddany
Cat and the Bell (1938) Marsales
Cat and the Canary (1927) Riesenfeld
Cat and the Canary (1939) Toch
Cat and the Fiddle (1934) Stothart
Cat and the Mermouse (1949) Bradley
Cat Ballou (1965) De Vol
Cat Burglar (1961) Bregman
Cat Came Back (1936) Spencer, N.
Cat Came Back (1944) Scheib
Cat Carson Rides Again (1952) Sharples, Winston
Cat-Choo (1951) Sharples, Winston
Cat Concerto (1947) Bradley
Cat Creeps (1930) Roemheld
Cat Creeps (1946) Sawtell
Cat Feud (1958) Franklyn
Cat Fishin' (1947) Bradley
Cat Happy (1950) Scheib
Cat in the Act (1957) Sharples, Winston
Cat Meets Mouse (1942) Scheib
Cat Nap Pluto (1947) Wallace
Cat Napping (1951) Bradley
Cat o' Nine Ails (1948) Sharples, Winston
Cat People (1943) Webb
Cat-Tails for Two (1953) Stalling
Cat Tamale (1951) Sharples, Winston
Cat-Tastrophy (1949) Calker
Cat That Hated People (1948) Bradley
Cat Trouble (1947) Scheib
Cat Women of the Moon (1953) Bernstein, E.
Cat's Bah (1953) Stalling
Cat's Me-Ouch (1964) Poddany
Cat's Meow (1957) Bradley
Cat's Nightmare (1931) Churchill
Cat's-Paw (1934) Newman
Cat's Paw (1958) Franklyn
Cat's Revenge (1954) Scheib
Cat's Tale (1941) Stalling
Cat's Tale (1951) Scheib
Catalina Caper (1967) Long, J.

Catalina Interlude (1948) Van Cleave
Catch as Catch Can (1931) Shield
Catch as Cats Can (1947) Stalling
Catered Affair (1956) Previn, A.
Catherine the Great (1934) Toch
Catman of Paris (1946) Butts
Catnip Capers (1940) Scheib
Catnip Gang (1949) Scheib
Catnipped (1932) Dietrich
Catnipped (1946) Kilfeather
Cats A-Weigh (1952) Stalling
Cats and Bruises (1965) Lava
Cats and Dogs (1932) Dietrich
Cats in a Bag (1936) Scheib
Catskill Honeymoon (1950) Olshanetsky
Catsup (1967) Bjom
Cattle Drive (1951) Rosen, M.
Cattle Empire (1958) Sawtell
Cattle King (1963) Sawtell
Cattle Queen (1950) Calker
Cattle Queen of Montana (1954) Forbes
Cattle Town (1952) Lava
Cattlemen's Days (1944) Jackson, H.
Catty Cornered (1952) Stalling
Catty-Cornered (1966) Brandt
Caught (1949) Hollander
Caught in the Draft (1941) Young, V.
Caught Plastered (1931) Schertzinger
Cause for Alarm (1951) Previn, A.
Caution, Danger Ahead (1952) Shilkret, N.
Cavalcade (1933) De Francesco
Cavalcade of Archery (1945) Dunn
Cavalcade of Egyptian Sports (1949) Lava
Cavalcade of San Francisco (1940) Bakaleinikoff, C.
Cavalier (1928) Riesenfeld
Cavalry Scout (1951) Skiles
Cave Man (1934) Stalling
Caveman Inki (1949) Stalling
Cease Fire! (1954) Tiomkin
Ceiling Hero (1940) Stalling
Ceiling Zero (1936) Kaun
Celebration Days (1947) Jackson, H.
Cell 2455, Death Row (1955) Bakaleinikoff, M.
Cellbound (1955) Bradley
Censored (1944) Stalling
Centennial Sports (1952) Lava
Centennial Summer (1946) Newman
Central Airport (1933) Kaun
Central Market (196?) Markowitz
Central Park (1932) Heindorf
Central Park (Trailer, 1932) Kaun
Certain Smile (1958) Newman
Cervantes (1968) Baxter
Chad Hanna (1940) Buttolph, David
Chafed Elbows (1967) O'Horgan
Chaim Soutine (1968) Bernstein, C.
Chain Gang (1930) Churchill
Chain Letters (1935) Scheib
Chain Lightning (1950) Buttolph, David
Chain of Evidence (1956) Skiles
Chained (1934) Stothart
Chained for Life (1951) Vars
Chairman (1969) Goldsmith
Challenge (1948) Rosen, M.
Challenge of Six Billion (1968) Kaplan, E.
Challenge—Science Against Cancer (1950) Applebaum
Challenge the Wild (1954) Skiles
Challenge to Lassie (1949) Previn, A.
Challenging Careers in Chemistry (1962) Kleinsinger
Chamber of Horrors (1966) Lava
Champ (1931) Scheib
Champ for a Day (1953) Butts
Champ of Champions (1943) Shilkret, J.
Champagne for Caesar (1950) Tiomkin
Champagne for Two (1947) Van Cleave
Champagne Waltz (1937) Boutelje
Champion (1949) Tiomkin
Champion of Justice (1944) Scheib
Champions Carry On (1943) De Francesco
Champions of the Future (1944) Jackson, H.
Champions of Tomorrow (1950) Lava
Champions Training Champions (1943) Lava
Chance to Be Somebody (196?) Duffy
Chances (1931) Mendoza
Chandu, the Magician (1932) Brunelli
Chang (1927) Riesenfeld
Change for the Better (1966) Clements
Change of Habit (1969) Goldenberg
Change of Heart (1934) De Francesco
Change of Mind (1969) Ellington
Changed Identity (1941) Hayton
Changes (1970) Baker, Alan
Changing Image (196?) Duffy
Changing of the Guard (1936) Roemheld
Chansons Populaire (1944) Applebaum
Chaplin's Art of Comedy (1966) Breeskin
Chapman Report (1962) Rosenman
Chappaqua (1966) Shankar
Charade (1963) Mancini
Charge at Feather River (1953) Steiner, M.
Charge of the Lancers (1953) Morton
Charge of the Light Brigade (1936) Steiner, M.
Charity? (1916) Hein
Charles Burchfield: Fifty Years of His Art (1966) Muczynski
Charley's Aunt (1930) Lapham
Charley's Aunt (1941) Mockridge
Charlie Chan at the Opera (1936) Maxwell
Charlie Chan at the Wax Museum (1940) Mockridge
Charlie Chan at Treasure Island (1939) Kaylin
Charlie Chan Carries On (1931) Kaylin
Charlie Chan in Honolulu (1939) Kaylin
Charlie Chan in Panama (1940) Kaylin
Charlie Chan in Paris (1935) Kaylin

Charlie Chan in Rio (1941) Mockridge
Charlie Chan in the Secret Service (1944) Hajos
Charlie Chan's Courage (1934) Buttolph, David
Charlie Cuckoo (1939) Marsales
Charlie McCarthy and Mortimer Snerd in Sweden (1950) Jackson, H.
Charlie McCarthy, Detective (1939) Skinner, F.
Charlie, the Lonesome Cougar (1967) Marks
Charlie's Mother-in-Law (1963) Calkera
Charly (1968) Shankar
Charm Bracelet (1939) De Nat
Charming Sinners (1929) Hajos
Charro (1969) Montenegro
Charter (1960) Laderman
Chartroose Caboose (1960) Calker
Chase (1946) Michelet
Chase Me, Charlie (1948) Breeskin
Chaser (1938) Ward, E.
Chaser on the Rocks (1965) Lava
Chasing Rainbows (1930) Axt
Chasing Rainbows (1947) Shilkret, N.
Chasing the Sun (1956) Jackson, H.
Chasing Through Europe (1929) Kay, Arthur
Chasing Trouble (1940) Kay, Edward
Chasing Yesterday (1935) Colombo
Chastity (1969) Bono
Chata (1947) Tullis
Chatterbox (1943) Scharf, W.
Che! (1969) Schifrin
Cheaper by the Dozen (1950) Mockridge
Cheaters (1945) Scharf, W.
Cheating Blondes (1933) Zahler
Cheating Cheaters (1934) Ward, E.
Check Your Guns (1948) Greene, W.
Checkered Coat (1948) Kay, Edward
Checkered Flag (1926) Hoffman, M.
Checkered Flag (1963) Simms
Cheechako—Tale of Alaska (1953) Shores
Cheers for Miss Bishop (1941) Ward, E.
Cheese Burglar (1946) Sharples, Winston
Cheese Chasers (1950) Stalling
Cheese It, the Cat! (1957) Stalling
Cheese-Nappers (1938) Churchill
Chef Donald (1941) Wolcott
Chelsea Through the Magnifying Glass (1938) Bowles
Cherokee Strip (1937) Jackson, H.
Cherokee Strip (1940) Leipold
Cherokee Uprising (1950) Kay, Edward
Cherry Blossom Time in Japan (1936) Grever
Cherry, Harry & Raquel (1969) Loose
Chesapeake Bay Retriever (1936) Blitzstein
Chetniks! (1943) Friedhofer
Chew-Chew Baby (1945) Calker
Chew Chew Baby (1958) Sharples, Winston
Chewin' Bruin (1940) Stalling
Cheyenne (1947) Steiner, M.
Cheyenne Autumn (1965) North
Cheyenne Days (1953) Lava
Cheyenne Kid (1933) Steiner, M.
Cheyenne Kid (1940) Lange, J.
Cheyenne Social Club (1970) Scharf, W.
Cheyenne Takes Over (1947) Greene, W.
Chicago (1927) Copping
Chicago Calling (1952) Roemheld
Chicago Deadline (1949) Young, V.
Chicago, the Beautiful (1948) Nussbaum
Chick and Double Chick (1946) Sharples, Winston
Chick Carter, Detective (1946) Zahler
Chicken a la King (1937) Timberg
Chicken Every Sunday (1949) Newman
Chicken in the Rough (1950) Dubin
Chicken Jitters (1939) Stalling
Chicken Little (1943) Wallace
Chicken Reel (1933) Dietrich
Chicken-Wagon Family (1939) Kaylin
Chief Charlie Horse (1956) Wheeler
Chief Crazy Horse (1955) Skinner, F.
Child Is Born (1939) Roemheld
Child Is Waiting (1962) Gold
Child of Divorce (1946) Harline
Child Psykolojiky (1941) Timberg
Child Sockology (1953) Sharples, Winston
Child Went Forth (1941) Eisler
Childish Things (1969) Greene, J.
Children Must Learn (1940) Stewart, F.
Children of Dreams (1931) Mendoza
Children of Israel (1967) Gould, S.
Children of Russia (1946) Forrell
Children of the Ritz (1929) Shilkret, N.
Children of the World (196?) Duffy
Children Without (1964) Wykes
Children's Hour (1961) North
Children's Letters to God (1969) Kleinsinger
Children's Village (1948) Shilkret, N.
Chile, Land of Charm (1937) Shilkret, J.
Chili Corn Corny (1965) Lava
Chili Weather (1963) Lava
Chiller Dillers (1968) Greene, W.
Chilly and the Woodchopper (1967) Greene, W.
Chilly Chums (1967) Greene, W.
Chilly Willy in The Legend of Rockabye Point (1955) Wheeler
Chimp & Zee (1968) Lava
China (1931) Dietrich
China (1931) Scheib
China (1943) Young, V.
China Carries On (1945) De Francesco
China Clipper (1936) Kaun
China Doll (1958) Vars
China Gate (1957) Steiner, M.
China Girl (1942) Friedhofer
China Jones (1958) Franklyn
China Plate (1931) Churchill
China Seas (1935) Stothart
China Seas (Trailer, 1935) Ward, E.
China Shop (1933) Harline
China Sky (1945) Harline

China Strikes Back (1937) North
China's Little Devils (1945) Tiomkin
China's Old Man River (1930) Axt
Chinaman's Chance (1933) Denni
Chinatown After Dark (1931) Zahler
Chinatown Champs (1944) Jackson, H.
Chinatown Mystery (1932) De Nat
Chinatown Nights (1929) Hajos
Chinese Cat (1944) Laszlo
Chinese Checkers (1963) Geesin
Chinese Dressmaking (1959) Kupferman
Chinese Firecrackers (1959) Kupferman
Chinese Nightingale (1935) Bradley
Chinese Ring (1947) Kay, Edward
Chinese Training Pilot (1942) Hayton
Chinese Village (1958) Smith, A.L.
Chip 'n' Dale (1947) Wallace
Chip Off the Old Block (1944) Russell, L.
Chips Ahoy (1955) Wallace
Chips Off the Old Block (1942) Bradley
Chisum (1970) Frontiere
Chitty Chitty Bang Bang (1968) Kostal
Chloe (1934) Henninger
Chocolate Soldier (1941) Stothart
Cholly Polly (1942) Worth, P.
Choo-Choo Amigo (1945) Smith, P.
Choose Your Weppins (1935) Steiner, G.
Choosing Canines (1953) Mamorsky
Chop Suey (1930) Scheib
Choppers (1961) Pellegrini
Chosen Prince (1917) Weinstock
Chow Hound (1944) Stalling
Chow Hound (1950) Stalling
Chris Columbo (1938) Scheib
Chris Columbus, Jr. (1934) Dietrich
Christine Jorgensen Story (1970) Sawtell
Christmas Carol (1938) Waxman
Christmas Comes But Once a Year (1936) Timberg
Christmas Eve (1947) Roemheld
Christmas Holiday (1944) Salter
Christmas in Australia (1945) Terr
Christmas in Connecticut (1945) Hollander
Christmas in July (1940) Shuken
Christopher Bean (1933) Stothart
Christopher Crumpet (1953) Bruns
Christopher Crumpet's Playmate (1955) Farnon
Christopher Strong (1933) Steiner, M.
Chubasco (1968) Lava
Chucky Lou—The Story of a Woodchuck (1948) Frye
Chuka (1967) Stevens, L.
Chuka (Trailer, 1967) Van Cleave
Chumlum (1964) MacLise
Chump at Oxford (1940) Hatley
Chump Champ (1950) Bradley
Churchill's Island (1941) Agostini
Ciao (1967) Summerlin
Cigarette Girl (1947) Gertz
Cilly Goose (1944) Sharples, Winston
Cimarron (1930) Steiner, M.
Cimarron (1960) Waxman
Cincinnati Kid (1965) Schifrin
Cinder Alley (1934) De Nat
Cinderella (1930) De Nat
Cinderella (1933) Scheib
Cinderella (1949) Wallace
Cinderella (1966) Delugg
Cinderella Goes to a Party (1942) Worth, P.
Cinderella Horse (1949) Jackson, H.
Cinderella Jones (1946) Hollander
Cinderella Meets Fella (1938) Stalling
Cinderella Swings It (1943) Sawtell
Cinderella's Feller (1940) Jackson, H.
Cinderfella (1960) Scharf, W.
Cindy and Donna (1970) Ragland
CinemaScope Parade (1954) Newman
Cinerama Holiday (1955) Gould, M.
Circle of Fire (1940) Ussachevsky
Circumstantial Evidence (1945) Buttolph, David
Circus (1959) Clark, R.
Circus Baby (1956) Kleiner
Circus Clown (1934) Roemheld
Circus Comes to Clown (1947) Sharples, Winston
Circus Days (1935) Scheib
Circus Daze (1937) Bradley
Circus Girl (1937) Hajos
Circus Horse (1947) Jackson, H.
Circus Kid (1928) Zuro
Circus Memories (1963) Breske
Circus on Ice (1954) Agostini
Circus Time (1931) De Nat
Circus Today (1940) Stalling
Circus Town (1948) Lava
Circus Wakes Up (1949) Mamorsky
Circus World (1964) Tiomkin
Cisco Kid and the Lady (1939) Kaylin
Cisco Kid in Old New Mexico (1945) Glasser
Cisco Kid Returns (1945) Glasser
Citadel of Crime (1941) Feuer
Citizen Kane (1941) Herrmann
City (1939) Copland
City Across the River (1949) Scharf, W.
City Beneath the Sea (1953) Stein, H.
City for Conquest (1940) Steiner, M.
City Girl (1930) Kay, Arthur
City Kitty (1952) Sharples, Winston
City Lights (1931) Chaplin, C.
City Limits (1934) Wallace
City of Bad Men (1953) Mockridge
City of Beautiful Girls (1950) Sharples, Winston
City of Chance (1940) Kaylin
City of Children (1949) Kopp, R.
City of Fear (1959) Goldsmith
City of Little Men (1938) Ward, E.
City of Missing Girls (1941) Hatley
City of Paradox (1944) De Francesco
City of Shadows (1955) Butts
City of Silent Men (1942) Erdody

City of Tanguy (1965) Keane
City Pastorale (1946) North
City Slicker (1938) De Nat
City Slicker (1951) Scheib
City Story (1954) Forbes
City Streets (1931) Hajos
City Streets (1938) Cutner
City That Never Sleeps (1953) Butts
City Week End (1947) De Francesco
City Without Jews (1928) Kurtz
City Without Men (1943) Raksin
Civilization (1916) Schertzinger
Clambake (1967) Alexander, J.
Clancy Street Boys (1943) Kay, Edward
Clarence, the Cross-Eyed Lion (1965) Armbruster
Clash by Night (1952) Webb
Claudelle Inglish (1961) Jackson, H.
Claudia (1943) Newman
Claudia and David (1946) Mockridge
Claws for Alarm (1953) Stalling
Claws in the Lease (1963) Lava
Clay (1964) Saltonstall
Clay Pigeon (1949) Sawtell
Clean Pastures (1937) Stalling
Clean Sweep (1967) Sharples, Winston
Clean Waters (1945) Carbonara
Cleaning House (1938) Lewis
Clear All Wires (1933) Axt
Clear Iron (1952) Craig, E.
Clearing the Way (1948) Rathaus
Cleopatra (1934) Kopp, R.
Cleopatra (1963) North
Cleopatra's Playground (1951) Shilkret, N.
Cliff Dwellers (1962) Manson
Climate of New York (1948) Flanagan
Climax (1944) Ward, E.
Climbing the Peaks (1943) De Francesco
Clinic of Stumble (1947) Tucker
Clint Clobber's Cat (1957) Scheib
Clipped Wings (1938) Kilenyi
Clipped Wings (1953) Skiles
Clippety Clobbered (1966) Lava
Clive of India (1935) Newman
Cloak and Dagger (1946) Steiner, M.
Cloak and Stagger (1956) Scheib
Clobber's Ballet Ache (1959) Scheib
Clock (1945) Bassman
Clock Cleaners (1937) Smith, P.
Clock Goes Round and Round (1937) De Nat
Clock Watcher (1944) Wallace
Clockmaker's Dog (1955) Scheib
Close Call for Ellery Queen (1942) Zahler
Close Harmony (1929) Leipold
Close Shave (1937) Scheib
Close to My Heart (1951) Steiner, M.
Close-Up (1948) Moross
Clown (1931) Dietrich
Clown (1952) Rose
Clown and the Kid (1962) LaSalle
Clown of the Jungle (1946) Wallace
Clown on the Farm (1952) Sharples, Winston
Clowning (1931) Scheib
Clowns Never Laugh: The Work of Walt Kuhn (1967) Muczynski
Club Havana (1945) Jackson, H.
Club Life in the Stone Age (1940) Scheib
Club Sandwich (1931) Scheib
Clues to Adventure (1949) Kopp, R.
Cluny Brown (1946) Mockridge
Clutching Hand (1936) Zahler
Coal Black and de Sebben Dwarfs (1943) Franklyn
Coal Face, Canada (1943) Applebaum
Coal Gas (1946) Applebaum
Coast Guard (1939) Parrish
Cobbs and Robbers (1953) Bradley
Cobra Strikes (1948) Glasser
Cobra Woman (1943) Ward, E.
Cobweb (1955) Rosenman
Cobweb Hotel (1936) Timberg
Cock-a-Doodle Dino (1957) Sharples, Winston
Cock-a-Doodle Dog (1950) Bradley
Cockatoos for Two (1947) Kilfeather
Cockeyed Cavaliers (1934) Webb
Cockeyed Cowboys of Calico County (1970) Murray
Cockeyed Miracle (1946) Snell
Cock-Eyed News (1930) Leipold
Cock o' the Walk (1935) Malotte
Cock of the Air (1932) Newman
Cocktail Hour (1933) Schertzinger
Cocky Bantam (1943) Kilfeather
Cocky Cockroach (1932) Scheib
Cocoanut Grove (1938) Leipold
Cocoanuts (1929) Tours
Code of Silence (1960) Pierce, Alex
Code of the Cactus (1939) Lange, J.
Code of the Fearless (1939) Lange, J.
Code of the Outlaw (1942) Feuer
Code of the Prairie (1944) Dubin
Code of the Saddle (1947) Kay, Edward
Code of the Secret Service (1939) Kaun
Code of the Silver Sage (1950) Wilson, S.
Code of the Streets (1939) Skinner, F.
Code of the West (1947) Sawtell
Code Two (1953) Colombo
Codfish Balls (1930) Scheib
Coffins on Wheels (1941) Amfitheatrof
Cohens and Kellys in Africa (1930) Roemheld
Cohens and the Kellys in Scotland (1930) Roemheld
Cold Romance (1949) Scheib
Cold Storage (1950) Dubin
Cold Turkey (1951) Smith, P.
Cold War (1950) Dubin
Cold Wind in August (1961) Fried
Cole Younger, Gunfighter (1958) Skiles
Collector (1965) Jarre
Colleen (1936) Roemheld

College (1931) Dietrich
College (1963) Katz, F.
College Capers (1953) Shefter
College Climbers (1947) Shilkret, N.
College Coach (1933) Kaun
College Confidential (1960) Elliott, Dean
College Days (1926) Burton
College Holiday (1936) Skiles
College Humor (1933) Leipold
College Love (1929) Zahler
College Queen (1946) Van Cleave
College Rhythm (1934) Satterfield
College Scandal (1935) Hollander
College Spirit (1932) Scheib
College Swing (1938) Jenkins
Colleges at War (1942) Kubik
Collegiate (1936) Hollander
Colonel Effingham's Raid (1945) Mockridge
Colonial Naturalist (1965) Kaplan, S.
Colonial Printer (1952) Price, Herman
Color and Light No. 1 (1950) Muller
Color and Texture in Aluminum Finishes (1957) Lewin
Color Lithography, an Art Medium (1955) Kent
Color Study (1969) Austin
Colorado Ambush (1951) Kay, Edward
Colorado Ranger (1950) Greene, W.
Colorado Serenade (1946) Hajos
Colorado Sundown (1952) Butts
Colorado Territory (1949) Buttolph, David
Colorado Trout (1944) Jackson, H.
Colorful Caracao (1939) Bakaleinikoff, C.
Colorful Colorado (1944) Nussbaum
Colorful Holland (1950) Nussbaum
Colorful Islands—Madagascar and Seychelles (1936) Shilkret, J.
Colorful North Carolina (1941) Nussbaum
Colossus of New York (1958) Van Cleave
Colourful Cairo (1936) White, L.
Colt .45 (1950) Lava
Colt Comrades (1943) Sawtell
Column South (1953) Stein, H.
Comanche (1956) Gilbert, H.
Comanche Station (1960) Bakaleinikoff, M.
Comanche Territory (1950) Skinner, F.
Comancheros (1961) Bernstein, E.
Combat (1941) Wheeler
Combat America (1944) Stothart
Combat Fatigue (1946) Dessau
Combat Patrol (1944) Lava
Combat Squad (1953) Dunlap
Come and Get It (1936) Newman
Come Back, Little Sheba (1953) Waxman
Come Back to Erin (1968) Kirk
Come Blow Your Horn (1963) Riddle
Come Blow Your Horn (Trailer, 1963) Van Cleave
Come Clean (1931) Shield
Come Fill the Cup (1951) Heindorf
Come Fill the Cup (Trailer, 1951) Lava
Come Fly With Me (1963) Murray
Come In, Jupiter (1955) von Haden
Come Live with Me (1941) Stothart
Come Next Spring (1955) Steiner, M.
Come On (1956) Dunlap
Come On Marines! (1934) Rainger
Come On, Rangers (1938) Lava
Come One, Come All! (1970) Kenzie
Come Out Fighting (1945) Kay, Edward
Come Ride the Wild Pink Horse (1967) Marini
Come September (1961) Salter
Come Spy with Me (1966) Bowers, R. C.
Come to the Stable (1949) Mockridge
Come with Me My Brother (1962) Schmidt, K.
Comedians (1967) Rosenthal
Comedy of Terrors (1964) Baxter
Comedy Tale of Fanny Hill (1963) Collette
Comet Over Broadway (1938) Roemheld
Comic (1969) Elliott, J.
Comic Book Land (1949) Scheib
Comin' Round the Mountain (1949) Sharples, Winston
Coming Attractions (1970) Conrad
Coming Out Party (1934) Friedhofer
Coming Out Party (1962) Greene, W.
Coming Snafu (1943) Stalling
Command (1954) Tiomkin
Command Decision (1949) Rozsa
Commando Cody (1953) Wilson, S.
Commando Duck (1944) Wallace
Commandos Strike at Dawn (1943) Gruenberg
Common Clay (1930) Kay, Arthur
Common Law (1931) Lange
Communications (1947) De Francesco
Communications Primer (1953) Bernstein, E.
Commuting for Adventure (1964) Gross
Company of Killers (1970) Hazard
Company She Keeps (1950) Harline
Compressed Hare (1961) Franklyn
Compromised (1931) Mendoza
Compulsion (1959) Newman, L.
Computer Age (1968) Barron
Computer Day at Midvale (1965) Bernstein, E.
Computer Glossary (1967) Bernstein, E.
Computer Wore Tennis Shoes (1969) Brunner
Comrade X (1940) Kaper
Concealment of Vehicles (1943) Lava
Concept of Intensive Coronary Care (1969) Robinson, E.
Concert Kid (1934) De Nat
Concerto in B Flat Minor (1942) Kilfeather
Condemned (1929) Riesenfeld
Coney Island (1943) Mockridge
Coney Island Holiday (1954) Jackson, H.
Coney Island Honeymoon (1944) Jackson, H.
Coney Island, U.S.A. (1950) North
Confederate Honey (1940) Stalling
Confederate Ironclad (1912) Simon, W.
Confession (1937) Roemheld

Confessions of a Co-ed (1931) Leipold
Confessions of a Nazi Spy (1939) Steiner, M.
Confessions of a Nazi Spy (Trailer, 1939) Deutsch
Confessions of a Wild Pair (1961) Deline
Confessions of an Opium Eater (1962) Glasser
Confidence (1933) Dietrich
Confidence Girl (1952) Cailliet
Confidential Agent (1945) Waxman
Confidentially Connie (1953) Rose
Confirm or Deny (1941) Buttolph, David
Conflict (1936) Jackson, H.
Conflict (1945) Hollander
Confrontation (1968) Laderman
Confusions of a Nutzy Spy (1943) Stalling
Congo (1944) Bowles
Congo (1945) Jackson, H.
Congo Crossing (1956) Mancini
Congo Jazz (1930) Marsales
Congo Maisie (1940) Ward, E.
Congolaise (1950) Segáll
Connecticut Yankee (1931) Kay, Arthur
Connecticut Yankee at King Arthur's Court (1920) Rapée
Connecticut Yankee in King Arthur's Court (1949) Young, V.
Connecticut Yankee in King Arthur's Court (Trailer, 1949) Lilley
Connection (1962) Redd
Conquer by the Clock (1942) Webb
Conquering Horde (1931) Leipold
Conqueror (1916) Schertzinger
Conqueror (1955) Young, V.
Conquerors (1932) Steiner, M.
Conquest (1937) Stothart
Conquest of Space (1955) Van Cleave
Conquest of Ungava (1953) Gardner
Conrad in Quest of His Youth (1920) Riesenfeld
Conrad, the Sailor (1942) Stalling
Conservation Road (1947) De Francesco
Consolation Marriage (1931) Steiner, M.
Conspiracy (1930) Webb
Conspiracy (1939) Tours
Conspiracy in Kyoto (1953) Heiden
Conspirators (1944) Steiner, M.
Constable (1940) Timberg
Constant Nymph (1943) Korngold
Contender (1944) Glasser
Continental Holiday (1955) Lava
Contra la Corriente (1935) Aguilar
Contrary Condor (1944) Smith, P.
Control of Filariasis in Tahiti (1950) Lund
Convention City (Trailer, 1933) Kaun
Convict Concerto (1954) Wheeler
Convict Stage (1965) LaSalle
Convicted (1950) Duning
Convicts 4 (1962) Rosenman
Coo Coo Bird (1947) Calker
Coo-Coo Bird Dog (1949) Calker
Coo-Coo, the Magician (1933) Stalling
Coocoonut Grove (1936) Stalling
Coogan's Bluff (1968) Schifrin
Cookie Carnival (1935) Harline
Cookin' with Gags (1955) Sharples, Winston
Cool and Groovy (1956) Mancini
Cool and the Crazy (1958) Kraushaar
Cool Cat (1967) Lava
Cool Cat Blues (1960) Sharples, Winston
Cool Hand Luke (1967) Schifrin
Cool Ones (1967) Freeman, E.
Cool Wind (1964) Kupferman
Cool World (1964) Waldron
Cooper's Craft (1967) Bennett, N.
Cop Hater (1957) Glasser
Copacabana (1947) Ward, E.
Copenhagen (1937) Shilkret, J.
Copenhagen Crusade (1965) Carmichael
Copenhagen Pageantry (1947) De Francesco
Copper (1965) Abramson
Copper Canyon (1950) Amfitheatrof
Copper Sky (1957) Kraushaar
Copper, the Oldest Modern Metal (1962) Merriman
Cops Is Tops (1955) Sharples, Winston
Copters and Cows (1956) Jackson, H.
Copy Cat (1941) Timberg
Coquette (1929) Riesenfeld
Corbit-Sharp House (1965) Bazelon
Corn Chips (1950) Wallace
Corn Is Green (1945) Steiner, M.
Corn on the Cop (1965) Lava
Corn Plastered (1950) Stalling
Corn's Hidden Enemies (196?) Forrell
Corner (1915) Beynon
Cornered (1945) Webb
Corny Concerto (1943) Stalling
Coronado (1935) Satterfield
Coronation (1965) Coulter
Coroner Creek (1948) Schrager
Corpse Came C.O.D. (1947) Duning
Corpse Vanishes (1942) Lange, J.
Corregidor (1943) Erdody
Corridor (1970) Riley
Corsair (1931) Newman
Corsican Brothers (1941) Tiomkin
Corvette K-225 (1943) Buttolph, David
Cosmic Man (1959) Sawtell
Cosmo Jones in Crime Smasher (1943) Kay, Edward
Cossacks (1930) Axt
Cotton Comes to Harlem (1970) MacDermot
Cottonpickin' Chickenpickers (1967) Kauer
Couch (1961) Perkins
Cougar Country (1970) Loose
Count Down Under (1964) Epstein
Count Me Out (1938) Stalling
Count of Monte Cristo (1934) Newman
Count the Hours (1953) Forbes
Count Three and Pray (1955) Duning
Count Yorga, Vampire (1970) Marx, W.

Count Your Blessings (1959) Waxman
Countdown (1968) Rosenman
Counter-Attack (1945) Gruenberg
Counter Attack (1960) Sharples, Winston
Counterfeit (1936) Jackson, H.
Counterfeit Cat (1949) Bradley
Counterfeit Killer (1968) Jones
Counterfeit Traitor (1961) Newman
Counterfeiters (1948) Gertz
Counterplot (1959) Sawtell
Counterpoint (1968) Kaper
Countess of Monte Cristo (1934) Ward, E.
Countess of Monte Cristo (1948) Scharf, W.
Country Beyond (1936) Bassett, R. H.
Country Boy (1935) Spencer, N.
Country Cousin (1936) Harline
Country Coyote Goes Hollywood (1964) Bruns
Country Doctor (1936) Mockridge
Country Fair (1941) Glickman, M.
Country Girl (1954) Young, V.
Country Mouse (1935) Spencer, N.
Country School (1931) Dietrich
Country Store (1937) Dietrich
County Fair (1934) Dietrich
County Fair (1950) Caswell
County Hospital (1932) Shield
Courage of Black Beauty (1957) Alperson
Courage of Lassie (1946) Bradley
Courageous Australia (1942) De Francesco
Courageous Dr. Christian (1940) Lava
Court Jester (1956) Schoen
Court-Martial of Billy Mitchell (1955) Tiomkin
Courtin' Trouble (1948) Kay, Edward
Courtneys of Curzon Street (1947) Collins
Courtship of Andy Hardy (1942) Snell
Courtship of Eddie's Father (1962) Stoll
Courtship to Courthouse (1946) Shilkret, N.
Covenant (1965) Oliveros
Covenant with Death (1967) Rosenman
Cover Girl (1944) Dragon
Cover Me Babe (1969) Karlin
Cover-Up (1949) Salter
Covered Pushcart (1949) Scheib
Covered Trailer (1939) Lava
Covered Wagon (1923) Riesenfeld
Covered Wagon Days (1940) Sawtell
Covered Wagon Raid (1950) Wilson, S.
Covered Wagon Trails (1940) Lange, J.
Cow Country (1953) Kay, Edward
Cow-Cow Boogie (1943) Calker
Cow Dog (1956) Lava
Cow's Husband (1931) Steiner, G.
Coward (1915) Nurnberger
Cowardly Watchdog (1966) Timmens
Cowards (1970) Lerner
Cowboy (1944) Goossens
Cowboy (1954) Brandt
Cowboy (1958) Duning
Cowboy (1966) Almeida
Cowboy and the Blonde (1941) Mockridge
Cowboy and the Lady (1938) Newman
Cowboy and the Prize Fighter (1949) Kraushaar
Cowboy and the Senorita (1944) Skiles
Cowboy Canteen (1944) Leipold
Cowboy Cavalier (1948) Kay, Edward
Cowboy Commandos (1943) Sanucci
Cowboy Crazy (1950) Sharples, Winston
Cowboy from Brooklyn (1938) Deutsch
Cowboy from Sundown (1940) Sanucci
Cowboy Needs a Horse (1956) Smith, P.
Cowboy Quarterback (1939) Jackson, H.
Cowboy's Holiday (1951) Agostini
Cowboys from Texas (1939) Torbett
Coy Decoy (1941) Stalling
Coy Decoy (1963) Wheeler
Crack in the Mirror (1960) Jarre
Crack-Up (1936) Kaylin
Crack-Up (1946) Harline
Cracked Ice (1938) Stalling
Cracked Nuts (1931) Steiner, M.
Cracked Quack (1951) Stalling
Crackpot Cruise (1939) Marsales
Crackpot King (1946) Scheib
Crackpot Quail (1941) Stalling
Cradle of a Nation (1947) Nussbaum
Cradle of Liberty (1946) De Francesco
Cradle of the Republic (1948) Lava
Cradle Song (1933) Harling
Craig's Wife (1936) Bassett, R. H.
Crash (1932) Harling
Crash (1970) Manson
Crash (Trailer, 1932) Kaun
Crash Dive (1943) Buttolph, David
Crashing Las Vegas (1956) Skiles
Crashing Thru (1949) Kay, Edward
Crashout (1955) Stevens, L.
Crawling Hand (1963) Skiles
Crazy Cruise (1942) Stalling
Crazy Knights (1944) Kay, Edward
Crazy Mixed-up Pup (1955) Wheeler
Crazy Over Daisy (1949) Wallace
Crazy Over Horses (1951) Kay, Edward
Crazy Quilt (1966) Schickele
Crazy with the Heat (1947) Wallace
Crazy World of Laurel and Hardy (1965) Fielding
Crazylegs (1953) Stevens, L.
Crazytown (1954) Sharples, Winston
Creation (1949) Geller
Creation of the Humanoids (1962) Kay, Edward
Creature from the Black Lagoon (1954) Salter
Creature Walks Among Us (1956) Mancini
Creeper (1948) Rosen, M.
Creeping Terror (1964) Kopp, F.
Crest of the Wave (1954) Rozsa
Crime Against Joe (1956) Dunlap
Crime and Punishment, U.S.A. (1959) Gilbert, H.
Crime by Night (1944) Lava
Crime Doctor (1943) Bakaleinikoff, M.

Crime Doctor's Courage (1945) Castelnuovo-Tedesco
Crime Doctor's Man Hunt (1946) Sawtell
Crime Doctor's Strangest Case (1943) Michelet
Crime Doctor's Warning (1945) Sawtell
Crime in the Streets (1956) Waxman
Crime of Passion (1957) Dunlap
Crime of the Century (1933) Leipold
Crime School (1938) Steiner, M.
Crime Wave (1954) Buttolph, David
Crime Without Passion (1934) Tours
Crime, Inc. (1945) Greene, W.
Criminal Court (1946) Sawtell
Criminals of the Air (1937) Oakland
Crimson Canary (1945) Fairchild
Crimson Ghost (1946) Glickman, M.
Crimson Key (1947) Butts
Crimson Kimono (1959) Sukman
Crisis (1916) Mowschine
Crisis (1950) Rozsa
Criss Cross (1948) Rozsa
Critic's Choice (1963) Duning
Crockett-Doodle-Do (1959) Franklyn
Crocodile Tears (1965) Brubeck, D.
Crooked Circle (1932) Burton
Crooked River (1950) Greene, W.
Crooked Road (1940) Lava
Crooked Way (1949) Forbes
Crooked Web (1955) Bakaleinikoff, M.
Croon Crazy (1933) Sharples, Winston
Crooner (1932) Heindorf
Crop Chasers (1939) Kilfeather
Crosby, Columbo and Vallee (1932) Marsales
Cross and the Switchblade (1970) Carmichael
Cross Country Cruise (1934) Roemheld
Cross Country Detours (1940) Stalling
Cross Country Romance (1940) Webb
Cross Currents (1915) Raynes
Cross My Heart (1947) Dolan
Cross of Lorraine (1943) Kaper
Crossed Trails (1948) Kay, Edward
Crosseyed Bull (1944) Smith, P.
Crossfire (1947) Webb
Crossroads (1942) Kaper
Crossroads of the World (1956) Lava
Crosswinds (1951) Cailliet
Crow's Feat (1961) Franklyn
Crowd Roars (1932) Kaun
Crowd Roars (1938) Ward, E.
Crowd Snores (1932) Dietrich
Crowded Out (1958) Maasz
Crowded Paradise (1956) Broekman
Crowded Sky (1960) Rosenman
Crowin' Pains (1962) Wheeler
Crowing Pains (1947) Stalling
Crowning Experience (1960) Dunlap
Crucible of Life (1918) McKenna
Crucifixion (1955) Kremenliev
Cruel Tower (1956) Dunlap
Cruise (1966) Carter
Cruise Cat (1952) Bradley
Cruise of the Eagle (1958) Wallace
Cruise of the Zaca (1952) Jackson, H.
Cruisin' Down the River (1953) Duning
Crumley Cogwheel (1961) Sharples, Winston
Crusades (1935) Kopp, R.
Cry Baby Killer (1958) Fried
Cry Blood, Apache (1970) Kaplan, E.
Cry Danger (1950) Dunlap
Cry for Happy (1961) Duning
Cry Havoc (1944) Amfitheatrof
Cry in the Night (1956) Buttolph, David
Cry of Battle (1963) Markowitz
Cry of the Banshee (1970) Baxter
Cry of the City (1948) Newman
Cry Terror! (1958) Jackson, H.
Cry Tough (1959) Almeida
Cry Vengeance (1954) Dunlap
Cry Wolf (1947) Waxman
Crying Wolf (1947) Scheib
Crystal Ball (1942) Young, V.
Crystal Brawl (1957) Sharples, Winston
Crystal Gazebo (1932) De Nat
Crystal Gazer (1941) Kilfeather
Crystal Growing (1959) Barron
Crystal of Energy (1948) Applebaum
Cuando Canta la Ley (1939) Moraweck
Cuba Calling (1944) Jackson, H.
Cuba, Land of Adventure and Sport (1943) Jackson, H.
Cuba, the Land of Rhumba (1933) Shilkret, N.
Cuban Fireball (1951) Wilson, S.
Cuban Love Song (1931) Stothart
Cuban Pete (1946) Rosen, M.
Cubby's Stratosphere Flight (1934) Sharples, Winston
Cuckoo Bird (1939) Scheib
Cuckoo Clock (1950) Bradley
Cuckoo I. Q. (1941) Worth, P.
Cuckoo Murder Case (1931) Stalling
Cue Ball Cat (1950) Bradley
Cult of the Cobra (1955) Lava
Cummington Story (1945) Copland
Cupid Gets His Man (1936) Sharples, Winston
Cured Duck (1945) Wallace
Curio Shop (1933) De Nat
Curious Female (1969) Phillips, S.
Curious George Rides a Bike (1958) Kleiner
Curious Puppy (1939) Stalling
Curley (1947) Roemheld
Curly Top (1935) Friedhofer
Curse of Eve (1917) Gottschalk
Curse of Her Flesh (1968) Aden
Curse of the Cat People (1944) Webb
Curse of the Faceless Man (1958) Fried
Curse of the Fly (1965) Shefter
Curse of the Living Corpse (1963) Holcombe
Curse of the Swamp Creature (1966) Stein, R.

Curse of the Undead (1959) Gertz
Curtain Call (1940) Webb
Curtain Call at Cactus Creek (1950) Scharf, W.
Curtain Call: The Art of Degas (1952) Belasco
Curtain Razor (1948) Stalling
Curtain Time (1948) Van Cleave
Curucu, Beast of the Amazon (1956) Kraushaar
Custer of the West (1967) Segáll
Custer's Last Stand (1936) Zahler
Customers Wanted (1939) Timberg
Cute Recruit (1941) Kilfeather
Cyborg 2087 (1966) Dunlap
Cycle Savages (1969) Styner
Cyclone Kid (1942) Feuer
Cyclops (1957) Glasser
Cynara (1932) Newman
Cynthia (1947) Kaper
Cynthia (Trailer, 1947) Kopp, R.
Cyrano de Bergerac (1950) Tiomkin
Czar of Broadway (1930) Roemheld
Czechoslovakia (1948) Applebaum
Czechoslovakia 1968 (1969) Bernstein, C.
Czechoslovakia on Parade (1938) Shilkret, J.

D' Fightin' Ones (1961) Franklyn
D'Artagnan (1916) Nurnberger
D-Day (1946) Palange
D-Day, the Sixth of June (1956) Murray
D.I. (1957) Buttolph, David
D.O.A. (1950) Tiomkin
Dad Minds the Baby (1947) Lava
Daddy, Darling (1970) Hazzard, T.
Daddy Duck (1947) Wallace
Daddy Long Legs (1931) Friedhofer
Daddy Long Legs (1955) Mockridge
Daddy-'O' (1959) Williams, J.
Daddy's Gone A-Hunting (1969) Williams, J.
Daddy's Little Darling (1955) Scheib
Daffy Dilly (1948) Stalling
Daffy Doc (1938) Stalling
Daffy Doodles (1945) Stalling
Daffy Duck and Egghead (1937) Stalling
Daffy Duck Hunt (1949) Stalling
Daffy Duck in Hollywood (1938) Stalling
Daffy Duck Slept Here (1947) Stalling
Daffy Duckaroo (1942) Stalling
Daffy Rents (1966) Gertz
Daffy the Commando (1943) Stalling
Daffy's Diner (1966) Greene, W.
Daffy's Inn Trouble (1961) Franklyn
Daffy's Southern Exposure (1942) Stalling
Daffydilly Daddy (1945) Sharples, Winston
Daisy Kenyon (1947) Raksin
Dakota (1945) Scharf, W.
Dakota Incident (1956) Butts
Dakota Kid (1951) Wilson, S.
Dakota Lil (1950) Tiomkin
Dallas (1950) Steiner, M.
Dalton Gang (1949) Greene, W.
Dalton Girls (1957) Baxter
Daltons Ride Again (1945) Skinner, F.
Daltons' Women (1950) Greene, W.
Dam Busters (Trailer, 1955) Lava
Damascus and Jerusalem (1936) White, L.
Dames (1934) Roemheld
Damn Citizen (1957) Mancini
Damn Yankees (1958) Heindorf
Damned (1968) Jarre
Damned Don't Cry (1950) Amfitheatrof
Damsel in Distress (1937) Bennett, R. R.
Dan (1914) Klein, Manuel
Dance Charlie Dance (1937) Jackson, H.
Dance Demonstration (1954) Wilson, J.
Dance Girl Dance (1933) Zahler
Dance, Girl, Dance (1940) Ward, E.
Dance Hall (1941) Mockridge
Dance Hall Racket (1955) Ruddy
Dance in the Sun (1953) Gilbert, R.
Dance of Life (1929) Leipold
Dance of Life (1930) Duke
Dance of the Weed (1941) Bradley
Dance with Me, Henry (1956) Dunlap
Dancer's World (1957) McCosh
Dancers (1930) Talbot
Dancers in the Dark (1932) Pasternacki
Dancers of the Deep (1953) Mockridge
Dancing Bear (1937) Scheib
Dancing Co-Ed (1939) Ward, E.
Dancing in Manhattan (1944) Castelnuovo-Tedesco
Dancing in the Dark (1949) Mockridge
Dancing Lady (1933) Silvers
Dancing Masters (1943) Lange
Dancing on a Dime (1940) Young, V.
Dancing on the Ceiling (1937) Vaughan
Dancing Pirate (1936) Newman
Dancing Romeo (1944) Terr
Dancing Shoes (1949) Scheib
Dancing Sweeties (1930) Copping
Dandy (1970) Dee
Dandy in Aspic (1968) Jones
Dandy Lion (1940) Timberg
Danger Ahead (1940) Lange, J.
Danger Is My Business (1950) Lava
Danger—Love at Work (1937) Mockridge
Danger on the Air (1938) Salter
Danger Signal (1945) Deutsch
Danger Street (1947) Calker
Danger Zone (1951) Shefter
Dangerous (1936) Roemheld
Dangerous Blondes (1943) Lawrence, Earl
Dangerous Business (1946) Castelnuovo-Tedesco
Dangerous Charter (1962) Dale
Dangerous Curves (1929) Harling
Dangerous Dan McFoo (1939) Stalling
Dangerous Holiday (1937) Colombo
Dangerous Intruder (1945) Hajos
Dangerous Lady (1941) Wheeler

Dangerous Millions (1946) Calker
Dangerous Mission (1954) Webb
Dangerous Money (1946) Kay, Edward
Dangerous Nan McGrew (1930) Bergunker
Dangerous Paradise (1930) Leipold
Dangerous Partners (1945) Snell
Dangerous Passage (1944) Laszlo
Dangerous Profession (1949) Hollander
Dangerous Waters (1936) Waxman
Dangerous When Wet (1953) Stoll
Dangerous Woman (1929) Hajos
Dangerous Years (1947) Kraushaar
Dangerously They Live (1941) Lava
Dangerously Yours (1933) De Francesco
Dangers of the Arctic (1932) Hoffman, M.
Dangers of the Canadian Mounted (1948) Glickman, M.
Daniel Boone (1936) Riesenfeld
Daniel Boone, Jr. (1960) Scheib
Daniel in the Lions' Den (1948) Rosen, M.
Danish Sport Delights (1953) Lava
Danny Boy (1946) Greene, W.
Dante Dreamer (1957) Sharples, Winston
Dante's Inferno (1935) Friedhofer
Danube (1958) Wallace
Daphni: Virgin of the Golden Laurels (1951) Brubeck, H.
Darby O'Gill and the Little People (1959) Wallace
Darby's Rangers (1958) Steiner, M.
Dare, Birthplace of America (1952) Mason, W.
Daredevil Drivers (1938) Jackson, H.
Daredevil Droopy (1951) Bradley
Daredevils of the Red Circle (1939) Lava
Daredevils of the West (1943) Glickman, M.
Daredevils on Wheels (1949) Jackson, H.
Daring Caballero (1949) Glasser
Daring Game (1967) Bruns
Daring Miss Jones (1948) Hajos
Daring Young Man (1935) Lange
Daring Young Man (1942) Leipold
Dark Alibi (1946) Kay, Edward
Dark Angel (1935) Newman
Dark at the Top of the Stairs (1960) Steiner, M.
Dark City (1950) Waxman
Dark Command (1940) Young, V.
Dark Delusion (1947) Snell
Dark Hazard (1934) Kaun
Dark Horse (1946) Salter
Dark Intruder (1965) Schifrin
Dark Mirror (1946) Tiomkin
Dark Mountain (1944) Stahl
Dark Odyssey (1961) Rosenthal
Dark Passage (1947) Waxman
Dark Passage (Trailer, 1947) Lava
Dark Past (1949) Duning
Dark Rapture (1938) Rochetti
Dark Shadows (1944) Shilkret, N.
Dark Skies (1929) Zahler
Dark Streets (1929) Leonardi
Dark Streets of Cairo (1940) Salter
Dark Venture (1955) Palange
Dark Victory (1939) Steiner, M.
Dark Waters (1944) Rozsa
Darkened Rooms (1929) Hajos
Darker Than Amber (1970) Parker
Darkest Africa (1936) Kay, Arthur
Darling Lili (1969) Mancini
Darling, How Could You! (1951) Hollander
Dartmouth Days (1934) Axt
Date Bait (1960) Carras
Date for Dinner (1947) Scheib
Date to Skate (1938) Timberg
Date with Judy (1948) Stoll
Date with the Falcon (1941) Sawtell
Daughter of Don Q (1946) Glickman, M.
Daughter of Her People (1933) Hochman
Daughter of Rosie O'Grady (1942) Jackson, H.
Daughter of Rosie O'Grady (1950) Buttolph, David
Daughter of the Dragon (1931) Kopp, R.
Daughter of the Gods (1916) Bowers, R. H.
Daughter of the Sun God (1962) Baxter
Daughter of the Tong (1939) Zahler
Daughter of the West (1949) Gertz
Daughters Courageous (1939) Steiner, M.
Davey Cricket (1965) Greene, W.
David and Bathsheba (1951) Newman
David and Lisa (1962) Lawrence, M.
David and the Giant (1955) Hayes
David Copperfield (1935) Stothart
David Harum (1934) Buttolph, David
Davy Crockett and the River Pirates (1956) Bruns
Davy Crockett, Indian Scout (1950) Sawtell
Davy Crockett, King of the Wild Frontier (1955) Bruns
Davy Jones' Locker (1934) Stalling
Dawg Gawn (1958) Sharples, Winston
Dawn at Socorro (1954) Skinner, F.
Dawn Express (1942) Zahler
Dawn of Better Living (1945) Smith, P.
Dawn on the Great Divide (1943) Kay, Edward
Dawn Patrol (1930) Dunn
Dawn Patrol (1938) Steiner, M.
Dawn to Dawn (1933) Macpherson
Day After Day (1940) Stewart, F.
Day at Hollywood Park (1947) Lava
Day at Santa Anita (1937) Jackson, H.
Day at the Beach (1938) Lewis
Day at the Fair (1948) Jackson, H.
Day at the Fair (1964) Chou Wen-chung
Day at the Races (1937) Waxman
Day at the Zoo (1939) Stalling
Day Dreams (1933) Scharf, W.
Day in Death Valley (1944) Nussbaum
Day in June (1944) Scheib
Day in the Country (1953) Shefter
Day in the Life of Manolete (1968) Almeida
Day Mars Invaded Earth (1962) LaSalle
Day Nurse (1932) Dietrich

Day of Fear (1957) Arnaud
Day of Fury (1956) Gertz
Day of the Bad Man (1957) Salter
Day of the Dead (1957) Almeida
Day of the Evil Gun (1968) Alexander, J.
Day of the Fight (1951) Fried
Day of the Fox (1956) Castelnuovo-Tedesco
Day of the Nightmare (1965) Brummer
Day of the Outlaw (1959) Courage
Day of the Painter (1960) Manson
Day of Triumph (1954) Amfitheatrof
Day on Treasure Island (1939) Bakaleinikoff, C.
Day the Bookies Wept (1939) Morton
Day the Earth Stood Still (1951) Herrmann
Day the World Ended (1955) Stein, R.
Day to Live (1931) Scheib
Day with the Boys (1969) Mention
Daydreamer (1966) Laws
Days in My Father's House (1968) Evans
Days of '76 (1945) Jackson, H.
Days of a Tree (1956) Kleinsinger
Days of Dylan Thomas (1965) Duffy
Days of Glory (1944) Amfitheatrof
Days of Jesse James (1939) Lava
Days of Old Cheyenne (1943) Glickman, M.
Days of Our Years (1956) Jackson, H.
Days of Sin and Nights of Nymphomania (1965) Craig, G.
Days of Thrills and Laughter (1961) Royal
Days of Wilfred Owen (1965) Lewine
Days of Wine and Roses (1962) Mancini
Daytime Reconnaisance Patrol (1943) Lava
Dayton's Devils (1968) Skiles
De Sade (1969) Strange
Dead Don't Dream (1948) Kraushaar
Dead End (1937) Newman
Dead End Cats (1947) Scheib
Dead End Kids on Dress Parade (1939) Jackson, H.
Dead Heat on a Merry-Go-Round (1966) Phillips, S.
Dead Man's Eyes (1944) Sawtell
Dead Man's Gold (1948) Greene, W.
Dead Man's Gulch (1943) Glickman, M.
Dead Man's Trail (1952) Kraushaar
Dead March (1937) Rapée
Dead Men Tell (1941) Raksin
Dead Men Walk (1943) Erdody
Dead or Alive (1944) Zahler
Dead Reckoning (1947) Skiles
Dead Ringer (1964) Previn, A.
Dead to the World (1961) Byrd, C.
Deadline (1948) Sanucci
Deadline at Dawn (1946) Eisler
Deadline for Danny (1954) Lavry
Deadline for Murder (1946) Schrager
Deadline—U.S.A. (1952) Mockridge
Deadly Affair (1967) Jones
Deadly Companions (1961) Skiles
Deadly Duo (1962) LaSalle
Deadly Game (1941) DiMaggio
Deadly Is the Female (1949) Young, V.
Deadly Mantis (1957) Gertz
Deadly Sins (1965) McDowell
Deadwood Dick (1940) Zahler
Deadwood Thunderball (1969) Goodwin
Dealers in Death (1934) Stahl
Dear Brat (1951) Van Cleave
Dear Brigitte (1965) Duning
Dear Heart (1965) Mancini
Dear Myrtle (1954) Skinner, F.
Dear Old Switzerland (1944) Scheib
Dear Ruth (1947) Dolan
Dear Uncle (1953) Poddany
Dear Wife (1950) Lilley
Death from a Distance (1935) Cutner
Death in Small Doses (1957) Miller, R.
Death Kiss (1933) Burton
Death of a Champion (1939) Leipold
Death of a Gunfighter (1969) Nelson, O.
Death of a Salesman (1951) North
Death of a Scoundrel (1956) Steiner, M.
Death on the Diamond (1934) Axt
Death Rides the Range (1940) Porter
Death Takes a Holiday (1934) Roder
Death Valley (1946) Mayfield
Death Valley Gunfighters (1949) Wilson, S.
Death Valley Manhunt (1943) Glickman, M.
Death Valley Rangers (1943) Sanucci
Deathwatch (1966) Fried
December 7th (1943) Newman
Deception (1921) Riesenfeld
Deception (1946) Korngold
Decision at Sundown (1957) Roemheld
Decision Before Dawn (1951) Waxman
Decision for Chemistry (1953) North
Decision of Christopher Blake (1948) Steiner, M.
Declaration of Independence (1938) Jackson, H.
Decoy (1946) Kay, Edward
Deduce, You Say! (1956) Franklyn
Deep Adventure (1957) Jackson, H.
Deep Boo Sea (1952) Sharples, Winston
Deep Freeze Squeeze (1964) Wheeler
Deep in My Heart (1954) Deutsch
Deep Inside (1968) Marini
Deep Sea Doodle (1960) Scheib
Deep Six (1958) Buttolph, David
Deep Valley (1947) Steiner, M.
Deep Waters (1948) Mockridge
Deerslayer (1957) Sawtell
Defense Against Invasion (1943) Wolcott
Defiant Giant (1966) Sharples, Winston
Defiant Ones (1958) Gold
Delicate Delinquent (1957) Bregman
Delicious (1931) Gershwin
Delightful Rogue (1930) Steiner, M.
Delightfully Dangerous (1945) Gould, M.
Delinquent Daughters (1944) Zahler
Delinquents (1957) Palange

Deliverance (1919) Goetzl
Delta Factor (1970) Kraushaar
Deluge (1933) Burton
Dementia (1953) Antheil
Dementia 13 (1963) Stein, R.
Demetrius and the Gladiators (1954) Waxman
Demo Derby (1965) Korb
Denmark 43 (1970) Hovey
Denver & Rio Grande (1952) Sawtell
Denver Kid (1948) Butts
Deported (1950) Scharf, W.
Deputy Droopy (1955) Bradley
Deputy Marshal (1949) Merrick
Der Fuehrer's Face (1942) Wallace
Derby Day (1952) Collins
Derelict (1930) Hajos
Desert Bandit (1941) Feuer
Desert Fox (1951) Amfitheatrof
Desert Fury (1947) Rozsa
Desert Hawk (1944) Zahler
Desert Hawk (1950) Skinner, F.
Desert Hell (1958) Kraushaar
Desert High-Jinks (1950) Mamorsky
Desert Justice (1936) Zahler
Desert Killer (1953) Lava
Desert Legion (1953) Skinner, F.
Desert Lights (1948) De Francesco
Desert Nights (1929) Axt
Desert of Lost Men (1951) Wilson, S.
Desert Passage (1952) Sawtell
Desert Playground (1944) Jackson, H.
Desert Pursuit (1952) Kay, Edward
Desert Rats (1953) Harline
Desert Raven (1965) LaSalle
Desert Sands (1955) Dunlap
Desert Song (1943) Roemheld
Desert Song (1953) Steiner, M.
Desert Warrior (1961) Michelet
Desert Wonderland (1942) De Francesco
Design for Correction (1963) Dahl
Design for Death (1948) Sawtell
Design for Dreaming (1966) Kleinsinger
Design for Leaving (1953) Stalling
Design for Living (1933) Leipold
Design for Scandal (1941) Waxman
Designing Woman (1957) Previn, A.
Designs on Jerry (1955) Bradley
Desirable (1934) Roemheld
Desirable (Trailer, 1934) Kaun
Desire (1936) Hollander
Desire in a Public Dump (1958) Kraft
Desire in the Dust (1960) Dunlap
Desire Is Fire (1967) Ivers
Desire Me (1947) Stothart
Desire Under the Elms (1958) Bernstein, E.
Désirée (1954) North
Desistfilm (1954) Tenney
Desk for Billie (1956) Bergsma
Desk Set (1957) Mockridge
Desperado (1954) Kraushaar
Desperadoes (1943) Leipold
Desperadoes' Outpost (1952) Wilson, S.
Desperados Are in Town (1956) Sawtell
Desperate (1947) Sawtell
Desperate Chance for Ellery Queen (1942) Zahler
Desperate Heart (1950) Segáll
Desperate Hours (1955) Amfitheatrof
Desperate Journey (1942) Steiner, M.
Desperate Moment (1926) Hoffman, M.
Despoilers (1916) Gottschalk
Destination 60,000 (1957) Glasser
Destination Big House (1950) Wilson, S.
Destination Gobi (1953) Kaplan, S.
Destination Inner Space (1966) Dunlap
Destination Magoo (1954) Maury
Destination Meat Ball (1952) Wheeler
Destination Moon (1950) Stevens, L.
Destination Murder (1950) Gertz
Destination Tokyo (1944) Waxman
Destination Unknown (1933) Harling
Destiny (1944) Tansman
Destroyer (1943) Collins
Destructors (1968) Dunlap
Destry (1954) Skinner, F.
Destry Rides Again (1939) Skinner, F.
Detective (1968) Goldsmith
Detective Kitty O'Day (1944) Kay, Edward
Detective Story (1951). See p. 8
Detour (1945) Erdody
Detour to Danger (1946) Zahler
Detouring America (1939) Stalling
Detouring Thru Maine (1950) Sharples, Winston
Devil and Miss Jones (1941) Webb
Devil and the Deep (1932) Hand
Devil at 4 O'Clock (1961) Duning
Devil Bat's Daughter (1946) Steinert
Devil Boats (1944) Lava
Devil Dancer (1927) Bassett, R.
Devil Dogs of the Air (1935) Kaun
Devil-Doll (1936) Waxman
Devil in Velvet (1968) Fuller, L.
Devil Is a Woman (1935) Leipold
Devil Is Driving! (1937) Nussbaum
Devil May Care (1930) Axt
Devil May Hare (1953) Franklyn
Devil of the Deep (1938) Scheib
Devil of the Matterhorn (1932) White, L.
Devil on Horseback (1936) Riesenfeld
Devil on Wheels (1947) Cadkin
Devil Pays Off (1941) Glickman, M.
Devil Thumbs a Ride (1947) Webb
Devil to Pay (1931) Newman
Devil to Pay! (1960) Werle
Devil with Hitler (1942) Ward, E.
Devil with Women (1930) Brunelli
Devil's 8 (1969) Curb
Devil's Angels (1967) Curb
Devil's Bargain (1970) Ivers

Devil's Bedroom (1964) Loose
Devil's Brigade (1968) North
Devil's Brother (1933) Shield
Devil's Canyon (1953) Amfitheatrof
Devil's Cargo (1948) Dessau
Devil's Doorway (1950) Amfitheatrof
Devil's Feud Cake (1962) Lava
Devil's Hairpin (1957) Van Cleave
Devil's Hand (1961) Ferguson
Devil's Holiday (1930) Goulding
Devil's in Love (1933) Zamecnik
Devil's Island (1939) Jackson, H.
Devil's Lottery (1932) Friedhofer
Devil's Mask (1946) Duning
Devil's Mistress (1966) Allen, B.
Devil's Partner (1961) Stein, R.
Devil's Playground (1933) Merkur
Devil's Saddle Legion (1937) Jackson, H.
Devil's Sisters (1966) Jacobs, A.
Devil's Squadron (1936) Jackson, H.
Devotion (1946) Korngold
Di que me quieres (1938) Shilkret, N.
Dial 1119 (1950) Previn, A.
Dial M for Murder (1954) Tiomkin
Dial Red O (1955) Skiles
Diamond Head (1963) Williams, J.
Diamond Horseshoe (1945) Spencer, H.
Diamond Jim (1935) Waxman
Diamond Queen (1953) Sawtell
Diane (1955) Rozsa
Diary of a Bachelor (1964) Pleis
Diary of a Chambermaid (1946) Michelet
Diary of a High School Bride (1959) Stein, R.
Diary of a Madman (1963) LaSalle
Diary of a Racing Pigeon (1940) Jackson, H.
Diary of Anne Frank (1959) Newman
Dick Tracy (1937) Colombo
Dick Tracy (1946) Webb
Dick Tracy Meets Gruesome (1947) Sawtell
Dick Tracy Returns (1938) Colombo
Dick Tracy vs. Crime, Inc. (1941) Feuer
Dick Tracy vs. Cueball (1946) Sawtell
Dick Tracy's Dilemma (1947) Sawtell
Dick Tracy's G-Men (1939) Lava
Dick Whittington's Cat (1936) Stalling
Did You Hear the One About the Traveling Saleslady? (1967) Mizzy
Dig That Dog (1954) Wheeler
Dig That Uranium (1955) Skiles
Dillinger (1945) Tiomkin
Dime to Retire (1954) Franklyn
Dime with a Halo (1963) Stein, R.
Dimension 5 (1966) Dunlap
Dimitri Works in Black Wax (1953) Liebling
Dimples (1936) Mockridge
Dinah East (1970) Nash
Ding Dog Daddy (1942) Stalling
Ding Dong Doggie (1937) Timberg
Ding Dong Williams (1945) Harline
Dinky (1935) Roemheld
Dinky Finds a Home (1946) Scheib
Dinner at Eight (1933) Axt
Dino (1957) Fried
Dinosaurus! (1960) Stein, R.
Dionysus (1963) Ito
Diplomaniacs (1933) Steiner, M.
Diplomatic Courier (1952) Kaplan, S.
Dippy Diplomat (1945) Calker
Dipsy Gypsy (1941) Raksin
Dirty Dingus Magee (1970) Alexander, J.
Dirty Dozen (1967) De Vol
Dirty Girls (1965) Hart
Dirtymouth (1970) Vardi
Disarmament Conference (1931) De Nat
Disaster (1948) Lubin
Disbarred (1939) Carbonara
Disc Jockey (1951) Hazard
Disciple (1915) Nurnberger
Discontented Canary (1934) Bradley
Discover Greyhound America (1966) Siegel, S.
Discovery in a Landscape (1969) Giuffre
Disembodied (1957) Skiles
Disgraced (1933) Leipold
Disguise the Limit (1960) Sharples, Winston
Dish Ran Away with the Spoon (1933) Marsales
Dishonored (1931) Hajos
Dishonored Lady (1947) Dragon
Disillusioned Blue Bird (1944) Worth, P.
Disneyland, U.S.A. (1956) Wallace
Disobedient Mouse (1938) Marsales
Disorderly Orderly (1964) Lilley
Dispatch from Reuter's (1940) Steiner, M.
Dispatch from Reuter's (Trailer, 1940) Jackson, H.
Displaced Persons (1948) Landau, S.
Dispossessed (1970) Wilson, T.
Disputed Passage (1939) Hollander
Disraeli (1929) Mendoza
Dissent Illusion (1963) Bottje
Distant Drums (1951) Steiner, M.
Distant Trumpet (1964) Steiner, M.
Dive Bomber (1941) Steiner, M.
Divide and Conquer (1943) Lava
Dividends for the Future (1947) Craig, E.
Divine Lady (1929) Copping
Diving Dandies (1946) De Francesco
Divorce (1945) Kay, Edward
Divorce American Style (1967) Grusin
Divorce Las Vegas Style (1970) Mann, Bobby
Divorce of Lady X (1938) Rozsa
Dixiana (1930) Steiner, M.
Dixie (1943) Dolan
Dixie Dugan (1942) Lange
Dixie Fryer (1960) Franklyn
Dixie Jamboree (1944) Schrager
Dixieland Droopy (1954) Bradley
Dixieland Jamboree (1946) Jackson, H.
Dizzy Acrobat (1943) Calker
Dizzy Dames (1935) Jackson, H.

Dizzy Dinosaurs (1952) Sharples, Winston
Dizzy Dishes (1955) Sharples, Winston
Dizzy Ducks (1936) De Nat
Dizzy Dwarf (1934) Dietrich
Dizzy Kitty (1941) Calker
Dizzy Newsreel (1943) Worth, P.
Dizzy Red Riding Hood (1931) Steiner, G.
Do a Good Deed (1935) Dietrich
Do Not Disturb (1965) Newman, L.
Do Not Fold, Staple, Spindle, or Mutilate (1967) Brubeck, D.
Do Not Throw Cushions Into the Ring (1970) Carras
Do or Diet (1953) Sharples, Winston
Do You Know What the Army Air Force Is? (1947) Rose
Do You Love Me (1946) Buttolph, David
Do You Remember (1945) De Francesco
Dobbin Steps Out (1950) Mamorsky
Doc's Last Stand (1961) Poddany
Docks of New Orleans (1948) Kay, Edward
Docks of New York (1945) Kay, Edward
Doctor (1934) Riesenfeld
Doctor and the Girl (1949) Kopp, R.
Doctor and the Playgirl (1965) Mendel
Doctor "B" (1957) Brant
Doctor Bull (1933) Kaylin
Doctor Doolittle (1967) Newman, L.
Doctor Jerkyl's Hide (1953) Stalling
Doctor Oswald (1935) Dietrich
Doctor Rhythm (1938) Jenkins
Doctor X (1932) Kaun
Doctor, You've Got to Be Kidding! (1966) Hopkins, K.
Doctor Zhivago (1965) Jarre
Doctor's Orders (1930) Shield
Doctor's Secret (1929) Burns, S.
Doctors Don't Tell (1941) Glickman, M.
Doctors' Wives (1931) Kaylin
Dodge City (1939) Steiner, M.
Dodge City Trail (1936) Still
Dodsworth (1936) Newman
Dog and the Bone (1937) Scheib
Dog, Cat and Canary (1945) Kilfeather
Dog Collared (1949) Stalling
Dog Daze (1937) Stalling
Dog Gone Modern (1938) Stalling
Dog Gone South (1950) Stalling
Dog-Gonedest Dog (1952) Mamorsky
Dog-House (1943) Terr
Dog House (1952) Bradley
Dog in a Mansion (1940) Scheib
Dog in the Orchard (1941) Jackson, H.
Dog Meets Dog (1942) Kilfeather
Dog of Flanders (1959) Sawtell
Dog of the Wild (1949) Laszlo
Dog Pounded (1953) Stalling
Dog Scents (1954) Grundman
Dog Show (1934) Scheib
Dog Show (1950) Scheib
Dog Show-Off (1948) Sharples, Winston
Dog Snatcher (1931) De Nat
Dog Snatcher (1952) Lava
Dog Tales (1958) Franklyn
Dog Tax Dodgers (1948) Calker
Dog That Cried Wolf (1953) Wheeler
Dog Tired (1942) Stalling
Dog Trouble (1942) Bradley
Dog Watch (1945) Wallace
Dog's Best Friend (1959) Sawtell
Dog's Dream (1941) Scheib
Doggone Cats (1947) Stalling
Doggone Clever (1948) Shilkret, N.
Doggone People (1960) Franklyn
Doggone Tired (1949) Bradley
Dogie Round Up (1944) Lava
Dognapper (1934) Lewis
Dogs You Seldom See (1940) Jackson, H.
Doin' Their Bit (1942) Hayton
Doing Impossikible Stunts (1940) Timberg
Doing Their Bit (1942) Scheib
Doing What's Fright (1959) Sharples, Winston
Doll Face (1946) Buttolph, David
Dollar Dance (1941) Applebaum
Dolly Sisters (1945) Buttolph, David
Dominion of Sports (1946) Jackson, H.
Domino Kid (1957) Bakaleinikoff, M.
Don Daredevil Rides Again (1951) Wilson, S.
Don Donald (1936) Smith, P.
Don Juan (1926) Axt
Don Juan Quilligan (1945) Raksin
Don Q, Son of Zorro (1925) Wilson, M.
Don Quixote (1934) Stalling
Don Ricardo Returns (1946) Steinert
Don Winslow of the Coast Guard (1942) Rosen, M.
Don's Fountain of Youth (1953) Dubin
Don't Axe Me (1957) Franklyn
Don't Bet on Blondes (1935) Kaun
Don't Drink the Water (1969) Williams, P.
Don't Fence Me In (1945) Butts
Don't Forget to Write (1954) Lava
Don't Gamble with Strangers (1946) Kay, Edward
Don't Get Personal (1936) Waxman
Don't Get Personal (1942) Skinner, F.
Don't Give Up the Sheep (1953) Stalling
Don't Give Up the Ship (1959) Scharf, W.
Don't Go Near the Water (1957) Kaper
Don't Hustle an Ant with Muscle (1970) Goodwin
Don't Just Lay There (1970) Margulies
Don't Just Stand There! (1968) Perito
Don't Knock the Twist (1962) Karger
Don't Look Now (1936) Stalling
Don't Make Waves (1967) Mizzy
Don't Spill the Beans (1965) Timmens
Don't Worry, We'll Think of a Title (1966) LaSalle
Don't You Believe It (1943) Terr
Donald and Pluto (1936) Smith, P.
Donald and the Wheel (1961) Baker, Buddy
Donald Applecore (1951) Dubin

Donald Duck and the Gorilla (1944) Wallace
Donald Gets Drafted (1942) Smith, P.
Donald in Mathmagic Land (1959) Baker, Buddy
Donald's Better Self (1938) Wallace
Donald's Camera (1941) Harline
Donald's Cousin Gus (1939) Wallace
Donald's Crime (1945) Plumb
Donald's Day Off (1944) Smith, P.
Donald's Decision (1942) Wallace
Donald's Diary (1953) Plumb
Donald's Dilemma (1947) Wallace
Donald's Dog Laundry (1940) Wallace
Donald's Double Trouble (1946) Wallace
Donald's Dream Voice (1947) Wallace
Donald's Garden (1942) Wallace
Donald's Gold Mine (1942) Wallace
Donald's Golf Game (1938) Wallace
Donald's Happy Birthday (1948) Wallace
Donald's Lucky Day (1938) Wallace
Donald's Nephews (1938) Wallace
Donald's Ostrich (1937) Wallace
Donald's Penguin (1938) Wallace
Donald's Snow Fight (1942) Wallace
Donald's Tire Trouble (1942) Wallace
Donald's Vacation (1940) Wallace
Dondi (1961) Morgan, T.
Donovan's Brain (1953) Dunstedter
Donovan's Reef (1963) Mockridge
Doolins of Oklahoma (1949) Duning
Doomed Caravan (1941) Leipold
Doomed to Die (1940) Kay, Edward
Doomsday (1938) Scheib
Door (1967) Terry, C.
Door Will Open (1939) Snell
Doors (1963) Valentine
Doorway to the Past (1969) Kaplan, S.
Dopey Dick, the Pink Whale (1957) Wheeler
Dorothy Vernon of Haddon Hall (1924) Schertzinger
Dos Más Uno, Dos (1934) Buttolph, David
Dot and the Line (1965) Poddany
Double Alibi (1940) Skinner, F.
Double-Barrelled Detective Story (1965) Kupferman
Double Chaser (1942) Stalling
Double-Cross-Country Race (1951) Sharples, Winston
Double Cross Roads (1930) Lipschultz
Double Crossbones (1950) Skinner, F.
Double Deal (1939) DiMaggio
Double Deal (1950) Michelet
Double Dribble (1946) Wallace
Double Dynamite (1951) Harline
Double Exposure (1944) Laszlo
Double Indemnity (1944) Rozsa
Double Jeopardy (1955) Butts
Double Life (1948) Rozsa
Double Man (1967) Freeman, E.
Double or Mutton (1954) Franklyn
Double or Nothing (1937) Young, V.
Double Rhythm (1946) Lilley
Double-Stop (1968) Davis, D.
Double Trouble (1915) Breil
Double Trouble (1941) DiMaggio
Double Trouble (1966) Alexander, J.
Double Wedding (1937) Ward, E.
Dough for the Do-Do (1948) Stalling
Dough Ray Me-ow (1948) Stalling
Doughboys (1931) Axt
Doughboys in Ireland (1943) Leipold
Doughgirls (1944) Deutsch
Doughnuts (1963) Glickman, L.
Dover (1942) Kubik
Dover Boys (1942) Stalling
Down Among the Sheltering Palms (1952) Lange
Down and Dirty (1969) Phillips, R.
Down Argentine Way (1940) Mockridge
Down Beat Bear (1956) Bradley
Down Dakota Way (1949) Butts
Down in "Arkansaw" (1938) Torbett
Down in San Diego (1941) Amfitheatrof
Down Laredo Way (1953) Wilson, S.
Down Liberty Road (1956) Koff
Down Memory Lane (1949) Kaplan, S.
Down Mexico Way (1941) Glickman, M.
Down Missouri Way (1946) Hajos
Down on the Levee (1933) Scheib
Down Singapore Way (1946) Dunn
Down South (1931) De Nat
Down Stream Highway (1950) Mamorsky
Down Texas Way (1942) Kay, Edward
Down the Fairway (1945) De Francesco
Down the Nile (1949) Lava
Down the Stretch (1936) Jackson, H.
Down the Wyoming Trail (1939) Sanucci
Down Three Dark Streets (1954) Sawtell
Down to Earth (1932) Gerstenberger
Down to Earth (1947) Roemheld
Down to Mirth (1959) Sharples, Winston
Down to the Sea (1936) Kay, Arthur
Down to the Sea in Ships (1922) Gilbert, Henry
Down to the Sea in Ships (1949) Newman
Down to Their Last Yacht (1934) Webb
Down with Cats (1943) Scheib
Downhearted Duckling (1954) Bradley
Downhill Racer (1969) Hopkins, K.
Dr. Blue Bird (1936) De Nat
Dr. Broadway (1942) Dolan
Dr. Chicago (1970) Ashley
Dr. Christian Meets the Women (1940) Bakaleinikoff, C.
Dr. Cyclops (1940) Malotte
Dr. Devil and Mr. Hare (1963) Lava
Dr. Ehrlich's Magic Bullet (1940) Steiner, M.
Dr. Gillespie's Criminal Case (1943) Amfitheatrof
Dr. Gillespie's New Assistant (1942) Amfitheatrof
Dr. Gloom and Dr. Cheer (1952) Hood
Dr. Goldfoot and the Bikini Machine (1965) Baxter

Dr. Goldfoot and the Girl Bombs (1966) Baxter
Dr. Ha Ha (1966) Timmens
Dr. Jekyll and Mr. Hyde (1920) Riesenfeld
Dr. Jekyll and Mr. Hyde (1932) Hand
Dr. Jekyll and Mr. Hyde (1941) Waxman
Dr. Jekyll and Mr. Mouse (1947) Bradley
Dr. Masher (1969) Potts
Dr. Monica (1934) Roemheld
Dr. Renault's Secret (1942) Raksin
Dr. Rhinestone's Theory (1967) Timmens
Dr. Socrates (1935) Kaun
Dr. Terror's Gallery of Horrors (1967) Skiles
Dracula's Castle (1969) Hulette
Dracula's Daughter (1936) Roemheld
Draegerman Courage (1936) Roemheld
Draft Horse (1942) Stalling
Draftee Daffy (1944) Stalling
Draftsmen of Dreams (1947) De Francesco
Drafty, Isn't It? (1957) Franklyn
Drag (1929) Copping
Drag-a-Long Droopy (1954) Bradley
Dragnet (1947) Gertz
Dragnet (1954) Schumann
Dragon Around (1954) Wallace
Dragon Murder Case (1934) Kaun
Dragon Seed (1944) Stothart
Dragon's Gold (1953) Glasser
Dragonfly Squadron (1953) Dunlap
Dragonwyck (1946) Newman
Dragoon Wells Massacre (1957) Dunlap
Dragstrip Girl (1957) Stein, R.
Dragstrip Riot (1958) Carras
Dramatic School (1938) Waxman
Drango (1957) Bernstein, E.
Draw Me a Telephone (1967) Small
Dream Girl (1948) Young, V.
Dream Girl (Trailer, 1948) Lilley
Dream Kids (1944) Kilfeather
Dream No More (1949) Adomian
Dream of Kings (1969) North
Dream Street (1921) Silvers
Dream Walking (1950) Scheib
Dream Wife (1953) Salinger
Dreamboat (1952) Mockridge
Dreamer (1970) Kingsley
Dreaming Out Loud (1940) Moraweck
Dreamnapping (1966) Timmens
Dreams (1940) Amfitheatrof
Dreams of Glass (1970) Freebairn-Smith
Dreams on Ice (1939) De Nat
Dreams That Money Can Buy (1948) Applebaum
Dress Reversal (1965) Timmens
Dressed to Kill (1941) Mockridge
Dressed to Thrill (1935) Brunelli
Dribble Drabble (1968) Timmens
Drifter (1967) Lauber
Driftin' Kid (1941) Sanucci
Driftin' River (1946) Hajos
Drifting Along (1946) Kay, Edward
Driftwood (1947) Scott, N.
Drilling for Girls in Texas (1954) Craig, E.
Drinks on the Mouse (1953) Sharples, Winston
Drip-Along Daffy (1950) Stalling
Drip Dippy Donald (1947) Wallace
Drippy Mississippi (1951) Sharples, Winston
Drive a Crooked Road (1954) Duning
Driving Scene (196?) Duffy
Drooler's Delight (1949) Calker
Droopy Leprechaun (1957) Bradley
Droopy's Double Trouble (1951) Bradley
Droopy's Good Deed (1951) Bradley
Dropouts Anonymous (1965) Hilton
Drum (1938) Rozsa
Drum (1952) Davenport
Drum Beat (1954) Young, V.
Drum Up a Tenant (1962) Sharples, Winston
Drummer Girl of Vicksburg (1912) Simon, W.
Drums Across the River (1954) Stein, H.
Drums Along the Mohawk (1939) Newman
Drums in the Deep South (1951) Tiomkin
Drums of Africa (1963) Mandel
Drums of Fu Manchu (1940) Feuer
Drums of India (1948) Lava
Drums of Jeopardy (1931) Burton
Drums of Love (1928) Cadman
Drums of the Congo (1942) Rosen, M.
Drums of the Desert (1940) Kay, Edward
Drunkard (1935) Zahler
Dry Martini (1928) Rapée
Du Pont Story (1950) Merrick
DuBarry Was a Lady (1943) Amfitheatrof
Dublin and Nearby (1930) Axt
Duchess of Idaho (1950) Stoll
Duck Amuck (1951) Stalling
Duck Doctor (1952) Bradley
Duck Dodgers in the 24th 1/2 Century (1952) Stalling
Duck, Duck (1970) Ussachevsky
Duck Fever (1955) Scheib
Duck Hunt (1937) Dietrich
Duck Pimples (1945) Wallace
Duck! Rabbit, Duck! (1952) Stalling
Duck Soup (1933) Leipold
Duck Soup to Nuts (1944) Stalling
Ducking the Devil (1957) Franklyn
Ducks (1970) Burroughs
Ducksters (1949) Stalling
Ducktators (1942) Stalling
Dude Cowboy (1941) Sawtell
Dude Duck (1950) Smith, P.
Dude Goes West (1948) Tiomkin
Dude Ranch Buckaroos (1943) Jackson, H.
Dude Rancheroos (1949) Jackson, H.
Dudes Are Pretty People (1942) Ward, E.
Duel at Diablo (1966) Hefti
Duel at Silver Creek (1952) Stein, H.
Duel in the Sun (1946) Tiomkin
Duel Personality (1966) Elliott, Dean

Duffy (1968) Freeman, E.
Duffy of San Quentin (1954) Dunlap
Duffy's Tavern (1945) Dolan
Duke Comes Back (1937) Colombo
Duke of Chicago (1949) Wilson, S.
Duke of the Navy (1942) Zahler
Duke of West Point (1939) Tours
Duke Steps Out (1929) Axt
Dulcy (1940) Kaper
Dumb Cluck (1937) Lessner
Dumb Girl of Portici (1916) Schmidt, A.
Dumb Like a Fox (1941) Kilfeather
Dumb Like a Fox (1964) Greene, W.
Dumb Patrol (1931) Marsales
Dumb Patrol (1963) Lava
Dumb-Bell of the Yukon (1946) Wallace
Dumb-Hounded (1943) Bradley
Dumbconscious Mind (1942) Worth, P.
Dumbo (1941) Churchill
Dummy (1929) Hajos
Dumpson's Place (1963) Faliks
Dune Bug (1969) Goodwin
Dunwich Horror (1970) Baxter
Dust Be My Destiny (1939) Steiner, M.
Dust Is Dying (1961) Kleinsinger
Dustcap Doormat (1958) Scheib
Dutch Guiana (1942) De Francesco
Dutch Treat (1930) Scheib
Dutch Treat (1956) Sharples, Winston
Dutch Treat in Sports (1952) Jackson, H.
Duty and the Beast (1943) Worth, P.
Dwightiana (1959) Ito
Dybbuk (1937) Heifetz
Dying to Live (1948) De Francesco
Dylan Thomas' A Child's Christmas in Wales (1962) Heckman
Dynamite (1929) Axt
Dynamite (1930) Axt
Dynamite (1949) Calker
Dynamite Canyon (1941) Sanucci

Each Dawn I Crow (1948) Stalling
Each Dawn I Die (1939) Steiner, M.
Eadie Was a Lady (1945) Duning
Eager Beaver (1945) Stalling
Eagle (1949) Hoffman, M.
Eagle and the Hawk (1933) Leipold
Eagle and the Hawk (1950) Schrager
Eagle Squadron (1942) Skinner, F.
Eagles of the Navy (1943) Jackson, H.
Eames Lounge Chair (1956) Bernstein, E.
Earl Carroll Sketchbook (1946) Scott, N.
Earl Carroll Vanities (1945) Scharf, W.
Earl of Chicago (1940) Heymann
Earl of Puddlestone (1940) Lava
Early Bird (1938) De Nat
Early Bird and the Worm (1936) Bradley
Early Bird Dood It! (1942) Bradley
Early Birds (1961) Brant
Early Expressionists (1965) Andrews, J.
Early to Bed (1941) Wallace
Early to Bet (1950) Stalling
Early Worm Gets the Bird (1939) Stalling
Earth Is Born (1957) Schuman
Earth vs. the Flying Saucers (1956) Bakaleinikoff, M.
Earth vs. the Spider (1958) Glasser
Earthbound (1940) Newman
Earthquakers (1943) Kubik
Earthworm Tractors (1936) Jackson, H.
East by North (1947) Applebaum
East Is East (1956) Jackson, H.
East Is West (1930) Roemheld
East Lynne (1931) Bassett, R. H.
East of Eden (1955) Rosenman
East of Java (1935) Waxman
East of Sumatra (1953) Stein, H.
East of the River (1940) Deutsch
East Side Kids (1940) Porter
East Side of Heaven (1939) Skinner, F.
East Side Sadie (1929) Secunda
East Side, West Side (1949) Rozsa
Easter Parade (1948) Salinger
Easter Yeggs (1946) Stalling
Eastern White Pine (1960) Kleinsinger
Easy Come, Easy Go (1947) Webb
Easy Come, Easy Go (1967) Lilley
Easy Life (1944) Carbonara
Easy Living (1937) Jenkins
Easy Living (1949) Webb
Easy Peckin's (1952) Stalling
Easy to Look At (1945) Skinner, F.
Easy to Love (1933) Roemheld
Easy to Love (1953) Stoll
Easy to Take (1936) Stone
Easy to Wed (1946) Green, J.
Eat Me Kitty Eight to the Bar (1942) Scheib
Eatin' on the Cuff (1942) Stalling
Ebb Tide (1937) Young, V.
Ecce Homo—Behold the Man (1965) Wilding-White
Echo Mountain (1936) Jackson, H.
Echo of an Era (1957) Amram
Echo of Youth (1919) Simon, W.
ECS (1961) Collette
Ecstasies of Women (1969) Allen, B.
Eddie Cantor Story (1954) Buttolph, David
Eddy Duchin Story (1956) Duning
Edgar Runs Again (1940) Scheib
Edge of Darkness (1943) Waxman
Edge of Doom (1950) Friedhofer
Edge of Eternity (1959) Amfitheatrof
Edge of Hell (1956) Gold
Edge of the Abyss (1915) Schertzinger
Edge of the City (1956) Rosenman
Edison, the Man (1940) Stothart
Educated Fish (1937) Timberg
Education for Death (1942) Wallace

Edward, My Son (1949) Rozsa
Eegah! (1962) Price, Henry
Egg and I (1947) Skinner, F.
Egg and Jerry (1956) Bradley
Egg Collector (1940) Stalling
Egg Cracker Suite (1943) Calker
Egg Hunt (1940) Kilfeather
Egg Scramble (1949) Stalling
Egg-Yegg (1945) Kilfeather
EGGcited Rooster (1951) Stalling
Egghead Rides Again (1937) Stalling
Eggnapper (1961) Poddany
Eggs (1970) Jones
Eggs Don't Bounce (1943) Timberg
Egyptian (1954) Newman
Egyptian Melodies (1931) Churchill
Eight Bells (1935) Jackson, H.
Eight Girls in a Boat (1934) Lewis, Harold
Eight Iron Men (1952) Stevens, L.
Eighteen and Anxious (1957) Stevens, L.
El Caballero de la Noche (1932) Bassett, R. H.
El Cid (1961) Rozsa
El Condor (1970) Jarre
El Diablo Rides (1939) Lange, J.
El Dorado (1966) Riddle
El Paso (1949) Calker
El Paso Stampede (1953) Wilson, S.
El Príncipe Gondolero (1931) Kopp, R.
El Rey de los Gitanos (1933) Kaylin
El Terrible Toreador (1929) Stalling
El Trovador de la Radio (1938) Riesenfeld
El Ultimo Varon Sobre la Tierra (1933) Friedhofer
Eleanor Roosevelt Story (1965) Laderman
Electrical Power (1939) Snell
Electronic Mouse Trap (1946) Scheib
Electronica (1960) Sharples, Winston
Elements of the Film (1965) Klein, Martin
Elephant Mouse (1951) Scheib
Elephant Never Forgets (1935) Timberg
Elephant Stampede (1951) Kraushaar
Elephant Walk (1954) Waxman
Eli Eli (1931) Secunda
Eli Eli (1940) Secunda
Eliza on the Ice (1944) Scheib
Eliza Runs Again (1938) Scheib
Ellen in Windowland (1958) Frank
Ellery Queen and the Murder Ring (1941) Zahler
Ellery Queen and the Perfect Crime (1941) Zahler
Ellery Queen, Master Detective (1940) Zahler
Ellery Queen's Penthouse Mystery (1941) Zahler
Ellis Island (1936) Zahler
Elmer and Elsie (1934) Leipold
Elmer Elephant (1936) Harline
Elmer Gantry (1960) Previn, A.
Elmer, the Great Dane (1935) Dietrich
Elmer's Candid Camera (1940) Stalling
Elmer's Pet Rabbit (1940) Stalling
Elopement (1951) Mockridge
Embarrassing Moments (1934) Ward, E.
Embraceable You (1948) Lava
Emergency Call (1933) Webb
Emergency Hospital (1956) Dunlap
Emergency Landing (1941) Porter
Emergency Squad (1939) Shuken
Emergency Wedding (1950) Heymann
Emma Belle Sweet (1962) Kleinsinger
Emperor Jones (1933) Tours
Emperor Waltz (1948) Young, V.
Emperor's Candlesticks (1937) Waxman
Emperor's Horses (1952) Lava
Emperor's New Clothes (1953) Lees
Empire State (1945) De Francesco
Employees' Entrance (1933) Kaun
Empty Holsters (1937) Jackson, H.
Enchanted Cottage (1945) Webb
Enchanted Forest (1945) Malotte
Enchanted Islands (1951) Jackson, H.
Enchanted Square (1947) Sharples, Winston
Enchanted Valley (1947) Cailliet
Enchantment (1948) Friedhofer
Encounter and Response (1965) Nelson, O.
End of St. Petersburg (1928) Stothart
End of the Road (1960) Macero
Endowing Our Future (1957) Brant
Enemies of Women (1923) Peters
Enemy Agents Meet Ellery Queen (1942) Zahler
Enemy Bacteria (1945) Calker
Enemy Below (1957) Harline
Enemy General (1960) Bakaleinikoff, M.
Enemy of the Law (1945) Zahler
Enemy of Women (1944) Guttmann
Energetically Yours (1957) Murray
Energy on the Move (1964) Lambro
Enforcer (1951) Buttolph, David
English Farm Family (1952) Forrell
English Outings (1949) Jackson, H.
Ensign Pulver (1964) Duning
Enter Arsene Lupin (1944) Rosen, M.
Enter Laughing (1967) Jones
Enter Madame! (1935) Roemheld
Envelope Jive (1962) Rubenstein
Environmental Sanitation (1946) Smith, P.
Equestrian Acrobatics (1937) Snell
Equinox (1970) Mendoza-Nava
Erik the Conqueror (1963) Baxter
Ernest Hemingway's Adventures of a Young Man (1962) Waxman
Ernst Thaelmann: Fighter Against Fascism (1934) Adomian
Erotica (1961) Morgan, T.
Errand Boy (1961) Scharf, W.
Escapade (1935) Kaper
Escapade in Japan (1957) Steiner, M.
Escape (1940) Waxman
Escape by Night (1937) Colombo
Escape from Crime (1942) Lava
Escape from Fort Bravo (1953) Alexander, J.
Escape from Red Rock (1957) Baxter

Escape from San Quentin (1957) Almeida
Escape from Zahrain (1961) Murray
Escape in the Desert (1945) Deutsch
Escape Me Never (1947) Korngold
Escape to Burma (1955) Forbes
Escape to Glory (1940) Heymann
Escape to Paradise (1939) Young, V.
Escort West (1959) Vars
Eskimo (1934) Axt
Eskimo Trails (1940) Rochetti
Espionage (1937) Axt
Espionage Agent (1939) Deutsch
Et Tu Otto (1962) Sharples, Winston
Eternal Harvest (1958) Kleinsinger
Eternal Jew (1933) Kay, Al
Eternal Love (1929) Riesenfeld
Eternal Sea (1955) Bernstein, E.
Eternally Yours (1939) Janssen
Europe in the Raw (1963) Skiles
Evangeline (1929) Riesenfeld
Eve and the Merman (1965) Roth
Eve Knew Her Apples (1945) Duning
Eve of St. Mark (1944) Mockridge
Evelyn Prentice (1934) Bassett, R. H.
Evening in a Jewish Camp (1931) Secunda
Events (1969) Oliveros
Events (1970) Gale
Ever in My Heart (1933) Kaun
Ever Since Eve (1934) Buttolph, David
Ever Since Eve (1937) Roemheld
Ever Since Venus (1944) Plumb
Everglade Raid (1958) Wheeler
Everglades Adventure (1948) De Francesco
Evergreen Empire (1939) Rochetti
Every Day's a Holiday (1938) Shuken
Every Dog Has His Day (1952) Lava
Every Girl Should Be Married (1948) Harline
Every Moment Thine (1955) Laszlo
Every Night at Eight (1935) Hollander
Every Sparrow Must Fall (1964) Kroculick
Everybody Dances (1956) Jackson, H.
Everybody Sing (1937) Dietrich
Everybody Sing (1938) Axt
Everybody's Dancin' (1950) Glasser
Everybody's Handicapped (1953) Applebaum
Everybody's Hobby (1939) Jackson, H.
Everybody's Old Man (1936) Buttolph, David
Everything But the Truth (1956) Stein, H.
Everything Happens at Night (1939) Buttolph, David
Everything I Have Is Yours (1952) Rose
Everything's Ducky (1961) Green, B.
Everything's on Ice (1939) Filippi
Everywhere in the World (1942) Agostini
Evidence (1929) Dunn
Evil Eye (1964) Baxter
Evil Eye Conquers (1933) Vincent, P.
Evolution of a Shadow (1964) Stock
Exalted Flapper (1929) Kay, Arthur
Exception and the Rule (1964) Ivey
Excess Baggage (1928) Axt
Ex-Champ (1939) Skinner, F.
Exchanges I (1969) Stallings
Exclusive (1937) Leipold
Exclusive Story (1936) Ward, E.
Excuse My Dust (1951) Stoll
Executive Suite (1954). See p. 8
Exile (1931) Heywood
Exile (1948) Skinner, F.
Exile Express (1939) Parrish
Exiled to Shanghai (1937) Colombo
Exodus (1960) Gold
Exotic Mexico (1942) Nussbaum
Expanding World Relationships (1946) Smith, P.
Expensive Husbands (1937) Roemheld
Experiment Alcatraz (1950) Gertz
Experiment in Terror (1962) Mancini
Experiment Perilous (1944) Webb
Expert (1932) Harling
Explorer (1931) Scheib
Explorers of the World (1931) Wachtel
Explosion (1970) Kaplan, S.
Explosive Generation (1961) Borne
Explosive Mr. Magoo (1958) Wilson, S.
Exposed (1938) Skinner, F.
Exposed (1947) Gold
Exposure (1959) Lewis, John
Expressionist Revolt (1957) Chudacoff
Exterminator (1945) Scheib
Extinct Pink (1969) Goodwin
Extraordinary Seaman (1968) Jarre
Extravagance (1930) Burton
Eye (1942) Applebaum
Eye Creatures (1965) Stein, R.
Eye for an Eye (1966) Kraushaar
Eye in Space (1957) Bazelon
Eye of an Artist (1956) George
Eye of the Cat (1969) Schifrin
Eyes Have It (1945) Smith, P.
Eyes in Outer Space (1959) Bruns
Eyes in the Night (1942) Hayton
Eyes of Texas (1948) Butts
Eyes of the Jungle (1953) Gertz
Eyes of the Navy (1940) Amfitheatrof
Ezra Jack Keats (1970) Freedman

Fabiola (1923) Henneman
Fabulous Bastard from Chicago (1969) Saint-Sanez
Fabulous Dorseys (1947) Shuken
Fabulous Fireworks Family (1959) Scheib
Fabulous Fraud (1948) Franklyn, R.
Fabulous Joe (1947) Roemheld
Fabulous Senorita (1952) Wilson, S.
Fabulous Suzanne (1946) Lange
Fabulous Texan (1947) Collins
Face Behind the Mask (1941) Cutner
Face in the Crowd (1957) Glazer
Face in the Rain (1963) Markowitz

Face in the Sky (1933) Brunelli
Face of a Fugitive (1959) Goldsmith
Face of Marble (1946) Kay, Edward
Face of Youth (1951) Luckhardt
Face to Face (1952) Friedhofer
Face to Face—Walt Whitman: A Hundred Years Hence (1968) Alexander, W.
Faces (1968) Ackerman
Faces and Fortunes (1960) Macero
Faces in the Fog (1944) Dubin
Faces of America (1965) Kupferman
Facing Your Danger (1945) Dunn
Facts of Life (1960) Harline
Fade In (1968) Lauber
Fagin's Freshmen (1939) Stalling
Fahrenheit 451 (1967) Herrmann
Failure at Fifty (1939) Amfitheatrof
Fair and Worm-er (1946) Stalling
Fair-Haired Hare (1950) Stalling
Fair Today (1941) Calker
Fair Warning (1930) Kay, Arthur
Fair Weather Fiends (1946) Calker
Fair Wind to Java (1953) Young, V.
Fairway Champions (1949) Mamorsky
Faithful in My Fashion (1946) Shilkret, N.
Faithless (1932) Axt
Fala (1943) Terr
Falcon in Mexico (1944) Harline
Falcon in San Francisco (1945) Sawtell
Falcon Out West (1944) Webb
Falcon's Adventure (1947) Sawtell
Falcon's Alibi (1946) Gold
Fall (Fashion Forecast) (1938) Rochetti
Fall Guy (1945) Terr
Fall Guy (1947) Kay, Edward
Fall In (1943) Ward, E.
Fall of a Nation (1916) Herbert
Fall of Babylon (1919) Gottschalk
Fall of the House of Usher (1959) Wilder
Fall of the House of Usher (1960) Baxter
Fall of the Roman Empire (1964) Tiomkin
Fall Out—Fall In (1943) Smith, P.
Fallen Angel (1945) Raksin
Fallen Sparrow (1943) Webb
Fallguy (1962) Mendoza-Nava
Falling Hare (1943) Stalling
False Alarm (1933) De Nat
False Colors (1943) Sawtell
False Faces (1932) Burton
False Hare (1963) Lava
False Madonna (1931) Leipold
False Paradise (1948) Kraushaar
Family Circus (1951) Gold
Family Honeymoon (1948) Skinner, F.
Family Jewels (1965) King
Family Next Door (1939) Skinner, F.
Family Planning (1967) Baker, Buddy
Family Secret (1951) Duning
Famous Ferguson Case (1932) Kaun
Famous Movie Dogs (1940) Jackson, H.
Famous Ride (1960) Scheib
Fan (1949) Amfitheatrof
Fancy Pants (1950) Van Cleave
Fancy Plants (1967) Timmens
Fandango (1970) Toscana
Fang and Claw (1935) Sharples, Winston
Fangs of the Arctic (1953) Kay, Edward
Fangs of the Wild (1954) Dunlap
Fanny (1960) Sukman
Fanny Foley Herself (1931) Steiner, M.
Fanny Hill (1969) Pitts
Fanny in the Lion's Den (1933) Scheib
Fanny's Wedding Day (1933) Scheib
Fantastic Plastic Machine (1969) Betts
Fantastic Voyage (1966) Rosenman
Fantasy of Siam (1947) De Francesco
Fantasy of the Sky (1956) Romeo
Far Country (1954) Skinner, F.
Far Frontier (1949) Butts
Far Horizons (1955) Salter
Far Sound (1962) Lackey
Fare Play (1932) De Nat
Farewell to Arms (1933) Harling
Farewell to Yesterday (1950) Applebaum
Fargo (1952) Kraushaar
Fargo Kid (1940) Leipold
Farm Battle Lines (1943) Forrell
Farm Foolery (1949) Sharples, Winston
Farm Frolics (1941) Stalling
Farm Front (1942) Arnell
Farm of Tomorrow (1954) Bradley
Farm Petroleum Safety (1954) Shores
Farmer (1931) Dietrich
Farmer Al Falfa and the Runt (1936) Scheib
Farmer Al Falfa's 20th Anniversary (1936) Scheib
Farmer Al Falfa's Ape Girl (1932) Scheib
Farmer Al Falfa's Bedtime Story (1932) Scheib
Farmer Al Falfa's Birthday Party (1932) Scheib
Farmer Al Falfa's Prize Package (1936) Scheib
Farmer and the Belle (1951) Sharples, Winston
Farmer Takes a Wife (1935) Buttolph, David
Farmer Takes a Wife (1953) Mockridge
Farmer Tom Thumb (1940) De Nat
Farmer's Daughter (1940) Young, V.
Farmer's Daughter (1947) Harline
Farmer's Other Daughter (1965) Pierce, V.
Farmers at War (1943) Forrell
Farming Fools (1936) Dietrich
Farmyard Symphony (1938) Harline
Fashion Horizons (1965) Mottola
Fashion Model (1945) Kay, Edward
Fashioned for Action (1948) De Francesco
Fashions for Tomorrow (1945) Jackson, H.
Fashions in Love (1929) Potoker
Fashions of 1934 (1934) Roemheld
Fashions of Yesteryear (1949) De Francesco
Fast and Furious (1939) Amfitheatrof
Fast and Furry-ous (1948) Stalling

Fast and the Furious (1954) Gerens
Fast Buck Duck (1962) Lava
Fast Company (1929) Carbonara
Fast Company (1938) Axt
Fast Company (1953) Colombo
Fast on the Draw (1950) Greene, W.
Fast Ones (1958) Bath
Fast Workers (1933) Axt
Faster, Pussycat! Kill! Kill! (1966) Sawtell
Fastest Guitar Alive (1966) Karger
Fastest Gun Alive (1956) Previn, A.
Fastest with the Mostest (1959) Franklyn
Fat Black Pussycat (1963) Bader
Fat Man (1951) Skinner, F.
Fat People, Skinny People (1968) Mulligan
Fatal Hour (1940) Kay, Edward
Fatal Kiss (1947) Smith, P.
Fatal Lady (1936) Young, V.
Fate Is the Hunter (1964) Goldsmith
Father Brown, Detective (1934) Roemheld
Father Goose (1964) Coleman, C.
Father Is a Bachelor (1950) Morton
Father Is a Prince (1940) Dunn
Father Knows Best (1935) Dietrich
Father Makes Good (1950) Kay, Edward
Father Nile (1931) Maloof
Father Noah's Ark (1933) Harline
Father of the Bride (1950) Deutsch
Father Steps Out (1941) Kay, Edward
Father Takes a Wife (1941) Webb
Father Takes the Air (1951) Kay, Edward
Father Was a Fullback (1949) Mockridge
Father's Day Off (1952) Smith, P.
Father's Lion (1951) Dubin
Father's Little Dividend (1951) Sendrey
Father's Son (1931) Copping
Father's Son (1941) Jackson, H.
Father's Week-End (1953) Dubin
Father's Wild Game (1950) Kay, Edward
Fathers Are People (1951) Smith, P.
Fathomless (1969) Lewin
Faust (1926) Axt
Fazil (1927) Bassett, R. H.
Fazil (1928) Rapée
F.B.I. Code 98 (1964) Jackson, H.
F.B.I. Girl (1951) Calker
FBI Story (1959) Steiner, M.
FDR—Hyde Park (1952) Landau, I.
Fear (1946) Kay, Edward
Fear and Desire (1953) Fried
Fear in the Night (1947) Schrager
Fear No More (1961) Glass, Paul
Fear Strikes Out (1957) Bernstein, E.
Fearless Fagan (1952) Kopp, R.
Fearless Frank (1969) Kupferman
Fearmakers (1958) Gertz
Feast and Furious (1952) Sharples, Winston
Feather Bluster (1957) Franklyn
Feather Dusted (1954) Franklyn
Feather Finger (1966) Greene, W.
Feather in His Hare (1946) Stalling
Feathered Bullets (1951) Shilkret, N.
Feathered Serpent (1949) Kay, Edward
Featherweight Champ (1953) Scheib
Federal Agent at Large (1950) Wilson, S.
Federal Agents vs. Underworld, Inc. (1948) Wilson, S.
Federal Fugitives (1941) Colombo
Federal Man (1950) Calker
Federal Man Hunt (1938) Feuer
Feed My Sheep (1957) Gates, C.
Feed the Kitty (1938) Churchill
Feed the Kitty (1951) Stalling
Feedin' the Kiddie (1956) Bradley
Feelin' Good (1966) Korb
Feeling All Right (1949) Applebaum
Feet First (1930) Lapham
Feline Frame-Up (1953) Stalling
Felineous Assault (1958) Sharples, Winston
Felix the Cat and the Goose That Laid the Golden Egg (1936) Sharples, Winston
Felix the Fox (1948) Scheib
Fella with the Fiddle (1937) Stalling
Fellow Americans (1942) Levant
Female Animal (1957) Salter
Female Animal (1970) Pitts
Female Jungle (1956) Carras
Female on the Beach (1955) Stein, H.
Females Is Fickle (1940) Timberg
Feminine Touch (1941) Waxman
Fence Riders (1950) Kay, Edward
Ferdinand the Bull (1938) Malotte
Fernand Leger in America (1943) Varèse
Festival Days (1955) Jackson, H.
Festival of Judo (1956) Monachelli
Feud (1936) Scheib
Feud of the Range (1939) Sanucci
Feud There Was (1938) Stalling
Feud with a Dude (1968) Lava
Feudin' Fools (1952) Kay, Edward
Feudin', Fussin' and A-Fightin' (1948) Stevens, L.
Feudin' Hillbillies (1948) Scheib
Fever Heat (1968) Mendoza-Nava
Fever in the Blood (1961) Gold
Few Quick Facts (#1) (1944) Bradley
Few Quick Facts (#2) (1944) Bradley
Few Quick Facts (#3) (1944) Bradley
Few Quick Facts (#4) (1944) Bradley
Few Quick Facts (#5) (1944) Bradley
Few Quick Facts (#8) (1944) Bradley
Fiberglass Chairs (1970) Collette
Fiddle Faddle (1959) Sharples, Winston
Fiddler (1930) De Nat
Fiddlesticks (1931) Stalling
Fiddlin' Around (1962) Sharples, Winston
Fiddlin' Fun (1934) Sharples, Winston
Fido Beta Kappa (1954) Sharples, Winston
Field and Scream (1954) Bradley

Field Mouse (1941) Bradley
Fiend of Dope Island (1961) Peterson
Fiend Who Walked the West (1958) Sawtell
Fiercest Heart (1961) Gertz
Fiesta (1941) Ward, E.
Fiesta (1947) Green, J.
Fiesta Fiasco (1967) Lava
Fiesta for Sports (1953) Lava
Fiesta Time (1945) Kilfeather
Fiesta Time (1950) Sharples, Winston
Fifth Column Mouse (1943) Stalling
Fifth Freedom (1963) Wing
Fifty-First Dragon (1954) Klatzkin
Fifty Year Barter (1937) Zahler
Figaro and Cleo (1943) Smith, P.
Figaro and Frankie (1946) Wallace
Fight, Fish, Fight (1941) Dunn
Fight for Life (1940) Gruenberg
Fight to the Finish (1947) Scheib
Fight: Science Against Cancer (1951) Applebaum
Fighter (1952) Gomez
Fighter Attack (1953) Skiles
Fighter Squadron (1948) Steiner, M.
Fightin' Pals (1940) Timberg
Fighting 69th (1940) Deutsch
Fighting 69th 1/2 (1940) Stalling
Fighting Athletes (1948) Lava
Fighting Back (1948) Calker
Fighting Bill Carson (1945) Sanucci
Fighting Caravans (1931) Leipold
Fighting Chance (1955) Butts
Fighting Coast Guard (1951) Buttolph, David
Fighting Dan McCool (1912) Komroff
Fighting Dervishes of the Desert (1912) Simon, W.
Fighting Devil Dogs (1938) Colombo
Fighting Engineers (1943) Jackson, H.
Fighting Father Dunne (1948) Webb
Fighting Fools (1949) Kay, Edward
Fighting Frontier (1942) Sawtell
Fighting Guardsman (1945) Sawtell
Fighting Kentuckian (1949) Antheil
Fighting Lady (1944) Buttolph, David
Fighting Lawman (1953) Kraushaar
Fighting Man of the Plains (1949) Sawtell
Fighting Marines (1935) Kay, Arthur
Fighting Mustang (1948) Sanucci
Fighting O'Flynn (1948) Skinner, F.
Fighting President (1933) Rochetti
Fighting Prince of Donegal (1966) Bruns
Fighting Ranger (1948) Kay, Edward
Fighting Redhead (1949) Calker
Fighting Seabees (1944) Scharf, W.
Fighting Stallion (1950) Wheeler
Fighting Tarpon (1948) Shilkret, N.
Fighting Thoroughbreds (1939) Feuer
Fighting Tools (1943) Stalling
Fighting Trouble (1956) Bregman
Fighting Valley (1943) Zahler
Fighting Vigilantes (1947) Greene, W.
Fighting with Kit Carson (1933) Zahler
File on Thelma Jordan (1949) Young, V.
Filet Meow (1966) Elliott, Dean
Filipino Sports Parade (1944) Lava
Film as an Art (1966) Crooks
Film Fan (1939) Stalling
Film for Hooded Projector (1963) Manupelli
Film Made to Music Written by Paul Bowles (1939) Bowles
Film Magazine of the Arts (1963) de Hirsch
Film Parade (1934) Zahler
Film Record of the Eucharistic Congress (1926) Rapée
Fin 'n Catty (1943) Stalling
Fin 'n Feathers (1945) Jackson, H.
Fincho (1957) Laszlo
Find the Blackmailer (1943) Roemheld
Finders Keepers (1951) Salter
Fine Feathered Fiend (1960) Sharples, Winston
Fine Feathered Frenzy (1954) Wheeler
Fine Feathered Friend (1942) Bradley
Fine Madness (1966) Addison
Fingerman (1955) Dunlap
Fingerprints Don't Lie (1951) Shefter
Fingers at the Window (1942) Kaper
Finian's Rainbow (1968) Heindorf
Finn and Hattie (1931) Rainger
Finnegan's Flea (1958) Sharples, Winston
Finney (1969) Reynolds
Fire Alarm (1936) Spencer, N.
Fire Brigade (1927) Axt
Fire Bugs (1930) Steiner, G.
Fire Chief (1940) Smith, P.
Fire! Fire! (1932) Bradley
Fire in Cities (1961) Brant
Fire Plug (1937) De Nat
Fire Trap (1936) Zahler
Fireball (1950) Young, V.
Fireball 500 (1966) Baxter
Firebird (1934) Kaun
Firebrand (1962) LaSalle
Firecreek (1967) Newman
Fired Wife (1943) Skinner, F.
Firefly (1937) Stothart
Firehouse Honeymoon (1932) Malotte
Fireman (1931) Dietrich
Fireman, Save My Child (1932) Harling
Fireman, Save My Child (1935) Scheib
Fireman, Save My Child (1954) Lava
Fireman's Bride (1931) Scheib
Firemen's Brawl (1953) Sharples, Winston
Firemen's Picnic (1937) Lessner
First 100 Years (1965) Siegel, S.
First Aid (1942) Snell
First Aiders (1944) Wallace
First as a Child (1948) Applebaum
First Baby (1936) Kaylin
First Bad Man (1955) Bradley
First Comes Courage (1943) Toch

First Hundred (1954) Keller
First Hundred Years (1938) Axt
First Impression (1964) Boyell
First Lady (1937) Steiner, M.
First Legion (1951) Sommer
First Love (1939) Skinner, F.
First Noel (1961) Marks
First Offenders (1939) Parrish
First Robin (1939) Scheib
First Snow (1935) Scheib
First Snow (1947) Scheib
First Swallow (1942) Bradley
First Texan (1956) Webb
First Time (1952) Hollander
First Time (1969) Hopkins, K.
First to Fight (1967) Steiner, F.
First Traveling Saleslady (1956) Gertz
First Woman Into Space (1965) Skiles
First World War (1934) Rochetti
First Yank Into Tokyo (1945) Harline
First Year (1932) Friedhofer
Fish and Chips (1962) Greene, W.
Fish and Slips (1961) Franklyn
Fish Are Where You Find Them (1956) Jackson, H.
Fish Follies (1940) De Nat
Fish Fry (1944) Calker
Fish Hooked (1960) Poddany
Fish Tales (1936) Spencer, N.
Fisherman (1931) Dietrich
Fisherman's Nightmare (1947) De Francesco
Fisherman's Wharf (1939) Young, V.
Fishermen's Luck (1945) Scheib
Fishin' Around (1931) Lewis
Fishing Bear (1940) Bradley
Fishing by the Sea (1947) Scheib
Fishing for Fun (1949) Bradley
Fishing Made Easy (1941) Scheib
Fishing Tackler (1957) Sharples, Winston
Fishing the Florida Keys (1947) Dunn
Fistic Mystic (1946) Sharples, Winston
Fistic Mystic (1969) Lava
Fit for a King (1937) Morton
Fit to Be Tied (1952) Bradley
Fit to Be Toyed (1958) Sharples, Winston
Fitzwilly (1967) Williams, J.
Five (1951) Russell, H.
Five and Dime (1933) Dietrich
Five Bold Women (1960) Calker
Five Came Back (1939) Webb
Five Chinese Brothers (1958) Kleiner
Five Finger Exercise (1962) Moross
Five Gates to Hell (1959) Dunlap
Five Graves to Cairo (1943) Rozsa
Five Guns to Tombstone (1960) Sawtell
Five Guns West (1954) Bregman
Five Hundred Horses (1955) Craig, E.
Five Little Peppers in Trouble (1940) Cutner
Five Miles West (1957) Ralf
Five Minutes to Live (1961) Kauer
Five of a Kind (1938) Rose, G.
Five Pennies (1959) Stevens, L.
Five Puplets (1935) Scheib
Five Short Films (1963) Manupelli
Five the Hard Way (1969) Curb
Five Weeks in a Balloon (1962) Sawtell
Fix That Clock (1964) Sharples, Winston
Fixed Bayonets! (1951) Webb
Fixer (1968) Jarre
Fixer Dugan (1939) Webb
Fizzicle Fizzle (1964) Sharples, Winston
Flag of Humanity (1940) Jackson, H.
Flag Speaks (1940) Snell
Flamboyant Arms (1959) Scheib
Flame (1947) Roemheld
Flame and the Arrow (1950) Steiner, M.
Flame and the Fire (1966) Colicchio
Flame and the Flesh (1954) Stoll
Flame Barrier (1958) Fried
Flame of Barbary Coast (1945) Butts
Flame of Calcutta (1953) Vaughan
Flame of New Orleans (1941) Skinner, F.
Flame of the Islands (1955) Riddle
Flame of the West (1945) Sanucci
Flame of Youth (1949) Wilson, S.
Flame Within (1935) Kern
Flaming Bullets (1945) Zahler
Flaming Creatures (1963) Conrad
Flaming Feather (1951) Sawtell
Flaming Frontier (1926) Riesenfeld
Flaming Frontier (1958) Bath
Flaming Signal (1933) Zahler
Flaming Star (1960) Mockridge
Flamingo Road (1949) Steiner, M.
Flap (1970) Hamlisch
Flareup (1969) Baxter
Flash Gordon (1936) Vaughan
Flashing Guns (1947) Kay, Edward
Flat Foot Fledgling (1952) Scheib
Flat Top (1952) Skiles
Flatbush, Florida (1950) Sharples, Winston
Flaxy Martin (1949) Lava
Flea Circus (1954) Bradley
Flea for Two (1955) Wheeler
Flea in Her Ear (1968) Kaper
Flebus (1957) Pintoff
Fleet That Came to Stay (1945) Engel
Fleet's In (1942) Shuken
Fleets of Stren'th (1942) Timberg
Flesh (1932) Newman
Flesh and Fantasy (1943) Tansman
Flesh and Fury (1952) Salter
Flesh and the Devil (1927) Axt
Flesh and the Spur (1956) Stein, R.
Flesh Eaters (1964) Stein, J.
Flesh Merchant (1955) Price, W.
Flicker (1966) Conrad
Flight (1960) Almeida
Flight 6 (1944) Applebaum

Flight Angels (1940) Roemheld
Flight at Midnight (1939) Feuer
Flight Command (1940) Waxman
Flight for Freedom (1943) Webb
Flight from Destiny (1941) Roemheld
Flight Lieutenant (1942) Heymann
Flight Nurse (1953) Young, V.
Flight of Birds (1966) Bath
Flight of the Lost Balloon (1961) Borne
Flight of the Phoenix (1965) De Vol
Flight That Disappeared (1961) LaSalle
Flight to Fame (1938) Cutner
Flight to Hong Kong (1956) Glasser
Flight to Mars (1951) Skiles
Flight to Nowhere (1946) Mayfield
Flight to Tangier (1953) Sawtell
Flim-Flam Man (1967) Goldsmith
Flip Flap (1948) Sharples, Winston
Flipper (1963) Vars
Flipper Frolics (1952) Scheib
Flipper's New Adventure (1964) Vars
Flirtation (1934) Riesenfeld
Flirtation Walk (1934) Roemheld
Flirting Widow (1930) Reiser
Flirting with Fate (1938) Young, V.
Flirty Birdy (1945) Bradley
Flivver Flying (1945) Dunn
Float Like a Butterfly, Sting Like a Bee (1969) Baker, M.
Flood (1931) Brunelli
Flood Tide (1957) Mancini
Floor Flusher (1954) Sharples, Winston
Flop (1951) Lewin
Flop Goes the Weasel (1943) Stalling
Flop House (1932) De Nat
Flop Secret (1952) Scheib
Flora (1948) Calker
Flora (1965) Ito
Floral Japan (1937) Grever
Florentine Dagger (1935) Kaun
Florian (1940) Waxman
Florida Aflame (1955) Craig, E.
Florida Cowhands (1951) Shilkret, N.
Florida, Land of Flowers (1940) Rochetti
Florida Special (1936) Bradshaw
Flower Arrangements of Williamsburg (1953) Horst
Flower Drum Song (1961) Newman
Flowers for Madame (1936) Spencer, N.
Flowing Gold (1940) Deutsch
Fluffy (1964) Gertz
Fly (1958) Sawtell
Fly-Away Baby (1937) Jackson, H.
Fly Fishing (1940) Dunn
Fly in the Ointment (1943) Worth, P.
Fly's Last Flight (1949) Sharples, Winston
Flying Bear (1941) Bradley
Flying Blind (1941) Tiomkin
Flying Cat (1951) Bradley
Flying Circus (1968) Lava
Flying Cups and Saucers (1949) Scheib
Flying Deuces (1939) Leipold
Flying Disc Man from Mars (1950) Wilson, S.
Flying Fever (1941) Scheib
Flying Fists (1931) Stalling
Flying Fleet (1929) Axt
Flying Fontaines (1959) Bakaleinikoff, M.
Flying Fortress (Trailer, 1942) Lava
Flying G-Men (1939) Cutner
Flying Gunners (1943) De Francesco
Flying High (1931) Axt
Flying Horseshoes (1953) Mamorsky
Flying Hunters (1934) Axt
Flying Irishman (1939) Webb
Flying Jalopy (1943) Wallace
Flying Jeep (1947) Smith, P.
Flying Leathernecks (1951) Webb
Flying Missile (1950) Duning
Flying Mouse (1934) Churchill
Flying Oil (1935) Scheib
Flying Padre (1951) Shilkret, N.
Flying Saucer (1949) Calker
Flying Serpent (1946) Erdody
Flying Sorceress (1956) Bradley
Flying South (1937) Scheib
Flying South (1947) Scheib
Flying Sportsman in Jamaica (1947) Jackson, H.
Flying Sportsman in the West Indies (1945) Jackson, H.
Flying Squirrel (1954) Wallace
Flying Stewardess (1940) Rochetti
Flying Tigers (1942) Young, V.
Flying Torpedo (1916) Raynes
Flying Turtle (1953) Wheeler
Flying Wild (1941) Lange, J.
Flying with Music (1942) Ward, E.
Foaled for Fame (1949) De Francesco
Focus on a Century of Communications (1964) Martin, R.
Fodder and Son (1957) Wheeler
Fog Island (1945) Hajos
Fog Over Frisco (1934) Kaun
Foghorn Leghorn (1948) Stalling
Foiled Again (1932) Dietrich
Foiled Again (1935) Scheib
Folies Bergere (1935) Newman
Folk Artist of the Blue Ridge (1963) Repine
Follow Me (1969) Phillips, S.
Follow Me, Boys! (1966) Bruns
Follow Me Quietly (1949) Raab
Follow That Dream (1961) Salter
Follow That Woman (1945) Laszlo
Follow the Arrow (1938) Allen, W.
Follow the Band (1943) Skinner, F.
Follow the Boys (1944) Harline
Follow the Boys (1963) Courage
Follow the Fleet (1936) Steiner, M.
Follow the Game Trails (1951) Mamorsky

Follow the Leader (1944) Kay, Edward
Follow the Sun (1951) Mockridge
Follow Thru (1930) Duke
Follow Thru with Sam Byrd (1944) Shilkret, J.
Follow Your Heart (1936) Riesenfeld
Foney Fables (1942) Stalling
Food and Magic (1943) Lava
Food for Feudin' (1949) Smith, P.
Food Will Win the War (1942) Smith, P.
Food, Weapon of Conquest (1945) Applebaum
Foofle's Picnic (1959) Scheib
Foofle's Train Ride (1959) Scheib
Fool Coverage (1951) Stalling
Fool There Was (1915) Gay
Fool's Advice (1932) Ward, E.
Foolish Bunny (1938) De Nat
Foolish Duckling (1952) Scheib
Foolish Wives (1922) Romberg
Fools (1970) Rogers
Fools for Scandal (1938) Deutsch
Foot Brawl (1965) Greene, W.
Football (1935) Scheib
Football (Now and Then) (1953) Plumb
Football Bugs (1936) De Nat
Football Fan (1949) Sharples, Winston
Football Fanfare (1946) De Francesco
Football Fever (1937) Dietrich
Football Finesse (1948) De Francesco
Football Royal (1955) Jackson, H.
Football Thrills (1938) Snell
Football Thrills, No. 10 (1947) Bradley
Football Thrills, No. 12 (1949) Bradley
Football Thrills, No. 14 (1951) Wolcott
Football Thrills, No. 15 (1952) Bradley
Football Thrills of 1938 (1939) Snell
Football Thrills of 1939 (1940) Snell
Football Thrills of 1940 (1941) Snell
Football Thrills of 1941 (1942) Snell
Football Thrills of 1942 (1943) Terr
Football Thrills of 1943 (1944) Terr
Football Thrills of 1944 (1945) Terr
Football Thrills of 1945 (1946) Terr
Football Toucher Downer (1937) Timberg
Footlight Glamour (1943) Leipold
Footlight Rhythm (1948) Van Cleave
Footlight Serenade (1942) Henderson, C.
Footlights and Fools (1929) Reiser
Footloose Heiress (1937) Jackson, H.
Footsteps in the Dark (1941) Hollander
Footsteps in the Night (1957) Skiles
For Ages 10 to Adult (1966) Rudin
For All Time (1958) Forrell
For Beauty's Sake (1940) Buttolph, David
For Better or Nurse (1945) Sharples, Winston
For Every Child (1953) Forbes
For God and Country (1943) Kaplan, S.
For Heaven's Sake (1950) Newman
For Love of Ivy (1968) Jones
For Love or Money (1939) Previn, C.
For Love or Money (1963) De Vol
For Me and My Gal (1942) Edens
For Men Only (1951) Curtin
For Pete's Sake (1966) Carmichael
For Scent-imental Reasons (1948) Stalling
For Singles Only (1968) Karger
For the Dead (1965) Higgins
For the First Time (1959) Stoll
For the Love of Mary (1948) Skinner, F.
For the Love of Rusty (1947) Skiles
For Those Who Think Young (1964) Fielding
For Whom the Bell Tolls (1943) Young, V.
For Whom the Bulls Toil (1953) Dubin
For You I Die (1947) Sawtell
Forbid Them Not (1961) Berres
Forbidden (1953) Skinner, F.
Forbidden Adventure (1931) Kopp, R.
Forbidden Desert (1957) Jackson, H.
Forbidden Fire (1919) Schertzinger
Forbidden Island (1958) Laszlo
Forbidden Jungle (1950) Calker
Forbidden Planet (1956) Barron
Forbidden Trails (1942) Kay, Edward
Forbin Project (1970) Colombier
Force of Arms (1951) Steiner, M.
Force of Evil (1949) Raksin
Force of Impulse (1961) Liebman
Forced Landing (1941) Tiomkin
Forecast—Continued Prosperity (1952) Van Camp
Foreign Affair (1948) Hollander
Foreign Agent (1942) Kay, Edward
Foreign Correspondent (1940) Newman
Forest (1965) Applebaum
Forest Commandos (1945) Dunn
Forest Fantasy (1952) Sharples, Winston
Forest in a Museum (1962) Kleinsinger
Forest Murmers (1963) Kaun
Forest Rangers (1942) Young, V.
Forever Amber (1947) Raksin
Forever and a Day (1943) Collins
Forever, Darling (1955) Kaper
Forever Female (1953) Young, V.
Forever Yours (1944) Tiomkin
Forged Passport (1939) Feuer
Forget Me Not (1965) Moross
Forgotten (1958) Bergsma
Forgotten Commandments (1932) Hand
Forgotten Faces (1936) Leipold
Forgotten Girls (1940) Feuer
Forgotten Island (1947) Shilkret, N.
Forgotten Step (1938) Snell
Forgotten Treasure (1943) Castelnuovo-Tedesco
Forgotten Victory (1939) Amfitheatrof
Forgotten Village (1941) Eisler
Forgotten Woman (1939) Skinner, F.
Forgotten Women (1949) Kay, Edward
Form Evolution (1949) Rosenman
Forms in Space: The Art of Sculpture (1949) Pitton

Fort Algiers (1953) Michelet
Fort Apache (1948) Hageman
Fort Bowie (1958) Baxter
Fort Courageous (1965) LaSalle
Fort Defiance (1951) Sawtell
Fort Dobbs (1958) Steiner, M.
Fort Dodge Stampede (1951) Wilson, S.
Fort Massacre (1958) Skiles
Fort Osage (1951) Skiles
Fort Utah (1967) Haskell
Fort Vengeance (1953) Dunlap
Fort Worth (1951) Buttolph, David
Fort Yuma (1955) Dunlap
Fortress Japan (1944) Applebaum
Fortress of Faith (1959) Gustafson.
Fortress of Freedom (1955) Jackson, H.
Fortress of the Dead (1965) Kauer
Fortune Cookie (1966) Previn, A.
Fortune Hunters (1946) Scheib
Fortune in Two Old Trunks (1947) Kilenyi
Fortune Teller (1934) Roemheld
Fortunes of Captain Blood (1950) Sawtell
Forty Guns (1957) Sukman
Forty Little Mothers (1940) Stringer
Forty-Niners (1954) Kraushaar
Forty Thieves (1932) Scheib
Forty Thieves (1944) Leipold
Forward Commandos (1942) Agostini
Forward March Hare (1952) Stalling
Foul Ball Player (1940) Sharples, Winston
Foul Hunting (1947) Wallace
Fountain (1934) Steiner, M.
Fountain of Faith (1961) Bartlett
Fountainhead (1949) Steiner, M.
Four Against Fate (1952) Collins
Four Boys and a Gun (1957) Glasser
Four Dark Hours (1937) Rozsa
Four Daughters (1938) Steiner, M.
Four Days' Wonder (1936) Previn, C.
Four Devils (1928) Rapée
Four Faces West (1948) Sawtell
Four Feathers (1929) Peters
Four Feathers (1939) Rozsa
Four Frightened People (1934) Hajos
Four Girls in Town (1956) North
Four Guns to the Border (1954) Stein, H.
Four Horsemen of the Apocalypse (1921) Gottschalk
Four Horsemen of the Apocalypse (1961) Previn, A.
Four Hours to Kill! (1935) Roemheld
Four in the Afternoon (1951) Smith, W.
Four Jills in a Jeep (1944) Friedhofer
Four Men and a Prayer (1938) Toch
Four Mothers (1941) Roemheld
Four Poster (1952) Tiomkin
Four Skulls of Jonathan Drake (1959) Dunlap
Four Sons (1928) Rapée
Four Sons (1940) Buttolph, David
Four Wheels, No Brakes (1955) Farnon
Four Wives (1940) Steiner, M.
Four's a Crowd (1938) Roemheld
Fourteen Hours (1951) Newman
Fourth Opinion (1956) Fletcher
Fowl Brawl (1947) Kilfeather
Fowl Play (1937) Timberg
Fowl Weather (1952) Stalling
Fowled Up Falcon (1960) Wheeler
Fowled Up Party (1957) Wheeler
Fox (1967) Schifrin
Fox and the Duck (1945) Scheib
Fox and the Grapes (1941) Kilfeather
Fox and the Rabbit (1935) Dietrich
Fox Hunt (1931) Churchill
Fox Hunt (1950) Scheib
Fox in a Fix (1949) Stalling
Fox Pop (1942) Stalling
Fox Terror (1957) Stalling
Foxed by a Fox (1955) Scheib
Foxes of Harrow (1947) Buttolph, David
Foxey Flatfoots (1946) Kilfeather
Foxfire (1955) Skinner, F.
Foxy by Proxy (1950) Stalling
Foxy Duckling (1947) Stalling
Foxy Fox (1935) Scheib
Foxy Hunter (1937) Timberg
Foxy Pup (1937) Kilfeather
Foxy Terrier (1935) Sharples, Winston
Fractured Friendship (1964) Greene, W.
Fractured Leghorn (1949) Stalling
Fragile (1948) Marshall, D.
Fragments (1967) Evans
Fraidy Cat (1942) Bradley
Framed (1939) Skinner, F.
Framed (1947) Skiles
Framed Cat (1950) Bradley
Frame-Up (1938) Scheib
Francis (1950) Skinner, F.
Francis Covers the Big Town (1952) Skinner, F.
Francis Goes to the Races (1951) Skinner, F.
Francis Goes to West Point (1952) Stein, H.
Francis in the Haunted House (1956) Mancini
Francis in the Navy (1955) Lava
Francis Joins the WACs (1954) Gertz
Frank Buck's Jungle Cavalcade (1941) Shilkret, N.
Frank Duck Brings 'Em Back Alive (1946) Wallace
Frankenstein (1931) Kaun
Frankenstein—1970 (1958) Dunlap
Frankenstein Meets the Wolf Man (1942) Salter
Frankenstein's Cat (1942) Scheib
Frankenstein's Daughter (1958) Carras
Frankie and Johnnie (1936) Young, V.
Frankie and Johnny (1966) Karger
Fraternity for Life (1965) Kenton
Fraud Fighters (1949) Shilkret, N.
Fraulein (1958) Amfitheatrof
Freckles (1960) Vars
Freddie Steps Out (1946) Zahler

Freddie the Freshman (1932) Marsales
Free and Easy (1930) Axt
Free and Easy (1941) Amfitheatrof
Free, Blonde and 21 (1940) Kaylin
Free Enterprise (1948) Scheib
Free for All (1949) Skinner, F.
Free Love (1930) Roemheld
Free Love Confidential (1967) Rubag
Free, White and 21 (1963) Johnson, J.
Freedom and You (1962) Lava
Freedom to Learn (1954) Kleinsinger
Freeloading Feline (1960) Poddany
Freeway Fracus (1964) Wheeler
Freewayphobia, No. 1 (1964) Bruns
Freight Fright (1965) Timmens
Freighters of Destiny (1931) Lange
French Fried (1930) Scheib
French Key (1946) Laszlo
French Leave (1948) Kay, Edward
French Line (1953) Scharf, W.
French Rarebit (1950) Poddany
French Without Dressing (1965) Bath
Frenchie (1950) Salter
Frenchman's Creek (1944) Young, V.
Fresh Airedale (1945) Stalling
Fresh Fish (1939) Stalling
Fresh from the West (1955) Wheeler
Fresh Hare (1942) Stalling
Fresh Laid Plans (1950) Smith, P.
Fresh Vegetable Mystery (1939) Timberg
Fresh Water Champs (1951) Mamorsky
Fresh Yeggs (1950) Sharples, Winston
Freshman Year (1938) Skinner, F.
Freud (1962) Goldsmith
Freudy Cat (1963) Lava
Friday the 13th (1953) Scheib
Fried Chicken (1930) Scheib
Friend at the Door (1950) Applebaum
Friend in Tweed (1964) Sharples, Winston
Friend Indeed (1937) Axt
Friend or Phoney (1952) Sharples, Winston
Friendly Enemies (1942) Moraweck
Friendly Ghost (1945) Sharples, Winston
Friendly Neighbors (1940) Torbett
Friendly Persuasion (1956) Tiomkin
Friendly Towns (1956) Manson
Friends and Lovers (1931) Schertzinger
Friends of Mr. Sweeney (1934) Jerome
Fright (1957) Davies
Fright from Wrong (1956) Sharples, Winston
Fright to the Finish (1954) Sharples, Winston
Frightday the 13th (1953) Sharples, Winston
Frighty Cat (1958) Sharples, Winston
Frigid-Hare (1948) Stalling
Frisco Jenny (Trailer, 1933) *Kaun*
Frisco Kid (1935) Kaun
Frisco Sal (1945) Ward, E.
Frisco Tornado (1950) Wilson, S.
Frog and the Princess (1944) Scheib
Frog Legs (1962) Sharples, Winston
Frog Pond (1938) Kilfeather
Frog Went A-Courtin' (1961) Kleiner
Froggy Froggo Duo (1970) Goodwin
Frogmen (1951) Mockridge
From A to Z-Z-Z (1955) Stalling
From Dime to Dime (1960) Sharples, Winston
From Eight to Five (1963) Richardson, B.
From Every Horizon: A Tone Poem to New York (19??) Dello Joio
From Hand to Mouse (1945) Stalling
From Headquarters (1929) Reiser
From Headquarters (1933) Kaun
From Heir to Heir (1960) Franklyn
From Hell It Came (1957) Calker
From Hell to Borneo (1964) Kauer
From Hell to Heaven (1933) Kopp, R.
From Hell to Texas (1958) Amfitheatrof
From Here to Eternity (1953) Duning
From Here to There (1964) Alexander, J.
From Inner Space (1961) Williams, G.
From Liverpool to Stratford (1949) Mayfield
From Mad to Worse (1957) Sharples, Winston
From Nags to Witches (1966) Sharples, Winston
From Scratch (1966) Osborn
From Sea to Shining Sea (1969) Vardi
From Singapore to Hong Kong (1940) Craig, E.
From the Earth to the Moon (1958) Forbes
From the Ends of the Earth (1939) Ward, E.
From the Ground Up (1955) Kleinsinger
From the Ridge to the River (1955) Kleinsinger
From the Terrace (1960) Bernstein, E.
From This Day Forward (1946) Harline
Front Page Woman (1935) Roemheld
Frontier Agent (1948) Kay, Edward
Frontier Badmen (1943) Salter
Frontier Crusader (1940) Porter
Frontier Days (1945) Jackson, H.
Frontier Feud (1945) Sanucci
Frontier Fugitives (1945) Zahler
Frontier Gal (1945) Skinner, F.
Frontier Gambler (1956) Dunlap
Frontier Gun (1958) Dunlap
Frontier Investigator (1949) Wilson, S.
Frontier Marshal (1939) Kaylin
Frontier Phantom (1951) Greene, W.
Frontier Revenge (1948) Greene, W.
Frontier Scout (1938) Nussbaum
Frontier Town (1937) Sanucci
Frontier Uprising (1961) Sawtell
Frontier Vengeance (1940) Feuer
Frontier Woman (1956) Greene, W.
Frontiers (1960) Epstein
Frontiers of '49 (1938) Zahler
Frontiers Unlimited (1951) Van Camp
Frontiersman (1938) Carbonara
Frozen Feet (1939) Scheib
Frozen Frontier (1956) Jackson, H.
Frozen Fun (1948) Shilkret, N.

Frozen Justice (1929) Kay, Arthur
Frozen North (1941) Scheib
Frozen River (1929) Silvers
Frozen Sparklers (1967) Timmens
Fuddy Duddy Buddy (1951) Lava
Fudget's Budget (1954) Bruns
Fugitive (1947) Hageman
Fugitive from a Prison Camp (1940) Zahler
Fugitive from Justice (1940) Jackson, H.
Fugitive from Sonora (1943) Glickman, M.
Fugitive in the Sky (1936) Jackson, H.
Fugitive Kind (1960) Hopkins, K.
Fugitive Lovers (1934) Axt
Fugitive of the Plains (1943) Erdody
Fugitive Sheriff (1936) Zahler
Fugitive Valley (1941) Sanucci
Fugitives for a Night (1938) Webb
Full Confession (1939) Webb
Full of Life (1957) Duning
Fulla Bluff Man (1940) Timberg
Fuller Brush Girl (1950) Roemheld
Fuller Brush Man (1948) Roemheld
Fun and Fancy Free (1947) Wallace
Fun at the Fair (1952) Sharples, Winston
Fun for All (1944) De Francesco
Fun House (1936) Dietrich
Fun in Acapulco (1963) Lilley
Fun on a Weekend (1947) Cailliet
Fun on Furlough (1959) Sharples, Winston
Fun Time (1944) Schrager
Funderful Suburbia (1962) Sharples, Winston
Funniest Man in the World (1967) Hague
Funny Bunny Business (1942) Scheib
Funny Face (1957) Courage
Funny Girl (1968) Scharf, W.
Funny Little Bunnies (1934) Churchill
Funnyman (1968) Schickele
Funshine State (1949) Sharples, Winston
Furies (1950) Waxman
Fur-Lined Foxhole (1961) Wernick
Further Perils of Laurel and Hardy (1967) Parker
Further Prophecies of Nostradamus (1942) Snell
Fury (1936) Waxman
Fury at Furnace Creek (1948) Raksin
Fury at Showdown (1957) Sukman
Fury in the Pacific (1945) Engel
Fusion (1967) Nikolais
Fuss and Feathers (1943) De Francesco
Future Champs (1949) De Francesco
Future Tense (1957) Manson
Futz (1969) O'Horgan
Fuz (1967) Sharples, Winston
Fuzzy Pink Nightgown (1957) May

G Man Jitters (1939) Scheib
"G" Men (1935) Kaun
"G" Men (Trailer, 1949) Lava
G-Men Never Forget (1947) Glickman, M.
G-Men vs. the Black Dragon (1943) Glickman, M.
G. I. Blues (1960) Lilley
G. I. Holiday (1955) Jackson, H.
G. I. Honeymoon (1945) Kay, Edward
G. I. Jane (1951) Greene, W.
G. I. Joe (1945) Applebaum
G. I. Pink (1968) Greene, W.
G. I. Sports (1944) Shilkret, J.
G. I. War Brides (1946) Gold
Gabby Goes Fishing (1941) Timberg
Gabby's Diner (1961) Poddany
Gabriel Churchkitten (1944) Sharples, Winston
Gabriel Over the White House (1933) Axt
Gaby (1956) Salinger
Gag and Baggage (1952) Sharples, Winston
Gag Buster (1957) Scheib
Gaily, Gaily (1969) Mancini
Gal Who Took the West (1949) Skinner, F.
Galahad Jones (1951) Kraushaar
Galaxia (1960) Sharples, Winston
Gallant Bess (1946) Kopp, R.
Gallant Blade (1948) Duning
Gallant Hours (1960) Wagner, R.
Gallant Journey (1946) Skiles
Gallant Lady (1934) Newman
Gallant Lady (1942) Zahler
Gallant Legion (1948) Glickman, M.
Gallant Sons (1940) Snell
Gallopin' Gals (1940) Bradley
Gallopin' Gaucho (1928) Stalling
Galloping Ghost (1931) Zahler
Galvani and Volta, an Early Debate in Science (1963) Humphreys, N.
Gambit (1967) Jarre
Gambler from Natchez (1954) Newman, L.
Gambler Wore a Gun (1961) Shefter
Gambler's Choice (1944) Glickman, M.
Gamblers (1929) Reiser
Gamblers (1970) Morris
Gambling (1934) Tours
Gambling House (1951) Webb
Gambling Lady (1934) Kaun
Gambling on the High Seas (1940) Jackson, H.
Game (1967) Chaitkin
Game Birds (1949) Semmler
Game of Death (1945) Sawtell
Games (1967) Matlovsky
Gamesters (1920) Eames
Gander at Mother Goose (1940) Stalling
Gandy Goose and the Chipper Chipmunk (1948) Scheib
Gandy the Goose (1938) Scheib
Gandy's Dream Girl (1944) Scheib
Gang Buster (1931) Leipold
Gang Busters (1955) Aurandt
Gang War (1928) Zuro
Gang War (1940) Porter
Gang War (1958) Dunlap
Gang's All Here (1941) Kay, Edward
Gang's All Here (1943) Lange

Gangs of Chicago (1940) Lava
Gangs of New York (1938) Colombo
Gangs of Sonora (1941) Feuer
Gangs of the Waterfront (1945) Glickman, M.
Gangster (1947) Gruenberg
Gangster's Boy (1938) Kay, Edward
Gangsters of the Frontier (1944) Zahler
Gangway for Tomorrow (1943) Webb
Garden Gaities (1935) De Nat
Garden Gopher (1950) Bradley
Garden Murder Case (1936) Axt
Garden of Allah (1916) Breil
Garden of Allah (1936) Steiner, M.
Garden of Eden (1954) McBride, R.
Garden of Evil (1954) Herrmann
Garden of the Moon (1938) Roemheld
Gardens of the Sea (1947) De Francesco
Garment Jungle (1957) Stevens, L.
Gas (1944) Stalling
Gas House Kids (1946) Erdody
Gas House Kids Go West (1947) Sommer
Gas House Kids in Hollywood (1947) Glasser
Gaslight (1944) Kaper
Gaslit Nineties (1932) Vincent, P.
Gaston Go Home (1958) Scheib
Gaston Is Here (1957) Scheib
Gaston's Baby (1957) Scheib
Gaston's Easel Life (1958) Scheib
Gaston's Mama Lisa (1959) Scheib
Gateway (1938) Maxwell
Gateway to a Miracle (1967) Garlock
Gathering of Eagles (1963) Goldsmith
Gathering of Evil (1969) Spice
Gaucho (1928) Kay, Arthur
Gauchos of the Pampas (1948) Lava
Gay Amigo (1949) Glasser
Gay Anties (1946) Stalling
Gay Blades (1946) Butts
Gay Bride (1934) Bassett, R. H.
Gay Caballero (1932) Bassett, R. H.
Gay Caballero (1940) Maxwell
Gay Cavalier (1946) Kay, Edward
Gay Deceivers (1969) Phillips, S.
Gay Desperado (1936) Newman
Gay Diplomat (1931) Steiner, M.
Gay Divorcee (1934) Steiner, M.
Gay Falcon (1941) Sawtell
Gay Intruders (1948) Kraushaar
Gay Knighties (1941) von Ottenfeld
Gay Purr-ee (1962) Lindsey
Gay Rio (1942) De Francesco
Gay Sisters (1942) Steiner, M.
Gay Vagabond (1941) Feuer
Gazebo (1959) Alexander, J.
Gee Whiz-z-z-z-z-z-z! (1955) Stalling
Geisha Boy (1958) Scharf, W.
Geisha Girl (1952) Glasser
Gem of the Ocean (1946) Lava
Gems from Gemini (1966) Timmens
Gems of M.G.M. (1930) Wineland
Gene Autry and the Mounties (1950) Leipold
Gene Krupa Story (1959) Stevens, L.
General (1930) Axt
General Crack (1929) Dunn
General Died at Dawn (1936) Janssen
General Spanky (1936) Hatley
General with the Cockeyed Id (1962) Goldsmith
Generation (1969) Grusin
Genesis (1962) Surinach
Genesis of an Idea (1960) Shinberg
Genie with the Light Pink Fur (1966) Greene, W.
Genius at Work (1946) Sawtell
Gente Alegre (1931) Leipold
Gentle Annie (1944) Snell
Gentle Gangster (1943) Zahler
Gentle Giant (1967) Matlovsky
Gentle Julia (1936) Kaylin
Gentleman After Dark (1942) Tiomkin
Gentleman at Heart (1942) Bradshaw
Gentleman from Arizona (1939) Bakaleinikoff, C.
Gentleman from Dixie (1941) Sanucci
Gentleman from Indiana (1915) Beynon
Gentleman from Texas (1946) Kay, Edward
Gentleman Jim (1942) Roemheld
Gentleman Joe Palooka (1946) Kay, Edward
Gentleman's Agreement (1947) Newman
Gentleman's Gentleman (1941) Smith, P.
Gentlemen Are Born (1934) Roemheld
Gentlemen Prefer Blondes (1953) Schaefer, H.
Gentlemen with Guns (1946) Zahler
Geography Lesson (1931) Snell
George Grosz' Interregnum (1960) Glass, Paul
George Raft Story (1961) Alexander, J.
George Town, Pride of Penang (1941) Bakaleinikoff, C.
George Washington Carver Story (1959) Collette
George Washington Slept Here (1942) Deutsch
George Washington's Railroad (1935) Shilkret, N.
George White's 1935 Scandals (1935) Friedhofer
George White's Scandals (1934) Friedhofer
George White's Scandals (1945) Webb
Georgie (1956) Kleiner
Georgie and the Dragon (1951) Gold
Gerald McBoing Boing (1951) Kubik
Gerald McBoing Boing on Planet Moo (1956) Gold
Gerald McBoing Boing's Symphony (1953) Gold
Geraldine (1929) Gromon
Geraldine (1953) Butts
Germ (1954) Norlin
Geronimo! (1940) Carbonara
Geronimo (1962) Friedhofer
Geronimo and Son (1966) Sharples, Winston
Geronimo Jones (1970) Shapiro
Get-Away (1941) Amfitheatrof
Get Going (1943) Salter
Get Hep to Love (1942) Previn, C.
Get Lost (1956) Wheeler
Get Lost! Little Doggy (1964) Wheeler

Get Outta Town (1960) Holman
Get Rich Quick (1935) Ward, E.
Get Rich Quick (1951) Smith, P.
Get-Rich-Quick Porky (1937) Stalling
Get Yourself a College Girl (1964) Karger
Getting Ahead (1965) Sharples, Winston
Getting Gertie's Garter (1945) Friedhofer
Getting Straight (1970) Stein, R.
Ghosks Is the Bunk (1939) Timberg
Ghost and Mr. Chicken (1966) Mizzy
Ghost and Mrs. Muir (1947) Herrmann
Ghost and the Guest (1943) Zahler
Ghost Breakers (1940) Toch
Ghost Catchers (1944) Ward, E.
Ghost Chasers (1951) Kay, Edward
Ghost Comes Home (1940) Snell
Ghost Diver (1957) Sawtell
Ghost Goes Wild (1947) Dubin
Ghost Guns (1944) Kay, Edward
Ghost in the Invisible Bikini (1966) Baxter
Ghost of Dragstrip Hollow (1959) Stein, R.
Ghost of Frankenstein (1942) Salter
Ghost of Hidden Valley (1946) Zahler
Ghost of Honor (1957) Sharples, Winston
Ghost of the China Sea (1958) Laszlo
Ghost of the Town (1952) Sharples, Winston
Ghost Ship (1943) Webb
Ghost Talks (1928) Stamper
Ghost Town (1936) Zahler
Ghost Town (1944) Scheib
Ghost Town (1956) Dunlap
Ghost Town Frolics (1938) Churchill
Ghost Town Law (1942) Kay, Edward
Ghost Town Renegades (1947) Greene, W.
Ghost Treasure (1941) Hayton
Ghost Valley Raiders (1940) Sawtell
Ghost Wanted (1940) Stalling
Ghost Writers (1958) Sharples, Winston
Ghosts on the Loose (1943) Kay, Edward
Giant (1956) Tiomkin
Giant Claw (1957) Bakaleinikoff, M.
Giant from the Unknown (1958) Glasser
Giant Gila Monster (1959) Marshall, J.
Giant of Norway (1939) Snell
Giantland (1933) Churchill
Giants in the Land (1956) Robinson
Giddy Gadgets (1961) Sharples, Winston
Giddyap (1950) Raksin
Giddy-Yapping (1944) Kilfeather
Gideon's Trumpet (1965) Manson
Gidget (1959) Morton
Gidget Goes Hawaiian (1961) Duning
Gidget Goes to Rome (1963) Williams, J.
Gift (1962) Schuller
Gift from Dirk (1954) Mamorsky
Gift of Gab (1934) Ward, E.
Gift of Gag (1955) Sharples, Winston
Gift of Love (1958) Newman
Gift Wrapped (1951) Stalling
Gifts (1970) Henderson, S.
Gifts from the Air (1936) De Nat
Gigantis the Fire Monster (1959) Sawtell
Gigi (1958) Salinger
Gigolette (1935) Rochetti
Gilda (1946) Friedhofer
Gilded Lily (1935) Satterfield
Gildersleeve's Ghost (1944) Sawtell
Ginger (1935) Kaylin
Ginger (1946) Kay, Edward
Ginger Bread Boy (1934) Dietrich
Girl, a Guy and a Gob (1941) Webb
Girl and the Gambler (1939) Webb
Girl at the Ironing Board (1934) Spencer, N.
Girl Can't Help It (1956) Harline
Girl Crazy (1932) Steiner, M.
Girl Crazy (1943) Stoll
Girl Downstairs (1938) Axt
Girl from 10th Avenue (1935) Roemheld
Girl from Alaska (1942) Feuer
Girl from Avenue A (1940) Mockridge
Girl from Calgary (1932) Malotte
Girl from God's Country (1940) Lava
Girl from Havana (1940) Feuer
Girl from Jones Beach (1949) Buttolph, David
Girl from Mandalay (1936) Kay, Arthur
Girl from Manhattan (1948) Roemheld
Girl from Mexico (1939) Webb
Girl from Missouri (1934) Axt
Girl from Monterey (1943) Merrick
Girl from Rio (1939) Kay, Edward
Girl from San Lorenzo (1950) Glasser
Girl from Scotland Yard (1937) Shuken
Girl Game (1963) Bazelon
Girl Habit (1931) Green, J.
Girl Happy (1964) Stoll
Girl He Left Behind (1956) Webb
Girl in 313 (1940) Buttolph, David
Girl in 419 (1933) Leipold
Girl in Black Stockings (1957) Baxter
Girl in Every Port (1952) Webb
Girl in Gold Boots (1968) Carras
Girl in Lover's Lane (1960) Stein, R.
Girl in the Case (1944) Leipold
Girl in the Case (1934) Wallace
Girl in the Glass Cage (1929) Reiser
Girl in the Red Velvet Swing (1955) Harline
Girl in the Woods (1957) Glasser
Girl in White (1952) Raksin
Girl Missing (1933) Kaun
Girl Most Likely (1957) Riddle
Girl Named Tamiko (1962) Bernstein, E.
Girl Next Door (1953) Mockridge
Girl o' My Dreams (1934) Ward, E.
Girl of My Dreams (1918) Beynon
Girl of the Golden West (1930) Leonardi
Girl of the Golden West (1938) Stothart
Girl of the Limberlost (1945) Gold
Girl of the Night (1960) Kaplan, S.

Girl of the Ozarks (1936) Carbonara
Girl of the Port (1930) Webb
Girl of the Rio (1932) Steiner, M.
Girl on a Landscape (1966) Hibbard
Girl on the Bridge (1951) Byrns
Girl on the Front Page (1936) Roemheld
Girl on the Spot (1945) Sawtell
Girl Rush (1944) Harline
Girl Said No (1937) Kay, Arthur
Girl, the Body, and the Pill (1967) Wellington
Girl Trouble (1942) Newman
Girl Who Came Back (1935) Cutner
Girl Who Had Everything (1953) Previn, A.
Girl Who Knew Too Much (1969) Greene, J.
Girl with an Itch (1958) Kauer
Girl Without a Room (1933) Hajos
Girl's Best Years (1937) Kopp, R.
Girls About Town (1931) Rainger
Girls and Flowers (1946) Jackson, H.
Girls and Gags (1946) De Francesco
Girls in Chains (1943) Erdody
Girls in Prison (1956) Stein, R.
Girls in the Night (1953) Mancini
Girls of Pleasure Island (1953) Murray
Girls of the Big House (1945) Dubin
Girls on Probation (1938) Jackson, H.
Girls on the Beach (1965) Usher
Girls on the Loose (1958) Vars
Girls Preferred (1944) De Francesco
Girls Town (1959) Alexander, V.
Girls! Girls! Girls! (1962) Lilley
Girls' Dormitory (1936) Maxwell
Girls' School (1938) Stone
Girls' Town (1942) Zahler
Girlsapoppin (1963) Glasser
Git! (1965) Lambro
Git Along Li'l Duckie (1955) Sharples, Winston
Give a Girl a Break (1953) Previn, A.
Give and Tyke (1957) Bradley
Give Me a Sailor (1938) Leipold
Give Me Your Heart (1936) Roemheld
Give My Regards to Broadway (1948) Mockridge
Give Us the Earth! (1947) Lava
Give Us This Night (1936) Korngold
Glacier Fishing (1950) Mamorsky
Glacier Park and Waterton Lakes (1942) Nussbaum
Glad Rag Doll (1929) Copping
Gladiator (1938) Young, V.
Glamor in Sports (1945) Jackson, H.
Glamour (1934) Jackson, H.
Glamour Boy (1941) Young, V.
Glamour for Sale (1940) Oakland
Glamour Girl (1948) Bakaleinikoff, M.
Glamour in Tennis (1952) Jackson, H.
Glamour Street (1948) Shilkret, N.
Glamour Town (1947) Jackson, H.
Glass Alibi (1946) Laszlo
Glass Bottom Boat (1966) De Vol
Glass Key (1935) Roemheld
Glass Key (1942) Young, V.
Glass Menagerie (1950) Steiner, M.
Glass Slipper (1938) Scheib
Glass Slipper (1955) Kaper
Glass Sphinx (1968) Baxter
Glass Wall (1953) Stevens, L.
Glass Web (1953) Stein, H.
Glee Worms (1936) De Nat
Glenn Miller Story (1953) Mancini
Glimpses of Argentina (1952) Nussbaum
Glimpses of Australia (1939) Shilkret, N.
Glimpses of Austria (1938) Shilkret, J.
Glimpses of California (1946) Nussbaum
Glimpses of Florida (1941) Bakaleinikoff, C.
Glimpses of Guatemala (1946) Nussbaum
Glimpses of Java and Ceylon (1937) Shilkret, N.
Glimpses of Kentucky (1940) Bakaleinikoff, C.
Glimpses of Morocco and Algiers (1951) Kirk
Glimpses of New Brunswick (1938) Shilkret, J.
Glimpses of New Scotland (1947) Nussbaum
Glimpses of Old England (1949) Nussbaum
Glimpses of Ontario (1942) Nussbaum
Glimpses of Peru (1937) Shilkret, J.
Glimpses of Picturesque Java (1936) White, L.
Glimpses of the U.S.A. (1959) Bernstein, E.
Glimpses of Washington State (1940) Bakaleinikoff, C.
Global Affair (1963) Frontiere
Global Morality (19??) Trythall
Gloom Chasers (1935) De Nat
Gloria's Romance (1916) Kern
Glorifying the American Girl (1929) Tours
Glorious Betsy (1928) Mendoza
Glory (1955) Perkins
Glory Alley (1952) Stoll
Glory of Their Times (1970) Bazelon
Glory Stompers (1967) Curb
Gnome-Mobile (1967) Baker, Buddy
Go Away Stowaway (1967) Lava
Go Fly a Kit (1956) Franklyn
Go for Broke (1951) Colombo
Go Getter (1937) Kaun
Go Go Amigo (1965) Lava
Go Into Your Dance (1935) Kaun
Go, Johnny, Go! (1959) Klatzkin
Go, Man, Go! (1954) North
Go Naked in the World (1960) Deutsch
Go West (1940) Stoll
Go West, Big Boy (1931) Scheib
Go West, Young Lady (1941) Leipold
Go West, Young Man (1936) Stoll
Goal Rush (1946) Sharples, Winston
Gobs and Gals (1952) Wilson, S.
Gobs of Fun (1950) Sharples, Winston
God Is My Co-Pilot (1945) Waxman
God Is My Partner (1957) Dunlap
God, Man, and Devil (1950) Secunda
God's Country (1946) Mayfield
God's Country and the Man (1937) Sanucci

God's Country and the Woman (1936) Steiner, M.
God's Gift to Women (1931) Mendoza
God's Little Acre (1958) Bernstein, E.
Goddess (1958) Thomson
Goddess of Love (1960) Michelet
Goddess of Spring (1934) Harline
Godless Girl (1928) Riesenfeld
Gods of the Road (1955) Powell, E.
Gog (1954) Sukman
Goggle Fishing Bear (1948) Bradley
Goin' to Heaven on a Mule (1934) Spencer, N.
Goin' to Town (1935) Satterfield
Goin' to Town (1944) Moraweck
Going, Going, Gosh! (1951) Stalling
Going Highbrow (1935) Kaun
Going His Way? (1955) Morey
Going Hollywood (1933) Stothart
Going Home (1962) Kay, U.
Going My Way (1944) Dolan
Going My Way (Trailer, 1950) Young, V.
Going Places (1938) Roemheld
Going Steady (1958) Bakaleinikoff, M.
Going to Blazes (1933) Dietrich
Going to Blazes (1948) Lava
Going Up (1962) Kaplan, E.
Gold Diggers in Paris (1938) Roemheld
Gold Diggers of '49 (1936) Spencer, N.
Gold Diggers of 1935 (1935) Roemheld
Gold Diggers of 1937 (1936) Roemheld
Gold Diggers of Broadway (1929) Mendoza
Gold Dust Gertie (1931) Mendoza
Gold Dust Oswald (1935) Dietrich
Gold Fever (1952) Richards, J.
Gold Getters (1935) De Nat
Gold Guitar (1966) Middlebrooks
Gold Is Where You Find It (1938) Steiner, M.
Gold Mine in the Sky (1938) Colombo
Gold of the Seven Saints (1961) Jackson, H.
Gold Raiders (1951) Borisoff
Gold Rush (1925) Chaplin, C.
Gold Rush (1942) Chaplin, C.
Gold Rush '68 (1968) Muri
Gold Rush Daze (1939) Stalling
Gold Rush Maisie (1940) Snell
Goldbrick (1943) Stalling
Golden Age of Comedy (1950) Steiner, G.
Golden Arrow (1936) Roemheld
Golden Blade (1953) Stein, H.
Golden Boy (1939) Young, V.
Golden Breed (1968) Curb
Golden Calf (1930) Friedhofer
Golden Claw (1915) Nurnberger
Golden Dawn (1930) Dunn
Golden Earrings (1947) Young, V.
Golden Eggs (1941) Harline
Golden Eye (1948) Kay, Edward
Golden Fleecing (1940) Snell
Golden Gate (1967) Gottlieb
Golden Girl (1952) Newman
Golden Gloves (1940) Hollander
Golden Gloves (1944) Shilkret, J.
Golden Gloves Story (1950) Lange, A.
Golden Harvest (1933) Lewis, Harold
Golden Hen (1946) Scheib
Golden Hoofs (1941) Mockridge
Golden Horde (1951) Salter
Golden Horses (1946) De Francesco
Golden Hunch (1945) Terr
Golden Idol (1954) Skiles
Golden Leaf (1955) Lewin
Golden Mistress (1954) Kraushaar
Golden Positions (1970) Hughes
Golden Stallion (1949) Scott, N.
Golden State (1948) Sharples, Winston
Golden Tomorrow (1955) Jackson, H.
Golden Touch (1935) Churchill
Golden Trail (1940) Sanucci
Golden Twenties (1950) Shaindlin
Golden West (1932) Lange
Golden West (1939) Scheib
Golden Yeggs (1949) Stalling
Goldie (1931) Bassett, R. H.
Goldie Gets Along (1933) Jackson, H.
Goldilocks and the Jivin' Bears (1944) Stalling
Goldilocks and the Three Bares (1963) Gillette
Goldilocks and the Three Bears (1934) Dietrich
Goldilocks and the Three Bears (1939) Bradley
Goldimouse and the Three Cats (1959) Franklyn
Goldseeker (1956) Cooper, P.
Goldstein (1965) Kupferman
Goldwyn Follies (1938) Newman
Golf Chumps (1939) De Nat
Golf Doctor (1947) Shilkret, N.
Golf Nuts (1930) Scheib
Golfers (1936) Dietrich
Goliath and the Barbarians (1959) Baxter
Goliath and the Dragon (1960) Baxter
Goliath II (1959) Bruns
Gondola Eye (1963) Lewin-Richter
Gone are the Days! (1963) Cowen
Gone Batty (1953) Stalling
Gone Fishin' (1952) Jackson, H.
Gone with the Wave (1965) Schifrin
Gone with the Wind (1939) Steiner, M.
Gonzales' Tamales (1957) Stalling
Goo, Goo, Goliath (1953) Stalling
Good and Guilty (1961) Sharples, Winston
Good Companions (1933) Friedhofer
Good Deed Daly (1955) Scheib
Good Earth (1937) Stothart
Good Egg (1939) Stalling
Good Fairy (1935) Roemheld
Good Fellows (1943) Shuken
Good Girls Go to Paris (1939) Harline
Good Guys and the Bad Guys (1969) Lava
Good Humor Man (1950) Roemheld
Good Intentions (1930) Brunelli
Good Little Monkeys (1935) Bradley

Good Luck, Mr. Yates (1943) Leipold
Good Morning, Judge (1943) Rosen, M.
Good Morning, Miss Dove (1955) Harline
Good Mousekeeping (1952) Scheib
Good Neighbor Sam (1964) De Vol
Good News (1947) Salinger
Good Night Elmer (1940) Stalling
Good Noose (1962) Lava
Good Old Corn (1945) Lava
Good Old Irish Tunes (1941) Scheib
Good Old Soak (1937) Ward, E.
Good Sam (1948) Dolan
Good Scout (1934) Stalling
Good Scouts (1938) Wallace
Good Scream Fun (1958) Sharples, Winston
Good Snooze Tonight (1962) Sharples, Winston
Good Speech for Gary (1953) Dennison
Good Sport (1931) Bassett, R. H.
Good Time for a Dime (1941) Harline
Good Time Henry (1934) Jackson, H.
Good Times (1967) Bono
Good Will to Men (1955) Bradley
Goodbye Charlie (1964) Previn, A.
Goodbye, Columbus (1969) Fox, C.
Goodbye in the Mirror (1965) Blagman
Good-bye Kiss (1928) Bierman
Good-Bye Love (1933) Roder
Good-bye, Miss Turlock (1948) Franklyn, R.
Goodbye, Mr. Chips (1969) Williams, J.
Good-bye Mr. Moth (1942) Calker
Goodbye, My Fancy (1951) Heindorf
Goodbye, My Lady (1956) Almeida
Goodbye to Captain Hook (1966) Ashley
Goode Knight (1934) Sharples, Winston
Goodie, the Gremlin (1961) Sharples, Winston
Goodie's Good Deed (1963) Sharples, Winston
Good-Night Rusty (1943) de Packh
Goofy and Wilbur (1939) Smith, P.
Goofy Gardener (1957) Poddany
Goofy Gondolas (1934) De Nat
Goofy Goofy Gander (1950) Sharples, Winston
Goofy Gophers (1946) Stalling
Goofy Groceries (1941) Stalling
Goofy Gymnastics (1948) Wallace
Goofy Movies No. 1 (1933) de Packh
Goofy Movies No. 2 (1934) Axt
Goofy News Views (1945) Kilfeather
Goofy's Freeway Troubles (1965) Bruns
Goofy's Glider (1940) Wolcott
Goonland (1938) Timberg
Goons from the Moon (1951) Scheib
Goony Golfers (1948) Scheib
Goopy Gear (1932) Marsales
Goose and the Gander (1935) Roemheld
Goose Flies High (1938) Scheib
Goose Goes South (1941) Bradley
Goose Is Wild (1963) Calker
Gopher Goofy (1942) Stalling
Gopher Spinach (1954) Sharples, Winston
Gopher Trouble (1936) Dietrich
Gorgeous Hussy (1936) Stothart
Gorilla (1939) Buttolph, David
Gorilla Hunt (1939) Kilfeather
Gorilla Man (1943) Lava
Gorilla My Dreams (1947) Stalling
Got It Made (1961) Kaplan, S.
Government Agents vs. Phantom Legion (1951) Wilson, S.
Government Girl (1943) Harline
Goya (1956) Almeida
Goya (1956) Gomez
Gracie Allen Murder Case (1939) Carbonara
Graduate (1967) Grusin
Graduation Exercises (1935) De Nat
Grain that Built a Hemisphere (1942) Plumb
Gramps to the Rescue (1963) Sharples, Winston
Granaderos del Amor (1934) Kaylin
Grand Canary (1934) De Francesco
Grand Canyon (1949) Glasser
Grand Canyon, Pride of Creation (1944) Nussbaum
Grand Canyon Trail (1948) Scott, N.
Grand Canyonscope (1954) Wallace
Grand Central Murder (1942) Hayton
Grand Hotel (1932) Axt
Grand Jury Secrets (1939) Young, V.
Grand Prix (1966) Jarre
Grand Slam (1933) Kaun
Grand Uproar (1933) Scheib
Grandad of Races (1950) Jackson, H.
Grandfather's Clock (1934) Sharples, Winston
Grandfather's Follies (1944) Arnaud
Grandma Moses (1950) Martin, H.
Grandma's Pet (1932) Dietrich
Grandpa Called It Art (1944) Shilkret, N.
Grandpa Goes to Town (1940) Sawtell
Granite Hotel (1940) Timberg
Granny Get Your Gun (1940) Jackson, H.
Grape Nutty (1949) Calker
Grapes of Wrath (1940) Newman
Grass (1926) Riesenfeld
Grass Eater (1961) Mendoza-Nava
Grass Is Always Greener (1949) Lava
Grass: The Big Story (1953) Kleinsinger
Grasshopper (1970) Goldenberg
Grasshopper and the Ants (1934) Harline
Grateful Gus (1958) Sharples, Winston
Gray Hounded Hare (1948) Stalling
Great American Broadcast (1941) Mockridge
Great American Divide (1942) Craig, E.
Great American Mug (1945) Terr
Great American Pastime (1956) Alexander, J.
Great Bank Robbery (1969) Riddle
Great Big Bunch of You (1933) Marsales
Great Big Thing (1968) Prince, R.
Great Bird Mystery (1932) De Nat
Great Carrot Train Robbery (1968) Lava
Great Caruso (1951) Green, J.

Great Catherine (1968) Tiomkin
Great Chase (1962) Adler
Great Cheese Mystery (1941) Worth, P.
Great Commandment (1939) Salter
Great Dan Patch (1949) Schrager
Great Day in the Morning (1956) Stevens, L.
Great Day's Coming (1944) Shilkret, N.
Great Dictator (1940) Chaplin, C.
Great Escape (1963) Bernstein, E.
Great Expectations (1934) Ward, E.
Great Experiment (1934) De Nat
Great Flamarion (1945) Laszlo
Great Garrick (1937) Deutsch
Great Gatsby (1949) Dolan
Great Gildersleeve (1943) Sawtell
Great Guns (1932) Dietrich
Great Guns (1941) Buttolph, David
Great Guy (1937) Skiles
Great Heart (1938) Snell
Great Impersonation (1935) Roemheld
Great Imposter (1960) Mancini
Great Jesse James Raid (1953) Shefter
Great Jewel Robber (1950) Lava
Great John L. (1945) Young, V.
Great Lakes (1946) Anderson
Great Lie (1941) Steiner, M.
Great Locomotive Chase (1956) Smith, P.
Great Love (1918) Gottschalk
Great Lover (1949) Lilley
Great Man (1956) Stein, H.
Great Man Votes (1939) Webb
Great Man's Lady (1942) Young, V.
Great McGinty (1940) Hollander
Great Meadow (1931) Axt
Great Meddler (1940) Amfitheatrof
Great Mike (1944) Zahler
Great Missouri Raid (1951) Sawtell
Great Moment (1944) Young, V.
Great Morgan (1945) Terr
Great Mr. Nobody (1941) Deutsch
Great O'Malley (1936) Roemheld
Great Piggy Bank Robbery (1946) Stalling
Great Plane Robbery (1940) Zahler
Great Plane Robbery (1950) Kay, Edward
Great Profile (1940) Mockridge
Great Race (1965) Mancini
Great Rights (1963) Fried
Great Rupert (1950) Stevens, L.
Great Sinner (1949) Kaper
Great Sioux Massacre (1965) Powell, E.
Great Sioux Uprising (1953) Stein, H.
Great Space Adventure (1964) Skiles
Great St. Louis Bank Robbery (1959) Segáll
Great Stone Face (1968) Hague
Great Swindle (1941) Zahler
Great Train Robbery (1941) DiMaggio
Great Train Robbery (1941) Feuer
Great Unfenced (1963) Muczynski
Great Victor Herbert (1939) Lange
Great Waltz (1938) Tiomkin
Great Who-Dood-It (1952) Wheeler
Great Wilderness (1950) Skiles
Great Ziegfeld (1936) Lange
Greater Movie Season (1936) Ward, E.
Greatest Gift (1942) Malotte
Greatest Good (1950) Lloyd, N.
Greatest Man in Siam (1944) Calker
Greatest Question (1919) Pesce
Greatest Show on Earth (1952) Young, V.
Greatest Story Ever Told (1965) Newman
Greatest Treasure (1947) Hamilton, W.
Greed (1925) Axt
Greedy for Tweety (1957) Franklyn
Greedy Gabby Gator (1963) Greene, W.
Greedy Humpty Dumpty (1936) Timberg
Greek Mirthology (1954) Sharples, Winston
Greeks Had a Word for Them (1932) Newman
Green Archer (1940) Zahler
Green Berets (1968) Rozsa
Green Dolphin Street (1947) Kaper
Green-Eyed Blonde (1957) Stevens, L.
Green Fields (1937) Heifetz
Green Fire (1954) Rozsa
Green Goddess (1923) Breil
Green Goddess (1929) Copping
Green Gold (1956) Jackson, H.
Green Grass of Wyoming (1948) Mockridge
Green Hell (1939) Skinner, F.
Green Light (1937) Steiner, M.
Green Line (1944) Scheib
Green Mansions (1959) Kaper
Green Mountain Land (1950) MacNeil
Green Pastures (1936) Korngold
Green Pastures (Trailer, 1936) Jackson, H.
Green Promise (1949) Schrager
Green Slime (1968) Fox, C.
Green Swamp (1916) Furst
Green Years (1946) Stothart
Green Years (Trailer, 1946) Terr
Greene Murder Case (1929) Hajos
Greener Hills (1939) Snell
Greener Yard (1948) Wallace
Greenie (1942) Kaplan, S.
Greentree Thoroughbred (1952) Dello Joio
Greenwich Village (1944) Buttolph, David
Greenwich Village Story (1963) Gubernick
Greetings (1968) Kaz, E.
Greetings Bait! (1943) Stalling
Grey, White and Blue (1943) Lava
Greyhound and the Rabbit (1940) De Nat
Greys (1963) Mumma
Grid Rules (1938) Snell
Gridiron Flash (1934) Colombo
Gridiron Glory (1929) Rodemich
Gridiron Greatness (1947) De Francesco
Grim Pastures (1944) Applebaum
Grin and Bear It (1954) Wallace
Grin and Share It (1956) Bradley

Gripes (1943) Stalling
Grizzly Golfer (1951) Curtin
Grocer and the Dragon (1955) Wilder
Grocery Boy (1932) Churchill
Groom Wore Spurs (1950) Lange
Groovie Movie (1944) Terr
Ground Hog Play (1956) Sharples, Winston
Grounds for Marriage (1950) Kaper
Group (1966) Gross
Growing Pains (1953) Scheib
Growing Years (1951) Bazelon
Gruesome Twosome (1945) Stalling
Gruesome Twosome (1967) Wellington
Grumpy (1930) Hajos
Guadalcanal Diary (1943) Buttolph, David
Guam (1945) Palange
Guarded Treasure (1957) Hamilton, W.
Guerilla Girl (1953) Bossick
Guerillas in Pink Lace (1964) Kauer
Guess What Happened To Count Dracula (1970) Roberts, D.
Guess What We Learned in School Today? (1970) MacKay
Guess Who? (1965) Greene, W.
Guess Who's Coming to Dinner (1967) De Vol
Guest (1951) Newman
Guest in the House (1944) Janssen
Guest Wife (1945) Amfitheatrof
Guests of Honour (1945) Applebaum
Guide for the Married Man (1967) Williams, J.
Guided Mouse-ille (1966) Poddany
Guided Muscle (1955) Stalling
Guilt of Janet Ames (1947) Duning
Guilty (1947) Schrager
Guilty Bystander (1950) Tiomkin
Guilty Men (1945) Agostini
Guilty of Treason (1950) Friedhofer
Gullible Canary (1942) Kilfeather
Gulliver Mickey (1934) Churchill
Gulliver's Travels (1939) Young, V.
Gulliver's Travels Beyond the Moon (1966) Delugg
Gumshoe Magoo (1958) Brandt
Gun Battle at Monterey (1957) Miller, R.
Gun Belt (1953) Gertz
Gun Brothers (1956) Gertz
Gun Code (1940) Porter
Gun Dog Life (1940) Jackson, H.
Gun Duel in Durango (1957) Sawtell
Gun Fever (1958) Dunlap
Gun Fight (1961) Sawtell
Gun for a Coward (1956) Skinner, F.
Gun Fury (1953) Bakaleinikoff, M.
Gun Glory (1957) Alexander, J.
Gun Grit (1936) Zahler
Gun Hawk (1963) Haskell
Gun in His Hand (1945) Terr
Gun Law Justice (1949) Kay, Edward
Gun Play (1951) Sawtell
Gun Runner (1949) Kay, Edward
Gun Runner (1969) DeKnight
Gun Runners (1958) Stevens, L.
Gun Smugglers (1949) Sawtell
Gun Street (1961) LaSalle
Gun Talk (1947) Kay, Edward
Gun the Man Down (1956) Vars
Gun to Gun (1944) Jackson, H.
Gunfight at Comanche Creek (1963) Skiles
Gunfight at Dodge City (1959) Salter
Gunfight at the O. K. Corral (1957) Tiomkin
Gunfight in Abilene (1967) Rogers
Gunfighter (1950) Newman
Gunfighters (1947) Schrager
Gunfighters of Abilene (1959) Dunlap
Gunfire (1950) Glasser
Gung Ho! (1943) Skinner, F.
Gunga Din (1939) Newman
Gunman (1952) Kraushaar
Gunman from Bodie (1941) Kay, Edward
Gunman's Walk (1958) Duning
Gunmen of Abilene (1950) Wilson, S.
Gunn (1967) Mancini
Gunners and Guns (1935) Zahler
Gunning for Justice (1948) Kay, Edward
Guns Don't Argue! (1957) Dunlap
Guns, Girls and Gangsters (1959) Bregman
Guns in the Dark (1937) Zahler
Guns of August (1964) Kaplan, S.
Guns of Fort Petticoat (1957) Bakaleinikoff, M.
Guns of Hate (1948) Sawtell
Guns of Navarone (1961) Tiomkin
Guns of the Black Witch (1961) Stein, R.
Guns of the Law (1944) Zahler
Guns of the Magnificent Seven (1969) Bernstein, E.
Guns of the Pecos (1936) Jackson, H.
Guns of the Timberland (1960) Buttolph, David
Guns of the Trees (1961) Dlugoszewski
Gunsight Ridge (1957) Raksin
Gunslinger (1956) Stein, R.
Gunslingers (1950) Kay, Edward
Gunsmith of Williamsburg (1969) Thayer
Gunsmoke (1953) Stein, H.
Gunsmoke in Tucson (1958) Cutner
Gunsmoke Mesa (1944) Zahler
Guy, a Gal, and a Pal (1945) Skiles
Guy Named Joe (1944) Stothart
Guy Who Came Back (1951) Harline
Guys and Dolls (1955) Mockridge
Gym Jam (1950) Sharples, Winston
Gym Jams (1938) De Nat
Gymnastic Rhythm (1952) Wolcott
Gypsy (1963) Perkins
Gypsy Colt (1954) Kopp, R.
Gypsy Fiddler (1933) Scheib
Gypsy Holiday (1948) Lilley
Gypsy Life (1945) Scheib
Gypsy Moth (1953) Kleinsinger
Gypsy Night (1935) Bassett, R. H.
Gypsy Wildcat (1944) Ward, E.

H. M. Pulham, Esquire (1941) Kaper
H2O (1931) McPhee
Habit of Happiness (1916) Riesenfeld
Hail, Hero! (1969) Moross
Hail Notre Dame (1946) Shilkret, N.
Hail the Conquering Hero (1944) Heymann
Hail the Woman (1921) Guterson
Hair Cut-Ups (1952) Scheib
Hair Raising Hare (1945) Stalling
Hair-Raising Tale (1965) Sharples, Winston
Hair Today, Gone Tomorrow (1954) Sharples, Winston
Hair-Trigger Casey (1936) Zahler
Hairless Hector (1941) Scheib
Hairy Ape (1944) Michelet
Haiti, Land of Dark Majesty (1941) Bakaleinikoff, C.
Half a Hero (1953) Sawtell
Half a Sixpence (1967) Kostal
Half Angel (1951) Mockridge
Half Baked Alaska (1965) Greene, W.
Half-Breed (1952) Sawtell
Half-Fare Hare (1956) Stalling
Half Naked Truth (1932) Steiner, M.
Half Past Midnight (1948) Calker
Half-Pint Palomino (1953) Bradley
Half-Pint Pygmy (1948) Bradley
Half Way to Heaven (1929) Lucas, G.
Halfway to Heaven (1944) Schrager
Hallelujah, I'm a Bum (1933) Newman
Hallelujah the Hills (1963) Kupferman
Hallelujah Trail (1965) Bernstein, E.
Halliday Brand (1957) Wilson, S.
Halloween (1931) De Nat
Halls of Anger (1970) Grusin
Halls of Montezuma (1951) Kaplan, S.
Hallucination Generation (1966) Segáll
Halt, Who Grows There? (1967) Sharples, Winston
Ham and Eggs (1933) Dietrich
Ham in a Role (1948) Stalling
Hamateur Night (1938) Stalling
Hams That Couldn't Be Cured (1942) Calker
Hand (1942) Applebaum
Hand and Clay: A Celebration (1970) Kudo
Hand of Death (1961) Burke
Handle with Care (1932) Brunelli
Handle with Care (1943) Applebaum
Handle with Care (1958) Courage
Handle with Care (1964) Mendoza-Nava
Hands (1928) Blitzstein
Hands Across the Border (1943) Glickman, M.
Hands Across the Table (1935) Roemheld
Hands of a Stranger (1962) LaSalle
Hands Tell the Story (1950) Lava
Handwritten (1959) Ito
Handwritten Word (1952) Hosmer
Handy Andy (1934) Buttolph, David
Hang 'Em High (1968) Frontiere
Hanging of Jake Ellis (1969) Singman
Hanging Tree (1959) Steiner, M.
Hangman (1959) Sukman
Hangman (1964) Hovey
Hangmen Also Die! (1943) Eisler
Hangover Square (1945) Herrmann
Hannah Lee (1953) Dunlap
Hans Christian Andersen (1952) Scharf, W.
Hansel and Gretel (1933) Scheib
Hansel and Gretel (1951) Timmerman
Hansel and Gretel (1952) Scheib
Happening (1967) De Vol
Happiest Man on Earth (1941) Amfitheatrof
Happiest Millionaire (1967) Elliott, J.
Happily Buried (1939) Snell
Happiness Ahead (1934) Roemheld
Happy and Lucky (1938) Scheib
Happy Anniversary (1957) Kaplan, S.
Happy Birthday (1938) De Nat
Happy Birthday, Davy (1970) Hanagan
Happy Butterfly (1934) De Nat
Happy Circus Days (1942) Scheib
Happy Cobblers (1952) Scheib
Happy Days (1936) Stalling
Happy Ending (1969) Legrand
Happy Faces (1941) Lava
Happy Family (1935) De Nat
Happy Go Ducky (1956) Bradley
Happy Go Lucky (1936) Hajos
Happy Go Lucky (1943) Dolan
Happy Go Lucky (1947) Scheib
Happy-Go-Nutty (1944) Bradley
Happy Haunting Grounds (1940) Scheib
Happy Holidays (1940) De Nat
Happy Holidays (1949) Lava
Happy Holland (1952) Scheib
Happy Land (1943) Mockridge
Happy Landing (1938) Mockridge
Happy Landing (1949) Scheib
Happy Scouts (1938) Churchill
Happy Time (1952) Tiomkin
Happy Times and Jolly Moments (1943) Lava
Happy Tots (1939) De Nat
Happy Years (1950) Harline
Happytots' Expedition (1940) De Nat
Harbor Lights (1963) Sawtell
Harbor of Missing Men (1950) Wilson, S.
Hard-Boiled Canary (1941) Boutelje
Hard Boiled Egg (1948) Scheib
Hard Boiled Mahoney (1947) Kay, Edward
Hard Brought Up, a Child Welfare Story (1954) Applebaum
Hard Contract (1969) North
Hard, Fast and Beautiful (1951) Webb
Hard Man (1957) Bakaleinikoff, M.
Hard Road (1970) Mendoza-Nava
Hard Rock Harrigan (1935) Riesenfeld
Hard to Get (1929) Reiser
Hard to Get (1938) Roemheld
Hard Way (1943) Roemheld

Harder They Fall (1956) Friedhofer
Hardship of Miles Standish (1940) Stalling
Hardys Ride High (1939) Snell
Hare-abian Nights (1958) Franklyn
Hare and Hounds (1940) Scheib
Hare-Brained Hypnotist (1942) Stalling
Hare-Breadth Finish (1956) Scheib
Hare-Breadth Hurry (1963) Lava
Hare Brush (1954) Franklyn
Hare Conditioned (1945) Stalling
Hare Do (1947) Stalling
Hare Force (1944) Stalling
Hare Grows in Manhattan (1947) Stalling
Hare-less Wolf (1957) Franklyn
Hare Lift (1951) Stalling
Hare Mail (1931) Dietrich
Hare Remover (1945) Stalling
Hare Ribbin' (1944) Stalling
Hare Splitter (1948) Stalling
Hare Tonic (1945) Stalling
Hare Trigger (1945) Stalling
Hare Trimmed (1952) Stalling
Hare-um Scare-um (1939) Stalling
Hare-way to the Stars (1957) Franklyn
Hare We Go (1949) Stalling
Haredevil Hare (1947) Stalling
Harem Girl (1952) Vaughan
Harlem Follies (1955) Prince, H.
Harlem Globetrotters (1951) Morton
Harlem on the Prairie (1938) Porter
Harlem Rides the Range (1939) Porter
Harlem Sketches (1935) Antheil
Harlem Wednesday (1958) Carter
Harlow (1965) Hefti
Harlow (1965) Riddle
Harmful Effects of Tobacco (1959) Amram
Harmony at Home (1929) Kaylin
Harmony Lane (1935) Kay, Arthur
Harmony of Nature and Man (1970) Bernstein, E.
Harness Racing (1947) Lava
Harold and the Purple Crayon (1969) Carroll
Harold Lloyd's Funny Side of Life (1963) Scharf, W.
Harold Lloyd's World of Comedy (1962) Scharf, W.
Harper (1966) Mandel
Harpoon (1948) Cailliet
Harried and Hurried (1965) Lava
Harriet Craig (1950) Duning
Harrigan's Kid (1943) Amfitheatrof
Harry Happy (1963) Sharples, Winston
Harum Scarum (1965) Karger
Harvest (1967) Rosmini
Harvest Melody (1943) Chernis
Harvest of the Sea (1947) De Francesco
Harvest Time (1940) Scheib
Harvests for Tomorrow (1941) Finckel
Harvey (1950) Skinner, F.
Harvey Girls (1945) Salinger
Harvey Middleman, Fireman (1965) Pintoff
Has Anybody Seen My Gal (1952) Stein, H.
Hash House Blues (1931) De Nat
Hashimoto-San (1959) Scheib
Hassle in a Castle (1965) Wheeler
Hast Any Philosophy in Thee? (1950) Michalsky
Haste Makes Waste (1946) Wheeler
Hasty But Tasty (1969) Goodwin
Hasty Hare (1951) Stalling
Hasty Heart (trailer) (1949) Buttolph, David
Hat-Box Mystery (1947) Calker
Hat Check Girl (1932) Lange
Hat Check Honey (1944) Skinner, F.
Hatari (1961) Mancini
Hatch Up Your Troubles (1949) Bradley
Hatchet Man (1932) Kaun
Hate (1917) Hahn
Hatful of Dreams (1945) Wheeler
Hatful of Rain (1957) Herrmann
Hatteras Honkers (1942) Dunn
Haul in One (1956) Sharples, Winston
Haunted Cat (1951) Scheib
Haunted Harbor (1944) Dubin
Haunted House (1928) Bergunker
Haunted House (1929) Stalling
Haunted House (1940) Kay, Edward
Haunted Mouse (1941) Stalling
Haunted Mouse (1965) Poddany
Haunted Palace (1963) Stein, R.
Haunted Ranch (1943) Sanucci
Haunted Trails (1949) Kay, Edward
Havana Rose (1951) Wilson, S.
Have a Heart (1934) Bassett, R. H.
Have Figure, Will Travel (1963) Bath
Have Rocket, Will Travel (1959) Bakaleinikoff, M.
Have You Got Any Castles (1938) Stalling
Having Wonderful Crime (1944) Harline
Having Wonderful Time (1938) Webb
Hawaii (1966) Bernstein, E.
Hawaii Calls (1938) Riesenfeld
Hawaii—USA (1967) Vardi
Hawaiian Aye Aye (1963) Lava
Hawaiian Birds (1936) Timberg
Hawaiian Holiday (1937) Smith, P.
Hawaiian Memories (1945) Jackson, H.
Hawaiian Sports (1951) Jackson, H.
Hawaiians (1970) Mancini
Hawk of Powder River (1947) Greene, W.
Hawk of the Wilderness (1938) Lava
Hay Foot (1941) Ward, E.
Hay Ride (1937) Scheib
Hay Rube (1954) Wheeler
Hazard (1948) Skinner, F.
He Can't Make It Stick (1943) Kilfeather
He Couldn't Say No (1937) Jackson, H.
He Dood It Again (1943) Scheib
He Hired the Boss (1942) Buttolph, David
He Laughed Last (1956) Morton
He Learned About Women (1932) Leipold
He Married His Wife (1940) Spencer, H.

He Ran All the Way (1951) Waxman
He Rides Tall (1963) Gertz
He Stayed for Breakfast (1940) Heymann
He Walked by Night (1948) Raab
He Was Her Man (1934) Kaun
He Was Her Man (1937) Stalling
He Who Gets Slapped (1924) Axt
Headin' East (1937) Kilenyi
Headin' for God's Country (1943) Glickman, M.
Headin' for the Rio Grande (1936) Sanucci
Headin' North (1930) Bibo
Heading for Heaven (1948) Borne
Headless Horseman (1934) Stalling
Headline Hunters (1955) Butts
Headquarters (19??) Loboda
Health Farm (1936) Scheib
Heap Big Hepcat (1960) Poddany
Heap Hep Injuns (1950) Sharples, Winston
Hear Me Good (1957) Shuken
Heart Is a Lonely Hunter (1968) Grusin
Heart Is a Rebel (1965) Carmichael
Heart of a Champion (1952) Jackson, H.
Heart of a Neighborhood (1956) Townsend
Heart of an Empire (1956) Jackson, H.
Heart of Mexico (1942) De Francesco
Heart of New York (1932) Kaun
Heart of Paris (1949) Lava
Heart of Spain (1937) North
Heart of the Golden West (1942) Glickman, M.
Heart of the North (1938) Deutsch
Heart of the Rockies (1951) Scott, N.
Heart to Heart (1949) Lava
Heartaches (1947) Cadkin
Heartbreak (1931) Friedhofer
Hearts and Glowers (1960) Scheib
Hearts Divided (1936) Roemheld
Hearts in Bondage (1936) Riesenfeld
Hearts in Exile (1929) Copping
Hearts of Men (1928) True
Hearts of the World (1918) Nurnberger
Heat Lightning (1934) Kaun
Heat's Off (1967) Timmens
Heat's On (1943) Leipold
Heaven Can Wait (1943) Newman
Heaven on Earth (1931) Kaun
Heaven Only Knows (1947) Roemheld
Heaven Scent (1955) Franklyn
Heaven to Betsy (1956) Norlin
Heaven with a Barbed Wire Fence (1939) Kaylin
Heaven with a Gun (1969) Mandel
Heavenly Body (1944) Kaper
Heavenly Days (1944) Harline
Heavenly Harmonies (1953) Chase
Heavenly Music (1943) Shilkret, N.
Heavenly Puss (1949) Bradley
Heckling Hare (1941) Stalling
Hector's Hectic Life (1948) Sharples, Winston
Hedge Hoppers (1944) Shilkret, J.
Hedonistic Pleasures (1969) Herth
Hedy (1965) Cale
Hei Tiki (1935) Potoker
Heidi (1937) Toch
Heir Bear (1953) Bradley
Heir-Conditioned (1955) Franklyn
Heir Restorer (1958) Sharples, Winston
Heir to Trouble (1935) Zahler
Heiress (1949) Copland
Heldorado (1946) Butts
Helen Keller in Her Story (1955) Lewis, M.
Helen Keller Story (1969) Bernstein, C.
Helen Morgan Story (1957) Heindorf
Helen of Troy (1956) Steiner, M.
Helicopter (1944) Scheib
Hell and High Water (1933) Hand
Hell and High Water (1954) Newman
Hell Below (1933) Axt
Hell Bent for Election (1944) Robinson
Hell Bent for Leather (1960) Gertz
Hell Bound (1957) Baxter
Hell Canyon Outlaws (1957) Gertz
Hell Harbor (1930) Berton
Hell in the Heavens (1934) De Francesco
Hell in the Pacific (1968) Schifrin
Hell Is for Heroes (1961) Rosenman
Hell on Devil's Island (1957) Gertz
Hell on Frisco Bay (1956) Steiner, M.
Hell Ship Mutiny (1957) Sawtell
Hell Squad (1958) Richardson, J.
Hell to Eternity (1960) Stevens, L.
Hell with Heroes (1968) Jones
Hell's Angels '69 (1969) Bruno
Hell's Angels (1930) Riesenfeld
Hell's Angels on Wheels (1967) Phillips, S.
Hell's Belles (1969) Baxter
Hell's Bells (1929) Stalling
Hell's Bloody Devils (1970) McGinnis
Hell's Fire (1934) Stalling
Hell's Five Hours (1958) Carras
Hell's Half Acre (1954) Butts
Hell's Heroes (1929) Perry
Hell's Hinges (1916) Schertzinger
Hell's Horizon (1955) Roemheld
Hell's Kitchen (1939) Roemheld
Hell's Outpost (1954) Butts
Hellcats of the Navy (1957) Bakaleinikoff, M.
Helldorado (1934) De Francesco
Heller in Pink Tights (1960) Amfitheatrof
Hellfighters (1968) Rosenman
Hellfire (1949) Butts
Hellgate (1952) Dunlap
Hello Aloha (1951) Dubin
Hello, Annapolis (1942) Leipold
Hello, Baby (1950) Kilpatrick
Hello, Dolly! (1969) Hayton
Hello Down There (1968) Sendrey
Hello, Frisco, Hello (1943) Buttolph, David
Hello, Sister! (1933) Lange
Hello, Sucker (1941) Skinner, F.

Hellzapoppin' (1941) Skinner, F.
Help! My Snowman's Burning Down (1964) Mulligan
Helpful Genie (1951) Scheib
Helping Grandma (1930) Shield
Helping Paw (1941) De Nat
Helpless Hippo (1953) Scheib
Helter Shelter (1955) Wheeler
Helter Swelter (1950) Sharples, Winston
Henhouse Henery (1948) Stalling
Henpecked Duck (1941) Stalling
Henpecked Hoboes (1946) Bradley
Henpecked Rooster (1944) Timberg
Henry Aldrich, Boy Scout (1944) Heymann
Henry Aldrich, Editor (1942) Shuken
Henry Aldrich for President (1941) Scharf, W.
Henry Aldrich Gets Glamour (1943) Dolan
Henry Aldrich Haunts a House (1943) Carbonara
Henry Aldrich Plays Cupid (1944) Heymann
Henry Aldrich Swings It (1943) Sawtell
Henry Aldrich's Little Secret (1944) Leipold
Henry and Dizzy (1942) Harline
Henry Browne, Farmer (1943) Forrell
Henry James' Memories of Old New York (1959) Ito
Henry's Social Splash (1934) Jackson, H.
Henry, the Rainmaker (1949) Kay, Edward
Hep Cat (1942) Stalling
Hep Cat Symphony (1948) Sharples, Winston
Hep Mother Hubbard (1955) Scheib
Her Adventurous Night (1946) Rosen, M.
Her and She and Him (1970) Hall
Her Bodyguard (1933) Jackson, H.
Her Cardboard Lover (1942) Waxman
Her First Beau (1941) Shuken
Her First Egg (1931) Scheib
Her First Romance (1940) Stone
Her First Romance (1951) Duning
Her Highness and the Bellboy (1945) Stoll
Her Husband Lies (1937) Stone
Her Husband's Affairs (1947) Duning
Her Husband's Secretary (1937) Jackson, H.
Her Jungle Love (1938) Stone
Her Kind of Man (1946) Waxman
Her Lucky Night (1945) Fairchild
Her Man (1930) Zuro
Her Master's Voice (1936) Roemheld
Her Name Was Ellie, His Name Was Luke (1966) Springer, R.
Her Primitive Man (1944) Ward, E.
Her Private Life (1929) Reiser
Her Second Mother (1940) Secunda
Her Secret (1933) Erickson
Her Sister's Secret (1946) Sommer
Her Twelve Men (1954) Kaper
Her Wedding Night (1930) Hand
Herald of the Skies (1937) Zahler
Hercules (1955) Kleiner
Hercules in New York (1970) Balamos
Here at Home (1943) Shilkret, N.
Here by the Water's Edge (1960) Cowell
Here Come the Girls (1953) Murray
Here Come the Jets (1959) Dunlap
Here Come the Marines (1952) Kay, Edward
Here Come the Nelsons (1951) Stein, H.
Here Come the WAVES (1944) Dolan
Here Comes Carter (1936) Jackson, H.
Here Comes Cookie (1935) Hollander
Here Comes Happiness (1941) Jackson, H.
Here Comes Kelly (1943) Kay, Edward
Here Comes Mr. Jordan (1941) Hollander
Here Comes the Band (1935) Ward, E.
Here Comes the Cavalry (1941) Jackson, H.
Here Comes the Circus (1946) De Francesco
Here Comes the Groom (1934) Hand
Here Comes the Groom (1951) Lilley
Here Comes Trouble (1948) Roemheld
Here I Am a Stranger (1939) Buttolph, David
Here Is Germany (1945) Tiomkin
Here Is My Heart (1934) Leipold
Here Today, Gone Tamale (1959) Franklyn
Here We Go Again (1942) Webb
Here We Go Again (1952) Jackson, H.
Here's to Good Old Jail (1938) Scheib
Here's to Romance (1935) De Francesco
Hereford Heritage (196?) Forrell
Heritage of the Desert (1939) Young, V.
Heritage Restored (1962) Kleinsinger
Heritage We Guard (1940) Craig, E.
Herman Melville's Moby Dick (1955) Mohaupt
Herman the Catoonist (1953) Sharples, Winston
Hero for a Day (1939) Previn, C.
Hero for a Day (1952) Scheib
Hero on Horseback (1956) Jackson, H.
Hero's Island (1962) Frontiere
Heroes (1943) Lava
Heroes at Leisure (1939) Axt
Heroes Die Young (1960) Pellegrini
Heroes for Sale (1933) Kaun
Heroes of the Hills (1938) Feuer
Heroes of the Range (1936) Zahler
Heroes of the Saddle (1940) Feuer
Heroes of the Street (1922) Edwards
Heroina (1965) Palmieri
Herr Meets Hare (1944) Stalling
Herring Murder Mystery (1944) Kilfeather
Hers to Hold (1943) Skinner, F.
Hey Boy! Hey Girl! (1959) Van Cleave
Hey Diddle Diddle (1935) Scheib
Hey-Hey Fever (1935) Bradley
Hey, Let's Twist! (1961) Glover, H.
Hey, Rookie (1943) Leipold
Hey There, It's Yogi Bear (1964) Paich
Hi, Beautiful! (1944) Skinner, F.
Hi Diddle Diddle (1943) Boutelje
Hi-Fi Jinx (1962) Sharples, Winston
Hi, Gaucho! (1935) Malotte
Hi-Ho Rodeo (1945) Shilkret, J.

Hi-Jacked (1950) Dunlap
Hi, Mom! (1970) Kaz, E.
Hi, Neighbor! (1942) Glickman, M.
Hi, Nellie! (1934) Kaun
Hi Ya, Sailor (1943) Rosen, M.
Hiawatha (1952) Skiles
Hiawatha's Rabbit Hunt (1941) Stalling
Hiccup Hound (1963) Sharples, Winston
Hic-cup Pup (1954) Bradley
Hick, a Slick and a Chick (1947) Stalling
Hick Chick (1946) Bradley
Hidden City (1950) Caswell
Hidden Danger (1948) Kay, Edward
Hidden Enemy (1940) Kay, Edward
Hidden Eye (1945) Snell
Hidden Guns (1956) Idriss
Hidden Hand (1942) Lava
Hidden Heart (1953) Forbes
Hidden Master (1940) Snell
Hidden Power (1939) Zahler
Hidden Treasures (1951) Elliott, V.
Hidden Valley Outlaws (1944) Glickman, M.
Hidden World (1958) Rosenman
Hide and Go Sidney (1959) Scheib
Hide and Peak (1956) Sharples, Winston
Hide and Seek (1966) Krainin
Hide and Shriek (1955) Sharples, Winston
Hide-Out (1930) Roemheld
Hide-Out (1934) Axt
Hideaway Girl (1936) Hollander
Higgins Family (1938) Lava
High and the Flighty (1955) Stalling
High and the Mighty (1954) Tiomkin
High Arctic (1965) Kupferman
High Barbaree (1947) Stothart
High Conquest (1947) Moraweck
High Cost of Loving (1957) Alexander, J.
High Diving Hare (1947) Stalling
High Explosive (1943) Amfitheatrof
High Flyers (1937) Webb
High Hat (1936) Wallace
High Lonesome (1950) Schrager
High Noon (1952) Tiomkin
High Note (1959) Franklyn
High Over the Borders (1942) Giannini
High Powered (1945) Laszlo
High-Powered Rifle (1960) Glasser
High Pressure (1932) Kaun
High School (1940) Rose, G.
High School Caesar (1960) Carras
High School Confidential (1958) Glasser
High School Hellcats (1958) Stein, R.
High School Hero (1946) Kay, Edward
High Sierra (1941) Deutsch
High Society (1955) Skiles
High Society (1956) Green, J.
High Society Blues (1930) Kaylin
High Stakes (1931) Steiner, M.
High Tide (1947) Schrager
High Time (1960) Mancini
High Voltage (1929) Zuro
High Wall (1948) Kaper
High, Wide and Handsome (1937) Bennett, R. R.
High, Wild and Free (1968) Mendoza-Nava
Higher and Higher (1943) Webb
Highland Games (1949) Jackson, H.
Highlights and Shadows (1938) Hanson, H.
Highlights of the Past (1933) Vincent, P.
Highway (1958) Hollister
Highway 13 (1949) Kraushaar
Highway 301 (1950) Lava
Highway Dragnet (1954) Kay, Edward
Highway Highlights (1948) Carbonara
Highway Mania (1946) Shilkret, N.
Highway Runnery (1965) Lava
Highway Slobbery (1964) Sharples, Winston
Highway Snobbery (1936) De Nat
Highway West (1941) Lava
Highwayman (1951) Gilbert, H.
Hilda Crane (1956) Raksin
Hildur and the Magician (1969) Andrews, J.
Hillbilling and Cooing (1955) Sharples, Winston
Hillbilly (1935) Dietrich
Hillbilly Blitzkrieg (1942) Sawtell
Hillbilly Hare (1950) Stalling
Hillbillys in a Haunted House (1967) Borne
Hills of Home (1948) Stothart
Hills of Oklahoma (1950) Wilson, S.
Hills of Old Wyoming (1937) Zahler
Hip Hip Olé (1964) Sharples, Winston
Hippety Hopper (1948) Stalling
Hippie Revolt (1967) Bähler
Hippydrome Tiger (1968) Lava
Hips, Hips, Hooray! (1934) Webb
Hired Gun (1957) Glasser
Hired Wife (1934) Henninger
Hired Wife (1940) Skinner, F.
His Better Elf (1958) Wheeler
His Bitter Half (1949) Stalling
His Brother's Ghost (1945) Sanucci
His Brother's Wife (1936) Waxman
His Butler's Sister (1943) Salter
His Day Off (1938) Scheib
His Double Life (1933) Rochetti
His Family Tree (1935) Colombo
His Girl Friday (1939) Cutner
His Glorious Night (1929) Barrymore
His Hare Raising Tale (1950) Stalling
His Kind of Woman (1951) Harline
His Land (1969) Carmichael
His Majesty O'Keefe (1954) Tiomkin
His Majesty, the Scarecrow of Oz (1914) Gottschalk
His Mouse Friday (1951) Bradley
His Woman (1931) Tours
Hiss and Make Up (1943) Stalling
Histadruth (1945) Rathaus
Historic Cape Town (1946) De Francesco

Historic Maryland (1942) Nussbaum
History Is Made at Night (1937) Newman
History of Balloons (1944) Bradley
History's Brew (1962) Paris
Hit and Run (1957) Steininger
Hit 'Im Again (1952) Jackson, H.
Hit of the Show (1928) Zuro
Hit Parade (1937) Colombo
Hit Parade of 1941 (1940) Scharf, W.
Hit Parade of 1943 (1943) Scharf, W.
Hit Parade of 1951 (1950) Butts
Hit the Deck (1955) Stoll
Hit the Hay (1945) Skiles
Hit the Ice (1943) Sawtell
Hitch Hike Lady (1936) Kay, Arthur
Hitch-Hiker (1939) Scheib
Hitch-Hiker (1953) Stevens, L.
Hitch Hikers (1947) Scheib
Hitch in Time (1955) Franklyn
Hitler (1961) Salter
Hitler Gang (1944) Buttolph, David
Hitler Lives? (1945) Lava
Hitler's Children (1943) Webb
Hitler's Madman (1943) Shilkret, N.
Hittin' the Trail (1937) Sanucci
Hittin' the Trail to Hallelujah Land (1931) Marsales
Hitting a New High (1937) Shilkret, N.
Hobbies (1941) Amfitheatrof
Hobby Horse-Laffs (1942) Stalling
Hobo Bobo (1947) Stalling
Hobo Gadget Band (1939) Stalling
Hobo's Holiday (1963) Sharples, Winston
Hockey Champ (1939) Wallace
Hockey Homicide (1945) Smith, P.
Hockey Stars' Summer (1951) Agostini
Hocus Focus Powwow (1968) Lava
Hoe to It (1944) Applebaum
Hoedown (1950) Leipold
Hold Anything (1930) Marsales
Hold Back the Dawn (1941) Young, V.
Hold Back the Night (1956) Salter
Hold Back Tomorrow (1955) Cutner
Hold Me Tight (1933) Bassett, R. H.
Hold On! (1965) Karger
Hold That Baby (1949) Kay, Edward
Hold That Blonde! (1945) Heymann
Hold That Ghost (1941) Salter
Hold That Girl (1934) Buttolph, David
Hold That Hypnotist (1957) Skiles
Hold That Kiss (1938) Ward, E.
Hold That Line (1952) Kay, Edward
Hold That Pose (1950) Smith, P.
Hold That Rock (1956) Wheeler
Hold the Lion, Please (1942) Stalling
Hold Your Horsepower (1945) Smith, P.
Hold Your Horses (1954) Jackson, H.
Hole Idea (1954) Franklyn
Hole in the Head (1959) Riddle
Hole in the Wall (1929) Carbonara
Holiday (1930) Zuro
Holiday (1938) Cutner
Holiday Affair (1949) Webb
Holiday for Drumsticks (1948) Stalling
Holiday for Lovers (1959) Harline
Holiday for Shoestrings (1945) Stalling
Holiday for Sinners (1952) Colombo
Holiday for Sports (1947) Jackson, H.
Holiday Highlights (1940) Stalling
Holiday in Havana (1949) Fontaine
Holiday in Mexico (1946) Stoll
Holiday in South Africa (1947) De Francesco
Holiday Inn (1942) Dolan
Holiday Land (1934) De Nat
Holiday on Horseback (1945) Jackson, H.
Holiday Rhythm (1950) Shefter
Holiday with Light (1965) Pockriss
Holland Days (1934) Scheib
Holland Off Guard (1965) Andriessen
Hollow Triumph (1948) Kaplan, S.
Hollywood and Vine (1945) Hatley
Hollywood Barn Dance (1947) Greene, W.
Hollywood Boulevard (1936) Stone
Hollywood Bowl (1938) Churchill
Hollywood Canine Canteen (1945) Stalling
Hollywood Canteen (1945) Roemheld
Hollywood Capers (1936) Spencer, N.
Hollywood Cavalcade (1939) Schrager
Hollywood Daffy (1946) Stalling
Hollywood Detour (1942) Worth, P.
Hollywood Diet (1932) Scheib
Hollywood Extra (1936) Ward, E.
Hollywood Goes Krazy (1932) De Nat
Hollywood Graduation (1938) De Nat
Hollywood Hotel (1937) Roemheld
Hollywood Matador (1942) Calker
Hollywood Nudes Report (1963) Karmen
Hollywood or Bust (1956) Scharf, W.
Hollywood Party (1934) Axt
Hollywood Picnic (1937) De Nat
Hollywood Revue (1929) Lange
Hollywood Stadium Mystery (1938) Colombo
Hollywood Steps Out (1941) Stalling
Hollywood Story (1951) Skinner, F.
Hollywood: Style Center of the World (1940) Snell
Hollywood Sweepstakes (1939) De Nat
Hollywood Thrillmakers (1954) Garf
Hollywood Trouble (1935) Jackson, H.
Hollywood Varieties (1950) Glasser
Hollywood Wonderland (1947) Jackson, H.
Holt of the Secret Service (1941) Zahler
Holy Matrimony (1943) Mockridge
Holy Oath (1937) Stillman
Holy Terror (1937) Rose, G.
Hombre (1966) Rose
Home Before Dark (1958). See p. 8
Home Defense (1943) Smith, P.
Home from the Hill (1959) Kaper
Home Front (1943) Stalling

Home Guard (1941) Scheib
Home in Indiana (1944) Friedhofer
Home in Oklahoma (1946) Dubin
Home Life (1962) Scheib
Home Made Home (1950) Dubin
Home of the Brave (1949) Tiomkin
Home of the Danes (1947) De Francesco
Home on the Range (1940) Bradley
Home on the Range (1942) Shilkret, J.
Home on the Range (1946) Butts
Home Sweet Homewrecker (1962) Wheeler
Home Sweet Homicide (1946) Buttolph, David
Home Town Olympics (1936) Scheib
Home Town Story (1951) Forbes
Home Tweet Home (1949) Stalling
Homecoming (1929) Hajos
Homecoming (1948) Kaper
Homeless Flea (1940) Bradley
Homeless Hare (1949) Stalling
Homeless Pup (1937) Scheib
Homer on the Range (1964) Sharples, Winston
Homesteader Droopy (1954) Bradley
Homesteaders (1953) Kraushaar
Homesteaders of Paradise Valley (1947) Glickman, M.
Homestretch (1947) Raksin
Homicidal (1961) Friedhofer
Homicide (1949) Lava
Homicide Bureau (1938) Cutner
Hondo (1953) Friedhofer
Honduras Hurricane (1938) Lewis
Honey Harvester (1948) Wallace
Honey-Mousers (1956) Franklyn
Honey's Money (1962) Franklyn
Honeychile (1951) Young, V.
Honeyland (1935) Bradley
Honeymoon (1930) Duke
Honeymoon (1947) Harline
Honeymoon Ahead (1945) Skinner, F.
Honeymoon Deferred (1940) Salter
Honeymoon for Three (1941) Roemheld
Honeymoon Hotel (1934) Spencer, N.
Honeymoon Hotel (1964) Scharf, W.
Honeymoon in Bali (1939) Hollander
Honeymoon Lodge (1943) Skinner, F.
Honeymoon Machine (1961) Harline
Honeymoon of Terror (1961) Carras
Honeymoon's Over (1939) Kaylin
Hong Kong (1951) Cailliet
Hong Kong Affair (1958) Forbes
Hong Kong Confidential (1958) Sawtell
Hong Kong, the Hub of the Orient (1937) Shilkret, N.
Honky Tonk (1929) Reiser
Honky Tonk (1941) Waxman
Honolulu (1939) Waxman
Honolulu (1950) Segáll
Honor Among Lovers (1931) Green, J.
Honor of the Family (1931) Mendoza
Honor's Altar (1916) Gottschalk
Honorable Mountain (1955) Laszlo
Hoodlum (1951) Calker
Hoodlum Empire (1952) Scott, N.
Hoodlum Priest (1961) Markowitz
Hoodlum Saint (1946) Shilkret, N.
Hoodoo Ann (1916) Riesenfeld
Hook & Ladder Hokum (1933) Rodemich
Hook (1962) Adler
Hook and Ladder No. 1 (1932) Scheib
Hook, Line and Sinker (1939) Scheib
Hook, Line and Sinker (1969) Stabile
Hook, Lion and Sinker (1949) Smith, P.
Hooked (1957) Dunlap
Hooked Bear (1956) Wallace
Hooked Generation (1968) Martell
Hookworm (1945) Smith, P.
Hooky Spooky (1957) Sharples, Winston
Hoola Boola (1941) Knudson
Hoop-la (1933) De Francesco
Hooray for Love (1935) Colombo
Hoosier Holiday (1943) Glickman, M.
Hootenanny Hoot (1963) Karger
Hop and Go (1943) Stalling
Hop Harrigan (1946) Zahler
Hop, Look, and Listen (1947) Stalling
Hop on the Melrose Distillers Bandwagon (1964) Johnson, Harold
Hop Skip and a Chump (1942) Stalling
Hopalong Casualty (1960) Franklyn
Hope Is Eternal (1964) Segáll
Hope That Jack Built (1957) Bazelon
Hopeful Donkey (1943) Scheib
Hoppy Days (1960) Franklyn
Hoppy Go Lucky (1951) Stalling
Hoppy Serves a Writ (1942) Sawtell
Horizons of Hope (1954) Poddany
Horizons of Tomorrow (1947) De Francesco
Horizons West (1952) Stein, H.
Horizontal Lieutenant (1961) Stoll
Horn Blows at Midnight (1945) Waxman
Horning In (1964) Sharples, Winston
Horror (1933) David, W.
Horror of Party Beach (1963) Holcombe
Horse and Buggy Days (1949) Jackson, H.
Horse Feathers (1932) Leipold
Horse Fly Fleas (1947) Stalling
Horse Hare (1959) Franklyn
Horse in the Gray Flannel Suit (1968) Bruns
Horse on the Merry-Go-Round (1938) Kilfeather
Horse Soldiers (1959) Buttolph, David
Horse with the Flying Tail (1960) Lava
Horse with the Human Mind (1946) Kopp, R.
Horses! Horses! Horses! (1942) Jackson, H.
Horse's Tale (1954) Wheeler
Horsefly Opera (1941) Scheib
Horton Hatches the Egg (1942) Stalling
Hostage (1966) Mendoza-Nava
Hostages (1943) Young, V.

Hostile Country (1950) Greene, W.
Hostile Guns (1967) Haskell
Hot and Cold (1933) Dietrich
Hot and Cold Penguin (1955) Wheeler
Hot Angel (1958) Markowitz
Hot Blood (1956) Baxter
Hot Car Girl (1958) Tjader
Hot Cargo (1946) Laszlo
Hot Cars (1956) Baxter
Hot Cross Bunny (1948) Stalling
Hot Dog (1930) Steiner, G.
Hot Dogs on Ice (1938) De Nat
Hot Erotic Dreams (1967) Cotton
Hot Feet (1931) Dietrich
Hot Foot Lights (1945) Kilfeather
Hot Heiress (1931) Rosebrook
Hot Lead (1951) Sawtell
Hot Money (1935) Shield
Hot Money (1936) Jerome
Hot News (1953) Skiles
Hot Noon (1953) Wheeler
Hot on Ice (1938) Ward, E.
Hot Pepper (1933) Spielter, W.
Hot Rhythm (1944) Kay, Edward
Hot Rod (1950) Kay, Edward
Hot Rod Action (1969) Curb
Hot Rod and Reel (1958) Franklyn
Hot Rod Gang (1958) Stein, R.
Hot Rod Girl (1956) Courage
Hot Rod Huckster (1954) Wheeler
Hot Rod Hullabaloo (1966) Lawrence, Elliot
Hot Rod Rumble (1957) Courage
Hot Rods (1953) Scheib
Hot Rods to Hell (1966) Karger
Hot Sands (1934) Scheib
Hot Saturday (1932) Leipold
Hot Shots (1956) Skiles
Hot Spell (1936) Scheib
Hot Spell (1958) North
Hot Spot (1945) Stalling
Hot Spur (1968) Martin, Denny
Hot Summer Game (1965) Mendoza-Nava
Hot Summer Night (1957) Previn, A.
Hot Time on Ice (1967) Greene, W.
Hotcha Melody (1935) De Nat
Hotel (1967) Keating
Hotel Berlin (1945) Waxman
Hotel Continental (1932) Burton
Hotel for Women (1939) Mockridge
Hotel Imperial (1939) Hageman
Hotel Is Born (1956) Meakin
Hotel Paradiso (1966) Rosenthal
Hotlip Jasper (1945) Wheeler
Hotsy Footsy (1952) Rogers
Hottentot (1922) Cohen, S.
Hottentot (1929) Reiser
Houdini (1953) Webb
Hound About That (1961) Sharples, Winston
Hound and the Rabbit (1937) Bradley
Hound Dog Man (1959) Mockridge
Hound for Pound (1962) Sharples, Winston
Hound for Trouble (1950) Stalling
Hound Hunters (1947) Bradley
Hound of the Baskervilles (1939) Maxwell
Hound That Thought He Was a Raccoon (1960) Baker, Buddy
Houndabout (1959) Sharples, Winston
Hounding the Hares (1948) Scheib
Hour Before the Dawn (1944) Rozsa
Hour of the Gun (1967) Goldsmith
House (1961) Ashley
House Across the Bay (1940) Janssen
House Across the Street (1949) Lava
House—After Five Years of Living (1955) Bernstein, E.
House Busters (1952) Scheib
House by the River (1950) Antheil
House Cleaning (1933) De Nat
House Cleaning Blues (1937) Timberg
House Divided (1931) Bibo
House Hunting Mice (1947) Stalling
House Is Not a Home (1964) Weiss
House of a Thousand Candles (1936) Kay, Arthur
House of Bamboo (1955) Harline
House of Dark Shadows (1970) Cobert
House of Dracula (1945) Lava
House of Errors (1942) Zahler
House of Fear (1944) Sawtell
House of Frankenstein (1944) Salter
House of Hashimoto (1960) Scheib
House of Horror (1929) Reiser
House of Magic (1937) Dietrich
House of Numbers (1957) Previn, A.
House of Rothschild (1934) Newman
House of Sand (1962) Jones, W.
House of Science (1962) Bernstein, E.
House of Strangers (1949) Amfitheatrof
House of the Child (1953) Forrell
House of the Damned (1963) Vars
House of the Seven Gables (1940) Skinner, F.
House of Tomorrow (1949) Bradley
House of Wax (1953) Buttolph, David
House of Wax (Trailer, 1953) Steiner, M.
House of Women (1961) Jackson, H.
House on 56th Street (1933) Kaun
House on 92nd Street (1945) Buttolph, David
House on Bare Mountain (1962) Martel
House on Cedar Hill (1953) Johnson, Hall
House on Haunted Hill (1958) Dexter
House on Telegraph Hill (1951) Kaplan, S.
House That Jack Built (1939) De Nat
Houseboat (1958) Duning
Housekeeper's Daughter (1939) Filippi
Housewife (1934) Roemheld
Housewife Herman (1938) Scheib
Housing Problem (1946) Scheib
How Do I Know It's Sunday? (1934) Spencer, N.
How Doooo You Do (1946) Jackson, H.

How Green Is My Spinach (1950) Sharples, Winston
How Green Was My Valley (1941) Newman
How Near to the Angels (1956) Gates, C.
How Now Boing Boing (1954) Bruns
How Russians Play (1946) Forrell
How Sweet It Is! (1968) Williams, P.
How the West Was Won (1962) Newman
How to Be a Detective (1952) Dubin
How to Be a Sailor (1943) Smith, P.
How to Be Very, Very Popular (1955) Mockridge
How to Become a Citizen of the United States (1938) Bowles
How to Catch a Cold (1951) Smith, P.
How to Commit Marriage (1969) Lilley
How to Dance (1953) Dubin
How to Fish (1942) Smith, P.
How to Have an Accident at Work (1959) Wallace
How to Have an Accident in the Home (1956) Marks
How to Hold Your Husband—Back (1941) Snell
How to Keep Cool (1953) Scheib
How to Make a Doll (1968) Wellington
How to Make a Monster (1958) Dunlap
How to Make It (1969) Baxter
How to Marry a Millionaire (1953) Mockridge
How to Murder Your Wife (1965) Hefti
How to Play Baseball (1942) Smith, P.
How to Play Football (1944) Smith, P.
How to Play Golf (1944) Wallace
How to Relax (1953) Scheib
How to Save a Marriage and Ruin Your Life (1967) Legrand
How to Sleep (1953) Plumb
How to Steal a Million (1966) Williams, J.
How to Stuff a Wild Bikini (1965) Baxter
How to Stuff a Woodpecker (1960) Wheeler
How to Succeed in Business Without Really Trying (1967) Riddle
How to Succeed with Sex (1970) Hamilton
How to Swim (1942) Smith, P.
How War Came (1941) Wheeler
How Wet Was My Ocean (1940) Scheib
How's Crops? (1934) Sharples, Winston
Howard (1965) Murtaugh
Howards of Virginia (1940) Hageman
Howdy, Partner (1956) Jackson, H.
Howling Success (1954) Scheib
Huckleberry Finn (1931) Leipold
Hucksters (1947) Hayton
Hud (1962) Bernstein, E.
Hud (Trailer, 1962) Kraft
Hudson's Bay (1941) Newman
Huey's Ducky Daddy (1953) Sharples, Winston
Huk! (1956) Glasser
Hula Happy (1956) Jackson, H.
Hula Heaven (1937) Rainger
Hula Hula Land (1949) Scheib
Hullabaloo (1940) Bassman
Human Body (1945) Smith, P.
Human Comedy (1943) Stothart
Human Desire (1954) Amfitheatrof
Human Element (1963) Bazelon
Human Jungle (1954) Salter
Human Side (1934) Kay, Arthur
Humoresque (1920) Riesenfeld
Humoresque (1947) Waxman
Humpty Dumpty (1935) Stalling
Hunchback of Notre Dame (1923) Riesenfeld
Hunchback of Notre Dame (1939) Newman
Hungarian Goulash (1930) Scheib
Hungarian Rhapsody (1929) Peters
Hunger Strife (1960) Wheeler
Hungry Wolf (1942) Bradley
Hunky and Spunky (1938) Timberg
Hunt the Man Down (1951) Sawtell
Hunted (1947) Kay, Edward
Hunter (1931) Dietrich
Hunter's Paradise (1942) Dunn
Hunters (1958) Sawtell
Hunters of the Deep (1954) Antheil
Hunting Big Game in Africa with Gun and Camera (1923) Severi
Hunting Dogs at Work (1942) Lava
Hunting Season (1935) Sharples, Winston
Hunting the Devil Cat (1944) Dunn
Hunting the Fox (1949) Lava
Hunting the Hard Way (1941) Dunn
Hurdler (1969) Fuller, J.
Hurdy-Gurdy Hare (1948) Stalling
Hurricane (1938) Newman
Hurricane (1969) Kleinsinger
Hurricane Express (1932) Zahler
Hurricane Smith (1941) Skiles
Hurricane Smith (1952) Sawtell
Hurricane's Challenge (1938) Ludwig
Hurry, Charlie, Hurry (1941) Webb
Hurry Sundown (1966) Montenegro
Husband's Holiday (1931) Leipold
Husband's Holiday (1935) Jackson, H.
Hush . . . Hush, Sweet Charlotte (1964) De Vol
Hush Money (1931) Knight, G.
Hush My Mouse (1945) Stalling
Hustler (1961) Hopkins, K.
Hyde and Go Tweet (1959) Franklyn
Hyde and Hare (1955) Stalling
Hypo-Chondri-Cat (1949) Stalling
Hypnotic Eye (1960) Skiles
Hypnotic Eyes (1933) Scheib
Hypnotic Hick (1953) Wheeler
Hypnotized (1932) Ward, E.
Hypnotized (1952) Scheib
Hypnotizing for Love (1932) Vincent, P.
Hysterical Highspots in American History (1941) Calker
Hysterical History (1953) Sharples, Winston

I Accuse My Parents (1944) Zahler
I Am a Fugitive from a Chain Gang (1932) Kaun
I Am a Thief (1935) Kaun
I Am an Alcoholic (1947) Shilkret, N.
I Am an American (1944) Lava
I Am Suzanne! (1933) Hollander
I Am the Law (1938) Parrish
I Beheld His Glory (1953) Gertz
I Believed in You (1934) Kaylin
I Bombed Pearl Harbor (1961) Greene, W.
IBM at the Fair (1965) Bernstein, E.
I Bury the Living (1958) Fried
I Can Get It for You Wholesale (1951) Kaplan, S.
I Cheated the Law (1949) Kay, Edward
I Confess (1953) Tiomkin
I Conquer the Sea! (1936) Kay, Arthur
I Could Go On Singing (1963) Lindsey
I Couldn't Marry (1955) DeBey
I Cover Big Town (1947) Calker
I Cover the Underworld (1955) Butts
I Cover the Waterfront (1933) Newman
I Crave Your Body (1967) Paul, M.
I Died a Thousand Times (1955) Buttolph, David
I Don't Care Girl (1953) Spencer, H.
I Don't Scare (1956) Sharples, Winston
I Dood It (1943) Bassman
I Dream of Jeanie (1952) Armbruster
I Dream Too Much (1935) Steiner, M.
I Drink Your Blood (1970) Pitts
I Escaped from the Gestapo (1943) Harling
I Found a Dog (1949) Laszlo
I Found Stella Parish (1935) Roemheld
I Gopher You (1953) Stalling
I Got Plenty of Mutton (1944) Stalling
I Haven't Got a Hat (1935) Spencer, N.
I, Jane Doe (1948) Roemheld
I Killed Geronimo (1950) Calker
I Killed That Man (1941) Lange, J.
I Killed Wild Bill Hickok (1956) Calker
I Like It That Way (1934) Ward, E.
I Like Mountain Music (1933) Marsales
I Like Soap Because . . . (1949) Shilkret, N.
I Like Your Nerve (1931) Mendoza
I Live for Love (1935) Roemheld
I Live in Grosvenor Square (1945) Collins
I Live My Life (1935) Tiomkin
I Live on Danger (1942) Rich
I Love a Mystery (1945) Castelnuovo-Tedesco
I Love a Parade (1933) Marsales
I Love a Soldier (1944) Dolan
I Love Melvin (1953) Stoll
I Love My Husband, But (1946) Terr
I Love My Wife (1970) Schifrin
I Love That Man (1933) Kaun
I Love to Singa (1936) Spencer, N.
I Love Trouble (1947) Duning
I Love You Again (1940) Waxman
I Love You, Alice B. Toklas! (1968) Bernstein, E.
I Love You, Do Not Be Afraid (1963) Manupelli
I Loved a Woman (1933) Kaun
I Loved You Wednesday (1933) De Francesco
I, Marquis de Sade (1967) Kaplan, E.
I Married a Communist (1949) Harline
I Married a Doctor (1936) Roemheld
I Married a Savage (1949) Scoloff
I Married a Witch (1942) Webb
I Married a Woman (1956) Mockridge
I Married Adventure (1940) Carbonara
I Married an Angel (1942) Stothart
I Met Him in Paris (1937) Bradshaw
I Met My Love Again (1938) Roemheld
I, Mobster (1958) Fried
I Must See You Regarding a Matter of the Utmost Urgency (1963) Manupelli
I Never Changes My Altitude (1937) Timberg
I Never Sang for My Father (1970) Gorgoni
I Only Have Eyes for You (1937) Stalling
I Passed for White (1960) Williams, J.
I Remember Mama (1948) Webb
I Remember the Glory: The Art of Botticelli (1952) Belasco
I Ring Doorbells (1946) Erdody
I Sailed to Tahiti with an All Girl Crew (1968) Springer, P.
I Saw What You Did (1965) Alexander, V.
I Sell Anything (1934) Jerome
I Shot Billy the Kid (1950) Glasser
I Shot Jesse James (1949) Glasser
I-Ski Love-Ski You-Ski (1936) Timberg
I Stand Accused (1938) Feuer
I Stole a Million (1939) Skinner, F.
I Take This Woman (1931) Rainger
I Take This Woman (1940) Kaper
I Taw a Putty Tat (1947) Stalling
I, the Jury (1953) Waxman
I Wake Up Screaming (1941) Mockridge
I Walk Alone (1947) Young, V.
I Walked with a Zombie (1943) Webb
I Wanna Be a Life Guard (1936) Timberg
I Wanna Be a Sailor (1937) Stalling
I Wanna Play House (1936) Spencer, N.
I Want a Divorce (1940) Young, V.
I Want My Mummy (1966) Sharples, Winston
I Want to Be an Actress (1937) De Nat
I Want to Live (1958) Mandel
I Want You (1951) Harline
I Wanted Wings (1941) Young, V.
I Was a Communist for the FBI (1951) Steiner, M.
I Was a Convict (1939) Feuer
I Was a Male War Bride (1949) Mockridge
I Was a Prisoner on Devil's Island (1941) Parrish
I Was a Teenage Frankenstein (1957) Dunlap
I Was a Teenage Thumb (1962) Lava
I Was a Teenage Werewolf (1957) Dunlap
I Was an Adventuress (1940) Buttolph, David
I Was an American Spy (1951) Kay, Edward

I Was Framed (1942) Jackson, H.
I Wish I Had Wings (1933) Marsales
I Won't Play (1944) Lava
I Wonder Who's Kissing Her Now (1947) Buttolph, David
I Wonder Why (1964) Elliott, Don
I Wouldn't Be in Your Shoes (1948) Kay, Edward
I'd Climb the Highest Mountain (1951) Kaplan, S.
I'd Give My Life (1936) Leipold
I'd Love to Take Orders from You (1936) Spencer, N.
I'd Rather Be Rich (1964) Faith
I'll Be Damned (1967) Rosenboom
I'll Be Doggoned (1957) Jackson, H.
I'll Be Seeing You (1944) Amfitheatrof
I'll Be Skiing Ya (1947) Sharples, Winston
I'll Be Yours (1947) Skinner, F.
I'll Cry Tomorrow (1956) North
I'll Get By (1950) Mockridge
I'll Give a Million (1938) Mockridge
I'll Name the Murderer (1936) Johnston, G.
I'll Never Crow Again (1941) Timberg
I'll Remember April (1944) Skinner, F.
I'll See You in My Dreams (1951) Heindorf
I'll Sell My Life (1941) Hatley
I'll Take Sweden (1965) Haskell
I'll Tell the World (1945) Akridge
I'll Wait for You (1941) Kaper
I'm a Big Shot Now (1936) Spencer, N.
I'm Cold (1955) Wheeler
I'm from Arkansas (1944) Wheeler
I'm from Missouri (1939) Leipold
I'm from the City (1938) Webb
I'm Just a Jitterbug (1939) Marsales
I'm Just Curious (1944) Timberg
I'm Just Wild About Jerry (1965) Poddany
I'm No Angel (1933) Jackson, H.
I'm No Fool as a Pedestrian (1960) Baker, Buddy
I'm No Fool Having Fun (1960) Dubin
I'm No Fool in Water (1960) Baker, Buddy
I'm No Fool with a Bicycle (1960) Dubin
I'm No Fool with Electricity (1960) Bruns
I'm No Fool with Fire (1960) Dubin
I'm Still Alive (1940) Webb
I've Always Loved You (1946) Scharf, W.
I've Got Ants in My Plans (1969) Goodwin
I've Got This Problem (1969) Rubenstein
I've Got to Sing a Torch Song (1933) Spencer, N.
I've Got Your Number (1934) Kaun
I've Lived Before (1956) Stein, H.
Ice Antics (1939) Snell
Ice-Capades (1941) Feuer
Ice-Capades Revue (1942) Scharf, W.
Ice Carnival (1941) Scheib
Ice Follies of 1939 (1939) Waxman
Ice House (1969) Kauer
Ice Palace (1960) Steiner, M.
Ice Pond (1939) Scheib
Ice Scream (1957) Sharples, Winston
Ice Skippers (1947) Shilkret, N.
Ice Station Zebra (1968) Legrand
Icebreaker (1951) Fried
Iceland (1942) Harline
Iceland—Land of the Vikings (1933) Shilkret, N.
Iceman Ducketh (1963) Lava
Ickle Meets Pickle (1942) Scheib
Idea Girl (1946) Skinner, F.
Identity Unknown (1945) Chernis
Idiot's Delight (1939) Stothart
Idols of Clay (1920) Riesenfeld
If a Man Answers (1962) Salter
If Cats Could Sing (1950) Scheib
If He Hollers, Let Him Go! (1968) Sukman
If I Had a Million (1932) Leipold
If I Were Free (1933) Webb
If I Were King (1938) Hageman
If I'm Lucky (1946) Mockridge
If It's Tuesday, This Must Be Belgium (1969) Scharf, W.
If Winter Comes (1923) Rapée
If Winter Comes (1947) Stothart
If You Don't Watch Out (1950) Dubin
If You Knew Susie (1948) Fairchild
If You Leave Me I Will Kill Myself (1963) Manupelli
Igloo (1932) Burton
Igloo for Two (1955) Scheib
Illegal (1955) Steiner, M.
Illegal Traffic (1938) Leipold
Illusion (1929) Hajos
Illustrated Man (1969) Goldsmith
Image (1964) Carlos
Image in the Snow (1948) Weber
Image in Time (1957) Ashley
Image of Love (1964) Laderman
Image of the City (1969) Fried
Images (1967) Rood
Imagination (1943) Worth, P.
Imago (1970) Schifrin
Imitation of Life (1934) Roemheld
Imitation of Life (1959) Skinner, F.
Immoral Mr. Teas (1959) Lasko, Edward
Immoral West—and How It Was Lost (1962) Skiles
Immortal Blacksmith (1944) Terr
Immortal Sergeant (1942) Buttolph, David
Impact (1949) Michelet
Impasse (1969) Springer, P.
Impatient Patient (1942) Franklyn
Impatient Years (1944) Skiles
Imperfect Lady (1947) Young, V.
Imperial Delhi (1938) Shilkret, J.
Important Business (1944) Terr
Impossible Possum (1954) Bradley
Impossible Years (1968) Costa
Imposter (1944) Tiomkin
Impractical Joker (1937) Timberg
Impression of John Steinbeck (1969) Raposo
Impressionable Years (1952) Mamorsky

In a Clock Store (1931) Churchill
In a Lonely Place (1950) Antheil
In Caliente (1935) Kaun
In Cold Blood (1967) Jones
In Darkest Florida (1954) Craig, E.
In Dutch (1945) Wallace
In Early Arizona (1938) Zahler
In Enemy Country (1968) Lava
In Fast Company (1946) Kay, Edward
In Fourteen Hundred Ninety-Two (1954) Lava
In Harm's Way (1965) Goldsmith
In Lewis and Clark's Footsteps Across Montana (1967) Tureck
In Like Flint (1967) Goldsmith
In Love and War (1958) Friedhofer
In Love With Life (1934) Zahler
In Mizzoura (1914) Klein, Manuel
In My Gondola (1936) De Nat
In Name Only (1939) Webb
In Old Amsterdam (1949) Nussbaum
In Old California (1929) Young, V.
In Old California (1942) Buttolph, David
In Old Chicago (1938) Mockridge
In Old Colorado (1941) Leipold
In Old Kentucky (1920) Beynon
In Old Kentucky (1935) Lange
In Old Mexico (1938) Stone
In Old Missouri (1940) Feuer
In Old Montana (1939) Zahler
In Old Monterey (1939) Sawtell
In Old Oklahoma (1943) Scharf, W.
In Old Sacramento (1946) Maxwell
In Old Santa Fe (1945) Jackson, H.
In Our Hands (1959) McPhee
In Our Time (1944) Waxman
In, Out, Up, Down, Under, Upside Down (1970) Burroughs
In Paris Parks (1954) Davenport
In Person (1935) Webb
In Search of Lost Worlds (1970) Bernstein, E.
In Society (1944) Skinner, F.
In the Aleutians (1945) Stalling
In the Bag (1956) Bruns
In the Bishop's Carriage (1913) Breil
In the Clutches of Death (1932) Vincent, P.
In the Forest (1960) Kleiner
In the Good Old Summertime (1949) Stoll
In the Headlines (1929) Copping
In the Heat of the Night (1967) Jones
In the Land of Diamonds (1953) Nussbaum
In the Meantime, Darling (1944) Mockridge
In the Money (1958) Skiles
In the Name of Freedom (1950) Clayton, J.
In the Navy (1941) Skinner, F.
In the Next Room (1930) Reiser
In the Nicotine (1961) Sharples, Winston
In the Pink (1967) Greene, W.
In the Pink of the Night (1969) Greene, W.
In the Street (1953) Kleiner
In the Valley of the Rhine (1953) Nussbaum
In the Year of the Pig (1968) Addiss
In the Zoo (1933) Dietrich
In This Corner (1948) Glasser
In This Our Life (1942) Steiner, M.
In Tune with Tomorrow (1939) Steiner, G.
In Venice (1933) Scheib
In Wonderland (1931) Dietrich
Inca Gold (1943) Terr
Incendiary Blonde (1945) Dolan
Incident (1948) Kay, Edward
Incident (1967) Knight, T.
Incident in a Glass Blower's Shop (1969) Hess
Incident in an Alley (1962) LaSalle
Incredible Journey (1963) Wallace
Incredible Mr. Limpet (1964) Perkins
Incredible Shrinking Man (1957) Gertz
Incredible Stranger (1942) Malotte
Incredibly Strange Creatures Who Stopped Living and Became Crazy Mixed-Up Zombies (1964) Price, Henry
Incubus (1966) Frontiere
Indestructible Man (1956) Glasser
India on Parade (1937) Shilkret, J.
Indian Agent (1948) Sawtell
Indian Fighter (1955) Waxman
Indian Life (1918) Elliott, V.
Indian Paint (1965) Skiles
Indian Serenade (1937) De Nat
Indianapolis Speedway (1939) Deutsch
Indians Are Coming (1930) Perry
Indiscreet (1931) Newman
Industrial Workers (1943) Applebaum
Industrial Workers of Central Canada (1940) Applebaum
Infantry Blues (1943) Stalling
Inferior Decorator (1947) Wallace
Inferior Decorator (1965) Sharples, Winston
Infernal Machine (1933) Kaylin
Inferno (1953) Sawtell
Inflation (1944) Raksin
Information Machine (1958) Bernstein, E.
Informer (1935) Steiner, M.
Inga (1968) Pitts
Ingagi (1930) Gage
Inherit the Wind (1960) Gold
Inheritance (1964) Kleinsinger
Injun Trouble (1938) Stalling
Injun Trouble (1951) Scheib
Injun Trouble (1969) Lava
Inki and the Lion (1941) Stalling
Inki and the Minah Bird (1943) Stalling
Inki at the Circus (1947) Stalling
Inner Circle (1946) Glickman, M.
Inner Sanctum (1948) Klatzkin
Innertube Antics (1944) Bradley
Innocent Affair (1948) Salter
Innocent Island (1934) Bowles
Innocents of Paris (1929) Leipold

Inquiry (1962) Bazelon
Inquisit Visit (1961) Sharples, Winston
Insect to Injury (1956) Sharples, Winston
Insects as Carriers of Disease (1945) Wallace
Inside Cackle Corners (1951) Calker
Inside Connecticut (1958) Kleiner
Inside Daisy Clover (1965) Previn, A.
Inside Harvester (1952) Kyte
Inside Job (1946) Skinner, F.
Inside Nazi Japan (1942) Applebaum
Inside Passage (1941) Bakaleinikoff, C.
Inside Story (1939) Mockridge
Inside Story (1948) Scott, N.
Inside Straight (1951) Hayton
Inside the Lines (1930) Webb
Inside the Mafia (1959) Glasser
Inside the Walls of Folsom Prison (1951) Lava
Inspector General (1949) Green, J.
Inspiration (1931) Axt
Insultin' the Sultan (1934) Stalling
Insurance Against Fire Losses (1952) Kraushaar
Interference (1929) Harling
Interim (1953) Tenney
Interior Guard Duty (1943) Lava
Interlude (1957) Skinner, F.
Intermezzo, a Love Story (1939) Steiner, M.
International Crime (1938) Kilenyi
International House (1933) Rainger
International Lady (1941) Moraweck
International Settlement (1937) Bassett, R. H.
International Squadron (1941) Lava
International Woodpecker (1957) Wheeler
Internes Can't Take Money (1937) Stone
Interns (1962) Stevens, L.
Interplay (1970) Burroughs
Interrupted Melody (1955) Deutsch
Intimacy (1966) Hormel
Into the Clouds (1944) Lava
Into the Good Ground (1949) Babbitt
Into Your Dance (1935) Spencer, N.
Intolerance (1916) Breil
Intrigue (1947) Forbes
Introduction to Feedback (1960) Bernstein, E.
Intruder (1959) Byrd, C.
Intruder (1962) Stein, H.
Intruder in the Dust (1949) Deutsch
Intruders (1947) Scheib
Invader (1955) Applebaum
Invaders from Mars (1953) Kraushaar
Invasion (1941) Rapée
Invasion of the Animal People (1962) Pierce, Arthur
Invasion of the Body Snatchers (1956) Dragon
Invasion of the Saucer Men (1957) Stein, R.
Invasion of the Star Creatures (1962) Cookerly
Invasion, U.S.A. (1952) Glasser
Invention Convention (1953) Sharples, Winston
Invisible Agent (1942) Salter
Invisible Atom (1958) Laderman
Invisible Boy (1957) Baxter
Invisible Enemy (1938) Colombo
Invisible Ghost (1941) Lange, J.
Invisible Informer (1946) Glickman, M.
Invisible Invaders (1959) Dunlap
Invisible Man (1933) Roemheld
Invisible Man Returns (1940) Salter
Invisible Man's Revenge (1944) Salter
Invisible Menace (1937) Kaun
Invisible Mouse (1947) Bradley
Invisible Moustache of Raoul Dufy (1955) Laszlo
Invisible Ray (1936) Waxman
Invisible Stripes (1939) Roemheld
Invisible Wall (1947) Butts
Invisible Woman (1940) Skinner, F.
Invitation (1952) Kaper
Invitation to a Gunfighter (1964) Raksin
Invitation to Happiness (1939) Hollander
Invitation to Lust (1966) Herman
Invitation to New York (1956) Mendelsohn
Invitation to the Dance (1956) Previn, A.
Involuntary Control (1969) Rosenboom
Ireland or Bust (1932) Scheib
Ireland—the Emerald Isle (1934) Shilkret, N.
Irene (1940) Collins
Irish Eyes Are Smiling (1944) Mockridge
Irish Gringo (1935) Budrow
Irish in Us (1935) Roemheld
Irish Luck (1939) Kay, Edward
Irish Stew (1930) Scheib
Irish Sweepstakes (1934) Scheib
Irma La Douce (1963) Previn, A.
Iron Claw (1941) Zahler
Iron Horse (1924) Rapée
Iron Major (1943) Webb
Iron Man (1951) Rosen, M.
Iron Mask (1929) Riesenfeld
Iron Mistress (1952) Steiner, M.
Iron Mountain Trail (1953) Wilson, S.
Iron Strain (1915) Nurnberger
Iroquois Trail (1950) Schrager
Irritability (1945) Engel
Is Everybody Happy? (1943) Leipold
Is It Always Right to Be Right? (1970) Heller
Is My Face Red? (1932) Steiner, M.
Is Paris Burning? (1966) Jarre
Is There a Doctor in the Mouse? (1964) Poddany
Isadora (1968) Jarre
Island (1959) Cobert
Island Fling (1947) Sharples, Winston
Island in the Sky (1953) Friedhofer
Island of Doomed Men (1940) Carbonara
Island of Lost Men (1939) Leipold
Island of Lost Women (1959) Kraushaar
Island of Love (1963) Duning
Island of the Blue Dolphins (1964) Sawtell
Island of the Lost (1967) Bruns
Islands of the Sea (1959) Wallace
Islands of the Sea (1968) Bourgois

Isle of Caprice (1969) Goodwin
Isle of Destiny (1940) Bakaleinikoff, C.
Isle of Forgotten Sins (1943) Erdody
Isle of Fury (1936) Jackson, H.
Isle of Lost Ships (1929) Reiser
Isle of Missing Men (1942) Kay, Edward
Isle of Paradise (1932) Bradford
Isle of Pingo Pongo (1938) Stalling
Isle of Romance (1945) De Francesco
Isle of Sports (1951) Mamorsky
Isle of Tabu (1945) Schrager
Isle of the Dead (1945) Harline
Isle of Women (1964) White, D.
Isn't It Romantic? (1948) Lilley
Isn't Life Wonderful (1925) Silvers
Israel (1959) Bernstein, E.
Israel (1965) Schickele
Israel, an Adventure (1958) Kroll
Israel Today (1960) Starr, J.
Istanbul (1956) Gertz
It Ain't Hay (1943) Skinner, F.
It All Came True (1940) Roemheld
It Came from Beneath the Sea (1955) Bakaleinikoff, M.
It Came from Outer Space (1953) Mancini
It Can't Be Done (1947) Franklyn, R.
It Comes Up Love (1942) Skinner, F.
It Conquered the World (1956) Stein, R.
It Could Happen to You (1937) Colombo
It Could Happen to You (1947) Sharples, Winston
It Grows on Trees (1952) Skinner, F.
It Had to Be You (1947) Roemheld
It Happened at the World's Fair (1962) Stevens, L.
It Happened in Brooklyn (1947) Green, J.
It Happened in Flatbush (1942) Buttolph, David
It Happened in New York (1935) Wallace
It Happened in Paris (1932) Shilkret, N.
It Happened in Springfield (1945) Lava
It Happened on Fifth Avenue (1947) Ward, E.
It Happened One Night (1934) Jackson, H.
It Happened to Crusoe (1941) De Nat
It Happened to Jane (1959) Duning
It Happened Tomorrow (1944) Stolz
It Happens Every Spring (1949) Harline
It Happens Every Thursday (1953) Stein, H.
It Happens on Rollers (1941) Lava
It Looks Like Rain (1945) Shilkret, N.
It Must Be Love (1940) Scheib
It Should Happen to You (1954) Hollander
It Shouldn't Happen to a Dog (1946) Buttolph, David
It Started with a Kiss (1959) Alexander, J.
It Started with Eve (1941) Salter
It! The Terror from Beyond Space (1958) Sawtell
It's a Big Country (1951) Deutsch
It's a Bikini World (1967) Curb
It's a Date (1940) Skinner, F.
It's a Dog's Life (1942) Kaplan, S.
It's a Dog's Life (1955) Bernstein, E.
It's a Gift (1934) Leipold
It's a Grand Old Nag (1947) Alexander, J.
It's a Great Feeling (1949) Jackson, H.
It's a Great Life (1929) Axt
It's a Great Life! (1935) Leipold
It's a Greek Life (1936) Sharples, Winston
It's a Hap-Hap-Happy Day (1941) Timberg
It's a Joke, Son! (1947) Levin
It's a Living (1957) Scheib
It's a Mad, Mad, Mad, Mad World (1963) Gold
It's a Pleasure (1945) Lange
It's a Small World (1935) Lange
It's a Small World (1950) Hajos
It's a Wonderful Life (1947) Tiomkin
It's a Wonderful World (1939) Ward, E.
It's All in the Stars (1946) Scheib
It's All in Your Mind (1938) Altschuler
It's All Yours (1937) Parrish
It's Always Fair Weather (1955) Previn, A.
It's an Ill Wind (1939) Stalling
It's Everybody's War (1942) Lange
It's for the Birdies (1962) Sharples, Winston
It's for the Birds (1967) Timmens
It's Got Me Again (1932) Marsales
It's Great to Be Alive (1933) Friedhofer
It's Great to Be Young (1946) Duning
It's Hummer Time (1949) Stalling
It's In the Air (1935) Axt
It's In the Bag (1945) Heymann
It's In the Stars (1938) Snell
It's Love I'm After (1937) Roemheld
It's Murder She Says (1945) Stalling
It's Nice to Have a Mouse Around the House (1964) Lava
It's Nifty to Be Thrifty (1944) Timberg
It's Not Just You, Murray! (1964) Coll
It's Not My Body (1970) Herman
It's Only Money (1962) Scharf, W.
It's the Farmers' Business (1962) Kleinsinger
It's the Ward Teachers (1956) Gates, C.
It's Tough to Be a Bird (1969) Bruns
It's Up to You (1941) Robinson
It's Your Life, Brother (1947) Colombo
It's Your War Too (1944) Lava
Italian Holiday (1955) Jackson, H.
Italian Job (1969) Jones
Italian Memories (1956) Jackson, H.
Italy (1951) Jackson, H.
Italy Rebuilds (1947) Forrell
Itch (1965) Sharples, Winston
Itch in Time (1943) Stalling
Item 72-D (1970) Leichtling
Ivanhoe (1952) Rozsa
Ivory Knife (1965) Bazelon
Ivy (1947) Amfitheatrof
Iwo Jima (1946) Palange

Jacaré (1942) Rozsa
Jack and Old Mac (1956) Bruns

Jack and the Beanstalk (1931) Steiner, G.
Jack and the Beanstalk (1933) Stalling
Jack and the Beanstalk (1952) Roemheld
Jack Armstrong (1947) Zahler
Jack Frost (1934) Stalling
Jack Johnson (1970) Davis, M.
Jack Levine (1964) Brant
Jack London (1943) Rich
Jack the Giant Killer (1962) Sawtell
Jack the Ripper (1958) Rugolo
Jack-Wabbit and the Beanstalk (1943) Stalling
Jack's Shack (1934) Scheib
Jackass Mail (1942) Amfitheatrof
Jackie Robinson Story (1950) Gilbert, H.
Jackson Pollock (1951) Feldman
Jacktown (1962) Provenzano
Jade Box (1930) Perry
Jade Mask (1944) Kay, Edward
Jaguar (1955) Alexander, V.
Jaguas (1942) Rathaus
Jail Bait (1954) Curtin
Jail Birds (1932) Bradley
Jail Birds (1934) Scheib
Jail Break (1946) Scheib
Jail Busters (1955) Skiles
Jail House Blues (1941) Skinner, F.
Jail Keys Made Here (1965) Brubeck, D.
Jailbreak (1936) Kaun
Jailbreakers (1960) Brummer
Jailhouse Rock (1957) Alexander, J.
Jaipur, the Pink City (1938) Shilkret, J.
Jalna (1935) Colombo
Jalopy (1953) Skiles
Jamaica (1946) De Francesco
Jamaica Run (1953) Cailliet
Jamboree (1957) Hefti
James Brothers of Missouri (1949) Wilson, S.
James Dean Story (1957) Stevens, L.
Jane (1915) Beynon
Jane Eyre (1944) Herrmann
Janice Meredith (1925) Taylor, D.
Janie (1944) Roemheld
Janie Get Your Gun (1965) Greene, W.
Janie Gets Married (1946) Hollander
Japan (1958) Wallace
Japan and the World Today (1950) Bassman
Japanese Beetle (1957) Kleinsinger
Japanese Family (1950) Forrell
Japanese House (1955) Lloyd, N.
Japanese Lanterns (1935) Sharples, Winston
Japanese War Bride (1952) Lange
Jason and the Argonauts (1963) Herrmann
Jasper and the Beanstalk (1945) Wheeler
Jasper and the Choo-Choo (1943) von Ottenfeld
Jasper and the Haunted House (1942) von Ottenfeld
Jasper and the Watermelons (1942) von Ottenfeld
Jasper Goes Fishing (1943) de Packh
Jasper Goes Hunting (1944) de Packh
Jasper in a Jam (1946) Wheeler
Jasper National Park (1952) Nussbaum
Jasper Tell (1945) Wheeler
Jasper's Boobytraps (1945) Wheeler
Jasper's Close Shave (1945) Wheeler
Jasper's Derby (1946) Wheeler
Jasper's Minstrels (1945) Wheeler
Jasper's Music Lesson (1943) Martyn
Jasper's Paradise (1944) de Packh
Java Journey (1938) Shilkret, J.
Jay Walker (1956) May
Jayhawkers! (1959) Moross
Jazz Age (1929) Filippi
Jazz Fool (1929) Stalling
Jazz Mad (1931) Scheib
Jazz of Lights (1954) Barron
Jazz Rhythm (1930) De Nat
Jazz Singer (1927) Silvers
Jazz Singer (1953) Steiner, M.
Jazzoo (1968) Lake, O.
Jealous Lover (1933) Scheib
Jealousy (1945) Eisler
Jeanne Eagels (1957) Duning
Jeep (1938) Timberg
Jeep-Herders (1945) Zahler
Jeepers Creepers (1939) Feuer
Jeepers Creepers (1939) Stalling
Jennie (1940) Mockridge
Jennie Gerhardt (1933) Leipold
Jennie, Wife/Child (1968) Hatcher
Jennifer (1953) Gold
Jenny (1970) Small
Jenny and the Poet (1964) Ashley
Jenny Lind (1931) Axt
Jenny's Birthday Book (1956) Kleiner
Jeopardy (1953) Tiomkin
Jerky Turkey (1945) Bradley
Jerry and Jumbo (1953) Bradley
Jerry and the Goldfish (1951) Bradley
Jerry and the Lion (1950) Bradley
Jerry's Cousin (1951) Bradley
Jerry's Diary (1949) Bradley
Jerry-Go-Round (1965) Poddany
Jerry, Jerry, Quite Contrary (1966) Elliott, Dean
Jerusalem (1962) Carmichael
Jerusalem, City of Peace (1931) Maloof
Jesse and James (1931) Scheib
Jesse James (1939). See p. 8
Jesse James, Jr. (1942) Feuer
Jesse James Meets Frankenstein's Daughter (1966) Kraushaar
Jesse James Rides Again (1947) Glickman, M.
Jesse James' Women (1954) Greene, W.
Jest of Honor (1934) Sharples, Winston
Jet Attack (1958) Stein, R.
Jet Cage (1962) Lava
Jet Job (1952) Kay, Edward
Jet Over the Atlantic (1959) Forbes
Jet Pilot (1957) Kaper

Jet Pink (1967) Greene, W.
Jet Propulsion (1945) Smith, P.
Jet Terminal (1961) Kleinsinger
Jewel of the Baltic (1949) De Francesco
Jewel of the Pacific (1942) De Francesco
Jewel Robbery (1932) Kaun
Jewels of Brandenburg (1947) Calker
Jewels of Iran (1944) De Francesco
Jewish Melody (1931) Secunda
Jewish Melody (1940) Secunda
Jezebel (1938) Steiner, M.
Jiggs and Maggie in Court (1948) Kay, Edward
Jiggs and Maggie in Jackpot Jitters (1949) Kay, Edward
Jiggs and Maggie in Society (1947) Kay, Edward
Jiggs and Maggie Out West (1950) Kay, Edward
Jigsaw (1949) Stringer
Jigsaw (1968) Jones
Jim the Man (1967) Granelli
Jim Thorpe—All-American (1951) Steiner, M.
Jimmy and Sally (1933) Lange
Jimmy Jones (1943) Applebaum
Jimmy the Gent (1934) Kaun
Jingle Bells (1931) Scheib
Jingle, Jangle, Jingle (1948) Lilley
Jingle, Jangle, Jungle (1950) Sharples, Winston
Jinx Money (1948) Kay, Edward
Jitterbug Follies (1939) Lewis
Jitterbug Jive (1950) Sharples, Winston
Jitterbugs (1943) Harline
Jittery Jester (1958) Wheeler
Jivaro (1954) Stone
Jive Junction (1943) Erdody
Joan Lowell, Adventure Girl (1934) Sharples, Winston
Joan of Arc (1948) Friedhofer
Joan of Ozark (1942) Glickman, M.
Joan of Paris (1942) Webb
Joan the Woman (1916) Furst
Joaquin Murrieta (1938) Snell
Job for a Gob (1955) Sharples, Winston
Joe (1970) Scott, B.
Joe and Ethel Turp Call on the President (1939) Ward, E.
Joe Butterfly (1957) Mancini
Joe Dakota (1957) Salter
Joe Glow, the Firefly (1941) Stalling
Joe Louis Story (1953) Bassman
Joe Palooka, Champ (1946) Laszlo
Joe Palooka in Fighting Mad (1948) Kay, Edward
Joe Palooka in Humphrey Takes a Chance (1950) Kay, Edward
Joe Palooka in The Big Fight (1949) Kay, Edward
Joe Palooka in The Counterpunch (1949) Kay, Edward
Joe Palooka in The Knockout (1947) Kay, Edward
Joe Palooka in The Squared Circle (1950) Kay, Edward
Joe Palooka in Triple Cross (1951) Calker
Joe Palooka Meets Humphrey (1950) Kay, Edward
Joe Smith, American (1942) Amfitheatrof
Joe's Lunch Wagon (1934) Scheib
Johann Mouse (1953) Bradley
John and Mary (1969) Jones
John F. Kennedy: Years of Lightning, Day of Drums (1966) Herschensohn
John Goldfarb, Please Come Home! (1964) Williams, J.
John Henry and the Inky-Poo (1946) Wheeler
John Loves Mary (1949) Buttolph, David
John Meade's Woman (1937) Hollander
John Nesbitt's Passing Parade (1938) Snell
John Paul Jones (1959) Steiner, M.
John, the Drunkard (1944) Merkur
Johnny Allegro (1949) Duning
Johnny Angel (1945) Harline
Johnny Apollo (1940) Mockridge
Johnny Belinda (1948) Steiner, M.
Johnny Come Lately (1943) Harline
Johnny Comes Flying Home (1946) Buttolph, David
Johnny Concho (1956) Riddle
Johnny Cool (1963) May
Johnny Dark (1954) Salter
Johnny Doesn't Live Here Any More (1944) Harling
Johnny Doughboy (1942) Scharf, W.
Johnny Eager (1941) Kaper
Johnny Guitar (1954) Young, V.
Johnny Holiday (1950) Waxman
Johnny O'Clock (1947) Duning
Johnny One-Eye (1950) Forbes
Johnny Reno (1965) Haskell
Johnny Rocco (1958) Kay, Edward
Johnny Smith and Poker-Huntas (1938) Stalling
Johnny Tiger (1966) Green, J.
Johnny Tremaine (1957) Bruns
Johnny Trouble (1957) De Vol
Johnstown Flood (1946) Scheib
Joker Is Wild (1957) Scharf, W.
Jolifou Inn (1955) Applebaum
Jolly Good Felons (1934) Sharples, Winston
Jolly Good Furlough (1943) Timberg
Jolly Little Elves (1934) Dietrich
Jolly, the Clown (1957) Sharples, Winston
Jolson Sings Again (1949) Duning
Jolson Story (1946) Skiles
Jonah and the Highway (1957) Gertz
Jones Family in Hollywood (1939) Rose, G.
Jones Family in On Their Own (1940) Kaylin
Jones Family in Quick Millions (1939) Rose, G.
Jones Family in Young as You Feel (1940) Kaylin
Joniko and the Kush Ta Ka (1969) Curtin
Jonker Diamond (1936) Axt
Jordan Is a Hard Road (1915) Raynes
José Come Bem (The Unseen Enemy) (1945) Smith, P.
Joseph and His Brethren (1952) Mamorsky
Joseph in Egypt (1952) Mamorsky
Joseph in the Land of Egypt (1932) Hochman

Josette (1938) Scharf, W.
Joshua in a Box (1970) Andes
Journal of a Crime (1934) Roemheld
Journal of a Crime (Trailer, 1934) Kaun
Journey for Margaret (1942) Waxman
Journey Into Light (1951) Dunlap
Journey Into Medicine (1946) Brant
Journey to Denali (1942) Craig, E.
Journey to Shiloh (1967) Gates, D.
Journey to the Center of the Earth (1959) Herrmann
Journey to the Center of Time (1967) Skiles
Journey to the Lost City (1960) Michelet
Journey to the Sea (1956) Jackson, H.
Journey to the Seventh Planet (1961) Stein, R.
Journey to the Stars (1962) Schuller
Journey to Yesterday (1944) Terr
Joy House (1964) Schifrin
Joy in the Morning (1964) Herrmann
Joy of Living (1938) Bennett, R. R.
Joy of Living: The Art of Renoir (1952) Belasco
Joy Ride (1958) Skiles
Joys of Jezebel (1970) Lance
Juarez (1939) Korngold
Jubal (1956) Raksin
Jubilee Trail (1954) Young, V.
Judge (1949) Lanham
Judge Hardy's Children (1938) Snell
Judge Priest (1934) Kaylin
Judge Steps Out (1949) Harline
Judgment at Nuremberg (1961) Gold
Judith (1965) Kaplan, S.
Judo Kudos (1968) Timmens
Juggler (1953) Antheil
Juggler of Our Lady (1957) Scheib
Juke Box Jamboree (1942) Calker
Juke Box Rhythm (1959) Morton
Juke Girl (1942) Deutsch
Julia Misbehaves (1948) Deutsch
Julie (1956) Stevens, L.
Julius Caesar (1953) Rozsa
Julius Caeser (1950) Becker
Jumbo (1962) Stoll
Jump Into Hell (1955) Buttolph, David
Jumpin' Jupiter (1954) Stalling
Jumping Beans (1930) Scheib
Jumping Jacks (1952) Lilley
Jumping Off Place (1951) Mamorsky
Jumping with Toy (1957) Sharples, Winston
June Bride (1935) Scheib
June Bride (1948) Buttolph, David
Jungle (1914) Klein, Manuel
Jungle Book (1942) Rozsa
Jungle Book (1967) Bruns
Jungle Captive (1944) Sawtell
Jungle Cat (1959) Wallace
Jungle Close-Ups (1947) De Francesco
Jungle Flight (1947) Calker
Jungle Gents (1954) Skiles
Jungle Girl (1941) Glickman, M.
Jungle Goddess (1948) Gertz
Jungle Headhunters (1950) Sawtell
Jungle Heat (1957) Baxter
Jungle Hell (1955) Carras
Jungle Jitters (1934) Stalling
Jungle Jitters (1938) Stalling
Jungle Jive (1944) Calker
Jungle Jumble (1932) Dietrich
Jungle Land (1943) De Francesco
Jungle Man (1941) Colombo
Jungle Man Killers (1948) Lava
Jungle Patrol (1948) Lange
Jungle Princess (1936) Stone
Jungle Raiders (1945) Zahler
Jungle Rhythm (1929) Stalling
Jungle Siren (1942) Porter
Jungle Terror (1949) Lava
Jungle Thrills (1944) Jackson, H.
Jungle Woman (1944) Sawtell
Junior G-Men of the Air (1942) Rosen, M.
Junior Jive Bombers (1944) Lava
Junior Miss (1945) Buttolph, David
Junior Prom (1946) Zahler
Jupiter's Darling (1955) Rose
Just a Clown (1934) Scheib
Just a Cute Kid (1940) Jackson, H.
Just a Little Bull (1940) Scheib
Just Across the Street (1952) Stein, H.
Just Ask Jupiter (1938) Scheib
Just Between Us (1961) Stein, R.
Just Dog (1932) Lewis
Just Ducky (1953) Bradley
Just for Fun (1950) Lava
Just for Sport (1952) Lava
Just for the Hell of It (1968) Wellington
Just for You (1952) Friedhofer
Just Imagine (1930) Friedhofer
Just Like Heaven (1930) Burton
Just My Luck (1935) Zahler
Just Off Broadway (1942) Raksin
Just Plane Beep (1965) Lava
Just the Bear Facts Ma'am (1955) Craig, E.
Just This Once (1952) Rose
Just We Two (1934) Jackson, H.
Justine (1969) Goldsmith

Kaleidoscope Jazz Chair (1960) Marx, D.
Kali (1967) Malik
Kangaroo (1952) Kaplan, S.
Kangaroo Courting (1954) Bruns
Kangaroo Kid (1938) De Nat
Kangaroo Steak (1930) Scheib
Kannibal Kapers (1935) De Nat
Kansan (1943) Carbonara
Kansas City Confidential (1952) Sawtell
Kansas City Kitty (1944) Duning
Kansas Cyclone (1941) Sawtell
Kansas Pacific (1953) Sendrey
Kansas Raiders (1950) Rosen, M.

Kansas Territory (1952) Kraushaar
Kansas Terrors (1939) Lava
Karamoja (1954) Gold
Karl Knaths' Cape Cod (1955) Jencks
Karnival Kid (1929) Stalling
Kathleen (1941) Waxman
Kathleen Mavourneen (1930) Riesenfeld
Kathryn Reed Story (1966) Williams, J.
Kathy O' (1957) Skinner, F.
Katie Did It (1951) Skinner, F.
Katie's Lot (1961) Phillips, S.
Katnip Kollege (1938) Stalling
Katnip's Big Day (1959) Sharples, Winston
Katnips of 1940 (1934) De Nat
Keep 'Em Growing (1943) Scheib
Keep 'Em Slugging (1943) Skinner, F.
Keep Punching (1939) Norman, Lee
Keep the Cool, Baby (1967) Sharples, Winston
Keep Your Grin Up (1955) Sharples, Winston
Keep Your Powder Dry (1945) Snell
Keeper of the Bees (1947) Sawtell
Keeper of the Flame (1942) Kaper
Keeper of the Lions (1937) Dietrich
Keeping Company (1940) Amfitheatrof
Keeping Up with Krazy (1962) Sharples, Winston
Kelly and Me (1956) Mancini
Kelly the Second (1936) Hatley
Kelly's Heroes (1970) Schifrin
Kenji Comes Home (1949) Kendrick
Kennel Murder Case (1933) Kaun
Kentuckian (1955) Herrmann
Kentucky Basketeers (1946) Shilkret, N.
Kentucky Belle (1931) Dietrich
Kentucky Blue Streak (1935) Zahler
Kentucky Derby Story (1949) Shilkret, N.
Kentucky Jubilee (1951) Greene, W.
Kentucky Kernels (1934) Webb
Kentucky Moonshine (1938) Mockridge
Kentucky Rifle (1955) Gertz
Kept Husbands (1931) Steiner, M.
Kettles in the Ozarks (1955) Mancini
Kettles on Old MacDonald's Farm (1957) Mancini
Key Largo (1948) Steiner, M.
Key to the City (1950) Kaper
Key Witness (1960) Wolcott
Keyhole (1933) Harling
Keys of the Kingdom (1944) Newman
Keystone Hotel (1935) Jackson, H.
Khyber Patrol (1954) Gertz
Kibitzer (1930) Harling
Kick in Time (1940) Timberg
Kickapoo Juice (1945) Kilfeather
Kickin' the Conga 'Round (1942) Timberg
Kid Comes Back (1937) Raksin
Kid Dynamite (1943) Kay, Edward
Kid from Borneo (1933) Shield
Kid from Brooklyn (1946) Dragon
Kid from Cleveland (1949) Scott, N.
Kid from Kansas (1941) Salter
Kid from Kokomo (1939) Deutsch
Kid from Left Field (1953) Newman, L.
Kid from Mars (1960) Sharples, Winston
Kid from Santa Fe (1940) Porter
Kid from Spain (1933) Newman
Kid from Texas (1939) Axt
Kid from Texas (1950) Skinner, F.
Kid Galahad (1937) Roemheld
Kid Galahad (1962) Alexander, J.
Kid Glove Killer (1942) Hayton
Kid in Upper 4 (1944) Kaplan, S.
Kid Millions (1934) Newman
Kid Monk Baroni (1952) Gilbert, H.
Kid Nightingale (1939) Jackson, H.
Kid Rides Again (1943) Erdody
Kid Sister (1945) Glasser
Kid'n' Africa (1933) Zahler
Kid's Last Ride (1941) Sanucci
Kiddie Koncert (1948) Calker
Kiddie League (1959) Poddany
Kiddie Revue (1936) Dietrich
Kiddie's Kitty (1955) Franklyn
Kiddin' the Kitten (1951) Stalling
Kidnapped (1938) Maxwell
Kidnapped (1948) Kay, Edward
Kids in the Shoe (1935) Steiner, G.
Kiki (1931) Newman
Kiko and the Honey Bears (1936) Scheib
Kiko Foils the Fox (1936) Scheib
Kiko's Cleaning Day (1937) Scheib
Kill (1968) Alexander, E.
Kill a Dragon (1967) Springer, P.
Kill or Be Killed (1950) Hajos
Kill the Umpire (1950) Roemheld
Killer at Large (1947) Glasser
Killer Dill (1947) Thompson, J.
Killer Is Loose (1956) Newman, L.
Killer Leopard (1954) Skiles
Killer McCoy (1947) Snell
Killer Shark (1950) Kay, Edward
Killer Shrews (1959) Bluestone
Killer That Stalked New York (1950) Salter
Killer's Kiss (1955) Fried
Killers (1946) Rozsa
Killers (1964) Steiner, F.
Killers at Bay (1954) Craig, E.
Killers from Space (1953) Compinsky
Killers of the Swamp (1952) Jackson, H.
Killers Three (1968) Curb
Killing (1956) Fried
Killing of Sister George (1968) Fried
Kilroy Was Here (1947) Kay, Edward
Kim (1950) Previn, A.
Kind Lady (1935) Ward, E.
Kind Lady (1951) Raksin
Kindly Scram (1943) Worth, P.
Kinestasis 60 (1970) Garson
King: A Filmed Record . . . Montgomery to Memphis (1970) Perkinson

King and Four Queens (1956) North
King and I (1956) Newman
King and the Chorus Girl (1937) Heymann
King Creole (1958) Scharf, W.
King Dinosaur (1955) Garf
King for a Day (1940) Timberg
King Klunk (1933) Dietrich
King Kong (1933) Steiner, M.
King Looney XIV (1935) Scheib
King Midas, Junior (1942) Worth, P.
King Neptune (1932) Lewis
King of Burlesque (1936) Mockridge
King of Chinatown (1939) Leipold
King of Hockey (1936) Jackson, H.
King of Jazz (1930) Dietrich
King of Kings (1927) Riesenfeld
King of Kings (1961) Rozsa
King of Madison Avenue (1967) Raim
King of the Archers (1943) Dunn
King of the Bandits (1947) Kay, Edward
King of the Bullwhip (1950) Greene, W.
King of the Carnival (1948) Jackson, H.
King of the Carnival (1955) Butts
King of the Cowboys (1943) Glickman, M.
King of the Everglades (1946) Dunn
King of the Forest Rangers (1946) Glickman, M.
King of the Gamblers (1948) Glickman, M.
King of the Grizzlies (1969) Baker, Buddy
King of the Ice (1964) Manson
King of the Islands (1936) Vaughan
King of the Jungle (1933) Hand
King of the Khyber Rifles (1953) Herrmann
King of the Kongo (1929) Zahler
King of the Lumberjacks (1940) Lava
King of the Mounties (1942) Glickman, M.
King of the Newsboys (1938) Colombo
King of the Roaring '20's (1961) Waxman
King of the Rocket Men (1949) Wilson, S.
King of the Royal Mounted (1940) Feuer
King of the Sierras (1938) Riesenfeld
King of the Stallions (1942) Sanucci
King of the Turf (1939) Tours
King of the Underworld (1939) Roemheld
King of the Wild (1931) Zahler
King of the Wild Horses (1947) Steinert
King of the Wild Stallions (1959) Skiles
King of the Zombies (1941) Kay, Edward
King Richard and the Crusaders (1954) Steiner, M.
King Salmon (1941) Dunn
King-Size Canary (1947) Bradley
King Solomon's Mines (1950) Rozsa
King Tut's Tomb (1950) Scheib
King Zilch (1933) Scheib
King's Daughter (1934) Scheib
King's Jester (1935) De Nat
King's Pirate (1967) Ferraro
King's Thief (1955) Rozsa
King's Vacation (1933) Kaun
Kings Go Forth (1958) Bernstein, E.
Kings of the Outdoors (1951) Jackson, H.
Kings of the Rockies (1949) Lava
Kings of the Sun (1963) Bernstein, E.
Kings of the Turf (1941) Dunn
Kings of the Wild Waves (1964) Podolor
Kings Row (1942) Korngold
Kings Up (1934) Dietrich
Kingdom of the Wild (1947) Dunn
Kipling's Women (1960) Glasser
Kismet (1920) Edouarde
Kismet (1930) Rosebrook
Kismet (1944) Stothart
Kismet (1955) Previn, A.
Kiss (1929) Axt
Kiss and Make-Up (1934) Rainger
Kiss and Tell (1945) Heymann
Kiss Before Dying (1956) Newman, L.
Kiss Before the Mirror (1933) Harling
Kiss for Corliss (1949) Heymann
Kiss Her Goodbye (1959) Richards, J.
Kiss in the Dark (1948) Steiner, M.
Kiss Me Again (1931) Mendoza
Kiss Me Cat (1951) Stalling
Kiss Me Deadly (1955) De Vol
Kiss Me Kate (1953) Previn, A.
Kiss Me, Stupid (1964) Previn, A.
Kiss of Death (1947) Buttolph, David
Kiss of Fire (1955) Salter
Kiss of Her Flesh (1968) Aden
Kiss the Blood Off My Hands (1948) Rozsa
Kiss the Boys Goodbye (1941) Young, V.
Kiss Them for Me (1957) Mockridge
Kiss Tomorrow Goodbye (1950) Dragon
Kiss Tomorrow Goodbye (Trailer, 1950) Lava
Kisses for Breakfast (1941) Deutsch
Kisses for Breakfast (Trailer, 1941) Jackson, H.
Kisses for My President (1964) Kaper
Kissin' Cousins (1964) Karger
Kissing Bandit (1948) Stoll
Kit Carson (1940) Ward, E.
Kit for Kat (1947) Stalling
Kitten Sitter (1949) Scheib
Kitten with a Whip (1964) Stalling
Kittens' Mittens (1940) Churchill
Kitty (1945) Young, V.
Kitty Caddy (1947) Calker
Kitty Coronered (1955) Sharples, Winston
Kitty Foiled (1948) Bradley
Kitty Foyle (1940) Webb
Kitty Gets the Bird (1941) Kilfeather
Kitty Kornered (1946) Stalling
Kliou (1935) Roemheld
Klondike Annie (1936) Young, V.
Klondike Casanova (1946) Sharples, Winston
Klondike Fury (1942) Kay, Edward
Klondike Kate (1943) Glasser
Klondike Kid (1932) Churchill
Knickerbocker Holiday (1944) Heymann

Knife Thrower (1951) Biviano
Knight for a Day (1945) Wallace
Knight-Mare Hare (1955) Franklyn
Knight of the Plains (1938) Zahler
Knight Without Armour (1937) Rozsa
Knights for a Day (1936) Dietrich
Knights Must Fall (1949) Stalling
Knights of the Range (1940) Leipold
Knights of the Round Table (1953) Rozsa
Knighty Knight Bugs (1957) Franklyn
Knock Knock (1940) Marsales
Knock on Any Door (1949) Antheil
Knock on Wood (1954) Young, V.
Knockout (1941) Jackson, H.
Know Your Ally: Britain (1943) Jackson, H.
Know Your Enemy—Japan (1945) Tiomkin
Know Your Money (1940) Snell
Knowing's Not Enough (1956) Norlin
Knute Rockne—All American (1940) Roemheld
Kol Nidre (1939) Secunda
Kona Coast (1968) Marshall, J.
Konga, the Wild Stallion (1939) Parrish
Kongo-Roo (1946) Kilfeather
Korea Patrol (1950) Gerens
Kozmo Goes to School (1961) Sharples, Winston
Krakatoa (1945) Scheib
Krakatoa, East of Java (1968) De Vol
Krazy Spooks (1933) De Nat
Krazy's Bear Tale (1939) De Nat
Krazy's Magic (1938) De Nat
Krazy's News Reel (1936) De Nat
Krazy's Race of Time (1937) De Nat
Krazy's Shoe Shop (1939) De Nat
Krazy's Waterloo (1934) De Nat
Kremlin Letter (1969) Drasnin
Kress Collection (1957) Baksa
Kristopher Kolumbus, Jr. (1939) Stalling
Kronos (1957) Sawtell
Kukan, the Battle Cry of China (1942) Craig, E.
Ku-Ku-Nuts (1945) Kilfeather

L'Amour the Merrier (1957) Sharples, Winston
L'il an Jil (1936) De Nat
La Boheme (1926) Axt
La Cautivadora (1931) Gama
La Ciudad de Cartón (1934) Kaylin
La Conga Nights (1940) Skinner, F.
La Cruz y la Espada (1934) Kaylin
La Ley del Harem (1931) Friedhofer
La Melodía Prohibida (1933) Kaylin
La Petite Parade (1959) Sharples, Winston
La Savate (1938) Axt
La Tosca (1921) Riesenfeld
La Ultima cita (1936) Stahl
La Vida Bohemia (1938) Borisoff
Lab School (1967) Markowitz
Labyrinth (1955) Maneri
Lad in Bagdad (1938) Stalling
Lad: A Dog (1961) Roemheld

Laddie (1940) Webb
Laddy and His Lamp (1963) Sharples, Winston
Ladies Courageous (1944) Tiomkin
Ladies in Distress (1938) Colombo
Ladies in Love (1936) Mockridge
Ladies in Retirement (1941) Toch
Ladies in Waiting (1948) Shilkret, N.
Ladies Love Brutes (1930) Potoker
Ladies Man (1947) Webb
Ladies Must Live (1940) Jackson, H.
Ladies Must Love (1933) Jackson, H.
Ladies of the Big House (1931) Leipold
Ladies of the Chorus (1949) Duning
Ladies of the Jury (1932) Steiner, M.
Ladies of Washington (1944) Mockridge
Ladies Should Listen (1934) Satterfield
Ladies They Talk About (Trailer, 1933) Kaun
Ladies' Day (1943) Webb
Ladies' Man (1931) Hand
Ladies' Man (1961) Scharf, W.
Lady and Gent (1932) Leipold
Lady and the Bandit (1951) Duning
Lady and the Lug (1940) Jackson, H.
Lady and the Mob (1939) Bradshaw
Lady and the Monster (1944) Scharf, W.
Lady and the Tramp (1955) Wallace
Lady at Midnight (1948) Erdody
Lady Be Careful (1936) Leipold
Lady Be Good (1941) Stoll
Lady Bodyguard (1943) Sawtell
Lady Chaser (1946) Greene, W.
Lady Confesses (1945) Zahler
Lady Eve (1941) Shuken
Lady Fights Back (1944) Shilkret, N.
Lady for a Day (1933) Jackson, H.
Lady for a Night (1942) Buttolph, David
Lady from Cheyenne (1941) Skinner, F.
Lady from Chungking (1943) Zahler
Lady from Louisiana (1941) Glickman, M.
Lady from Shanghai (1948) Roemheld
Lady Gambles (1949) Skinner, F.
Lady Gangster (1942) Lava
Lady Godiva of Coventry (1955) Skinner, F.
Lady Godiva Rides (1969) Weiner
Lady Has Plans (1941) Harline
Lady in a Cage (1963) Glass, Paul
Lady in a Jam (1942) Skinner, F.
Lady in Cement (1968) Montenegro
Lady in Question (1940) Moraweck
Lady in Red (1936) Spencer, N.
Lady in the Dark (1944) Dolan
Lady in the Death House (1944) Gray
Lady in the Iron Mask (1952) Tiomkin
Lady in the Lake (1946) Snell
Lady in the Lake (Trailer, 1946) Kopp, R.
Lady Is Willing (1942) Harling
Lady Killer (1933) Kaun
Lady Luck (1946) Harline
Lady Marines (1951) Shilkret, N.

Ladybug, Ladybug (1963) Cobert
Lady, Let's Dance (1944) Kay, Edward
Lady Objects (1938) Cutner
Lady of Burlesque (1943) Lange
Lady of Chance (1929) Axt
Lady of Secrets (1936) Still
Lady of the Lake (1930) Shilkret, N.
Lady of the Pavements (1929) Riesenfeld
Lady of the Tropics (1939) Waxman
Lady on a Train (1945) Rozsa
Lady or the Tiger? (1942) Kaplan, S.
Lady Pays Off (1951) Skinner, F.
Lady Play Your Mandolin (1931) Marsales
Lady Possessed (1951) Scott, N.
Lady Said No (1945) Smith, P.
Lady Says No (1952) Lange
Lady Surrenders (1930) Roemheld
Lady Takes a Chance (1943) Webb
Lady Takes a Flyer (1957) Stein, H.
Lady Takes a Sailor (1949) Steiner, M.
Lady Wants Mink (1952) Wilson, S.
Lady Who Dared (1931) Reiser
Lady With a Past (1932) Lewis, Harold
Lady with Red Hair (1940) Roemheld
Lady with the Lamp (1951) Collins
Lady Without Passport (1950) Raksin
Lady's from Kentucky (1939) Shuken
Lady's Profession (1933) Leipold
Lafayette Escadrille (1958) Rosenman
Lake Placid Serenade (1944) Scharf, W.
Lake Texoma (1951) Shilkret, N.
Lakewood Learns to Live (1956) Marsh
Lamb (1915) Breil
Lamb in a Jam (1945) Sharples, Winston
Lambert, the Sheepish Lion (1951) Dubin
Lambs Will Gamble (1930) De Nat
Lament (1951) Lloyd, N.
Lamentation (1943) Horst
Lamplighter (1937) Churchill
Lancer Spy (1937) Maxwell
Land (1941) Arnell
Land Beyond the Law (1937) Jackson, H.
Land of 10,000 Lakes (1945) De Francesco
Land of Alaska Nellie (1940) Bakaleinikoff, C.
Land of Auld Lang Syne (1950) Mayfield
Land of Everyday Miracles (1952) Jackson, H.
Land of Fun (1941) De Nat
Land of Hunted Men (1943) Sanucci
Land of Legend (1954) Newman
Land of Lost Watches (1951) Sharples, Winston
Land of Orizaba (1942) Nussbaum
Land of Promise (1935) Carbonara
Land of Romance (1947) Dunn
Land of the Book (1967) Marais
Land of the Incas (1937) Shilkret, J.
Land of the Lawless (1947) Kay, Edward
Land of the Lost (1948) Sharples, Winston
Land of the Lost Jewels (1950) Sharples, Winston
Land of the Mayas (1946) Nussbaum
Land of the Midnight Fun (1939) Stalling
Land of the Outlaws (1944) Kay, Edward
Land of the Pharaohs (1955) Tiomkin
Land of the Quintuplets (1942) Nussbaum
Land of the Six Guns (1940) Lange, J.
Land of the Sleeping Fire (1952) Axom
Land of the Taj Mahal (1952) Nussbaum
Land of the Trembling Earth (1952) Lava
Land of the Zuider Zee (1951) Nussbaum
Land of Tradition (1950) Nussbaum
Land of White Alice (1960) Pinkham
Land Unknown (1957) Salter
Landing of the Pilgrims (1940) Scheib
Landlord (1970) Kooper
Landscape of the Norse (1949) De Francesco
Language of Faces (1961) Ito
Language of the Film (1965) Klein, Martin
Lapis (1966) Shankar
Lapland (1957) Wallace
Laramie Trail (1944) Glickman, M.
Larceny (1948) Stevens, L.
Larceny in Her Heart (1946) Erdody
Larceny, Inc. (1942) Deutsch
Las Fronteras del Amor (1934) Kaylin
Las Vegas Nights (1941) Scharf, W.
Las Vegas Shakedown (1955) Kay, Edward
Las Vegas Story (1952) Harline
Las Vegas, Frontier Town (1946) Jackson, H.
Lasers and Atoms (1965) Bazelon
Lash (1930) Mendoza
Lash of the Penitentes (1936) Zahler
Lassie Come Home (1943) Amfitheatrof
Last Alarm (1940) Zahler
Last Angry Man (1959) Duning
Last Bandit (1949) Butts
Last Challenge (1967) Shores
Last Chapter (1966) Heifetz
Last Command (1955) Steiner, M.
Last Crooked Mile (1946) Dubin
Last Days of Pompeii (1913) Clark, P.
Last Days of Pompeii (1935) Webb
Last Egyptian (1914) Gottschalk
Last Frontier (1956) Harline
Last Frontier Uprising (1947) Glickman, M.
Last Gangster (1937) Ward, E.
Last Gentleman (1934) Newman
Last Hungry Cat (1961) Franklyn
Last Hunt (1956) Amfitheatrof
Last Indian (1938) Scheib
Last Installment (1945) Terr
Last Lesson (1942) Shilkret, N.
Last Mail (1933) Sharples, Winston
Last Man (1965) Karlin
Last Man on Earth (1924) Rapée
Last Man on Earth (1964) Sawtell
Last Mile (1932) Burton
Last Mile (1959) Alexander, V.
Last Moment (1966) Michaelides
Last Mouse of Hamelin (1955) Scheib

Last Musketeer (1952) Butts
Last of Mrs. Cheyney (1929) Axt
Last of Mrs. Cheyney (1937) Axt
Last of the Badmen (1957) Sawtell
Last of the Comanches (1952) Duning
Last of the Desperadoes (1956) Dunlap
Last of the Duanes (1930) Kaylin
Last of the Duanes (1941) Buttolph, David
Last of the Fast Guns (1958) Salter
Last of the Mobile Hotshots (1970) Jones
Last of the Mohicans (1920) Kay, Arthur
Last of the Mohicans (1932) Zahler
Last of the Mohicans (1936) Webb
Last of the Pagans (1935) Axt
Last of the Redmen (1947) Gertz
Last of the Secret Agents? (1966) King
Last of the Wild Horses (1948) Glasser
Last of the Wild West (1951) Sawtell
Last Outpost (1935) Kaun
Last Outpost (1951) Cailliet
Last Performance (1929) Perry
Last Ride (1944) Lava
Last Round-Up (1934) Hand
Last Round-Up (1943) Scheib
Last Round-Up (1947) Dubin
Last Shot You Hear (1968) Shefter
Last Straw (1934) Scheib
Last Summer (1969) Simon, J.
Last Sunset (1961) Gold
Last Time I Saw Archie (1961) Comstock
Last Time I Saw Paris (1954) Salinger
Last Train from Gun Hill (1959) Tiomkin
Last Voyage (1960) Schrager
Last Voyage (1960) Stone, Andrew & Virginia
Last Wagon (1956) Newman, L.
Last Will and Testament of Tom Smith (1943) Jenkins
Last Woman on Earth (1960) Stein, R.
Late George Apley (1947) Mockridge
Latin Lovers (1953) Stoll
Laugh a Day (1951) Lava
Laugh Your Blues Away (1942) Belasco
Laughing Anne (1953) Collins
Laughing at Danger (1940) Kay, Edward
Laughing at Life (1933) Zahler
Laughing Boy (1934) Stothart
Laughing Gas (1931) Stalling
Laughing Gravy (1931) Shield
Laughing Till It Hurt: The Comedy of Charles Chaplin (1968) Hazzard, P.
Laughter (1930) Duke
Laughter Through Tears (1933) Secunda
Laundromat Symphony (19??) Trythall
Laura (1944) Raksin
Laurel and Hardy's Laughing 20's (1965) Alquist
Laurel-Hardy Murder Case (1930) Shilkret, N.
Law and Audrey (1952) Sharples, Winston
Law and Lead (1937) Zahler
Law and Order (1932) Broekman
Law and Order (1950) Scheib
Law and Order (1953) Rosen, M.
Law and the Lady (1951) Dragon
Law Comes to Gunsight (1947) Kay, Edward
Law Comes to Texas (1939) Zahler
Law in Her Hands (1936) Roemheld
Law in Her Hands (Trailer, 1936) Kaun
Law Men (1944) Kay, Edward
Law of the Badlands (1945) Jackson, H.
Law of the Badlands (1950) Sawtell
Law of the Golden West (1949) Wilson, S.
Law of the Lash (1947) Glasser
Law of the Lawless (1963) Dunlap
Law of the Pampas (1939) Young, V.
Law of the Panhandle (1950) Kay, Edward
Law of the Timber (1941) Wheeler
Law of the Tropics (1941) Jackson, H.
Law of the Valley (1944) Kay, Edward
Law of the West (1949) Kay, Edward
Law Rides Again (1943) Sanucci
Law West of Tombstone (1938) Webb
Lawless (1950) Merrick
Lawless Breed (1952) Stein, H.
Lawless Code (1949) Kay, Edward
Lawless Cowboys (1951) Kraushaar
Lawless Rider (1954) De Saxe
Lawless Riders (1935) Zahler
Lawless Street (1955) Sawtell
Lawless Valley (1938) Webb
Lawrence of Arabia (1962) Jarre
Lawton Story of the Prince of Peace (1949) Kay, Edward
Lawyer (1970) Dodds
Lawyer Man (1932) Kaun
Lay That Rifle Down (1955) Butts
Lazy Hunter (1946) Jackson, H.
Lazy Little Beaver (1947) Scheib
Lazy River (1934) Axt
Lazybones (1934) Steiner, G.
Le Escape Goat (1966) Greene, W.
Le Pig-Al Patrol (1967) Greene, W.
Leading Edge (1967) Raksin
Leaf (1962) Katz, F.
League of Frightened Men (1937) Parrish
Leak in the Dike (1965) Sharples, Winston
Leaky Faucet (1959) Scheib
Learn and Live (1942) Steinert
Learn and Live (1945) Lava
Learning Tree (1969) Parks
Leather Burners (1942) Kaylin
Leather Pushers (1930) Roemheld
Leatherneck (1929) Filippi
Leatherneck (1929) Zuro
Leathernecking (1937) Levant
Leave Her to Heaven (1946) Newman
Leave It to Henry (1949) Kay, Edward
Leave It to the Marines (1951) Shefter
Leave Us Chase It (1947) Calker
Leave Well Enough Alone (1939) Timberg

Leaven for the Cities (19??) Kayden
Lecoque (1964) Glasser
Lecture on Camouflage (1944) Stalling
Leech Woman (1959) Gertz
Left Hand of God (1955) Young, V.
Left Handed Gun (1958) Courage
Legend of Aku-Aku, the Mysterious Land of Easter Island (1961) Laszlo
Legend of Coyote Rock (1945) Wallace
Legend of El Dorado (1956) Jackson, H.
Legend of Jimmy Blue Eyes (1964) Buckner
Legend of Lobo (1962) Wallace
Legend of Lylah Clare (1968) De Vol
Legend of Rudolph Valentino (1961) Semmler
Legend of Soupspoon (1962) Weinman
Legend of the Boy and the Eagle (1967) Marks
Legend of the Thirsting Stones (1950) Fried
Legend of Tom Dooley (1959) Stein, R.
Legendary Champions (1967) Chapin, S.
Leghorn Blows at Midnight (1948) Stalling
Leghorn Swoggled (1950) Poddany
Legion of the Lawless (1940) Sawtell
Lemon Drop Kid (1934) Satterfield
Lemon Drop Kid (1951) Young, V.
Lena Rivers (1932) Burton
Lend a Paw (1941) Harline
Leningrad—the Gateway to Soviet Russia (1932) Shilkret, N.
Lentil (1958) Kleiner
Leo the Last (1970) Myrow
Leopard Man (1943) Webb
Leopard Men of Africa (1940) Dietrich
Leprechaun's Gold (1949) Sharples, Winston
Les Boys (1965) Sharples, Winston
Les Girls (1957) Deutsch
Les Miserables (1925) Riesenfeld
Les Miserables (1935) Newman
Les Miserables (1952) North
Less Than the Dust (1916) Howe
Lest We Forget (1918) Beynon
Let Freedom Ring (1939) Lange
Let It Be Me (1936) Spencer, N.
Let Katie Do It (1916) Furst
Let No Man Write My Epitaph (1960) Duning
Let Us Live (1939) Rathaus
Let's Ask Nostradamus (1953) Kopp, R.
Let's Be Happy (1957) Sendrey
Let's Be Ritzy (1934) Ward, E.
Let's Dance (1950) Dolan
Let's Do It Again (1953) Duning
Let's Eat (1932) Dietrich
Let's Face It (1943) Dolan
Let's Get Tough (1942) Lange, J.
Let's Go (1937) De Nat
Let's Go Boating (1949) Lava
Let's Go Camping (1946) Dunn
Let's Go Collegiate (1941) Kay, Edward
Let's Go Fishing (1944) Jackson, H.
Let's Go Gunning (1945) Dunn
Let's Go Navy (1951) Kay, Edward
Let's Go Places (1929) Kay, Arthur
Let's Go Steady (1945) Duning
Let's Go Swimming (1947) Jackson, H.
Let's Go to Art School (1954) Colvig
Let's Live a Little (1948) Heymann
Let's Live Again (1948) Kraushaar
Let's Look at the Birds (1955) Craig, E.
Let's Make It Legal (1951) Mockridge
Let's Make Love (1960) Hagen
Let's Make Music (1941) Webb
Let's Sing Again (1936) Riesenfeld
Let's Stalk Spinach (1951) Sharples, Winston
Let's Stick Together (1952) Wallace
Let's Talk Turkey (1939) Bakaleinikoff, C.
Letter (1940) Steiner, M.
Letter for Evie (1945) Bassman
Letter from Aldershot (1940) Agostini
Letter from an Unknown Woman (1948) Amfitheatrof
Letter from Australia (1944) Lee, D.
Letter from Bataan (1942) Amfitheatrof
Letter from Cairo (1941) De Francesco
Letter of Introduction (1938) Skinner, F.
Letter to a Rebel (1948) Shilkret, N.
Letter to Three Wives (1949) Newman
Letty Lynton (1932) Axt
Lew Lehr Makes the News (1944) De Francesco
Li'l Abner (1940) Moraweck
Li'l Abner (1959) Lilley
Libeled Lady (1936) Axt
Liberation of L. B. Jones (1970) Bernstein, E.
Library of Congress (1945) North
Lickety-Splat (1961) Franklyn
Lieutenant Wore Skirts (1955) Mockridge
Life at Stake (1955) Baxter
Life Begins (Trailer, 1932) Kaun
Life Begins at Eight-Thirty (1942) Newman
Life Begins at Forty (1935) Kaylin
Life Begins for Andy Panda (1939) Marsales
Life in the Andes (1952) Nussbaum
Life in the Balance (1966) Diamond
Life of Emile Zola (1937) Steiner, M.
Life of Gauguin (196?) Katz, F.
Life of Her Own (1950) Kaper
Life of Jimmy Dolan (1933) Kaun
Life of John Bunyan (1912) Altschuler
Life of Riley (1949) Skinner, F.
Life of the Party (1937) Webb
Life of Thomas Edison (1945) Hatley
Life of Vergie Winters (1934) Steiner, M.
Life on the Thames (1950) Nussbaum
Life Returns (1934) Wallace
Life to Life (1958) Shepard
Life with Father (1947) Steiner, M.
Life with Feathers (1945) Stalling
Life with Fido (1942) Scheib
Life with Henry (1941) Hollander
Life with Tom (1953) Bradley

Lifeboat (1944) Friedhofer
Lifeguard (1951) Beckman
Lifeline (1947) Applebaum
Lifelines (1960) Ito
Light! (1965) Lawrence, Elliot
Light and Power (1947) De Francesco
Light Fantastic (1964) Liebman
Light House Keeping (1932) De Nat
Light in the Forest (1958) Smith, P.
Light in the Window: The Art of Vermeer (1952) Belasco
Light Is What You Make It (1945) Smith, P.
Light of the World (1951) Keefer
Light of Western Skies (1930) Midgely
Light of Western Stars (1940) Young, V.
Light Reflections (1948) Muller
Light That Failed (1940) Young, V.
Light Touch (1951) Rozsa
Lighter Than Hare (1960) Franklyn
Lighthouse (1947) Gold
Lighthouse Keeping (1946) Wallace
Lighthouse Keeping Blues (1964) Greene, W.
Lighthouse Mouse (1955) Franklyn
Lightnin' (1930) Kay, Arthur
Lightnin' in the Forest (1948) Glickman, M.
Lightning Express (1930) Perry
Lightning Raiders (1945) Zahler
Lightning Strikes Twice (1951) Steiner, M.
Lightning Strikes West (1940) Porter
Lightning Warrior (1931) Zahler
Lights Fantastic (1942) Stalling
Lights of Old Santa Fe (1944) Butts
Lights Out (1942) Scheib
Lights Out in Europe (1940) Janssen
Like It Is (1968) Porée
Like It Is (1970) Rogers
Likely Story (1947) Harline
Lilac Time (1928) Copping
Lilac Time (1928) Shilkret, N.
Lili (1953) Kaper
Lilies of the Field (1963) Goldsmith
Liliom (1930) Fall
Lilith (1964) Hopkins, K.
Lillian Russell (1940) Mockridge
Lilly Turner (1933) Heindorf
Lilly Turner (Trailer, 1933) Kaun
Lily and the Rose (1915) Breil
Limehouse Blues (1934) Leipold
Limelight (1952) Chaplin, C.
Lincoln in the White House (1939) Jackson, H.
Lincoln Speaks at Gettysburg (1953) Forrell
Linda and Abilene (1969) Regan
Linda, Be Good (1948) Mason, J.
Line (1957) Resnick
Line of Apogee (1967) Ussachevsky
Line of Screammage (1956) Sharples, Winston
Lines of Communication (1964) Deutsch, H.
Lineup (1958) Bakaleinikoff, M.
LINK (1967) Roberts, A.
Lion and the Horse (1952) Steiner, M.
Lion and the Mouse (1943) Scheib
Lion and the Mouse (1954) Pinsky, M.
Lion Around (1949) Wallace
Lion Down (1950) Smith, P.
Lion Hunt (1938) Scheib
Lion Hunt (1949) Scheib
Lion Hunters (1951) Skiles
Lion in the Roar (1956) Sharples, Winston
Lion Is in the Streets (1953) Waxman
Lion Tamer (1934) Sharples, Winston
Lion, the Griffin, and the Kangaroo (1952) Kay, U.
Lion's Busy (1949) Stalling
Lion's Busy (1961) Sharples, Winston
Lion's Friend (1934) Scheib
Lions for Sale (1941) Dunn
Lions Love (1969) Byrd, J.
Lions on the Loose (1941) Bradley
Lippold's The Sun (1965) Diamond
Liquidator (1965) Schifrin
Lisbon (1956) Riddle
Lisette (1961) Baxter
List of Adrian Messenger (1963) Goldsmith
Listen, Darling (1938) Axt
Listen Soldier (1944) Applebaum
Litho (1961) Hamilton
Litterbug (1961) Baker, Buddy
Little Accident (1939) Skinner, F.
Little Anglers (1952) Scheib
Little Archer (1949) Jackson, H.
Little Audrey Riding Hood (1955) Sharples, Winston
Little Bantamweight (1938) Bradley
Little Beau Pepe (1951) Stalling
Little Beau Porky (1936) Stalling
Little Beaux Pink (1968) Greene, W.
Little Big Horn (1951) Dunlap
Little Big Man (1970) Hammond
Little Big Shot (1935) Roemheld
Little Bird Told Me (1934) Sharples, Winston
Little Bit of Heaven (1940) Skinner, F.
Little Blabbermouse (1940) Stalling
Little Black Sambo (1935) Stalling
Little Blue and Little Yellow (1961) Cohrssen
Little Blue Blackbird (1938) Marsales
Little Boo-Peep (1953) Sharples, Winston
Little Boy Blue (1933) Scheib
Little Boy Blue (1936) Bakaleinikoff, C.
Little Boy Blue (1936) Stalling
Little Boy Boo (1953) Stalling
Little Boy Lost (1953) Young, V.
Little Boy with a Big Horn (1953) Bruns
Little Brother Rat (1939) Stalling
Little Brown Jug (1948) Sharples, Winston
Little Buck Cheeser (1937) Bradley
Little Buckaroo (1938) De Nat
Little Caesar (1930) Mendoza
Little Cesario (1941) Bradley
Little Cheeser (1936) Bradley

Little Colonel (1935) Mockridge
Little Cut Up (1949) Sharples, Winston
Little Dreamer (1968) Stein, R.
Little Dutch Mill (1934) Steiner, G.
Little Dutch Plate (1936) Spencer, N.
Little Foxes (1941) Willson
Little Friend (1934) Toch
Little Fugitive (1953) Manson
Little Giant (1946) Fairchild
Little Goldfish (1939) Bradley
Little Gravel Voice (1942) Bradley
Little Hiawatha (1937) Malotte
Little House (1952) Smith, P.
Little Iodine (1946) Steinert
Little Isles of Freedom (1943) Lava
Little Jack Horner (1937) Zahler
Little Johnny Jet (1953) Bradley
Little Johnny Jones (1929) Dunn
Little Lambkin (1940) Timberg
Little Lamby (1937) Timberg
Little Lion Hunter (1939) Stalling
Little Lord Fauntleroy (1921) Gottschalk
Little Lord Fauntleroy (1936) Steiner, M.
Little Lost Sheep (1939) De Nat
Little Maestro (1937) Lannin
Little Man, What Now? (1934) Kay, Arthur
Little Match Girl (1937) De Nat
Little Men (1934) Riesenfeld
Little Men (1941) Webb
Little Minister (1934) Steiner, M.
Little Miss Big (1946) Salter
Little Miss Marker (1934) Rainger
Little Miss Nobody (1936) Kaylin
Little Miss Thoroughbred (1938) Jackson, H.
Little Mister Jim (1946) Bassman
Little Mole (1941) Bradley
Little Moth's Big Flame (1938) De Nat
Little Nellie Kelly (1940) Stoll
Little Nobody (1936) Steiner, G.
Little Ol' Bosko and the Cannibals (1937) Bradley
Little Ol' Bosko and the Pirates (1937) Bradley
Little Ol' Bosko in Bagdad (1937) Bradley
Little Old New York (1923) Peters
Little Old New York (1940) Newman
Little Orphan (1949) Bradley
Little Orphan Airedale (1947) Stalling
Little Orphan Annie (1938) Forbes
Little Orvie (1940) Sawtell
Little Pancho Vanilla (1938) Stalling
Little Phantasy on a 19th-Century Painting (1946) Applebaum
Little Pioneer (1937) Jackson, H.
Little Princess (1939) Mockridge
Little Problems (1951) Scheib
Little Quacker (1949) Bradley
Little Ranger (1938) Snell
Little Red Hen (1934) Stalling
Little Red Hen (1955) Scheib
Little Red Lighthouse and the Great Gray Bridge (1956) Kleiner
Little Red Riding Rabbit (1944) Stalling
Little Red Rodent Hood (1951) Stalling
Little Red School Mouse (1949) Sharples, Winston
Little Red Schoolhouse (1936) Zahler
Little Red Walking Hood (1937) Stalling
Little Rover (1935) De Nat
Little Runaway (1952) Bradley
Little Rural Riding Hood (1949) Bradley
Little School Mouse (1954) Bradley
Little Shepherd of Kingdom Come (1960) Vars
Little Smokey (1953) Kleinsinger
Little Soap and Water (1935) Timberg
Little Star of Bethlehem (1961) Kleinsinger
Little Stranger (1936) Timberg
Little Theatre (1941) Kilfeather
Little 'Tinker (1948) Bradley
Little Tough Guy (1938) Skinner, F.
Little Tough Guys in Society (1938) Skinner, F.
Little Tough Mice (1939) Marsales
Little Trail (1930) De Nat
Little Whirlwind (1941) Wallace
Little White Lie (1945) Terr
Little Wise Quacker (1952) Bradley
Little Witch (1945) Simeone
Little Women (1933) Steiner, M.
Little Women (1949) Deutsch
Little Woody Riding Hood (1962) Wheeler
Littlest Bully (1960) Scheib
Littlest Diplomat (1938) Jackson, H.
Littlest Hobo (1958) Stein, R.
Littlest Outlaw (1954) Lava
Littlest Rebel (1935) Mockridge
Live a Little, Love a Little (1968) Strange
Live Fast, Die Young (1958) Wilson, S.
Live, Love and Learn (1937) Ward, E.
Live Wires (1946) Kay, Edward
Lively Set (1964) Darin
Lives of a Bengal Lancer (1935) Roemheld
Living Desert (1953) Smith, P.
Living Ghost (1942) Sanucci
Living in a Big Way (1947) Hayton
Living It Up (1954) Scharf, W.
Living on Velvet (1935) Roemheld
Living Swamp (1955) Sawtell
Living with Lions (1948) Jackson, H.
Lizzie (1957) Stevens, L.
Llano Kid (1939) Young, V.
Lloyd's of London (1936) Mockridge
Loaded Pistols (1948) Morton
Loan Shark (1952) Roemheld
Loan Stranger (1942) Calker
Lobstertown (1947) De Francesco
Local Boy Makes Good (1931) Mendoza
Locked On (1961) Meakin
Locket (1946) Webb
Locks of Sault Ste. Marie (1955) Bassett, L.
Loco Lobo (1947) Kilfeather

Lodger (1944) Friedhofer
Log Jam (1952) Gart
Log Jammed (1959) Wheeler
Log Rollers (1953) Scheib
Logos (1957) Jacobs, H.
Lolita (1961) Riddle
Lollipop Cover (1965) Raksin, R.
London Blackout Murders (1942) Scharf, W.
London Bridge Is Falling Down (1969) Lewin
London by Night (1937) Axt
London Derriere (1967) Greene, W.
London of William Hogarth (1956) Voegeli
Lone Chipmunks (1954) Wallace
Lone Cowboy (1933) Hand
Lone Gun (1954) Gertz
Lone Hand (1953) Stein, H.
Lone Mountie (1938) De Nat
Lone Ranger (1938) Colombo
Lone Ranger (1956) Buttolph, David
Lone Ranger and the Lost City of Gold (1958) Baxter
Lone Rider Ambushed (1941) Lange, J.
Lone Rider Crosses the Rio (1941) Lange, J.
Lone Rider Fights Back (1941) Lange, J.
Lone Rider in Cheyenne (1942) Lange, J.
Lone Rider in Frontier Fury (1941) Lange, J.
Lone Rider in Ghost Town (1941) Lange, J.
Lone Rider in Texas Justice (1942) Lange, J.
Lone Star (1951) Buttolph, David
Lone Star Moonlight (1946) Glickman, M.
Lone Star Pioneers (1939) Zahler
Lone Star Raiders (1940) Feuer
Lone Star Ranger (1941) Mockridge
Lone Star State (1948) Sharples, Winston
Lone Stranger and Porky (1938) Stalling
Lone Texan (1958) Dunlap
Lone Texas Ranger (1945) Glickman, M.
Lone Wolf in London (1947) Gertz
Lone Wolf in Mexico (1947) Gertz
Lone Wolf Keeps a Date (1940) Cutner
Lone Wolf Meets a Lady (1940) Cutner
Lone Wolf Returns (1936) Jackson, H.
Lone Wolf Spy Hunt (1939) Nussbaum
Lone Wolf Strikes (1940) Cutner
Lone Wolf Takes a Chance (1941) Cutner
Lonely Are the Brave (1962) Goldsmith
Lonely by the Sea (1954) Shologon
Lonely Crime (1958) Martino
Lonely Hearts Bandits (1950) Wilson, S.
Lonely Man (1957) Van Cleave
Lonely Night (1952) Powell, M.
Lonely Wives (1931) Gromon
Lonelyhearts (1958) Salinger
Lonesome Ghosts (1937) Malotte
Lonesome Lenny (1946) Bradley
Lonesome Mouse (1943) Bradley
Lonesome Ranger (1965) Greene, W.
Lonesome Stranger (1940) Bradley
Lonesome Trail (1945) Sanucci
Lonesome Trail (1955) Klatzkin
Lonesome Trailer (1936) Jackson, H.
Long Day's Journey Into Night (1962) Previn, A.
Long Gray Line (1954) Duning
Long-Haired Hare (1949) Stalling
Long Haul (1963) Nelson, R.
Long, Hot Summer (1958) North
Long John Silver (1954) Buttolph, David
Long, Long Trail (1929) Perry
Long, Long Trailer (1954) Deutsch
Long Lost Father (1934) Colombo
Long Night (1947) Tiomkin
Long Rope (1961) Sawtell
Long Shadow (1968) Lackey
Long Voyage Home (1940) Hageman
Long Wait (1954) Castelnuovo-Tedesco
Long Way from Nowhere (1970) Schifrin
Longest Day (1962) Jarre
Longest Night (1936) Ward, E.
Longhorn (1951) Kraushaar
Lonnie (1963) Cooper, B.
Look for the Silver Lining (1949) Buttolph, David
Look in Any Window (1961) Shores
Look Out Sister (1949) Jordan
Look Park (1970) Druckman
Look Who's Laughing (1941) Webb
Looking Down at London (1946) Mayfield
Looking for Danger (1957) Skiles
Looking for Love (1964) Stoll
Looking for Trouble (1934) Newman
Looking Forward (1933) Axt
Looking Forward (1962) Buttolph, David Heyman
Loony Baloonists (1936) De Nat
Loony Tom (1951) Brubeck, H.
Loophole (1954) Dunlap
Looping the Loop (1929) Riesenfeld
Loose Ankles (1930) Reiser
Loose in London (1953) Skiles
Loose in the Caboose (1947) Sharples, Winston
Loose Nut (1945) Calker
Looters (1955) Roemheld
Lord Jeff (1938) Ward, E.
Lord Jim (1965) Kaper
Lord Love a Duck (1966) Hefti
Lord of the Jungle (1955) Skiles
Lorelei (1931) Scheib
Lorna Doone (1951) Duning
Los Angeles—Wonder City of the West (1935) Shilkret, N.
Losers (1970) Phillips, S.
Lost and Foundling (1944) Stalling
Lost and Foundry (1937) Timberg
Lost Angel (1943) Amfitheatrof
Lost Battalion (1919) Breil
Lost Battalion (1961) Stein, R.
Lost Boundaries (1949) Applebaum
Lost Canyon (1942) Sawtell
Lost Chick (1935) Bradley
Lost City (1935) Zahler
Lost Command (1966) Waxman

Lost Continent (1951) Dunlap
Lost Dream (1949) Sharples, Winston
Lost Flight (1970) Frontiere
Lost Honeymoon (1947) Heymann
Lost Horizon (1937) Tiomkin
Lost in a Harem (1944) Shilkret, N.
Lost in Alaska (1952) Mancini
Lost in the Night (1955) Laszlo
Lost Lady (1934) Roemheld
Lost Lake (1946) De Francesco
Lost, Lonely and Vicious (1958) David, F.
Lost Man (1969) Jones
Lost Missile (1958) Fried
Lost Moment (1947) Amfitheatrof
Lost Patrol (1934) Steiner, M.
Lost Squadron (1932) Steiner, M.
Lost Volcano (1950) Caswell
Lost Weekend (1945) Rozsa
Lost World (1925) Copping
Lost World (1960) Sawtell
Lost World Revisited (1967) Muri
Lost Zeppelin (1929) Willson
Lot in Sodom (1933) Siegel, L.
Lottery Bride (1930) Riesenfeld
Lottery Lover (1935) Lange
Louisa (1950) Skinner, F.
Louisiana (1947) Kay, Edward
Louisiana Hussy (1960) Greene, W.
Louisiana Purchase (1941) Dolan
Louisiana Springtime (1945) De Francesco
Louisiana Story (1948) Thomson
Louisiana Territory (1953) Bassman
Louisiana's Koasati (1955) Klauss
Louvre Come Back to Me (1962) Franklyn
Lovable Cheat (1949) Hajos
Love (1928) Axt
Love Affair (1939) Webb
Love Among the Millionaires (1930) Jackson, H.
Love and Curses (1938) Stalling
Love and Kisses (1965) Loose
Love and Learn (1947) Steiner, M.
Love and Sacrifice (1936) Schwartz, A.
Love Before Breakfast (1936) Waxman
Love Begins at Twenty (1936) Jackson, H.
Love Birds (1934) Roemheld
Love Bug (1968) Bruns
Love Crazy (1941) Snell
Love Doctor (1929) Hajos
Love Doctors (1970) David, M.
Love Finds Andy Hardy (1938) Snell
Love Flower (1920) Pesce
Love from a Stranger (1947) Salter
Love God? (1969) Mizzy
Love Goddesses (1965) Faith
Love Happy (1950) Ronell
Love Has Many Faces (1964) Raksin
Love, Honor, and Behave (1938) Roemheld
Love, Honor and Goodbye (1945) Webb
Love Hunger (1965) Simon, T.
Love in a Cottage (1940) Scheib
Love in a Goldfish Bowl (1961) Haskell
Love in Bloom (1935) Roemheld
Love-Ins (1967) Karger
Love in the Afternoon (1957) Waxman
Love in Truro (1963) Mumma
Love Is a Carousel (1970) Gary
Love Is a Headache (1938) Ward, E.
Love Is a Many-Splendored Thing (1955) Newman
Love Is Better Than Ever (1951) Hayton
Love Is Blind (1957) Scheib
Love Is On the Air (1937) Jackson, H.
Love Krazy (1932) De Nat
Love Laughs at Andy Hardy (1946) Snell
Love Letters (1945) Young, V.
Love Me Forever (1935) Schertzinger
Love Me Like I Do (1970) Singman
Love Me, Love My Mouse (1966) Poddany
Love Me or Leave Me (1955) Stoll
Love Me Tender (1956) Newman, L.
Love Me Tonight (1932) Leipold
Love Merchant (1966) Cove
Love Moods (1952) Rose, W.
Love Nest (1951) Mockridge
Love of Living—at the Kahala Hilton (1964) Howell
Love of Sunya (1927) Rubini
Love on the Run (1936) Waxman
Love Parade (1930) Leipold
Love Racket (1930) Reiser
Love Rebellion (1967) Marini
Love Slaves of the Amazon (1957) Wilson, S.
Love Statue (1966) Stallworth
Love-Tails of Morocco (1931) Axt
Love That Brute (1950) Mockridge
Love That Pup (1949) Bradley
Love Thy Neighbor (1940) Young, V.
Love Time (1934) Kaylin
Love Under Fire (1937) Lange
Love with the Proper Stranger (1963) Bernstein, E.
Love's Intrigue (1940) Lava
Love's Labor Won (1948) Scheib
Lovelorn Leghorn (1950) Poddany
Lovely to Look At (1952) Dragon
Lovely Way to Die (1968) Hopkins, K.
Lover Come Back (1946) Salter
Lover Come Back (1961) De Vol
Lover of Camille (1924) Guterson
Lover's Oath (1925) Cadman
Lovers and Lollipops (1956) Manson
Lovers and Other Strangers (1970) Karlin
Loves of an Actress (1928) Hajos
Loves of Carmen (1927) Bassett, R. H.
Loves of Carmen (1948) Castelnuovo-Tedesco
Loves of Edgar Allan Poe (1942) Buttolph, David
Loves of Pharaoh (1922) Riesenfeld
Lovesick (1937) Lessner
Loving (1970) Segáll
Loving You (1957) Scharf, W.

Lt. Robin Crusoe, U.S.N. (1966) Brunner
Lucia (1963) Carmichael
Luck of Ginger Coffey (1964) Segáll
Luck of the Irish (1948) Mockridge
Luckiest Girl in the World (1936) Roemheld
Luckiest Guy in the World (1947) Terr
Lucky Boy (1929) Riesenfeld
Lucky Cisco Kid (1940) Mockridge
Lucky Cowboy (1944) Shuken
Lucky Devils (1933) Steiner, M.
Lucky Dog (1956) Scheib
Lucky Duck (1940) Scheib
Lucky Ducky (1948) Bradley
Lucky Jordan (1943) Deutsch
Lucky Losers (1950) Kay, Edward
Lucky Lulu (1944) Sharples, Winston
Lucky Me (1954) Heindorf
Lucky Night (1939) Waxman
Lucky Number (1950) Smith, P.
Lucky Partners (1940) Tiomkin
Lucky Pigs (1939) De Nat
Lucky Pink (1968) Greene, W.
Lucky Stiff (1949) Roemheld
Lucky Swede (1936) Jackson, H.
Lucy Gallant (1955) Van Cleave
Lullaby (1963) Horn
Lullaby Land (1933) Harline
Lullaby of Bareland (1964) Sullivan, I.
Lullaby of Broadway (1951) Jackson, H.
Lulu at the Zoo (1944) Timberg
Lulu Belle (1948) Russell, H.
Lulu Gets the Birdie (1944) Sharples, Winston
Lulu in Hollywood (1944) Timberg
Lulu's Birthday Party (1944) Timberg
Lulu's Indoor Outing (1944) Sharples, Winston
Lulu's Love (1936) Steiner, G.
Lumber Camp (1937) Dietrich
Lumber Champ (1933) Dietrich
Lumber Jack and Jill (1949) Sharples, Winston
Lumber Jack-Rabbit (1953) Stalling
Lumber Jerks (1955) Franklyn
Lumberjack (1944) Sawtell
Lummox (1930) Riesenfeld
Lunch with a Punch (1952) Sharples, Winston
Lure of Bali (1964) Skiles
Lure of the Islands (1942) Kay, Edward
Lure of the Swamp (1957) Dunlap
Lure of the Wasteland (1939) Sanucci
Lure of the Wilderness (1952) Waxman
Lured (1947) Michelet
Lust for Gold (1949) Duning
Lust for Life (1956) Rozsa
Lustful Turk (1968) Allen, B.
Lusty Men (1952) Webb
Luv (1967) Mulligan
Luxury Liner (1933) Kaun
Luxury Liner (1948) Deutsch
Lydia (1941) Rozsa
Lydia Bailey (1952) Friedhofer
Lyin' Hunter (1937) De Nat
Lyin' Lion (1949) Scheib
Lyin' Mouse (1937) Stalling
Lying Lips (1939) Shilkret, J.

M (1951) Michelet
Ma and Pa Kettle at Home (1954) Stein, H.
Ma and Pa Kettle at Waikiki (1955) Mancini
Ma and Pa Kettle on Vacation (1953) Stein, H.
Ma Barker's Killer Brood (1960) Kauer
Macabre (1958) Baxter
Macademy Awards (1949) Sharples, Winston
Macao (1952) Collins
Macbeth (1951) Girvin
Machete (1958) Sawtell
Machine Gun Kelly (1958) Fried
Machine Gun Mama (1944) Glickman, M.
Machismo—40 Graves for 40 Guns (1970) Preisner
Macho Callahan (1970) Williams, P.
Mackenna's Gold (1969) Jones
Mackerel Moocher (1962) Poddany
Mackinac Island (1944) Nussbaum
Macomber Affair (1947) Rozsa
Mad About Music (1938) Previn, C.
Mad as a Mars Hare (1963) Lava
Mad at the World (1955) Stevens, L.
Mad Doctor (1933) Lewis
Mad Doctor (1940) Young, V.
Mad Dog (1932) Lewis
Mad Dog Coll (1961) Phillips, S.
Mad Empress (1939) Roemheld
Mad Genius (1931) Mendoza
Mad Hatter (1940) De Nat
Mad Hatter (1947) Calker
Mad Holiday (1936) Axt
Mad House (1934) Scheib
Mad King (1932) Scheib
Mad Love (1935) Tiomkin
Mad Maestro (1939) Bradley
Mad Magician (1954) Lange
Mad Martindales (1942) Buttolph, David
Mad Miss Manton (1938) Webb
Mad Monster Party (1967) Laws
Mad Parade (1931) Leipold
Mad Room (1969) Grusin
Mad Wednesday (1946) Heymann
Madam Satan (1931) Axt
Madame Bovary (1949) Rozsa
Madame Butterfly (1933) Harling
Madame Curie (1943) Stothart
Madame Du Barry (Trailer, 1934) Kaun
Madame DuBarry (1934) Roemheld
Madame Racketeer (1932) Leipold
Madame Sans-Gêne (1925) Riesenfeld
Madame Spy (1934) Roemheld
Madame X (1929) Axt
Madame X (1937) Snell
Madame X (1966) Skinner, F.
Madcap Magoo (1955) Castillo

Made for Each Other (1939) Friedhofer
Made in Paris (1965) Stoll
Made on Broadway (1933) Axt
Madeira, Isle of Romance (1938) Shilkret, J.
Madeline (1952) Raksin
Mademoiselle Fifi (1944) Heymann
Madero of Mexico (1942) Kaplan, S.
Madhattan Island (1947) Sharples, Winston
Madigan (1968) Costa
Madison Avenue (1961) Sukman
Madison Square Garden (1932) Lewis, Harold
Madonna of Avenue A (1929) Silvers
Madonna of the Desert (1948) Glickman, M.
Madonna's Secret (1946) Dubin
Maeva (1961) Ito
Mag (1958) Marx, D.
Magazine Magic (1946) McBride, R.
Magic (1953) Fletcher
Magic Beans (1939) Marsales
Magic Carpet (1951) Morton
Magic Cloak of Oz (1914) Gottschalk
Magic Face (1951) Gilbert, H.
Magic Fire (1955) Korngold
Magic Fish (1934) Scheib
Magic Fluke (1949) Castillo
Magic Fountain (1961) Belasco
Magic Garden of Stanley Sweetheart (1970) Styner
Magic Hat (1952) Hovey
Magic in the Sun (1956) Jackson, H.
Magic Key (1950) Curtin
Magic Michael (1960) Kleiner
Magic of Youth (1945) De Francesco
Magic on a Stick (1945) Terr
Magic Pear Tree (1968) Almeida
Magic Pencil (1940) Scheib
Magic Prison (1969) Laderman
Magic Shell (1941) Scheib
Magic Slipper (1948) Scheib
Magic Sword (1962) Markowitz
Magic Tide (1961) Ferguson
Magic Town (1947) Webb
Magic Tree (1970) Wagner, T.
Magical Maestro (1951) Bradley
Magicalulu (1945) Sharples, Winston
Magician Mickey (1937) Malotte
Magician's Daughter (1938) Snell
Magicians (1968) Austin
Magnetic Monster (1953) Sanford, B.
Magnificence in Trust (1966) Glasser
Magnificent Ambersons (1942) Herrmann
Magnificent Brute (1936) Maxwell
Magnificent Doll (1946) Salter
Magnificent Dope (1942) Mockridge
Magnificent Fraud (1939) Boutelje
Magnificent Lie (1931) Leipold
Magnificent Matador (1955) Kraushaar
Magnificent Obsession (1935) Waxman
Magnificent Obsession (1954) Skinner, F.
Magnificent Rogue (1946) Scott, N.
Magnificent Roughneck (1956) Dunlap
Magnificent Seven (1960) Bernstein, E.
Magnificent Yankee (1950) Raksin
Magoo (1956) Comstock
Magoo Beats the Heat (1956) Farnon
Magoo Breaks Par (1957) Cutkomp
Magoo Express (1955) Comstock
Magoo Goes Skiing (1954) Maury
Magoo Goes West (1956) Comstock
Magoo Makes News (1955) Farnon
Magoo Saves the Bank (1957) Farnon
Magoo Slept Here (1953) Gold
Magoo's Canine Mutiny (1956) Curtin
Magoo's Check Up (1955) Farnon
Magoo's Cruise (1958) Farnon
Magoo's Glorious Fourth (1957) Elliott, Dean
Magoo's Lodge Brother (1959) Meakin
Magoo's Masquerade (1957) Murray
Magoo's Masterpiece (1953) Bruns
Magoo's Moose Hunt (1957) Farnon
Magoo's Private War (1957) Farnon
Magoo's Problem Child (1956) Farnon
Magoo's Puddle Jumper (1956) Elliott, Dean
Magoo's Three-Point Landing (1958) Farnon
Magoo's Young Manhood (1958) Elliott, Dean
Magpie Madness (1948) Scheib
Mahatma Gandhi—20th Century Prophet (1953) Koff
Mahnomen, Harvest of the North (1960) Pilhofer
Maid in China (1938) Scheib
Maid of Salem (1937) Young, V.
Mail Dog (1947) Wallace
Mail Order Bride (1963) Bassman
Mail Pilot (1933) Lewis
Main Street After Dark (1944) Bassman
Main Street, Canada (1945) Applebaum
Main Street Lawyer (1939) Lava
Main Street on the March! (1942) Amfitheatrof
Main Street to Broadway (1953) Ronell
Main Street Today (1944) Raksin
Maine Sail (1949) De Francesco
Maintain the Right (1940) Snell
Maisie (1939) Ward, E.
Maisie Gets Her Man (1942) Hayton
Maisie Goes to Reno (1944) Snell
Maisie Was a Lady (1941) Snell
Majesty of Yellowstone (1948) De Francesco
Major and the Minor (1942) Dolan
Major Dundee (1965) Amfitheatrof
Major Google (1936) De Nat
Major Lied Till Dawn (1938) Stalling
Majority of One (1961) Steiner, M.
Make a Wish (1937) Riesenfeld
Make Believe Revue (1935) De Nat
Make Haste to Live (1954) Bernstein, E.
Make Me a Star (1932) Leipold
Make Mine Freedom (1948) Smith, P.
Make Mine Laughs (1949) Webb
Make Mine Monica (1949) Sharples, Winston

Make Mine Music (1946) Wolcott
Make Way for Ducklings (1955) Kleiner
Make Way for Tomorrow (1937) Young, V.
Make Your Own Bed (1944) Roemheld
Making Friends (1936) Timberg
Making Good (1932) Dietrich
Making Mounties (1951) Agostini
Making of the River (1955) Bricken
Making the Grade (1929) Rapée
Malaya (1949) Kaper
Male Animal (1942) Roemheld
Male Vanity (1952) Shilkret, N.
Malibu Beach Party (1940) Stalling
Malice in Slumberland (1942) Kilfeather
Maltese Bippy (1969) Riddle
Maltese Falcon (1941) Deutsch
Mama Loves Papa (1931) Shield
Mama Loves Papa (1945) Harline
Mama Runs Wild (1938) Colombo
Mama Steps Out (1937) Ward, E.
Mama's New Hat (1939) Lewis
Mamba (1930) Tandler
Mammy (1930) Silvers
Man About Town (1939) Hollander
Man Afraid (1957) Mancini
Man Against a Fungus (1955) Applebaum
Man Against Hunger (1955) Townsend
Man Alive (1945) Harline
Man Alive (1952) Lees
Man Alone (1955) Young, V.
Man and His Job (1943) Applebaum
Man and the Bird (1956) Baker, Bill
Man and the Moment (1929) Brunelli
Man at Large (1941) Buttolph, David
Man Behind the Gun (1952) Buttolph, David
Man Betrayed (1941) Glickman, M.
Man Called Adam (1966) Carter
Man Called Dagger (1967) Stein, R.
Man Called Flintstone (1966) Paich
Man Called Gannon (1968) Grusin
Man Called Horse (1970) Rosenman
Man Called Peter (1955) Newman
Man Crazy (1953) Gold
Man-Eater of Kumaon (1948) Salter
Man from Bitter Ridge (1955) Gertz
Man from Button Willow (1965) Stoll
Man from Colorado (1948) Duning
Man from Dakota (1940) Snell
Man from Del Rio (1956) Steiner, F.
Man from Down Under (1943) Snell
Man from Frisco (1944) Skiles
Man from Galveston (1964) Buttolph, David
Man from God's Country (1958) Skiles
Man from Guntown (1935) Zahler
Man from Headquarters (1942) Kay, Edward
Man from Laramie (1955) Duning
Man from Missouri (1946) De Francesco
Man from New Orleans (1948) Lava
Man from O.R.G.Y. (1970) Bernstein, C.
Man from Oklahoma (1945) Butts
Man from Planet X (1951) Koff
Man from Rainbow Valley (1946) Glickman, M.
Man from Sonora (1951) Kay, Edward
Man from Texas (1939) Sanucci
Man from Texas (1948) Robinson
Man from the Alamo (1953) Skinner, F.
Man from the Black Hills (1952) Kraushaar
Man from the Diners' Club (1963) Phillips, S.
Man from the Rio Grande (1943) Glickman, M.
Man from Thunder River (1943) Glickman, M.
Man from Wyoming (1930) Hajos
Man from Yesterday (1932) Leipold
Man Hunt (1933) Jackson, H.
Man Hunt (1936) Kaun
Man Hunt (1938) Marsales
Man Hunt (1941) Buttolph, David
Man Hunt (Trailer, 1936) Roemheld
Man I Love (1947) Steiner, M.
Man I Married (1940) Buttolph, David
Man I Marry (1936) Previn, C.
Man in Half Moon Street (1944) Rozsa
Man in Space (1956) Bruns
Man in the 5th Dimension (1964) Carmichael
Man in the Barn (1937) Snell
Man in the Gray Flannel Suit (1956) Herrmann
Man in the Iron Mask (1939) Moraweck
Man in the Net (1959) Salter
Man in the Saddle (1951) Duning
Man in the Shadow (1957) Stein, H.
Man in the Trunk (1942) Mockridge
Man in the Vault (1955) Vars
Man in the Water (1963) Loose
Man Is Armed (1956) Butts
Man Killers (1943) Dunn
Man Machine Meets Machine Man (1968) Bresnick
Man-Made Miracles (1954) Baxter
Man Made Monster (1941) Salter
Man Nobody Knows (1925) Savine
Man of a Thousand Faces (1957) Skinner, F.
Man of Conflict (1953) Glasser
Man of Conquest (1939) Young, V.
Man of Courage (1943) Zahler
Man of Iron (1935) Kaun
Man of the People (1937) Ward, E.
Man of the West (1958) Harline
Man of the World (1931) Hand
Man of Tin (1940) De Nat
Man of Two Worlds (1934) Kaun
Man on a String (1960) Duning
Man on a Tightrope (1953) Waxman
Man on Fire (1957) Raksin
Man on the Eiffel Tower (1949) Michelet
Man on the Flying Trapeze (1954) Maury
Man on the Land (1951) Lava
Man on the Prowl (1957) Gold
Man on the Rock (1938) Snell
Man or Gun (1958) Garf

Man-Proof (1937) Waxman
Man to Remember (1938) Webb
Man-Trap (1961) Stevens, L.
Man Trouble (1930) Bassett, R. H.
Man Wanted (1932) Kaun
Man Who Broke the Bank at Monte Carlo (1935) Mockridge
Man Who Came Back (1930) Kay, Arthur
Man Who Came to Dinner (1942) Hollander
Man Who Changed the World (1941) Amfitheatrof
Man Who Cheated Himself (1950) Forbes
Man Who Dared (1933) Kaylin
Man Who Dared (1939) Deutsch
Man Who Dared (1946) Duning
Man Who Had Power Over Women (1970) Mandel
Man Who Knew Too Much (1956) Herrmann
Man Who Lost Himself (1941) Salter
Man Who Played God (Trailer, 1932) Kaun
Man Who Reclaimed His Head (1934) Roemheld
Man Who Shot Liberty Valance (1962) Mockridge
Man Who Talked Too Much (1940) Roemheld
Man Who Understood Women (1959) Dolan
Man Who Walked Alone (1945) Hajos
Man Who Wouldn't Die (1942) Raksin
Man Who Wouldn't Talk (1940) Kaylin
Man with a Cloak (1951) Raksin
Man with a Thousand Hands (1953) Lava
Man with My Face (1951) McBride, R.
Man with the Golden Arm (1955) Bernstein, E.
Man with the Gun (1955) North
Man with the Steel Whip (1954) Butts
Man with Two Faces (1934) Kaun
Man with Two Lives (1942) Sanucci
Man Without a Country (1925) Rapée
Man Without a Country (1938) Jackson, H.
Man Without a Star (1955) Stein, H.
Man's Best Friend (1941) Calker
Man's Best Friend (1951) Dubin
Man's Castle (1933) Harling
Man's Favorite Sport? (1963) Mancini
Man's Greatest Friend (1938) Ward, E.
Man's Man (1929) Cupero
Man's Paradise (1938) Reiser
Man's Pest Friend (1945) Sharples, Winston
Man's World (1942) Leipold
Manchurian Candidate (1962) Amram
Mandalay (1934) Roemheld
Mandrake the Magician (1939) Cutner
Manhandled (1949) Calker
Manhattan Heartbeat (1940) Mockridge
Manhattan Melodrama (1934) Axt
Manhattan Merry-Go-Round (1937) Colombo
Manhattan Moon (1935) Hajos
Manhattan Rhythm (1935) Steiner, G.
Manhunt in the Jungle (1958) Jackson, H.
Manhunt of Mystery Island (1945) Glickman, M.
Manila Calling (1942) Mockridge
Mannequin (1938) Ward, E.
Manpower (1941) Deutsch
Manpower (1942) Kubik
Manslaughter (1930) Hajos
Mantel of Protection (1955) Kleiner
Mantis in Lace (1968) Lance
Mantrap (1943) Glickman, M.
Many a Slip (1931) Roemheld
Many Rivers to Cross (1955) Mockridge
Many Tanks (1942) Timberg
Mara Maru (1952) Steiner, M.
Mara of the Wilderness (1965) Bluestone
Maracaibo (1958) Almeida
Marauders (1947) Kraushaar
Marauders (1955) Sawtell
March On, America (1942) Jackson, H.
March On, Marines (1940) Jackson, H.
Marco Polo (1962) Baxter
Mardi Gras (1943) Leipold
Mardi Gras (1958) Newman, L.
Mare Nostrum (1926) Axt
Margie (1946) Newman
Margin for Error (1943) Harline
Marianne (1929) Axt
Marie Antoinette (1938) Stothart
Marie Galante (1934) Lange
Marina del Rey (1967) Bernstein, C.
Marine Anniversary (1944) Lava
Marine Battleground (1966) Mendoza-Nava
Marine Circus (1939) Snell
Marine Raiders (1944) Webb
Mariners Ahoy (1954) Jackson, H.
Marines Fly High (1940) Webb
Marines in the Making (1943) Terr
Marines, Let's Go! (1961) Gertz
Marius (1931) Gromon
Marjorie Morningstar (1958) Steiner, M.
Mark (1963) McPartland
Mark of the Lash (1948) Greene, W.
Mark of the Renegade (1951) Skinner, F.
Mark of the Vampire (Trailer, 1935) Ward, E.
Mark of the Whistler (1944) Castelnuovo-Tedesco
Mark of the Witch (1970) Thomas
Mark of Zorro (1920) Axt
Mark of Zorro (1940) Newman
Marked for Murder (1945) Zahler
Marked Money (1928) Zuro
Marked Trails (1944) Sanucci
Marked Woman (1937) Kaun
Marksman (1953) Kraushaar
Marlowe (1968) Matz
Marnie (1964) Herrmann
Marriage by Contract (1928) Baer
Marriage-Go-Round (1960) Frontiere
Marriage Humor (1933) Zahler
Marriage Is a Private Affair (1944) Kaper
Marriage on the Rocks (1965) Riddle
Marriage Playground (1929) Harling
Marriage Wows (1949) Sharples, Winston
Married and in Love (1940) Lange
Married Bachelor (1941) Amfitheatrof

Married Before Breakfast (1937) Snell
Married in Hollywood (1929) Kay, Arthur
Marry-Go-Round (1943) Sharples, Winston
Marry Me Again (1953) Kraushaar
Marry the Boss's Daughter (1941) Mockridge
Marry the Girl (1928) Hoffman, M.
Marry the Girl (1937) Roemheld
Marry the Girl (Trailer, 1937) Jackson, H.
Marrying Kind (1952) Friedhofer
Mars (1931) Dietrich
Mars Needs Women (1964) Stein, R.
Marshal of Cedar Rock (1953) Wilson, S.
Marshal of Cripple Creek (1947) Glickman, M.
Marshal of Heldorado (1950) Greene, W.
Marshal of Mesa City (1939) Sawtell
Marshal of Reno (1944) Dubin
Marshal's Daughter (1953) Calker
Martian Thru Georgia (1962) Lava
Martin Luther, His Life and Time (1924) Spielter, H.
Marty (1955) Webb
Martyrs of the Alamo (1915) Breil
Marusia (1938) Prydatekych
Marvin Digs (1967) Lantz
Mary Burns, Fugitive (1935) Roemheld
Mary Jane's Pa (1935) Roemheld
Mary Lou (1948) Dubin
Mary Mary (1963) Perkins
Mary of Scotland (1936) Shilkret, N.
Mary Poppins (1964) Kostal
Mary Regan (1921) Beynon
Mary Stevens, M.D. (1933) Kaun
Mary Visits Poland (1946) Forrell
Mary's Little Lamb (1935) Stalling
Maryjane (1968) Curb
Maryland (1940) Buttolph, David
MASH (1969) Mandel
Mask (1961) Applebaum
Mask of Comedy (1960) Sutton, J.
Mask of Diijon (1946) Hajos
Mask of Dimitrios (1944) Deutsch
Mask of Fu Manchu (1932) Axt
Mask of Nippon (1942) Agostini
Mask of the Avenger (1951) Castelnuovo-Tedesco
Mask of the Dragon (1951) Shefter
Masked Marvel (1943) Glickman, M.
Masked Raiders (1949) Sawtell
Masks of the Devil (1928) Axt
Masque Raid (1937) De Nat
Masquerade in Mexico (1945) Young, V.
Masquerader (1933) Newman
Mass Mouse Meeting (1943) Worth, P.
Massacre (1934) Kaun
Massacre River (1949) Leipold
Master Minds (1949) Kay, Edward
Master of the World (1961) Baxter
Master Race (1944) Webb
Master Will Shakespeare (1936) Stothart
Mata Hari (1932) Axt
Match Kid (1933) De Nat
Match King (1932) Kaun
Matchmaker (1958) Deutsch
Mathematica (1961) Bernstein, E.
Matinee Mouse (1966) Elliott, Dean
Matinee Wives (1970) Howard
Mating Game (1959) Alexander, J.
Mating of Millie (1948) Heymann
Mating Season (1951) Lilley
Mating Urge (1958) Wilson, S.
Matrimony (1915) Nurnberger
Matter of Consequence (1966) Keane
Maverick (1952) Kraushaar
Maverick Queen (1956) Young, V.
Maw and Paw (1953) Wheeler
Mawas (1929) Dugan
Maya Through the Ages (1949) Tullis
Mayaland Safari (1964) White, D.
Mayan Secrets (1958) Baxter
Maybe Darwin Was Right (1942) Jackson, H.
Maybe It's Love (1934) Roemheld
Mayflower (1935) Scheib
Mayflower Story (1959) Lewin
Mayor of 44th Street (1942) Webb
Mayor of Hell (1933) Kaun
Maytime (1937) Stothart
Maze (1953) Skiles
Mazel Tov, Jews (1941) Secunda
McConnell Story (1955) Steiner, M.
McDougal's Rest Farm (1947) Scheib
McFadden's Flats (1935) Leipold
McGuerins from Brooklyn (1942) Ward, E.
McHale's Navy (1964) Fielding
McHale's Navy Joins the Air Force (1965) Fielding
McLintock! (1963) De Vol
McMasters (1970) Perkinson
Me and the Colonel (1958) Duning
Me Musical Nephews (1942) Timberg
Me, Natalie (1969) Mancini
Meanest Man in the World (1942) Mockridge
Meaning of Modern Art (1967) Laderman
Meat/Rack (1970) Skinner, D.
Meatless Flyday (1943) Stalling
Meatless Tuesday (1943) Calker
Mechanical Bird (1951) Scheib
Mechanical Cow (1932) Dietrich
Mechanical Cow (1937) Scheib
Mechanical Handy Man (1937) Dietrich
Mechanical Man (1932) Dietrich
Mechanical Principles (1931) McPhee
Mechanics of Love (1955) Gruen
Mechanix Illustrated No. 3 (1940) Jackson, H.
Mechanix Illustrated No. 4 (1940) Jackson, H.
Mechanized Patrol (1943) Lava
Medal for Benny (1945) Young, V.
Medicine Show (1933) De Nat
Meditation (1968) Zekley
Mediterranean Blues (1934) Maloof
Mediterranean Ports of Call (1941) Shilkret, J.

Medium Cool (1969) Bloomfield
Meet Boston Blackie (1941) Cutner
Meet Doctor Christian (1939) Nussbaum
Meet John Doe (1941) Tiomkin
Meet John Doughboy (1941) Stalling
Meet King Joe (1949) Smith, P.
Meet Me at the Fair (1952) Rosen, M.
Meet Me in Las Vegas (1956) Stoll
Meet Me in St. Louis (1944) Salinger
Meet Me on Broadway (1946) Duning
Meet Miss Bobby Socks (1944) Duning
Meet Mother Magoo (1956) Castillo
Meet Nero Wolfe (1936) Jackson, H.
Meet the Chump (1941) Salter
Meet the Fleet (1940) Jackson, H.
Meet the Missus (1937) Webb
Meet the Missus (1940) Feuer
Meet the People (1944) Hayton
Meet the Stewarts (1942) Shuken
Meeting at a Far Meridian (1966) Ronell
Melissa: The Total Female (1970) Casarini
Melodies Old and New (1941) Snell
Melody (1953) Dubin
Melody and Moonlight (1940) Feuer
Melody Comes to Town (1941) Hatley
Melody Cruise (1933) Steiner, M.
Melody for Machines (1963) Rood
Melody for Three (1941) Bakaleinikoff, C.
Melody for Two (1937) Roemheld
Melody Lane (1941) Skinner, F.
Melody Lingers On (1935) Newman
Melody Parade (1943) Kay, Edward
Melody Time (1948) Daniel
Melody Trail (1935) Zahler
Member of the Wedding (1953) North
Memories and Melodies (1935) Ward, E.
Memories of Australia (1943) Shilkret, N.
Memories of Columbus (1945) De Francesco
Memories of Europe (1941) Amfitheatrof
Memphis Belle (1944) Kubik
Men (1950) Tiomkin
Men Against the Arctic (1955) Wallace
Men Against the Sky (1940) Tours
Men and Dust (1940) Stewart, F.
Men and Ships (1940) Kubik
Men Are Like That (1930) Harling
Men Are Such Fools (1932) Harling
Men Are Such Fools (1938) Roemheld
Men for the Fleet (1942) De Francesco
Men in Exile (1937) Jackson, H.
Men in Her Diary (1945) Rosen, M.
Men in Her Life (1941) Raksin
Men in War (1957) Bernstein, E.
Men in White (1934 trailer) Axt
Men of Boys Town (1941) Stothart
Men of Chance (1932) Steiner, M.
Men of Science (1952) Grundman
Men of Steel (1938) Snell
Men of Texas (1942) Ward, E.
Men of the Fighting Lady (1954) Rozsa
Men of the Navy (1942) Smith, P.
Men of the Shooting Stars (1949) Shilkret, N.
Men of the Sky (1931) Mendoza
Men of the Sky (1942) Jackson, H.
Men of Tomorrow (1945) Lava
Men of West Point (1942) De Francesco
Men on Call (1930) Kaylin
Men on Her Mind (1944) Zahler
Men Wanted (1940) Jackson, H.
Men with Wings (1938) Harling
Men Without Names (1935) Leipold
Men Without Skirts (1930) Zahler
Men Without Souls (1940) Cutner
Men Without Women (1929) Brunelli
Men, Women and Children (1954) Kleinsinger
Menu (1933) Axt
Merbabies (1938) Bradley
Mercy Island (1941) Feuer
Merely Mary Ann (1931) Fall
Merely Mary Ann (trailer) (1931) Brunelli
Merida and Campeche (1945) Nussbaum
Merlin the Magic Mouse (1967) Lava
Mermaids of Tiburon (1962) LaSalle
Merrill's Marauders (1962) Jackson, H.
Merrily We Go to Hell (1932) Kopp, R.
Merrily We Live (1938) Hatley
Merry Andrew (1958) Riddle
Merry Cafe (1936) De Nat
Merry Chase (1950) Scheib
Merry Dog (1932) Dietrich
Merry Dwarfs (1929) Stalling
Merry Frinks (1934) Kaun
Merry-Go-Round of 1938 (1937) Henderson, C.
Merry Kittens (1935) Sharples, Winston
Merry Mannequins (1937) Kilfeather
Merry Minstrel Magoo (1958) Ellenhorn
Merry Monahans (1944) Salter
Merry Mouse Cafe (1941) Worth, P.
Merry Mutineers (1936) De Nat
Merry Old Soul (1933) Dietrich
Merry Old Soul (1935) Spencer, N.
Merry Widow (1925) Axt
Merry Widow (1934) Stothart
Merry Widow (1952) Blackton
Merry Wives of Reno (1934) Roemheld
Merton of the Movies (1947) Snell
Mesa of Lost Women (1953) Curtin
Meshes of the Afternoon (1959) Ito
Mesquite Buckaroo (1939) Sanucci
Mess Production (1945) Sharples, Winston
Message to Gracias (1963) Lava
Messed Up Movie Makers (1966) Scheib
Messenger of Peace (1950) Colombo
Metamorphosis (1951) Chudacoff
Metamorphosis (1970) Ross
Method and Maw (1962) Sharples, Winston
Mexicali Rose (1939) Feuer
Mexicali Shmoes (1958) Franklyn

Mexican Baseball (1947) Scheib
Mexican Boarders (1961) Franklyn
Mexican Cat Dance (1963) Lava
Mexican Hayride (1948) Scharf, W.
Mexican Joy Ride (1947) Stalling
Mexican Jumping Beans (1940) Jackson, H.
Mexican Maize (1962) Duffy
Mexican Majesty (1944) De Francesco
Mexican Manhunt (1953) Kay, Edward
Mexican Mousepiece (1966) Lava
Mexican Sea Sports (1945) Dunn
Mexican Spitfire (1940) Sawtell
Mexican Spitfire Out West (1940) Webb
Mexican Spitfire's Elephant (1942) Webb
Mexican Sportland (1944) Gama
Mexicana (1945) Scharf, W.
Miami Expose (1956) Bakaleinikoff, M.
Miami Maniacs (1955) Scheib
Mice Follies (1954) Bradley
Mice Follies (1959) Franklyn
Mice in Council (1934) Scheib
Mice Meeting You (1950) Sharples, Winston
Mice Paradise (1951) Sharples, Winston
Mice Will Play (1938) Stalling
Mice-Capades (1952) Sharples, Winston
Miceniks (1960) Sharples, Winston
Michael O'Halloran (1937) Colombo
Michael O'Halloran (1948) Moraweck
Michael Shayne, Private Detective (1941) Mockridge
Michigan Kid (1947) Salter
Michigan Ski-Daddle (1945) Dunn
Mickey (1948) Skiles
Mickey and the Seal (1948) Wallace
Mickey Down Under (1947) Wallace
Mickey in Arabia (1932) Churchill
Mickey One (1965) Sauter
Mickey Plays Papa (1934) Churchill
Mickey the Kid (1939) Feuer
Mickey's Amateurs (1937) Wallace
Mickey's Big Chance (1953) Marsh
Mickey's Birthday Party (1941) Wolcott
Mickey's Choo Choo (1929) Stalling
Mickey's Circus (1936) Smith, P.
Mickey's Crusaders (1931) Zahler
Mickey's Delayed Date (1947) Wallace
Mickey's Elephant (1936) Malotte
Mickey's Fire Brigade (1935) Lewis
Mickey's Follies (1929) Stalling
Mickey's Gala Premier (1933) Churchill
Mickey's Garden (1935) Harline
Mickey's Golden Rule (1931) Zahler
Mickey's Good Deed (1932) Lewis
Mickey's Grand Opera (1936) Harline
Mickey's Kangaroo (1935) Lewis
Mickey's Man Friday (1935) Lewis
Mickey's Mechanical Man (1933) Harline
Mickey's Mellerdrammer (1933) Churchill
Mickey's Pal Pluto (1933) Churchill
Mickey's Parrot (1938) Wallace
Mickey's Polo Team (1936) Churchill
Mickey's Rival (1936) Harline
Mickey's Service Station (1935) Harline
Mickey's Steam-Roller (1934) Lewis
Mickey's Surprise Party (1939) Wallace
Mickey's Trailer (1938) Wallace
Microscopic Mysteries (1932) Axt
Midas Run (1969) Bernstein, E.
Middle East (1959) Forrell
Middle of the Night (1959) Bassman
Middleton Family at the New York World's Fair (1939) Ludwig
Midnight (1939) Hollander
Midnight (1945) Palange
Midnight Alibi (1934) Roemheld
Midnight at Maxim's (1915) Simon, W.
Midnight Club (1933) Rainger
Midnight Court (1937) Raksin
Midnight Frolics (1938) Kilfeather
Midnight Graduate (1970) Mendoza-Nava
Midnight Lace (1960) Skinner, F.
Midnight Limited (1940) Zahler
Midnight Madonna (1937) Stoll
Midnight Manhunt (1945) Laszlo
Midnight Mary (1933) Axt
Midnight Serenade (1947) Lilley
Midnight Shadow (1939) Lange, J.
Midnight Snack (1941) Bradley
Midnight Story (1957) Salter
Midnight Sun (1931) Kaun
Midnight Warning (1932) Zahler
Midstream (1929) Riesenfeld
Midsummer Mush (1933) Hatley
Midsummer Night's Dream (1935) Korngold
Midtown Madness (1969) Kynard
Mighty (1929) Potokor
Mighty Barnum (1935) Newman
Mighty Hunters (1940) Stalling
Mighty Joe Young (1949) Webb
Mighty Jungle (1964) Baxter
Mighty Manhattan, New York's Wonder City (1949) Kirk
Mighty Marlin (1949) Shilkret, N.
Mighty McGurk (1946) Snell
Mighty Mouse and the Hep Cat (1946) Scheib
Mighty Mouse and the Kilkenny Cats (1945) Scheib
Mighty Mouse and the Magician (1948) Scheib
Mighty Mouse and the Pirates (1945) Scheib
Mighty Mouse and the Two Barbers (1944) Scheib
Mighty Mouse and the Wolf (1945) Scheib
Mighty Mouse at the Circus (1944) Scheib
Mighty Mouse Meets Bad Bad Bill Bunion (1945) Scheib
Mighty Mouse Meets Deadeye Dick (1947) Scheib
Mighty Mouse Meets Jekyll and Hyde Cat (1944) Scheib
Mighty Niagara (1943) Nussbaum

Mighty Termite (1961) Sharples, Winston
Mighty Treve (1937) Raksin
Mike Makes His Mark (1955) Lloyd, N.
Mike Mulligan and His Steam Shovel (1956) Kleiner
Mike the Masquerader (1959) Sharples, Winston
Mild Cargo (1934) Sharples, Winston
Mild West (1947) Sharples, Winston
Mildred Pierce (1945) Steiner, M.
Military Law (1943) Applebaum
Milk and Money (1936) Stalling
Milk for Baby (1938) Scheib
Milkman (1950) Rosen, M.
Milkman (1931) De Nat
Milkman (1932) Bradley
Milky Waif (1946) Bradley
Milky Way (1936) Young, V.
Milky Way (1940) Bradley
Miller's Daughter (1934) Spencer, N.
Millerson Case (1947) Gertz
Millie (1931) Lange
Millie's Daughter (1947) Morton
Million Dollar Baby (1941) Hollander
Million Dollar Cat (1944) Bradley
Million Dollar Kid (1943) Kay, Edward
Million Dollar Legs (1932) Leipold
Million Dollar Legs (1939) Leipold
Million Dollar Mermaid (1952) Deutsch
Million Dollar Pursuit (1951) Wilson, S.
Million Dollar Ransom (1934) Ward, E.
Million Dollar Weekend (1948) Ohman
Millionaire (1931) Reiser
Millionaire Droopy (1956) Bradley
Millionaire for Christy (1951) Young, V.
Millionaire Hobo (1939) De Nat
Millionaire Playboy (1940) Sawtell
Millionaires in Prison (1940) Webb
Million-Hare (1962) Lava
Millions in the Air (1935) Bradshaw
Millions of Cats (1955) Kleiner
Mind Reader (1933) Kaun
Mind Your Own Business (1937) Shuken
Minding the Baby (1931) Steiner, G.
Minding the Baby (1932) De Nat
Miner (1930) De Nat
Miner's Daughter (1950) Kubik
Miner's Ridge (1970) Neff
Miners Forty Niners (1951) Sharples, Winston
Minesweeper (1943) Glickman, M.
Mini-Skirt Mob (1968) Baxter
Mini Squirts (1967) Sharples, Winston
Ministry of Fear (1944) Young, V.
Miniver Story (1950) Rozsa
Minnesota Document (1938) Verrall
Minnesota Story (1964) Semmler
Minnesota, Land of Plenty (1942) Nussbaum
Minstrel Man (1944) Grofé
Minstrel Show (1932) De Nat
Mint Men (1960) Scheib
Minute and 1/2 Man (1959) Scheib
Miracle (1953) Keefer
Miracle (1959) Bernstein, E.
Miracle at Lourdes (1939) Snell
Miracle at Your House (1965) Lowe
Miracle in a Cornfield (1947) Kopp, R.
Miracle in the Caribbean (1956) Jackson, H.
Miracle in the Rain (1956) Waxman
Miracle Kid (1941) Wheeler
Miracle Makers (1941) Dunn
Miracle Man (1919) Riesenfeld
Miracle Man (1932) Harling
Miracle of Hydro (1941) Lava
Miracle of Living (1947) Applebaum
Miracle of Morgan's Creek (1944) Shuken
Miracle of Our Lady of Fatima (1952) Steiner, M.
Miracle of Salt Lake (1938) Snell
Miracle of Sister Beatrice (1939) Antonini
Miracle of Sound (1940) Amfitheatrof
Miracle of the Bells (1948) Harline
Miracle of the Bulb (1958) Forrell
Miracle of the Hills (1959) Sawtell
Miracle of the White Stallions (1963) Smith, P.
Miracle on 34th Street (1947) Mockridge
Miracle on Main Street (1939) Salter
Miracle Rider (1935) Zahler
Miracle Worker (1962) Rosenthal
Miracles for Sale (1939) Axt
Miraculous Journey (1948) Erdody
Mirage (1965) Jones
Miramagic (1953) Barron
Mirele Efros (1939) Heifetz
Mirror in the Mountains (1957) Manson
Misadventures of Merlin Jones (1963) Baker, Buddy
Misbehaving Ladies (1931) Copping
Misconduct (1966) Karmen
Misfits (1961) North
Misguided Missile (1957) Wheeler
Misleading Lady (1932) Green, J.
Miss Annie Rooney (1942) Calker
Miss Body Beautiful (1954) Michelet
Miss Glory (1936) Spencer, N.
Miss Grant Takes Richmond (1949) Roemheld
Miss Mink of 1949 (1949) Merrick
Miss Pinkerton (1932) Kaun
Miss Polly (1941) Ward, E.
Miss Robin Crusoe (1953) Bernstein, E.
Miss Sadie Thompson (1953) Duning
Miss Susie Slagle's (1946) Amfitheatrof
Miss Tatlock's Millions (1948) Young, V.
Miss V from Moscow (1942) Zahler
Misses Stooge (1935) Shield
Missile to the Moon (1959) Carras
Missing Corpse (1945) Hajos
Missing Daughters (1933) Tuchman
Missing Daughters (1939) Morgan, F.

Missing Evidence (1939) Salter
Missing Lady (1946) Kay, Edward
Missing Link (1927) Rapée
Missing Links (1916) Breil
Missing Mouse (1952) Plumb
Missing Witnesses (1937) Kaun
Missing Women (1951) Wilson, S.
Mission in Morocco (1959) Kauer
Mission Mars (1968) Kalajian
Mission of the Bells (1955) Yeaworth
Mission Over Korea (1953) Bakaleinikoff, M.
Mission to Moscow (1943) Steiner, M.
Mission Trail (1946) Nussbaum
Mississippi Gambler (1942) Skinner, F.
Mississippi Gambler (1953) Skinner, F.
Mississippi Hare (1949) Stalling
Mississippi Rhythm (1949) Kay, Edward
Mississippi Swing (1941) Scheib
Mississippi Traveler (1955) Jackson, H.
Missouri Outlaw (1941) Feuer
Missouri Traveler (1957) Marshall, J.
Missourians (1950) Wilson, S.
Mister 880 (1950) Kaplan, S.
Mister and Mistletoe (1955) Sharples, Winston
Mister Antonio (1929) Zahler
Mister Big (1943) Schoen
Mister Buddwing (1965) Hopkins, K.
Mister Cinderella (1936) Hatley
Mister Cory (1957) Stein, H.
Mister Kingstreet's War (1970) Sukman
Mister Roberts (1955) Waxman
Mister Scoutmaster (1953) Mockridge
Mistigri (1931) Gromon
Misty (1961) Sawtell
Misunderstood Giant (1959) Scheib
Mite Makes Right (1948) Sharples, Winston
Mixed Master (1955) Franklyn
Mixed-Up Women (1955) Shefter
Mme. Olga's Massage Parlor (1965) St. Jean
Mme. Sans-Gêne (1912) Breil
Moana (1926) Bradford
Moans and Groans (1935) Scheib
Mob (1951) Duning
Moby Duck (1965) Lava
Model and the Marriage Broker (1952) Mockridge
Model Is Born (1948) Sharples, Winston
Model Wife (1941) Salter
Modeling for Money (1938) Axt
Models, Inc. (1952) Gilbert, H.
Modern Arms and Free Men (1950) Shaindlin
Modern Guatemala City (1945) Nussbaum
Modern Hero (1934) Roemheld
Modern Hero (Trailer, 1934) Kaun
Modern Inventions (1937) Wallace
Modern Madrid (1930) Axt
Modern Marriage (1950) Kay, Edward
Modern Mexico City (1942) Nussbaum
Modern New Orleans (1940) Bakaleinikoff, C.
Modern Red Riding Hood (1935) Scheib
Modern Times (1936) Chaplin, C.
Modernizing Marketing Facilities (1955) Kleinsinger
Mohawk (1955) Alperson
Mojave Firebrand (1944) Glickman, M.
Mokey (1942) Hayton
Mole People (1956) Roemheld
Molly (1951) Van Cleave
Molly and Me (1929) Riesenfeld
Molly and Me (1945) Mockridge
Molly Maguires (1970) Mancini
Molly Moo-Cow and Rip Van Winkle (1935) Sharples, Winston
Molly Moo-Cow and Robinson Crusoe (1936) Sharples, Winston
Molly Moo-Cow and the Butterflies (1935) Sharples, Winston
Molly Moo-Cow and the Indians (1935) Sharples, Winston
Mom and Dad (1944) Kay, Edward
Moment in Love (1957) Lloyd, N.
Moment to Act (196?) Raksin
Moment to Moment (1966) Mancini
Moments That Made History (1944) Terr
Mommy Loves Puppy (1940) Timberg
Mondo Bizarro (1966) Van Lattman
Mondo Hollywood (1967) Curb
Money and Banking (1968) Poddany
Money and the Woman (1940) Kaun
Money from Home (1954) Harline
Money, Goods and Prices (1944) Applebaum
Money in My Pocket (1962) Hormel
Money Jungle (1967) Dunlap
Money Madness (1948) Erdody
Money to Burn (1939) Feuer
Money Trap (1965) Schaefer, H.
Money, Women and Guns (1958) Stein, H.
Monika (1955) Baxter
Monitors (1969) Kaz, F.
Monkey Business (1931) Leipold
Monkey Business (1952) Harline
Monkey Doodles (1960) Sharples, Winston
Monkey Love (1935) De Nat
Monkey Meat (1930) Scheib
Monkey on My Back (1957) Sawtell
Monkey Wretches (1935) Dietrich
Monkeys, Go Home! (1966) Brunner
Monkey's Paw (1932) Steiner, M.
Monkey's Uncle (1965) Baker, Buddy
Monkey-Tone News (1947) De Francesco
Monolith Monsters (1957) Gertz
Monroe Doctrine (1939) Jackson, H.
Monsieur Beaucaire (1924) Riesenfeld
Monsieur Beaucaire (1946) Dolan
Monsieur Verdoux (1947) Chaplin, C.
Monster and the Ape (1945) Zahler
Monster and the Girl (1941) Carbonara

Monster from Green Hell (1957) Glasser
Monster from the Ocean Floor (1954) Brummer
Monster Maker (1944) Glasser
Monster of Ceremonies (1966) Wheeler
Monster That Challenged the World (1957) Roemheld
Monster Walks (1932) Zahler
Monsters of the Deep (1941) Dunn
Monstrosity (1963) Kauer
Montage IV (1962) Ivey
Montage V: How to Play Pinball (1965) Ivey
Montana (1950) Buttolph, David
Montana Belle (1951) Scott, N.
Montana Desperado (1951) Kay, Edward
Montana Incident (1952) Kraushaar
Monte Carlo (1926) Rapée
Monte Carlo (1930) Harling
Montmartre Madness (1939) Shilkret, N.
Montreal by Night (1947) Applebaum
Monument to the Dream (1968) Wykes
Moods in Motion (1954) MacLaine
Moon and Sixpence (1942) Tiomkin
Moon Is Blue (1953) Gilbert, H.
Moon Is Down (1943) Newman
Moon Over Burma (1940) Young, V.
Moon Over Harlem (1939) Heywood
Moon Over Her Shoulder (1941) Mockridge
Moon Over Miami (1941) Mockridge
Moon Over Montana (1946) Sanucci
Moon Pilot (1961) Smith, P.
Moon's Our Home (1936) Carbonara
Moonfleet (1955) Rozsa
Moonlight for Two (1932) Marsales
Moonlight in Hawaii (1941) Skinner, F.
Moonlight Masquerade (1942) Feuer
Moonlight Murder (1936) Ward, E.
Moonlight on the Prairie (1935) Jackson, H.
Moonlighter (1953) Roemheld
Moonlighting Wives (1966) Free
Moonplay (1962) Ito
Moonrise (1948) Lava
Moonshine War (1970) Karger
Moontide (1942) Mockridge
Moonwolf (1966) Price, Henry
Moose Hunt (1931) Lewis
Moose Hunters (1937) Smith, P.
Moose on the Loose (1952) Scheib
Mopping Up (1943) Scheib
More About Nostradamus (1940) Zador
More Dead Than Alive (1969) Springer, P.
More Kittens (1936) Churchill
More Pep (1936) Timberg
More Pigs (1943) Applebaum
More Power to America (1946) Carbonara
More Power to the American Farmer (1946) Carbonara
More Than a Secretary (1936) Tiomkin
More Than Meets the Eye (1952) Selinsky
More Than Meets the Eye (1964) Cacioppo
More Than Words (1969) Robinson
More the Merrier (1943) Harline
More Trifles of Importance (1941) Amfitheatrof
Morituri (1965) Goldsmith
Mormon Trails (1943) De Francesco
Morning for Jimmy (1960) Taylor, B.
Morning Glory (1933) Steiner, M.
Morocco (1930) Hajos
Morocco Nights (1934) Kaun
Morris, the Midget Moose (1950) Smith, P.
Mortal Storm (1940) Kaper
Moscow Strikes Back (1942) Tiomkin
Moses (1954) Elliott, C.
Moses and His People (1952) Mamorsky
Moses and the Ten Commandments (1952) Mamorsky
Moses in Egypt (1952) Mamorsky
Moses Soyer—Paintings in a Low Voice (1963) Martin, David
Mosquito (1945) Scheib
Mosquito and Malaria (1942) Smith, P.
Moss Rose (1947) Buttolph, David
Most Dangerous Game (1932) Steiner, M.
Most Dangerous Man Alive (1961) Forbes
Motel Confidential (1967) Gigagusky
Moth and the Flame (1938) Malotte
Moth and the Spider (1935) Scheib
Mother and the Law (1919) Gottschalk
Mother Carey's Chickens (1938) Tours
Mother Didn't Tell Me (1950) Mockridge
Mother Goose a Go-Go (1966) Kauer
Mother Goose Goes Hollywood (1938) Plumb
Mother Goose in Swingtime (1939) De Nat
Mother Goose Land (1933) Steiner, G.
Mother Goose Nightmare (1945) Scheib
Mother Goose on the Loose (1942) Calker
Mother Goose's Birthday Party (1950) Scheib
Mother Hen's Holiday (1937) De Nat
Mother Hubba-Hubba Hubbard (1947) Kilfeather
Mother Is a Freshman (1949) Newman
Mother Knows Best (1928) Rapée
Mother Machree (1928) Rapée
Mother Pluto (1936) Harline
Mother Was a Rooster (1962) Franklyn
Mother Wore Tights (1947) Buttolph, David
Mother's Cry (1930) Mendoza
Mother's Day (1948) Brubeck, H.
Motive for Revenge (1935) Zahler
Motl, the Operator (1939) Secunda
Motor Mania (1950) Smith, P.
Motor Patrol (1950) Caswell
Motorcycle Gang (1957) Glasser
Motoring in Mexico (1942) Nussbaum
Motorpsycho (1965) Sawtell
Moulin Rouge (1929) Littau
Moulin Rouge (1934) Newman
Mount Vernon (1949) North
Mountain (1956) Amfitheatrof
Mountain Ears (1939) De Nat

Mountain Fighters (1943) Jackson, H.
Mountain Justice (1936) Kaun
Mountain Moonlight (1941) Glickman, M.
Mountain Music (1937) Leipold
Mountain Rhythm (1939) Feuer
Mountain Rhythm (1941) Glickman, M.
Mountain Road (1959) Moross
Mountain Romance (1938) Scheib
Mourning Becomes Electra (1947) Hageman
Mouse and Garden (1950) Scheib
Mouse and Garden (1960) Franklyn
Mouse and the Lion (1953) Wheeler
Mouse Blanche (1962) Sharples, Winston
Mouse Cleaning (1948) Bradley
Mouse Comes to Dinner (1945) Bradley
Mouse Divided (1951) Stalling
Mouse Exterminator (1939) De Nat
Mouse for Sale (1955) Bradley
Mouse from H.U.N.G.E.R. (1967) Elliott, Dean
Mouse in Manhattan (1945) Bradley
Mouse in the House (1947) Bradley
Mouse in the House (1967) Greene, W.
Mouse Mazurka (1948) Stalling
Mouse Meets Bird (1952) Scheib
Mouse Meets Lion (1940) De Nat
Mouse Menace (1946) Stalling
Mouse Menace (1953) Scheib
Mouse-merized Cat (1946) Stalling
Mouse of Tomorrow (1942) Scheib
Mouse on 57th Street (1959) Franklyn
Mouse-Placed Kitten (1958) Franklyn
Mouse-Taken Identity (1957) Stalling
Mouse That Jack Built (1958) Franklyn
Mouse Trapeze (1955) Sharples, Winston
Mouse Trapped (1959) Poddany
Mouse Trappers (1941) Churchill
Mouse Trek (1967) Sharples, Winston
Mouse Trouble (1944) Bradley
Mouse Wreckers (1947) Stalling
Mousetro Herman (1956) Sharples, Winston
Mouseum (1956) Sharples, Winston
Mousewarming (1952) Stalling
Mousie Come Home (1946) Calker
Mousieur Herman (1955) Sharples, Winston
Mouth (1942) Applebaum
Mouthpiece (1932) Kaun
Move (1970) Hamlisch
Move Over, Darling (1963) Newman, L.
Movie Crazy (1932) Newman
Movie Daze (1934) Hatley
Movie Mad (1931) Bradley
Movie Madness (1951) Scheib
Movie Phoney News (1938) Churchill
Movie Star, American Style (1966) Greene, J.
Movie Struck (1933) De Nat
Movietone Follies of 1930 (1930) Lipschultz
Moving Aweigh (1944) Sharples, Winston
Moving Day (1936) Malotte
Moving Finger (1963) Vann
Mr. Ace (1946) Roemheld
Mr. & Mrs. Is the Name (1935) Spencer, N.
Mr. and Mrs. North (1941) Amfitheatrof
Mr. & Mrs. Smith (1941) Ward, E.
Mr. Belvedere Goes to College (1949) Newman
Mr. Belvedere Rings the Bell (1951) Mockridge
Mr. Blabbermouth! (1942) Amfitheatrof
Mr. Blandings Builds His Dream House (1948) Harline
Mr. Bug Goes to Town (1941) Harline
Mr. Charmley Meets a Lady (1956) Castelnuovo-Tedesco
Mr. Chump (1938) Jackson, H.
Mr. Deeds Goes to Town (1936) Jackson, H.
Mr. District Attorney (1941) Feuer
Mr. District Attorney (1947) Gilbert, H.
Mr. District Attorney in the Carter Case (1941) Feuer
Mr. Dodd Takes the Air (1937) Deutsch
Mr. Doodle Kicks Off (1938) Webb
Mr. Duck Steps Out (1940) Wolcott
Mr. E. from Tau Ceti (1963) Clayton, W.
Mr. Flagmaker (1942) Cowell
Mr. Fore by Fore (1944) Kilfeather
Mr. Hex (1946) Kay, Edward
Mr. Hobbs Takes a Vacation (1962) Mancini
Mr. Imperium (1951) Kaper
Mr. Lemon of Orange (1931) Talbot
Mr. Lucky (1943) Webb
Mr. Money Gags (1957) Sharples, Winston
Mr. Moocher (1944) Kilfeather
Mr. Moto in Danger Island (1939) Kaylin
Mr. Moto Takes a Vacation (1939) Kaylin
Mr. Moto's Last Warning (1939) Raksin
Mr. Mouse Takes a Trip (1940) Harline
Mr. Muggs Rides Again (1945) Kay, Edward
Mr. Muggs Steps Out (1943) Kay, Edward
Mr. Music (1951) Lilley
Mr. Peabody and the Mermaid (1948) Dolan
Mr. Reckless (1948) Lubin
Mr. Robinson Crusoe (1932) Newman
Mr. Sardonicus (1961) Dexter
Mr. Skeffington (1944) Waxman
Mr. Skitch (1933) De Francesco
Mr. Smith Goes to Washington (1939) Tiomkin
Mr. Soft Touch (1949) Roemheld
Mr. Strauss Takes a Walk (1942) von Ottenfeld
Mr. Texas (1951) Carmichael
Mr. Trull Finds Out (1940) Menotti
Mr. Universe (1950) Tiomkin
Mr. Walkie Talkie (1952) Klatzkin
Mr. Whitney Had a Notion (1949) Kopp, R.
Mr. Winkle Goes to War (1944) Dragon
Mr. Winlucky (1967) Timmens
Mr. Wise Guy (1942) Lange, J.
Mr. Wong in Chinatown (1939) Kay, Edward
Mr. Wong, Detective (1938) Kay, Edward
Mrs. Jones' Rest Farm (1949) Scheib
Mrs. Lady Bug (1940) Bradley

Mrs. Mike (1949) Steiner, M.
Mrs. Miniver (1942) Stothart
Mrs. O'Leary's Cow (1938) Scheib
Mrs. O'Malley and Mr. Malone (1950) Deutsch
Mrs. Parkington (1944) Kaper
Mrs. Wiggs of the Cabbage Patch (1934) Leipold
Mrs. Wiggs of the Cabbage Patch (1942) Young, V.
Much Ado About Mousing (1964) Poddany
Much Ado About Mutton (1947) Sharples, Winston
Much Ado About Nothing (1940) Scheib
Much Ado About Nutting (1952) Stalling
Mucho Mouse (1956) Bradley
Muchos Locos (1965) Stein, H.
Mugger (1958) Glasser
Muggy-Doo Boycat (1963) Sharples, Winston
Mumbo Jumbo (1969) Goodwin
Mummy (1932) Dietrich
Mummy's Boys (1936) Webb
Mummy's Curse (1944) Sawtell
Mummy's Ghost (1943) Skinner, F
Mummy's Hand (1940) Skinner, F.
Mundo Depravados (1967) Ballantine
Munster, Go Home! (1966) Marshall, J.
Mural: Midwest Metropolis (1960) Siegel, S.
Murder a la Mod (1968) McDowell
Murder Among Friends (1941) Mockridge
Murder at Dawn (1932) Zahler
Murder at Midnight (1931) Burton
Murder at the Vanities (1934) Roder
Murder by an Aristocrat (Trailer, 1936) *Kaun*
Murder by Contract (1958) Botkin
Murder by Television (1935) Wallace
Murder, He Says (1945) Dolan
Murder, He Says (Trailer, 1945) Schrager
Murder in Mississippi (1965) Lesko
Murder in Swingtime (1937) DiMaggio
Murder in the Air (1940) Lava
Murder in the Big House (1942) Jackson, H.
Murder in the Blue Room (1944) Lava
Murder in the Clouds (1934) Heindorf
Murder in the Fleet (1935) Marquardt
Murder in the Music Hall (1946) Scharf, W.
Murder in Trinidad (1934) Buttolph, David
Murder, Inc. (1960) De Vol
Murder Is My Beat (1955) Glasser
Murder Is My Business (1946) Erdody
Murder, My Sweet (1945) Webb
Murder of Dr. Harrigan (1935) Kaun
Murder on a Honeymoon (1935) Colombo
Murder on Lenox Avenue (1941) Heywood
Murder on the Blackboard (1934) Steiner, M.
Murder on the Waterfront (1943) Jackson, H.
Murder on the Yukon (1940) Lange, J.
Murder Over New York (1940) Mockridge
Murder Will Out (1930) Reiser
Murder Without Tears (1953) Kay, Edward
Murderers' Row (1966) Schifrin
Murders in the Zoo (1933) Kopp, R.
Muscle Beach (1948) Robinson
Muscle Beach Party (1964) Baxter
Muscle Beach Tom (1956) Bradley
Muscle Maulers (1946) De Francesco
Muscle Tussle (1952) Stalling
Muscles and the Lady (1948) Shilkret, N.
Museum (1930) De Nat
Museum Piece (1969) Johnston, B.
Music Box Kid (1960) Sawtell
Music Circus (1951) Sharples, Winston
Music for a Film on the Yale Library (1956) Porter, Q.
Music for Madame (1937) Shilkret, N.
Music for Millions (1944) Michelet
Music for Ploesti (1956) Cowell
Music from the Mountains (1948) Curtin
Music Goes 'Round (1936) Jackson, H.
Music Hath Charms (1936) Dietrich
Music in Manhattan (1944) Harline
Music in My Heart (1939) Cutner
Music in the Air (1934) Waxman
Music Is Magic (1935) Rose, G.
Music Land (1935) Harline
Music Made Simple (1938) Snell
Music Man (1948) Kay, Edward
Music Man (1961) Heindorf
Music Mice-tro (1967) Lava
Music, Music Everywhere (1936) Lucas, C.
Music of Williamsburg (1960) Forrell
Musical Doctor (1932) Timberg
Musical Farmer (1932) Churchill
Musical Justice (1931) Timberg
Musical Madness (1951) Scheib
Musical Masterpieces (1946) Terr
Musical Mexico (1945) Jackson, H.
Musical Moments from Chopin (1947) Calker
Musical Mountaineers (1939) Timberg
Musicalulu (1946) Sharples, Winston
Mustang (1959) Kraushaar
Mutiny (1952) Tiomkin
Mutiny Ahead (1935) Zahler
Mutiny in the Big House (1939) Kay, Edward
Mutiny on the Bounty (1935) Stothart
Mutiny on the Bounty (1962) Kaper
Mutiny on the Bunny (1948) Stalling
Mutt 'n Bones (1944) Kilfeather
Mutt in a Rut (1949) Sharples, Winston
Mutt in a Rut (1958) Franklyn
Mutts About Racing (1957) Bradley
Muzzle Tough (1953) Stalling
My American Wife (1936) Hollander
My Best Gal (1944) Skiles
My Bill (1938) Jackson, H.
My Blood Runs Cold (1965) Duning
My Body Hungers (1967) Free
My Boy Johnny (1944) Scheib
My Brother Talks to Horses (1946) Kopp, R.
My Buddy (1944) Butts
My Bunny Lies Over the Sea (1948) Stalling

My Country 'Tis of Thee (1951) Lava
My Cousin Rachel (1952) Waxman
My Daddy the Astronaut (1967) Sharples, Winston
My Darling Clementine (1946) Buttolph, David
My Dear Miss Aldrich (1937) Snell
My Dear Secretary (1948) Roemheld
My Dog Buddy (1960) Marshall, J.
My Dream Is Yours (1949) Jackson, H.
My Fair Lady (1964) Previn, A.
My Father's House (1947) Brant
My Favorite Blonde (1942) Buttolph, David
My Favorite Brunette (1947) Dolan
My Favorite Duck (1943) Stalling
My Favorite Spy (1942) Webb
My Favorite Spy (1951) Young, V.
My Favorite Wife (1940) Webb
My Foolish Heart (1949) Young, V.
My Forbidden Past (1950) Hollander
My Friend Flicka (1943) Newman
My Friend Irma (1949) Webb
My Friend Irma Goes West (1950) Harline
My Friend the Monkey (1939) Timberg
My Gal Loves Music (1944) Ward, E.
My Gal Sal (1942) Mockridge
My Garden Japan (1967) Britton
My Geisha (1961) Waxman
My Girl Tisa (1948) Steiner, M.
My Girlfriend's Wedding (1969) Kooper
My Green Fedora (1935) Spencer, N.
My Gun Is Quick (1957) Skiles
My Heart Belongs to Daddy (1943) Shuken
My Japan (1946) Palange
My Kingdom for a Cook (1943) Leipold
My Lady's Garden (1934) Scheib
My Lady's Past (1929) Riesenfeld
My Life with Caroline (1941) Heymann
My Lips Betray (1933) Friedhofer
My Little Buckaroo (1937) Stalling
My Little Chickadee (1940) Skinner, F.
My Little Duckaroo (1954) Franklyn
My Love Came Back (1940) Roemheld
My Man and I (1952) Buttolph, David
My Man Godfrey (1936) Previn, C.
My Man Godfrey (1957) Skinner, F.
My Man Jasper (1945) Wheeler
My May (1965) Ashley
My Name Is Han (1948) Lloyd, N.
My Name is Mary Brown (1955) Johnson, M.
My Name Is Paul (1968) Mulhoberac
My Old Kentucky Home (1946) Scheib
My Old Town (1948) Franklyn, R.
My Own True Love (1949) Dolan
My Own True Love (Trailer, 1949) Van Cleave
My Own United States (1948) Lava
My Pal (1947) Laszlo
My Pal Gus (1952) Harline
My Pal Trigger (1946) Butts
My Pal Wolf (1944) Heymann
My Past (1931) Mendoza
My Past (foreign version, 1931) Reiser
My People's Dream (1934) Hoffman, M.
My Pop, My Pop (1940) Sharples, Winston
My Reputation (1946) Steiner, M.
My Silent Love (1949) Sharples, Winston
My Sin (1931) Green, J.
My Sister Eileen (1942) Cutner
My Sister Eileen (1955) Duning
My Sister's Business (1970) Levine, E.
My Six Convicts (1952) Tiomkin
My Six Loves (1962) Scharf, W.
My Son (1939) Olshanetsky
My Son Is a Criminal (1939) Parrish
My Son John (1952) Dolan
My Son, My Son! (1940) Ward, E.
My Son, the Hero (1943) Erdody
My Third Wife (1968) Tosco
My Tomato (1943) Terr
My Valet (1915) Furst
My Weakness (1933) Lange
My Wife's Best Friend (1952) Harline
My Wife's Relatives (1939) Feuer
My Wild Irish Rose (1947) Steiner, M.
My World Dies Screaming (1958) Calker
Mysteries of the Deep (1959) Wallace
Mysterious Ceylon (1949) Lava
Mysterious Cowboy (1952) Scheib
Mysterious Desperado (1949) Sawtell
Mysterious Doctor (1943) Lava
Mysterious Doctor Satan (1940) Glickman, M.
Mysterious Dr. Fu Manchu (1929) Potoker
Mysterious Intruder (1946) Duning
Mysterious Island (1929) Lamkoff
Mysterious Island (1961) Herrmann
Mysterious Jug (1937) Dietrich
Mysterious Lady (1930) Axt
Mysterious Miss X (1939) Lava
Mysterious Mr. Moto (1938) Maxwell
Mysterious Mr. Valentine (1946) Glickman, M.
Mysterious Package (1960) Scheib
Mysterious Rider (1938) Carbonara
Mysterious Stranger (1948) Scheib
Mystery Broadcast (1943) Glickman, M.
Mystery House (1937) Jackson, H.
Mystery in Mexico (1948) Sawtell
Mystery in Swing (1940) DiMaggio
Mystery in the Moonlight (1948) Scheib
Mystery Lake (1953) Lava
Mystery Man (1944) Sawtell
Mystery Mountain (1934) Zahler
Mystery of Edwin Drood (1935) Ward, E.
Mystery of Mr. Wong (1939) Kay, Edward
Mystery of Mr. X (1934) Axt
Mystery of the Hooded Horsemen (1937) Sanucci
Mystery of the Wax Museum (1933) Kaun
Mystery of the Yellow Room (1919) Riesenfeld
Mystery Plane (1939) Sanucci
Mystery Ranch (1932) Friedhofer
Mystery Range (1949) De Saxe

Mystery Sea Raider (1940) Malotte
Mystery Street (1950) Kopp, R.
Mystery Submarine (1950) Rosen, M.
Mystic India (1944) De Francesco
Mysto Fox (1946) Kilfeather

N. P. Patients (1944) Engel
N. Y., N. Y. (1958) Forrell
Nabonga (1944) Stahl
Naked Alibi (1954) Salter
Naked and the Dead (1958) Herrmann
Naked Angels (1969) Zappa
Naked City (1948) Rozsa
Naked Dawn (1955) Gilbert, H.
Naked Eye (1956) Bernstein, E.
Naked Gun (1956) Greene, W.
Naked Hills (1956) Gilbert, H.
Naked in the Sun (1957) Rosenthal
Naked Jungle (1954) Amfitheatrof
Naked Kiss (1964) Dunlap
Naked Paradise (1957) Stein, R.
Naked Runner (1966) Sukman
Naked Sea (1954) Almeida
Naked Spur (1953) Kaper
Naked Street (1955) Gold
Naked Witch (1961) Plagens
Name of the Game Is Kill! (1968) Phillips, S.
Namu the Killer Whale (1966) Matlovsky
Nana (1934) Newman
Nancy Drew and the Hidden Staircase (1939) Roemheld
Nancy Drew—Detective (1938) Roemheld
Nancy Drew—Reporter (1939) Roemheld
Nancy Drew—Trouble Shooter (1939) Roemheld
Nancy Goes to Rio (1950) Salinger
Nancy Steele Is Missing (1937) Buttolph, David
Nanking (1959) Kupferman
Nanook of the North (1922) Axt
Nanook of the North (1947) Schramm
Napoleon Blown-Aparte (1966) Lava
Napoleon Bunny-Part (1956) Stalling
Narcissus (1956) Hovhaness
Narcotics Story (1958) Laszlo
Narcotics Trade (1964) Pope
Narrow Corner (1933) Kaun
Narrow Margin (1952). See p. 8
Nashville Rebel (1966) Blanford
Nasty Quacks (1945) Stalling
Natalka Poltavka (1936) Shvedoff
Natchez Trace (1961) Greene, W.
Nation Aflame (1937) Kilenyi
Nation Builders (1941) Agostini
Nation Is Born (1947) Shilkret, N.
Nation on Skis (1948) Jackson, H.
National Barn Dance (1944) Schrager
National Fisheries Center and Aquarium (1967) Collette
National Gallery of Art, Washington, D.C. (1958) Zornig
National Parks—A Road for the Future (1968) Stein, R.
National Rebuild (1947) Applebaum
National Velvet (1944) Stothart
Native Land (1942) Blitzstein
Natural Wonders of the West (1938) Shilkret, J.
Natural Wonders of Washington State (1939) Bakaleinikoff, C.
Nature's Half Acre (1951) Smith, P.
Nature's Playmates (1962) Brady
Nature's Strangest Creatures (1959) Dubin
Nature's Workshop (1933) Dietrich
Naughty Baby (1928) Carbonara
Naughty But Mice (1939) Stalling
Naughty But Mice (1947) Sharples, Winston
Naughty But Nice (1939) Roemheld
Naughty Marietta (1935) Stothart
Naughty Nanette (1945) Schrager
Naughty Neighbors (1939) Stalling
Naughty Nineties (1945) Fairchild
Naughty Nudes (1965) Woode
Naughty Twenties (1951) Jackson, H.
Nautical But Nice (1944) Jackson, H.
Navajo (1951) Stevens, L.
Navajo Kid (1945) Zahler
Navajo Run (1964) Loose
Navajo Trail (1944) Kay, Edward
Navajo Trail Raiders (1949) Wilson, S.
Navigator (1924) Axt
Navy Blue and Gold (1937) Ward, E.
Navy Blues (1930) Axt
Navy Blues (1941) Roemheld
Navy Bound (1951) Kay, Edward
Navy Comes Through (1942) Webb
Navy Gets Rough (1943) Jackson, H.
Navy Nurse (1945) Lava
Navy Secrets (1939) Kay, Edward
Navy Way (1944) Stahl
Navy Wife (1935) Buttolph, David
Navy Wife (1956) Salter
Nazi Agent (1942) Amfitheatrof
Nazis Strike (1942) Webb
Nazty Nuisance (1942) Ward, E.
Neanderthal Man (1953) Glasser
Neapolitan Mouse (1954) Bradley
Near Sighted and Far Out (1964) Sharples, Winston
Nearly Eighteen (1943) Kay, Edward
Nearlyweds (1957) Sharples, Winston
'Neath Brooklyn Bridge (1942) Kay, Edward
'Neath Canadian Skies (1946) Mayfield
'Neath the Bababa Tree (1931) Scheib
Neck and Neck (1942) Scheib
Negro Soldier (1944) Tiomkin
Neighbor Next Door (1951) Lava
Neighborhood Story (1954) Nelson, R.
Neighboring Shore (1960) Levy, M.
Neighbors in the Night (1949) Sharples, Winston

Nell's Yells (1939) Kilfeather
Nellie, the Indian Chief's Daughter (1938) Churchill
Nellie, the Sewing Machine Girl (1938) Churchill
Nelly's Folly (1961) Franklyn
Neptune Nonsense (1936) Sharples, Winston
Neptune's Daughter (1914) Bowers, R. H.
Neptune's Daughter (1949) Stoll
Neptune's Daughters (1942) De Francesco
Neptune's Playground (1948) De Francesco
Nero (1922) Rapée
Nerve of Some People (1954) Craig, E.
Nevada Badmen (1951) Caswell
Nevada City (1941) Feuer
Nevada Smith (1965) Newman
Nevadan (1950) Morton
Never a Dull Moment (1943) Salter
Never a Dull Moment (1950) Hollander
Never a Dull Moment (1968) Brunner
Never Alone (1958) Katz, F.
Never Bug an Ant (1969) Goodwin
Never Fear (1949) Stevens, L.
Never Give a Sucker an Even Break (1941) Previn, C.
Never Love a Stranger (1958) Scott, Raymond
Never Say Die (1939) Roder
Never Say Goodbye (1946) Hollander
Never Say Goodbye (1955) Skinner, F.
Never So Few (1959) Friedhofer
Never Sock a Baby (1939) Timberg
Never Steal Anything Small (1958) Mancini
Never Too Late (1965) Rose
Never Trust a Gambler (1951) Morton
Never Wave at a WAC (1953) Bernstein, E.
New Car (1931) Bradley
New Deal (1933) Dietrich
New Dimensions (1968) Lackey
New England Folk Painter, Erastus Salisbury Field (1968) Repine
New Faces Come Back (1946) Applebaum
New Faces of 1937 (1937) Webb
New Fields in the Old Dominions (1949) Marshall, C.
New Frontier (1939) Lava
New Girl (1959) Scott, Tony
New Hampshire (1940) Palmer, S.
New Homestead (1937) De Nat
New Horizons (1940) Jackson, H.
New Horizons (1958) Baksa
New Interns (1964) Hagen
New Kind of Love (1963) Stevens, L.
New Look Is the Anxious Look (1959) Overton
New Mexico (1951) Moraweck
New Moon (1931) Axt
New Moon (1940) Stothart
New Neighbor (1953) Plumb
New Orleans (1929) Riesenfeld
New Orleans Uncensored (1955) Bakaleinikoff, M.
New Pioneers (1950) Koff
New Shoes (1936) Ward, E.
New Spirit (1942) Applebaum
New Spirit (1942) Wallace
New Tobaccoland, U.S.A. (1947) Mamorsky
New Tools for Learning (1952) Kraushaar
New Venezuela (1954) Harline
New Ways of Seeing (1954) Fine
New Wine (1941) Rozsa
New World of Stainless Steel (1960) Norlin
New York 100 (1967) Bazelon
New York City (1948) Jackson, H.
New York, City of Magic (1958) Kay, U.
New York City—the Most (1968) Kaplan, S.
New York Confidential (1955) Mullendore
New York Eye and Ear Control (1964) Cherry
New York: The Anytime City (1966) Martin, R.
New York Town (1941) Shuken
New York University (1952) Powell, M.
Newcomer (1938) Scheib
Newcomers (1953) Agostini
News Hound (1955) Sharples, Winston
News Hounds (1947) Kay, Edward
News Oddities (1940) De Nat
Newsboys Home (1938) Skinner, F.
Next Ten (1957) Meakin
Next Time I Marry (1938) Webb
Next Time We Love (1936) Waxman
Next Voice You Hear (1950) Raksin
Niagara (1953) Kaplan, S.
Niagara Falls (1941) Ward, E.
Niagara Fools (1956) Wheeler
Nice Doggy (1952) Scheib
Nice Girl? (1941) Skinner, F.
Nice Girl Like Me (1969) Williams, P.
Nice Women (1931) Bibo
Nick Carter, Master Detective (1939) Amfitheatrof
Nick's Coffee Pot (1939) Scheib
Nifty Nineties (1941) Wolcott
Night and Day (1946) Steiner, M.
Night and the City (1950) Waxman
Night Angel (1931) Goulding
Night at Earl Carroll's (1940) Young, V.
Night at the Opera (1935) Stothart
Night at the Troc (1939) DiMaggio
Night Before Christmas (1933) Harline
Night Before Christmas (1941) Bradley
Night Before the Divorce (1942) Harline
Night Cargo (1935) Zahler
Night Club Girl (1944) Skinner, F.
Night Descends on Treasure Island (1939) Bakaleinikoff, C.
Night Editor (1946) Castelnuovo-Tedesco
Night Flight (1933) Stothart
Night for Crime (1942) Zahler
Night Freight (1955) Kay, Edward
Night Has a Thousand Eyes (1948) Young, V.
Night Hawk (1938) Feuer

Night Holds Terror (1955) Cailliet
Night in a Music Hall (1939) DiMaggio
Night in Casablanca (1946) Janssen
Night in Hollywood (1953) Green, P.
Night in New Orleans (1942) Sawtell
Night in Paradise (1946) Skinner, F.
Night Into Morning (1951) Dragon
Night Is Young (1935) Stothart
Night Life in Chicago (1948) Nussbaum
Night Life in the Army (1942) Scheib
Night Life in Tokyo (1960) Scheib
Night Life of the Bugs (1936) Dietrich
Night Life of the Gods (1935) Morton
Night Must Fall (1937) Ward, E.
Night of Adventure (1944) Harline
Night of Evil (1962) Holop
Night of January 16th (1941) Carbonara
Night of June 13th (1932) Leipold
Night of Nights (1939) Young, V.
Night of the Blood Beast (1958) Laszlo
Night of the Generals (1967) Jarre
Night of the Grizzly (1966) Stevens, L.
Night of the Hunter (1955) Schumann
Night of the Quarter Moon (1959) Glasser
Night Parade (1930) Webb
Night Passage (1957) Tiomkin
Night People (1954) Mockridge
Night Plane from Chungking (1943) Carbonara
Night Raiders (1952) Kraushaar
Night Ride (1930) Perry
Night Riders (1939) Lava
Night Riders of Montana (1951) Wilson, S.
Night Runner (1957) Stein, H.
Night Shift (1942) Blitzstein
Night Song (1947) Stevens, L.
Night They Raided Minsky's (1968) Strouse
Night Tide (1961) Raksin
Night Time in Nevada (1948) Butts
Night to Remember (1942) Heymann
Night Train to Memphis (1946) Butts
Night Train to Mundo Fine (1966) Bath
Night Unto Night (1949) Waxman
Night Waitress (1936) Webb
Night Walker (1964) Mizzy
Night Watch (1928) Bierman
Night Watch: The Art of Rembrandt (1952) Belasco
Night Watchman (1938) Stalling
Night Wind (1948) Kraushaar
Night Without Sleep (1952) Mockridge
Night Work (1930) Zuro
Night World (1932) Newman
Nightfall (1956) Duning
Nightingale (1914) Klein, Manuel
Nightingale (1930) Levey
Nightmare (1942) Skinner, F.
Nightmare (1956) Gilbert, H.
Nightmare Alley (1947) Mockridge
Nightmare in the Sun (1964) Glass, Paul
Nightmare of a Goon (1942) Borne
Nikki, Wild Dog of the North (1961) Wallace
Nine from Little Rock (1964) Phillips, B.
Nine Girls (1944) Leipold
Nine Lives Are Not Enough (1941) Lava
Nine Variations on a Dance Theme (1966) Robinson, M.
Nineteen Trees (1960) Hosseini
Ninotchka (1939) Heymann
Nitwits (1935) Webb
Nit-Witty Kitty (1951) Bradley
Nix on Hypnotricks (1941) Timberg
No Barking (1953) Stalling
No Buddy Atoll (1945) Stalling
No, But I Saw the Movie (1961) Daum
No Defense (1929) Dunn
No Dejes la Puerta Abierta (1933) Kaylin
No Down Payment (1957) Harline
No Escape (1953) Shefter
No Exceptions (1943) Buttolph, David
No Exit (1962) Ussachevsky
No Greater Glory (1934) Bassett, R. H.
No Greater Sin (1941) Kay, Edward
No Handouts for Mrs. Hedgepeth (1968) Earls
No Hands on the Clock (1941) Sawtell
No Holds Barred (1952) Kay, Edward
No Hunting (1954) Wallace
No Ifs, Ands or Butts (1954) Sharples, Winston
No Leave, No Love (1946) Stoll
No Man of Her Own (1950) Friedhofer
No Man's Land (1964) Mendoza-Nava
No Man's Woman (1955) Butts
No Minor Vices (1948) Waxman
No More Ladies (1935) Ward, E.
No Mutton fer Nuttin' (1943) Timberg
No Name on the Bullet (1959) Stein, H.
No News Is Good News (1943) Terr
No! No! A Thousand Times No!! (1935) Steiner, G.
No, No, Nanette (1930) Copping
No, No, Nanette (1940) Collins
No One Man (1932) Rainger
No Other Choice (1964) Epstein
No Parking Hare (1953) Stalling
No Pets Allowed (1952) Jackson, H.
No Place for a Lady (1943) Zahler
No Place Like Home (1946) Stringer
No Place Like Rome (1936) Kopp, R.
No Place Like Rome (1953) Sharples, Winston
No Place to Go (1939) Roemheld
No Place to Hide (1956) Gilbert, H.
No Questions Asked (1951) Stevens, L.
No Room for the Groom (1952) Skinner, F.
No Room for Wilderness? (1968) Tracey
No Sad Songs for Me (1950) Duning
No Sail (1945) Wallace
No Sleep for Percy (1955) Scheib
No Smoking (1951) Smith, P.

No Teacher Alone (1957) Gillis
No Time for Comedy (1940) Roemheld
No Time for Flowers (1952) Gilbert, H.
No Time for Love (1943) Young, V.
No Time for Sergeants (1958) Buttolph, David
No Time to Be Young (1957) Bakaleinikoff, M.
No Way Out (1950) Newman
Noah's Ark (1929) Reiser
Noah's Ark (1959) Bruns
Noah's Outing (1932) Scheib
Nob Hill (1945) Buttolph, David
Nobody Lives Forever (1946) Deutsch
Nobody's Baby (1937) Hatley
Nobody's Children (1940) Parrish
Nobody's Darling (1943) Scharf, W.
Nobody's Perfect (1968) Gertz
Nocturne (1947) Harline
None But the Brave (1965) Williams, J.
None But the Lonely Heart (1944) Eisler
None Goes His Way Alone (1957) Applebaum
None Shall Escape (1944) Toch
Nonsense Newsreel (1953) Scheib
Noose for a Gunman (1960) Shefter
Noose Hangs High (1948) Schumann
Nora Prentiss (1947) Waxman
Norma (1970) Barber
Normal Love (1964) Conrad
Norman Normal (1967) Lava
North by Northwest (1959) Herrmann
North Carolina, Variety Vacationland (1950) Mason, W.
North of Nome (1936) Zahler
North of the Border (1946) Mayfield
North of the Sahara (1954) Jackson, H.
North of the Yukon (1939) Cutner
North Pal (1953) Sharples, Winston
North Star (1943) Copland
North to Alaska (1960) Mockridge
North to the Klondike (1942) Skinner, F.
North West Mounted Police (1940) Young, V.
North Woods (1931) Dietrich
Northern Mites (1960) Sharples, Winston
Northern Patrol (1953) Kay, Edward
Northern Pursuit (1943) Deutsch
Northern Rampart (1946) Shilkret, N.
Northward, Ho! (1940) Amfitheatrof
Northwest Hounded Police (1946) Bradley
Northwest Mousie (1953) Sharples, Winston
Northwest Outpost (1947) Armbruster
Northwest Passage (1940) Stothart
Northwest Passage (1943) Applebaum
Northwest Rangers (1942) Amfitheatrof
Northwest Stampede (1948) Sawtell
Northwest Territory (1951) Kay, Edward
Northwest Trail (1945) Sanucci
Northwest U.S.A. (1945) Lloyd, N.
Norway Replies (1944) Shaindlin
Norwood (1970) de Lory
Nose (1966) Seletsky
Nosotros (1962) Kay, U.
Nostradamus (1938) Snell
Nostradamus and the Queen (1953) Kopp, R.
Nostradamus IV (1944) Shilkret, N.
Nostradamus Says So (1953) Kopp, R.
Not a Ladies' Man (1942) Leipold
Not as a Stranger (1955) Antheil
Not by Chance (1957) Bergsma
Not Damaged (1930) Lipschultz
Not Enough (1968) Shankar
Not Exactly Gentlemen (1931) Brunelli
Not Ghoulty (1959) Sharples, Winston
Not of This Earth (1957) Stein, R.
Not Tonight Henry (1961) Borne
Not Wanted (1949) Stevens, L.
Not With MY Wife, You Don't! (1966) Williams, J.
Notes to You (1941) Stalling
Nothing But a Man (1964) Kirk, W.
Nothing But the Tooth (1947) Stalling
Nothing But Trouble (1944) Shilkret, N.
Nothing Sacred (1937) Levant
Nothing to Sneeze At (1960) Murphy, M.
Notorious (1946) Webb
Notorious Affair (1930) Copping
Notorious Cleopatra (1970) Lance
Notorious Daughter of Fanny Hill (1966) More
Notorious Elinor Lee (1940) Shilkret, J.
Notorious Gentleman (1935) Roemheld
Notorious Landlady (1962) Duning
Notorious Sophie Lang (1934) Leipold
Nova Scotia (1945) De Francesco
Novelty Shop (1936) De Nat
Now, Hare This (1957) Franklyn
Now Hear This (1962) Lava
Now I'll Tell (1934) Friedhofer
Now That April's Here (1958) Bath
Now That Summer Is Gone (1938) Stalling
Now, Voyager (1942) Steiner, M.
Nude on the Moon (1962) Hart
Nudes on Tiger Reef (1965) Karmen
Nuisance (1933) Axt
Number of Things (1960) Elliott, Don
Number One (1969) Frontiere
Nun and the Sergeant (1962) Fielding
Nun's Story (1959) Waxman
Nuptiae (1969) Harrison
Nurse Edith Cavell (1939) Collins
Nurse Maid (1932) Stalling
Nurse Mates (1940) Timberg
Nurse to Meet Ya (1955) Sharples, Winston
Nurse's Secret (1941) Lava
Nursery Crimes (1943) Worth, P.
Nursery Rhyme Mysteries (1943) Terr
Nutrition (1943) Applebaum
Nuts and Volts (1963) Lava
Nutty Network (1939) Scheib
Nutty News (1942) Stalling

Nutty Pine Cabin (1942) Calker
Nutty Professor (1963) Scharf, W.
Nymphs of the Lake (1944) De Francesco

O'er the Ramparts We Watched (19??) Loboda
O'Shaughnessy's Boy (1935) Axt
O, My Darling Clementine (1943) Skiles
O-Solar-Meow (1966) Poddany
O. Henry's Full House (1952) Newman
O.K. End Here (1963) Coleman, O.
O.S.S. (1946) Amfitheatrof
Objective, Burma! (1945) Waxman
Obliging Young Lady (1941) Webb
Obmaru (1953) Dunham
Ocean Bruise (1965) Sharples, Winston
Ocean's Eleven (1960) Riddle
Oceans of Love (1956) Scheib
Odd Ant Out (1970) Goodwin
Odd Couple (1968) Hefti
Odds Against (1966) Shapiro
Odds Against Tomorrow (1959) Lewis, John
Odds and Ends (1959) Jacobs, H.
Ode on a Grecian Urn (1954) Brant
Ode to Victory (1943) Shilkret, N.
Odette (1950) Collins
Odor of the Day (1948) Stalling
Odor-able Kitty (1944) Stalling
Odyssey (1912) Selden
Odyssey (1964) Laderman
Of Earth and Fire (1968) Bazelon
Of Feline Bondage (1965) Poddany
Of Fox and Hounds (1940) Stalling
Of Human Bondage (1934) Steiner, M.
Of Human Bondage (1946) Korngold
Of Human Hearts (1938) Stothart
Of Love and Desire (1963) Stein, R.
Of Men and Demons (1970) Jones
Of Mice and Magic (1953) Sharples, Winston
Of Mice and Men (1940) Copland
Of Mice and Menace (1954) Sharples, Winston
Of Rice and Hen (1952) Stalling
Of Sea and Ships (1966) Reichert
Of the Same Gender (1968) Starr, P.
Of Thee I Sting (1946) Stalling
Of This We Are Proud (1946) Carbonara
Off Limits (1953) Van Cleave
Off the Record (1939) Deutsch
Off the Record (Trailer, 1939) Jackson, H.
Off to China (1936) Scheib
Off to the Opera (1952) Scheib
Off to the Races (1954) Lava
Off We Glow (1952) Sharples, Winston
Office Boy (1932) Bradley
Office Love-In, White Collar Style (1968) Gigagusky
Office Wife (1930) Reiser
Officer Duck (1939) Wallace
Officer Pooch (1941) Bradley
Often an Orphan (1948) Stalling
Oh Dad, Poor Dad, Mamma's Hung You in the Closet and I'm Feelin' So Sad (1967) Hefti
Oh Dem Watermelons (1965) Reich
Oh, for a Man (1930) Brunelli
Oh Gentle Spring (1942) Scheib
Oh, Men! Oh, Women! (1957) Mockridge
Oh Sailor Behave (1930) Leonardi
Oh! Susanna (1933) Scheib
Oh! Susanna (1951) Butts
Oh, Teacher (1932) Dietrich
Oh, What a Night (1944) Kay, Edward
Ohio Story (1965) Roznyai
Oil Can Mystery (1933) Scheib
Oil Can—and Does (1940) Bennett, T.
Oil for Aladdin's Lamp (1941) Colombo
Oil for the Lamps of China (1935) Roemheld
Oiltown, U.S.A. (1952) Carmichael
Oily American (1953) Stalling
Oily Bird (1954) Sharples, Winston
Oily Hare (1951) Stalling
Okay for Pictures (1946) Lava
Okay for Sound (1946) Lava
Okay, Jose (1936) Jackson, H.
Okey Dokey Donkey (1958) Sharples, Winston
Oklahoma! (1955) Deutsch
Oklahoma Annie (1952) Scott, N.
Oklahoma Badlands (1948) Glickman, M.
Oklahoma Blues (1948) Kay, Edward
Oklahoma Justice (1951) Kraushaar
Oklahoma Kid (1939) Steiner, M.
Oklahoma Renegades (1940) Sawtell
Oklahoma Territory (1958) Glasser
Oklahoma Woman (1956) Stein, R.
Oklahoman (1957) Salter
Old Acquaintance (1943) Waxman
Old Age Pension (1935) Dietrich
Old Army Game (1943) Smith, P.
Old Bangum (1956) Townsend
Old Barn Dance (1938) Colombo
Old Blackout Joe (1942) Worth, P.
Old Dark House (1932) Broekman
Old Dog Tray (1935) Scheib
Old Fashioned Girl (1949) Gilbert, H.
Old Fashioned News Reel (1933) Vincent, P.
Old-Fashioned Way (1934) Leipold
Old Fire Horse (1939) Scheib
Old Frontier (1950) Wilson, S.
Old Glory (1939) Stalling
Old Grey Hare (1944) Stalling
Old Heidelberg (1915) Breil
Old Hickory (1940) Jackson, H.
Old Homestead (1935) Jackson, H.
Old Homestead (1942) Glickman, M.
Old House (1936) Bradley
Old Hutch (1936) Axt
Old Ironsides (1927) Riesenfeld
Old Kentucky Hounds (1934) Zahler
Old King Cole (1933) Churchill
Old Los Angeles (1948) Gold

Old MacDonald Duck (1941) Harline
Old MacDonald Had a Farm (1945) Sharples, Winston
Old Maid (1939) Steiner, M.
Old Man and the Flower (1962) Pintoff
Old Man and the Sea (1958) Tiomkin
Old Mill (1937) Harline
Old Mill Pond (1936) Bradley
Old Mother Clobber (1958) Scheib
Old Mother Hubbard (1935) Stalling
Old Natchez on the Mississippi (1940) Bakaleinikoff, C.
Old Nest (1921) Swinnen
Old New Mexico (1940) Bakaleinikoff, C.
Old New Orleans (1940) Bakaleinikoff, C.
Old Oaken Bucket (1941) Scheib
Old Oklahoma Plains (1952) Wilson, S.
Old-Order Amish (1959) Behrens
Old Overland Trail (1953) Butts
Old Pioneer (1934) Bradley
Old Plantation (1935) Bradley
Old Rockin' Chair Tom (1948) Bradley
Old San Francisco (1927) Riesenfeld
Old Sequoia (1945) Wallace
Old Shell Game (1948) Sharples, Winston
Old Shep (1934) Axt
Old Smokey (1938) Wheeler
Old South (1940) Amfitheatrof
Old Swimmin' Hole (1940) Kay, Edward
Old Testament Series: Moses, Leader of God's People (1958) Nussbaum
Old Vamps for New (1930) Zahler
Old Wives for New (1918) Gottschalk
Old Yeller (1957) Wallace
Ole Rex (1961) Bagley
Olga's Girls (1964) Otis
Olio for Jasper (1946) Wheeler
Olive Oyl and Water Don't Mix (1942) Timberg
Olive Oyl for President (1948) Sharples, Winston
Olive's Boithday Presink (1941) Timberg
Olive's Sweepstake Ticket (1941) Timberg
Oliver! (1968) Green, J.
Ollie the Owl (1962) Sharples, Winston
Olympic Champ (1941) Smith, P.
Olympic Class (1948) De Francesco
Olympic Elk (1951) Smith, P.
Olympic Water Wizards (1948) De Francesco
Omaha Trail (1942) Snell
Omar Khayyam (1957) Young, V.
Omoo-Omoo, the Shark God (1949) Glasser
On a Clear Day You Can See Forever (1970) Riddle
On Again—Off Again (1937) Webb
On an Island with You (1948) Stoll
On Borrowed Time (1939) Waxman
On Dangerous Ground (1951) Herrmann
On Fighting Witches (1966) Cherry
On Guard (1969) Bernstein, C.
On Her Bed of Roses (1966) Greene, J.
On Ice (1935) Lewis
On Moonlight Bay (1951) Steiner, M.
On Our Merry Way (1948) Roemheld
On Probation (1935) Stewart, C.
On Stage Everybody (1950) Van Cleave
On-Stream (1955) Lava
On Such a Night (1937) Toch
On the Avenue (1937) Mockridge
On the Beach (1959) Gold
On the Bowery (1957) Mills, C.
On the Double (1961) Stevens, L.
On the Farm (1932) Carbonara
On the Isle of Samoa (1950) Morton
On the Level (1930) Lipschultz
On the Loose (1951) Harline
On the Night of the Fire (1939) Rozsa
On the Old Spanish Trail (1947) Glickman, M.
On the Riviera (1951) Hagen
On the Road to Monterrey (1944) Nussbaum
On the Shores of Nova Scotia (1947) Nussbaum
On the Sound (1963) Gryce
On the Spot (1940) Kay, Edward
On the Sunny Side (1941) Mockridge
On the Threshold of Space (1956) Murray
On the Town (1949) Salinger
On the Waterfront (1954) Bernstein, L.
On This Mountain (1965) Mendoza-Nava
On Trial (1939) Kaun
On Watch (1949) Engel
On with the Show (1929) Copping
On Your Back (1930) Lipschultz
On Your Own (1943) Jackson, H.
On Your Toes (1939) Roemheld
Once a Doctor (1936) Roemheld
Once a Lady (1931) Kopp, R.
Once a Sinner (1930) Kay, Arthur
Once a Thief (1950) Michelet
Once a Thief (1964) Schifrin
Once Before I Die (1966) Vardi
Once in a Blue Moon (1935) Antheil
Once More, My Darling (1949) Firestone
Once Over (1964) Sharples, Winston
Once Over Lightly (1938) Snell
Once Over Lightly (1944) Lava
Once There Was a City (1969) Kaplan, S.
Once Upon a Honeymoon (1942) Dolan
Once Upon a Horse (1958) Skinner, F.
Once Upon a Rhyme (1950) Sharples, Winston
Once Upon a Sunday (1957) Fenyo
Once Upon a Time (1944) Hollander
Once Upon a Time (1969) Piserchio
Once Upon a Wintertime (1944) Sack
Once Upon the Wabash (1953) Norlin
Once You Kiss a Stranger (1969) Fagas
One Against the World (1939) Amfitheatrof
One and Only Genuine, Original Family Band (1968) Elliott, J.
One-Armed Bandit (1939) Churchill
One Body Too Many (1944) Laszlo

One Cab's Family (1952) Bradley
One Crowded Night (1940) Webb
One Desire (1955) Skinner, F.
One Droopy Knight (1957) Bradley
One Exciting Adventure (1934) Roemheld
One Exciting Night (1922) Pesce
One Exciting Week (1946) Butts
One-Eyed Jacks (1960) Friedhofer
One Fine Day (1967) Lee, B.
One Foot in Heaven (1941) Steiner, M.
One Foot in Hell (1960) Frontiere
One Froggy Evening (1955) Franklyn
One Funny Knight (1957) Sharples, Winston
One Girl's Confession (1953) Divina
One Gun Gary in the Nick of Time (1939) Scheib
One Ham's Family (1943) Bradley
One Heavenly Night (1930) Tours
One Hour Late (1934) Satterfield
One Hour with You (1932) Leipold
One Hundred and One Dalmatians (1960) Bruns
One Hundred Men and a Girl (1937) Skinner, F.
One Hundred Million Dollars a Day (1967) Martin, R.
One in a Million (1937) Buttolph, David
One Last Fling (1949) Buttolph, David
One Law for Both (1917) Beynon
One Mad Kiss (1930) Brunelli
One Man Navy (1941) Scheib
One Man's Law (1940) Feuer
One Man's Lifetime (1951) Merrick
One Man's Way (1964) Markowitz
One Meat Brawl (1947) Stalling
One Mile from Heaven (1937) Kaylin
One Million B.C. (1940) Heymann
One Minute to Zero (1952) Young, V.
One More River (1934) Harling
One More Spring (1935) Buttolph, David
One More Time (1931) Marsales
One More Tomorrow (1946) Steiner, M.
One Mother's Family (1939) Bradley
One Mouse in a Million (1939) Scheib
One Mysterious Night (1944) Sawtell
One Naked Night (1963) McIntyre
One New York Night (Trailer, 1935) Ward, E.
One Night in Lisbon (1941) Young, V.
One Night in the Tropics (1940) Skinner, F.
One Night of Love (1934) Schertzinger
One Note Tony (1947) Scheib
One of the Family (1962) Sharples, Winston
One Potato, Two Potato (1964) Fried
One Quack Mind (1951) Sharples, Winston
One Rainy Afternoon (1936) Newman
One Romantic Night (1930) Riesenfeld
One Spring Day (1970) Bernstein, C.
One Step Ahead of My Shadow (1933) Marsales
One Sunday Afternoon (1933) Leipold
One Sunday Afternoon (1949) Buttolph, David
One-Tenth of a Nation (1940) Harris, R.
One Third of a Nation . . . (1939) Shilkret, N.
One Thrilling Night (1942) Sanucci
One Too Many (1951) Shefter
One Touch of Venus (1948) Ronell
One, Two, Three (1961) Previn, A.
One Way Passage (1932) Harling
One Way Street (1950) Skinner, F.
One Way Ticket to Hell (1956) Drasnin
One Way to Love (1945) Skiles
One Way Wahine (1965) Hanson, J.
One Weak Vacation (1962) Sharples, Winston
One Week in October (1963) Hopkins, K.
One Woman Idea (1929) Kay, Arthur
One World or None (1947) Applebaum
Onionhead (1958) Buttolph, David
Only Angels Have Wings (1939) Tiomkin
Only Game in Town (1968) Jarre
Only One New York (1964) Delugg
Only Saps Work (1930) Rainger
Only the Brave (1930) Harling
Only the Valiant (1951) Waxman
Ontario—Land of Lakes (1949) Nussbaum
Oompahs (1951) Sherman
Op, Pop, Wham and Bop (1965) Sharples, Winston
Open House (1953) Scheib
Open Secret (1948) Gilbert, H.
Open the Door and See All the People (1964) Wilder
Open Up That Golden Gate (1952) Lava
Open Your Eyes (1965) Raim
Opened by Mistake (1940) Leipold
Opera Caper (1967) Sharples, Winston
Opera Night (1935) Scheib
Opera School (1952) Applebaum
Operation A-Bomb (1952) Applebaum
Operation Bikini (1963) Baxter
Operation Bottleneck (1961) Sawtell
Operation CIA (1965) Dunlap
Operation Cold Feet (1957) Wheeler
Operation Dames (1959) Markowitz
Operation Eichmann (1961) Borisoff
Operation Haylift (1950) Garcia
Operation Jack Frost (1950) Mamorsky
Operation Mad Ball (1957) Duning
Operation Mexico (1952) Kraushaar
Operation Pacific (1951) Steiner, M.
Operation Petticoat (1959) Rose
Operation Rabbit (1950) Stalling
Operation Sawdust (1953) Wheeler
Operation Secret (1952) Webb
Operation Shanghai (1966) Greene, W.
Operation Snafu (1945) Stalling
Operation Underground (1946) Lopez
Operations Wildlife (1948) Marshall, C.
Operator 13 (1934) Axt
Opportunity America (1953) Van Camp
Opposite Sex (1956) Stoll
Opry House (1929) Stalling
Optical Poem (1938) Snell
Opus Op (1967) Macero

Orange Blossoms for Violet (1952) Jackson, H.
Orchestra Wives (1942) Harline
Orchids to Charlie (1941) Antheil
Orchids to You (1935) Lange
Ordeal by Ice (1945) Applebaum
Orders from Tokyo (1945) Colombo
Oregon Passage (1958) Dunlap
Oregon Trail (1959) Dunlap
Oregon Trail Scouts (1947) Glickman, M.
Oresteia of Aeschylus (1955) Hallstrom
Organ Grinder (1933) Marsales
Orgia (1967) Ito
Orgy of the Dead (1965) Mendoza-Nava
Orient Express (1934) Friedhofer
Oriental Evil (1952) Glasser
Oriental Paradise (1937) Grever
Orozco Murals: Quetzalcoatl (1962) Newman, T.
Orphan Duck (1939) Scheib
Orphan Egg (1953) Scheib
Orphans of the Storm (1921) Gottschalk
Orphans of the Street (1938) Feuer
Orphans' Benefit (1934) Churchill
Orphans' Benefit (1941) Churchill
Orphans' Picnic (1936) Malotte
Oscar (1966) Faith
Osmosis (1948) Brant
Ostrich Egg and I (1956) Poddany
Ostrich Feathers (1937) Lessner
Other City (1957) Strouse
Other Love (1947) Rozsa
Other Men's Wives (1919) Schertzinger
Ohter Men's Women (1931) See p. 8
Other Woman (1942) Lange
Other Woman (1954) Gold
Otto Nobetter and the Railroad Gang (1957) Simmons
Ounce of Pink (1965) Lava
Our African Frontier (1943) Dunn
Our Alaskan Frontier (1944) Jackson, H.
Our Battle-Wagons Are Rolling (1942) Smith, P.
Our Betters (1933) Kaun
Our Daily Bread (1934) Newman
Our Dancing Daughters (1928) Axt
Our Frontier in Italy (1944) Lava
Our Funny Finny Friends (1949) Sharples, Winston
Our Gang Follies of 1938 (1937) Hatley
Our Hearts Were Growing Up (1946) Young, V.
Our Hearts Were Young and Gay (1944) Heymann
Our Heritage (1965) Palmer, S.
Our Leading Citizen (1939) Carbonara
Our Little Girl (1935) Brunelli
Our Magic Land (1957) Kleinsinger
Our Man Flint (1965) Goldsmith
Our Miss Brooks (1956) Webb
Our Modern Maidens (1929) Axt
Our Neighbors—the Carters (1939) Young, V.
Our Northern Neighbour (1944) Agostini
Our Old Car (1946) Terr
Our Relations (1936) Shield
Our Schools Have Kept Us Free (1964) Kleinsinger
Our Town (1940) Copland
Our Very Own (1949) Young, V.
Our Vines Have Tender Grapes (1945) Kaper
Our Vines Have Tender Grapes (Trailer, 1945) Terr
Our Wife (1941) Shuken
Out Again, In Again (1948) Scheib
Out and Out Rout (1966) Lava
Out California Way (1946) Scott, N.
Out-Foxed (1949) Bradley
Out of Darkness (1941) Amfitheatrof
Out of Darkness (1956) Carlson
Out of Evil (1950) Rathaus
Out of It (1969) Small
Out of Scale (1951) Smith, P.
Out of Sight (1966) de Lory
Out of the Blue (1947) Dragon
Out of the Desert (1956) Jackson, H.
Out of the Ether (1933) De Nat
Out of the Fog (1941) Roemheld
Out of the Frying Pan Into the Firing Line (1942) Smith, P.
Out of the Night (1945) Erdody
Out of the Past (1947) Webb
Out of the Ruins (1946) Applebaum
Out of the Tiger's Mouth (1962) Wells
Out of the Woods (1955) Kleinsinger
Out of This Whirl (1959) Sharples, Winston
Out of This World (1945) Simeone
Out-of-Towners (1969) Jones
Out on a Limb (1950) Dubin
Out to Punch (1956) Sharples, Winston
Out West with the Hardys (1938) Snell
Out West with the Peppers (1940) Cutner
Outbreak (1949) Brant
Outcast (1928) Schertzinger
Outcast (1937) Toch
Outcast (1954) Butts
Outcast Souls (1927) Hoffman, M.
Outcasts of Poker Flat (1952) Friedhofer
Outcasts of the City (1958) Sukman
Outdoor Living (1944) Jackson, H.
Outer Space Visitor (1959) Scheib
Outlaw (1941) Young, V.
Outlaw Brand (1948) Kay, Edward
Outlaw Country (1948) Greene, W.
Outlaw Deputy (1935) Zahler
Outlaw Gold (1950) Kay, Edward
Outlaw Queen (1956) Kauer
Outlaw Roundup (1944) Zahler
Outlaw Trail (1944) Sanucci
Outlaw Treasure (1954) Calker
Outlaw Women (1951) Greene, W.
Outlaw's Daughter (1954) Kraushaar
Outlaw's Son (1957) Baxter
Outlaws Is Coming (1965) Dunlap
Outlaws of Boulder Pass (1943) Lange, J.
Outlaws of Cherokee Trail (1941) Skiles
Outlaws of Pine Ridge (1942) Glickman, M.

Outlaws of Santa Fe (1944) Glickman, M.
Outlaws of Stampede Pass (1943) Kay, Edward
Outlaws of Texas (1950) Kay, Edward
Outlaws of the Desert (1941) Leipold
Outlaws of the Plains (1946) Zahler
Outlaws of the Rockies (1945) Skiles
Outpost (1942) Scheib
Outpost (1944) Stalling
Outpost in Morocco (1949) Michelet
Outrage (1950) Sawtell
Outrage (1964) North
Outriders (1950) Previn, A.
Outriders (1963) Hoffman, D.
Outside Dope (1965) Sharples, Winston
Outside of Paradise (1938) Colombo
Outside the 3-Mile Limit (1940) Zahler
Outside the Law (1930) Roemheld
Outside These Walls (1939) Morgan, F.
Outsider (1961) Rosenman
Over 18, . . . and Ready! (1969) Bath
Over 21 (1945) Skiles
Over Exposed (1956) Bakaleinikoff, M.
Over-Exposed (1969) Porée
Over My Dead Body (1942) Mockridge
Over the Andes (1944) Nussbaum
Over the Border (1950) Kay, Edward
Over the Goal (1937) Roemheld
Over the Hill (1920) Rapée
Over the Santa Fe Trail (1947) Gertz
Over the Seas to Belfast (1946) Mayfield
Over the Wall (1937) Jackson, H.
Over the Wall (1944) Jackson, H.
Overdrive (1967) Ashley
Overland Express (1938) Kilenyi
Overland Mail Robbery (1943) Glickman, M.
Overland Pacific (1954) Gertz
Overland Riders (1946) Zahler
Overland Stagecoach (1943) Erdody
Overland Telegraph (1951) Sawtell
Overland Trails (1948) Kay, Edward
Overland with Kit Carson (1939) Cutner
Overseas Roundup (1945) Jackson, H.
Overseas Roundup No. 2 (1945) Jackson, H.
Overseas Roundup No. 3 (1945) Jackson, H.
Overture to Glory (1940) Olshanetsky
Overture to Tomorrow (1966) Bazelon
Overture to William Tell (1947) Calker
Owl and the Pussy Cat (1939) Scheib
Owl and the Pussycat (1934) Scheib
Owl and the Pussycat (1970) Halligan
Owly to Bed (1959) Sharples, Winston
Ox-Bow Incident (1942) Mockridge
Oxford Student (1952) Forrell
Oyster and Virginia (1948) Marshall, C.
Ozzie Ostrich Comes to Town (1937) Scheib

P. J. (1967) Hefti
Pace That Thrills (1952) Sawtell
Pacific Blackout (1941) Carbonara
Pacific Frontier (1942) Lava
Pacific Island (1949) Horst
Pacific Liner (1939) Bennett, R. R.
Pacific Paradise (1960) Shefter
Pacific Rendezvous (1942) Snell
Pacific Sports (1955) Jackson, H.
Pack Up Your Troubles (1932) Shield
Pack Up Your Troubles (1939) Kaylin
Package for Jasper (1944) Diamond, L.
Pad (and How to Use It) (1966) Garcia
Paddle to the Sea (1966) Applebaum
Paddle Your Own Canoe (1950) Jackson, H.
Paddy (1970) Rubinstein, J.
Paddy O'Day (1936) Kaylin
Paddy the Next Best Thing (1933) De Francesco
Pagan (1929) Axt
Pagan Love Song (1950) Deutsch
Pagan Moon (1931) Marsales
Page Miss Glory (1935) Roemheld
Paid in Full (1914) Klein, Manuel
Paid in Full (1950) Young, V.
Paint Pot Symphony (1949) Scheib
Paint Your Wagon (1969) Riddle
Painted Angel (1929) Reiser
Painted Desert (1931) Gromon
Painted Hills (1951) Amfitheatrof
Painted Stallion (1937) Hajos
Painted Veil (1934) Stothart
Painted Woman (1932) Friedhofer
Painter and the Pointer (1945) Calker
Painting (1962) Taubman
Painting the Clouds with Sunshine (1951) Jackson, H.
Pair of Sneakers (1969) Goodwin
Pajama Game (1957) Heindorf
Pajama Party (1931) Shield
Pajama Party (1964) Baxter
Pal, Canine Detective (1949) Laszlo
Pal from Texas (1939) Lange, J.
Pal, Fugitive Dog (1950) Laszlo
Pal Joey (1957) Duning
Pal's Adventure (1948) Laszlo
Pal's Gallant Journey (1950) Laszlo
Pal's Return (1948) Laszlo
Pale-Face (1933) Denni
Paleface (1948) Young, V.
Paleface (Trailer, 1948) Schrager
Paleface Pup (1931) Boutelje
Pale Horseman (1946) Brant
Palestine at War (1942) Wolpe
Palm Beach Story (1942) Young, V.
Palm Springs (1936) Leipold
Palm Springs Weekend (1963) Perkins
Palmetto Quail (1946) Grundman
Palmour Street (1950) Applebaum
Palmy Days (1931) Newman
Palomino (1950) Leipold
Pals (1933) Sharples, Winston
Pals of the Pecos (1941) Feuer
Pals of the Saddle (1938) Feuer

Pampas Sky Targets (1952) Stringer
Pan (1937) Bauer
Panama (1946) Anderson
Panama Flo (1932) Lewis, Harold
Panama Hattie (1942) Stoll
Panama Lady (1939) Webb
Pan-Americana (1945) Harline
Pancho (1960) Kleiner
Pancho (1967) Kaplan, S.
Pancho Villa Returns (1950) Breeskin
Pancho's Hideaway (1964) Lava
Pandora (1934) Scheib
Pandora's Box (1943) Scheib
Paneless Window Washer (1937) Timberg
Panhandle (1948) Dunn
Panhandling on Madison Avenue (1964) Sharples, Winston
Panic in the City (1968) Dunlap
Panic in the Streets (1950) Newman
Panic in Year Zero! (1962) Baxter
Panic Is On (1931) Shield
Panther Girl of the Kongo (1955) Butts
Panther's Claw (1942) Zahler
Pantry Pirate (1941) Harline
Papa Gets the Bird (1940) Bradley
Papa's Day of Rest (1951) Scheib
Papa's Delicate Condition (1963) Lilley
Papa's Little Helpers (1951) Scheib
Paper Bullets (1941) Lange, J.
Paper Hanger (1932) De Nat
Paper Hangers (1937) Scheib
Paper Lion (1968) Kellaway
Papillote (1964) Fran
Papoose on the Loose (1961) Wheeler
Pappy's Puppy (1955) Stalling
Parachute Battalion (1941) Webb
Parachute Jumper (1933) Warren
Parachute Jumper (Trailer, 1933) Kaun
Parachute Nurse (1942) Leipold
Parachute to Paradise (1969) Evans
Parade of the Wooden Soldiers (1933) Steiner, G.
Paradine Case (1947) Waxman
Paradise Alley (1962) Steininger
Paradise for Buster (1952) Glasser
Paradise for Three (1938) Ward, E.
Paradise—Hawaiian Style (1965) Lilley
Paramount on Parade (1930) Jackson, H.
Paratroop Command (1958) Stein, R.
Paratroops (1943) Kubik
Pardners (1956) De Vol
Pardon My Gun (1930) Zuro
Pardon My Past (1945) Tiomkin
Pardon My Sarong (1942) Skinner, F.
Pardon My Stripes (1942) Glickman, M.
Pardon Our Nerve (1939) Rose, G.
Pardon Us (1931) Shield
Pardoner's Tale (1954) Muller
Parent Trap (1961) Smith, P.
Paris After Dark (1943) Friedhofer
Paris Blues (1961) Ellington
Paris Bound (1929) Alexander, A.
Paris Calling (1941) Hageman
Paris Follies of 1956 (1955) De Vol
Paris Holiday (1958) Lilley
Paris Honeymoon (1939) Rainger
Paris in Spring (1935) Hollander
Paris in the Spring (1947) Van Cleave
Paris Interlude (1934) Axt
Paris Model (1953) Glasser
Paris on Parade (1938) Shilkret, J.
Paris Playboys (1954) Skiles
Paris-Underground (1945) Tansman
Paris—When It Sizzles (1963) Riddle
Park Avenue Pussycat (1955) Scheib
Park Row (1952) Dunlap
Park Your Baby (1939) De Nat
Parking Space (1933) Dietrich
Parlez Vous Woo (1956) Sharples, Winston
Parnell (1937) Axt
Parole (1936) Previn, C.
Parole Fixer (1940) Carbonara
Parole, Inc (1948) Laszlo
Parrish (1961) Steiner, M.
Parrotville Fire Department (1934) Sharples, Winston
Parrotville Old Folks (1935) Sharples, Winston
Parrotville Post Office (1935) Sharples, Winston
Parson and the Outlaw (1957) Sodja
Parson of Panamint (1941) Leipold
Parson of Panamint (1916) Stickles
Part Time Pal (1947) Bradley
Part Time Wife (1930) Bassett, R. H.
Partners in Time (1946) Moraweck
Partners of the Sunset (1948) Kay, Edward
Partners of the Trail (1944) Kay, Edward
Party (1968) Mancini
Party Fever (1938) Snell
Party Girl (1958) Alexander, J.
Party Lines (1947) Steiner, G.
Party Smarty (1951) Sharples, Winston
Pass the Biscuits Mirandy! (1943) Calker
Passage from Hong Kong (1941) Lava
Passage to Marseille (1944) Steiner, M.
Passage West (1951) Merrick
Passages from "Finnegans Wake" (1966) Kaplan, E.
Passion (1920) Axt
Passion (1920) Rapée
Passion (1954) Forbes
Passion in Hot Hollows (1969) Marini
Passion Street, U.S.A. (1964) Emenegger
Passkey to Danger (1946) Glickman, M.
Passport to Alcatraz (1940) Zahler
Passport to Destiny (1944) Webb
Passport to Hell (1932) Friedhofer
Passport to Nowhere (1947) Shilkret, N.
Past Perfumance (1954) Franklyn
Pastoral (1956) Townsend

Pastoral Panoramas (1950) Nussbaum
Pastry Panic (1951) Scheib
Pastry Town Wedding (1934) Sharples, Winston
Pat and Mike (1952) Raksin
Patch Mah Britches (1935) De Nat
Patch of Blue (1965) Goldsmith
Patchwork Girl of Oz (1914) Gottschalk
Patent Leather Kid (1927) Copping
Paths of Glory (1957) Fried
Patient in Room 18 (1937) Kaun
Patient Porky (1940) Stalling
Patria (1916) Bowers, R. H.
Patrick the Great (1944) Salter
Patriot (1928) Savino
Patriotic Pooches (1943) Scheib
Patriotic Popeye (1957) Sharples, Winston
Patrolling the Ether (1944) Shilkret, N.
Patsy (1964) Raksin
Patterns of Progress (1960) Kaplan, S.
Patton (1969) Goldsmith
Paul Bunyan (1958) Bruns
Paula (1952) Duning
Paunch 'n Judy (1940) De Nat
Pawnbroker (1965) Jones
Pawnee (1957) Sawtell
Paw's Night Out (1955) Wheeler
Pay Day (1944) Stalling
Pay or Die (1960) Raksin
Paying the Piper (1947) Stalling
Payment Deferred (1932) Axt
Payment on Demand (1951) Young, V.
Payoff (1935) Roemheld
Payoff (1943) Dant
Peace Conference (1935) De Nat
Peace for a Gunfighter (1967) Ellis, D.
Peace in the Valley (1964) Sheff
Peace on Earth (1939) Bradley
Peaceful Neighbors (1939) De Nat
Peacemaker (1956) Greeley
Peacemeal (1967) Hamilton
Peace-Time Football (1946) Scheib
Peach-o-Reno (1931) Steiner, M.
Peaches and Cream (1964) Masagni
Peachy Cobbler (1950) Bradley
Peacock Alley (1929) Willson
Pearl (1947) Diaz Conde
Pearl of Death (1944) Sawtell
Pearl of the South Pacific (1955) Forbes
Pearls of the Pacific (1957) Jackson, H.
Peck o' Trouble (1951) Stalling
Peck Up Your Troubles (1945) Stalling
Peck Your Own Home (1960) Sharples, Winston
Peck's Bad Boy (1934) Riesenfeld
Peck's Bad Boy with the Circus (1938) Young, V.
Pecos Pest (1955) Bradley
Peculiar Penguins (1934) Harline
Pedro and Lorenzo (1956) Sharples, Winston
Peekaboo (1957) Sharples, Winston
Pee-kool-yar Sit-chee-ay-shun (1944) Kilfeather
Peeks at Hollywood (1945) Jackson, H.
Peep in the Deep (1940) De Nat
Peep in the Deep (1946) Sharples, Winston
Peeping Penguins (1937) Timberg
Peer Gynt (1915) Beynon
Peer Gynt (1915) Stickles
Peg Leg Pete (1932) Scheib
Peg Leg Pete the Pirate (1935) Scheib
Peg o' My Heart (1933) Stothart
Peggy (1916) Schertzinger
Peggy (1950) Scharf, W.
Peking (1959) Kupferman
Peking Express (1951) Tiomkin
Pelican and the Snipe (1943) Wallace
Pen Point Percussion (1951) Applebaum
Penalty (1941) Snell
Pendulum (1969) Scharf, W.
Penelope (1966) Williams, J.
Penguin for Your Thoughts (1956) Sharples, Winston
Penguin Parade (1938) Stalling
Penguin Pool Murder (1932) Steiner, M.
Penitentes (1915) Breil
Pennies from Heaven (1936) Still
Pennsylvania: Keystone of the Nation (1960) Hopkins, K.
Penny Antics (1955) Sharples, Winston
Penny Pals (1962) Sharples, Winston
Penny Serenade (1941) Harling
Penrod and His Twin Brother (1938) Jackson, H.
Penrod and Sam (1931) Mendoza
Penrod and Sam (1937) Jackson, H.
Penrod's Double Trouble (1938) Jackson, H.
Pent-House Mouse (1963) Poddany
Penthouse Rhythm (1944) Fairchild
People Against O'Hara (1951) Dragon
People Are Bunny (1959) Franklyn
People Are Funny (1946) Schrager
People Between (1947) Applebaum
People Born in September (1929) Shilkret, N.
People Next Door (1970) Sebesky
People of Russia (1943) Nussbaum
People of the Cumberland (1937) North
People on Paper (1945) Terr
People Soup (1969) Lavsky
People Without Fear (1953) Forrell
People Without Place (1954) Laszlo
People's Choice (1946) Zahler
Pepe (1960) Green, J.
Peppermint Tree (1954) Fuller, D
Pére Facts (1968) Rosenboom
Perfect Crime (1928) Zuro
Perfect Furlough (1958) Skinner, F.
Perfect Marriage (1946) Hollander
Perfect Set-Up (1936) Ward, E.
Perfect Snob (1941) Mockridge
Perfect Specimen (1937) Roemheld
Perfect Strangers (1950) Harline
Perfect Tribute (1935) Axt

Performance (1970) Nitzsche
Perilous Holiday (1946) Sawtell
Perilous Journey (1953) Young, V.
Perilous Waters (1948) Schrager
Perils of Nyoka (1942) Glickman, M.
Perils of Pauline (1947) Dolan
Perils of Pauline (1967) Mizzy
Perils of Pearl Pureheart (1949) Scheib
Perils of the Jungle (1941) Lava
Perils of the Royal Mounted (1942) Zahler
Period of Adjustment (1962) Murray
Perri (1957) Smith, P.
Perry Popgun (1961) Sharples, Winston
Person to Bunny (1959) Franklyn
Personal Cleanliness (1945) Smith, P.
Personal Maid's Secret (1935) Jackson, H.
Personal Property (1937) Waxman
Personalities (1942) Hayton
Personality Kid (1934) Kaun
Personality Kid (1946) Steinert
Persons in Hiding (1939) Leipold
Persuader (1957) Carmichael
Pertaining to Marin (1953) Lewin
Peru (1944) Lloyd, N.
Pest in the House (1947) Stalling
Pest Pilot (1941) Timberg
Pest Pupil (1957) Sharples, Winston
Pest That Came to Dinner (1947) Stalling
Pestilent City (1965) Goldman, P.
Pests for Guests (1954) Franklyn
Pests of the West (1949) Smith, P.
Pesty Guest (1965) Greene, W.
Pet Peeve (1954) Bradley
Pet Problems (1954) Scheib
Pet Shop (1932) De Nat
Pet Store (1933) Harline
Pete Hothead (1952) Curtin
Pete Kelly's Blues (1955) Heindorf
Pete Roleum and His Cousins (1939) Eisler
Peter Ibbetson (1935) Toch
Peter Pan (1952) Wallace
Petrified Dog (1948) Schaeffer, P.
Petrified Forest (1936) Kaun
Petrified River—The Story of Uranium (1956) Forrell
Petticoat Fever (1936 trailer) Axt
Petticoat Politics (1941) Feuer
Pettin' in the Park (1934) Spencer, N.
Petty Girl (1950) Duning
Petunia Natural Park (1938) Lewis
Peyton Place (1957) Waxman
Phantom (1943) Zahler
Phantom Cowboy (1941) Feuer
Phantom Empire (1935) Zahler
Phantom from 10,000 Leagues (1955) Stein, R.
Phantom from Space (1953) Lava
Phantom Gold (1938) Zahler
Phantom Killer (1942) Sanucci
Phantom Moustacher (1961) Sharples, Winston
Phantom of 42nd Street (1945) Hajos
Phantom of Chinatown (1940) Kay, Edward
Phantom of the Horse Opera (1961) Wheeler
Phantom of the Opera (1925) Breil
Phantom of the Opera (1943) Ward, E.
Phantom of the Rue Morgue (1954) Buttolph, David
Phantom of the West (1931) Zahler
Phantom President (1932) Leipold
Phantom Raiders (1940) Snell
Phantom Rancher (1940) Porter
Phantom Ranger (1938) Porter
Phantom Rider (1945) Glickman, M.
Phantom Ship (1936) Spencer, N.
Phantom Speaks (1945) Plumb
Phantom Stagecoach (1957) Bakaleinikoff, M.
Phantom Stallion (1954) Butts
Phantom Tollbooth (1969) Elliott, Dean
Phantoms, Inc. (1945) Terr
Pharaoh's Curse (1957) Baxter
Phenix City Story (1955) Sukman
Phffft (1954) Hollander
Philadelphia Story (1940) Waxman
Philbert (1963) Jackson, H.
Philharmaniacs (1953) Sharples, Winston
Philip Evergood (1952) Ames
Philo Vance Returns (1947) Glasser
Philo Vance's Gamble (1947) Levin
Phone Call from a Stranger (1952) Waxman
Phoney Baloney (1945) Kilfeather
Phoney Express (1932) Bradley
Phoney Express (1962) Poddany
Phony News Flashes (1955) Scheib
Phynx (1970) Stoller
Pianissimo (1963) Popkin
Picador Porky (1937) Stalling
Piccadilly Incident (1946) Collins
Piccadilly Jim (1936) Axt
Pick a Pet (1955) Craig, E.
Pick a Star (1937) Morton
Pick-Necking (1933) Scheib
Pick Up (1933) Rainger
Pickled Pink (1965) Lava
Pickup (1951) Byrns
Pickup on South Street (1953) Harline
Picnic (1948) Gold
Picnic (1956) Duning
Picnic Panic (1935) Sharples, Winston
Picnic Panic (1946) Kilfeather
Picnic with Papa (1952) Scheib
Pictura (1951) Adomian
Picture in Your Mind (1949) Forrell
Picture Mommy Dead (1966) Drasnin
Picture of Dorian Gray (1945) Stothart
Picture Snatcher (1933) Heindorf
Pictures in Pure Light (1957) Eto
Picturesque (1939) Shilkret, J.
Picturesque Massachusetts (1942) Nussbaum
Picturesque Patzcuaro (1942) Nussbaum
Pie in the Eye (1948) Jackson, H.

Piece of Wood (1957) Kleinsinger
Pieces of Dreams (1970) Legrand
Pied Piper (1933) Harline
Pied Piper (1942) Newman
Pied Piper of Basin Street (1944) Calker
Pied Piper of Guadalupe (1961) Franklyn
Pied Piper Porky (1939) Stalling
Piegan Medicine Lodge (1959) Humphreys, A.
Pier 5 Havana (1959) Shefter
Pier 13 (1940) Mockridge
Pier 23 (1951) Shefter
Piernas de Seda (1935) Kaylin
Pierre of the Plains (1914) Klein, Manuel
Pierre of the Plains (1942) Hayton
Pig-a-Boo (1952) Sharples, Winston
Pig in a Pickle (1954) Wheeler
Pigeon Holed (1956) Wheeler
Pigeon Patrol (1942) Calker
Pigs! (1967) Sahl
Pigs in a Polka (1943) Stalling
Pigs Is Pigs (1937) Stalling
Pigs Is Pigs (1953) Wallace
Pigs' Feat (1963) Sharples, Winston
Pigskin Capers (1930) Scheib
Pigskin Parade (1936) Buttolph, David
Piker's Peak (1957) Stalling
Pilgrim Lady (1946) Butts
Pilgrim Popeye (1951) Sharples, Winston
Pilgrim Porky (1940) Stalling
Pilgrimage (1933) Bassett, R. H.
Pilgrimage Play (1950) Colombo
Pill Peddlers (1952) Scheib
Pillars of the Sky (1956) Lava
Pillow of Death (1945) Skinner, F.
Pillow Talk (1959) De Vol
Pillow to Post (1945) Hollander
Pilot #5 (1943) Hayton
Pin Feathers (1933) Dietrich
Pin Games (1947) Shilkret, N.
Pin Up Girl (1944) Mockridge
Pinch Hitter (1925) Schertzinger
Pinch Singer (1936) Shield
Pineapple Country, Hawaii (1961) Roberts, T.
Pink and Blue Blues (1952) Lees
Pink-a-Boo (1966) Greene, W.
Pink-a-Rella (1969) Greene, W.
Pink Blueprint (1966) Lava
Pink Elephants (1937) Scheib
Pink Ice (1965) Lava
Pink-In (1970) Greene, W.
Pink in the Clink (1968) Greene, W.
Pink Jungle (1968) Freeman, E.
Pink of the Litter (1967) Greene, W.
Pink Panther (1964) Mancini
Pink Pest Control (1969) Greene, W.
Pink Phink (1964) Lava
Pink Pistons (1966) Lava
Pink, Plunk, Plink (1966) Greene, W.
Pink Tail Fly (1965) Lava
Pink Valiant (1968) Greene, W.
Pinkadilly Circus (1968) Greene, W.
Pinkfinger (1965) Lava
Pinknic (1967) Greene, W.
Pinky (1949) Newman
Pinocchio (1940) Harline
Pinocchio (1969) Scott, J.
Pins and Cushions (1946) De Francesco
Pinto Bandit (1944) Zahler
Pinto Canyon (1940) Lange, J.
Pioneer Days (1930) Lewis
Pioneer Justice (1947) Greene, W.
Pioneer Marshal (1949) Wilson, S.
Pioneer Trail (1938) Zahler
Pioneers (1941) Sanucci
Pioneers of the West (1940) Feuer
Pip-Eye, Pup-Eye, Poop-Eye and Peep-Eye (1942) Timberg
Pipe Dreams (1938) Bradley
Pipito's Serenade (1946) Smith, P.
Pirate (1948) Hayton
Pirate Ship (1933) Scheib
Pirate Treasure (1934) Roemheld
Pirate's Gold (1956) Scheib
Pirates of Monterey (1947) Rosen, M.
Pirates of the Skies (1939) Skinner, F.
Pirates of Tortuga (1961) Sawtell
Pirates on Horseback (1941) Malotte
Pistol Harvest (1951) Sawtell
Pit and the Pendulum (1961) Baxter
Pitcairn Island Today (1935) Axt
Pitchin' Woo at the Zoo (1944) Timberg
Pitfall (1948) Forbes
Pittsburgh (1942) Skinner, F.
Pixie Land (1938) Marsales
Pixie Picnic (1948) Calker
Pixillation (1970) Lewin
Pizza Tweety-Pie (1957) Franklyn
Pizzicato Pussycat (1955) Franklyn
Place in the Sun (1949) Mackay
Place in the Sun (1951) Waxman
Place to Live (1941) Diamond
Plainsman (1937) Antheil
Plainsman (1966) Williams, J.
Plainsman and the Lady (1946) Antheil
Plan for Destruction (1943) Shilkret, N.
Plane Crazy (1928) Stalling
Plane Daffy (1944) Stalling
Plane Dippy (1936) Spencer, N.
Plane Goofy (1940) Scheib
Plane Nuts (1933) Axt
Planet Mouseola (1960) Sharples, Winston
Planet of the Apes (1967) Goldsmith
Plastered in Paris (1966) Lava
Plastic Dome of Norma Jean (1970) Legrand
Plastic Haircut (1963) Reich
Plastics Inventor (1944) Wallace
Platinum High School (1960) Alexander, V.
Play Ball (1932) Scheib

Play Ball (1933) Stalling
Play Ball (1937) Scheib
Play Girl (1932) Harling
Play Girl (1941) Sawtell
Play Safe (1936) Timberg
Playboy of Paris (1930) Jackson, H.
Playful Pan (1931) Lewis
Playful Pelican (1948) Calker
Playful Pest (1943) Kilfeather
Playful Pluto (1934) Churchill
Playful Polar Bears (1938) Timberg
Playful Pup (1937) Dietrich
Playful Puss (1953) Scheib
Playgirl (1954) Skinner, F.
Playground (1965) Kaplan, E.
Playing Politics (1936) De Nat
Playing the Pied Piper (1941) Kilfeather
Playlands of Michigan (1949) Nussbaum
Playmates (1941) Webb
Playmates of the Sea (1952) Mamorsky
Playthings of Desire (1934) Henninger
Playtime in Hawaii (1941) De Francesco
Playtime in Rio (1948) Jackson, H.
Playtime in Scandinavia (1948) De Francesco
Playtime Pals (1956) Jackson, H.
Playtime's Journey (1946) De Francesco
Please Believe Me (1950) Salter
Please Don't Eat the Daisies (1960) Rose
Please Murder Me! (1956) Glasser
Pleased to Eat You (1950) Sharples, Winston
Pleasure Cruise (1933) Brunelli
Pleasure of His Company (1961) Newman
Pleasure Seekers (1965) Newman, L.
Pledge to Bataan (1945) Lava
Plenty Below Zero (1943) Kilfeather
Plenty of Money and You (1937) Stalling
Plop Goes the Weasel (1954) Stalling
Plot Against Harry (1969) Lewin
Plot Sickens (1961) Sharples, Winston
Plots Thicken (1944) Applebaum
Plough and the Stars (1937) Webb
Plow Boy (1929) Stalling
Plow That Broke the Plains (1936) Thomson
Plows, Planes and Peace (1941) Craig, E.
Plugger (1941) Applebaum
Plumber (1933) Dietrich
Plumber (1967) Sharples, Winston
Plumber of Seville (1956) Poddany
Plumber's Helpers (1953) Scheib
Plumbing Is a Pipe (1938) Timberg
Plunder of the Sun (1953) Diaz Conde
Plunder Road (1957) Gertz
Plunderers (1948) Butts
Plunderers (1960) Rosenman
Pluto and the Armadillo (1942) Smith, P.
Pluto and the Gopher (1949) Wallace
Pluto at the Zoo (1942) Wallace
Pluto, Junior (1942) Harline
Pluto's Blue Note (1947) Wallace
Pluto's Christmas Tree (1952) Dubin
Pluto's Dream House (1940) Harline
Pluto's Fledgling (1947) Wallace
Pluto's Heart Throb (1949) Wallace
Pluto's Housewarming (1946) Wallace
Pluto's Judgment Day (1935) Churchill
Pluto's Kid Brother (1945) Wallace
Pluto's Party (1952) Wallace
Pluto's Playmate (1941) Smith, P.
Pluto's Purchase (1947) Wallace
Pluto's Quin-Puplets (1937) Smith, P.
Pluto's Surprise Package (1948) Wallace
Pluto's Sweater (1948) Wallace
Plutopia (1950) Dubin
Plymouth Adventure (1952) Rozsa
Plywood Panic (1953) Wheeler
Pocketful of Miracles (1961) Scharf, W.
Poem of Life (1953) Winslow
Poem Posters (1967) Handy
Poet and Peasant (1946) Calker
Poetry of Polymers (1966) Gould, G.
Point Blank (1967) Mandel
Pointed Heels (1929) Harling
Pointer (1939) Smith, P.
Points on Arrows (1941) Jackson, H.
Poland (1965) Schickele
Polar Fright (1966) Greene, W.
Polar Pals (1939) Stalling
Polar Pest (1944) Bradley
Polar Pests (1958) Wheeler
Polar Playmates (1946) Kilfeather
Polar Trappers (1938) Smith, P.
Police Dog Story (1960) Sawtell
Police Dogged (1956) Scheib
Police Nurse (1963) LaSalle
Politicians (1970) Bath
Polka-Dot Puss (1949) Bradley
Polly Wants a Doctor (1943) Kilfeather
Pollyanna (1960) Smith, P.
Polo Joe (1936) Jackson, H.
Polo with the Stars (1941) Jackson, H.
Pond and the City (1963) Bazelon
Pony Express (1925) Riesenfeld
Pony Express (1953) Sawtell
Pony Express Days (1940) Jackson, H.
Pony Soldier (1952) North
Pooch Parade (1940) De Nat
Poop Deck Pirate (1961) Poddany
Poop Goes the Weasel (1955) Sharples, Winston
Poopdeck Pappy (1940) Timberg
Poor Elmer (1938) De Nat
Poor Fish (1933) Lannin
Poor Little Butterfly (1938) De Nat
Poor Little Me (1935) Bradley
Poor Little Rich Girl (1936) Mockridge
Poor Little Witch Girl (1965) Sharples, Winston
Poor Rich (1934) Roemheld
Pop Always Pays (1940) Sawtell
Pop Corn Story (1950) Curtin

Pop Goes Your Heart (1935) Spencer, N.
Pop 'Im Pop (1949) Stalling
Pop-Pie a la Mode (1945) Sharples, Winston
Popalong Popeye (1952) Sharples, Winston
Popcorn (1931) Scheib
Popcorn and Politics (1961) Sharples, Winston
Popeye and the Pirates (1947) Sharples, Winston
Popeye for President (1956) Sharples, Winston
Popeye Makes a Movie (1950) Sharples, Winston
Popeye Meets Hercules (1948) Sharples, Winston
Popeye Meets Rip Van Winkle (1941) Timberg
Popeye's 20th Anniversary (1954) Sharples, Winston
Popeye's Mirthday (1953) Sharples, Winston
Popeye's Pappy (1952) Sharples, Winston
Popeye's Premiere (1949) Sharples, Winston
Popeye, the Ace of Space (1953) Sharples, Winston
Popeye the Sailor Meets Ali Baba's Forty Thieves (1937) Timberg
Popeye the Sailor Meets Sindbad the Sailor (1936) Timberg
Popi (1969) Frontiere
Poppin' the Cork (1933) Scharf, W.
Poppy (1936) Hollander
Poppycock! (1966) Woldin
Popsicle (1969) Dragon, D.
Population Explosion (1967) Coleman, O.
Porgy and Bess (1959) Previn, A.
Pork Chop Hill (1959) Rosenman
Porkuliar Piggy (1944) Kilfeather
Porky & Daffy (1938) Stalling
Porky and Gabby (1937) Stalling
Porky and Teabiscuit (1939) Stalling
Porky at the Crocadero (1937) Stalling
Porky Chops (1947) Stalling
Porky in Egypt (1938) Stalling
Porky in the Northwoods (1936) Stalling
Porky in Wackyland (1938) Stalling
Porky Pig's Feat (1943) Stalling
Porky the Fireman (1938) Stalling
Porky the Giant Killer (1939) Stalling
Porky the Gob (1939) Stalling
Porky the Rainmaker (1936) Spencer, N.
Porky the Wrestler (1936) Stalling
Porky's Aunt (1941) Stalling
Porky's Badtime Story (1937) Stalling
Porky's Baseball Broadcast (1940) Stalling
Porky's Bear Facts (1941) Stalling
Porky's Building (1937) Stalling
Porky's Cafe (1942) Stalling
Porky's Double Trouble (1937) Stalling
Porky's Duck Hunt (1937) Stalling
Porky's Five and Ten (1938) Stalling
Porky's Garden (1937) Stalling
Porky's Hare Hunt (1938) Stalling
Porky's Hero Agency (1937) Stalling
Porky's Hired Hand (1940) Stalling
Porky's Hotel (1939) Stalling
Porky's Last Stand (1939) Stalling
Porky's Midnight Matinee (1941) Stalling
Porky's Movie Mystery (1939) Stalling
Porky's Moving Day (1936) Stalling
Porky's Naughty Nephew (1938) Stalling
Porky's Party (1938) Stalling
Porky's Pastry Pirates (1942) Stalling
Porky's Pet (1936) Spencer, N.
Porky's Phoney Express (1937) Stalling
Porky's Picnic (1939) Stalling
Porky's Pooch (1941) Stalling
Porky's Poor Fish (1940) Stalling
Porky's Poppa (1937) Stalling
Porky's Poultry Plant (1936) Stalling
Porky's Preview (1941) Stalling
Porky's Prize Pony (1941) Stalling
Porky's Railroad (1937) Stalling
Porky's Road Race (1937) Stalling
Porky's Romance (1937) Stalling
Porky's Snooze Reel (1940) Stalling
Porky's Spring Planting (1938) Stalling
Porky's Super Service (1937) Stalling
Porky's Tire Trouble (1939) Stalling
Port of Hate (1939) Lange, J.
Port of Hell (1954) Kay, Edward
Port of Lost Dreams (1934) Zahler
Port of Missing Mice (1945) Scheib
Port of New York (1946) Shulman
Port of New York (1949) Kaplan, S.
Port of Seven Seas (1938) Waxman
Port Sinister (1952) Glasser
Portia on Trial (1937) Colombo
Portland Expose (1957) Dunlap
Portrait in Black (1960) Skinner, F.
Portrait in Terror (1965) Stein, R.
Portrait of a Genius (1943) Terr
Portrait of Europe (1960) Baksa
Portrait of Jennie (1949) Tiomkin
Portrait of Mexico (1962) Baksa
Portrait of the West (1948) De Francesco
Portraits for Eternity (1963) Hibbard
Portraits, Self-Portraits, and Still Lifes (1969) Ashley
Portugal (1957) Wallace
Posse Cat (1953) Bradley
Possessed (1931) Maxwell
Possessed (1947) Waxman
Possibilities of Agam (1967) Pinsky, D.
Possum Pearl (1957) Sharples, Winston
Post No Bills (1967) Gross
Post Office (1968) Tcherepnin
Post War Inventions (1945) Scheib
Postal Inspector (1936) Vaughan
Postman Always Rings Twice (1946) Bassman
Postman Didn't Ring (1942) Raksin
Pot o' Gold (1941) Forbes
Pot-Pourri (1968) Zekley
Potions and Notions (1966) Sharples, Winston
Potted Psalm (1946) Campbell

Poultry Pirates (1938) Lewis
Pound (1970) Cuva
Pound of Flesh (1952) Girvin
Pour (1969) Bresnick
Powder River Rustlers (1949) Wilson, S.
Power (1967) Rozsa
Power Among Men (1959) Thomson
Power and the Glory (1933) Zamecnik
Power and the Land (1940) Moore, D.
Power and the Prize (1956) Kaper
Power Behind the Nation (1947) Lava
Power Dive (1941) Bakaleinikoff, C.
Power of Life (1938) Stillman
Power of the Press (1943) Sawtell
Power of the Whistler (1945) Sawtell
Power of Thought (1948) Scheib
Power Unlimited (1945) Machan
Powers Girl (1943) Silvers
Powers of Ten (1968) Bernstein, E.
Practical Pig (1939) Smith, P.
Practical Yolk (1965) Greene, W.
Practically Yours (1944) Young, V.
Practice Makes Perfect (1940) De Nat
Prairie (1948) Steinert
Prairie Badmen (1946) Zahler
Prairie Chickens (1943) Ward, E.
Prairie Express (1947) Kay, Edward
Prairie Law (1940) Sawtell
Prairie Outlaws (1948) Greene, W.
Prairie Pals (1943) Lange, J.
Prairie Pioneers (1941) Feuer
Prairie Rustlers (1945) Zahler
Prairie Swingaroo (1937) DiMaggio
Prairie Thunder (1937) Jackson, H.
Preface to a Life (1950) Rathaus
Preferred List (1933) Webb
Prehistoric Perils (1951) Scheib
Prehistoric Porky (1940) Stalling
Prehistoric Women (1950) Kraushaar
Pre-Hysterical Man (1948) Sharples, Winston
Prejudice (1949) Gertz
Prelude (1968) Ruff
Prelude to an Afternoon with the Dentist (1963) Darreg
Prelude to War (1942) Harline
Premature Burial (1962) Stein, R.
Prescription for Percy (1954) Scheib
Prescription for Romance (1937) Previn, C.
Presenting Lily Mars (1943) Stoll
President Vanishes (1935) Riesenfeld
President's Analyst (1967) Schifrin
President's Country (1965) Tiomkin
President's Lady (1953) Newman
President's Mystery (1936) Riesenfeld
Press On Regardless (1967) Lauber
Pressure Point (1962) Gold
Prestige (1932) Lange
Prest-o Change-o (1939) Stalling
Pretender (1947) Dessau
Pretoria to Durban (1952) Nussbaum
Pretty Baby (1950) Buttolph, David
Pretty Boy Floyd (1960) Sanford, W.
Pretty Poison (1968) Mandel
Price of a Life (1968) Shapiro
Price of Fear (1956) Roemheld
Price of Power (1916) Raynes
Price of Victory (1942) Amfitheatrof
Pride and Prejudice (1940) Stothart
Pride and the Passion (1957) Antheil
Pride of St. Louis (1952) Lange
Pride of the Blue Grass (1939) Jackson, H.
Pride of the Blue Grass (1954) Skiles
Pride of the Bowery (1940) Lange, J.
Pride of the Marines (1945) Waxman
Pride of the Navy (1939) Feuer
Pride of the Plains (1943) Glickman, M.
Pride of the Yankees (1942) Harline
Pride of the Yard (1954) Scheib
Prime Minister (1941) Roemheld
Prime Time (1960) Rubenstein
Primitive Pitcairn (1936) Axt
Primitive Pluto (1949) Wallace
Primordium (1968) Shankar
Primrose Path (1940) Heymann
Prince and the Pauper (1937) Korngold
Prince, King of Dogs (1935) Snell
Prince of Foxes (1949) Newman
Prince of Players (1955) Herrmann
Prince Valiant (1954) Waxman
Prince Violent (1961) Franklyn
Prince Who Was a Thief (1951) Salter
Princely India (1949) Lava
Princess and the Magic Frog (1965) Allen, B.
Princess and the Pirate (1944) Rose
Princess and the Plumber (1930) Lipschultz
Princess Comes Across (1936) Leipold
Princess in the Tower (1956) Fried
Princess O'Hara (1935) Morton
Princess O'Rourke (1943) Hollander
Princess of the Dark (1917) Schertzinger
Princess of the Nile (1954) Newman, L.
Priorities on Parade (1942) Young, V.
Prison Break (1938) Sanucci
Prison Nurse (1938) Colombo
Prison Ship (1945) Castelnuovo-Tedesco
Prisoner of Japan (1942) Erdody
Prisoner of Shark Island (1936) Bassett, R.
Prisoner of the Harem (1912) Simon, W.
Prisoner of War (1954) Alexander, J.
Prisoner of Zenda (1913) Breil
Prisoner of Zenda (1922) Axt
Prisoner of Zenda (1937) Newman
Prisoner of Zenda (1952) Salinger
Prisoners in Petticoats (1950) Wilson, S.
Private Affairs of Bel Ami (1947) Milhaud
Private Detective (1939) Dunn
Private Detective (Trailer, 1939) Jackson, H.
Private Detective 62 (1933) Kaun

Private Eye Pooch (1955) Wheeler
Private Eye Popeye (1954) Sharples, Winston
Private Eyes (1953) Skiles
Private Hell 36 (1954) Stevens, L.
Private Life of a Cat (1945) Forrell
Private Life of Don Juan (1934) Toch
Private Life of Helen of Troy (1927) Copping
Private Life of Sherlock Holmes (1970) Rozsa
Private Lives (1931) Axt
Private Lives of Adam and Eve (1959) Alexander, V.
Private Lives of Elizabeth and Essex (1939) Korngold
Private Navy of Sgt. O'Farrell (1968) Sukman
Private Number (1936) Mockridge
Private Pluto (1943) Wallace
Private Scandal (1931) Zahler
Private Snafu vs. Malaria Mike (1944) Stalling
Private Snuffy Smith (1942) Schrager
Private War of Major Benson (1955) Lava
Private Worlds (1935) Roemheld
Private's Affair (1959) Mockridge
Prize (1963) Goldsmith
Prize Guest (1939) Scheib
Prize Pest (1950) Stalling
Problem Child (1938) Churchill
Problem Girls (1953) Glasser
Procession (1960) Kayden
Prodigal (1955) Kaper
Producers (1967) Morris
Product of the Imagination (1958) Norlin
Prof. Offkeysky (1940) Scheib
Prof. Small and Mr. Tall (1943) Kilfeather
Professional Soldier (1936) Bassett, R. H.
Professionals (1966) Jarre
Professor Lust (1967) Ammon
Professor Tom (1948) Bradley
Profile of an Alcoholic (1959) De Lane
Project Moon Base (1953) Gilbert, H.
Project X (1967) Van Cleave
Projections in Indian Art (1959) Baksa
Promise (1967) Cunningham
Promise Her Anything (1965) Murray
Promises to Keep (1969) Schulman
Promises! Promises! (1963) Borne
Proper Time (1959) Manne
Prophet Without Honor (1939) Snell
Prospecting Bear (1941) Bradley
Prospecting for Petroleum (1948) Wheeler
Prosperity (1932) Axt
Prosperity Blues (1932) De Nat
Protek the Weakerist (1937) Timberg
Proud and Profane (1956) Young, V.
Proud Ones (1956) Newman, L.
Proud Rebel (1958) Moross
Proud Years (1956) Vito
Proudest Girl in the World (1944) Applebaum
Proudly She Marches (1943) Applebaum
Proudly We Serve (1944) Lava
Prowler (1951) Murray
Prowlers of the Everglades (1952) Smith, P.
Psychedelic Pink (1968) Greene, W.
Psycho (1960) Herrmann
Psycho a Go-Go! (1965) McGinnis
Psychological Testing (1962) Sharples, Winston
Psych-Out (1968) Stein, R.
PT 109 (1963) Lava
Public Affair (1962) Greene, J.
Public Deb No. 1 (1940) Buttolph, David
Public Defender (1931) Steiner, M.
Public Enemies (1941) Feuer
Public Enemy (1931) Mendoza
Public Enemy's Wife (1936) Kaun
Public Hero No. 1 (1935) Ward, E.
Public Opinion (1935) Zahler
Public Opinion Polls (1947) Smith, P.
Public Pigeon No. 1 (1956) Rose
Public Wedding (1937) Jackson, H.
Puce Moment (1949) Halper
Puddin' Head (1941) Scharf, W.
Puddy the Pup and the Gypsies (1936) Scheib
Puddy the Pup in the Book Shop (1937) Scheib
Puddy's Coronation (1937) Scheib
Pudgy and the Lost Kitten (1938) Timberg
Pudgy Picks a Fight (1937) Timberg
Pudgy Takes a Bow-Wow (1937) Timberg
Pudgy the Watchman (1938) Timberg
Pueblo Boy (1947) Stringer
Pueblo Pluto (1948) Wallace
Puerto Rico (1947) Applebaum
Puff Your Blues Away (1931) Timberg
Puffs and Bustles (1933) Vincent, P.
Pufnstuf (1970) Fox, C.
Pull My Daisy (1959) Amram
Pump Trouble (1954) Surinach
Pumpkin Coach (1960) Kayden
Punch and Judo (1951) Sharples, Winston
Punch Trunk (1952) Stalling
Punchy de Leon (1950) Castillo
Punchy Pooch (1962) Calker
Puny Express (1951) Wheeler
Pup on a Picnic (1955) Bradley
Puppet Love (1944) Timberg
Puppet Murder Case (1935) De Nat
Puppet Show (1936) Dietrich
Puppet's Dream (1961) Katz, F.
Puppy Love (1933) Churchill
Puppy Tale (1953) Bradley
Pups' Christmas (1936) Bradley
Pups' Picnic (1936) Bradley
Pure and Simple (1930) Zahler
Puritan Passions (1923) Converse
Purity Squad (1945) Terr
Purloined Pup (1946) Wallace
Purple Gang (1960) Dunlap
Purple Heart (1944) Newman
Purple Heart Diary (1951) Duning
Purple Hills (1961) LaSalle

Purple Mask (1955) Roemheld
Purple Turtle (1961) Wernick
Purple V (1943) Glickman, M.
Purple Vigilantes (1938) Colombo
Purr-Chance to Dream (1967) Brandt
Pursued (1934) Friedhofer
Pursued (1947) Steiner, M.
Pursuit (1935) Stothart
Pursuit of Happiness (1934) Satterfield
Push Back the Edge (1954) Agostini
Push Button Kitty (1952) Bradley
Pusher (1959) Scott, Raymond
Pushover (1954) Morton
Puss 'n' Boats (1966) Brandt
Puss 'n Boos (1954) Sharples, Winston
Puss 'n Booty (1943) Stalling
Puss 'n Toots (1942) Bradley
Puss Gets the Boot (1940) Bradley
Puss in Boots (1931) Shilkret, N.
Puss in Boots (1934) Stalling
Puss-Cafe (1949) Smith, P.
Pussycat, Pussycat, I Love You (1970) Schifrin
Put on the Spout (1931) Scheib
Put-Put Pink (1968) Greene, W.
Put-Put Troubles (1940) Wallace
Putney Swope (1969) Cuva
Puttin' on the Dog (1944) Bradley
Puttin' Out the Kitten (1937) De Nat
Putty Tat Trouble (1950) Stalling
Puzzle of a Downfall Child (1970) Small
Pygmalion (1938) Axt
Pygmy Hunt (1938) Lewis

Quack a Doodle Doo (1950) Sharples, Winston
Quack, Quack (1931) Scheib
Quack Shot (1953) Stalling
Quacker Tracker (1967) Perkins
Quackodile Tears (1961) Franklyn
Quail Hunt (1935) Dietrich
Quaint Quebec (1949) De Francesco
Quaint St. Augustine (1939) Bakaleinikoff, C.
Quality and Promise (1967) Wykes
Quality in Photographic Lenses (1954) Morley
Quality Street (1937) Webb
Quantez (1957) Stein, H.
Quantrill's Raiders (1958) Skiles
Quarter Horses (1946) Anderson
Quarterback (1940) Leipold
Que Puerto Rico (1963) Elliott, Don
Quebec (1951) Van Cleave
Quebec Camera Hunt (1953) Mendelsohn
Quebec in Summertime (1949) Nussbaum
Quebec, Path of Conquest (1942) Agostini
Queen Bee (1955) Duning
Queen Christina (1934) Stothart
Queen Elizabeth (1912) Breil
Queen for a Day (1951) Friedhofer
Queen Kelly (1931) Tandler
Queen of Blood (1966) Stein, R.
Queen of Broadway (1943) Erdody
Queen of Burlesque (1946) Greene, W.
Queen of Destiny (1938) Collins
Queen of Hearts (1934) Stalling
Queen of Outer Space (1958) Skiles
Queen of Sheba (1921) Rapée
Queen of Sheba (1953) Carmichael
Queen of the Amazons (1946) Zahler
Queen of the Mob (1940) Hollander
Queen of the Yukon (1940) Kay, Edward
Queen Was in the Parlor (1932) Marsales
Queen's Guard (1955) Jackson, H.
Queen's Kittens (1938) Marsales
Queens of Beauty (1955) Mancini
Quentin Durward (1955) Kaper
Quentin Quail (1945) Stalling
Quest for Freedom (1966) Katz, F.
Quest of the Lost City (1954) Sawtell
Question Tree (1961) Laderman.
Quetzalcoatl (1952) Paddock
Quick and the Dead (1963) Mendoza-Nava
Quick, Before It Melts (1964) Rose
Quick Facts on Fear (1944) Plumb
Quick Gun (1964) LaSalle
Quick on the Vigor (1950) Sharples, Winston
Quicksand (1950) Gruenberg
Quiet Gun (1957) Dunlap
Quiet Man (1952) Young, V.
Quiet One (1948) Kay, U.
Quiet, Please (1939) Jackson, H.
Quiet Please! (1945) Bradley
Quiet, Please, Murder (1942) Lange
Quiet Revolution (1967) Mendoza-Nava
Quincannon, Frontier Scout (1956) Baxter
Quintupland (1938) Shilkret, N.
Quo Vadis? (1925) Copping
Quo Vadis (1951) Rozsa

R'coon Dawg (1950) Smith, P.
R. P. M. (1970) Botkin, Jr.
Rabbit Every Monday (1950) Stalling
Rabbit Fire (1950) Stalling
Rabbit Hood (1949) Stalling
Rabbit Hunt (1938) Marsales
Rabbit of Seville (1949) Stalling
Rabbit Punch (1947) Stalling
Rabbit Punch (1955) Sharples, Winston
Rabbit Rampage (1954) Franklyn
Rabbit Romeo (1957) Franklyn
Rabbit, Run (1970) Lava
Rabbit Seasoning (1951) Stalling
Rabbit Stew and Rabbits Too (1969) Lava
Rabbit Transit (1946) Stalling
Rabbit Trap (1959) Marshall, J.
Rabbit's Feat (1960) Franklyn
Rabbit's Kin (1951) Stalling
Rabbitson Crusoe (1955) Franklyn
Race Rider (1947) Jackson, H.
Race Street (1948) Webb

Racers (1955) North
Rachel and the Stranger (1948) Webb
Rachel, Rachel (1968) Moross
Racing Blood (1954) Kay, Edward
Racing Fever (1964) Jacobs, A.
Racing Lady (1937) Webb
Racing Sleuths (1947) Shilkret, N.
Racing Thrills (1950) Lava
Racing World (1968) Ellington
Racing Youth (1932) Bibo
Rack (1956) Deutsch
Racket (1951) Sawtell
Racket Buster (1948) Scheib
Racket Busters (1938) Deutsch
Racket Busters (Trailer, 1938) Jackson, H.
Racket Man (1944) Cutner
Racketeer Rabbit (1946) Stalling
Racketeers in Exile (1937) Nussbaum
Rackets (1945) Applebaum
Rackety Rax (1932) Lange
Radar (1945) Palange
Radar Men from the Moon (1952) Wilson, S.
Radar Patrol vs. Spy King (1949) Wilson, S.
Radar Secret Service (1950) Garcia
Radio City Revels (1938) Bennett, R. R.
Radio Girl (1932) Scheib
Radio Hams (1939) Snell
Radio Operator (1942) Steinert
Radio Rhythm (1931) Dietrich
Radio Scout (1935) Ward, E.
Radio Stars on Parade (1945) Webb
Radio, Take It Away! (1947) Sharples, Winston
Raffles (1940) Young, V.
Rag Doll (1935) Sharples, Winston
Rage at Dawn (1955) Sawtell
Rage in Heaven (1941) Kaper
Rage of Paris (1938) Skinner, F.
Rage to Live (1965) Riddle
Raggedy Ann and Raggedy Andy (1941) Timberg
Raging Tide (1951) Skinner, F.
Rags to Riches (1941) Glickman, M.
Ragtime Bear (1949) Castillo
Ragtime Romeo (1931) Stalling
Rah Rah Ruckus (1964) Calker
Raid (1954) Webb
Raiders (1952) Mancini
Raiders (1964) Stevens, M.
Raiders from Beneath the Sea (1964) Levine, H.
Raiders of Sunset Pass (1943) Glickman, M.
Raiders of the Border (1944) Kay, Edward
Raiders of the Desert (1941) Salter
Raiders of the Range (1942) Feuer
Raiders of the Seven Seas (1953) Sawtell
Raiders of the South (1947) Kay, Edward
Raiding the Raiders (1945) Scheib
Rail Rodents (1954) Sharples, Winston
Railroad Rhythm (1937) De Nat
Railroad Rhythms (1954) White, R.
Railroad Special Agent (1951) Grundman
Railroaded (1947) Levin
Railroaded (1968) Glass, Philip
Rails Into Laramie (1954) Stein, H.
Rain (1932) Newman
Rain Drain (1966) Timmens
Rain People (1969) Stein, R.
Rainbow (1929) Littau
Rainbow Chasers (1951) Shilkret, N.
Rainbow Island (1944) Webb
Rainbow Man (1929) Gottschalk
Rainbow on the River (1936) Riesenfeld
Rainbow Over Texas (1946) Maxwell
Rainbow Over the Range (1940) Sanucci
Rainbow Over the Rockies (1946) Sanucci
Rainbow 'Round My Shoulder (1952) Duning
Rainbow Trail (1931) Brunelli
Rainbow Valley (1959) Bernstein, E.
Rainbow Valley: The Story of a Forest Ranger (1954) Kleinsinger
Rainmaker (1956) North
Rainmakers (1935) Webb
Rainmakers (1951) Scheib
Rains Came (1939) Newman
Rains of Ranchipur (1955) Friedhofer
Rainshower (1965) Marais
Raintree County (1957) Green, J.
Rainy Day (1940) Bradley
Raisin in the Sun (1961) Rosenthal
Raising of Lazarus (1948) Rosen, M.
Rally 'Round the Flag, Boys! (1958) Mockridge
Ramona (1916) Bierman
Ramona (1928) Riesenfeld
Ramona (1936) Newman
Rampage (1963) Bernstein, E.
Ramparts We Watch (1940) De Francesco
Ramrod (1947) Deutsch
Ranch in White (1946) Jackson, H.
Rancho in the Sky (1946) DiMaggio
Rancho Notorious (1952) Friedhofer
Random Harvest (1942) Stothart
Range Beyond the Blue (1947) Hajos
Range Busters (1940) Sanucci
Range Justice (1949) Kay, Edward
Range Land (1949) Kay, Edward
Range Law (1944) Kay, Edward
Range Renegades (1948) Kay, Edward
Range War (1939) Young, V.
Ranger Courage (1936) Zahler
Ranger of Cherokee Strip (1949) Wilson, S.
Rangers of Fortune (1940) Hollander
Rangers Ride (1948) Kay, Edward
Rangers Step In (1937) Zahler
Rangers Take Over (1943) Zahler
Rangers' Round-Up (1938) Porter
Rango (1931) Hajos
Ransom! (1955) Alexander, J.
Rare Breed (1966) Williams, J.
Rascal (1969) Baker, Buddy

Rasputin and the Empress (1933 trailer) Axt
Rasputin and the Empress (1933) Stothart
Rasslin' Match (1934) Sharples, Winston
Rasslin' Round (1934) Stalling
Rat (1937) Collins
Rat Fink (1965) Stein, R.
Rat Pfink and Boo Boo (1966) Price, Henry
Rat Race (1960) Bernstein, E.
Ration Bored (1943) Calker
Ration fer the Duration (1943) Timberg
Rationing (1944) Castelnuovo-Tedesco
Raton Pass (1951) Steiner, M.
Rattled Rooster (1948) Stalling
Ravaged Earth (1942) Kilenyi
Raven (1935) Vaughan
Raven (1942) Timberg
Raven (1963) Baxter
Raw Deal (1948) Sawtell
Raw Edge (1956) Gertz
Raw Wind in Eden (1958) Salter
Raw! Raw! Rooster (1956) Stalling
Rawhide (1951) Kaplan, S.
Rawhide Trail (1958) Brummer
Rawhide Years (1955) Skinner, F.
Raymie (1960) Stein, R.
Razor's Edge (1946) Newman
Razzberries (1931) Scheib
REA Story (1960) Kleinsinger
Reaching for the Moon (1931) Newman
Reaching for the Moon (1933) Steiner, G.
Reaching for the Sun (1941) Young, V.
Readin', Ritin', and Rhythmetic (1948) Sharples, Winston
Reading and Riding (1947) Shilkret, N.
Reading, Writhing and 'Rithmetic (1964) Sharples, Winston
Ready for Love (1934) Satterfield
Ready for the People (1964) Perkins
Ready on Arrival (1967) Lackey
Ready, Set, Zoom! (1954) Stalling
Ready, Willing, and Able (1937) Roemheld
Ready, Woolen and Able (1959) Franklyn
Real Glory (1939) Newman
Real Gone Woody (1954) Wheeler
Real Thing (1966) Coleman, O.
Really Important Person (1947) Terr
Really Scent (1958) Franklyn
Realm of the Redwoods (1949) De Francesco
Reap the Wild Wind (1942) Young, V.
Rear Gunner (1943) Jackson, H.
Rear Window (1954) Waxman
Reason and Emotion (1943) Smith, P.
Rebecca (1940) Waxman
Rebecca of Sunnybrook Farm (1917) Beynon
Rebecca of Sunnybrook Farm (1932) Lange
Rebel City (1953) Kraushaar
Rebel in Paradise (196?) Katz, F.
Rebel in Town (1956) Baxter
Rebel Rabbit (1947) Stalling
Rebel Rousers (1970) Loose
Rebel Set (1959) Dunlap
Rebel Without a Cause (1955) Rosenman
Rebel Without Claws (1961) Franklyn
Rebellious Daughters (1938) Zahler
Rebound (1931) Lange
Recess (1969) Henderson, L.
Reckless (1935) Virgil
Reckless Age (1944) Skinner, F.
Reckless Driver (1946) Calker
Reckless Hour (1931) Mendoza
Reckless Living (1938) Skinner, F.
Reckless Moment (1949) Salter
Reckless Ranger (1937) Zahler
Reckless Roads (1935) Zahler
Reckless Way (1936) Johnston, G.
Recreation (1946) North
Recruit (1941) Harline
Recruiting Daze (1940) Prince, H.
Red Badge of Courage (1951) Kaper
Red Canyon (1949) Scharf, W.
Red Carpet (1955) Kleiner
Red Cross (1948) Vincent, J.
Red Dance (1928) Rapée
Red Danube (1949) Rozsa
Red Desert (1949) Greene, W.
Red Dragon (1945) Kay, Edward
Red Garters (1954) Lilley
Red-Headed Baby (1931) Marsales
Red Headed Monkey (1950) Scheib
Red, Hot and Blue (1949) Lilley
Red Hot Music (1937) Scheib
Red Hot Rangers (1947) Bradley
Red Hot Rhythm (1929) Zuro
Red Hot Riding Hood (1943) Bradley
Red Hot Tires (1935) Jerome
Red House (1947) Rozsa
Red Kite (1965) Applebaum
Red Light (1949) Tiomkin
Red Line 7000 (1965) Riddle
Red Men on Parade (1940) Bakaleinikoff, C.
Red Menace (1949) Scott, N.
Red Mountain (1951) Waxman
Red Planet Mars (1952) Merrick
Red Pony (1949) Copland
Red Riding Hood Rides Again (1942) Kilfeather
Red Riding Hoodlum (1957) Wheeler
Red Riding Hoodwinked (1955) Franklyn
Red River (1948) Tiomkin
Red River Range (1938) Lava
Red River Renegades (1946) Glickman, M.
Red River Shore (1953) Butts
Red Runs the River (1963) Gustafson
Red Salute (1935) Newman
Red Skies of Montana (1952) Kaplan, S.
Red Snow (1952) Borisoff
Red Stallion (1947) Hollander
Red Stallion in the Rockies (1949) Cailliet
Red Sundown (1955) Salter

Red Tomahawk (1966) Haskell
Red Wagon (1945) Harling
Red, White and Black (1970) Phillips, S.
Red, White and Boo (1955) Sharples, Winston
Reddy Made Magic (1946) Calker
Redeemer (1965) Raksin
Redemption (1930) Axt
Redhead (1941) Sawtell
Redhead and the Cowboy (1951) Buttolph, David
Redhead from Manhattan (1943) Grau
Redhead from Wyoming (1953) Stein, H.
Redskin (1929) Zamecnik
Reducing Creme (1934) Stalling
Redwood Forest Trail (1950) Wilson, S.
Redwood Sap (1951) Wheeler
Reef and Beyond, or Darrow's Scope (1967) Lerman
Reflections of New York (1963) Elliott, Don
Reflections of Paris (1964) Elliott, Don
Reform Candidate (1915) Beynon
Reform School Girl (1957) Stein, R.
Reformed Wolf (1954) Scheib
Reformer and the Redhead (1950) Raksin
Refugee Story (1962) Byrd, C.
Registered Nurse (1934) Roemheld
Reg'lar Fellers (1941) DiMaggio
Reg'lar Kids (1935) Jackson, H.
Reign of Terror (1949) Kaplan, S.
Reivers (1969) Williams, J.
Relativity (1966) Tepper
Relentless (1948) Skiles
Reluctant Astronaut (1967) Mizzy
Reluctant Dragon (1941) Churchill
Reluctant Pup (1953) Scheib
Remains to Be Seen (1953) Alexander, J.
Remarkable Andrew (1942) Young, V.
Remarkable Mr. Pennypacker (1958) Harline
Remedy for Riches (1940) Bakaleinikoff, C.
Remember? (1939) Ward, E.
Remember Last Night? (1935) Waxman
Remember Pearl Harbor! (1942) Glickman, M.
Remember the Day (1941) Mockridge
Remember the Night (1940) Hollander
Rendezvous (1935) Axt
Rendezvous (1965) Small
Rendezvous 24 (1946) Lange
Rendezvous with Annie (1946) Dubin
Renegade Girl (1946) Calker
Renegade Ranger (1938) Webb
Renegade Trail (1939) Leipold
Renegades (1930) Kay, Arthur
Renegades (1946) Sawtell
Renfrew of the Royal Mounted (1937) Kay, Arthur
Renfrew on the Great White Trail (1938) Porter
Reno (1939) Webb
Repeat Performance (1947) Antheil
Replay (1970) Strouse
Report on Japan (1946) Stringer
Report to Judy (1945) Engel
Report to the People (1942) Terry, R.
Reprisal! (1956) Bakaleinikoff, M.
Reptilicus (1962) Baxter
Reputation (1921) Riesenfeld
Requiem for a Gunfighter (1965) Stein, R.
Requiem for a Heavyweight (1962) Rosenthal
Rescue (1929) Riesenfeld
Rescue Dog (1946) Wallace
Resisting Enemy Interrogation (1944) Rose
Rest Resort (1937) Dietrich
Restitution (1918) Read
Restless Breed (1957) Alperson
Restless Ones (1965) Carmichael
Restless Sax (1931) De Nat
Restless Sea (1964) Bruns
Restless Years (1958) Skinner, F.
Resurrection (1927) Burton
Resurrection (1931) Tiomkin
Resurrection of Broncho Billy (1970) Carpenter, J.
Retreat (19??) Loboda
Retreat, Hell! (1952) Lava
Return from Nowhere (1944) Shilkret, N.
Return from the Sea (1954) Dunlap
Return No More (1964) Korn
Return of Doctor X (1939) Kaun
Return of Dracula (1958) Fried
Return of Frank James (1940) Buttolph, David
Return of Gilbert and Sullivan (1952) Murray
Return of Jack Slade (1955) Dunlap
Return of Jesse James (1950) Grofé
Return of Monte Cristo (1946) Moraweck
Return of October (1948) Duning
Return of Peter Grimm (1935) Colombo
Return of Rin Tin Tin (1947) Erdody
Return of Rusty (1946) Duning
Return of the Ape Man (1944) Kay, Edward
Return of the Bad Men (1948) Sawtell
Return of the Cisco Kid (1939) Scharf, W.
Return of the Fly (1959) Sawtell
Return of the Frontiersman (1950) Buttolph, David
Return of the Lash (1947) Greene, W.
Return of the Plainsman (1952) Andrews, D.
Return of the Rangers (1943) Zahler
Return of the Seven (1966) Bernstein, E.
Return of the Terror (1934) Kaun
Return of the Texan (1952) Kaplan, S.
Return of the Vampire (1943) Castelnuovo-Tedesco
Return of Wildfire (1948) Glasser
Return to Paradise (1953) Tiomkin
Return to Peyton Place (1961) Waxman
Return to Treasure Island (1954) Sawtell
Return to Warbow (1958) Bakaleinikoff, M.
Reunion (1936) Buttolph, David
Reunion in France (1942) Waxman
Reunion in Paris (1955) Craig, E.
Reunion in Vienna (1933) Axt
Reveille with Beverly (1943) Leipold
Revenge (1928) Riesenfeld

Revenge of the Creature (1955) Lava
Revenge of the Zombies (1943) Kay, Edward
Revolt at Fort Laramie (1957) Baxter
Revolt in the Big House (1958) Kay, Edward
Revolt of Mamie Stover (1956) Friedhofer
Revolutionary (1970) Small
Revolving Door (1968) Shapiro
Reward (1965) Bernstein, E.
Rhapsody in Blue (1945) Steiner, M.
Rhapsody in Rivets (1941) Stalling
Rhapsody in Wood (1947) Burns, R.
Rhapsody of Steel (1959) Tiomkin
Rhapsody Rabbit (1946) Stalling
Rheumatic Fever (1947) Applebaum
Rhino! (1963) Schifrin
Rhubarb (1951) Van Cleave
Rhythm in the Bow (1935) Spencer, N.
Rhythm in the Clouds (1937) Colombo
Rhythm in the Ranks (1941) von Ottenfeld
Rhythm Inn (1951) Kay, Edward
Rhythm Jamboree (1940) Rosen, M.
Rhythm of a Big City (1948) Lava
Rhythm of the Rio Grande (1940) Sanucci
Rhythm of the Saddle (1938) Colombo
Rhythm on the Range (1936) Leipold
Rhythm on the River (1940) Young, V.
Rhythm Parade (1942) Kay, Edward
Rhythm Round-Up (1945) Sawtell
Rhythms of a Big City (1931) Levey
Rice (1963) Bazelon
Rich Are Always With Us (1932) Harling
Rich Man's Folly (1931) Leipold
Rich Man, Poor Girl (1938) Axt
Rich, Young and Pretty (1951) Rose
Richard the Lion-Hearted (1923) Axt
Riches of the Earth (1954) Applebaum
Richest Man in Town (1941) Shuken
Ricochet Romance (1954) Lava
Riddle of Rhodesia (1948) De Francesco
Ride a Crooked Mile (1938) Stone
Ride a Crooked Trail (1958) Wilson, S.
Ride a Violent Mile (1957) Kraushaar
Ride a White Horse (1952) Jackson, H.
Ride Back (1957) De Vol
Ride Beyond Vengeance (1966) Markowitz
Ride Clear of Diablo (1953) Stein, H.
Ride 'Em Cowboy (1941) Skinner, F.
Ride 'Em Cowgirl (1939) DiMaggio
Ride Him, Bosko (1933) Marsales
Ride in the Whirlwind (1966) Drasnin
Ride Kelly Ride (1941) Maxwell
Ride Lonesome (1959) Roemheld
Ride On, Vaquero (1941) Raksin
Ride Out for Revenge (1958) Stevens, L.
Ride, Ranchero, Ride (1948) Jackson, H.
Ride, Ryder, Ride (1949) Calker
Ride the High Country (1962) Bassman
Ride the Man Down (1952) Freeman, N.
Ride the Pink Horse (1947) Skinner, F.
Ride the Wild Surf (1964) Phillips, S.
Ride, Vaquero! (1953) Kaper
Rider from Tucson (1950) Sawtell
Rider on a Dead Horse (1962) Hooven
Riders from Nowhere (1940) Lange, J.
Riders in the Sky (1949) Leipold
Riders of Black Mountain (1940) Porter
Riders of Death Valley (1941) Rosen, M.
Riders of the Andes (1951) Shilkret, N.
Riders of the Black Hills (1938) Colombo
Riders of the Dawn (1937) Sanucci
Riders of the Dawn (1945) Sanucci
Riders of the Deadline (1943) Sawtell
Riders of the Dusk (1949) Kay, Edward
Riders of the Frontier (1939) Sanucci
Riders of the Pony Express (1949) Kraushaar
Riders of the Purple Sage (1931) Bassett, R. H.
Riders of the Purple Sage (1941) Mockridge
Riders of the Range (1949) Sawtell
Riders of the Rio Grande (1943) Glickman, M.
Riders of the Rockies (1937) Sanucci
Riders of the Sage (1939) Sanucci
Riders of the Timberline (1941) Leipold
Riders to the Stars (1954) Sukman
Ridin' Down the Trail (1947) Kay, Edward
Ridin' on a Rainbow (1941) Glickman, M.
Ridin' the Cherokee Trail (1941) Lange, J.
Ridin' the Rails (1951) Mamorsky
Riding Hannefords (1946) Jackson, H.
Riding High (1943) Bradshaw
Riding High (1950) Young, V.
Riding High (Trailer, 1950) Van Cleave
Riding Into Society (1940) Jackson, H.
Riding on Air (1937) Morton
Riding Shotgun (1954) Buttolph, David
Riding the California Trail (1947) Kay, Edward
Riding the Rails (1938) Timberg
Riding the Sunset Trail (1941) Sanucci
Riding the Wind (1954) Shilkret, N.
Riff Raff (1936) Ward, E.
Riff Raffy Daffy (1948) Stalling
Riffraff (1947) Webb
Right Approach (1961) Frontiere
Right Cross (1950) Raksin
Right Hand of the Devil (1963) Bath
Right of Way (1931) Reiser
Right Off the Bat (1958) Sharples, Winston
Right Timing (1942) Lava
Right to Live (1935) Kaun
Right to Live (1961) Lindahl
Right to Love (1930) Harling
Right to Romance (1933) Webb
Right to the Heart (1942) Harline
Right Way (1939) Jackson, H.
Rim of the Canyon (1949) Dubin
Rimfire (1949) Greene, W.
Ring (1952) Gilbert, H.
Ring Masters (1969) Lerman
Ring of Fear (1954) Dunlap

Ring of Steel (1942) Gould, M.
Ring of Terror (1962) Cairncross
Ringading Kid (1962) Sharples, Winston
Rings Around the World (1966) Belasco
Rings on Her Fingers (1942) Harline
Ringside (1949) Greene, W.
Ringside Maisie (1941) Snell
Rio (1939) Skinner, F.
Rio Bravo (1959) Tiomkin
Rio Conchos (1964) Goldsmith
Rio Grande (1950) Young, V.
Rio Grande Patrol (1950) Sawtell
Rio Grande Raiders (1946) Glickman, M.
Rio Grande Ranger (1936) Zahler
Rio Lobo (1970) Goldsmith
Rio Rita (1929) See p. 10
Rio Rita (1942) Stothart
Rio the Magnificent (1932) Shilkret, N.
Riot (1968) Komeda
Riot in Cell Block 11 (1954) Gilbert, H.
Riot in Rhythm (1950) Sharples, Winston
Riot on Sunset Strip (1967) Karger
Riot Squad (1941) Sanucci
Rip Van Winkle (1934) Scheib
Rippling Romance (1945) Worth, P.
Riptide (1934) Stothart
Rise and Fall of Legs Diamond (1960) Rosenman
Rise and Shine (1941) Buttolph, David
Rise of Duton Lang (1955) Farnon
Ritzy Hotel (1932) De Nat
Rival Romeos (1950) Scheib
River (1929) Baron, M.
River (1937) Thomson
River Changes (1956) Webb
River Gang (1945) Salter
River Lady (1948) Sawtell
River of No Return (1954) Harline
River of Romance (1929) Hajos
River Ribber (1946) Kilfeather
River Run (1952) Mamorsky
River's Edge (1957) Forbes
River's End (1940) Vaughan
Riverboat Rhythm (1946) Webb
Riverrun (1970) Greene, R.
Riveter (1940) Wallace
Riviera Days (1950) Lava
Riviera Revelries (1955) Jackson, H.
Road (1968) Baker, E.
Road Back (1937) Tiomkin
Road Demon (1938) Rose, G.
Road Gang (1936) Roemheld
Road Gang (Trailer, 1936) Kaun
Road House (1948) Newman
Road Hustlers (1968) Colicchio
Road Show (1941) Stoll
Road to Andalay (1964) Lava
Road to Bali (1953) Lilley
Road to Carolina (1965) Duffy
Road to Denver (1955) Butts
Road to Glory (1936) Bassett, R. H.
Road to Happiness (1942) Kay, Edward
Road to Morocco (1942) Young, V.
Road to Reno (1931) Leipold
Road to Reno (1938) Henderson, C.
Road to Rio (1947) Dolan
Road to Singapore (1940) Young, V.
Road to the Big House (1947) Kraushaar
Road to Utopia (1946) Harline
Road to Zanzibar (1941) Young, V.
Roadblock (1951) Sawtell
Roadracers (1958) Markowitz
Roamin' Roman (1964) Wheeler
Roaming Through Arizona (1944) Nussbaum
Roaming Through Michigan (1950) Nussbaum
Roaming Through Northern Ireland (1949) Mayfield
Roar of the Crowd (1953) Skiles
Roar of the Dragon (1932) Steiner, M.
Roar of the Iron Horse (1951) Leipold
Roar of the Press (1941) Kay, Edward
Roarin' Guns (1936) Wallace
Roaring City (1951) Shefter
Roaring Game (1951) Agostini
Roaring Guns (1944) Jackson, H.
Roaring Twenties (1939) Roemheld
Roaring Westward (1949) Kay, Edward
Robber Kitten (1935) Churchill
Robber's Roost (1955) Dunlap
Robbers' Roost (1932) Bassett, R. H.
Robby Bluewood (1968) Eaton
Robe (1953) Newman
Robert Kennedy Remembered (1968) Wykes
Roberta (1935) Steiner, M.
Robin and the 7 Hoods (1964) Riddle
Robin Goodhood (1970) Goodwin
Robin Hood (1922) Schertzinger
Robin Hood (1933) Scheib
Robin Hood Daffy (1957) Franklyn
Robin Hood in an Arrow Escape (1936) Scheib
Robin Hood Makes Good (1939) Stalling
Robin Hood of El Dorado (1936) Stothart
Robin Hood of Monterey (1947) Kay, Edward
Robin Hood of Texas (1947) Scott, N.
Robin Hood of the Pecos (1941) Glickman, M.
Robin Hood Winked (1948) Sharples, Winston
Robin Hood, Jr. (1934) Stalling
Robin Hoodlum (1948) Castillo
Robin Hoodwinked (1957) Bradley
Robin Hoodwinked (1967) Sharples, Winston
Robin Hoody Woody (1962) Wheeler
Robin Rodenthood (1955) Sharples, Winston
Robinson Crusoe (1936) Luz
Robinson Crusoe Isle (1934) Dietrich
Robinson Crusoe on Mars (1964) Van Cleave
Robinson Crusoe's Broadcast (1938) Scheib
Robinson Crusoe, Jr. (1941) Stalling
Robot Monster (1953) Bernstein, E.
Robot Rabbit (1952) Stalling
Robot Ringer (1962) Sharples, Winston

Robot Rival (1964) Sharples, Winston
Rock-a-Bye Baby (1958) Scharf, W.
Rock-a-Bye Bear (1952) Bradley
Rock-a-Bye Gator (1962) Poddany
Rock a Bye Pinky (1966) Greene, W.
Rock All Night (1957) Ram
Rock Island Trail (1950) Butts
Rock 'n' Rodent (1967) Brandt
Rock, Pretty Baby (1957) Mancini
Rock River Renegades (1942) Sanucci
Rockabilly Baby (1957) Dunlap
Rocket Racket (1962) Wheeler
Rocket Squad (1955) Franklyn
Rocket to Mars (1946) Sharples, Winston
Rocket-Bye Baby (1956) Franklyn
Rockets Bursting in Air (1945) Palange
Rocketship X-M (1950) Grofé
Rockhound Magoo (1957) Elliott, Dean
Rockin' in the Rockies (1945) Sawtell
Rocky (1948) Kay, Edward
Rocky Eden (1951) Agostini
Rocky Mountain (1950) Steiner, M.
Rocky Mountain Big Game (1942) Dunn
Rocky Mountain Grandeur (1937) Shilkret, N.
Rocky Mountain Rangers (1940) Feuer
Rocky Mountain River Thrills (1953) Mamorsky
Rodent to Stardom (1967) Lava
Rodeo (1952) Skiles
Rodeo (1969) Rosmini
Rodeo Dough (1931) De Nat
Rodeo King and the Senorita (1951) Wilson, S.
Rodeo Romeo (1946) Sharples, Winston
Rodeo Round-up (1941) Jackson, H.
Rodeo Roundup (1954) Lava
Rodney (1951) McBride, R.
Roger Touhy, Gangster (1944) Friedhofer
Rogue River (1950) Sawtell
Rogue Song (1930) Axt
Rogue's Gallery (1968) Haskell
Rogue's March (1952) Colombo
Rogues of Sherwood Forest (1950) Castelnuovo-Tedesco
Rogues' Gallery (1945) Zahler
Rogues' Regiment (1948) Amfitheatrof
Roll On Texas Moon (1946) Butts
Roll, Thunder, Roll! (1949) Kraushaar
Roll Wagons Roll (1940) Sanucci
Roller Derby Girl (1949) Sharples, Winston
Rollin' Home to Texas (1940) Sanucci
Rollin' Plains (1938) Sanucci
Rollin' Westward (1939) Sanucci
Rolling Caravans (1938) Zahler
Rolling Down the Great Divide (1942) Lange, J.
Rolling Home (1946) Calker
Rolling Stones (1936) Scheib
Rolling Thrills (1949) Shilkret, N.
Roman Holiday (1953) Young, V.
Roman Legion-Hare (1955) Franklyn
Roman Scandals (1933) Newman
Romance (1930) Axt
Romance (1932) Scheib
Romance and Dance (1947) Jackson, H.
Romance in Manhattan (1935) Colombo
Romance in the Air (1936) Jackson, H.
Romance in the Dark (1938) Young, V.
Romance in the Rain (1918) Hamilton, p. 363
Romance of Happy Valley (1937) Jackson, H.
Romance of Louisiana (1937) Jackson, H.
Romance of Robert Burns (1937) Vaughan
Romance of Rosy Ridge (1947) Bassman
Romance of the Fjords (1947) De Francesco
Romance of the Potato (1939) Amfitheatrof
Romance of the Redwoods (1939) Morgan, F.
Romance of the Rio Grande (1941) Mockridge
Romance of the West (1935) Jackson, H.
Romance of the West (1946) Franklin
Romance on the High Seas (1948) Hollander
Romance on the Run (1938) Colombo
Romance Road (1937) Jackson, H.
Romantic Nevada (1943) Nussbaum
Romantic Riviera (1951) Kirk
Romantic Rumbolia (1949) Smith, P.
Rome Adventure (1962) Steiner, M.
Romeo and Juliet (1933) Scheib
Romeo and Juliet (1936) Stothart
Romeo in Rhythm (1940) Bradley
Romola (1924) Gottschalk
Roof Top Razzle-Dazzle (1964) Greene, W.
Roof Tops of New York (1961) Liebman
Roogie's Bump (1954) Engel
Rookie (1959) Dunlap
Rookie Bear (1941) Bradley
Rookie Cop (1939) Webb
Rookie Revue (1941) Stalling
Rookies in Burma (1943) Grau
Rookies on Parade (1941) Glickman, M.
Room and Bird (1951) Poddany
Room and Board (1943) Kilfeather
Room and Bore (1962) Wheeler
Room and Wrath (1956) Wheeler
Room for One More (1952) Steiner, M.
Room Runners (1932) Bradley
Room Service (1938) Webb
Room That Flies (1954) Craig, E.
Roosevelt Story (1947) Robinson
Roots in the Earth (1940) Bowles
Rooty Toot Toot (1952) Moore, P.
Rope (1948) Buttolph, David
Rope of Flesh (1965) Price, Henry
Rope of Sand (1949) Waxman
Rosalie (1937) Stothart
Rose Bowl (1936) Leipold
Rose Bowl Story (1952) Skiles
Rose Marie (1936) Stothart
Rose Marie (1954) Stoll
Rose of Cimarron (1952) Kraushaar
Rose of the Rancho (1936) Friedhofer
Rose of the Rio Grande (1938) Riesenfeld

Rose of the Yukon (1949) Wilson, S.
Rose of Washington Square (1939) Rose, G.
Rose Tattoo (1955) North
Roseanna McCoy (1949) Buttolph, David
Rosemary's Baby (1968) Komeda
Roses Are Red (1947) Schrager
Rosie (1967) Murray
Rosita (1923) Gottschalk
Rotate the Body in All Its Planes (1961) Partch
Rough and Tumbleweed (1961) Poddany
Rough Night in Jericho (1967) Costa
Rough Riders (1927) Riesenfeld
Rough Riders of Durango (1951) Wilson, S.
Rough Riders' Round-Up (1939) Lava
Rough Riding (1954) Bradley
Rough Riding Hood (1965) Wheeler
Rough Romance (1930) Brunelli
Rough, Tough and Ready (1945) Skiles
Roughly Speaking (1945) Steiner, M.
Roughly Squeaking (1946) Stalling
Roughshod (1949) Webb
Round Trip (1947) Applebaum
Round Trip to Mars (1957) Wheeler
Round Up (1941) Young, V.
Rounders (1964) Alexander, J.
Roustabout (1964) Lilley
Rover's Rangers (1943) Lava
Rover's Rescue (1940) Scheib
Rover's Rival (1937) Stalling
Row, Row, Row (1930) Steiner, G.
Rowdy Raccoons (1953) Craig, E.
Roxie Hart (1942) Newman
Royal African Rifles (1953) Dunlap
Royal Box (1930) Levey
Royal Cat Nap (1957) Bradley
Royal Divorce (1938) Collins
Royal Duck Shoot (1948) Lava
Royal Flesh (1970) Mendoza-Nava
Royal Four-Flusher (1947) Sharples, Winston
Royal Good Time (1934) Sharples, Winston
Royal Journey (1951) Applebaum
Royal Mounties (1954) Lava
Royal Purple (1961) Henderson, S.
Royal Scandal (1945) Newman
Royal Wedding (1951) Sendrey
Royalty of the Range (1947) De Francesco
Rubber River (1947) Jackson, H.
Rubáiyat of Omar Khayyám (1922) Cadman
Ruby Gentry (1952) Roemheld
Rugged Bear (1953) Wallace
Ruggles of Red Gap (1935) Roemheld
Rulers of the Sea (1939) Hageman
Rules and Laws (1951) Townsend
Ruling Voice (1931) Mendoza
Rumba (1935) Rainger
Rumble on the Docks (1956) Bakaleinikoff, M.
Rumors (1943) Stalling
Run, Angel, Run! (1969) Phillips, S.
Run, Appaloosa, Run (1965) Shores
Run for Cover (1955) Jackson, H.
Run for the Hills (1953) Kraushaar
Run for the Sun (1956) Steiner, F.
Run Home Slow (1965) Zappa
Run of the Arrow (1957) Young, V.
Run, Run, Sweet Road Runner (1965) Lava
Run Sheep Run (1936) Bradley
Run Silent, Run Deep (1958) Waxman
Runaround (1931) Steiner, M.
Runaround (1946) Skinner, F.
Runaway Daughters (1956) Stein, R.
Runaway Girl (1966) LaSalle
Runaway Mouse (1953) Scheib
Running for Sheriff (1954) Taylor, R.
Running Target (1956) Gold
Running the Keyes (1949) Mamorsky
Running Water on the Farm (1946) Carbonara
Rupert the Runt (1940) Scheib
Rural Hungary (1939) Bakaleinikoff, C.
Rural Nurse (1946) North
Rural Sweden (1938) Shilkret, J.
Rushing Roulette (1965) Lava
Russia and the West (1963) Cutner
Russian Consumer (1968) Gould, S.
Russian Dressing (1933) De Nat
Russian Rhapsody (1944) Stalling
Russians Are Coming The Russians Are Coming (1966) Mandel
Rustlers (1949) Sawtell
Rustlers of Devil's Canyon (1947) Glickman, M.
Rustlers on Horseback (1950) Wilson, S.
Rustlers' Ransom (1950) Rosen, M.
Ruthless (1948) Janssen
Ryan's Daughter (1970) Jarre

S-73 (Sofa Compact) (1954) Bernstein, E.
Saadia (1953) Kaper
Sable Lorcha (1915) Breil
Sabotage (1939) Feuer
Sabotage Squad (1942) Leipold
Saboteur (1942) Skinner, F.
Sabre Jet (1953) Gilbert, H.
Sabrina (1954) Hollander
Sabu and the Magic Ring (1957) Skiles
Sad Horse (1959) Sawtell
Sad Little Guinea Pigs (1938) De Nat
Sad Sack (1957) Scharf, W.
Saddle Legion (1950) Sawtell
Saddle Mountain Roundup (1941) Sanucci
Saddle Pals (1947) Glickman, M.
Saddle Silly (1941) Stalling
Saddle-Sore Woody (1964) Greene, W.
Saddle the Wind (1957) Bernstein, E.
Saddle Up (1947) Jackson, H.
Saddlemates (1941) Feuer
Sadie Hawkins Day (1944) Kilfeather
Sadie McKee (1934) Axt
Sadismo (1967) Baxter
Sadler's Wells Ballerina (1952) Forrell

Safari (1940) Hollander
Safari Drums (1953) Skiles
Safari So Good (1947) Sharples, Winston
Safe at Home! (1962) Alexander, V.
Safe in Hell (Trailer, 1931) Schrager
Safety First (195?) Janssen
Safety Is Golden (1966) Hastings
Safety Second (1950) Bradley
Safety Spin (1953) Curtin
Saga of Hemp Brown (1958) Stein, H.
Saga of Windwagon Smith (1961) Bruns
Sagebrush and Silver (1941) De Francesco
Sagebrush Law (1942) Sawtell
Sahara (1943) Rozsa
Sahara Hare (1954) Franklyn
Saigon (1948) Dolan
Sail a Crooked Ship (1962) Duning
Sail Ho (1941) Dunn
Sailing Zero (1964) Sharples, Winston
Sailor Beware (1951) Lilley
Sailor Mouse (1938) Marsales
Sailor Takes a Wife (1945) Green, J.
Sailor's Holiday (1944) Leipold
Sailor's Home (1936) Scheib
Sailor's Lady (1940) Kaylin
Sailor's Sweetheart (1931) Secunda
Sails Aloft (1943) De Francesco
Sails of Acapulco (1952) Mamorsky
Saint in Palm Springs (1941) Webb
Saint Louis: Gateway to the West (1966) Feierabend
Saint of Devil's Island (1962) Botkin
Saint Strikes Back (1939) Webb
Saint Takes Over (1940) Webb
Saint's Double Trouble (1940) Webb
Sainted Sisters (1948) Van Cleave
Saintly Sinners (1961) LaSalle
Sal of Singapore (1928) Zuro
Sally (1930) Leonardi
Sally and Saint Anne (1952) Skinner, F.
Sally of the Sawdust (1925) Silvers
Salmon Fishing (1945) Shilkret, J.
Salmon Yeggs (1958) Wheeler
Salome (1918) Rubinstein, G.
Salome (1922) Marcelli
Salome (1953) Duning
Salome, Where She Danced (1945) Ward, E.
Salt Lake Diversions (1943) Bakaleinikoff, C.
Salt of the Earth (1954) Kaplan, S.
Salt Water Daffy (1941) Calker
Salt Water Tabby (1947) Bradley
Salt Water Taffy (1930) Scheib
Salty McGuire (1937) Scheib
Salty O'Rourke (1945) Dolan
Saludos Amigos (1942) Wolcott
Salute for Three (1943) Young, V.
Salute to France (1944) Weill
Salute to the Marines (1943) Hayton
Salvage (1942) Kreutz
Sam Whiskey (1969) Gilbert, H.
Samar (1961) Zimmerman
Samba-Mania (1948) Van Cleave
Samoa (1956) Wallace
Sampan Family (1949) Forrell
Samson (1914) Kreider
Samson and Delilah (1949) Young, V.
Samson and the Seven Miracles of the World (1962) Baxter
Samson Scrap (1960) Sharples, Winston
San Antone (1953) Butts
San Antone Ambush (1949) Wilson, S.
San Antonio (1946) Steiner, M.
San Diego, I Love You (1944) Salter
San Fan See (1963) Brackman
San Fernando Valley (1944) Glickman, M.
San Francisco (1936) Stothart
San Francisco Conference (1946) Gould, M.
San Francisco Docks (1940) Salter
San Francisco, Metropolis of the West (1941) Craig, E.
San Francisco, San Francisco, San Francisco (1965) Tjader
San Francisco Story (1952) Dunlap
San Francisco—Pacific Gateway (1947) Shilkret, N.
San Pietro (1945) Tiomkin
San Quentin (1937) Roemheld
San Quentin (1946) Sawtell
Sanctuary (1961) North
Sand (1949) Amfitheatrof
Sand Castle (1961) Wilder
Sand, or Peter and the Wolf (1969) Riesman
Sand Pebbles (1966) Goldsmith
Sandman Tales (1933) De Nat
Sandpiper (1965) Mandel
Sands of Iwo Jima (1949) Young, V.
Sandy Claws (1954) Stalling
Sangaree (1953) Cailliet
Sangaree (Trailer, 1953) Van Cleave
Santa Claus Conquers the Martians (1964) Delugg
Santa Fe (1951) Sawtell
Santa Fe Marshal (1940) Leipold
Santa Fe Passage (1955) Butts
Santa Fe Scouts (1943) Glickman, M.
Santa Fe Stampede (1938) Lava
Santa Fe Trail (1940) Steiner, M.
Santa Fe Uprising (1946) Glickman, M.
Santa's Christmas Circus (1966) Jenks
Santa's Surprise (1947) Sharples, Winston
Santa's Workshop (1932) Churchill
Santiago (1956) Buttolph, David
Sap from Syracuse (1930) Green, J.
Sappho Darling (1968) Price, Henry
Sappy Homiens (1956) Rogers
Saps at Sea (1940) Hatley
Saps in Chaps (1942) Stalling
Sarah and Son (1930) Potoker
Saratoga (1937) Ward, E.
Saratoga Trunk (1946) Steiner, M.

Sardinia (1956) Wallace
Sarge Goes to College (1947) Kay, Edward
Sarong Girl (1943) Kay, Edward
Saskatchewan (1954) Mancini
Sassy Cats (1933) De Nat
Satan Bug (1965) Goldsmith
Satan in High Heels (1962) Lowe
Satan Met a Lady (1936) Kaun
Satan's Cradle (1949) Glasser
Satan's Sadists (1969) Hatcher
Satan's Waitin' (1953) Stalling
Satisfied Customers (1954) Scheib
Satisfied Saurians (1949) De Francesco
Saturday (1970) Ivers
Saturday Evening Puss (1949) Bradley
Saturday Night Bath in Apple Valley (1965) Wakefield
Saturday Night Kid (1929) Leipold
Saturday's Children (1929) Reiser
Saturday's Children (1940) Deutsch
Saturday's Hero (1951) Bernstein, E.
Savage (1952) Sawtell
Savage Drums (1951) Calker
Savage Eye (1959) Rosenman
Savage Frontier (1953) Wilson, S.
Savage Girl (1932) Zahler
Savage Gold (1933) Bradford
Savage Horde (1950) Butts
Savage Sam (1963) Wallace
Savage Seven (1968) Curb
Savage Splendor (1949) Sawtell
Savage Wild (1970) Mendoza-Nava
Saved by the Bell (1950) Sharples, Winston
Savoy in the Alps (1940) Craig, E.
Saw Mill Mystery (1937) Scheib
Sawdust Paradise (1928) Carbonara
Saxon Charm (1948) Scharf, W.
Say Ah, Jasper (1944) von Ottenfeld
Say It in French (1938) Shuken
Say Nothing About This to Anyone (1963) Manupelli
Say One for Me (1959) Harline
Sayonara (1957) Waxman
Scalp Treatment (1952) Wheeler
Scalp Trouble (1939) Stalling
Scalphunters (1968) Bernstein, E.
Scandal at Scourie (1953) Amfitheatrof
Scandal for Sale (1932) Broekman
Scandal in Paris (1946) Eisler
Scandal, Inc. (1956) Sawtell
Scandal Sheet (1931) Hajos
Scandal Sheet (1952) Duning
Scandal Street (1938) Leipold
Scapegoat (1958) Kaper
Scaramouche (1923) Axt
Scaramouche (1952) Young, V.
Scared Crows (1939) Timberg
Scared Stiff (1945) Laszlo
Scared Stiff (1953) Stevens, L.
Scared to Death (1946) Mayfield
Scaredy Cat (1948) Stalling
Scarf (1951) Gilbert, H.
Scarface (1932) Tandler
Scarlet Claw (1944) Sawtell
Scarlet Clue (1945) Kay, Edward
Scarlet Coat (1955) Salinger
Scarlet Dawn (1932) Roder
Scarlet Dawn (Trailer, 1932) Kaun
Scarlet Empress (1934) Leipold
Scarlet Horseman (1946) Rosen, M.
Scarlet Hour (1956) Stevens, L.
Scarlet Letter (1926) Axt
Scarlet Pumpernickel (1948) Stalling
Scarlet Seas (1928) Hajos
Scarlet Street (1945) Salter
Scars of Jealousy (1923) Cohen, S.
Scary Crows (1937) De Nat
Scary Time (1960) Glanville-Hicks
Scat Cats (1956) Bradley
Scattergood Baines (1941) Bakaleinikoff, C.
Scattergood Meets Broadway (1941) Tiomkin
Scattergood Pulls the Strings (1941) Bakaleinikoff, C.
Scattergood Rides High (1942) Sawtell
Scattergood Survives a Murder (1942) Sawtell
Scene of the Crime (1949) Previn, A.
Scenic Grandeur (1941) Amfitheatrof
Scenic Oregon (1943) Nussbaum
Scenic Sweden (1948) De Francesco
Scent-imental Over You (1947) Stalling
Scent-imental Romeo (1949) Stalling
Scent of the Matterhorn (1961) Franklyn
Scholastic England (1948) Mayfield
School Birds (1937) Scheib
School Days (1932) Bradley
School Daze (1942) Scheib
Schoolboy Dreams (1940) De Nat
Schooner the Better (1946) Kilfeather
Science Friction (1963) Greene, W.
Science Friction (1970) Goodwin
Scotch Highball (1930) Scheib
Scotland Yard (1930) Kay, Arthur
Scotland Yard (1941) Mockridge
Scotland Yard Investigator (1945) Maxwell
Scottie Finds a Home (1935) Sharples, Winston
Scottish Miner (1952) Forrell
Scoundrel (1935) Antheil
Scout Fellow (1951) Sharples, Winston
Scout with the Gout (1947) Sharples, Winston
Scouting for Trouble (1960) Sharples, Winston
Scoutmaster Magoo (1958) Farnon
Scouts to the Rescue (1955) Scheib
Scram (1932) Shield
Scrambled Aches (1956) Stalling
Scrambled Eggs (1939) Marsales
Scrap for Victory (1943) Scheib
Scrap Happy Daffy (1943) Stalling
Scrap the Japs (1942) Timberg

Scrappily Married (1945) Sharples, Winston
Scrappy Birthday (1949) Calker
Scrappy's Added Attraction (1939) De Nat
Scrappy's Art Gallery (1934) De Nat
Scrappy's Auto Show (1933) De Nat
Scrappy's Band Concert (1937) De Nat
Scrappy's Boy Scouts (1936) De Nat
Scrappy's Camera Troubles (1936) De Nat
Scrappy's Dog Show (1934) De Nat
Scrappy's Expedition (1934) De Nat
Scrappy's Ghost Story (1935) De Nat
Scrappy's Music Lesson (1937) De Nat
Scrappy's News Flashes (1937) De Nat
Scrappy's Party (1933) De Nat
Scrappy's Playmates (1938) De Nat
Scrappy's Pony (1936) De Nat
Scrappy's Relay Race (1934) De Nat
Scrappy's Rodeo (1939) De Nat
Scrappy's Side Show (1939) De Nat
Scrappy's Television (1934) De Nat
Scrappy's Theme Song (1934) De Nat
Scrappy's Toy Shop (1934) De Nat
Scrappy's Trailer (1935) De Nat
Scrappy's Trip to Mars (1938) De Nat
Scratch a Tiger (1970) Goodwin
Scratch Harry (1970) Lauber
Scream in the Dark (1943) Glickman, M.
Screaming Eagles (1956) Sukman
Screaming Mimi (1958) Bakaleinikoff, M.
Screaming Skull (1958) Gold
Screwball (1943) Calker
Screwball Football (1939) Stalling
Screwball Sports (1956) Jackson, H.
Screwball Squirrel (1944) Bradley
Screwdriver (1941) Calker
Screwy Truant (1945) Bradley
Scrooge McDuck and Money (1967) Marks
Scrub Me Mama with a Boogie Beat (1941) Calker
Scuba Duba Do (1966) Timmens
Scudda-Hoo! Scudda-Hay! (1948) Mockridge
Sculpture by Lipton (1954) Feldman
Sculpture in Minnesota (19??) Carpenter, V.
Scum of the Earth! (1963) Ortiz
Sea Around Us (1953) Sawtell
Sea Chase (1955) Webb
Sea-Food Mamas (1944) De Francesco
Sea for Yourself (1941) Amfitheatrof
Sea God (1930) Hajos
Sea-Going Smoke Eaters (1953) McBride, R.
Sea Hawk (1924) Axt
Sea Hawk (1924) Copping
Sea Hawk (1940) Korngold
Sea Hornet (1951) Butts
Sea Hound (1947) Sawtell
Sea in Your Future (1970) Evans
Sea Legs (1930) Rainger
Sea of Contention (1967) Lackey
Sea of Grass (1946) Stothart
Sea of Lost Ships (1953) Butts
Sea Racketeers (1937) Colombo
Sea Raiders (1941) Rosen, M.
Sea Salts (1948) Wallace
Sea Scouts (1939) Wallace
Sea Sirens (1946) De Francesco
Sea Sports of Tahiti (1954) Lava
Sea Tiger (1952) Kay, Edward
Sea Wolf (1930) Kaylin
Sea Wolf (1941) Korngold
Seal Island (1948) Wallace
Seal Skinners (1939) Lewis
Sealed Cargo (1951) Webb
Sealed Orders (1914) Levy, S.
Sealed Verdict (1948) Friedhofer
Sealskins (1932) Shield
Seapreme Court (1954) Sharples, Winston
Search (1964) Roznyai
Search for Beauty (1934) Leipold
Search for Bridey Murphy (1956) Webb
Search for Danger (1949) Hajos
Search for Paradise (1957) Tiomkin
Search Into Darkness (1962) Foss
Searchers (1956) Steiner, M.
Searching Eye (1960) Bland
Searching Eye (1964) Alexander, J.
Searching Wind (1946) Young, V.
Searchlight on the Nations (1947) Applebaum
Seas Beneath (1931) Brunelli
Seasick Sailors (1951) Scheib
Seaside Adventure (1951) Scheib
Seats of the Mighty (1914) Smyth
Seattle, Gateway to the Northwest (1940) Bakaleinikoff, C.
Sebastian (1967) Goldsmith
Second Chance (1947) Butts
Second Chance (1950) Forbes
Second Chance (1953) Webb
Second Chorus (1941) Shaw
Second Face (1950) Kraushaar
Second Fiddle (1939) Mockridge
Second Fiddle to a Steel Guitar (1965) Williams, A.
Second Floor Mystery (1930) Kaylin
Second Greatest Sex (1955) Mancini
Second Hand Wife (1932) Lipschultz
Second Honeymoon (1937) Mockridge
Second Sight (1952) Shilkret, N.
Second Time Around (1961) Fried
Second Woman (1951) Nussbaum
Seconds (1966) Goldsmith
Secret Agent of Japan (1942) Harline
Secret Agent Woody Woodpecker (1967) Greene, W.
Secret Beyond the Door (1948) Rozsa
Secret Bride (1934) Kaun
Secret Call (1931) Kopp, R.
Secret Code (1942) Zahler
Secret Command (1944) Sawtell
Secret Enemies (1942) Jackson, H.

Secret Evidence (1941) Kay, Edward
Secret Fury (1950) Webb
Secret Garden (1949) Kaper
Secret Heart (1946) Kaper
Secret Invasion (1964) Friedhofer
Secret Land (1948) Kaper
Secret Life of an American Wife (1968) May
Secret Life of Walter Mitty (1947) Raksin
Secret of Convict Lake (1951) Kaplan, S.
Secret of Deep Harbor (1961) LaSalle
Secret of Madame Blanche (1933) Axt
Secret of My Success (1965) Cailliet
Secret of Santa Vittoria (1969) Gold
Secret of the Fjord (1942) De Francesco
Secret of the Incas (1954) Buttolph, David
Secret of the Purple Reef (1960) Bregman
Secret of the Sacred Forest (1970) Gilbert, H.
Secret of the Wastelands (1941) Leipold
Secret of the Whistler (1946) Gilbert, H.
Secret Service (1931) Steiner, M.
Secret Service in Darkest Africa (1943) Glickman, M.
Secret Service of the Air (1939) Kaun
Secret Sinners (1933) Zahler
Secret Thief (1956) Brant
Secret Ways (1961) Williams, J.
Secret Weapon (1943) Jackson, H.
Secrets (1933) Newman
Secrets of a Co-Ed (1943) Zahler
Secrets of a Nurse (1938) Skinner, F.
Secrets of a Secretary (1931) Green, J.
Secrets of a Sorority Girl (1946) Hajos
Secrets of an Actress (1938) Roemheld
Secrets of Life (1956) Smith, P.
Secrets of Scotland Yard (1944) Maxwell
Secrets of the Reef (1956) Elliott, C.
Secrets of the Underground (1942) Scharf, W.
Security Risk (1954) Kay, Edward
Seducers (1962) Lindsey
See America Thirst (1930) Roemheld
See Here, Private Hargrove (1944) Snell
See My Lawyer (1944) Akridge
See Naples and the Island of Ischia (1951) Flanagan
See the World (1934) Scheib
See Ya Later Gladiator (1968) Lava
Seed (1931) Roemheld
Seeds of Destiny (1946) Machan
Seein' Red, White 'n' Blue (1943) Timberg
Seeing Ceylon (1952) Nussbaum
Seeing El Salvador (1945) Nussbaum
Seeing Eye (1941) Dunn
Seeing Eye (1952) Lava
Seeing Ghosts (1948) Scheib
Seeing Hands (1943) Terr
Seeing Stars (1932) De Nat
Seeing the World; A Visit to New York (1936) Bowles
Seesaw and the Shoes (1945) Terr
Self Control (1938) Wallace
Self-Defense (1942) Kaplan, S.
Self-Made Mongrel (1945) Sharples, Winston
Sellout (1951) Buttolph, David
Senator Was Indiscreet (1948) Amfitheatrof
Send Me No Flowers (1964) De Vol
Senior Prom (1958) Alexander, V.
Señor Droopy (1949) Bradley
Señor Jim (1936) Tulane
Senorella and the Glass Huarache (1963) Lava
Senorita from the West (1945) Fairchild
Sensations of 1945 (1944) Merrick
Senses (1967) Szabo
Sentimental Journey (1946) Mockridge
Separate Tables (1958) Raksin
September Affair (1951) Young, V.
September in the Rain (1937) Stalling
September Storm (1959) Kraushaar
Sequoia (1935) Stothart
Serenade (1956) Heindorf
Serene Siam (1937) Shilkret, N.
Serenity (1962) Hartman
Sergeant Deadhead (1965) Baxter
Sergeant Madden (1939) Axt
Sergeant Mike (1944) Castelnuovo-Tedesco
Sergeant Murphy (1937) Jackson, H.
Sergeant Rutledge (1960) Jackson, H.
Sergeant Ryker (1968) Williams, J.
Sergeant York (1941) Steiner, M.
Sergeants 3 (1962) May
Serpent of the Nile (1953) Bakaleinikoff, M.
Servant of Mankind (1940) Amfitheatrof
Servant of the People (1937) Vaughan
Servants' Entrance (1934) Friedhofer
Service De Luxe (1938) Henderson, C.
Service with a Smile (1964) Sharples, Winston
Seven Angry Men (1955) Brandt
Seven Brides for Seven Brothers (1954) Deutsch
Seven Cities of Antarctica (1958) Smith, P.
Seven Cities of Gold (1955) Friedhofer
Seven Days Ashore (1944) Webb
Seven Days in May (1964) Goldsmith
Seven Days Leave (1930) Leipold
Seven Days' Leave (1942) Webb
Seven Doors to Death (1944) Zahler
Seven Faces (1929) Lipschultz
Seven Guns to Mesa (1958) Stevens, L.
Seven Hills of Rome (1957) Stoll
Seven Keys to Baldpate (1930) Webb
Seven Keys to Baldpate (1935) Colombo
Seven Keys to Baldpate (1947) Sawtell
Seven Little Foys (1955) Lilley
Seven Men from Now (1956) Vars
Seven Sinners (1940) Skinner, F.
Seven Sweethearts (1942) Waxman
Seven Thieves (1959) Frontiere
Seven Ways from Sundown (1960) Gertz

Seven Were Saved (1947) Calker
Seven Wise Dwarfs (1941) Wallace
Seven Women (1965) Bernstein, E.
Seven Women from Hell (1961) Dunlap
Seven Wonders of the World (1956) Raksin
Seven Year Itch (1955) Newman
Seventeen (1940) Bradshaw
Seventh Cross (1944) Webb
Seventh Heaven (1937) Buttolph, David
Seventh Sin (1957) Rozsa
Seventh Victim (1943) Webb
Seventy Times Seven (1960) Botkin
Sex and the Lonely Woman (1967) Bath
Sex and the Single Girl (1964) Hefti
Sex Kittens Go to College (1960) Elliott, Dean
Sex Life of the Common Film (1938) Bowles
Sexploiters (1965) Karmen
Sh! The Octopus (1937) Roemheld
Sh-h-h-h-h (1955) Wheeler
Shack Out on 101 (1955) Dunlap
Shadow (1940) Zahler
Shadow in the Sky (1951) Kaper
Shadow of a Doubt (1942) Tiomkin
Shadow of a Woman (1946) Deutsch
Shadow of Doubt (1935) Bassett, R. H.
Shadow of Doubt (Trailer, 1935) Ward, E.
Shadow of Suspicion (1944) Zahler
Shadow of Terror (1945) Hajos
Shadow of the Eagle (1932) Zahler
Shadow of the Law (1930) Potoker
Shadow of the Thin Man (1941) Snell
Shadow on the Wall (1949) Previn, A.
Shadow on the Window (1957) Duning
Shadow Over Italy (1956) Gustafson
Shadow Returns (1946) Kay, Edward
Shadow Valley (1947) Greene, W.
Shadowed (1946) Castelnuovo-Tedesco
Shadows (1922) Gottschalk
Shadows (1959) Mingus
Shadows of the Orient (1937) Zahler
Shadows of the West (1949) Kay, Edward
Shadows of Tombstone (1953) Butts
Shadows on the Range (1946) Kay, Edward
Shadows on the Sage (1942) Glickman, M.
Shadows on the Stairs (1941) Kaun
Shadows Over Chinatown (1946) Kay, Edward
Shady Lady (1945) Lava
Shaggy (1948) Kraushaar
Shaggy Dog (1959) Smith, P.
Shake Hands with Murder (1944) Zahler
Shake Your Powder Puff (1934) Spencer, N.
Shake, Rattle, and Rock! (1956) Courage
Shakespearian Spinach (1940) Sharples, Winston
Shakiest Gun in the West (1967) Mizzy
Shall We Dance (1937) Shilkret, N.
Sham Battle Shenanigans (1942) Scheib
Shame, Shame, Everybody Knows Her Name (1969) Craig, G.
Shamrock and Roll (1969) Lava
Shamrock Hill (1949) Gilbert, H.
Shane (1953) Young, V.
Shanghai (1935) Hollander
Shanghai Chest (1948) Kay, Edward
Shanghai Cobra (1945) Kay, Edward
Shanghai Express (1932) Harling
Shanghai Gesture (1941) Hageman
Shanghai Lady (1929) Perry
Shanghai Madness (1933) Zamecnik
Shanghai Story (1954) Butts
Shanghaied (1934) Churchill
Shanghaied Shipmates (1936) Spencer, N.
Shanty Where Santy Claus Lives (1933) Marsales
Shantytown (1943) Scharf, W.
Shape Ahoy (1945) Sharples, Winston
Shark River (1953) Gertz
Sharkfighters (1956) Moross
Sharpshooters (1938) Rose, G.
Shaving Muggs (1953) Sharples, Winston
She (1935) Steiner, M.
She Beast (1966) Ferraro
She Couldn't Say No (1940) Jackson, H.
She Couldn't Say No (1954) Webb
She Creature (1956) Stein, R.
She Demons (1958) Carras
She Devil (1957) Sawtell
She-Devils on Wheels (1968) Wellington
She Done Him Right (1933) Dietrich
She Done Him Wrong (1933) Leipold
She Freak (1967) Allen, B.
She Gets Her Man (1935) Hajos
She Gets Her Man (1945) Skinner, F.
She Gods of Shark Reef (1958) Stein, R.
She Goes to Vassar (1961) Leonard
She Goes to War (1929) Altschuler
She Had to Eat (1937) Rose, G.
She Knew All the Answers (1941) Heymann
She Learned About Sailors (1934) Buttolph, David
She Loved a Fireman (1937) Jackson, H.
She Loves Me Not (1934) Satterfield
She Married a Cop (1939) Feuer
She Was an Acrobat's Daughter (1937) Stalling
She Went to the Races (1945) Shilkret, N.
She-Wolf of London (1946) Lava
She Wore a Yellow Ribbon (1949) Hageman
She Wouldn't Say Yes (1945) Skiles
She Wrote the Book (1946) Fairchild
She's a Soldier Too (1944) Castelnuovo-Tedesco
She's a Sweetheart (1944) Duning
She's Back on Broadway (1953) Buttolph, David
She's Dangerous (1937) Raksin
She's for Me (1943) Russell, L.
She's Working Her Way Through College (1952) Jackson, H.
Shed No Tears (1948) Kraushaar
Sheep Ahoy (1953) Franklyn
Sheep Dog (1948) Wallace

Sheep in the Deep (1961) Franklyn
Sheep in the Meadow (1939) Scheib
Sheep Shape (1946) Sharples, Winston
Sheep Wrecked (1957) Bradley
Sheepish Wolf (1942) Stalling
Sheepish Wolf (1963) Sharples, Winston
Sheepman (1958) Alexander, J.
Sheik (1938) Bradford
Sheik Steps Out (1937) Colombo
Shell Shock (1964) Mendoza-Nava
Shell-Shocked Egg (1948) Stalling
Shelter (196?) Raksin
Shenandoah (1965) Skinner, F.
Shep Comes Home (1948) Greene, W.
Shepherd of the Hills (1941) Carbonara
Shepherd of the Hills (1963) Skiles
Shepherd of the Ozarks (1942) Glickman, M.
Shepherd of the Seven Hills (1934) White, L.
Sheriff of Medicine Bow (1948) Kay, Edward
Sheriff of Sage Valley (1943) Lange, J.
Sheriff of Wichita (1949) Wilson, S.
Sherlock Holmes (1932) Bassett, R. H.
Sherlock Holmes and the Voice of Terror (1942) Skinner, F.
Sherlock Holmes in the Singular Case of the Plural Green Mustache (1965) Bernstein, E.
Sherman Was Right (1932) Scheib
Shield for Murder (1954) Dunlap
Shiloh—Portrait of a Battle (1956) Haggh
Shinbone Alley (1970) Kleinsinger
Shine On, Harvest Moon (1944) Roemheld
Shining Hour (1938) Waxman
Shining Victory (1941) Steiner, M.
Ship A-Hooey (1954) Sharples, Winston
Ship Ahoy (1942) Stoll
Ship Ahoy (Trailer, 1942) Hayton
Ship Cafe (1935) Satterfield
Ship from Shanghai (1930) Axt
Ship Is Born (1943) Lava
Ship of Fools (1965) Gold
Shipmates Forever (1935) Kaun
Ships and Men (1944) Applebaum
Shipwreck (1931) Dietrich
Shipwrecked Brothers (1933) Scheib
Shipyard Symphony (1943) Scheib
Shir Hashirim (1935) Rumshinsky
Shishkabugs (1962) Lava
Shock (1946) Buttolph, David
Shock Corridor (1963) Dunlap
Shock Treatment (1964) Goldsmith
Shocking Miss Pilgrim (1946) Raksin
Shocking Pink (1965) Lava
Shockproof (1949) Duning
Shoe Must Go On (1960) Sharples, Winston
Shoe Shine Boy (1944) Kaplan, S.
Shoe Shine Jasper (1947) Wheeler
Shoeflies (1965) Sharples, Winston
Shoemaker and the Elves (1934) De Nat
Shoes (1961) Pintoff
Shoes of the Fisherman (1968) North
Shoot Out at Big Sag (1962) Loose
Shoot-Out at Medicine Bend (1957) Webb
Shoot to Kill (1947) Calker
Shoot Yourself Some Golf (1942) Lava
Shootin' Stars (1960) Sharples, Winston
Shooting (1965) Markowitz
Shooting High (1940) Kaylin
Shooting of Caribou Lou (1967) Greene, W.
Shooting of Dan McGoo (1945) Bradley
Shooting of Dan McGrew (1966) Shearing
Shooting Straight (1930) Webb
Shop Angel (1932) Burton
Shop Around the Corner (1940) Heymann
Shop, Look, and Listen (1940) Stalling
Shopworn Angel (1929) Bergunker
Shopworn Angel (1938) Ward, E.
Short Grass (1950) Kay, Edward
Short in the Saddle (1963) Wheeler
Short Snorts on Sports (1948) Calker
Shortenin' Bread (1950) Sharples, Winston
Shot and Bothered (1965) Lava
Shot in the Dark (1941) Lava
Shot in the Dark (1964) Mancini
Shotgun (1955) Brandt
Should Husbands Work? (1939) Lava
Should Ladies Behave? (1933) Axt
Shove Thy Neighbor (1957) Scheib
Show Biz Bugs (1957) Franklyn
Show Boat (1936) Bennett, R. R.
Show Boat (1951) Deutsch
Show Business (1944) Harline
Show Folks (1928) Zuro
Show Girl (1928) Carbonara
Show Kids (1934) Ward, E.
Show-Off (1946) Snell
Show People (1928) Axt
Showboat Serenade (1944) Leipold
Showdown (1940) Leipold
Showdown (1950) Wilson, S.
Showdown at Boot Hill (1958) Harris, A.
Showdown at Sunup (1949) Glasser
Showing Off (1931) De Nat
Showman (1930) De Nat
Shriek (1933) Dietrich
Shrike (1955) Skinner, F.
Shrines of Yucatan (1945) Nussbaum
Shuffle Off to Buffalo (1933) Marsales
Shulamith (1931) Goldfaden
Shut My Big Mouth (1942) Leipold
Shut Up . . . I'm Crying (1970) Charles
Shuteye Popeye (1952) Sharples, Winston
Shutter Bug (1963) Wheeler
Shutter Bugged Cat (1967) Elliott, Dean
Si See Sunni (1967) Felciano
Siam (1954) Wallace
Sick, Sick Sidney (1958) Scheib
Sick Transit (1965) Sharples, Winston
Sickle or the Cross (1949) Colombo

Side Street (1930) Steiner, M.
Side Street (1949) Hayton
Side Streets (1934) Roemheld
Sidelong Glances of a Pigeon Kicker (1970) Williams, P.
Sideshow (1950) Kay, Edward
Sidney's Family Tree (1958) Scheib
Siege at Red River (1954) Mockridge
Siege of Petersburg (1912) Simon, W.
Siegfried (1925) Riesenfeld
Sierra (1950) Scharf, W.
Sierra Baron (1958) Sawtell
Sierra Journey (1947) Borisoff
Sierra Passage (1950) Kay, Edward
Sierra Stranger (1957) Courage
Sighet, Sighet (1967) Giuffre
Sight for Squaw Eyes (1962) Sharples, Winston
Sign of Plexiglas (1959) Lewin
Sign of the Cross (1932) Kopp, R.
Sign of the Cross (1944) Young, V.
Sign of the Pagan (1954) Skinner, F.
Sign of the Ram (1948) Salter
Sign of the Wolf (1941) Kay, Edward
Sign of Zorro (1958) Lava
Signed, Sealed and Clobbered (1958) Scheib
Signpost to Murder (1964) Murray
Sikhs of Patiala (1945) De Francesco
Silence (1931) Leipold
Silencers (1966) Bernstein, E.
Silent Call (1961) Aurandt
Silent Conflict (1948) Calker
Silent Crisis (1964) Wolff, F.
Silent Enemy (1930) Midgely
Silent Raiders (1954) Bernstein, E.
Silent Screamer (1967) Mendoza-Nava
Silent Snow, Secret Snow (1964) Kleinsinger
Silent Tweetment (1946) Kilfeather
Silent Witness (1943) Kay, Edward
Silent Witness (1962) Kauer
Silk Express (1933) Kaun
Silk Stockings (1957) Salinger
Silly Billies (1936) Webb
Silly Hillbilly (1949) Sharples, Winston
Silly Science (1960) Sharples, Winston
Silly Seals (1938) Churchill
Silver Blades (1955) Lava
Silver Bullet (1942) Salter
Silver Chalice (1955) Waxman
Silver City (1951) Sawtell
Silver City Bonanza (1951) Wilson, S.
Silver Cord (1933) Steiner, M.
Silver Dollar (1933) Roder
Silver Dollar (Trailer, 1933) Perry
Silver Lining (1931) Zahler
Silver Lode (1954) Forbes
Silver on the Sage (1939) Leipold
Silver Queen (1942) Young, V.
Silver Raiders (1950) Kay, Edward
Silver Range (1946) Kay, Edward
Silver River (1948) Steiner, M.
Silver Skates (1943) Merrick
Silver Skates (1943) Seidel
Silver Stallion (1941) Sanucci
Silver Star (1955) Klatzkin
Silver Streak (1945) Scheib
Silver Threads (1937) Zahler
Silver Threads Among the Gold (1915) Levi
Silver Trails (1948) Kay, Edward
Silver Wings (1944) De Francesco
Simple Simon (1935) Stalling
Simple Siren (1945) Kilfeather
Simple Things (1952) Smith, P.
Sin of Jesus (1961) Feldman
Sin of Nora Moran (1933) Roemheld
Sin Takes a Holiday (1930) Zuro
Sin Town (1942) Salter
Sinbad the Sailor (1935) Stalling
Sinbad the Sailor (1946) Webb
Since Life Began (1961) Wilder
Since You Went Away (1944) Steiner, M.
Sincerely Yours (1955) Heindorf
SINderella and the Golden Bra (1965) Szarvas
Sing a Jingle (1943) Skinner, F.
Sing Again of Michigan (1951) Sharples, Winston
Sing and Be Happy (1937) Rose, G.
Sing Another Chorus (1941) Skinner, F.
Sing, Baby, Sing (1936) Mockridge
Sing Boy Sing (1958) Newman, L.
Sing, Cowboy, Sing (1937) Sanucci
Sing, Dance, Plenty Hot (1940) Feuer
Sing for Your Supper (1941) Dragon
Sing Me a Love Song (1936) Roemheld
Sing Me a Song of Texas (1945) Duning
Sing Me Goodbye (1950) Sharples, Winston
Sing or Swim (1948) Sharples, Winston
Sing Sing Song (1931) Scheib
Sing While You Dance (1946) Duning
Sing While You're Able (1937) Kay, Edward
Sing You Sinners (1938) Malneck
Sing Your Way Home (1945) Webb
Singapore (1947) Amfitheatrof
Singapore and Jahore (1938) Shilkret, N.
Singapore Woman (1941) Deutsch
Singer of Naples (1934) Kaun
Singin' in the Corn (1946) Sommer
Singin' in the Rain (1952) Hayton
Singing Blacksmith (1938) Weinberg
Singing Cowgirl (1939) DiMaggio
Singing Dude (1940) Jackson, H.
Singing Earth (1948) Kleiner
Singing Fool (1928) Silvers
Singing Guns (1950) Scott, N.
Singing Kid (1936) Roemheld
Singing Marine (1937) Roemheld
Singing Nun (1966) Sukman
Singing Sheriff (1944) Akridge
Single Room Furnished (1968) Sheldon
Single Standard (1929) Axt

Sinister Journey (1948) Calker
Sinister Stuff (1934) Sharples, Winston
Sink or Swim (1952) Scheib
Sink Pink (1965) Lava
Sinkin' in the Bathtub (1930) Marsales
Sinner Take All (1936) Ward, E.
Sinners in Paradise (1938) Wallace
Sinners in the Sun (1932) Leipold
Sins of Ambition (1917) Beynon
Sins of Jezebel (1953) Shefter
Sins of Man (1936) Friedhofer
Sins of Rachel Cade (1961) Steiner, M.
Sins of the Fathers (1928) Riesenfeld
Sinthia, the Devil's Doll (1970) Price, Henry
Sioux City Sue (1946) Dubin
Sioux Me (1939) Stalling
Sioux Me (1965) Wheeler
Sir Irving and Jeames (1956) Sharples, Winston
Siren of Atlantis (1948) Michelet
Siren of Bagdad (1953) Leipold
Siren of Seville (1924) Guterson
Sirocco (1951) Antheil
Sis Hopkins (1941) Scharf, W.
Sissy Sheriff (1966) Wheeler
Sister Kenny (1946) Tansman
Sisters (1938) Steiner, M.
Sit Tight (foreign version 1931) Dunn
Sit Tight (1931) Rosebrook
Sitka and Juneau, a Tale of Two Cities (1940) Bakaleinikoff, C.
Sittin' on a Backyard Fence (1934) Spencer, N.
Sitting Bull (1954) Kraushaar
Sitting Pretty (1948) Newman
Situation Hopeless—But Not Serious (1965) Byrns
Sitzmarks the Spot (1950) Agostini
Siva (1933) Bowles
Six Bridges to Cross (1955) Stein, H.
Six-Gun Gospel (1943) Kay, Edward
Six Gun Man (1946) Zahler
Six Gun Mesa (1950) Kay, Edward
Six-Gun Rhythm (1939) Porter
Six-Gun Serenade (1947) Sanucci
Six Hours to Live (1932) Brunelli
Six of a Kind (1934) Leipold
Six, Seven and Eight-Year Olds (1957) McElheny
Sixteen Fathoms Deep (1934) Wallace
Sixty Glorious Years (1938) Collins
Skabenga (1955) Skiles
Skaterdater (1966) Curb
Skating Lady (1946) Shilkret, N.
Skeleton Dance (1929) Stalling
Skeleton Frolic (1937) De Nat
Ski Aces (1945) De Francesco
Ski Belles (1947) Shilkret, N.
Ski Birds (1939) Amfitheatrof
Ski Crazy (1955) Vars
Ski Fascination (1966) Golson
Ski Fever (1969) Styner
Ski for Two (1944) Calker
Ski in the Sky (1951) Agostini
Ski-Lark in the Rockies (1951) Mamorsky
Ski-Napper (1964) Greene, W.
Ski on the Wild Side (1967) Allen, B.
Ski Party (1965) Usher
Ski Patrol (1940) Skinner, F.
Ski Skill (1937) Axt
Ski Slopes (1944) De Francesco
Ski Troop Attack (1960) Katz, F.
Ski Valley (1956) Jackson, H.
Ski Whizz (1944) Jackson, H.
Ski's the Limit (1949) Sharples, Winston
Skidoo (1968) Nilsson
Skin Deep (1922) Cohen, S.
Skin Deep (1929) Dunn
Skin Deep in Love (1967) Greene, B.
Skinfolks (1964) Greene, W.
Skipalong Rosenbloom (1951) Gertz
Skipper Surprised His Wife (1950) Kaper
Skippy (1931) Leipold
Skippy and the 3 R's (1953) Kleinsinger
Skirts Ahoy! (1952) Stoll
Skullduggery (1970) Nelson, O.
Skunked Again (1936) Scheib
Sky Bride (1932) Leipold
Sky Devils (1932) Newman
Sky Dragon (1949) Kay, Edward
Sky Full of Moon (1952) Sawtell
Sky Giant (1938) Webb
Sky High (1951) Shefter
Sky House (1950) Compinsky
Sky Is Falling (1947) Scheib
Sky Larks (1934) Dietrich
Sky Liner (1949) Kraushaar
Sky Murder (1940) Snell
Sky Parade (1936) Leipold
Sky Pirate (1970) Trentham
Sky Princess (1942) von Ottenfeld
Sky Sailing (1940) Lava
Sky Science (1943) Terr
Sky Scrappers (1957) Sharples, Winston
Sky Thrills (1948) De Francesco
Sky Trooper (1942) Churchill
Sky's the Limit (1943) Harline
Sky's the Limit (1965) Timmens
Skydivers (1963) Bath
Skylark (1941) Young, V.
Skyline (1931) Brunelli
Skyscraper (1959) Macero
Skyscraper Caper (1968) Lava
Slammin' Sammy Snead (1951) Shilkret, N.
Slander (1956) Alexander, J.
Slander House (1938) Zahler
Slap Happy (1950) Lava
Slap Happy Hunters (1941) Scheib
Slap Happy Lion (1947) Bradley
Slap Happy Pappy (1940) Stalling
Slaphappy Valley (1939) Marsales
Slap-Hoppy Mouse (1956) Stalling

Slapsie Maxie's (1939) Jackson, H.
Slattery's Hurricane (1949) Mockridge
Slaughter on Tenth Avenue (1957) Gilbert, H.
Slaughter Trail (1951) Calker
Slave Girl (1947) Rosen, M.
Slave Ship (1937) Newman
Slaves (1969) Scott, B.
Slaves of Babylon (1953) Vars
Slay It with Flowers (1943) Kilfeather
Sleep Happy (1951) Wheeler
Sleep, My Love (1948) Schrager
Sleep Walker (1942) Harline
Sleepers East (1934) Buttolph, David
Sleepers West (1941) Mockridge
Sleeping Beauty (1958) Bruns
Sleeping City (1950) Skinner, F.
Sleeping Princess (1939) Marsales
Sleepless Night (1948) Scheib
Sleepy Lagoon (1943) Scharf, W.
Sleepy Time Donald (1946) Wallace
Sleepytime Gal (1942) Glickman, M.
Sleepy Time Possum (1950) Stalling
Sleepy-Time Squirrel (1954) Bradley
Sleepy-Time Tom (1951) Bradley
Slender Thread (1965) Jones
Sleuth But Sure (1956) Sharples, Winston
Slick Chick (1962) Franklyn
Slick Hare (1946) Stalling
Slicked-Up Pup (1951) Bradley
Slide, Donald, Slide (1948) Wallace
Slide, Kelly, Slide (1927) Axt
Slide, Nellie, Slide (1936) Vaughan
Slight Case of Larceny (1953) Colombo
Slight Case of Murder (1938) Roemheld
Slightly Daffy (1944) Stalling
Slightly Dangerous (1943) Kaper
Slightly French (1949) Duning
Slightly Honorable (1940) Janssen
Slightly Scarlet (1930) Hajos
Slightly Scarlet (1955) Forbes
Slim (1937) Steiner, M.
Slim Carter (1957) Stein, H.
Sling Shot 6 7/8 (1951) Wheeler
Slink Pink (1969) Greene, W.
Slip Us Some Redskin (1951) Sharples, Winston
Sliphorn King of Polaroo (1945) Calker
Slippery When Wet (1959) Shank
Slippy McGee (1948) Glickman, M.
Sloppy Jalopy (1952) Raksin
Slow But Sure (1934) Scheib
Slumberland Express (1936) Dietrich
Small Hours (1962) Hart
Small Sawmill (1954) Kleinsinger
Small Town Girl (1936) Stothart
Small Town Girl (1953) Previn, A.
Smart Alecks (1942) Kay, Edward
Smart as a Fox (1946) Lava
Smart Blonde (1936) Roemheld
Smart Girls Don't Talk (1948) Buttolph, David
Smart Guy (1943) Kay, Edward
Smart Money (1931) Mendoza
Smart Politics (1948) Kay, Edward
Smart Woman (1948) Gruenberg
Smartest Girl in Town (1936) Shilkret, N.
Smarty Cat (1955) Bradley
Smash-Up (1947) Skinner, F.
Smashing the Money Ring (1939) Kaun
Smashing the Rackets (1938) Tours
Smashing the Spy Ring (1938) Stone
Smile, Darn Ya, Smile (1931) Marsales
Smile of Recife (1963) Kopp, F.
Smile Pretty, Say Pink (1966) Lava
Smiles (1964) Giuffre
Smilin' Through (1941 trailer) Amfitheatrof
Smilin' Through (1941) Stothart
Smiling Ghost (1941) Kaun
Smith! (1969) Brunner
Smith College (1953) Wilson, J.
Smithsonian Institution (1965) Bernstein, E.
Smitten Kitten (1952) Bradley
Smoke Eaters (1947) Shilkret, N.
Smoke Lightning (1933) Lange
Smoke Signal (1955) Lava
Smoked Hams (1947) Calker
Smoky (1933) Buttolph, David
Smoky (1946) Raksin
Smoky (1966) Stevens, L.
Smoky Joe (1945) Scheib
Smoky River Serenade (1947) Bakaleinikoff, M.
Smoky Trails (1939) Sanucci
Smooth as Silk (1946) Gold
Smooth Sailing (1947) Van Cleave
Smuggled Cargo (1939) Feuer
Smuggler's Cove (1948) Kay, Edward
Snafu (1945) Sawtell
Snafuperman (1944) Stalling
Snake Pit (1948) Newman
Snap Happy (1945) Sharples, Winston
Snap Happy Traps (1946) Kilfeather
Snappy Snapshots (1952) Scheib
Sneak, Snoop and Snitch (1940) Timberg
Sneak, Snoop and Snitch in Triple Trouble (1941) Timberg
Sneezing Weasel (1937) Stalling
Sniffer Soldiers (1942) Lava
Sniffles and the Bookworm (1939) Stalling
Sniffles Bells the Cat (1940) Stalling
Sniffles Takes a Trip (1940) Stalling
Sniper (1952) Antheil
Sniper's Ridge (1961) LaSalle
'Sno Fun (1951) Scheib
Snoopy Loopy (1960) Curtin
Snooze Reel (1951) Sharples, Winston
Snow Business (1951) Stalling
Snow Carnival (1949) Jackson, H.
Snow Creature (1954) Compinsky
Snow Dog (1950) Kay, Edward
Snow Eagles (1945) Jackson, H.

Snow Excuse (1966) Lava
Snow Follies (1939) Schwarzwald
Snow Foolin' (1949) Sharples, Winston
Snow Frolics (1952) Lava
Snow Gets in Your Eyes (1938) Snell
Snow Man (1940) Scheib
Snow Man (1946) Scheib
Snow Man's Land (1939) Stalling
Snow Place Like Home (1948) Sharples, Winston
Snow Place Like Home (1965) Greene, W.
Snow Queen (1959) Skinner, F.
Snow Sports (1943) Lava
Snow Time (1932) De Nat
Snow Time for Comedy (1941) Stalling
Snow Trails (1942) De Francesco
Snow White and the Seven Dwarfs (1937) Churchill
Snow White and the Three Stooges (1961) Murray
Snowbody Loves Me (1964) Poddany
Snowed Under (1936) Roemheld
Snowfire (1958) Glasser
Snows of Kilimanjaro (1952) Herrmann
Snowtime (1938) Kilfeather
Snuffy's Party (1939) Churchill
Snuffy's Song (1962) Sharples, Winston
So Big (1953) Steiner, M.
So Big (Trailer, 1932) Kaun
So Dark the Night (1946) Friedhofer
So Dear to My Heart (1948) Smith, P.
So Does the Automobile (1939) Timberg
So Ends Our Night (1941) Gruenberg
So Evil My Love (1948) Young, V.
So Goes My Love (1946) Salter
So Little Time (1964) Carmichael
So Many Hands (1944) Sawtell
So Much for So Little (1949) Stalling
So Proudly We Hail! (1943) Rozsa
So Red the Rose (1935) Harling
So Sorry, Pussycat (1960) Scheib
So They May Walk (1947) Colombo
So This Is Love (1953) Steiner, M.
So This Is New York (1948) Tiomkin
So This Is Paris (1954) Mancini
So This Is Washington! (1943) Moraweck
So Well Remembered (1947) Eisler
So You Don't Trust Your Wife (1955) Lava
So You Love Your Dog (1953) Lava
So You Never Tell a Lie (1952) Lava
So You Think the Grass Is Greener (1956) Lava
So You Think You Can't Sleep (1954) Lava
So You Think You're a Nervous Wreck (1946) Lava
So You Think You're Allergic (1945) Lava
So You Think You're Not Guilty (1950) Lava
So You Want a Model Railroad (1955) Lava
So You Want a Raise (1950) Lava
So You Want a Television Set (1953) Lava
So You Want an Apartment (1947) Lava
So You Want to Be a Baby Sitter (1948) Lava
So You Want to Be a Bachelor (1951) Lava
So You Want to Be a Banker (1955) Lava
So You Want to Be a Cowboy (1951) Lava
So You Want to Be a Detective (1948) Lava
So You Want to Be a Gambler (1948) Lava
So You Want to Be a Gladiator (1955) Lava
So You Want to Be a Handyman (1951) Lava
So You Want to Be a Muscle Man (1949) Lava
So You Want to Be a Musician (1952) Lava
So You Want to Be a Paperhanger (1951) Lava
So You Want to Be a Plumber (1952) Lava
So You Want to Be a Policeman (1955) Lava
So You Want to Be a Salesman (1947) Lava
So You Want to Be a V.P. (1955) Lava
So You Want to Be an Actor (1949) Lava
So You Want to Be an Heir (1954) Lava
So You Want to Be in Pictures (1947) Lava
So You Want to Be in Politics (1948) Jackson, H.
So You Want to Be on a Jury (1955) Lava
So You Want to Be on the Radio (1948) Jackson, H.
So You Want to Be Popular (1948) Lava
So You Want to Be Pretty (1956) Lava
So You Want to Be Your Own Boss (1954) Lava
So You Want to Build a House (1948) Lava
So You Want to Buy a Used Car (1951) Lava
So You Want to Enjoy Life (1952) Lava
So You Want to Get It Wholesale (1952) Lava
So You Want to Get Rich Quick (1949) Lava
So You Want to Go to a Convention (1952) Lava
So You Want to Go to a Night Club (1955) Lava
So You Want to Hold Your Husband (1950) Lava
So You Want to Hold Your Wife (1947) Lava
So You Want to Keep Your Hair (1947) Lava
So You Want to Know Your Relatives (1954) Lava
So You Want to Learn to Dance (1953) Lava
So You Want to Move (1950) Lava
So You Want to Play the Horses (1946) Lava
So You Want to Play the Piano (1956) Lava
So You Want to Throw a Party (1950) Lava
So You Want to Wear the Pants (1952) Lava
So You Won't Talk? (1940) Harline
So You're Going on a Vacation (1947) Lava
So You're Going to Be a Father (1947) Lava
So You're Going to Have an Operation (1950) Lava
So You're Going to the Dentist (1952) Lava
So You're Having In-Law Trouble (1949) Lava
So You're Having Neighbor Trouble (1954) Lava
So You're Taking In a Roomer (1954) Lava
So Young, So Bad (1950) Stringer
So Your Wife Wants to Work (1956) Lava
So's Your Aunt Emma! (1942) Kay, Edward
Soak the Old (1940) Amfitheatrof
Soap Box Derby (1948) Lava
Soapy Opera (1952) Scheib
Soaring Over the Everglades (1954) von Ottenfeld
Social Error (1935) Zahler
Social Lion (1930) Jackson, H.
Social Lion (1954) Wallace
Social Register (1934) Shilkret, N.
Social Security Story (1962) Nelson, R.

Society Doctor (1935) Bassett, R. H.
Society Dog Show (1939) Wallace
Society Lawyer (1939) Ward, E.
Society Man (1953) Craig, E.
Society of the Cincinnati (1960) Bales
Sock-a-Bye Kitty (1950) Sharples, Winston
Sock-a-Doodle-Do (1951) Stalling
Sockeroo (1940) Jackson, H.
Socko in Morocco (1954) Wheeler
Soda Poppa (1931) De Nat
Sodom and Gomorrah (1962) Rozsa
Sofi (1967) Ferguson
Soft Ball Game (1936) Dietrich
Soft Pad (1970) Collette
Soil (1939) Eisler
Soil (195?) Janssen
Sojourn in Havana (1940) Craig, E.
Sol Madrid (1967) Schifrin
Soldier and the Lady (1937) Shilkret, N.
Soldier Brothers of Susanna (1912) Simon, W.
Soldier in the Rain (1963) Mancini
Soldier of Fortune (1955) Friedhofer
Soldier Old Man (1932) De Nat
Soldiers in White (1941) Lava
Soldiers of Fortune (1914) Klein, Manuel
Soldiers of Fortune (1919) Pryor
Soldiers of the Soil (1943) Harling
Soldiers Three (1951) Deutsch
Solid Gold Cadillac (1956) Duning
Solid Ivory (1948) Calker
Solid Serenade (1946) Bradley
Solid Tin Coyote (1966) Lava
Solitary Refinement (1965) Sharples, Winston
Sombrero (1953) Arnaud
Sombrero Kid (1942) Glickman, M.
Some Came Running (1958) Bernstein, E.
Some Kind of a Nut (1969) Mandel
Some Like It Hot (1959) Deutsch
Some of the Best (1949) Cutner
Some Sort of Cage (1964) Bernstein, E.
Some Time Soon (1937) Snell
Somebody Loves Me (1952) Van Cleave
Somebody Up There Likes Me (1956) Kaper
Someone to Remember (1943) Scharf, W.
Something for Everyone (1970) Kander
Something for Mrs. Gibbs (1964) Maltby
Something for the Birds (1953) Kaplan, S.
Something for the Boys (1944) Mockridge
Something for the Girls (1962) Wernick
Something in the Wind (1947) Green, J.
Something New Under the Sun (1959) Robinson
Something of Value (1957) Rozsa
Something Old, Something New (1948) De Francesco
Something to Live For (1952) Young, V.
Something to Shout About (1943) Leipold
Something to Sing About (1937) Alderman
Something Wild (1961) Copland
Something You Didn't Eat (1945) Plumb
Somewhat Secret (1939) Snell
Somewhere I'll Find You (1942) Kaper
Somewhere in Egypt (1943) Scheib
Somewhere in the Night (1946) Buttolph, David
Somewhere in the Pacific (1943) Scheib
Somewhere, U.S.A. (1944) Terr
Son Comes Home (1936) Leipold
Son of a Bad Man (1949) Greene, W.
Son of Ali Baba (1952) Stein, H.
Son of Belle Starr (1953) Skiles
Son of Billy the Kid (1949) Greene, W.
Son of Dr. Jekyll (1951) Sawtell
Son of Dracula (1943) Salter
Son of Flubber (1962) Bruns
Son of Frankenstein (1939) Skinner, F.
Son of Fury (1941) Newman
Son of God's Country (1948) Butts
Son of Kong (1933) Steiner, M.
Son of Lassie (1945) Stothart
Son of Monte Cristo (1940) Ward, E.
Son of Paleface (1952) Murray
Son of Rusty (1947) Gertz
Son of Sinbad (1955) Young, V.
Son of the Guardsman (1946) Zahler
Son of the Navy (1940) Kay, Edward
Son of the Renegade (1953) Calker
Son of Zorro (1947) Glickman, M.
Son-Daughter (1932) Stothart
Song a Day (1936) Timberg
Song and Dance Man (1936) Rose, G.
Song and the Silence (1969) Cohen, N.
Song Is Born (1947) Friedhofer
Song o' My Heart (1930) Brunelli
Song of Arizona (1946) Butts
Song of Bernadette (1943) Newman
Song of India (1949) Laszlo
Song of Mid-America (1951) van Grove
Song of My Heart (1947) Nussbaum
Song of Nevada (1944) Glickman, M.
Song of Revolt (1937) Cutter
Song of Russia (1944) Stothart
Song of Scheherazade (1947) Rozsa
Song of Songs (1933) Hajos
Song of Sunshine (1945) De Francesco
Song of Surrender (1949) Young, V.
Song of Texas (1943) Glickman, M.
Song of the Birds (1949) Sharples, Winston
Song of the Buckaroo (1938) Sanucci
Song of the Caballero (1930) Perry
Song of the City (1937) Axt
Song of the Drifter (1948) Kay, Edward
Song of the Eagle (1933) Lewis, Harold
Song of the Flame (1930) Mendoza
Song of the Gringo (1936) Sanucci
Song of the Islands (1942) Buttolph, David
Song of the Open Road (1944) Previn, C.
Song of the Saddle (1936) Jackson, H.
Song of the Sarong (1945) Ward, E.
Song of the Scaffold (1959) Becker

Song of the Sierras (1946) Sanucci
Song of the South (1946) Amfitheatrof
Song of the Thin Man (1947) Snell
Song of the Trail (1936) Zahler
Song of the Wasteland (1947) Kay, Edward
Song of Victory (1942) Kilfeather
Song Shopping (1933) Steiner, G.
Song to Remember (1944) Rozsa
Song Without End (1960) Sukman
Songs and Saddles (1938) Zahler
Songs of Erin (1951) Scheib
Sonny Boy (1929) Silvers
Sonora Stagecoach (1944) Sanucci
Sons o' Guns (1936) Roemheld
Sons of Courage (1946) De Francesco
Sons of Katie Elder (1965) Bernstein, E.
Sons of Liberty (1939) Jackson, H.
Sons of the Desert (1933) Hatley
Sons of the Pioneers (1942) Feuer
Sons of the Plains (1938) Jackson, H.
Sons of the Sea (1942) Roemheld
Sorcerer (196?) Katz, F.
Sorority Girl (1957) Stein, R.
Sorority House (1939) Webb
Sorrowful Jones (1949) Dolan
Sorrows of Satan (1927) Riesenfeld
Sorry, Wrong Number (1948) Waxman
SOS Coast Guard (1937) Colombo
S.O.S. Icicle (1933) Dietrich
S.O.S.Tidal Wave (1939) Feuer
Souls at Sea (1937) Harling
Souls in Conflict (1954) Carmichael
Souls of Sin (1949) Glover, H.
Sound and the Fury (1959) North
Sound of Fury (1950) Friedhofer
Sound of Laughter (1963) Waldman
Sound of Music (1965) Kostal
Sound Off (1952) Duning
Soup Song (1931) Stalling
Soup to Mutts (1939) Marsales
Soup's On (1947) Wallace
Sour Grapes (1950) Scheib
Sour Gripes (1963) Sharples, Winston
Sour Puss (1940) Stalling
Sourpuss in Dingbat Land (1949) Scheib
South America (1960) Forrell
South American Sports (1942) Jackson, H.
South of Caliente (1951) Butts
South of Dixie (1944) Skinner, F.
South of Monterey (1946) Kay, Edward
South of Monterrey (1946) Dunn
South of Pago Pago (1940) Ward, E.
South of Panama (1941) Colombo
South of Rio (1949) Wilson, S.
South of Santa Fe (1942) Glickman, M.
South of St. Louis (1949) Steiner, M.
South of Suez (1940) Hollander
South of Tahiti (1941) Skinner, F.
South of the Border with Disney (1942) Plumb
South of the Himalayas (1956) Jackson, H.
South of the Rio Grande (1945) Kay, Edward
South Pacific (1958) Newman
South Pole or Bust (1934) Scheib
South Pole Pals (1966) Greene, W.
South Sea Rose (1929) Brunelli
South Sea Sinner (1950) Scharf, W.
South Sea Woman (1953) Buttolph, David
South Seas Adventure (1958) North
Southbound Duckling (1955) Bradley
Southern California Holiday (1951) Jackson, H.
Southern Cross (1953) Morey
Southern Exposure (1934) Rosoff
Southern Fried Hospitality (1960) Poddany
Southern Fried Rabbit (1952) Stalling
Southern Horse-pitality (1935) Scheib
Southern Rhythm (1932) Scheib
Southern Yankee (1948) Snell
Southerner (1945) Janssen
Southside 1-1000 (1950) Sawtell
Southwest Passage (1954) Lange
Souvenirs of Death (1948) Franklyn, R.
Soviet Russia Through the Eyes of an American (1935) Krummel
Space Children (1958) Van Cleave
Space Kid (1966) Sharples, Winston
Space Monster (1964) Skiles
Space Mouse (1959) Wheeler
Space Rendezvous (1966) Nikolais
Spanish Affair (1957) Amfitheatrof
Spanish Earth (1937) Blitzstein
Spanish Main (1945) Eisler
Spanish Revolt of 1836 (1912) Simon, W.
Spare the Child (1955) Farnon
Spare the Rod (1953) Scheib
Spare the Rod (1953) Wallace
Spark Plug (1936) De Nat
Spartacus (1914) Altschuler
Spartacus (1960) North
Spartan Mother (1912) Simon, W.
Spawn of the North (1938) Tiomkin
Speak Easily (1932) Axt
Speaking of Animals (1941) Wheeler
Speaking of the Weather (1937) Stalling
Special Agent (1935) Kaun
Special Agent (1949) Cailliet
Spectacle Maker (1934) Stothart
Specter of the Rose (1946) Antheil
Spectrum (1961) Ceely
Speed (1936) Ward, E.
Speed Crazy (1959) LaSalle
Speed Lovers (1968) Palmer, C.
Speed Sub-Zero (1954) Jackson, H.
Speed to Spare (1948) Calker
Speedway (1929) Axt
Speedway (1968) Alexander, J.
Speedy Ghost to Town (1967) Lava
Speedy Gonzales (1955) Stalling
Spell of the Circus (1930) Perry

Spellbinder (1939) Dunn
Spellbound (1945) Rozsa
Spellbound Hound (1950) Castillo
Spelling and Learning (1950) Thompson, D.
Spencer's Mountain (1963) Steiner, M.
Spendthrift (1936) Carbonara
Spider (1931) Friedhofer
Spider (1945) Buttolph, David
Spider Baby (1968) Stein, R.
Spider Returns (1941) Zahler
Spider Talks (1932) Scheib
Spider Woman (1943) Salter
Spider Woman Strikes Back (1946) Rosen, M.
Spider's Web (1938) Cutner
Spieler (1928) Zuro
Spies (1943) Stalling
Spills for Thrills (1940) Jackson, H.
Spinach fer Britain (1943) Timberg
Spinach Packin' Popeye (1944) Sharples, Winston
Spinach vs Hamburgers (1948) Sharples, Winston
Spinning Mice (1935) Sharples, Winston
Spinout (1966) Stoll
Spiral Road (1962) Goldsmith
Spiral Staircase (1945) Webb
Spirit in the Tree (1968) Lewin
Spirit Is Willing (1966) Mizzy
Spirit of '43 (1943) Smith, P.
Spirit of Culver (1939) Skinner, F.
Spirit of Lafayette (1919) Orlando
Spirit of St. Louis (1957) Waxman
Spirit of Stanford (1942) Leipold
Spirit of West Point (1947) Forbes
Spirit of Youth (1938) Zahler
Spiritualist (1948) Laszlo
Spite Flight (1933) Stalling
Spite Marriage (1929) Stahlberg
Spitfire (1934) Kaun
Splendid Hazard (1920) Gottschalk
Splendor (1935) Newman
Splendor in the Grass (1961) Amram
Splendor in the Sand (1967) Quincy
Split (1968) Jones
Split Second (1953) Webb
Spoilers (1914) Stronach
Spoilers (1930) Hajos
Spoilers (1942) Salter
Spoilers (1955) Mancini
Spoilers of the North (1947) Glickman, M.
Spoilers of the Plains (1951) Butts
Spook and Span (1958) Sharples, Winston
Spook Busters (1946) Kay, Edward
Spook Chasers (1957) Skiles
Spook No Evil (1953) Sharples, Winston
Spook Town (1944) Zahler
Spooking About Africa (1957) Sharples, Winston
Spooking of Ghosts (1959) Sharples, Winston
Spooking with a Brogue (1955) Sharples, Winston
Spooks Run Wild (1941) Lange, J.
Spooky Swabs (1957) Sharples, Winston
Sport Chumpions (1941) Stalling
Sport of Kings (1947) Bakaleinikoff, M.
Sport of Millions (1949) Jackson, H.
Sportickles (1958) Sharples, Winston
Sporting Blood (1940) Waxman
Sporting Chance (1931) Zahler
Sporting Courage (1953) Lava
Sporting Dogs (1942) Jackson, H.
Sporting Irish (1956) Jackson, H.
Sporting Suwannee (1950) Mamorsky
Sports Coverage (1948) Shilkret, N.
Sports Down Under (1948) Jackson, H.
Sports Go to War (1945) Jackson, H.
Sports New and Old (1949) Lava
Sports of the Southwest (1953) Jackson, H.
Sportsman's Holiday (1955) Jackson, H.
Sportsman's Memories (1944) Terr
Sportsman's Playground (1947) Jackson, H.
Sportsmen of the Far East (1949) Lava
Spotlight on Indo-China (1940) De Francesco
Spotlight on Mexico (1949) Sawtell
Spotlight Scandals (1943) Kay, Edward
Spree for All (1946) Sharples, Winston
Spree Lunch (1957) Sharples, Winston
Spring Comes to Niagara (1949) Agostini
Spring Festival (1937) De Nat
Spring Fever (1951) Scheib
Spring in the Park (1934) Dietrich
Spring Is Here (1930) Copping
Spring Is Here (1932) Scheib
Spring Madness (1938) Axt
Spring Night (1935) Achron
Spring of Our Faith (1952) Mason, W.
Spring Parade (1940) Salter
Spring Reunion (1957) Spencer, H.
Spring Song (1949) Sharples, Winston
Spring Styles (Fashion Forecast) (1939) Rochetti
Spring Tonic (1935) Brunelli
Springfield Rifle (1952) Steiner, M.
Springtime (1929) Stalling
Springtime for Clobber (1957) Scheib
Springtime for Henry (1934) Brunelli
Springtime for Pluto (1944) Wallace
Springtime for Thomas (1946) Bradley
Springtime in Holland (1935) Jackson, H.
Springtime in Holland (1956) Jackson, H.
Springtime in Texas (1945) Sanucci
Springtime in the Netherlands (1951) Nussbaum
Springtime in the Rockage (1940) Timberg
Springtime in the Rockies (1937) Colombo
Springtime in the Rockies (1942) Henderson, C.
Springtime in the Sierras (1947) Glickman, M.
Springtime Serenade (1935) Dietrich
Spunky Skunky (1952) Sharples, Winston
Spy (1931) Brunelli
Spy Chasers (1955) Skiles
Spy Hunt (1950) Scharf, W.
Spy in Black (1939) Rozsa
Spy Ship (1942) Lava

Spy Smasher (1942) Glickman, M.
Spy Swatter (1967) Lava
Spy Train (1943) Kay, Edward
Spy Who Came (1969) Herman
Spy Who Came In for the Olds (1966) Martin, R.
Spy Who Came In from the Cold (1965) Kaplan, S.
Spy with My Face (1966) Stevens, M.
Squad Car (1960) Daniels
Square Dance 1: Take a Little Peek (1954) Long, N.
Square Dance 2: Split the Ring (1954) Long, N.
Square Dance Jubilee (1949) Greene, W.
Square Dance Katy (1950) Kay, Edward
Square Jungle (1955) Roemheld
Square Root of Zero (1964) Kaplan, E.
Square Shootin' Square (1955) Wheeler
Square Shoulders (1929) Zuro
Squatter's Rights (1946) Wallace
Squaw Man (1931) Stothart
Squaw-Path (1967) Sharples, Winston
Squawkin' Hawk (1942) Stalling
Squeak in the Deep (1966) Greene, W.
Squeaker (1937) Rozsa
Squeeze (1963) Hollister
Squirrel (1944) Applebaum
Squirrel Crazy (1950) Scheib
St. Benny the Dip (1951) Stringer
St. Francis of Assisi (1964) Klein, Martin
St. Louis Blues (1939) Bradshaw
St. Louis Blues (1958) Riddle
St. Louis Kid (1934) Kaun
St. Valentine's Day Massacre (1967) Steiner, F.
Stablemates (1938) Ward, E.
Stage Door (1937) Webb
Stage Door Canteen (1943) Rich
Stage Door Cartoon (1945) Stalling
Stage Door Magoo (1955) Farnon
Stage Fright (1940) Stalling
Stage Fright (Trailer, 1950) Lava
Stage Hoax (1952) Wheeler
Stage Mother (1933) Silvers
Stage Struck (1948) Kay, Edward
Stage Struck (1936) Roemheld
Stage Struck (1950) Scheib
Stage Struck (1958) North
Stage to Blue River (1951) Kraushaar
Stage to Chino (1940) Sawtell
Stage to Mesa City (1947) Greene, W.
Stage to Thunder Rock (1963) Dunlap
Stage to Tucson (1950) Sawtell
Stagecoach (1939) Leipold
Stagecoach (1966) Goldsmith
Stagecoach Buckaroo (1941) Rosen, M.
Stagecoach Days (1938) Zahler
Stagecoach Driver (1951) Kraushaar
Stagecoach Express (1942) Feuer
Stagecoach Kid (1949) Sawtell
Stagecoach to Dancer's Rock (1962) Steininger
Stagecoach to Denver (1946) Glickman, M.
Stagecoach to Fury (1956) Dunlap
Stagecoach War (1940) Leipold
Stairway to Light (1945) Terr
Stakeout! (1962) Downing
Stake Out on Dope Street (1958) Markowitz
Stalag 17 (1953) Waxman
Stalking Moon (1968) Karlin
Stallion Road (1947) Hollander
Stamboul Quest (1934) Axt
Stampede (1949) Kay, Edward
Stan (1937) Riesenfeld
Stand at Apache River (1953) Skinner, F.
Stand By All Networks (1942) Leipold
Stand By for Action (1942) Hayton
Stand-In (1937) Roemheld
Stand Up and Cheer! (1934) Lange
Stand Up and Fight (1939) Axt
Standing Room Only (1944) Dolan
Stanley and Livingstone (1939) Silvers
Star (1952) Young, V.
Star! (1968) Hayton
Star Bright (1944) Schrager
Star Dust (1940) Buttolph, David
Star for a Night (1936) Maxwell
Star in the Dust (1956) Skinner, F.
Star in the Night (1945) Lava
Star Is Bored (1956) Franklyn
Star Is Born (1937) Steiner, M.
Star Is Born (1954) Heindorf
Star Is Hatched (1937) Stalling
Star Maker (1939) Newman
Star of Midnight (1935) Steiner, M.
Star of Texas (1953) Kraushaar
Star Spangled City (1946) Lava
Star Spangled Rhythm (1942) Dolan
Star Witness (1931) Reiser
Starbuilders (1963) Kauer
Starfighters (1964) Paul, S.
Stark Fear (1963) Fisher
Starlet (1969) Allen, B.
Starlift (1951) Jackson, H.
Starlight Over Texas (1938) Sanucci
Stars and Stripes Forever (1952) Newman
Stars Are Singing (1953) Young, V.
Stars in My Crown (1950) Deutsch
Stars Look Down (1941) Amfitheatrof
Stars on Horseback (1943) Lava
Stars on Parade (1944) Sawtell
Stars Over Arizona (1937) Sanucci
Stars Over Broadway (1935) Roemheld
Stars Over Texas (1946) Hajos
Start Cheering (1937) Parrish
Starting from Hatch (1953) Sharples, Winston
Starting Line (1947) Applebaum
State Department—File 649 (1949) Cailliet
State Fair (1933) De Francesco
State Fair (1945) Powell, E.
State Fair (1962) Newman
State of the Union (1948) Young, V.
State's Attorney (1932) Steiner, M.

Station West (1948) Roemheld
Stay Away, Joe (1968) Marshall, J.
Steal Wool (1957) Franklyn
Steamboat on the River (1944) De Francesco
Steamboat Round the Bend (1935) Kaylin
Steel Against the Sky (1941) Lava
Steel by Stopwatch (1962) Roznyai
Steel Claw (1961) Zimmerman
Steel Fist (1952) Kay, Edward
Steel Helmet (1951) Dunlap
Steel Jungle (1956) Buttolph, David
Steel Lady (1953) Lange
Steel—Man's Servant (1938) Armbruster
Steel Trap (1952) Tiomkin
Steel Workers (1937) Dietrich
Steelhead Fighters (1942) De Francesco
Steeltown (1944) Schuman
Steeple Jacks (1951) Scheib
Steeplechase (1933) Churchill
Steeplechasers (1946) Shilkret, N.
Stella (1950) Mockridge
Stella Dallas (1926) Rosen, H.
Stella Dallas (1937) Newman
Step by Step (1946) Sawtell
Step Lively (1944) Harline
Stepchild (1947) Silva, M.
Steppin' Pretty (1945) De Francesco
Stepping Sisters (1931) Bassett, R. H.
Stepping Stones (1932) De Nat
Steps Towards Art (1969) Kimmel
Sterile Cuckoo (1969) Karlin
Stevedores (1937) Dietrich
Stewardesses (1969) Mendoza-Nava
Stick to Your Guns (1941) Leipold
Sticks and Stones (1970) Frontiera
Stiletto (1969) Ramin
Still Going Places (1955) Vito
Sting of Death (1966) Jacobs, A.
Stingaree (1934) Steiner, M.
Stockholm, Pride of Sweden (1937) Shilkret, J.
Stoked—The Surfer Generation (1967) Richards, E.
Stolen Harmony (1935) Leipold
Stolen Heaven (1938) Leipold
Stolen Holiday (1937) Roemheld
Stolen Hours (1963) Lindsey
Stolen Life (1946) Steiner, M.
Stolen Paradise (1941) Shilkret, N.
Stone Age (1931) Dietrich
Stone Soup (1955) Kleiner
Stones of Eden (1965) Alto
Stooge (1953) Lilley
Stooge for a Mouse (1950) Stalling
Stop Driving Us Crazy (1959) Golson
Stop, Look, & Hasten! (1953) Stalling
Stop! Look and Laugh (1952) Lava
Stop! Look! and Laugh! (1960) Duning
Stop, Look and Listen (1949) Scheib
Stop, Look and Love (1939) Rose, G.
Stop That Cab (1951) Sentesi
Stop, You're Killing Me (1952) Buttolph, David
Stopover Tokyo (1957) Sawtell
Stork Bites Man (1947) Kraushaar
Stork Club (1945) Dolan
Stork Market (1931) De Nat
Stork Market (1949) Sharples, Winston
Stork Naked (1954) Franklyn
Stork Raving Mad (1958) Sharples, Winston
Stork Takes a Holiday (1937) De Nat
Stork's Holiday (1943) Bradley
Stork's Mistake (1942) Scheib
Storm (1939) Henderson, C.
Storm (1943) Shilkret, N.
Storm at Daybreak (1933) Axt
Storm Center (1956) Duning
Storm Fear (1955) Bernstein, E.
Storm of Strangers (1970) Hovey
Storm Over Bengal (1938) Feuer
Storm Over Lisbon (1944) Maxwell
Storm Over the Andes (1935) Roemheld
Storm Over Tibet (1951) Stevens, L.
Storm Over Wyoming (1949) Sawtell
Storm Rider (1957) Baxter
Storm Warning (1940) Raksin
Storm Warning (1951) Amfitheatrof
Stormy (1935) Roemheld
Stormy Seas (1932) Bradley
Stormy, the Thoroughbred with an Inferiority Complex (1953) Lava
Stormy Weather (1943) Mockridge
Story About Ping (1955) Kleiner
Story Book Kiddles (1967) Collette
Story of a Brownie Troop (1950) Forrell
Story of a Dog (1945) Lava
Story of a Girl Scout Troop (1950) Forrell
Story of a Three Day Pass (1968) Baker, M.
Story of a Woman (1970) Williams, J.
Story of Alexander Graham Bell (1939) Toch
Story of Alfred Nobel (1939) Snell
Story of Anyburg U.S.A. (1956) Dubin
Story of Bob and Sally (1948) Rosen, M.
Story of Colonel Drake (1954) Laszlo
Story of Doctor Carver (1938) Axt
Story of Dr. Jenner (1939) Snell
Story of Dr. Wassell (1944) Young, V.
Story of George Washington (1965) Sharples, Winston
Story of Life (1948) Kilenyi
Story of Louis Pasteur (1936) Roemheld
Story of Mankind (1957) Sawtell
Story of Ruth (1960) Waxman
Story of Seabiscuit (1950) Buttolph, David
Story of Temple Drake (1933) Kaun
Story of the DE-733 (1945) Amfitheatrof
Story of the Pope (1946) Craig, E.
Story of the Vatican (1941) De Francesco
Story of Three Loves (1953) Rozsa
Story of Vernon and Irene Castle (1939) Bennett, R. R.

Story of Will Rogers (1952) Young, V.
Story on Page One (1959) Bernstein, E.
Story Tellers of the Canterbury Tales (1954) Linn
Story That Couldn't Be Printed (1939) Snell
Stowaway (1932) Broekman
Stowaway Woody (1963) Wheeler
Stowaways (1949) Scheib
Straight and Narrow (1970) Conrad
Straight Is the Way (1934) Axt
Straight Shooter (1940) Wallace
Straight Shooters (1946) Wallace
Strait-Jacket (1963) Alexander, V.
Stranded (1935) Roemheld
Strange Adventure (1956) Butts
Strange Affair (1944) Skiles
Strange Affair of Uncle Harry (1945) Salter
Strange Alibi (1941) Jackson, H.
Strange Bargain (1949) Hollander
Strange Bedfellows (1965) Harline
Strange Cargo (1940) Waxman
Strange Case of Clara Deane (1932) Leipold
Strange Case of Doctor Rx (1942) Skinner, F.
Strange Confession (1945) Skinner, F.
Strange Death of Adolph Hitler (1943) Lava
Strange Destiny (1945) Terr
Strange Faces (1938) Skinner, F.
Strange Fascination (1952) Divina
Strange Gamble (1948) Kraushaar
Strange Glory (1938) Snell
Strange Holiday (1945) Jenkins
Strange Impersonation (1946) Laszlo
Strange Intruder (1956) Dunlap
Strange Journey (1946) Schrager
Strange Justice (1932) Schertzinger
Strange Lady in Town (1955) Tiomkin
Strange Love of Martha Ivers (1946) Rozsa
Strange Love of Molly Louvain (1932) Kaun
Strange Lovers (1963) Barker
Strange Mr. Gregory (1945) Kay, Edward
Strange Mrs. Crane (1948) Smith, P.
Strange One (1960) Hopkins, K.
Strange Rampage (1967) Strokin
Strange Testament (1941) Amfitheatrof
Strange Triangle (1946) Buttolph, David
Strange Victory (1948) Diamond
Strange Voyage (1946) Moraweck
Strange Wives (1934) Ward, E.
Strange Woman (1946) Dragon
Stranger (1946) Kaper
Stranger at My Door (1956) Butts
Stranger from Pecos (1943) Kay, Edward
Stranger from Santa Fe (1945) Sanucci
Stranger in the Lighthouse (1951) Jackson, H.
Stranger in Town (1932) Harling
Stranger in Town (1943) Amfitheatrof
Stranger on Horseback (1955) Dunlap
Stranger on the Third Floor (1940) Webb
Stranger Rides Again (1938) Scheib
Stranger Wore a Gun (1953) Bakaleinikoff, M.
Strangers in Love (1932) Kopp, R.
Strangers in the City (1962) Prince, R.
Strangers of the Evening (1932) Burton
Strangers on a Train (1951) Tiomkin
Strangers When We Meet (1960) Duning
Strangled Eggs (1960) Franklyn
Strangler (1964) Skiles
Strangler of the Swamp (1946) Steinert
Strategic Air Command (1955) Young, V.
Strategy of Terror (1969) Murray
Stratford Adventure (1954) Applebaum
Stratos-Fear (1933) Stalling
Stratton Story (1949) Deutsch
Strawberry Blonde (1941) Roemheld
Strawberry Roan (1948) Bakaleinikoff, M.
Strawberry Statement (1970) Freebairn-Smith
Strawhat Cinderella (1949) Sharples, Winston
Streamline Empress (1935) Kay, Arthur
Streamlined Donkey (1941) De Nat
Streamlined Greta Green (1937) Stalling
Street (1953) Shores
Street Angel (1928) Rapée
Street Cat Named Sylvester (1952) Stalling
Street Corner (1948) Katz, B.
Street of Chance (1930) Leipold
Street of Chance (1942) Buttolph, David
Street of Darkness (1958) Worth, F.
Street of Memories (1940) Buttolph, David
Street of Missing Men (1939) Feuer
Street of Shadows (1946) Stringer
Street of Sinners (1957) Glasser
Street of Women (1932) Harling
Street Scene (1931) Newman
Streetcar Named Desire (1951) North
Streets of Laredo (1949) Young, V.
Streets of New York (1939) Kay, Edward
Strictly Dishonorable (1951) Hayton
Strictly Dynamite (1934) Webb
Strife with Father (1948) Stalling
Strike It Rich (1948) Schrager
Strike Me Pink (1936) Newman
Strike Up the Band (1940) Stoll
Strikes to Spare (1948) Shilkret, N.
String Bean Jack (1938) Scheib
Strip (1951) Stoll
Strip Tease Murder Case (1950) Prince, H.
Stripper (1963) Goldsmith
Strolling Thru the Park (1949) Sharples, Winston
Stronger Than Desire (1939) Ward, E.
Stronghold (1952) Diaz Conde
Structures (1968) Pinkham
Struggle (1931) Scheib
Struggle for Life (1935) Tandler
Struggle for Life (1944) Dunn
Stubborn Mule (1939) Marsales
Stud Farm (1969) Hayward
Student Prince (1954) Stoll
Student Prince in Old Heidelberg (1928) Axt
Student Tour (1934) Bassett, R. H.

Studio Murder Mystery (1929) Hajos
Studs Lonigan (1960) Goldsmith
Study in Scarlet (1933) Burton
Stuff for Stuff (1948) Applebaum
Stuffie (1940) Snell
Stump Run (1960) Dunlap
Stunt Men (1960) Scheib
Stunt Pilot (1939) Sanucci
Stupid Cupid (1944) Stalling
Stupidstitious Cat (1947) Sharples, Winston
Stupor Duck (1955) Stalling
Stupor Salesman (1948) Stalling
Style & Class (1931) Lubin
Style of the Stars (1947) De Francesco
Subject Was Roses (1968) Pockriss
Sublimated Birth (1964) Lewin-Richter
Submarine (1928) Baron, M.
Submarine Alert (1943) Rich
Submarine Base (1943) Dant
Submarine Command (1951) Buttolph, David
Submarine D-l (1937) Steiner, M.
Submarine Eye (1917) Lake, M.L.
Submarine Patrol (1938) Maxwell
Submarine Raider (1942) Leipold
Submarine Seahawk (1958) Laszlo
Substitution and Conversion (1943) Tiomkin
Subterraneans (1960) Previn, A.
Suburbia Confidential (1966) Gigagusky
Success at Any Price (1934) Kaun
Successful Calamity (1932) Kaun
Successful Failure (1934) Vaughan
Such Men Are Dangerous (1930) Brunelli
Sucker Bait (1943) Amfitheatrof
Sudan (1945) Rosen, M.
Sudden Danger (1955) Skiles
Sudden Fear (1952) Bernstein, E.
Sudden Fried Chicken (1946) Sharples, Winston
Sudden Money (1939) Leipold
Suddenly (1954) Raksin
Suddenly It's Spring (1947) Young, V.
Suddenly It's Spring! (1944) Sharples, Winston
Sued for Libel (1939) Webb
Suez (1938) Mockridge
Suez (1956) Stanleigh
Suffer Little Children (1945) Applebaum
Suffer Little Children (1962) Bazelon
Sufferin' Cats! (1943) Bradley
Sugar and Spies (1966) Greene, W.
Sugarfoot (1950) Steiner, M.
Suicide Battalion (1958) Stein, R.
Suicide Fleet (1931) Lange
Sullivans (1944) Mockridge
Sullivan's Empire (1967) Schifrin
Sullivan's Travels (1941) Shuken
Sultan Pepper (1934) Sharples, Winston
Sultan's Birthday (1944) Scheib
Sultan's Cat (1931) Scheib
Sultan's Daughter (1944) Hajos
Summer (1930) Stalling
Summer and Smoke (1961) Bernstein, E.
Summer Children (1967) Markowitz
Summer Holiday (1947) Salinger
Summer Love (1957) Mancini
Summer Magic (1963) Baker, Buddy
Summer Place (1959) Steiner, M.
Summer Sequence (1954) Scott, Tom
Summer Stock (1950) Salinger
Summer Storm (1944) Hajos
Summer Time (1931) Scheib
Summer Trails (1946) De Francesco
Summertime (1935) Stalling
Summit (1963) Butens
Summoning of Everyman (1956) Epstein
Sun (1970) Burroughs
Sun Also Rises (1957) Friedhofer
Sun Comes Up (1948) Previn, A.
Sun Never Sets (1939) Skinner, F.
Sun Sets at Dawn (1950) Stevens, L.
Sun Shines Bright (1953) Young, V.
Sun Valley Fun (1948) Jackson, H.
Sun Valley Serenade (1941) Mockridge
Sunbonnet Blue (1937) Stalling
Sunbonnet Sue (1945) Kay, Edward
Sunday Clothes (1931) De Nat
Sunday Dinner for a Soldier (1944) Newman
Sunday Go to Meetin' Time (1936) Spencer, N.
Sunday in New York (1963) Nero
Sunday Lark (1964) Segáll
Sunday on the Range (1953) Carmichael
Sunday Punch (1942) Snell
Sunday Sinners (1941) Heywood
Sundown (1941) Rozsa
Sundown Jim (1942) Mockridge
Sundown Kid (1942) Glickman, M.
Sundown on the Prairie (1939) Sanucci
Sundowners (1949) Schrager
Sundowners (1960) Tiomkin
Sunflight (1966) Miller, A.
Sunflower (1965) Pintoff
Sunflower (1970) Mancini
Sunken Treasures (1936) Scheib
Sunny (1941) Collins
Sunny Italy (1950) Scheib
Sunny Side of the Street (1951) Duning
Sunny South (1931) Dietrich
Sunny South (1933) Scheib
Sunrise (1927) Bassett, R. H.
Sunrise (1927) Rapée
Sunrise at Campobello (1960) Waxman
Sunset Blvd. (1950) Waxman
Sunset Carson Rides Again (1948) Sanucci
Sunset in El Dorado (1945) Butts
Sunset in the Pacific (1946) Lava
Sunset in the West (1950) Butts
Sunset on the Desert (1942) Feuer
Sunset Pass (1933) Leipold
Sunset Pass (1946) Sawtell
Sunset Strip Case (1938) Riesenfeld

Sunset Trail (1939) Carbonara
Sunshine Makers (1935) Sharples, Winston
Super Lulu (1947) Sharples, Winston
Super Mouse Rides Again (1943) Scheib
Super-Rabbit (1943) Stalling
Super Salesman (1947) Scheib
Super Snooper (1951) Stalling
Superman (1941) Timberg
Superman and the Mole-Men (1951) Calker
Superman in Billion Dollar Limited (1942) Timberg
Superman in Destruction, Inc. (1942) Timberg
Superman in Electric Earthquake (1942) Timberg
Superman in Jungle Drums (1943) Timberg
Superman in Secret Agent (1943) Timberg
Superman in Showdown (1942) Timberg
Superman in Terror on the Midway (1942) Timberg
Superman in The Arctic Giant (1942) Timberg
Superman in The Bulleteers (1942) Sharples, Winston
Superman in The Eleventh Hour (1942) Timberg
Superman in The Japoteurs (1942) Timberg
Superman in The Magnetic Telescope (1942) Timberg
Superman in The Mechanical Monsters (1941) Timberg
Superman in The Mummy Strikes (1943) Timberg
Superman in The Underground World (1943) Timberg
Superman in Volcano (1942) Timberg
Supermarket (1964) Manson
Supernatural (1933) Hajos
Support Your Local Sheriff! (1969) Alexander, J.
Suppose They Gave a War and Nobody Came (1970) Fielding
Suppressed Duck (1965) Lava
Sure Cures (1946) Terr
Surf (1963) Engleman
Surf and Seaweed (1931) Blitzstein
Surf and Sound (1954) Sharples, Winston
Surf Bored (1953) Sharples, Winston
Surf-Bored Cat (1967) Elliott, Dean
Surf Party (1963) Haskell
Surfers (1967) Hamilton, Frank
Surrender (1931) Bassett, R. H.
Surrender (1950) Scott, N.
Survival 1967 (1968) Bazelon
Susan and God (1940) Stothart
Susan Lenox (1931) Axt
Susan Slade (1961) Steiner, M.
Susan Slept Here (1954) Harline
Susan's Wonderful Adventure (1955) MacIsaac
Susanna Pass (1949) Wilson, S.
Susannah of the Mounties (1939) Maxwell
Susie Steps Out (1946) Borne
Susie, the Little Blue Coupe (1952) Smith, P.
Suspect (1945) Skinner, F.
Suspense (1946) Amfitheatrof
Suspicion (1941) Waxman
Sutter's Gold (1936) Waxman
Suva, Pride of Fiji (1940) Bakaleinikoff, C.
Suzy (1936) Axt
Svengali (1931) Mendoza
Svengali's Cat (1946) Scheib
Svengarlic (1931) De Nat
Swab the Duck (1956) Sharples, Winston
Swallow the Leader (1948) Stalling
Swamp Fire (1946) Schrager
Swamp Water (1941) Buttolph, David
Swamp Woman (1941) Lange, J.
Swamp Women (1956) Holman
Swan (1925) Riesenfeld
Swan (1956) Kaper
Swanee River (1939) Schrager
Sweater Girl (1942) Young, V.
Sweeney Steps Out (1943) Lava
Sweepings (1933) Steiner, M.
Sweepstakes Winner (1939) Jackson, H.
Sweet Adeline (1935) Roemheld
Sweet and Low (1947) Van Cleave
Sweet and Low-Down (1944) Mockridge
Sweet and Sourdough (1969) Goodwin
Sweet and the Bitter (1967) Dunlap
Sweet Bird of Youth (1961) Woodbury
Sweet Charity (1968) Coleman, C.
Sweet Genevieve (1947) Gertz
Sweet Kitty Bellairs (1930) Dunn
Sweet Love, Bitter (1967) Waldron
Sweet Music (1935) Kaun
Sweet November (1968) Legrand
Sweet Ride (1967) Rugolo
Sweet Rosie O'Grady (1943) Mockridge
Sweet Sioux (1937) Stalling
Sweet Smell of Sex (1965) O'Horgan
Sweet Smell of Success (1957) Bernstein, E.
Sweetheart of Sigma Chi (1933) Ward, E.
Sweetheart of Sigma Chi (1946) Kay, Edward
Sweetheart of the Fleet (1942) Leipold
Sweetheart of the Navy (1937) Skiles
Sweetheart Serenade (1943) Ward, E.
Sweethearts (1938) Stothart
Sweethearts and Wives (1930) Leonardi
Sweethearts on Parade (1953) Armbruster
Sweetie (1929) Harling
Swell Guy (1946) Skinner, F.
Swim and Live (1945) Feuer
Swimcapades (1945) Jackson, H.
Swimmer (1968) Hamlisch
Swimmer Take All (1952) Sharples, Winston
Swing Banditry (1936) Bassman
Swing Cleaning (1941) Timberg
Swing Ding Amigo (1966) Greene, W.
Swing Fever (1943) Stoll
Swing High (1930) Zuro
Swing High, Swing Low (1937) Young, V.
Swing It Soldier (1941) Rosen, M.
Swing, Monkey, Swing! (1937) De Nat

Swing Out the Blues (1944) Leipold
Swing Parade of 1946 (1946) Kay, Edward
Swing Shift Cinderella (1945) Bradley
Swing Shift Maisie (1943 trailer) Amfitheatrof
Swing Shift Maisie (1943) Hayton
Swing, Sister, Swing (1938) Skinner, F.
Swing Social (1940) Bradley
Swing That Cheer (1938) Colombo
Swing Time (1936) Bennett, R. R.
Swing Wedding (1937) Bradley
Swing Your Lady (1937) Deutsch
Swing Your Partner (1943) Calker
Swing Your Partner (1943) Glickman, M.
Swinger (1966) Paich
Swingin' Affair (1963) Kauer
Swingin' Along (1961) Morton
Swingin' Summer (1965) Betts
Swingin' West (1963) Byrd, C.
Swinging Into Step (1944) Lava
Swingtail (1969) Fox, J.C.
Swiss Cheese (1930) Scheib
Swiss Cheese Family Robinson (1947) Scheib
Swiss Family Robinson (1940) Collins
Swiss Miss (1938) Hatley
Swiss Miss (1951) Scheib
Swiss Movements (1931) De Nat
Swiss Ski Yodelers (1940) Scheib
Swiss Tease (1947) Calker
Switzerland (1955) Smith, P.
Switzerland Sportland (1952) Jackson, H.
Switzerland Today (1947) Shilkret, N.
Swooner Crooner (1944) Stalling
Swooning the Swooners (1945) Scheib
Sword and the Flute (1959) Shankar
Sword and the Stone (1963) Bruns
Sword in the Desert (1949) Skinner, F.
Sword of Monte Cristo (1951) Kraushaar
Sword of the Avenger (1948) von Ottenfeld
Sword of Venus (1952) Koff
Swordsman (1947) Friedhofer
Sworn Enemy (1936) Ward, E.
Sydney, Pride of Australia (1938) Shilkret, N.
Sylvia (1964) Raksin
Sylvia (Trailer, 1964) Van Cleave
Sylvia Scarlett (1936) Webb
Sylvia's Girls (1965) Gillette
Symmetry (1967) Forrell
Symphony in Motion (1961) Lasko, Emil
Symphony in Slang (1951) Bradley
Symphony in Snow (1941) De Francesco
Symphony of Living (1935) Zahler
Symphony of Six Million (1932) Steiner, M.
Synanon (1965) Hefti
Syncopation (1942) Stevens, L.
Synthetic Sin (1928) Shilkret, N.
System (1953) Buttolph, David

T Is for Tumbleweed (1958) Katz, F.
Tabasco Road (1957) Stalling
Table Tennis Topnotchers (1944) Shilkret, J.
Taboos of the World (1965) Baxter
Tabu (1931) Riesenfeld
T'ai Chi Ch'uan (1970) Johnson, T.
Taffy and the Jungle Hunter (1965) Rogers
Tahiti Nights (1944) Glickman, M.
Tahitian (1956) Lund
Tail End (1938) Churchill
Take a Giant Step (1959) Marshall, J.
Take a Giant Step (1969) Friedman
Take a Letter, Darling (1942) Young, V.
Take Care of My Little Girl (1951) Newman
Take Her by Surprise (1967) Bath
Take Her, She's Mine (1963) Goldsmith
Take It Big (1944) Schrager
Take It or Leave It (1944) Mockridge
Take Me (1968) Geesin
Take Me Back to Oklahoma (1940) Sanucci
Take Me Naked (1966) Aden
Take Me Out to the Ball Game (1949) Edens
Take Me to Town (1953) Stein, H.
Take Me to Your Gen'rul (1962) Sharples, Winston
Take One False Step (1949) Scharf, W.
Take the Air (1940) Jackson, H.
Take the Heir (1930) Coopersmith
Take the High Ground! (1953) Tiomkin
Take the Money and Run (1969) Hamlisch
Taken for a Ride (1931) De Nat
Taking Care of Baby (1934) Axt
Tale in a Tea Cup (1948) Applebaum
Tale of a Dog (1959) Scheib
Tale of a Shirt (1933) Scheib
Tale of the Navajos (1948) Adomian
Tale of the Northern Lights (1960) Clayton, W.
Tale of the Vienna Woods (1934) Bradley
Tale of Truthful George (1964) Segáll
Tale of Two Cafés (1946) Schrager
Tale of Two Cities (1935) Stothart
Tale of Two Kitties (1942) Stalling
Tale of Two Mice (1945) Stalling
Talent for Disaster (1960) Glassner
Talent Scout (1937) Jackson, H.
Talented Beauties (1949) De Francesco
Tales of Manhattan (1942) Kaplan, S.
Tales of Robin Hood (1951) Klatzkin
Tales of Terror (1962) Baxter
Tales of the Black Forest (1957) Lava
Tales of the East (1940) Rochetti
Talisman (1966) Mendoza-Nava
Talk About a Lady (1946) Skiles
Talk About a Stranger (1952) Buttolph, David
Talk of the Town (1942) Hollander
Talking Car (1953) Marsh
Talking Dog (1956) Wheeler
Talking Horse Sense (1959) Sharples, Winston
Talking Magpies (1946) Scheib
Tall, Dark and Handsome (1941) Mockridge
Tall in the Saddle (1944) Webb
Tall Man Riding (1955) Sawtell

Tall Men (1955) Young, V.
Tall Story (1960) Mockridge
Tall Stranger (1957) Salter
Tall T (1957) Roemheld
Tall Tale Teller (1954) Scheib
Tall Target (Trailer,1951) Kopp, R.
Tall Texan (1953) Shefter
Tall Timber Tale (1951) Scheib
Tally-Hokum (1965) Sharples, Winston
Talpa (1956) Adomian
Taming (1968) Aimée
Taming of the Shrew (1929) Riesenfeld
Taming the Cat (1948) Scheib
Tammy and the Bachelor (1957) Skinner, F.
Tammy and the Millionaire (1967) Marshall, J.
Tammy Tell Me True (1961) Faith
Tampico (1944) Raksin
Tanbark Champions (1947) De Francesco
Tanganyika (1954) Salter
Tanga-Tika (1953) Baxter
Tangier (1946) Rosen, M.
Tangier Incident (1953) Kay, Edward
Tangled Angler (1942) Worth, P.
Tangled Destinies (1932) Zahler
Tangled Television (1940) De Nat
Tangled Travels (1944) Kilfeather
Tango (1936) Vaughan
Tank Battalion (1958) LaSalle
Tank Commando (1959) Stein, R.
Tanks a Million (1941) Ward, E.
Tanks Are Coming (1941) Jackson, H.
Tanks Are Coming (1951) Lava
Tap Roots (1948) Skinner, F.
Tapline in Arabia (196?) Elliott, Don
Tappy Toes (1968) McDowell
Tar with a Star (1949) Sharples, Winston
Tara the Stone-Cutter (1955) May
Tarantella (1940) Gerschefski
Tarantula (1955) Stein, H.
Taras Bulba (1962) Waxman
Target (1952) Sawtell
Target Berlin (1944) Applebaum
Target Dead Ahead (1945) Palange
Target Earth (1954) Dunlap
Target for Today (1942) Steinert
Target Snafu (1944) Stalling
Target Unknown (1951) Rosen, M.
Target Zero (1955) Buttolph, David
Tarnished (1950) Wilson, S.
Tarnished Angel (1938) Tours
Tarnished Angels (1957) Skinner, F.
Tarnished Lady (1931) Duke
Tars and Spars (1946) Skiles
Tarts and Flowers (1950) Sharples, Winston
Tarzan and His Mate (1934) Stothart
Tarzan and the Amazons (1945) Sawtell
Tarzan and the Great River (1967) Loose
Tarzan and the Huntress (1947) Sawtell
Tarzan and the Jungle Boy (1967) Loose
Tarzan and the Leopard Woman (1945) Sawtell
Tarzan and the Mermaids (1948) Tiomkin
Tarzan and the She-Devil (1953) Sawtell
Tarzan and the Slave Girl (1950) Sawtell
Tarzan and the Valley of Gold (1966) Alexander, V.
Tarzan of the Apes (1918) Elliott, V.
Tarzan, the Ape Man (1959) Rogers
Tarzan the Tiger (1929) Perry
Tarzan Triumphs (1943) Sawtell
Tarzan's Desert Mystery (1943) Sawtell
Tarzan's Fight for Life (1958) Gold
Tarzan's Hidden Jungle (1955) Sawtell
Tarzan's Magic Fountain (1948) Laszlo
Tarzan's Peril (1951) Michelet
Tarzan's Revenge (1938) Riesenfeld
Tarzan's Savage Fury (1952) Sawtell
Task Force (1949) Waxman
Taste of Blood (1967) Wellington
Taste of Catnip (1966) Greene, W.
Tattered Dress (1957) Skinner, F.
Tattooed Police Horse (1964) Lava
Tattooed Stranger (1950) Shulman
Taxi (1953) Harline
Taxi 13 (1928) Zuro
Taxi! (Trailer, 1932) Perry
Taxi, Mister (1943) Ward, E.
Taxi-Turvy (1954) Sharples, Winston
Taza, Son of Cochise (1953) Skinner, F.
T-Bird Gang (1958) Manne
T-Bone for Two (1942) Wallace
Tea and Sympathy (1956) Deutsch
Tea for Two (1950) Jackson, H.
Tea for Two Hundred (1948) Wallace
Teachers Are People (1952) Wallace
Teacher's Pest (1932) Dietrich
Teacher's Pest (1950) Sharples, Winston
Teacher's Pet (1958) Webb
Teahouse of the August Moon (1956) Chaplin, S.
Tear Gas Squad (1940) Jackson, H.
Tears of an Onion (1938) Timberg
Tears of the Moon (1955) Creston
Tease for Two (1965) Lava
Techno-Cracked (1933) Bradley
Technology, Phooey (1969) Goodwin
Technoracket (1933) De Nat
Teddy, the Rough Rider (1940) Jackson, H.
Tee Bird (1959) Wheeler
Tee for Two (1945) Bradley
Teen Age Tars (1948) Shilkret, N.
Teenage Caveman (1958) Glasser
Teenage Doll (1957) Greene, W.
Teenage Gang Debs (1966) Karmen
Teenage Monster (1957) Greene, W.
Teenage Mother (1967) Karmen
Teenage Rebel (1956) Harline
Teenage Rebellion (1967) Curb
Teenage Thunder (1957) Greene, W.
Teeny Weeny Meany (1966) Greene, W.

Tel (1950) Glanville-Hicks
Telephone and the Farmer (1951) Kleinsinger
Television Spy (1939) Leipold
Tell It to a Star (1945) Dubin
Tell It to the Judge (1949) Heymann
Tell Me a Badtime Story (1963) Sharples, Winston
Tell Me in the Sunlight (1967) Andersen
Tell Me That You Love Me, Junie Moon (1969) Springer, P.
Tell No Tales (1939) Axt
Tell-Tale Heart (1941) Kaplan, S.
Tell Tale Heart (1953) Kremenliev
Tell Them Willie Boy Is Here (1969) Grusin
Telling Stories to Children (1959) Shetler
Tembo (1952) Sweeten
Temperamental Lion (1940) Scheib
Tempest (1927) Riesenfeld
Temple Tower (1930) Lipschultz
Temptation (1946) Amfitheatrof
Temptress (1926) Luz
Ten Commandments (1923) Riesenfeld
Ten Commandments (1956) Bernstein, E.
Ten Days in Paris (1939) Rozsa
Ten Days to Tulara (1958) Adomian
Ten Gentlemen from West Point (1942) Mockridge
Ten Little Farmers (1947) Applebaum
Ten Little Indians (1946) Applebaum
Ten Minutes to Live (1932) Heywood
Ten North Frederick (1958) Harline
Ten Pin Aces (1943) Shilkret, J.
Ten Pin Terrors (1953) Scheib
Ten Tall Men (1951) Buttolph, David
Ten Thousand Bedrooms (1957) Stoll
Ten Wanted Men (1955) Sawtell
Ten Who Dared (1960) Wallace
Tenant's Racket (1963) Greene, W.
Tender Comrade (1943) Harline
Tender Hearts (1955) Gold
Tender Is the Night (1961) Herrmann
Tender Trap (1955) Alexander, J.
Tender Years (1947) Kilenyi
Tenderfoot Trail (1946) Anderson
Tennessee Champ (1954) Salinger
Tennessee Johnson (1942) Stothart
Tennessee's Partner (1955) Forbes
Tennis Chumps (1949) Bradley
Tennis Racquet (1948) Wallace
Tennis Town (1947) Jackson, H.
Tension (1949) Previn, A.
Tension at Table Rock (1956) Tiomkin
Tenth Avenue Angel (1947) Kopp, R.
Tepee for Two (1963) Wheeler
Teresa (1951) Applebaum
Termites from Mars (1953) Wheeler
Terra Sancta: A Film of Israel (1969) Muczynski
Terrible Troubadour (1933) Dietrich
Terrier Stricken (1952) Stalling
Terrified! (1963) Andersen
Terror (1963) Stein, R.
Terror Aboard (1933) Hand
Terror at Midnight (1956) Butts
Terror Faces Magoo (1959) Marcellino
Terror from the Year 5000 (1958) DuPage
Terror in a Texas Town (1958) Fried
Terror in the City (1965) Mersey
Terror in the Haunted House (1958) Calker
Terror in the Jungle (1968) Baxter
Terror of Tiny Town (1938) Kilenyi
Terrors on Horseback (1946) Zahler
Terry and the Pirates (1940) Zahler
Terry of the Times (1930) Perry
Terry the Terror (1960) Sharples, Winston
Tess of the D'Urbervilles (1913) Breil
Tess of the Storm Country (1922) Breil
Tess of the Storm Country (1932) De Francesco
Tess of the Storm Country (1960) Sawtell
Test of Violence (1969) Glass, Paul
Test Pilot (1938) Waxman
Test Pilot Donald (1950) Smith, P.
Tetched in the Head (1935) De Nat
Tevya (1939) Secunda
Tex Rides with the Boy Scouts (1937) Sanucci
Texan Meets Calamity Jane (1950) De Saxe
Texans (1938) Carbonara
Texas (1941) Cutner
Texas Across the River (1966) De Vol
Texas Bad Man (1953) Kraushaar
Texas, Brooklyn, and Heaven (1948) Lange
Texas Carnival (1951) Rose
Texas City (1952) Kraushaar
Texas Gun Fighter (1932) Bibo
Texas Hemisphere (1968) Schickele
Texas Kid (1943) Kay, Edward
Texas Lady (1955) Sawtell
Texas Lawmen (1951) Kraushaar
Texas Longhorns (1967) Sawtell
Texas Manhunt (1942) Lange, J.
Texas Marshal (1941) Lange, J.
Texas Masquerade (1943) Sawtell
Texas Rangers (1936) Carbonara
Texas Rangers Ride Again (1940) Leipold
Texas Redheads (1948) Shilkret, N.
Texas Renegades (1940) Lange, J.
Texas Romance, 1909 (1964) Schmidt, H.
Texas Terrors (1940) Feuer
Texas, the Big State (1951) Jackson, H.
Texas to Bataan (1942) Sanucci
Texas Today (1967) Sawtell
Texas Tom (1950) Bradley
Texas Trouble Shooters (1942) Sanucci
Texoprint (1957) Esposito
Textile Industry (1948) Carbonara
Texture in Painting (1963) Erb
Thank Your Lucky Stars (1943) Roemheld
Thanks for the Memory (1938) Bradshaw
Thar She Blows (1953) Lava
Thar She Blows (1969) Allen, B.
That Brennan Girl (1946) Antheil

That Certain Age (1938) Skinner, F.
That Certain Feeling (1956) Lilley
That Certain Woman (1937) Steiner, M.
That Cold Day in the Park (1969) Mandel
That Darn Cat (1965) Brunner
That Forsyte Woman (1949) Kaper
That Funny Feeling (1965) Darin
That Gang of Mine (1940) Porter
That Girl from Paris (1936) Shilkret, N.
That Hagen Girl (1947) Waxman
That Hamilton Woman (1941) Rozsa
That Kind of Woman (1958) Amfitheatrof
That Lady in Ermine (1948) Newman
That Man from Tangier (1953) Firestone
That Man Rickey (1952) Shilkret, N.
That Man's Here Again (1937) Jackson, H.
That Midnight Kiss (1949) Previn, C.
That Mothers Might Live (1938) Snell
That Night in Rio (1941) Newman
That Night with You (1945) Salter
That Tender Touch (1969) Saxon
That Texas Jamboree (1946) Skiles
That They May See (1965) Klein, Martin
That Touch of Mink (1962) Duning
That Uncertain Feeling (1941) Heymann
That Way with Women (1947) Hollander
That Wonderful Urge (1948) Mockridge
That's Bully (1949) Lava
That's My Baby (1944) Chernis
That's My Boy (1951) Harline
That's My Man (1947) Salter
That's My Mommy (1955) Bradley
That's My Pup! (1953) Bradley
That's No Lady—That's Notre Dame (1966) Greene, W.
That's Right—You're Wrong (1939) Webb
That's the Spirit (1945) Salter
That's Why I Left You (1943) Terr
Theatre (1957) Lees
Theatre and Your Community (1969) Kreutz
Theft of Fire (1962) DiMase
Their Dizzy Day (1944) Jackson, H.
Their Last Bean (1939) Scheib
Their Little World (1958) Beattie
Their Mad Moment (1931) Fall
Their Own Desire (1930) Axt
Them! (1954) Kaper
Then and Now (1941) Jackson, H.
Theodora Goes Wild (1936) Still
There Ain't No Such Animal (1942) Lava
There Auto Be a Law (1952) Stalling
There Goes Kelly (1945) Kay, Edward
There Goes My Heart (1938) Hatley
There Is a Season (1953) Powell, M.
There They Go-Go-Go! (1956) Stalling
There Was a Crooked Man . . . (1970) Strouse
There's a Girl in My Heart (1949) Gilbert, H.
There's Always a Woman (1938) Parrish
There's Always Tomorrow (1934) Kay, Arthur
There's Always Tomorrow (1955) Stein, H.
There's Gold in Them Thrills (1956) Craig, E.
There's Good Boos Tonight (1948) Sharples, Winston
There's Music in Your Hair (1941) De Nat
There's No Business Like Show Business (1954) Newman
There's One Born Every Minute (1942) Skinner, F.
There's Something About a Soldier (1934) Steiner, G.
There's Something About a Soldier (1943) Leipold
There's Something About a Soldier (1943) Worth, P.
There's That Woman Again (1938) Harline
These Glamour Girls (1939) Ward, E.
These Thousand Hills (1958) Harline
These Three (1936) Newman
These Wilder Years (1956) Alexander, J.
They All Come Out (1939) Snell
They All Kissed the Bride (1942) Heymann
They All Like Boats (1952) Mamorsky
They Asked for It (1939) Skinner, F.
They Call Me MISTER Tibbs (1970) Jones
They Came to Blow Up America (1943) Friedhofer
They Came to Cordura (1959) Siegmeister
They Dare Not Love (1941) Belasco
They Died with Their Boots On (1942) Steiner, M.
They Drive by Night (1940) Deutsch
They Fly Through the Air (1952) Jackson, H.
They Gave Him a Gun (1937) Romberg
They Got Me Covered (1942) Harline
They Had to See Paris (1929) Lipschultz
They Just Had to Get Married (1932) Dietrich
They Knew What They Wanted (1940) Newman
They Live Again (1938) Snell
They Live by Night (1948) Harline
They Made Her a Spy (1939) Webb
They Made Me a Criminal (1939) Steiner, M.
They Made Me a Killer (1946) Laszlo
They Meet Again (1941) Bakaleinikoff, C.
They Met in Argentina (1941) Moraweck
They Met in Bombay (1941) Stothart
They Ran for Their Lives (1967) Kraushaar
They Rode West (1954) Sawtell
They Saved Hitler's Brain (1963) Hulette
They Seek Adventure (1956) Koff
They Shall Have Music (1939) Newman
They Shoot Horses, Don't They? (1969) Green, J.
They Went That-a-Way (1949) Salter
They Were Expendable (1945) Stothart
They Won't Believe Me (1947) Webb
They Won't Forget (1937) Deutsch
They're Off (1947) Wallace
Thick Pucker (1965) Reich
Thief (1952) Gilbert, H.
Thief of Bagdad (1924) Wilson, M.
Thief of Bagdad (1940) Rozsa
Thief of Damascus (1952) Leipold
Thieves Fall Out (1941) Roemheld

Thieves' Highway (1949) Mockridge
Thin Ice (1937) Buttolph, David
Thin Man (1934) Axt
Thin Man Goes Home (1944) Snell
Thin Man Goes Home (Trailer, 1944) Terr
Thing (1951) Tiomkin
Thing of Beauty (1966) Kay, U.
Thing That Couldn't Die (1958) Mancini
Think (1964) Bernstein, E.
Think Before You Pink (1969) Greene, W.
Think Fast, Mr. Moto (1937) Bassett, R. H.
Think or Sink (1967) Sharples, Winston
Thinnest Slice (1949) Wedberg
Third Day (1965) Faith
Third Dimensional Murder (1940) Snell
Third Finger, Left Hand (1940) Snell
Third of a Man (1962) Matlovsky
Third Victory Loan (1945) Applebaum
Third Voice (1960) Mandel
Thirteen Women (1932) Steiner, M.
Thirteenth Chair (1929) Axt
Thirteenth Hour (1947) Morton
Thirty Day Princess (1934) Leipold
Thirty Seconds Over Tokyo (1944) Stothart
This Above All (1942) Newman
This Could Be the Night (1957) Stoll
This Day and Age (1933) Jackson, H.
This Earth Is Mine (1959) Friedhofer
This Gun for Hire (1942) Buttolph, David
This Happy Feeling (1958) Skinner, F.
This Is a Life? (1955) Franklyn
This Is a Test (19??) Trythall
This Is America (1933) Riesenfeld
This is Baseball (1954) Palmer, S.
This Is Blitz (1942) Agostini
This Is Cinerama (1953) Steiner, M.
This Is Heaven (1929) Riesenfeld
This Is Israel (1963) Kleinsinger
This Is It (1944) Buttolph, David
This Is Kilmer (1957) Forrell
This Is Korea (1951) Young, V.
This Is My Affair (1937) Maxwell
This Is My Alaska (1969) LaSalle
This Is My Love (1954) Waxman
This Is New York (1962) Kleiner
This Is Not a Test (1962) McRitchie
This Is Nylon (1948) Merrick
This Is Russia (1957) Stein, H.
This Is the Army (1943) Heindorf
This Is the Bowery (1941) Amfitheatrof
This Is the Life (1935) Buttolph, David
This Is the Life (1943) Skinner, F.
This Is the Night (1932) Harling
This Is Tomorrow (1943) Shilkret, N.
This Is Venice (1964) Glickman, L.
This Is Your Army (1954) Shaindlin
This Is Your Enemy (1943) Jackson, H.
This Is Your Forest (1955) Kleinsinger
This Island (1970) Giuffre
This Island Earth (1955) Stein, H.
This Land Is Mine (1943) Perl
This Little Piggie Went to Market (1934) Steiner, G.
This Love of Ours (1945) Salter
This Man Is Mine (1934) Webb
This Man's Navy (1945) Shilkret, N.
This Moving World (1949) Colombo
This Property Is Condemned (1966) Hopkins, K.
This Rebel Breed (1960) Rose
This Reckless Age (1932) Leipold
This Side of Heaven (1934) Axt
This Side of the Law (1950) Lava
This Sporting World (1949) Lava
This Thing Called Love (1941) Heymann
This Time for Keeps (1942) Hayton
This Time for Keeps (1947) Stoll
This Was Paris (1942) Deutsch
This Was Paris (Trailer, 1942) Roemheld
This Way Please (1937) Leipold
This Way to Nursing (1948) Palmer, S.
This Woman Is Dangerous (1952) Buttolph, David
This Woman Is Mine (1941) Hageman
Thomas Crown Affair (1968) Legrand
Thoroughbreds (1944) Dubin
Thoroughbreds Don't Cry (1937) Axt
Thoroughly Modern Millie (1967) Bernstein, E.
Those Beautiful Dames (1935) Spencer, N.
Those Calloways (1964) Steiner, M.
Those Endearing Young Charms (1945) Webb
Those Redheads from Seattle (1953) Shuken
Those We Love (1932) Burton
Those Were the Days (1940) Young, V.
Those Were Wonderful Days (1934) Spencer, N.
Those Who Dance (1950) Jackson, H.
Thou Shalt Not Kill (1939) Feuer
Thought of Food (1943) Agostini
Thousand and One Nights (1945) Skiles
Thousand Clowns (1965) Walker
Thousand Days (1942) Agostini
Thousand Million Years (1954) Applebaum
Thousand Pleasures (1968) Aden
Thousand Smile Check-Up (1960) Scheib
Thousands Cheer (1943) Stothart
Threat (1949) Sawtell
Threat (1960) Stein, R.
Three (1969) Rosenthal
Three Bad Sisters (1956) Dunlap
Three Bears (1934) Scheib
Three Bears (1935) Stalling
Three Bears (1939) Scheib
Three Bears (1945) Applebaum
Three Bears in a Boat (1943) Steiner, G.
Three Bites of the Apple (1966) Manson
Three Blind Mice (1938) Maxwell
Three Blind Mice (1945) Applebaum
Three Blind Mouseketeers (1936) Malotte
Three Blondes in His Life (1960) Brummer
Three Brave Men (1957) Salter
Three Brothers (1944) Stalling

Three Caballeros (1944) Wolcott
Three Came Home (1950) Friedhofer
Three Came to Kill (1960) Sawtell
Three Cheers for Love (1936) Boutelje
Three Cheers for the Irish (1940) Deutsch
Three Coins in the Fountain (1954) Young, V.
Three Comrades (1938) Waxman
Three Cornered Moon (1933) Leipold
Three Dances (1965) McDowell
Three Daring Daughters (1948) Stothart
Three Daughters (1949) Olshanetsky
Three Desperate Men (1951) Glasser
Three Faces East (1925) Riesenfeld
Three Faces East (1930) Lamkoff
Three Faces of Eve (1957) Dolan
Three Faces West (1940) Young, V.
Three for Breakfast (1947) Wallace
Three for Jamie Dawn (1956) Scharf, W.
Three for the Show (1955) Duning
Three Girls Lost (1931) Bassett, R. H.
Three Godfathers (1936) Axt
Three Guns for Texas (1968) Garcia
Three Guys Named Mike (1951) Kaper
Three Hearts for Julia (1943) Stothart
Three Hours to Kill (1954) Sawtell
Three Husbands (1950) Gilbert, H.
Three in the Saddle (1945) Zahler
Three Is a Crowd (1950) Scheib
Three Kids and a Queen (1935) Waxman
Three Kisses (1955) Craig, E.
Three Lazy Mice (1935) Dietrich
Three Little Bops (1957) Rogers
Three Little Girls in Blue (1946) Buttolph, David
Three Little Pigs (1933) Churchill
Three Little Pups (1954) Bradley
Three Little Wolves (1936) Churchill
Three Little Woodpeckers (1964) Greene, W.
Three Little Words (1950) Previn, A.
Three Live Ghosts (1929) Riesenfeld
Three Live Ghosts (1936) Axt
Three Lives (1953) Lava
Three Lives of Thomasina (1963) Smith, P.
Three Loves (1931) Kilenyi
Three Married Men (1936) Leipold
Three Men from Texas (1940) Young, V.
Three Men in White (1944) Shilkret, N.
Three Men on a Horse (1936) Jackson, H.
Three Minnies (1949) Wheeler
Three Musketeers (1921) Gottschalk
Three Musketeers (1933) Zahler
Three Musketeers (1935) Steiner, M.
Three Musketeers (1939) Maxwell
Three Musketeers (1948) Stothart
Three Nuts in Search of a Bolt (1964) Moody
Three of a Kind (1944) Kay, Edward
Three on a Couch (1966) Brown, Louis
Three on a Honeymoon (1934) Kaylin
Three on a Ticket (1947) Cadkin
Three on the Trail (1936) Sargent
Three Orphan Kittens (1935) Churchill
Three Outlaws (1956) Dunlap
Three Passions (1929) Riesenfeld
Three Pigs (1949) Calker
Three R's Go Modern (1947) De Francesco
Three Ring Circus (1954) Scharf, W.
Three Ring Fling (1958) Wheeler
Three Russian Girls (1944) Harling
Three Sailors and a Girl (1953) Heindorf
Three Secrets (1950) Buttolph, David
Three Smart Girls (1936) Roemheld
Three Smart Girls Grow Up (1939) Skinner, F.
Three Sons (1939) Webb
Three Sons o' Guns (1941) Jackson, H.
Three Stooges Go Around the World in a Daze (1963) Dunlap
Three Stooges in Orbit (1962) Dunlap
Three Stooges Meet Hercules (1962) Dunlap
Three Strangers (1946) Deutsch
Three Stripes in the Sun (1955) Duning
Three Texas Steers (1939) Lava
Three Violent People (1957) Scharf, W.
Three Weeks of Love (1965) Jackson, C.
Three Wise Fools (1946) Kaper
Three Wise Fools (Trailer, 1946) Terr
Three Wise Guys (1936) Axt
Three's a Crowd (1933) Marsales
Threshold (1970) Martinez
Thrift Plan (1945) Applebaum
Thrifty Cubs (1952) Scheib
Thrifty Pig (1941) Wallace
Thrill Killers (1965) Price, Henry
Thrill of a Lifetime (1938) Jenkins
Thrill of a Romance (1945) Stoll
Thrill of Brazil (1946) Arnaud
Thrill of Fair (1951) Sharples, Winston
Thrill of It All (1963) De Vol
Throne for a Loss (1966) Sharples, Winston
Through Normandy to Mont St. Michel (1936) White, L.
Through the Colorado Rockies (1943) Nussbaum
Throw a Saddle on a Star (1946) Lawrence, Earl
Throwing the Bull (1944) Nussbaum
Throwing the Bull (1946) Scheib
Thru Different Eyes (1942) Mockridge
Thru the Mirror (1936) Churchill
Thugs with Dirty Mugs (1939) Stalling
Thumb Fun (1950) Stalling
Thumbs Up (1943) Scharf, W.
Thunder (1929) Axt
Thunder Afloat (1939) Ward, E.
Thunder Bay (1953) Skinner, F.
Thunder Below (1932) Krumgold
Thunder Birds (1942) Buttolph, David
Thunder in Carolina (1960) Greene, W.
Thunder in Dixie (1965) Lawrence, Elliot
Thunder in God's Country (1951) Wilson, S.
Thunder in the City (1937) Rozsa
Thunder in the East (1953) Friedhofer

Thunder in the Night (1935) Kaylin
Thunder in the Pines (1948) Cailliet
Thunder in the Sun (1959) Mockridge
Thunder in the Valley (1947) Mockridge
Thunder Island (1963) Sawtell
Thunder of Drums (1961) Sukman
Thunder of the Sea (1938) Gable
Thunder on the Hill (1951) Salter
Thunder Over Arizona (1956) Butts
Thunder Over Mexico (1933) Riesenfeld
Thunder Over the Plains (1953) Buttolph, David
Thunder Pass (1954) Kay, Edward
Thunder River Feud (1942) Sanucci
Thunder Road (1958) Marshall, J.
Thunder Town (1946) Zahler
Thunderbirds (1952) Young, V.
Thunderbolt (1929) Hajos
Thunderbolt (1945) Kubik
Thunderhead (1945) Mockridge
Thundering Caravans (1952) Wilson, S.
Thundering Herd (1933) Hajos
Thundering Jets (1958) Gertz
Thundering Trail (1951) Greene, W.
Thundering Trails (1943) Glickman, M.
Thy Neighbor's Wife (1953) Divina
Tick . . . Tick . . . Tick (1969) Styner
Tick, Tock, Tuckered (1944) Stalling
Ticket to Tomahawk (1950) Mockridge
Tickle Me (1965) Scharf, W.
Ticklish Affair (1963) Stoll
Tide of Empire (1929) Axt
Tiger by the Tail (1970) Greene, J.
Tiger Fangs (1943) Zahler
Tiger Makes Out (1967) Rogers
Tiger Shark (1932) Kaun
Tiger Trouble (1944) Smith, P.
Tiger Walks (1964) Baker, Buddy
Tiger Woman (1944) Dubin
Tiger's Tail (1964) Sharples, Winston
Tight Spot (1955) Duning
Tijuana Story (1957) Bakaleinikoff, M.
Tijuana Toads (1969) Goodwin
'Til We Meet Again (1940) Roemheld
Till the Clouds Roll By (1946) Salinger
Till the End of Time (1946) Harline
Till We Meet Again (1936) Hollander
Till We Meet Again (1944) Buttolph, David
Tillie the Toiler (1941) Lawrence, Earl
Tillie's Punctured Romance (1941) Kilenyi
Timber (1941) Wallace
Timber Fury (1950) Kraushaar
Timber Queen (1944) Stahl
Timber Stampede (1939) Webb
Timber Trail (1948) Glickman, M.
Timberjack (1954) Young, V.
Timbuktu (1958) Fried
Time for Beanie (1952) Jenkins
Time for Decision (1966) Elliott, Dean
Time for Decision (1969) Bernstein, C.
Time for Killing (1967) Alexander, V.
Time for Love (1935) Timberg
Time Gallops On (1952) Scheib
Time Limit (1957) Steiner, F.
Time Machine (1960) Garcia
Time of the Heathen (1961) Hiller
Time of the Locust (1968) Feldman
Time of the West (1966) Wykes
Time of Their Lives (1946) Rosen, M.
Time of Wonder (1961) Kleiner
Time of Your Life (1948) Dragon
Time Out for Play (1945) De Francesco
Time Out of Mind (1947) Amfitheatrof
Time Out of War (1954) Hamilton, Frank
Time Piece (1965) Sebesky
Time Stood Still (1956) Jackson, H.
Time, the Place, and the Girl (1929) Reiser
Time, the Place, and the Girl (1946) Hollander
Time to Kill (1942) Raksin
Time to Love and a Time to Die (1958) Rozsa
Time to Play (1967) Bucci
Time to Sing (1968) Karger
Time Travelers (1964) LaSalle
Times Square Lady (1935) Ward, E.
Timetable (1956) Scharf, W.
Timid Pup (1940) De Nat
Timid Rabbit (1937) Scheib
Timid Scarecrow (1953) Scheib
Timid Tabby (1956) Bradley
Timid Toreador (1940) Stalling
Tin Can Tourist (1937) Scheib
Tin Pan Alley (1940) Newman
Tin Pan Alley Cat (1960) Scheib
Tin Pan Alley Cats (1943) Stalling
Tin Star (1957) Bernstein, E.
Tingler (1959) Dexter
Tip on a Dead Jockey (1957) Rozsa
Tip-Off (1931) Lange
Tips on Trips (1943) Terr
Tire Trouble (1942) Scheib
Tired and Feathered (1965) Lava
Tish (1942) Snell
Titanic (1953) Kaplan, S.
Titian (1947) Bergsma
Tito's Guitar (1942) Worth, P.
T-Men (1948) Sawtell
To Be Alive (1967) Amram
To Be Alive! (1964) Forrell
To Be as One (1961) Raksin
To Be or Not to Be (1942) Heymann
To Bee or Not to Bee (1951) Lava
To Beep or Not to Beep (1963) Lava
To Boo or Not to Boo (1951) Sharples, Winston
To Catch a Thief (1955) Murray
To Catch a Woodpecker (1957) Wheeler
To Duck or Not to Duck (1943) Stalling
To Each His Own (1946) Young, V.
To Hare Is Human (1956) Franklyn
To Have and Have Not (1945) Waxman

To Hell and Back (1955) Lava
To Ingrid My Love, Lisa (1969) Lauber
To Itch His Own (1957) Stalling
To Kill a Mockingbird (1963) Bernstein, E.
To Market, to Market (1969) Lewin
To Mary—With Love (1936) Mockridge
To My Unborn Son (1943) Terr
To Please a Lady (1950) Kaper
To Save One Life (1952) Weinberg
To Spring (1936) Bradley
To the Coast of Devon (1950) Nussbaum
To the Ends of the Earth (1948) Duning
To the Fair (1964) Forrell
To the Rescue (1932) Dietrich
To the Shores of Hell (1966) Schaefer, William
To the Shores of Iwo Jima (1945) Lava
To the Shores of Tripoli (1942) Newman
To the Victor (1948) Buttolph, David
Toast of New Orleans (1950) Stoll
Toast of New York (1937) Shilkret, N.
Tobacco Road (1941) Buttolph, David
Tobor the Great (1954) Jackson, H.
Tobruk (1967) Kaper
Toby Tortoise Returns (1936) Harline
Toby Tyler (1959) Baker, Buddy
Toccata for Toy Trains (1957) Bernstein, E.
Today I Hang (1942) Lange, J.
Today We Live (1933) Axt
Together Again (1944) Heymann
Together in the Weather (1946) Wheeler
Toilers (1928) Riesenfeld
Tokio Jokio (1943) Stalling
Tokyo After Dark (1958) Courage
Tokyo File 212 (1951) Glasser
Tokyo Joe (1949) Antheil
Tokyo Rose (1945) Schrager
Toll Bridge Troubles (1942) Kilfeather
Toll of the Desert (1935) Zahler
Toltec Mystery (1964) White, D.
Tom and Chérie (1955) Bradley
Tom and Jerry in the Hollywood Bowl (1950) Bradley
Tom Brown of Culver (1932) Broekman
Tom Brown's School Days (1940) Collins
Tom, Dick and Harry (1941) Webb
Tom Sawyer (1930) Leipold
Tom Sawyer, Detective (1938) Carbonara
Tom Thumb (1934) De Nat
Tom Thumb (1936) Stalling
Tom Thumb in Trouble (1940) Stalling
Tom Thumb's Brother (1941) Kilfeather
Tom, Tom, the Piper's Son (1934) Scheib
Tom Turk and Daffy (1944) Stalling
Tom Turkey and His Harmonica Humdingers (1940) Bradley
Tom's Photo Finish (1956) Bradley
Tomahawk (1951) Salter
Tomahawk Trail (1956) Baxter
Tomboy (1940) Kay, Edward
Tomboy and the Champ (1961) Shores
Tombstone (1942) Carbonara
Tombstone Canyon (1932) Burton
Tom-ic Energy (1964) Poddany
Tomorrow (1961) Chou Wen-chung
Tomorrow and Tomorrow (1932) Hand
Tomorrow Is Another Day (1951) Amfitheatrof
Tomorrow Is Another Day (Trailer, 1951) Lava
Tomorrow Is Forever (1945) Steiner, M.
Tomorrow John Jones (1944) Shilkret, N.
Tomorrow, the World! (1944) Applebaum
Tomorrow We Diet (1950) Dubin
Tomorrow We Live (1942) Erdody
Tomorrow's Citizens (1947) Applebaum
Tom-Tom Tomcat (1952) Stalling
Tongues of Men (1915) Beynon
Tonight and Every Night (1945) Skiles
Tonight for Sure! (1961) Coppola
Tonight Is Ours (1933) Hajos
Tonight or Never (1931) Newman
Tonight We Raid Calais (1943) Mockridge
Tonight We Sing (1953) Newman
Tonka (1958) Wallace
Tonto Basin Outlaws (1941) Sanucci
Tony Rome (1967) May
Too Busy to Work (1939) Rose, G.
Too Hop to Handle (1955) Franklyn
Too Hot to Handle (1938) Waxman
Too Late Blues (1961) Raksin
Too Late for Tears (1949) Butts
Too Late the Hero (1970) Fried
Too Many Blondes (1941) Skinner, F.
Too Many Girls (1940) Bassman
Too Many Husbands (1940) Hollander
Too Many Parents (1936) Carbonara
Too Many Winners (1947) Levin
Too Many Women (1942) Wheeler
Too Much Harmony (1933) Roemheld
Too Much Johnson (1938) Bowles
Too Much, Too Soon (1958) Gold
Too Soon to Love (1959) Stein, R.
Too Weak to Work (1943) Timberg
Too Young to Kiss (1951) Kaper
Too Young to Know (1945) Roemheld
Tools of Telephony (1956) Meakin
Toonerville Picnic (1936) Sharples, Winston
Toonerville Trolley (1936) Sharples, Winston
Toot, Whistle, Plunk and Boom (1953) Dubin
Tooth or Consequences (1947) Calker
Top (1965) Specht
Top Cat (1960) Sharples, Winston
Top Figure Champs (1949) Mamorsky
Top Gun (1955) Gertz
Top Man (1943) Skinner, F.
Top o' the Morning (1949) Dolan
Top of the Town (1937) Skinner, F.
Top of the World (1955) Glasser
Top Secret Affair (1957) Webb
Top Sergeant (1942) Salter

Top Sergeant Mulligan (1928) True
Top Speed (1930) Leonardi
Topa Topa (1938) Kilenyi
Topaz (1968) Jarre
Topaze (1933) Webb
Topeka (1953) Kraushaar
Topper (1937) Hatley
Topper Returns (1941) Heymann
Topper Takes a Trip (1939) Friedhofer
Tops (1969) Bernstein, E.
Tops in the Big Top (1945) Sharples, Winston
Tops with Pops (1957) Bradley
Topsy Turkey (1948) Calker
Topsy TV (1957) Scheib
Tora! Tora! Tora! (1970) Goldsmith
Torch (1950) Diaz Conde
Torch Singer (1933) Rainger
Torch Song (1953) Deutsch
Torchy Blane in Chinatown (1939) Jackson, H.
Torchy Blane in Panama (1938) Jackson, H.
Torchy Blane—Playing with Dynamite (1939) Jackson, H.
Torchy Gets Her Man (1938) Jackson, H.
Torchy Runs for Mayor (1939) Jackson, H.
Toreadorable (1953) Sharples, Winston
Tormented (1960) Glasser
Torn Curtain (1966) Addison
Torn Curtain (1966) Herrmann
Tornado (1943) Rich
Tornado Range (1948) Greene, W.
Torpedo Alley (1952) Kay, Edward
Torpedo Boat (1942) Rich
Torrent (1926) Axt
Torrid Toreador (1942) Scheib
Torrid Zone (1940) Deutsch
Tortilla Flaps (1957) Franklyn
Tortilla Flat (1942) Waxman
Tortoise and the Hare (1935) Churchill
Tortoise Beats Hare (1941) Stalling
Tortoise Wins Again (1946) Scheib
Tortoise Wins by a Hare (1943) Stalling
Tot Watchers (1957) Bradley
Totem—The World of Nikolais (1963) Nikolais
Tots of Fun (1952) Sharples, Winston
Touch of Evil (1958) Mancini
Touch of Her Flesh (1967) Aden
Touch of the Times (1949) Van Slyck
Touchdown (1931) Leipold
Touchdown Army (1938) Leipold
Touchdown Demons (1940) Scheib
Touchdown Highlights (1954) Craig, E.
Touchdown Mickey (1932) Churchill
Touché and Go (1957) Franklyn
Touché, Pussy Cat! (1954) Bradley
Tough Assignment (1949) Glasser
Tough Egg (1936) Scheib
Tough Guy (1936) Axt
Tough Kid (1939) Kay, Edward
Toughest Gun in Tombstone (1958) Dunlap
Toughest Man Alive (1955) Kay, Edward
Toughest Man in Arizona (1952) Butts
Touring Northern England (1950) Nussbaum
Tournament of Roses (1954) Mockridge
Tovarich (1937) Steiner, M.
Toward a Better Life (1965) McCurdy
Toward the Unknown (1956) Baron, P.
Towed in a Hole (1933) Shield
Tower of London (1939) Skinner, F.
Tower of London (1962) Andersen
Towers (1957) Cutkomp
Town Mouse and the Country Mouse (1949) Calker
Town Musicians (1956) Kleinsinger
Town Tamer (1965) Haskell
Town Went Wild (1944) Carbonara
Town Without Pity (1961) Tiomkin
Towne Hall Follies (1935) Dietrich
Toy Shoppe (1934) Dietrich
Toy Tiger (1956) Mancini
Toy Tinkers (1949) Smith, P.
Toy Town Hall (1936) Stalling
Toy Trouble (1941) Stalling
Toy Wife (1938) Ward, E.
Toyland (1932) Scheib
Toyland Broadcast (1934) Bradley
Toyland Premiere (1934) Dietrich
Toys in the Attic (1963) Duning
Toys Will Be Toys (1949) Sharples, Winston
Track and Field Quiz (1945) Terr
Track of the Cat (1954) Webb
Tracking the Sleeping Death (1938) Snell
Trade Winds (1938) Newman
Trader Horn (1931) Axt
Trader Hornee (1970) Allen, B.
Trader Mickey (1932) Lewis
Trader Tom of the China Seas (1954) Butts
Traffic (1932) Carbonara
Traffic in Crime (1946) Glickman, M.
Traffic with the Devil (1946) Lava
Tragedy at Midnight (1942) Feuer
Tragedy of Big Eagle Mine (1913) Simon, W.
Tragedy of the Desert (1912) Simon, W.
Tragic Magic (1962) Wheeler
Trail Blazers (1953) Kay, Edward
Trail Guide (1951) Sawtell
Trail of '98 (1929) Axt
Trail of Robinhood (1950) Scott, N.
Trail of Terror (1943) Zahler
Trail of the Lonesome Pine (1936) Carbonara
Trail of the Mounties (1947) Glasser
Trail of the Silver Spurs (1941) Sanucci
Trail of the Vigilantes (1940) Salter
Trail of the Yukon (1949) Kay, Edward
Trail Riders (1942) Sanucci
Trail Street (1947) Sawtell
Trail to Mexico (1946) Sanucci
Trail to San Antone (1947) Glickman, M.
Trail's End (1949) Kay, Edward
Trailblazer Magoo (1954) Comstock

Trailer Horn (1949) Smith, P.
Trailer Life (1937) Scheib
Trailer Thrills (1937) Dietrich
Trailin' West (1936) Jackson, H.
Trailin' West (1949) Colombo
Trailing Danger (1947) Kay, Edward
Trailing Double Trouble (1940) Sanucci
Trailing the Killer (1932) Potoker
Train (1964) Jarre
Train Busters (1943) Agostini
Train to Tombstone (1950) Glasser
Trained Hoofs (1935) Axt
Training Pigeons (1936) Timberg
Traite du Rossignol (1970) Druckman
Traitor Within (1942) Glickman, M.
Trans Atlantic (1952) Kubik
Transatlantic (1931) Bassett, R. H.
Transatlantic Merry-Go-Round (1934) Newman
Trans-Canada Express (1944) Applebaum
Transgression (1931) Steiner, M.
Transit (1945) Carbonara
Transmission of Disease (1945) Smith, P.
Transplanters (1969) Macero
Transportation (1945) Carbonara
Transportation USA (196?) Elliott, Don
Transylvania 6-5000 (1963) Lava
Trap (1946) Kay, Edward
Trap Happy (1946) Bradley
Trap Happy Porky (1945) Stalling
Trapeze Artist (1934) De Nat
Trapeze Pleeze (1960) Scheib
Trapped (1949) Kaplan, S.
Trash Program (1962) Sharples, Winston
Trauma (1962) Collette
Travel Door (1969) McGlohon
Travel Squawks (1938) De Nat
Travelaffs (1958) Sharples, Winston
Traveling Executioner (1970) Goldsmith
Traveling Saleslady (1935) Kaun
Traveling Saleswoman (1950) Leipold
Treachery Rides the Range (1936) Jackson, H.
Treachery Rides the Trail (1949) Jackson, H.
Treasure Island (1934) Stothart
Treasure Jest (1945) Kilfeather
Treasure of Lost Canyon (1951) Skinner, F.
Treasure of Monte Cristo (1949) Glasser
Treasure of Pancho Villa (1955) Stevens, L.
Treasure of Ruby Hills (1955) Kay, Edward
Treasure of the Golden Condor (1953) Kaplan, S.
Treasure of the Sierra Madre (1948) Steiner, M.
Treasure Runt (1932) De Nat
Tree (1969) Hopkins, K.
Tree Bank (1956) Kleinsinger
Tree-Cornered Tweety (1955) Franklyn
Tree Farm (1951) Lava
Tree for Two (1943) Worth, P.
Tree for Two (1951) Stalling
Tree in a Test Tube (1943) Craig, E.
Tree Is a Tree Is a Tree? (1962) Sharples, Winston
Tree Medic (1955) Wheeler
Tree Surgeon (1944) Bradley
Tree's a Crowd (1958) Wheeler
Tree's Knees (1931) Marsales
Trent's Last Case (1952) Collins
Trespasser (1929) Zuro
Trespasser (1947) Glickman, M.
Trial (1955) Amfitheatrof
Trial Marriage (1929) Filippi
Trial of Donald Duck (1947) Wallace
Trial of Mr. Wolf (1941) Stalling
Trial of Vivienne Ware (1932) Friedhofer
Trial Without Jury (1950) Wilson, S.
Tribute to a Bad Man (1956) Rozsa
Trick for Trick (1933) Bassett, R. H.
Trick or Cheat (1966) Sharples, Winston
Trick or Treat (1952) Smith, P.
Trick or Tree (1961) Sharples, Winston
Trick or Tweet (1958) Franklyn
Tricky Business (1942) Scheib
Trifles of Importance (1940) Amfitheatrof
Trifles That Win Wars (1943) Terr
Trigger Fingers (1946) Kay, Edward
Trigger, Jr. (1950) Butts
Trigger Law (1944) Sanucci
Trigger Pals (1939) Porter
Trigger Treat (1960) Sharples, Winston
Triggerman (1948) Kay, Edward
Trilogy (1969) Kupferman
Trip (1967) Sharples, Winston
Trip for Tat (1960) Franklyn
Trip Thru a Hollywood Studio (1935) Ward, E.
Trip to Sportland (1948) Jackson, H.
Triple Justice (1940) Sawtell
Triple Trouble (1948) Scheib
Triple Trouble (1950) Kay, Edward
Triplet Trouble (1952) Bradley
Tripoli (1950) Cailliet
Triumph Without Drums (1941) Hayton
Trocadero (1944) Chernis
Trojan Horse (1946) Scheib
Trolley Ahoy (1936) Sharples, Winston
Trolley Troubles (1931) Dietrich
Trolling for Strikes (1944) De Francesco
Trombone Trouble (1944) Wallace
Trooper Hook (1957) Fried
Tropic Fury (1939) Skinner, F.
Tropic Holiday (1938) Jenkins
Tropic of Scorpio (1968) Herth
Tropic Zone (1953) Cailliet
Tropical Africa (1961) Lloyd, N.
Tropical Fish (1933) Scheib
Tropical Heat Wave (1952) Wilson, S.
Tropical Masquerade (1948) Van Cleave
Tropical Noah's Ark (1952) Katz, E.
Tropical Sportland (1943) Lava
Trouble Along the Way (1953) Steiner, M.
Trouble Chasers (1945) Kay, Edward
Trouble Date (1960) Sharples, Winston

Trouble for Two (1936) Waxman
Trouble in Paradise (1932) Harling
Trouble in Sundown (1939) Webb
Trouble in Texas (1937) Sanucci
Trouble in the Glen (1954) Young, V.
Trouble Indemnity (1950) Curtin
Trouble Makers (1948) Kay, Edward
Trouble Preferred (1948) Cailliet
Trouble with Angels (1966) Goldsmith
Trouble with Girls (1969) Strange
Trouble with Harry (1955) Herrmann
Trouble with Women (1947) Young, V.
Troublemaker (1964) Coleman, C.
Truant Officer Donald (1941) Harline
Truant Student (1958) Wheeler
Truce Hurts (1948) Bradley
Truck Busters (1943) Jackson, H.
Truck That Flew (1943) de Packh
Trucker's Girl (1970) Levine, E.
Truckload of Trouble (1949) Scheib
True Boo (1952) Sharples, Winston
True Confession (1937) Hollander
True Gang Murders (1961) Martin, G.
True Glory (1945) Blitzstein
True Grit (1969) Bernstein, E.
True Peace (1952) Silva, G.
True Story of Jesse James (1957) Harline
True Story of Lynn Stuart (1958) Bakaleinikoff, M.
True Story of the Civil War (1957) Gold
True to Life (1943) Young, V.
True to the Army (1942) Dolan
True to the Navy (1930) Jackson, H.
Trumpet Blows (1934) Rainger
Truth About Mother Goose (1957) Bruns
Truth About Murder (1946) Harline
Try and Catch Me! (1947) Sharples, Winston
Tsientsien (1959) Kupferman
Tubal-Cain (1934) Willis
Tubby the Tuba (1947) Wheeler
Tuberculosis (1945) Smith, P.
Tucson (1949) Calker
Tucson Raiders (1944) Glickman, M.
Tue. Afternoon (1968) Swansen
Tuesday in November (1945) Thomson
Tuesday's Child (1955) Engel
Tugboat Annie (1933) Marquardt
Tugboat Annie Sails Again (1940) Deutsch
Tugboat Annie Sails Again (Trailer, 1940) Jackson, H.
Tugboat Granny (1956) Franklyn
Tugboat Mickey (1940) Wallace
Tulips Shall Grow (1942) von Ottenfeld
Tulsa (1949) Glanville-Hicks
Tulsa (1949) Skinner, F.
Tumbledown Ranch in Arizona (1941) Sanucci
Tumbleweed (1953) Mancini
Tumbleweed Trail (1942) Lange, J.
Tumbleweed Trail (1946) Hajos
Tumbleweeds (1939) Bradford
Tuna Clipper (1949) Kay, Edward
Tundra (1936) Kay, Arthur
Tunisian Victory (1944) Tiomkin
Tupapaoo (1938) Snell
Turkey—A Nation in Transition (1962) Ramsier
Turkey Dinner (1936) Dietrich
Turn Back the Clock (1933) Stothart
Turn Off the Moon (1937) Leipold
Turn-Tale Wolf (1951) Stalling
Turnabout (1940) Morton
Turning the Fables (1960) Sharples, Winston
Turtle Scoop (1961) Sharples, Winston
Tusk, Tusk (1960) Scheib
Tuttles of Tahiti (1942) Webb
Tuxedo Junction (1941) Glickman, M.
T.V.A. (1945) Shulman
TV Fuddlehead (1959) Sharples, Winston
T.V. of Tomorrow (1953) Bradley
TV or No TV (1962) Sharples, Winston
Tweet and Lovely (1959) Franklyn
Tweet and Sour (1955) Franklyn
Tweet Dreams (1959) Franklyn
Tweet Music (1951) Sharples, Winston
Tweet Tweet Tweety (1950) Stalling
Tweet Zoo (1956) Franklyn
Tweetie Pie (1947) Stalling
Tweety and the Beanstalk (1956) Franklyn
Tweety's Circus (1954) Franklyn
Tweety's S.O.S. (1950) Stalling
Twelve Chairs (1970) Morris
Twelve Crowded Hours (1939) Bennett, R. R.
Twelve Hours to Kill (1960) Dunlap
Twelve O'Clock and All Ain't Well (1941) Scheib
Twelve O'Clock High (1949) Newman
Twenty Plus Two (1961) Fried
Twenty Years After (1944) Snell
Twice Blessed (1945) Snell
Twice Told Tales (1963) LaSalle
Twilight for the Gods (1958) Raksin
Twilight in the Sierras (1950) Wilson, S.
Twilight of Honor (1963) Green, J.
Twilight on the Prairie (1944) Skinner, F.
Twilight on the Rio Grande (1947) Maxwell
Twilight on the Trail (1941) Leipold
Twin Beds (1942) Tiomkin
Twin Flappers (1927) Kurtz
Twin Tripletts (1935) Shield
Twinkle in God's Eye (1955) Alexander, V.
Twinkle, Twinkle, Little Telestar (1965) Timmens
Twinkletoes Gets the Bird (1941) Timberg
Twist All Night (1962) Greene, W.
Twist Around the Clock (1962) Karger
Twisted Nerve (1969) Herrmann
Two Against the World (1936) Kaun
Two Before Zero (1962) Siegel, S.
Two Blondes and a Redhead (1947) Duning
Two Bright Boys (1939) Skinner, F.
Two by Two (1965) Sharples, Winston
Two Chips and a Miss (1951) Dubin

Two Crows from Tacos (1956) Stalling
Two Dollar Bettor (1951) Gertz
Two Down and One to Go! (1945) Tiomkin
Two-Faced Woman (1942) Kaper
Two-Fisted Justice (1942) Sanucci
Two Flags West (1950) Friedhofer
Two for the Road (1966) Mancini
Two for the Seesaw (1962) Previn, A.
Two for the Zoo (1941) Timberg
Two Gals and a Guy (1951) Kubik
Two Girls and a Sailor (1944) Stoll
Two Girls on Broadway (1940) Raksin
Two Gophers from Texas (1947) Stalling
Two Gun Goofy (1952) Smith, P.
Two Gun Justice (1938) Kilenyi
Two-Gun Lady (1956) Klatzkin
Two Gun Man (1931) Burton
Two-Gun Mickey (1934) Harline
Two Gun Rusty (1944) de Packh
Two Guns and a Badge (1954) Kraushaar
Two Guys from Milwaukee (1946) Hollander
Two Guys from Texas (1948) Hollander
Two Headed Giant (1939) Scheib
Two Heads on a Pillow (1934) Riesenfeld
Two Hearts in Wax Time (1935) Ward, E.
Two in a Crowd (1936) Roemheld
Two Kinds of Women (1932) Leipold
Two Latins from Manhattan (1941) Lawrence, Earl
Two Lazy Crows (1936) De Nat
Two Little Bears (1961) Vars
Two Little Indians (1953) Bradley
Two Little Lambs (1935) Dietrich
Two Little Pups (1936) Bradley
Two Lost Worlds (1950) Borisoff
Two Lovers (1928) Riesenfeld
Two Loves (1961) Kaper
Two-Man Submarine (1944) Castelnuovo-Tedesco
Two Men and a Maid (1929) Riesenfeld
Two Million Rooms (1946) Grundman
Two Mouseketeers (1952) Bradley
Two Mrs. Carrolls (1947) Waxman
Two Nymphs of the Well (1953) Jaffe
Two of a Kind (1951) Duning
Two on a Guillotine (1964) Steiner, M.
Two Rode Together (1961) Duning
Two Scents Worth (1955) Franklyn
Two Seconds (1932) Harling
Two Sisters (1938) Rumshinsky
Two Sisters from Boston (1946) Salinger
Two Smart People (1946) Bassman
Two Thoroughbreds (1939) Webb
Two Thousand Maniacs! (1964) Lewis, Herschell
Two Tickets to Broadway (1951) Scharf, W.
Two Tickets to London (1943) Skinner, F.
Two Tickets to Paris (1962) Glover, H.
Two Ton Baby Sitter (1960) Scheib
Two Too Young (1936) Shield
Two Weeks in Another Town (1962) Raksin
Two Weeks Off (1929) Reiser
Two Weeks to Live (1943) Moraweck
Two Weeks Vacation (1952) Wallace
Two Weeks with Love (1950) Stoll
Two Wise Maids (1937) Hajos
Two Yanks in Trinidad (1942) Leipold
Two Years Before the Mast (1946) Young, V.
Two's a Crowd (1949) Stalling
Twonky (1953) Meakin
Tycoon (1947) Harline
Typhoon (1940) Hollander

U.C.L.A. Story (1950) Merrick
Ugly American (1963) Skinner, F.
Ugly Dachshund (1965) Bruns
Ugly Dino (1940) Timberg
Ugly Duckling (1939) Malotte
Ultimate Degenerate (1969) Aden
Un Capitán de Cosacos (1934) Kaylin
Una Viuda Romántica (1933) Kaylin
Unashamed (1938) Chapin, F.
Unbearable Bear (1943) Stalling
Unbearable Salesman (1957) Wheeler
Unbeliever (1918) Hutton
Uncertain Glory (1944) Deutsch
Uncertain Lady (1934) Ward, E.
Unchained (1955) North
Unchained Goddess (1958) Kraushaar
Uncle Donald's Ants (1952) Dubin
Uncle Joey (1941) Scheib
Uncle Joey Comes to Town (1941) Scheib
Uncle Moses (1932) Polonsky
Uncle Tom's Bungalow (1937) Stalling
Uncle Tom's Cabaña (1947) Bradley
Uncle Tom's Cabin (1928) Riesenfeld
Uncle Tomcat's House of Kittens (1967) Davis, H.
Uncle Vanya (1958) Janssen
Uncommon Clay (1952) Hoffman, M.
Unconditional Surrender (1945) Engel
Unconquered (1947) Young, V.
Uncultured Vulture (1947) Kilfeather
Undead (1956) Stein, R.
Undefeated (1969) Montenegro
Under a Flag of Truce (1912) Simon, W.
Under Arizona Skies (1946) Kay, Edward
Under California Stars (1948) Glickman, M.
Under Capricorn (trailer) (1949) Buttolph, David
Under Carib Skies (1957) Jackson, H.
Under Colorado Skies (1947) Glickman, M.
Under-Cover Man (1932) Hand
Under Cover of Night (1937) Axt
Under Eighteen (1931) Kaun
Under Fiesta Stars (1941) Glickman, M.
Under Fire (1957) Dunlap
Under Mexicali Stars (1950) Wilson, S.
Under My Skin (1950) Amfitheatrof
Under Nevada Skies (1946) Glickman, M.
Under-Pup (1939) Skinner, F.
Under Suspicion (1930) Kaylin
Under Texas Skies (1940) Lava

Under the Counter Spy (1954) Wheeler
Under the Gun (1950) Rosen, M.
Under the Little Big Top (1952) Jackson, H.
Under the Pampas Moon (1935) Mockridge
Under the Red Robe (1924) Peters
Under the Shedding Chestnut Tree (1942) Kilfeather
Under the Spreading Blacksmith Shop (1942) Calker
Under the Tonto Rim (1947) Sawtell
Under the Yum Yum Tree (1963) De Vol
Under Two Flags (1936) Mockridge
Under Water Spear Fishing (1945) Jackson, H.
Under Western Skies (1945) Sawtell
Under Your Spell (1936) Maxwell
Undercover Agent (1939) Kay, Edward
Undercover Doctor (1939) Young, V.
Undercover Maisie (1947) Snell
Undercover Man (1942) Sawtell
Undercover Man (1949) Duning
Undercurrent (1946) Stothart
Underdog (1932) Dietrich
Underdog (1943) Zahler
Underground (1941) Deutsch
Underground Rustlers (1941) Sanucci
Undersea Girl (1957) Courage
Undertaker and His Pals (1966) White, J.
Undertow (1930) Perry
Underwater City (1962) Stein, R.
Underwater Warrior (1957) Sukman
Underwater! (1954) Webb
Underworld Story (1950) Rose
Underworld, U.S.A. (1961) Sukman
Undying Monster (1942) Raksin
Unearthly (1957) Vars
Unexpected Father (1939) Skinner, F.
Unexpected Pest (1955) Stalling
Unexpected Riches (1942) Kaplan, S.
Unexpected Uncle (1941) Collins
Unfaithful (1931) Hajos
Unfaithful (1947) Steiner, M.
Unfaithfully Yours (1948) Mockridge
Unfamiliar Sports (1952) Lava
Unfinished Business (1941) Waxman
Unfinished Dance (1947) Stothart
Unfinished Dance (Trailer, 1947) Kopp, R.
Unforgiven (1960) Tiomkin
Unfortunate Bride (1932) Shryer
Unguarded Hour (1936) Axt
Unguarded Moment (1956) Stein, H.
Unholy Garden (1931) Newman
Unholy Night (1929) Axt
Unholy Partners (1941) Snell
Unholy Three (1930) Axt
Unholy Wife (1957) Amfitheatrof
Unicorn in the Garden (1953) Raksin
Unidentified Flying Objects (1956) Gold
Uninvited (1944) Young, V.
Uninvited Pest (1943) Bradley
Uninvited Pests (1946) Scheib
Union in the Mill (1952) Epstein
Union Pacific (1939) Leipold
Union Station (1950) Roemheld
United Action (1939) Robinson
United Nations Day (1959) Brant
United Way (1954) Kleinsinger
United We Stand (1942) De Francesco
Unknown (1946) Steinert
Unknown Guest (1943) Tiomkin
Unknown Island (1948) Kraushaar
Unknown Man (1951) Salinger
Unknown Ranger (1936) Zahler
Unknown Terror (1957) Kraushaar
Unknown World (1951) Gold
Unmarried (1939) Leipold
Unmasked (1950) Wilson, S.
Unmentionables (1963) Lava
Unnatural History (1959) Franklyn
Unpopular Mechanic (1936) Dietrich
Unruly Hare (1944) Stalling
Unsafe and Seine (1966) Greene, W.
Unsana Takoff (1931) Secunda
Unseen (1945) Toch
Unshrinkable Jerry Mouse (1964) Poddany
Unsinkable Molly Brown (1964) Arnaud
Unsure-Runts (1946) Kilfeather
Unsuspected (1947) Waxman
Unsuspected (1952) Mamorsky
Untamed (1930) Axt
Untamed (1940) Axt
Untamed (1955) Waxman
Untamed Breed (1948) Duning
Untamed Frontier (1952) Salter
Untamed Fury (1947) Laszlo
Untamed Heiress (1954) Wilson, S.
Untamed Women (1952) Kraushaar
Untamed Youth (1957) Baxter
Until They Sail (1957) Raksin
Unto Thyself Be True (1949) Colombo
Untrained Seal (1936) De Nat
Unveiling Algeria (1940) Craig, E.
Unwelcome Guest (1945) Bradley
Up a Tree (1955) Wallace
Up and Over—Exploring on the Stegel (1969) Mendoza-Nava
Up for Murder (1931) Roemheld
Up Goes Maisie (1945) Snell
Up in Arms (1944) Steiner, M.
Up in Central Park (1948) Green, J.
Up in Mabel's Room (1944) Michelet
Up in Smoke (1957) Skiles
Up in the Air (1940) Kay, Edward
Up in the Cellar (1970) Randi
Up 'n' Atom (1947) Kilfeather
Up Is Down (1969) Boyell
Up Pops the Devil (1931) Leipold
Up the Down Staircase (1967) Karlin
Up the River (1938) Kaylin

Up to Mars (1930) Steiner, G.
Up Your Teddy Bear (1970) Jones
Upperworld (1934) Kaun
Ups an' Downs Derby (1950) Sharples, Winston
Ups and Downs (1956) Craig, E.
Ups'n Downs (1931) Marsales
Upstanding Sitter (1948) Stalling
Upswept Hare (1952) Stalling
Uptight (1968) Jones, B.
Uptown New York (1932) Burton
Uranium Blues (1955) Scheib
Uranium Fever (1955) Jackson, H.
Urbanissimo (1967) Carter
Urubu (1948) Glasser
USA: The Seventh Generation (1966) Herschensohn
Utah (1945) Butts
Utah Kid (1930) Burton
Utah Trail (1938) Sanucci
Utah Wagon Train (1951) Wilson, S.
Utopia of Death (1940) Amfitheatrof

V.I.P.s (1963) Rozsa
VE-VJ (1945) Applebaum
Vacation Days (1947) Kay, Edward
Vacation Daze (1935) Ward, E.
Vacation from Love (1938) Ward, E.
Vacation in Reno (1946) Sawtell
Vacation Magic (1947) De Francesco
Vacation—Two Weeks a Year (1947) De Francesco
Vacation with Play (1951) Sharples, Winston
Vagabond King (silent, 1930) Leipold
Vagabond King (sound, 1930) Potoker
Vagabond King (1956) Young, V.
Valentine for Marie (1965) Ito
Valentino (1951) Roemheld
Valerie (1957) Glasser
Valiant Hombre (1949) Glasser
Valiant Is the Word for Carrie (1936) Hollander
Valiant Tailor (1934) Stalling
Valiant Venezuela (1939) Bakaleinikoff, C.
Valley (1940) Jackson, H.
Valley of Blossoms (1942) De Francesco
Valley of Decision (1945) Stothart
Valley of Fear (1947) Kay, Edward
Valley of Gwangi (1969) Moross
Valley of Headhunters (1953) Bakaleinikoff, M.
Valley of Hunted Men (1942) Glickman, M.
Valley of Mystery (1967) Elliott, J.
Valley of the Dolls (1967) Williams, J.
Valley of the Dragons (1961) Raksin, R.
Valley of the Giants (1938) Friedhofer
Valley of the Kings (1954) Rozsa
Valley of the Redwoods (1960) Bregman
Valley of the Sun (1942) Sawtell
Valley of the Sun (1954) Jackson, H.
Valley of the Tennessee (1944) Lloyd, N.
Valley of the Zombies (1946) Plumb
Valley of Vanishing Men (1942) Zahler
Valley Town (1940) Blitzstein
Vampire (1957) Fried
Vanessa: Her Love Story (1935) Stothart
Vanessa: Her Love Story (Trailer, 1935) Ward, E.
Vanishing American (1926) Riesenfeld
Vanishing American (1955) Butts
Vanishing Duck (1957) Bradley
Vanishing Frontier (1932) Zahler
Vanishing Legion (1931) Zahler
Vanishing Outpost (1951) Greene, W.
Vanishing Prairie (1954) Smith, P.
Vanishing Private (1942) Wallace
Vanishing Virginian (1941) Amfitheatrof
Vanishing Westerner (1950) Wilson, S.
Vanquished (1953) Cailliet
Variable Studies (1965) Deutsch, H.
Varieties on Parade (1951) Greene, W.
Variety Girl (1947) Lilley
Variety Time (1948) Sawtell
Varley (1953) Applebaum
Varsity Show (1937) Roemheld
Vegetable Vaudeville (1951) Sharples, Winston
Veils of Bagdad (1953) Mancini
Velvet Touch (1948) Harline
Vendetta (1942) Amfitheatrof
Vendetta (1950) Webb
Venetian Affair (1966) Schifrin
Venezuela (1945) North
Venezuela (1955) Jackson, H.
Venezuelan Adventure (1967) Cambern
Vengeance (1964) Kraushaar
Vengeance Valley (1951) Kopp, R.
Ventriloquist Cat (1950) Bradley
Venus and Adonis (1935) Bowles
Vera Cruz (1954) Friedhofer
Verbena trágica (1939) Zahler
Verboten (1959) Sukman
Verdict (1946) Hollander
Vertigo (1958) Herrmann
Very Eye of Night (1958) Ito
Very Honorable Guy (1934) Kaun
Very Special Favor (1965) Mizzy
Very Thought of You (1944) Waxman
Very Young Lady (1941) Buttolph, David
Vibrations (1969) McVane
Vice Raid (1959) Shefter
Vice Squad (1931) Rainger
Vice Squad (1953) Gilbert, H.
Vicious Breed (1957) Baxter
Vicious Circle (1948) Dessau
Vicious Viking (1966) Greene, W.
Vicious Years (1950) Lange
Vicki (1953) Harline
Victoria the Great (1937) Collins
Victors (1963) Kaplan, S.
Victory (1941) Hollander
Victory Loan News Clips (1942) Applebaum
Victory Quiz (1942) Amfitheatrof
Victory Through Air Power (1943) Plumb

Victory Vehicles (1943) Wallace
Victory Vittles (1942) Snell
Viet Flakes (1966) Tenney
View from Pompey's Head (1955) Bernstein, E.
View from the People Wall (1964) Bernstein, E.
Vigil in the Night (1940) Newman
Vigilante Hideout (1950) Wilson, S.
Vigilante Terror (1953) Kraushaar
Vigilantes Are Coming (1936) Kay, Arthur
Vigilantes of Boomtown (1947) Glickman, M.
Vigilantes Return (1947) Skinner, F.
Viking (1929) Axt
Viking Women and the Sea Serpent (1958) Glasser
Villa (1958) Sawtell
Villa Rides (1968) Jarre
Village Barber (1931) Stalling
Village Barn Dance (1940) Feuer
Village Blacksmith (1933) Scheib
Village Blacksmith (1938) Scheib
Village of the Giants (1965) Nitzsche
Village of the Poor (1954) Strassburg
Village Smithy (1936) Stalling
Village Smithy (1941) Wolcott
Village Smitty (1931) Stalling
Village Specialist (1932) Bradley
Village Tale (1935) Colombo
Villain Still Pursued Her (1937) Scheib
Villain Still Pursued Her (1940) Tours
Villain's Curse (1932) Scheib
Vintage (1957) Raksin
Violated (1953) Mottola
Violators (1957) Lawrence, Elliot
Violence (1947) Kay, Edward
Violent Men (1954) Steiner, M.
Violent Midnight (1963) Holcombe
Violent Ones (1967) Skiles
Violent Road (1958) Stevens, L.
Violent Saturday (1955) Friedhofer
Violets in Spring (1936) Vaughan
Violinist (1959) Pintoff
Virgin President (1968) Ito
Virgin Queen (1955) Waxman
Virgin Sacrifice (1959) Sawtell
Virginia (1941) Shuken
Virginia City (1940) Steiner, M.
Virginia Judge (1935) Leipold
Virginian (1929) Hajos
Virginian (1946) Amfitheatrof
Virtuous Sin (1930) Hajos
Virtuous Wives (1918) Spitalny
Visit to a Small Planet (1959) Harline
Visiting Italy (1951) Kirk
Visiting St. Louis (1944) Nussbaum
Visiting Vera Cruz (1946) Nussbaum
Visiting Virginia (1947) Mayfield
VistaVision Visits Austria (1956) Jackson, H.
VistaVision Visits Gibraltar (1956) Jackson, H.
VistaVision Visits Hawaii (1955) Jackson, H.
VistaVision Visits Spain (1958) Jackson, H.
Visual Variations on Noguchi (1953) Dlugoszewski
Vital Victuals (1934) Axt
Vitamin G-Man (1943) Kilfeather
Vitamin Hay (1941) Timberg
Vitamin Pink (1966) Lava
Viva Buddy (1934) Spencer, N.
Viva Cuba (1956) Jackson, H.
Viva Las Vegas (1963) Stoll
Viva Max! (1969) Montenegro
Viva Mexico (1941) Amfitheatrof
Viva Villa! (1934) Stothart
Viva Willie (1934) Stalling
Viva Zapata! (1952) North
Vivacious Lady (1938) Webb
Vogues of 1938 (1937) Young, V.
Voice Beneath the Sea (1956) Poddany
Voice in the City (1968) Byrd, C.
Voice in the Mirror (1958) Mancini
Voice in the Wind (1943) Michelet
Voice of Action (1942) Agostini
Voice of Bugle Ann (1936) Roemheld
Voice of Israel (1931) Goldfaden
Voice of the Forest (1961) Kleinsinger
Voice of the Hurricane (1964) Freebairn-Smith
Voice of the Turkey (1950) Sharples, Winston
Voice of the Turtle (1947) Steiner, M.
Voice of the Whistler (1945) Castelnuovo-Tedesco
Voice of Truth (1945) Palange
Voice That Thrilled the World (1943) Jackson, H.
Voices of Venice (1951) Kirk
Volcano Is Born (1943) De Francesco
Volga Boatman (1926) Bassett, R. H.
Volga Boatman (1926) Riesenfeld
Voltaire (1933) Kaun
Volunteer Organist (1914) Newcomer
Von Ryan's Express (1965) Goldsmith
Voo-Doo Boo-Boo (1962) Calker
Voodoo in Harlem (1938) Churchill
Voodoo Island (1957) Baxter
Voodoo Man (1944) Kay, Edward
Voodoo Woman (1956) Calker
Voyage Four (1964) Brant
Voyage from Tahiti (1967) Sharples, Win
Voyage to a Prehistoric Planet (1965) Stein, R.
Voyage to America (1964) Thomson
Voyage to the Bottom of the Sea (1961) Sawtell

Wabash Avenue (1950) Mockridge
Wabbit Trouble (1941) Stalling
Wabbit Who Came to Supper (1942) Stalling
WAC from Walla Walla (1952) Butts
Wackiest Ship in the Army (1961) Duning
Wackiki Wabbit (1943) Stalling
Wacky Blackout (1942) Stalling
Wacky-Bye Baby (1948) Calker
Wacky Wabbit (1942) Stalling
Wacky Weed (1946) Calker
Wacky Wigwams (1942) Worth, P.
Wacky Wild Life (1940) Stalling

Wacky World of Mother Goose (1967) Laws
Wacky World of Numburrs (1968) Rogers
Wacky Worm (1941) Stalling
Waco (1952) Kraushaar
Waco (1966) Haskell
Waggily Tale (1957) Franklyn
Wagon Heels (1945) Stalling
Wagon Master (1950) Hageman
Wagon Tracks West (1943) Glickman, M.
Wagon Train (1940) Sawtell
Wagon Wheels (1934) Leipold
Wagon Wheels West (1943) Jackson, H.
Wagons Roll at Night (1941) Roemheld
Wagons West (1952) Skiles
Wagons Westward (1940) Feuer
Wags to Riches (1949) Bradley
Waif's Welcome (1936) Sharples, Winston
Waikiki Wedding (1937) Shuken
Wait Till the Sun Shines, Nellie (1952) Newman
Wait Until Dark (1967) Mancini
Waiting (1952) Varner
Wakamba (1955) Jackson, H.
Wake Island (1942) Buttolph, David
Wake Me When It's Over (1960) Mockridge
Wake of the Red Witch (1949) Scott, N.
Wake Up and Dream (1934) Jackson, H.
Wake Up and Dream (1946) Mockridge
Wake Up and Live (1937) Mockridge
Wake Up the Gypsy in Me (1933) Marsales
Walk (1962) Hollister
Walk a Crooked Mile (1948) Sawtell
Walk Don't Run (1966) Jones
Walk East on Beacon (1952) Applebaum
Walk in the Deep (1955) Craig, E.
Walk in the Spring Rain (1970) Bernstein, E.
Walk in the Sun (1945) Rich
Walk Like a Dragon (1960) Dunlap
Walk on the Wild Side (1962) Bernstein, E.
Walk Softly, Stranger (1949) Hollander
Walk Tall (1960) Aurandt
Walk the Angry Beach (1961) Marx, W.
Walk the Dark Streets (1956) Dunlap
Walk the Proud Land (1956) Salter
Walking Dead (1936) Kaun
Walking Down Broadway (1938) Glover, J.
Walking Hills (1949) Morton
Walking My Baby Back Home (1953) Mancini
Walking on Air (1936) Shilkret, N.
Walking Target (1960) Shefter
Walky Talky Hawky (1946) Stalling
Wall of Flesh (1968) Marini
Wall of Noise (1963) Lava
Wall Street Cowboy (1939) Lava
Wall Street Impressions (1961) Arel
Wallaby Jim of the Islands (1937) Kay, Arthur
Wallflower (1941) De Nat
Wallflower (1948) Hollander
Walls Came Tumbling Down (1946) Skiles
Walls of Gold (1933) Kaylin
Walls of Jericho (1948) Newman
Wanda (1969) Quick
Wanderer (1926) Riesenfeld
Wanderer of the Wasteland (1945) Sawtell
Wanderers of the West (1941) Sanucci
Wanderers' Return (1951) Jackson, H.
Wandering Footsteps (1925) Hoffman, M.
Wandering Here and There (1944) Nussbaum
Wandering Jew (1933) Hochman
Wandering Jew (1933) Riesenfeld
Wandering Through Wales (1948) Mayfield
Wanted a Master (1936) Axt
Wanted: Dead or Alive (1951) Kraushaar
Wanted: No Master (1939) Lewis
War (1968) Watts
War Against Mrs. Hadley (1942) Snell
War and Pieces (1963) Lava
War Arrow (1954) Stein, H.
War Brides (1916) Bowers, R. H.
War Comes to America (1945) Tiomkin
War Days (1945) Engel
War Dogs (1942) Sanucci
War Dogs (1943) Bradley
War Drums (1957) Baxter
War for Men's Minds (1943) Applebaum
War Hunt (1962) Shank
War Is Hell (1961) Stein, R.
War Lord (1965) Moross
War Mamas (1931) Shield
War of the Colossal Beast (1958) Glasser
War of the Satellites (1958) Greene, W.
War of the Worlds (1953) Stevens, L.
War Paint (1953) Lange
War Party (1965) LaSalle
War Wagon (1967) Tiomkin
Warhol (1964) Young, L.
Warkill (1967) Kauer
Warlock (1959) Harline
Warming Up (1928) Carbonara
Warning Shadow (1953) Forrell
Warning Shot (1966) Goldsmith
Warpath (1951) Sawtell
Warrior's Husband (1933) Zamecnik
Warriors 5 (1962) Stein, R.
Wartime Housing (1943) Applebaum
Washington Masquerade (1932) Axt
Washington Melodrama (1941) Snell
Washington Story (1952) Salinger
Wasp Woman (1959) Katz, F.
Watch for Joe (1951) Greeley
Watch on the Rhine (1943) Steiner, M.
Watch Out for Witchweed (1963) Kleinsinger
Watch the Birdie (1950) Stoll
Watch the Birdie (1958) Wheeler
Watch the Birdie . . . Die! (1968) Bath
Watchdog (1939) Scheib
Watchdog (1945) Scheib
Water Babies (1935) Harline
Water Babies (1945) Jackson, H.

Water Birds (1952) Smith, P.
Water—Friend or Enemy (1943) Plumb
Water Jockey Hi-Jinks (1951) Mamorsky
Water Rustlers (1939) DiMaggio
Water Speed (1949) Mamorsky
Water Sports (1941) Lava
Water, Water Every Hare (1950) Stalling
Water Wizards (1949) Jackson, H.
Water Wonderland (1949) Jackson, H.
Waterfront (1928) Carbonara
Waterfront (1939) Roemheld
Waterfront (1944) Zahler
Waterfront at Midnight (1948) Lubin
Waterhole #3 (1967) Grusin
Waterloo Bridge (1931) Burton
Waterloo Bridge (1940) Stothart
Watermelon Man (1970) Van Peebles
WAVE, a WAC and a Marine (1944) Rich
Wave of the Flag (1955) Jackson, H.
Wavelength (1967) Wolff, T.
Waves of Change (1970) Johns
Wax Works (1934) Dietrich
Way Back (1964) DiPasquale
Way Back Home (1931) Steiner, M.
Way Back When a Nag Was Only a Horse (1940) Timberg
Way Back When a Night Club Was a Stick (1940) Timberg
Way Back When a Razzberry Was a Fruit (1940) Sharples, Winston
Way Back When a Triangle Had Its Points (1940) Timberg
Way Back When Women Had Their Weigh (1940) Timberg
Way Down East (1920) Silvers
Way Down East (1935) Friedhofer
Way Down South (1939) Young, V.
Way Down Yonder in the Corn (1943) Kilfeather
Way in the Wilderness (1940) Snell
Way of a Gaucho (1952) Kaplan, S.
Way of a Ship (1965) Reichert
Way of All Flesh (1940) Young, V.
Way of All Pests (1941) De Nat
Way of Peace (1947) von Ottenfeld
Way of the Padres (1948) De Francesco
Way Out (1966) Kaiser
Way Out of the Wilderness (1968) Bond
Way Out West (1937) Hatley
Way to Love (1933) Rainger
Way to the Gold (1957) Newman, L.
Way . . . Way Out! (1966) Schifrin
Way We Live Now (1970) Sassover
Way West (1967) Kaper
Wayward (1932) Green, J.
Wayward Bus (1957) Harline
Wayward Canary (1932) Lewis
Wayward Girl (1957) Kraushaar
Wayward Hat (1960) Scheib
Wayward Pups (1937) Bradley
We Are Not Alone (1939) Steiner, M.
We Are the Marines (1942) Shaindlin
We Did It (1936) Timberg
We Give Pink Stamps (1965) Lava
We Go Fast (1941) Mockridge
We Have Our Moments (1937) Henderson, C.
We Like it Here (1966) Kennedy
We Live Again (1934) Newman
We Must Have Music (1941) Hayton
We Refuse to Die (1942) Amfitheatrof
We Shall Return (1963) Summerlin
We the Animals Squeak (1941) Stalling
We Went to College (1936) Axt
We Were Dancing (1942) Kaper
We Were Strangers (1949) Antheil
We Who Are Young (1940) Kaper
We're a Team (19??) Loboda
We're Going to Be Rich (1938) Maxwell
We're in the Honey (1948) Sharples, Winston
We're in the Money (1933) Marsales
We're In the Money (1935) Roemheld
We're No Angels (1955) Hollander
We're Not Dressing (1934) Jackson, H.
We're Not Married! (1952) Mockridge
We're on Our Way to Rio (1944) Sharples, Winston
We're on the Jury (1937) Webb
We're Rich Again (1934) Webb
We've Never Been Licked (1943) Skinner, F.
Weakly Reporter (1944) Stalling
Weapons for Victory (1943) De Francesco
Wearing of the Grin (1951) Poddany
Weary River (1929) Silvers
Weasel Stop (1955) Franklyn
Weather Magic (1965) Timmens
Weaver (1967) Andrews, J.
Web (1947) Salter
Web of Danger (1947) Glickman, M.
Wedding Bells (1933) De Nat
Wedding Belts (1940) Timberg
Wedding Knight (1966) Sharples, Winston
Wedding March (1928) Zamecnik
Wedding Night (1935) Newman
Wedding Party (1969) McDowell
Wedding Present (1936) Skiles
Wedding Yells (1942) Lava
Weddings and Babies (1960) Manson
Wee Bit of Scotland (1949) Mayfield
Wee Cooper o' Fife (1947) Steiner, G.
Wee Men (1947) Sharples, Winston
Wee Willie Winkie (1937) Newman
Wee-Willie Wildcat (1953) Bradley
Week Ends Only (1932) Lange
Week-End at the Waldorf (1945) Green, J.
Week-End in Havana (1941) Newman
Week-End Marriage (1932) Harling
Week-End Pass (1944) Skinner, F.
Weekend for Three (1941) Webb
Weekend Love (1969) Lance

Weekend of Fear (1966) Lockwood
Weekend Pass (1961) Marx, W.
Weekend with Father (1951) Skinner, F.
Weekend with the Babysitter (1970) Ragland
Weenie Roast (1931) De Nat
Weird Woman (1944) Sawtell
Welcome Little Stranger (1941) Scheib
Welcome Soldier (1944) Applebaum
Welcome Stranger (1947) Dolan
Welcome to Hard Times (1966) Sukman
Welding (1945) Carbonara
Well (1951) Tiomkin
Well Done (1945) Engel
Well Groomed Bride (1946) Webb
Well Oiled (1947) Calker
Well Worn Daffy (1965) Lava
Well-Rowed Harvard (1942) De Francesco
Wells Fargo (1937) Young, V.
Wells Fargo Days (1944) Jackson, H.
Wells Fargo Gunmaster (1951) Wilson, S.
Werewolf of London (1935) Hajos
West of Carson City (1939) Salter
West of Cimarron (1941) Feuer
West of Eldorado (1949) Kay, Edward
West of Laramie (1949) Skinner, F.
West of Pinto Basin (1940) Sanucci
West of Shanghai (1937) Roemheld
West of Texas (1943) Zahler
West of the Alamo (1946) Sanucci
West of the Brazos (1950) Greene, W.
West of the Pecos (1945) Sawtell
West of the Pesos (1959) Franklyn
West of the Rio Grande (1944) Kay, Edward
West of the Rockies (1941) Lava
West of Wyoming (1950) Kay, Edward
West of Zanzibar (1928) Axt
West Point of the Air (1935) Maxwell
West Point of the Air (Trailer, 1935) Ward, E.
West Point of the South (1936) Maxwell
West Point on the Hudson (1942) Nussbaum
West Point Story (1950) Jackson, H.
West Point Widow (1941) Leipold
West Side Kid (1943) Glickman, M.
West Side Story (1961) Chaplin, S.
West to Glory (1947) Hajos
Westbound (1959) Buttolph, David
Westbound Stage (1940) Sanucci
Western Courage (1950) Rosen, M.
Western Crossing (1943) Ludwig
Western Cyclone (1943) Erdody
Western Daze (1941) Raksin
Western Frontier (1935) Zahler
Western Jamboree (1938) Lava
Western Mail (1942) Sanucci
Western Pacific Agent (1950) Glasser
Western Renegades (1949) Kay, Edward
Western Trail (1936) Scheib
Western Union (1941) Buttolph, David
Westerner (1940) Tiomkin
Westinghouse in Alphabetical Order (1965) Bernstein, E.
Westward (1970) Hieronymous
Westward Bound (1943) Sanucci
Westward Ho (1942) Feuer
Westward Ho the Wagons (1956) Bruns
Westward Passage (1932) Kaun
Westward the Women (1951) Alexander, J.
Westward Trail (1947) Greene, W.
Westward Whoa (1936) Spencer, N.
Wet Blanket Policy (1948) Calker
Wet Hare (1962) Franklyn
Wet Knight (1932) Dietrich
Wet Paint (1946) Wallace
Wet Parade (1932) Axt
Wetback Hound (1956) Lava
Wetbacks (1956) Baxter
Whacks Museum (1933) De Nat
Whalers (1938) Malotte
Wharf Angel (1934) Roemheld
What a Blonde (1945) Harline
What a Knight (1932) De Nat
What a Life (1939) Leipold
What a Lion! (1938) Lewis
What a Little Sneeze Will Do (1941) Scheib
What a Man! (1944) Kay, Edward
What a Night (1935) Scheib
What a Way to Go! (1964) Riddle
What a Widow! (1930) Zuro
What a Woman (1943) Leipold
What About Daddy? (1942) Snell
What Am I Bid? (1967) Freeman, E.
What Becomes of the Children? (1936) Zahler
What Did You Do in the War, Daddy? (1966) Mancini
What Do You Say to a Naked Lady? (1970) Karmen
What Do You Think? No. 3 (1938) Snell
What Ever Happened to Aunt Alice? (1969) Fried
What Ever Happened to Baby Jane? (1962) De Vol
What Every Woman Knows (1934) Stothart
What Happens at Night (1941) Scheib
What Is a Man? (1958) Ericson
What Is a Painting? (1961) Holcombe
What Is a Tree? (1965) Scharf, S.
What It Takes (1959) Glasser
What It Takes to Make a Star (1945) De Francesco
What Makes Daffy Duck? (1948) Stalling
What Makes Us Tick (1952) Poddany
What Men Want (1930) Roemheld
What Next (1970) Cacioppo
What Next, Corporal Hargrove? (1945) Snell
What, No Men? (1935) Jerome
What, No Spinach? (1936) Timberg
What Price Fleadom (1948) Bradley
What Price Glory (1926) Bassett, R. H.
What Price Glory (1926) Rapée
What Price Glory (1952) Newman
What Price Hollywood? (1932) Steiner, M.
What Price Porky (1938) Stalling

What Time Is It Now? (1967) Manson
What, Who, How (1957) Watt
What's a Nice Girl Like You Doing in a Place Like This? (1963) Coll
What's Brewin' Bruin? (1947) Stalling
What's Buzzin' Buzzard (1943) Bradley
What's Buzzin' Cousin? (1943) Leipold
What's Cookin' Doc? (1944) Stalling
What's Cookin? (1941) Calker
What's Hatchin'? (1948) Jackson, H.
What's My Lion? (1961) Franklyn
What's New Pussycat? (1965) Bacharach
What's Opera Doc? (1957) Franklyn
What's Peckin' (1965) Wheeler
What's So Bad About Feeling Good? (1968) De Vol
What's Sweepin' (1953) Wheeler
What's Up, Doc? (1949) Stalling
What's Up, Tiger Lily? (1966) Lewis, Jack
What's Your I. Q.? (1940) Zahler
Wheat Country (1959) Applebaum
Wheat Smut Control (1952) Wheeler
Wheel of Ashes (1970) Robertson
Wheel of Life (1929) Potoker
Wheeler Dealers (1963) De Vol
When a Girl's Beautiful (1947) Dubin
When a Man Loves (1926) Hadley
When Asia Speaks (1944) Agostini
When Comedy Was King (1959) Royal
When Dad Was a Boy (1933) Vincent, P.
When Fish Fight (1954) Jackson, H.
When G.I. Johnny Comes Home (1945) Sharples, Winston
When Gangland Strikes (1956) Alexander, V.
When Hell Broke Loose (1958) Glasser
When I Grow Up (1951) Moross
When I Yoo Hoo (1936) Spencer, N.
When in Rome (1952) Dragon
When Knighthood Was in Flower (1922) Peters
When Knights Were Bold (1941) Scheib
When Ladies Meet (1933) Axt
When Ladies Meet (1941) Kaper
When Lightning Strikes (1934) Zahler
When Love Is Young (1937) Skinner, F.
When Magoo Flew (1955) Curtin
When Mousehood Was in Flower (1953) Scheib
When Strangers Marry (1944) Tiomkin
When the Boys Meet the Girls (1965) Karger
When the Cat's Away (1929) Stalling
When the Cat's Away (1935) Bradley
When the Clock Strikes (1961) LaSalle
When the Daltons Rode (1940) Skinner, F.
When the Girls Take Over (1962) Oakland
When the Lights Go On Again (1944) Harling
When Tomorrow Comes (1939) Skinner, F.
When We Grow Up (1951) Robinson
When Were You Born (1938) Kaun
When Willie Comes Marching Home (1950) Newman
When Winter Calls (1942) De Francesco
When Worlds Collide (1951) Stevens, L.
When You're in Love (1937) Newman
When You're Smiling (1950) Duning
When's Your Birthday? (1937) Leipold
Where All Roads Lead (1956) Jackson, H.
Where Angels Go . . . Trouble Follows! (1967) Schifrin
Where Are Your Children? (1944) Kay, Edward
Where Danger Lives (1950) Webb
Where Do We Go from Here? (1945) Raksin
Where East Is East (1929) Axt
Where Is My Child? (1937) Stillman
Where It's At (1969) Golson
Where Love Has Gone (1964) Scharf, W.
Where the Boys Are (1960) Stoll
Where the Buffalo Roam (1938) Sanucci
Where the Heart Is (1953) Gart
Where the North Begins (1947) Glasser
Where the Sidewalk Ends (1950) Mockridge
Where the Trade Winds Play (1953) Lava
Where the West Begins (1938) Lange, J.
Where There's Life (1947) Young, V.
Where Time Is a River (1965) Peaslee
Where Time Stands Still (1945) Nussbaum
Where Trails End (1942) Sanucci
Where Were You When the Lights Went Out? (1968) Grusin
Where Winter Is King (1954) Jackson, H.
Where's Charley? (1952) Heindorf
Where's Jack? (1969) Bernstein, E.
Where's Poppa? (1970) Elliott, J.
Which Is Witch (1948) Stalling
Which Is Witch (1958) Sharples, Winston
Which Way to the Front? (1970) King
While I Run This Race (1967) Byrd, C.
While Paris Sleeps (1932) Kay, Arthur
While the City Sleeps (1928) Axt
While the City Sleeps (1956) Gilbert, H.
While the Patient Slept (1935) Kaun
Whip (1928) Bergunker
Whip Hand (1951) Sawtell
Whiplash (1949) Waxman
Whipsaw (1935) Ward, E.
Whirlpool (1950) Raksin
Whirlpool (Trailer, 1950) Newman
Whirlwind (1951) Leipold
Whisperin' Bill (1933) Axt
Whispering Footsteps (1943) Glickman, M.
Whispering Ghosts (1942) Harline
Whispering Shadow (1933) Zahler
Whispering Skull (1944) Zahler
Whispering Smith (1949) Deutsch
Whispering Winds (1929) Riesenfeld
Whispers (1941) Amfitheatrof
Whispers (196?) McDowell
Whistle at Eaton Falls (1951) Applebaum
Whistle for Willie (1965) Galbraith
Whistle in the Night (1947) Shilkret, N.
Whistle Stop (1946) Tiomkin
Whistler (1944) Moraweck

Whistling Hills (1951) Kraushaar
Whistling in Brooklyn (1943) Bassman
Whistling in Dixie (1942) Hayton
Whistling in the Dark (1933) Axt
Whistling in the Dark (1941) Kaper
White Angel (1936) Roemheld
White Banners (1938) Steiner, M.
White Bondage (1937) Vaughan
White Cargo (1942) Kaper
White Christmas (1954) Lilley
White Christmas (Trailer, 1954) Van Cleave
White Cliffs of Dover (1944) Stothart
White Cockatoo (1935) Kaun
White Eagle (1941) Zahler
White Fang (1936) Friedhofer
White Feather (1955) Friedhofer
White Flood (1940) Eisler
White Goddess (1953) Gertz
White Gorilla (1945) Zahler
White Heat (1949) Steiner, M.
White Hell of Pitz Palu (1930) Roemheld
White House (1946) Shilkret, N.
White Hunter (1936) Maxwell
White Legion (1936) Riesenfeld
White Lightning (1953) Skiles
White Orchid (1954) Diaz Conde
White Parade (1934) De Francesco
White Phantom (1949) Glasser
White Pongo (1945) Erdody
White Rooster (1953) Martino
White Rose (1923) Breil
White Safari (1946) Applebaum
White Sails (1941) Jackson, H.
White Savage (1943) Skinner, F.
White Shadows in the South Seas (1928) Axt
White Sister (1923) Breil
White Sister (1933) Stothart
White Slave Ship (1962) Baxter
White Squaw (1956) Bakaleinikoff, M.
White Tie and Tails (1946) Rosen, M.
White Tower (1950) Webb
White Wilderness (1958) Wallace
White Witch Doctor (1953) Herrmann
White Woman (1933) Hajos
Whiz Quiz Kid (1963) Sharples, Winston
Who Buys Your Livestock? (1951) Calker
Who Done It? (1942) Skinner, F.
Who Is Hope Schuyler? (1942) Raksin
Who Killed Aunt Maggie? (1940) Feuer
Who Killed Cock Robin? (1935) Churchill
Who Killed Cock-Robin? (1933) Scheib
Who Killed Rover? (1930) Axt
Who Killed Teddy Bear? (1965) Calello
Who Killed Who? (1943) Bradley
Who Says I Can't Ride a Rainbow! (1970) Scott, B.
Who Scent You? (1959) Franklyn
Who Was That Lady? (1960) Previn, A.
Who's Afraid of Virginia Woolf? (1966) North
Who's Been Sleeping in My Bed? (1963) Duning
Who's Cookin' Who? (1946) Calker
Who's Crazy? (1965) Coleman, O.
Who's Enchanted? (1962) Sullivan, J.
Who's Got the Action? (1962) Duning
Who's Guilty? (1945) Zahler
Who's Kitten Who? (1950) Stalling
Who's Minding the Mint? (1967) Schifrin
Who's Minding the Store? (1963) Lilley
Who's Superstitious? (1943) Terr
Who's Who in the Jungle (1945) Scheib
Who's Who in the Zoo (1942) Stalling
Who's Who in the Zoo (1955) Jackson, H.
Who's Zoo in Hollywood (1941) Kilfeather
Whoa, Be Gone! (1957) Franklyn
Wholly Smoke (1938) Stalling
Whoopee! (1930) Newman
Whoopee Party (1932) Churchill
Whoops! I'm a Cowboy (1937) Timberg
Why Daddy? (1944) Terr
Why Do I Dream Those Dreams? (1934) Spencer, N.
Why Girls Leave Home (1945) Greene, W.
Why Man Creates (1968) Alexander, J.
Why Mules Leave Home (1934) Scheib
Why Must I Die? (1960) LaSalle
Why Play Leap Frog? (1949) Smith, P.
Why Vandalism? (1955) Varges
Wichita (1955) Salter
Wicked (1931) Bassett, R. H.
Wicked Die Slow (1968) Schwartz, R.
Wicked Dreams of Paula Schultz (1968) Haskell
Wicked Wolf (1946) Scheib
Wicked Woman (1934) Axt
Wicked Woman (1954) Baker, Buddy
Wicket Wacky (1951) Wheeler
Wicky, Wacky Romance (1939) Scheib
Wide Open Faces (1938) Riesenfeld
Wide Open Spaces (1947) Wallace
Wide Open Spaces (1950) Scheib
Wide Open Town (1941) Leipold
Widening Circle (1964) Smith, R.
Wideo Wabbit (1956) Stalling
Widow from Monte Carlo (1936) Roemheld
Wife, Husband and Friend (1939) Maxwell
Wife of Monte Cristo (1946) Dessau
Wife Takes a Flyer (1942) Heymann
Wife vs. Secretary (1936) Stothart
Wife Wanted (1946) Kay, Edward
Wigwam Whoopee (1948) Sharples, Winston
Wilbur the Lion (1947) Wheeler
Wild 90 (1968) Brown, C.
Wild About Hurry (1959) Franklyn
Wild and the Innocent (1959) Salter
Wild and Wonderful (1964) Stevens, M.
Wild and Woody (1948) Calker
Wild and Woolfy (1945) Bradley
Wild and Woolly (1931) Axt
Wild and Woolly (1932) Dietrich
Wild and Woolly Hare (1959) Franklyn

Wild and Woozy West (1942) Worth, P.
Wild Angels (1966) Curb
Wild Beauty (1946) Skinner, F.
Wild Bill Hickok Rides (1942) Jackson, H.
Wild Blue Yonder (1951) Young, V.
Wild Boar Hunt (1940) Jackson, H.
Wild Boys of the Road (1933) Kaun
Wild Bunch (1969) Fielding
Wild Cargo (1934) Sharples, Winston
Wild Chase (1965) Lava
Wild Company (1930) Kaylin
Wild Country (1947) Hajos
Wild Dakotas (1956) Dunlap
Wild Frontier (1947) Glickman, M.
Wild Geese Calling (1941) Buttolph, David
Wild Girl (1932) Zamecnik
Wild Gold (1934) Buttolph, David
Wild Goose Chase (1950) Mamorsky
Wild Guitar (1962) O'Day
Wild Gypsies (1969) Brummer
Wild Hare (1940) Stalling
Wild Harvest (1947) Friedhofer
Wild Harvest (1961) Sawtell
Wild Heritage (1958) Vars
Wild Honey (1942) Bradley
Wild Horse Ambush (1952) Wilson, S.
Wild Horse Mesa (1932) Leipold
Wild Horse Mesa (1947) Sawtell
Wild Horse Range (1940) Lange, J.
Wild Horse Rodeo (1937) Colombo
Wild Horse Rustlers (1943) Erdody
Wild Horse Stampede (1943) Sanucci
Wild Horse Valley (1940) Lange, J.
Wild Horses (1943) Terr
Wild in the Country (1961) Hopkins, K.
Wild in the Streets (1968) Baxter
Wild Is My Love (1963) Holcombe
Wild Is the Wind (1958) Tiomkin
Wild Life (1959) Scheib
Wild Man of Borneo (1941) Snell
Wild North (1952) Kaper
Wild on the Beach (1965) Haskell
Wild One (1953) Stevens, L.
Wild Orchids (1929) Axt
Wild Over You (1952) Stalling
Wild Party (1929) Leipold
Wild Party (1956) Bregman
Wild Racers (1968) Curb
Wild Rebels (1967) Jacobs, A.
Wild River (1960) Hopkins, K.
Wild Scene (1970) Mendoza-Nava
Wild Seed (1965) Markowitz
Wild Stallion (1952) Skiles
Wild Turkey (1947) Shilkret, N.
Wild Water Champions (1950) Jackson, H.
Wild Waves (1929) Stalling
Wild Weed (1949) Kraushaar
Wild West (1946) Hajos
Wild Wheels (1969) Hatcher
Wild Wife (1953) Stalling
Wild, Wild Winter (1966) Long, J.
Wild, Wild World (1959) Franklyn
Wild Youth (1961) LaSalle
Wildcat (1942) Rich
Wilderness Canoe Country (1949) Heaps
Wilderness of Zin (1958) Rosenberg
Wilderness River Trail (1952) Leonard
Wilful Willie (1942) Scheib
Will Do Mousework (1956) Sharples, Winston
Will It Happen Again? (1948) Craig, E.
Will Penny (1967) Raksin
Will Success Spoil Rock Hunter? (1957) Mockridge
Will to Win (1951) Lava
Willem de Kooning (1966) Feldman
William Fox Movietone Follies of 1929 (1929) Kay, Arthur
William Tell (1934) Dietrich
Williamsburg in the American Heritage (1957) Price, Herman
Williamsburg Restored (1951) Lloyd, N.
Williamsburg, the Story of a Patriot (1957) Herrmann
Willie and Joe in Back at the Front (1952) Mancini
Willie the Kid (1952) Gold
Willoughby's Magic Hat (1943) Worth, P.
Willow Run (1942) Bennett, R. R.
Willy (1963) Carras
Willy McBean and His Magic Machine (1965) Forrell
Wilson (1944) Newman
Wily Weasel (1937) Dietrich
Wimmin Is a Myskery (1940) Timberg
Win, Place and Showboat (1950) Sharples, Winston
Winchester '73 (1950) Scharf, W.
Wind (1928) Axt
Wind (1970) Burroughs
Wind Across the Everglades (1958) Sawtell
Windblown Hare (1948) Stalling
Windflowers (1968) Mekas
Windjammer (1958) Gould, M.
Window (1949) Webb
Window Cleaners (1940) Smith, P.
Window Pains (1966) Greene, W.
Window Shopping (1938) De Nat
Windsong (1958) Partch
Windward Way (1938) Shilkret, N.
Windy (1935) Snell
Wine of Morning (1955) Schmoll
Wine, Women and Horses (1937) Jackson, H.
Wing and a Prayer (1944) Friedhofer
Winged Horse (1932) Dietrich
Winged Idol (1915) Nurnberger
Winged Victory (1944) Rose
Wings (1927) Zamecnik
Wings for the Eagle (1942) Hollander
Wings for Victory (1942) Applebaum
Wings in the Dark (1935) Roemheld

Wings of a Continent (1941) Agostini
Wings of Chance (1961) Andersen
Wings of Defense (1942) De Francesco
Wings of Eagles (1957) Alexander, J.
Wings of Steel (1941) Jackson, H.
Wings of the Hawk (1953) Skinner, F.
Wings of the Navy (1939) Roemheld
Wings of the Wind (1947) De Francesco
Wings of Youth (1940) Agostini
Wings Over Canada (1945) Applebaum
Wings Over Honolulu (1937) Raksin
Wings Over the Pacific (1943) Kay, Edward
Wings to the North (1954) Craig, E.
Wings to the Word (1951) Mamorsky
Wink of an Eye (1958) Gold
Winner by a Hare (1953) Sharples, Winston
Winner Take All (1932) Harling
Winner Take All (1939) Kaylin
Winner Take All (1948) Kay, Edward
Winner Take All (Trailer, 1932) Perry
Winner's Circle (1944) Jackson, H.
Winner's Circle (1948) Cailliet
Winnie the Pooh and the Blustery Day (1967) Baker, Buddy
Winnie the Pooh and the Honey Tree (1965) Baker, Buddy
Winning (1969) Grusin
Winning Basketball (1946) Anderson
Winning of Barbara Worth (1926) Henkel
Winning Team (1952) Buttolph, David
Winning the West (1946) Scheib
Winning Ticket (1935) Maxwell
Winning Ticket (1938) Lewis
Winning Your Wings (1942) Jackson, H.
Wins Out (1932) Dietrich
Winter (Fashion Forecast) (1938) Rochetti
Winter A-Go-Go (1965) Betts
Winter Carnival (1939) Janssen
Winter Draws On (1948) Sharples, Winston
Winter Geyser (1968) Collette
Winter Holiday (1946)
Winter in Eskimo Land (1941) De Francesco
Winter Meeting (1948) Steiner, M.
Winter Paradise (1954) Lava
Winter Storage (1948) Wallace
Winter Wonderland (1947) Dessau
Winter Wonders (1951) Jackson, H.
Winterset (1936) Shilkret, N.
Wintertime (1943) Lange
Wiretapper (1955) Carmichael
Wise Little Hen (1934) Harline
Wise Owl (1940) Kilfeather
Wise Quackers (1948) Stalling
Wise Quacking Duck (1943) Stalling
Wise Quacks (1939) Stalling
Wise Quacks (1952) Scheib
Wiser Sex (1932) Green, J.
Wish and Ticino (1963) Bluestone
Wish You Were Here (1950) Lava
Wistful Widow of Wagon Gap (1947) Schumann
Witch Crafty (1955) Wheeler
Witch's Cat (1948) Scheib
Witch's Tangled Hare (1959) Franklyn
Witchcraft (1916) Beynon
Witching Hour (1934) Leipold
Witchmaker (1969) Mendoza-Nava
With a Song in My Heart (1952) Newman
With Byrd at the South Pole (1930) Baer
With Love and Kisses (1936) Kay, Edward
With One Voice (1954) Forrell
With Rod and Gun in Canada (1945) Jackson, H.
With Rod and Reel on Anticosti Island (1943) Jackson, H.
With Six You Get Eggroll (1968) Mersey
With the Marines at Tarawa (1943) Jackson, H.
With These Hands (1950) Mamorsky
Within Man's Power (1954) Bruch
Within These Walls (1945) Buttolph, David
Within These Walls (1951) Curtin
Without Each Other (1962) Tiomkin
Without Honor (1949) Steiner, M.
Without Love (1945) Kaper
Without Reservations (1946) Webb
Without Time or Reason (1961) Sharples, Winston
Without Warning (1952) Gilbert, H.
Witness for the Prosecution (1957) Malneck
Witness to Murder (1954) Gilbert, H.
Wives and Lovers (1963) Murray
Wives Under Suspicion (1938) Henderson, C.
Wizard of Arts (1941) Timberg
Wizard of Baghdad (1960) Gertz
Wizard of Clubs (1953) Mamorsky
Wizard of Gore (1970) Wellington
Wizard of Oz (1939) Stothart
Wolf at the Door (1933) De Nat
Wolf Call (1939) Kay, Edward
Wolf Chases Pigs (1942) Worth, P.
Wolf Dog (1958) Bath
Wolf Hunters (1949) Kay, Edward
Wolf in Cheap Clothing (1936) Scheib
Wolf in Sheik's Clothing (1948) Sharples, Winston
Wolf Larsen (1958) Dunlap
Wolf Man (1941) Skinner, F.
Wolf of New York (1940) Lava
Wolf of Wall Street (1929) Hajos
Wolf Song (1929) Carbonara
Wolf! Wolf! (1934) Dietrich
Wolf! Wolf! (1944) Scheib
Wolf's Pardon (1947) Scheib
Wolf's Side of the Story (1938) Scheib
Wolf's Tale (1944) Scheib
Woman (1918) Riesenfeld
Woman Accused (1933) Kopp, R.
Woman Between (1931) Schertzinger
Woman Chases Man (1937) Newman
Woman Disputed (1928) Riesenfeld
Woman Doctor (1939) Lava
Woman from Monte Carlo (1932) Kaun

Woman from Moscow (1928) Hajos
Woman Hunt (1961) Vars
Woman I Love (1937) Webb
Woman in Green (1945) Dessau
Woman in Red (1935) Kaun
Woman in Room 13 (1932) Friedhofer
Woman in the Dark (1951) Wilson, S.
Woman in the House (1942) Hayton
Woman in the Window (1944) Friedhofer
Woman in White (1948) Steiner, M.
Woman Obsessed (1959) Friedhofer
Woman of Affairs (1928) Axt
Woman of Distinction (1950) Heymann
Woman of Experience (1931) Lange
Woman of Paris (1923) Gottschalk
Woman of Paris (1923) Stahlberg
Woman of the North Country (1952) Butts
Woman of the Town (1943) Rozsa
Woman of the Year (1942) Waxman
Woman on the Beach (1947) Eisler
Woman on the Run (1950) Lange
Woman Racket (1930) Axt
Woman Rebels (1936) Webb
Woman They Almost Lynched (1953) Wilson, S.
Woman to Woman (1929) Zahler
Woman Trap (1929) Hajos
Woman Who Came Back (1945) Plumb
Woman Who Dared (1933) Zahler
Woman's Devotion (1956) Baxter
Woman's Face (1941 trailer) Amfitheatrof
Woman's Face (1941) Kaper
Woman's Secret (1949) Hollander
Woman's Vengeance (1948) Rozsa
Woman's World (1954) Mockridge
Women (1939) Ward, E.
Women Are Like That (1937) Roemheld
Women Are Trouble (1936) Ward, E.
Women at War (1943) Lava
Women Everywhere (1930) Brunelli
Women from Headquarters (1950) Wilson, S.
Women in Bondage (1943) Kay, Edward
Women in Sports (1943) Lava
Women in War (1940) Feuer
Women Love Once (1931) Rainger
Women Men Marry (1937) Ward, E.
Women of All Nations (1931) Bassett, R. H.
Women of Pitcairn Island (1956) Dunlap
Women of Russia (1968) Gould, S.
Women of the Prehistoric Planet (1966) Stein, R.
Women of Tomorrow (1949) Jackson, H.
Women Without Names (1940) Carbonara
Women Women Women Moira (1970) Fox, D.
Wonder Dog (1948) Wallace
Wonder Eye (1947) Applebaum
Wonder Gloves (1951) Maury
Wonder Man (1945) Roemheld
Wonder of Women (1929) Lange
Wonderful Country (1959) North
Wonderful Life (1951) Forbes
Wonderful World of the Brothers Grimm (1962) Harline
Wonders of Araby (1956) Lava
Wonders of Arkansas (1962) Ellis, R.
Wonders of Dallas (1962) Gohman
Wonders of Kentucky (1965) Vaughn
Wonders of Manhattan (1956) Bock
Wonders of New Orleans (1957) Kleinsinger
Wonders of Philadelphia (1962) Gohman
Wonders of the Sea (1941) De Francesco
Wood Goes to War (1943) Nussbaum
Wood Nymph (1916) Breil
Wood-Peckin' (1943) Timberg
Wooden Indian (1948) Scheib
Wooden Shoes (1933) De Nat
Woodland (1932) Scheib
Woodland Cafe (1937) Harline
Woodland Manners (1952) Kleinsinger
Woodman Spare That Tree (1942) Kilfeather
Woodman Spare That Tree (1950) Scheib
Woodpecker from Mars (1956) Wheeler
Woodpecker in the Moon (1959) Wheeler
Woodpecker in the Rough (1952) Wheeler
Woodpecker Wanted (1964) Wheeler
Woods Are Full of Cuckoos (1937) Stalling
Woody and the Beanstalk (1965) Greene, W.
Woody Dines Out (1945) Calker
Woody Meets Davy Crewcut (1956) Wheeler
Woody the Giant Killer (1948) Calker
Woody Woodpecker (1941) Calker
Woody Woodpecker Polka (1952) Wheeler
Woody's Clip Joint (1964) Calker
Woody's Kook-Out (1961) Calker
Woolen Under Where (1962) Lava
Word for the Greeks (1951) Kirk
Words and Music (1948) Hayton
Working for Peanuts (1953) Wallace
Working Girls (1931) Rainger
Working Man (Trailer, 1933) Kaun
Works of Calder (1950) Cage
World and the Flesh (1932) Hand
World at War (1942) Kubik
World Changes (1933) Kaun
World Dances (1954) Borisoff
World for Ransom (1954) De Vol
World Friendship (1949) Forrell
World in His Arms (1952) Skinner, F.
World in My Corner (1956) Mancini
World in Revolt (1934) Schwarzwald
World Is Ours (1939) Snell
World Moves On (1934) De Francesco
World of Beauty (1955) Mancini
World of Henry Ford (1963) Kaplan, S.
World of Henry Orient (1964) Bernstein, E.
World of Mosaic (1956) Hemmer
World of Pleasure (1964) Roemheld
World of Susie Wong (1960) Duning
World Premiere (1941) Young, V.
World, the Flesh and the Devil (1958) Rozsa

World Was His Jury (1958) Bakaleinikoff, M.
World Within (1935) Sharples, Winston
World Without End (1956) Stevens, L.
World's Affair (1933) De Nat
World's Fair Encounter (1964) Carmichael
World's Greatest Sinner (1962) Zappa
World's Most Beautiful Girls (1952) Mancini
Worm Turns (1936) Smith, P.
Worm's Eye View (1939) De Nat
Wormwood Star (1955) Harlan
Worship, a Family's Heritage (1962) Wernick
Worst Woman in Paris? (1933) De Francesco
Worthington (1966) Small
Wot's All th' Shootin' Fer (1940) Scheib
Woton's Wake (1962) McDowell
Wotta Knight (1947) Sharples, Winston
Wrangler's Roost (1941) Sanucci
Wreck of the Hesperus (1944) Scheib
Wreck of the Mary Deare (1959) Duning
Wrecking Crew (1942) Rich
Wrecking Crew (1969) Montenegro
Wrestling Wrecks (1953) Wheeler
Written on the Wind (1956) Skinner, F.
Wrong Man (1957) Herrmann
Wrong Road (1937) Colombo
Wrong Son (1950) Kopp, R.
WUSA (1970) Schifrin
Wuthering Heights (1939) Newman
Wynken, Blynken and Nod (1938) Harline
Wyoming (1940) Snell
Wyoming (1947) Scott, N.
Wyoming Mail (1950) Lubin
Wyoming Outlaw (1939) Lava
Wyoming Roundup (1952) Kraushaar
Wyoming Wildcat (1941) Feuer

X-15 (1961) Scott, N.
X—The Man with X-Ray Eyes (1963) Baxter
Xmas (1962) Steinert
XXX Medico (1940) Amfitheatrof

Y (1963) Calahan
Yambaó (1956) Adomian
Yank at Eton (1942) Kaper
Yank at Oxford (1938) Ward, E.
Yank in Libya (1942) Zahler
Yank in London (1945) Collins
Yank in the R.A.F. (1941) Newman
Yank in Viet-Nam (1964) LaSalle
Yank on the Burma Road (1942) Amfitheatrof
Yankee Buccaneer (1952) Rosen, M.
Yankee Dood It (1956) Franklyn
Yankee Doodle Bugs (1954) Franklyn
Yankee Doodle Daffy (1943) Stalling
Yankee Doodle Dandy (1942) Heindorf
Yankee Doodle Donkey (1944) Timberg
Yankee Doodle Goes to Town (1939) Snell
Yankee Doodle Home (1939) Shilkret, N.
Yankee Doodle Mouse (1944) Bradley
Yankee Doodle Swing Shift (1942) Calker
Yankee Fakir (1947) Laszlo
Yankee Girl (1915) Beynon
Yankee Painter: The Work of Winslow Homer (1964) Muczynski
Yankee Pasha (1954) Salter
Yankee Ski Doodle (1948) De Francesco
Yanks Ahoy (1943) Ward, E.
Yanks Are Coming (1943) Zahler
Yaqui Drums (1956) Kay, Edward
Yarn About Yarn (1941) Scheib
Ye Happy Pilgrims (1934) Dietrich
Ye Olde Minstrels (1941) Snell
Ye Olde Songs (1932) Scheib
Ye Olde Swap Shoppe (1940) Kilfeather
Ye Olde Toy Shop (1935) Scheib
Ye Olden Days (1933) Churchill
Year of the Mouse (1965) Poddany
Year Toward Tomorrow (1966) Lewin
Yearling (1946) Stothart
Yellow Cab Man (1950) Bradley
Yellow Canary (1963) Hopkins, K.
Yellow Dust (1936) Colombo
Yellow Fin (1951) Kay, Edward
Yellow Jack (1938) Axt
Yellow Mountain (1954) Mancini
Yellow Rose of Texas (1944) Skiles
Yellow Sky (1948) Newman
Yellow Ticket (1931) Bassett, R. H.
Yellow Tomahawk (1954) Baxter
Yellowneck (1955) Rosenthal
Yellowstone (1936) Vaughan
Yellowstone Cubs (1963) Smith, P.
Yellowstone Kelly (1959) Jackson, H.
Yellowstone Legend (1952) Enos
Yellowstone Park (1936) Shilkret, J.
Yellowstone Park (1950) Andriessen
Yelp Wanted (1931) De Nat
Yes, My Darling Daughter (1939) Roemheld
Yes Sir, Mr. Bones (1951) Greene, W.
Yes Sir, That's My Baby (1949) Scharf, W.
Yesterday and Today (1953) Daniel
Yesterday in Fact (1963) Schuller
Yesterday, Today, and Forever (1949) Colombo
Yesterday's Heroes (1940) Mockridge
Yin-Yang (1968) Zekley
Yodeling Yokels (1931) Marsales
Yokel Boy (1942) Glickman, M.
Yokel Boy Makes Good (1938) Churchill
Yokel Duck Makes Good (1943) Scheib
Yokohama Yankee (1954) Scheib
Yolanda (1924) Peters
Yolanda and the Thief (1945) Hayton
Yoo Hoo! I'm a Bird (1966) Raim
Yosemite the Magnificent (1941) Shilkret, J.
You and Me (1938) Weill
You Are France to Me (1963) Lawrence, Elliot
You Are What You Eat (1968) Simon, J.
You Belong to Me (1934) Roder

You Belong to Me (1941) Hollander
You Came Along (1945) Young, V.
You Can Beat the A-Bomb (1950) Kraushaar
You Can't Beat the Law (1943) Kay, Edward
You Can't Buy Everything (1934) Axt
You Can't Cheat an Honest Man (1939) Skinner, F.
You Can't Escape Forever (1942) Deutsch
You Can't Escape Forever (Trailer, 1942) Roemheld
You Can't Fool a Camera (1940) Amfitheatrof
You Can't Fool Your Wife (1940) Webb
You Can't Get Away with Murder (1939) Roemheld
You Can't Have Everything (1937) Scharf, W.
You Can't Ration Love (1944) Heymann
You Can't Run Away from It (1956) Duning
You Can't Take It With You (1938) Tiomkin
You Can't Win (1952) Keefer
You, Chicago! (1951) Wolff, F.
You Don't Know What You're Doing (1931) Marsales
You Gotta Stay Happy (1948) Amfitheatrof
You Have to Run Fast (1961) LaSalle
You Hit the Spot (1945) Schrager
You, John Jones (1943) Green, J.
You Never Can Tell (1951) Salter
You Only Live Once (1937) Newman
You Ought to Be in Pictures (1940) Stalling
You Said a Mouseful (1958) Sharples, Winston
You Said a Mouthful (1932) Harling
You Were Meant for Me (1948) Mockridge
You Were Never Duckier (1948) Stalling
You Were Never Lovelier (1942) Harline
You'll Find Out (1940) Webb
You'll Never Walk Alone (1953) Waring
You're a Big Boy Now (1966) Prince, R.
You're a Sap, Mr. Jap (1942) Timberg
You're a Sweetheart (1937) Henderson, C.
You're a Trooper (1955) Craig, E.
You're an Education (1938) Stalling
You're In the Army Now (1941) Jackson, H.
You're in the Navy Now (1951) Mockridge
You're My Everything (1949) Newman
You're Never Too Young (1955) Scharf, W.
You're Not Built That Way (1936) Timberg
You're Only Young Once (1937) Snell
You're Telling Me (1934) Leipold
You're the One (1941) Boutelje
You're Too Careless with Your Kisses (1933) Marsales
You've Got to Be Smart (1967) Worth, S.
Young Americans (1967) Byers
Young and Beautiful (1934) Kay, Arthur
Young and Beautiful (1943) Lava
Young and Dangerous (1957) Dunlap
Young and Evil (1962) Adomian
Young and Healthy (1933) Marsales
Young and the Brave (1963) Stein, R.
Young and Willing (1942) Young, V.
Young Animals (1968) Baxter
Young at Heart (1955) Heindorf
Young Bess (1953) Rozsa
Young Billy Young (1969) Manne
Young Captives (1958) Markowitz
Young Daniel Boone (1950) Kay, Edward
Young Desire (1930) Perry
Young Dillinger (1965) Rogers
Young Doctors (1961) Bernstein, E.
Young Don't Cry (1957) Antheil
Young Donovan's Kid (1931) Steiner, M.
Young Dr. Kildare (1938) Snell
Young Eagles (1930) Leipold
Young Fury (1964) Dunlap
Young Guns (1956) Skiles
Young Guns of Texas (1962) Sawtell
Young Ideas (1943) Bassman
Young Immortal: The Art of Raphael (1952) Belasco
Young in Heart (1938) Waxman
Young Jesse James (1960) Gertz
Young Land (1957) Tiomkin
Young Lions (1958) Friedhofer
Young Lovers (1964) Kaplan, S.
Young Man of Manhattan (1930) Mendoza
Young Man with a Horn (1950) Steiner, M.
Young Man with Ideas (1952) Rose
Young Man's Bride (1968) Harper
Young Mr. Lincoln (1939) Newman
Young People (1940) Mockridge
Young Philadelphians (1959) Gold
Young Racers (1963) Baxter
Young Runaways (1968) Karger
Young Savages (1961) Amram
Young Sinner (1965) Manne
Young Stranger (1957) Rosenman
Young Swingers (1963) Levine, H.
Young Tom Edison (1940) Ward, E.
Young Warriors (1967) Rosen, M.
Young Widow (1946) Dragon
Youngblood Hawke (1964) Steiner, M.
Younger Brothers (1949) Lava
Youngest Profession (1943) Snell
Your Cheatin' Heart (1964) Karger
Your Child Is a Genius! (1947) Brown, H.
Your Community (1956) Brant
Your Last Act (1941) Hayton
Your National Gallery (1943) Bales
Your Safety First (1957) Poddany
Your Share in Tomorrow (1957) Forrell
Your Union (1964) Lackey
Your Voice and Vote (1964) Lackey
Yours, Mine and Ours (1968) Karlin
Youth Aflame (1945) Sanucci
Youth Dances (1959) Meeker
Youth Gets a Break (1940) Moore, D.
Youth of Russia (1934) Stillman
Youth on Parade (1942) Scharf, W.
Youth on Parole (1937) Colombo
Youth on Trial (1945) Skiles

Youth Runs Wild (1944) Sawtell
Youth Takes a Fling (1938) Previn, C.
Youth Will Be Served (1940) Mockridge
Youthful Cheaters (1923) Smith, E.
Yugoslav Farm Family (1964) Moore, F.
Yugoslavia (1962) Lloyd, N.
Yukon Flight (1940) Porter
Yukon Gold (1952) Kay, Edward
Yukon Manhunt (1951) Kay, Edward
Yukon Patrol (1942) Feuer
Yukon Vengeance (1954) Kay, Edward
Yule Laff (1962) Sharples, Winston

Z Is for Zoo (1970) Burroughs
Zamba (1949) Kraushaar
Zamboanga (1937) Kilenyi
Zander the Great (1925) Schertzinger
Zanzibar (1940) Skinner, F.
Zaza (1939) Hollander
Zebra in the Kitchen (1965) Barker
Zenobia (1939) Hatley
Zero Hour (1957) Dale
Zero in the Universe (1966) Cherry
Zero the Hero (1954) Sharples, Winston
Zero, the Hound (1941) Timberg
Zero to Sixth (1960) Henderson, S.
Ziegfeld Follies (1946) Edens
Ziegfeld Girl (1941) Stothart
Zig Zag (1970) Nelson, O.
Zip 'n Snort (1960) Franklyn
Zipping Along (1952) Stalling
Zis Boom Bah (1941) Lange, J.
Zodiac Couples (1970) Bagley
Zombies (1964) Norman, Lon
Zombies of Mora Tau (1957) Bakaleinikoff, M.
Zombies of the Stratosphere (1952) Wilson, S.
Zombies on Broadway (1945) Webb
Zontar: The Thing from Venus (1966) Stein, R.
Zoo in Budapest (1933) Zamecnik
Zoom and Bored (1957) Stalling
Zoom at the Top (1962) Franklyn
Zoot Cat (1944) Bradley
Zorro Rides Again (1937) Colombo
Zorro's Fighting Legion (1939) Lava
Zotz! (1962) Green, B.
Zula Hula (1937) Timberg
Zululand (1947) De Francesco